THE WAR
ILLUSTRATED

WE REJOICED AND PAID HOMAGE IN LONDON'S GREAT VICTORY PARADE

On June 8, 1946, H.M. the King took the salute at the mighty parade of victorious British, Imperial, Dominion and Allied Forces. Here, Civil Defence contingents pass the Houses of Parliament.

Direct colour photograph by Pictorial Press

THE WAR
Illustrated

Complete Record of the Conflict
by Land and Sea and in the Air

Edited by

Sir JOHN HAMMERTON

Editor of The War Illustrated 1914-1919 ; World War ; I Was There ! , **etc.**

Volume Ten

This TENTH AND FINAL VOLUME contains the issues numbered 231 to 255, covering the period April 1946 to April 1947. Hostilities in the main having ceased, there was much " winding-up " to record in picture and print : of a world in travail, of bewildered peoples groping for real peace and just settlements in an atmosphere charged with the fearfulness of the developing Atomic Age.

Introduction of several new features of outstanding interest became possible : the retelling of great stories of the war in the light of subsequent revelations ; reports, more closely detailed than previously possible, of outstanding operations on land and sea and in the air ; achievements of our crack regiments, H.M. ships, R.A.F. squadrons and army divisions ; descriptions by on-the-spot observers of widely diverse post-war conditions in Europe's wartime capitals.

Full measure we gave to gay and impressive celebrations of the Victory Parade in London on June 8, 1946, when famed leaders passed by, and representatives of Home and Empire units who had borne the burden and heat of battle. Four months later we recorded the Judgement at Nuremburg : climax of the greatest trial in history, when Justice overtook those Nazi leaders who constituted Hitler's Old Guard and the curtain fell on all that grim and sordid drama. We followed with lively interest meetings of the United Nations First General Assembly in New York, of its subsidiary U.N.E.S.C.O. in Paris and the World Food Conference in Copenhagen.

It is to us a matter of not inconsiderable pride that in the long wartime production of THE WAR ILLUSTRATED there occurred no break in publication. It took the Peace to interrupt our orderly sequence. The fuel crisis of early 1947 entailed urgent and drastic national conservation of power, resulting in our temporary suspension in company with British periodicals in general. Our break occurred after the publication of No. 252, one month elapsing before the appearance of the next number. We were in our stride again when opportunity came, at last, to picture the signing of the peace treaties with five ex-enemy states, preliminary to the framing of the German and Austrian treaties by the " Big Four " in conference at Moscow—the outcome of their momentous deliberations anxiously awaited by all peace-hungry mankind.

Published 2000
Cover Design © 2000
TRIDENT PRESS INTERNATIONAL
ISBN 1-58279-109-0 Single Edition
Printed in Croatia

General Index to Volume Ten

THIS Index is designed to give ready reference to the whole of the literary and pictorial contents of THE WAR ILLUSTRATED. Individual subjects and persons of importance are indexed under their own headings, while references are included to general subjects such as Casualties; Housing. Page Numbers in italics indicate illustrations.

Aachen, teacher shortage at, 351
Aandalsnes, R. Marines at, 43
Abdiel, H.M.S., sunk, 220
Abdul Illah, in Trans-Jordan, 215
Abdullah I, K. of Trans-Jordan, 215
Aberdeen (Maryland), 100-ton tank at, 480
Abyssinia, E. Africans in, 275
Acasta, H.M.S., sunk, 292
Accra, W. African port, 104
——wounded Africans at, 691
Achates, H.M.S., sunk, 739
Achenbach, S.S. Sgt. Gunther, 539-41
Acireale, D.L.I. at, 429
Acker, M. Van, Belgian premier, 436
Acoustic Torpedo, success, 489
Adair, Maj.-Gen. Sir Allan H.S, 8, 10
——commands Guards Armoured Division, 524
Adams, Cpl. A. J., B.E.M., 456
Adamson, Guardsman, of Irish Guards, 364
Addis Ababa, Allies enter, 243
——capture, E. Africans at, 275
Addiscombe, bomb removed from, 450
Addu Atoll, Illustrious at, 159
——R. Marines in, 43
Aden, Moonstone at, 330
——strategic importance, 54
Adkins, Derek, on "Bomber Offensive," 724
Admiral Graf Spee, prisoners of, 413-14, 443
Admiral Hipper (ship), complete loss, 194
——and Glorious, 292
——and Glowworm, 678
——as raider, 451
Aegean Sea, Dodecanese in, 495-98
Afghanistan, joins U.N., 617
Africa, colonies' efforts, 147
——E., British Legion in, 639
——and Central, British colonies in, 83
——troops for Victory Parade, 135
——W. Africans defend, 243
——N., Black Watch in, 235-36, 237
————Buffs in, 556, 557
————D.C.L.I. in, 203
————Desert Rats in, 90
————D.L.I. in, 427, 428, 430
————D. of Wellington's in, 491
————Grenadiers in, 7, 9
————H.A.C. in, 395, 396, 397
————H.L.I. in, 651, 652
————Irish Guards in, 363, 364
————R.E.s in, 713, 715
————Recce in, 108
————R. Signals in, 331, 333
————78th Div. in, 460
————Suffolk Regt. in, 780
————Welsh Guards in, 747
——Partition of, 243
——W., British colonies in, 104
——troops for victory parade, 160
African Pioneer Corps, 243, 307
Afridi, H.M.S., R. Marines in, 43
Agnew, Capt. W. G., R.N., and Vanguard, 32, 97
Airborne Division (1st), war record, 596
——(6th), Black Watch with, 236
————war record, 602
Airborne Troops, Allied, at Arnhem, 217-19
——British, Arnhem memorial, 390
——Chindits, Burma, 314-16
——German, in Crete, 578, 580
Aircraft, Australia's shortage, 195
——drop supplies, 613
——Japanese factory, conversion, 290
——tested, Farnborough, 13
Aircrews, new badges for, 521
Airfield Construction Groups, of R.E.s, 713, 717
Air Force, German, Goering creates, 499

Air Force (cont.)
——Royal, bomb Walcheren, 543
—— — in Cocos Is., 283
—— — good will mission to U.S., 265
—— — Mauritians with, 627
—— — memorial, London, 402
—— — Sharrild, 357
—— — new badges for, 521
—— — No. 8 Squadron, 285
—— — 10 Squadron, 508
—— — 20 Squadron, 317
—— — 35 Squadron, 476
—— — 43 Squadron, 540
—— — 56 Squadron, 122
—— — 57 Squadron, 572
—— — 60 Squadron, 189
—— — 61 Squadron, 604
—— — 62 Squadron, 348
—— — 65 Squadron, 634
—— — 72 Squadron, 670
—— — 78 Squadron, 698
—— — 81 Squadron, 252
—— — 102 Squadron, 60
—— — 117 Squadron, 410
—— — 149 Squadron, 730
—— — 215 Squadron, 383
—— — 216 Squadron, 77
—— — 230 Squadron, 444
—— — 240 Squadron, 220
—— — 250 Squadron, 766
—— — 460 Squadron, 792
—— — 609 Squadron, 156
—— — and S. Nazaire raid, 67
—— — Signals unit, 334
—— — transports, S. France, 633
—— — West Indians in, 755
——U.S. Army, latest troop-carriers, 325
Air Force Regt. R., in Cocos Is., 282, 284
—— — — in Cos, 497
—— — — in Jerusalem, 756
—— — — patrol Berlin, 681
—— — — war record, 75-78
Air Force Volunteer Reserve, R., of Ceylon, 627
Air Formation Signals, 334
Air Landing Reconnaissance Squadron (1st), 108, 110
Airmen, Allied, Bahamas memorial, 546
Air Ministry, guide-flare on, 399
Airport, of Lisbon, 626
Air Raids, on Cyprus, 214
Air Raid Shelters, and atomic bombs, 319
—— — Berlin, demolition, 788
—— — caves as, Dover, 415
—— — demolished, London, 128
—— — German, figures, 127
—— — as hospital, 116
—— — as store, 197
Air Training Scheme, in Ceylon, 627
Akabo R., Africans cross, 307
Ala, Hussein, on Security Council, 56
Alamein, El, anniversary gathering, 486
——battlefield, 679
——Black Watch at, 236
——Buffs at, 555, 556
——D.L.I. at, 428
——50th Div. at, 300
——Green Howards at, 620
——H.A.C. at, 395, 397
——Household Cavalry at, 299
——John Kerr at, 569-70
——Recce at, 108
——R. Signals at, 331
Alanbrooke, F M Viscount, at opening of Parliament, 519
——in Victory Parade, 164, 175, 186
Albania, Tirana the capital, 278
Albert Canal, Household Cavalry cross, 302
Albert Hall, Alamein reunion in, 486
Aldershot, Cameronians at, 523
——internment camp at, 322
Aleutian Is., submarine earthquake in, 232
Alexander, F/M Viscount, and Cassino, 484
——home life, 21

Alexander, F./M. (cont.)
——to Irish Guards, 363
——in Victory Parade, 165, 175, 179
Alexander, Rt. Hon. A. V., and D.E.M.S., 246
——at Peace Conference, 306, 313, 326
Alexandra, H.R.H. Princess, 175, 179
Alexandria, British vacate, 757
Alexandrine, Queen, 359
Algiers, Black Watch at, 237
A Lighters, supply Tobruk, 253-54
Alison, Col., U.S.A.A.F., 314
Allen, Lt.-Col. F. E., 140, 142
Allfrey, Lt.-Gen. Sir Charles, 264
Allied Armies' Graves Registration Command, 296
Allied Control Commission : see Control Commission
Allied Control Council, in session, 56
Allied Forces Mascot Club, 190
Allies, sign peace treaties, 751-753
All Saints' Day, in Bayeux cemetery, 562
Alpen, battle of, Cameronians at, 526
Alpuget F/O J. A. d', over Sumatra, 789
Altmark (ship), Keating's account, 414, 443-44
——prisoners rescued, 445
Aluminium, for houses, 470, 584
Amba Alagi, Worcestershires at, 683
Americans, French memorials to, 406
——Havre memorial, 425
Amiens, Peace of, and Ceylon, 627
Amman, king enthroned at, 215
Ammunition, E. Lancs carry, 141
——explosion, Haenigsen, 197
——Japanese, dumped in Pacific, 242
——train explosion, Savernake, 242
Amritsar, riots in, 775
Amsterdam, Churchill in, 98
——liberation, 675-76
Andaman Is., and Ceylon, 627
Anders, Gen. Wladyslaw, 214
Anderson, Clinton P., 244
Anderson Lt.-Gen. Sir Kenneth, on African troops, 691
——Black Watch with, 236
——in N. Africa, 611-12
Andros, Force 133 at, 412
" And So to Work," exhibition, 692
Anglo-French Pact, signed, 741
Anhvi, evacuation ship, 122
Animals, numbers used in war, 607
Annand, 2nd Lt. R. W., V.C., 427
Anson, H.M.S., returns home, 320
Antananarivo, E. Africans at, 275
Anti-aircraft Batteries, of R. Marines, 43
Anti-aircraft Cruiser, design, 232
Anti-aircraft Guns, Japanese, 52
—— — R.A.F. Regt. manhandle, 78
Anti-invasion Exercises, Green Howards in, 619
Anti-tank Detachment, of D.C.L.I., 205
Anti-tank Guns, British, at Calais, 34
—— — at Cassino, 483
—— — of E. Lancs Regt., 141
—— — Tunisia, 610
—— — German, Tebourba, 612
Anti-tank Rifles for D.L.I., 427
Antwerp, E. Lancs at, 139, 141
——liberation, H.L.I. at, 651
Anzio, Buffs at, 558
——Cameronians at, 523
——D. of Wellington's at, 491
——Green Howards at, 619, 621

Anzio (cont.)
——Grenadier Guards at, 8
——Grenville off, 570-72
——Inniskilling Fus. at, 460, 462
——Irish Guards at, 363
——Recce at, 107, 108, 110
Aouina, El, raids on, 54
Apes, in Gibraltar, 183
Aphoven, H.L.I. at, 654
Aprons, white, of R.W.F., 581
Aqueducts, Italian, parachutists and, 547-48
Arab Legion, successes, 214
—— — for Victory Parade, 134
Arabs, and Jewish ex-Servicemen, 294
Aragon, Louis, French poet, 310
Arakan, British drive into, 249-50
——flying visual control-posts in, 699-702
——Marines in, 46
Ardennes, battle of, E. Lancs and, 139
——Black Watch and, 238
——R.A.F. Regt. and, 78
——Recce and, 110
Ardent, H.M.S., sunk, 292
Arethusa, H.M.S., war record, 712
Argenlieu, Adm. d', 201
Argenta Gap, H.A.C. at, 396
Argonaut, H.M.S., 234
Argyll and Sutherland Highlanders, 737
Arkell, George, in Rorqual, 377-78
Ark Force, Black Watch with, 235
Ark Royal, H.M.S., and Bismarck, 451
——and Norway evacuation, 292
Armour, British, at Cassino, 483
——on Imphal-Tamu Road, 59
Armoured Cars, British, Berlin, 681
—— — Marmon Harrington, 299, 300
—— — British staff, 582
—— — Staghound, for Household Cavalry, 299, 300
Armoured Corps, R., in Normandy landings, 228
—— — 7th Division with, 780
—— — in Victory Parade, 167, 169
Armoured Division (7th), war record, 90
——(11th), war record, 100
Armoured Support Group, of R. Marines, 46
Armoured Unit, of R.A.F. Regt., 77
—— — of Recce, 110
Armourers, R.A.F., in Burma, 701
Armstrong, Cdr. H. T., R.N., 452
Army, British, battlefronts show, 582
——in Germany, plastic coins, 322
——new badges for, 521
——new Royal regiments, 718, 723
——walking-out uniform, 256
——Russian, rear establishments' work, 415
——U.S., Tunisia results, 612
Army Dental Corps, now Royal, 721, 723
Army Educational Corps, now Royal, 720-21, 723
Army Mechanical Demonstration Column, 417
Army Service Corps, R., Cypriots with, 214
——dumps Japanese ammunition, 242
—— — and opium runners, 509-10
—— — in recruiting campaign, 417
Arneke, Gloucestershire Regt. at, 267
Arnemuiden, Allies occupy, 652

Arnhem, anniversary, 390
——D.C.L.I. and, 203
——5th R.I.D.G. at, 588
——1st (Airborne) Div. at, 555
——49th Div. at, 268
——Gloucesters enter, 267
——Household Cavalry at, 302
——Irish Guards at, 366
——Recce at, 110
——R. Signals at, 334
——schoolchildren visit, 358
——Taylor on, 217-19
——Worcestershires at, 684
Arnim, Gen. J. Sixt von, Indians take, 5
—— — surrenders, 611
—— — in Tunisia, 612
Arno R., Buffs cross, 558
Arnold, Capt. F. J. H., M.C., 139
Arras, British G.H.Q at, 697
Arromanches, " Mulberry " B at, 771
——memorial at, 671
——now Port Winston, 559
——state-owned site, 671
Art, in Prague, 660
Artillery, Royal, at Alamein, 569-70
—— — in Malaya, 636-37
—— — Montgomery on, 371
Artillery Road, in Burma, 60
Art Treasures, found at Wesel, 319
——German, rehousing, 197
Ascension Is., importance, 104
Asdic, and U-boat war, 489
Ashton, Sgt., D.C.M., of Irish Guards, 363
Asia, S.E., Japanese surrender in, 381-83
Assam, Ordnance Field Park in, 665
Assault Craft, British, at Tamatave, 761
Atallah, Gen., and Cairo Citadel, 264
Athabaskan, H.M.C.S., 638, 639
Athens, H.L.I. in, 651
——Independence Day in, 1
——in 1946, 198, 199
Atherstone, H.M.S., 67-68
Athlone, E. of, at Victory Parade, 179
Atlantic, battle of, McMurtrie on, 489
Atlantic Ocean, British colonies in, 104
Atlantic Wall, Commandos breach, 790-92
Atlantis (hospital ship), 292
Atomic Bomb, Bikini tests, 232-33
——Hiroshima casualties, 127
——on Hiroshima, effects, 274
——probable effects, 319
——under-water explosion, 336-37
A.T.S., from Ceylon, 134
——in Victory Parade, 187
Attlee, Rt. Hon. Clement R., and coal nationalization, 664
—— — and Colossus, 293
—— — and Commonwealth Conference, 130
—— — at Gort memorial service, 33
—— — home life, 86
—— — on " invasion " of 1940, 567
—— — at Peace Conference, 289, 303, 305, 306, 313
—— — and S. Africa's gifts, 490
—— — at Victory Parade, 175, 179, 185, 186
Attlee, Mrs., with French children, 490
—— — at Northolt, 303
Auchinleck, Gen. Sir Claude, with H.A.C., 397
Audacity, H.M.S., escort carrier, 489
Augusta, Allies bombard, 601, 602
Aunay-sur-Odon, 5th R.I.D.G. in, 589
——prefabricated town, 770
Aurora, H.M.S., and invasion of Sicily, 601
—— — at Levitha, 43
—— — war record, 458
Austen, Maj.-Gen. Godwin, 243

Australia, demobilization in, 383
—Greek urn for, 607
—R. Navy in, 72
—saved from Japs, 195-96
—war orphans for, 351
Australians, Commandos, raid Singapore, 387-89
—in Crete, 579
—defend Singapore, 259-60
—how they took Sattelberg, 707-08
—in N. Guinea, 196
—in Tokyo, *207*
Austria, Buffs in, *558*
—Inniskilling Fus. in, 460, *462*
—peace-treaty discussions, *773*
Automatic Weapons, infra-red sight for, *777*
Auxiliary Military Pioneer Corps, of Palestine, 214
A.V.R.E., assault vehicles, 713
Avro York, at Lisbon, 626
Aziz, Hosain, and U.N., *617*

B

Baarland, Cameronians take, 524
Bachequera, H.M.S., 31
Bacon, John, William III statue, 79
Bader, Group Capt. Douglas, and battle of Britain, 153-54, 511
— — — anniversary, *401*
Badges, new, for Army and R.A.F., *521*
Bad Harzburg, rest camp, 698-99
Badoglio, Marshal Pietro, and armistice terms, 100
— —and peace demonstrations, 99
Baerlein, Henry, on Luxemburg, 372
Bagnold, Lt.-Col. Ralph A., and L.R.D.G., 603
Bailey (sculptor), and Nelson's column, *82*
Bailey Bridges, numbers built, 713, 717
— —over Rapido, 484
— —over Rhine, *716*
Baillie-Grohman, Vice-Adm. M. T., in Kiel, 398
Baker, Driver A. J., B.E.M., 456
Baker, Maj. S. E., on D. of Wellington's Regt., 491-94
Bakes, F/O G. L., 789
Balaena, whaling ship, *728*
Ball, Capt. Albert, V.C., 122, 189
Ballard, Lt.-Cdr. A. H., R.N.R., *31*
Ballet, in Belgrade, 564
Balloon Barrage, Dowding on, 403
Balmoral, air liner, *386*
Balmoral Concert Party, *237*
Baltic States, domestic workers from, *490*
Banana Ridge, D. of Wellingtons at, 491
Bananas cultivation and transport, *23*
Band, of D.C.L.I., 206
—of Irish Guards, at Piedmonte, *366*
Bandits, on Ledo Road, 765
Bandsmen, R.M., duties, 43
Bangkok, R.E.'s bridge at, *263*
Bangkok-Moulmein Rly: see Burma-Siam
Bank Notes, looted, Frankfort, *680*
B.A.O.R., in Berlin, *197*
— — —families join, *424*
— — — —wives and children of, 415
Barbados, war difficulties, 147
Barbed Wire, for export, *706*
Barber, Maj.-Gen. C. M., 142
Barbero, M., hotel-proprietor, 634
Barberry, S.S. sunk, 121
Barce, L.R.D.G.'s raid on, 604
Bardia Bill, gun, 253-54
Barentu, H.L.I. at, 651
—Worcestershires at, 683
Bare Ridge, battle of, Buffs at, 556
Barges, as homes, Walcheren, 317
Barham, H.M.S., *Hotspur* and, 74
Barjot, Adm. Pierre, 232
Barker, Lt.-Gen. Sir Evelyn, in Kiel, 398
— — —in King David Hotel, *295*
— — — —MacMillan succeeds, *490*
Barker, Len, Commando raids on Singapore, 387-88
Barnabas, St., a Cypriot, 214
Barnett, Pte F., B.E.M., 456
Baron, L/Cpl. M.M., 364
Barossa (ship), burned, 795
Barrandov, film studio at, 660
Barre, Gen., in N. Africa, 611
Bartelsee, Klein, British prisoners at, *670*, 671
Bartlet, Lt., of Irish Guards, 363
Bartolomeo Colleoni (ship), 618
Bassingbourne, orbit meter at, *386*
Bastille Day, in Metz, *261*
Basutoland, war effort, 307
Batavia, memorial to British dead, *229*
Bates, Cpl. S., V.C., 492
Bathurst, W. African port, 104
Bauxite, colonies produce, 147
Bayeux, cemetery at, *562*
—De Gaulle in, *201*
—Y.M.C.A. at, *560*
Baynton, Sec. Off. Percy 127, 415
B.C.O.F., holidays for, 415
— — — —wives and families of, 415
Beach Obstacles, on Norman coast, *227*
Beale, Capt. R. G. A., of Recce, *108*
Bear, as Polish mascot, *545*
Bearman, Capt. J. B., in Verdun, *507*
Bearman, Maj. L. L., with Ordnance sub-park, 665-67
Beattie, Lt.-Cdr. S. H., V.C., 67
Beaufighters, with Home Fleet, *517*
Beaulieu, parachute descent at, *325*
Bech, M., Foreign Min. of Luxemburg, 372
Bechuanaland Protectorate, war effort, 307
Bed, air-conditioned, *422*
Beer, Prague brews, 660
Beeson, Sgt., escape bid, 285-87
Beet, Lt. Trevor Agar, R.N., *41*
B.E.F., saved from Dunkirk, *2*, *3*
Belfast, Gloucestershire Regt. in, *267*
Belfast, H.M.S., war record, *778*
Belgium, H.L.I. in, 651
—Resistance in, 604-06
Belgrade, Mihailovich's trail, *230*
—in 1946, *564*, *565*
Belisha Beacon, travels, 378-80
Bell, of *Illustrious*, on exhibition, *630*
—as memorial, Lympstone, *46*
Bell, Don, in Santo Tomas, 124
Bell, Capt. F. S., R.N., in *Anson*, 320
Bell, S. in *Royal Daffodil*, *649*
Bellinger, Adm., U.S.N., and Pearl Harbour, 419
Bellona, H.M.S., at Narvik, *210*
— —in Thames, *181*
Bemba Tribe, chief's loyal message, 14
Bengal, H.M.I.S., war record, *746*
Benghazi, cemetery at, *516*
—Mauritius Pioneers at, *627*
Benham, J. in *Royal Daffodil*, *649*
Benneville, Worcestershires in, *686*
Bentley Priory, Fighter Command H.Q., *510*
Beny Bocage, Le, 302
Beppu, thermal region, 575
Berbera, Black Watch at, 235
Berengaria of Navarre, 214
Bergen, *Theseus* at, *208-09*, *224*
Bergues Canal, E. Lancs. on, 139
Berkhamsted Castle, London statues at, 79, 81
Berlin, Allied airmen's graves in, 607
—Black Market in, 764-65
—demolition in, *788*
—Desert Rats in, 90
— —milestone in, *455*
—D.L.I. in, 430
—Four-Power Allied Control Council in, *258*
—German prisoners' return, *454*
—Grenadiers in, 10
—Hitler's victory monument, *425*
—Indians in, *197*
—R.A.F. Regt. in, *681*
—remembers Nazi victims, *424*
—today, 115, *116-17*
—in winter, *648*
Berlin Conference, and Partition of Africa, 243
Bermuda, importance, 104
—share in victory, 755
Berneville, R. Signals at, *331*
Barney-Ficklin, Maj.-Gen. H. P. M., 36
Bernhard, Prince, at Victory Parade, 179, 186
Bernieres, reconstruction in, *559*
Berry, Gunner W. H., in Malaya, 636-37
— —prisoner of Japs, 446-47
Berry, John, portrait by, *593*
Bessborough, E. of, 439
Best, Cameronians take, 526
—H.L.I. at, *653*
Bethnal Green, new flats in, *374*
Béthouart, Gen., at Narvik, *210*
Beveland, S., Cameronians on, 524, 526
Bevin, Rt. Hon. Ernest, and Commonwealth Conference, *130*
— — —at Lake Success, *585*
— — —meets Sidky Pasha, *490*
— — —at Moscow conference, *773*
— — —in New York, *513*, *617*
— — —in Paris, *70*, *101*
— — —illness, 289
— — —private life, *438*
— — — —signs peace treaties, *751*
— — — —and Treaty of Dunkirk, *741*
Bewley, Cyril, death, 484
Bhagat, Lieut., V.C., 714
Bhor, Sir J., at Peace Conference, *306*
Bickerton, H.M.S. torpedoed, *667*, 668
Bicycles, for Black Watch, *236*
—in Copenhagen, 532, *533*
—valves vulcanized, *466*
Bidault, Georges, at ballet, Paris, *326*
— —in Moscow, *773*
— —in Paris, *70*, *101*
— —at Peace Conference, 289, *305*, 313
— —and peace treaties, *752-53*
— —and Treaty of Dunkirk, *741*
— —and U.N.E.S.C.O., *566*
Biddle, Cpl. Arthur, with L.R.D.G., 603-04
Biddle, Francis, at Nuremberg, 431
Biddle, Lt.-Col. R. A., D.S.O., *270*
Bièvres, Resistance camp at, 606
Biggin Hill, Memorial Chapel at, *400-01*
— — —burned out, *600*
Biggs, Maj. K. A., G.C., 456
Bikini, atom bomb at, 232-33, *336-37*
Billy, R.W.F. goat, *101*
Bir el Harmat, D.C.L.I. at, 203
Bir-el-Tamar, H.L.I. take, 651
Birkett, Mr. Justice, at Nuremberg, *431*, 435
Birthday Cake, for Y.M.C.A. canteen, *416*
Bishop, Capt. W. A., V.C., 189
Bisley, Tedder at, 276
Bismarck (ship), *King George V* and, 428
—sinking of, 451-52
Bittern, H.M.S., Marines in, 43
Bjornsson, Hon. Sveinn, President of Iceland, 694
Black Billy, pit pony, *450*
Black Market, in Belgium, 478
— —in Berlin, 764-65
— —in Bucharest, 628
— —in Budapest, 19
— —in Finland, 342
— —in Greece, 193
— —not in Oslo, 404
— —not in Sofia, 468
— —in Paris, 310
— —in Prague, 660
— —in Rome, 786, *787*
— —in Vienna, 51
Blackmore, Capt. R. R. G., with Dagger Division, 58-61, 441-42
Black Sea Fleet, Doenitz on, 740
Black Watch, at Alamein, 569
— —in British Somaliland, 275
— —in Crete, 579
— —war record, 235-38
Blade Force, in Tunisia, *610*, 611-12
Bladel, E. Lancs at, 139
Blakang Mati, prisoners in, 92
Blaking, Maj., in war trial, *230*
Blamey, Gen. Sir Thomas, 195, 196
Blandy, Vice-Adm. W. H. P., 232
Blane, Lady, at Waterloo canteen, *416*
Blaskowitz, F/M Johannes, strength of Army, 675
Bleckede, Cameronians at, 523
Block, Denise Madeline, 631
Blondeau, Dr., at Winterburg, 26
Blue Nile Province Police, 307
Bluenose, Order of, 27
Blue Trains, "Telcom" units, 534
Blum, Léon, and U.N.E.S.C.O., *566*
Bocket, H.L.I. at, 654
Boer, Mr. de, of Dutch Resistance, 676
Bofors Guns, British, at Dunkirk, *473*
— —of Green Howards, Italy, *621*
— —of *Grenville*, *572*
— —R.A.F. Regt. and, 75, 77
Bogomolov, Mr., signs peace treaty, *752*
Bois Halbout, E. Lancs at, 139
Bols, Maj.-Gen. Eric, and Rhine crossing, 323
— —and 6th Airborne Div., 602
Bolsover Colliery, troops at, *745*
Boltenstern, Gen. von, *384*
Bombardons, of Mulberry, 772
Bomb Disposal, by German P.O.W., *450*
— —by R.E.s, *714*, *717*
Bombs, Japanese, as mines, *715*
—radio-controlled, *Grenville* and, 638-39
Bon, C., Black Watch at, 236
— —Recce at, 108
Bonaventure, H.M.S., *351*
Bône, Allies occupy, 612
—1st Parachute Brigade at, 556
—port wrecked, *610*
Bonneville, 5th R.I.D.G. at, *589*
Booby-traps, in Belgium, 254
Borgund (steamer), and *Glorious*, 292
Borie, Raymond, as P.O.W., 668-69
Bormann, Martin, and Hitler, 659
— —sentence, 432, 435
Borneo, British N., a Crown Colony, *467*
Bottomley, A/M Sir Norman and good will mission, *265*
— —to No. 35 Squadron, 353
Bougainville, Fijians in, 467
Boulogne, Irish Guards at, 363
—R. Marines at, 43
Bouvines, Suffolk Regt. at, *780*
Bovallsand, granite for monument at, *425*
Bovell, Capt. H. C., and *Bismarck*, 451-52
Bovet, Russian architect, 596
Bowman, Lt. George, and Amsterdam's liberation, 675-76
Boyd, Vice-Adm. Sir Denis, *615*
Boyd, C.S.M. J., of H.L.I., 652
Bradford, Lt.-Col. at S. Valéry cemetery, *238*
Brash, Albanian youth union, 278, *279*
Bratislava, exhibition in, *630*
—liberation anniversary, *38*
Braun, Prof. von, and V-weapons, 124
Braun, Eva, Hitler and, *659*
Brauning, Adm., *384*
Bread, British, production, *87*
—rationed, Albania, 278
— —Portugal, 624
—rationing, reasons for, *244*
Breendonck, prison camp at, *606*
Bremen, attack on, Cameronians at, 526
—damage at, 639
—D.C.L.I. at, 206
Bren Carriers, of Cameronians, Germany, *525*
— —Egyptian, Alexandria, *757*
— —of Gloucesters, Nisper, *270*
— — —Green Howards overhaul, *620*
— —for Household Cavalry, *301*
— —on Ijssel, *676*
— —of R. Hampshires, *722*
Bren Gun, of Cameronians, Italy, *524*
Bresle, R., Black Watch on, *235*
Brest, ships escape from, 131-33
Bricks, for houses, *12*
—sorting, Berlin, *648*
Bridgend, harvest at, *384*
Bridge-layers, on Churchill tanks, 228
Bridges, of Budapest, destroyed, *18*, 19
—on Burma-Siam Rly., *347*
—destroyed, Belgrade, *565*
— —Corinth Canal, *471*
— —Vienna, *50*
—factory for, Czernowitz, 630
—reopened, Cologne, *114*
—wrecked, Berlin, *117*
Bridging Tanks, in Victory Parade, *170*
Brind, Cdre Patrick, 452
Britain, Battle of, anniversary celebrations, *399-402*
— —Bader on, 153-54, *155*
— —and invasion of Britain, 567
— —from underground, 510-11
— —Roll of Honour, *674*
Britain Can Make It Exhibition, *422-23*
British Empire, share in victory, 14
British (3rd) Division, the Ironsides, 492
British (78th) Division, war record, 460
British Legion, in E. Africa, 639
British Monarch (tanker), on fire, 795
British Zone, displaced persons in, 671
— —Norwegian troops for, *674*
— —policing frontier, *711*, *736*
— —war damage in, 543
Britten, Maj., in Burma, 442
Brno, devastation in 660
Broadlands, Mountbatten home, *53*
Broadway, jungle airstrip, 314, 316
Bromley, Maj. W., on V-weapons, 125
Brown, Dep. Chief Cyril, G.M., *127*
Brown, John & Co., built *Vanguard*, *112-13*
Brown, Capt. J. W., of H.L.I., 652
Browne, Maj. P. F. W., exploit, *16-17*
Browning, Maj.-Gen. F. A. M., 556
Bruges, Fortinbras at, 478
Brunei, war gifts, 467
Brunsrerk, Cameronians at, 524
Brunt, Capt. J. H. C., V.C., 718
Brussels, Grenadiers in, 8
—Irish Guards reach, 364
—liberation, 50th Div. and, 300
— —Household Cavalry at, 302
—today, 436-37
Bruyelle, Gloucestershire Regt. at, 267
Bucharest, in 1947, *628*, *629*
Buckingham Palace Dutch horses at, *297*
— —H.A.C. on guard, *395*
— —Naik Kamal Ram, V.C. at, *608*
Buckley, Christopher, on Cassino, 483
Buckley, Kenneth J., in Falklands, 762-64
Buckmaster, Col. Maurice, 381
Bucknall, Maj.-Gen. G. C., 36
Budalin, Gloucesters at, *270*
Budapest, bridges destroyed at, *18*
—Danube fleet returns to, *630*
—in 1946, *19*
Buffs, The, Palestine troops with, 214
— —war record, 555-58
Bugler, Marine, in *Vanguard*, *112*
Bulat Is., Commandos at, *389*
Bulbs, for Britain, from Holland, *85*
—Dutch, for miners, *514*
Bulford, H.A.C. at, 395
Bulgaria, peace treaty signed, *751-53*
—proclaims republic, *468*, *469*
Bulldozers, on Ledo Road, *59*
Bumi R., Australians cross, 707
Burden, Lt.-Col. G. W. of E. Lancs Regt., 139
Burma, Africans in, 691
—airborne troops for, 314-16
—Allied agents in, 285
—Black Watch in, 236
—Buffs in, *558*
—Cameronians in, 523
—Campaign in, Giffard and, 595
— —official account, *531*
—D.L.I. in, 430
—D. of Wellington's in, 491
—E. Lancs. in, *139*, 142
—Flying Visual Control Posts in, 699-702
—Gloucestershire Regt. in, 267, *268*, *270*
—Green Howards in, 619, *622*
—Indian Div. in, 441-42
—Inniskilling Fusiliers in, *459*
—Japs repatriated from, *262*
—jungle replica, London, *582*
—Ordnance Field Parks in, 665-667
—R.A.F. Regt. in, *78*
—R.E.s in, 713, *714*, *715*
—Recce in, *110*
—roads of, *59*
—R. Marines in, 44, *45*, 46
—R. Signals in, *332*
—Suffolks in, 779
—Worcestershires in, *685*, 686
Burma-Siam Rly., memorial to victims, 703
— — —prisoners work on, 93, 345-47
Burnett, Rear Adm. R. L. in *Belfast*, 778
— —and *Onslow*, *740*
Burrell, Maj. F. G., M.C., decorated, *685*
Burroughs, Adm. Sir Harold, *725*
Burton, Sir Geoffrey, and Mulberry, 772
Burton, Pte. R. H., V.C., 492
Busk-Wood, Capt. W. G., in *Duchess of York*, *57*, *58*
Buthidaung, Africans occupy, 691
Buxtehude, German naval H.Q. at, *590*
Buzzard, Capt. A. W., R.N., in *Glory*, 537-38
Byrnes, James F., Bevin and *438*
— —in N. York, *513*
— —in Paris, *70*, *101*, *326*
— —at Peace Conference, *303*, *306*, 313
— —on Security Council, *56*
— —signs peace treaties, 751

C

Cable & Wireless, Ltd., war service, *534*
Cables, for telephones, R. Signals lay, *333*, *334*
Cadogan, Sir Alexander, *56*

Caen, Allied armour round, *91*
—bombing south of, *89*
—British schoolboys at, *439*
—devastation in, 560-61
—today, *146*
Caernarvon, and R. Welch Fusiliers, *42*
Cailleville, Black Watch at, 238
Cairo, citadel returned to Egypt, *264*
—Household Cavalry in, 299
Caissons, for Mulberry, Marchwood, *733*
Calais, defence of, 34-36
—R. Marines at, 43
Calcutta, investiture at, *685*
Caldwell, Surg. Lt. Cdr. E. D., R.N., in *Royal Oak*, 281-82
Caldwell, Samuel, and Canterbury's stained glass, *693*
Caledon, H.M.S., Hyde in, 761
Calvert, Brig. Gen. M., in Burma, 314, 316
Camel Corps, at Amman, *215*
Camera, for aircraft, Burma, *701*
Cameron Highlanders, at Tobruk, *683*
Cameronians, war record, 523-26
Cammaerts, Emile, on Brussels today, 436
Camouflage, for aircraft, Burma, *701*
—for Irish Guards' tank, *365*
—R.E.'s and, 714
Campbell, H.M.S. and *Scharnhorst*, 132
Campbell, Sec. Ldr. Alec, G.M., *127*
Campbell, Sir Hugh, in Lisbon, 99
Campbell, Brig. Jock, V.C., 395
Campbell, Capt. Robert, raids Rommel's H.Q., 515
Campbeltown, H.M.S., at S. Nazaire, 67-68
Canadian Army (1st), Black Watch with, 236
Canadian Hussars (1st) and D.D. Tanks, 228
Canadians, free Amsterdam, 675-76
—in Normandy, 189, 190
Canarias (ship) and *Bismarck* casualties, 452
Canary, Montgomery's pet, 66
Canberra, H.M.A.S., sunk, 196
Canberra, V2 for, *706*
Canea, defence of, 580
Cang, J., on Moscow today, 596
— —on Warsaw, 500
Cannes, Messent in, 634
Canoes, British submersible, *645*
—of Solomon Islanders, war use, *563*
Canteens, mobile, from W. Indies, 755
—N A A F I., Hamburg, *424*
—Y.M.C.A., Waterloo station, *416*
Canterbury, Archbishop of, on Churchill, *321*
Canterbury Cathedral, stained glass restored, *693*
Capuzzo, Buffs take, 555
Carboni, Gen., and armistice, 100
Cardinall, Sir Alan, 762
Caribbean Sea, Mahan on, 104
Carless, Pte. F., grave, *296*
Carlisle, Horses' Rest Home at, *450*
Carpenter, Cpl. W. H., in Burma, *666*
Carrier-pigeons, memorial to, *421*
— —R. Signals use, *333*, 334
Carroceto, Grenadier Guards at, 8
—Irish Guards at, 363
Carswell, Chief Steward H. in *Empire Tide*, *27*
— —in Malta convoy, 474-76
Carton de Wiart, V.C., Gen., and Italian armistice, 99
Casey, L/Cpl. and Exeter bombs, *63*
Cassel, Gloucestershire Regt. at, 267
Cassibile, armistice signed at, 99, 100
Cassino, Black Watch at, 236
—Buffs at, 558
—capture of, 482-84
—Cyprus Regt. at, 214
—D.C.L.I. at, 203
—Grenadier Guards at, 8
—Polish cemetery at, *482*
—78th Div. at, 460
—Welsh Guards at, 748
—wireless at, 331
Castellano, Gen. G., 99, 100
Casualties, Allied, at Valetta, *55*
—**British,** N.E.I., 639
— —at S. Nazaire, 68
—**German** civilian, 223
—H.A.C., at Knightsbridge, 395
—of Irish Brigade, Italy, 462
—**Japanese,** at Guadalcanal, 196
—of Jewish Brigade, 214
Casualties *(cont.)*
—in R. Navy, 190
—of 6th Airborne, Rhine crossing, 324
—U.K. total, 179
Catacomb, camouflaged, N. Africa, *333*
Catalina, sights *Bismarck*, 451-52
—sinks last U-boat, 489
Catania, D.L.I. at, 429, 430
Catapult Launching Device, in *Empire Tide*, *27*
Catroux, Gen. Georges, *201*
Cattle, German, treatment, 115
Caumont, Cameronians at, 526
Cavan, F/M Earl of, *363*
Caves, of Dover, as shelters, *415*
Cement-Mixer, of R.E.'s, *713*
Cemetery, Allied, at Alamein, *679*
— —in Normandy, *562*
—British, Benghazi, *516*
— —in Holland, *296*
— —at Narvik, *210*
— —at Oosterbeek, *390*
—Hamme, Luxemburg, *261*
—St. Valéry, *26*
Cenotaph (London), Arnhem anniversary at, *390*
—new inscription, *518*
—Victory Parade passes, *167*, *168*
Centuripe, Buffs at, 558
—Inniskilling Fus. at, *461*, 462
Ceylon, African troops in, 691
—agricultural students from, *544*
—Hyde in, 761
—M.N.B.D.O. in, 44
—represented, Victory Parade, *134*
—share in victory, 627
—strategic importance, 83
—supplies Malaya, 789-90
war effort, 147
Ceylon Defence Force, 627
Chadwick, Sapper, and Exeter bombs, *63*
Chadwick, Brig. C. A. H., *102*
Chadwick, Sir James, 232
Chambon, Pte. Evelyn, *507*
Champion de Crespigny, Air V/M H. V., *551*
Changi, barracks as prison, 90
—liberation, 92, 93
Changing of Guard, in British Zone, *711*
Chaplain, as teacher, Germany, *551*
Chapman, Maj., in Cyprus, 412
Chapman, Cpl. E. T., V.C., 100
Charles I, statue returns to London, *65*, *80-81*
Charlton, Guardsman E., V.C., 366, *457*
Charlton, Flt. Lieut. F. F. R., over Sumatra, 789
Chase-me-Charlie, radio-controlled bomb, 638-39
Chatham, Norwegian destroyers at, *453*
—R.N. Dockyard at, 383
Cheduba Is., Marines at, 43, *45*
Cheltenham, prefabricated houses, *374*, *470*
Cherbourg, British wireless truck at, *156*
—Buffs evacuated from, 555
—Cameronians evacuated from, 526
Chertsey, ploughing match at, *448*
Chibaken Agricultural Experimental Institute, *550*
Chifley, Rt. Hon. J.B., *130*
Children, Austrian, in England, *490*
—French, in Sussex, *490*
Chilvers Coton, Church damaged, *514*
Chimney, felling, Hamburg, *454*
Chimney-sweep, helps prisoners, *350*
China, British engines for, *514*
Chindits, Black Watch with, 236
—effect on Burma Campaign, 531
—glider-borne, 314-16
—Nigerian Brigade with, 691
Chindwin R., Dagger Division crosses, 58-61
— —gliders cross, 316
— —Gloucesters cross, 270
— —R.E.'s bridge, *714*
— —R. Marines on, 44
— —Worcestershires cross, 686
Chinese, in Malaya, 339
Chin Kee On, " Malaya Upside Down," 259
Chitimukula, Chief, loyal message, 14
Chobry, H.M.T., Irish Guards in, 363
Chowne, Lt. Albert, V.C., *103*
Christian X, K. of Denmark, *359*
Christmas, at Tobruk, *253*
Christmas Card, from H.A.C., *398*
Christmas Is., Japanese occupy, 282
Chrysanthemum, H.M.S., and D.E.M.S., *246*
Churchill, Mary, at Patton's grave, *261*
Churchill, Capt. Peter Morland, 381
Churchill, Rhona, on Athens, *198*
Churchill, Rt. Hon Winston, at Alamein reunion, *486*
— —and battle of Britain, 403
— —and *Bismarck*, 451
— —and Dunkirk, 4
— —on fall of Singapore, 259
— —at Gort memorial service, *33*
— —with H. L. I., *652*
— —Holland honours, *98*
— —home life, *191*
— —and invasion of Normandy, *227*
— —and Italian armistice, 99
— —at Metz, *261*
— —and Mulberry Harbour, 771
— —on Palmyra, 299
— —and parachute troops, 547
— —on *Royal Oak*, 281
— —at Victory Parade, *175*, 179, *185*, 186
— —as Warden of Cinque Ports, *321*, *328*
Churchill-Roosevelt Club, Lido, *272-73*
Churchill Tanks, as bridge-layers, 228
— —with tank ramp, *257*
Cinema, landing craft as, *354*
Cinque Ports, Churchill as Warden, *321*, *328*
Citrine, Lord, and bulbs for miners, *514*
City of Singapore, S.S., 574
Civil Affairs Teams, in Paris, 507-09
Civil Defence, in Malta, 183
— —in Victory Parade, *168*
Civilians, German, casualties, 223
—leave Kota Bharu, *637*
Civitavecchia, flour unloaded at, *655*
Clark, Gen. Mark, at Moscow Conference, *773*
— —and Rome Victory March, 492, *493*
Clay, Maj. W. E., on Green Howards, 619-22
Clayton, R.S.M. John, in Aegean, *412*
Clémenceau, Georges, De Gaulle at grave, *201*
Clemens, Capt., with Solomon Islanders, *563*
Cleopatra, H.M.S., off Malaya, 382
Cléry, D. of Wellington's at, *491*
Cleve, D.C.L.I. at, 206
Clothing, shortage, Denmark, 532
— —Norway, 404
— —Paris, 310, *311*
Clydach, wooden houses at, *374*
Clyde, Firth of, *Iron Duke* in, *322*
Clydebank, *Vanguard* at, *32*, *112-113*
Coal, Belgian production, 436
—British shortage, *744-45*
—French production, 310
—German shortage, 511
—Norwegian shortage, 404
Coal Board, National, takes over, *664*
Coal-miners, in Victory Parade, *168*
Coal Mines, British, mechanized, *656-57*
— —State takes over, *664*
Coastal and Fishing Fleet, German, *551*
Coastal Command, and battle of Atlantic, 439
— —and *Scharnhorst*, 131-33
Cockayne, Sqd-Ldr., M. H. D., on R.A.F. Regt., 75-78
Coconuts, in Ceylon, 147
Cocos Is., secret garrison in, 282-84
Codrington, H.M.S., bombed, 126-27
Coffee, for Finland, 342, *343*
Coins, plastic, for B.A.O.R., *322*
Colban, Mme Erik, *453*
Colban, Erik, and destroyers for Norway, *453*
Colditz, Borie at, 668
Coldstream Guards, free Irish Guards, *365*
— —in Tobruk, 683
Cole, Lt. Col. Howard N., " Heraldry in War," 255
Cole, Capt. Leslie, painting by, *594*
Collar Studs, manufacture, 466
Collins, Maj. A. J. R., on 2nd Household Cavalry Regt., 300-02
Collins, Maj. P. B., in Normandy, 89-90
Colman, Hilda, at Bayeux, *560*
Cologne, Cathedral repaired, *47*
—South Bridge reopened, *114*
Colombo, air raids on, 627
—*Illustrious* at, 158
—importance, 83
—Press ship at, *534*
Colonial Office, Inquiries and Casualty Department, 319
Colonies, British, war stores, 147
Colossus, H.M.S., lent to French Navy, *293*
Colvin, Col. R. B. R., on Grenadier Guards, 7
Comacchio, L., Marines at, 46
Combat-Cargo Task Force, 531
Combe, Capt. S., of Irish Guards, 363
Combined Food Board, becomes Emergency Food Council, *244*
Combined Operations, Grenadiers in, 9
— —Marines with, 43
Comines Canal, Black Watch on, 235
Commandos, Allied, on Symi, 410-13
—Australian, raid Singapore, 387-89
—British, in Madagascar, *30*
— —at St. Nazaire, 67-68
—Fijian, 467
—memorial to, Westminster Abbey, *425*
—raid Rommel's H.Q., 515-16
—R. Marine, achievements, 44-46
— — —breach Atlantic Wall, 790-92
— — —and Sicilian invasion, 643-44
— — —at Walcheren, 250-53
—use infra-red rays, *777*
Commons, House of, rebuilding, *769*
— —and Valetta hospital, 241
Commonwealth, H.M.S., naval shore base, Japan, 609, *615*
Commonwealth Conference, in London, *130*
Communications, of Berlin, restoring, *648*
Concentration Camps, Austrian children from, *490*
Concrete, for houses, Britain, *470*
Condor, German bomber, *58*
Confectionery Shop, Belgrade, *565*
Conges, H.L.I. at, *651*
Connally, Senator, in Paris, *70*
Conolly, Adm. R. L., *487*
Control Commission, allocates reparations, 575
— —in Berlin, 115
— —civilians for, 543
Convoys, British, balloons for, *489*
—to Russia, adventures, 27-29, *739*, 740
— —*Belfast* with, *778*
— —Marines with, *45*
Cook, Lt., raids Rommel's H.Q., 516
Cook, Chief Warden, A. H., and bombing of Tower, 93-95
— —on VI on London, 348-49
Cooper, Rt. Hon. A. Duff, meets Prime Minister, *303*
— —signs peace treaties, *752*
Copenhagen, invasion anniversary, *39*
—in 1946, 532-33
—World Food Conference at, *359*
Coral Sea, battle of, 195
Corfu, channel swept, *614*
Corinth Canal, clearing, *471*
Cork and Orrery, Adm. of the Fleet, E. of, 291
Cormeilles, Allied armour in, *91*
—Black Watch at, *238*
—Highland Div's H.Q., 89, 90
Cornford, Alderman F. J., *379*, 380
Corvettes, British, in Trieste, *118*
Cos Is., D.L.I. in, 430
— —Dodecanese Is., *496-97*
— —R.A.F. Regt. in, 75
Cossack, H.M.S., and *Altmark*, *443*, 444, 445
Cotton, Uganda's production, 147
Courageous, H.M.S., sunk, 220, 291
Courrier Bay, landings at, 761
Courseulles, state-owned site, 671
—V Day at, *189*, 190
Couve de Murville, M., in N. York, *513*, *617*
— —in Paris, *70*
Coventry, makes Ferguson tractors, *706*
Coventry Cathedral, service in, 549
Cowan, Maj. Gen. D. T., *111*
Craig, Wing. Cdr. A. J. L., *265*
Creasy, Rear-Adm. G. E., R.N., *335*
Crediton, Bishop of, 46
Crete, Black Watch in, 235
—bomb fence in, *64*
—Cypriot troops in, 214
—defence of, Gwynn on, 578-580
—M.N.B.D.O. in, 43
Cripps, Rt. Hon. Sir Stafford, on Irish Brigade, 462
Crist, Capt. L. Edson, *487*
Croft, Gwen, and Mulberry Harbour, 733-34
" Cromwell," invasion code word, 567
Cross, L/Cpl., M.M., of Irish Guards, 363
Crossing Sweepers, the 15th (Scottish) Division, 142
Crosskeys, British 2nd Div., *20*
Crosslé, Maj. J. R. C., in Burma, 249-50
— —on R. Inniskilling Fusiliers, 459-62
Crouch, Lt. R. N., in *Thunderbolt*, 219-20
Crowther, K., in *Eddystone*, 572
Croziers, H.M.S., for Norway, *453*
Crystal, H.M.S., for Norway, *453*
Cully, Brig. J. J., *339*
Cummings, A. J., at **Peace** Conference, 313
Cunliffe, Capt. R. L. B., R.N., 410
Cunningham, Adm. Lord, on Bikini experiment, 232
— —in Victory Parade, *164*, *165*, *175*, 186
Cunningham, Gen. Sir Alan, Epstein's bust of, *593*
— —in Kenya, 243
Curtis, P/O C. E., in *Mauritius*, 601-03
Cuxhaven, Welsh Guards at, *750*
Cyprus, D.L.I. in, *428*
—Green Howards in, *620*
—Household Cavalry in, 299, *301*
—importance to Britain, 54
—war effort, 214
Czernowitz, bridge-making factory at, *630*

D

Dagger Arms, The, *442*
Dagger Division, in Burma, 58-61, 441-42
— —Worcestershires with, 686
Daily Telegraph, The, on Victory Parade, 174, 179
Dakotas, carry supplies, *613*
—transport Chindits, 314-16
—as transports, *633*
Dale, Capt., of Punjabis, *646*
Dalewood (collier), Willcocks in, 574
Dalrymple-Hamilton, Capt. F. H. G., R.N., 451-52
Daly, Capt. G. F. K., and Italian aqueducts, 547-48
Dances, of Dodecanese Is., *498*
Danube Canal, at Vienna, *50*, 51
Danube Fleet, Hungarian, returned, *630*
Dar-es-Salaam, Tanganyika port, 83
Darwin, Port, Japanese attacks on, 794-95
— — —graves in, *195*
Dau, Capt., of *Altmark*, 414, 443-44
Davidson, Lt. D. N., R.N.V.R., 387
Davies, Sec. Off. N. H. P., in *Tricula*, 634, 635
Davis, Capt. W. E., R.N., in *Mauritius*, 601
D-Day, British equipment exhibited, *630*
— —Holman on, 227-28
— —Recce on, 110
— —R. Signals and, 334
D.D. Tanks, on D-Day, 228
Deane-Drummond, Lt. A. J., and Italian aqueducts, 547-48
Decorations, campaign, making, *450*
—French, for British leaders, *674*
Decoy, for Krupps, 159
Deedes, Gen. Sir Charles, *308*
Defensively Equipped Merchant Ships, memorial, *246*
Dehydration, in Kenya, 147
Delhi, new Assembly at, *616*
—New, Wavell at, *213*
Demobilization, in Australia, 383
—figures, 255, 639
—Fortinbras on, 478-79
—of U.S. Navy, 415
Democracy, Askari and, 14
Demolition, in Berlin, *788*
—in Hamburg, *341*

Demolition Teams, on Normandy beaches, 228
Dempsey, Gen. Sir Miles, to 15th Div., 142
——and 53rd Div., 396
——and H.L.I. colours, *392*
——in Victory Parade, *165*
D.E.M.S., army in, 572-74
Dendre R., Grenadiers hold, 7
Denmark, German refugees in, 639
—Iceland separated from, 694
—invasion anniversary, *39*
—R.A.F. honoured in, *357*
—war memorials, *658*
Deptford, *Royal Daffodil* at, 649
Depth-charges, for sunk ships, *48-49*
Derbyshire, Lt., of K.O.Y.L.I., *308*
Derbyshire Yeomanry (2nd), with Recce, 110
Derrick, Sgt. Thomas, V.C., 708
Desert Rats, last milestone, *455*
——and liberation of Ghent, 669-70
——7th Armoured Div., 90
Desmond, Eileen, in Vichy France, 574-75
Destroyers, and Dunkirk evacuation, 2, 3-4
Detmar, Charles, trial, *230*
Deutsch Eylau, Sadgrove at, 793-94
Devonport, bell from, for New Plymouth, *514*
—*Implacable* arrives at, *208*
Devonshire, H.M.S., and *Glorious*, 292
Diadem, H.M.S., in Thames, *181*
Diamare, Abbot, of Cassino, 483
Dick, Sir W. Reid, and Roosevelt memorial, *546*
Dickin Medal, for dogs, 671
Dicks, Cmdre R. M., and Italian armistice, *99*
Didessa R., battle of, 243
Diego Suarez, captured, 31
——E. Lancs. at, 139
——*Illustrious* at, 159
——Inniskilling Fusiliers at, 459
Dieppe, Canadian memorial at, *329*
—Marine Commandos at, 44
Dilli, Japanese air-base, 794
Dimitrov, M. Georgi, *468*
Dinghies, R.A.F., in Victory Parade, *169*
Dinwoodie, Sqd.-Ldr. H., G.C., *706*
Disabled, rehabilitation, 692
Dispatch Rider, of D.C.L.I., *205*
——of R. Signals, *334*
Displaced Persons, and Black Market, 765
Divers, in Corinth Canal, *471*
Divine, A. D., on Blade Force, 611-12
——on Dunkirk, 3-4
——on Pearl Harbour, 419-20
Djebel Bou Aoukas, Irish Guards at, 363, 729
Djedeida, Blade Force at, 611
Dobson, Capt. M. G. Y., 252
Docks, of Lisbon, *623*
Dockyards, R.N., peacetime work, *383*
Dodecanese Is., British troops for, *514*
——scenes in, *495-98*
Doenitz, Adm. Karl, on naval failure, 739-40
——and Operation Sealion, 567
——sentenced, *432-33*, 435
Dogs, Dickin Medal for, 671
—as spies, Okegem, 318-19
—in Victory Parade, *168*, 190
Dominic-Browne, Brig. E., with E. Lancs. Regt., *142*
Donaldson, Capt. E. M., 386
Donbaik, Inniskilling Fus. at, 459
—Japanese at, 249
Dongas Is., Commandos at, 387, *388*
Donnedieu de Vabres, Prof., *431*
Doodle-bugs : See VI
Doric Star, S.S., *Graf Spee* and, 413
Dorling, Capt. Taprell, R.N., 489
Dornberger, Gen., and V-weapons, 124
Dornier, down in London, 153, *154*
Dorsetshire, H.M.S., and *Bismarck*, 451-52
Dortmund, railway repaired at, *102*
Dortmund-Ems Canal, Cameronians on, 526
——5th R.I.D.G. on, 590
——H.L.I. on, *653*
——reopened, *530*
Douglas, Lewis William, *738*
Douglas, Marshal of R.A.F., Sir Sholto, and Allied Control Council, *258*
Douglas *(cont.)*
——in Berlin, *197*
——in British Zone, *551*
——C.-in-C., B.A.O.R., *66*
——on No. 117 Squadron, 410
Dover, Churchill at, *321*, *328*
—Dunkirk men at, *2*
—Fire Brigade's exploits, 126-27
—jams German radar, *710*
—last month of bombardment, 414-15
Dowding, Air C/M Lord, and battle of Britain anniversary, *401*
——at Bentley Priory, 511
——dispatch, 403
Dowell, Fireman, death, 415
Dower, Gandar, on African Askari, 275
Dragoon Guards (4/7th), and D.D. tanks, 228
——(5th), amalgamate with Inniskilling Dragoons, 587
Driel, Polish parachutists at, 219
Drierwagen, Cameronians take, 524
Drierwalde, Cameronians take, 526
Dring, W., paintings by, *593*, *594*
Drum Major, Indian, in Tokyo, *193*
Drums, of R. Scots, *647*
—of Suffolks, restored, *782*
Dryad, H.M.S., Naval Room, *335*
Duchess of York, S.S., sinking of, 57-58
" **Ducks,**" ammunition thrown from, *102*
—carry Japanese ammunition, *242*
—in Normandy landings, 228
—in Victory Parade, *169*
Duke, Flt.-Lieut. R. W. E., in Arakan, 699, *700*, 702
Duke of Cornwall's L.I., war record, 203-06
Duke of Wellington's Regt., war record, 491-94
Duke of York Column, London, *80*
Dunbar-Nasmith, Adm. Sir Martin, V.C., *246*
Dunera, H.M.T., Inniskilling Fus. in, 461
Dunkerley, Lt.-Col. A. J., *137*
Dunkirk, Black Watch at, 235, *236*, 238
—Buffs at, 555
—Cameronians at, 523
—capture, " Dukes " at, *494*
—Cypriot muleteers at, 214
—D.C.L.I. at, 203
—D.L.I. at, 427
—E. Lancs. and, 139
—Gloucestershire Regt. at, 267
—evacuation, *473*
—50th Div. at, 300
—5th R. Inniskilling D.G.s at, 587
—H.L.I. at, 651
—Inniskilling Fusiliers at, 459
—a planned miracle, 2-4
—port reopened, *338*
—retreat to, Suffolks in, 779
——Tewson on, 697-98
—R. Signals at, 154-57
—Worcestershires at, 686
Dunkirk, Treaty of, *741*
Dunn, Capt. Edwin, at Walcheren, 252
Dunn, James, in Paris, *70*
Duns, Poles at, *545*
Dupont, Capt. R. J. M., drawing by, *441*
Durban, *Illustrious* at, 159
Durban Castle, S.S., as transport, 643
Durham Light Infantry, war record, 427-30
Durrant, Sgt. Tom, V.C., 68
Düsseldorf, travel office, *530*
Dust, in Burma, 665
Dyes, Ceylon makes, 147
Dyle R., D.L.I. on, 427
——Grenadiers defend, 7

E

Eagle Squadron, *403*
Eardley, Sgt. G. H., V.C., 100
Earl Haig's Appeal Fund, poppies for, *450*, 479
Easonsmith, Maj. Jake, 604
East Africans, in Burma, 691
——First Battles, 275
East African Scouts, 275
East Anglian District, new badge, *521*
Eastern Fleet, *Illustrious* with, 157-59
East Kent Regt. R. : see Buffs
East Lancashire Regt., in Madagascar, 31
————war record, 139-42
East River (N.Y.), Lancasters cross, *265*
East Surrey Regt., in Tunisia, 612
E-boats, *Grenville* rams, 570-72
Eccles, Lt.-Col. T. A., of E. Lancs. Regt., 142
Echt, H.L.I. at, *653*
Echternach, Allies hold, 372
Eddystone, S.S., Willcocks in, 572-73
Ede, " Dukes " at, *494*
Edelbach, Bòrie at, 668
Edelsten, Vice-Adm., in *Anson*, 320
Edmonton, new houses in, *12*
Education, in British Zone, 511
" Egg-crates," sea-mine-detonating craft, 674
Egret, H.M.S., sunk, *638*, 639
Egypt, British evacuation, *264*, *757*
—defence of, D.C.L.I. and, 203
Eighth Army, at Alamein, *571*
——at Cassino, 483-84
——H.A.C. with, 396, *397*
——Household Cavalry with, 299
——Inniskilling Fusiliers with, 459
Eindhoven, Guards Armoured Division at, *10*
—welcomes B.L.A., 217
Eisenbeck, Gen., helps with harvest, *384*
Eisenhower, Gen. Dwight D., and *Dryad's* map, *335*
——and Italian armistice, 100
——report, synopsis, 211
——Victory message, 174
——visits Tower, 348
——welcomes Montgomery, *385*
Elbe, R., frozen, *716*
Electric Cleaners, by bomb-rack machinery, *465*
Electricity, rationed, Rome, 786
Electric Power, in Iceland, 694
Elephants, on Ledo Road, *59*
—at Moulmein pagoda, *271*
Elias, D. M., on Ledo Road, 765
Elizabeth, Queen, statue, *600*
Elizabeth, H.M. Queen, and Dutch horses, *297*
——and Lt. R. G. Walker, 62, 63
——at opening of Parliament, 519
——in Thames pageant, 188
——and Victory Parade, *162*, 174, *175*, *179*, 185
Elizabeth, H.R.H. Princess, and Grenadier Guards, 7, *10*
——launches *Vanguard*, 113
——on Remembrance Day, 518
——in Thames pageant, 188
——at Victory Parade, *162*, 174, *175*, *179*, 186
Elms, Gordon, of R. Sussex Regt., 698
Elst, B.L.A. welcomed by, 217
Elsterhorst, hospital at, *27*
Eluard, French poet, 310
Emborio, village of Niceros, *498*
Emden (ship), sunk in N. Keeling Is., 284
Emergency Food Council, International, 244
Empire Baltic, Landing Ship Tank, *418*
Empire Day, in Tokyo, *193*, *207*
Empire Ridley, S.S., salvages Pluto, *407*
Empire Tide, S.S., in Archangel convoy, *27*
Ems R., Cameronians cross, *525*, 526
Enckell, M. Karl, at Peace Conference, *327*
——signs peace treaty, *753*
Enfidaville, 50th Div. at, 300
Engineers, Indian, in Cocos Is., *283*
—Royal, Berlin demolition, *788*
——in Hamburg, *454*
——in Malaya and Siam, *263*
——and mine clearance, 254-55
——in Normandy landings, 228
——rebuild Cologne bridge, *114*
——war record, 713-17
——Canadian at Wilhelmshaven, *255*
England, Sgt.-Maj. J. P., 253
Englishcombe, Montgomery's flag at, *743*
Enkereind, Buffs decorated at, *556*
Enterprise, U.S.S., at Midway, 195
Epstein, Jacob, busts by, *593*
Erbie, Montgomery's canary, 66
Erdely, Eugène, on Prague, 660
Erebus, H.M.S., off Sicily, 601-03
——at Walcheren, 46, 250
Eros, statue, Caen, *561*
Ervine-Andrews, Capt. H. M., V.C., 139
Escaut R., Buffs on, 555
Esja, mountains, Iceland, 694
Esmonde, Lt.-Cdr. E., and *Bismarck*, 451-52
——and *Scharnhorst*, 132, 133
Essential Service Labour Corps, in Ceylon, 627
Esserden, Black Watch take, 238
Estoril, Casino at, *625*
Ethiopians, for Victory Parade, *135*
Evacuation, of Kota Bharu, *637*
Evans, Lieut., of D. of Wellington's, 494
Evans, Pte. Albert, H.L.I., 654
Evans, Maj.-Gen. G. C., 684
Evatt, Rt. Hon. Dr. H. V., at Commonwealth Conference, *130*
——at Peace Conference, *306*, *313*, *326*
Evzones, on Independence Day, *1*
—in Victory Parade, *166*, 186
Exeter, H.M.S., *40*
Exeter, unexploded bombs at, *62-63*
Exmouth (training ship), now *Worcester*, *687-90*
Exports, British, increase, *226*

F

Factories, Russian, change over, 671
Fairchild C-82, troop carrier, *325*
Falaise, reconstruction in, *143*
Falaise Gap, Recce in, 110
Falestoh, Worcestershires at, 683
Falkland Islands, strategic importance, 104
——in wartime, 762-64
Falls, A/B B. A., with Commandos, 387-88
Falmouth, *Thrasher* at, *73*
Famagusta, harbour improved, 214
Fancourt, Maj. G. V., at Nijmegen, 494
Far East, R. Signals in, 334
Fareham, *Dryad* at, *335*
Farnborough, aircraft tested at, *13*
Faroe Is., R. Marines occupy, 43
Farrandock (collier), Willcocks in, 574
Faviell, Lt.-Col., D.S.O., 348
Fawzi Bey, Household Cavalry and, 299
Federated Malay Straits, history, 339
Feisal, K. of Iraq, at Victory Parade, *175*, 179, 186
Fenwick, F/O C., in *Empire Tide*, *27*
Ferguson Tractors, manufacture, 706
Festing, Maj.-Gen. F. E., and Japan Occupation Troops, *111*
——and 36th Div., 186
F.F.I., and liberation of Paris, 507-09
Fierlinger, Dr., on liberation anniversary, *38*
Fifth Column, in Calais, 35
——in Malaya, 339
Fifth Division, British, war record, 36
Figgess, Lt.-Col. G., receives drum, *647*
Fighter Command, Bentley Priory H.Q., *510*
——and *Scharnhorst*, 132
Fiji, share in victory, 467
—strategic importance, 83
Filgate, Lt.-Col., O.B.E., 742
Films, in Prague, 660
Findly, Brig. C. M., on W. Africans, 691
Finland, peace treaty signed, *751-53*
Finschhafen, Australians at, 707, *708*
Fireworks, on V Night, *178*, *188*
First Army, British, in Tunisia, 610-12
Fish, Iceland exports, 694
Fisher, Capt., and Dunkirk evacuation, 3
Fish Meal, preparation, *503*
FitzGerald, Maj. D. J. L., on Irish Guards, 363-66, 729-31
Flags, for signalling, Cyprus, *620*
—for Victory Day, *136*
Flail Tanks, in Victory Parade, *170*
Fleet Air Arm, R. Marines with, 43
———at Trincomalee, 157
Flemish National Movement, 604
Fléri, Cameronians in, *524*
Flood Lighting, on Victory Day, *136*, *172*
Flores, (sloop), off Sicily, 602
Floridia, Cameronians take, 523
Flour, for Italy, *655*
Flower, Capt. Dick, at Walcheren, 252
Flowers, for sale, Helsinki, *342*
Flushing, Commandos take, 252
Flying Bombs : *see* VI
Fly-past, at Victory Parade, 179, *180*, 185
——Victory Parade seen from, *171*
Folkestone, 5th R. Inniskilling D.Gs. at, *587*
Fondouk, Welsh Guards at, 748
Fontaine Etoupefour, D.C.L.I. take, 203
Fonthill Gifford, Irish Guards at, *363*
Food, shortage, Brussels, 436
——Paris, 310
—world shortage, *87*
Food & Agriculture Organization, of U.N., *359*
Food Coupons, Belgian, *606*
Foot, Rt. Hon. Isaac, and bell for New Plymouth, *514*
Football, for British P.O.W, *477*
Foote, Maj. J. W., V.C., *457*
Footwear, for British zone, 639
Forbes, Adm. of the Fleet Sir Charles, 291
Force 133, in Aegean, 410-13
Ford, Capt. C. M., of *Queen Elizabeth*, *770*
Foreign Legion, Household Cavalry and, 299
Foreign Ministers, in N. York, *513*, *617*
——in Moscow, *773*
——Paris Conference, *70*
Forests, of Finland, wealth, 342
Forman, Pte., of Worcestershire Regt., *686*
Formidable, H.M.S., suicide plane on, *766*
Formosa, British prisoners in, 446
Forrest, Maj. A., on V-weapon factory, 124-26
Fort Garry Horse, 228
Forth, H.M.S., and *Thunderbolt*, 219, 220
Fortinbras, John, at Bad Harzburg, 698-99
——on Berlin's Black Market, 764-65
——demobilized, 478-79
——on Lidice, *355*
——on Operation Clean-up, 254-55
Fourteenth Army, No. 20 Squadron with, 317
Foxholes, of Twin Knobs, 249-50
Fox-Pitt, Brig. W. A. F. L., 747
Fraiteur, Col. de, *738*
France, Buffs in, *555*
—collapse, and Singapore, 259
—Commemoration Day, *201*
—" Dukes " in, *492*
—fall of, and Britain's Life-Line, 54
—H.L.I. in, *651*, 654
—memorial stones in, *406*
—Recce welcomed in, *109*
—S., parachute troops in, 633-34
—Worcestershires in, 684, *686*
Franco-British Society, and public schools, *439*
Frank, Hans, sentenced, *432-33*, 435
Frank, Dr. Karl Hermann, trial and death, *355*
Frankfort, Nazi loot at, *680*
Franklin Delano Roosevelt, U.S.S., *322*
Franklyn, Lt.-Gen. Sir H. E., and D.L.I., 427
——and 5th Division, 36
Franz Josef I, monument, Vienna, *50*
Freetown, W. African port, 104
French, Narvik memorial to, *425*
French, Sgt. J., of E. Lancs. Regt., 139
Freyberg, Gen. Sir Bernard, V.C., Buffs with, 558
——on Cassino, 484
——in Crete, 579-80
——in Trieste, 118
Frick, Wilhelm, sentenced, *432-433*, *434*, 435
Fritzsche, Hans, acquitted, *432-433*, *434*, 435
Frog Men, British, at S. Ives, *225*
——R. Marines with, 46
Fuel, shortage, Budapest, 19
——Paris, 310
Fuel Crisis, in G. Britain, *744-45*
Fulton, Sgt. Taylor, and Himmler's secrets, 539-41
Funk, Walter, sentenced, *432-33*, *434*, 435
Furious, H.M.S., *106*
Furnes, British withdrawal from, 473-74
Furness, Lt. the Hon. C., V.C., *103*, 747
Fusiliers, R., H. A C. with, 395
Fyfe, Hamilton, on " In Darkest Germany," 783

G

Gabain, Ethel, painting by, *594*
Gale, Maj.-Gen. R. N., 602
Galileo Galilei (submarine), *Moonstone* and, 330
Gallaghan, Pte. W., H.L.I., *654*
Gallagher, Pte. D., B.E.M., 456
Gambia, W. African territory, 243
Gander, L. Marsland, on Cassino, 483-84
——on liberation of Amsterdam, 675-76

Gander *(cont.)*
——on Rhine Crossing, 323-24
——on Victory Parade, 174, 179, 186
Gander Airfield, Lancasters at, *265*
Gangelt, 5th R.I.D.G. at, *590*
Gardens, as war memorials, *105*
Gardiner, Lieut., D.L.I., Catania surrenders to, 430
Gardiner, Col. W. T., in Rome, 100
Gardner, Charles, on Campaign in Burma, 531
Gareloch, Mulberry parts at, *733*, *771*
—R.E.s make, 717
Garigliano, R., Cameronians on, 523
——Grenadier Guards at, 8
——Inniskilling Fusiliers at, 460
Garland (destroyer), rescues Heinson, *121*
Garngoch Colliery, Nationalization, 664
Gasperi, Alcide de, presents Italy's case, *327*
Gatow, Berlin suburb, *681*
—Montgomery at, *66*
—Sir S. Douglas at, *66*
Gatwick, Sir S. Douglas at, 66
Gaulle, Gen. Charles De, on Commemoration Day, *201*
——at Ile de Seine, *360*
Gay, M. Francisque, *71*
Gazala, D.L.I. at, 428
Gazala Line, Green Howards in, 619, 620
Gee, Pte. J., H.L.I., *654*
Geilenkirchen, Cameronians at, 524, 526
—D.C.L.I. at, *205*
Geldern, E. Lancs at, 142
Gemas, fighting at, 259
Genese, Maj. C. C. S., of E. Lancs, 139
Geneva Convention, and prisoners' work, 671
George III, statue returns to London, *80-81*
George VI, H.M. King, birthday celebrations, Kiel, *398*
——with Black Watch, 236, *237*
——and Britain Can Make It, 422, 423
——with Cameronians, *523*
——at Cenotaph, *518*
——and Dutch horses, 297, 450
——and Lt. R. G. Walker, 62, 63
——opens Parliament, 519
——and Stoker Piggott, 220
——in Thames pageant, 188
——Victory Day message, *136*
——and Victory Parade, *162*, 174, *175*, *179*, 185
George, K. of Greece, at Victory Parade, *175*
George Cross, for Malta, 183
George Medals, winning the first, 126-27
Georgiev, Col Kimon, Bulgarian premier, *468*
Gerbrandy, Prof. P. S., on The Hague, *148*
Gerlach, Herr, in the Tower, 95
Germany, British and U.S. zones merged, 479, 585
—British zones in, *197*, *551*
—coal shortage in, 511
—failure at sea, 739-40
—Finland sides with, 342
—food for British zone, 479
—Irish Guards in, *365*, 366
—peace treaty discussions, *773*
—relief for British zone, 575
—reparations for Britain, *600*
German Zonal Search Bureau, 543
Gestapo, in Belgium, 604-06
—French, members tried, *230*
—Goering founds, 499
—in Walcheren, 542-43
Ghent, 5th R. Inniskilling D.Gs. in, 587
—H.L.I. at, 654
—liberation, 669-70
Ghilks, Ldg.-Fmn., at Dover, 415
Gibraltar, Black Watch in, *236*
—importance to Britain, 54, *55*
—Suffolk Regt. in, *781*
—at war, 183
Gibraltar Defence Force, *134*
Gibson, Sir J. W., and Mulberry, 772
Giel, tragedy at, 254
Giffard, Gen. Sir George, claim to fame, *595*
Gilbert and Ellice Islands, 563
Gillard, Frank, at Eindhoven, 217
Gipsies, Rumanian, *628*
Giraud, Gen. H. H., and D.C.L.I., *203*
——meets Churchill, Metz, *261*
Givath Saul, troops search, *520*
Gizo, bombed, Kennedy and, 563
Glasgow, locomotive works, 226
Glasgow Highlanders (1st) H.L.I. Territorials, 651, 652, *653*
Glencorse, R. Scots' depot, 647
Gliders, dump, Arnhem, *358*
Glières, Plâteau des, Maquis at, *71*
Gloire (cruiser), and *Laconia*, *734*, *735*
Glorious, H.M.S., sunk, 131, 291-92
Glory, H.M.S., repatriates prisoners, 537-38
Gloucester, H.R.H. Duke of, 267
Gloucestershire Regt., war record, 267-70
——(5th) and Recce, 107
Glowworm, H.M.S., and *Hipper*, 194
——last fight, German photos, *678*
Glubb, Brig. J. B., in Trans-Jordan, 214
Gneisenau, escape, 131-33
—and *Glorious*, 291-92
—as raider, 451
Goats, and atom bomb test, *233*
—in Japan, *290*
—of Malta, killed, 183
—of R. Lincolnshire Regt., *722*
—R.W.F. mascot, *42*, *101*, *581*
Gobyin Chaung, Gloucesters at, 270
Goch, Black Watch at, 238
Godliman, Sub-Conductor F.W., M.B.E., 456
Goering, F/M Hermann, bullet-proof car, 582
——and Operation Sealion, 567
——sentenced, *432-33*, *434*, 435
——Sutherland on, *499*
Gogni, Worcestershires at, 683
Gold Coast, war effort, 147
——W. African territory, 243
Gold Coast Regt., story, 243
Gollancz, Victor, "In Darkest Germany," 783
Gombault, Georges, on Paris, 310
Gona, Japanese land at, 196
Gondar, capture, E. Africans at, 275
Gooch, Maj. R. E. S., in Western Desert, *300*
Goods Wagons, German, repaired, 223
Gooseberries, artificial harbours, 228, *772*
Gordon, Capt. C. G. M., on 1st Household Cavalry Regt., 299-300
Gordon, J. C., on Bucharest, *628*
Gordon-Bennett, Maj.-Gen., in Singapore, 259-60
Gorman, Lt., M.C., in Normandy, 364
Gort, F/M Viscount, V.C., and Dunkirk, 3.
——funeral, *11*
——liaison officer with, 697-98
——on Malta's goats, 183
——memorial service to, *33*
Gort Line, construction, 7, 9
Gothic Line, Cypriots in, 214
——H.A.C. in, 395
——Household Cavalry in, 300.
Goubellat Plain, Inniskilling Fus. on, 462
Gouin, Félix, on Commemoration Day, *201*
Gould, P/O T., V.C., 73
Gourlie, Norah, on Reykjavik, 694
Gourock, *Sobieski* at, 492
Grand Canal, British Military police on, *288*
Grapes, harvest, Luxemburg, *372*
Graph, H.M.S., formerly *U.570*, *489*
Grave, Guards Armoured Div. in, *217*
Gravel Pits, prisoners work in, 670-71
Gravely, Col. T. B., on Royal Signals, 331-34
——on Signals at Dunkirk, 154-57
Graves, British, at Narvik, *210*
——in Netherlands, 296
—Japanese, Darwin, *195*
—of Patton, Hamme, *261*
—of prisoners, Burma-Siam Rly., *346*
—in Tokyo, *290*
Graves, Charles, The Thin Red Lines, 534
Gray, Lt. R. H., R.C.N., V.C., *457*
Grazebrook, Lt.-Col. R. M., on Gloucestershire Regt., 267-70
Great Britain, bread for, *87*
——change-over in, *463-66*
——Dutch gratitude to, *85*
——exports rise, *226*
——fuel crisis in, *744-45*
——German reparations for, *600*
——Hitler plans invasion, 567
——imported meat for, *309*
——Life-Line in Middle East, 54
——in Malaya, 339
Great Britain *(contd.)*
——milk supply, *375*
——rations bread, 244
——trade exhibition, *422-23*
Great Eastern Tank Ramp, *257*
Greece, Buffs in, 558
—Cypriot troops in, 214
—evacuation, Crete and, 579
—Independence Day in, *1*
—the Isles of, *495-98*
—present condition, 198
—in Victory Parade, *166*
Greenhithe, *Worcester* at, *687-690*
Green Howards, war record, 619-22
Greenwell, R.S.M., of H.L.I., *392*
Greenwich, concrete houses at, *470*
Gregory, Bernard, in Normandy, 190
Gregson-Ellis, Maj.-Gen., P. G. S., 36, 697
Grenadier Guards, at Dunkirk, 473-74
——at Louvain, 302
——war record, 7
Grenville, H.M.S., off Anzio, 570-72
——and Kamikaze pilots, 766-767
——and radio-controlled bomb, 638-39
Griffin, Maj. C. W., of E. Lancs. Regt., 139
Griffin, Murray, paintings, *754*
Griffin, Vice-Adm. Robert H., *52*
Griffith, Second Engineer, in *Empire Tide*, 28
Griffiths, Brig. F. A. V. Copland, 747-48
Grigg, Rt. Hon. Sir James, on Sir G. Giffard, *595*
Grimblemont, E. Lancs. take, 140
Grineau, Bryan de, drawing by, *16-17*
Grogan, Brig. Gen. G. W. St. G., V.C., *684*
Gromyko, Andrei, walks out, *56*
Groza, Petru, Rumanian premier, 629
Grundy, Black Watch mascot, *236*
G.S. Walden (M.V.) adventure, 606-07
Guadalcanal, Clemens in, *563*
—fight for, 196
—Fijians in, 467
Guard, Changing of, Hamburg, *110*
Guards Armoured Division, and Arnhem operations, *217*, 218-19
———formation, 7, *10*
———Household Cavalry with, 300, 302
———Irish Guards in, 363, 364
———in Normandy, 8
———war record, 524
———Welsh Guards with, 747
Guards' Chapel, bombed, 348
Gubbio, Household Cavalry at, 299
Guiana, British, bauxite from, 147
Guinea, French, wrecked seamen in, 223
Gulzar, H.M.S., bombed, 127
Gundel, Sgt., of Irish Guards 364
Guns, Allied, by air, *325*
—**British**, at Alamein, *569*
——in Falklands, *762*
——R.M. clean, *45*
——25-pdr., Knightsbridge, 397
—redundant, at Park Royal, *37*
—**U.S.**, T-28, *480*
Gurkhas, in Burma, 441-42
—at Cassino, 483, 484
—at Medicina, 16
—in Victory Parade, *129*, 186
Gusev, M., at Moscow Conference, *773*
Gustav Line, Cassino and, 483-84
——D.C.L.I. at, 203
Guthrie, Robin, portrait by, *595*
Gwynn, Maj.-Gen. Sir Charles, on defence of Crete, 579-80
Gyongyossi, M., at Peace Conference, *327*
——signs peace treaty, *753*

H

H 49, Piggott in, 219, 220
Haakon VII, K., and French memorial, Narvik, *425*
——and Green Howards, 622
Habo Patrol, 131-33
Hacohen, David, released, *520*
Haecht, Suffolk's drums at, *782*
Haenigsen, explosion at, *197*
Hagana, terrorist activities, *215*
Hagen, shelter as store, *197*
Hague, The, Churchill in, *98*
——today, 148, *149*
Haifa, *San Dimitrio* at, *520*
Haile Selassie, Emp., 243
Halsey, Adm., U.S.N., at Guadalcanal, 196
——in S. Pacific, 195
Halsey, Adm. Sir William, on Trafalgar Day, *481*
Hamburg, damage at, 639
—E. Lancs. and, *140*, 142
—Elbe frozen at, *716*
—5th R.I.D.G. at, 590
—housing problem in, *551*
—N.A.A.F.I. gift shop, *102*, *424*
—and Nuremberg trials, *454*
—Recce in, *110*
—reconstruction in, *341*
—U-boats scuttled, *354*
Hamilton, Lt.-Col. C. D., D.S.O., 494
Hamilton, Gen. Sir Ian, *738*
Haminkeln, 6th Air Landing Brigade at, 324
Hamm, British raids on, 223
Hammah, El, H.A.C. at, 395
Hammamet, Irish Guards at, *364*
Hamme, cemetery, *261*
Hammerton, Sir John, farewell to readers, 796
Hammocks, in Trafalgar Sq., *173*
Hampshire Regt., now Royal, 718, *722*
———in Tunisia, *611*, *612*
Hann, Capt. D., and Italian armistice, 99
Hannibal, and Cassino, 483
Hanno, and W. Africa, 243
Hara-kiri, knife for, *151*
Harar, Africans in, 243
Harding, Lt.-Gen. Sir John, in Trieste, 118
Harding, Lt.-Col. R. P., and 5th R. Inniskilling D. Gs., 587-90
Hare-Scott, Kenneth, on Australians at Sattelberg, 707-08
——on Berlin, 115
——on Rommel's H.Q., 515-16
Harmer, Chief-Off. Ernest, G.M., *127*
Harper, Cpl. J. W., V.C., 268
Harper, Coder S. D., on Japanese surrender, 381-83
Harriman, Averill, at Peace Conference, *306*, *313*
Harris, Marshal of R.A.F. Sir Arthur, "Bomber Offensive," 724
——private life, *119*
Harris, Rev. S. B., as teacher, *551*
Harrow School, Worcestershires at, *684*
Hart, Brig.-Gen. Franklin A., in Victory Parade, *164*
Hart, Sqd.-Ldr. Leonard, in Burma, 314-16
Hart Force, in Tunisia, 612
Hartington, Marchioness of, Portal and, *535*
Hartley, A. C., and Pluto, 407
Harvest, British, Germans and, *384*
—Gloucesters help with, 269
Harvey, Maj.-Gen. C. O., and 8th (Indian) Div., 717
Harvey, Capt. Frank Willis, in *Empire Tide*, *27*, 28
Harvey, Group-Capt. L. G., 547
Harwood, Commodore H. H., R.N., in *Exeter*, 40
Harz Mts., underground factory in, *124-26*
Hastings, transport plane, *386*
Hatton, Sgt. C., of E. Lancs Regt., 139
Hat Trick, in P.O.W. Camp, 349-50
Havay, U.S. memorial, *406*
Havel, L., Berlin, *681*
Haverman, Mrs. Margaret, in Walcheren, 542-43
Havert, Cameronians near, *525*
Havre, Le, Black Watch at, 235, 238
—capture, H.A.C. at, *398*
—Gloucestershire Regt. at, 267
—U.S. memorial at, *425*
Hawkesworth, Lt.-Gen., funeral, *781*
Haydon, Capt. Peter, at Walcheren, 252
Headlines, history in, 22, *69*
Hedgehog, anti-submarine, weapon, 489
Heinson, Seaman Harry, adventure, *121*
Helmet, for street musician, *116*
Helmstedt, zone frontier at, *711*, *736*
Helsinki, in 1946, *342*, *343*
Henderson, Capt. I. A., in Western Desert, *300*
Henin-Liétard, Black Watch H.Q., *235*
Herakles, S.S., with coffee for Finland, 342
Heraklion, airstrip at, 579
—Black Watch at, 235
—bombed, *578*, 580
Heraldry in War, 255
Herbert, Lt. J., R.N.V.R., in *Grenville*, 570-72, 638-39
——on Kamikaze planes, 766-67
Hereward, H.M.S., and *Bonaventure*, *350*, 351
Hermanville, Allied cemetery at, *562*
Hero, H.M.S., and *Medway*, 220, 221
Herring, from drifter to table, *502*, *503*
Hertogenbosch, E. Lancs at 139, *140*
—5th R.I.D.G. at, 588, 590
—Recce at, *109*
Hess, Rudolf, sentenced, *432-33*, 435
——in Tower, 95
Hewitt, Adm. H. K., and 12th U.S.N. Squadron, *322*
——in Victory Parade, *164*
Hewlett, Frank, in Santo Tomas, 124
Heydrich, Reinhard, death, 355
Hickinbotham, Inspector H., *514*
High Commission Territories, war service, 307
Highland Division (51st) at Alamein, 569-70
——Black Watch with, 235
——at S. Valéry-en-Caux, *248*
——war record, 332
Highland L. I., in Cairo, *264*
——new colours for, *392*
——war record, 651-54
Highway Six, Monte Cassino and, 483, 484
Hilary, H.M.S., Holman in 227-28
——Vian in, 643
Hill 122 (Normandy), today, *560-61*
Hill 212, Irish Guards' memorial, 729
Hillebrand, Dutch patriot, 542-543
Hillingdon, "shutter" houses at, *470*
Himalaya Mts., supplies for outposts, 613
Himmler, Heinrich, secrets discovered, 539-41
——treachery, Hitler and, 659
Hirohito, as democratic monarch, *550*
Hiroshima, casualties, 127
—devastation at, *274*
Hitler, Adolf, Goering joins, 499
——and invasion of Britain, 567
——and Italy, 99
——and Lidice, 355
——and naval failure, 739-40
——new light on, 659
——planned victory monument, *425*
——and Prien, *282*
——and surface raiders, 452
Hoare, Sir Samuel, 99
Hobart, Maj.-Gen., P. C. S., 90
Hochheid, D.C.L.I. take, 206
Hodgson, Col. W. R., on Security Council, *56*
Hoey, Maj. Charles, V.C., 718
Hogue, La, bombed, 89
Holborn, *Indefatigable's* ensign for, *418*
Holidays, in Czechoslovakia, 660
—public, for B.C.O.F., 415
Holland: see Netherlands
Holland, Vice-Adm. L. E., 451
Hollis, Capt. Mark, of H.L.I., 651
Hollis, Sgt.-Maj. S. E., V.C., 622
Holman, Gordon, on invasion of Normandy, 227-28
Holt, Lt.-Col. A. V., on Black Watch, 235-38
Homburg, frontier sign at, *630*
Home Fleet, British, autumn exercises, *517*
Home Guard, Cypriot, 214
——and Green Howards, 622
——Maltese, 183
Home Market, British, workers for, 543
Hongkong, Japan Occupation Troops at, *111*
—prison camp in, *15*
—R. Marines in, 44
—share in victory, 467
—war production, 147
Honour, Roll of, *88*, *120*, *152*, *185*, *216*, *247*, *280*, *312*, *344*, *376*, *408*, *440*, *472*, *504*, *536*, *568*, *598-99*, *632*, *662-63*, *696*, *726-27*, *760*, *784-85*
Honourable Artillery Company, war record, 395-98
Hood, H.M.S., sunk, 451, 452
Hopsten, Cameronians at, 526
Horlington, Brig., in Alexandria, *757*
Hornet, U.S.S., at Midway, 195
Horrocks, Gen. Sir Brian G., and Worcestershire Regt., *684*
Horsa Gliders, for Rhine crossing, 323, *324*
Horses, Holland's gift of, 297 *450*

Horton, Adm. Sir Max, 220
Hoschrid Wood, Cameronians in, 524
Hospital, air-raid shelter as, Berlin, *116*
—for children, Helsinki, 342, *343*
—Grenadiers in, 7
Hotels, for B.C.O.F., Japan, 575
Hot Springs, in Iceland, 694
Hotspur, H.M.S., 74
Hotton, Black Watch at, *238*
Hounslow, Army Mechanical Demonstration Column at, *417*
Household Cavalry, at Arnhem, 219
——Dutch horses for, *297*, *450*
——in Victory Parade, *162*
——war record, 299-302
Houses, aluminium, erection, *584*
—new British types, *374*
Housey Housey, Inniskillings play, *459*
Housing, Berlin problem, *648*
—in Britain, *12*, *374*, *470*
—Bucharest difficulties, 628
—Norwegian shortage, 404
—Paris shortage, 310
—Poplar's effort, *84*
Rome's problem, 786
Hoven, D.C.L.I. at, 206
Howe, H.M.S., recruits in, *393*
Hoxha, Gen. Enver, *279*
Hughes, Chief Engineer, in *Empire Tide*, 28
Hughes, Third Butcher, in *Duchess of York*, 57
Hull, Cordell, and Pearl Harbour, 419, 420
Hull, Maj.-Gen. R. A., and 5th Division, 36
Hume, Peter, on fall of Singapore, 259-60
Hungary, peace treaty signed, *751-53*
Hunt, Air Cdre. A. W., 282
Hunter, Cpl. Tom, V.C., memorial to, *46*
Huntly, Marquis and Marchioness of, 248
Hunton, Gen. Sir Thomas, Commandent-Gen., R.M., *43*
Huntsman, S.S., *Graf Spee* and, 414, 443
Hurribombers, in Burma, 700, *701*, 702
Hurricane, speed, Dowding on, 403
Hussars (13/18th), and D.D. tanks, 228
Hussey, Lt.-Cdr. W. F. C., D.S.C., R.N., 725
Huston, A/B A. W., with Commandos, 387-88
Huxley, Dr. Julian, Director-General of U.N.E.S.C.O., *566*
Huysmanns, Camille, Belgian statesman, 436
Hyde, M. C., in *Illustrious*, 157-59
——in Indian Ocean, 761-62
——off Salerno, 409-10
Hynde, H., and Col de Fraiteur, *738*

I

I Brahim, Gen. Abdul Azim, *757*
Ibu, Fijians at, 467
Iceland, 49th Div. in, 268
—joins U.N., *617*
—Reykjavik the capital, *694-95*
Ide, Capt. John, U.S.N., *335*
Identity Card, examined, Teheran, *719*
Ijssel, R., Bren carriers on, *676*
Illingworth, Frank, on first George medals, 126-27
——on Dover's ordeal, 414-15
Illustrious, H.M.S., bell exhibited, *630*
——off Madagascar, 761-62
——in Pacific, 157-59
——off Salerno, 409-10
——war record, *488*
Imperial Guards (Japanese), in Singapore, 259
Imphal, epic of, 531
—R.A.F. Regt. at, 76
—Recce at, 110
Imphal-Tamu Road, *59*
Implacable, H.M.S., at Devonport, *208*
——to be broken up, 677
——at Sydney, 72
Incontro Monastery, D.C.L.I. take, 203, *204*
"In Darkest Germany," 783
Indefatigable, H.M.S., ensign for Holborn, *418*
Independence (carrier), atom bomb and, 232, *233*
India, British exports to, 226
—Buffs in, 558
—new assembly meets, *616*
—R.E.s in, 715
India *(contd.)*
—Victory Parade detachment, *161*
Indianapolis, U.S.S., sunk, 52
Indian Army, 4th Div. at Salonika, 5
Indian (4th) Division, war record, 620
— (5th)—war record, 654
— (7th)—war record, 684
— (8th)—war record, 717
— (19th)—war record, 748
— (25th)—war record, 782
Indian Ocean, British colonies in, 83
——Hyde in, 761-62
Indians, in Berlin, *197*
—at Cassino, 483-84
—defend Singapore, 259
—in Mauritius, 627
—in Tokyo, *641*, *646*
—for Victory Parade, *129*, *135*
Indies, W., food production in, 147
——importance, 104
Indomitable, H.M.S., off Madagascar, 761
Infantry, Montgomery on, 371
Inflation, Belgium averts, 436
—in Budapest, 19
—in Greece, 198
Infra-red Rays, operational use, *777*
Ingleton, Maj. R. N., R.M., with Commandos, 388
Inniskilling Dragoon Guards, R. (5th), war record, 587-90
Inniskilling Dragoons, 587
Inniskilling Fusiliers, R., return home, 742
———war record, 459-62
———(1st), at Mayu Ridge, 249-50
Interpreters, for World Food Conference, *359*
Invasion, of Great Britain, Attlee on, 567
Invasion Barge, Heinson on, 121
Iorabaiwa, Japanese halted at, 196
Ios Nicolas, Greek caïque, *412*
Iran, Inniskilling Fusiliers in, 459, *460*
Iraq, Buffs in, 558
—Household Cavalry in, 299
—Regent of, at Victory Parade, *175*
—in Victory Parade, *134*
Irish Fusiliers, R., in Malta, *557*
Irish Guards, at Diebel Bou Aoukaz, 729-31
——war record, 363-66
Iron Duke, H.M.S., to be broken up, *322*
——war record, *298*
Ironside, F/M W. E. I., 698
Ironsides, 3rd (British) Div., 492
Iroquois, H.M.C.S., *266*
Irrawaddy R., R. Marines on, 44
——Worcestershires cross, 686
Iserlohn, N.A.A.F.I. at, *551*
Isernia, Cameronians take, 523
Island, The, at Arnhem, 218, 219
Ismay, Gen. Sir Hastings, at Victory Parade, *175*
Italy, becomes republic, *200*
—British parachute attack on, 547-48
—Buffs in, *557*, 558
—Cameronians in, 523, *524*
—D.C.L.I. in, 203, *204*
—Desert Rats in, 90
—D.L.I. in, 430
—D. of Wellington's in, 491
—1st (Airborne) Div. in, 556
—food for, *655*
—Green Howards in, 619, *621*
—Grenadier Guards in, 7-9
—H.A.C. in, 395, 396
—H.L.I. in, 654
—Household Cavalry in, 299
—Inniskilling Fusiliers in, 459
—invasion of, Recce and, 108
—Jewish Brigade in, 214
—Marines in, 44, 46
—peace treaty signed, *751-53*
—R.A.F. Regt. in, 75, *76*, *77*
—R.E.s in, *715*, 717
—R. Leicesters in, *720-21*
—R. Signals in, *332*
—secrets of armistice, 99
—and the Sudan, 307
—Suffolk Regt. in, 780
—and Tirana, 278
—and Trieste, *231*
—Welsh Guards in, 748, *749*
Itzehoe, memorial to Nazi victims, *424*
Iwakuni, B.C.O.F. in, *290*

J

Jakobs, Josef, shot, 94
Jamaica, food production in, 147
—Spitfire fund, 14
Japan, B.C.O.F. wives for, 415
—as democracy, *550*
—Five-Year Plan for, 447
—leave hotels in, 575
Japan *(contd.)*
—Occupation Troops for, *111*
—today, *290*
—treatment of prisoners, *754*
—trooping the Colour in, *581*
Japanese, attempt on Australia, 195-96, 794-95
—surrender, S.E. Asia, 381-83
Jaquot, Major Henry, 189-90
Java, V.C.P. in, *700*
Javelin, H.M.S., war record, *522*
Jean, Prince, of Luxemburg, 372
Jebb, Gladwyn, in Paris, *70*
Jeep Railway, Burma, *531*
Jeeps, repairing, Pinwe, *666*
Jerusalem, Household Cavalry in, 299, *300*
—King David Hotel blown up, *295*
—station searched, *520*
—terrorist work in, *756*
Jervis Bay, H.M.S., survivors' reunion, *706*
Jet, dog, in Victory Parade, *168*
Jet Engines, against snow, *744*
Jet Planes, new British, *386*
Jews, ex-Servicemen, at Kfar-Kisch, *294*
—war service, 214
Jinnah, Mr., in London, *616*
Jodl, F/M Alfred, sentenced, *432-33*, 435
"Joe's Bridge," over Escaut Canal, 366
Joessing Fjord, *Cossack* and *Altmark* in, *443*, *444*, *445*
Johore Bahru, Anti-Japanese Army at, *339*
——Japanese surrender at, *526*
Johore Causeway, Japanese repair, *260*
Jollain Merlin, Gloucestershire Regt. at, 267
Jones, A/B A. W., with Commandos, 387-88
Jones, Purser Claude, in *Laconia*, 702-03, 734-35
Joseph, Dr. Bernard, released, *520*
Juba R., Africans force, 243
Juba Line, E. Africans break, 275
Juliana, Princess, at Victory Parade, *175*, 179
Juniper (trawler), sunk, 292
Junkers, invade Crete, *578*, *580*
—88, down, Naples, 76
Jupiter (ship), at Dunkirk, *338*

K

Kaiser Wilhelm Canal, 5th R.I.D.G. on, *590*
Kaladan R., W. Africans on, 691
Kalemyo, Africans take, 691
Kalewa, Africans take, 691
Kaliningrad, settlers in, 575
Kaltenbrunner, Ernst, sentenced, *432-33*, 435
Kamikaze (destroyer), and Japanese surrender, *383*
Kamikaze Pilots, Herbert on, 766-67
Kampen, Bren carriers near, *676*
Kanchanaburi, Burma-Siam Rly. at, *347*
Kangaroo (car), D.L.I. in, *430*
—at Medicina, 16
—in Normandy, 89
Kannyu, prisoners' graves at, *346*
Karamea, S.S., V2 on, *706*
Karanja, H.M.S., off Madagascar, *31*
Karatine, dehydration plant at, 147
Kardelj, M. Edouard, in Paris, *326*
Karelians, in Helsinki, 342
Karlshorst, trotting races at, *116*
Karlsruhe (ship), *Truant* and, 586
Kassassin, Household Cavalry at, 299
Kauffmann, Henrik, at World Food Conference, *359*
Kay, Sgt. D. A., G.M. for, 456
Kazassov, M., Bulgarian Min. of Information, 468
Keating, James, in *Altmark*, 443-44
——in *Graf Spee*, 413-14
Keigwin, Lieut., at Djebel Bou Aoukaz, 730
Keitel, F/M Wilhelm, sentenced, *432-33*, 435
Kelly, H.M.S., Mountbatten in, 219
Kempthorne, H.M.S., and *Bickerton*, 668
Kendrick, Pte. F., at Helmstedt, *736*
Keneally, L/Cpl. J. P., V.C., 363, *730*
Kenna, Pte. Edward, V.C., *103*
Kennard, Lieut., D.S.O., of Irish Guards, 363
Kennard, Michael F., on Mulberry Harbour, 771-73
Kennedy, Maj., of Irish Guards, 364
Kennedy, Capt., in Solomon Is. 563
Kensington Gardens, troops camp in, *134-35*, *136*
Kent, H.R.H. Duchess of, at Victory Parade, *175*, *179*, 186
Kenya, strategic importance, 83
—war effort, 275
Kenya Regt., 275
Kephalos, Cos, *497*
Keren, H.M.S., and capture of Madagascar, 31
Keren, battle of, H.L.I. at, 651
——Worcestershires at, 683
Kerminshah, Household Cavalry in, 299
Kerr, Capt. Ralph, R.N., and *Bismarck*, 451
Kerugoya, dehydration plant at, 147
Kesselring, F/M Albert, on Dunkirk, 4
Keyes, Lt.-Col. Geoffrey, V.C., raids Rommel's H.Q., 515
Keyes, Adm. Sir Roger, at G.H.Q., 698
Keys, Ceremony of, cancelled, 95
Kfar-Kisch, ex-Servicemen found, *294*
Khyber Pass, Nehru attacked in, *527*
Kiel, cinema landing craft at, *354*
—H.A.C. in, *398*
—*Hipper* at, *194*
Kiel Canal, 5th R.I.D.G. on, 590
Kikoku Maru, *Bengal* and, *746*
Kilindini, Kenya port, 83
Kilts, pressing, N. Africa, *237*
Kimmel, Adm. Husband, 419, 420
Kimmins, Cdr. Anthony, R.N., 183
King, S/Ldr. Rev. Cecil, *400-01*
King, Rt. Hon. W. L. Mackenzie, and Canadian memorial, *329*
——at Commonwealth Conference, *130*
——at Peace Conference, *306*, *326*
——at Victory Parade, *175*, 186
King George V., H.M.S., in autumn exercises, *517*
——and *Bismarck*, 451-52
——war record, *428*
King's African Rifles, in Somaliland, 275
———on Sudan frontier, 307
———in Victory Parade, *135*
King's (Liverpool) Regt. (1st) with Chindits, 314
King's Own Malta Regt., war service, 183
King's Own Yorkshire L.I., at Minden, *308*
King's Royal Rifles, in Calais, 35
Kingston, Brigadier, in Syria, 299
Kirk, Rear-Adm. Alan G., 228
Kisch, Brig. F. H., village named for, *294*
Kismayu, E. Africans at, 275
Kitchen, all-electric, *422*
—of aluminium house, *584*
—for prefabricated houses, *470*
Kite, H.M.S., war record, *182*
Kite Balloons, for convoys, *489*
Kiwi, H.M.N.Z.S., war record, *682*
Klang Bridge, Malaya, *263*
Kloppenburg, D.C.L.I. at, 206
Knife, Japanese, for hara-kiri, *151*
Knightsbridge (N. Africa), H.A.C. at, 395, 397
—Recce at, 107
—Worcestershires at, 683
Knitsley (collier), Willcocks in, 574
Knud, Prince, of Denmark, *359*
Knudsen, O. F., on Oslo, 404
Koenig, Gen. Joseph, and Allied Control Council, *258*
——in Victory Parade, *164*
Kohima, D.L.I. at, 430
—epic of, 531
—Recce at, 110
—relief, 2nd Div. and, 20
Koivula, Reino, on Helsinki, 342
Kokoda, fighting for, 196
Kommandatura, of Berlin, 115
Koniev, Marshal, at Moscow Conference, *773*
Königsberg: see Kaliningrad
Königswartha, hospital at, 27
Kormoran (ship), *Sydney* and, 618
Kosanovic, M. Sava, *326*
Kota Bharu, Japanese land at, *636*
Koudekerke, flooded, 542-43
Krait (ship), Commandos in, 387-88, *389*
Kramer, Capt., and Pearl Harbour, 420
Kretschmer, Capt., German **submarine** commander, captured, 489
Krupps, decoy for, *159*
Kuala, H.M.S., sunk, 345
Kuala Lumpur, street-fighting in, *637*
Kufra, L.R.D.G. at, 603
Kulichev, M., at Peace Conference, *327*
Kunikawa Maru, *Bengal* and, *746*
Kure, *Commonwealth* at, 609, *615*
Kuriers, bomb *Duchess of York*, 57-58

L

Labour, Icelandic shortage, 694
Labour Party, British, and Schumacher, *585*
Laconia, S.S., sunk, 702-03, 734-35
Lacoutorf, Tech.-Sgt. E., in Tokyo, *646*
Lae, Australians take, 707
Lagos, *Nigeria* at, *577*
—W. African port, 104
Lahore, riots in, *775*
Lake, Maj. F. J., of E. Lancs. Regt., 139
Lakes, battle of the, 275
Lake Success, U.N. committees at, *617*
——U.N. Conference at, *585*
Lampard, Lt., of Irish Guards, 366
Lampedusa, R.A.F. Regt. in, 75
Lancashire Fusiliers, in Tunisia, 612
Lancashire Parachute Battalion (13th), *190*
Lancasters, and battle of Britain anniversary, 399
—bomb Westkapelle, 250
—good will mission to U.S., *265*
—over St. Paul's, *355*
—in Victory fly-past, *180*
—in war museum, *552*
Lanciano, Green Howards at, *621*
Landi Kotal, Nehru attacked at, *527*
Landing Craft, Allied, Captain addresses crew, *643*
——for Sicily, *642*, *644*
——**British**, off Madagascar, *30*
——broken up, Mortlake, *418*
——**German**, as cinema, *354*
——**Japanese**, Kota Bharu, *636*
——as Press ship, 534
Landing Craft Obstruction Clearance Unit, Frogmen with, *225*
————Marines with, 46
Landing Ship Tank, *Empire Baltic* as, 418
Lane, C.Q.M.S., of K.O.Y.L.I., *308*
Langmaid, Lt. Cdr. R., R.N.; painting by, *350*
Langrune, Commandos at, 792
Langsdorff, Capt. Hans, of *Graf Spee*, *413*, 414, 443
——grave, *575*
——at Montevideo, *575*
Lanyon, Marine F. W., at Walcheren, 252
Larcom, Capt. C. A. A., R.N., and *Bismarck*, 451-52
Latimer, H.M.S., now *Empire Ridley*, *407*
Lattre de Tassigny, Gen. J. J. de, *201*
Laugher, Lt.-Col. F. F., at Caernarvon, 42
Lawrence, Lord Justice, at Nuremberg, *431*, 435
Lawrence, A/B C., on *A Lighters*, 253-54
Laycock, Maj. Gen. Robert, and Commandos, 515
——in Crete, 580
Layton, Adm. Sir Geoffrey, *165*
L.C.G. (T.), not for D-Day, 228
L.C.T., Japanese ammunition in, 242
L.D.V., D.L.I. and, 427
Leach, Capt. J. C., R.N., 451
Leaflets, Allied, on Saigon, 346
—British, on Walcheren, 543
League of Nations, and Trans-Jordan, 214
Leberecht Maass (destroyer), sunk, 740
Ledo, E. Lancs. airborne from, 139, 142
—Gloucesters at, 270
Ledo Rd., hunting bandits on, 765
——work on, *59*
Ledringhem, Gloucestershire Regt. at, 267
Ledward, Gilbert, Westminster Abbey memorial, *425*
Lee, Rear-Adm., U.S.N., at Guadalcanal, 196
Lee, Sub Lt. (A) E., and *Scharnhorst*, *131*
Lee, Lt.-Col. J. M., D.S.O., 718
Leeman, Lt. Wayne, and Himmler's secrets, 539
Leese, Gen. Sir Oliver, at Cassino, 484
——decorates Burrell, *685*

Leicester, Brig. "Jumbo," 250
Leicestershire Regt., in Crete, 579
——now Royal, 718, 720-21
Leigh, Maj. W. H. Gerard, in Western Desert, 300
Leipzig (ship), scuttled, 354
Leith, *Altmark* prisoners at, 444, 445
Lemonnier, Adm., Peace delegate, 326
Lenin, portrait, Vienna, 50
Lentini, bombarded and taken, 601-02
Leontic, Dr., in Paris, 326
Leopold III, K. of the Belgians, Cammaerts on, 436
——Col.-in-Chief, R.I.D.G., 587
Leros, Buffs in, 558
—Dodecanese Is., 495
Leroy, Pte., and Himmler's secrets, 539-40
Lessay, today, 144-45
Letpadan, Gloucesters at, 268
Lever, Rev. Clifford, at Calais, 35-36
Levitha, Marines take, 43
Lewis Guns, for D.E.M.S., 573
Lexington, U.S.S., sunk, 195
Leyden University, honours Churchill, 98
Liardet, Maj.-Gen. Sir Claude, 75
Liberation, Order of, ceremonies, 201
Liberators, in Cocos Is., 284
Liberty Ships, at Hamburg, 341
——repatriate Japanese, 262
Libya, H.L.I. in, 652
Lidice, Truth About, 355-56
Lido, British troops at, 272-73
Lids, Britain makes, 464
Lie, Trygve, at Peace Conference, 313
Light Transport, at Alamein, 571
Lille, Michel memorial at, 600
Lincolnshire Regiment, now Royal, 718, 722
Line S.E. Patrol, 131-33
Lines of Communication, in N. Africa, 611
———R.E.'s and, 713
Lingevres, D.L.I. at, 430
—R.A.F. Regt. at, 78
Lisbon, Italian peace overtures in, 99
—*Roosevelt* at, 322
—war story, 623-26
Lisieux, today, 145
Lively, H.M.S., memorial to, 723
Liverpool, *Lively* memorial, 725
Li Wo, H.M.S., exploit, 631, 671
Lloyd, Air V/M Sir Hugh P., 186
Lloyd, Lt.-Col. J., death, 473
Lobnitz and Co., Ltd., and Mulberry, 771
Locomotives, British, for China, 514
—British export, 226
Loire R., S. Nazaire docks on, 67-68
Loise, H.M.S., hit, 415
London, H.M.S., 362
London, air-raid shelters demolished, 128
—"And So to Work" Exhibition, 692
—Army's show in, 582
—and Battle of Britain, 155
———anniversary, 399-402
Britain Can Make It, 422-23
—Commonwealth Conference in, 130
—demobilization centres in, 479
—Dornier down in, 153, 154
—first flying bombs on, 348-49
—flowers on blitzed sites, 277
—Garden of Remembrance, 105
—Guard changed at Whitehall, 300, 302
—mines exhibited, 322
—opening of Parliament, 519
—pigeons' memorial, 421
—Remembrance Day in, 518
—statues return, 65, 79-82
—Victory Parade in, 161-92
———preparations, 129, 134-35, 136
—Welsh exhibition in, 759
London Bridge, Victory Parade on, 170
London Division (56th), war record, 428
London International Telephone Exchange, 85
London Scottish (1st), colours laid up, 673
Long Range Desert Group, 603-604, 605
Long Range Penetration Brigade, Cameronians with, 523
————Recce as, 110
Longstop Hill, Buffs take, 558
Lonsdale, Lt.-Cdr. R. P., R.N., in *Seal*, 41
Loot, German, Allies' deal with, 680
Lord, Flt.-Lt. D. S. A., V.C., 103
Lorries, German, in British Zone, 711
Lorries *(cont.)*
—as home, Hamburg, 551
Louvain, Grenadiers relieve, 10
—Household Cavalry at, 302
Lowestoft, *Martello* at, 418
Lowland Division (52nd), war record, 364
Lübeck, Borie at, 668
Luca, stone quarry at, 241
Lucknow, Defence of, D.C.L.I. and, 203
Ludendorff Bridge, students see, 530
Luetjens, Vice-Adm., death, 452
Lugard, Lord, in W. Africa, 243
Lumsden, Lt.-Col. "Bertie," 643
Lundy, H.M.S., clears channels, 48-49
Lüneburg, D.C.L.I. band at, 206
Lunga Point, battle of, 196
Lushnja, National Congress at, 278
Luttrell, Col. Francis, 619
Luxemburg, Churchill a freeman, 261
—today, 372-73
Lympstone, Cpl. Hunter's memorial, 46
Lyon, Maj. Ivor, Commando leader, 387-88

M

Maas R., Cameronians cross, 526
——5th R.I.D.G. on, 588
——Suffolk Regt. on, 781
McAll, R. Kenneth, in Pootung Camp, 505-06
MacArthur, Gen. Douglas, and Japanese prisoners, 262
——protects Australia, 195
Macartney, Maj. Roy, Australia saved from Japs, 195-96
——on raids on Darwin, 794-95
Macbeth, prisoners produce, 27
M'Call, Naval Telegraphist J. A., on Burma-Siam Rly., 345-47
McClean, Rev. N., and H.L.I. colours, 392
McCreery, Lt.-Gen. Sir Richard, and R. Norfolk's colours, 514
——in Victory Parade, 165
McCudden, Maj. J. T. B., V.C., 122
McCulloch, Maj.-Gen. Sir Andrew, on H.L.I., 651-54
MacDonald, Rt. Hon. Malcolm, 467
Macdonald, Roderick, death, 484
McGrath, Father, on Bathurst Is., 795
Machine Gun Corps, London memorial, 82
Mack, John D., on Sofia, 468
Mackay, H.M.S., and *Scharnhorst*, 132
Mackensen, Gen. Eberhard von, trial, 546
Mackey, Cpl. J. B., V.C., 103
Macmillan, Maj.-Gen. G.H.A., 142, 737
——for Palestine, 490
Macmillan, Rt. Hon. Harold, 100
McMillan, Richard, on V Day in Normandy, 189-90
——at Walcheren, 317-18
Macmullen, Maj.-Gen. H. T., on East Lancs. Regt., 139-41
McMurtrie, Francis E., on Atom Bomb, 232
——on battle of Atlantic, 489
——on escape of *Scharnhorst*, 131-33
——on Germany's naval failure, 739-40
——on sinking of *Bismarck*, 451-52
——of *Glorious*, 291-92
McNarney, Gen. Joseph T., and Allied Control Council, 258
——in Victory Parade, 164
Mac Ships, in Atlantic battle, 489
Madagascar, Cameronians in, 523
—capture of, 30-31, 761, 762
—E. Africans in, 275
—E. Lancs. in, 139
—Inniskilling Fusiliers in, 459
—Mauritians in, 627
—R. Marines in, 43
—strategic importance, 83
Madol, H. R., on Copenhagen today, 532
Magforce, Cameronians with, 523
Magic, U.S. organization, 419
Mahan, Adm. A. T., 104
Mahe, in Seychelles, 83
Maisey, Pte. Peter, at St. Valéry, 25, 26
Maison Neuve Regt., at Walcheren, 652
Majunga, Allies take, 762
—E. Africans at, 275
Malacca, history, 339
Malaita, wireless in, 563
Malaria, war on, Burma, 531
Malaya, British 2nd Div. in, 20
—Buffs in, 558
—Cameronians in, 523
—Japanese enter, 636-37
——occupation, Usill on, 339
—opium-running in, 509-10
—R.E.'s triumphs in, 263
Malayan Police Force, in Victory Parade, 134
Malays, Anti-Japanese army, 339
Maleme, Crete airfield, 579, 580
Malta, Buffs in, 555, 556, 557
—D.L.I. at, 428
—*Illustrious* returns to, 409
—importance to Britain, 54, 55
—reconstruction in, 239-41
—submarine reinforces, 377-78
—victory parade contingent, 137
—at war, 183
Malta Artillery, R., 183
Manchester Regt., in Singapore, 90
Mandalay, capture, Africans and, 691
—Dagger Division at, 442
—Recce in, 110
—Worcestershires at, 686
Mandated Territories, history, 14
Mandra, riots in, 775
Manila, concentration camp in, 122-24
—*Glory* at, 537
Manipur Rd., traffic on, 58
Mann, George, and pigeons' memorial, 421
Mannerheim, F/M Gustav, birthday celebration, 343
Manpower, Colonies and, 14
Manxman, H.M.S., lays mines, 131
——war record, 554
Maoris, in Crete, 580
Maquis, memorial service for, 71
Marble Arch (Libya), L.R.D.G. at, 603
Marcello (submarine), sunk, 489
Marchwood, Mulberry caissons at, 733
Marda Pass, battle of, Africans in, 243
Mareth Line, D.L.I. in, 428
——50th Div. at, 300
——Green Howards in, 620
——Grenadier Guards in, 7
Margaret, H.R.H. Princess, and Dutch horses, 297
——in Thames pageant, 188
——at Victory Parade, 162, 174, 175, 179, 186
Margarine, production method, 150
Margate, Belisha beacon from, 379
Marienburg, British prisoners at, 477
Marine Corps, U.S., in Victory Parade, 166
Mariner, H.M.S., on ice-guard, 744
Marines, German, in Amsterdam, 675-76
—**Japanese**, standard captured, 196
—**Royal**, in Madagascar, 31
——in Nauplia, 485
——and *San Dimitrio*, 520
——and Sicilian invasion, 642-644
——in *Vanguard*, 112
——in Victory Parade, 176-77
——war record, 43-46
See also Commandos
— **U.S.**, free Omori, 447
——at Guadalcanal, 196
Maris, Jacob, and Arnhem memorial, 391
Marlin, American machine-gun, 574
March, A/B F. W., with Commandos, 387
Marsh, Cdr. "Tiger," in *Medway*, 220
Marshall, Gen. George, and Pearl Harbour, 420
——in Moscow, 773
Marshall, Roy, in *Bonaventure*, 351
Martello, H.M.S., closed down, 418
Martin, Gen., and Pearl Harbour, 419
Martin, Lt.-Gen. H. G., and Eisenhower's report, 211
——on Montgomery's report, 371
Martin, P. H., in *Bickerton*, 667-68
Martin-Bellinger Report, 419, 420
Martino, Don, at Cassino, 483
Mary, H.M. Queen, opens Garden of Remembrance, 105
——and S. James's Park bomb, 96
——and Victory Parade, 162, 174, 175, 179
Mary, H.R.H. Princess Royal, 175, 179, 331
Marzin, M., Mayor of Ile de Seine, 360
Masaryk, M. Jan, signs peace treaty, 752
Mashona, H.M.S., sunk, 452
Massey, Mrs. Vincent, and *Iroquois*, 266
Massigli, M., welcomes French children, 490
Massingham, Hugh, on Victory Parade, 185-86
Master Aircrew, new badge, 521
Mateur, sniper at, 610
Mathieu, Col. Paul, memorial to, 559
Matilda Tanks, at Sattelberg, 707, 708
Matsuoka, Yosuke, death, 230
Matthews, Freeman, at Peace Conference, 306
Matthews, Sgt. J. H., G.M. for, 456
Maubeuge, French prisoners at, 668
Mauchamps, Clémenceau's grave at, 201
Maund, Capt. L. E. H., R.N., and *Bismarck*, 451-52
Mauretania, S.S., released from service, 479
Mauritius, H.M.S., and invasion of Sicily, 601-03
Mauritius, share in victory, 627
—strategic importance, 83
Maw, Clifford, in *Viking Star*, 222-23
Max Schultz (destroyer), sunk, 740
Maymyo, the Dagger Arms, 442
Mayu Peninsula, Inniskilling Fus. at, 459
Mayu Ridge, Crosslé at, 249-50
Meat, imported, 309
Mechanized Division, of R. Navy, 163
Medals, R. Mint makes, 450
Medan, P.O.W. at, 790
Medicina, battle for, 16-17
Mediterranean Sea, British colonies in, 54
——Colonies' war effort, 214
Mediterranean Fleet, visits Greece, 485
Medjez-el-Bab, Black Watch at, 236
——1st Army at, 610, 611, 612
Medway, H.M.S., at Alexandria, 377
——sunk, 220, 221
Meidob, war gifts, 307
Meiktila, Ordnance Field Park at, 667
—R.A.F. Regt. at, 76
Melbourne, *Taurus* at, 72
Melons, at Lisbon docks, 623
—for Recce, Mandalay, 110
Melos, Force 133 and, 412
Menan R., R.E's bridge, 263
Mentmore, Charles I statue at, 65
Merapas Is., Commandos on, 388
Merchantman, sunk, 222
Merchant Navy, *Worcester* cadets for, 687-90
Mercier, Pte. Georgette, 507
Merema, Worcestershires at, 686
Mergui, M'Call at, 345
Meriel, Louis, at Courseulles, 190
Mersa Matruh, Buffs at, 555, 556
——D.L.I. at, 428
——H.L.I. at, 651
——supplies from, for Tobruk, 253-54
Messent, Roger, parachutes into France, 633-34
Messervy, Maj.-Gen. F. W., 684
Messina, Allies take, 603
Meteor Plane, on Horse Guards Parade, 386
Metz, Churchill at, 261
Michel, Capt., memorial, 600
Michelet, M., and *Colossus*, 293
Middle East, Australians return from, 195
——Britain's Life-Line in, 54
——Cameronian pipers in, 526
Middleton, Capt. Paul E., 507
Midway Is., Japanese designs on, 195
Mihailovich, Gen. D., trial, 230
Milestones, commemorative, France, 406
—Desert Rats' last, 455
Military Police, British, in Venice, 288
——in Vienna, 50
Military Police, Corps of, now Royal, 719, 723
Milk, British supply, 375
Milk Marketing Board, work, 375
Milne Bay, defence, 195, 196
Milnes, Lt.-Col. F. A., at Minden, 782
Minden, K.O.Y.L.I. celebrate at, 308
Minden *(cont.)*
—Suffolks at, 782
Miners, Dutch bulbs for, 514
Mines, clearance, 254-55
—cleared from Russia, figures, 255
—detection, Studland Bay, 352
—enemy shipping sunk by, 159
—magnetic, first in British waters, 322
—R.Es clear, 714
Minesweepers, at Dunkirk, 4
—for Sheerness, 418
—in Thames, 181
Mine-sweeping, in Corfu Channel, 614
Mingaladon, Gloucesters at, 267
Minneriya, airstrip at, 789
Mint, R., makes medals, 450
Minyat Baku, signallers at, 20
Mitchel Field, R.A.F. Lancasters at, 265
Mitchell, Pte. G. A., V.C., 428
Mittelwerke, underground factory, 124-26
M.N.B.D.O., marines in, 43
——at Suda Bay, 579
Moffatt, Brig. J., on Symi, 411
Mogadishu, Africans reach, 243
Mogok, E. Lancs at, 142
—Gloucesters at, 270
Mohanbari, freight planes load at, 613
Mol, Mynheer, Mrs. Haverman and, 542
Molenberg, H.L.I. take, 651
Molotov, Viatcheslav, in N. York, 513
——at Moscow Conference, 773
——in Paris, 70, 101, 326
——at Peace Conference, 304, 306, 313
——and U.N. Assembly, 617
Mombasa, Hyde at, 761, 762
Mongmit, Gloucesters at, 270
Monnington, W. T., painting by, 732
Montanari, Signor Franco, 99
Montevarchi, D.C.L.I. at, 203, 204
Montgomery, F/M Viscount, at Alamein gathering, 486
——on capture of Centuripe, 461, 462
——decorates Biddle, 270
——Dunkirk prophecy, 474
——and E. Lancs Regt., 139
——Eisenhower on, 211
———welcomes, 385
——farewell to B.A.O.R., 66
——flag at Englishcombe, 743
——and Guards Armoured Division 8, 9
——in Moscow, 705, 709
——and new W.O. badge, 521
——report on operations in N.W. Europe, 371
——on R. Signals, 334
——and spy-dogs, 318-19
——with Stalin, 674
——and 3rd Div., 492
——in Victory Parade, 165, 179 186
Montgomery, Guardsman, of Irish Guards, 364
Monywa, Cameronians at, 523
—Gloucesters at, 270
Mook, fighting at, 217
Mook, Dr. Van, and Batavia memorial, 229
Moonstone, H.M.S., war record, 330
Moorhouse, Flt.-Lieut. S., in Cocos Is., 282-84
——over Sumatra, 789-90
Moorman, William, R.N., in *Moonstone*, 330
Moreh, Ordnance Field Park at, 665
Morell, Dr., Hitler's doctor, 659
Morette, Maquis memorial service, 71
Moriarty, L/Cpl, D.C.M., of Irish Guards, 364
Morris, C/O K. J., in *Tricula*, 634, 635
Morrison, Maj. E. M., of E. Lancs Regt., 140
Morrison, Rt. Hon. Herbert, on V1, 348
Morrison, Ian, on fall of Singapore, 260
Mortar Detachments, of Gloucesters, Burma, 268
——of Recce, Anzio, 107
Mortar Team, of Green Howards, Anzio, 621
Mortlake, invasion craft at, 418
Moscow, Foreign Ministers in, 773
—Montgomery in, 705, 709
—today, 596, 597
Motor Buses, in Warsaw, 500
Motor-cars, British export, 226
——at Lisbon docks, 623
——in Paris, numbers, 310
Motor Launches, for military police, Venice, 288
——at S. Nazaire, 67-68

Mouen, Worcestershires take, 684
Moulmein, pagoda shifts, *271*
Moulton, Lt.-Col. Jim, at Walcheren, 252
Mountain Warfare, British exhibit, *582*
Mountbatten, Adm. Viscount, and Burma campaign, 531
——on Ceylon, 83
——and Giffard, 595
——home life, *53*
——H.Q. in Ceylon, 627
——in *Kelly*, 219
——R.A.F. Regt. salutes, *78*
——as Viceroy, *738*
——and Victory Parade, *162, 165, 175*
Mountbatten, Viscountess in Singapore, 93
Moys, Capt. J. D., at Walcheren, 252
M.T.B.s, and *Scharnhorst*, 132, *133*
Muar, guarding rice at, *20*
—Japanese take, 259
Muar R., fighting on, 259
Muddle, Company Officer George, 414-15
Mulberries, artificial harbours, 228
—building of, 771-73
—cutting up, *546*
—in exhibition, *630*
—Gwen Croft on, 733-34
—relic, Southampton, *208-09*
—R.E.s and, 717
—for Walcheren, *317*
—as war memorial, 671
Mules, ford Burma river, 249
—with Green Howards, *621*
Mule Transport Companies, of R.A.S.C., 214
Mullenheim, Lt.-Cdr. Freiherr von, 452
Mumbles, " egg-crates " at, *674*
Municipal Elections, in Germany, *424*
Munster, Provincial Advisory Council at, *102*
Murdoch, Sir Keith, 260
Murphy, John, and Odette Sansom, 381
Murphy, R. D., and Italian armistice, 100
Murphy, Sir William L., and Nassau memorial, *546*
Musgrove, Sgt. Leslie, 250
Mushroom Farm, airborne troops at, 323
Musician, street, Berlin, *116*
Muslim League, and Constituent Assembly, 616
Myitche, Ordnance Field Park at, 666
Myitkyina, E. Lancs airborne to, 139, 142
—Gloucesters at, 270
Myitson, Buffs at, *558*
—Gloucesters at, 270
Mynarski, P/O C., V.C., *457*
Myola, recaptured, 196
Myrtle, H.M.S., wreck destroyed, *48-49*

N

N.A.A.F.I., gift shop, Hamburg, *102, 424*
—at Iserlohn, *551*
—supplies Buffs, N. Africa, *556*
Naba, E. Lancs. at, 142
Nabob, Escort Carrier, torpedoed, 667-68
Namsos, R. Marines at, 43
Napier, Lt.-Cdr. L. W., in *Rorqual*, *378*
Naples, Bay of, Ju 88 in, 76
——*Grenville* in, *570*
—capture, 46th Div. and, 250
—R.E.s reconstruct, 717
Napoleon I, and Malta, 183
Narbada (sloop), off Arakan, 700
Nares, Maj.-Gen. E. P., in Berlin, 115
Narvik, French memorial at, *425*
—memorial services at, *210*
Nash, Rt. Hon. Walter, *130*
Nassau (Bahamas), airmen's memorial, *546*
National Anthems, prisoners sing, 668
National Equine Defence League, and Black Billy, *450*
National Fire Service, in Victory Parade, *168, 169*
National Republican Guards, of Portugal, *624*
Nauplia, Marines beat " retreat " on, *485*
Navy, Chinese, R.N. trains, *776*
—**Free French,** de Gaulle and, *360*
—**French,** *Colossus* for, *293*
—**German,** broken up, *354*
—**Italian,** Doenitz on, 740
—**Royal,** autumn exercises, *517*
——casualties, 190
——and Crete, 579, 580
——Frenchmen with, *360*
——and German radar, *710*
Navy, Royal *(cont.)*
——lays up flags, *361*
——numbers restored, 287
——saves Malta, 183
——Signals units, 334
——in Thames, *181*
——trains Chinese sailors, *776*
——in Victory Parade, *163, 176-77*, 186, *192*
——**Norwegian,** British submarines for, 511
—**U.S.,** demobilization, 415
——Pearl Harbour losses, *420*
Navy League, Trafalgar Day wreath, *481*
Nazism, memorial to victims, *424*
Nehru, Pandit Jawaharlal, attack on, *527*
——in London, *616*
Nelson, H.M.S., and Japanese surrender, *382*
——war record, *650*
Nelson, Adm. Lord Navy League remembers, *481*
Nelson's Column, cleaning, *82*
Neosho, U.S.S., sunk, 195
Neptune (ship), burned, 795
Netherlands, British war graves in, *296*
—bulbs from, *85, 514*
—gift of horses from, *297*
—gratitude to Britain, *85*
—honour Churchill, *98*
—remember Arnhem, *390-91*
—in Victory Parade, *166*
—Welsh Guards in, 747
Netherlands, E. Indies, British leave, 639
———supplied by air, 789-90
Netherlands War Graves Committee, *296*
Neurath, Constantin, sentenced, *433-34*, 435
Newfoundland, H.M.S., off Sicily, 602
New Guinea, Australians in, 707-08
——campaign in, 196
——Fijians in, 467
New Hebrides, share victory, 563
Newman, Lt.-Col. A. C., V.C., on St. Nazaire raid, 67-68
New Plymouth, Devonport bell for, *514*
Newspapers, in Budapest, 19
—gipsies sell, Bucharest, *628*
—sold at Nuremberg, *435*
New York, Foreign Ministers in, *513*
——Lancasters visit, *265*
——Security Council at, *56*
——U.N. Assembly at, *617*
New Zealanders, at Cassino, 483-84
——in Crete, 578-80
——with L.R.D.G., 603-04
Niceros, Dodecanese Is., *498*
Nicholls, L/Cp. H., V.C., 7
Nicholson, Guardsman, D.C.M., of Irish Guards, 363
Nicholson, Maj.-Gen. C. G. G., Japanese surrender to, *526*
Nicholson, Marine Donald, at Walcheren, 252
Nicholson, Col. W. N., on R. Suffolk Regt., 779-82
Nicobar Islands, *Illustrious* at, 158
Nigeria, H.M.S., at Lagos, *577*
Nigeria, air bases in, 104
—W. African territory, 243
Nigeria Regt., war record, 243
Nijmegen Bridge, battle for, 217, *218*
——" Dukes " at, 494
——Grenadiers at, 10
——Welsh Guards cross, 750
Nijmegen Salient, British graves in, *296*
——Gloucesters in, *270*
——held by 49th Div., 268
——H.L.I. in, 652
Nikitchenko, Maj.-Gen., at Nuremberg, *431*
Nilaveli, rest camp at, 159
Nineteen Thirty-nine-Forty-five Star, making, *450*
Nisper, Gloucesters at, *270*
Nockolds, Roy, painting by, *732*
Noise, in Prague, 660
Nordhausen, underground factory near, 124-26
Norfolk, H.M.S. and *Bismarck*, 451
Norfolk Regt. R. (1st), new colours for, *514*
Norman, Wing-Cdr. Sir Nigel, and parachute troops, 547-548
Normandy, Allied invasion of, 227-28
——50th Div. at, 300
——R.A.F. Regt. and, 76, *78*
——R. Marines and, 44
——R. Signals and, 334
——U-boats and, 489
—battle of, Eisenhower on, 211
—Black Watch in, 236, *238*
—break through in, 89-90
Normandy *(cont.)*
—D.C.L.I. in, 203, *205*
—Desert Rats in, 90
—D.L.I. in, *430*
—49th Div. in, 268
—51st Div. in, 332
—5th R. Inniskilling D.G.s in, 587, *588, 589*
—Gloucestershire Regt. in, 267
—Green Howards in, 619, *622*
—H.A.C. in, 396, 398
—H.L.I. in, 654
—Household Cavalry in, 302
—Irish Guards in, 364, *366*
—R.E.s in, *717*
—R. Hampshires in, *722*
—state-owned sites in, 671
—Suffolk Regt. in, 779
—today, *143-46, 559-62*
—V Day on beaches, *189*
—Welsh Guards in, 748, *750*
North Cape, naval battle off, *739, 740*
Northcott, Lt.-Gen. John, in Tokyo, *207*
Northern Rhodesia Regt., 275
North Midland Division (46th), war record, 250
Northolt, P.M. leaves from, *303*
North Shore Regt., in Normandy, 792
Northumberland Fusiliers (4th), and Recce, 107
Northumbrian Division (50th), D.L.I. with, 427
——Green Howards with, 619
——war record, 300
Norton, Lt. G., V.C., 250, 718
Norway, aliens repatriated, 383
—Allies evacuate, 291
—British destroyers for, *453*
—D. of Wellingtons for, *492*
—49th Div. in, 268
—Green Howards in, 619, 622
—Irish Guards in, 363
—R. Marines in, *43*
—traitors in, figures, 159
—in Victory Parade, *166*
Norway, Crown Prince and Princess, at Victory Parade, *175*, 179
Norwegians, for Germany, *674*
Noto, Black Watch in, *236*
Nottinghamshire Yeomanry, and D.D. Tanks, 228
Noumea, U.S. naval base, 195
Nuisance, A/B Just, dog, 159
Nuremberg Trials, figures, 415
——Hamburg and, *454*
——Judgement at, *431-34, 435*
Nurses, at Alamein gathering, 486
Nyhavn, sailors' memorial, *658*
Nyohaung, Africans take, 691

O

Oakley-Hill, D. R., on Tirana, 278
Obbov, M., signs peace treaty, *753*
Observer Corps, R., Dowding on, 403
——reorganized, 671
Occupation Troops, for Japan, 111
O'Connor, Gen. Sir Richard, in Victory Parade, *165*
Odiham, Eagle Squadron at, *403*
Odon R., H.L.I. on, 654
Oerlikon Gun, in *Bellona*, *181*
——instruction in, *573*
Officers, German, help with harvest, *384*
Oil Pioneer (tanker), sunk, 292
Okegem, spy-dogs of, 318-19
Okshitkon, E. Lancs. at, 142
Old, Brig., U.S.A.A.F., in Burma, 316
Oldale, L/Sgt., M.M., H.L.I., 654
Olive Oil, rationed, Italy, *787*
Olympia (London), clothing depot at, *479*
Omagh, Inniskillings return to, *742*
Omaha Beach, state-owned, 671
Omnibuses, British, in Holland, *296*
—in Paris, 310, *311*
Omo R., battle of, 243
Omori, Christmas pantomime at, *446*
—liberation, 447
Ondina (ship), with *Bengal*, *746*
O'Neill, L/Cpl. Paddy, of E. Lancs. Regt., 139
Onishi, Adm., and Pearl Harbour, 419
Ons Jongen, Luxemburg society, 372
Onslow, H.M.S., off North Cape, *739, 740*
——war record, *394*
Oosterbeek, Airborne memorial at, *391*
——Troops' cemetery, *390*
—garrison rescued, 219
Operation Chariot, S. Nazaire raid, 68
Operation *(cont.)*
—Clean-up, 254-55
—Dynamo, 3, 156-57
—Fuller, 131-33
—Honeybee, 351
—Neptune, 227-28
—Nipoff, *262*
—Overlord, 227-28
—Sealion, invasion of Britain, 567
—Squirt, on V Night, *188*
—Torch, difficulty, 611
—Totalize, La Hogue, 89
—Varsity, 323-24
—Zipper, Malayan D-Day, 383
Operations Room, of Fighter Command H.-Q., 510-11
Opium, smuggling, Malaya, 509-510
Orama (transport), sunk, 292
Orbit Meter, use, *386*
Ordnance Field Parks, in Burma, 665-67
Organ, Green Howards capture, *621*
Orion, H.M.S., and invasion of Sicily, 601
Orkney Is., new roads for, *528-29*
Orlando, Friedl, on Italian armistice, 99
Orontes, S.S., Indians leave in, *5*
Orr, Sir John Boyd, in Copenhagen, *359*
——at food conference, *244*
Ortutay, Gyula, and Budapest radio, 19
Orvieto, 78th Div. at, 460
Osborn, C.S.M. J. R., V.C., *457*
Oslo, to-day, 404, *405*
Osnabrück, R. Marines at, *44*
Oss, food-dump captured, 219
Oste, R., Household Cavalry cross, 300
O'Sullivan, G. P., and Belgian Resistance, 604-06
Ottley, H.L.I. at, *652*
Otter-Bay (Panjang Is.), *387*
Oudendijk, reconstruction in, *318*
Overhoff, Major, in Amsterdam, 676
Overloon, Suffolk Regt. at, 779, *780*
Owen, Lt.-Col. Frank, on Burma Campaign, 531
Owen Stanley Mts., retreat over, 196
Oxen, German use, 698, 699
—threshing with, Cos, *497*
Oxford, Portal a D.C.L., *535*
Oxford & Bucks L.I., 324
Oxspring, R. W., in battle of Britain, 511

P

Pacific Ocean, British colonies in, 83
——Japanese ammunition dumped in, *242*
Pacific Packs, for German children, 351
Packet : See Fairchild C-82
Pack Transport Companies, Cypriot, 214
Paddy Fields, in Japan, *550*
Padua, " telcom." unit in, 534
Page, Lt. R., A.I.F., with Commandos, 387-88
Paget, Gen. Sir Bernard, and Recce, *108*, 110
Pakistan, rioting over, *775*
Palazzolo, H.A.C. in, *396*
Palel-Tamu Road, *59*
Palestine, 1st Household Cavalry Regt. in, *299*
—importance to Britain, 54
—Jewish ex-Servicemen in, *294*
—martial law in, *774*
—unrest in, *215, 520*
—war effort, 147, 214
Palestine Infantry Companies, 214
Palestine Potash Co., barges searched, 215
Paletwa, Africans take, 691
Pallice, La, *Scharnhorst* at, 131
Palmach, terrorist activities, *215*
Palmer, Lt.-Col. Eric, at Walcheren, 252
Palmyra, Household Cavalry at, 299
Pamir (barque), war prize, *704*
Pampas, S.S., 27, 474-76
Pandit, Mrs., in U.N. Assembly, *617*
Panjang Is., Commandos on, *387*
Pantomime, by prisoners, Omori, *446*
Papen, Franz von, acquitted, *432-33, 434*, 435
Parachute, as signal, Arnhem, *219*
Parachute Regt. (4th), in Tel Aviv, *215*
Parachute Troops, British, first attack by, 547-48
——demonstration, Beaulieu, *325*
Parachute Troops *(cont.)*
——dummy, Madagascar, 31, 761, *762*
——Green Howards as, 619
——Gurkhas as, 442
——Westminster Abbey memorial, *425*
Parc de Boislande, " Dukes " at, 492
Paris, Bevin in, *438*
—Foreign Ministers' Conference, *70*
—Gestapo trial in, *230*
—liberation, Capt. Stone and, 507-09
—naval exhibition in, *630*
—Peace Conference in, *289, 303-06, 313, 314, 326-27*
—peace treaties signed in, *751-53*
—today, 310-11
—U.N.E.S.C.O. conference in, *566*
—Victory Parade, *101*
—Welsh Guards in, *747*
Park, Air C/M Sir Keith, and battle of Britain anniversary, *401*
——Dowding on, 403
Parker, Judge J. J., at Nuremberg, *431*
Parkes, Lt.-Col. J., of Worcestershires, *683*
Parkes, Messrs. Jos and Son, and Mulberry Harbour, 771
Park Royal, redundant guns at, *37*
Parliament, British, state opening, *519*
—Houses of, flood-lighting for, *136*
——rebuilding, 769
Parrish, Sgt., and Exeter bombs, 62, *63*
Partridge, Pte. F. J., V.C., *103*
Patani, Japanese air base, 259
Paterno, Allies enter, 602
Paterson, 2nd Lieut. G. W., with parachute troops, 548
Patmos, Dodecanese Is., *495*
Patourel, Maj. H. W. Le, V.C., 718
Patterson, Capt. A., D.S.O., in *Royal Daffodil*, *649*
Patterson, C.S.M. A., of K.O.Y.L.I., *308*
Patterson, Capt. W. R., R.N., and *Bismarck*, 451-52
Patton, Gen. George S., grave, *261*
——in Luxemburg, 372
Paul, St., on Cyprus, 214
Paungde, Gloucesters at, 270
Pavlov, M., in Paris, *70*
Payne, Air Cdre L. G. S., and Dowding's dispatch, 403
Peace Conference, delegates to, *326-27*
——in Paris, *289, 303-06, 313, 314*
Peace Treaties, signed, *751-53*
Pearce, Sgt. J. E., on fall of Singapore, 90-93
Pearl Harbour, amazing facts, 419-20
——*Glory* at, 538, 539
Pears, Charles, pictures by, *591, 739*
Pearson, Capt. and Qmr. O. H., of D.L.I., 427
Peary, U.S.S., bombed, 795
Pegasus, H.M.S., and *Royal Oak*, 282
Pegu, Cameronians in, 523
—Ordnance Field Park at, 667
Pembroke, C., lighthouse at, *763*
Penang, Britain leases, 339
—British evacuation, 339
Penelope, H.M.S., Marine band in, 43
Penshurst, Gort buried at, *11*
Percival, Gen. A. E., in Singapore, 260
Pereira, Maj. H. P. E., on Worcestershires, 683-86
Péronne, wine van skids at, 269
Persia, Cameronians in, 523
—Household Cavalry in, 299, *301*
—R.E.s in, *714*
—Security Council and, *56*
Petard, H.M.S., and Japanese surrender, 381-83
Petrignano, D.C.L.I. take, 203
Petroleum, colonies produce, 147
Phillips, Capt. A. J. L., R.N., and *Bismarck*, 451
Phillips, Lt.-Col. C. F., at Walcheren, 252-53
Phillips, Adm. Sir Tom, and Singapore, 259
Phipps, Brig. C. C., on R.E.s, 713-17
Phoenix, caissons for Mulberry, 772
Piat, of Irish Guards, *366*
Piccadilly, Burma landing-ground, *316*
Picchi, Fortunato, with parachute troops, *548*

Piccolo, Monte, Welsh Guards at, 748, 749
Picton, Sir Thomas, and E. Lancs. Regt., 140
Piedmonte, Irish Guards' band at, 366
Pierre-Emmanuel, French poet, 310
Piggott, Stoker, narrow escapes, 219-20
Pill-box, as home, Westkapelle, 672
Pilot Message, and Pearl Harbour, 419
Pilots, British, battle of Britain, 155
—German, wounded, 155
Pinbaw, Gloucesters at, 270
Pinwe, jeep repairs at, 666
Pinwe R., bridges repaired, 715
Pioneer, H.M.S., at Melbourne, 72
Pioneer Companies, Cypriot, 214
Pioneer Corps, now Royal, 719, 723
Pioneers, in Calais, 35
—from Mauritius, 627
—of R.W.F., 101
Piorun (destroyer), and *Bismarck*, 451
Pipe Major, of 1st Punjabis, 641
Pipers, of Argyll and Sutherland Highrs., 737
—and *Balmoral*, 386
—of Black Watch, 236
—of Cameronians, 526
—of Highland Division, 248
—of H.L.I., Libya, 652
—of Inniskilling Fusiliers, 742
—of R.I.F., Malta, 557
—in Victory Parade, 179
Pitcairn Island, 14, 563
Pit Ponies, Black Billy, 450
Pizey, Capt. C. T. M., and *Scharnhorst*, 132, 133
Plasma, war use, 383
Plastics, for peace purposes, 465
Platt, Gen. Sir William, in Africa, 243
——on E. African Infantry, 275
——in Sudan, 307
Plawski, Cdr. E., commander of *Piorun*, 451
Plessis Grimault, Le, D.C.L.I. at, 203
Ploughing, by German P.O.W., Normandy, 560
—prize team, 448
"Plumbers, The," 1st Guards Brigade, 7
Pluto, R.E.'s and, 717
—salvage from, 407
Plymouth, Garden of Remembrance, 105
—S. Andrew's, flood-lit, 172
Plymouth Argylls, in Singapore, 44
Point 63, D.C.L.I. at, 203
Point 204, Buffs at, 555
Pola, passes to Yugoslavia, 758
Poland, deaths, etc., in, 287
Poles, bear mascot of, 545
—at Cassino, 482-84
Police, Black Watch as, Sicily, 236
—British, train army officers, 514
—Danish, memorial to, 658
—German, at Aldershot, 322
—Palestine, in Jerusalem, 520
—of Prague, 660
Polish Army and Resettlement Corps, figures, 671
Polish Parachute Brigade, at Arnhem, 219
Polo, Mountbatten and, 53
Pompong, Commandos at, 388
Pontoons, for Mulberry, 771
Ponza, R.A.F. Regt. in, 75
Pootung Camp, Dr. McAll in, 505-06
Popa, Mt., R.E.s at, 714
——Worcestershires on, 685
Poplar, housing effort, 84
Poppies, for Remembrance Day, 450, 479
Pork, in Czechoslovakia, 660
Portal, Marshal of R.A.F. Viscount, and battle of Britain anniversary, 400
——private life, 535
——in Victory Parade, 164, 175, 186
Port-en-Bessin, Marines take, 46
Port Harcourt, W. African port, 104
Portland, Training Battleship Squadron at, 393
Port Louis, Mauritius, 83
Port Moresby, defence, 195, 196
Ports, R.E.s make, 717
Portsmouth, *Anson* at, 320
—*Colossus* handed over at, 293
—flags laid up at, 361
—*Implacable* at, 677
—*Warspite* at, 677
Port Stanley, capital of Falklands, 762, 763
Portugal, neutrality, 623
Port Winston, formerly Arromanches, 559
Posters, of Variety Show, Omori, 446
Post Office, war honours, 511
Pottery, in Cos, 496-97
Pourville, Canadians at, memorial, 329
Pownall, Gen. Sir H., with Gort, 697
Prague, in 1947, 660, 661
Prefabricated Houses, in Palestine, 520
——in Poplar, 84
——various types, 374
Premesques, Command Post at, 698
Prendergast, Lt.-Col. G. L., and L.R.D.G., 604
Prendergast, Pte. J. W., B.E.M., 456
President, H.M.S., D.E.M.S. in, 246
Preston, Adm. Sir Lionel, 3
Prestwick, *Balmoral* at, 386
Pretoria Castle, S.S., now *Warwick Castle*, 770
Price, Nancy, and pigeons' memorial, 421
Prien, Capt., death, 489
——sinks *Royal Oak*, 282
Priest Guns, for H.A.C., 395, 396, 397
Prince Charles (steamer), 478
Prince of Wales, H.M.S., and *Bismarck*, 451, 452
——sunk, 259
Princess Royal, H.R.H., 175, 179
——with R. Signals, 331
Prinz Eugen (ship), with *Bismarck*, 451
——at Brest, 131
Prison Camps, German, Borie in, 668-69
——Hongkong, 15
Prisoners-of-War, Allied, on Burma-Siam Rly., 345-47
———*Glory* repatriates, 537-38
———in Malaya, 754
———supplies by air for, 789-790
——**British,** in Germany, 476-478
———hat trick in camp, 349-50
——**French,** at Maubeuge, 668
——**German,** and bomb disposal, 450
——— of British air-trooper, 323
———and Chilvers Coton church, 514
———clear snow, 744
——— destroy ammunition, 102
———of H.L.I., 653
———of Irish Guards, 364, 730
———new concessions, 511
———in Normandy, 560
———repatriation, 454, 479
———of R.I.D.G., 589
———Russia releases, 447
———statistics, 607
———Schumacher with, 585
——**Italian,** in Sicily, 642
——**Japanese,** Malaya, 20
———repatriation, 262
Pritchard, Maj. T. A. C., and Italian aqueducts, 547-48
Production, peacetime, in Britain, 463-66
Prome, Cameronians at, 523
Propaganda, Russian, in Belgrade, 564
Prosser, Lt. R. E., 711
Pryce-Jones, Alan, on Vienna today, 51
Puffin, H.M.S., to be scrapped, 546
Pugsley, Capt. A. F., 250
Punjab, rioting in, 775
Punjab Regt. (1st) in Tokyo, 641, 646
Punjabi, H.M.S., 428
Punjab Squadron (56), war record, 122
Purbeck, H.M.S., and Studland Bay clearance, 352
Pursuivant, H.M.S., Port Stanley, 762, 763
Pyawbwe, British convoy at, 666
"Pygmalion" (Shaw), in Moscow, 596
Pyrethrum, insecticide from, 147

Q

Quatre Bras, E. Lancs. at, 140
Quebec Conferences, and Mulberry Harbour, 771, 772
Queen Elizabeth, H.M.S., with Eastern Fleet, 157, 158, 159
Queen Elizabeth, S.S., Supreme Soviet in, 770
——and *Vanguard*, 112-13
Queen Mary, S.S., anchor chains, 766
Queen's Own Cameron Highlanders, for Japan, 111
————(2nd) in Trieste, 118
Queen Victoria's Rifles, in Calais, 35

R

Races, at Karlshorst, 116
Radar, German, Dover jams, 710
—effect on Germany, 287
Radio, in Budapest, 19
Radio Car, for L.R.D.G., 603
Radio Sets, Dutch, Germans seize, 542
Radio Station, Allied, on Symi, 410
Radlett, air display at, 386
Raeder, Grand-Adm. Erich, and Germany Navy, 739
——and Operation Sealion, 567
——sentence, 432-33, 435
Rafferty, Lt. John, and Amsterdam's liberation, 675-76
Raffles, Sir Stamford, founds Singapore, 339
Railways, Chinese, British engines for, 514
—German, repaired, 102
—for jeeps, Burma, 531
—R.E.s construct, 714, 717
Raimondo, Signor, alias Castellano, 99
Rajah, H.M.S., as troopship, 24
Rajput Regt. (1/7th), at Twin Knobs, 249
Ram, Naik Kamal, V.C., in London, 608
Ramillies, H.M.S., off Madagascar, 31, 43
Ramree Is., Africans at, 691
——Marines at, 43
——R.A.F. Regt. at, 76, 78
Ramsay, Vice-Adm. Sir Bertram, and Dunkirk, 3-4
——and invasion of Normandy, 227
——and R. Signals, 156
——and Walcheren assault, 250
Rangoon, capture, Africans and, 691
—D. of Wellington's at, 491
—evacuation, Gloucesters and, 268
—first air raid on, 268
—Japs repatriated from, 262
—mobile wireless unit at, 534
—R.A.F. Regt. at, 76, 78
Rangoon R., Marines on, 46
Ranville, D-Day anniversary at, 190
Rapido R., Allies cross, 483, 484
Raqqa, Household Cavalry at, 299, 300
Rationing, of bread, causes, 244
—in Bulgaria, 468
—in Czechoslovakia, 660
—in Denmark, 532
—in Finland, 342
—in Oslo, 404
Rations, for Indian Army, 442
Ratmalana, air raid on, 627
Rauray, 49th Div. take, 268
Ravenstein, Gen. von, on Libyan Desert, 603
Rawalpindi, H.M.S., 131
Rawlings, Leo, drawings by, 636-37
R.C.M., Radio Countermeasures, 710
Rebori, Capt., in Burma, 316
Reconnaissance Corps, Green Howards with, 619
——war record, 107-10
——(43rd), formerly 5th Gloucesters, 267
Reconstruction, Greek aversion from, 198
—of ports, by R.Es, 715
—in Warsaw, 500, 501
Recruiting Campaign, by A.M.D.C., 417
Recruits, R.N., in *Howe*, 393
—W. Indian, 755
Red Cross, helps prisoners, 26
——and Valetta hospital, 241
Red Eagles, 4th Indian Div., 5
Redfern, John, in Amsterdam, 675-76
Redhill, and Operation Dynamo, 156
Red Sea, British supply route, 54
Rees, Black Watch take, 238
Rees, Maj.-Gen. T. Wynford, and Dagger Division, 58, 61, 748
Referendum, on Italian monarchy, 200
Refugees, in Denmark, 532, 639
Regent's Park, Dutch bulbs in, 85
Rehabilitation, of disabled persons, 692
Reichswald Forest, Cameronians in, 526
——E. Lancs in, 140
Remagen, French students at, 530
Remembrance Day (1946), 518
——poppies for, 450, 479
Rennie, Maj.-Gen. T. G., death, 238
Renown, H.M.S., 202, 291
——trains Chinese sailors, 776
Renwick, Lt. J., of H.L.I., 652
Reparations, allocation, 575
—for Britain, from Germany, 600
Repulse, H.M.S., sunk, 259
Resistance, Dutch, in Amsterdam, 676
—in Solomons, 563
Retimo, airstrip at, 579, 580
"Retreat," beaten in Malta, 557
——in Nauplia, 485
Reykjavik, in 1947, 694, 695
Rheine, Cameronians take, 525
Rhine, battle of, D.C.L.I. in, 203
Rhine R., Airborne Crossing of, 323-24
——from Arnhem, 358
——Cameronians cross, 526
——crossing, Black Watch at, 238
———clean-up after, 255
———5th R.I.D.G. at, 590
———H.A.C. at, 398
———H.L.I. at, 654
———Household Cavalry at, 300, 302
———Marines at, 46
———R. Signals and, 331
——present-day scenes, 530
——R.E.s bridge, 715
Rhino Ferry, on Normandy beaches, 228
Rhodes, Dodecanese Is., 495, 496-97
—Force 133 on, 412
Rhodesia, N., war effort, 275
Rhodesia, S., in Victory Parade, 175
Ribbentrop, Joachim von, sentenced, 432-33, 435
Rice, Ceylon cultivates, 147
—guarded, Muar, 20
Rice Corps, R.I.A.S.C., 58
Richard I., and Cyprus, 214
Richards, Capt., R.A.S.C., 242
Richards, Capt. Stephen, and Himmler's secrets, 539-41
Richardson, Third Off. J. R., in *Tricula*, 634-35
Richelieu (ship), and *Colossus*, 293
Richmond (Yorks), Green Howards' Memorial Chapel, 622
Riddell, Maj. J. W., 593
Riddell-Webster, Gen., and Dunkirk, 3
Rideau Hall, Alexander's home, 21
Ridgway, Bernard T., in Arakan, 699-702
——on opium-running, 509-10
Ridgway, Maj.-Gen. M. B., and Rhine crossing, 323-24
Rifle Brigade, in Calais, 35
Rio San Juan (ship), 635
Ritchie, Lt.-Gen. N. M., 396
River Plate, battle of, Falkland Isles and, 104
Rizeigat Tribe, give horses, 307
Roads, British prisoners work on, 671
—of Burma, 59
—watch on, by L.R.D.G., 603, 605
Robb, A/M Sir John, 401
Roberts, H.M.S., at Walcheren, 46, 250, 252
Roberts, C.S.M. G. J., in Symi 410-13
Roberts, Maj.-Gen. G. P. B., and 11th Armoured Div. 100
——at Minden, 308
Roberts, Lt. P. S. W., V.C., 73
Roberts, Cpl. R., and Batavia memorial, 229
Robertson, Lt.-Gen. H. C. H., in Japan, 581
Robinson, Commodore, U.S.N., 335
Robson, W/O, in Japanese factory, 290
Rock, Maj. J. F., and parachute troops, 547
Rocket Propulsion, over tank obstacles, 257
Rockets, atom-carrying, experiments, 232
Rodney, H.M.S., and *Bismarck*, 451-52
——at Scapa, 291
Roer R., 5th R.I.D.G. on, 588
Rogerson, Staff-Sgt. S. G., G.C., 456
Rolfe, Lilian, 631
Rome, Cameronian pipers in, 526
—"Dukes" lead Victory March, 492, 493
—elections in, 200
—Inniskillings in, 462
—in 1946, 786, 787
Romita, Giuseppe, 200
Rommel, F/M Erwin, at Geoffrey Keyes' funeral, 516
——H.Q. raided, 515-16
Ronta, "Dukes" at, 493
Rooks, Maj.-Gen. W., and Italian armistice, 99
Roope, Lt.-Cdr. G. B., R.N., V.C., 194
Roosevelt, Franklin D., and Invasion of Normandy, 227
——and Italian armistice, 99
——memorial statue, 546
———donations for, 576
——on Pearl Harbour, 419
Rorqual, H.M.S., history, 136
——reinforces Malta, 377-78
Rose, Sub.-Lt. (A) W. B., and *Scharnhorst*, 131
Rosenberg, Alfred, sentenced, 432-33, 435
Ross, Lt. H. R., with Commandos, 388
Rotherham, Cdr. G. A., R.N., 451
Rothermere, S.S., sunk, 573
Rotten Row, Dutch horses in, 450
Roubaix, 5th R. Inniskilling D.G.s at, 587
Royal Albert Dock, new cranes at, 583
Royal Artillery: see Artillery
Royal Daffodil, R.N. releases, 649
Royal Fusilier, S.S., in convoy, 573
Royal Oak, H.M.S., sunk, 281-82, 528-29
Royal Scots (2nd), drum returned, 647
Royal Signals, at Dunkirk, 154-57
——new badge, 521
——war record, 331-34
Royal Sovereign, H.M.T., Royal Inniskilling Fusiliers in, 459
Royal Ulsterman, H.M.S., 31
Rubber, Ceylon cultivates, 147
—wild, colonies produce, 147
Rule Britannia, for 3rd Grenadier Guards, 7.
Rumania, peace treaty signed, 751-53
Rundstedt, F/M Gerd von, on conquest of Norway, 654
——counter-offensive, R.A.F. Regt. and, 78
——on invasion secrecy, 227
——in London, 770
Russell, Maj.-Gen. D., and 8th (Indian) Div., 717
Russell, Lt.-Col. J. D., of H.L.I., 651
Russia convoys to, adventures, 27-29
——figures, 159
—factories change over, 671
—Finland makes peace with, 342
—and World Food Conference, 359
Ruyter, Adm. de, burial place, 675
Ruzyn, Czech airfield, 660
Rybalko, Marshal, Montgomery and, 705
Ryder, Gen., and Cassino, 483
Ryder, Cdr. R. E. D., V.C., 67
Ryukaku (carrier), sunk, 195

S

Saar, French Customs in, 630
Saar R., Black Watch on, 235
Sabang, *Illustrious* at, 158, 159
Sachar, Bhim Sen, 775
Sadgrove, Charles J., as P.O.W., 349-50, 476-78, 670-71, 793-94
Saigon, Allied leaflets on, 346
—*Gloire* at, 734
Sailors, Danish, memorial to, 658
St. Aubin, Marines land at, 790-92
St. Columba's (London), London Scottish colours in, 673
St. David (hospital ship), at Malta, 55
St. Helena, importance, 104
St. Ives, Frog Men at, 225
St. James, H.M.S., in autumn exercises, 517
St. James's Park, bomb in, 96
St. John of Jerusalem, Knights of, in Malta, 183
St. Lô, today, 144
St. Louis, welcomes Lancasters, 265
St. Martin-des-Besaces, Irish Guards at, 366
St. Nazaire, raid on, 67-68
St. Nicholas, Welsh Guards at 747, 748
St. Patrick's Day, at Anzio, 462
St. Paul's Cathedral, Lancasters over, 353
St. Pierre-le-Viger, cemetery at, 238
St. Symphorien, victory milestone at, 406
St. Valéry-en-Caux, Black Watch at, 235, 238
——cemetery at, 238
——51st Div. at, 25-27, 332

St. Valéry-en-Caux *(cont.)*
——recaptured, 238, *248*
Salazar, Dr., and Portuguese neutrality, 623
Salerno, D. of Wellington's at, 491
—46th Div. at, 250
—Marine Commandos at, 44
—naval action off, 409-10
—Recce at, 108
Salonika, 4th Indian Div. at, *5*
Salote, Queen of Tonga, 467
Saltley, coal at, *745*
Salvation Army, war work, 703
Sandbanks, Suffolk Regt. at, *779*, 780
Sandhurst, H.M.S., bombed, 126-127
Sandhurst, end of R.M.C., *512*
San Dimitrio (ship), at Haifa, *520*
Sand Seas, in Libyan Desert, 603
Sangars (shelters), at Cassino, 483
Sangro R., Buffs on, 558
San Remo, Treaty of, 214
Sansom, Mrs. Odette, G.C. for, *381*
Santo Tomas, concentration Camp, Manila, 122-24
Sanzenbacher, Feldwebel, in Walcheren, 542-43
Sappers and Miners, in Burma, 60
Saratoga, U.S.S., with Eastern Fleet, *157*, 158, 159
Sasebo, Japanese submarine base, *52*
Sassoferrato, Household Cavalry at, 299
Sattelberg, Australians take, 707-08
Sauckel, Fritz, sentenced, 432-33, 435
Saumarez, H.M.S., mined, *614*
Saundby, A/M R.H.M.S., 186
Saunder, H.M.S., 253
Savage, A/B W. A., V.C., 68
Save R., at Belgrade, *565*
Savernake, explosion at, *456*
Savo Is., battle of, 196
Scandrett, Richard, on White Russia, 447
Scapa Flow, defence, and new roads, *528-29*
——*Royal Oak* at, *281*
Scarf, Sqn. Ldr. A. S. K., V.C., *457*
Scarlet Beach, Australians at, 707
Scarlett, Maj.-Gen. the Hon. P. G., 555
Schacht, Hjalmar, acquitted, *432-33*, *434*, 435
Scharnhorst (ship), escape, 131-33
—and *Glorious*, 291-92
—as raider, 451
Schepke, Capt., death, 489
Scheveningen, Gerbrandy on, 148, *149*
Schirach, Baldur von, sentenced, *432-33*, 435
Schnorkel, success, 489
Schools, Japanese, children rear goats, *290*
Schreiber, Lt.-Gen. Sir E. C. A., and Suffolk Regt., *779*
Schroeder, Lt.-Col., surrenders Amsterdam, 676
Schumacher, Dr. Kurt, *585*
Schuman, M., at Metz, *261*
Schwarzhuber, Johann, 631
Scotland, new roads in, *528-29*
Scots Guards, at Uelzen, 654
Scott, Capt., M.C., of H.L.I., 654
Scott, Rev. R. F. V., D.D., *673*
Scott, Lt.-Col. W. P., in Burma, 314
Scottish Division (15th), war record, 142
Scottish Rifles : *see* Cameronians
Scrubber, electric, in *Theseus*, *209*
S.E.A.C., Cocos Is. base, 282-84
Seafires, of *Theseus*, *209-09*
Seaforth Highlanders of Canada, 643
Seagrim, Lt.-Col. D. A., V.C., 622
Sea Island Cotton, uses, 147
Seal, H.M.S., truly story, *41*
Sealion, H.M.S., in Brest, 131
Sea Lions, in Falklands, *763*
Sea-Mine-Detonating Craft, for demolition, 674
Searchlight Regt., (66th), 267
Searchlights, for Chinese railways, *514*
—German, across Channel, *591*
—of Gibraltar, *55*
Second Escort Group, achievements, 489
Seine, Ilede, De Gaulle at, *360*
Seine R., Cameronians cross, 526
——5th R.I.D.G. cross, *588*
Selarang, prisoners at, 93
Sendall, Maj. W. R., on R. Marines, 43-46
Sendall, Maj. *(cont.)*
——on Marines at Atlantic Wall, 790-92
——on Marines in Sicily, 643-44
——at Walcheren, 250-53
Sennelager, R. Norfolks at, *514*
Sentry, British, at Helmstedt, *736*
—naval, Tokyo, *609*
—Portuguese, *624*
Seventy-Eighth Division, disbandment garden-party, *558*
Sewing-machine, electric, *422*
Seychel'es, share in victory, 627
—strategic importance, 83
Seychelles Pioneer Corps, for victory parade, *135*
Seyss-Inquart, Arthur, sentenced, *432-33*, *435*
Sham Shui Po, prison camp, *15*
Shapiro, L. S. B., and Himmler's secrets, 539-41
Sharp, Sidney W., in liberated Ghent, 669-70
Sharrild, R.A.F. memorial at, *357*
Shaving, for D.L.I., *428*
Shaw, Sir John, in Jerusalem bomb outrage, *295*
Sheep Dog, R.M.P. tend, 719
Sheerness, minesweepers for, *418*
Sheffield, H.M.S., and *Bismarck*, 451
Sheffield, change-over in, *463*
Shepherd, Lt.-Col. W. S., and Viking badge, *521*
Shepley, F. L., on Rome today, 786
Shepway, Grand Court of, *328*
Sherbrooke, Capt. R. St. V., V.C., 394, 739-40
Shertok, Moshe, released, *520*
Sherwood Rangers, at Tripsrath, 652
Shinwell, Rt. Hon. Emanuel, *664*
Ship, aerial torpedo sinks, *28*
Shipping, Axis, sunk by mines, 159
—Finnish, Allies return, 342
Shoeblacks, Portuguese, *624-25*
Short, Gen. Walter, and Pearl Harbour, 420
Short, Capt. E. W., on D.L.I., 427-30
Shotley, *Puffin* at, *546*
Shropshire, H.M.A.S., in Capt. Cook Dock, *553*
Shuttlewood, Guardsman A. A., at Furnes, 473-74
——on German spy-dogs, 318-319
Shwebo, Gloucesters at, 270
—Worcestershires at, 686
Shwedaung, Gloucesters at, 270
Shweli R., Buffs on, *558*
Siam, R.E.s triumphs in, *263*
Siang Valley, supplies for, *613*
Sibbert, Lt.-Col. F. R., *647*
Sicily, Black Watch in, *236*
—Buffs in, 558
—Cameronians in, 523, *524*
—D.L.I. in, 429, 430
—50th Div. in, 300
—1st (Airborne) Div. in, 556
—Green Howards in, 619, 622
—H.A.C. in, 395
—Inniskilling Fusiliers in, 459, *461*, 462
—invasion, 51st Div. in, 332
——*Mauritius* at, 601-03
——Marines in, 642-44
——R.A.F. Regt. and, 75
—Marine Commandos in, **44**
—Recce in, 108
—R.E.s in, 717
—R. Hampshire Regt. in, 722
—78th Div. in, 460
Sick Bay, of *Commonwealth*, *615*
——of *Worcester*, *690*
Siddall, Lt. D. R., 494
Sidi Nsir, Hampshires at, 611
Sidi Rafa, Rommel's H.Q. at, *515*, *516*
Sidky Pasha, in London, *490*
Sidney, Maj. W. P., V.C., 8
Siebengebirge, tug passes, *530*
Sierra Leone, troops from, Victory Parade, *135*
——W. African territory, 243
Signallers, British, Malaya, *20*
—Chinese, R.N. trains, *776*
—of H.L.I., truly, *654*
Signalling, by flag, Cyprus, 620
—in *Worcester*, *688*
Signposts, at Stonehenge Camp, *685*
—in W. Desert, *719*
Sigurdsson, Jon, Icelandic patriot, *695*
Sikhs, for victory parade, *129*
"Silver Phantom," *Aurora*, *458*
Simeto R., Cameronians on, 523
——D.L.I. cross, *429*
Simpson, Gen. W. H., decorates Buffs, *556*
Sims, U.S.S., sunk, 195
Singapore, British cars for, *226*
—Commando raids on, 387-89
– fall, Usill on, 339
Singapore *(cont.)*
—liberation, news sent, *534*
—R.A.F. Regt. in, *78*
—R. Marines in, *44*
—Suffolk Regt. in, 780
—surrender of, 90-93
—why the Cease-Fire sounded, 259-60
Singh, Jemadar, in Tokyo, *646*
Singh, Jemadar Ram Sarup, V.C., *457*
Singh, Havildar Umrao, V.C., *129*
Singhu, Worcestershires at, 686
Singora, Japanese air base, 259
Sinhalese, in Ceylon, *627*
Sinker, Lt.-Col, D.S.O., 718
Sinthe, Ordnance Field Park at, 666
Sittang R., D. of Wellington's at, 491
Skeats, T. C., in *G. S. Walden*, *606-07*
"Skins, The," R. Inniskilling Fusiliers, 742
Skvorzov, Lt. A. V., drawings by, *15*
Slavery, abolition, Mauritius, 627
Slave Trade, in W. Africa, 243
Slim, Gen. Sir William, and Burma campaign, 531
——and Cameronians, 523
——on E. Africans, 691
——private life, *151*
——in Victory Parade, *165*, 186
Slit Trenches, British, Cassino, *483*
——D.C.L.I. in, *204*
——R. Hampshires in, *722*
Slovakia, liberation anniversary, *38*
Smith, Dr., in Santo Tomas, 122
Smith, G. in *Royal Daffodil*, *649*
Smith, Lt. Gilbert, on Tanks for Tobruk, *61*
Smith, Maj.-Gen. W. Bedell, and Italian armistice, 99, 100
——at Peace Conference, *306*
Smoke Screen, destroyers lay, *517*
Smuts, F/M J. C., brings S. African gifts, *490*
——at Commonwealth Conference, *130*
——private life, *340*
——at Victory Parade, *175*, 186
Snaefell Glacier, from Reykjavik, 694
Snell, L. S., on D.C.L.I., 203-06
Snipers, British, in Tunisia, *610*
—cleared from Cassino, *483*
—5th Column, in Calais, 35
Snow, in Britain, *744-45*
—in Italy, *621*
Sobieski (ship), D. of Wellington's in, *492*
Sofia, in 1946, *468*, *469*
Sokolovsky, Gen. Vasily, *258*
Solomon Is., campaign in, 196
——share in victory, *563*
Somaliland, British, Black Watch in, 235
——E. Africans in, 275
Somaliland Camel Corps, 275
Somerville, Vice-Adm. Sir James, and *Bismarck*, 451
——and Dunkirk, 4
——in Mediterranean, 54
——in Victory Parade, 186
Somme Day, E. Lancs celebrate, *142*
Soragna, Márchese di, signs peace treaty, *753*
Sorbonne, The, U.N.E.S.C.O. in, *566*
Sorrell, Alan, painting by, *592-93*
South Africa, gifts for Britain from, *490*
South Africans, memorial, Alamein, *679*
South African War, veterans of, *738*
Southampton, Mulberry Harbour parts at, *546*
—*Triumph* at, *208-09*
Southern Venturer, whaling ship, *212*
Southwick Park, *Dryad* at, *335*
Southwood, Viscount, gave Garden of Remembrance, *105*
Sparrow, Capt. Oswald, in *Tricula*, 634, 635
Spee, Adm. von, off Falklands, 104
Speer, Albert, sentenced, *432-433*, 435
Spencer, Capt. Paul, at Walcheren, 253
Spencer, Ldg.-Smn. Victor, D.S.M., 631
Spendlove, A/B Albert, D.S.M., 631
Sphakia, evacuation, Marines and, 43
Spies, dogs as, 318-19
—shot at Tower, 94
Spirit of Winship, light aircraft, 699
Spitfire Mark I, in War Museum, *552*
Spitfires, in Cocos Is., *283*
—in Japan, *290*
—in Victory Fly-past, *180*
Spokane, U.S.S., in Thames, *487*
Sports, Britain caters for, *423*
Spree R., Palace Bridge wrecked, *117*
Squid, anti-submarine weapon, 489
Stacpoole, Maj. Derek de, death, 252
Stade, Household Cavalry take, 300
Staghound, armoured car, in Ghent, *669*
Stag K., H.M.S., 253
Stalag XXB., Sadgrove in, 793-794
Stalin, Marshal Josef, Montgomery meets, *674*
——portrait, Vienna *50*
Stalin Tanks, Montgomery and, *705*
Stamps, British victory, *190*
—French, for Peace Conference, *304-05*
——and U.N.E.S.C.O., *566*
—new German, *424*
—Polish, commemorate Cassino, *484*
Standard, of Japanese Marines, *196*
Stanier, Col. Sir Alexander, Bart., 747
Stanley, Col. Oliver, in W. Indies, *755*
Stanley-Clarke, Lt., of Irish Guards, 366
Stanmore, Bentley Priory, *510*
Stanton, Sub.-Lt. R. G. G., R.N.R., D.S.O., 631
Starcevich, Pte. T., V.C., *103*
Star Dale (aircraft), at Lisbon, *626*
Starr, Brig.-Gen. R. E., in Tokyo, *646*
Starr, Capt. W. B. S., in *Tairoa*, 413-14
Stars and Stripes, in Santo Tomas, 123
Stavanger (destroyer), formerly *Crystal*, *453*
Steam-rollers, British export, *226*
Steele, Capt. Gordon, V.C., R.N., 690
Steele, Lt.-Gen. Sir James, with Buffs, *558*
Sten Gun, of British air-trooper, *323*
Stephenson, Dr., in Santo Tomas, 122
Sternbeck, Father, at Lidice, 355
Stettinius, Edward, on Security Council, *56*
Stirling Castle, A. & S. Highlanders at, *737*
Stirlings, cross Rhine, *324*
Stokers, Chinese, R.N. trains, *776*
Stokes, Pte. J., V.C., 492
Stone, Capt. L. E., in liberated Paris, 507-09
Stonehenge Camp, signpost at, *685*
Stoops, Lt. I. M., in *Rorqual*, *378*
Stopford, Lt.-Gen. Sir Montagu, 229
Stopper Patrol, 131-33
Store, shelter as, Hagen, *197*
Stork, H.M.S., and *Chobry*, 363
Strachey, John, at food conference, 244
Straits Settlements, constituents, 339
Strange, Wing-Cdr. L. A., 547
Stranraer, new port at, 717
Stratemeyer, Lt.-Gen. G. E., and visiting Lancasters, *265*
Straussler, Nicholas, and D.D. tanks, 228
Street-fighting, in Kuala Lumpur, *637*
Streicher, Julius, sentenced, *432-33*, *434*, 435
Stretcher-bearers, German, dogs with, *319*
——of H.L.I., Conges, *651*
Strickland, Mabel, on the Maltese, 183
Strikes, in Athens, 198
Stripey, *Warspite's* cat, *677*
Strong, Brig. K. W., and Italian armistice, 99, 100
Stubbs, Capt., of *Doric Star*, 414
Studland Bay, mines cleared at, *352*
Sturdee, Adm. Sir Doveton, 104
Sturgeon, H.M.S., at S. Nazaire, *67*
Subar, Commandos at, 387
Submarines, British, for Norway, 511
—Japanese, destruction, *52*
—midget, infra-red rays for, *777*
Suda Bay, bombed, *578*, 579
Sudan, D.C.L.I. in, *205*
—Worcestershires in, 683
Sudan Defence Force, and Italy, 307
———for victory parade, *134*
Sudeland, Cameronians take, 524
Sueur, Hubert Le, Charles I statue, *65*, *80-81*
Suez, H.L.I. at, *392*
Suez Canal, *Rajah* in, *24*
Suffolk, H.M.S. and *Bismarck*, 451
Suffolk Regiment, war record, 779-82
Suffren, Cdre., on Ceylon, 83
Sugar-beet, Gloucesters harvest, *269*
Suggit, L/Sgt. H. V., escape bid, 285-87
Suicide Planes, Japanese, in action, *766*, *767*
Suliman the Magnificent, attacks Malta, 183
Sumatra, Malay Kingdom in, 339
—mercy planes over, 789-90
Sunday Times The, on battle of Britain, 403
Sunderland Flying Boat, and *Marcello*, 489
———in Victory Fly-past, *180*
Supermarine E10/44, jet plane, *386*
Supplies, by air, Himalaya, *613*
———for P.O.W., Sumatra, 789-90
Support Craft, Marines and, 44, 46
Supreme Soviet, members in Britain, 770
Surabaya, as F.A.A. target, 159
—V.C.P. in, *700*
Sutherland, Hugh, on Goering, *499*
Sutlej, H.M.I.S., at Hiroshima, 274
Swansea, and Arethusa, *712*
Swaziland, war effort, 307
Sweden, help Norway, 404
—joins U.N., *617*
—wooden houses from, *374*
Sweets, for German children, 639
Swinton, Rt. Hon. Viscount, and W. African importance, 104
Swordfish, and *Scharnhorst's* escape, 131-33
Sydney, H.M.A.S., and *Emden*, 284
——war record, *618*
Sydney, Captain Cook Dock, *553*
—*Implacable* at, 72
Syfret, Adm. Sir Neville, C.-in-C. Home Fleet, *517*
Symi, Allied occupation, 410-13
—Dodecanese Is., *495*
Syracuse, Allies take, 601
Syria, Black Watch in, 235
—D.L.I. in, 428, 430
—Household Cavalry in, 299
Szabo, Tania, *640*
Szabo, Mme Violette, G.C., *631*

T

Tabor, Mt., from Kafr-Kisch, *294*
Tabori, Paul, on Belgrade today, 564
——on Budapest, *19*
Taffy, R.W.F. mascot, *42*
Tagus, R., *Roosevelt* in, *322*
Tairoa, *Graf Spee* and, 413-14
Taite, Maj. Hamish, in Amsterdam, 675-76
Takamatsu, Prince and Princess, *290*
Takoradi, W. African port, 104
Talaai, Lieut. Henry, of Tongan Voluntary Defence Force, 467
Talamba (hospital ship), sunk, 601
Talisman, H.M.S., Piggott in, 220
Tamatave, British land at, *761*, 762
Tamils, in Ceylon, *627*
—in Malaya, 339
Tanganyika, strategic importance, 83
Tangoucha, capture, Inniskillings at, *462*
Tank Bridges, in Normandy landings, 228
Tank Obstacles, device against, *257*
Tank Regt. R., E. Lancs battalion in, 139
—— (4th), for Tobruk, *61*
Tanks, A.V.R.E., 713
—British, D. of Wellington's with, *491*
——at Ede, *494*
——at Nijmegen, *218*
—dummy, R.E.s make, *714*
—German, R.E.s demolish, *715*
—Grenadiers give up, *10*
—of Guards Armoured Division, *10*
—of Irish Guards, camouflaged, *365*

Tanks *(cont.)*
—Italian, at Alamein, *555*
—Montgomery on, 371
—for Tobruk, 61
—U.S. 100-ton, *480*
—in Victory Parade, *169*
Taplow, barbed wire at, *706*
Taranto, battle of, *Illustrious* at, *488*
—R.E.s at, *714*
Tarnopolski, Sgt. J., *711*
Tartar, H.M.S., and *Mashona,* 452
Task Forces, for invasion of Normandy, 227-28
Tasman Sea, *Pamir* in, *704*
Tatarescu, M., at Peace Conference, *327*
——signs peace treaty, *753*
Tatchell, C.Q.M.S., of K.O.Y.L.I., *308*
Tatlock, Sapper, and Exeter bombs, *63*
Taukkyan, Gloucesters at, 268
—Ordnance Field Park at, 666
Taungi, Gloucesters take, 270
Taurus, H.M. submarine, at Melbourne, 72
Tavoy, M'Call at, 345
Taylor, Lieut. J. L., at Arnhem, 217-19
——on Recce, 107-10
Taylor, Flt.-Lt. J. T., in Burma, *701*
Taylor, Brig.-Gen. Maxwell, in Rome, 100
Tea, production, *245*
Teachers, German shortage, 351
Teak Trees, felling, Burma, 60
Tebarka, Allies occupy, 612
Tebourba, German A. A. gun at, *612*
Tedder, Marshal of R.A.F., Baron, and battle of Britain anniversary, *402*
——private life, *276*
——Q. Wilhelmina to, *85*
——in Victory Parade, *165*
Teheran, Household Cavalry in, 299
—R.M.P. in, *719*
Teheran Conference, Buffs guard, 558
Tel Aviv, martial law in, *774*
——unrest in, *215*
Telecommunications, story, *534*
Telephone Exchange, regimental, of Suffolks, *780*
Telephones, plastic instruments, *465*
—R. Signals and, *331*
Tempests, and V1s, *732*
Tennie La Sorte, Grenadier Guards at, 9
Tennis Balls, from bomber factory, *466*
Termoli, Inniskillings at, 462
—Marine Commandos at, 44
Terneuzen, Cameronians at, 524
Trepeshev, Gen., Bulgarian deputy-premier, *468*
Terrible (ship), at Narvik, *210*
Terry, Sgt., raids Rommel's H.Q., 516
Tewson, Peter, with F/M Lord Gort, 697-98
Thames R., colliers in, *745*
——*Spokane* in, *487*
——V1 in, *348*
——on V Night, *178, 188*
——warships in, *181*
——wreck disposal in estuary, *418*
Thanbyuzayat, railhead, 345
Theatre, in Bulgaria, 468
—in Paris, 310
—in Prague, 660
Theron, Maj.-Gen. François, in Paris, *326*
Theseus, H.M.S., at Bergen, *208-209, 224*
Thirty-Sixth Division (British), war record, 186
Thom, Maj. W. W., and Belisha beacon, *380*
Thomas, Lt.-Gen. G., opens Cologne bridge, *114*
Thompson, Actg. P/O A. W., C.G.M., 631
Thompson, Musician H. T., in *Bonaventure, 351*
Thompson, Lt. (A) L. F., R.N.V.R., and V1s, 731-32
Thorburn, Lt.-Col., of H.L.I., 651
Thorn, British P.O.W. at, *477*
Thor Thors, and U.N., *617*
Thrasher, H.M. submarine, end of, *73*
Threshing, in Cos, *497*
Thumeries, conscripts trained at, 269
Thunderbolt, H.M.S., Piggott in, 219
Thury, R.E.s clear highway, *717*
Tiger Moth, facts about, 447
Tigre (destroyer), *Manxman* as, 554
Tildy, President, of Hungary, 19
Tillin, Ordnance Field Park at, 666
Tilney, Lt.-Col. H. A. R., on Medicina, 16
Tirana, 278, 279
Tirpitz (ship), pursuit of, *667-668*
—St. Nazaire and, 67, 68
—at Trondheim, 131
Tito, Marshal, in Belgrade, 564, *565*
——salary, 564
Tiwana, Sir Khizar Hayat Khan, 306
Tmimi, H.A.C. at, *395*
Tobruk, Black Watch at, 235
—Buffs at, 555
—D.L.I. at, 428
—supplies for, 253-54
—tanks for, 61
—Worcestershires at, *683*
Tojo, Gen. Hideki, trial, *230*
Tokyo, Empire Day in, *193, 207*
—naval sentry in, *609*
—P/W camps in, *446-47*
—Punjabis in, *641, 646*
—R. Scots' drum in, *647*
—U.S. huts in, *290*
—war trials in, *230*
Tommy-gun, instruction in, *720*
Tonga, share in victory, 467
—war contribution, 14
Torbay, H.M.S., Commandos in, 515
Torpedo, aerial, sinks ship, *28*
—Italian human, *552*
Torpello (ship), blown up, 602
Tottenham, Cdr. (S) E. L., in *Illustrious,* 410
Toungoo, Gloucesters at, *268*
—Ordnance Field Park at, *665,* 667
Tournai, transit camp at, *478, 479*
Tovey, Adm. Sir John, and *Bismarck,* 451-52
Tower of London, bombed, 93-95
——and V1s, 348-49
——Victory Parade passes, *169*
Toys, Britain makes, *422, 464-65*
Tracer Shells, off Salerno, *410*
Tractors, unloaded, Helsinki, *342*
Trafalgar Day, Navy League wreath, *481*
Trafalgar Square, floodlit, *172*
——Roosevelt memorial collecting office, *576*
——on Victory morning, *173*
Traffic Control, in Prague, *660*
Tragino R., aqueducts over, *547,* 548
Traitors, Norwegian, figures, 159
Traitor's Gate, damaged, *95*
Trams, in Bucharest, 629
Tramways, of Berlin, reconstruction, *648*
Transjordan, importance to Britain, 54
——independence, 214, *215*
—war effort, 214
Trans-Jordan Frontier Force, 214
Transport, in Berlin, 115
—British, at Pyawbwe, *666*
—of Green Howards, overhauling, *620*
—by mule, Burma, *249*
—Paris improvement, 310
—Rome shortage, 786, *787*
—in Warsaw, *500*
Transport Command, 216 Squadron, *77*
Transport Planes, of R.A.F., S. France, *633*
Transport Services, in Victory Parade, *168*
Trawlers, at Dunkirk, 2
Treml, Dr. Franz, at Lidice, 356
Trenchard, Marshal of R.A.F., Lord, *402*
Trent, Sqd.-Ldr L. H., V.C., *457*
Trevor-Roper, Maj. H. R., on Hitler, 659
Trewin, J. C., on V-night, 188-89
Tribal Class Destroyers, Mountbatten and, 53
Tricula, M. V., adventure, 634-35
Trieste, Allied parade in, *118*
—demonstrations in, *231*
Trincomalee, air raid on, 627
—*Illustrious* at, 157, 158, 159
—importance, 83
Trinidad, petroleum from, 147
Tripoli, Buffs in, 556
Tripolitania, Black Watch in, *237*
Tripsrath, H.L.I. at, 652
—Worcestershires take, 684
Triumph, H.M.S., awaits parachute troops, 547
——at Southampton, *208-09*
Troarn, Suffolk Regt. at, *781*
Trocquer, M. Le, on V Day, *189*
Trondheim (destroyer), formerly *Croziers, 453*
Troon, invasion practice at, 643
Trooping the Colour, in Japan, *581*
Tropic Sea (ship), *Truant* and, *586*
Trottobas, Capt. Michael, memorial, *600*
"Trout Line," Marines in, 46
Truant, H.M.S., to be broken up, *600*
——war record, *586*
Trucks, Japanese, in Singapore, *93*
Truman, President Harry, and atom bomb, 232
Tuck, Stanford, in battle of Britain, 511
Tufnell, Lt. K., of E. Lancs. Regt., 140
Tug Argan Gap, E. Africans at, 275
Tulkarm, Household Cavalry at, *299*
Tunbridge Wells, Bevin at, *438*
Tunis, capture, H.A.C. at, 395
Tunisia, Blade Force in, *610, 611-12*
—D.C.L.I. in, 203
—D.L.I. in, 430
—Grenadier Guards in, 7
—Pioneers in, *719*
—R.E.s in, *715*
—Suffolk Regt. in, 780
Tunnels, prisoners make, 668-69
Turkey, and Trans-Jordan, 214
Turley-George, Flt. Lt. D. R., in *Empire Tide,* 27
Turner, Capt. C. B., on Belisha beacon, 378-80
Twin Knobs, British hold, 249-250
Twinnge, E. Lancs. at, 142
Two Tree Hill, Inniskilling Fus. at, *460*
Two Years' Plan, for Czechoslovakia, 660
Tynedale, H.M.S., at S. Nazaire, 67-68
Tyneside Scottish (1st) with Black Watch, 235, 236

U

U-570, surrenders, 489
U-boat Campaign, McMurtrie on, 489
U-boats, crew casualties, 159
——*Empire Tide* and, 29
——numbers destroyed, 190
——S. Nazaire base, 67
——uncompleted, scuttled, *354*
Uelzen, Cameronians take, *525*
—H.L.I. at, 654
Uganda, H.M.S., and invasion of Sicily, 601
Uganda, cotton production, 147
—importance, 83
Ulster Rifles, R., and Rhine crossing, 324
Umberto II, K., leaves Italy, *200*
Unden, Besten, and U.N., *617*
Underground Movement, in Holland, 542
U.N.E.S.C.O., Paris conference, *566*
Unfederated Malay States, history, 339
Union Jack, lowered, Alexandria, *757*
——Cairo, *264*
Union Jack, Army newspaper, *367-70*
United Nations, end of 1st Assembly, *617*
——Security Council, 56
————and Trieste, 231
United States of America, awards to Buffs, *556*
————Lancasters' good will mission to, *265*
————in Victory Parade, *166*
Unknown Warrior, tomb, Berlin, *116*
————Rome, *786*
U.N.R.R.A., and Albania, 278
————in Cos, 497
————in Greece, 198
————helps Italy, *655*
————Iceland a member, 694
————and White Russia, 447
————and Yugoslavia, 564
Upton, Clive, painting by, *592*
Urquhart, Sgt. Philip, and Himmler's secrets, 539-41
Usill, Harley V., Africa's share in victory, 691
——on Atlantic Colonies, 104
——Britain's Life-Line in Middle East, 54
——on British W. Indies and Bermuda, 755
——Ceylon, Mauritius and the Seychelles, 627
——on Cyprus, Palestine and Trans-Jordan, 214
——on Empire and Victory, *14*
——First Battles of E. Africans, 275
————of W. Africans, 243
Usill, Harley *(cont.)*
——Gibraltar and Malta at war, 183
——Hongkong, Borneo, Fiji, and Tonga, 467
——on Indian Ocean and Pacific Colonies, 83
——Malaya and Singapore Summing-up, 339
——on Solomons and other Pacific isles, 563
——on Sudan and other African territories, 307
——War Stores of British Colonies, 147
Usk, Institute of Agriculture, *544*
Utah Beach, state-owned, 671
——today, *144-45*
Uzzell, Jack, ploughman, *448*

V

V1, first on London, 348-49
——night-fighters and, 731-32
——R.A.F. Regt. and, 76
——Tempests destroy, *732*
——in war Museum, *552*
V2, for Australia, *706*
—the Tower and, 349
Valentine Tanks, scissors bridges on, 228
Valetta, casualties at, *55*
—parade contingent in, *137*
—reconstruction in, *239, 240-41*
Valiant, H.M.S., and Norway evacuation, 291, 292
Valkenswaard Cemetery, *296*
Vandeleur, Lt.-Col. J. O. E., of Irish Guards, 366
Vanguard, H.M.S., battle honours, 97
——at Clydebank, *32*
——for trials, *112-13*
Vangunu Is., Kennedy in, 563
Variety Show, poster, Omori, *446*
Vassilievsky, Marshal, Montgomery with, *709*
V Day, cost, 287
Velchev, Gen., Bulgarian war minister, 468
Velden Officers' Club, garden party at, *558*
Vellasco, Dr., on Security Council, *56*
Venafro, bombed, 484
Venice, British Military Police in, *288*
—"Union Jack" published, *367-70*
Venning, Gen. Sir Walter K., *203*
Venray, Suffolk Regt. at, *781*
Verdun, Civil Affairs Team at, *507*
Verity, Capt. Hedley, death, 619
Verney, Maj.-Gen. G. L., 669
Verson, D.C.L.I. take, 203
Ver-sur-Mer, D-Day in, 189-90
Vesselhovede, Welsh Guards at, 750
Vian, Adm. Sir Philip, R.N., and *Bismarck,* 451-52
——in *Cossack,* 444
——in *Illustrious,* 486
——and invasion of Normandy, 227
——new appointment, 449
——and Sicilian invasion, 643
——in Victory Parade, 186
Vibo Valentia, Marine Commandos at, 44
Vick, Chief-Eng. Ernest E., *57*
Vickers Viking, at Lisbon, *626*
Vichy Govt., N. Africa resistance, 611
Victor Emmanuel III, K., abdication, *200*
——and armistice terms, 100
Victorious, H.M.S., and *Bismarck,* 451
Victory Parade, in London, 161-92
——arrivals for, *129, 134-35*
Vienna, compulsory labour in, 351
—D.L.I. in, 430
—life today, 50-51
Viking Star (ship), sunk, crew's adventures, *222*
Villers Bocage, E. Lancs Regt. at, 139, *141*
——5th R.I.D.G. at, 587, *588*
Villers-Bretonneux, Australian memorial at, 351
Villers-le-Sec, ploughing at, *560*
Vincent, Maj. J. T. E., at Walcheren, 252
Vindictive, H.M.S., and Norway evacuation, 291
Vis, H.L.I. in, 652
Vishinsky, A., in Paris, *70*
——at Peace Conference, *306,* 313
Vistula R., at Warsaw, *501*
Visual Control Posts, in Burma, 699-702
Vital, Sgt., and Himmler's secrets, 539-41
Vitosha, Mt., outside Sofia, 468
Vivacious, H.M.S., and *Scharnhorst,* 132
Volage, H.M.S., mined, 614
Volchkov, Lt.-Col., at Nuremberg, *431*
Volunteer American Field Service, in Victory Parade, *169*
V-sign, Churchill gives, *185*
——Indians give, *5*
——in Madagascar, *30*
Vulture, Monte, aqueducts, attack on, 547-48
V-weapons, underground factory for, 124-26

W

W.A.A.F., at R.A.F. memorial, *402*
Wadara, Gold Coast Brigade at, 243
Wadi Akarit, 51st Div. at, 332
Wageningen, surrender conference at, 675
Wahagnies, Tewson at, 697
Wak, El, raid on, 243
Wakeford, Major R., V.C., 718
Wakenshaw, Pte. A. H., V.C., 428
Wake-Walker, Rear-Adm. W. F., and *Bismarck,* 451-52
Walcheren, Cameronians on, 524, 526
—H.L.I. at, 651
—ordeal of, 542-43
—re-afforestation, 543
—reclaimed, 317-18
—R. Marines at, *45,* 46, 250-53
Wales, manufactures, *759*
Walker, A/B, in *Grenville,* 572
Walker, Capt. F. J., R.N., 182, 489
Walker, Maj. G. Goold, on H.A.C., 395-98
Walker, Lt. Ronald G., G.M., and Exeter's bombs, 62-63
Walrus Aircraft, for whaling, *728*
War Artists, *15-17, 591-94, 754*
Warburton, F/O A., 547
Warburton-Lee, Capt. B. A.W. V.C., grave, *210*
War Crimes, figures, 703
War Crimes Trials, figures, 543
War Criminals, Hungarian, trials, 19
Ward, Eileen M., and Mulberry, 733
War Memorials, in Denmark, *658*
War Museum, Imperial, re-opened, *552*
War Office, new badge, *521*
War Savings, in Ceylon, 627
Warsaw, British airmen's graves in, 607
—today, *500, 501*
Warspite, H.M.S., at Malta, *409*
——off Salerno, 409, *410*
——off Sicily, *602*
——to be broken up, *677*
——at Walcheren, 46, 250, 252
——war record, 6
Warwick Castle, S.S., in peace and war, *770*
Washing Machines, instead of bombers, *465*
Washington, food conference at, *244*
—Montgomery's arrival, *385*
Wasungen, hospital at, 26
Water, shortage, Singapore, 260
Water-point, at Benghazi, *627*
Waters, Elsie and Doris, 444
Water Supply, R.E.s and, 715
Watson, L/Cpl., and Italian aqueducts, 548
Watson, Maj. G. F., in Belfast, *267*
Wau, fighting for, 196
Wavell, F/M Viscount, and Arakan drive, *249*
——and Burma Campaign, 531
——and Crete, *579,* 580
——Epstein's bust of, *593*
——and 4th Div., 620
——and Giffard, 595
——in London, *616*
——in private life, *213*
——in Singapore, 260
Waveney, H.M.S., and *Gloire, 734*
Webb-Carter, Lt.-Col. B. W., 492
Weech, Trooper, of 4th R. Tank Regt., 61
Weezen, Municipal elections at, *424*
Weismann, Hauptsturmfuehrer, at Lidice, 355
Welch Fusiliers, R., freedom of Caernarvon, *42*
————in Japan, *581*
————in Paris parade, *101*
Wellington Barracks, chapel bombed, 348
Wellington Bombers, factory, makes washing-machines, *465*

Wells, Lieut. J. L., R.N.V.R., in *Glory*, 537-38
Welsh Division (53rd), war record, 396
Welsh Guards, at Boulogne, 363
——in Calais, 35
——war record, 747-50
Welshman, H.M.S., lays mines, 131
Welsh Regt., in Crete, 579
Wenceslas, monument in Prague, 660
—Square, 661
Weseke, D.L.I. at, 430
Wesel, art treasures at, 319
Weser R., Cameronians cross, 526
Wessex Division (43rd), war record, 206
West African Frontier Force, R., war record, 243
West African Pioneers, in Middle East, 243
West African Reconnaissance Regt., 691
West Africans, in Burma, 691
——first battles, 243
West African Way, in Burma, 691
Western Desert, Green Howards in, 619
——H.L.I. in, 651
——Household Cavalry in, 299, 300
——R.A.F. Regt. in, 75
——R.E.s in, 714
——R.M.P. in, 719
——R. Signals in, 331, 333
Western Front, Gloucesters on, 269
West Indies, British, share in victory, 755
Westkapelle, pill-box home in, 672
——R. Marines at, 46, 250-53
Westminster Abbey, Gort memorial service at, 33
——Roll of Honour for, 674
——Services' memorial, 425

Westminster (South) Area Committee, 745
Weston, Maj.-Gen. E. C., R.M., in Crete, 579-80
Weston - Super - Mare, prefabs made at, 584
Westphalia, Provincial Advisory Council of, 102
West Riding Division (49th), graves, Holland, 296
——war record, 268
West Riding Squadron (609), of R.A.F., 156
West Wall, demolition, 254
West Yorkshire Regt., badge, 20
——(11th), in Falklands, 762
Weymouth, adopts *Rorqual*, 138
Whale Oil, production, 212
Whaling, aircraft help, 728
Wheat, Canadian, at Hamburg, 341
White, Brig. Sir Bruce, and Mulberry, 771
Whitehill Colliery, mechanization in, 656-57
White Russia, devastation in, 447
Whitshed, H.M.S., and *Scharnhorst*, 132
Whitworth, Adm. Sir William, at Narvik, 210
Wholey, Mrs. Ethel, in Santo Tomas camp, 122-24
Wight, I. of, Black Watch in, 236
Wilcocks, Capt. G. H., of Irish Guards, 366
Wilder, Capt. N. P., with L.R.D.G., 604
Wilhelmina, Q., and Arnhem memorial, 391
——with Churchill, 98
——escape, Irish Guards and, 363
——R. Marines and, 43
——presents horses, 297
Wilhelmshaven, demolition at, 255

Wilkinson, Norman, painting by, 443
Wilkinson, Lt. Thomas, V.C., R.N.R., 631, 671
Willcocks, A. J., on D.E.M.S., 572-74
William I, statue, Falaise, 143
William III, statue returns to London, 79
William, H.R.H. Prince, Lord L. Mountbatten with, 53
Williams, Douglas, on Victory Parade, 174
William Thorpe Colliery, N.C.B. flag at, 664
Willis, Vice-Adm. Sir A. U., at Salerno, 409
Wilmott, Lt., in *Talisman*, 220
Wilsey, Brigadier, D.S.O., 494
Wilson, A. J., on British parachute attack, 547
——at Fighter Command Ops Room, 510-11
Wilson, F/M Lord Maitland, and D.C.L.I., 203
——in Victory Parade, 175, 186
Wilton Park, Schumacher at, 585
Winant, John, and visiting Lancasters, 265
Windsor Castle, flood-lit, 172
Wind Tunnel, for aircraft testing, 13
Wine, Gloucesters salvage, Péronne, 269
Wingate, Gen. Orde, Black Watch with, 236
——and Burma campaign, 531
——and Chindits, 314-16
Winterburg, hospital at, 26
Wireless, at Dunkirk, 154-57
—for war, R. Signals and, 331, 334
—for Worcestershires, Burma, 685
Wireless Set, portable, at Arnhem, 334
——No. 10, R. Signals and, 334
Witt, Judge de, in Santo Tomas, 124

Wolde, Aklilu Abt., 306
Wolf Pack System, in U-boat war, 489
Wolverine, H.M.S., and *Chobry*, 363
Women, German, clear Berlin, 116
—of Kenya, war effort, 275
Women's Auxiliary Services (Burma), for Japan, 111
Wood, Prof. F. Derwent, M.G.C. memorial, 82
Wood, Peter, at Walcheren, 252
Woodworth, Cpl., and Exeter bombs, 63
Woolwich Arsenal, makes medals, 450
Woolton, Frank A., painting by, 592-93
Worcester, H.M.S., at Dunkirk, 686
——life in, 687-90
——and *Scharnhorst*, 132, 133
Worcestershire Regt., war record, 683-86
Working Party, German, on Norman coast, 227
World Food Conference, at Copenhagen, 359
World Friendship Association, visits under, 358
Worsley, Lt. John, painting by, 591
Worther See, ammunition sunk in, 102
Wounded, of D.L.I., Normandy, 430
——German, on Rhine, 323
——of H.L.I., 653
——W. African, from Burma, 691
Woztek, Pte., Polish bear mascot, 545
Wreck Disposal Fleet, in Thames estuary, 418
Wrecks, depth-charges used for, 48, 49
Wright, C.S.M. Peter, V.C., 428

Wyatt, M. C., George III statue, 80-81
Wylie, Sgt., D.C.M., death, 364

X

Xanten, D.C.L.I. at, 206

Y

Yamamoto, Adm. Isoruku, 419
Yamashita, Gen. Tomoyukai, at Singapore, 260
Yamato, (ship), and Pearl Harbour, 419
Yarmouth, herring fisheries at, 503
Yenanyaung, Cameronians at, 523
——Gloucesters at, 270
——Inniskilling Fusiliers at, 459
Ye-u, Gloucesters at, 270
Y.M.C.A., at Bayeux, 560
——Waterloo canteen, 416
York and Lancaster Regt., in Crete, 579
Yorktown, U.S.S., at Midway, 195
Ypres-Comines Canal, Cameronians on, 523
Yugoslavia, Pola passes to, 758
—and Trieste, 231.

Z

Zanussi, Gen., Italian, peace overtures, 99
Zeban, Worcestershires take, 683
Zero Plane, destroyed, Port Darwin, 795
Zetten, 49th Div. at, 268
Zog I, K. of Albania, 278, 279
Zouteland, Commandos take, 252
Zulu, H.M.S., and *Medway*, 220, 221
Zutphen, Gloucestershire Regt. at, 267

I Was There: the Human Story of 1939-1946

A Clerk Takes a Jump Into France, 633
Action Stations Off Salerno, 409
Adrift on an Invasion Barge, 121
A Frigate in Search of the Tirpitz, 667
At a Place They Called El Alamein, 569
Back to the Normandy Beaches, 189
Battle of Britain, 153
Battle of Britain From Underground, 510
Beacon That Went to Battle, 378
Berlin's Black Market as I Knew It, 764
Brisk Battle of Wits in Stalag XXB, 793
Captured by the Admiral Graf Spee, 413
Charmed Life in H.M. Submarines, 219
Chased by a Radio-Controlled Bomb, 638
Chasing Japs with Smoke and Fire, 699
Chief Engineer of a Floating Volcano, 57
Chief Steward in Battle Malta-Bound, 474
Commando Beach-Party at Madagascar, 31
Crippled 800 Miles From Land, 606
Death Lurked in the Wake of Battle, 254
Devil's Workshop Under the Harz, 124
Dover's Ordeal in the 49th Month, 414
Eight Hundred Drowned This Night, 281
Escape Bid in German Uniform, 285
First Into Liberated Paris, 506
First to Meet the Japanese in Malaya, 636
Flying Mercy Missions Over Sumatra, 789

Frenzied Italians Rushed Our Boats, 702
From the Philippines to Canada, 537
Goodbye to Bonaventure, 351
"Guest" of the Japs in Tokyo, 446
Guests of the Sea Wolves, 734
Hat Trick in a German P.O.W. Camp, 349
Hounds of Okegem Betrayed Us, 318
How They Surrendered in S.E. Asia, 381
How We Paid Tribute, 185
I Crash-Landed on Burma's Broadway, 314
I Fought the Germans Underground, 604
I Lent a Hand With Mighty Mulberry, 733
In Burma, With the 19th Indian Division, 441
In Ghent With R.A.S.C. Troop-Carriers, 669
In Singapore When the Japs Pounced, 90
I Sailed With the Carrier Illustrious, 157
I Swam for Life Through Black Oil, 634
"I Will Lead You Again," Said Monty, 473
Jap Suicide Pilots in Action, 766
King of an Island in the Aegean, 410
Knocking Around in the Indian Ocean, 761
Last Weeks in Jap-Held Manila, 122

Let's Give the Nazi Devil His Due, 476
Liaison Officer With Lord Gort, 697
Mighty Thrust for Arnhem, 219
Night-Fighter Versus Flying Bombs, 731
Night of Our Year-Old Victory, 188
Normandy Breakthrough, 89
On the Road from Assam to Rangoon, 665
On the Trail of the Opium-Runners, 509
Our Badge Was the Venomous Scorpion, 603
Rebirth of Walcheren as an Island, 317
Rounded-Up By Gestapo Gunmen, 381
Seventy-Two Hours' Blissful Leave, 698
Signals Helped at Dunkirk, 154
Slave on a Japanese Railway, 347
Tanks Versus Submarines on Way to Tobruk, 61
Terror that Came to Darwin, 794
The Army Served in D.E.M.S., 572
They Made Me Wield a Pick in Germany, 670
They Snatched Us From a Hell Ship, 443
Through Arctic Seas to Russia, 27
Through Fire and Flood in Walcheren, 542
To Malta by Submarine, 377
Tower of London Under Fire, 93
Twenty-One Nations Meet to Make Peace, 313
Twin Knobs Foxholes, 249

'Twixt Riven Halves of a Flaming Hull, 570
"Up the Micks!" at Djebel Bou Aoukaz, 729
Waited Six Years to Collect It, 478
Wartime Life in the Lonely Falklands, 762
We Battled With Exeter's Unexploded Bombs, 62
We Breached the Atlantic Wall, 790
We Covered the Landings in Sicily, 601
We Found Himmler's Buried Secrets, 539
We Hunted Bandits on the Ledo Road, 765
We Navigated the African Bush, 222
We Ran the Gauntlet of Bardia Bill, 253
We Sang the Marseillaise in Prison, 668
We Stormed the Walcheren Batteries, 250
When France Fell My Luck Went With It, 574
When the Doodle-Bugs Came to London, 348
Winning the First George Medals, 126
Wise Pootung Pete of Shanghai Camp, 505
With Dagger Division's Guns to the Chindwin, 58
With the 51st Division at St. Valery, 25
World's Most Secret Garrison, 282

Great Stories of the War Retold

Dunkirk Was a "Planned" Miracle, 3
The Last Stand at Calais, 35
What Happened at St. Nazaire, 67
Secrets of the Italian Armistice, 99
Why Scharnhorst and Gneisenau Escaped, 131
How Australia Was Saved From the Japs, 195
The Invasion of Normandy, 227

Why the "Cease Fire" Sounded at Singapore, 259
The Tragedy of H.M.S. Glorious, 291
The Airborne Crossing of the Rhine, 323
The Truth About Lidice, 355
Australian Commando Raids on Singapore, 387
The Amazing Facts About Pearl Harbour, 419

"The Bismarck Has Been Sunk," 451
Cassino: Ypres of the Second Great War, 483
The Daring Raid on Rommel's H.Q., 515
The First Attack by British Parachutists, 547
Was the Defence of Crete a Turning-Point? 579

Blade Force's Gallant Failure was Invaluable, 611
How the Marines Went in at Sicily, 643
The Dramatic Liberation of Amsterdam, 675
How the Australians Took Sattelberg, 707
How Germany Came to Grief at Sea, 739
The Building of Mulberry Harbour, 771

Our Empire's Proud Share in Victory

Introductory, 14
Britain's Life Line in the Middle East, 54
Indian Ocean and Pacific Colonies, 83
Colonial Guardians of the Atlantic, 104
War Stores of the British Colonies, 147

How Gibraltar and Malta Went to War, 183
Cyprus, Palestine and Trans-Jordan, 214
First Battles of the West Africans, 243
First Battles of the East Africans, 275

Sudan and Other African Territories, 307
Malaya and Singapore Summing Up, 339
Hongkong, Borneo, Fiji and Tonga, 467
Solomons and Other Pacific Islands, 563

Ceylon, Mauritius and the Seychelles, 627
East and West Africans in Burma, 691
British West Indies and Bermuda, 755

Records of the Regiments: 1939-1945

The Black Watch, 235
The Buffs, 555
The Cameronians (Scottish Rifles), 523
The Duke of Cornwall's Light Infantry, 203
The Duke of Wellington's Regiment, 491
The Durham Light Infantry, 427

The East Lancashire Regiment, 139
The Gloucestershire Regiment, 267
The Green Howards, 619
The Grenadier Guards, 7
The Highland Light Infantry, 651
The Honourable Artillery Company, 395

The Household Cavalry, 299
The Irish Guards, 363
The Reconnaissance Corps, 107
The Royal Air Force Regiment, 75
The Royal Engineers, 713
The Royal Inniskilling Fusiliers, 459

The 5th Royal Inniskilling Dragoon Guards, 587
The Royal Marines, 43
The Royal Signals, 331
The Suffolk Regiment, 779
The Welsh Guards, 747
The Worcestershire Regiment, 683

Divisional Records

British 2nd Division, 20
British 5th Division, 36
7th Armoured Division, 90
11th Armoured Division, 100
15th (Scottish) Division, 142
British 36th Division, 186
43rd (Wessex) Division, 206

46th (North Midland) Division, 250
49th (West Riding) Division, 268
50th (Northumbrian) Division, 300
51st (Highland) Division, 332
52nd (Lowland) Division, 364
53rd (Welsh) Division, 396

56th (London) Division, 428
78th (Indian) Division, 460
3rd (British) Division, 492
Guards Armoured Division, 524
1st Airborne Division, 556
6th Airborne Division, 602

4th (Indian) Division, 620
5th (Indian) Division, 654
7th (Indian) Division, 684
8th (Indian) Division, 717
19th (Indian) Division, 748
25th (Indian) Division, 782

Royal Air Force Squadrons

No. 1 (Fighter) Squadron, 4
No. 102 (Bomber) Squadron, 60
No. 216 Squadron (Transport Command), 77
No. 56 (Punjab) Squadron, 122
No. 609 (West Riding) Squadron, 156
No. 60 (Fighter-Bomber) Squadron, 189

No. 240 (G.R.) Squadron, 220
No. 81 (Fighter) Squadron, 252
No. 8 Squadron, 285
No. 20 Squadron, 317
No. 62 Squadron, 348
No. 215 Squadron, 383
No. 117 Squadron, 410

No. 230 Squadron, 444
No. 35 Squadron, 476
No. 10 Squadron, 508
No. 43 Squadron, 540
No. 57 Squadron, 572
No. 61 Squadron, 604

No. 65 Squadron, 634
No. 72 Squadron, 670
No. 78 Squadron, 698
No. 149 Squadron, 730
No. 250 Squadron, 766
No. 460 Squadron, 792

His Majesty's Ships

H.M.S. Arethusa, 713
H.M.S. Argonaut, 234
H.M.S. Aurora, 458
H.M.S. Belfast, 778
H.M.I.S. Bengal, 746
H.M.S. Exeter, 41
H.M.S. Furious, 106

H.M.S. Hotspur, 74
H.M.S. Illustrious, 488
H.M.S. Iron Duke, 298
H.M.C.S. Iroquois, 267
H.M.S. Javelin, 522
H.M.S. King George V, 426

H.M.S. Kite, 182
H.M.N.Z.S. Kiwi, 682
H.M.S. London, 362
H.M.S. Manxman, 554
H.M.S. Moonstone, 331
H.M.S. Nelson, 650

H.M.S. Onslow, 394
H.M.S. Renown, 203
H.M.S. Rorqual, 138
H.M.A.S. Sydney, 618
H.M.S. Truant, 586
H.M.S. Warspite, 6

Europe's Wartime Capitals in 1946 and 1947

Athens, 198
Belgrade, 564
Berlin, 115
Brussels, 436
Bucharest, 628

Budapest, 19
Copenhagen, 532
Helsinki, 342
Luxemburg, 372
Moscow, 596

Oslo, 404
Paris, 310
Prague, 660
Reykjavik, 694
Rome, 786

Sofia, 468
The Hague, 148
Tirana, 278
Vienna, 51
Warsaw, 500

Photogravure Sections

Life-Near-Death in a Hongkong Prison Camp, 15
Top-Speed Battle for Medicina, 16-17
Budapest's Beautiful Bridges are Broken Down, 18
Past Glory to be Restored to Cologne Cathedral, 47
Shattering Sunken Wrecks by Depth-Charge Clears Britain's Obstructed Shipping-Lanes, 48-49
Life in Austria's Once-Gay Capital Revives But Slowly, 50
Home-Coming of London's War-Exiled Statues,
From Country Castle back to Town Square, 79
Famous Evacuees in Bronze Return To Their Old Places in London's Scene, 80-81
In Memory of Valiant Exploits, 82
Occupation Troops Ready for Japan, 111
Britain's £11,000,000 H.M.S. Vanguard Passes Down the Clyde to Her Trials, 112-13
Reopening of South Bridge at Cologne, 114
Historic Normandy Two Years after D-Day
William the Conqueror Still Mounted in Falaise, 143
Utilitarian New Replaces Picturesque Old Where the Battletide flowed in Normandy, 144-45
Calm in the Sunshine Now Lies Caen, 146
At The Victory Parade Saluting Base in the Mall, 175
London's Memorable Day of Gay Pageantry, 176
Imposing Columns of 21,000 Men and Women, 177

Night Blaze of Fireworks over London s River, 178
Empire Forces Celebrate Empire Day in Tokyo, 207
Our Largest and Fastest Carrier Comes Home, 208
H.M.S. Theseus With Her Seafires Visits Norway, 209
In Remembrance of Our Fallen at Narvik, 210
Gallant Malta Rebuilds her Shattered Streets, 239
Healing Malta's Architectural Wounds With Stone from Her Ancient Quarries, 240-41
R.A.S.C. Dumps Jap Ammunition in the Pacific, 242
Moulmein's Pagoda is Moving Down Hill, 271
" Millionaires' Beach " on an Adriatic Shore, Now for the Relaxation of " Other Ranks ", 272-273
Atom Bomb Aftermath in Hiroshima, 274
Paris Peace Conference: Opening Scenes, 303
'Five Peace Conferences in One,' 304-305
Representing Seven of the Peace-Seeking Peoples, 306
Where Eisenhower Watched on D-Day, 335
Amazing Demonstration of Disruptive Genius—World's First Underwater Atomic Bomb Explosion, 336-337
Dunkirk Port Reopened to Navigation at Last, 338
Venice as a News Centre for Our Troops News-Hungry Servicemen Kept Abreast of Events, 367

Here the Latest News Becomes the Printed Word On Paper Barge-Borne Down the Grand Canal, 368-369
Over an Italy-Wide Network " U.J." Starts Out, 370
Britain Pays Tribute to ' The Few,' 399
Remembering the Fallen in the Battle of Britain—" Hinge on Which Our Lives and Future Turned," 400-401
To the Honour and Glory of Our Air Forces, 402
Justice Overtakes the Nazi Leaders, 431
Hitler's " Old Guard " On Trial for Their Lives Hear the Verdicts the World Has Awaited, 432-433
Surprises for Some on the Day of Reckoning, 434
Britain's Swift Change-Over to Peace Production, 463
Our Machines of War now Hum to the Tune of a Mighty Drive to Bring Back Prosperity, 464-465
Little Things that Mean So Much to All of Us, 466
" The Isles of Greece, the Isles of Greece . . .," 495
Scenes in the Long-Lost Islands of Greece That Have Now Been Restored to the Motherland, 496-497
Time and Mood for Joyous Living, 498
Ambushed in Khyber Pass, 527
New Roads to Scotland's Farthest Isles that Grew Out of Threats to Scapa Flow, 528-529
. . . And Quiet Flows the Rhine !, 530
Present Day Scenes along Normandy's Invaded Coast, 559

In the Footsteps of the Invasion Army, 560
Where Time has Stood Still in Normandy, 561
The Peace that Came at Last When Battle Passed, 562
Our Last Display of Wartime Art, 591-594
Lisbon's Story can Now be Told, 623
The Daily Round in Portugal's Capital, 624
Where Europe Gambled as Europe Bled, 625
Airport of Lisbon a Great World-Junction, 626
Relieving the Bread Line in Hungry Italy, 655
Mechanical Working of Britain's Coal Fields to Meet the Urgent Needs of Vital Industry, 656-657
They Upheld Name and Fame of Denmark, 658
Life in Britain's Largest Training Ship Afloat, 687
Cadets Trained in the Ways of the Sea, 688
Young Seadogs Work Hard and Play Hard, 689
Home of 200 Cadets, 690
War Service of the New " Royals," 719
Uplift and Instruction in Intervals of War, 720
Time off from Battle to Visit the Dentist, 721
Lincolns and Hampshires, 722
Five Peace Treaties Signed at Last, 751
Ceremony in Paris Seals Solemn Pacts with States that Waged War as Hitler's Satellites, 752-753
Japanese Nightmare, 754

Cover Subjects

One Hundred and Twenty-fifth Anniversary of Greek Independence, 1
H.M.S. Vanguard for Royal Visit to Africa, 32
Mr. Attlee and Mr. Winston Churchill leaving the Abbey, 33
A Bomb-fenced Road in the Island of Crete, 64
Charles I returns to London, 65
Queen Mary at St. James's Park Bomb Site, 96
First Commander of H.M.S. Vanguard, 97
V Day Parade Clear-up in Trafalgar Square, 128
India's Colourful Contingent for London's Victory Parade, 129
From West Africa for London's V Day March, 160
India's Detachment in the Victory Parade, 161
Navy "Ducks" Invade London's East End, 192

First Empire Day since Defeat of Japan, 193
Good Companions Aboard Our Carrier Theseus, 224
Frog Men Emerging from Sea at St. Ives, Cornwall, 225
The New Uniform for All Ranks of Our Army, 256
Great Eastern Tank Ramp, 257
Red Caps in Venice Patrol the Grand Canal, 288
Britain's Prime Minister addressing the Paris Peace Conference, 289
Home from the Far East is H.M.S. Anson, 320
Mr. Churchill as Lord Warden of the Cinque Ports, 321
Extracting Death from Dorset's Studland Bay, 352
Lancaster Bombers of No. 35 Squadron over St. Paul's, London, 353
German Prisoners Assist Our Harvest Home, 384

Field-Marshal Montgomery and General Eisenhower, 385
Forces Canteen at Waterloo Keeps a Birthday, 416
Army Mechanical Demonstration Column, 417
Preparing for Our Third Post-War Harvest, 448
Vice-Admiral Sir Philip Vian at the Admiralty, 449
U.S. 100-ton Tank that Never Went to War, 480
Admiral Sir William Halsey at Nelson's Column, 481
R.M. College Colours Are Laid Up for Ever, 512
Four Foreign Ministers in New York, 513
From Ceylon to Learn our Farming Craft, 544
Bear Mascot of the Polish Army, 545
Tribute to "A Man Who Loved the People," 576
Nigeria's Namesake at Lagos, 577

V.C. from India Views Wonders of London, 608
Guarding the Imperial Palace, Tokyo, 609
Daughter of One Faithful Unto Death, 640
Pipe Major of the 5th Bn. the 1st Punjab Regt., 641
German Strongpoint Becomes Dutch Home, 672
Colours of 1st Bn. The London Scottish, 673
Full-Rigged Prize of War in Tasman Sea, 704
Field-Marshal Montgomery at the Stalin Military Academy, 705
British-Soviet Frontier Post in Germany, 736
Argyll and Sutherland Highlanders at Stirling Castle, 737
Troopship Queen Mary is Being Demobbed, 768
Scaffolding on Site of the New House of Commons, 769

Maps and Plans

Africa, N., Blade Force in, 612
Bikini Atoll, 233
Burma, airborne invasion, 314
Cassino, 483

Crete, 579
Europe, sinking of the Glorious, 291
Far East, Bangkok-Moulmein Rly 345

Italy, first parachute attack, 548
New Guinea, Finschhafen and Operations round, 708

Pacific Ocean, course of Krait, 388
St. Nazaire, Commando Raid, 68
Trieste, 231
Walcheren Island, 542

Special Drawings and Diagrams

Banana Production, 23
Britain's Bread Supply, 87
Britain's Milk Supply, 375
Herring Industry, 502

Last action of H.M.S. Hereward, by Lt.-Cdr. R. Langmaid, R.N., 350
Indian Division in Burma, by R. J. M. Dupont, 441

Margarine Manufacture, 150
Meat Ration from Overseas, 309
Suggit and Beeson's escape, Germany, 286-87

Tea Production, 245
Whale Oil Production, 212
Why the Scharnhorst and Gneisenau escaped, 131-33

Errata and Addenda

P. 279. Caption, line 7, should read: " in the left foreground are the changing rooms and halls attached to the Stadium."

P. 592. Artist's name of top left-hand picture should be Clive Uptton.
P. 614. Caption to photograph 2 : for H.M.S. Saumarez read H.M.S. Volage.

Printed in Great Britain by The Amalgamated Press, Ltd., London

Vol 10 *The War Illustrated* Nº 231

SIXPENCE

APRIL 26, 1946

I WAS THERE

ONE HUNDRED AND TWENTY-FIFTH ANNIVERSARY OF GREEK INDEPENDENCE was celebrated in traditional style on March 25, 1946. A salute of twenty salvos from Greek warships in Piraeus harbour heralded the commemoration of the first raising of the Greek flag after centuries of Turkish rule. Headed by the Evzones in the picturesque kilted dress of the warriors who fought against the Turks in 1821, the annual procession is parading in Constitution Square, Athens.

Photo, Central Press

Edited by Sir John Hammerton

NO. 232 WILL BE PUBLISHED FRIDAY, MAY 10

Seamen From Every Walk of Life Came Forward

FROM THE LIVING HELL OF DUNKIRK the salvation of the B.E.F. in May-June 1940 was accomplished by nearly 1,000 craft and (in the Admiralty's words) " seamen from every walk of life who came forward to assist their brother seamen of the Royal Navy." Dunkirk harbour (1) under a pall of smoke from the blazing town after intense bombing and shelling by the Germans. A trawler (2) heads for England crammed with troops. British and French arriving at Dover in a destroyer (3). See also facing page.

PAGE 2   *Photos, The News Chronicle, Topical, G.P.U.*

Dunkirk Was a 'Planned' Miracle

By A. D. DIVINE, D.S.M.
Author of
'Dunkirk'; 'Destroyers' War'

Out of Dunkirk a legend has grown. It is a legend that may be conveniently divided into four parts : the first that this, the greatest rescue of an army ever accomplished in history, was achieved by a mass of small boats spontaneously appearing on the narrow and dangerous seas off the beaches of Northern France ; the second that it was achieved in an absolute calm ; the third that fog shielded boats and men from the wrath of the Germans ; and the fourth that the thousands of men rescued waded off the beaches to their salvation.

All these things are true—in part. Together they give a completely erroneous picture of the whole. Nothing can take from the men who manned the small boats the glory of their achievement ; but this story of the small boats has robbed the men of the bigger ships—the destroyers, the Fleet minesweepers, the cross-Channel steamers—who did by far the greater part of the triumphant " lifting," of their due share in the honours of Dunkirk.

Why the Evacuation Was Necessary

It blinds the ordinary man to a proper appreciation of the amazing, often desperate, organization that lay behind the rescue ; to the energy, the effort and the imagination of the staff at Dover ; and, above all, to the genius of the late Sir Bertram Home Ramsay, then Vice-Admiral, Dover. Dunkirk has been called a miracle. It was—a miracle of clear thinking, incisive planning and the utilization of inadequate forces in circumstances which have no parallel in all the superb record of our history.

The evacuation of the British Expeditionary Force under the late Gen. Lord Gort became necessary the moment the German Army broke across the Meuse on May 14, 1940. That necessity was not appreciated at the time. None of us had then had time to measure the weakness of France, the corruption of her body politic and the incompetence of her army. But the crossing of the Meuse in itself constituted a threat to the lines of communication of the British Army, which lay across Belgium and Northern France to Le Havre.

On May 15 the War Office intimated to the Ministry of Shipping that it might be necessary almost at once to switch the main line of supply from Le Havre to the nearer Channel ports. Three days later the spearhead of the German advance was in Amiens. On May 19 another meeting was held at the War Office, under General Riddell-Webster, to settle the problems of the new supply. The swiftly changing situation had brought other matters to the fore.

As a secondary item on the agenda the question of evacuating superfluous personnel was considered. At the very bottom of the agenda was a tentative question—" the hazardous evacuation of very large forces." This was dismissed as unlikely. Yet the situation was deteriorating so rapidly that even now one remains almost breathless at the speed of events. Even while the meeting was sitting Dunkirk port was declared out of operation owing to bomb damage ; the Belgian ports were compromised by the German thrust to the north, and from Amiens the German Army, coiled like a steel spring, was thrusting out ominously towards the Channel.

On May 20 another conference of all parties concerned was called at Dover and continued at the War Office the following day. The problem of " emergency evacua-tion across the Channel of very large forces " had moved up from last place on the agenda to a place very near the top. At that meeting a skeleton plan was evolved which envisaged the use of Calais, Boulogne and Dunkirk simultaneously *if* the necessity should arise. " Allowing for moderate (enemy) interference " it was estimated that the capacity of the arrangements provided for in this plan would permit of the evacuation of 10,000 men from each port in each twenty-four hours, using cross-Channel steamers.

Partly as a result of this meeting, a special staff was created at Dover to deal with the immediate problems of the area. This staff was housed in what was known as the " Dynamo Room," a portion of the underground system below Dover Castle. From the name of its accommodation the plan was called " Operation Dynamo."

In connexion with the change of the supply line and the other obvious necessities of the situation which had arisen in Holland immediately after May 10 and had continued as the German plan developed, there were gathered in Dover or in the Downs at that time the cross-Channel steamers Biarritz,

BOARDING A DESTROYER at Dunkirk— one of the 38 which, taking part in this great evacuation, brought away over 91,000 of the 337,000 men. PAGE 3 *Photo, The Times*

Mona's Queen, Canterbury, Maid of Orleans, King George V, Queen of the Channel, King Orry, Mona's Isle and St. Helier, while at Southampton there were ready Normannia, Manxmaid, Royal Daffodil, Royal Scot, Archangel and Lorina. In addition to these there were another fourteen ships of similar type ready at call at Southampton, and the Navy had accumulated in the Downs twelve drifters and six small coasters.

At the War Office meeting Captain Fisher, Director of Coastwise and Short Sea Shipping, suggested the use of British self-propelled barges and in particular of the flat-bottomed Dutch coasters that had come to England on the fall of the Dutch ports. Forty-five of these were requisitioned in the Thames and at Poole, and speedily manned by naval crews from Portsmouth and from Chatham barracks.

At the same time the Ministry of Shipping initiated a survey of all shipping in British harbours, and Sea Transport Officers at Harwich, London, Newhaven, Southampton, Poole and Weymouth were instructed to obtain records of all small ships up to 1,000 tons, including paddle-steamers, pleasure craft and so on, capable of carrying troops.

It was on the basis of this material that the staff of the Dynamo Room began its work. In the five days that passed between this meeting and the inception of Operation Dynamo they built from this small but firm beginning the immense fleet of the deliverance. Behind them the whole vast naval machine had come into operation. On the very day that the Germans had crossed the Meuse, Admiral Sir Lionel Preston, Director of the Small Vessels Pool, had promulgated an Order which was broadcast by the B.B.C.—remember this was an Order, not a request.

It required all owners of pleasure craft from 30 feet to 110 feet in length to send in at once particulars of their vessels. The great bases provided crews for ships suddenly earmarked for the purpose by the Dover Command. The responsible departments at the Admiralty made it possible for repair ships and salvage vessels to be moved towards the area. Stores, equipment and, above all, fuel of half a dozen different kinds were dispatched to Dover and the small ports of the area.

Increasingly Desperate Situation

And across, through and over all this work of preparation came the difficulties and disasters of that black week. Boulogne fell, and of the regular flotilla of destroyers that operated out of Dover there was one ship only left undamaged. Destroyers were put out of action off Dunkirk and off Calais. The French lost three in the area in this period. The precious cross-Channel ships suffered loss and damage. Calais was invested and by-passed, the Belgian Army was in parlous condition.

The situation was so ·desperate that the High Command decided to throw the First Canadian Division into Flanders—an order that was countermanded only after the loading had actually begun. Yet through the chaos of circumstance, the terrible confusion of battered communications and inadequate news, the staff of the Dynamo Room continued its operations until at 6.57 p.m. on Sunday, May 26, Operation Dynamo was initiated by a signal from Admiral Sir Bertram Ramsay.

The weather on this Sunday was good, but there was in the whole fantastic picture of Dunkirk on that day small ground for further consolation. The perimeter was by no means secure. Dunkirk port, despite heroic repair measures, was finally out of operation. There was left the open beach from Gravelines to Nieuport and the single out-jutting finger of the Dunkirk Mole. The plan that had been outlined so optimistically on May 21 was already buried under the accumulations of disaster.

There could be no orderly evacuation of 10,000 men from each of three ports per day. There could only be a desperate improvised thing from the pitiful facilities that remained. On Friday evening, May 24, Mr. Churchill, coming from a meeting of the War Cabinet and the naval and military authorities, warned the House of Commons and the nation "to prepare for hard and heavy tidings." We know now that some of the best judges expected that those tidings would be nothing less than a report to the nation of the loss of the British Army. Twenty thousand was the figure which many experts believed to be the utmost that could be snatched off that naked coast. Yet 337,000 men came safe from Dunkirk. How ?

Census of Small Craft Was Ready

They came because behind the rescue were five days of the most intensive and brilliant planning in all the story of naval achievement. Between them the Admiralty, the Ministry of Shipping and Admiral Ramsay had brought the ships to Dover. But ships cannot operate without fuel ; warships cannot operate without ammunition ; small boats cannot operate without men, without ropes, without anchors, without repair facilities for delicate petrol engines, without food, without charts, without swept channels and buoys and sea marks. All these things were behind Dover—all these things as well as the courage, the spirit and the self-sacrifice of the men who took the ships across.

The first tentative movements showed that a multitude of small craft would be essential if men were to be lifted from the sand. Immediately the foresight of the Small Vessels Pool proved its value. The census of small craft was ready to hand. From the office of the Pool, borrowed from other departments, borrowed from the great bases, officers went out to select and dispatch small craft from the ports. From the Ministry of Shipping, from its representatives in the ports, information and energetic assistance came. The flow of boats that was to make the armada of deliverance was not spontaneous. It was part of a plan devised against a desperate necessity.

It grew beyond that plan as the self-same spirit that brought the small ships of the Channel out against the Spanish Armada woke anew in the yachting harbours of the little ports from Norfolk to Teddington, from Teddington to Devon and beyond. It sent to the narrow channel between the sandbanks and the shore that lines the coast from Calais to the Scheldt, motor-boats and barges, river ferries and fire floats, fishing craft and lighters and sludge boats and oyster dredgers.

The work these small craft did is beyond praise. I, who was with them, would be the very last to detract in any way from their achievement. But, tremendous though their work was, it is essential in making a picture of the Dunkirk operation as a whole to record it in conjunction with the work of the rest of the ships.

Let us consider figures for a moment. The destroyers—thirty-eight of them, almost five flotillas—were thrown in to Dunkirk as ship after ship, flotilla after flotilla, was wrecked, battered, sunk. These thirty-eight ships between them brought away 91,624 men, substantially more than a quarter of the total rescued. The Fleet minesweepers lifted 30,942, the paddle-minesweepers 18,838, the

British-manned Dutch skoots 20,284. No precise total exists for the seventy-nine smaller minesweeping craft and anti-submarine trawlers, for the three special service ships—the famous Eagles of the Thames—the nineteen flare-burning drifters, the eleven patrol yachts, the host of boom defence and harbour patrol and boarding vessels that were drawn from the ranks of the Royal Navy, but the figure is immense.

The figures which do exist credit the four main naval categories with 161,688, almost precisely half of the total lifted, and at a moderate estimate at least another 40,000 can be added to that for the miscellaneous naval craft. The cross-Channel steamers have the second highest record in all the liftings, with a total of 61,867. French naval vessels, the four French cross-Channel ships and coasters

are credited with 30,000. These totals come to approximately 300,000 men, and to them must be added figures for the many coasting steamers and similar craft that took part in the operation. It is sufficiently clear from this that the picture of an army coming back from the Continent in yachts and motor-boats is scarcely justifiable.

The cold light of figures cannot be used to evaluate heroism. Nothing in this, as I have said, detracts in any way from the work of the "little ships." An enormous number of men were brought safe to Margate and Ramsgate and to Dover by yachts and barges and fishing craft. A very much greater work was accomplished off the beaches where probably something between 60,000 and 70,000 men were ferried off to destroyers, skoots and cross-Channel steamers lying in the deep water.

But it is none the less clear that the mainstay of the deliverance was the destroyers, the personnel ships, the trawlers, drifters and coasters that used the ruins of the harbour and of Dunkirk Mole. Though precise figures are not, and never can be, available, the generally accepted estimate is that over the Mole itself between 250,000 and 270,000 men embarked to safety.

There remains the question of the weather. There was fog, but it was a night fog only and lasted for short periods. There was also smoke from the burning oil storage areas and the haze of battle. These things brought relief occasionally to the hard-pressed ships and men, but the daily list of our losses alone is sufficient to dissipate the German story that the escape was made under cover of an impenetrable pall.

Field-Marshal Kesselring at the Nuremberg trials a short while ago said, "And I say now that it (the great catastrophe of Dunkirk) would have been much greater if bad weather had not kept us back two days." It is not easy to see what was in the Field-Marshal's mind. Nowhere during that week was the weather bad enough to delay land operations. The record of attacks shows that it was not sufficient to save us from the air. It would appear that the Field-Marshal was falling back on the weather legend as an excuse for the German failure.

A Breaking Sea on Vital Beaches

What of the wind ? It is true that there was no heavy gale during the nine days of Dunkirk, such as was to blow four years later for three June days on the beaches of Normandy. But on Friday, May 31, there was a strong northerly breeze that set up on the vital beaches to the east of the Mole a breaking sea sufficient to beach almost every small boat that was ferrying. Had it not been for the brilliant working of the Small Vessels Pool and the Dover authorities on the other shore, the boat loading would that day have come to an end. As it was, reinforcements were found, prepared and manned in sufficient numbers to counterbalance the difficulties of the weather.

Dunkirk, as I have said, was a miracle, a miracle of many facets—no one of them greater than the courage, the devotion, and the desperate unwearying exertion of the men who manned the ships from open boats to destroyers. But bright among these facets must always be reckoned the work of organization, the initiative, the drive and energy of the staffs, the genius of Admiral Ramsay and the brilliant assistance of Admiral Somerville. It was a miracle because out of these things and under a pressure such as perhaps has never been put on men so placed before, there was welded out of divergent interests, unprepared *matériel*, amateur seamen and inadequate equipment, a force sufficient to the greatest individual task of the War.

Motto : " First in All Things."

No. I (FIGHTER) SQUADRON

ONE of the oldest R.A.F. regular squadrons, No. I has a proud record in two wars. Its history can be traced back to 1894. It is a direct descendant of the balloon factory formed in that year, and No. I (Airship) Company, Air Battalion, Royal Engineers, formed on April I, 1911. When the airships were handed over to the Navy, No. I Squadron was reorganized into an aeroplane squadron, in May 1914, under the command of Capt. C. A. H. Longcroft. During its service in France in the 1914-18 war the Squadron destroyed a total of 200 enemy aircraft.

Following the invasion of France and the Low Countries in May 1940, No. I Squadron destroyed 100 German aircraft. Later, in the Battle of Britain, its record was outstanding, culminating in its heavy night attack on London on May 10-11, 1941, when a total of 33 enemy aircraft was brought down. No. I Squadron played a great part in that battle in the night skies. Flying Hurricanes, with only visual aid, it destroyed seven bombers and damaged another two, thus setting the seal on its great efforts during the Battle of Britain.

APART from activities in France and the Battle of Britain it was engaged against the Scharnhorst, Gneisenau, Prinz Eugen and their escorts, when its pilots opened fire at a range of 100 yards. It was in action against the flying bomb when, equipped with Spitfire IXs, it was credited with the destruction of 47½ of these missiles. It attacked enemy lines of communication, transport, ships, rolling stock, and escorted heavy bombers in attacks on targets in the Ruhr, Holland and Belgium. Equipped with Tempests the Squadron also defended Southern England during the " little blitz," bringing its total bag of enemy aircraft to over 250. Three years ago it was presented with the King's Standard in commemoration of twenty-five years' R.A.F. service.

Many distinguished officers have served with it, including the late Air Marshal Sir W. G. H. Salmond, its first Commander in France ; Air Chief Marshal Sir E. R. Ludlow Hewitt (as a Captain); and Wing-Commander T. A. F. Maclachlan, D.S.O., D.F.C. and Bar, Fighter Command's one-armed " ace " night-fighter pilot.

Still flying with Fighter Command, the history and traditions of No. I Squadron are an inspiration to all future fighter pilots of the Royal Air Force.

India's Famed Red Eagles Homing from Salonika

4th INDIAN DIVISION veterans embarked on the Orontes at Salonika, Greece, in February 1946. Their happy frame of mind is expressed on all faces (top). Amidst handwaving one gives the " V " sign (left). The passing from the Mediterranean scene of this Division recalls how much is owed to those who carried the striking head-gear and the red eagle flash (above) 50,000 miles, from the Western Desert to Abyssinia, back again to Tunisia, Italy and Greece. First of India's Expeditionary Force to leave India in the summer of 1939, and the last to return, in six years of campaigning it accounted for 100,000 prisoners, including General von Arnim, Commander of the Axis forces in N. Africa, suffered 25,000 casualties and had its gallantry rewarded 1,000 times. V.C.s were awarded to Subadar Lalahadur Thapa (see page 123 Vol. 7) ; Coy. Havildar-Major Chhelu Ram (see page 599, Vol. 8) ; Naik Yeshwant Ghadge (see page 599, Vol. 8) ; and Sher Bahadur Thapa, the last three posthumously.

Photos, British Official

HIS MAJESTY'S SHIPS

H.M.S. Renown

Motto: " Guardian of Ancient Renown "

A SHIP of 32,000 tons, launched on the Clyde in 1916, the Renown is the only remaining battle cruiser in the Royal Navy. She has a main armament of six 15-inch guns. From 1920 to 1922 the Renown was employed on special service, taking the Prince of Wales on official visits to the United States, Australia, New Zealand, India and Japan. Five years later our present King and Queen, then Duke and Duchess of York, went to Australia in her.

In 1936-39 the ship was completely rebuilt and re-engined at a cost of over £3,000,000, equal to the original expense of construction. Her first action after recommissioning was with the German battleships Scharnhorst and cruiser Admiral Hipper, off Northern Norway, in April 1940. After the Scharnhorst had been hit the enemy vessels managed to break off the engagement under cover of heavy weather. Not long afterwards the Renown became the flagship of Sir James Somerville in the Western Mediterranean. After engaging two Italian battleships at long range off Sardinia, she took part in the bombardment of Genoa. (See pages 219 and 309, Vol. 4.) In May 1941 she was one of the ships engaged in rounding up the German battleship Bismarck.

It was in the Renown that Mr. Churchill returned from the United States in 1943. A little later she joined the Eastern Fleet, but was back in home waters in 1945. The first meeting with German naval representatives to arrange for the surrender of enemy forces in Norway was held in the Renown at Rosyth on May 7, 1945; and on August 2 following, the King received President Truman on board her at Plymouth. (See page 267, Vol. 9.) Few ships have had so many associations with distinguished personages.

Photo, P. A. Vicary

The Grenadier Guards

By Authority of the Officer Commanding
Col. R. B. R. COLVIN, D.S.O.

O^N September 3, 1939, when Great Britain declared war on Germany, the strength of the Regiment stood at three service battalions and a training battalion at Windsor. Early in 1940 a Holding Battalion, whose duty it was to mount public duties and also provide drafts for the service battalions, was formed in London.

The three service battalions went over to the Continent with the British Expeditionary Force in September—the 1st and 2nd Battalions in the 3rd Division, commanded by General Montgomery, and the 3rd Battalion in the 1st Division, commanded by General Alexander. And, save for a few weeks patrolling by the 3rd Battalion in the Maginot Line, they spent the next seven months peacefully on the Belgian frontier constructing a defensive line, known as the Gort Line, from which it was destined that they were never to fire a shot.

The German armies invaded the Low Countries on May 10, 1940, and during the next day the 1st and 2nd Battalions motored into Belgium to take over the defence of a sector of the River Dyle near Louvain. Here, three days later, the first elements of the invading army encountered them, and were held. For two more days there was no movement either forward or back, but on the 17th news came that the French line had been turned on the south, and the British fell back to avoid being outflanked.

Three Battalions Fought Side by Side

So the retreat began, and the battalions of the Regiment marched back through Belgium, halting every few days to fight a rearguard action. They held the enemy at the River Dendre, where the three battalions, for the first time in their history, found themselves fighting side by side in the line, although in different divisions. And they held the enemy at the Scheldt, where in a counter-attack a corporal of the 3rd Battalion, L-Cpl. H. Nicholls, alone, and armed with a Bren gun, silenced three machine-gun posts and killed numbers of the enemy, for which he was awarded the V.C. (See portrait in page 183, Vol. 9.)

At last, on May 20, the 1st and 2nd Battalions marched into Furnes, seven miles from the sea, and prepared to hold the canal south of the town until all the British troops had been evacuated from Dunkirk. All that night the retreating divisions poured through, and next day the bridges were blown behind them. For two more days they held on against repeated German attacks, and in the early hours of June 1 the forward positions of the 1st and 2nd Battalions were abandoned and they withdrew to the beaches, to be taken on board ships of all classes lying off La Panne—the last British troops to leave that coast. Meanwhile, farther to the south, the 3rd Battalion had been playing their part in the final rearguard action of the B.E.F. On the same day they were embarked for home from Dunkirk.

W^{ITH} the fall of France began a period of reconstruction. The whole of North-Western Europe was overrun, and before any of it could be regained British troops would have to be landed again by the Royal Navy on a coast over 2,000 miles long that was now in enemy hands. The 3rd Battalion of the Regiment was one of the first units of the Army to begin training with this end in view, and this battalion's new role was one of historical significance.

The Regiment was raised in Flanders in 1656 under Lord Wentworth as a bodyguard to King Charles II, a refugee on the Continent since his defeat at Worcester in 1650. On his restoration ten years later the King raised a regiment under Colonel John Russell which, together with Wentworth's, became known as the "Royal Regiment of Guards." This, in 1685, became the "First Regiment of Foot Guards." In 1815, to commemorate achievements at Waterloo, it was given the present proud title of "First or Grenadier Regiment of Foot Guards."

In the wars against the Dutch in the latter half of the 17th century, the companies which later formed the 3rd Battalion served and fought on board ships of the Royal Navy, prior to the formation of a Corps of Marines, and in memory of this service Rule Britannia is played to this day by the drums of the battalion at Tattoo. In 1941, after a lapse of nearly three centuries, Rule Britannia" was again played on the quarter-deck of one of H.M. ships, in which the 3rd was training in combined operations.

In the same year, while the whole Regiment was still in England, three new battalions were formed, and after much doubtful speculation as to the possible adaptability of guardsmen to tank warfare the idea of a Guards Armoured Division became a reality. Two battalions were chosen to be converted to armour, and two were motorized; two remained to perpetuate the infantry tradition of the Regiment. Early in 1942 H.R.H. The Duke of Connaught died, and in his place H.M. the Colonel-in-Chief honoured his First Guards by the appointment as their Colonel of H.R.H. Princess Elizabeth.

The 6th Motor Battalion, now the youngest battalion in the Regiment, was the first to go overseas. Leaving England in June 1942 they sailed by the Old East Indian trade route round the Cape of Good Hope and came under the command of the 201st Guards Brigade in Syria. And early in the next year they motored over 2,000 miles to Tunisia to join the 8th Army at the Battle of Medenine. Ten days later, on March 16, the Brigade, with the Grenadier and Coldstream Guards leading, attacked by moonlight up the feature known as the Horseshoe, overlooking Mareth.

The attack was pushed home, and the companies gained the heights. But in the morning it was found that on account of the formidable and unexpected minefields no support could be brought up to them ; stranded without ammunition, food, or heavy weapons, the 6th Battalion was ordered by the Divisional Commander to retire. The casualties had been heavy and the attack in its immediate aims unsuccessful, but it opened the way to the final breach of the Mareth Line.

How "The Plumbers" Got Their Name

After all the months of combined training, the 3rd Battalion landed peacefully behind the 1st Army at Algiers, in the 1st Guards Brigade, and during the early months of 1943 were in action on so many occasions and in so many different gaps in the 1st Army line where German thrusts might have broken through that this Brigade earned the local nickname of "The Plumbers." At the beginning of May came the last offensive, which cleared the Germans from North Africa. After a short period of rest and refitting in the area of Constantine the Battalion started to prepare itself for the next task.

The 5th Battalion had advanced with 24th Guards Brigade and, after bitter fighting, captured Jebel Bou Aoukaz, the hill feature which was the keystone to the defences of Tunis. On May 3 the 201st Guards Brigade crossed over to the 1st Army front, and in the push which carried them past Tunis and across the base of the Cape Bon Peninsula to the sea the 3rd and 6th Battalions fought in the same division and led the Army's advance until the final German surrender.

The story of the Grenadiers in Italy is woven into the whole pattern of the succeed-

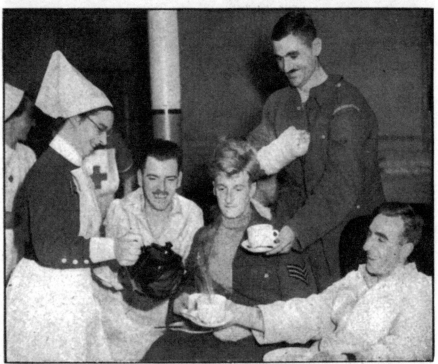

RECOVERING IN HOSPITAL IN ENGLAND early in 1940. **The 1st and 2nd Battalions of the Grenadier Guards** first encountered the invading Germans at the River Dyle, near Louvain, Belgium, in May of that year, more than seven months after their arrival on the Continent. Previously casualties had been sustained in training. PAGE 7 *Photo, Associated Press*

ing offensives which carried the 5th and 8th Armies up the entire length of the Italian Peninsula and into Southern Austria. The 6th Battalion landed in Italy in divisional reserve at Salerno in September 1943, and in the months that followed continued to be engaged in hard fighting, culminating in the two strenuous assaults up the six-hour climb to the summit of Monte Camino and the final crossing of the Garigliano River.

In the New Year the 5th were on the Anzio beach-head. They landed on the first day —January 22—and for three days all was quiet. Thereafter followed a fortnight of the fiercest and most critical fighting of the whole War. The straggling village of Carroceto was the scene of one long continuous battle by night and by day, and on the flat and muddy downland, overlooked from the north by the German mounted observation posts, the casualties of the battalion in the beach-head were unbearably heavy.

On February 7, the enemy made at dusk a tank attack which broke through on the left of the battalion position, and two companies were surrounded. By midnight, Battalion Headquarters itself was threatened, and in the fighting which followed Major W. P. Sidney, though wounded and losing blood, drove back almost unaided on three separate occasions parties of the enemy who were attacking Battalion Headquarters ; for this action he was later awarded the V.C. (See portrait on page 760, Vol. 7, THE WAR ILLUSTRATED) The battalion was withdrawn from the beach-head a month later, having lost 31 officers and over 600 men. So heavy, indeed, had been the casualties suffered by the 5th and 6th Battalions that in March 1944 the 6th returned to England and was subsequently disbanded.

The spring came with the 3rd Battalion entrenched among the ruins of Cassino. At last Cassino fell, and the advance which had been halted so long rolled northward again.

Major-General Sir ALLAN H. S. ADAIR, C.B., D.S.O., M.C., commanded the Guards Armoured Division in Normandy until it reverted to its traditional role of infantry on June 9, 1945. *Photo, British Official*

As the spring changed to summer, Rome and Florence fell ; the 3rd Battalion with the 6th Armoured Division, and the 5th with the South African 6th Armoured Division, played their part in the great advance.

1st and 2nd Battalions in Brussels

In April 1945 the 5th Battalion returned home and, after parading before H.R.H. the Colonel the day before V Day, was disbanded. Only the 3rd Battalion remained to represent the Grenadiers in the occupation of Southern Austria in May 1945 ; but meantime the War had entered its last phase, and for nearly a year British soldiers had once again been fighting in North-Western Europe.

The Guards Armoured Division did not sail for Normandy until nearly three weeks after the first landings had been made, and it was not till August 28, after some heavy fighting around Caen, that Field-Marshal Sir Bernard Montgomery chose it to take the lead in the final advance along the road to Germany. By September 2 Douai was reached, 20 miles from the Belgian frontier. And by the evening of the next day a battalion of the Welsh Guards and the 1st and 2nd Battalions of the Grenadiers had driven through to Brussels.

In the city German opposition had almost ceased, but the enthusiasm of the citizens brought the advance to a standstill. Every street was thronged with the populace, every house decked with loyal emblems. Night fell, illuminated by a full moon and the flames of the burning Palais de Justice.

CARRYING THE ASSAULT ACROSS ITALY'S MOUNTAINS, Grenadier Guardsmen are making their way to forward positions on the 5th Army Front. Grenadiers served throughout the Italian campaign, taking part in some of the fiercest engagements with the 5th and 8th Armies, on the Garigliano, the Anzio beach-head and at Cassino. PAGE 8 *Photo, British Official*

With the Grenadiers in France and N. Africa

3rd BATTALION OF THE REGIMENT was destined to be one of the first units of the British Army to be trained in Combined Operations, after Dunkirk. Some of the troops are seen resting at G.H.Q., Tennie La Sorte, France, where during the B.E.F. assembly period in the early days of 1940 they prepared for the coming conflict. With the 1st and 2nd Battalions the 3rd assisted in building the Gort Line, and for a time patrolled the British sector of the Maginot Line. In 1942 the 3rd Battalion landed in Algeria with the 1st Guards Brigade, and later fought through Italy—to represent the Regiment in the occupation of Southern Austria in May 1945. *Photo, British Official*

WITH THE 1st AND 8th ARMIES IN NORTH AFRICA, the Regiment suffered heavy casualties, particularly when assaulting the Horseshoe on March 16, 1943, from positions overlooking Mareth. Field-Marshal Lord Montgomery, then General commanding the 8th Army, is seen (left) on his way to inspect Grenadier positions in this area. A Guards officer (right) observes shell-bursts in a wood to which the Germans had withdrawn near Medjez-el-Bab, on the 1st Army Front in Tunisia.

Photos, British Official

TANK SQUADRON LEADER briefs his troop leaders before engaging the enemy in an attack near Eindhoven. Guards Armoured Division tanks led the assault on the Nijmegen Bridge, Holland, on September 19, 1944.
Photo, British Official

On the day after, the Grenadiers relieved Louvain, the scene of their first action in the War; and there remained to be accomplished an operation which, had it been successful, would, by carrying the impetus of the British advance to the Zuider Zee, have cut off all the German forces in North-West Holland. On September 17, two U.S. Airborne Divisions were dropped to seize the bridges over the River Meuse at Grave and the Rhine (Waal) at Nijmegen. The bridge over the Neder Rhein (or Lek) at Arnhem, farther north, was the objective of the 1st British Airborne Division.

Fighting for the Nijmegen Bridge

On the 19th, led by the 1st and 2nd Battalions of the Grenadiers, the Guards Armoured Division crossed the Meuse, which was in American hands; by evening the 1st Battalion had reached a cross-roads three hundred yards south of the Nijmegen Bridge. The attack on the bridge began at eight o'clock the following morning, and throughout the day the Grenadiers fought their way street by street towards the fort guarding the approaches.

It was dusk before the final assault was made. In the glare of flames in the burning town of Nijmegen a troop of tanks of the 2nd Battalion charged forward from the shelter of the fort, their guns firing. The first tank crossed right over and reached the far bank: the three tanks following were all hit but the

fifth came safely across. The superstructure continued to be defended most bitterly, the enemy firing even from the topmost girders. But in a short while a troop of Sappers were able to go down into the explosive chambers in the buttresses and neutralize the charges, and the great bridge over the Rhine was captured undamaged.

Great Ceremonial Parade in Berlin

With the arrival of winter the fighting became of a more static nature, and the final offensive which was utterly to crush Germany's military power did not commence until the end of March 1945. The 1st and 2nd Battalions with the Armoured Division fought their way north. The 4th Battalion, which had previously taken part at Caumont in the breakout from the Normandy bridgehead, was placed under command of the outstanding 6th Airborne Division and they struck due east through Minden. This was the formation with its Churchill tanks which led the advance of the British 2nd Army across Germany. By the cessation of hostilities on May 8 the 1st and 2nd Battalions had reached the neighbourhood of Cuxhaven on the North Sea, whilst the 4th Battalion was near Lübeck on the Baltic.

ON June 9, 1945, the Guards Armoured Division said goodbye to its armour in a farewell parade before Field-Marshal Montgomery, and its own Commander, General Allan Adair, C.B., D.S.O., M.C., himself a Grenadier, and reverted once more to its traditional role of infantry. With the occupation of Germany the 1st Battalion was sent to Berlin under command of the 7th Armoured Division, for a great ceremonial parade. The battalion marched past their G.O.C. carrying their Colours—for the first time since 1939 and for the first time in history in the capital city of the German people.

H.R.H. PRINCESS ELIZABETH, wearing on her hat the regimental badge, inspecting a battalion of the Grenadier Guards during a tour of the Southern Command in 1943. On her 16th birthday, April 21, 1942, the Princess had been appointed as their Colonel, by H.M. the Colonel-in-Chief, in succession to her great-great-uncle, the Duke of Connaught, who died early in the same year.
Photo, British Official

A Great Grenadier Goes to His Long Rest

THE FUNERAL OF FIELD-MARSHAL THE VISCOUNT GORT, V.C., who died in London on March 30, 1946, aged 59, took place on April 5, at **Penshurst, Kent.** As the coffin was unloaded villagers and members of the Services lined the road ; a guard of honour was mounted by the Grenadier **Guards.** Commanding the 1st Battalion of this Regiment (see facing page) Lord Gort won the V.C. in 1918. He was C.-in-C. of the B.E.F. 1939–40 ; **Governor and C.-in-C. Gibraltar, 1941, and Malta 1942–44 ;** High Commissioner for Palestine 1944–45. *Photo, John Topham*

Housing the Homeless: Brick Dwellings Go Up

FIRST OF 350 post-war permanent houses to be built by Edmonton Borough Council, London, was "opened" officially on April 6, 1946. It is one of four ready for occupation on the Hoe Lane site, and 64 are to be completed by August, local men being employed. Some of the 100 workers have been out of the Services only a few weeks, under the Class B release scheme. Costing the council about £1,000 each, these houses are for letting only.

Walls of the four completed houses going up in October 1945, when building began (1). A stage further—window-frames in position (2). The roof on—tiling in progress (3). The four-in-one block finished (4). The built-in pantry is a special feature (5).

Exclusive to
THE WAR ILLUSTRATED

Raging Gale Tests for R.A.F. Model Aircraft

SCALE MODELS, of aircraft are tested in a scientifically constructed and equipped "tunnel" at the Royal Aircraft Establishment, Farnborough, Hants; any atmospheric conditions can be reproduced. Performance is watched (1) through a window.

COOLING PIPES (2) beneath the tunnel. Control panel (3) regulating atmospheric conditions. The huge tunnel in course of construction (4); it houses a 4,000 h.p. fan producing "gales" of more than 600 m.p.h.

Photos, R.A.F. Official, Fox

Our Empire's Proud Share in Victory

FULLY REVEALED FOR THE FIRST TIME

By Harley V. Usill

WHEN the last stroke of Big Ben sounded at 11 o'clock on Sunday, September 3, 1939, Great Britain and her Colonial Empire were at war with Germany. Each of the self-governing Dominions, with the sole exception of Eire which opted to remain neutral, made its own separate declaration of war, since by the Statute of Westminster they were no longer bound by an Act of the British Government.

The magnificent response of the Dominions to the call to defend a common way of life, however, does not fall within the scope of this series of articles; here we are concerned to record the great contribution to victory of more than 60,000,000 people of every race, colour and creed who comprise the British Colonial Empire and Mandates.

The mandated territories became British dependencies after the war of 1914-1918, and were surrendered, not to the League of Nations, as a number of people suppose, but to the "Principal Allied and Associated Powers." The Sovereignty of these territories was by that act transferred to those Powers jointly. The Powers then allocated to certain of their number the various ex-German Colonies. The question whether in so doing they transferred the Sovereignty over these territories to each Mandatory Power or whether the Sovereign Power is still vested in the Allied and Associated Powers as a whole could only be settled by international jurists, but for all practical purposes these territories are now part and parcel of the country to which they were allocated.

In a Colonial Empire thus spread all over the world it is not surprising to find striking differences between the forty odd territories of which it is composed, ranging from lands of ancient culture like Cyprus, once given by Antony to Cleopatra as a gift, to the hinterland of East Africa unknown to Western Europe until the last century. To these extremes must be added many differences in political systems and standards of life.

WHAT would be the reaction of these varying peoples to the decision to go to war to defend Poland, that had been taken many thousands of miles away in London; how would they respond to an appeal to join in a war against an enemy whose remoteness removed him from consideration as an immediate menace to the day-to-day affairs of village or town life? The loyal answer was not long in coming, but in assessing the motive for each response it is as well to avoid generalizations. Here, for instance, is one of the many messages of loyalty and offers of help which literally poured into Downing Street from the Colonial Empire within a few hours of the declaration of war. It is from Chitimukula, the Paramount Chief of the Bemba tribe in Northern Rhodesia, and reads:

"I, Chief Chitimukula, Paramount Chief of the Bemba tribe, on behalf of my Sub-Chiefs and people, send greetings to His Excellency the Governor and assure him of our loyalty, co-operation and wholehearted support in this time of war. We are sad to think that again there is the necessity of war but happy to think that Great Britain is fighting to save a smaller nation from persecution. On this account my people are willing and ready to offer their services in defence of this country and the Empire in whatever way may be required. Many of my people are now enrolled in the Northern Rhodesian Regiment as soldiers and porters. This is tangible evidence of our loyalty to our King."

This Chief was evidently quite clear in his own mind on one, at least, of the causes of the war. The following, however, is probably more typical of the attitude of the African "man-in-the-street." An East African askari (soldier), after listening to a lecture in which

FROM an educational point of view nothing that we have published, or could present to our readers, exceeds in interest or in importance this series of articles surveying the whole marvellous effort and value of the British Colonial Empire (as distinct from the self-governing Dominions) throughout the War. Written by an authority on Colonial affairs, the Editor hopes that his readers will follow the course of Mr. Usill's brilliant and immensely informative narrative of an aspect of the Empire's supreme effort in saving the world for Civilization, an effort little appreciated by the British themselves, largely unknown to their American allies, totally unknown to the entire population of Soviet Russia.—THE EDITOR.

the subject of the defence of democracy was mentioned as a primary war objective, enquired what this democracy was. He explained that he had joined the army to fight for "Kingie Georgie" as he understood that "Kingie Georgie" had gone to war and he suggested that if he was also expected to fight for democracy, he ought perhaps to have his pay increased! This personal loyalty to the King is a predominant motive throughout much of the Colonial Empire, and except among the more sophisticated there is, as yet, little appreciation of rival ideologies.

HARLEY V. USILL

WHATEVER the activating motive for loyalty may have been, response was staggering. In all, the Colonies voluntarily contributed in gifts and loans over £30,000,000. They subscribed to buy squadrons of aircraft, and it was a colony, Jamaica, that started the idea of Spitfire funds. They contributed generously to buy mobile canteens to serve people bombed out of their homes in Great Britain, and little Pitcairn Island, which has only 189 inhabitants, made and sent to the U.K. several hundred walking-sticks for wounded soldiers; finally there is the case of Tonga, a small island Kingdom in the Pacific, which wanted to make a war contribution, but was told that the sum offered was too generous. The reply was to increase the sum and to insist upon its acceptance.

This unstinted generosity extended throughout the whole period of the war, and it is significant to record that expressions of loyalty, support and confidence were most frequent during the dark days following Dunkirk. This brief statement of facts provided a clear answer to those critics (like Ribbentrop and some of our own intellectuals) who said that Colonial peoples were so dissatisfied with British rule that they would take the first opportunity to break away from it. At the same time, it constitutes an additional challenge to Great Britain to ensure that the Colonies receive the maximum help in the difficult tasks which lie ahead.

Apart from these spontaneous expressions of loyalty and generosity, which will be dealt with in greater detail when we come to consider individual Colonies, the contribution of the Colonial Empire to the total war effort can be considered under three main heads.

When Hitler started the war, after several years of preparation, he had all the additional advantage of fighting on interior lines. He was able to invade one country after another, and to march his armies, with comparatively little resistance, almost where he wished on the Continent of Europe. But unless he could break out of his land-locked fortress he could not in the long run win the war.

Strategic Importance of Colonies

It was Britain's task to keep him contained in Europe, to keep her own communications open, to feed her people, and to gather and convert the raw materials of war until she and the Allies could summon enough strength to strike. In this general pattern of strategy the Colonies played a vital part. They formed, with the self-governing Dominions, India and Burma, an outer circle which, though dented here and there, enabled Great Britain and, later, Russia, to confine Hitler in an inescapable stranglehold.

The fortresses of Malta and Gibraltar, the ports of Freetown, Aden, Colombo and Mombasa fitted into the general plan, and as the war progressed and spread so the importance of the Colonies increased, e.g. the granting of bases in the West Indies to the United States, the existence of a great block of British territory in East Africa which was to prove so valuable in the first African Campaign, the value when France collapsed of West African territories as a naval base and for air communications between Britain, America and North Africa, and of Trincomalee in Ceylon as an alternative base after the fall of Singapore.

In fact, the strategic disposition and loyal support of the Colonies helped to prevent the Axis Powers from achieving their major plan—the meeting of the Germans and the Japanese on the banks of the Nile.

Sources of Raw Materials

Many products essential to the war effort came from the British Colonies. In addition to the setting-up of dehydration plants for the supply of rations for troops in the Middle East, East and Central Africa contributed sisal, pyrethrum, rubber, wheat, maize, tea, tobacco, sugar, cotton, oil seeds, quinine, hides and copper. West Africa was mainly responsible for maintaining our supply of the essential ingredients for margarine and soap in the form of palm oil, palm kernels and groundnuts, while iron ore from Sierra Leone, manganese and bauxite from the Gold Coast and tin from Nigeria added further valuable contributions to the limitless demands of the Allies for the sinews of war. From Ceylon came rubber, tea and copra. The West Indies island of Trinidad exploited to the full her rich deposits of petroleum.

The Contribution of Manpower

The utilization of Colonial manpower took three main forms. First there was the recruitment of workers for the many increased production drives, a service which became particularly important in those Colonies which were called upon to make good some of the losses resulting from the Japanese invasions. Then there was the raising of local Defence Forces which had the valuable effect of freeing a large number of British troops for service elsewhere. And, finally, the recruitment and training of those Regiments and Pioneer Corps which served with such distinction on various battlefronts

This brief survey will serve to indicate the importance of the British Colonial war effort, and in succeeding articles we will develop certain themes and cover, as far as practicable, the efforts of individual, or groups of, Colonies.

Life-near-Death in a Hongkong Prison Camp

From the time of the town's capture by the Japanese, on December 25, 1941, until August 1945, white prisoners in Hong-kong lived in appalling conditions. Of all the Red Cross food parcels sent, no one captive received more than seven throughout the whole period. Brutality was commonplace: an Allied officer (top left) is being beaten with a heavy stick. At Sham Shui Po camp, on the waterfront, almost without hope officers sat and watched the sunset every evening (top right), or gathered in a hut for lectures and mutual discussion (bottom) in an effort to dispel intolerable boredom.

Drawings by Lieut. A. V. Skvorzov, of the Hongkong Volunteer Defence Corps; exclusive to THE WAR ILLUSTRATED

Top-Speed Battle for Medicina

THE incident depicted in this spirited drawing by Bryan de Grineau commemorates the great gallantry, initiative and fine leadership shown by Major P. F. W. Browne, D.S.O., M.C., 14/20 King's Hussars, Commanding "C" Squadron of that Regt., at the culmination of a hard day's fighting, which is described for THE WAR ILLUSTRATED by Lieut.-Col. H. A. R. Tilney, O.B.E., commanding 14/20 King's Hussars.

14/20 Hussar Regimental Group, comprising 14/20 H., "A" Squadron, 2 R.T.R., and 2/6 Gurkha Rifles, was advanced guard to 43 Gurkha Lorried Infantry Bde. Group during the final offensive in Italy, and the town of Medicina was its first main objective. From the crossing of the river Sillaro on the morning of April 16, 1945, 14/20 H. Group fought its way slowly forward.

BY the evening "C" Squadron, supported by "B" Company 2/6 Gurkha Rifles, carried in "Kangaroos" of a troop of "A" Squadron and who were advanced guard to 14/20 H. Group, had neared the town. Though more than a third of its effective Sherman Tanks had been put out of action, Major Browne led "C" Squadron and his supporting "Kangaroos" at top speed for Medicina.

He charged his own tank down the main street, and in doing so outstripped those supporting him when this street became blocked by the blazing remains of a self-propelled German gun and a collapsed house. Major Browne's tank succeeded in reaching the railway station at the eastern edge, and there was knocked out by one of several Bazooka teams. "B" Company, closely supported by remaining tanks of "C" Squadron, rapidly started cleaning-up, and with the entry of other companies in "Kangaroos" closely supported by "B" Squadron, the complete capture of Medicina was effected with extremely small loss.

Exclusive to
THE WAR ILLUSTRATED

Budapest's Beautiful Bridges are Broken Down

The fight for Budapest, finally occupied by the Russians on February 13, 1945, was one of the bitterest on the Eastern Front, the German and Hungarian garrison fiercely contesting every street. Of the bridges across the Danube the only one now operating between Buda and Pest is the new Kossuth Bridge (1), named after the 19th-century Hungarian patriot. The Lanchid chain bridge (2) was built by British engineers in 1845. Remains of the Francis Joseph Bridge, with Mount Gellert on the Buda bank (3), and the Elizabeth Bridge (4) claimed to be the most beautiful in Europe. See also facing page.

Europe's Wartime Capitals in 1946

BUDAPEST

By PAUL TABORI

THE siege of Budapest in December 1944–February 1945 lasted almost seven weeks and left it a shattered city. It had been already plundered by the retreating Germans, and it was looted again by the desperate Hungarian Nazis and the 30,000 criminals whom the Germans had set free, after burning the police archives. Budapest today, fifteen months after the siege, is the ruined capital of a ruined country which has a long and arduous path to climb before it can return even to a shadow of its former beauty and gaiety.

Eighty per cent of hilly Buda, on the western bank of the Danube, has been destroyed. The Royal Castle is an empty shell. About 50 per cent of Pest, on the opposite (eastern) bank, has been devastated. Raw materials, machinery, labour are all woefully lacking. There is a Russian occupation army of 1,000,000, which mainly lives off the land. And while the free and democratic elections have brought an overwhelming victory of the moderate Smallholders' Party and the coalition government has united the best brains of the country, the physical obstacles are too great for a quick recovery.

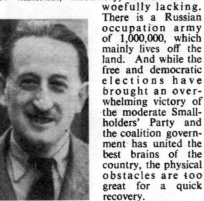

PAUL TABORI

When I arrived in Budapest the pound stood at 250,000 pengoes, exactly 10,000 times its pre-war rate. When I left, inflation had worsened and the pound was about 2,000,000 pengoes. Today, I believe, it is 20,000,000. Torn thousand-pengoe notes —40 pounds at the pre-war rate—are swept in the gutter. A newspaper cost 1,000 pengoes, a tram ticket 500. Food was scarce, and fuel almost unobtainable. By a special effort electricity was maintained, as darkness would have immensely strengthened the crime wave which already caused about a dozen murders and two or three hundred armed robberies *every night.* Gas supplies were cut to one hour in the morning and one in the evening. Trams ran from 10 a.m. to 10 p.m., but there were no buses, and the few cars you saw in the streets belonged to the members of the Allied missions and to high state officials. Hansom cabs and growlers had returned after 30 years; there was no set fare: you had to bargain, and the charges changed from hour to hour.

THE lovely bridges of Budapest—the oldest of them designed by the Clark brothers, two Scotsmen—had been blown up wantonly by the Germans. (When they destroyed them, the Russians were already on both sides of the Danube and it served no military purpose at all.) The Russians built two pontoon bridges which, however, had to be opened every time shipping was passing up and down the river. "Maggie" and "Elsie," as the indestructible Budapest wit baptized them, were near the original Margaret and Elizabeth bridges. Both of them were swept away in the first rush of the ice floes. Luckily by that time, working day and night, the Hungarians had finished their first permanent bridge, ugly but serviceable, named after Kossuth, the great hero of their war of independence in the 19th century. Otherwise Buda and Pest would have been completely cut off from one another for the rest of the winter.

PAUL TABORI is an old contributor to "The War Illustrated," having written an important series of articles in Volume Six. An eminent Budapes journalist, as his father had been; a master of many languages, his "Epitaph for Europe" made a name for him in England and he has since become one of our best-selling novelists, while his serious studies of international affairs have firmly established him in both British and American journalism.

Russian soldiers were much in evidence everywhere. They travelled on the yellow trams, bargained in the shops for the few articles left to sell, queued up in front of the cinemas and sat in the shabby parks. They drove fast and furiously along the main boulevards. They were well dressed and well fed. As few Hungarians could speak their language, there was not much intercourse between them and the population.

The greatest problem of Budapest was fuel. Even the hospitals and clinics had no coal, and doctors had to operate by dipping their fingers from time to time into a small bowl of hot water warmed over a spirit lamp. Many patients died because of the cold. Infant mortality was up to 40 per cent. Yet in spite of all, Budapest was making tremendous efforts to recover. The rubble had been cleared away from the streets, though every day houses were still collapsing often burying people who sought shelter in them. The housing shortage was acute; the average occupancy of rooms three to five people.

Problems of Coal, Light and Food

Architects were preparing plans for rebuilding the whole city, for extending the underground railway—the first but still the shortest in Europe—and to clear away the slums which have, ironically, escaped destruction. Lovely St. Margaret's Island which had four swimming pools, half-a-dozen hotels and restaurants, was completely devastated by the Germans who held out there for weeks. The famous rose trees were uprooted, the buildings burned to the ground. Now an entirely new health resort is being planned which would be able to accommodate 10,000 people in first-class hotels. New streets are to be opened in Pest, and the two principal railway stations, both of which have suffered heavily, are to be replanned and enlarged.

What makes Budapest perhaps unique among the post-war capitals of the Balkans is her brilliantly active intellectual life. With the exception of two, all the theatres have escaped serious damage and all of them are open. There is no coal to heat them; but people flock to the performances dressed in various layers of clothing, carrying rugs and comforters. Performances start early, so that they can get home before darkness falls. The playwrights whose works are produced include J. B. Priestley, Aldous Huxley, Charles Morgan; there are revivals of Shakespeare and Molière, and for the first time several Soviet dramatists receive a hearing. The actors and actresses often go on provincial tours because in that way they can pick up a little food; they measure their success not by the applause but by the bacon or flour they can bring back.

There are more daily papers in Budapest than in London, though newsprint is still short and they are restricted to four pages, with six for their Sunday editions. Weeklies are also appearing in great numbers and sell very well. Reuters news service is distributed by the Official News Agency and there is no visible censorship. Budapest Radio is still handicapped by the weakness of its transmitter—the two strong transmitters of Lakihegy were blown up by the Germans—but Gyula Ortutay, President of the Hungarian Radio, told me that they hoped to have their equipment rebuilt. Broadcasts go out for 20 hours every day, and there is no interference from the Allied or Russian side with the programmes. I gave an improvised radio interview myself, without a script.

Music, too, is flourishing in the ruined capital. The Opera House has daily performances and there is a concert almost every day. The cabarets of Budapest, which are really small theatres presenting sketches and solo artists, are also open. But the largest concert hall of all is occupied with more serious business; in the main hall of the Academy of Music the Hungarians are staging their war criminal trials, which are regularly broadcast. People fight for seats to see the Hungarian quislings, the murderers of forced labour and concentration camps, face their judges. This is the finest and most rewarding spectacle for them: to watch their tormentors writhe and wilt under the relentless questioning of the prosecutors. Once or twice policemen had difficulty in saving the accused from being lynched.

LIFE is Spartan and hard in the former "Queen of the Danube." Most people have to walk long distances, as the trams are overcrowded. There is much queueing, especially at bakers' shops, for few people have enough gas to bake their bread at home as was their wont before the war and the bakers do it for them, not having bread of their own to sell.

There is a black market, of course, in which everything from cigarettes to motor cars can be bought. Opposite the National Theatre dozens of young boys and elderly men sell cigarettes, saccharine and cakes made of maize and sweetened with molasses. Almost everybody is in the black market, for it is the only way of making a living. But considering the devastation and the uncertain future, the people of Budapest are cheerful and optimistic. "We have our soil and we have our brains," as President Tildy told me. "That is enough!"

STARVING HUNGARIANS in Budapest besiege a train to take them to the country districts in desperate search of food. See also facing page.
Photo, Planet New

'Crosskeys' Well Occupied in Malaya

Colours : White Keys on Black

BRITISH 2ND DIVISION

ONE of the original formations of the Regular Army, the British 2nd Division—the Crosskeys—under the command of Major-General H. C. Loyd, landed with the first contingent of the B.E.F. in France in September 1939. In May and June 1940 it was heavily engaged until Dunkirk, when it was evacuated to Britain. The Division then became part of the Home Forces until 1942, when it was transferred to India, and underwent training in amphibious warfare.

Of its subsequent brilliant achievements, none deserves record more than the relief of Kohima and the liberation of Mandalay. Rushed from its training area in India, in April 1944, the Division, commanded by Major-General J. M. L. Grover, M.C., fought its way through the Japanese besieging Kohima and sustained the remnants of the garrison. In one of the bloodiest battles ever fought it hurled back the enemy's last desperate attempt to take the town, and finally cleared it on May 14, 1944, thus removing the direct threat to India.

FROM June 2, 1944, in a southward advance from Kohima, the Division routed the enemy along the Imphal-Kohima road and linked up with IV Corps on June 22. It chased the Japanese to the Chindwin River, taking over the bridge-head from the East Africans at Kalewa, and expanding it in preparation for the British all-out offensive to liberate Burma.

The Chindwin was crossed on December 16, 1944, and within 20 days the Division (since July under the command of Major-General C. G. G. Nicholson, C.B.E., D.S.O.) advanced 130 miles to take the airfields at Shwebo on January 6, 1945, and the town of Shwebo the following day. This remarkable feat of endurance under adverse conditions laid the foundations for the capture of Mandalay. The Division held the Japanese 10 miles west of the city, around Sagaing, their crossing of the Irrawaddy on February 25 being bitterly opposed. Having forced the enemy to pull troops from other sectors it fell to the Division not to capture Mandalay but, together with the 20th Indian Division, to seal the enemy's escape routes in the west and south while the 19th Indian Division advanced from the north to take the city on March 12, 1945.

FOR the 2nd Division this was a fitting climax to a year's hard fighting. It had halted the Jap on the threshold of India, thrown him into the jungle, hunted and chased him to the Chindwin and then to the Irrawaddy. After the surrender of Japan, August 15, 1945, the 2nd Division combined with the British 36th Division.

SINCE ITS DEPLOYMENT in the Bahru-Johore area, following the surrender of Japan, the British 2nd Division has performed military and civil tasks aimed at the rehabilitation of Malaya. Guarding the Government rice store at Muar (1), where Malayans load rice for the civilian population, thousands of whom are being saved from starvation by the British Military Administration. The ignominy of defeat is brought home to this Japanese prisoner (2), under the watchful eye of a lance-corporal, painting the stone-carved badge of the West Yorkshire Regiment at their H.Q. at Muar. Signallers rest from their labours at their lonely station at Minyat, Baku (3). The Divisional H.Q. at Johore was the scene of a ceremonial parade on Feb. 21, 1946, when Admiral Lord Louis Mountbatten presented awards to nine officers and eight men of the Division.

Photos, British Official

Our War Leaders in Peacetime
FIELD-MARSHAL
ALEXANDER

HAROLD Rupert Leofric George Alexander—Field-Marshal Viscount Alexander of Tunis—as Governor-General is the King's representative in Canada, and as he has the simplicity and directness of manner appreciated by Canadians he is likely to be " accepted " everywhere there very readily. He sailed to the Dominion with his wife and family, to take up his appointment (in succession to the Earl of Athlone), on April 5, 1946.

" I've always wanted to live in Canada," he said, "and no humbug about it. But I never thought I'd be Governor-General, and I hope they like me." There is certainly no humbug (one of his favourite expressions) about Alexander. Though his name was among the best-known of all during the years of war as that of a brilliant military leader and planner, he is simple and retiring, and in leisure hours loved to look after the hens scratching among the leaves at Rideau Hall, his Georgian home on the edge of Windsor Forest. In the study there he spent hours reading about Canada, between helping to pack and answering batteries of questions from his children about their home-to-be.

Born in Ulster, in 1891, the third son of the Earl of Caledon, Alexander married in 1931 Lady Margaret Diana Bingham, daughter of the Earl of Lucan. Now he turns with half-derogatory remarks every reference to his success as a war leader ; and although her eyes deny her words Lady Margaret backs him up by saying, " Alec is just an ordinary family man, you know."

Local people grew accustomed to see the general who helped to defeat the Axis strolling around in an old pair of grey flannel trousers with his two sons and one daughter or romping with ten-year-old Shane and his younger boy, Brian. An athlete, Alexander has enjoyed many a week-end walking in Windsor Forest or shooting over the stubble, often by himself. Water-colour painting and botany are among his hobbies, and he is a member of White's and the Guards' Clubs.

AT Rideau Hall he spent much time answering shoals of letters from men who served under him in North Africa and Italy. " The War Office has put a room at my disposal," he said. " It's good of 'em, you know, for I'm not doing much for them these days and I couldn't run an office on my own—not on my salary, when I have to buy such a lot of kit for Canada."

With the children growing up, he gives the impression of being satisfied with the family life normal to most happily married people. He himself went to Harrow and Sandhurst, but his sons will not necessarily follow their father's example. The boys can go to Harrow, he says, but there's no reason why they should not be educated in Canada.

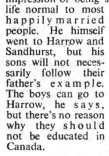

IN HIS LEISURE HOURS, at home in England, Field-Marshal Viscount Alexander of Tunis found time to interest Brian (top), one of his three children, in the action of his Luger pistol—a souvenir from Italy. No mean exponent of the art of water-colours, he shows Lady Alexander his painting of Lake Como, Italy (oval), done in company with Mr. Churchill. Strolling in the grounds of his home on the edge of Windsor Forest, Berkshire (bottom), with his wife and son, Brian, just before the family sailed for Canada.

Photos, Sport & General, Illustrate

The Daily ~~Cen~~ and Morning Post

Imperial

LONDON, MONDAY, SEPTEMBER 4, 1939

GREAT BRITAIN AT WAR

THE KING'S MESSAGE

5 CRUISERS ... **THE SPEE** ...

AWAIT

48-Hour Ultim...

The ★ **Star**

LATE SPECIAL

THE LONDONER'S EVENING PAPER

NAZI ARMY INVADES DENMARK & NORWAY

BOMB RAIDS ON OSLO

Evening Standard

FINAL NIGHT EXTRA

This is the Gin Gordon's

NAZIS INVADE HOLLAND, BELGIUM, LUXEMBURG: FRENCH TOWNS BOMB...

British Troops in Heavy Fig...

BELGIAN ARMY SURRENDERS

LEOPOLD GIVES UP

The ★ **Star**

LATE FINAL

THE LONDONER'S EVENING PAPER

335,000 MEN BROUGHT FROM JAWS OF DEATH —CHURCHILL

GERMAN TROOPS ENTER PARIS

FRENCH RETIRE TO SAVE CITY

The ★ **Star**

LATE FINAL

R.A.F. RECORD BAG—185 IN A DAY

Goering Loses

News **Chronicle**

Late London Edition

NAZIS INVADE YUGO-SLAVIA, GREE...

IN ACTION IN Addis Taken: 70...

Push in a...

Daily Express

NEW YORK

BERLIN

VICHY

WAVELL CUTS RETREAT OF BENGHAZI ARMY

"Double, double, toil and

The Daily Tel

1,500 TROOPS IN AIR ATTACK ON CRETE

NEARING NEW ZEALAND BATTLE-DRESS

FIRST INVASION GLID...

LATE FINAL

BISMARCK IS SUNK IN ATLANTIC

NAVY AVENGE THE HOOD IN W...

LONGEST SEA BATTLE

Hitler's newest 35,00...

has been ...

News **Chronicle**

LATE LONDON EDITION

GERMANY ATTACKING RUSSIA

...anians Join Nazi ...Mile Front

Churchill Pledges All British Ai...

FIRST AID

Daily Express

YEAST-VITE
The Lightning Pick-Me-Up

On the 826th day of the battle, war speeds right round the world

JAPS DECLARE WAR

'We fight Britain and America from dawn'

News **Chronicle**

LATE LONDON EDITION

PREMIER ANNOUNCES FALL OF SINGAPORE

Daily T

Tobruk Falls: Enemy Forces Are in Bardia

Britain's Food: How The Bananas Come to Us

FOOD VALUE OF FULLY RIPE BANANA

NATURE'S BACTERIA-PROOF WRAPPER

MOISTURE 75·6
SUGARS 20·4
PROTEIN 1·2
STARCH 1·2
FIBRE ·6
FAT ·2
MINERALS ·8

1 GREEN FROM TREE
2 GREEN TIP
3 YELLOW RIPE
4 FULLY RIPE BROWN FLECKED

SUSPENDED DURING FIVE YEARS OF WAR, shipments of bananas have recently begun to arrive again in Britain. Though their distribution is at present restricted to those under 18 years of age they will eventually become available to all. This drawing, compiled with the co-operation of Messrs. Elders & Fyffes, Ltd., shows how this welcome addition to our frugal post-war diet reaches Britain.

Bananas flourish in all moist tropical areas such as the Caribbean. In Jamaica 200 to 300 bunches per acre are produced. The plant attains a height of between 20 and 30 ft. in its 14 months of growth, and after the crop has been harvested the trees are cut down and left to rot on the ground, forming rich humus to feed the next crop.

In the background are shown early stages of planting and growth. The blossom (A) first appears when the tree is about 11 months old, and within three or four months the crop is ready. The banana at this stage is green—it is never allowed to ripen on the plant. Harvesting is carried out by teams of three men: the cutter, using a

long-handled knife (B), nicks the trunk, and the fruit is caught on the shoulder of the "backer" (C). The third man (D) severs the stem—average weight 35 to 40 pounds—with his machete, and the load is carried on muleback (E) to one of the many light tramways (F), thence to the main railway (G) and the port. Overhead wires (H) are often used to bring crops over marshy ground or water.

A refrigerated and ventilated vessel (K) is used for carrying bananas; carefully packed to avoid bruising, they are kept at a temperature of around 53 degrees Fahrenheit during the voyage. On arrival at the British port the cargo is unloaded by means of a mechanical elevator (L) into specially conditioned railway vans. Still green, the bananas are placed in ripening-rooms (M) at a temperature of between 65 and 70 degrees; ripening from stage 1 to stage 3 takes five to seven days. Stage 4 is best for eating, the starch in the fruit having now become fruit sugar.

Specially drawn for THE WAR ILLUSTRATED *by* Haworth

Aircraft Carrier Rajah Brings the Troops Home

SPEEDIER REPATRIATION OF BRITISH TROOPS resulted from the conversion of aircraft carriers of the Royal Navy to troopships. One of the first to assume this role was H.M.S. Rajah seen (1, left) passing another carrier while navigating the Suez Canal on the homeward journey. An accordion player (2) entertains on the flight deck, below which is the spacious hangar filled with bunks (3), ample ventilation being afforded by the lowered aircraft lift at the top end. The flight deck (4) lends itself admirably to exercise and sports.

Photos, British Official

I Was With the 51st Division at St. Valery

Private Peter Maisey, East Surrey Regiment, was captured when Rommel's Armoured Corps swept remnants of the 51st Division into the French town of St. Valery-en-Caux, in June 1940. He tells of a month-long forced march, a voyage in the black holds of coal barges, then by cattle-truck to the prison camp and, finally, repatriation.

EXPECTING opportunities of mass embarkation on that evening of June 9, 1940, troops lined up, ten deep, from the quay to the outskirts of the town. Chaos reigned throughout the night. Burning houses gave a fantastic appearance to the scene. Thousands of men—most of us had lost touch with our units — huddled in pouring rain, staring out to sea, wondering whether or not the Navy was there to take us off. Stray, half-crazed horses floundered about. Countermanded orders, rumours and false alarms added to the confusion.

Pte. PETER MAISEY

In the morning I joined a number of men carrying wounded along the beaches towards a solitary French cargo boat that lay off-shore about a mile from the town. High cliffs overshadowed us. Germans had control of the cliff top, and in spite of our errand they took pot-shots whenever we appeared in view dodging around land-slides and boulders.

When I was half-way to the boat and still with hope of escape, the Germans opened fire with a French field gun, blowing the boat out of the water with their second round. Then they systematically shelled every vessel in sight. Escape now was obviously out of the question. The town had already fallen. Some officers with us hoisted a white sheet and the whole column turned about, heading back to St. Valery and the prison camps.

The first German I saw was a small, cheerful individual who told us not to worry, as France had fallen, England would capitulate in a week, and we should then be sent home. I wonder what he is thinking now! The day was spent by the Germans in rounding up stray parties of men who had attempted to dodge through their lines to the south. Very few got away.

The Germans Withheld Even Water

We were roughly searched and collected in a field, hungry because there had been no organized food supplies for several days. I was lucky enough to have my water-bottle half full of rum. That evening we were marched two or three kilometres to the grounds of a large farm, where we were herded together and left for the night. The next day we started to march.

For weeks we marched through northern France, Belgium, and part of Holland, a period of intolerable physical exhaustion. The Germans gave us practically nothing to eat—we lived on what we could pick up from the gardens and fields that we passed. The few French civilians whom we saw during the first two weeks were sympathetic but had nothing to give us except water, and on several occasions the Germans forbade even that.

Later, we passed through large towns; St. Pol was the first that I can remember. Here the civilians gave us everything they could—bread, wine, soup, soap, towels, and all manner of things they could lay hands on. France had just signed an armistice. The women were weeping. Things looked black.

During the whole of the march the weather was boiling hot by day and mistily cold by night. Through most of Holland we were transported on a local railway. The Dutch gave us a great ovation, throwing bottles of milk and pea soup and bread on to the trucks as we passed.

We Longed for a Breath of Air

Then came the coal barges. One hundred of us at a time were stuffed into the dirty black holds. The decks were filled with men, so that those unfortunate enough to be below could not get above for a breath of fresh air. We had just enough room to lie down together with our legs in an awful tangle. In this suffocating atmosphere, with a loaf apiece, we spent four days.

Getting off the barges, we set foot on German soil for the first time—nearly a month after capture. Trains of cattle-trucks were waiting to take us to various stalags. This journey lasted thirty-six hours. Stalag XIC, **Bad Salza**, was being built by Poles when we arrived. Long marquee tents with a miserable sprinkling of straw over the ground served to accommodate the whole party for three days, during which time we were de-loused, bathed, given a number, photo-

graphed, searched, interrogated, and allocated to various working parties.

Again we boarded cattle-trucks, a form of transport we learned to hate. The doors were locked for the whole forty-eight-hour journey, and the slot-like windows were heavily wired. Sixty men were in each truck, many suffering with acute diarrhoea, all half-dead with fatigue and hunger.

The party to which I had been allocated, some two hundred strong, were bundled off the train at Eisenach, a small town in middle Germany, surrounded by wooded hills. We marched through the main station and along the high road; a remarkable crowd, lousy again, ragged, thin, yet with enough energy to sing and comment on the aloof crowd.

OUR camp was perched on the side of a hill. The red, wooden huts with green window-boxes and white window frames looked very pleasant from outside. Inside they were filthy. Two large huts provided sleeping accommodation for us, a smaller one for the guards. There was a cook-house, a hut for coal and potatoes, a bath-house and primitive lavatories.

The night we arrived we were given imitation coffee, and we found it to be as bad as its reputation—made, I believe, from acorns, and almost without taste unless cooked in the proportion of half coffee to half water, when it did develop a flavour, but so appalling that even the Germans winced. Each hut was partitioned into rooms that held thirty-five men. There were no separate beds; box-like shelves ran the length of each wall, containing straw palliasses on which we slept shoulder to shoulder.

Reveille that first morning was at six; for the rest of the summer it was at four-thirty. We were given one quarter of a civilian loaf, margarine and a small portion of sausage, which we thought a very handsome breakfast until later we found that it had to do also for lunch and tea. Plus a bowl of soup, this constituted a day's whole ration.

BENEATH THESE CLIFFS AT ST. VALERY men of the 51st Division made their perilous way towards rescue ships, in June 1940. In the Maginot Line on May 10, and ordered west, the Division was cut off by the Germans at this point near Dieppe and a large part of it was forced to surrender when ammunition gave out. PAGE 25 *Photo, New York Times Photos*

LITTERED BEACHES at St. Valery still bore witness months later to the grim ordeal through which the 51st Division had heroically passed.
Photo, Associated Press

That morning civilian contractors arrived to claim bunches of prisoners for work on different sections of a road being constructed nearby. Work started at seven in the morning and continued until six in the evening, with two half-hour breaks. As some of the parties had four or five kilometres to walk there was not much leisure. The unluckiest spent thirteen hours out of twenty-four away from camp. We were given Saturday afternoon and Sunday free, to begin with ; but soon we were fighting hard for our stipulated one day's rest in seven.

THE work was unskilled labouring: loading and unloading lorries of sand, rubble and broken stone, digging trenches, laying drain pipes, levelling land and handling cut stone for bridge building. For two months we scarcely knew each other's names : sheer exhaustion made conversation impossible. Then the apples ripened in orchards adjacent to our work and we stole them in quantities ; the soup thickened a little

and our condition improved. Life became coloured with songs, mouth-organ music, jokes and arguments. A sort of passive resistance developed against German bullying. Impromptu concerts were organized.

Winter came. Very suddenly the country was covered with dry snow, winds became vicious, temperatures fell to minus thirty and lower. An issue of old Polish military great-coats did nothing to keep the cold out. In lieu of socks we were given pieces of rag to wrap round our feet. When the soles completely disappeared from our boots, wooden clogs appeared. The power of the commandant was absolute. We had no appeal, until Swiss and American Red Cross representatives visited the camp some nine months later.

Over Christmas for a month the weather made road-work impossible ; instead, we cleared snow from paths and the main streets of Eisenach. At the beginning of February

IN STALAG IVa to which some of the captured Division were sent. Private Peter Maisey, who tells his story here, is seated at the extreme left.

1941 rain and cold, damp winds replaced snow. We restarted our road work, often drenched to the skin, miserably cold and hungry. On April 10, unmistakable symptoms of tuberculosis forced the Germans to send me to a prisoner of war hospital at Wasungen.

Red Cross Parcels Saved My Life

I did no more work in Germany. It is significant that in spite of my disease I was envied by the other men, because of the indefinite rest I should be getting. Wasungen Lazarett was a disused mill. It consisted of two large, barn-like buildings with various outlying structures, all on their last legs, surrounded with barbed wire and called a hospital. Inside, the wards were revolting ; wooden floorboards, ages-old, caked with filth ; crumbling plaster walls ; wooden beds, in most cases double tiered and far too many in each ward. Food was worse in quality than at the working camp, for the Germans argue that non-workers need less nourishment. Luckily for us Red Cross food parcels started to arrive, saving my life and the lives of thousands of other sick men.

As there was no form of treatment for my complaint they decided after three months to send me to another hospital. Winterburg Lazarett was a step up the social scale for prisoners. It was a dance hall, on top of a small hill with pine and birch trees that we could sit under. My ward used to be

IN THE CEMETERY AT ST. VALERY, graves of those who fell in 1940 were visited by some of their comrades of the 51st Division who, returning to France as victors, liberated the town, on September 2, 1944, and thus avenged the tragedy that had befallen the Division four years earlier. See also illus. page 562, Vol. 8. *Photo, British Official*

the skittle alley, dark but airy and not over-crowded. Most wonderful of all, we had spring beds. Here I received expert treatment from Dr. Blondeau, a Parisian T.B. specialist, who was responsible for the saving of dozens of British lives during his two years' imprisonment there.

This hospital being smaller and in pleasant surroundings had an atmosphere physically and spiritually conducive to convalescence. The guards were easily persuaded to buy us commodities such as paper, pen-knives, razor blades and matches, with bribes of cocoa or chocolate. One little Saxon became very fond of "housey-housey."

In December 1941, after four months of comparative comfort, the whole hospital was moved to Konigswartha, a small village in Saxony. This hospital was already full, and we were accommodated in a new wooden barrack. This was bisected by a corridor with small rooms on either side containing twelve beds—four single, four two-tiered. There were beds for one hundred and twenty men, a wash-room with one small tap, and the usual flushless lavatories. This was our sanatorium—for patients who had chest trouble, mostly tuberculosis. We lived there for over a year.

During that time our interests expanded. We staged seven different shows. Book parcels arrived, and we soon had a library of nearly two thousand volumes. A choir was organized, sometimes a little breathless, but always willing. A magazine appeared at

odd intervals. A Toc-H group started. Gramophones and records came from the Red Cross. Bridge tournaments were taken very seriously. Our greatest achievement was a presentation of Macbeth. Three months' work rehearsing, making costumes from dyed sacking, painting decorations on newspaper and cardboard: it was a triumph of improvisation.

Towards the end of 1942 the Germans' attitude began to change perceptibly. The swing-over began. Our food and cigarette parcels shook the German complacency. The war news worried them. For the first time our protests produced tangible results, and the sanatorium was again moved, this time to a better site.

Elsterhorst, the last hospital I was in, consisted of brick huts with excellent sanitary arrangements, a small football pitch and a large sandy enclosure. This move was negotiated in April 1943. Then the period of repatriation rumours commenced, stories too easily believed by nostalgic, weary men. At last, in October, we were told to pack our bags. One memorable Sunday morning we were paraded by the gate with our sealed luggage. The Swastika waved over our heads for the last time as lorries rushed us out of the gate and down to the station.

Nine days later we disembarked at Liverpool. It all happened as quickly as that. A three-day train journey through Germany, in comfortable carriages; the ferry boat to Sweden; a six-hour journey by rail through Sweden, then the hospital boat to England.

Our Fight Through Arctic Seas to Russia

As Chief Steward of the Empire Tide of the Royal Mail Line, in convoy for Archangel in 1942, Horace Carswell mixed other excitements with the suddenly assumed role of surgeon--and gained the Lloyds War Medal for Bravery at Sea to add to his D.S.M., M.M. and B.E.M.

My old floating home, S.S. Pampas of the Royal Mail Line, lay at Malta bombed into scrap-iron as I drew £42 for lost kit and went to spend my "survivor's leave" with relatives at Reading —where the biscuits used to come from. Before that leave had expired, the pavements began to pall and I got the hankering to feel a deck under my feet again. As I was not in the Reserve Pool of seafarers, I made my own arrangements and joined the S.S. Empire Tide of the Royal Mail Line as Chief Steward, and learnt that the ship was due to leave for America to load a general cargo for Russia.

We sailed on May 10, 1942, and the Atlantic crossing was curiously peaceful.

The cargo was taken aboard at an American port, and the ship then proceeded to Reykjavik in Iceland. From the Icelandic port we set out on the long voyage to Archangel in the White Sea, in convoy with thirty-seven merchant ships accompanied by an escort of twelve cruisers, destroyers and corvettes.

The season was midsummer by the time we were over the Arctic Circle steaming on a nor'-easterly course for the Barents Sea, and daylight had lengthened to about twenty hours. Three days out from Reykjavik the first German air-scout came nosing along, a Focke-Wulf 190 from one of the bases in enemy-occupied Norway. It flew round the convoy at a respectful distance and made

off, but other aircraft, like birds of ill-omen arrived to shadow our ships in turn.

The after-glow of the sun mellowed the sky even at midnight, and almost uninterrupted daylight and clear weather made reconnaissance easy for the Hun. Crews of the warships and cargo-carriers were on their toes continually in anticipation of attack, for all the indications were that the convoy taking vital munitions and stores for the Russkies was not likely to remain unmolested for long.

Bells Ringing "Action Stations"

Yet we managed to keep cheerful. At least, the threat from the Jerries did not prevent some of us, in Arctic seas for the first time, from being initiated in the Order of the Bluenose. The initiation was a bit

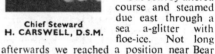

different from the ceremony of greeting King Neptune when crossing the Equator: a feature was that each new "Bluenose" was presented with a coloured certificate duly signed by "Neptunus Rex, Ruler of the Raging Main" and his consort "Aurora Borealis, Queen of His Majesty's Northern Provinces."

Chief Steward
H. CARSWELL, D.S.M.

Our convoy altered course and steamed due east through a sea a-glitter with floe-ice. Not long afterwards we reached a position near Bear Island, which is roughly midway between the north coast of Norway and Spitzbergen. This was the zone of greatest danger, lying as it did within easy range of the German air-bases and, as everyone expected, the alarm bells were soon ringing for "Action Stations."

The enemy's assault was launched on the grand scale. Between forty and fifty Jerries came racing in from all directions—a combined force of bombers, fighter-bombers and torpedo-carrying planes that filled the Arctic sky with the thunder of high-powered engines. It was the Fourth of July. With unconscious irony, the winged squadrons of the Reich began a rip-snorting celebration of Independence Day in the tough Nazi manner by slamming bombs and cannon-shells at two American ships which were in the convoy. In less than a minute, battle was raging over a wide area of the ice-dappled sea, with

S.S. EMPIRE TIDE (left), on which Chief Steward Horace Carswell served on the convoy-run to Russia in 1942, was fitted with a catapult launching device for fighter aircraft. Captain Frank Willis Harvey, master of the ship (extreme right), chatting to the two Hurricane pilots, Flt.-Lt. D. R. Turley-George and F/O C. Fenwick, was awarded the D.S.O. for the superb manner in which he handled his vessel. *Photos. British Official*

all hell let loose in a holocaust of flame, thunder and smoke. A ship on the Empire Tide's port quarter erupted like a volcano and disappeared in the frigid depths. Two or three others began to lose way, then listed and settled deeply from the impacts of bombs and the deadly " fish."

The sea spurted in columns of foam. Fragments of ice from the shattered floes spattered our decks. Warships and merchantmen combined to fill the sky with the fury of high-explosives, and the rain of steel made you thankful for a tin " battle bowler," inadequate protection though it was. The only notes of real music in this devil's concerto were the whine of stricken Jerry planes spiralling into the sea.

For handling and fighting his ship that day, Captain Frank Willis Harvey, master of the Empire Tide, was awarded the D.S.O. Our skipper was grand ; he was an inspiration to us all. By cool courage and quick decision he met each emergency as it arose, outwitting the Huns time and again by superb seamanship and well-directed gunfire. Throughout the whole attack Chief Engineer Hughes and Second Engineer Griffith remained in the engine-room, ensuring the utmost possible speed under conditions of great stress. They, too, earned decorations for their devotion to duty during this and subsequent ordeals.

A Shout in the Din of Gunfire

While the battle was at its height I stood on deck and thought to myself. " This is about as hot as the party we had on the Malta convoy." Then I heard an agonized shout sandwiched in the din of gunfire, and quickly looked up. It came from the gun position on the ship's " monkey island," and I was just in time to see a lad sag limply across the bullet-proof screen.

Something had to be done for the chap. Everyone seemed to have a job on his hands just then except me. So, despite a bit too much weight for lively exertion, I managed to bounce up the bridge-ladder and the extension leading to the isolated platform to look after him. The victim belonged to the Royal Navy, one of the few R.N. ratings borne in the Empire Tide for gunnery duties, and he had caught " a proper fourpenny-one " in the thigh.

LUCKILY my shoulders are broad, and the old knees sound for all my fifty-odd years, though a Chief Steward doesn't get the healthful exercise of hauling on ropes and scrubbing decks enjoyed (more or less) by deckhands. However, I managed to hoist this matelot across my back, fireman-fashion, and carry him down the ladders without taking a nose-dive. It was with no little relief that I got him below, what with the scrap iron flying about, and the ship bucketing from bombs exploding uncomfortably close.

Our ship had no doctor on board. I cast a weather-eye over the victim and decided something else must be done smartly, or he would soon be slipping his cables. This wasn't a one-man job, though. I summoned the pantryman and a few others of the First Aid party, and made ready to do a spot of surgery which, as events proved, might well have daunted a Harley Street surgeon.

But ignorance is bliss—at least, I was happily unaware from my amateurish examination of what the emergency operation entailed. What knowledge I had of surgery and medicine was of the elementary order, but I had confidence in myself—although unwarranted in the circumstances—and, was not lacking in the " bedside manner."

" There's nothing to worry about, son," I assured the patient. " I'll soon fix you up all right." The bluejacket was not so easy of mind. His lurid remarks betokened pain

and resentment when I probed the gaping wound in his thigh and the ship lurched to the concussion of a bursting bomb close alongside. Amid the renewed din of gunfire. I remarked : " You've picked up a bit of metal in this leg of yours, that's all. I'll winkle it out in two shakes of a cod's tail."

HIT BY AN AERIAL TORPEDO this merchant ship in convoy to Russia sank near Bear Island in the Arctic. *Photo, Associated Press*

The haggard gunner squirmed in the grip of the orderlies. " Y-you mind what you're playing at," he spluttered ; and emphasized his anxiety with a few seamanlike expletives. He had good reason for uneasiness. A skilled naval surgeon, as I came to realize, would not have relished the task ; indeed, my own serenity was ruffled somewhat when I was able to diagnose the injury more thoroughly. It certainly shook me to find a small-calibre unexploded shell from an Oerlikon gun embedded in the chap's thigh ! The thing had to be extracted and the wound properly dressed or the patient would pass out. Unfortunately, there were no anaesthetics in the medicine chest of the Empire Tide, and our surgical instruments were the sort of things you might expect to find in a carpenter's tool-box. However, I took the necessary precautions according to the text-books, and got on with the job. Then, having dug the live shell out, I put sixteen stitches in the wound while the luckless victim alternately gritted his teeth and bellowed pungent opinions of the proceedings. I gave a sigh of relief.

" Like taking a tooth out," I murmured. It did not surprise me that the matelot was overflowing with sweat rather than gratitude.

" Y-you ought to have been a something

butcher !" he ground out. I passed him an enamel mug.

" Here, son—put this tot of rum down the hatch. You're the best patient I've had on this voyage." It did not seem necessary to add that he was also the first ! And he was not the last. Several other casualties came to my hands, for it was over a week before the services of a qualified doctor could be obtained. Apart from rendering first aid, the after-care of cases included repeated dressing of wounds to prevent sepsis.

That aerial attack on July 4, 1942, began at 4.30 p.m., and continued for some time with unabated fury. The Huns suffered severely for initial successes, but further sorties were made and the surviving warships and merchantmen had to fight grimly for their headway through the Barents Sea. It was just one of the many battles that convoys had to wage through that "white hell" of the Arctic to take supplies to our Russian allies. A heavy price was paid with the lives of British, American and Norwegian seamen for the delivery of a large proportion of the vital cargoes. The sacrifice in our own convoy can be judged by the fact that only nine merchant ships out of thirty-seven made the round trip unscathed.

With Toes and Fingers Gangrenous

The white route to Russia was certainly no picnic in those days when the Luftwaffe was riding the skies in strength. Things were bad enough in "the Med" when your ship was scuppered, but if you took to the boats or went overboard in these icy seas your ordeal was a sight worse and chance of survival considerably less.

The going was so tough that our captain decided to make for temporary haven at Novaya Zemlya, the long island which, if you look at a map, rears up like a disturbed caterpillar from the north Russian coast. On the way, we picked up 148 survivors from lifeboats adrift—men suffering from exposure and frost-bitten hands and feet. This rescue work provided me with plenty to do ; in fact, I was landed with a job occupying twenty-four hours a day looking after these "orphans of the storm."

Once we had gained shelter, radio signals were made. These brought a plane post-haste from the mainland, and a Russian lady doctor took charge of the casualties, and a few of the severely wounded were flown to Archangel for hospital treatment. Among these was my patient, the naval gunner, the chap who had gritted his teeth and sworn a little when I dug the live shell out of him.

Many of the others were in bad shape, but had to be left in my care. Unfortunately some had landed on another island before being rescued, and had built fires and toasted their toes. The safe method in a below-zero climate is to rub snow on partly frozen extremities, and the result of their mistake was that toes and fingers became gangrenous and needed drastic treatment.

IN making Moller Bay, where we anchored, the Empire Tide struck an uncharted rock, and the master, chief engineer and second engineer had another tough job on their hands, although all were greatly exhausted through lack of sleep. But the ship was repaired and refloated, and later we set off unescorted on the last leg of the voyage to Archangel. Land had been dropped below the horizon far astern when the look-out in the crow's-nest aroused our interest by a report to the bridge :

" Object on the starboard bow, sir !" Captain Harvey altered course two points to bring the object ahead, and he and the First Officer focused their glasses while the distance was being closed. Without the aid of binoculars, I could see nothing more than what looked like a long stick and three

WILL you please tell your newsagent, well in advance, when you are going away from home for your summer holiday so that he can reserve your copies of THE WAR ILLUSTRATED until your return.

ATTACKING FROM ALL DIRECTIONS, flying low to avoid A.A. gun-fire, enemy aircraft swoop on an Allied convoy sailing the Northern route to Russia. Two of the ships have been picked out as targets for bombs and aerial torpedoes. One of the aircraft (left foreground) coming out of its dive appears to be touching the tip of a mast, while high above floats the freighter's barrage balloon. U-boats intensified the ordeals of the convoys, as told in Chief Steward Horace Carswell's story.
Photo, Associated Press

chunks of wood floating nearby. On closer inspection they proved to be the foremast and stern of a sinking ship and three lifeboats manned by survivors.

Another "object" loomed into view, and drew near the boats. It was the green-grey conning-tower and hull of a U-boat. This neighbourhood was not so healthy ! Our captain altered course and ordered "Full ahead" on the engines, and these turn-tail tactics must have been unspeakably galling to him. No one would have taken a crack at that U-boat with more zest than Captain Harvey, but all our ammo had been expended in the bitter fighting.

THE submarine hove-to within a few oars' lengths of the lifeboats, and did not appear to take offensive action against the men, though it was difficult for us to see exactly what was happening. Meanwhile, the wreck sank slowly, and the U-boat made off.

"We're going to pick those blokes up !" I heard someone remark. None of us doubted that Captain Harvey would go back after he had led the U-boat commander to suppose he had scurried to shelter. Every man aboard the Empire Tide appreciated that humane decision, though many an anxious eye scanned the sea for a periscope or the bubbling wake of a steel "fish." There was a chance that the Jerry had come back stealthily to keep watch on those lifeboats, which he might regard as bait to attract further prey. But no attack was made.

The crew of the torpedoed ship were got aboard, some of them suffering from frost-bite due to immersion in the icy water before being hauled into the boats. So I received more patients for my shipboard "hospital."

Some of the survivors told us that the Jerries had given them water and biscuits to add to the normal lifeboat rations, and the German commander, who spoke English fluently, had advised a course to a haven in Novaya Zemlya. "You are not Bolsheviks," he said. "Why do you come to the help of these Russians ?" To which a British officer answered : "Because they are our allies in this war you Germans started !"

The U-boat commander glared coldly. "Britain and France declared war on the Fatherland," he snapped ; but conveniently avoided any reference to Hitler's savage invasion of Poland despite repeated warnings from the Allies. It appeared, too, that the German had boasted of his sinking of other merchant ships sailing independently for

CHIEF STEWARD CARSWELL behaved with outstanding courage in the face of great danger when a gunner was wounded during the action with enemy aircraft. He made his way to the gun position and carried the gunner down to the ship's hospital. There he inserted sixteen stitches in the man's leg while the attack on the vessel was proceeding. But for the prompt action and skill of Mr. Carswell the wounded man might have lost his life.—Extract from Lloyd's List and Shipping Gazette, No. 40310.

Archangel after the battle of the Barents Sea On learning this, our captain decided to make a wide sweep of the area in case other hapless crews were adrift, and the search resulted in the rescue of survivors from two other torpedoed vessels. From this and other warnings, there appeared to be small hope of the Empire Tide making a lone voyage to Archangel in safety. So we ran back to Moller Bay where, by good fortune, we found four corvettes and an equal number of merchant ships that had arrived after various misadventures. A small convoy was formed, and without further interference we reached Archangel to deliver our cargoes.

AT the time, some 2,000 British and Allied seamen—survivors from aircraft and U-boat attack—were housed in the Intourist Club, a huge ·logwood building surmounted by the Union Jack and Soviet flag. Our arrival with munitions and supplies was greeted cordially by Russian officials, but there were no wild demonstrations of welcome by the people. After our ship had made a call at Molotov, a new port about forty miles from Archangel, a convoy of twelve ships was formed for the homeward voyage. Again we had to run the gauntlet of the Polar route, and were frequently attacked by hostile aircraft and finally by a U-boat pack. Eight merchant ships and one corvette were lost, and of the whole convoy only one escort and two cargo-carriers—the Empire Tide and Ocean Freedom—reached the homeland in safety from that Arctic hell.

How We Outwitted the Japs in the Indian Ocean

FIFTH LARGEST ISLAND IN THE WORLD, with an area of 241,000 square miles, Madagascar in 1942 was under Vichy French administration, and the Allies feared a Japanese move against this strategic base in the Indian Ocean, off the east coast of Africa. First steps to prevent its vital anchorages and airfields falling into enemy hands were taken by the British on May 5, as told in the facing page. Two of our assault landing craft are seen heading for the shore (1) and, later, Commandos making their way around a hill-side (2) on a mopping-up expedition. A native woman fruit-vendor (3) is amused by a British soldier whose fingers are indicative of victory.   PAGE 30   *Photos, British Official*

My Commando Beach-Party at Madagascar

The naval base of Diego Suarez was captured in 48 hours, on May 5-7, 1942, in a combined attack by British Army and Naval forces. Joint Principal Beach Master in the assault landings was Lieut.-Commander A. H. Ballard, D.S.C. and Bar, R.N.R. The newspapers called him "The man who had five D-Days"—and here is his story of one of them. See also facing page.

BY good fortune and what is called "the exigencies of the Service" I have had a variety of jobs with the Royal Navy, and consequently little boredom. The high spots were the landings. I suppose it was somewhat unusual for any one individual to take part successively in the amphibious invasions of Norway, Madagascar, North Africa, Normandy and Holland — and with nothing worse than leg wounds on two occasions. It was just my luck.

Lieut.-Commander A. H. BALLARD, D.S.C. and Bar, R.N.R.

Those of us aboard H.M.S. Keren, an assault ship in a southbound convoy from a British port in the spring of 1942, had no idea of what was brewing, and merely presumed we were bound for the Far East. I was in command of a beach party of Commandos, and shortly before the convoy reached Durban "hush-hush" lectures were given to me and other officers on an amphibious operation for the capture of Rangoon. Afterwards, charts of Trincomalee and the approaches to the Irrawaddy were issued, and we were told to take them to our cabins and look after them carefully. Needless to say, stewards and orderlies on board the Keren and other ships saw some of the charts and got wise to the operation. The "news" reached shore, as it was intended to do; and no doubt, in due course, the Japanese received warning to "Watch Rangoon!"

At Durban I was transferred to the Keren's sister-ship H.M.S. Karanja, and appointed J.P.B.M. (Joint Principal Beach Master). Then, after the judicious leakage of the false news, we were briefed in strictest secrecy for the real operation—that of seizing Madagascar by a surprise assault. This large island, off the east coast of Africa and on the ocean highway to Asia, was being administered by the Vichy French at the time and the Allies feared, with good reason, that the Japanese might seize this strategical base. Which was the reason the Allies decided to jump in first.

THE attacking force was divided into two convoys, the slow ships leaving early and the fast convoy with assault ships following, to rendezvous off the north-east coast of Madagascar on the evening of May 4. Formation was taken up outside a string of islets and reefs, which present a barrier pierced only by narrow and tricky channels. The Vichy French assumed an amphibious attack from the west was impracticable by craft larger than fishing-boats, and so concentrated most of their forces to the east where, at the psychological time, a feint attack was made by British warships and aircraft.

All appeared quiet on the island. For a time, the armada proceeded dead slow whilst a destroyer went in and dropped dan-buoys to indicate the passage through a deep-water channel in the reef. On each of these dan-buoys glowed a blue light, visible for two miles after dark in clear weather. The navigational dangers were considerable, despite the guiding lights, but the assault ships and a supporting cruiser went through

the channel and quietly dropped their hooks at an anchorage inside the reef.

Small assault landing craft, carried on the big ships, were lowered gently, and all was ready for the landings, timed for 4 a.m.—about two hours before dawn in the tropics—on selected parts of the Madagascar coast: known as Red, White and Green beaches for purposes of the operation. The sea was calm. A full moon enabled us to see the rugged coast of the island about eight miles from where we were assembled for the assault. Conditions, in short, were more or less ideal, for the ships could not be seen from the shore.

The naval Beach Master, my opposite number, was of equal rank but senior to me (Royal Naval Reserve) by reason of his being a regular R.N. officer. In his boat he had an assortment of military ranks—artillery, transport, signal and liaison officers—and my command consisted of an equal number in duplicate of his party. With typical British flair for apt description, his crowd was known officially as the First Eleven and mine as the Second Eleven. I rendezvoused with the assault craft conveying the Third Commandos (military) and two companies of the East Lancashire Regiment.

We Reached Shore at Zero Hour

Waiting for "the balloon to go up" is one of the nerve-trying ordeals of war; but previous to the period of suspense a sailing boat had come from the shore with two Englishmen who proved to be our "fifth column" from Madagascar. They gave us information about the dispositions of the Vichy French forces and other conditions ashore that proved not only useful but comforting. With a heart-felt sense of relief we got under way and sped toward the shore to arrive on the beaches at zero hour.

My own craft and several others headed northward and had to cover a distance of twelve miles to Red Beach, where the troops leaped ashore without encountering opposition and immediately dashed to the capture of the first objectives. Two French officers showed resistance in the Observation Post of a heavy battery and were killed by tommy-gun fire. Over 60 French troops then surrendered to the Commandos, while other troops followed the telegraph wires over rugged country to the barracks, where 108 Vichy French soldiers were taken.

Having landed my party I went alongside H.M.S. Royal Ulsterman to collect other units, then led an attack on an additional

beach that I located and which subsequently proved to be the best for landing military supplies in quantity. My special party of transport and other officers comprising the Second Eleven were still in the assault craft, to wait aboard until I decided the right time and place to land them.

On this second approach to the shore, the Vichy enemy displayed a "certain liveliness." Machine-gun bullets lashed the sea into feathers of foam, and several penetrated the hull of the assault craft. The Second Eleven—poor devils!—had nothing to do but lie low and assume that air of nonchalance becoming to British officers under fire. From my perch above the assault craft it was easy for me to locate some of the machine-gun nests ashore and direct the landing of other craft to the best advantage. There was hot fighting on this new beach before our troops moved inland.

Having seen this attack well under way, I was able to proceed with my next job, which was to patrol inshore and find a suitable spot to beach H.M.S. Bachequera, loaded with artillery. On this survey along twelve miles of coast the wind freshened and the sea became so choppy that the Second Eleven heartily wished themselves "facing the bowling" ashore.

That assault craft behaved like a fractious mule; in the rougher weather it did almost everything except sit up and beg. Twice it bucked me into the sea, and on the second occasion I was hauled out the worse for a couple of cracked ribs sustained by striking against the hull on falling overboard. However, there was neither time nor opportunity to get treatment until two days later, when a naval surgeon applied a strapping.

OPERATIONS ashore were going well. A destroyer raced into the harbour of Diego Suarez and landed 50 Royal Marines, who swept irresistibly through the town of Antsirane. H.M.S. Ramillies and other warships bombarded the east coast, and aircraft dropped dummy paratroops in boiler-suits.

The urgent need as I patrolled the coast in the assault craft was to get reinforcements ashore and the heavier stuff in the shape of artillery and half-track vehicles. To this end the Bachequera had to be beached, and after a close survey I went out to the anchorage to report to the Senior Naval Officer of Landings that I had found a suitable beach. "Good show!" he said. "There's your ship. Take her in."

I went aboard the Bachequera and managed to ram her aground without damage and get the artillery ashore, and I was switched almost immediately to the task of landing munitions and stores in the Red Beach area. For three weeks after the Vichy surrender I held an executive post ashore, flying the White Ensign over the bungalow requisitioned for my headquarters.

H.M.S. KARANJA, the assault ship to which Lieut.-Commander A. H. Ballard transferred at Durban, was later sunk, in 1942, while taking part in the North African landings. Before the War the Karanja was a passenger and cargo liner (9,891 tons) on the British India Steam Navigation Co. mail service between Bombay and Durban.

Photo, British Official

H.M.S. Vanguard for Royal Visit to Africa

Photo, G.P.U.

BRITAIN'S NEWEST BATTLESHIP, in which the Royal Family will sail to South Africa in February 1947, the Vanguard is seen at Clydebank. Princess Elizabeth will attend the commissioning service and dedication of the ship's chapel at Greenock on May 12, 1946. Estimated displacement 42,500 tons, the Vanguard mounts eight 15-in. guns. Her first commander will be Captain W. G. Agnew, C.B., C.V.O., D.S.O. and Bar, R.N., gunnery expert, whose exploits in command of the cruiser Aurora in the Mediterranean in 1941-42 made him famous.

Printed in England and published every alternate Friday by the Proprietors, THE AMALGAMATED PRESS, LTD., The Fleetway House, Farringdon Street, London, E.C.4. Registered for transmission by Canadian Magazine Post. Sole Agents for Australia and New Zealand : Messrs. Gordon & Gotch, Ltd. ; and for South Africa : Central News Agency, Ltd.—April 26, 1946. S.S. *Editorial Address :* JOHN CARPENTER HOUSE, WHITEFRIARS, LONDON, E.C.4.

BRITAIN'S LEADERS IN WAR AND PEACE, the Rt. Hon. Winston S. Churchill (right), and the Rt. Hon. Clement R. Attlee, Prime Minister, leaving Westminster Abbey, London, after the memorial service to Field-Marshal the Viscount Gort, V.C., on April 10, 1946. The service, conducted by Canon A. C. Don, was also attended by high-ranking officers of the Royal Navy, the Army and the R.A.F., and by representatives of Malta, Gibraltar and Palestine. See also page II.
Photo, P.A.-Reuter

Edited by Sir John Hammerton

Calais After the Siege : Dauntless in Defeat

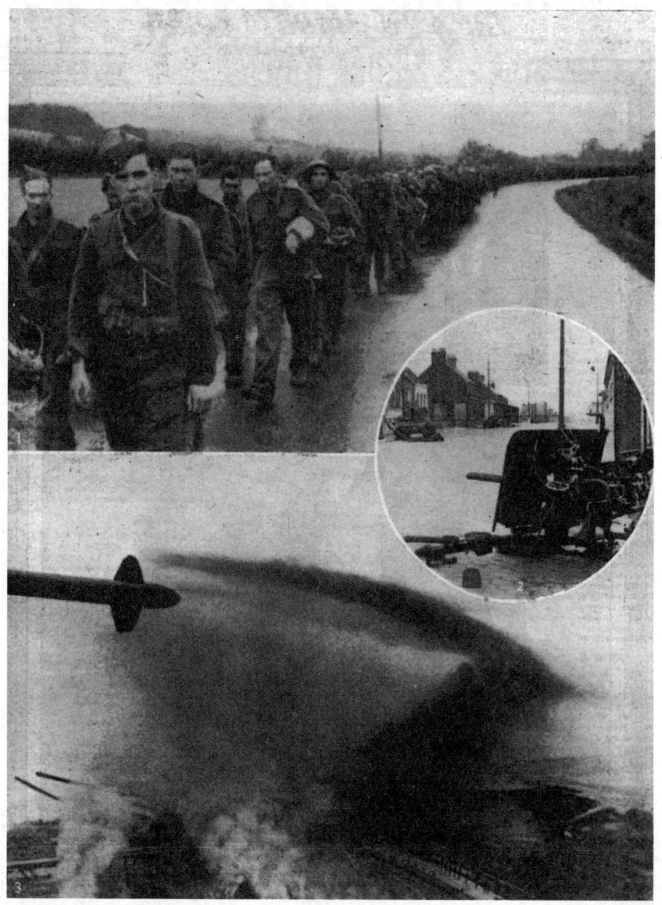

UNCONQUERABLE IN THEIR SOULS though Calais had fallen, after a fight beyond reason, the last round of ammunition expended, expressions of these British troops (1) marching away to captivity tell the story of their indomitable courage. Equipment of the defenders, including an anti-tank gun (2), lay shattered in the battle-torn streets when the Germans occupied the town on May 26, 1940. Burning and smoke-wreathed, the wharves (3) took heavy punishment from relays of dive-bombers. See facing page.

PAGE 34

Photos, Associated Press

The Last Stand at Calais

By Rev. CLIFFORD LEVER
Author of On My Heart Too

BREAKFAST in our comfortable château just outside Ardre was a pleasant meal on that lovely May morning in 1940. Even the Adjutant seemed quite serene, despite the rumours: "Boulogne has fallen." . . . "St. Omer is captured." . . . "The Germans are heading your way for Calais." . . . and so on. As we had no official information none of us took these rumours seriously. They were too fantastic; they just didn't make sense!

But sense was bludgeoned into our disbelieving minds by a sudden, shattering roar of gunfire. We rushed on to the veranda. In the valley, two miles away, we could see yellow fumes of cordite rising slowly into the still air. And to our ears came the harsh clattering of tanks and a bedlam of cannon-fire.

Into a cloudless blue sky roared a formation of dive-bombers that began to peel off into screaming attack. Another moment and our Hurricanes and Spitfires were attacking them. To our incredulous eyes the air became filled with whirling, twisting, diving, fire-spitting death. Flaming planes crashed to earth; others limped off in clouds of smoke. Parachutes floated calmly down. Then the sky emptied again save for an intricate pattern of vapour-trails; but the noise of battle continued in the valley.

CLIFFORD LEVER, C.F.

It was all as sudden as that! We goggled at each other. A telephone screeched, and a voice, commandingly insistent, said, "Everybody to R.H.Q. . . . immediately." A few minutes more and we found ourselves in our *own* little hell. Enough only need be said of our isolated action to give the picture of many similar actions that were taking place or had taken place all over the countryside around Calais. Sufficient to relate that a column of German tanks, men and field-guns, assisted by spotting-planes and parachuted snipers, were held up for a whole day by a handful of clerks, cooks, batmen and officers comprising the R.H.Q., who barricaded themselves, with ration-lorries, inside the rectangular farmyard which was Headquarters, and fought like veterans.

Victims of Fifth Column Snipers

The end, of course, was a foregone conclusion. But we denied the enemy the satisfaction of capture. For, as the evening came on, and screened by the smoke from the now blazing farm-buildings about us, we slipped out of our garrison, waded waist-high along a nearby dyke and safely reached the main road that led north to Calais. In a weary "crocodile" we marched the nine miles to the outer perimeter of the town amid whining shells and the bursting of explosives. We found the railway-siding, canal and dykes which formed this perimeter sparsely manned by platoons of the K.R.R.s. We entered Calais.

We could hear the sounds of battle away to the west of the town, and learned that partial siege had already been laid by the enemy two days before. Gunners, Pioneers, R.E.s and a few Welsh Guards who had trickled back from shattered Boulogne had held the west side of Calais until reinforced by untried units of K.R.R.s, Queen Victoria's Rifles and the Rifle Brigade. These had arrived that morning and gone straight into action. The main fighting so far had been on that side of the town, as the Germans, moving up from the south, had not yet arrived. *We* knew they were on their way!

A ship loaded with ammunition, equipment and some tanks, accompanying these units, could not be off-loaded because of the failure of the electric power to the dock-cranes and the disappearance of the French dockers. (The ship, later, had to return to England still fully loaded save for a few tanks that had been manhandled on to the quay by our own men. These must have been the tanks we had heard in action that morning.) We were warned that it was necessary to be on the alert for Fifth Column snipers who had already killed some of our men.

AS we walked warily down the shattered streets, dodging flying slates, splintering glass and chunks of masonry, the last four tanks the garrison possessed passed us on their way out. Before we reached the end of the main thoroughfare the largest tank, battered and broken, was back again. The other three did not return. From this the inference was simple: the Germans from the south were now with us!

The shortage of men and ammunition soon became apparent. That night, as we crouched in a cellar while bombs rained on to the town, we could hear, between bomb-bursts, the chattering of rifle and Bren-gun fire becoming louder and nearer—so near that it meant the outer perimeter had been abandoned and we were now fighting on a shorter line to hold the inner perimeter.

Next morning the smouldering inferno of the night blazed up white-hot; an inferno that made Dante's a pale fantasy beside this fiendish, stinking hell. Rifle, Bren-gun, tank-gun and field-gun fire; crashing walls; flying slates and glass; men crawling from street-corner to street-corner, firing as they crawled; men blazing away through glassless windows at an enemy who seemed amazingly expert at this kind of battle; men fighting from flaming roof to flaming roof; bodies falling out of windows and from the roof-tops; streams of bullets smacking the cobbles and zipping past your crouching body; stretcher-bearers creeping along, ignoring their own danger in the greater purpose of mercy; water from burst mains flooding down the littered streets—water with a pinky tinge as it lapped around your feet; red-hot dust choking lungs and nostrils. All this and, over all, the cataclysmic din and that insidious awareness of death that blacks out reason and leaves only naked instinct to motivate one's actions.

Pioneers Held the Inner Bridges

The trained infantry units were now fighting bitterly—fanatically—on the inner perimeter which half-circled the town, every shrinking yard claiming its percentage of life. The Pioneers—old veterans of Mons and some, I swear, of Mafeking—toothlessly grinned as they held the inner bridges and stopped loose-roving tanks by the sheer rate of their Bren-gun firing. (These were cunning old men who neatly piled up German dead to make fire-parapets for themselves.) Gunners and R.E.s, now turned infantry, blazed away with their unfamiliar rifles. Time and time again the Nazis broke before them.

In roared the dive-bombers . . . ineffectually. The fighting was too close-contained. They sheered off, to wait until the situation cleared. Slowly, as the terrible days and nights vaguely punctuated this unrespited agony, the situation did clear. It was inevitable. You cannot fight tanks and armour for ever with rifles, Bren-guns and anaemic anti-tank rifles, especially if you are so few in number that you cannot get any relief save the snatched moment of twitching sleep. No matter how high your courage or how tenacious your obstinacy, rations that become more and more frugal and ammunition that dwindles without replenishment will make the end inevitable. Street by street, square by square, the area of the town held by us shrank. It was all so simple—for the Germans!

Two German tanks at one end of a street two at the other with no tanks to oppose them—then their infantry would fight a way with sub-machine guns and grenades into the first house of the street, blast a hole through

THE TOWN HALL AT CALAIS with its well-known clock tower as it is today. After the siege of 1940—described above—from 1941 to 1943 this ancient French town was the frequent target of R.A.F. bombers and long-range guns sited at Dover, and again saw heavy fighting when the Canadian Army recaptured it in 1944.

　　　Photo, Planet News

the internal wall into the next, and the next, and the next. Slowly our men, fighting on every floor, on every roof, would expend their ammunition. There would be no replenishment. Vainly they would charge, collectively and individually, with butt, bayonet and often with bare fist—the ending was always the same : into the street finally, to find the two ends sealed off by four enemy tanks. It was all so ruthlessly efficient, so logically achieved.

The Nazi flag fluttered from the tall tower of the Town Hall. That meant that half the town had now fallen. The fighting concentrated on and around The Citadel where Brigade Headquarters still desperately held out. Around the docks and near the medical-post in the railway station, over the shattered bridges, on the smashed lock-gates the battle went on. Every previously abandoned vehicle on the quay (and there were many) became a flaming point of resistance until the ammunition ran out.

" So British . . . I Salute You ! "

Until the ammunition ran out . . . The same monotonous theme ! If ever banner could have been unfurled over the blazing, splendid ruins of Calais, on its scroll could truly have been written in letters of unfading blood, "We fought on until the ammunition was spent."

The whole town suddenly became very quiet. We were startled by the unfamiliar silence. We wondered what it could mean. Some of our optimists started to cheer; they thought we had won. It soon became known, however, that the Germans had sent an emissary, under a white flag, to ask for our surrender.

That silence was very brief. The inferno blazed up again. The answer had been given. Weary as they were, every man cheered and the rattle of rifle-fire became more defiant than ever—with a new, inspired defiance. It was magnificent, but short-lived. Slowly, on that final Sunday morning, as the dive-bombers, at last coming into their own, screamed down on to The Citadel, the rifle-fire died down until, apart from an occasional shot, the whole town stilled into silence. Finally, even the occasional shot ceased and nothing could be heard save the crackling of flames in the sunshine. It was the end of the splendid epic that was Calais.

Squads of Germans with sub-machine guns at the ready crept cautiously about, rounding-up prisoners. German Red Cross personnel helped ours to carry away the wounded of both sides. Rations of stew were served out to friend and foe alike. As evening came on all the prisoners were lined up in the big square, all so very, very weary that many slept as they stood. The Germans, equally weary, grouped around, standing or sitting, gazing curiously on this ragged, tiny remnant of an Army which had defied their efficient might so long. They gazed curiously and with grudging admiration.

THREE German staff cars came up, and stopped. A General stood up in the second car and gazed long and steadily at our men. In his face of granite was a softening compassion and admiration. Nobody called out an order but, unconsciously, our men and the Germans, despite their weariness, stiffened into some semblance of attention. Somebody whispered, "It's Rommel !" Whether it was or not nobody could be sure ; it didn't matter. He spoke, in stilted, halting English, "Bloody, bloody fools ! . . . So magnificent . . . so hopeless. So British . . . so futile . . . but still . . . magnificent. I salute you !"

He gravely saluted to the front ; saluted to the half-right and again to the half-left and, still standing at the salute, passed out of sight as the cars moved on. Almost before he had gone the men, British and German alike, flopped down on to the hard cobbles of the square. As night drew her dark cloak about them, enemy and friend slept side by side in the uncaring abandon of utter exhaustion.

The days that followed almost beggar description. Long columns of exhausted prisoners were forced-marched fifteen kilometres a day through French villages whose inhabitants stood silent in the streets with tragic hopelessness. Many of our men were badly wounded, but if they could stagger along at all they were made to do so. One major, in particular, with rough bandaging round a bleeding hole in his back, limped along in a delirium of agony through all the never-ending hours of a stifling day until the angry, blasphemous protestations of our own men—risking being shot in voicing them—finally forced the Germans to send transport ; next day he and others like him were taken on ahead. The rest staggered on, footsore, and frantic with thirst, yet not permitted to stop for a gulp of cold water proffered by the pitying wayside peasants.

ON the third day it rained a little and eased the agony. Our men put on their gas-capes. The Germans were intrigued by these and gleefully took them. In fairness to the enemy let it be said that the treatment by these front-line fighting troops, though rough, was humane, and the meagre rations of soup doled out to our men were exactly of the same quality and quantity as their own. It was later, on the fourth or fifth day, when they were handed-over to the base-personnel, that our men felt the full harshness of bitter and gloating enmity.

The first night after this handing-over some of our men were comfortably housed in a brickworks ; too comfortably ! In the middle of the night the Commander of the Guard had them turned out and they were made to sleep in the storehouse on pyramids of brick. They lay, as best they could, on the sloping sides. If they slid down they were booted back by the guards ; if they protested they were prodded with loaded rifles or banged with the butts.

Finally, in some wayside railway station in Belgium, they were loaded into open cattle-trucks—crammed so tightly that it was impossible for them to sit or lie down. The next four days of the journey through Belgium and Germany into Poland were spent standing, all day, in blazing heat ; and at night, by contrast, in bitter cold. The nightmare journey at last ended and they were drafted off into the different forts in Poland that were to be their prison-camps. Here the conditions were appalling.

After a few weeks of this, when everybody was crawling with lice and bitten by bugs, our doctors firmly protested to the Camp Commandants, only to be blandly told that it was not worth while making any serious attempt to change the conditions as the War would soon be over now and our men repatriated ! It was only when England refused to give in and the War looked like going on for some time longer that the Germans got down to the problem of the prison-camps and made a real job of it.

To Await the Moment of Escape

Not all our men arrived in Poland. A few died on the way, but many more, not caring to spend the rest of the War in captivity, slipped out of the prisoner-columns as they passed through some familiar French village. There they sank into the background of peasant-life to await the moment of escape. One officer found a French farm intact, complete with cattle, pigs and poultry, and donning the clothes left behind by the hurriedly departed farmer he calmly ran the farm for some three months.

He even supplied the German Officers' Mess across the way with milk, butter and eggs. At last, being "tipped off" that the Germans were beginning to suspect his true identity, he left the farm ; cadged lifts on German military lorries to Cherbourg, and there, helped by friendly fishermen, finally got a boat across to England : to receive a Military Cross. In him is typified the real spirit of the epic that was Calais and of men who fought, refusing to be daunted and even when defeated remained unconquerable in their souls.

Colours : White " Y " on Brown

BRITISH 5TH DIVISION

RE-FORMED in France in October 1939, by the late Field-Marshal Lord Gort, V.C., the nucleus of the Division comprised three regular infantry brigades, and was commanded by Major-General (now Lieut.-General) H. E. Franklyn. Destined to a globe-trotting fighting existence it became known as the " Gipsy Division."

The Division fought on two fronts in 1940, two brigades in France and one in Norway. On the Western Front two noted actions were fought which materially assisted in the successful evacuation of the B.E.F., May-June 1940. The first was in the defence of Arras (May 21) and the second along the Ypres-Comines canal (May 27-28). In both, severe casualties were inflicted on the enemy, and sustained by the Division.

The other brigade, transferred to Norway, landed at Aandalsnes (April 23-24) and repulsed heavy attacks at Kram, 100 miles away (April 25). In a second battle at Otta (April 28) it again proved its superiority. After being withdrawn from Norway the Division rejoined in England, in October 1940.

EARLY in 1942 and now commanded by Major-General H. P. M. Berney-Ficklin, the " Gipsies " sailed for South Africa en route for Madagascar where two brigades, after landing on May 5, fought brilliantly and paved the way for the capture of Antsirane two days later. The third brigade had proceeded to India, where it was later joined by the other two, and the Division moved to Persia in face of the German threat to the Caucasus.

In January 1943 the Division went to Syria, trained for the invasion of Sicily and, landing south of Syracuse on July 10, 1943, took the town of Syracuse by nightfall, and Paterno later. With the 8th Army the Division, under the command of Major-General G. C. Bucknall, led the assault on Italy on September 3, 1943, and immediately captured Scilla. In nine months campaigning Muro was taken (September 25); Lupara, after a heavy engagement on the Biferno, in October ; and Forli (November 9). The Garigliano was crossed on January 18, 1944, with the 5th Army, and Minturno taken two days later. Commanded by Major-General P. G. S. Gregson-Ellis the Division became part of the bridge-head force at Anzio from March 1944, subsequently crossed the Moletta river and advanced until the fall of Rome on June 4, 1944. In this last phase Sgt. M. W. Rogers (2nd Wilts) earned a posthumous V.C. (portrait in page 376, Vol. 8).

AFTER refitting in Palestine the Division, now commanded by Major-General R. A. Hull, reappeared on the Western Front (April 1945) and assisted in driving the Germans across the Elbe and entered Lubeck. By VE Day the Division had completed a trek of 30,000 miles and won for itself a glorious reputation by its doggedness and fighting qualities.

Redundant Now: Not Again to be Fired in Anger?

IN NEATLY MARSHALLED RANKS hundreds of redundant guns stand mutely just beyond Park Royal Station, Middlesex, in a huge depot spreading from Western Avenue across the fields. Among them are some of the finest pieces of British artillery. In the foreground can be seen Bofors 40-mm. A.A. platforms. To the rear are the famous 25-pdr. field guns, and the 17-pdr. anti-tank guns designed originally to counteract the 88-mm. weapon mounted on the German heavy tanks, and later used by our Airborne forces.

Photo, Keystone

Slovakia Goes Gay on Year-Old Liberation Day

THROUGH THE STREETS OF BRATISLAVA, capital of Slovakia, on April 4, 1945, marched the people who for six years had been under Nazi "protection," like others in Bohemia and Moravia. The occasion, the first anniversary of the city's liberation by Russian troops, was marked by a speech delivered by Dr. Fierlinger, Prime Minister of the Czechoslovak Republic, in one of the city's squares (top), and by a procession of Slovak girls in picturesque and colourful national costume (bottom).

Photos, Keystone

Invasion Anniversary Remembered by Denmark

TWO MINUTES SILENCE WAS OBSERVED throughout Denmark on April 13, 1946, to commemorate the sixth anniversary of the German invasion (April 9, 1940) and in homage to those who lost their lives in the long and bitter struggle to free their country from Nazi tyranny. In the Town Hall Square, Copenhagen (top), crowds massed for the observance; many remained at the memorial cross (bottom), erected to those Danes who had suffered in enemy concentration camps.

Photos, New York Times Photos

HIS MAJESTY'S SHIPS

H.M.S. Exeter

Motto: "Ever Faithful"

LAUNCHED at Devonport in 1929, H.M.S. Exeter, of 8,390 tons, mounted six 8-in. guns as her main armament, and was thus the most powerful of the three British cruisers under Commodore H. H. Harwood which defeated the German pocket battleship Admiral Graf Spee in the Battle of the River Plate, December 13, 1939. In the earlier stages of the action the Exeter became the principal target for the enemy's 11-in. shells. On fire and with her guns mostly silenced, she was obliged to withdraw to execute temporary repairs at Stanley, Falkland Islands.

Completely refitted in this country in 1940, the Exeter was recommissioned for further foreign service. She was one of the five Allied cruisers which faced a superior Japanese squadron in the Battle of the Java Sea on February 27, 1942. With most of her boilers disabled and the greater part of her ammunition expended, she put back to Surabaya, but left again 24 hours later in company with two destroyers. Though her boilers were partially repaired by the superhuman exertions of the engineroom staff, she was again engaged by Japanese cruisers and destroyers on March 1, being so heavily damaged as to be incapable of movement. Soon after being abandoned by her surviving officers and men she sank.

This glorious fighting record recalls the stubborn resistance which a previous Exeter offered to several enemy ships at the Battle of Sadras(also in the Eastern seas)160 years before.

Truth About the Submarine Seal Revealed at Last

MYSTERY surrounded the fate of one of Britain's newest minelaying submarines when in May 1940 the Admiralty announced that "H.M. submarine Seal is overdue and must be presumed to be lost. Foreign reports suggest that some of her crew may be prisoners of war." The Times Naval Correspondent commented, "The mention of 'foreign reports' probably refers to an account, published in Germany and Sweden on May 6, of the capture of prisoners from a disabled British submarine in the Kattegat by a German seaplane. The German report went on to describe how the submarine was subsequently taken in tow by a German minesweeper and captured, but that part of it was probably fictitious."

Lieut.-Commander R. P. LONSDALE, R.N.

Six years were to pass before details of the loss of the 1,520-ton Seal became generally known—as the result of two courts-martial convened at Portsmouth: the first on April 9, 1946, when 27-years-old Lieut. Trevor Agar Beet, R.N. (now of H.M.S. Victory) faced charges of failing to sink the ship to prevent her falling into the hands of the enemy, and was honourably acquitted.

In evidence, Lieut.-Commander Rupert Philip Lonsdale, R.N., who was in command of the Seal from April 29 to May 5, 1940—and, with his men, from then on for five years a prisoner of war—told how they left the Humber on April 29 on a minelaying expedition in the Kattegat and were attacked by a hostile aircraft but suffered no damage. Later, having successfully laid her mines, the Seal was proceeding out of the Kattegat when she struck a mine.

Tense Drama on Bed of the Sea

The mine exploded and the Seal, 20 per cent flooded, hit the bottom of the sea-bed and lay there with her bows up, at an angle of 18 degrees. Strenuous but futile efforts were at once made to close a water-tight door through which water was cascading in. Oil and water were pumped out of the tanks, to lighten the submarine. All this, the Lieut.-Commander said, "made continuous and ever-increased demands on the physical and mental capacities of the crew." The men were dizzy, and panting for breath.

There occurred then a never-to-be-forgotten scene. The Commander summoned all hands, and together, as the Seal lay crippled and helpless on the sea-bed, officers and 60 men repeated the Lord's Prayer. Eventually the motors started again and the submarine surfaced, after having been submerged for 22 hours. Code books and other secret documents were placed in weighted bags and thrown overboard and periscope and Asdic detecting gear were smashed. Four at a time the crew went to the conning tower for air; but some of their number were in a comatose condition, unable to move.

Helpless as she lay on the surface, the Seal came in for further attack by German aircraft. Now the engines failed altogether to respond, and when the main motors were switched on they blew up. It was impossible for any of the crew to go on deck; those who attempted it were subjected to streams of machine-gun bullets. The odds were too tremendous to continue, and the Commander hoisted a white sheet from the

bridge—but not until the first Arado seaplane had been joined by two others and (it was stated in evidence) Lieut.-Commander Lonsdale himself had fired at them with Lewis guns, until the guns jammed, as shown in our artist Haworth's spirited impression.

One of the seaplanes came down close to the Seal, and the Commander was ordered to leave the submarine and swim over to the aircraft. Finally, all the crew were taken aboard a German trawler and the Seal taken in tow, reaching Denmark only just afloat.

AFTER the Commander had left the ship, everybody aboard (said Lieut. Beet, in evidence) thought she was in a sinking condition and would go down; and a depth-charge set in the Seal would go off when she sank. In these circumstances it did not occur to him to hasten the sinking. This grim story from the past so far brought to light, the Court was cleared whilst the judges came to a decision.

When the Court reassembled, the position of the sword, which (in accordance with Naval tradition) had lain lengthwise on the judge's table throughout the hearing, had been changed. As Lieut. Beet re-entered he

saw the hilt pointing towards him, and with a smile the President of the Court returned the sword to its owner.

The following day Lieut.-Commander Lonsdale faced the court-martial on charges that he had failed to take immediate action to engage the enemy aircraft that attacked the Seal, and had failed to take steps to see that the submarine was sunk when it appeared possible that she might fall into enemy hands. He also was honourably acquitted.

Lieut. TREVOR AGAR BEET, R.N.

Of matters concerning the Seal which may still remain unsolved there is the mystery of the submarine's final disposal by the enemy. Close investigation has revealed that she was never used operationally by the Germans, but no trace of her has been found in German and Danish U-boat yards.

Caernarvon's Freedom for Royal Welch Fusiliers

THE 13th CENTURY CASTLE was the setting for freedom presentation of the Freedom of Caernarvon Borough to the 6th Battalion Royal Welch Fusiliers on April 11, 1946. The Battalion, now stationed in Düsseldorf, Germany, was represented by a detachment led by the Commanding Officer, Lieut. Col. F. F. Laugher, who is here seen addressing the assembly during the ceremony. "Taffy," the Regiment's famous mascot (right) was among those present.

Photos, Topical

The Royal Marines

By Major W. R. SENDALL

Everywhere the Fleet has been, Royal Marines serving as ships' detachments have also been in action—manning between a quarter and a third of the armament of every ship, from a cruiser to a battleship. In all the big actions of the Second Great War in which such ships have been engaged—the River Plate, Matapan, the destruction of the Bismarck and the Scharnhorst, the battles in the Java Sea and the Pacific—the Royals have formed a substantial part of the ships' companies, their detachments numbering from 60 to over 250 according to the class of ship. Royal Marine officers serving with the Fleet Air Arm distinguished themselves in actions from the days of Norway and Taranto to attacks on the Japanese.

The ships' detachments are also trained to act as a land striking force under the Naval Commander-in-Chief. Marines from the cruisers Sheffield and Glasgow made up the major part of the first British force to land in Norway in 1940, forming a bridgehead at Namsos for an Army expedition. At Aandalsnes a few days later Marines from the battleships Barham, Nelson and Hood landed to discharge a similar task, and also remained to cover the final evacuation as a rearguard. Another force of sea-service Marines carried out a swift occupation of the Faroe Islands to forestall the enemy.

At the Hook of Holland, Boulogne and Calais, when the German armoured scythe was sweeping all before it, parties of Royal Marines carried out special tasks. At the Hook they covered the escape of Queen Wilhelmina and her Government. At Boulogne they protected a naval demolition party destroying harbour facilities while the Germans were in the outskirts of the town. At Calais they landed for the same purpose, and most of them remained to take part in the now immortal defence.

In Madagascar in 1942 the Marines of H.M.S. Ramillies made a daring landing in

NO comparable unit of the Armed Forces can lay claim to such a variety of War service as the Corps of Royal Marines. They have been everywhere and done nearly everything. Their badge is the Globe itself, surrounded by laurel, awarded to them more than 100 years ago as a symbol of their universal service. They have borne it not only by sea and land but under the sea and in the air, in every theatre of War from the River Plate to the North Cape, from Hongkong to Iceland.

the rear of the defences that expedited the capture of the naval base of Diego Suarez. In the Aegean in 1944 H.M.S. Aurora's Marines captured the island of Levitha. And in 1945 a force drawn from the East Indies Fleet chased the Japanese out of Cheduba island off the Burma coast, later re-embarking to take their place at the guns for the bombardment of Ramree.

THAT, briefly, is the record of the soldiers of the Fleet. In the main their story is that of the ships in which they serve, and as a fighting ship is a highly integrated team it would be impossible, even if it were desirable, to attempt to disentangle the story of one particular component. But among those not to be forgotten are the Royal Marine bandsmen, the fighting musicians, who man the fire control instruments—the nerves of a ship of war—when Action Stations sounds. Perhaps their best story is that of H.M.S. Penelope's band who for two days played to the men unloading a precious cargo in Valetta harbour, Malta, while the Stukas screamed down on them incessantly. While the bombs burst around they played steadfastly from a lighter to keep up the spirits of those at work.

The ships' detachments, though still the basic role of the Corps, are at present only a minority, the great majority of Marines having served in the wide and varied field of Combined Operations. Around the tiny nucleus left at the end of 1939 after the Fleet's

General Sir THOMAS HUNTON, K.C.B., a Jutland veteran, Commandant-General of the Royal Marines since 1943. He retired from the Service in April 1946. *Photo, Associated Press*

requirements had been met, a Royal Marine Brigade and the first Mobile Naval Base Defence Organization were built. The former was the first British amphibious assault force to be formed during the War; the latter was an elaborate organization to establish and defend advanced bases for the Fleet in any part of the world.

A battalion from the Brigade was dispatched, after the invasion of Norway, to forestall the enemy in Iceland, and within a week of receiving its warning order was deployed in that island over a front of 70 miles. Throughout the desperate summer of 1940 the R.M. Brigade stood by for action as the only force in Britain capable of counter-invasion role. In the autumn it sailed to take part in the Dakar operation which, to the great disappointment of the Marines, was broken off before they had an opportunity to show their mettle.

Record Bag of Enemy Aircraft

The Mobile Naval Base Defence Organization (M.N.B.D.O.) was deployed in Home Defence of Great Britain—which, of course, is the world's greatest naval base—manning anti-aircraft and coast defence guns. The Marine anti-aircraft batteries claimed a record bag of enemy planes, one Regiment shooting down 98 and one battery alone claiming 44 in 40 days, figures which have never been excelled. With the Germans mounting long-range guns at Calais, the Royal Marines manned two great naval guns and a pair of long-range guns on railway mountings near Dover, to counter them. Their two original guns—Winnie and Pooh—remained in action constantly until 1944, when they fired their last rounds across the Channel in support of the Canadian attack on the Boulogne-Calais area.

Early in 1941 the M.N.B.D.O. sailed for Crete, to establish a defended anchorage for the Fleet at Suda Bay. When only a portion of the Organization had landed, the German airborne invasion broke upon the island. The Marines, all specialists (such as A.A. and Coast gunners, signallers, etc.), took to their rifles and fought in the rearguard that covered the evacuation from Sphakia. Their splendid performance was an outstanding justification of the Corps training policy: that every Marine, no matter for what specialist role he may be destined, is trained to be a first-class infantry soldier, this taking precedence of all else.

The first M.N.B.D.O. reformed in the Middle East after its heavy losses in Crete. Its component units were employed far and wide in many different functions, in particular the fortification of Addu Atoll, a

AMONG THE FIRST BRITISH TROOPS TO LAND IN NORWAY in 1940, these Royal Marines went ashore at Namsos to seize and hold a bridge-head for the Army. Their ships, H.M.S. Bittern and Afridi, were sunk after the evacuation. At a South Coast port, one of them wears a French sailor's hat as a souvenir. *Photo, Topical*

ROYAL MARINE COMMANDOS ENTER OSNABRÜCK STATION, in April 1945. Among the first to cross the Rhine (1st Cdo Brigade was in the spearhead of the British crossing), when Field-Marshal Montgomery unleashed his last offensive, they went on to clear this big industrial town whose capture opened the way into the Hanover plain. Later, Marines took part in the first crossings of the rivers Weser, Aller and the Elbe, where they seized bridge-heads for our armour to pass through. *Photo, Sport & General*

remote group of tiny coral islands in the Indian Ocean, as a defended anchorage for our ships against the Japanese menace. When the Japs entered the war the A.A. batteries of the M.N.B.D.O. were deployed in defence of Ceylon, taking heavy toll of enemy aircraft in the raids of Easter 1942 on Colombo and Trincomalee.

Besides their part in the naval actions, Marines ashore helped to meet the Jap eruption. A tiny detachment fought gallantly in Hongkong. After the loss of their fine ships, the R.M. detachments of H.M.S. Prince of Wales and Repulse formed with the remnants of a battalion of the Argyll and Sutherland Highlanders a composite unit known as the Plymouth Argylls, and as such played a distinguished part in the last defence of Singapore.

In Burma, a small band of volunteers detached by the M.N.B.D.O. in Ceylon, manned an improvised flotilla of river craft on the Irrawaddy, which protected the flank of the Army during the famous withdrawal from Burma. They fought ashore and afloat under the White Ensign on the Irrawaddy, and later the Chindwin, until the Army retired across the latter river, when they destroyed their craft and marched back over the mountains to India, having lost nearly half their numbers in action.

AT home, 1942 saw the beginning of two roles that were to be of great importance to the Corps: the formation of the first Royal Marine Commando and the manning by Marines of the armament of a new type of craft for Combined Operations, the Support Craft, designed to give fire support to landing operations from closer inshore than destroyers could venture. These craft distinguished themselves in their first action at Dieppe, and were used in ever-increasing

numbers in every major amphibious operation subsequently. No. 40 R.M. Commando also saw its first action at Dieppe, where it suffered severe casualties attempting a landing on a beach swept by German fire.

The Commando role was, of course, traditional in the Royal Marines, but the prior demands of the M.N.B.D.O.'s and the expansion of the R.M. Brigade into a Division had previously absorbed the whole of the Corps' slender manpower. Now to No. 40 R.M. Commando was added another —No. 41; and both these units were engaged in the invasion of Sicily, where they were the first to land from the sea, striking at coast defences on the flank of the 8th Army in a night landing that was a complete success.

At Termoli They Avenged Dieppe

The Support Craft were engaged off the Sicilian beaches while the Marines of the second M.N.B.D.O. were also there, their A.A. batteries being deployed first in defence of Malta during the mounting of the invasion and later in defence of the naval anchorage at Augusta, while the Coast Artillery component manned captured Italian batteries at Syracuse and Augusta. Other units were employed in the supply and maintenance of the 15th Army Group.

When the assault on the Italian mainland was launched the Royal Marine Commandos and the Support Craft were again in the van. No. 40 Commando made assault landings at Vibo Valentia, and later, in company with Army Commandos, at Termoli on the Adriatic coast, where they took part in a bold move to outflank the German line facing the 8th Army. The Marines surprised a German parachute regiment in the town of Termoli and took their revenge for Dieppe in the street fighting which followed. At Salerno,

No. 41 Commando landed with an Army Commando to seize and hold the Vietri defile on the main road from Salerno to Naples. For four days they repelled attack after attack from crack troops of the German Hermann Goering Division, until the main Army forces fought their way up to the pass from the beaches. Later they suffered bitter casualties in another desperate battle to stem a German drive for the beach in the neighbourhood of a small village called Pigoletti.

BACK at home in the summer of 1943 attention was focused on the coming invasion in the West. It was decided that the Royal Marine Division, which was too lightly armed to be suitable for Continental warfare, should be split up into six new Commandos—Nos. 42, 43, 44, 45, 46 and 47 —while the balance of the troops, supplemented by men of the M.N.B.D.O.s as they returned to the United Kingdom, should be formed into crews for vast fleets of minor landing craft that would be required for the Normandy operation. The number of Support Craft was also greatly increased, the smallest of them—the L.C.S.(M)—being entirely taken over by Marines.

Two of the new Commandos—42 and 44 —departed for the Far East, while 41 in Italy was relieved by No. 43, 41 returning to re-form for a task in the invasion. Early in 1944 another R.M. Commando—No. 48— was formed from the 7th Battalion R.M., which had served in Sicily first as the nucleus of a beach unit and later in the line in the battle for Catania. All were concentrating now on their invasion tasks.

About 20,000 Marines went into action in Normandy, ashore or afloat, over ten thousand of them on D-Day itself. Two-thirds of the assault craft that carried in the first waves of infantry were manned by

The Soldiers of the Fleet in Diverse Roles

IN THE STEAMING JUNGLE OF BURMA or the icy Arctic seas the Royal Marine has to be equally at home. In tropical kit, this Marine (1) points to the scar on the neck of a native who was rescued when a R.M. striking force drove the Japs from Cheduba Island, off the Burma coast, on January 26, 1945. The man had been hanged by the Japs—but survived. Duty at the guns of battleships and cruisers took Marines with the Russian convoys through the depths of Northern winter : cleaning guns on the snow-strewn deck of a light cruiser (2) in April 1943. R.M. Commandos (3) who stormed the great German batteries which dominated the Scheldt estuary sight the lighthouse tower of Walcheren, where they made their historic landing at dawn on November 1, 1944.   PAGE 45   *Photos, British Official*

Marines, and the whole of the huge fleet of tiny craft in the "Build-up" Squadrons, many of which crossed the Channel under their own steam—no small feat in the prevailing weather conditions, when heavily loaded. R.M. Commandos were in action ashore, their outstanding achievements being the capture of Port-en-Bessin, the storming of strong-points such as Langrune, Petit-Enfer and Douvres Radar station, and the clearing of the river Mue valley. Later they helped to hold the left flank of the Allied bridge-head east of the river Orne, alongside Army Commandos and Airborne troops.

MANY Marines were operating in the naval forces, some at the guns of battleships and cruisers, others in Support Craft which, after supporting the assault, took their place in the "Trout Line"—the line of ships and craft that covered the assault area at sea from incursions of German midget submarines, explosive motor boats, and other mosquito craft during the covering action known as the Battle of Seine Bay.

Many, too, were among the "frogmen"—the Landing Craft Obstruction Clearance units that broke a way through the underwater barriers erected by the enemy to stop our landing craft. Another unexpected Royal Marine role was the R.M. Armoured Support Group, the first Marine formation ever to use tanks; these took part in the assault as a novel type of amphibious assault artillery. As the Royal Navy occupied ports and the famous Mulberry was established, many Marines were employed on vital transport and communications work in the naval base organization.

The R.M. Commandos fought on the flank until after Falaise, when they took part in the advance to the Seine. After the fall

of Antwerp, 4th Commando Brigade, consisting of three R.M. and one Army Commando, began planning and training for their part in the attack on Walcheren—which opened the estuary of the Scheldt to our ships. The amphibious assault on the Westkapelle Dyke in Walcheren was the outstanding Marine operation of the War. Three Royal Marine Commandos landed in the gap blown in the famous dyke by Lancasters of the R.A.F. to storm the great batteries by means of which the Germans dominated the estuary.

The assault was covered by the Assault Squadron, Eastern Flank, a large Support Craft force with many Royal Marines at the guns, as well as the battleship H.M.S. Warspite and the monitors Erebus and Roberts. The Support Craft fought an amazing duel at point-blank range with the big German guns in a rmouredcasemates, suffering severe casualties but sufficiently subduing the enemy fire to enable the three R.M. Commandos to get ashore in the gap. One after another the batteries fell to the determined attacks of the Marines, till the R.M. Commandos linked up with No. 4 Army Commando that had been the spearhead of the Army attack across the river against Flushing. With this junction the sea-way up the Scheldt was effectively cleared for our minesweepers.

Up the Rangoon River to the City

Later, 1st Commando Brigade was in the spearhead of the British crossing of the Rhine. No. 46 R.M. Commando was the first unit across at Wesel. These Marines continued in the great drive through Germany, helping to win bridge-heads across the rivers Weser, Aller and finally the Elbe.

Meanwhile, in the Italian theatre, after

taking part in the crossing of the Garigliano and Anzio, Nos. 40 and 43 R.M. Commandos crossed over to the Dalmatians for an exciting spell of amphibious warfare among the islands, co-operating with Marshal Tito's partisans in some hard and bitter fighting. They returned to join, with the remainder of the 2nd Commando Brigade, in the fierce action on the shores of Lake Comacchio that was the prelude to the 8th Army's final offensive, in the course of which battle Corporal Tom Hunter of No. 43 R.M. Commando won the V.C. (portrait in page 376, Vol. 9).

IN the Far East, 44 R.M. Commando was engaged in the Arakan early in 1944, harassing Japanese lines of communication from the sea. In 1945 both the Royal Marine Commandos in that theatre took part in the series of landings at Akyab, Myebon and Kangaw, which brought the Arakan fighting to a victorious close. Royal Marines in landing craft also took part in these operations. Over 900 Marines manned landing craft in the force that made the longest run in assault craft in history—up the Rangoon river to the reoccupation of that city.

This very rapid sketch of Royal Marine operations during the Second Great War has not paused to mention such episodes as the canoe raid up the Gironde to destroy enemy ships near Bordeaux (see illus. page 623, Vol. 9), the performance of R.M. anti-aircraft batteries shooting down a record number of flying bombs in defence of London and Antwerp, of the R.M. officers with the Airborne forces in Normandy, of the Landing Craft Marines who turned themselves into infantry again to take part in the final battles of North-West Germany and the occupation of the great German naval ports.

DEDICATION OF MEMORIAL TO Cpl. TOM HUNTER, of No. 43 R.M. Commando, the only Royal Marine to whom a V.C. was awarded during the War (for magnificent courage on the shores of Lake Comacchio), took place on March 12, 1946, at the R.M. Depot, Lympstone, Devon, where he did his initial training. The Bishop of Crediton is seen dedicating a ship's bell, which will be struck every half-hour, day and night, in the Corporal's memory. See portrait in page 376, Vol. 9.

Photo, P.A.-Reuter

Past Glory to be Restored to Cologne Cathedral

In Allied air raids on Germany's third largest city the Cathedral received fourteen hits—due to its close proximity to the main railway station and the Hohenzollern Bridge. Part of the roof of the north transept (1 and 3), with station and city beyond. A view from the south-east (2). Half of the roof had been covered with zinc by March 1946. Temporary repairs to the building—which was one of the finest examples of Gothic architecture in Europe—will be effected by the year-end.

Shattering Sunken Wrecks by Depth-Charge—

Legacy of six years of total warfare, many submerged vessels present a menace to shipping today. When salving of these wrecks is impracticable depth-charges are dropped to blow them to pieces. Engaged in the clearance of channels leading to the Thames is the Sheerness-based 450-ton trawler H.M.S. Lundy, here seen operating, together with a cutter, above the sea-bed hulk of the minesweeper Myrtle, a 550-ton trawler which fell victim to a mine on June 14, 1940.

—Clears Britain's Obstructed Shipping-Lanes

The wreck having been located by the cutter, by means of echo sounding apparatus, fifteen depth-charges, involving 5,600 lb. of T.N.T., are prepared (1), and lowered from H.M.S. Lundy to the cutter (2), from whose bows they are then suspended (3). The cutter proceeds to the buoy-marked area (4) above the wreck, leaving the Lundy at a safe distance, drops the charges and with a shattering roar and uprush of water (5) the Myrtle is disintegrated—a menace no more.

Life in Austria's Once-Gay Capital Revives But Slowly

All eyes turn in admiration as mounted members of the British Corps of Military Police (1) patrol past the burnt-out Opera House (seen also at 4) in the Inner City of Vienna, occupied by the Four Powers jointly. At the Soviet H.Q. are displayed (2) portraits of Lenin (left) and Stalin, with the Red Star in between. A monument of the Emperor Franz Josef I (1830–1916) still stands amid the ruins (3). Spanning the Danube Canal, which divides Vienna, this bridge (5) was completely destroyed by the Germans. Strenuous efforts are being made to speed the flow of traffic. See also facing page.

Europe's Wartime Capitals in 1946

VIENNA

by ALAN PRYCE-JONES

**formerly Lieut.-Colonel on
General McCreery's staff in Austria**

〰〰〰〰

It was a year ago, in April 1945, that the first Russian troops entered Vienna and penetrated unopposed as far as the Ring, in a taxi. That was only a reconnaissance, it is true, if of an unconventional kind, and there was plenty of fighting before the capital of Austria was captured ; still, at that time much of it was undamaged, and when, two months later, the first Allied mission to Marshal Tolbukhin drove in from Carinthia we had only the vaguest notion of what we were likely to find.

There had been a spate of rumours, owing to the fact that no official observers had been allowed into Vienna so far. Ugly stories had spread about. As usual, no tale was altogether true. But what nobody had foretold was the astonishing and, I believe, sincere welcome we received from the Viennese.

ALAN PRYCE-JONES
Photo, Hugh Cecil

Our little convoy of staff cars had passed through the ruined industrial wilderness of Wiener Neustadt and over the dreary road by which Vienna is entered from the south. Suddenly we reached the Ring and there, beside the old Imperial gardens, stopped in the middle of a Viennese crowd, all exclaiming "At last they are here !" with embarrassing enthusiasm. It was an absurd situation, many times to be repeated in those early days of liberation.

The crowd flocked around, the Russians looked on with more or less benevolent indifference, and the handful of Allied officers, remembering the rules against fraternization, tried to show a detached interest in the battered architecture around them. But it was no good. The Viennese liked us and were determined we should know it. And so for weeks wherever a British soldier appeared a crowd tried, much to his confusion, to treat him as a saviour.

They turned to us with touching faith in the British Empire to bring back normal circumstances of daily life with a wave of the wand. And indeed the reality was grim. Picture a city which has been heavily bombed —the overall damage was assessed by the Russians at over 20 per cent of the whole built-up area, much of it done during the autumn and winter raids—then captured after intermittent street fighting, set on fire by the Germans in retreat, and finally looted by its own underworld, with some help from the conquerors. It had been left without water, gas or electricity except in limited areas. Not all the dead were buried.

The wonder is that there was no breakdown. I remember being told at the city hall that within a week the municipality had been ordered back to work, and that even the collection of rates and taxes had not been held up for more than that week. The main obstacle to be overcome was that there were practically no civilian vehicles at all.

Medical supplies were running out ; for weeks on end the banks and shops were shut ; the tiny sums which could be withdrawn from the savings banks were useless, and any distribution of goods inside the city broke down almost as a matter of course, in spite of a rationing system which looked reasonably fair on paper. Yet somehow there was no total breakdown. And for this miracle the Viennese must thank not only the Russians, who during the time when they were the sole occupying force showed considerable powers of improvising first-aid measures, but a really exceptional team of local administrators, many of them quite without experience of office, and some just out of concentration camps.

Nevertheless, the task was almost unbelievably hard. To run a city without vehicles is bad enough ; when there are no post-office facilities and few telephones it becomes next to impossible. Added to these physical difficulties was the overriding fact that pretty well everyone in a responsible position had been a Nazi, even if a half-hearted one. Some were arrested ; the Russians, however, had so much on their hands that no scientific purge was carried out. The thorough purging of all public life at the outset would have meant still greater chaos ; but the absence of any thorough purging, even if inevitable, has led to a world of recrimination since.

It was autumn, 1945, before the occupying forces took up their stations in Vienna beside the Russians, and only then was real work started to clear the city of wreckage. Here again unexpected difficulties arose. The ration scales were so low that there was not available labour with the strength to undertake heavy work. Even the British headquarters in the palace of Schoenbrunn could not be repaired to a time-schedule. By November there were still no windows in whole blocks of the palace.

Fantastic Prices Still Rising

Far more, therefore, did the Viennese themselves go without. And though the food situation has improved since the early days, especially so far as distribution is concerned, it is still wofully insufficient for anything above bare existence. Proof of this is the case of an old English governess I know who returned to this country at Christmas. In three months of British rationing she put on over two stones in weight.

Of course there was always the black market. This had flourished under the Germans and at first dwindled under Russian occupation. During the summer, however, it became the only means of doing any shopping whatever. Anything could be bought in the black market, from a ton of coke to a pound of coffee, but at steadily rising prices. For instance, in June butter cost 800 marks, or £20 a pound ; by October the price had doubled. Luxury articles fetched enormous sums. An Austrian friend of mine was seriously advised to invest the legal equivalent of £300 in a secondhand typewriter as an altogether exceptional bargain—a sum which he could only scrape together by first selling a winter suit and an overcoat. Prices are still rising.

Gradually, however, some appearance of surface normality has been restored to the city. The trams work — many of them— the underground railway is functioning again ; there is less danger every week of some burnt-out façade in a main street collapsing on to passers-by. It is no longer unsafe to walk alone at nights, and the sudden appearance of energetic, but unlawful,

visitors to remove the radio, some carpets, and all clothing, need no longer be reckoned with as a likely possibility.

But no real resumption of ordinary life is possible until Vienna can again function as the capital of a united country. Until that day, business must remain at a standstill, and no solution to the problems of housing, reconstruction and unemployment can be attempted ; even the final eradication of Nazi elements is made immeasurably more difficult owing to the division of the city into national zones. And what a work will remain to be done !

A large part of the centre of the town will have to be rebuilt, including the main shopping street. On both sides of the Danube Canal (see facing page) an area as long as London's Oxford Street and several blocks deep has been destroyed. The industrial suburbs are largely in ruins, including many great blocks of workers' flats. Almost every public building, notably the Cathedral, will need complete reconstruction.

The Vicious Circle of Misery

Housing will be one of the first problems to be tackled. Overcrowding at present is extremely severe, in spite of a big drop in population. The battered houses are crammed with people, living as best they can behind boarded windows and under leaky roofs. Luckily the winter has been bearable, otherwise there must have been a grim toll of deaths from cold and hunger, for only a very small minority can offset these discomforts by warm clothes or a good fire. The fortunate ones are those who, in the general breakdown of civilized life, happened to be overlooked by the looters.

The people you see on the streets, therefore, are a drab crowd. Any hoarded stocks have been eaten by now—though it must be remembered that Vienna did not know any privations until the last months of the war. The general lack of food in Europe is reflected in a growing shortage of all essentials, and the eyes of the crowd are lack-lustre as they saunter past the empty shops. Only in the theatres and concert-halls do they revive. The Viennese passion for music and the stage is the one emotion strong enough to conquer the misery of the outside world.

This misery goes in a vicious circle ; as long as there is no food there can be no work done, and until work is begun there can be no food. One of the most striking features of the country around Vienna, and especially in the food-producing lands to the east, is its utter emptiness. There seem to be neither people nor beasts. So that while the housing problem is being tackled inside the city, the equally serious problem of restocking the farmlands will have to be undertaken.

The requisitioning which has been going on for nearly a year has stripped most of the factories of their equipment. Apart from manual labour, therefore, there is hardly any work to be had ; and since the wreckage has still not been cleared, even from main thoroughfares, despite the efforts of local authorities, it is evident that on present rations sustained heavy work is impossible.

The Viennese have always liked taking life easily, and, in addition, one has the feeling today that they have no incentive to work while the Occupying Armies bear the full responsibility for keeping Austria on its feet. Money is certainly useless, for there is nothing to buy. From a haircut to house-carpentry any service can be obtained much more easily for half a dozen cigarettes than for a handful of schillings.

Japanese Submarines Towed to a Shameful Doom

FROM THEIR BASE AT SASEBO twenty-four Jap submarines were recently towed into the deep waters of the Pacific and there sunk by destroyers of the United States Navy, this operation forming part of the Allied programme for the complete destruction of Japanese naval power. All Japan's remaining warships are to be scuttled, with the exception of 38 destroyers being distributed among the four Allied powers— Britain, U.S.A., Russia and China.

Assembled in a creek (1) near the formerly important base, preparatory to commencing this last voyage; among them is the notorious 158, on which Vice-Admiral Robert H. Griffin, Commander of Naval Activities, Japan, is seen (2) examining an A.A. gun. The 158 sank the U.S. cruiser Indianapolis shortly before the end of hostilities, in August 1945, after the cruiser had successfully discharged her cargo of atomic bomb material. Charges of T.N.T., and direct hits from the guns of the American destroyers deputed to this task, ended the 158's career for all time (3).

Photos, L.N.A

Our War Leaders in Peacetime
MOUNTBATTEN

BORN in Windsor, Berkshire, in 1900, "Dickie" Mountbatten—Rear-Admiral Lord Louis Mountbatten, Supreme Allied Commander South-East Asia—was brought up in the Naval tradition. Second cousin of His Majesty the King, the son of Admiral of the Fleet the Marquis of Milford Haven, he was a naval cadet at 12, and at 14 saw action as a midshipman in Beatty's flagship H.M.S. Lion.

And keenly as ever today, whether engaged on Service matters or at home with the girl (Miss Edwina Ashley, daughter of Lord Mount Temple) he married twenty-four years ago, and their two young daughters, Patricia and Pamela, he studies naval matters.

The Mountbattens have a town house in Westminster, London; a country house at Romsey, Hampshire; and a castle in Co. Sligo, Ireland, where, before the War, they entertained the great names in the land. At his country residences Mountbatten used to shoot, fish, ride, and drive a car. He likes outdoor pastimes, but he is also keen on study and reading and spends hours poring over technical books.

ALL his life he has been making notes and committing his conclusions to writing. His friends pull his leg about this propensity, but from it has grown a number of books, pamphlets and manuals on a variety of subjects, for writing is among his favourite recreations. His notes on destroyer design are reflected in the new-type bridge fitted to the Tribal class and later destroyers. Mountbatten evolved this masterpiece in naval construction in his spare time. Also he has worked out several developments in naval radio technique.

Mountbatten is particularly interested in radio; ever since he passed out first in the Long Course at the Royal Naval Signal School 21 years ago it has been his main hobby. He wrote the first Admiralty Handbook on Wireless Telegraphy, and this he is constantly bringing up to date. But it is five years now since he spent any length of time among his technical books at his London home.

He concerns himself with a new subject so enthusiastically that he becomes an acknowledged expert in it; polo, for instance, at which as a player he has but limited success. He just does not possess the natural qualities for this exacting game; but having arrived at that conclusion, he studied the game scientifically and then sat down and wrote: "Introduction to Polo." His own polo did not benefit to any extent; but the book by "Marco" became a standard work.

When Lord Louis returns home the Royal and Ancient Golf Club of St. Andrews will see him, and once again he will appear at the Royal Motor Yacht Club. Yachting is another subject on which he has written authoritatively. Meanwhile, the man who directed the war in Burma is making notes on military government and colonial administration.

REAR-ADMIRAL LORD LOUIS MOUNTBATTEN shoulders his cousin, Prince William, son of the Duke of Gloucester, Governor-General of Australia (1). At Broadlands, home of Lord and Lady Louis, at Romsey, Hampshire (2), Pamela strolls with her parents in the grounds (3). As sailor-sportsman, after a polo match (4). *Photos, British Official, Associated Press, Topical*

BRITAIN'S LIFE-LINE in the MIDDLE EAST

By HARLEY V. USILL

IN this, the second of his series of articles on the British Colonies in the War, the author treats of the vital part played by their strategic disposition. He shows how the Mediterranean colonies of Gibraltar, Malta and Cyprus, the Mandated Territories of Palestine and Trans-Jordan, and the Red Sea outpost of Aden kept the Middle East defence position intact, despite furious Axis attempts to break into it.

FROM the very day that war was declared, in 1939, Great Britain had to face the two-fold problem of creating and maintaining an impregnable island fortress at the same time as she was waging war wherever Germany and, later, the Axis Powers might decide to strike. Her task, as we shall show later, was made much more difficult after the fall of France, and necessitated a radical change in her initial strategic plan. But in every phase of the war the strategic disposition of the Colonial Empire played a vital part.

The weakness of Britain's position lay in her reliance on long lines of communication for the reception of the raw materials of war, including the food without which she could not remain the spearhead of resistance, and also in the enormous difficulties she experienced in transporting and maintaining her forces overseas. It was essential, therefore, that she should keep intact her lines of communication with the outside world; and, if one or more were broken, be in a position to change her tactics accordingly. The Colonial Empire was able to give her that indispensable mobility of action.

Imperial Defence and Middle East

At the outbreak of war the main arteries of the British Empire ran through the Mediterranean, the Red Sea, and across the Indian Ocean. They were served primarily by shipping, but a secondary, although growing form of communication was provided by air transport whose main lines of development ran considerably north of the Mediterranean, across the Levant, Iraq and Persia, to India and beyond. Along this vital axis Britain had developed in the course of centuries essential defensive positions, the maintenance of which depended mainly on sea power.

These comprised Gibraltar, Malta, Cyprus, the Suez area, Aden and Socotra, Mauritius, India, Burma, Malaya and Singapore. This was an effective line of communication, particularly when there was added the flanking possessions of France. In the Mediterranean, too, France could add half of the North African coastline and the hinterland of Syria and the Lebanon. In the Indian Ocean she could contribute Madagascar, and beyond India, French Indo-China formed with Malaya and Burma a compact bastion for the defence of the Dutch East Indies and against Japanese penetration into the Indian Ocean. All this was altered at a blow when France fell in 1940, and it was then the value of those British Colonial territories which come within this sphere became so apparent.

The Mediterranean Colonies

Britain's sole remaining possession on the Continent of Europe—Gibraltar—stands guarding the entrance to the Mediterranean. The Rock has always played an important part in British naval strategy, the main function being to allow free access to all ships of the Royal and Merchant Navies, and those of other friendly Powers. This function, however, was seriously upset by the fall of France and the entry of Italy into the war, events which necessitated the division of the Mediterranean into two defensive zones—the Eastern and the Western.

In the Western zone Gibraltar continued to play an important part; a British destroyer force guarded the vital Straits, and Force H, as it was called, assembled at Gibraltar under the command of Admiral Sir James Somerville for the defence of the western Mediterranean, or for operations in the Atlantic.

The island of Malta (with Gozo) lies in the narrowest part of the Mediterranean, about 58 miles from the nearest point of Sicily, and about 180 miles from the nearest point of the mainland of Africa. It stands at the junction of the sea routes from Gibraltar to Alexandria and the Suez Canal, and from Sicily to Tripolitania, and until the entry of Italy into the war the island was only on the fringe of hostilities, but from then on Malta became a vital link in the Allies' defence line. The official account of the Air Battle of Malta says:

"The island was not a single weapon wielded as an isolated arm; it had an integral part to play in Mediterranean strategy as a whole. . . . Every theatre of war in the Mediterranean was within range of its aircraft, and not the least important task of its pilots was to watch from their central position all the movements of the enemy. The battles in the Mediterranean hinged upon supplies, on the capacity of both sides to reinforce themselves across a limited area of sea and across desert land. ' The geographical situation of the island was vital to the Allies in the supply conflict; but for Malta, Rommel in 1942 might well have pressed on to Alexandria."

At all costs, then, Malta had to be kept from enemy hands, and great were the risks and losses involved in this vital task. When the siege of Malta had been lifted, the island turned to a fury of assault on enemy bases. El Aouina (airfield of Tunis) was raided by night and day; farther to the east the Malta bombers attacked Tripoli; to the north they ranged over the airfields and ports of Sicily and Italy. This hard-pressed island was not only getting its revenge but its very existence as a base for air operations spelt the death knell of Axis dreams in North Africa.

THE island of Cyprus, too, has played an important part in the strategy of the Eastern Mediterranean. Situated some 240 miles north of Egypt, 60 miles west of Syria and 40 miles south of Turkey, her occupation by enemy forces would have had a most serious effect upon the whole Mediterranean situation. Real threats to Cyprus did not develop until 1941, when the Allied evacuation of Greece and then of Crete, 350 miles to the west, brought the island into the main Middle East defence line. At one time it looked as if Cyprus might become the main point of Axis attack, but hostilities in Russia, and the British occupation of Syria, stabilized the position in the Eastern Mediterranean.

In 1942 the Middle East was again threatened, and Cyprus became important as a forward base against the enemy forces in Greece, Crete and Rhodes. It was then that Mr. Churchill named Cyprus as a part of the line through the Middle East which safeguarded the Allied communications with Turkey, Iraq and Russia.

AGAINST considerable odds the British maintained control of the eastern basin of the Mediterranean, but it was essential to Hitler's main strategic plan that this hold should be broken. While, then, the reinforced Italians with Rommel's Afrika Korps were to strike back in North Africa, Germany herself planned to overrun the Balkans, press down the British-controlled eastern basin, and from there exert pressure against Turkey.

Meanwhile, Russia was to be attacked, and the main weight of the German land forces, diverted from the postponed invasion of Britain, was to be driven eastwards to the Caucasus and beyond. Simultaneously, a successful African drive would establish an Axis domination from Europe to the Persian Gulf. A major part in the defeat of these plans was played by the British Mandated territories of Palestine and Trans-Jordan.

From bases in these two territories advances were made into Syria, and at the end of a five weeks' campaign the occupation of the Levant States was complete. Then followed the race against time to control Iran, which was won when the British reached Teheran and the Russians got to Tabriz; by the success of these two campaigns the main structure of security in the landward areas of the Middle East was complete.

It is impossible to exaggerate the disastrous effects which would have fallen on all the Allies if this German plan had been successful. Against such an aggregation of power as would then have faced them, Britain and America would have been in the utmost peril. Events in the Middle East in general, and in the Mediterranean in particular, were critical for the progress of the whole struggle for world power, and in the successful issue of that struggle Gibraltar, Malta and Cyprus, and the two British Mandates of Palestine and Trans-Jordan played a vital part.

How Aden Guarded the Back Door

After the fall of France and the entry of Italy into the war, the sea route to India and the Far East via the Suez Canal and the Red Sea was to all intents and purposes unusable and Great Britain was compelled to send most of her convoys round the Cape. There remained to Aden, however, a very important function to perform in regard to the whole Middle East defence scheme. While Britain retained possession of Aden (and Port Sudan) the initial successes of the Italians, particularly after the fall of British Somaliland, were not so serious as they might have been.

They were on the wrong side of the Red Sea, but if they had been able to capture Aden they would have had unhampered access to Saudi Arabia and thus constituted a very real threat to the eastern basin of the Mediterranean and the whole Middle East position. As it was, Aden was used in 1941 as one of the jumping-off grounds for the recapture of British Somaliland, and when British troops landed at Berbera the Italians marched out as quickly as possible.

THE fact that Aden virtually dominated the entrance to the Red Sea, even during the Italian occupation of British Somaliland, enabled British reinforcements from India to reach Port Sudan, and it was from here that General Platt launched his attack on Kassala and crossed the Sudan border into Eritrea. In the campaign which followed he was helped by naval and air forces based on Aden.

The Abyssinian campaign, in which the African Colonies played such a magnificent part, is the subject of another article, but neither this nor the campaigns in Iraq and Syria could have been waged successfully unless the Red Sea had remained a safe supply route. That was the strategic background to Aden's part in the war, a background which will become even clearer as we consider the Colonies in the Indian Ocean.

It is equally true that if the Mediterranean and Middle East campaigns had not been fought to a successful conclusion our position in the Far East might have been irreparably undermined. With the initial Japanese success the position was bad enough; but, in other circumstances, the Japanese might have reached Africa and thus formed a junction with the Germans on the Nile.

Our Mediterranean Bastions: Gibraltar and Malta

COLONIES WHOSE STRATEGIC POSITION PLAYED A VITAL PART in maintaining the Allied Middle East defence line, especially after the fall of France and the entry of Italy into the war, included Gibraltar and Malta. Searchlights probed for enemy raiders over the " Rock," gun flashes marking the A.A. positions (top). In Grand Harbour, Valetta, Malta (bottom), casualties from Sicily were disembarked from the St. David, the first hospital ship to arrive there, in the summer of 1943. See also facing page.

Photos, British Official

United Nations Security Council Debates Persia

PERSIA'S CASE AGAINST RUSSIA, opened by the Security Council of the U.N.O., at New York, on March 27, 1946, provided a dramatic episode when the Russian delegate, Mr. Andrei Gromyko, walked out following the rejection of his proposal for the hearing to be postponed until April 10. Persia intimated that the presence of Soviet troops on her soil after March 2, 1946, constituted a threat to the country's security. During the hearing a treaty was signed between the two countries, on April 5, Russia undertaking to remove her troops by May 6. Persia withdrew her complaint on April 15, but the Council decided to retain the case on its agenda until May 6.

HUSSEIN ALA, PERSIAN DELEGATE, seated second from right (1) at horseshoe table, addresses the Security Council ; the vacant chair (extreme left) had been occupied by Mr. Andrei Gromyko. Hussein Ala (2) presents the Persian case. Sir Alexander Cadogan (3, left), U.K. and Mr. Edward Stettinius, U.S. Mr. Gromyko leaves (4). Members voting on the motion to shelve the dispute until May (5), (left to right, front row), Sir A. Cadogan, Mr. Stettinius, Mr. Byrnes (U.S.), Col. W. R. Hodgson (Australia) and Dr. Vellasco (Brazil).

Photos, Associated Press, Keystone

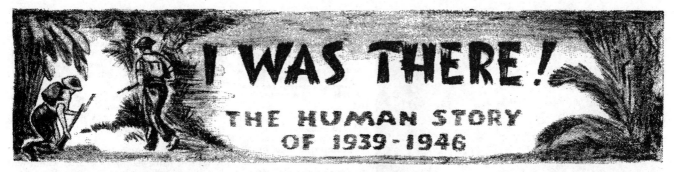

I Was Chief Engineer of a Floating Volcano

Awarded the O.B.E. for his share in the events narrated here, also the Lloyds Medal for Bravery at Sea, Ernest Edward Vick, of the Canadian Pacific Steamship Company's liner Duchess of York, relates how the ship, afire—with ammunition in the holds—after a German air attack ended her career in the North Atlantic on July 11, 1943.

THE 20,000-ton transport Duchess of York, commanded by Captain W. G. Busk-Wood, O.B.E., under whom I was serving as Chief Engineer, had left a Scottish port and was proceeding southward through the Bay of Biscay in a small convoy consisting of three other merchant ships, with two destroyers and one of the new frigates for escort. The notorious Bay was in genial mood, and the setting sun spread a cloth of gold over the smooth Atlantic swells.

Chief Engineer ERNEST E. VICK, O.B.E.

All was peaceful as a holiday-cruise, until with startling suddenness the strident blare of Klaxon horns gave warning for Action Stations. Nothing could be seen in that clear sunset sky, but hostile aircraft had been detected by the radar apparatus. Most of my day had been spent in the oily warmth of the engine-room, and I was in my cabin relaxing with a book and cigar after an excellent dinner. It was just another "alert," I supposed, and on going below to my post on the starting-platform I had no premonition that never again would I see the inside of that spacious cabin with its soft carpet, modern furniture, books, photographs and all the small personal treasures that made it a home from home.

Those of us in the engine-room and stoke-holds deep below the waterline saw nothing, of course, of the earlier phases of what was an unusually daring and persistent enemy air attack. Five Focke-Wulf Kuriers, long-range Atlantic bombers, came flying in at about 10,000 feet, then fanned out and swooped from different directions upon the large merchantmen that offered such tempting prey. The first sticks of bombs crashed into the sea perilously near two vessels of the convoy. The sky flamed and thundered with bursting shells from our ack-ack guns, but the German pilots manoeuvred with skill and came roaring down several times in power-dives to unload their deadly cargoes.

With a deafening explosion two large bombs now struck the Duchess of York simultaneously, and the precise time of the disaster was recorded automatically as all the electric clocks in the ship stopped at the moment of impact. Serious casualties occurred. Among other effects was the destruction of the main switchboard; instantly the engine-room and stokeholds were plunged in darkness. Soon two fires broke out and flame swept through the debris.

The bombs struck the ship with barely a second's warning to those of us below.

Instinctively I flung up my left arm to shield my face, and both the hand and arm became deeply pitted with scraps of flying metal that otherwise might have blinded me. Fumes came from the decks above, water cataracted through the hatch from the fractured fire-mains, and the reserve tank emptied itself over the engine-room gratings.

All communication to Captain Busk-Wood on the bridge was broken—telegraph, telephones and voice-pipes. The forced lubrication pumps were put out of action, and this stoppage automatically operated the safety controls and stopped the engines. Agitated voices sounded amid the plash of seawater and the dull roar of the blaze spreading rapidly. The heart of the Duchess of York had ceased to beat, and her dead body was in process of cremation.

I HAD no time to heed either an injured left arm or the discomfort of being drenched to the skin. A rapid survey had to be made and certain emergency repairs effected, if possible. So I switched on a pressure torch and groped my way to the main switchboard. The thing lay spread over the deck in chunks of debris, and tests applied to the lubrication pumps proved them to be totally useless. Meantime, the attack by the enemy Kuriers continued in the face of heavy defensive fire from the convoy. Three minutes after the Duchess of York had been stricken, a thunderous explosion sounded the doom of a second big merchant ship.

A further rapid survey convinced me that the engine-room and adjacent compartments would soon become a death-trap. So, unable to communicate with the Captain, I assumed responsibility for ordering my entire staff to clear out before the spreading fire between-decks cut off all means of escape. When all others had gone, I gave a last look at my engines, from which the life had been drained, then clambered up an iron ladder and emerged on the B-deck alleyway.

Only ten minutes had passed since the bombs had found their target, but already a barrier of fire athwartships prevented anyone from going for'ard along this deck. Looking in that direction I saw one of my subordinates, clad in a blue boiler-suit and fantastically illuminated by the flames. I shouted out to him, "How are conditions in the boiler-rooms?"

Made a Bridge of His Own Body

He bawled an answer above the roar and crackle of burning woodwork. "All lights have gone and the forced draught fans have stopped. One steam-pipe burst. I've shut off the oil supply to the furnaces!" He did not mention then that he had been badly scalded by the steam-pipe bursting. Nor did I learn till later that another member of our crew, Third Butcher Hughes, had made a bridge of his own body to enable many shipmates to climb over him to safety. Many other heroic deeds were performed that tragic evening while officers and men strove to stem the fire with inadequate means and to save life both before and after the Captain had given the order to abandon ship.

Unable to go for'ard, I found a way to the open deck by means of a companion ladder aft. It was good to breathe the sea-air! For a moment or two I paused to survey the

THE DUCHESS OF YORK, whose "heart ceased to beat" after two German bombs struck the vessel simultaneously, disrupting all communication with Captain W. G. Busk-Wood on the bridge and sending flames racing along the decks, as graphically described by her Chief Engineer. Survivors were rescued by a British destroyer. *Photo, Topical*

FOCKE-WULF CONDOR, prototype of the Focke-Wulf Kurier, employed by the Germans for attacking Allied vessels in the Atlantic, is here seen circling over a U.S. merchantman before America entered the war in 1941. *Photo, Associated Press*

dramatic scene. A merchant ship was stopped half-a-mile distant, with flames licking her tophamper and masts, and with several lifeboats in the water alongside. A destroyer, weaving patterns of white foam, was smearing the sky with the vomit of her guns, and the rest of the convoy were streaking southward belching clouds of covering smoke. More smoke was writhing from the strained upper deck as I went for'ard and climbed to the navigating bridge to report to Captain Busk-Wood. Then the threatening roar of aero-engines sounded.

"Look out !" the Captain shouted. "Here they come again ! Take cover !" Three Kuriers dived upon us. More bombs screamed down and crashed into the sea, and the Germans zoomed skyward, miraculously unharmed by the destroyer's gun-fire.

Worried lest anyone had been left in the engineers' quarters and adjoining compartments near the seat of the blaze, I retraced my steps aft and approached a mess-room on the port side. I turned the handle, the door flew open with a violence that hurled me flat on my back, and a storm of flame and smoke swept over the deck. No living man could be there, and after prolonged investigations elsewhere I went to rejoin the Captain while the lifeboats were being lowered and got away.

The task of abandoning ship was proceeding calmly, yet many men refused to leave and fought gamely for an hour in the forlorn hope of stemming the blaze—despite the risk that the ship might blow up on account of ammunition in the holds.

My decision to return to the bridge was made none too soon. By this time the ship was a floating volcano from which fire would erupt with cataclysmal fury directly the growing pressure of pent-up heat overcame the resistance of the strained upper deck. Part of that deck bulged ominously when I crossed it ; many of the seams had opened and were fringed by darting flames ; there were nests of fire over which I had to jump to regain the bridge ladder.

A few seconds later, when I stood beside Captain Busk-Wood again, deck-boards were upflung in smoking fragments, and the fire raged unchecked about the tophamper of the ship. Men still on the boat-deck were driven away by the heat, and two lifeboats burst into flame on the davits. The mainmast became a torch ; the after-funnel and deck-plating glowed white-hot ; the for'ard funnel, its paint peeled away, grew red in the furnace-heat. A continuous moan was emitted by the siren.

"You clear off, Chief," the Captain said to me. "There's a boat on the port side about to leave, and you may just about make it. I wish you luck !"

"And you, sir ?"

"I shall leave directly you have gone." A wall of flame had advanced to within ten feet of the bridge, and small-arms ammunition and signal rockets had become ignited to give a devil's pyrotechnic display. The boat to which I had been directed was full, and by another mischance that caused further delay I was the last man to leave the ship. I plunged into the sea and swam toward the destroyer a cable's length away—and the five Kuriers returned to make a final attack before leaving the scene, with only one of their number showing signs of damage.

It took the warship three and a half hours to collect us survivors, adrift all over the sea, while the two merchant ships blazed like beacons in the growing darkness of night. Then torpedoes were loosed at them both, and the crowded destroyer sped southward, leaving the shattered hulks to sink amid clouds of steam and smoke.

Thus did the Duchess of York meet her fate in the North Atlantic.

With Dagger Division's Guns to the Chindwin

Captain R. R. G. Blackmore, 115th Field Regt., R.A., recalls astonishing feats of road-making and serviceing by the 19th Indian Division during the 14th Army's final advance from North Burma, in the autumn of 1944, through some of the most difficult country in the world.

OUR Regiment was part of the Divisional Artillery of the 19th Indian Division, better known as the Dagger Division. Its commander was that Napoleon-like figure, Major-General T. W. Rees, D.S.O., M.C., affectionately known to all of us as "the Green Gremlin," "Dagger Rees," or just "Pete," and whose flamboyant scarlet silk scarf will always be remembered.

One day in the autumn of 1944 the Division found itself on the edge of the Naga Hills, north of the Imphal Plain, at approximately milestone 113 on the Manipur Road ; which was the jumping-off place for the Division on its great advance across the Chindwin to Shwebo, across the Irrawaddy to Mandalay and across the Sittang to the Mawchi Road and finally, "the Battle of the Breakthrough," in the Pegu Yomas and the end of the Japanese campaign in Burma.

Driving 8-ton Lorries at 40 m.p.h.

The Manipur Road runs from the railway line at Dimapur through Kohima to Imphal. And what a road it was ! Before the War it was a mere cart-track. By 1944 it was a tarmac main road which curled around mountains, skirted precipices, took hairpin bends in its stride and declared to the world that the Army engineers could make a road anywhere. Down it there moved incessantly, day and night, thousands of lorries carrying all the supplies of five Divisions— ammunition, food, petrol, medical and canteen stores, amenities, guns, reinforcements, aircrews, coolies to work on the road, everything and everyone ; nursing Sisters and pressmen, visiting officers from other theatres, Staff Officers from G.H.Q., and E.N.S.A. artists from home. All, in fact, that goes to make a modern army went down the Manipur Road.

The drivers of these "Rice Corps" vehicles —so-called because rice is one of the main items of the Indian Army's food, and as a pronunciation of R.I.A.S.C., abbreviation for the Royal Indian Army Service Corps—

were Indians, men of the villages who had offered their services voluntarily, with the other 2,000,000 who flocked to the Colours.

Many of them, when they joined the Army, had never been in a motor vehicle, far less driven one, but they were eager to learn and they eventually contributed their share to victory by many weary hours of concentrated effort up and down the Manipur Road.

Captain R. R. G. BLACKMORE

They hoped to get four hours sleep in every 36 hours. They did not drive in convoy but were organized for "loose" or "free" running. Each driver and his relief driver accepted the responsibility of getting his load from the railhead to the correct dump in Imphal as quickly as possible.

Their speed was terrifying—men who had never driven anything faster than a bullock cart carrying a few maunds (a maund is 80 lb.) were taking three-ton, five-ton, eight-ton lorries filled to capacity over more than 100 miles of tortuous mountain roads at speeds which often touched forty miles per hour. As it was free running there were no restrictions against passing, and time and again my jeep was left standing by a huge lorry which, piloted by a confident Madrasi or Sikh, appeared to be possessed with magical ability to hold the road.

I imagined that dozens of lorries must be lost over the side of the slope. But I was wrong. Accidents were few and far between, which is in itself an argument in favour of the protective beneficence of the Gods of Ind, or the training of these men, or both. Or was it that they knew that the men down there, down on the road, were fighting for

Capt. W. G BUSK-WOOD, O.B.E., commanded the Duchess of York on her tragic last voyage, in 1943.

Photo by courtesy of Canadian Pacific Railway

Battling With the Nightmare Roads of Burma

ON THE WINDING IMPHAL-TAMU MOUNTAIN ROAD British armour (1) proceeded with no great hindrance after Sappers and Miners had toiled to convert the fair-weather track to a main supply route for 14th Army troops then closing in on Mandalay from the north-west. Jeeps and trucks during monsoon fighting struggled through treacherous mud of the Palel-Tamu Road (2). Elephants and bulldozers worked side by side (3) to drive the Ledo Road forward to junction with the Burma Road. See also facing page.   PAGE 59   *Photos, British and Indian Official, Keystone.*

their lives? They are proud men, these Indians, and no right-thinking man of any forward unit could deny that these "Rice Corps Wallahs" were risking their lives from minute to minute in their feverish haste to get the munitions of war to the front.

I visited a Naga village in the company of a colonel who had spent much of his service in the district and spoke the language. This village was perched on the top of a spur of a mountain and was surrounded by a stockade, the entrance being blockaded at night by thorns. When we entered everyone vanished, leaving a few dogs to greet us. We walked to the centre and in a few moments the Head Man appeared and welcomed us. Near to where we were standing was a large barn-like building in which I learned the adolescents of the village lived until they married. At one end of this "lodge" was the skin of a tiger on a bamboo frame, which the men of the village had slaughtered.

By this time curiosity was getting the better of fear and we found ourselves the centre of a small group of children, while the women emerged one by one and went on with their work. The women had their hair done in a quaint style, cut in a stiff fringe all the way round. Their dress consisted of several strings of highly coloured beads, a short blouse, and a length of cotton cloth wound round their middle as a skirt.

3 Hours by Jeep to do 18 Miles

The men also wore beads, but their sole garment was a black loincloth with black bands of the same material round the legs above and below the knee and above the elbow. They carried a blanket over one shoulder and a bow and several arrows. One had a magnificent pillarbox-red blanket presented as a gift from the King-Emperor for specially valuable services rendered to our Forces. On inquiry I discovered that the men of this village and the neighbouring villages had acted as guides and scouts to our Forces and had also indulged in sniping the Japs with their arrows; in the jungle, where visibility is short, an arrow is quieter and, if the man who draws the bow is a good shot, just as effective as a rifle.

The Dagger Division had been trained to fight in the jungle, to do combined operations and to be airborne, and at this stage no one knew when, where or how we should attack the Japs. Then, one day, the orders came and we moved forward down the Manipur Road to Imphal, thence to Palel, then up on to the mountains which separate Palel from the Kabaw Valley. Earlier in the year there had been fierce fighting in this area when the 20th Indian Division fell back to take part in the defence of Imphal. These hills were even more trouble to the Sappers and Miners, (the Indian Engineers) than the Naga Hills, but the indefatigable men triumphed.

THE road was not tarmac or in any way so grand as the Manipur Road, but they got round difficulties by making two routes, one on each side of each hill, and having one-way traffic, and if you kept to about ten m.p.h. there was no real danger of falling down the hillside. The work was still going on as we went over the road, the Sappers and Miners working day and night assisted by the women and children of the Nagas and scores of coolies from India and Assam.

At the eastern end of the mountains we found the small town of Tamu, but instead of proceeding straight on down to the Chindwin we turned north up a track through the teak forest to the Taret river. It was not a good track; in a jeep it took approximately three hours to go 18 miles. We were now in the Kabaw valley, and we heard that groups of B.T.A., the Burma Traitor Army, were operating in the area and that occa-

sional Jap patrols came across the Chindwin. There were reports of attacks on lone men and we were cautioned not to go about singly. Near where we camped we found a deserted Jap vehicle park; our mechanics got busy, and soon each Battery had a large three-tonner in working order.

We were next told that we must cut a road over the hills from the Taret river valley near Thanan to the Chindwin, so we all became pioneers swinging the pick, or engineers blowing the rocks and big trees. It was during this period that I first saw Burmese woodmen at work with their elephants. Teak trees are magnificent. They stand straight and tall for a hundred feet or more and the wood is, I suppose, as tough as any. The Burmese woodmen tackle them

Motto: "Attempt and Achieve."
102 (BOMBER) SQUADRON

DURING its service in France in the war of 1914-1918 No. 102 Squadron dropped a total of 368 tons of bombs. It was originally formed at Hingham, Norfolk, in 1917, and was disbanded in 1919. It was re-formed at Worthy Down, Hants, in 1935, and during the Second Great War was equipped with aircraft as a result of gifts from Ceylon, becoming one of the "named" squadrons of the R.A.F. It was also adopted by the Lancashire town of Morecambe. In 1942 Halifax bombers replaced the Whitleys used in the early part of the war, and the record number of twenty aircraft from the squadron took part in the first 1,000-bomber attack on Cologne.

From Sept. 4, 1939, when three Whitleys dropped propaganda leaflets over the Ruhr, to its final sortie against Heligoland before the German capitulation, the squadron dropped nearly 14,200 tons of bombs on targets in the Reich and enemy-occupied territory and laid nearly 2,000 mines in hostile waters. On D-Day, 102 Squadron dropped over three hundred 1,000-lb. and 500-lb. bombs on a coastal gun battery. Its crews carried 134,250 gallons of petrol without mishap in support of the airborne operations at Arnhem. And in the great day and night attacks on Duisburg in the closing stages of the war some of its pilots made two round trips in twenty-four hours.

ITS personnel were awarded five D.S.O.s, 115 D.F.C.s, two bars to the D.F.C., and also 34 D.F.M.s. Group-Captain G. L. Cheshire, V.C., D.S.O., D.F.C. (portrait in page 599, Vol. 8), gained the immediate award of his D.S.O. with 102 Squadron for his attack (he was then a Pilot Officer) on a target in the Ruhr on the night of Nov. 12/13, 1940. He was later awarded the D.F.C. for operations with 102 Squadron.

It has had a distinguished list of Commanding Officers, including Wing-Commander G. W. Holden, D.S.O., D.F.C., who after winning the D.F.C. for his part in the great daylight attack on Brest led his squadron to Turin on the night of November 20, 1942, and stayed over the town throughout the attack to make a special report; Wing-Commander (now G/Capt.) S. J. Marchbank, D.F.C., who was in command during the D-Day operations; and W/Cdr. L. D. Wilson, D.F.C., A.F.C.

The history of 102 Squadron typifies the great work of Bomber Command air and ground crews which contributed so much to the defeat of Germany.

with what appear to be most inadequate weapons but are really astonishingly efficient. The axe they use has a helve not quite as long as ours, and only as thick as a man's thumb and made of bamboo; its head is a piece of teak fashioned into the shape of a cow's horn, and on the point of the horn is a small steel blade with not more than three inches of cutting edge. Before the blows from this light-weight axe the largest teak trees bow to the ground.

Records in Big Boulder-Shifting

The road we built from the Taret valley over the hills to the Chindwin gave us great pride although we were responsible for relatively only a small portion of it. Our orders were to make a road without a surface suitable for vehicles up to nine tons gross weight, to move one way in good weather. There was a road already in existence, but it was so narrow and steep that we could not take the guns over it. The Engineer officers surveyed the new cut, and then all the units detailed for the work drew lots. We were lucky and drew the lot which involved making the first section of the road on the lowest part of the hill. It was hard work, but most satisfying.

WE laboured from 7.30 a.m. to 4.30 p.m. each day with a short break for lunch, hacking the road out of a steep hillside and throwing the soil over the edge. Often there were large boulders, five or six feet through, which had to be moved. Soon we were all engaged in a competition to create records in boulder-shifting. When we pushed one over it would go crashing down the hillside, flattening even biggish trees before its headlong rush. Fate alone determined where and when it would stop and who or what should be broken by it. We were assisted by Sappers and Miners for the more tricky problems; they showed us how to use ammanol and gelignite and we had some exciting moments blowing huge cotton trees and solid rock faces.

After a fortnight of road-making we had orders to move. My battery went first—and we were the first vehicles to use the new cut, which we christened Artillery Road. The total distance to our destination on the banks of the Chindwin was only 12 miles, but it took us 13 hours. It was a night of nightmares. The first portion of the road, say about four miles, was easy enough. Then things started happening. The way was so steep that my jeep could not pull its trailer up.

So we had to unload the trailer, take the jeep up and then ferry the big accumulators and other heavy gear to the top, a distance of about half a mile. The surface was clay, and the heavy dew made it so slippery that even in Army boots, studded as they are, you could hardly keep your feet. Gun tractors with their heavy loads were winched slowly from corner to corner, and slowly we pushed on.

Half Over the Valley of Death

At one point the new cut had not been completed and we had to use the old original road. Here the hill was exceptionally steep, the road running round it on a ledge which had been cut out of the hillside, so that the nearside was a sheer face of soil and on the other side a drop of 30 feet, then steep rocky hillsides going down to an invisible bottom.

At this point all the gun detachments dismounted and the drivers, quite alone, took the guns over. They gently brushed the nearside of their vehicles against the hill; but even so only half of their off-side wheels were on the road, the other half being suspended over what seemed to be the Valley of Death. But they were good drivers, and gently they coaxed the heavy vehicles and trailers and guns over a very unpleasant 100 yards of road and then on again.

Even when daylight came, after what seemed a lifetime of night and trouble, all was not well, because the road down by the Chindwin passed over a place where a small tributary ran into the big river. We had to ford this, and as it was not monsoon season the bed of the stream was almost dry; it looked easy until we got off the firm ground into the soft, silvery sand. Before we knew what was happening we were bellied in it, and were extricated only with the help of two elephants and a Sikh with a small bulldozer.

crews sun-bathing on the canvas hatch covers, with our escort wheeling overhead. But towards evening our fighters left.

Just before dark a gunner, Trooper Weech, asked permission to mount his Besa heavy machine-gun on deck. He unshipped it from his tank in the hold and brought it up, and as there was no suitable fitting for such a heavy weapon he lashed it to a steel stanchion, then saw to a supply of ammunition. The gun was very unwieldy, and it was not easy to get high elevation; but it worked. When the moon came up the bombers returned; for two hours they dropped bombs around us but never a sight did we get of a plane.

None Left Alive on the Deck

About one in the morning I was on the little bridge, trying to cheer myself up by chatting to the captain, and watching the other two lighters wallowing along, when suddenly the lighter farthest from us fired a burst from its pom-pom. It seemed odd to us that the tracers didn't go up in the air but along the water. The captain at once put up his night-glasses. "There's something over there—I think it's an E-boat!" he said. I stared and saw a dim, long shape moving across the bows of the farthest lighter, and a white light ticked from it. The signalman beside us read the message. "He's asking for our numbers, sir," he said. "What! In white light?" asked the captain. (Our own craft signalled in blue light, I learned later). "He's a Jerry, for sure!" He turned and told the port pom-pom to train on the dark shape. The signalman, his voice showing his excitement, said, "No. 18 reports enemy submarine, sir. He's going to ram!"

We heard the noise of a heavy-calibre gun, quickly followed by the explosion of a shell. The submarine had opened fire. It was then ahead of the centre lighter and coming towards us. It fired again, and hit No. 13, farthest from us. No. 18 had altered course and was bearing down on the submarine, sparks shooting up from the exhaust funnel. But the more manoeuvrable submarine evaded the clumsy lighter and, still shooting, came closer to us. We could clearly see the conning-tower and the long shape of the gun forward of it. Suddenly there was a stream of tracer, and a fast rattle—our Besa had opened fire. The bullets swept the forward part of the submarine and the gun stopped firing. Now our gunner concentrated, and we heard streams of armour-piercing bullets rattling on the conning-tower. Two-pounder pom-pom shells were bursting there, too. By now the submarine was not more than 100 yards from us. There could not have been anyone left alive on the deck, and in a moment or two it had sheered off in the darkness to our stern. We took evasive action, at our full nine knots, with a plume of sparks showering from our stumpy exhaust.

Major-General T. WYNFORD REES, D.S.O., M.C. (centre), commander of 19th Indian ("Dagger") Division, with some of his officers and men at Mandalay, Burma, in March 1945. Right, the Division's famous badge.

Tanks versus Submarine on the Way to Tobruk

During the months of Tobruk's siege, from April to December 1941, reinforcements and supplies were regularly sent in by the sea route from Egypt. How one detachment of tanks from the Western Desert Force, loaded on lighters, slowly battled their way to the beleaguered garrison under air and submarine attacks is told by Lieut. Gilbert Smith, 4th Royal Tank Regiment.

IN the bars of Cairo and in tented messes in the Western Desert there was talk, during September 1941, of a coming autumn offensive. The 4th Royal Tank Regiment, equipped with Matildas, was in the area south of Matruh, when suddenly there came an operational order for us to reinforce Tobruk's garrison. A hundred miles west of Halfaya Pass, the most easterly German position, Tobruk fortress was in the sixth month of its siege.

We moved down to Mersa Matruh on September 30 by squadrons, and embarked in lighters—blunt-bowed, flat-bottomed, nine-knot craft, powered by high-octane petrol motors. Each could carry four tanks. My troop went aboard one afternoon, spending two perspiring hours running our four tanks up the bow ramps and manoeuvring them inside for quick unloading. We sailed at about five in the evening, in company with two other lighters—Nos. 13 and 18.

All that evening we chugged our way slowly west. About nine o'clock we saw a flight of German bombers en route for Mersa, but they left us alone, and happily we watched the sun sizzle out on the horizon. The night was deliciously dark until eleven, when a large and hateful moon came up—and soon we heard the buzz of an aircraft. The 2-pounder pom-poms were manned, and after ten minutes' suspense the aircraft went away. An hour or so later he came back with others, and we were bombed, off and on, all night. One bomb landed just under our stern: the little lighter lifted, the propellers raced, there was a deluge of water, and the lights went out. We were certainly surprised and pleased to find ourselves still afloat—but speed had to be reduced slightly.

On we ploughed up Bomb Alley, past Sollum, which was German-held, with aircraft always above us. Now and then we could hear the brief noise of a motor ticking over as a plane glided slowly down over our phosphorescent wake, then a quick whistling rush and the crash of a bomb. They dropped all round us, but did no damage apart from a few strained plates. We were uncomfortably conscious of our high-octane petrol tanks covered only by thin mild-steel plating!

Dawn came, and the attacks stopped. All that day we went on, seeing an odd aircraft, and getting more and more nervous, though the R.A.F. had promised us fighter cover past that part of the coast which was thick with enemy aerodromes. At 12.30 a single enemy recce plane came and had a look at us, and from then on the tension was considerable. At 1.40 the look-out reported a squadron of enemy aircraft coming up to port, very high. Our hearts sank, and I'm afraid we cursed the R.A.F. We knew we had no chance at all from daylight bombing, with our inadequate A.A. protection, and we also knew that one small bomb was enough to sink us.

The formation flew past us, turned, and came back. Suddenly the lookout cried: "Aircraft coming up on the starboard quarter!" and we looked up. There was our escort—twelve beautiful Hurricanes—and hastily we apologized to the R.A.F. The German bombers saw them too, and turned off and beat it southward very quickly indeed. The rest of the day was enjoyable enough—just chugging along, the tank

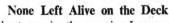
Lieut. GILBERT SMITH

AN hour later we made contact again with No. 18, but could get no reply from 13 on the radio. We had seen her hit, and we felt upset about our friends on her—and the tanks, too. We knew how badly they were wanted in Tobruk. At 3 o'clock we saw two dim green lights to shorewards. They were the markers for the Tobruk harbour bar. We went in and unloaded in the middle of one of the biggest air-raids Tobruk had ever had. It was tricky work getting the clumsy tanks out of the narrow bow and one of mine became jammed half-out, with the result that it pulled the lighter up the beach with it.

The men guiding the drivers in pitch darkness were showered with fragments of the barrage, but we rolled off, up through the shattered town, shaken but whole. Two days later No. 13 turned up. She had turned back to Mersa Matruh, damaged, and with casualties. Of the three lighters which brought my squadron along to Tobruk not one survived the trip back.

We Battled with Exeter's Unexploded Bombs

Lieut. Ronald G. Walker, G.M., Royal Engineers, Section Officer of a Bomb Disposal Section of R.E.s based at Plymouth, in May 1942, describes how he dug up and dealt with stray bombs—and was presented to Their Majesties the King and Queen for his high-speed work on the railway line.

AT 5.30 on the morning of May 4, 1942, the phone rang in my quarters at Plymouth and I was told, " There is a bomb on the railway line just outside Exeter Station. Will you come ? " Our life consisted of a series of mad rushes, clearing bombs for a few days, then spells of boredom doing odd jobs. This was one of the rushes !

I hastily dressed, and roused Taffy, my batman-driver, who had so many things to

Lieut. RONALD G. WALKER, G.M.

say about Hitler and the Luftwaffe and the war in general that he was fully clothed long before he had finished. ' A few days previously Exeter had suffered a raid and there had been three or four unexploded bombs for us to deal with, and to save travelling time I had billeted my Section in the city ; so on this day working-parties were already standing-by awaiting our arrival. And as we were exempted from all speed limits and traffic restrictions whilst on priority bombs, so we managed to complete the 40-mile journey and contact the railway officials at St. David's Station, Exeter, within an hour. After a short walk along the track we found the bomb-hole, at the junction of the lines, on the embankment by St. Thomas's goods yard. The hole was about 30 inches in diameter, which gave us a clue as to what lay at the bottom of it.

Avoiding Unnecessary Casualties

We judged it to be a 500 kilogram general-purpose bomb, which is approximately four feet long and 18 inches in diameter—the larger diameter of the hole being accounted for by the bomb wobbling during flight and as it hit the ground. We used a long stick to try to touch it, but the bomb had curved in its downward path and we could not get round the bend. However, it was possible to estimate its position and for our excavation we marked out a shaft six-foot square.

This was done by my Section Sergeant— Sergeant Parrish—and myself, the remainder of the working-party remaining behind the brick wall of the goods yard weigh-bridge house about 70 yards away, outside the danger area. The procedure of limiting the number of persons actually around the bomb was always observed to avoid unnecessary casualties should an explosion occur whilst preliminary work was in progress.

The setting-out of the shaft completed, the remainder of the party came up and work commenced with the removal of two rails and half-a-dozen sleepers which were in the way. The working party consisted of one N.C.O. and three sappers, the N.C.O. in a Bomb Disposal Section doing his share of all digging and timbering. We had three shifts in the 24 hours : from 6 a.m. to 2 p.m., 2 p.m. to 10 p.m., and 10 p.m. till 6 a.m. This was our normal method of working on a priority bomb when speed was vital. I arranged with the local barracks to have a cook on duty at all hours to prepare hot meals for the men before and after leaving the job. Meanwhile, sandwiches were provided, and enormous quantities of tea brewed by the lorry driver who was sanding by with his vehicle.

It did not take long to move the rails, then two of the men commenced digging. The other two were busy carrying timber from a stack in the goods yard to the site ; as the line was on an embankment the soil would be too loose to hold on its own, so we would have to timber the sides as we went down.

The digging was carried out by the men working in pairs, one with a pick and one with a shovel, for a 20-minute spell, then the other pair took over for 20 minutes, an arrangement which could be maintained throughout the eight-hour shift. As the hole became deeper there was room for only one man on the bottom, and he threw the soil on to a staging half-way up, a man on the staging throwing on to the surface, and one on top shovelling the soil away so that the ground round the shaft was kept clear.

We Decided to Operate Immediately

As we dug down so the timbering was placed—planks (" runners ") varying from eight to 12 feet long and nine inches by one and a half inches section, positioned vertically against the sides of the shaft and held in place by " walings " of nine-inch by four timber which formed horizontal frames wedged against the runners. As we went deeper so the runners were lowered and other frames put in at approximately four-foot intervals. It was on one of these frames that the staging was supported.

Whilst this was going on I had a look around, and saw a small greenhouse (which had collapsed) about 20 yards away in a back garden at the foot of the embankment. I decided to investigate, and found that a bomb had fallen through the greenhouse roof. On probing, I felt something hard about five feet down. I sent Taffy to collect another squad, complete with tools, and they got busy on the debris to clear a working space. This second bomb complicated matters, because the explosion of one would almost certainly cause the detonation of the other and casualities would be doubled. However, our work had to continue.

About two o'clock in the afternoon I received a message from the Exeter Control Centre that another unexploded bomb had been found, in a public convenience about a mile away ; this was causing a large area to be evacuated, and would I go over ?

Photo, Western Times

This piece of news was brought to me on the railway line by a police messenger. I left instructions with the N.C.O.s on the railway job as to where I was going, and Taffy and I rushed over in the car to this latest incident.

There was the bomb with its nose buried and the remainder sticking up in the air. We decided to operate immediately. The roads were closed, and my driver took the truck along to a safe spot around the corner and informed the policeman on duty what was happening, whilst I got busy on the bomb, first clearing away some of the bricks and rubble so that I could identify the fuse. After a few minutes' fiddling with the latter, which was now nicely exposed in the side of the bomb, I was able to announce all clear. On reaching the truck I found a crowd waiting for the news that they could return to their homes. I told the policeman that the bomb was now quite " dead " and that a squad would arrive later to collect it.

Back to the railway by four o'clock, to discover, much to my relief, that all was well and work proceeding smoothly ; by now, of course, the second party had taken over. I had one more call during the day. This concerned a small 50 kilogram bomb which had plunged through the roof of a house and a bedroom floor and was resting peacefully beside the fireplace in the dining-room. After a few minutes' work on the fuse I carried the bomb out on my shoulder, put it in the back of the truck— and that was that.

AT 10 o'clock the third party took over, and so into the night, when we had to use lights. As we had to observe the blackout as much as possible we fixed up a temporary timber framework over the top of the shaft and covered it with a tarpaulin from one of the lorries. This looked most unsafe, but it served the purpose. The lighting consisted of a couple of large electric hand-lamps borrowed from the local A.R.P. people.

1,000-lb. BOMB BEING RAISED at Exeter (left). The fuse had broken, and T.N.T. had to be melted out. Working-party consists of Sgt. Parrish, L/Cpl. Casey, Spr. Tatlock, Spr. Chadwick, Cpl. Woodworth. Looking down the shaft (above), showing method of timbering. The N.C.O. is holding part of tail fins which have just been recovered.

At 2.30 a.m., whilst I was in the shaft digging with the men, the party working at the greenhouse shouted that they had uncovered the bomb—a 500 kilogram (approximately 1,000 lb.). This meant ceasing work on both jobs, for the parties to take cover whilst I "drew its teeth." Fortunately all went well, and one party departed for bed, whilst the rest of us returned to work. Six o'clock came, and once more the parties changed. By now we were about 15 feet down and still had not touched what we were after. The railway officials paid us periodic visits to see how we were progressing, and about midday we touched what we thought was the bomb. It was another five feet down, making a total depth of 25 feet. Our work went on with renewed zest.

During the afternoon a G.W.R. official came along and, calling me aside, asked when I could get the bomb clear as Their Majesties the King and Queen were due to pass through in the Royal Train at 8 p.m. I promised it should be done by 6 p.m., which would leave two hours for the company's gang to fill in the excavation and relay the lines. It was agreed that an engine with truck and crane would be standing by half a mile up the line from 4 o'clock onwards. This I intended to call up to lift the bombs from the holes and take them down into the sidings in the goods yard, to be loaded on to our lorry for final disposal. By now excitement was tense, but when we uncovered what we had hoped was the bomb it proved to be only the tail fins left behind on its downward path. However, we could touch the bomb now, another three feet down, and on we went, racing against time.

Three feet to go and two hours to do it !

There was no time for timbering as we "rabbited" down. We were all absolutely exhausted. Picks and shovels seemed twice their normal weight. And when one of the men working at the bottom hit the timber above his head with his pick he muttered in a very weary voice, "Sorry, timber ! " A sure sign that we were all just about at the end of our tether !

At last we uncovered the base-plate, which was just inside our shaft, the nose of the bomb pointing away from it. This meant going down another two feet and tunnelling around the bomb—most awkward in this confined space, but we scratched the earth away somehow and finally reached the fuse in the side of the bomb case about midway between nose and base-plate. It was another 500 kilogram, partner to the one that had wrecked the greenhouse.

The party retired to the safety of the weigh-bridge house for a brew-up whilst I operated on the fuse and made the bomb safe for handling. When this was finished, one of the men went along to bring up the engine whilst the rest of us cleared more soil from around the bomb and loosened it ready for removal. The time was five minutes past six and we had excavated 28 feet, timbered the shaft and dealt with the bomb, besides

~~~ Roll of Honour ~~~

THE large number of photographs already received is now being prepared for reproduction, and the first page of our Roll of Honour will appear shortly. Meanwhile, those readers who sent stamped and addressed envelopes can be sure that their photographs will be returned in due course. No correspondence on this subject can be considered.

disposing of the other incidents, in 34 hours.

Up came our special train, the jib of the crane was swung over the hole and the hook lowered. Having made the bomb secure by wrapping the chain around it the weighty missile was hoisted up, swung round, and deposited in the truck. Now we turned our attention to the one which was still lying in the debris of the greenhouse and treated it in similar manner.

We Cheered as the Train Passed

The bombs clear, a party from the railway company shovelled back the soil, the timber being left in the hole for support, the lines were relaid, and within half an hour the first train rattled past. At that time we were rolling the bombs from the railway truck into our lorry, but we managed to raise a cheer as the train passed by. That night, Tuesday, I had a sorely needed wash, a shave and a meal—my first in comfort since the Sunday, as I had never left the job except for the short intervals to deal with the other incidents —and straightway went to bed.

The next few days were spent uneventfully in clearing up numerous other bombs in less important places, such as minor roads, parks and outlying districts ; one was in a sewage tank, which necessitated working waist-deep in the sludge. Fortunately, during this period we had the assistance of other Bomb Disposal Sections who had been drafted into the city. It was whilst I was hard at work—and plastered with mud— that I received a summons by dispatch rider to report at Exeter Station in half an hour to be presented to Their Majesties the King and Queen for my work on the line. Then back to our station, to await the next call.

A Bomb-Fenced Road in the Island of Crete

REMINDER OF ALLIED AIR ATTACKS on Crete during the period of German occupation is this fence of bombs (rendered harmless) edging a road there. The peasants now go leisurely about their accustomed daily tasks, with but occasional memories of the guerilla warfare they waged against the Huns for four years. When Allied troops arrived in May 1945 Cretan patriots, assisted by secretly landed British officers, had already cleared most of the island and penned the German garrison into one corner.

Photo, Associated Press

Printed in England and published every alternate Friday by the Proprietors, THE AMALGAMATED PRESS, LTD., The Fleetway House, Farringdon Street, London, E.C.4. Registered for transmission by Canadian Magazine Post. Sole Agents for Australia and New Zealand : Messrs. Gordon & Gotch, Ltd. ; and for South Africa : Central News Agency, Ltd.—May 10, 1946. S.S. *Editorial Address :* JOHN CARPENTER HOUSE, WHITEFRIARS, LONDON, E.C.4

Vol 10 *The War Illustrated* Nº 233

SIXPENCE

I WAS THERE

MAY 24, 1946

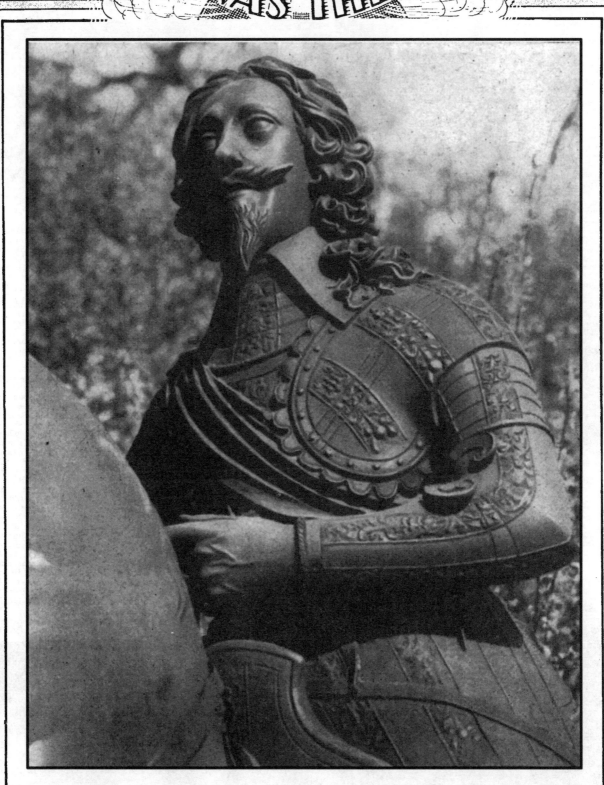

CHARLES I RETURNS TO LONDON from Lord Rosebery's Mentmore estate, in Buckinghamshire, to which the bronze equestrian figure, cast in 1633 by Hubert Le Sueur, had been removed in 1941 after receiving damage in air raids. It will be among the first of the Capital's statues to be restored to its plinth, in Trafalgar Square. Once before it had been "evacuated"—during Cromwell's Protectorate it was hidden away for safety, and re-erected after the Restoration of 1660. See also pages 79-82.

Edited by Sir John Hammerton

NO. 234 WILL BE PUBLISHED FRIDAY, JUNE 7

Monty's 'Great Debt to All British Soldiers'

TAKING LEAVE OF HIS COMMAND of the British Army of the Rhine, on May 2, 1946, to return to England to assume (in June) duties as Chief of the Imperial General Staff, Field-Marshal Viscount Montgomery of Alamein broadcast to the troops in Germany his appreciation at having commanded " . . . this great Army, the like of which our country can never before have put into the field . . . I can justly say the Army has been a fine example to the Germans. of the ideals for which we fought . . . I feel I have a great debt to all British soldiers and I shall take every opportunity of repaying it . . ." His successor as C.-in-C. B.A.O.R. is Marshal of the Royal Air Force Sir Sholto Douglas.

The Field-Marshal turned about to give a farewell salute as he entered the plane (1) at Gatow airfield, Berlin, where before his departure for England he inspected the Guard of Honour (2). His pet canary, "Erbie" (3), waited to be taken to his master's caravan home at Hindhead, Surrey.

Marshal. of the R.A.F. Sir Sholto Douglas inspected the Guard of Honour at Gatwick airport (4) before taking off for Germany, May 1, 1946; on arrival at Gatow airfield, Berlin (5).

Photos, British Official, Keystone, Associated Press, G.P.U. PAGE 66

What Happened at St. Nazaire

By
Lt.-Col. A. C. NEWMAN, V.C.

To appreciate the reasons for our attack on the docks at the German-occupied French town of St. Nazaire on March 27–28, 1942, it is necessary to consider the situation in Britain at the end of 1941. The U-boat campaign in the Atlantic was expected to reach its full strength before America could really get going and help to provide effective counter-measures. The Royal Navy was hard-pressed to protect the British life-line of convoys crossing the Atlantic, and any additional enemy weight in this quarter would be a contingency difficult to meet.

At this time it was learnt that the German battleship Tirpitz was lying in Norwegian waters and that she was likely to come out into the Atlantic to join in the campaign as a raider. If this was indeed so, anything that could be done to influence her to stay where she was would be of great value, even if such an action was only effective for the few months that were vital for America to be in a position to help our Navy.

It was as a result of this possible threat that the attack on St. Nazaire was considered in the spring of 1942. It was thought that if the Tirpitz was engaged, in all probability she would make for the dry dock there—the only one on the French Atlantic coast big enough to house her if she were knocked about and needed repairs. The destruction of this dock would therefore be likely to have the effect of keeping her in Norwegian waters, or of making her run the gauntlet of the Straits of Dover to get back to the naval base at Kiel. At the same time St. Nazaire was a very strong U-boat base, having a massively constructed concrete bunker, and any damage that could be done to it would assist to some extent the Allied anti-U-boat campaign.

Such were the main reasons for the raid and, in brief, this was the plan for carrying it out. A force of approximately 270 Commandos was to be landed in the Docks, 90 of whom were to carry out the demolition of all the essential dock machinery, gates and approach bridges ; the remainder were to destroy the gun crews and keep the area clear of enemy whilst the demolitions were taking place. They were to be conveyed there by light surface craft— M.L.s, carrying about 15 men in each—and in an old American destroyer, H.M.S. Campbeltown, which, with five tons of explosives in her bows, was to ram the outer dock gates. A delayed-action charge in the explosives would detonate them some hours later when the land demolitions had been completed. To create a diversion to the many dual-purpose enemy gun positions in the area, the R.A.F. were to carry out a raid on the docks throughout the action.

It was known that a large force of Germans was housed in the old French barracks just outside the town of St. Nazaire, so it was essential that the raid should be a surprise and the time ashore reduced to a minimum. The maximum time ashore was to be 1½ hours, and it was hoped this might be considerably reduced if all operations went well. The St. Nazaire docks lie some miles up the River Loire, and to get there it was necessary to run the gauntlet of many coastal batteries covering the estuary and river. So it was decided to carry the raid out at high tide, when there was just sufficient water covering the mud flats over which the destroyer and the M.L.s would cross, rather than to approach by the normal deep-water channel. High water was at half-past one on the night of March 28, 1942, and the landings were to be made at this time with, it was hoped, all away by 3 a.m.

On the morning of March 26 the force sailed from Falmouth, escorted by the destroyers H.M.S. Atherstone and Tynedale, these to cruise about outside the Loire estuary and give cover and assistance to the landing forces after the withdrawal and on the journey home. The passage to the Loire was uneventful, except for an attack on a U-boat which was seen at dawn on the 27th surfaced in the Bay of Biscay. After nightfall on the evening of the 27th, in close formation the convoy headed at high speed for the Loire estuary.

The Atherstone and the Tynedale had been left behind in the Bay and a sharp lookout was kept in the darkness for the pre-arranged navigational beacon in the mouth of the river, which was to be given by the submarine H.M.S. Sturgeon. With an intermittent light flashing from her conning tower she was to mark the entrance to the river, after which the convoy was to be directed on to their objectives up the river by a M.G.B. carrying the Force commanders.

A muffled " Good-bye and good luck ! " from the Sturgeon's conning tower as the convoy passed was the last link with home, and the operation was before us. Creeping across the mud flats had its anxieties. H.M.S. Campbeltown touched ground on two occasions, but by good fortune she managed to clear herself. Ahead could be seen the flak in the sky, telling us that the R.A.F. were there and the raid was on. How far we would be able to proceed up the river undetected was in the lap of the gods but, incredible though it seems, the Force was able to get within a few minutes of its objective

before searchlights picked us up and every enemy gun in the area was let loose at practically point-blank range. Tracer of all colours swept across the river. The Campbeltown was seen to be hit many times, but on she came, closely following the little motor gunboat. The shooting was not all one-sided. From every vessel a stream of missiles answered the enemy fire ; many searchlights were put out and many gun positions silenced. It was a great relief when immediately ahead could be seen the large dry-dock gate ; and, pulling over to starboard to allow the Campbeltown to pass on to her objective, the Force commanders were to see the first part of the operation successful as, breaking through an anti-submarine boom, the old destroyer crashed into the dock gate—fair and square in the middle. Her determined commander (Lt.-Cmdr. S. H. Beattie, V.C., R.N.) had taken her in at almost twice the specified speed. (Portrait in page 669, Vol. 5).

Almost before she had stopped the Commandos on board were swarming over her bows, which were stuck far into the dock gate, and were making towards their objectives. The M.L.s, however, were not having such a good time. Trying to land their Commandos at points which were closely protected by gun positions, many of them were hit. In some cases they were so close to the German pillboxes that the enemy were able to lob hand grenades into the vessels. It was not long before the river was a mass of burning craft. Petrol was flaming on the water and men were trying to swim ashore under intense enemy fire.

Ashore, intermittent explosions in the vicinity of the dry dock indicated that the demolitions were being carried out according to plan. One by one the small parties reported that their task had been completed, and proceeded to the pre-arranged point of re-embarkation. The big white pump-house close to the dock entrance went up in a cloud of smoke and flame, and for a minute the whole area was full of falling masonry and bricks. The winding houses that operated the opening and closing of the outer and inner dock gates were blazing, following big explosions in each. Many of the gun emplacements that had a few moments earlier been firing were now silent ; the crews had been destroyed and the guns smashed.

When all the demolition parties from the dry-dock area had reported, the fighting parties were withdrawn to the point where it had been arranged to re-embark the Force. On arrival here it was realized that getting away again was not going to be possible. The scene in the river was a nasty one. Burning M.L.s seemed to be everywhere, and heavy enemy gunfire across the river clearly indicated that it would be impossible for any M.L.s which survived from the gallant little fleet to reach the landing point, embark the Commandos and get away again.

In the river the Naval Commander in the motor gunboat (Cmdr. R. E. D. Ryder, V.C., portrait in page 627, Vol. 5) had tried everything to take off those ashore, but with the position in the river rapidly deteriorating

AFTER THE ST. NAZAIRE RAID many Commando survivors, left to their own resources, "went to ground" in the hope that escape would later be possible. The picketing of cross-roads and a systematic house-to-house search in the town by the Germans the following day (above) resulted in the capture of almost all of them.

it was necessary and right that such remaining craft as were left—all carrying many wounded men picked up from the river—should withdraw down the Loire. This, in itself, was a hazardous task, and it was carried out under continuous devastating fire by shore batteries who were by now thoroughly aware of what was happening and whose fire was accurate and heavy.

ONE little M.L. proceeding at full steam ahead down the river was engaged by a German destroyer and a lively action ensued. Running alongside each other a continuous interchange of fire was kept up between the two vessels, the much larger enemy destroyer causing heavy casualties on the unprotected M.L. With nearly all the men on board killed or wounded, the M.L. was called upon by the destroyer to surrender, but a burst of fire from a light automatic weapon on the M.L.'s deck told the German captain that there was still some fight left in the little British ship.

When the Campbeltown 'Went Up'

The very gallant firer of this weapon was the Commando Sergeant Tom Durrant, who although wounded many times, kept up his answer to the heavier German demand. Needless to say, in the end they were overpowered and those on board who remained alive taken prisoner. Sergt. Durrant, mortally wounded, was taken aboard to die a few hours later, and like his comrade, Able Seaman W. A. Savage, who gave his life on the M.G.B., firing his gun to the last, was awarded a posthumous Victoria Cross (portraits in page 185, Vol. 9 and page 28, Vol. 6). Those little ships that made the estuary reached home with colours flying. Attacked by enemy aircraft, one of which at least they shot down, they succeeded in making the double journey.

Back on shore the remaining Commandos had formed a defensive perimeter around the jetty side. With rapidly diminishing ammunition it was no place to stay. Close behind them was the as yet unexploded five tons of dynamite in the Campbeltown's bows. They were in the dock centre, to which point all German reinforcements would make, and space to manoeuvre was by now very limited. It was decided to form up into parties of about 20 and break out of the dock area into the town, do as much damage to the enemy as depleted ammunition would allow, and then attempt to get through to the open country beyond.

With luck their hope lay in making their way through France to Spain and home. Five of them managed it and sailed for home from Gibraltar ! The majority of the remainder managed to penetrate the enemy ring surrounding them and enter the town. In small groups they engaged the Germans in the streets, fighting their way as far as they could into the town of St. Nazaire. When ammunition ran out each group went to earth and, with daylight adding to their difficulties, hoped to remain hidden through the day and to escape the following night. But, carrying out a systematic house-to-house search, with all cross-roads picketed by automatic weapons, the Germans combed the town and one by one the parties of Commandos were taken prisoner.

THEY knew just what had happened when at about ten o'clock next morning there was a tremendous explosion from the dock area. At that time many high-ranking German officers were carrying out an examination of the Campbeltown, and it is known that when she went up many of them went up too, some 300 officers and men dying as a result of the explosion. H.M.S. Campbeltown had done her job ; the main entrance to the dry dock was completely destroyed, and every effort by the Germans to repair the dock was unsuccessful. Delayed-action torpedoes fired into the entrance gates to the lock through which the U-boats had to pass to their bunker caused heavy damage, and all the installations connected with the working of the dry dock had been successfully demolished.

Failure, however, had to be reported with regard to any damage that we had hoped to do to the bridges and entrance to the inner basin. The men whose task it was to destroy these objectives either lost their lives trying to reach them or, in the case of some, failed to be landed by their M.L.s at the dock side. But the main task was successful. And if as a result of this action the Tirpitz decided to stay in Norwegian waters, as indeed she did, then the raid as a whole may be considered successful.

German Divisions Were Recalled

Our casualties were high—34 Commando officers out of 44 and 178 other ranks out of 224 were left behind ; 34 naval officers and 151 ratings were killed or missing out of a total of 62 officers and 291 ratings. From the day the exploit was planned, when it was known as " Operation Chariot," until the day the small Force sailed from Falmouth, there never was a doubt in anyone's mind that it would be otherwise. Yet never did a more confident Force sail from its base to do a job that needed to be done.

The action at St. Nazaire had another far-reaching result. The Germans were surprised by it, and for a while they thought it was the opening of the Second Front. Their losses were very heavy, and there is no doubt that in the confusion during the darkness and also during the days that followed, many of their casualties were caused by their own guns. The French citizens in St. Nazaire had spontaneously joined in the fighting and had added considerably to the enemy confusion and discomfiture. As a result it is known that not only were the Germans unable to send away many Divisions which they had earmarked for the Russian front but there is evidence that some on the way were actually recalled. Thus the action did to some extent relieve pressure on our Allies.

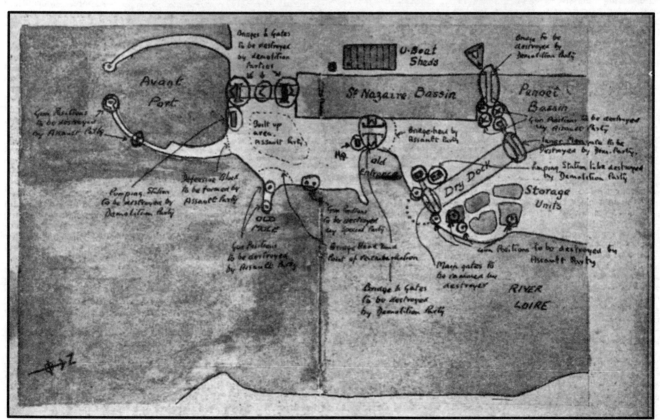

SKETCH PLAN OF THE ST. NAZAIRE OPERATIONS, drawn by Lieut.-Col. A. C. Newman, V.C., who led the Commandos in the attack described in these pages. Main objectives of the assault parties are shown, and though not all were achieved the raid was a success inasmuch that the damage inflicted to the installations and docks resulted in the German battleship Tirpitz remaining in Norwegian waters, and the retention in the area of a large number of German divisions earmarked for the Russian Front.

Chronicle

Sebastopol Falls After Eight Months

FIGHTING AT ALAMEIN — HAND-TO-HAND FIGHTING

The Daily Telegraph

SUCCESS OF COMMANDOS' INVASION TEST

HEAVY DAMAGE TO ENEMY IN 9 HOURS AT DIEPPE

42 NAZI PLANES
100 MORE

RUSSIAN

The Evening News

NEW LANDINGS IN AFRICA

ALLIES NOW 60 MILES FROM TUNISIA BORDER

The Desert Lullaby

R.A.F. STRIKE AT TARANTO
TORPEDO PLANES

PREMIER TAKES THE SALUTE

News Chronicle

TRIPOLI FALLS: TANKS RACE TO CUT RETREAT

Eighth Army Shelled City From Hill Tops As Axis Forces Fled

AFRICAN ASTROLOGY

Soviets Storm Salsk, Close On Armavir, Voroshilov

The Daily Tele

GERMANS' STALINGRAD C.-IN-C. SURRENDERS

16 GENERALS TAKEN PRISONER

RUSSIAN TR

DAILY EXPRESS

Burma despatch which was held up 10 days tells heroic story: 'Even convalescents fought'

SCRATCH FORCE HELD JAPS. AT KOHIMA

the dumps

DAILY EXPRESS

Montgomery points across the Strait—"There is Italy. Let us now knock her out of the war." And his troops are still pouring over

8th ARMY BRIDGEHEADS CUT 10 MILES INTO ITALY

Churchill

ROME FALLS: RESISTANCE RESISTANCE

Citizens welcom

Chronicle

WE INVADE

6 a.m. Air & Sea Land: On Normand: First Re

TANKS CRUSH THE

LATE EXTRA

Herald

ROBOT RAIDERS IN FORCE LAST NIGHT

Way Across Heart Of Peninsula

THIS IS IT

US Planes
Coast

Daily Mail

RUNDSTEDT OPENS ATTACK

Tanks Strike on 70-mile Front

Liberation

News Chronicle

HITLER DEAD

Doenitz, new Fuehrer, says: We figh

WEHRMACHT ORDERED TO MAINTAIN DISCIPLINE

News Chronicle

VICTORY ISSUE
May 8, 1945

TODAY IS V DAY

Today and tomorrow are national holiday. Churchill speaks at 3 p.m., the King at

East End and West End—neither waited

Daily Mail

Most terrifying weapon in history: Churchill's w

ATOMIC BOMB: JAPS GIVEN 48 HOURS TO SURRENDER

threaten Tokio: 'You can

DAILY EXPRESS

Attlee, at midnight, gives news that it is all over

PEACE ON EARTH

JAPS REPLY: We have the honour to surrender.

Foreign Ministers' Conference Opens in Paris

DELEGATES AT THE OPENING SESSION were Mr. Bevin (1) and his deputy on the council of Foreign Ministers, Mr. Gladwyn Jebb (2) ; Mr. Vishinsky (3), assistant Foreign Minister U.S.S.R., Mr. Molotov (4), Foreign Minister U.S.S.R., Mr. Pavlov (5), U.S.S.R. ; Mr. James Dunn (6), U.S.A., deputy to Mr. J. F. Byrnes ; Senator Connally, U.S.A. (7) ; Mr. J. F. Byrnes (8), U.S. Secretary of State ; M. Couve de Murville, France (9), deputy to French Foreign Minister, M. Bidault (10).   *Photo, New York Times Photos*

THE FOUR POWER CONFERENCE between the Foreign Ministers, Mr. Ernest Bevin (U.K.), Mr. J. F. Byrnes (U.S.A.), Mr. Molotov (U.S.S.R.), and M. Bidault (France), opened at the Luxembourg Palace, Paris, on April 25, 1946, to draft peace treaties with Italy and the former Axis satellite states. Quick decisions were made on points of procedure, and on the future of the Italian Navy—to be shared between the Big Four and Greece and Yugoslavia, Italy to retain only four cruisers.

Surprises came with Mr. Bevin's proposal that the former Italian colonies of Libya and Cyrenaica should be united into a Greater Libya ; and Mr. Byrnes proposed a 25-year Four Power pact for the disarmament of Germany and promised continued American interest in European affairs. Discussion on the Italian peace treaty, including the future of Trieste, and the Italo-Yugoslav frontier, produced a deadlock between the Western Powers and Russia. The shelving of the Italian peace treaty by the Ministers, and the focusing of their attention on treaties with Bulgaria, Hungary, Rumania and Finland, brought the first ten days of the Conference to a close.

BRITAIN'S FOREIGN MINISTER, the Rt. Hon. Ernest Bevin (1, left) with Mr. Gladwyn Jebb at the Conference table. The Russian delegation (2), left to right, Mr. Vishinsky, Mr. Molotov, and Mr. Pavlov ; the " U.R.S.S." on the table is the French form of U.S.S.R.   Mr. Bevin arriving at the Luxembourg Palace (3).   *Photos, Associated Press, New York Times Photos, Keystone*

France Pays Homage to Fallen Maquis Heroes

BENEATH THE CRUCIFORM SYMBOL OF THE FREE FRENCH, in the cemetery at Morette, the French Government, represented by M. Francisque Gay, recently honoured the memory of Maquis heroes of Plateau des Glières, where they fought to the last man when cornered by the Germans and were buried on the spot where they fell. Among the large gathering at the ceremony (above) were members of the Resistance Movement and representatives of the French Army.

Photo, Planet

Royal Navy Maintenance in Australian Ports

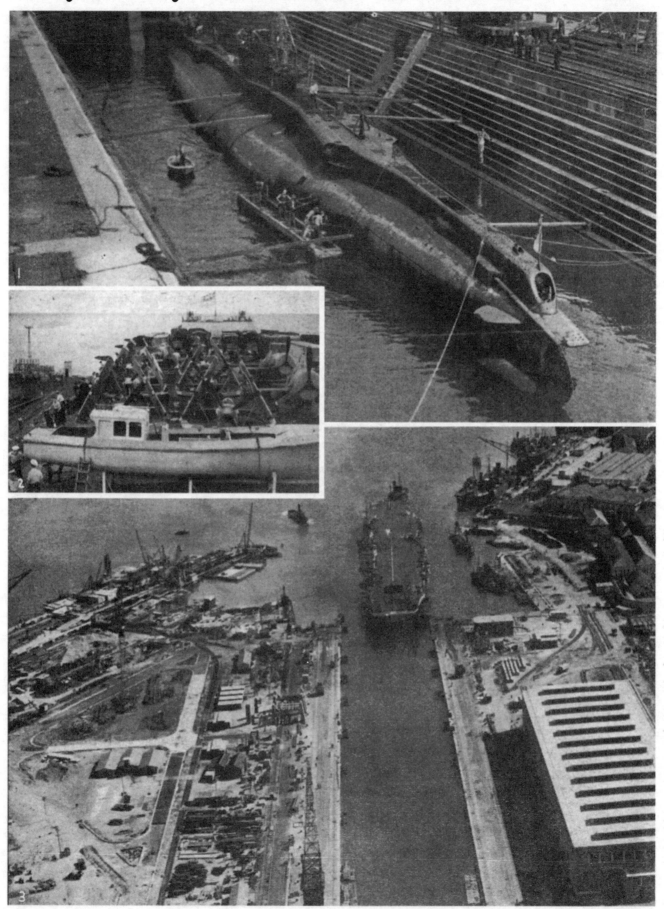

HELP FROM AUSTRALIA both in the war years and afterwards has not been confined to men, food and materials only : her maritime facilities have proved invaluable for the maintenance of ships of the Royal Navy. H.M. submarine Taurus (1) being overhauled in Williamstown Dock, at Melbourne, where H.M.S Pioneer (2), decks packed with repaired aircraft, is being prepared for passage to England. H.M.S. Implacable, British aircraft carrier (3), going for a refit into the great Captain Cook graving dock at Sydney. See also illus. page 43, Vol. 9.

Photos, Planet News

Last Days of H.M.S. Thrasher, V.C. Submarine

SLUMPED ON THE MUD OF RESTRONGUET CREEK, Falmouth, in April 1946, and waiting with her comrades Taku, Tribune and Trusty to be towed away for breaking up, was the famous Thrasher (1), her service days finished for ever. She figured in a remarkable episode in February 1942, when Lieut. P. S. W. Roberts, R.N., and Petty Officer T. Gould removed two unexploded German bombs from her gun-casing (inset) and for their heroism were each awarded the Victoria Cross (see illus. in page 59, Vol. 6). After refitting and recommissioning, the Thrasher prepared for sea again (2); alongside a submarine depot ship after patrol (3).

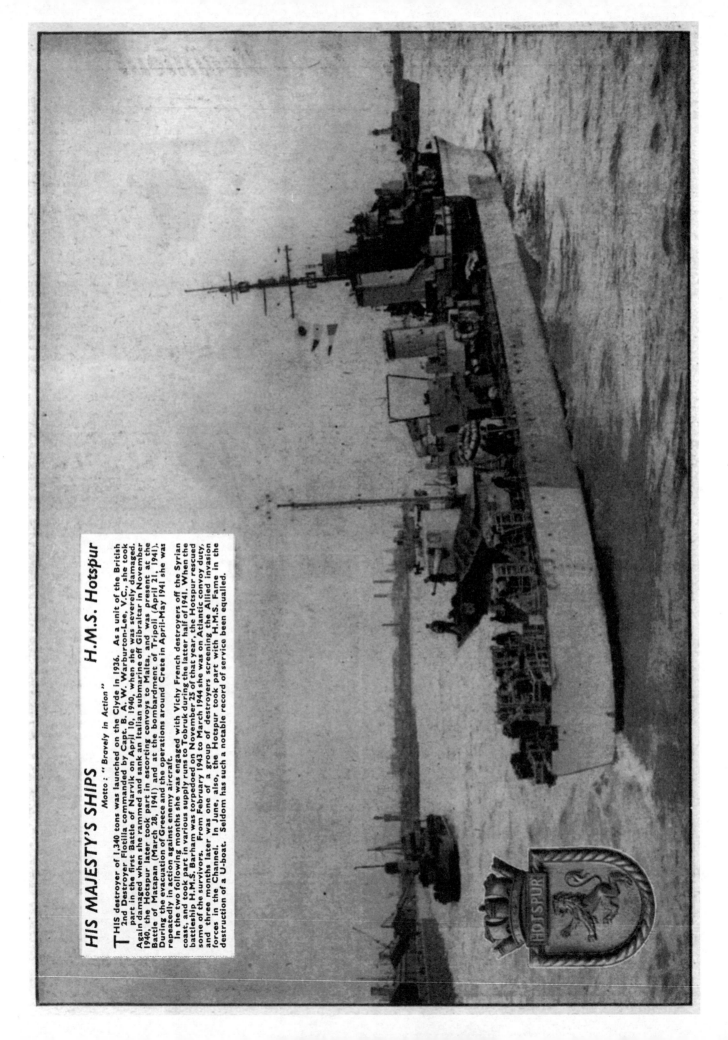

HIS MAJESTY'S SHIPS   H.M.S. Hotspur

Motto: "Bravely in Action"

THIS destroyer of 1,340 tons was launched on the Clyde in 1936. As a unit of the British 2nd Destroyer Flotilla commanded by Capt. B. A. W. Warburton-Lee, V.C., she took part in the first Battle of Narvik on April 10, 1940, when she was severely damaged. Again damaged when she rammed and sank an Italian submarine off Gibraltar in November 1940, the Hotspur later took part in escorting convoys to Malta, and was present at the Battle of Matapan (March 28, 1941) and at the bombardment of Tripoli (April 21, 1941). During the evacuation of Greece and the operations around Crete in April-May 1941 she was repeatedly in action against enemy aircraft.

In the two following months she was engaged with Vichy French destroyers off the Syrian coast, and took part in various supply runs to Tobruk during the latter half of 1941. When the battleship H.M.S. Barham was torpedoed on November 25 of that year, the Hotspur rescued some of the survivors. From February 1943 to March 1944 she was on Atlantic convoy duty, and three months later was one of a group of destroyers screening the Allied invasion forces in the Channel. In June, also, the Hotspur took part with H.M.S. Fame in the destruction of a U-boat. Seldom has such a notable record of service been equalled.

The Royal Air Force Regiment

by Squadron-Leader
M. H. D. COCKAYNE

From a nucleus of ground gunners who had first been enlisted into the R.A.F. after the fall of France, the R.A.F. Regiment was formed in February 1942. Those gunners had shared with the Army the responsibility of protecting airfields from ground and air attack, and had played their part in the Battle of Britain.

To assist with the training and organization of the newly-formed Regiment a number of senior Army officers and N.C.O. instructors were lent by the War Office, with Major-General C. F. Liardet, C.B., D.S.O., T.D., who had recently commanded the London Division, as the first Commandant.

The first task of the squadrons was to relieve the Army garrisons at airfields throughout the United Kingdom. These squadrons were to form a mobile striking force ready for immediate action, the defended localities on the airfields being manned meanwhile by station personnel all of whom were now being armed and trained to fight in defence of their station. By June 1942, 62 squadrons had taken the place of Army garrisons, and by September take-over was virtually complete.

Meanwhile, ten units of the Regiment were being specially trained for service overseas, and in November they landed with the Expeditionary Force in North Africa. In the Middle East newly organized Regiment units were ready to play their part when the advance from El Alamein began. In North Africa and the Western Desert they adapted their role to conditions very different from those at home. To provide the air support so necessary for the Army's rapid advance it was essential to occupy and protect each airfield immediately it was taken.

THE Regiment was called into being primarily to defend the airfields of the United Kingdom from threatened invasion. Rapidly adapting its role step by step in response to the changing needs of the R.A.F., its range of activities developed far beyond the original conception. It made extremely important contributions to the success of the major operations of the War by providing the R.A.F. with a force of trained fighting troops for the ground and air defence of its own airfields and relieving the Army of these commitments.

Major-General Sir Claude LIARDET, K.B.E., C.B., D.S.O., T.D., who became the R.A.F. Regiment's first Commandant on its formation in February 1942. *Photo, Fox*

Consequently the Regiment became much more mobile, moving well forward, clearing the airfields of any pockets of enemy, of minefields and obstructions, and giving protection to the air squadrons operating from them. In these theatres the armies moved on narrow fronts and their operations were fluid ; landing grounds and radar stations were frequently established to a flank and the defence of these had to be provided by the Regiment. From El Alamein to Tripoli and from Algiers to Cape Bon the Regiment gave valuable assistance to the Desert Air Force and Eastern Air Command, facilitating the provision of air cover for the forward troops by its rapid occupation and protection of advanced landing grounds.

In the spring of 1943 it was decided that the Regiment should relieve A.A. Command of responsibility for the light A.A. defence of airfields in the U.K., and by September the Regiment were manning 300 of the 40-mm. Bofors guns—to them an entirely new weapon. When the invasion of Sicily took place in July, squadrons of the Regiment from U.K., Middle East and North Africa took part. Two squadrons—one from U.K. and one from the Middle East—made beach landings to give A.A. protection to a coastal airfield. At the end of the Sicilian campaign the squadrons which had taken part moved into Italy, three being flown to forward airfields near Taranto. Others followed from the Middle East and North Africa.

Battle Experience in the Line

In September 1943 a light anti-aircraft squadron was flown to the Island of Cos, in the Aegean, to protect the forward airfields which were to be established there. The squadron was constantly in action against the low-level attacks which preceded the German landings on the island, and early in October, when German forces invaded Cos in strength, the Regiment gunners joined the Army units in resisting the invaders.

In Italy and the Central Mediterranean area it was decided to give Regiment Squadrons, when possible, the benefit of battle experience in the line alongside the Army. Such duties were admittedly outside the role for which the squadrons had been formed and trained but the experience gained was often of the greatest value. Two squadrons had occupied the island of Lampedusa during the operations which led up to the invasion of Sicily. There, in a sudden emergency, they organized the local fishing fleet to search for the crew of one of our bombers which had crashed in the sea, all of whom were eventually found.

Another sea-rescue occurred six months later, from the Island of Ponza, in the Tyrrhenian Sea, where a Regiment unit was protecting an R.A.F. radar station. An American vessel containing troops and prisoners was washed ashore on the rocks at the foot of a high cliff where heavy seas

FIRST ACTION of the Regiment occurred in the Western Desert, where it proved invaluable in occupying and protecting captured airfields in the Army's advance from Alamein to Tripoli. Waiting to go forward (left) on the edge of an enemy airfield.
Photo, British Official

months of training and preparation came to an end on June 6, 1944, and on that day the first squadrons, detailed to protect the bridge-head airfields, accompanied the invading forces across the Channel. The first units went ashore on D-Day + 1, and within a few hours of their landing were deployed on their appointed airfields in Normandy, engaging enemy aircraft.

At home a new form of attack from the air—the flying bomb—began on June 13, and the Regiment was quickly assisting A.A. Command in its defeat. In all, 51 A.A. squadrons were deployed along the south and south-east coasts, and there they stayed, manning their guns by day and night until October, when they were withdrawn to prepare for the move to the Continent, where the advancing armies were securing more airfields, requiring squadrons for their defence.

Clearing an Airstrip at Meiktila

In Air Command, South-East Asia, the defence personnel who had been absorbed into the Regiment on its formation had been reorganized and equipped. The Japanese offensive of early 1944 found Regiment units protecting the airfields in the Imphal plain, where operations were maintained at maximum intensity only by air supply and by constant vigilance against infiltration. Battle experience was gained by attachments to Army units engaged in long-range patrols, and this training proved its value when the offensive into Burma began and the airfields were moved forward as the Army advanced.

In January 1945, in this theatre, some units of the Regiment took part in the combined operation for the capture of Ramree Island while others were advancing on Rangoon. One of the latter particularly distinguished itself at Meiktila, in March, by clearing a considerable force of Japanese from an airstrip to enable the fighters to operate. A Regiment Squadron had been flown in after the capture of the airfield. It had only recently arrived in Burma and had not so far been in action. The Japanese were attacking fiercely and made a nightly withdrawal from the airfield necessary. It was impracticable to put a cordon around the airstrip, so a defensive "box" was established quite near it and manned each night by the squadron and a detachment of Indian troops.

One morning at dawn, after being heavily attacked during the night, the small Regiment

ON THE ITALIAN FRONT, after fighting in Sicily, squadrons of the R.A.F. Regiment occupied forward positions; defending H.Q. (above) situated in a cave within half a mile of the enemy lines. Wreckage of a German Ju 88 brought down in Naples Harbour (right) by the Regiment's A.A. gunners. *Photos, British Official*

were breaking. Rescue work was organized and carried out by the men of the Regiment under great difficulties, one officer losing his life in the attempt. Nearly all of the Americans and their prisoners were rescued and the American authorities later awarded their Soldier's Medal to two men of the rescue party. This same unit had another experience when it was ordered during the summer of 1944 to provide A.A. protection for Marshal Tito's headquarters in the mountains of Yugoslavia.

By the end of 1943 most of the Regiment squadrons in the U.K. were actively preparing to take part in the assault on the Continent, and as the preparations developed during the first five months of 1944 the danger of enemy attack on our airfields in Southern England increased. To guard against this danger a heavy concentration of Regiment A.A. units was made at these vital air bases. The

R.A.F. Soldiers in Overseas Action

Motto : " 216 Bearing Gifts "

NO. 216 SQUADRON
(TRANSPORT COMMAND)

WITH a long history, No. 216 Squadron owes its origin to a flight of four twin-engined Handley-Page bombers which was detached from No. 7 Naval Squadron in France towards the end of 1917 for inshore anti-submarine patrols off the North Yorkshire coast. On October 2, 1917, the flight was transferred to Manston as the nucleus of a bombing squadron— " A " Squadron, R.N.A.S.—for independent bombing operations, in co-operation with the R.F.C., against industrial areas in Southern Germany. On January 8, 1918, " A " Squadron became No. 16 Squadron R.N.A.S., and on April 1 it was renumbered No. 216 Squadron, R.A.F.

Between the wars No. 216 was engaged in mail, freight, passenger and troop transport operations between Egypt, Palestine and Iraq, and training in troop emplaning, casualty evacuation and supply dropping. On the outbreak of war in September 1939 the squadron was the only heavy Bomber-Transport squadron in the Middle East. Under Wing-Commander G. C. Gardner, its first task was the transfer of R.A.F. units to their war stations in the Middle East. It was re-equipped with Bombays at the end of 1939, and by December 1940 had finished its last bombing raid and was engaged solely in transport and airborne support duties. Its first large commitment was the evacuation of troops from Greece in 1941.

IN 1942 the squadron was re-equipped with Hudsons, and in October took part in diversionary operations in preparation for the break-through at El Alamein. During the early months of 1943 the advance was so rapid that the squadron was fully occupied in moving forward Fighter Wings, supplying ground forces and evacuating casualties. With the formation of R.A.F. Transport Command in 1943 the squadron undertook a number of new scheduled flights, and carried out paratroop training.

Early in 1944 the squadron, now flying Dakotas, went to Air Command, South-East Asia, to meet urgent air-supply demands of the Allied forces in the India-Burma theatre, and flew 3,422 operational hours, dropped over 600 tons of supplies, landed more than 1,500 tons of freight, carried 7,200 passengers and evacuated 508 casualties. A great compliment was paid to it by the Supreme Commander South-East Asia when Admiral Lord Louis Mountbatten wrote, " Thank you, 216 Squadron, for saving the situation in Imphal ! "

ON A NEWLY-CAPTURED AIRFIELD on the Adriatic coast of Italy in July 1944, men of the Regiment man a Bofors gun (above) and keep watch for sight of an enemy aircraft. Members of an armoured unit (below) patrol the perimeter of an airfield in Britain in 1942 ; mechanization had become essential for rapid movement to threatened points.   *Photos, British Official*

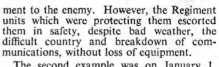

ment to the enemy. However, the Regiment units which were protecting them escorted them in safety, despite bad weather, the difficult country and breakdown of communications, without loss of equipment.

The second example was on January 1, 1945, when the Luftwaffe suddenly launched a determined attack on the forward airfields in Belgium and Holland. Formations of up to 50 fighters and fighter-bombers, approaching at tree-top height, attacked 11 airfields. By the end of the action, which lasted one and a half hours, the Bofors gunners of the Regiment defending these airfields had destroyed 27 and damaged 54 enemy aircraft.

The last days of hostilities in N.W. Europe provided a fitting climax to the activities of the Regiment in 2nd T.A.F. At dawn on May 5 nine columns composed of 11 squadrons moved ahead of the Army to take over all the airfields in the Schleswig-Holstein peninsula, accepting the surrender of over 20,000 Germans, 1,000 aircraft intact, and stores.

AT LINGEVRES, 10 km. south of Bayeux in Normandy, men of the R.A.F. Regiment clear wreckage of German aircraft from ground required for forward airfields. They landed on June 7, 1944. *Photo, British Newspaper Pool*

garrison of the "box" sent out a patrol to reconnoitre the landing strip and found that a strong Japanese force had taken up positions on and near it. While a tank and infantry counter-attack was being prepared the patrol gallantly held its ground, continuously engaging the enemy. When the strip was finally regained, 150 Japanese dead were counted. The losses of the Regiment patrol were seven killed and eight wounded.

THE campaign in North-West Europe provided two classic examples in which the Regiment fulfilled the role for which it was originally formed—that of protecting R.A.F. installations against ground and low-flying air attack in a defensive battle. The German counter-offensive which Von Rundstedt launched in the Ardennes in December 1944 found our radar units directly in its path and close to its starting-line. These units were, in consequence, in danger of being overrun and losing their secret technical equip-

AT SINGAPORE a detachment of the Regiment presented arms to Admiral Lord Louis Mountbatten, Supreme Allied Commander South-East Asia, at a ceremonial parade preceding the signing of the island's surrender by the Japanese on September 12, 1945. Units of the Regiment were some of the first troops to go ashore for the reoccupation. PAGE 78 *Photo, British Official*

ON A BURMESE BEACH they manhandled A.A. guns through a sea of mud for the final advance on Rangoon. *Photo, British Official*

Young officers found themselves in command of airfields containing 7,000 armed Luftwaffe personnel, and at the same time responsible for the welfare of large numbers of prisoners of war and displaced persons of many nationalities. With tact, firmness and good judgement the situation was mastered, and by May 10 the Regiment was relieved by 2nd Army and Air Disarmament Wings of the R.A.F. The operation demonstrated the value of a small force of trained units at the disposal of the R.A.F., and the ability of officers and airmen of the Regiment to deal with the most unexpected situations.

In the final advance at Rangoon through Central Burma the units of the Regiment moved forward with the air squadrons. They not only provided protection for our air and ground crews and aircraft from snipers and enemy patrols, but hunted down Japanese stragglers and saboteurs when they ventured near newly captured airstrips. It so happened that some of these airstrips were located directly in the escape line of the trapped Japanese Army. This necessitated our keeping our patrols in operation right up to and even after the official VJ Day. Later, when the British reoccupation of Singapore took place, R.A.F. Regiment units were among the first to go ashore, in September 1945, taking over the protection of Kalang airfield.

Home-Coming of London's War-Exiled Statues

From Country Castle back to Town Square

Removed to Berkhamsted Castle, Hertfordshire, to escape possible damage by air raids, the fine equestrian statue of King William the Third was returned to London on April 18, 1946. In a Ministry of Works storehouse in St. James's Park evidence of its lengthy retirement has been removed, and a final short journey saw it restored to its somewhat warworn site in St. James's Square, where it was originally placed in 1808.

An interesting point in the history of this statue of a British monarch who was born at The Hague (in 1650) is that 106 years elapsed between William the Third's death (in 1702) and its erection, though the pedestal had been in position in the Square since 1732. The bronze is the work of John Bacon. See also illus. in page 284, Vol. 6.

Exclusive to THE WAR ILLUSTRATED

79

Famous Evacuees in Bronze Return—

From wartime retreat at Mentmore Park, Bucks, King Charles the First was seen returning to Town on a truck (1) on April 5, 1946; the York Column (background) is surmounted by Westmacott's bronze statue of the Duke of York, second son of George the Third, which survived the Battle of London intact. Sliding backwards down a ramp (2) at the St. James's Park storehouse, King Charles and his mount reappears, as of old, at the top of Whitehall (3). See also illus. page 65.

Planet

—To Their Old Places in London's Scene

Back to the twelve-foot high pedestal at the junction of Cockspur Street and Pall Mall, off Trafalgar Square, came King George the Third and his charger on April 15. Stormy war-years safely passed in the seclusion of Berkhamsted Castle (in company with William the Third and other Important Personages), the statue by M. C. Wyatt is swung into the position (4) which it first occupied in 1837. Removal of the scaffolding (5) reveals it as it was in former days of peace (6).

81

In Memory of Valiant Exploits

Commemorating 14,000 of our men killed in the First Great War the Machine Gun Corps Memorial, designed by Professor F. Derwent Wood, R.A., was erected at Hyde Park Corner. The unveiling ceremony of the bronze statue of David on a pedestal of stainless marble was performed by the Duke of Connaught in May 1925; the Machine Gun Corps, created in October 1915, was disbanded in July 1922. When that war which was to end wars was followed by another and vastly more terrible conflict the Memorial was removed and housed in the Aldwych Tube Station beyond reach of the Luftwaffe's bombs. On April 5, 1946, the crated sections were once more disturbed—this time to be taken to the foot of the lift-shaft (1) for the ascent to open air and daylight. After a spell at Millbank, for necessary attentions, it will be reassembled at Hyde Park Corner. The Memorial as it was and is to be again (2).

The towering column with Bailey's statue of Nelson at its summit (3) remained unscathed in Trafalgar Square; steeplejacks are cleaning it. See also illus. in page 799, Vol. 9.

Photos, Fox, Keystone

INDIAN OCEAN AND PACIFIC COLONIES

By HARLEY V. USILL

THE Middle East, the cradle of civilization, might, but for the foresight of the British and almost superhuman endeavour, have become its grave. The fact that it did not become such a grave is due to the interlocking and flexible strategic character of the British Colonial Empire as a whole, and the point is brought home most clearly when we turn to the Indian Ocean.

The Battle of the Mediterranean was more in the nature of a series of holding actions to prevent domination of the area by the Axis Powers, but while these were going on the Indian Ocean provided the alternative route for the transport of men and materials to the various battlefronts in the Middle East.

The Great Importance of Ceylon

Undoubtedly one of the greatest prizes for an enemy to have captured in the Indian Ocean was Ceylon. In the words of the French commodore Suffren in 1782, "the importance of Ceylon is such that, if English troops captured the island, its recapture would be more important than all other conquests wherewith one could begin a war in India." Ceylon lies to the south-east of India, a few degrees north of the Equator. Its greatest length is 270 miles, its greatest width 140 miles, its area 25,352 square miles, or about half the size of England.

The defended port of Colombo on the west coast of the island is a major junction of trade routes by the Cape and Suez to India and the Far East, and was particularly important as a nodal point of communications when the Mediterranean route was virtually closed to Allied shipping. Trincomalee on the east, which Napoleon described as the finest harbour in the world, is the only British naval base, except Bombay, between Aden and Australia.

The occupation of Malaya and Burma by the Japanese brought Ceylon into the front line as a bastion of defence against further aggression, and in March 1942 the post of Commander-in-Chief, Ceylon, was created to ensure the proper co-ordination of all branches of defence. As the tide turned, however, Ceylon began to be developed as an offensive base ; supplies were accumulated from Great Britain, Australia and the United States, and Allied troops and aircraft poured into the island. Old aerodromes were enlarged and new ones hacked from the jungle.

In his Christmas broadcast in 1942, the Commander-in-Chief said, "Ceylon is the springboard from which to launch an attack against Japan, and our fighting men are being trained for the offensive." Sixteen months later, on April 16, 1944, Lord Louis Mountbatten moved his headquarters to Ceylon, and this island became the pivotal point for the operations which followed. The attack on Sumatra, for instance, was carried out by warships and carrier-borne aircraft based on Ceylon. But more about Ceylon later.

Mauritius and the Seychelles

Ships rounding the Cape on the route to the Red Sea and Suez, or serviceing the ports on the East African coast, were faced with the problem of extended lines of communication. These became increasingly dangerous when Japan entered the war and gained access to the Indian Ocean. To a considerable extent, however, the dangers were lessened by the strategical position in the Indian Ocean of Mauritius and the Seychelles.

Mauritius might well be described as the "Clapham Junction" of the Indian Ocean. Situated 500 miles east of the French-owned Madagascar, the island, comprising about 920 square miles, commands the route from the Cape to India and Ceylon, and ships based on Mauritius are also within striking distance

CONTINUING his explanations of the strategic importance of the British Colonial Empire, the author deals here with the supremely important islands in the Indian Ocean—alternative wartime route to the Middle East after the enemy had partially closed the Mediterranean. The strategic significance of the East and Central African groups of Colonies and British possessions in the Pacific is also dealt with in this article.

of the Cape route between Great Britain and Australia and New Zealand. The harbour at Port Louis is one of the best in the East, and is sufficiently spacious to receive a large number of ships.

During that part of the War when the Cape route was used to transport men and supplies to the battle zones in the Middle East by way of Aden and the Red Sea, and to Russia by way of the Persian Gulf, the strategical importance of Mauritius was very considerable, since its position enabled control to be maintained of a number of separate routes of supply and communication.

The Seychelles form a Colony which, with its dependencies of 92 islands, covers a total area of 156¼ square miles. It is distant from Mauritius 939, from Madagascar 600, and from Zanzibar 970 miles. The chief island, Mahe, has a safe and commodious harbour, and lies on the direct route from Cape Town via Mauritius to the Red Sea. Its importance was such that its garrison was considerably increased during the War.

East and Central African Groups

It can be argued that this group of Colonies belongs to both the Middle East and the Indian Ocean systems of defence, and for this reason it is perhaps less confusing to treat them as a separate region, at the same time showing how they are interlocked with both. The British Colonial territories in East and Central Africa consist of Kenya, Uganda, the Mandated Territory of Tanganyika, the island of Zanzibar, and Northern Rhodesia and Nyasaland. Altogether, with Southern Rhodesia and South Africa, they form an all-British block extending from the Cape to the borders of the Anglo-Egyptian Sudan, Abyssinia and the former Italian Somaliland. To complete the picture we must, of course, include British Somaliland, which faces Aden on the entrance to the Red Sea.

Kenya covers an area of about 220,000 square miles, or about 2½ times the size of Great Britain. To the north it borders the Anglo-Egyptian Sudan and Ethiopia, and to the east it has a land frontier with former Italian Somaliland and a coast line on the Indian Ocean. With such a long frontier with enemy territory, Kenya was in the front line from the day of the Italian declaration of war in June 1940. The direct threat of Italian aggression, however, was relatively quickly removed, but the fall of Singapore brought the Japanese menace close to Kenya's shores since, after the Japanese ships entered the Indian Ocean, the Eastern Fleet was withdrawn temporarily from Ceylon to the port of Kilindini.

For the most part, however, Kenya's strategic importance has lain in her position on the supply routes of the armies of Middle East, Kilindini becoming the principal port of call for vessels bringing men and supplies from the United Kingdom and the United States. It served, too, as the base from which communications with India, Ceylon, and the oil ports of the Persian Gulf were protected. Road and air communications with South Africa passed through Kenya.

The Uganda Protectorate covers an area of about 94,000 square miles, of which 14,000 square miles are water. It lies on the northern shore of Lake Victoria, while its eastern border is contiguous with Kenya. The strategic position of Tanganyika is best appreciated when it is remembered the trouble it caused in the 1914-1918 war when it was in German hands. An area of about 360,000 square miles, it borders Uganda and Kenya in the north, and Northern Rhodesia and Nyasaland in the south, with the port of Dar-es-Salaam giving access to the Indian Ocean. The 290,000 square miles of Northern Rhodesia and the 37,000 square miles of Nyasaland, neither with a port on the Indian Ocean, complete the link with Southern Rhodesia and South Africa.

EAST and Central Africa, then, were an integral part of the defensive and offensive systems of the Middle East, but after the fall of France the whole position was threatened by the uncertainty regarding Madagascar—that island more than a thousand miles long by 350 miles across at its widest point which, if captured by the enemy, could have severed our main lines of communication with Egypt, India, Persia and East Africa itself. The Madagascar campaign, then, which began with the capture of Diego Suarez in May, 1942, and ended with the signing of the agreement at Ambalvo on November 6, served to preserve intact the strategic usefulness of East Africa. In later articles we will deal with the great war effort of the individual Colonies, and particularly with the courage, endurance and loyalty of the troops of East Africa Command.

The strategic position of the units comprising the British Colonial Empire is again seen to advantage when we pass from the Indian to the Pacific Ocean. This positioning enabled the shock of the disaster in the Pacific to be absorbed without irreparable damage to the Allied cause. Normally Hongkong, Malaya, Singapore, Sarawak and the many other British possessions in the Pacific presented an impenetrable barrier to possible Japanese aggression, but the treacherous surrender of French Indo-China, and the Pearl Harbour disaster, upset the strategy on which Pacific defences were based.

Formed a Second Line of Defence

It was always assumed, and few would have been bold enough to have questioned the belief before the events, that the back door to Malaya would always be held by a friendly France, and that the United States Fleet would be available intact should the Japanese ever embark upon aggression. In the event, all the bravery in the world—and there was much displayed in these Colonies before they fell into enemy hands—could not save the situation. The subsequent failure of the Japanese to press home their advantage to a successful conclusion, however, was in large measure due to the strategic disposition of those Colonies which were called upon to form a second line of defence.

When the Japanese advance had reached its farthest limit, with bases in New Guinea, the Solomons and the Gilbert Islands, another British Colony, Fiji, assumed great strategic importance. It was at once in the front line, and was included for naval purposes in the Southern Pacific Command under a United States Admiral. The Fijian Islands are one of the groups which guard the sea routes from North America to New Zealand and Australia, and they also serve as a link to the north-east with Samoa and the American naval base at Pago Pago, to the south-west with the French Colony of New Caledonia, and to the west with the Anglo-French condominium of the New Hebrides.

Housing the Homeless: East London's Enterprise

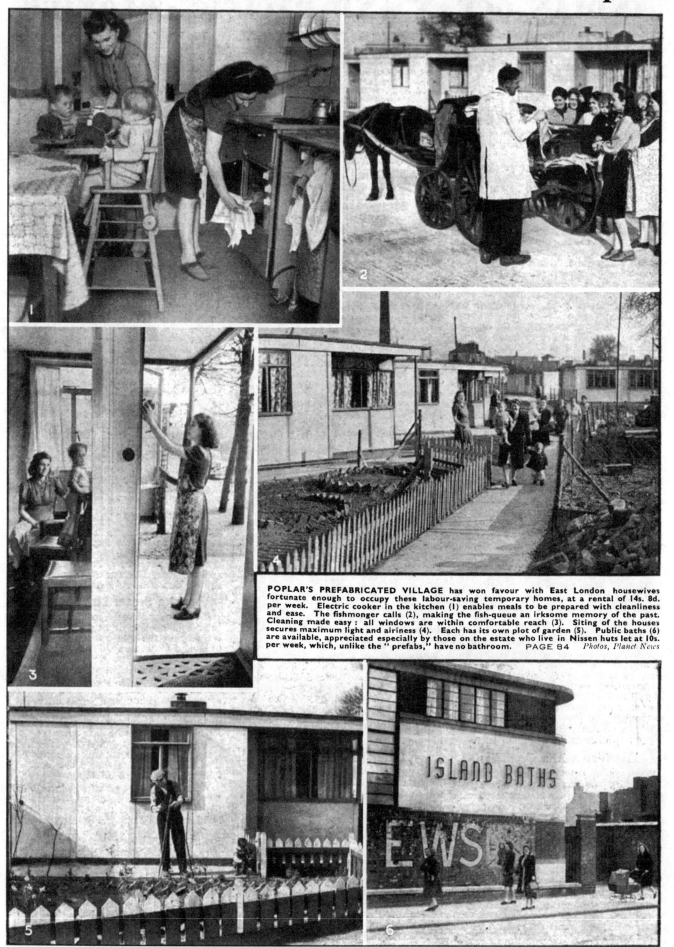

POPLAR'S PREFABRICATED VILLAGE has won favour with East London housewives fortunate enough to occupy these labour-saving temporary homes, at a rental of 14s. 8d. per week. Electric cooker in the kitchen (1) enables meals to be prepared with cleanliness and ease. The fishmonger calls (2), making the fish-queue an irksome memory of the past. Cleaning made easy : all windows are within comfortable reach (3). Siting of the houses secures maximum light and airiness (4). Each has its own plot of garden (5). Public baths (6) are available, appreciated especially by those on the estate who live in Nissen huts let at 10s. per week, which, unlike the " prefabs," have no bathroom.　PAGE 84　*Photos, Planet News*

ISLAND BATHS

EWS

'Our Friendship Will Be an Enduring One'

GRATITUDE TO BRITAIN for the wholehearted support and hospitality given to the Netherlands has been expressed eloquently in both words and gifts. Recently, telephone operators at The Hague presented a Delft plaque to their "sisters" at the International Exchange, London, in appreciation of their parcels to Holland. The plaque (above) bears the inscription, "Food, Peace and Freedom," and is displayed in the London International Exchange (right). A magnificent show of tulips in Regent's Park (below) and other London parks is the result of a generous gift of bulbs from the Netherlands. In a message to Marshal of the Royal Air Force, Lord Tedder, on April 26, 1946, Queen Wilhelmina summed up such gracious acts in the words, "Friendship between you and us . . . will be an enduring one." *Exclusive to* THE WAR ILLUSTRATED

Our War Leaders in Peacetime
ATTLEE

OF all our political leaders the Prime Minister is, perhaps, the least ostentatious. No. 10 Downing Street is his London address, and Chequers, in Buckinghamshire, his country residence ; but he was much more at home among his books in an ordinary house at Stanmore, on the outskirts of London.

Before he superseded Mr. Churchill as Prime Minister at No. 10 Downing Street, in July 1945 he travelled to Whitehall as often as not on the Underground, again as often as not smoking a pipe ; back home in the evening he settled down for a quiet smoke and read. He sold his Stanmore house a few months ago, and today affairs of State cut right across his personal interests.

Before the war Attlee spent his week-ends playing tennis and golf. And if he did not excel at either he had the stamina to play a good hard-court game, and the eye and balance to be more than an average golfer. Now, after five years in the Cabinet, his golf and tennis have become rusty and he contents himself largely with home interests—when opportunity offers.

Newsreel and newspaper give the world details of the Prime Minister's public life : speeches, banquets, conferences. But his private life has escaped the public gaze, largely because it is so very "ordinary." He enjoys the cinema, a game of cards, and a quiet evening with his wife—the fair-haired girl he married, Violet Millar, at a Hampstead church, 24 years ago. She is still his constant companion, but seldom appears in public life with him.

Janet, their eldest daughter, 22-years-old, is a Section Officer in the W.A.A.F. Martin, their 18-year-old son, comes home in Merchant Navy uniform when his ship docks in Britain. He wants to remain in the Merchant Service. Felicity, a year older, is training to

be a nurse. The youngest of the family, 15-year-old Alison, is still at school. When all four children are home the Attlees have a simple and quiet celebration.

Reading is among the Prime Minister's favourite recreations. Ever since he went to Haileybury from his father's home in Putney, where he was born sixty-three years ago, he has been reading, mainly on social matters. His over-riding interest has always been the welfare of his fellow mortals. His father was a solicitor, and Attlee, a Barrister-at-Law specializing in Company Law, was doing well when in his early thirties he left the Bar for social work in London's Mile End slums. There he lived for several years, lecturing at Toynbee Hall and taking part in local government affairs.

THE Attlees spend their time between London and the country. Weekdays find them in their self-contained flat at the top of No. 10 Downing Street. At week-ends Violet Attlee leaves a few hours before her husband to see that everything is shipshape at Chequers before he arrives for a little temporary relaxation.

IN THE STUDY of his former suburban home at Stanmore, Middlesex, Britain's Prime Minister pauses in his meditation on papers of State. In the garden (top left) Mr. Attlee found pleasant diversion from onerous tasks in mowing the lawn.

TEA TIME on this occasion was a family affair at Stanmore, where (left) sitting on the arm of her father's chair is 19-year-old Felicity Attlee. Martin, the only son, a cadet in the Merchant Service, stands next to Alison, youngest of the children. Mrs. Attlee, at the tea table, is seated next to the eldest daughter, Janet, who holds a commission in the W.A.A.F. As Prime Minister, the Rt. Hon. Clement Richard Attlee's residences are now at Downing Street, London, and Chequers, near Wendover in Buckinghamshire.

Photos, Topical

Britain's Food: The Battle for Daily Bread

	AVERAGE MONTHLY IMPORTS OF WHEAT AND FLOUR			
THOUSAND TONS	1937	1939	1942	1944
	403·6	442·0	290·6	235·3
	35·6	30·6	31·2	66·0

■ WHEAT
▨ FLOUR

| EXTRACTION RATE | 70% | 73% | 85% | 82½% |

HOME WHEAT PRODUCTION

ACREAGE TILLED FOR WHEAT
JUNE 1939	1,766,000
JUNE 1942	2,516,000
JUNE 1944	3,220,000

THE FLOUR MILLS

QUANTITY OF WHEAT HARVESTED
1939	1,645,000	TONS
1942	2,567,000	TONS
1944	3,138,000	TONS

MOBILE SUCTION PLANT

UNLOADING CANADIAN WHEAT

SECTION THROUGH A GRAIN OF WHEAT (ENLARGED)

OUTER SKIN OR BRAN
SEMOLINA
SCUTELLUM
GERM

5 SQ. YARDS OF GROUND YIELD 36,600 GRAINS OF WHEAT, GIVING 1½ LBS. OF FLOUR.

2 LB. LOAF

CONTENTS: CARBO-HYDRATES, PROTEINS, VITAMIN B₁, RIBOFLAVIN, NICOTINIC ACID AND IRON.

300,000 TONS FEEDING STUFFS
ANNUALLY
72 MILLION DOZEN EGGS ... OR ... 60,000 TONS OF PORK

SERIOUS WORLD WHEAT SHORTAGES have resulted in a reduction in weight of Britain's standard 1 lb. loaf to 14 oz., the 2 lb. loaf to 1¾ lb., and the 4 lb. loaf to 3½ lb. Announced by the Government on April 25, 1946, to take effect from May 5, this ensures the saving of 12 per cent of the 100,000 tons of flour used weekly to meet Britain's daily requirements of between 16 and 20 million loaves.

This diagram was compiled with the assistance of milling experts, our artist Haworth being given facilities to follow the processes of making wheat into flour at one of our modern mills. Arriving by ship or barge (1) the wheat is taken into the mill at the rate of 60 tons an hour by vacuum suction plant (2). Passing over magnets, which free it from any metallic substances, it is given a first sieve (3) to remove other impurities, then stored in large concrete or metal silos holding upwards of 50,000 tons (4), whence it is taken, as required, by means of moving bands and elevators to the disc separator (5), which removes barley and other seeds.

Next, it passes between saw-toothed rollers (6) which crack the wheat and loosen the outer bran from the inner semolina. The next move is to the plansifter dressers (7) which separate the bran from the semolina, the latter going to the purifiers (8), where it is graded ready for grinding into flour by chilled steel rollers, the grinding and sieving on centrifugal dressers (9) continuing until nothing is left behind but a fibrous substance known as weatings. The flour is automatically packed into bags for delivery (10).

At present a mixture of 10 per cent British and 90 per cent Manitoba (Canadian) wheat is being milled, and the "extraction rate" was recently raised from 80 per cent to 85 per cent—which means that the miller must extract 85 per cent of flour from every grain of wheat, retaining the most nutritious parts—situated in the germ, the scutellum, and the portion immediately adjoining the outer bran. This 5 per cent extraction increase means a loss to Britain of 300,000 tons annually of animal feeding stuffs.

Pte. E. BAKER
2nd S. Staffs Airborne R.
In action : Sicily. 9.7.43.
Age 23. (Lewisham)

Cpl. A. T. BARNETT
1/4 Essex Regt.,
In action: Athens. 15.12.44.
Age 19. (Leominster)

L/Cpl. B. BEECROFT
4th Suffolk Regt.
Died Jap Camp. 21.7.43.
Age 24. (Ipswich)

Pte. D. G. BRACHER
Royal Army Medical Corps.
In action: Walcheren.1.11.44.
Age 20. (Bristol)

L/Sgt. H. BULLARD
154/172 Field Regt., R.A.
Died N. Africa. 19.9.43.
Age 30. (Walthamstow)

B. J. BUTTERWORTH
Tele. Royal Navy.
In action : France. 25.6.44.
Age 19. (Milnrow)

Sgt. P. V. COOK
Royal Air Force.
In action : Belgium. July 43
Age 21. (Bromley)

Flt/Sgt. E. P. HAWKES
Royal Air Force.
In action : Caen. 6.6.44.
Age 20. (Putney)

Pte. E. HENRY
Durham Light Infantry.
In action : Caen. 9.8.44.
Age 28. (Chorlton-cum-Hardy)

Pte. T. W. HOLLICK
2nd King's Shropshire L.I.
In action : Beauville. 6.6.44
Age 20. (Birmingham)

Pte. J. J. R. HOOD
Royal Artillery, H.A.A.
In action : at sea. 7.1.43.
Age 22. (Leyton)

Rfn. W. H. NEATE
Cameronians
In action : Italy. Jan. 44.
Age 33. (Gosport)

O/S W. J. ODELL
H.M.S. Firedrake.
In action : at sea. 17.12.42.
Age 29. (Walthamstow)

Stoker C. OSBORN
H.M.S. Dunoo.i
In action : at sea. 30.4.40.
Age 19. (Long Eaton)

L/Cpl. J. OWEN
9th York & Lancs. Regt.
In action : Arakan. 12.1.45.
Age 27. (Runcorn)

Fusilier D. PEACOCK
Royal Scots Fusiliers
Action: Boschkant. 27.10.44.
Age 19. (Darlington)

Gnr. D. H. PILBEAM
18 Div. Royal Artillery.
Action: Singapore. 10.2.42.
Age 24. (Chertsey)

A/B C. PLANT
Royal Navy.
In action : Anzio. 23.1.44.
Age 27. (Cheddleton)

A. RIGGLESFORD
Stoker H.M.S. Hood.
In action. 24.5.41.
Age 20. (Bexhill-on-Sea)

Driver M. ROBERTS
Royal Army Service Corps.
Action: Dunkirk. 29.5.40.
Age 38. (Flint)

Pte. W. ROBERTS
5th Beds. & Herts. Regt.
Died P.O.W. Siam. 28.11.43.
Age 24. (Chingford)

L/Cpl. A. SALMON
Royal Engineers.
In action : Saigon. 26.2.42.
Age 33. (Rochester)

L/Cpl. E. E. SCOTT
7th K.O.S.B.
In action : Arnhem. 22.9.44.
Age 24. (Edgware)

A/B A. S. SEWELL
H.M.S. Charybdis.
Action: Channel. 23.10.43.
Age 46. (London)

Stkr. D. J. SUTTON
H.M.S. Calcutta.
In action : Crete. 1.6.41.
Age 22. (Nonington)

Gnr. T. SWINDELL
Royal Horse Artillery.
Middle East. 27.6.42.
Age 24. (Newcastle/Lyme)

Sapper T. N. TAYLOR
Royal Engineers.
In action : Sicily. 2.9.43.
Age 22. (Langley, B/ham).

Pte. G. THOMPSON
King's Own Scottish Bds.
Action: Walcheren. 2.11.44.
Age 20. (Liverpool)

Pte. W. THOMPSON
Royal Welch Fusiliers.
In action : Burma. 5.5.44.
Age 32. (Northwich)

Gnr. UNDERWOOD
72nd Field Battery, R.A.
Kasserine Pass. 22.2.43.
Age 35. (Sunningdale)

M. W. WALKER
L/Tele. H.M.S. Salmon.
Action: Norway. July 1940
Age 25. (Grange/Sands)

Pte. A. WAYMAN
King's Shropshire L.I.
Anzio. 20.2.44.
Age 25. (Sunderland)

Cpl. H. WHAIT
1st Leicester Regt.
West Wesel. 21.10.44.
Age 31. (Leicester)

Pte. K. C. WILSON
No. 2 Commando.
In action. 3.6.42.
Age 20. (Wood Green)

Sergt. WINTERBURN
R.A.F.V.R.
In action. 29.9.43.
Age 21. (Otley)

Sgt. J. WOODGATE
44th Reconnaissance Regt.
In action : Italy. 3.12.43.
Age 24. (Robertsbridge)

Pte. A. L. YOUNGS
1st Hertfordshire Regt.
Palestine. 24.4.45.
Age 27. (Hitchin)

A/B E. BROUGHTON
H.M.S. Carlisle.
In action : Crete. 22.5.41.
Age 21. (Hull).

I Saw the Normandy Break-Through

At the time of the tremendous events related here Major (then Lieut.) P. B. Collins, Reconnaissance Corps, was serving with the 51st Highland Division as an Air Photo Interpreter. Vividly he conveys the majesty and terror of the R.A.F. bombing and the gunfire which heralded the opening of our smashing advance towards the Low Countries in the summer of 1944.

My diary for August 7, 1944, reads: "All tee'd up for the big attack, and off now to see what I can see." The attack was to be the start of our final break-through from the Normandy beach-head and, more especially, from that corner east of the Orne River which was probably the toughest and most difficult sector of the whole campaign. Except for one brief respite, the 51st Highland Division, with whom I was serving, had been in that corner since the first few days of the Invasion.

At the time of that entry in my diary, Divisional H.Q. was near an old powder factory at Cormelles, a mile or two south-east of Caen. Ourselves the most easterly of the attacking formations, we had further British divisions on our left, on whom we would pivot in our great sweep to the east, before they began their advance. On our right, the great force of the Canadian and, beyond them, further British divisions, were also poised for that leap forward which was to lead before the end of the month to the German disaster of the Falaise Gap.

Major P. B. COLLINS

At the moment we were in a shell-torn, cratered wood, surrounded by a tremendous concentration of weapons of every sort—armour, guns, vehicles—and everywhere the patient infantry. As usual in this sector, life was punctuated by the whine and crump of occasional shells, for there was no part of our area that was yet out of enemy range, and we had done our usual digging-in as soon as we arrived, some hours previously.

Eight Columns of Armour Moving

Working as a photographic interpreter at divisional headquarters I had for weeks past been getting to know the ground over which our troops were to fight, up to the last minute watching and reporting on the development of the defences that lay out of sight over the ridge beyond Bourgebus and Tilly-la-Campagne. There, when driving up to our present location, we had seen the village disappear suddenly, obliterated in the dust and smoke of an enemy mortar attack; and there, now, I knew that our own troops were lying, waiting their turn to advance.

It was dusk when I left the camp and wandered out towards that ridge. On my right, quite near at hand, things were already on the move. Down what a few hours before had been a narrow, dusty track, the armour was beginning to advance. Eight columns deep it moved, a solid stream of tanks and carriers, S.P. guns and Kangaroos—those troop-carrying tank-hulls whose use set the standard of success for this operation. So dark was it now, and so thick the up-

flung dust, that it would seem impossible to see with normal vision through the driver's narrow slit in a Sherman tank. Yet on they went, nose to tail almost, each commander watching from the open turret-top and controlling his driver with brief orders over the inter-com. It was a crawling, ceaseless stream of metal. They moved slowly, first one column accelerating, then another, with a deadly purposefulness that told me that to walk in among that stream of armour, however slow its movement seemed, would be to court as sure a death as that administered by its individual guns.

I REACHED the top of the rise, and became conscious, above the roar of the armour, of another sound—the drone of the four-engined heavies of the R.A.F. Then, almost immediately, it began. At first, all I could see was the crimson streaming of the markers as they poured through the evening haze over the target area—the village of la Hogue, one of those difficult positions from which, with Tilly-la-Campagne farther west, Jerry had so obstinately refused to budge. Suddenly the air shook with frightful din. I had heard many bombardments, had seen the R.A.F. Lancasters at work at much closer quarters, but this was indescribably frightening. It was as though, down there in the haze of smoke and debris, a vast diabolical whip was being cracked, every crack bringing destruction and death.

For over half an hour I watched this terrible performance. Dark though it now was I could see the outlines of great pillars of smoke and ruin. Every few seconds came the crimson glare of a major explosion and, like long white tendrils, the streaming lines of more markers. This pulverizing

offensive of our heavy bombers indeed had been well named "Operation Totalize."

Away to the right, down in the valley at May-sur-Orne, a similar programme of timed destruction was in progress. I could hear no sound of this, though the flashes of the bigger bombs were occasionally visible, and I knew that the greatest, the most impressive "show" was yet to come—the artillery barrage. Now, and very suddenly, the whole horizon was ringed with flashes, red, yellow, orange and white. The briefest interval of complete stillness, and then the first bellow as the sound of the nearest guns reached me. Gradually, the noise intensified, finally becoming one ceaseless shattering roar.

Searchlights Sprang Into Life

This barrage covered the whole front, and as far as I could see in either direction the sky was alive with flashes. Behind, on the slopes of Mondeville and Faubourg de Vaucelles, that hard-won suburb of Caen, the medium guns—our famous "five-fives"—were at work, while the American Long Toms and our own heavies threw their weight from even farther back. A hundred yards to my right a troop of American S.P. field guns were firing, but their flashless charge left them almost invisible in the dark; only when the scene was lit by some other battery could I see the smoke curling upwards from their muzzles, which stuck up high out of the tank-like hull of their tracked mounting. On either flank single Bofors guns began to fire, not at hostile aircraft this time but to mark with their red tracer the lines of our axis for the advancing troops. The sole human sound in this bedlam was the occasional fire order from the commander of some gun crew.

And then, from all around, from every eminence and hill, searchlights sprang into life. Directed at a low angle on to the base of the clouds, they gave a semblance of uncanny moonlight to the entire battlefield. For a while yet the guns would roar their barrage, as the tanks and their infantry, achieving with the Kangaroos the surprise

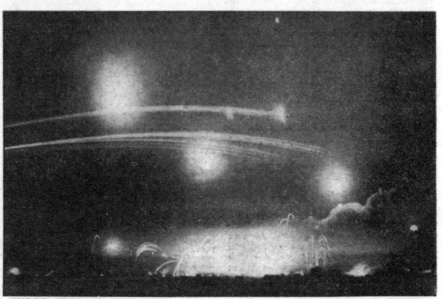

THE BOMBING SOUTH OF CAEN, on the night of August 7-8, 1942, which heralded the Allied break-through in Normandy, grew in intensity until it became "indescribably frightening," as told above. The tracer-filled sky over the German positions is viewed here at the commencement of the R.A.F. bombardment.

Photo, British Official

In Singapore When the Japs Pounced

Sergeant J. E. Pearce, 1st (Perak) Battalion, the Federated Malay States
Volunteer Force, tells how the threat of advancing Japanese troops early in
1942 took a sudden startling turn, entailing 1,200 days' loss of liberty for
our men. Dramatically there came another turning-point with the arrival
at Singapore, in 1945, of Allied aircraft and parachute troops.

Colours : Red Rat in White Circle
on Red Background.

7TH ARMOURED DIVISION

MOULDED in the Desert at Mersa Matruh, 1938, under the guidance of Maj.-Gen. P. C. S. Hobart, the 7th Armoured Division, familiarly known as the "Desert Rats," grew from an indifferent collection of armour to a force whose power was felt from Alamein to Berlin. In its first major battle, at Sidi Barrani in December 1940, the Division advanced to storm Tobruk on January 22, 1941, and later reached Benghazi.

The next two years saw fluctuating fortunes in which the "Desert Rats" were engaged against Rommel's Afrika Korps—at El Agheila in April 1941 ; in the "Battle Axe" offensive of June-July ; and at Sidi Rezegh in November, where V.Cs were gained by Maj.-Gen. "Jock" Campbell (portrait in page 512, Vol. 5) ; Lieut. G. Ward-Gunn (3 R.H.A.) ; and Rfn. J. Beeley (1 K.R.R.C.), the last two posthumously (portraits in page 694, Vol. 5).

In 1942 heavy losses were sustained on the Gazala Line in May ; at Ruweisat Ridge in June-July ; and defending Alamein from which the final British offensive was launched in October 1942 when the Division, breaking through and commencing the pursuit of the Afrika Korps, captured Benghazi for the third time, on November 20, and entered Tripoli on January 23, 1943. In Tunisia it took Sfax (April 10), and Enfidaville (April 20). Transferred from the 8th Army to the British 1st Army the Division was the first of the Allies to enter Tunis, on May 7, 1943, thus completing a 2,000-mile "swan" in six months.

BY-PASSING Sicily, the "Desert Rats" were the first British armour to land in Italy, at Salerno, September 1943. In bitter fighting some of the Division led the way round Vesuvius while others entered Naples on October 1. After fighting across the Volturno and along the Garigliano the Division was recalled to England to prepare for D-Day. It landed at Arromanches, Normandy, on June 6, 1944. It assisted in the assault on Caen (July 18) ; crossed the Seine (August 31), and later the Somme, to capture Ghent on September 10. After crossing the Rhine (March 27, 1945), the Division took Hamburg on May 3. The last chapter in the history of the "Desert Rats" was written in Berlin where, as occupational troops, Mr. Churchill paid the Division a glowing tribute.

COMMANDERS of the Division were Maj.-Gen. Sir M. O'M. Creagh (1939-41) ; Lieut.-Gen. W. H. E. Gott (1941-42) ; Maj.-Gen. "Jock" Campbell, V.C. (1942) ; Lieut.-Gen. F. W. Messervy (1942) ; Maj.-Gen. J. M. Renton (1942) ; Lieut.-Gen. Sir John Harding (1942-43) ; Maj.-Gen. G. W. E. J. Erskine (1943-44) ; and Maj.-Gen. L. O. Lyne (1944).

that was so essential, pushed down to their objective. As I picked my way back to camp in that eerie light I knew that "Operation Totalize" was truly under way.

It was only later, calling at the "Ops" lorry on my way to bed in the early hours, that I heard how successful it had been : how the first of the German defensive lines, their occupants driven below ground by our bombing and kept there by our gunfire, had let our tanks through in accordance with their usual plan, only to find that they had at the same time admitted the infantry ! Surrendering, the Germans left their second line to fight or run, as run they finally did, not stopping until they had reached the canals and rivers of the Low Countries.

ABOUT 4 p.m. on Sunday, February 15, 1942, Japanese troops were dangerously close to the Kallang Civil Airport. What was happening elsewhere on the Island was not known to the two companies of local Volunteers and the one company of the Manchester Regiment, who were retiring under heavy mortar fire along the East Coast Road. Orders were given to retire over Kallang Bridge and make a stand there, fighting to the last man and the last round. We got over the bridge where a large bus was overturned and the steel anti-tank barricade raised.

At 4.20 we were told to pile our arms—because the war was over ! Also we were told to destroy any papers that might be of use to the enemy, as we were now prisoners of war. We were then taken to a nearby Chinese school to await what the Future might bring forth. The school was old, dirty and insanitary, an awful contrast to the splendid aerodrome a few hundred yards away and on the construction of which so many millions of dollars had been spent.

The 'Poached Egg' Flag Appeared

An hour or so later a Japanese officer drove up, got out of his car, produced a large-scale map of Singapore, and addressed me in Nipponese. As I did not understand him and he spoke no English, he grunted, folded up his map and drove off. Such was my first contact with my new "hosts." A restless night passed, with harrowing, shamed thoughts going confusedly through our minds —and burrowing, unashamed insects going over our bodies.

Throughout the following day we did what we could to feed and clean ourselves. Numbers of Japanese troops in trucks passed up and down the road, showing few signs of their "glorious victory." The Japanese flag (known to us as the "poached egg") appeared at a number of houses, but there were no demonstrations. The Chinese near us continued to give us what help they could. Orders came that all the British troops were to go to the barracks at Changi on Tuesday morning.

Three trucks were available for my company, to carry the men's gear and also unfit personnel. The remainder had to march

the twelve miles, and they covered the distance in good style, arriving in Changi in well under four hours. Fortunately for me I was driving the first truck. Leaving at 7 a.m., the convoy was stopped at Kallang Air Port entrance by a Jap sentry. He looked at my watch and ring as if he would like to take them, as was the usual procedure. However, he transferred his curiosity to my identification disc, murmured a few words, stepped back, bowed and waved me on, And so began the first of the many moves we made under Japanese control.

The barracks at Changi were large and substantial and had suffered very little damage during the blitz. They were ideally situated near the sea, off which there was always a cooling breeze. As the number of men now to be accommodated was very much larger than in pre-war days, each was allowed about 6 feet by 4 feet of floor space. Optimism was still high, and we could not see ourselves being held for very long ; but we also realized that our requirements had to be necessities, as we had no room for storing kit or means for transporting it when we were shifted.

Inside the barbed wire we were still under our own administration, which meant that we had our own offices, cookhouses, stores and so on. Rations were supplied by the Japanese and consisted mostly of rice and green vegetables with occasional issues of fish or meat. A number of stores had been brought in by ourselves, chiefly tins of bully, milk, M & V, and vegetables. These, however,

LAYING DOWN ARMS in the courtyard of Raffles College, Singapore. On that fateful day in February 1942 the fighting for these British troops was over, but their captivity was to last until the end of the war itself.

With Allied Armour on the Battlefields of Caen

ON THE FIERCELY CONTESTED BATTLEFIELDS round Caen in Normandy—one heavy engagement is described by Major Collins in pages 89-90. In Cormeilles (1) liberated by the Allied Armies on August 24, 1944, an armoured car keeps roads covered while a Churchill tank burns in the background. Earlier in the month 1,000 R.A.F. bombers cleared the way for a break-through S.E. of Caen. British and Canadian armour move up (2). At Cormelles, H.Q. of the 51st (Highland) Division, on August 7, a troop commander issues rations to his tank crew (3). PAGE 9

LIBERATION DAY AT CHANGI PRISON, SINGAPORE, was heralded in August 1945 by Allied aircraft dropping parachute troops and supplies. Raising excited cheers at the gates of the gaol (where Sgt. Pearce spent part of his captivity) are some of the 6,700 British prisoners who, with 2,600 civilian internees, were numbered among the 37,000 captives of the Japanese at Singapore. Within three weeks of the Allied landing, on September 5, 1945, almost all of them were on their way home.

Photo, Topical

did not last long, and soon we were issuing one tin of bully to 22 men—three-fifths of an ounce each. The last of the milk was used at the rate of 48 men to a 1-lb. tin. Digestive troubles began immediately, owing to the sudden change of diet.

The water supply was out of action, so that it had to be hand-carried and consequently we were severely rationed. Firewood was obtained by felling trees in the camp area. The hygiene wallahs got down to their job, as did the medical staff, and in a short time the camp routine was running smoothly. As was so obvious through all the P.O.W. days, the harder the times the better the men pulled together. Gardeners, amateur and otherwise, began cultivating any spare ground. Many jeered at what looked like pessimism ; little did the majority think that 1,200 days would pass before we would be free again.

WAYS and means of making the meagre rations look and taste differently from just rice were devised, with extraordinary results. The Japanese did not trouble the camp as a whole ; what went on between our Command and theirs I do not know. As the camp was large in area a certain amount of freedom was possible. There was sea-bathing, and one could visit friends in other units. Rumours and false news items were continually passing around, so that our hopes rose and fell daily. Soon, however, the realists were in the majority and we settled down to routine. After about a couple of months the Japanese called for a working party of engineers to go to Singapore to help put the essential services in order again. Assurances were given that the men would not be employed in helping the Nipponese war effort ; in spite of which, from now on parties were continually being sent away on work that was definitely helping the enemy.

In mid-May, 500 of us—a mixture of British and Australians—were taken to Blakang Mati, an island fortress in Singapore harbour. Living tightly packed in two barrack blocks surrounded by wire that did not allow any walking space, we ran our own cookhouses, canteen and "Q" stores with goods provided by our "hosts." Blakang Mati was a Japanese bomb dump, and most of the work that had to be done was shifting bombs to and from Singapore. It was a curious coincidence that on five occasions during 1943-44 all men were carrying bombs to Singapore immediately after a large hospital ship had arrived in port. Although we did not actually load this ship, we were convinced that she was carrying arms to some base a few days' journey away.

Qualified men were picked to look after the Diesel power-house, the water supply and the Japanese motor and carpenter shops. Others acted as boatmen on the ferry service to and from Singapore. One fatigue that was popular was working in the Japanese cook-house and "Q" stores ; one always had the chance of acquiring an extra spot of food ! The building of a Japanese temple took up a lot of time. I presume it was some form of War Memorial. Anyhow, it was quite impressive when completed. Much of the work that we were made to do was, of course, very galling, and the average Japanese guard naturally took full advantage of his newly acquired powers to make things worse.

There were many unfortunate incidents, few of the boys coming through without some kind of beating. Much of the trouble arose through language difficulties, feigned or otherwise, and the natural desire of the fellows to sabotage the job as much as possible. Bombs were dropped into the sea

during loading and unloading, oil drums punctured, tools broken or lost ; in fact, as many difficulties as possible we put in the way of the Nips. As their army discipline is based on physical punishment for mistakes, the Japanese guards automatically used the same methods to correct their prisoners. Where and with what they suddenly and savagely struck was seldom considered.

Human Heads Displayed on Stands

The camp was healthy enough, the only deaths being due to accidents. After one drowning our officers held an inquiry in the barracks, as it was said that the guard had pushed the unfortunate Aussie into the sea and he was carried away by a swift tide. The Japanese said the Aussie had slipped. They decided to inquire into the matter on their own, and sent for the witnesses and the Australian major one night near eleven o'clock. The Australians refused to change their story, and were unmercifully beaten.

The major was told that his men were lying. His reply "My men do not tell lies!" so angered the Japs that the major was picked up and flung about the room. After more talk and kickings the Australians were sent back to their barracks. It is to be hoped that these Nips will be caught and brought to trial in Singapore.

It was toward the end of 1942 when I was over in Singapore collecting rations that I saw one method the Japanese employed to try to control their local enemies. On stands, outside the Station entrance, the Post Office and the Cathay Building, were the heads of half a dozen Asiatics who had been executed for being anti-Japanese. The stands bearing the heads carried large posters "telling the world"—as a warning. The main camp had been moved westward a few miles to Selarang, where the Gordons had lived prior to the outbreak of the war in the Far East. The main buildings became the hospital, the bungalows and married quarters being used as barracks. Once again the men were crowded, but as the buildings were not huge the atmosphere was different. Rations were far from what they should have been, but many new ideas had been put into practice. The variety of the cookhouse products was amazing. The gardens now covered about 150 acres and produced about 30 tons of vegetables per month. Although not of high quality these "greens and roots" helped in no small way to eke out the Japanese supplies, which were irregular in quantity and quality. Coconuts were also collected and helped to flavour the rice, but we could never get nearly enough. There was plenty of room to walk about if one had the time and energy. The shows at the theatres, the concerts, lectures and classes all helped to keep us cheery.

We Watched the Flying Fortresses

In November-December 1943 word began to come through telling of the awful conditions that existed in the Siamese and Burma camps where the workers on the Siam-Burma railway were living. Not long afterwards the first of the survivors arrived—all hospital cases, starved and ill. To describe the emaciated, ulcerous condition of these men is impossible. Unless seen it is well-nigh impossible to believe what the human body can withstand when the will to get through is there. These lads when able could still smile and joke, but the lack of medical supplies and invalid foods hampered their recovery grievously.

Early in 1944 there was a change in the Japanese command, which resulted in our camp being told to shift again. This move meant transferring the civil internees from Changi Gaol to a camp in Singapore, while we took over the gaol. The gaol itself was far from being big enough to hold the 10,000 of us, so that bamboo huts had to be built. Practically all the materials supplied by the Japanese had been used at least once before, and great credit is due to our men who transported and rebuilt the "hutted camp" outside the gaol walls.

Just over 4,000 men were put inside a building designed and built to hold some 600 convicts. The bamboo huts in addition to accommodating men were made into hospital wards. Numerous and remarkable were the medical and surgical feats performed by the doctors and surgeons in the most difficult of conditions and without anything like sufficient or proper materials.

Working parties went out daily to labour in the gardens, on the drome, or wherever the Nips required a job to be done. Aerodrome work was hard and distasteful, the guards mostly being a tough type. Many were the beatings. But much was forgotten when the

JAPANESE TRUCKS IN SINGAPORE, seen passing through Finlayson Square in 1942, packed with temporary conquerors. Believing that their triumph was a permanent one, there was to come a turning of the tables, with defeat in 1945, when their "poached egg" flag would be hauled down.

first Allied planes came and used the drome at Liberation time ! Most of us will never forget November 5, 1944, when the first Allied air raid took place. Daily after that we watched the skies, and often were rewarded with the sight of scores of Flying Fortresses doing a grand job of bombing at the docks or naval base.

As the Japanese realized that their spell of power was being seriously threatened, working parties from the camp were sent all over the island to dig tunnels to shelter the Jap troops. We knew this work would not last very long ; our news service continued to keep us up to date, so toward the middle of August 1945 we were not surprised when working parties were sent back into the gaol.

Then one day Allied planes came low over the gaol and dropped three parachutists and much-needed supplies on the drome, and we began to realize that our long wait was over. More men and supplies were landed, then the taking-over troops came ashore—and the Japanese guards disappeared. Under a most efficient R.A.P.W.I. organization, parties were soon arranged to begin the journey to Blighty. The unheralded visit of Lady Louis Mountbatten at that time came as a great surprise. Her enthusiastic friendliness and solicitude for the boys will be long remembered by all of us who survived.

bombs which fell near the White Tower, one within seven yards of it. The modern buildings nearby were badly blitzed, but the Norman building took it unflinchingly—except the windows.

On October 5, at 11.30 p.m., a stick of bombs was released over the Tower and Tower Hill, two falling on North Bastion. This building had suffered considerable damage on September 11, and now it collapsed like a pack of cards. Our only warder casualty throughout the War was killed here, also an old lady of 70. There were ten other occupants and two Alsatian dogs, and all had marvellous escapes. The area around was floodlit from the fires of a burst gas main on the hill ; metal from the main was flying about in all directions, and it was two hours before the fire-fighters were able to get the flames under control.

In the Tower of London Under Fire

Chief Warder A. H. Cook, D.C.M., M.M., B.E.M., of His Majesty's Tower of London, records its terrible ordeals from the start of the night-blitzing to the arrival there, as a prisoner, of Rudolf Hess, the Deputy Fuehrer. He presents vivid pen-pictures of the Capital standing out in flaming silhouette.

THE night-blitzing started on September 7, 1940, and although no bombs fell in the Tower on that occasion our public services were all affected. The electric light failed for several hours, we were without gas for seven weeks, and the water was filthy. The first high explosive fell in our Moat at 3.20 a.m. on September 11, near North Bastion ; and though there were no casualties, walls varying from eight to ten feet in thickness were cracked right through. Many incendiaries fell around Tower Hill and Great Tower Street on

September 16, and started several fires. At 3.40 a.m. on September 23, two H.E.s arrived. One hit the military quarters near the Officers' Mess, completely demolishing a portion of it and killing one soldier. The other fell on a warder's quarters at No. 4 The Casemates ; fortunately this warder was on night duty and his wife had gone to the shelter, otherwise they must both have been killed. The Conqueror's Keep had a very narrow escape at 9.35 p.m. on October 1, when the Tower rocked at the impact of two

Chief Warder A. H. COOK, D.C.M., M.M., B.E.M., of the Tower of London, author of these memories of days and nights of ferocious blitz during 1940-41. *Photo, Fox*

The next fell at 9.15 a.m. on October 10, between the Queen's Steps and Tower Pier, causing damage to the Byward Tower, and on this day an order was issued to all Yeomen Warders advising them to evacuate their families to the country. Tower Bridge had been put out of action, and remained so till the 14th. At 2.30 a.m. on October 15 a bomb fell on Tower Dock near the West Gate, demolishing and setting fire to the General Navigation Company's ticket office which was being used by the R.N.V.R. as a guard room. The sentry was badly injured, and two ratings sleeping in the hut were burned beyond recognition. Hostile planes were overhead most of the night, and the noise of bursting bombs intermingled with the barrage was terrific.

The night of Sunday, December 8, was decidedly unpleasant. Flares were dropped at 6.30 p.m. and it soon became evident that the enemy meant business. At 9.40 p.m. the Tower shook when a bomb hit the Port of London Authority building. Incendiaries which began to fall on the Tower about two hours later, and were all dealt with by the Warders and military, were immediately followed by H.E.s, one of which fell near the West Gate, killing a soldier and the Tower electrician, also injuring the landlord and landlady of the Tiger Inn nearby. The Middle and Byward Towers suffered much damage.

B Y midnight fires completely encircled us. To add to the inferno more incendiaries fell at 12.30 a.m., and there was an immediate rush to smother them. One had lodged on the roof of the miniature range, but a hurried message brought a Yeoman Warder with his trailer pump into action and the fire was under control in fifteen minutes. This miniature range had to be saved at all costs, for it was here that spies were shot in the Tower—and we did not wish to be deprived of this honour! The honour occurred only once—on August 15, 1941, when a German spy named Josef Jakobs was shot at 7.15 a.m. It gave us a certain amount of satisfaction to have preserved the range for his benefit.

While we were attending to incendiaries on that night of Dec. 8, 1940, a heavy bomb fell on Tower Hill, near the foundations of the Roman Wall, and scattered debris all over the place. A stone weighing 17 lb. came over the Moat and crashed through my skylight; an incendiary missed my other skylight by a foot. And so the night wore on, bombs crashing down unceasingly for eight hours. The east end of All Hallows Church had a direct hit, completely destroying the altar. Two also fell on the Children's Beach.

By dawn our poor old Tower looked in a pitiful plight, for hardly a portion of it had escaped the fury of the night. Most of its windows had been blown out, or were hanging awry. Glass was strewn everywhere. Doors were off their hinges, ceilings down, and blackout curtains torn to ribbons.

I Wanted to Shoot the Signaller

Our worst night to date was December 29, when Hitler tried to destroy the City of London by fire. The alert sounded at 6.8 p.m. and guns were in action as the German planes approached. By 6.30 many fires had started north of the Tower and around Wapping. Fifteen minutes later showers of incendiaries fell on the Tower, Tower Hill and all adjacent areas. Some were of an explosive type and had to be tackled warily. Others were burning themselves out around the Moat and on Tower Hill, giving a brilliant prominence to the whole of the Tower, the P.L.A. building, and Tower Bridge.

Many incendiaries had lodged on the roofs, and by 7 p.m. Skipper and East's buildings, opposite the West Gate, were afire. For three hours this was a blazing furnace. Fanned by a strong breeze nothing could stop the flames; the fire-fighters were helpless. At 7.15 an incendiary, which had fallen unobserved on the roof of the Sergeants' Mess, started a fire. A strong wind soon had this out of control in spite of the valiant efforts of the Tower fire-fighters. The whole building, comprising the Sergeants' Mess, Corporals' Room, complete N.A.A.F.I. Institutes, grocery bar, Q.M. office, stores, main guard room and the orderly room, was completely gutted—except for the orderly room.

Whilst patrolling the Casemates, about 7.30 p.m., I saw what appeared to be someone signalling in Morse from a top window of a house in Trinity Square. I watched for a while, in company with some soldiers, then I decided to go and investigate. I found two policemen on the hill, told them my story, and persuaded them to accompany me. There was a terrific din, and my throat was parched from the fumes of the bombs and smoke of the fires. Flares in the sky and fires on the ground had turned night into day, and it was obvious that whoever had been signalling had seen our approach and stopped. So not being able to verify my statement I returned disconsolately to the Tower.

An hour later the signalling started again. I tried to borrow a rifle or a Lewis gun and go on the ramparts to have a crack at that window; but no one seemed prepared to let me have either. Next morning the top floor of that house was ablaze, so I had the satisfaction of knowing there would be no more signalling from there.

The N.A.A.F.I. block was now a raging furnace. Fire hoses were being directed at it from the White Tower, but nothing would stay the flames' progress; only the thick walls of the White Tower saved it from destruction. At 8 p.m. fires were raging all along the river as far as the eye could see, both east and west, and flames were everywhere on Tower Hill. One started in the King's House, but was successfully dealt with; had it got a hold all the Tudor buildings on Tower Green would have been destroyed and many warders would have been rendered homeless.

T HE air appeared to be full of planes, yet at times there was little gun-fire. Only those who have been under continuous bombing know the comfort a heavy barrage can give. You get the satisfaction of knowing it is probably just as uncomfortable up there as it is down below. We hoped our fighters were up amongst them, as there were occasional bursts of M.G. fire. About 9 p.m. the blitzing began to ease up. At 11.25, when all seemed quiet, a bomb hurtled down, and five minutes later the Tower shook; this was probably a delayed action. The All Clear sounded at 11.40 p.m. Although of comparatively short duration (5 hours 32 minutes) the raid had been very severe.

From the ramparts facing the City we had a grandstand view of the fires. On the Hill great blocks of masonry were crashing. Firemen were everywhere, one moment silhouetted brilliantly by flames, the next completely blotted out by sparks or shadowed by a mantle of smoke. Against hopeless odds they struggled on in the glistening streets now running with water, or perched precariously at the top of their fire ladders. Sparks had settled in the ruins of Chapman's Buildings and, fanned by a strong breeze, soon added to the destruction, taking in the Mazawattee block. At 12.45 a.m. flames were rising double the height of these buildings and the heat could be felt as far away as the Brass Mount at the north-east corner of the Tower.

IN THE TOWER MOAT, drained and used as a parade ground, the first high explosive bomb fell on September 11, 1940. Beyond its crater (in centre of moat) is seen debris of the North Bastion, which collapsed "like a pack of cards" when struck by two bombs on October 5.

According to later reports over 1,500 fires were started that night, and the Tower and Tower Hill had more than their share. The N.A.A.F.I. at dawn was still burning furiously, also Trinity House. Many buildings in Byward Street and Great Tower Street were either gutted or badly damaged. The church of All Hallows was completely destroyed, also the Interpreter's House, and the Public Ledger printing press.

For over 700 years the "Ceremony of the Keys" had been carried out without a break, but it had to be cancelled this night, not by falling bombs but by reason of the N.A.A.F.I. block being a blazing furnace at 10 p.m. The men of the guard from whom the escort would have been drawn were too busy salvaging belongings from the guard room under the burning N.A.A.F.I. So for the first time in history the Ceremony was called off.

In the early hours of January 10, 1941, incendiaries fell around the S.E. corner, some in the Moat and on the wharf front, in the river and on Tower Bridge. They were all successfully dealt with. About 7.13 p.m. more fell, just missing the Tower. Six days later, at 3.47 a.m., things were rather quiet and I was resting on the settee when suddenly there were three explosions. The windows blew open, glass clattered down and debris could be heard falling. I went out to investigate, and what a grand night it was ! There had been a fall of snow, and the brilliant moon seemed to turn our grimy old Tower into a fairyland. But dark patches in the snow showed where debris had settled.

THESE bombs were definitely intended for Tower Bridge, but one fell on barges moored just west of the Bridge, setting them on fire and causing some casualties. There followed a quiet spell of exactly three months duration. The peaceful nights were broken on April 16. The alert sounded at 9.3 p.m., and soon enemy aircraft were dropping flares, of a chandelier type with twelve lights. These came down S.E. of the river, and, drifting in our direction, started one of our worst nights to date. Woolwich, Old Kent Road, and the Elephant and Castle direction appeared to be receiving the brunt of the initial attack, but later it developed everywhere, and the Tower was in the thick of it.

By 9.45 fires were burning everywhere. Suddenly there was a swish of a bomb, followed by a vivid flash and a terrific crack. Out came the window frames, followed by the familiar sound of breaking glass. Blackout blinds were torn to threads, and there were frantic shouts of "Put those ——— lights out !" For seven hours pandemonium continued. It was at its worst between 3 and 4 a.m. Planes were coming in from all directions. Sometimes the barrage was heavy, sometimes not a gun could be heard. The prowling enemy was dropping his loads of death wherever he wished.

Against a starlit sky the spires and tall buildings of tragic London stood out in silhouette, heavy billows of smoke rising as the flames shot up. The night was red, but the red turned to white where incendiaries were falling. Many bombs seemed to screech right over us, and their impact would shake the ground like a jelly. With dawn the old Tower came grimly to life, its sleepless residents beginning all over again the task of clearing-up.

The next night of horror was May 10, in my opinion the fiercest raid of the War. The alert sounded at 11 p.m. and lasted for 6 hours and 50 minutes. Guns were soon in action, but at no time was the barrage very heavy ; and for long periods not a gun could be heard, although the sky was full of aircraft. As 33 planes were brought down, 29 of them by our fighters, it must be presumed the sky was left clear for the latter. A good job they made of it ! At 11.23 the first bomb fell, and from then they were too numerous to record.

BOMB-DAMAGED CEILING ABOVE THE TRAITOR'S GATE is here being repaired. Dating (it is believed) from the reign of Henry the Third, the arched entrance, facing the Thames, was originally known as the Water Gate. It became Traitor's Gate by reason of the fact that State Prisoners were brought to the Tower by that entrance.
Photo, Planet News

Warders and military personnel pounced on all incendiaries, and although there must have been at least 100 on the Tower during that night, no serious fires were started. H.E. bombs, too, whistled down. At 2.30 a.m. there were four terrific crashes, which blasted out windows and brought ceilings tumbling everywhere. Tower Pier had received a direct hit and was no more. A naval boat anchored to the pier sank with the pier on top of it, drowning several naval ratings.

From the ramparts we could see warehouses in Lower Thames Street burning furiously, Great Tower Street and Seething Lane all afire. Trinity Square looked in a bad way, also the Minories, St. Catherine's Dock House, and buildings behind the Mint. Once more the Tower was surrounded by fire. The blazing buildings stood out in stark relief, tongues of flame leaping from one place to another, the moonlit sky frequently blotted out by huge rolling billows of black or brown or white smoke.

When dawn arrived, practically all streets around the Tower were closed. People wishing to get to the west had to make a long detour. Miles of firemen's hoses lay everywhere, like huge serpents, making roads practically impossible for traffic. Men of the National Fire Service were struggling valiantly with their stupendous tasks, their faces smoke-blackened, their eyes bloodshot, their clothing drenched. Proudly I raise my hat to them ! It was the last big raid by piloted aircraft and no more serious damage was done to the Tower.

On May 17, 1941, at about 10.30 a.m., a Me.109 was brought into the Tower, followed by several cars and outriders. We, the warders, wondered who on earth our visitor was. It proved to be none other than Rudolf Hess, the Deputy Fuehrer ! He was imprisoned in the King's House, in the room in which Herr Gerlach, German Consul for Iceland, had been imprisoned from June to September 1940. The arrival of Hess gave us plenty of scope for speculation. Had he turned traitor to his country ? Had he brought us peace terms ? We were still guessing when, on the third day after his arrival, he was removed to other and distant quarters.

NEW FACTS AND FIGURES

FAMILIES of imprisoned anti-Nazis were expected to pay 1s. 6d. a day for the upkeep of the prisoner. When the prisoner's head was cut off they had to pay £15 for the cost of execution. Detailed bills were sent in, including such items as the washing off of blood, and the final cleaning, states United Nations War Crimes Commission.

A TYPICAL statement of accounts sent by the Court's Cashier in Berlin on February 15, 1943, addressed to the heirs and successors of Anton Slavik, former Director of the Brno Broadcasting Station, for the attention of his widow Marie : charge for death sentence, 300 marks ; charge for defence counsel, 81·96 marks ; cost of transport, 33·60 marks : cost of imprisonment for 986 days, 1,479 marks ; cost of execution including fee, last wish, travelling expenses and printing of poster, 145·15 marks. Widow Slavik had to pay £103 5s. for the death of her husband !

WAR figures in the provincial areas of Cologne, issued by the Control Commission for Germany in April 1946, show 10,000 people killed ; 18,000 injured ; 43,000 totally bombed out ; 8,934 houses completely destroyed, 54,375 partly demolished ; 260 factories and 11 mines destroyed ; 672 farms destroyed, 3,089 partly damaged ; 3,000 head of cattle killed as well as 2,190 sheep, 2,100 pigs and 8,971 horses. Considerable damage was done to 620 miles of road, 200 miles of railway and 35 miles of tramways ; 65 railway stations, 117 railway bridges, 228 road bridges and eight railway tunnels were also destroyed. Figures for the population do not include Cologne city, as records of casualties there are missing.

NET estimated cost of the British control of north-western Germany in the next 12 months is £80,000,000. Actual expenditure will be closer to £130,000,000, but German exports are expected to bring in £50,000,000, says The Times (April 1946). Food must be imported for the 21,500,000 Germans under British control.

GERMAN birth-rate declined by only 761,000 in the first four years of the War, compared with a decrease of over 3,000,000 in the First Great War, states the International Committee for the Study of European Questions. Population of Germany has increased to roughly 72,000,000, including minorities returning to the Reich from Czechoslovakia and elsewhere. Also about 2,000,000 prisoners are still to go back.

IN Britain there are now 146,000 prisoners of war allocated for work on the land— 111,000 Germans and 35,000 Italians. Before the end of 1946 the Government intend to make the total up to 200,000. Most of the Italians will have been sent home by the end of this summer and the additional men will be Germans.

Queen Mary at St. James's Park Bomb Site

WITHIN A QUARTER-MILE OF BUCKINGHAM PALACE a 1,000-lb. German delayed action bomb, dropped in St. James's Park on April 16, 1941, suddenly began "ticking" at the bottom of the 30-ft. shaft where R.E.s were working to remove it on April 24, 1946. Containing 600 lb. of T.N.T., the bomb was electrically detonated two days later by No. 2 Bomb Disposal Squad. Within 15 minutes of the violent explosion H.M. Queen Mary, in residence at Marlborough House, was inspecting the crater, which was about 40 feet across.

Photo, Keystone

Printed in England and published every alternate Friday by the Proprietors, THE AMALGAMATED PRESS, LTD., The Fleetway House, Farringdon Street, London, E.C.4. Registered for transmission by Canadian Magazine Post. Sole Agents for Australia and New Zealand: Messrs. Gordon & Gotch, Ltd.; and for South Africa: Central News Agency, Ltd.—May 24, 1946   S.S.   *Editorial Address:* JOHN CARPENTER HOUSE, WHITEFRIARS, LONDON, E.C.4.

Vol 10 *The War Illustrated* N° 234

SIXPENCE

JUNE 7, 1946

I WAS THERE

1588 H.M.S. VANGUARD 1946

THE ARMADA	1588	LOWESTOFT	1665
CADIZ	1596	FOUR DAYS BATTLE	1666
THE KENTISH KNOCK	1652	ST JAMES DAY	1666
DUNGENESS	1652	BARFLEUR	1692
PORTLAND	1653	QUEBEC	1759
THE GABBARD	16	THE NILE	1798
THE TEXEL	1653	JUTLAND	1916

FIRST COMMANDER OF H.M.S. VANGUARD, Captain W. G. Agnew, C.B., C.V.O., D.S.O. and Bar, R.N., on her deck has for background the displayed battle honours of his ship's predecessors. The first Vanguard helped to destroy the Spanish Armada, in 1588 ; and this, our most powerful battleship, is the ninth to bear the honoured name. Her gunnery, damage control, and radar equipment are unexcelled. The most comfortable mess deck in the Navy, electric labour-saving devices, and other amenities combine to make her a "happy ship." See also illus. pages 112-113. *Photo, Central Press*

Edited by Sir John Hammerton

NO. 235 WILL BE PUBLISHED FRIDAY, JUNE 21

Honours in Holland for Winston S. Churchill

FIRST FOREIGN STATESMAN TO ADDRESS THE NETHERLANDS PARLIAMENT, at The Hague, Mr. Churchill began his visit to the country by creating this precedent on May 9, 1946. After receiving the honorary degree of Doctor of Law at Leyden University (1), he is seen with Queen Wilhelmina (2) on a balcony of the Royal Palace, Amsterdam, acknowledging the people's tribute; with Princess Juliana's and Prince Bernhard's children (3); addressing the Netherlands Parliament (4). Seated on the dais are Mrs. Churchill (right) and Mary Churchill (left). PAGE 98

Secrets of the Italian Armistice

by FRIEDL ORLANDO
Formerly engaged on British Government Intelligence work concerning Italian affairs

THE date was August 19, 1943. Darkness was falling on Lisbon when a taxi stopped outside the British Embassy. Out stepped two civilians who, after a furtive glance down the road, rushed into the building. Some time later another taxi arrived, bringing two high-ranking Allied officers. Immediately they were shown into the private rooms of the British Ambassador, Sir Hugh Campbell, who received them with great cordiality. Did they think they had been watched?

No, their whole journey since they left Algiers had gone according to plan. The German agents in Portugal were apparently too busy gambling and amusing themselves at the Estoril. The Ambassador introduced the two civilians to the two officers, who, without saying a word, answered only with a short bow. More would have been too much: the two civilians were The Enemy.

Not a month had passed since Italy had rid herself of the Fascist regime, but more than ever she had become involved in the German alliance. Hitler, who only a few weeks earlier had assured Mussolini that he had no troops to spare for the defence of Italy, had, after Mussolini's fall, sent division after division across the Alps. He was blackmailing the new Government and forcing the recalcitrant Italians to fight on in his war.

The Predicaments of Badoglio

The Allies had freed Sicily, and an invasion of the mainland would not be far off. Marshal Badoglio, the new Head of the Italian Government, knew that the Italian people wanted peace with the Allies at any price. After Mussolini's fall the whole population of Italy had come out into the streets and squares to demonstrate for peace. They had taken it for granted that the fall of Fascism meant also Italy's breaking away from the Nazi alliance. Badoglio, terrified of the German reaction, had managed to suppress these demonstrations by martial law.

But he realized that his Government had received from the people only a short lease of life and that, if he did not soon come to terms with the Allies, he would be swept away as Mussolini was before him. But what if he entered into negotiations with the Allies, and the Germans got wind of it? The Nazis would instal a rabid Fascist Government, and Italy's last hope of freedom would have vanished for good. Mussolini was still safely guarded by the King's Carabinieri, but Farinacci or some other Nazi stooge would always be at hand to preside over a quisling Government if the Germans so desired. These conflicting arguments in Badoglio's mind made him hesitate and waver for some weeks; meanwhile, German troops were comfortably establishing themselves in the country. At last, giving way to the heavy political pressure from inside, Badoglio decided to contact the Allies.

On August 12, a delegation of the Italian Foreign Office left Rome on their way to Lisbon. There they were to receive the staff of the Italian Embassy in Santiago de Chile who, since diplomatic relations between Chile and Italy had been broken off, were returning to Rome. Attached to the Foreign Office delegation was a certain Signor Raimondo, an official of the Ministry of Foreign Exchange. "Signor Raimondo," whose real name was General Giuseppe Castellano, did not know a word of English; he therefore made friends on the train with a young Foreign Office official, Franco Montanari, a graduate of Harvard, and they became inseparable.

At Madrid on August 15 Castellano presented himself to the British Ambassador.

After he had shown Sir Samuel Hoare a letter of introduction from the British Minister to the Vatican, he was received with great cordiality. On hearing about the purpose of General Castellano's mission Sir Samuel expressed great satisfaction and cabled to Quebec, where President Roosevelt and Mr. Churchill were just meeting.

Two days later, Castellano and Montanari arrived in Lisbon as inconspicuous civilians. The British Ambassador there immediately asked General Eisenhower to send two of his personal representatives to hear the Italian delegates' proposals. An American, Major-General Walter Bedell Smith, and an Englishman, Brigadier Kenneth W. Strong, arrived on behalf of the Commander-in-Chief,

SIGNING THE ITALIAN ARMISTICE on September 3, 1943, at Cassibile, Sicily, Maj.-Gen. W. Bedell Smith, Eisenhower's Chief of Staff, is watched by (left to right) Commodore R. M. Dicks, Royal Navy; Maj.-Gen. W. Rooks, U.S.A.; Captain D. Hann, Brigadier Strong's A.D.C.; General Castellano, Italy; Brigadier K. W. Strong in background; and Signor Montanari, Italy.

Mediterranean. Their meeting with Castellano and Montanari, on August 19, lasted from 10.30 in the evening to 7.30 in the morning. It might as well have been shorter, for General Eisenhower's delegates simply presented the Italians with twelve terms of surrender apparently prepared and decided upon some time previously. It was a matter of "take it or leave it," a demand, in fact, for unconditional surrender.

THE terms stipulated immediate cessation of hostilities, immediate end of all help to the Germans, release of Allied prisoners, handing over of all Italian territory as a base for future Allied operations, handing over of the Italian Fleet and Air Force, the recalling of all Italian troops abroad, and postponement of all discussions on economic and political matters. The only bright spot for the Italians was a telegram, dispatched a few hours earlier by President Roosevelt and Mr. Churchill, promising that Italy's lot would be improved according to the measure in which she contributed to the war effort of the United Nations.

General Castellano was flabbergasted. His orders were to explain to the Allies that Italy wanted to drive the Germans out of the country, and to ask for Allied help; in short, he was to establish some kind of military collaboration. He tried to explain to the Allied officers that even if the Italian Government would accept the terms of

surrender they would not be able to fulfil them. How could they surrender territory which, though nominally Italian, was practically in German hands? How could they recall their divisions in the Balkans when these were surrounded by German troops and, in view of their lack of supplies, could not even hope to fight their way out?

The Allied answer was that all that was required of Italy was the fulfilment of the terms to the best of her ability. In Castellano's arguments and objections the Allied officers saw but an attempt to bargain for advantages, a sign that the Italians did not really mean business. Eventually it was decided that Castellano should return to Rome and submit the terms to his Government. A reply should be sent by radio to Algiers not later than August 30. He was given a radio transmitting and receiving set.

The departure of the diplomatic train which was to bring the staff of the Santiago Embassy to Rome was delayed. For four more days Castellano and Montanari had to hide in Lisbon, haunted by the fear of being discovered by German agents. When they finally boarded the train on August 23, the sealed envelope containing the terms of surrender was handed to the Ambassador to Chile as a matter of precaution. The Italian Minister in Lisbon told him that the papers contained extremely important information of a financial and commercial nature. And, in his ignorance, the good man carried them through stretches of German-occupied France. On the journey to Lisbon the diplomatic train had run into heavy bombings, but there were no air attacks on the homeward journey. The Allies took care that Castellano should arrive safely in Rome!

For more than two weeks the Italian Government had had no sign of life from Castellano. Fearing that he had been caught by German agents they had dispatched another delegate, General Zanussi. He was accompanied by a distinguished Allied prisoner, General Carton de Wiart, V.C., whom the Italians had set free as a sign of their good faith. The idea was not a very happy one: General Carton de Wiart was a very notable figure, tall, with a big moustache and with only one arm and one eye. It was a miracle that the mission escaped German notice. Moreover, the appearance of another Italian delegate at Lisbon raised new suspicions in the minds of the Allies, and doubts as to the authenticity of the first one. They were dispelled only when, on

August 27, Algiers received a radio message announcing Castellano's arrival in Rome.

Two days passed, during which King Victor Emmanuel, Marshal Badoglio, the Chief of the General Staff and a few trusted advisers, considered the Allied terms. The majority of the Cabinet Ministers did not even know that Badoglio had been in touch with the Allies. On August 31, General Castellano, equipped with a Government memorandum, was again dispatched to the Allied side. He arrived in Sicily by plane, and was received by General Smith and Brigadier Strong, who drove him to an open camp at Cassibile, near Syracuse.

Germans Ignorant of Armistice

In a tent erected in an olive grove Castellano submitted Badoglio's memorandum: the Italian Government, it said, would have been glad to accept the terms as they stood; but in view of the fact that Italy was a German-occupied country they needed guarantees of Allied military assistance. They asked for an Allied landing in force north of Rome, on the very date the Armistice would be announced, because Italian forces could not hold the capital against a German onslaught. In addition, they wanted to be informed some time in advance of the Armistice announcement and of the exact spot of the landing.

The Allies were surprised at what seemed to them highly unjustified curiosity on the part of the Italian Government. Castellano was sent back to Rome with the reply that Allied plans had already been worked out and could neither be altered nor discussed with the Italians. It was also hinted to Castellano that, if his Government found it so difficult to make up their minds, perhaps the Allies would assist them with some bombing of Rome and thus speed the process.

So when Castellano returned again to Sicily he brought the news that Italy was ready to accept the terms unconditionally. In the afternoon of September 3, 1943, the Armistice between Italy and the United Nations was signed in the olive grove near Cassibile. General Smith signed for the Allied Commander-in-Chief, General Castellano for Marshal Badoglio. Present at the ceremony were General Eisenhower and the civilian representatives of the British and United States Governments, Mr. Harold Macmillan and Mr. R. D. Murphy. However, at the moment of signature, the civilians left the tent to underline the purely military character of the instrument. Afterwards, when the officers stepped out of the tent, each broke an olive branch from the tree that shadowed the entrance.

The Armistice was signed, but the Germans did not know it. Nor did the Italian people, nor the majority of the Government. The Allies had agreed with Castellano that it should be announced simultaneously by the Allied Commander-in-Chief and Marshal Badoglio. As the announcement was to coincide with the main Allied landing in Italy, date and hour were to be chosen by General Eisenhower. Marshal Badoglio would be informed only a few hours earlier. The proclamation to the Italian people and Armed Forces which he was to read on that occasion had already been drafted and, with a few modifications, had been approved by General Eisenhower. But the Italian Government was working under a dangerous illusion: Castellano had assured them that from conversations with Allied officers in Sicily he had gathered that the Armistice would not be made public before September 12 at the earliest.

However, on the 7th the Italians were informed by Allied H.Q. that two American officers were on their way to Rome. They were Brigadier-General Maxwell Taylor, vice-commander of the U.S. parachute forces, and Colonel W. T. Gardiner, of the U.S. Air

Forces. They would disembark at night near Gaeta, and were to be taken to Rome immediately under the pretext that they were two Allied airmen who had crashed in the sea and been rescued.

On their arrival in Rome the two Americans asked to be shown to the Commander of the Rome Area, General Carboni. They had come to place themselves under his command. For this was the Allied plan: the Armistice would be announced the next day, September 8; simultaneously there would be an Allied landing in force at a place which they were still not authorized to specify. What they could say, however, was that an entire American parachute division was ready to take Rome by assault and defend the city

Colours: Black Bull with Red Horns and Hoofs on Yellow Background

11TH ARMOURED DIVISION

FORMED in the years between Dunkirk' June 1940, and D-Day, June 1944' and trained mainly in N. Ireland, the Division became one of the Allied armoured spearheads in the liberation of Europe. Commanded by Major-General G. P. B. Roberts, the Division landed on the Normandy beach-head on June 13, 1944, and two weeks later, June 26-27, fought its way across the river Odon to Hill 112, drove the enemy from it and withstood counter-attacks before being withdrawn.

In its second action, July 18-20, east of Caen, the loss of 115 tanks in one day was sustained, but the battle proved a vital factor in the subsequent Allied break-out from the beach-head.

In the historic Falaise Gap phase the Division, heavily engaged throughout, fought along the entire length of the pocket, exploited a weakly-held enemy flank and captured Beny Bocage, August 1. The clearing of the pocket continued, and the Division took Vassy, Flers, Putanges and Briouze before a junction with the Americans at Argentan on August 19.

THE closing of the Falaise Gap and the crossing of the Seine was the signal for the Division to start its spectacular dash to capture Amiens and the bridges over the Somme, August 31. Antwerp, 96 miles away, was reached within the next 26 hours and captured intact on September 4. At this point the Division had covered 340 miles in six days.

At Arnhem the Division played a subordinate role, but to the south, at Overloon, its first V.C. was recorded, won by Sgt. G. H. Eardley, K.S.L.I., on October 16 (see illus. pages 578 and 664, Vol. 8). In Feb.-March 1945, in the Reichswald salient, the Division assisted in throwing the Germans back across the Rhine at Wesel, and after crossing the Rhine, March 28, the second V.C. was awarded, to Cpl. E. T. Chapman, Monmouthshire Regt., April 2 (portrait in page 376, Vol. 9), in a grim struggle on Teutoburger Wald, overlooking the Dortmund-Ems canal.

OVERCOMING bitter opposition on the rivers Weser and Aller, the Division encountered the horrors of Belsen. The first British troops to reach the Elbe, elements in another characteristic dash took 70,000 prisoners, including 27 generals, at Lubeck, which was captured on May 2. The Division's entry into Flensburg, the taking of the Dönitz Government (May 23) and William Joyce (Lord Haw-Haw), was the culmination of a fighting record studded with outstanding achievements. The Division was disbanded in Germany, in March 1946.

against the Germans. But it was imperative that Italian troops should hold all airports in and around Rome for three or four nights to enable the entire division to land.

General Carboni was shocked. It was the first time he had ever heard of such a plan. If, as General Taylor hinted, Castellano had suggested it, he must have done so on his own initiative and without any proper knowledge of the facts. And the facts were that all airports were virtually in German hands, that the Italian troops were insufficiently trained, that they had not enough petrol, and that their ammunition would last for only two hours' fighting. General Carboni also appeared to hope that the Germans, when hearing of the Armistice, might voluntarily retreat—provided, of course, they were not attacked. This was the kind of wishful thinking which at the time was shared by many Italian and Allied officers, and was largely the cause of the subsequent disaster.

At three o'clock on the morning of September 8 the two Americans asked to be led to Marshal Badoglio, who, roused from sleep, confirmed Carboni's views. But to him the greatest shock was the imminence of the Armistice announcement. Having banked on a later date the Italian High Command had not yet done anything to inform the various H.Q.s as to the imminent change of alliance, and no instructions had been issued. Again, it had been the fear of the Germans finding out too early which had prompted them to leave everything to the very last moment. But, it now appeared, the very last moment had already passed. How could they hope, in the few hours that were left, to reach all the outlying commands, all the ships at sea?

Shameful Flight to Allied Camp

Badoglio sent an S.O.S. to Eisenhower, asking him to postpone the announcement. "Do you think the delay will be granted?" somebody asked General Taylor after the message had been dispatched. "Only if they happen to be in a very good mood over there," was the answer. General Taylor himself sent a two-word message to Algiers, "Situation innocuous"—the latter being the word agreed upon in case a cancellation of the parachutists' plan became necessary; and the planes ready for the take-off were taxied back into their hangars.

When he received Badoglio's telegram General Eisenhower was apparently not in "a very good mood." And even if he had been it would probably have been quite impossible to stop the great seaborne operation, already in progress. At 6.30 p.m. he announced the Armistice on Radio Algiers. And after some renewed wavering and consultation with the King, Marshal Badoglio followed suit one hour later.

At midnight, the Germans attacked the Italian troops protecting the capital. Next morning, the King, Marshal Badoglio, the High Command and most of the Ministers, were on their shameful flight into the safety of the Allied camp. But the citizens of Rome, supported by disbanded soldiers, fought a hopeless battle for two more days. The Allied forces were far off, engaged in deadly struggle on the beaches of Salerno. In order to have air-cover they had landed far south of the capital and could do nothing for its protection. And, instead of attacking with fifteen divisions, as the Italians had hoped, they had landed with only four in face of vastly superior German forces.

It was a bad beginning all round. Understandable yet fatal distrust on the part of the Allies, fear mixed with wishful thinking on the part of Badoglio, had produced a disastrous result. For the Allies it heralded a drawn-out and most bitter campaign, and for Italy the most tragic period in her history.

Royal Welch Fusiliers in Paris Victory Parade

WATCHED BY THE "BIG FOUR" FOREIGN MINISTERS, Paris celebrated the Victory anniversary on May 12, 1946, with a military parade (3). At the Arc de Triomphe were (1, left to right) M. Bidault, France ; Mr. Molotov, U.S.S.R. ; Mr. Bevin, U.K.; Mr. Byrnes, U.S. Representing the British Army, the Royal Welch Fusiliers were led by their mascot, Billy, and the Pioneer section (2) wearing aprons and shouldering picks—a mark of distinction granted by the Duke of Connaught in 1886 and shared by no other British regiment. PAGE 101

First Move Towards Self-Government in the Ruhr

ESTABLISHING DEMOCRACY IN WESTPHALIA, Germany, including the Ruhr, is the task of the British Military authorities and the German Provincial Advisory Council. The first meeting of the Council (2), at Münster, May 1946, was attended by Brigadier C. A. H. Chadwick, C.B.E., seen (I) inspecting the Guard of Honour.

FOLLOWERS OF NAZI IDEOLOGY, who fought fanatically for its survival are now, under Allied supervision, destroying the foundations upon which it was built—arms and ammunition. German prisoners of war (3) heave boxes of small arms ammunition over the side of a British amphibian "Duck" into the deep waters of the Worther See, in Southern Austria. N.A.A.F.I. gift shop in Hamburg (4) is besieged by British troops anxious to buy presents for their relatives in Britain. These shops are part of N.A.A.F.I.'s overseas service, offering a variety of articles at reasonable cost and thus preventing the fleecing of troops by black market traders. Wreckage of bombed railway lines and rolling stock at Dortmund has been cleared aside and the track repaired (5). PAGE 102

V.C.s Won in Conflict With Germans and Japs

Lieut. ALBERT CHOWNE
With superb heroism and self-sacrifice this officer of the 2/2 Australian Infantry Battalion, on March 15, 1945, near Wewak, New Guinea, silenced two Japanese machine-gun posts and, although wounded, accounted for two more Japanese before being killed.

Pte. T. STARCEVICH
Firing his Bren gun from the hip, Pte. Starcevich, of the 2/43 Australian Infantry Battalion, rushed four enemy machine-gun posts at Beaufort, North Borneo, on June 28, 1945. He killed 12 Japanese, his action resulting in the Allied objectives being attained.

Cpl. J. B. MACKEY
Of the 2/3 Australian Pioneer Corps, this Australian (right) was awarded a posthumous V.C. for a heroic exploit east of Tarakan, Borneo, on May 12, 1945. With rifle, tommy gun and bayonet, single-handed, he assaulted a hill feature to wipe out two Japanese machine-gun posts.

Lieutenant the Hon. C. FURNESS
Although wounded, this officer of the Welsh Guards (below) circled a German position at Arras, in May 1940, inflicting heavy losses before his carrier was knocked out. He then continued in hand-to-hand combat until he was killed. But the enemy had to withdraw, enabling wounded to be evacuated.

Pte. F. J. PARTRIDGE
This rifleman of the 8th Australian Infantry Battalion (top right), wounded three times and weak from loss of blood, attacked Japanese bunkers at Bougainville, Solomon Is., on July 24, 1945. His outstanding gallantry ultimately saved two patrols from annihilation.

Flt.-Lieut. D. S. A. LORD, D.F.C.
Determined to complete his mission of dropping supplies to our men at Arnhem on September 19, 1944, this R.A.F. pilot (right) continued to fly his burning aircraft through intense A.A. fire until the last container had been dropped. He then ordered his crew to abandon the aircraft before he crashed in flames to his death.

Pte. EDWARD KENNA, 2/4 Australian Infantry Battalion
Purposely drawing enemy fire towards himself, standing erect and firing his Bren gun, Private E. Kenna engaged Japanese machine-gunners at Wewak, New Guinea, on May 15, 1945, until his ammunition was spent. Grasping a rifle and displaying bravery of the highest degree he shot two of the enemy with successive rounds. He is seen above being congratulated by nurses and patients whilst recovering from wounds.

COLONIAL GUARDIANS OF THE ATLANTIC

By HARLEY V. USILL

DURING the bitterest periods of the war the vital importance of the Atlantic life-line was appreciated by every family in hard-pressed Britain. Once again we shall find British Colonial territories making their invaluable contribution to the eventual victory of the United Nations. Since we finished our last article in the Pacific (see page 83), we will enter the Atlantic by rounding Cape Horn, to be faced immediately by the Falkland Islands occupying a major strategic position between these two great Oceans.

The Falkland Islands lie about 300 miles east and north of the Straits of Magellan, which, before the opening of the Panama Canal, was the route round Cape Horn connecting the Atlantic and Pacific Oceans, and the westward highway to Australia and New Zealand. In the war of 1914-1918, and again during the Second Great War, the Falkland Islands proved invaluable as a base for fuelling, for communications, and for keeping a watch on the South Atlantic.

It was in the Falklands that Admiral Sturdee's ships were coaling when on the morning of December 8, 1914, the German squadron under Admiral von Spee appeared, having two months before destroyed a British squadron in the Pacific. Now, in the Battle of the Falklands, Von Spee and his ships were destroyed by Admiral Sturdee. In December 1939, after the Battle of the River Plate which drove the German pocket battleship Admiral Graf Spee to self-destruction off Montevideo, the British cruisers Ajax, Achilles and Exeter went to the Falklands, the nearest British territory, to land their wounded.

The approximate area of the group of islands which make up the Colony and its dependencies is 4,618 square miles, and the two main islands, East Falkland and West Falkland, are divided by Falkland Sound. Around them are about 200 smaller islands, and the two groups of dependencies to the south: South Georgia, the South Orkneys and South Sandwich Islands, and South Shetlands and Grahamsland.

The British West Indian Colonies

Before we cross the Atlantic to West Africa to complete our survey of the strategic importance of the British Colonial Empire, we must travel up the long east coast-line of South America to the British West Indian Colonies. These are a number of islands dispersed among the autonomous states of Cuba, Haiti and the Dominican Republic, and the French, Dutch and American Dependencies which lie in a great semi-circle dividing the Atlantic from the Caribbean Sea. In addition, British Honduras (Central America) and British Guiana (South America) though strictly speaking not in the West Indies, are for convenience included.

The Caribbean Sea was described by Admiral Mahan of the U.S. Navy as "the strategic key to two great oceans, the Atlantic and the Pacific." The islands which enclose the Caribbean command the central Atlantic, the approaches to the Panama Canal, and the Gulf ports of the United States. They lie on the sea and air routes between Europe and Central and South America, and America and Africa, and provide naval and air bases essential for the security of these routes. With the entry of the United States into the war, in 1941, the burden for the defence of this area became a joint responsibility of the British and American navies and air forces. In 1940, in exchange for 50 over-age destroyers, the United States had obtained from Britain the lease of land for 99 years free of all rent to build bases in six British West Indian Colonies (see p. 277, Vol. 3).

TO complete his survey of the strategic interlocking of the British Colonial Empire, the author turns to the Atlantic. Here the southern tip of South America was guarded during the War by the Falkland Islands, and the Panama Canal by the West Indian colonies, while West Africa provided air bases and ports for the maintenance of the sea-route round the Cape, as well as supplying vital raw materials after the loss of Allied possessions in Asia.

The British West Indian Colonies consist of the Bahamas, Barbados, British Guiana, British Honduras, Jamaica, the Leeward Islands, Trinidad and Tobago, the Windward Islands, and, in lonely solitude, but not strictly part of the group, Bermuda. The latter has been transformed by the war from a tourist centre into a fortress. The group of coral islands which form the colony lie 600 miles off the North American mainland, 677 miles from New York, 713 miles from Halifax (Nova Scotia), and about the same distance from the Bahamas.

It thus occupies a key position in relation to the eastern seaboard of the North American mainland, and to trade routes between Europe, the United States and Canada, and between North America and the Caribbean Sea. During 1940, Bermuda was a calling port for Atlantic convoys. The whole area was strategically vital to the Allied war effort. We shall return later to deal with the Caribbean at war.

Great Air Bases in West Africa

British West Africa, comprising Nigeria, the Gold Coast, Sierra Leone, the Gambia and the Mandated Territories of the Cameroons and Togoland, covers an area of over 500,000 square miles. From being strategically unimportant before the war, these widely separated Colonies became quite unexpectedly, in mid-1940, strategically of vital importance. When France fell, in 1940, the West African Colonies became enclaves in Vichy-controlled territory with men of Vichy stationed in Dakar. With the closing of the Mediterranean the whole area became a front-line defence. Broadcasting on August 8, 1943, Lord Swinton, the Resident Minister in West Africa, said:

> After the fall of France, the only way to get aircraft quickly to the danger spots in the Middle East was to fly them overland from West Africa to Egypt. That meant building great air bases in West Africa, and making a chain of airfields right across Central Africa. It will give you some idea of the work involved if I tell you that in Nigeria alone, working always against time, 30 airfields had to be built and maintained with all the necessary control buildings, camps and workshops. The air victories from Alamein to Tunis were the result. Not only that, but this African highway became the route for aircraft for Russia, for India and for China. In the Gambia, also most westerly of our African colonies, we built great airfields. These airfields in their turn were to prove of vital importance. During the early months of the campaign in North-West Africa, practically every aircraft that flew from America to that battle front came by these airfields in the Gambia.

But it was not only in the construction and maintenance of air routes that these colonies played such a vital part. West Africa felt the closing of the Mediterranean in another way. Ships for the Middle East had now to follow the long route round the Cape, and West Africa had to help to protect, shepherd and victual them. The chief ports in British West Africa are Bathurst, Freetown, Takoradi, Accra, Lagos and Port Harcourt. Bathurst can accommodate smaller types of ocean-going vessels. Freetown, about 400

miles south of Bathurst, is one of the finest natural harbours on the West Coast.

At Takoradi there is a well-equipped artificial deep-water harbour, the only one between Sierra Leone and Nigeria capable of giving complete shelter for ocean-going ships of large size. Accra is an open roadstead. Lagos, the main port of Nigeria, has deep-water quays and provides considerable accommodation for ocean-going vessels, and both here and at Port Harcourt there is a floating dock. From all the main ports of West Africa, with the exception of Bathurst, which is served mainly by river facilities, there are railway communications with the principal inland towns and trading centres.

Kept the Factory Wheels Turning

Added strategic importance was given to West Africa by the loss of the mineral wealth and natural resources of Burma, Malaya and the Netherlands East Indies. Almost overnight West Africa was called upon to make good some of the loss. Tin from Nigeria, manganese and bauxite from the Gold Coast, and iron ore from Sierra Leone, helped to keep factory wheels turning in Britain and America, with the added assistance of diamonds from the Gold Coast and Sierra Leone for the machine-tool industry. There can be no doubt, then, about the strategic value of West Africa in the war.

Before leaving the Atlantic Ocean mention must be made of St. Helena and Ascension Island. The former is an island 700 miles south-east of Ascension and 1,200 miles from the coast of Portuguese West Africa. Prior to the opening of the Red Sea route it was a port of call for much shipping to and from India and other parts of the Far East. In the Second Great War it again became important because of its position on the Cape route. Ascension Island, 1,000 miles south of Sierra Leone, is a Dependency of St. Helena, and is an important cable station.

In this survey of the strategic importance of the British Colonial Empire, with an area of 2,250,000 square miles, and distributed so widely over the world's surface, we have not been able to mention each individual colony. Many of those which have not been included, however, will be dealt with when we come to consider other aspects of the Colonial Empire at war. In particular, we shall introduce the High Commission Territories of Basutoland, Bechuanaland and Swaziland, but these do not fall into the general picture of colonies which played a vital strategic part in the war.

WE have now traced the strategic importance of British Colonies and Mandated Territories in the Mediterranean, the entrance to which is guarded by Gibraltar and its back door by Aden. We have seen the importance of our possessions in the Indian Ocean as a jumping-off ground for the first African campaign, as a supply route for the whole of the Middle East, as a second line of defence after the fall of Malaya, and finally as bases for hitting back at the Japanese. We have seen how the Falklands guarded the southern tip of South America and the West Indian Colonies the vital Panama Canal. And, finally, we have placed the four West African Colonies in perspective in relation to the whole strategic pattern.

In peacetime these far-flung British Colonial territories were part and parcel of a British Commonwealth and Empire devoted to the arts of peace. When war came, their very existence and disposition enabled the life-lines of liberty to be kept open until the Allied nations could eventually muster the necessary strength to deliver the death blow to the aggressors.

Gardens Commemorate the People's Courage

THE MAGNIFICENT SPIRIT OF THOSE WHO ENDURED the war-years in London and Plymouth is commemorated by Gardens of Remembrance. Within the roofless framework of St. Andrew's Church, Plymouth (1), bombed in March 1941, lawns and gay flower-beds have taken the place of the pews of yore, providing a colourful and fragrant setting for peaceful summer services.

The forecourt of St. James's Church, Piccadilly, is the site of London's own Garden. After a dedication service conducted by the Bishop of London, Her Majesty Queen Mary, on May 12, 1946, unlocked the decorative wrought-iron gates (2) opening into the brightly planted enclosure (3) wherein are seats, in the Wren style, made from oak more than a century old. A board bears the inscription : "The Garden on this bomb-damaged site was given by the late Viscount Southwood on behalf of The Daily Herald to commemorate the courage and fortitude of the people of London in the Second World War, 1939-1945."

Photos, The War Illustrated, *Gill, Topical*

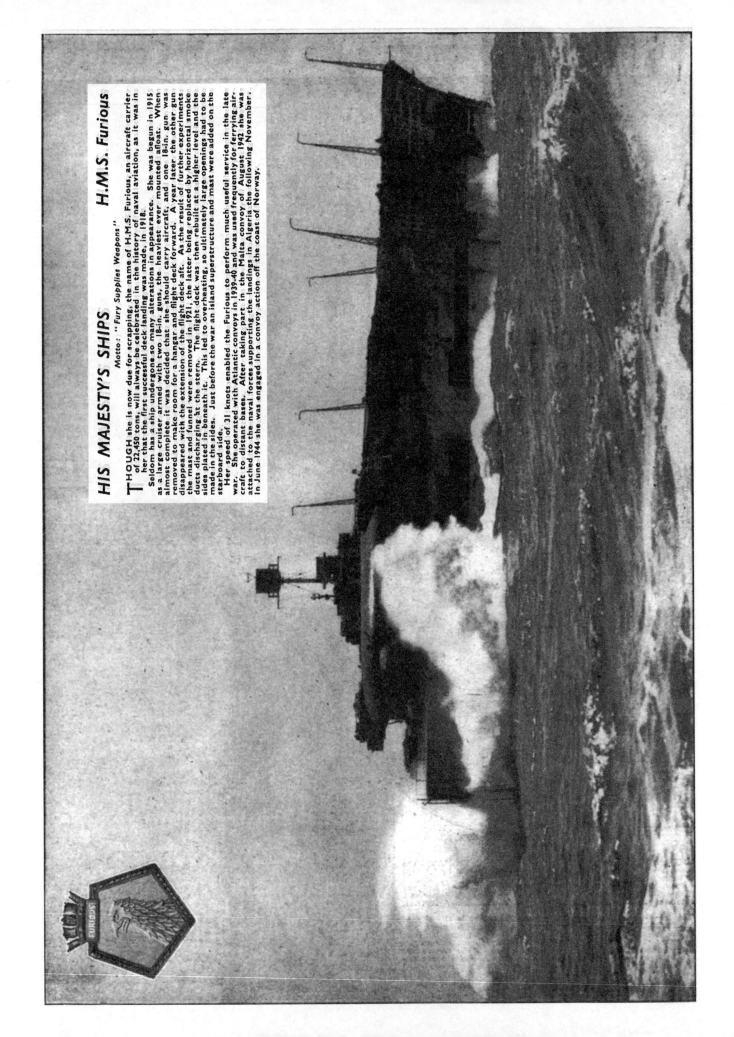

HIS MAJESTY'S SHIPS   H.M.S. Furious

Motto: "Fury Supplies Weapons"

THOUGH she is now due for scrapping, the name of H.M.S. Furious, an aircraft carrier of 22,450 tons, will always be celebrated in the history of naval aviation, as it was in her that the first successful deck landing was made, in 1918.

Seldom has a ship undergone so many alterations in appearance. She was begun in 1915 as a large cruiser armed with two 18-in. guns, the heaviest ever mounted afloat. When almost complete it was decided that she should carry aircraft, and one 18-in. gun was removed to make room for a hangar and flight deck forward. A year later the other gun disappeared with the extension of the flight deck aft. As the result of further experiments the mast and funnel were removed in 1921, the latter being replaced by horizontal smoke ducts discharging at the stern. The flight deck was then rebuilt at a higher level and the sides plated in beneath it. This led to overheating, so ultimately large openings had to be made in the sides. Just before the war an island superstructure and mast were added on the starboard side.

Her speed of 31 knots enabled the Furious to perform much useful service in the late war. She operated with Atlantic convoys in 1939-40 and was used frequently for ferrying aircraft to distant bases. After taking part in the Malta convoy of August 1942 she was attached to the naval forces supporting the landings in Algeria the following November. In June 1944 she was engaged in a convoy action off the coast of Norway.

The Reconnaissance Corps

by Lieut. J. L. TAYLOR

IN the autumn of 1940 the Reconnaissance Corps was an idea born of something near desperation. The Infantry Divisions, who had been served before Dunkirk by Mechanized Cavalry Regiments, were left without any reconnaissance arm at all when these Cavalry Regiments were taken for the fast-growing Armoured Divisions.

Experiments were made by some commanders in furnishing a reconnaissance unit from within the Division. It was soon clear that makeshift measures were inadequate :

reconnaissance had always been of prime importance in war and there was no reason to suppose that in the fast mobile warfare to come it was to be less important. On the contrary, it seemed that, as war itself became more swift, the more essential was quick and accurate information to the General's battle-map.

It was decided that reconnaissance was a job for experts, specially trained in a new technique required by new conditions. So the Reconnaissance Corps was formed as the " cat's whiskers " of the infantry, in the streamlined army being fashioned at high speed north of the Channel. The need was for a body of men of more than usual intelligence, endurance and enterprise. With every branch of the Army calling for the same

TWENTY Regiments of the new Corps were taking shape by the spring of 1941—in their time to serve with great distinction in the Far East, North Africa, Sicily, Italy, Greece, and in the sweep from Normandy and North Italy to the line of victory in Europe. Fighting for information, attacking, holding long front-line stretches, they could claim at the end that there was no more highly organized and efficient branch of the British Army than the " young " Reconnaissance Corps.

〜〜〜〜

thing, the Corps yet managed to lay a firm foundation of the right type of soldier.

Some came from the tough Brigade Anti-Tank companies, fresh from the star role in Belgium and France. Many were volunteers who liked the sound of the job. In some cases (that of the 5th Gloucestershire Regiment) infantry battalions with good records were converted en bloc. By the spring of 1941 the Corps was taking shape, and the nuclei were visible of the twenty regiments that, in their time, were to serve in the Far East, in North Africa, Sicily, Italy, Greece, and in the sweep from Normandy and North Italy to the line of victory in Europe.

A Reconnaissance Regiment was planned as a self-contained unit, fast moving on wheels and tracks, with a heavy punch in fire-power. It was visualized that information would frequently have to be fought for,

which turned out to be quite correct. A detailed wireless network covered the Regiment and linked it straight back to Division. By necessity, much of this, in the early days, was accepted by token, and had not materialized very far when the Corps first went into battle.

Not counting the luckless 18th Regiment, which arrived at Singapore, without its vehicles, just in time to be surrendered to the Japanese early in 1942, the first Regiment to go into action was the 50th. They were the old 4th Northumberland Fusiliers, who can claim to be the forerunners of the Corps since they operated experimentally in Belgium and France on reconnaissance work, largely with motor-cycles. At Knightsbridge (Libya), without their motor-cycles (not much use in the desert) and without much of the equipment which was on the production lines for Reconnaissance, they had no chance against the German armour which hit their defensive positions in May 1942.

That was part of the general bad start. From then on the Corps fought with continued success, learning the new job, calling for, and getting, ever improved equipment. There grew up, too, a remarkable morale. Reconnaissance work in the field had no room for passengers. Every man counted, was trusted, made decisions in tight corners— and by the nature of the job there were many tight corners. Then the Corps itself was comparatively small and drew from the same OCTU, Holding Regiment and Training Regiment. There was very quickly a strong

RECCE MORTAR DETACHMENT IN THE ANZIO BEACH-HEAD, Italy, fire into a gully at suspected German troop movements. Two members of the detachment are seen taking cover as the weapon dispatches its missile towards the enemy. In the swaying battle in the beach-head early in 1944 the 1st Reconnaissance Regiment demonstrated its fighting qualities and versatility as a " thin red line "—a role outside the purpose for which the Corps had been formed three years previously. *Photo, British Official*

CAPTAIN R. G. A. BEALE, M.C., of the 1st Reconnaissance Regiment (right) greets an American officer on the bridge marking the place of the Anglo-American link-up following the Allied break-out from the Anzio beach-head in May 1944. Captain (then Lieut.) Beale's own narrative of the exploit which gained him his decoration appears below. *Photo, British Official*

family feeling in Reconnaissance, for that reason. What exactly was the job ? Come with Captain (then Lieutenant) R. G. A. Beale, M.C., of the 1st Reconnaissance Regiment, on the armoured car outing from the Anzio beach-head early in 1944 which gained him his decoration. Dawn is just breaking.

" We rush the bridge and get over against light opposition. Observe an 88-mm. gun to my right. Lucky enough to get a direct hit on gun and crew with H.E. A mile farther on we see movement in a house 800 yards to the left. A Boche officer comes out. He is joined by six or seven more. We open with machine-guns and see two fall. The remainder run for the house. We next see half a dozen Boches running for some vehicles. We get three more. Push on, and my leading car captures a motor-cyclist D.R. who nearly falls off with surprise. His bulging dispatch case is just what we want.

" We edge round the next bend and come in sight of our main objective, a railway bridge over the road. A German sentry is leaning against the wall with his helmet off and his rifle by his side. He is obviously bored with life. He isn't much longer. He dies still leaning against the wall. By this time more troops are appearing. We have an excellent shoot as they run for cover up the bank. We back the cars round a corner out of sight, but still keeping the bridge under observation. Very soon we see a car ap-

proaching from a side road. It contains a German engineer officer and he is going to blow the bridge. My gunner kills him. Seven more men try to blow the bridge but they are all mown down.

" We are now ordered by wireless to visit another bridge about a quarter-mile farther on. I give my leading car covering fire. A grenade is thrown on him from the railway bridge, but bounces off the armour. As my own car goes through we get another grenade. A burst of Spandau fire spatters our armour. In the turret I do a 180 degrees traverse and see two men with grenades in their hands. If I let them off they will undoubtedly blow the bridge and we won't be able to return. We get clear and check up on our last mission. By now all hell has broken loose. Every type of weapon is being fired at us. We skid round and make with all speed for a more congenial atmosphere . . ."

Chasing the Boche Round Cap Bon

The patrol had plenty of excitement after that. It eventually saved the bridge for the passage of our own troops, and is one of the many such small actions which fit together to make the history of the Corps. The idea of having to fight for information was never far wrong. The Corps had seen a good deal of action before the Anzio beach-head. The 44th started a career of distinction with a nasty mine-lifting assignment at Alamein in the autumn of 1942. Later they had a better reconnaissance role in Tunisia.

The 56th Regiment came in at Algiers in November 1942, followed later in the campaign by the 46th, 1st and 4th. The 56th had the envy of the rest of the Corps for their opportunity, as first arrivals, to make the famous run from Algiers to within 20 miles of Tunis, in four days. These five Regiments all contributed to the victory in Tunisia, where the Corps finished strongly, in May 1943, by chasing the Boche at high speed round Cap Bon. The narrow mountain roads of Sicily, flanked with steep drops and lava walls, prevented cross-country movement in most places. The 5th Reconnaissance Regiment had a tough time of it there in the summer of 1943. The other Regiment in Sicily was the 56th.

The Reconnaissance Corps really started to go with the invasion of Italy. The 5th were recompensed with a most exciting dash up the west coast, being at one time 200 miles in front of the main body of the Division, meeting trains on peacetime schedules, one of which they captured and co-opted.

The 1st Air Landing Reconnaissance Squadron, later to drop at Arnhem, landed at Taranto, September 9, 1943, and raced up the east coast, with the 56th Regiment. At the same time the 46th and the 44th went in to the hot reception at Salerno. It was early in the next year that the 1st,

GENERAL SIR BERNARD C. T. PAGET, G.C.B., D.S.O., M.C., since 1943 Colonel-Commandant of the Reconnaissance Corps, talks to a member of one of the Corps units undergoing training in Palestine before taking part in the North African campaign. General Paget was at the time Commander-in-Chief Middle East. PAGE 108 *Photo, British Official*

Recce Corps on the Victory Trail in Europe

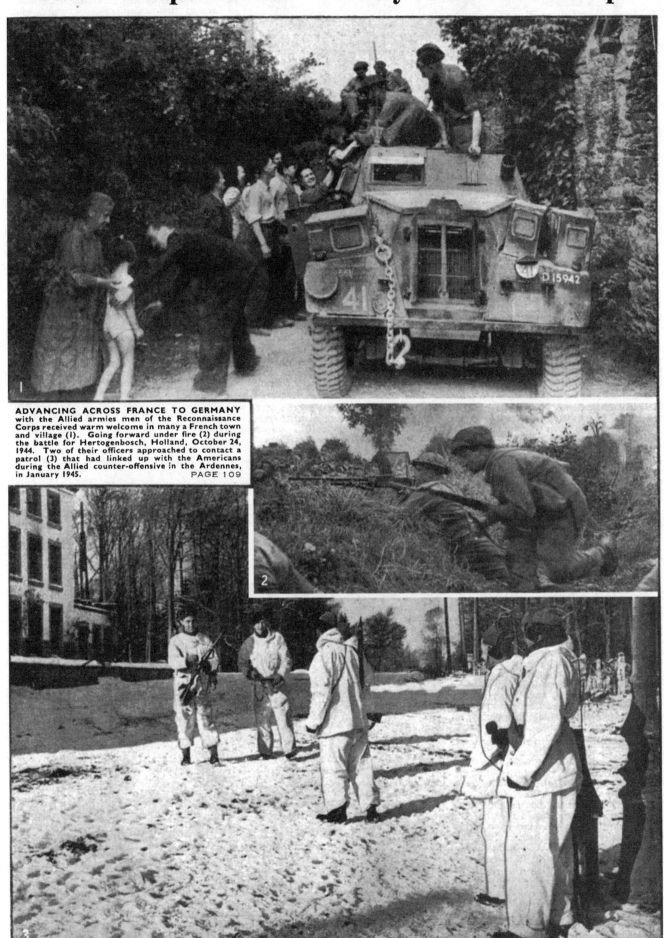

ADVANCING ACROSS FRANCE TO GERMANY with the Allied armies men of the Reconnaissance Corps received warm welcome in many a French town and village (1). Going forward under fire (2) during the battle for Hertogenbosch, Holland, October 24, 1944. Two of their officers approached to contact a patrol (3) that had linked up with the Americans during the Allied counter-offensive in the Ardennes, in January 1945. PAGE 109

TASTING THE FRUITS OF VICTORY had a double meaning for these men of the Reconnaissance Corps in the Far East. Enjoying melons, they also had the satisfaction of having played a big part in the fall of Mandalay, in March 1945. The 2nd Regiment had helped in the relief of Kohima, in May 1944, and Imphal in June, which preceded the final Allied advance. *Photo, British Official*

forgetting its specific role as a Reconnaissance unit, as many Regiments have cheerfully done in emergency, became the "thin red line" at Anzio. When the Italian campaign slowed up, the Regiments, now supplemented by the 4th, manned observation posts and patrolled for information.

Meanwhile, at home, D-Day was building. Seven Reconnaissance Regiments practised waterproofing, embarkation drill and the "break-through" role planned for the second phase of the operation. They were the 3rd, 15th Scottish, 43rd, 49th West Riding, 53rd Welsh, 59th and 61st Reconnaissance Regiments. From Normandy, where some of them, notably the 61st, greatly distinguished themselves on the beaches, all seven regiments got their break-through.

The run to the Seine, across the Belgian border and up to the line of the winter of 1944, was the perfect Reconnaissance task, a field day shared with the Armoured Recce Regiments. At different times each Regiment came into its own. For most of them contact with the enemy was continuous, and casualties on occasion were heavy. But the work done was a final justification of the idea born in the dark days of the war.

Among Floundering German Armies

The Infantry Divisions found that pursuit of the still cunning Boches was greatly aided by armoured tentacles feeling in front of the advance. When opposition was not too heavy the Reconnaissance Regiments cleared it out of the way in short sharp battles. Otherwise, troops of carriers and armoured cars pin-pointed and held the enemy for attack by larger forces.

That was the classic role. There were others. The 49th, early on, became embroiled with heavy tanks (and when one calls Reconnaissance "armoured," that did not mean against much more than small arms fire). Their Anti-Tank Troop and P.I.A.T.S. disposed of four in quick time. In the Falaise Gap, in August 1944, the 53rd set up something of a record by capturing 4,800 prisoners in 36 hours. The 52nd Lowland Regiment, of the Mountain Division, landed (ironically) in the flattest part of Holland, in September, just after the opening of the Eindhoven corridor, which was constantly being cut. One of their Squadrons fought to free it.

When winter came the mobility and high fire-power of the Reconnaissance Regiments enabled them to hold long stretches of the front. The 3rd were for several months

responsibile for an icy, inhospitable stretch of the river Maas, north-east of Helmond. The 49th had an equally gruelling winter, continually in contact with lively German patrols along the river west of Nijmegen, and in the "island"—the flooded tract north of Nijmegen on the road to Arnhem.

When Rundstedt achieved his "bulge," in December 1944, the 43rd, the 52nd, the 53rd and the 61st Reconnaissance Regiments were among the troops rushed south to deal with it. The part played by the 61st was especially gallant. They had just handed in all their vehicles prior to disbanding with their Division. Transport and fighting vehicles were thrown back at them in considerable chaos and hurry, and they went off to do their last job as well as they had done all their others. For similar "high-level" reasons the 59th Reconnaissance Regiment was also disbanded before the end.

The hard fight to the Rhine was a second edition of Normandy, but the break-through afterwards went faster and was thick with

incident as the Regiments found themselves among the floundering German armies which were uncertain whether to fight or surrender. In some places resistance was tough and the always hard-worked 15th Scottish did a fine job in the last lap. The 5th Regiment, brought up from Italy, also had a run in this campaign before the end.

No picture of the Corps' history is complete without mention of the 1st Air Landing Reconnaissance Squadron's brief but glorious stand at Arnhem in September 1944. The 2nd Derbyshire Yeomanry, though not officially in the Corps, served with the Regiments as the Reconnaissance unit of the Highland Division, and both sides are proud of the ties existing with this Regiment.

The Corps has also served in the Far East. The 45th Regt., before they could go into action in a reconnaissance role, were turned into a Long-Range Penetration Group under General Wingate and harried the Japanese deep in Burma when that part of the world was not shown as belonging to us. And no Reconnaissance Regiment has a longer, more gruelling or more glorious battle history than the 2nd Regiment. After two years of training in the Far East they were in the relief of Kohima, May 1944, and of Imphal in June, and were finally at the head of the advance which in 1945 opened the way to Mandalay and Rangoon.

Officers of the Corps have been distinguished with more than a dozen awards of the D.S.O. and nearly 100 awards of the Military Cross. The bravery of Other Ranks in the field—and Reconnaissance work requires much from the judgement and daring of junior leaders—has been recognized by the award of well over 160 Military Medals.

At home, the Holding Regiment was the 80th (later 38th), at Morecambe. The Reconnaissance Training Centre was at Catterick. General Sir Bernard C. T. Paget, G.C.B., D.S.O., M.C., has been Colonel-Commandant of the Corps since 1943. The "family," now with a disposition to put its feet on the mantelpiece and certainly with many hair-raising yarns to spin, owns a Reconnaissance Corps Comrades Association of over 14,000 members, with a big peace-time programme of reunion and mutual aid.

CHANGING OF THE GUARD outside the 53rd Division Headquarters in Hamburg, by men of the Corps who a few days previously had been engaged in hard fighting. Thus they carried from battlefield to parade the Corps' tradition for smartness and organization—and fighting—built up through a short but very active history. *Photo, British Official*

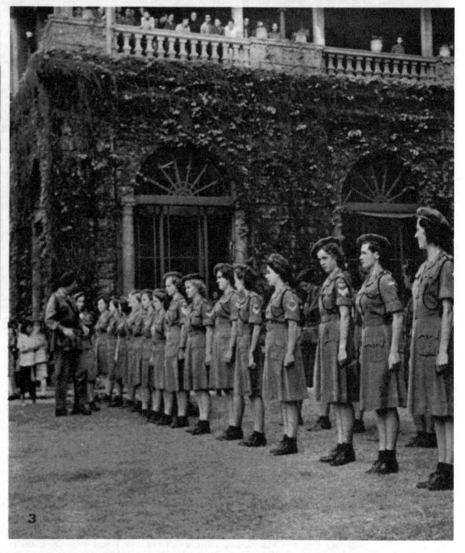

Occupation Troops Ready for Japan

First contingent of the British and Indian Occupation Troops for Japan marched through the streets of Kowloon, Hongkong, on March 23, 1946, before leaving for their Occupation duties. They were led by the Queen's Own Cameron Highlanders (1) carrying the King's and Regimental Colours, and the salute was taken by Major-General F. E. Festing, C.B.E., D.S.O., G.O.C. Land Forces Hongkong. Included in the march-past were members of the W.A.S.(B)—Women's Auxiliary Services (Burma)—seen parading for inspection (3). Major-General D. T. Cowan, C.B., C.B.E., D.S.O., M.C. (2, right), G.O.C. the British Indian Division, chats with Major-General Festing (left).

Photos, British Official

Britain's £11,000,000 H.M.S. Vanguard—

Through quiet rural scenery passes the 42,500-ton Vanguard (1), our latest and greatest battleship, 830 feet in length.   Piloted from the fitting-out basin at John Brown's Clydebank shipyard, on May 2, 1946, down the tricky 14-mile channel, she parted with her tugs at Greenock and sailed under her own power into the Estuary.   Seen, looking aft, are four of her eight 15-in. guns (2) with the ship's badge displayed on their tompions;   her secondary armament comprises sixteen 5·25-in. guns.

Photo

—*Passes Down the Clyde to Her Trials*

Press,

Princess Elizabeth launched the Vanguard in November 1944 (see illus. page 519, Vol. 8) and on May 12, 1946, revisited her for the blessing ceremony at Greenock, the ship then proceeding to carry out gunnery trials off the north of Ireland, followed by engine and steaming trials in the Firth of Clyde. Beneath her 15-in. guns a Marine bugler sounds off (3); the liner Queen Elizabeth is in the background, and again—being repainted—by the Vanguard's side (4). See also page 97.

Reopening of South Bridge at Cologne

Attacked by R.A.F. Typhoons, the South Bridge across the Rhine at Cologne was wrecked on January 6, 1945. Reconstruction was commenced, under the supervision of Royal Engineers, in June 1945, almost unprecedented floods and other difficulties—including the lifting of two large spans from the riverbed, and shortage of material and labour—delaying the work for some time. It was reopened to rail traffic on May 3, 1946, and renamed South Bridge by Lieut.-General G. Thomas, acting C.-in-C. of the B.A.O.R. A single track providing communication between the goods marshalling yards on the east and west sides of Cologne, a through route for passenger traffic, an important link between Germany and the Channel ports, it can take approximately 40 trains each way daily ; when permanently reconstructed it will be capable of taking 72. The bridge rebuilt (above), Lieut.-General Thomas cuts the tape (left) to let the first train run through.

Photos, New York Times Photos

Europe's Wartime Capitals in 1946

BERLIN

by
KENNETH HARE-SCOTT
Serving with the
Control Commission in Berlin

I AM writing in the heart of the city which a year ago (May 1, 1945) was enclosed in the iron grip of Russian encirclement. Today a visit to the outskirts of Berlin and beyond will still reveal the ferocity of that fighting, for the roads to Gatow, Potsdam and the Reich Autobahn pass through shell-torn woods. Overturned rusty vehicles are everywhere—on the pavements in the city, in the ditches and even crowning the rubble of shattered buildings.

The Allies working in Berlin, and in the four zones, are engaged upon the framing and implementation of an administration to last for many years. In Berlin the Army, commonly known as B.T.B. (British Troops Berlin), comprises the military garrison and generally administers the military aspects of control and development in the British sector. The Commander is Major-General E. P. Nares, and the formation includes battalions of the Dorsetshire Regiment and the Life Guards.

The Control Commission at Work

The executive administration of the British sector, coming under the control of B.T.B., rests with " Military Government," divided into several departments each closely linked with its corresponding number in the Control Commission which extends its authority not only to the British sector but throughout the whole of the British zone. In course of time the Control Commission, which is the civilian element of our administration in Germany, will expand whilst the military organization will correspondingly diminish. The quadripartite rule of Berlin is vested in the "Kommandatura"—a Council of the Four Powers, which designs the common policy for governing the capital.

Many officers who have been released from the Services and who have proved their worth whilst serving with the British Administration in Germany are returning to civilian appointments in the Control Commission. The work of the Commission is in many senses highly specialized and only through experience and experiment can the British plan, which is generally considered the best of the four Occupying Powers, be developed to provide a just and progressive administration.

The meeting-place for quadripartite Conferences and Committees is the A.C.A. (Allied Control Authority) Building in the American sector. Once the People's Court of the Nazi judicial system, the A.C.A. has seen many famous trials, including the Reichstag Fire trial and that of the high-ranking German officers who took part in the anti-Hitler plot in July 1944. Now Washington, Paris, Moscow and London, geographically miles apart, are brought together in this building through the work of the many Committees which determine the future administration of Germany.

EACH of the Four Powers has its administrative headquarters in its sector, the French at Frohnau, the Americans at Omgus, the British at Wilmersdorf and the Russians at Karlshorst (see illus. in page 116). Here the individual work of the Nation is carried out and national hospitality extended. There is a free and easy exchange of social intercourse, and the friendship and understanding which have resulted do much to facilitate the progress of unified government.

Berlin is a city of ruins, and it is expected that 20 or 30 years must elapse before the rubble is cleared and the way prepared for rebuilding (see illus. in page 117). So many houses have been severely damaged that it is a common sight to see home-made kitchen chimneys jutting through the walls in place of the normal chimney which ceased to exist when the upper part of the house "disappeared." A surprising number of shops still display their scanty and exorbitantly-priced wares at the foot of buildings gutted by fire or torn in the upper storeys by bomb or shell blast.

Among the very few articles which can be bought are various forms of woodwork, pictures, wrought iron lamps and ornaments, and a limited amount of perfume and cosmetics at fantastic prices. Clothing is very scarce and usually only sold by private bargain. Food is, of course, virtually unobtainable except on a ration card—the most precious possession of every Berliner. If lost it is nearly impossible to obtain another—a rule which has been rigidly enforced in order to curb black market activities and the cornering of vital supplies.

On the whole, Berliners show few signs of undernourishment—certainly none, as yet, of starvation. It may be that behind the walls some suffering is endured of which those who go about give no indication. The children look well and happy, and in the warm sunshine they play in the streets and gardens with all the life and laughter of children in England. There are exceptions—and occasional signs of physical malnutrition—but in no greater proportion (visibly) than in a large industrial town at home.

Derelict Areas Producing Food

Pavement cafés are appearing, and here the few uninteresting drinks allowed to Germans can be bought. Cigarettes and pipe tobacco are unobtainable, but the underground traffic in cigarettes needs few signposts to direct it along the channels of profitable barter, and so it is untrue to say that Berliners do not get a smoke occasionally. A postal service for Germans was introduced on April 1, 1946, within the four sectors of Berlin and with the outside world —except Spain and Japan. Telephone communication is allowed only to those engaged upon official (and approved) business.

Transport facilities are confined to trams—the usual Continental string of two or three linked together—and the Underground. Both are very overcrowded, owing to the shortage and antiquity of the equipment. There is no petrol ration for Germans, unless their duties are connected with Administrative Departments. Bicycles are plentiful on the streets ; and the horse-drawn conveyance is seen frequently, but this can last only as long as the under-fed horses survive.

In a city where devastation is as complete as it is possible to imagine—certainly eclipsing anything known in our cities at home—the work of the allotment holders, the ploughing of the Tiergarten and the extensive seed-sowing in the nurseries, combine to represent one of the most visibly constructive aspects of the work of the Military Government and Control Commission in the British sector. Land cultivation is proceeding at every point in the city where an open space exists, transforming derelict areas into the familiar patchwork landscape of the allotment garden, or, as in the case of the Tiergarten, a vast space now ploughed up for a crop of potatoes. A tour of the Berlin farms does not embrace the green pastureland of the Englishman's conception. They are smelly, sometimes dirty, promenades of busy thoroughfares and backyards. I visited four in the heart of the city, having in all a total of nearly 50 head of cattle. These live out their lifetime in stalls, and are fed on straw, potato and beet peelings. Their only exercise seems to be getting up and lying down, and as a result of this confined existence the quality of the milk is low, although the quantity varies considerably.

A FEW weeks ago an exhibition was opened in Schluter Strasse called "Heute im England" (In England Today). In an attractively arranged series of large photographs Berliners were shown the British way and conditions of life. A short film show, and a room devoted to the Empire, added interest to an exhibition which has drawn large daily attendances. Later, it will tour the main towns in the British zone. For entertainment the Germans have opera, ballet, and a number of theatres and cinemas, and also the zoo.

The living conditions of the British Service men and women, and civilians of the Control Commission, are on the whole good. Officers and Other Ranks live in blocks of flats or buildings suitably apportioned two or three to a room or flat. There are a number of messes, large and comfortably equipped, scattered throughout the British sector, and in the early days officers' messes were opened on the fringe of the Grunewald forest—later to be allotted to wives and families. There are several clubs which cater for different purposes, and Other Ranks make full use of the Rothwell Arms, the Winston, the Red Shield, the Bristol, and Marlborough —examples of places where people can relax and find all amenities for amusement.

Officers have the Embassy, a large house in its own grounds which during the War was the combined Embassy of Germany's satellite countries—and before that the home of a Berlin chain-store magnate—luxuriously furnished and with painted ceilings, tapestries and plenty of gilt. The Embassy is a popular place for dinner and dancing. Another is the Blue White—the Roehampton of Berlin, and once the city's select sports club. Here one can play tennis on any one of 16 courts, bathe, and dine but not dance.

No Normal Existence for Anyone

Working in Berlin's depressing surroundings, it is refreshing (and necessary) to escape sometimes, although living in the heart of the Russian zone precludes motor trips into the countryside. The two "lungs" where one can breathe fresh air, sail, swim and walk, are at Gatow for officers and the Southend for Other Ranks. Both are on the outskirts of the city, overlooking a large lake, well out of sight of Berlin's ruins, and set among surroundings of cornfields, woods and orchards. Ballet, opera, a theatre and cinemas complete the cycle of entertainment.

One cannot pretend that life in Berlin is a normal existence for anybody. It cannot be so for a long time to come, and it is more than ever necessary for those whose work for months and possibly years ahead will be in the city to create a way of living which will be consistent with our task of administration and the well-being of the British community. The first year has seen remarkable progress in the establishment of a sound administration and steady living conditions for our people. There have been and will be difficulties ; but they will not deter the authorities, and the reputation which the British people now enjoy in Berlin and in their zone will be enhanced as life settles down and the work of reconstruction proceeds.

BERLIN: After Thirteen Months of Peace

ORDER IS EMERGING OUT OF CHAOS, though even the women of Berlin must toil in order that all bomb debris shall be removed (1).   On the roof of an air-raid shelter, now used as a hospital, casualities convalesce (2).   In the Russian zone trotting races at Karlshorst (3) help to pass the time. The bomb damaged tomb of the 1914-18 Unknown Warrior is a reminder of other troublous times (4).   A street musician attracts attention with his helmet (5)—as worn by the Kaiser's Guards in the First Great War.   PAGE 116   *Photos, R. Hammond, Keystone, Associated Press, The Daily Mirror*

Remnants of Past Imperial Glory : BERLIN

SHELL OF THE REICHSTAG STANDS DESOLATE in the Tiergarten (top), lately the centre of Berlin's black market, and now ploughed for crops. Built in the 1880's, as seat of the Imperial Parliament, the Reichstag was gutted by fire in 1933, supposedly by Communists but actually through "arrangement" contrived by the Nazi Government. The famous Palace Bridge (bottom) over the River Spree, near the former Imperial Palace, was wrecked by the Germans in a desperate attempt to halt the Russian advance in April 1945. See also page 115. *Photos, Keystone*

ALLIED MILITARY FORCES PARADED THROUGH TRIESTE on May 2, 1946, to commemorate the first anniversary of two notable events—the surrender of the German armies in Italy to Field-Marshal Viscount Alexander, and the occupation of Trieste by New Zealanders under the command of General Sir Bernard Freyberg, V.C. The 2nd Battalion of the Queen's Own Cameron Highlanders, seen passing the saluting base on the Piazza Unita, with British corvettes in the background, formed a section of the parade that took three hours to pass Lieut.-General Sir John Harding, G.O.C. 13th Corps, who took the salute. Among the troops whom the citizens of the town acclaimed as successors to their liberators were veterans who had fought their way from Alamein through Sicily and Italy.

Photo, Associated Press

Our War Leaders in Peacetime
HARRIS

THE "Bomber" Harris who tinkers with a car or plays lightheartedly with his six-years-old daughter Jacqueline seems a very different person from Marshal of the R.A.F. Sir Arthur Harris, G.C.B., O.B.E., who controlled R.A.F. bomber fleets in Europe for three years. In uniform he was known as a strict disciplinarian.

The one-time Chief of Bomber Command (he retired early in 1946) favours a natural all-round life with a job for his hands as well as his head. He likes getting into the sun, preferably by the seaside or on a farm, for he has never forgotten the days when, as a tobacco planter in Rhodesia, he took both hot sun and hard work for granted. His tobacco plantation was a successful venture, and he says he would not have given it up but for the outbreak of war in 1914.

HIS main interest in engines dates from those days. In August 1914 he drove to an enlistment centre in one of the first cars to reach Rhodesia, and after a year in the 1st Rhodesian Regiment flew one of the earliest types of R.F.C. fighters. His interest in the internal combustion engine does not extend to motor-boats. The latter he considers "abominations," but of sailing he is very fond. The trouble is, he says, he has never been able to afford to buy a sailing boat large enough to house his family.

Born in 1892, Harris has been twice married, the first time in 1916. Twenty-two years later, with one son and two daughters, he married Thérèse Hearne. Their child, Jacqueline, is the image of her mother, and by all accounts when Jacqueline was a baby the man who invented "saturation bombing" handled her as adeptly as would any woman.

Today the family is in Rhodesia again, where Harris would like to settle. He now wants time for hobbies the war denied him. Big-game shooting was one of his pre-war sports. When in London, he was a member of the International Sportsmen's Club. Nowadays, at 54 years of age, he prefers watching animals to shooting them, although he says he could make a bit out of a gun as he did in the past, and that would help towards the boat he would like to acquire.

HIS interests are not restricted to outdoor sports. He likes reading, mainly on practical matters: before the war these included shooting, sailing, motoring and, of course, aeronautics. He is a stout champion of the cause of British Civil Aviation and wants to see Britain and South Africa linked by a first-class air service. He is not particularly interested in politics. But "Bomber" Harris helped to knock the world down, and now he wants to know how it is to be rebuilt, for which reason he has extended his reading to social subjects.

THE FORMER CHIEF OF BOMBER COMMAND with his six-years-old daughter Jacqueline (1). It's time off from war and time for a story, and Sir Arthur is glad of the change. With her parents in the garden, Jacqueline is undecided about the example of topiary art: is it a Teddy Bear (2) or just a cleverly trimmed shrub? Sir Arthur using the direct telephone line (3) between his house and Bomber Command Headquarters, and acting as his own chauffeur (4) on the way back to work. PAGE 119 *Photos, Picture Post, Keystone*

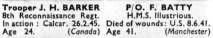

The
Roll of Honour
NCOS & MEN
1939—1946

Flt/Sgt. J. H. ASPDEN
Bomber Command, R.A.F.
Over Germany. 16.4.43.
Age 28. (Pontnewynydd)

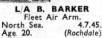

Readers of THE WAR ILLUSTRATED *who wish to submit photographs for inclusion in our Roll of Honour must fill in the coupon which appeared in No. 230. No portraits can be considered that are not accompanied by this coupon.*

L/A B. BARKER
Fleet Air Arm.
North Sea. 4.7.45.
Age 20. (Rochdale)

Trooper J. H. BARKER
8th Reconnaissance Regt.
In action : Calcar. 26.2.45.
Age 24. (Canada)

P/O. F. BATTY
H.M.S. Illustrious.
Died of wounds: U.S. 8.6.41.
Age 41. (Manchester)

Flt/Sgt. W. BRAND
9 Sqn., Royal Air Force.
In action : Bergen. 12.1.45.
Age 22. (Sheffield)

Gdn. G. F. BRICKWOOD
4th Bn. Coldstream Gds.
Action : Normandy. 30.7.44.
Age 21. (Swavesey)

Flt/Sgt. C. BRONHAM
Pathfinder Force, R.A.F.
In action : Stettin. 5.1.44.
Age 28. (Pontypridd)

Sgt. A/G. B. S. G. BUGG
Bomber Comd. R.A.F.V.R.
Action : Frankfurt. 10.4.43.
Age 20. (Tottenham)

Pte. H. J. CLARK
Royal West Kent Regt.
In action : Burma. 1.1.44.
Age 27. (London)

Pte. W. J. COUSINS
5th Essex Regt.
D. of wounds: Caen. 31.7.44.
Age 23. (Maldon)

Sgt. D. DART
Royal Air Force.
In action : Berlin. 27.1.44.
Age 20. (Blandford)

Tele. F. H. ELKES
H.M.S. Nith.
Off Normandy. 26.6.44.
Age 22. (Uttoxeter)

Tpr. R. A. O. FULLER
5th R. Inniskilling Drgn. Gds.
Action : Normandy. 21.8.44.
Age 18. (Caterham)

Pte. G. HARNBY
King's Own Royal Regt.
Died : Ceylon. 28.9.42.
Age 32. (W. Hartlepool)

A/B H. HART
Royal Navy.
Mediterranean. 1.9.44.
Age 38. (Willenhall)

Pte. N. HAZELHURST
South Stafford Regt.
D. of wounds: Bruges. 10.4.45.
Age 19. (Bilston)

Sgt. W. HEALEY
262 Coy., R.A.S.C.
Died of wounds. 13.4.45.
Age 30. (W. Hartlepool)

Pte. W. HUDSON
Royal Artillery.
Died of wounds. 28.7.44.
Age 28. (Edmonton)

Sgt. A/G. T. S. JAMES
Royal Air Force.
Over Hamburg. Nov. 43.
Age 31. (Shepherds Bush)

O S E. JENKS
Royal Navy.
Off Channel Is.. 23.10.43.
Age 17½. (Market Drayton)

Cpl. O. C. JONES
Royal Army Medical Corps.
West Africa. 26.3.41.
Age 22. (Cardiff)

L/Cpl. J. F. KITCHENER
Royal Marines.
In action: Antwerp. 23.2.45.
Age 21. (Stansted)

Fusilier A. LANE
Royal Welch Fusiliers.
Burma. 7.5.44.
Age 29. (Greenwich)

Flt/Sgt. H. LAWLEY
614 Sqn., R.A.F.
In action : Po'a. 21.2.45.
Age 22. (Brierley Hill)

V. G. LAWRENCE
Flt/Sgt. R.A.F.
Bombing ops. 28.8.42.
Age 19. (Gloucester)

Gnr. H. A. McCART
1st Maritime Regt., R.A.
In action : at sea. 9.3.43.
Age 21. (Belfast)

Rfn. N. McFARLAND
Royal Ulster Rifles.
In action : Ranville. 7.6.44.
Age 21. (Ilfracombe)

Pte. F. G. MASON
Royal Scots Fusiliers.
In action : Burma. 3.3.45.
Age 26. (Torquay)

Pte. H. W. MORRIS
6th Bn. R. W. Kent Regt.
In action : Cassino. 26.3.44
Age 22. (London)

Flt/Sgt. R. OSWALD
44 Rhodesia Sqn. R.A.F.
In action : France. 25.6.44.
Age 20. (Royton)

L/Cpl. L. OTTEWELL
3/4 Hampshire Regt.
Died : Italy. 15.9.44.
Age 23. (Heanor)

W. PANKHURST
Coder Royal Navy.
N. Atlantic. 23.9.43.
Age 34. (Newcastle/Lyme)

Fus. F. W. J. SEXTON
R. Inniskilling Fusiliers.
D. of wounds:Italy. 3.11.43.
Age 29. (Wimbledon)

Flt/Sgt. R. SMITH
467 Sqn., R.A.F.V.R.
Action: Wurzburg. 17.3.45.
Age 21. (Bournemouth)

Pte. F. C. STEPHENSON
Gordon Highlanders.
In action : Rees. 23.3.45.
Age 31. (Spilsby)

Pte. W. WALKER
King's Own Yorkshire L.I.
Died : Burma. 15.8.42.
Age 21. (Bradford)

Gdn. L. WIMBRIDGE
3rd Bn. Irish Guards.
Died of wounds. 9.8.44.
Age 31. (Yeovil)

Pte. E. W. WOOSNAM
East Lancashire Regt.
In action : Caen. 8.7.44.
Age 18. (Wallasey)

18 Days Adrift on an Invasion Barge

Homeward bound in November 1942 the S.S. Barberry was sunk by a German torpedo, and Merchant Navy Seaman Harry Heinson, flung into the Atlantic, found himself alone. Tersely he describes the long ordeal that followed. He was later awarded the British Empire Medal.

Mrs. HARRY HEINSON, whose portrait was the sole source of comfort and hope to her husband adrift and alone in the Atlantic.
Photo, Daily Mirror

SEVEN days out from New York and about 275 miles north-east of Newfoundland we ran into really bad weather, lost all our boats and rafts on the port side, and a 135-ton invasion barge we were carrying on deck was split to pieces. On November 26, 1942, the captain decided to turn back. A couple of hours after we had left the convoy a torpedo struck us.

I ran below and rang the alarm. On deck again, I happened to glance towards the stern—and there was a U-boat. I could see a man in the conning tower, quite clearly. But it was too late for our gunners to take a pot at her; for, there was no doubt about it, we were going down.

H. HEINSON, B.E.M.

I started to help lower one of the lifeboats, but there was a kink in the rope and it seemed we were going to be unlucky for the last time on this earth. I crawled back to the davit and managed to cut the rope, and as the boat, with its fifteen occupants, dropped clear, I was swept into the Barberry's well-deck by an enormous wave. The next I knew I was struggling in the water, thanking God for my lifebelt. At first I could see nothing; then I made out a log, about eighteen feet long. I struggled to it and hung on. Then I spotted part of our smashed-up invasion barge, and decided to abandon the log for the somewhat greater safety of that piece of wreckage.

The wind was with me, and as I reached the barge a big cabbage floated by. Almost unconsciously I grabbed it and tossed it aboard, and then clambered after it up the five-foot side. Now I felt fairly safe and I looked around for my comrades. Fifteen of them were in that lifeboat all right, and I was mighty glad that by cutting the rope as I had done I had given them a chance of being saved. I shouted, but they did not hear me. Then I heard the rattle of machine-gun fire and hastily I laid low. I thought it was the U-boat peppering away.

Presently I took stock of my surroundings. My bit of barge was no more than 15 feet by 10, and I found it difficult to stand upright because of the slope. Around the sides were lockers, and as darkness was falling I tore open one of the lids and removed some cases of stuff so that I could get some sort of shelter for the night. There was just enough room for me in that locker; but I had no sleep, for with the rolling of the barge cases were constantly bumping about.

The cases were painted grey on the outside, but the insides were unpainted. The notion came to me to break up about thirty of them and spread the unpainted insides uppermost over the deck—I figured they might be spotted by a chance R.A.F. plane and there would be possibilities of rescue. But most of the pieces as I laid them down were washed overboard, and at last, thoroughly worn out, I reckoned I would be safer if I returned to my two-foot wide locker. But it was impossible for me to stay there long.

It rained and snowed and was freezing cold. I was ravenously hungry—and suddenly remembered the cabbage. It had been washed overboard, but was still floating alongside. I fished it aboard and took a couple of bites. I don't think much of raw cabbage for a starving man, but it was better than nothing. I wondered if there might be anything eatable in the other lockers, and forced another open. No, there was nothing to eat, but there were several torches, plenty of cutlery, and some lubricating oil. The latter was a real find, and I stripped and rubbed it all over my body.

I Guessed the End Was About Due

Further locker-searching revealed two one-gallon jars of fresh water, and a pair of binoculars. But no food. As the interminable days and nights passed I became very weak. I had chewed all my buttons, even, and I guessed the end was about due. I tried to occupy myself at something, moving up and down my piece of barge, holding on to a bit of rope for safety. To counter the effects of snow and hail, which was constantly falling I continued to rub myself with oil, as best I could, every day. I tried to cheer myself up by looking at my wife's photograph, whenever there was enough light to see by, and imagining she was telling me to keep my chin up and I'd be rescued presently.

On December 13, a Sunday, I got tired of seeing and hearing bits of wood banging and floating about on the deck. Angrily I tossed one of them overboard, and in the early morning mist it seemed to me that it remained sticking up in the water. Fascinated, I threw in another piece. That too remained sticking-up. And then I realized I was beginning to "see things." It was certainly a nasty jolt!

A few minutes later I thought I saw a cross-spar—and then a submarine. I took a quick look through the binoculars. Nothing but a blur. But as I continued to look the blur came slowly nearer, and I realized it was a Polish destroyer. It turned out to be the Garland. A year seemed to pass before they threw me a rope. With difficulty I made it fast around myself and gave them the signal to haul away.

I was nearly all-in when they dragged me aboard, but I had just enough breath left to ask my rescuers to present the binoculars (which, somewhat to my own surprise, I found myself still clutching) to their captain. At first I was mistaken for a nigger, I was so smothered in oil. They took me to the ship's hospital and stripped me and put me to bed. I kept craving for something to eat. But the ship's doctor gave me only beef-tea.

POLISH DESTROYER GARLAND, appearing as a "blur which came slowly nearer," rescued seaman Heinson when he was "beginning to see things," on December 13, 1942. Twelve days later he was spending Christmas with his wife, who had been informed that her husband had been lost at sea.

Photo, British Official

On that same day (Sunday the 13th) the doctor came to me, at about two minutes to midnight, and asked me where my lifebelt was. I could see there was something wrong by the look on his face. He told me there was a submarine hanging around, and the lifebelt might be wanted. The night was pitch-black and the U-boat was surfaced, but it did not see the Polish destroyer, which had to swerve suddenly to avoid collision with it. Our crew let fly with one-pound shells and a 4·7-in. gun, then unloaded some depth-charges. And that was the end of the submarine. I like to think it was the same U-boat that had sent the old Barberry down !

The following Sunday we arrived at a north-Scotland port, where the Shipwrecked Mariners' Society gave me a complete rig-out. Meanwhile, my wife had been informed that I had been lost at sea and she had drawn the pension for five weeks, as I had been presumed dead. I took train to Euston, hoping I should arrive home before the telegram I had sent. And I did—by not more than seven minutes. I still marvel how I survived to spend that Christmas at home.

Our Last Weeks in Jap-Held Manila

In the concentration camp of Santo Tomas, Manila, were 3,700 civilian internees suffering under the oppression of the Japanese. The long ordeal, and the tension among prisoners and gaolers alike in the last week's before liberation (Jan.-Feb. 5, 1945), are recalled by Ethel Wholey, one of the British women who with her children spent three years there. See also story of Manila's recapture in page 665, Vol. 8.

"You'd better get out before it's too late, you'd better get out before it's too late." What is this strange, insistent tune that goes round and round in my brain ? Why, of course, it's our old radio churning out the morning reveille, and that's our radio announcer's way of telling us that "something's moving" in the islands. Maybe there are really landings on Mindoro. (U.S. troops landed there on December 15, 1944.)

Things are certainly becoming grim, and if we don't all get out this month it will be too late for most of us. We can't last

Mrs. ETHEL WHOLEY

much longer on 600 calories a day, and our stomachs are beginning to revolt against this ever-lasting lugao (soft rice) without sugar or milk. Two meals a day, and a midday one out of what you can save from breakfast — and, if you are in hospital, sometimes hot vegetable soup to help it down.

Surely something must happen soon. But we've been saying that in a crescendo or diminu-endo of hopefulness for the last three years. More than three years. It was December 3, 1941, when we left Shanghai as "reluctant evacuees" on board the Anhui, the official evacuation ship bound for Australia. Evacuations had always been unpopular, and this last exodus lived up to that reputation. However, the Consul thought it better to send as many women and children as possible out of Shanghai, for many reasons. The Yangtse had been blockaded for two years ; the Japanese were occupying the outside roads ; food was expensive, and meat, excepting buffalo meat, hard to obtain ; unpleasant "incidents" were increasing, and the dollar was rapidly depreciating in value.

Our ship was just one day outside of Hongkong when the Captain called us together for an important announcement. "Since last night we have been at war with Japan," he informed us. "Pearl Harbour was bombed by the Japanese. We were chased by a submarine. Every hour of the night we have been in danger. By the grace of God we are safe. Everybody will carry a lifebelt, and there will be no smoking on deck. Other orders will be issued later."

A few days passed, and our ship put into Manila Bay. Then came the dreadful occasion when the Japs attacked us from the air. The ships all around us were on fire,

and many bombs fell so near that we were thrown off our feet by the concussions. All that night we watched ships burning. The next day the Captain decided that he could not proceed farther with so many women and children on board, and gave orders that we should disembark at Pier 7, taking only our hand luggage.

So we arrived in Manila—450 refugees, dependent for food and shelter on the Red Cross of that city. And there we lived until the fateful January of 1942, when Manila having been declared an open city the Japanese came in through Paranaque. On January 5 the military police started collecting British and Americans for "two days ques-tioning." That was three years ago, and we are still here in the camp at Santo Tomas. Things are certainly grim. Our jokes are growing grim, too, but we do still joke, and that is something the Japs can never under-stand. Our favourite "joke," at the moment, is that if the Americans don't come soon they will be in time to bury the last internee.

'As One Skeleton to Another'

Dr. Smith comes along, more gaunt than ever. I smile as he approaches, for I think he looks like rows of cotton reels strung together with spindly arms and legs attached by some industrious but inartistic child. He makes a feint of lifting my bed to show how strong he is, and asks, "As one skeleton to another, how are we ?" I weigh five stone eight, and I think he doesn't weigh much more. Men are dying at the rate of ten a day and being carried out in rough wooden boxes, sometimes two in a box.

Dr. Stephenson is in gaol for signing certi-ficates, "Death due to malnutrition." Beri-beri and pellagra are rife. What a ghastly sickness the former is, accompanied so often by yellow jaundice. A woman has just been carried in. She is bright yellow, and her legs, arms and stomach are inflated like large, over-blown balloons. It is agony for her to move, and usually the heart is affected. There seems very little hope ; but the doctors are wonderful, they never give up.

Today everybody is worn out. Our sleep was disturbed when, in the middle of the night, a Japanese officer and men clumped through the ward, sabres trailing as usual. Their raucous voices roused us. We stiffened spasmodically as they gesticulated near us. They ordered our shutters to be closed, and kept so, regardless of the fact that we could get only very little air. Today they are sending workmen to nail them shut. They think we see too much. They're not far wrong about that ; they should hear us cheer when our boys get one of their planes ! (Heavy air attacks on the Manila area preceded Allied landings at Lingayen Jan. 9, 1945.)

I am so worried about my children that nothing else seems to matter. They are so haggard-looking, so old. Their translucent,

Motto: "What if the Heavens fall ?"

56 (PUNJAB) SQUADRON

FORMED in June 1916, the squadron went to France in the critical days of April 1917 when the enemy was making a final bid for air supremacy. It was more than a match for the Germans in aerial combat, and by the time of the Armistice (Nov. 1918) had downed 427 enemy aircraft. Its ranks included the famous V.C. aces Capt. Albert Ball and Major J. T. B. McCudden, who destroyed 44 and 50 German aircraft respectively.

No. 56 Squadron's arrival in France during the Second Great War was at an equally critical period—May 1940, when the Allied line was cracking under the German hammer-blows. On its first day in action the squadron destroyed seven German aircraft. Later its pilots helped to provide an air umbrella for the Dunkirk evacuation. In late 1941 the squadron was the first to re-equip with Typhoons, and in the following August carried out its first important operational assignment on these aircraft by helping to provide top cover for the Dieppe landings. During 1943 it carried out harassing attacks on the enemy's "Western Wall." In November the Typhoons were fitted with bombs, and the squadron attended to a wide range of targets in Northern France with devastating success. Eventually the pilots concentrated more and more on flying-bomb launching sites, which the Germans were feverishly building.

IN mid-May 1944 the squadron converted to Spitfire IXs, but at the end of June was re-equipped with the world's fastest low-altitude fighter—the Tempest. Strate-gically placed in what soon became known as "Doodle-Bug Alley" No. 56 destroyed more than 60 flying-bombs. Arnhem was the next landmark in its history. Its pilots effectively dealt with flak opposition as our airborne forces went in. Shortly after, the squadron returned once again to the Continent, this time as part of the 2nd Tactical Air Force. It hit hard and accurately at enemy transport, and in February 1945 accounted for no less than 90 locomotives.

While Montgomery's men forced a cross-ing north of the Wesel the "Fighting Fifty-Sixth" was one of the squadrons which patrolled the Rhine and, in the ensuing weeks, as our troops raced ahead, its pilots assisted in the disintegration of the German defences by non-stop strafing in front of our forward elements.

tightly-drawn skin, their lifeless eyes, show the havoc that hunger is making. They have fallen into a dull apathy, much worse than their former irritation. They do not laugh or joke any longer. This day, they sit silent and disinterested. "Hunger !" says my son presently, and never shall I forget the pent-up heartbreak in that young voice. "Hunger !" There is no doubt we are at the end of our tether, as they say in Lincoln-shire, my old home. How far away it seems ! As long as the kits (packages sent by our Home Government) lasted we could eke out our scanty allowance, but even with the most skilful manipulation we could not make them last for ever.

People have been doing wonderful things with roots and leaves for a long time. Now they are eating snails, frogs and cats—you can get cats skinned and prepared by an internee who has set up in business. He

Life in Manila's Notorious Santo Tomas Camp

CIVILIAN INTERNEES made shift for more than three years with the crude accommodation provided by the Japanese in Manila, as told in the facing page. Huts with roofs of dried grass and other vegetable fibre propped up on poles (1) in the courtyard of the Santo Tomas camp were terribly overcrowded; in the centre, internees are grouped about a charcoal brazier cooking an insufficient meal. When feeding arrangements had been somewhat improved women and men lined up to collect a meal, on a rough-and-ready cafeteria system (2). Twelve commandments displayed for all to see (3) kept the power of the Japs to punish—with death or otherwise—ever in the minds of the people. Emaciated and enfeebled, internees acclaimed the U.S. flag (4) on liberation day, in Feb. 1945.

Photos, Associated Press, Acme, Keystone
PAGE 123

Mrs. WHOLEY'S SON, photographed at the time of this story, beside a ramshackle shack—or nipa—in which many internees lived in Manila.

takes one-third of the meat and the skin in payment. He won't get much more business, as there is only one cat left in the camp and she is intelligent enough to elude capture.

A great blow has fallen upon us. Four of our committee men, for some time detained in the Jap gaol, have now been taken out, and, we fear, to that dread torture house Fort Santiago. Truly it can be said of that place, "All hope abandon, ye who enter here." We have seen men and women back from the Fort shattered in mind and body. They dare not speak of their experiences; their lips are sealed. One woman, a missionary, brought into hospital from Fort Santiago, told something of her experiences. The next night she was collected by armed guards. Even the walls have ears!

Forbidden to Look Up at the Sky

One thing gives us great satisfaction—the manifest uneasiness of the Japs. Ever since the Allied bombing started they have been growing more and more uneasy. Of course, they take it out of us in divers ways. Rules have been tightened up. Women are no longer allowed to read or knit during Roll Call, and all except the sick must stand. The bowing, also—our way of bowing does not meet the approval of the Japanese military. The monitors have been given lessons : hands straight by the sides, feet together, face the Jap sentry, and bow from the waist. It is wearisome now that people are so weak, especially as we must bow to every Jap.

Every time there is an announcement we know there is something disagreeable, though Don Bell, our radio announcer, has done much to keep up our morale. Pennies From Heaven was played when the first Allied bombs dropped on Manila. Smoke Gets in Your Eyes was played when cooking in shanties was forbidden, and Better Leyte Than Never, though made in connexion with a consignment of rice, told us when the Allies landed on Leyte. (October 20, 1944.)

Yes, the Japs are definitely uneasy. They have made themselves burrows in the earth, commonly called foxholes, and to these they have taken all their valuable documents, chiefly, one would imagine, complaints about

food, and suggestions that they should follow international law, since Judge de Witt fairly plastered their office with letters on that subject, until, because of his importunity, he was banished to Lôs Banos.

Evidently the foxholes do not come up to requirements, for visitors tell us that the Japs are taking out the papers and making a bonfire of them. For a long time they have been bringing trucks full of crates into the camp, and we have seen them burying barrels of petrol around the walls. Now they are drilling outside, and yelling.

Internees are being punished for receiving food unlawfully; the gaols are full of offenders —most of them offenders against the food regulations. One internee, a Chinese American, is there for refusing to sign the oath. He is the only man who didn't sign, and has been in gaol for three months. It is now a crime to look up at the sky, and internees if seen doing so are made to stand at the gate for hours as a punishment. The place is full of rumours, chiefly of kits, maybe because we need them so badly. (Further Allied landings took place on January 29, 1945.)

Suddenly, as we are lying wooing sleep, we hear cheers and shouting, and my neighbour exclaims wildly, " The Americans ! " Then a voice shouting, " Where is my wife ? " It is Frank Hewlett, of the Associated Press, who has come in with the first tanks. How we hug and kiss these boys of the First U.S. Cavalry Division ! But our difficulties are not yet over. There is constant rattle of gun-fire, for the Japs have planted machine-gun nests in the rooms in the Education Building, where there are 220 young children and other internees. Our boys cannot fire into them without endangering the children. At last, in order to avoid loss of life, we have

come to terms with our enemies—they are to be conducted out, with arms and ammunition, to within 100 yards of their own lines. How happy we are to see these jolly young boys of the First Cavalry, to hear something of what is happening in the outside world and to have food in abundance.

The Battle of Manila rages night and day over our heads. Charred fragments are blowing into the ward, and we are afraid of fire. Shrapnel is spattered all over the camp. One of our buildings has been struck by a shell, and there are many casualties. We are ordered to move down into the church for safety. We sleep on the floor for a week, then the main building is struck again. Many of our friends, among them one of our pastors, are killed, and more are injured. We are moved out to Quezon city.

Begged for Mercy but Mown Down

For twenty-one days the battle has raged and we have seen unforgettable sights, heard almost unbelievable stories of savagery as victims of these murderers are brought to the care of army nurses and doctors. Young girls, roped together, covered with petrol and burnt, women stabbed and mutilated as they ran from homes wantonly set on fire ; babies struck on the head, and mothers mowed down as they begged for mercy ; Swiss, Spanish, Germans, Filipinos, all slaughtered without discrimination ; whole families wiped out in this incredible orgy of blood.

During the battle a shell struck the Quezon Institute, but no one was injured. Now reports say that Intramuros, the scene of the last enemy organized resistance, has fallen, the Japs have retreated across the Pasig River. And Manila, that pearl of the Orient, is left broken, ruined, despoiled of her beauty.

Devil's Workshop Under the Harz

Major A. Forrest, 107 H.A.A. Regt., R.A., describes his visit in 1945 to a colossal V-weapons factory. To the north of Nordhausen, in Germany, this workshop in the belly of a mountain, excavated by slave labour, was the birthplace of rockets and doodle-bugs designed for our destruction.

"AROUND you," remarked the American soldier quietly, "lie the means of destroying England, perhaps the world !" Here, indeed, the Nazi war industrialists had conspired to turn the War after D-Day in Europe, June 6, 1944—to obliterate our British cities.

I stood, this June day of 1945, within the slave - excavated belly of a mountain, a sole Englishman surrounded by vaults filled with derelict infernal machines ; my feet on a causeway of limestone ; above me an impenetrable bomb-proof roof of rock 800 feet thick. I was in a catacomb created by modern war conditions where thousands of men and women had laboured to let loose hell on earth. And the

Major A. FORREST

contrast of Nature's mood outside added to my extreme discomfiture within.

There, under a blue sky devoid of clouds, and spreading over 90 square kilometres of magnificent forest scenery, lie the Harz mountains, a bountiful district of quiet verdant valleys with timbered and red-roofed villages, places which because of their seclusion and peace had been set aside as hospital and convalescent centres for Wehrmacht and Luftwaffe wounded.

Where I stood was the scene of Hitler's so-called invulnerable V1 and V2 weapons factory—the only combined Vergeltungswaffe (revenge weapon) installation ever brought into operation. It lies six kilometres to the north of Nordhausen, a town with several thousand inhabitants in the extreme south of the Harz district. Even with this information it is not easily tracked down. Those treeless, white-scarred terraces scaling the mountain's south-easterly face hint at nothing more sinister than surface limestone quarrying. With binoculars an observer might gain a different impression. Yet, on second thoughts, I doubt if even then he could pinpoint at the hill's base those tiny entrances into the rock so ingeniously camouflaged.

So unobtrusive are these four apertures, two on the north and two on the south flank, serving equally as exits and entrances, that not a single Allied bomb or shell pitched in the vicinity. Nor by the name of Mittel Werke, by which it was known alike by its directors, executives, S.S. personnel and slave labourers, does the factory give the outsider any clue as to its intentions.

THE Nazis' V-weapon output fell short of the total desired for war-winning blows chiefly as a result of the R.A.F.'s precision bombing. But here, immune from such interference, the rocket propulsion experts led by General Dornberger and Professor von Braun had promised their Fuehrer so massive an output of V2s (the 12-ton A-4 rocket weapon, as our scientists know it) that launchings against England could be effected and maintained at a rate of 1,000 a day ! Imagine, in any one period of 24 hours, a thousand of these missiles, technically long-range shells of great pulverizing power, plunging into the midst of London or Manchester or Edinburgh or Liverpool, with our A.A. and Fighter Defences (so brilliantly deployed against the V1), powerless to divert or destroy them !

Fortunately, the factory never came within appreciable measure of full production. It opened shop late in 1944, after 16 months of frenzied, slave-sweated hewing, during which 10,000,000 tons of rock must have been shifted, and huge power plants, air-conditioning apparatus, and several thousand machines, many on the S.S. Priority Secrets list, were installed. From then on, until its seizure —which was a most dramatic surprise to directors caught eating their luncheon sandwiches—by a combat group of the American 9th Army in April 1945, its examiners booked out an aggregate of approximately 1,800 V1s and 1,000 V2s. In the same period several hundred aero-engines for the Junkers Flugzeug and Motorenwerke firm had been manufactured within the third and least important sector of the factory.

Rockets With 3,000 Miles Range

As the outcome of one month's investigation into the machinery assembled here, an American scientific adviser, Major W. Bromley, declared as his belief that within six months after VE Day this factory would have been producing rocket weapons with not, as at the time, a 220-mile horizontal range but with a "carry" of 3,000 miles. Revenge weapons, that is, capable of flooring New York's skyscrapers !

As I walked in the greyness and gloom, with the American G.I. as a guide through these corridors, offices, workshops and factory lines, all now unoccupied, I became obsessed by the awful power of science when it is organized for death. During my excursions I discovered, though of course I did not cover the entire distance afoot, no less than 22 miles of subterranean tunnels comprising long main galleries used as assembly lines and delivery or supply lines, interlaced by a series of separate vaults or caverns, each serviced and set out as a workshop, each performing specialized tasks, each with its own roster of shift-masters and slave workers. Electricity, water and air-cooling systems infiltrated to every department, including offices and latrines offset in the rock walls of their respective vaults.

Most conspicuous were the two main shafts or galleries running parallel north and south. They pierced the mountain from flank to flank, travelling each a distance of 1¼ miles from daylight through darkness into daylight again. Then, intersecting these two parallel routes, like cross-pieces in a web, were 42 vaults described in the German as either Stollen or Halle. Each is an independent cave 500 yards long, 25 feet high, and about 36 feet wide. A few are double-deckers, divided for storage purposes into an upper and lower floor.

I SAW reinforced walls at the entrances and exits of the main galleries only. Here, to a penetration of 400 yards, the naked walls and ceilings had been covered by concrete and brick. As for the rest of the tunnelling, it is rough-hewn, unsupported, and drill marks score the limestone's face. There is one exception to be found in Halle 29, the V2 turbine and fuel pump assembly shop. Here, in token of the value put on the machinery and processing used, steel girders had been erected as protective ribs against roofs and walls— mighty girders with interlocking cross-pieces.

It was impressed on me that between 25,000 and 30,000 foreign workers had died in these chambers since excavations began in earnest in August 1943. Theirs was no simple death. Forced to operate the drills in these shafts and clear away the debris, with S.S. foremen using whips and wild dogs to herd them, they must have trembled at the slightest

falling off, knowing full well that it implied one fate only—the crematorium. Moreover, such was the atmosphere of thick limestone dust, in which they sweated, that thousands died from tuberculosis and other lung diseases, their illness aggravated by the infamous treatment meted out to them.

As stimulants to the lax or rebellious the S.S. staged mass hangings periodically, actually carried out inside the mountain. The factory's crane combined the functions of gallows and execution block. Workers themselves were compelled to act as hangmen of their fellow shift-workers, whilst the Nazis looked on. According to evidence of survivors at the local camp called Dora, a workers' compound just outside the mountain, with wooden huts, barbed wire, raised observation and spot-light towers and other conventional concentration-camp paraphernalia, deaths in this vicinity totalled thousands. The American liberation forces saw piles of rotting corpses.

The cold, artificial wind coursing out of the vents beneath the dazzling white arc lights, which were kept switched on for the benefit of American patrols and guards, never abated. I shivered and walked on. That the Nazis thought certain bodies worth at least temporary preservation was made clear when, at the entrance to a Halle, I came across a Red Cross sign, and on a wooden door the legend "Nordhausen Krankenhaus." Inside, I discovered a complete sick bay, consisting of a series of wooden cubicles, barren except for some very utilitarian chairs and beds. Here, special operatives received treatment. It was not healthy to stay too long in these plywood compartments, since typhus had been detected. The Americans had put up on a door their warning-off sign, "Off Limits to All Troops."

Halle 29 was impressive not only in size but in its contents. Here I found intact a whole series of V2 steam turbines and combustion units, each assembly housed in a steel framework which assisted fitment of the separate units ; overhead electrically-driven pulleys had operated, carrying the engines to their

assembly lines. I counted 53 steel cages in this girdered engine-room, then abandoned count. "The firework foundry," commented the G.I. laconically.

Close to this lies the Halle in which the V2s' cylindrical fuel tanks were stored, and at the time of my first visit many were still there : though emptied of their fuel—the "liberated" displaced workers saw to that ! They knew that each V2 was equipped, like the V1, with an alcohol fuel tank ; in the case of the V2, a 500-gallon container with a 40 per cent alcohol content. And on this so-called "buzz-bomb juice" they made whoopee, to their own detriment. The stuff, literally firewater, soon had its victims raving.

Lightness of Metal Amazed Me

Incidentally, each V2 when assembled carried two of these huge tanks, one containing alcohol as described, and the other liquid oxygen, a fuel load which, when combined, weighed eight tons, or three-quarters of the weight of the entire rocket. I was amazed to feel the lightness of the metal used for construction. One picked up a heavy-looking piece, such as a projectile's nose cap, and it almost floated in one's grip. Also astonishingly light-weight, in ratio to their size, were the sheet steel skins which encased these giant rocket-driven shells. These covers, enclosing the combustion unit with venturi, the two fuel tanks and part of the war-head, I estimated to be about 30 feet long and quite six feet in diameter. In one Halle I found four huge plants each of which automatically welded a V2 skin at speed.

Forced labourers in another workshop-tunnel used to do nothing but assemble V2 tail units. In the more westerly of the two main shafts I stumbled on presses and tool precision machines, hundreds of them. "Don't touch it, sir !" warned my guide. "It will cut your hands." I had bent down to pick up a bundle of attractive-looking, fleecy white wool, rolls of which littered this particular floor. It was glass wool, used extensively as insulating material. I owe it to the G.I.'s caution that I did not spend the day recovering glass splinters from my hand.

ROUGH-HEWN FROM THE ROCK, installed with the most up-to-date machinery, this eerie-looking workshop represented only one tiny corner of the monster organization within the Harz Mountains. Nearly 3,000 V-weapons had been produced there by the time the factory was seized by the American 9th Army in April 1945. PAGE 125 *Photo, U.S. Army Signal Corps*

In curiosity I turned over a number of Arbeitsbucher fur Auslander (work books for foreigners) ; in each of these identity books (one issued to each displaced national) was a foreword signed by the General Plenipotentiary for Work Production. Its English version runs as follows : "Like the German, so does the foreign worker by brawn and mind serve through his production in Greater Germany the New Order of Europe and the struggle that assures the welfare and happy future of peoples on the European Continent. The foreign worker must always be conscious of his task and his distinction. On these premises rest his position, his achievements and his personal integrity."

It was a happy relief when at the end of a main gallery I came out beneath a canopy of dark camouflage netting into sunlight and sweet air. I took several deep breaths— and thought of the R.A.F.'s intensified programme of strategic bombing, executed day and night, versus the German secret weapon programme bolstered up day and night by ever-increasing hordes of slave labourers ; of the master-stroke from the air that in a single raid smashed the £50,000,000 experimental station at Peenemunde, claiming 750 specialists among its victims and setting the V bomb plans back by at least six months.

Going back through the main easterly gallery I was hemmed in by railway tracks, aluminium air-conditioning tubes running in parallel lines on opposite sides of the roof, and by electric cables housed in a wooden duct under the road surface, conveying power to all the thousand and one machines in the factory. I noticed areas along the shaft where the drilling of new tunnels at right angles to its axis had begun. Actually, Mittel Werke's directors had schemed to drill two more main galleries, parallel with the two existing shafts, and link them by stalls and bays, so trebling the factory's working space. Suddenly I sighted a placard, its text underlined by a skull and cross-bones of the black pattern typical of German minefield notices. It announced "SICHERUNGEN ENTFERNEN IST SABOTAGE" (to withdraw safety devices is sabotage).

Towards the southern entrance I stumbled on another astonishing spectacle. Filling one side of the main gallery were the V1 assembly lines. It was bewildering to see mounted on wooden cradles, in all phases of advancement, scores of "doodle-bugs." Some were minus tail assemblies ; others deficient of compressed-air bottles or gyroscopic controls ; others had no nose-cap for protection of their war-heads. Not one had wings. The stove-pipe wings of metal or wood fabric (wooden wings were adopted only in the later stages of the weapon's deployment) travelled independently to be fitted, I believe, in the launching zones.

With no great effort I recalled the blazing jet trails of doodle-bugs at night. When we battled against them, 24 hours a day, in defence of Antwerp, I pictured no scene such as this : a procession of newly-born doodles worming out of their womb on wooden cradles from inside a mountain !

Outside, beneath the friendly sky again, I saw concrete roads, railway lines, a big miscellaneous collection of V1 and V2 parts, and the workers' squalid encampments. "No one slept in the factory. Work inside was continuous. The only sleep they allowed you was the one from which you don't get up," said a Polish girl, a former assistant in the electric-lamp accessory department.

Twelve thousand workers (I have confirmed this figure from other sources), she asserted, toiled here daily, their labour spread over three shifts. To be late or missing was answerable by torture or death. Each shift, functioning in each Halle or Stollen, had its own master responsible for the assembly and control of workers ; in the larger Halle there was also a "Halleleiter" (shop manager) accorded extra powers of control. Thus, until the Americans came, the mountain laboured ceaselessly, enduring a tumult in its belly with machines that screeched, thudded, drummed and sparkled amid thick clouds of dust floating in hot, stifling air. It must have been an ordered, pandemonium of hell.

Winning the First George Medals

Serving with the Auxiliary Fire Service at the time, Frank Illingworth graphically tells how the first three George Medals to be awarded were won by his comrades of the Dover Fire Brigade during German dive-bombing attacks on H.M. ships Sandhurst, Gulzar and Codrington in July 1940.

FIFTY Junkers 87 dive-bombers roared out of the clear morning skies into a hail of A.A. fire. The "boof" of Bofors mingled with the roar of the "heavies" and the chatter of machine-guns with A.A. mountings. Pocked with hundreds of shell bursts, the sky was alive with flying metal ; and one after another German wings lurched and crashed.

Before I could struggle into fire-fighting kit clouds of smoke soared from three burning warships, from oil storage tanks and a coal saith, and from the burning sea itself. It was 7.15 a.m. on July 27, 1940.

For some time we had anticipated a blitz on H.M.S. Sandhurst and the destroyer Codrington tied up alongside the supply ship in the inner harbour—the Camber—at Dover. A few hours before this early morning attack the Luftwaffe had been over in force. The R.A.F. had had no opportunity to interfere : defence rested with the shore batteries and guns of ships in the harbour. And if the barrage was such that the enemy lost much of his bombing accuracy at least one bomb had exploded sufficiently near the Codrington to break her back. But the Sandhurst had survived. Now the Luftwaffe was back to finish off the job.

The enemy crossed the coast at about 2,000 feet, wheeled behind Dover Castle and attacked out of the sun in steep dives. In a twinkling hell was let loose. As I pedalled to the fire station, heads popped from bedroom windows to cheer the destruction of a Junkers hit by two shells simultaneously. The Junkers exploded, and fell in the form of steel rain. On either

H.M.S. SANDHURST WITH THE DESTROYER CODRINGTON, anchored in the Camber, Dover Harbour, after the fire and bombing attack described here. Smoke is rising from burning oil, which spread over the water and enveloped the ships, endangering their ammunition. PAGE 126

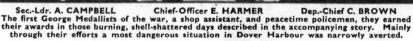

Sec.-Ldr. A. CAMPBELL   Chief-Officer E. HARMER   Dep.-Chief C. BROWN
The first George Medallists of the war, a shop assistant, and peacetime policemen, they earned their awards in those burning, shell-shattered days described in the accompanying story. Mainly through their efforts a most dangerous situation in Dover Harbour was narrowly averted.

side, two aircraft staggered and trailed black smoke-plumes towards the sea.

"Look !" a girl shrilled. "Three men have jumped out of that plane !" But they were bombs, and the attacking Junkers came hurtling past the cliffs in almost perpendicular power-dives. Bombs crashed into the Royal Naval auxiliary H.M.S. Gulzar, tied up in the Camber. Others exploded on the Eastern Arm. And H.M.S. Sandhurst was hit. By a miracle the supply ship survived the missile that entered one of her holds and, in the words of Warrant Engineer Fox, "did a kind of circular tour and then made its exit to explode on the jetty." But the Sandhurst was badly shaken ; her engine-room inlets burst, and she began to settle.

Wings Falling Out of the Skies

At the fire station we stood by, awaiting the call for assistance. Fascinated by the Junkers and the barrage few of us noticed the approach of R.A.F. formations, until suddenly dog fights broke out between Hurricanes and the Junkers' escorts, some 40 Messerschmitt 109s. Machine-guns added to the clatter of A.A. batteries and exploding bombs. Here and there wings fell out of the skies as Hurricanes chased the marauders into the guns of a second Hurricane formation waiting out to sea. Of the twenty-seven German planes shot down in this attack, I saw six plunge to destruction.

A vast column of smoke over the Camber confirmed that the enemy had accomplished at least part of his purpose, and at about 7.45 a.m. the "in" telephones shrilled at the Fire Station. The Chief, Ernie Harmer, and his deputy, Cyril Brown, were already on their units. Section-Leader Alec Campbell was, as usual, in the middle of the road "watching the fun," which he usually tried to deny us on the grounds that we "might cop a bit of shrapnel." As the machines turned into the street with bells clanging he swung aboard.

For close on two years we had trained for just such an event as now presented itself. The days of make-believe fires were over. This was the real thing, and some of us were nervous at the prospect of fire-fighting beneath an umbrella of enemy wings.

The scene at the Camber was far from reassuring. Fuel-oil flowed around the Sandhurst, and flames gripped the supply ship's stern and surrounded the burning destroyer's upper works. The grey-painted Gulzar, once the property of the Prince of Wales, sat on the bottom of the Camber, on fire, with streams of burning oil stretching towards the Sandhurst. Smoke poured from the supply ship, and from 200,000 tons of coal in the wharf-side saith. An oil pipe-line from the storage tanks was severed and from it flaming oil poured into and across the Camber. And overhead enemy wings were droning.

Chief-Officer Harmer took charge of the four fire-pumps. Just two words he uttered, "Get cracking !" And we "got cracking." The Gulzar was an obvious total loss, so we turned towards the Sandhurst ; indeed, Alec Campbell was already aboard, helping naval ratings to unload ammunition. With the deck red-hot and flames licking around the stern there was a good chance of the ammunition aboard going up. Furthermore, the destroyer Codrington was enveloped in flames and we didn't know if her torpedoes and ammunition had been removed. Thus there was a definite risk in boarding the Sandhurst alongside her, but the cry "Get the ammo away !" had to be answered.

Hoses were being run out. A tug drew into the Camber with a crew under Section-Officer P. Baynton. From the Eastern Arm Harmer yelled to him, "Throw your jets on to the Sandhurst's stern, Percy !" Other jets flung streams of white foam on to the burning sea, on to the Codrington, the Sandhurst and the fractured pipe-line. But still oil escaped and, burning, spread over the Camber. Faces were scorched. Men had to be relieved every few minutes.

In the meantime, Alec Campbell was in the Sandhurst's operating theatre, fighting on his own a fire that threatened to spread rapidly. Ernie Harmer, Cyril Brown and Hookins were amidships, directing the hoses. Cyril had lost his smile. Ernie, too, looked grim and Alec was as black as the ace of spades, But gradually the flames were

being beaten back, and we felt confident we were going to save the Sandhurst. Suddenly the air-raid warning "red" signal was given. Abandon ship ! The Luftwaffe was returning ! Sweating and cursing, Harmer ordered us to the shelters.

Air battles broke out afresh, and the flames began to spread again. Down by the stern, the Sandhurst's side-plates grew red hot and Harmer asked for permission to return to the ship. It was refused. But he persisted ; and ultimately the senior naval officer present grudgingly gave permission for selected volunteers to board her. Hookins, wearing breathing apparatus, tried to enter the stern hatchways, but intense heat drove him back. The decks were steaming, the side plates sizzling. Hoses were lowered down the hatchways and directed through the ports.

It took five hours to get the main oil fire under control. And at about 2 p.m. fresh columns of smoke told Dover that the flames were liable to assert themselves again. Aerial warfare swayed across the skies and renewed attack on the burning ships was anticipated. Percy Baynton said something about being "Caught like rats in a trap." But he and the rest remained at the hoses. By 3 p.m. the fire was well under control. The Sandhurst's engine-room hatches were torn off. It proved impossible to enter the poop before the late afternoon, but the flames were finally extinguished by 8 p.m.

TIRED, hungry, blackened, scorched, we returned to the station. We were no longer amateurs, but firemen—though no one for a moment imagined that three of our number were to be awarded the George Medal. It was weeks before a citation took us back to that flaming day at the end of July 1940. "In a recent large-scale attack by enemy bombers on Dover Harbour," the London Gazette said, "fires were started in ships and oil stores. Air raids continued throughout the day. All members of the Dover Fire Brigade and the Auxiliary Fire Service did excellent work in difficult and dangerous circumstances and the fires were extinguished. The individuals named volunteered to return to a blazing ship containing explosives, in which they fought the flames while enemy aircraft were in the vicinity." Their names were Ernie Harmer, peacetime policeman ; Cyril Brown, also of the police force ; and Alec Campbell, shopman in a hardware store—the first of the war's George Medallists.

NEW FACTS AND FIGURES

THE atomic bomb dropped on Hiroshima, August 6, 1945, resulted in 78,150 Japanese killed, 13,983 missing, 9,428 seriously injured, 27,997 slightly injured ; total 129,558. In addition, another 176,987 were rendered homeless or suffered sickness from after-effects : total of 306,545 thus affected by the bomb. These final casualty figures were announced by Allied H.Q. Tokyo on February 2, 1946.

IN the period from October 1, 1941, to March 31, 1946 (stated Mr. Attlee in the House of Commons on April 16, 1946), we supplied to the Soviet Union 5,218 tanks, of which 1,388 were from Canada ; also 7,411 aircraft, including 3,129 sent from the United States. The total value of military supplies dispatched amounted to approximately £308,000,000. We also sent about £120,000,000 of raw materials, foodstuffs, machinery, industrial plant, medical supplies and hospital equipment. Forty-one outward convoys went to Russia during the War.

FROM the winter of 1941 onwards, immensely strong air-raid shelters of reinforced concrete were built in Germany, states the International Committee for the Study of European Questions. With walls and roofs of a thickness of up to 9 feet 10 inches

they could resist even a direct hit. Düsseldorf had 24, Hanover 44, and Hamburg 157, one of which alone could shelter 60,000 persons. In Essen (in which only 320,000 inhabitants remained) 111 old mining tunnels, some of them shut down decades ago, were reopened, providing shelter for 240,000 people of this heavily-bombed Ruhr town.

SOUTH NORWAY was almost clear of landmines by April 1946 (according to the Norwegian State Information Service), except in the Stavanger district, where some areas were found to be still dangerous after German gangs had declared them free of mines. In Finmark, North Norway, however, mine clearance was still far from finished and had been delayed by winter frosts, which prevented work. It was expected that German gangs working under Norwegian control would be able to clear the rest of the minefields during the summer of 1946.

FIGURES published in Oslo on April 3, 1946, show that casualties among Germans engaged in mine clearance in Norway have been high—over ten per cent. The number of Germans killed totalled 500 out of 4,300. Casualties among Allied troops were two British killed and three injured, and six Norwegians killed and six injured.

V-Day Parade Clear-up in Trafalgar Square

AIR-RAID SHELTERS AROUND NELSON'S COLUMN were removed in preparation for the great parade on June 8, 1946. Their purpose served, they might have performed a final function as grandstands for a lucky few on the Day; but their removal was desired in the interests of all. Framed in an emergency exit of one of the shelters—with a busy pick demolishing the roof—is one of Landseer's four bronze lions at the base of the memorial to Nelson's last victory. Near the Column's summit is steeplejacks' scaffolding. (See also illus. in page 82.) *Photo, Planet News*

Printed in England and published every alternate Friday by the Proprietors, THE AMALGAMATED PRESS, LTD., The Fleetway House, Farringdon Street, London, E.C.4. Registered for transmission by Canadian Magazine Post. Sole Agents for Australia and New Zealand : Messrs. Gordon & Gotch, Ltd. ; and for South Africa : Central News Agency, Ltd.—June 7, 1946. S.S. *Editorial Address :* JOHN CARPENTER HOUSE WHITEFRIARS, LONDON, E.C.4.

Vol 10 *The War Illustrated* N° 235

SIXPENCE

I WAS THERE

JUNE 21, 1946

INDIA'S COLOURFUL CONTINGENT to London's Victory Parade on June 8, 1946, included nine detachments drawn from the Royal Indian Navy, Army and Air Force, and the band of the Royal Garhwal Rifles. Among them was Havildar Umrao Singh, V.C., of the Indian Artillery, seen smiling (centre) from the window of a railway carriage as he arrived at Euston Station. With him are a bearded Sikh (right) and one of the famous Gurkha Rifles (left). See also portrait in page 216, Vol. 9. *Photo P.A.-Reuter*

Edited by Sir John Hammerton

NO. 236 WILL BE PUBLISHED FRIDAY, JULY 5

Commonwealth Prime Ministers Meet in London

IN THE GARDEN OF No. 10 DOWNING STREET, residence of Britain's Prime Minister, during a recess in one of the sessions of the Commonwealth Conference the Rt. Hon. Ernest Bevin, Foreign Minister (1, left) chatted with Dr. H. V. Evatt, Australia's Minister of External Affairs, and (2) with the Rt. Hon. W. L. Mackenzie King, Prime Minister of Canada. The Rt. Hon. Walter Nash (3, left), Deputy Prime Minister of New Zealand, with the Rt. Hon. J. B. Chifley, Prime Minister of Australia. The Rt. Hon. Clement R. Attlee (4, left) with Field-Marshal the Rt. Hon. J. C. Smuts, South Africa.

THE COMMONWEALTH PRIME MINISTERS' CONFERENCE which opened in London on April 23, 1946, concluded on May 23. The discussions afforded opportunities for consultations between representatives of all the Dominions on matters of mutual interest, and included separate discussions between individual United Kingdom and Dominion Ministers on matters affecting one particular Dominion only. Under consideration were the draft peace treaties with Italy, the Balkan States and Finland ; the future of Germany ; security responsibilities and arrangements between the Commonwealth Governments on military affairs ; economic and welfare co-operation in the South Pacific and South-East Asia ; the British Government's proposal to withdraw forces from Egypt ; the Palestine Report ; and the future distribution of political influence in the eastern Mediterranean. Because of the informal nature of the talks " Agreements " and " Decisions " were purposely omitted from publicized reports. Existing methods of consultation between the Dominions were approved as being preferable to any rigid centralized machinery. The Dominion Prime Ministers attending are seen above. PAGE 130

Why 'Scharnhorst' and 'Gneisenau' Escaped

by
FRANCIS E. McMURTRIE
Specially Illustrated by C. Haworth

Towards the end of March 1941 the German battleships Scharnhorst and Gneisenau entered the port of Brest, France. Dispatched into the Atlantic on a commerce-raiding expedition, they narrowly escaped falling into a trap when the Admiralty took the precaution of adding battleships to the escorts of the more important convoys. Whether their retirement to Brest was due to damage, shortage of fuel or fear of encirclement, has never been made clear, but all three causes may have operated. Some two months later the heavy cruiser Prinz Eugen, which had parted company with her consort, the battleship Bismarck, after the latter's speed had been reduced by a torpedo hit, also took refuge in Brest. She was first sighted there, in dry-dock, during an air reconnaissance on June 4.

The Scharnhorst and Gneisenau were sister ships with an actual standard displacement of nearly 32,000 tons, though it had been given officially by the Germans as 26,000 tons. Similarly, their speed appears to have been a knot or two in excess of the nominal figure of 27 knots. Each mounted nine 11-in. guns in triple turrets. Together the two ships had been responsible for the destruction of the armed merchant cruiser Rawalpindi in October 1939, and had destroyed H.M.S. Glorious at the close of the Norwegian campaign in the following year.

Nominally a 10,000-ton cruiser, armed with eight 8-in. guns, the Prinz Eugen actually displaced considerably more. According to a recent report the correct figure is 19,550 tons, but this is probably the deep load displacement. Her speed appears to have been in excess of 32 knots, and she subsequently enjoyed the distinction of being the largest German warship to fall into the hands of the Allies intact.

'Operation Fuller' in Readiness

For month after month a series of bombing raids by the R.A.F. kept the enemy ships fully occupied in adding to their anti-aircraft defence and in devising fresh methods of camouflage, with an occasional shift of berth. On one occasion the Scharnhorst slipped out under cover of darkness and was located next day (July 23) at La Pallice, but that port proved a more uncomfortable haven under air attack than Brest, to which she soon returned. From that date until the middle of December all three ships remained in dock, and thenceforward at least one of them was usually in dock. But at the beginning of February 1942 all three were out of dock, apparently in seaworthy condition.

From the fact that a flotilla comprising two destroyers, five large torpedo boats and eight minesweepers, had appeared in Brest towards the end of January it seemed evident that a sortie was contemplated. The sudden arrival at Trondheim, in Norway, on January 23, of the big new battleship Tirpitz, sister of the Bismarck, suggested that the enemy were trying to divert attention from the group of ships lying at Brest.

Though it was possible that the three ships might return to commerce raiding into the Atlantic, or make for a Mediterranean port such as Genoa, it seemed far more likely that their destination was Wilhelmshaven or some other German base. In that event they would hardly take the hazardous route northabout the British Isles, where there was more chance of their being intercepted. This caused the Admiralty to forecast on February 2 that the ships would most probably proceed up Channel and through the Straits of Dover. This view was supported by recent enemy concentrations of light craft at various points along the coast from Le Havre to the Hook of Holland. A plan which had already been concerted between the Admiralty and the Air Ministry in April 1941 was therefore prepared for execution.

Under this plan, known as "Operation Fuller," the Commander-in-Chief at the Nore was ordered to arrange for six destroyers to be ready at six hours' notice in the Thames estuary. Six motor torpedo boats were to be in readiness for operations under the Vice-Admiral, Dover; and six Swordfish aircraft were ordered to move from Lee-on-Solent to Manston, in Kent, where they would come under the same command. The submarine Sealion was ordered to join two old submarines patrolling a line to the west of Brest.

Three night air patrols were organized by Coastal Command, these being the "Stopper" patrol, off the entrance to Brest; the "Line S.E." patrol, between Ushant and the Ile de Brehat; and the "Habo" patrol, between Havre and Boulogne. All these patrols were composed of Hudson aircraft fitted with A.S.V. radar gear of an elementary type compared with that now in use. A squadron-and-a-half of Beaufort torpedo-bombers was stationed at Thorney Island as a striking force,

and a further one-and-a-half squadrons were held ready at St. Eval, in Cornwall.

Between February 3 and 9, H.M.S. Manxman and H.M.S. Welshman laid 1,000 mines of both contact and magnetic types in six fields between Ushant and Boulogne, while Bomber Command laid 98 magnetic mines in five specified areas off the Frisian Islands. On February 8 the Commander-in-Chief, Coastal Command, ordered a squadron of torpedo-bombers, which had been stationed at Leuchars in Scotland, to proceed south as a reinforcement in view of the probability of the enemy ships coming up Channel. This had been increased by the arrival in Brest of two more German destroyers. On February 11 it was observed that still another pair of destroyers had appeared.

Clearly the critical moment was at hand. The submarine Sealion, exercising the discretion given to her captain by his orders, crept into Brest with the tide on the afternoon of the 11th, remaining there until the evening without seeing anything of the enemy ships. Undoubtedly the enemy chose this time for emergence on the basis of weather reports obtained by special flights made from Bergen and Brest westwards into the Atlantic. He knew that it was going to be cloudy, with poor visibility. Fortune now proceeded to play into his hands in more than one respect. "Stopper" patrol was undertaken by

ONE OF THE ILL-FATED SWORDFISH AIRCRAFT, piloted by Sub-Lieut. (A) W. B. Rose, R.N.V.R., releasing its torpedo in the desperate attempt on the German battleships Scharnhorst and Gneisenau in the English Channel, February 12, 1942. With reckless abandon Sub-Lieut. (A) E. Lee, standing, directs the attack as tracer bullets from Focke-Wulf 190s, with flaps and undercarriages down to retard speed, flash past the Swordfish.

RUNNING THE CHANNEL GAUNTLET, the German battleships Scharnhorst and Gneisenau (centre) as seen from one of their escorting warships, after steaming out from Brest on the evening of February 11, 1942. At the time the most sought-after enemy naval prize, and the most bombed, the "S and G," as they had become known, defied British air and sea attacks of some months' planning, by the Air Ministry and the Admiralty, the efficiency of which had been impaired by defective equipment on the specially detailed night air patrols.

three aircraft, which relieved each other at intervals. The first of the three, en route to the patrol area, found its A.S.V. equipment had become unserviceable, and as the fault could not be detected, returned to its base, where the crew transferred to another aircraft. This left a gap of three hours during which the entrance to Brest was unwatched. Still worse, the "Line S.E." patrol aircraft had a failure of its A.S.V. gear which caused it to return nearly two hours after leaving; during this time there was no effective reconnaissance, and a relief aircraft was not sent. Thus for practical purposes this patrol night as well have been nonexistent. "Habo" patrol was carried out without incident, but the enemy vessels did not reach this zone until after it had been withdrawn. Had they been operating with full efficiency, there is no doubt the "Stopper" and "Line S.E." patrols would have had every chance of picking up the German squadron when it left Brest.

From about 9.20 a.m. on February 12 the enemy tried hard to jam our radio direction-finding screen. Significance of this deliberate interference does not seem to have been appreciated for about two hours. By that time an order had already been issued by Fighter Command for a reconnaissance to be made over the Channel. The two Spitfires constituting this reconnaissance sighted what appeared to be a convoy of 20 to 30 vessels off Le Touquet. Landing at Hawkinge about 10.50, this was reported, a sergeant adding the useful note that he had spotted a ship with a tripod mast and heavy superstructure.

By the time this fact was elicited other aircraft had sighted and definitely identified the German ships, information reported shortly after 11. This news, together with instructions to attack, was received at 11.30

by Lieut.-Commander E. Esmonde, D.S.O., in command of the six Swordfish aircraft at Manston. Fighter protection for these was hurriedly arranged, but it was not until nearly an hour later that a single squadron of fighters arrived at Manston from Biggin Hill. Esmonde thereupon decided to carry out his attack without further delay.

By this time the enemy squadron was about 10 miles north of Calais. It was well protected by fighters, which attacked the Swordfish before they reached their target. Torpedoes were dropped by some of the six before all were brought down into the sea, but there is no evidence that they scored a hit. There were few survivors, Esmonde himself, who had won great distinction in the pursuit of the Bismarck in May 1941, losing his life. He received the posthumous award of the V.C. (portrait in page 567, Vol. 5).

16 of 39 Attacking Bombers Lost

Almost at the same time five motor torpedo boats from Dover sighted the enemy and discharged their torpedoes at ranges of from 3,000 to 5,000 yards. Again there is no reason to suppose that any hits were scored. In spite of the risks they were taking none of the m.t.b.s was sunk, their retreat being covered by some motor gunboats which arrived on the scene a little later. Three m.t.b.s from Ramsgate sighted some of the German small craft between 1 and 2 p.m., but were not able to get near enough to attack the large ships.

Between 3 and 5 p.m., seven Beauforts of Coastal Command from Thorney Island did their best to locate the enemy, and got near enough to drop torpedoes, but no results could be observed. One of the Beauforts was destroyed. Shortly after 4, nine Beauforts from Leuchars attacked, seven torpedoes

being released; again heavy anti-aircraft fire prevented observation of results. Meanwhile, 12 more Beauforts had reached Thorney Island from St. Eval and followed the others over the North Sea. Four German minesweepers were seen, but the rest of the squadron could not be found. Two of these aircraft were lost.

Five destroyers exercising off Harwich were luckier. These were H.M.S. Campbell, Mackay, Vivacious, Whitshed and Worcester, which proceeded in the reported direction of the enemy at their utmost speed. In order to make certain of gaining contact, Captain C. T. M. Pizey, commanding the flotilla, took the risk of crossing a minefield off the Maas. Shortly after 3.15 the enemy ships were sighted at a distance of 9½ miles. Regardless of the heavy fire that was opened upon him, Captain Pizey pressed to within 3,000 yards before three of his destroyers fired their torpedoes; one destroyer, the Worcester, got as close as 2,400 yards, though the Mackay was obliged to turn at about 5,000. The Worcester was the only ship hit, but managed to struggle into port with severe damage. Again there is no record of torpedo hits.

The final attack was made by 242 bombers, the majority of which were unable to locate the German squadron owing to low cloud and failing visibility. Only 39 contrived to carry out attacks, and 16 were lost. Fighter Command also sent out aircraft to the number of nearly 400. Of these, 102 made attacks on various enemy vessels; one small merchantman and a German coastal craft were sunk and at least 16 enemy aircraft brought down. Seventeen of our own fighters were lost. Mines laid by Bomber Command in concert with the Admiralty Torpedo and Mining Department caused damage to both the Scharnhorst and Gneisenau; the latter ship, indeed, received such serious injuries that she never proceeded to sea again.

It was considered by the Board of Inquiry into the whole circumstances (whose report was published recently) that, in view of the failure of two of the night patrols to function efficiently, a daylight reconnaissance down Channel to the westward should have been flown. Failure to send another aircraft to replace the one which had an A.S.V. failure on the "S.E. Line" patrol was criticized. No. 11 Fighter Group, it is suggested, "were not sufficiently alive to the fact that the German ships might be coming out at about this time" when reports of numerous enemy aircraft circling about to the northward of Le Havre appeared on their radio direction-finder plots. If the significance of the persistent radio interference by the enemy had been appreciated earlier, these plots might have been investigated and the ships detected sooner.

On the question of co-ordination between the Admiralty and Air Force, it is considered that all reasonable plans were made. Those in command of the various striking forces were naturally more concerned to delay the enemy in any way possible by immediate attacks than to risk losing the opportunity in the effort to arrange co-ordinated attacks. On February 4, when the "Fuller" scheme became operative, bomber forces were put in a state of two hours' readiness. Unfortunately, some days later, in spite of the Admiralty pointing out that with more

M.T.Bs MADE GREAT EFFORT to penetrate the powerful escort of enemy vessels shepherding the Scharnhorst and Gneisenau through the Straits of Dover. The action of these five small craft, which attacked with torpedoes at ranges of from 3,000 to 5,000 yards, was approved by the subsequent Admiralty Board of Inquiry.

favourable tides there was more rather than less danger of the ships coming out, this was altered to four hours' readiness. The Board of Inquiry thought Bomber Command should have informed the Admiralty of this.

Lieut.-Commander Esmonde's decision to deliver his Swordfish attack as soon as possible, without waiting for the arrival of a

larger fighting escort, was approved by the Board. That the torpedo bomber force of Beauforts was not used with maximum effect was a result of the failure to know in good time what the German ships were doing. The action of the motor torpedo boats and of Captain Pizey's destroyer flotilla received full approval. As regards mines, it is observed that "the work appears to have been skilfully done by the two Services in co-operation."

It is considered doubtful whether the forces employed to attack were sufficient to cripple the German ships, even if their movement out of Brest had been known at once. As the attack had to be made by day, the best prospect of disabling the ships lay with the bombers and torpedo-bombers.

Having been continuously employed on other duties, some of the crews of the Beaufort torpedo-bombers had not had sufficient training and experience for such an operation.

Owing to the low cloud, the bombers played a comparatively ineffective part in the battle. Evidence indicated that the training of the greater part of Bomber Command was not designed for effective attack on fast-moving warships by day. Bad visibility aided the motor torpedo boats, which could not otherwise have been expected to carry out their attack in broad daylight without loss. To sum up, the main reason for the failure to do more damage to the enemy was that he was not detected earlier.

H.M.S. WORCESTER was one of five British destroyers hurriedly dispatched from exercises off Harwich to intercept the Scharnhorst and Gneisenau on February 12, 1942. After manoeuvring through a minefield off the Maas the destroyer flotilla sighted the enemy, and the Worcester closed to within 2,400 yards—nearer than any other surface craft—to release her torpedoes. In this gallant but unsuccessful action heavy enemy fire caused severe damage to the Worcester, but she managed to struggle into port.

Overseas Units in the Great March-Past

ASSEMBLED IN LONDON for the June 8 procession in which Their Majesties The King and Queen and the Princesses Elizabeth and Margaret drove in a State landau were (1) men of the Arab Legion from Transjordan and a member of the Sudanese Defence Force, seen in the Kensington Gardens camp. There were men from Iraq (2), and this sergeant (3) from the Gibraltar Defence Force. From Ceylon came this sailor and A.T.S. (4). An inspector of the Malayan Police Force (5, left). Troops from Malaya, Borneo, Sarawak and Hongkong queued up for meals (6). PAGE 134

Camping in Kensington Gardens

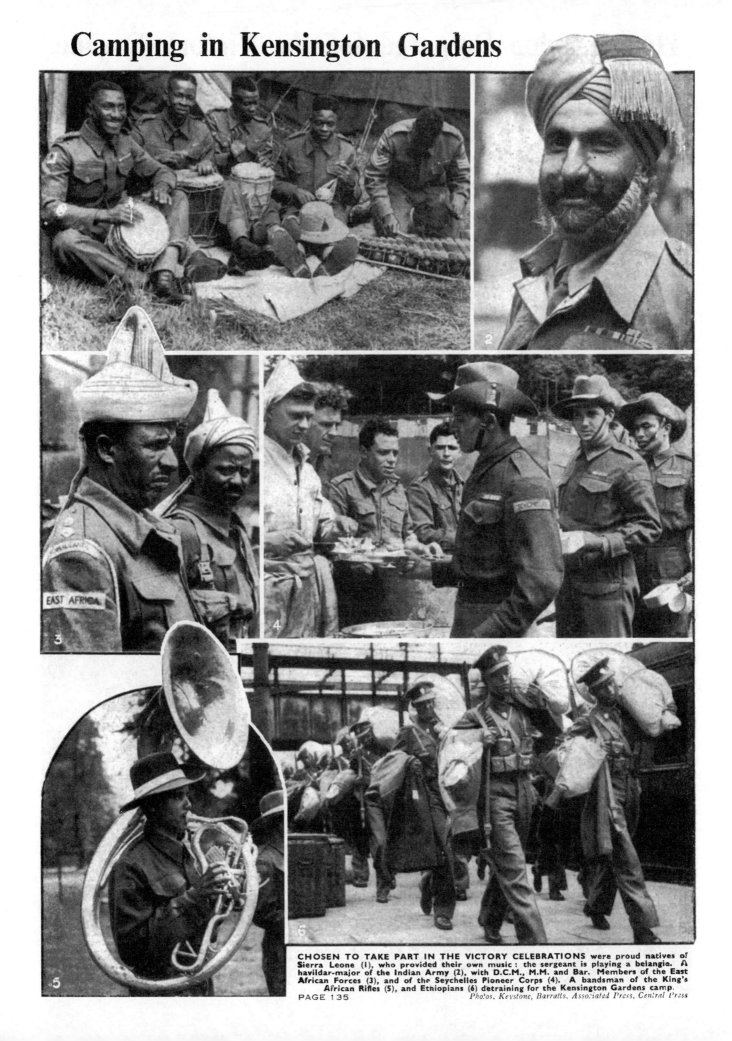

CHOSEN TO TAKE PART IN THE VICTORY CELEBRATIONS were proud natives of Sierra Leone (1), who provided their own music: the sergeant is playing a belangie. A havildar-major of the Indian Army (2), with D.C.M., M.M. and Bar. Members of the East African Forces (3), and of the Seychelles Pioneer Corps (4). A bandsman of the King's African Rifles (5), and Ethiopians (6) detraining for the Kensington Gardens camp.

Photos, Keystone, Barratts, Associated Press, Central Press

How London Prepared for the Victory Parade

8th June, 1946

TO-DAY AS WE CELEBRATE VICTORY, I send this personal message to you and all other boys and girls at school. For you have shared in the hardships and dangers of a total war and you have shared no less in the triumph of the Allied Nations.

I know you will always feel proud to belong to a country which was capable of such supreme effort; proud, too, of parents and elder brothers and sisters who by their courage, endurance and enterprise brought victory. May these qualities be yours as you grow up and join in the common effort to establish among the nations of the world unity and peace.

George R.I.

TO REGULATE THE TRAFFIC during Victory Week, June 8-15, 1946, crush gates were erected at points along the parade route, as at Duncannon Street, Charing Cross (1). Printed in six colours, 6,875,000 commemorative cards (2) bearing H.M. The King's special message to schoolchildren were distributed. Signs in Kensington Gardens (3) where Empire troops were accommodated. Floodlighting equipment at the Houses of Parliament (4) and on barges on the Thames (5). Rush orders for flags were executed (6). PAGE 136

Malta's Contingent Bids Au Revoir to Valetta

MARCHING THROUGH THE BOMB-SCARRED CAPITAL, some of the George Cross Island's defenders are seen on their way to Valetta's Palace Square, where they were reviewed before embarking for London to take part in the June Victory Parade. Comprising detachments of the fighting and civilian services, including three George Medallists, the contingent, totalling 134, was headed by Lieut.-Col. A. J. Dunkerley, O.B.E., who commanded one of the Royal Malta Artillery regiments during some of the most critical days of the siege.　　PAGE 137　　*Photo. Topical Press*

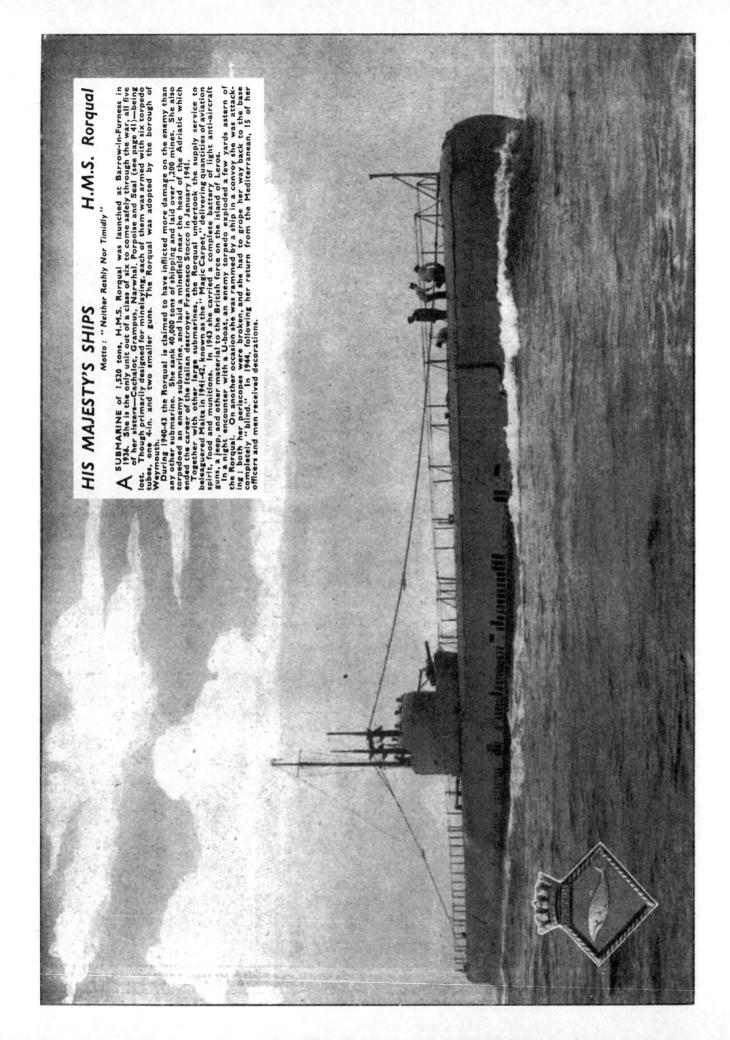

HIS MAJESTY'S SHIPS

H.M.S. Rorqual

Motto: "Neither Rashly Nor Timidly"

A SUBMARINE of 1,520 tons, H.M.S. Rorqual was launched at Barrow-in-Furness in 1936. She is the only unit out of a class of six to come safely through the war, all five of her sisters—Cachalot, Grampus, Narwhal, Porpoise and Seal (see page 41)—being lost. Though primarily designed for minelaying, each of them was armed with six torpedo tubes, one 4-in. and two smaller guns. The Rorqual was adopted by the borough of Weymouth.

During 1940-43 the Rorqual is claimed to have inflicted more damage on the enemy than any other submarine. She sank 40,000 tons of shipping and laid over 1,200 mines. She also torpedoed an enemy submarine, and laid a minefield near the head of the Adriatic which ended the career of the Italian destroyer Francesco Stocco in January 1941.

Together with other large submarines, the Rorqual undertook the supply service to beleaguered Malta in 1941-42, known as the "Magic Carpet," delivering quantities of aviation spirit, food and munitions. In 1943 she carried a complete battery of light anti-aircraft guns, a jeep, and other material to the British force on the island of Leros.

In a night encounter with a U-boat, an enemy torpedo exploded a few yards astern of the Rorqual. On another occasion she was rammed by a ship in a convoy she was attacking; both her periscopes were broken, and she had to grope her way back to the base completely "blind." In 1944, following her return from the Mediterranean, 15 of her officers and men received decorations.

The East Lancashire Regiment

by Major-General
H. T. MACMULLEN,
C.B., C.B.E., M.C.

THE first clash between autocracy and democracy came for the East Lancashire Regiment in the Second Great War when an over-bold member of a German patrol called out across the River Escaut, at Tournai, "Heil Hitler, you democratic swine!" The prompt reply from B Company was, "Go away, you square-headed So-and-so !" The order was not obeyed. Two Bren guns saw to that. This incident in Belgium took place on May 20, 1940.

Ten days later, when the situation had become critical on the famous retreat to Dunkirk, a battalion of the Regiment stood and fought on the Bergues Canal for three days, bereft of all transport save three carriers, supplied with only the ammunition that each man carried, and provisioned with only the rations that each happened to have in his haversack. During this battle Captain H. M. Ervine-Andrews won the first V.C. awarded to the Army in the Second Great War (portrait in page 139, Vol. 3).

With his company he held a blazing Belgian barn in the teeth of a critical flank attack which threatened to overrun the whole position. There can be no doubt that this defence saved the day on this sector of the line. On the same battleground Lance-Corporal Paddy O'Neill and his section refused to share an open Flanders field with anyone, and killed 40 of the 100 foemen who tried to fight their way in.

They Captured 'Boiled Halibut'

Back at home, three new battalions had been raised, but none of these was destined to fight the enemy under Regimental Colours. One was dubbed "Home Defence Only," another was converted to light anti-aircraft, the third changed its carriers for Churchill tanks and is now an honoured member of the Royal Tank Regiment. These changes did not take place until 1942, when the major threat of invasion had passed and it was possible to put into effect the General Staff's plans for bigger and brighter things.

FORMED in 1881 when the 30th Foot (raised in 1702) and the 59th Foot (raised in 1755) were linked to become respectively the 1st and 2nd Battalions East Lancashire Regiment. A 3rd (Special Reserve) Battalion and two Territorial Battalions were added in later years. The oldest Battle Honour is Gibraltar, 1704-5, gained by the 30th when still Marines ; and Canton, 1857, is a unique possession awarded only to the 59th. During the 1914-18 war the East Lancashires were expanded to seventeen battalions and fought with distinction in all the main theatres.

In 1942 another battalion of the Regiment sailed from a north-western port. Its destination was the big French naval base of Diego Suarez, situated on the northern tip of the Vichy-controlled island of Madagascar, and the battalion formed part of a special task force which had been ordered to seize it. This ticklish operation opened before dawn on May 5, 1942, when B Company was landed with No. 5 Commando and completely surprised a heavy battery on a commanding promontory guarding the entrance to the bay in which the assault convoy was to anchor. The remainder of the Battalion took part in the main landing and subsequent land attack on the key town of Antsirane. For his brilliant handling of the Battalion carriers in this action Captain F. J. H. Arnold was awarded the M.C. It was the Regiment's first experience of offensive action in the War.

When the British Army re-entered France in 1944 the Regiment was again represented, as at Dunkirk, by two battalions. One was soon to gain fame for itself. " Send my congratulations to Colonel Burden and the East Lancashires," wrote the Divisional General, " for their magnificent work in the capture of Bois Halbout." This small Norman town, by the way, received the nickname of " Boiled Halibut." When the attack was at its height Sergeant J. French wheeled his 6-pounder anti-tank gun up a street in full view of the enemy and blasted a German machine-gun nest out of the town hall at sixty yards' range. During a counter-attack Sergeant C. Hatton dashed up another street in a hail of Spandau fire, engaging a tank with his Piat gun and forcing it to retire.

The other battalion was not so fortunate. The attack to which it was committed on July 16, 1944, from Fontenay was doomed to failure from the start. In the heart of the dense Bocage country effective support from artillery and tanks was out of the question, and only one company, under the command of Major C. C. S. Genese, succeeded in reaching the final objective. July 16 had indeed been a black Sunday. Grappling with a determined foe in this tortured and twisted country had cost the Battalion over 250 casualties in killed and wounded. And that was not the end of its mortification.

On July 30 General Montgomery, as he was then, wrote to the Commanding Officer with characteristic straightforwardness, " I am afraid I have bad news for you, and so prefer to break it myself." There were not enough men to feed all infantry units in the Field, and it had therefore been decided, with regret, that the hammer of disbandment must fall on the anvil of Regimental pride, and as fine a Battalion as ever fought was not summoned again to answer roll call. So only one battalion was left to take part in the drive to Antwerp. It rode on tanks, guns, tractors and lorries, as well as on its own vehicles.

A Dash in Flame-throwing Tanks

Arrived in the Low Countries, fresh laurels awaited the Battalion. There was the storming and capture of Bladel, a small Dutch town over the Belgian border, on September 22, 1944, two intrepid company commanders, Majors C. W. Griffin and J. F. Lake, sweeping forward to an objective which the Germans had a particular reason for wanting to keep. This was followed on November 24 by Hertogenbosch, where a daring dash in armoured lorries and flame-throwing tanks failed to get through, but a quick appreciation by Lieut.-Colonel G. W. Burden produced an alternative plan which included a hazardous night advance across country intersected with dykes about 15 feet wide and whose muddy banks were lined with barbed wire. This dramatic change from armour to foot won another Battalion objective.

On December 17, 1944, the Battalion was suddenly summoned to the Ardennes. Its route to the threatened area took it through places steeped in the history of the Waterloo

THROUGH BURMESE SWAMPS, JUNGLE AND DESERT SCRUB, 2nd East Lancashires, of the 36th British Division, fought and pursued the retreating 53rd Japanese Division. A new era was opened in the Regiment's history when on August 6, 1944, the whole battalion was lifted by air from Ledo in Assam over the Patkai Hills to Myitkyina in N. Burma. Taking part in the advance from there towards Mandalay, men placed logs to form a stream-crossing (left). Advancing through sun-scorched scrub (right).
Photos, British Official

IN THE STREETS OF HERTOGENBOSCH, in Holland, men of the 1st Battalion the East Lancashire Regiment sought out the enemy tenaciously holding on to the town. The first assault, on November 24, 1944, had failed; but the following day, where armour had failed these men succeeded and another objective was won by the Battalion.
Photo, British Official

campaign. One of them was Quatre Bras, and as the troop-carrying vehicles rattled over the famous cross-roads they passed the very spot where the Regiment had fought in square nearly 130 years before and had caused Sir Thomas Picton to cry out that he would make the highest report of the Commanding Officer and the Regiment.

Now the inheritors of that report were on their way to a different battlefield and where it was to be proved that the same spirit still pervaded all ranks. In this Ardennes battle for six whole days everyone, from Rifle Section to Battalion H.Q., was exposed to the rigours of what has been described as the coldest spell for fifty years. There was not a vestige of protection against the weather, and

it can truthfully be said that exposure and exhaustion in this battle were even deadlier enemies than guns and machine-guns. The final objective was the village of Grimblemont. It had a special tactical significance because it dominated all escape for the enemy along the road from Marche to Laroche. It was stormed and captured by exhausted troops on January 7, 1945, despite as unpropitious a start as could well be imagined.

A 88-mm. shell landed on Battalion H.Q. as it was forming up for the advance, and killed the Adjutant, Intelligence Sergeant and Provost Corporal. The Arctic conditions, too, proved insuperable to the supporting tanks. When the time came, not one could cross the start-line and the assault companies

had to double out of the woods without the tanks to gain the smoke-screen laid to conceal them from enemy view. Yet these men, worn out by exposure and fatigue, plunged forward in the ever-deepening snow. When the two leading companies staggered into Grimblemont they could not muster fifty officers and men between them. At one time it seemed that they would never get there, until Lieutenant K. Tufnell and a Piat team gave fresh impetus to the attack by routing three Tiger tanks that barred the way.

WITH Von Rundstedt's diversion successfully frustrated the Battalion was hastily re-equipped for the Rhineland invasion, which had been postponed to February 8. A large force had been detailed for the capture of the Reichswald Forest redoubt, covering an area of forty square miles of closely planted firs. Of the Battalion's share in this battle it was written in the Liverpool Daily Post:

"They fought and plodded their way through nine miles of deep mud and black forest. I have not seen anything approaching these terrible conditions anywhere. My journey to these Lancashire men was a nightmare. Nothing could get forward that night that depended on wheels and tracks, but the men went on. The tracks vanished underfoot and they went on by compass. They had barely consolidated when the orders came through again, 'Push on!' All the time the orders were 'Push on!'"

In Regimental memories the Reichswald leaves three prominent landmarks. The brilliant leadership of a young C.O.—Lieut.-Colonel F. E. E. Allen—who was awarded a bar to the D.S.O. he had just gained in the Ardennes; the capture of a "captured" battery of four Russian 12·2cm. guns; an old-fashioned bayonet charge by C Company, led by Major E. M. Morrison, M.C.

"SHALL WE HAVE TO FIGHT FOR HAMBURG?" was on the lips of the East Lancashires, in this hitherto unpublished photograph, when, having reached the Valley of the Elbe, the Battalion moved along the highway leading to Germany's great seaport. But Hamburg fell without a fight, and at 6 a.m. on May 4, 1945, the companies started arriving to make secure the surrender of the city—the Hamburg Constabulary directing the various convoys to their destinations.
Photo, British Official

East Lancashires at Antwerp and Villers Bocage

ONLY ONE BATTALION OF THE REGIMENT WAS LEFT to take part in the drive to Antwerp : with a six-pounder anti-tank gun the 1st covered the approaches to Antwerp docks (top) after the port had fallen to the Allies, September 4, 1944. In the lower of these previously unpublished photographs. men of East Lancashires are carrying ammunition through a village near Villers Bocage at the beginning of August 1944. In this region the " Black Sunday " of July 16 cost the 5th Battalion over 250 casualties.

Photo, British Official

Emerging from the forest the Battalion took part in the southerly advance to link up with the American 9th Army. It had the distinction of being the first unit of General Crerar's Army to do so. This historic event took place at Geldern, and there was a momentary melée of great excitement during which the representatives of Britain, America and Germany had some difficulty in recognizing each other's "club colours." When its turn came to cross the Rhine the Battalion did so in the wake of the assaulting Divisions. Its final goal was the great port of Hamburg.

When, eventually, the Valley of the Elbe was reached the question on everyone's lips was, "Shall we have to fight for Hamburg?" As things turned out the answer was "No," and at 6 a.m. on May 4, 1945, the companies started arriving to make secure the surrender of the city. There was no "grand entry" about it. Dressed in white, the Hamburg Constabulary directed the traffic of the various convoys to their different destinations with the efficiency of the London Metropolitan Police. B Company's area included the broadcasting station, and its one regret, at the close of the hostilities, was that Lord "Haw-Haw" had only just vacated. His capture would have been just retribution for the message broadcast to the company across the banks of the Escaut five years before.

The war against Germany ended before the war against Japan, and the same sequence will be observed in this article. So we must recall

running south to Mandalay, and down it the 36th Division, to which the Battalion belonged, set off in pursuit of the retreating 53rd Japanese Division. The story of the pursuit is chiefly one of sharp small-scale engagements and battle patrols ranging deep into the heart of the jungle. But a big action was fought from November 9 to 12, 1944, when the Brigade was allotted the task of capturing Naba junction.

Mopping-Up in the Shan States

In the plan of attack the Commanding Officer, Lieut.-Colonel T. A. Eccles, was given the special mission of advancing down the axis of the Auktan-Indaw Road to capture the village of Okshitkon. The object was to draw off the enemy from his main position on the railway corridor, and to harass his left flank. The enemy had also been inspired with a similar idea and had assembled a considerable force in the Auktan area with the intention of attacking Mawlu, 13 miles up the corridor from Naba. The capture of Okshitkon was thus not achieved until the remainder of the Battalion, after bitter fighting, had succeeded in joining up with A Company, which had penetrated 1,500 yards behind the Japanese position after a most daring manoeuvre round his flank.

The task had been rendered doubly difficult by the unexpected Japanese concentration, but there were double laurels as well. Not only had the objective been captured but an

Colours: Red Lion on Yellow Circle surrounded by White Ring on Black Background

15TH (SCOTTISH) DIVISION

SUCCESSORS to the "Ladies of Hell" of the First Great War, the new 15th Division, the "Crossing Sweepers," so nicknamed for its part in "leaping" rivers, was formed mostly of Scottish Territorial troops, in Scotland in 1939, but did not see action until after D-Day, June 1944. Landing in Normandy on June 13 the Division, commanded by Maj.-Gen. G. H. A. Macmillan, took part in the "Battle of the Scottish Corridor," June 26, and elements advanced to secure two bridge-heads over the river Odon, capturing the town of Tourville on June 27.

Moved to Caumont on July 23 the Division swept through Sept Vents and Hervieux, to take the Bois de l'Homme early in August, "vital to the success of the whole Second Army plan," in the words of the Corps Commander. Heavy losses were sustained outside Estry, where Maj.-Gen. Macmillan was wounded; he was succeeded by Maj.-Gen. C. M. Barber. The Division when withdrawn evoked the tribute of the Army Commander, Gen. Sir Miles Dempsey: "You have set the very highest standard from the day you landed in Normandy."

ON the move again in "Operation Gallop," the Division reached the Seine where, on August 28, it embarked on one of its many river crossings to continue the advance in Northern France to enter Belgium. At Gheel, in mid-September, it hung on for a few days to a small bridge-head on the canal, where further praise was paid to it, this time by the German High Command, in an order to its own troops to "eliminate the bridge-head at all costs. You are fighting the crack 15th Division."

Entering Holland on September 20, it was heavily engaged around Best and Schijndel. In a whirlwind advance Tilburg was captured, on October 1, and from there the Division went to the support of the Americans in the Nijmegen salient, and helped to push the Germans back across the Peel marshes. Reaching the river Maas on November 26, Blerick was stormed and captured.

Spearhead of the offensive against the Siegfried Line, on February 8, 1945, the Division experienced bitter fighting but had taken Cleves and Goch before the end of the month. On March 24 it was one of the two Divisions to lead the assault across the Rhine—"a difficult task magnificently performed," wrote the Corps Commander to Maj.-Gen. Barber. After securing a crossing over the Yssel, Celle fell to the Division and Uelzen was captured on April 18. In a final assault the Elbe was crossed on April 29. The Division was disbanded on April 10, 1946.

CELEBRATING "SOMME DAY" on July 1, 1945, the 1st Battalion of the East Lancashires remembered those of the Regiment who fell in the famous battle in 1916. These previously unpublished photographs show the sounding of "Last Post" (above) and (right) the C.O., Lieut.-Col. F. F. E. Allen, D.S.O. and Bar, with Brigadier E. Dominic-Browne, O.B.E., who took the salute at the march-past.
Photos, British Official

the victorious battalion left behind in Madagascar. It did not return to the United Kingdom, but was moved on to India and from there to Burma, where it distinguished itself by a dogged and Lancashire-like resistance on the Arakan front. Then a new era was opened in Regimental history when the whole Battalion was lifted by air from Ledo in Assam to Myitkyina in North Burma.

This event took place on August 6, 1944, a few days after Myitkyina had fallen to an international army, composed mostly of Chinese, under command of the American General "Vinegar Joe" Stilwell. Its fall opened up the terminus of a railway corridor

enemy plan had been frustrated, a plan that might have had serious consequences for the rest of the Brigade fighting in the corridor. The sword of a Japanese officer, killed in this battle, is now a treasured Regimental trophy.

After entering Twinnge, on February 8, 1945, the 36th Division was switched eastwards for mopping-up operations in the Shan States. On March 20 the Battalion entered Mogok, the centre of the famous ruby mines, and after that it saw no more fighting with S.E.A.C. In its ranks were too many officers and men due for repatriation under the "Python" scheme and it was ordered back to India. On arrival, the Colours and Mess Plate were withdrawn from store in Bombay, and so the symbols of Peace came back once more to their proper resting-place.

William the Conqueror Still Mounted in Falaise

In the last stages of the Battle of the Falaise Gap—one of the bloodiest conflicts on the Western Front—ancient Falaise fell to Canadian troops on August 17, 1944. Still intact amidst debris in the Place de la Trinité is the bronze equestrian statue (top) of William the Conqueror, who was born in the castle whose ruins overlook the town—capital of his dukedom of Normandy. Almost totally destroyed was St. Gervais Church (bottom). Rubble has been sorted for use in reconstruction.

Utilitarian New Replaces Picturesque Old—

Once-important road centre on the right bank of the River Vire, St. Lo was already in ruins (1) when the U.S. 1st Army captured it on July 18, 1944. Now, two years after the Normandy beach landings (June 6), usable wreckage awaits incorporation in a new St. Lo. Captured on July 27, half the town of Lessay was destroyed : in the shadow of the bombed church a wooden chapel (2) serves the people, for whom temporary accommodation has been erected (3).

—Where the Battle-tide Flowed in Normandy

Medieval houses which made the streets of Lisieux picturesque were destroyed largely by fires started by the retreating Germans; the 15th-century St. Jacques Church (4) was gutted, and around it now are temporary shops. Thirty miles east of Caen, the town was cleared by August 25. Ironically, whilst beauty spots of Normandy have been reduced to rubble, German fortifications still stand on Utah Beach (5), one of the D-Day landing-places, on the Cotentin Peninsula.

Calm in the Sunshine Now Lies Caen

Some of the fiercest fighting following the D-Day landings raged round this most important road junction in Normandy. Eastern bastion of the German positions and desperately defended, Caen was captured by British and Canadian troops on July 9, 1944, after artillery and air bombardment had made it almost unrecognizable. Before they were driven out the Germans added to the destruction by wanton damage as well as military demolition. Eight thousand houses were destroyed or badly damaged; of the medieval wooden houses which gave it character and beauty only two remained. In orderly mounds (top) the stones of its old buildings await the bricklayers of the New Age; in the background is the Church of St. Jean. The 16th-century Hôtel d'Escoville (bottom) is but a jagged shell of memories.

Exclusive to THE WAR ILLUSTRATED

146

WAR STORES of the BRITISH COLONIES

By HARLEY V. USILL

IN a number of respects the great industrial and production effort of the British colonies was a vital contribution to the victory of the United Nations. It took three main forms : in the first place, each Colonial territory had to become as near as possible self-supporting as regards their own food supplies in order to minimize the use of shipping space for imports ; then they had to meet ever-increasing demands for certain foods and raw materials required for the total war effort ; and they had to supply foodstuffs and other commodities for armies operating in the various Colonial regions.

To perform this threefold task meant that a careful balance had to be struck between the utilization of land and labour, and between internal and external needs. Owing, however, to the general lack of industrial machinery in most Colonial territories, the main contribution consisted in the supply of food and raw materials rather than in the finished products of industry : Palestine, and for a time, Hongkong, provided exceptions.

Palestine's Magnificent Record

By remarkable development of a large number of small industries Palestine was able to meet many of the military requirements of the Middle East. Between 1939 and 1942 the number of industrial establishments in Palestine increased from 1,217 to 3,470, the gross output from a value of £8,842,000 to £36,828,000, and the persons engaged from 20,414 to 49,977. Manufactured goods supplied direct to the military authorities in 1942 were valued at £7,200,000.

Orders were placed for hundreds of thousands, and sometimes millions, of such articles as bottles, mess tins, stoves, pumps, electric cable, glass insulators, khaki drill uniforms, camouflage nets, tarpaulin tents, boots, bolts and nuts, and many other items. Another valuable contribution was the production of concentrated citrus juices essential to the health of troops in the Middle East. In addition to a variety of scientific and engineering articles, textiles and medical stores, production also included valuable chemicals. Sulphuric acid was produced to meet the requirements not only of Palestine but also Syria, Cyprus and Iraq. Palestine also manufactured superphosphate fertilizers and the important drug D.D.T.

HAD it not been for the intervention of the Japanese, Hongkong might well have competed successfully with Palestine for first place as an industrial colony. Her shipbuilding yards might have been of great value to the war effort, since in 1941 plans were in being for using them for the Royal Navy. The same year a mission from the Ministry of Supply were satisfied that Hongkong could manufacture heavy presses, minesweepers, Diesel truck engines, scientific instruments, hospital equipment, wireless and telephone apparatus, and chemicals. This project, however, was not to be realized.

Difficulties in the West Indies

The disasters of 1941-42 in the Far East cut the West Indies off from their chief sources for the supply of rice ; and the activities of enemy submarines in the Caribbean, combined with demands for shipping for the war fronts, led to a serious shrinkage in the amount of food reaching them. Throughout the West Indies, then, the main contribution on the production front developed into the most intensive drive for more food. The importance of this is seen by reference to Malta, where much shipping, at considerable risk, had to be employed to get food convoys through at all costs.

In making this drive many difficulties had to be overcome, and the final result was not

LEAVING his study of the strategic importance of the British Colonial Empire the author turns to the mighty industrial and production effort which the Colonies put forth during the War. More food for their own use and for armies operating in their territory, and more raw materials, were their chief objectives. How successfully these were attained is shown in the all-over picture presented here.

〜〜〜〜〜

brought about without much personal sacrifice. In Barbados an extension of the area under food crops meant a reduction in the acreage under sugar and cotton ; while in Grenada, St. Lucia and St. Vincent (Windward Islands) the demand for labour for the construction of the American bases affected the numbers available for agriculture. In British Guiana and Jamaica a shortage of petrol, spare parts and transport provided a constant difficulty in marketing. In spite of all, the production drive was a very real success. One example of achievement must suffice : the acreage registered under food in Jamaica increased from 80,000 acres in 1940 to more than 200,000 acres in 1943, with the result that the island was able to dispense with imports of rice.

Apart from this essential food drive, there was an intensification of the output of petroleum from Trinidad and bauxite from British Guiana. Sea Island cotton, used as a substitute for silk in barrage balloons and for war clothing and equipment, came from the Windward and Leeward Islands, while wild rubber was tapped in British Honduras, British Guiana and Trinidad.

Industries Developed in Ceylon

Ceylon is another example of an island Colony which had to turn to its own resources for the bulk of its food supplies, especially after the Japanese invasion of Burma cut her off from the main source of rice. By August 1943 more than 450,000 acres of land were brought under cultivation, principally with rice—an expansion which involved irrigation works on a large scale ; and by 1944 there were three Government rice mills, the largest of which produced about 25,000 bushels a month.

Supplementary foodstuffs production included yams, cereals, beans, fruits, sugar, ginger, chillies, onions and turmeric. Local fisheries were also developed. One of the difficulties involved in food drives in tropical countries is to persuade the people to change from one diet to another. After many centuries of a one-diet menu the stomach reacts violently against a sudden change.

Ceylon also possesses raw materials which were essential to the war effort. Before the war coconuts were, after tea, the most important of Ceylon's agricultural products, and on this industry several other industries are dependent, the main production being copra, coconut oil, desiccated coconut, coir, toddy and arrack. The needs of war called for a step-up in the by-products of the coconut, and new factories were established to cope with the increased demand. The presence of a large army in Ceylon led to the development of many other industries previously unknown to the country.

A steel-rolling mill was erected in 1941 to turn scrap metal into hoop iron, steel bars, nuts, bolts and rivets. A plywood factory, using locally-made glue, was opened in 1941, and textile mills to produce war materials from yarn imported from India followed in 1942, and later a bleaching and dyeing works was opened at Colombo. In connexion with the last the people of Ceylon

found plants from which to produce dyes previously imported from Germany. The fall of Malaya placed another burden upon Ceylon. There was at once an urgent demand to produce more rubber, and every effort was made to meet this, even to the extent of slaughter-tapping—that is, tapping the rubber trees so intensively as to exhaust the trees within two years. As a result, records in rubber production were reached during the critical years of 1941 and 1942.

Kenya, Uganda and Tanganyika in East Africa and Nigeria, the Gold Coast, Sierra Leone and the Gambia in West Africa, in addition to ensuring by local production the maximum of food, produced many essential commodities for the war effort. They provided nearly all the United Nations' requirements of pyrethrum (insecticide) and many thousands of tons of sisal, rubber, wheat, maize, tea, sugar, cotton, coffee, wool, flax, copra, minerals, timber, paper, quinine, oil seeds and hides.

Triumphant in E. and W. Africa

Our supplies of margarine, soap, lubricants and glycerine came very largely from an intensification of production of palm oil, palm kernels and ground nuts in West Africa ; iron ore came from Sierra Leone, manganese and peroxide from the Gold Coast and tin from Nigeria. In order to meet our copper requirements, Northern Rhodesia worked a twenty-four-hour day.

The African war effort was so completely all-out that it is invidious to make distinctions, and by choosing a few examples it is not intended to emphasize the contribution of one Colony as against another. One example of the way in which East and West Africa made the Allied victory possible was the setting-up of dehydration plants at Kerugoya and Karatine in Kenya. By May 1944 these factories were buying vegetables for dehydration from nearly 10,000 African farmers.

The factories were kept going twenty-four hours a day, and the task of training completely unskilled Africans to handle complicated machinery had to go on all the time. In addition, the African farmers were taught to raise seedlings in nurseries, to deal with pests and to lay out irrigation areas.

WITH campaigns being fought in malarial regions, the war against the mosquito was as important as against human enemies, and for that war an insecticide made from pyrethrum, a flower which looks like a daisy, is essential. Japan and the Caucasus were the normal sources of supply, but with these areas in the hands of the enemy Kenya was called upon to fill the gap. She also supplied consignments of seed to a number of Allied countries, including 20,000 lb. to Russia.

In addition to the export to Kenya for civil and military needs of nearly 100,000 head of livestock between 1939 and 1943, Uganda turned one of her main products, cotton, to several uses. New uses were found for cotton seed as a fertilizer, as a cattle feed and as fuel to replace coal. In 1942 25,000 tons of cotton seed were supplied to the United Kingdom to make vegetable oils.

One more example comes from West Africa. The Gold Coast, in addition to being called upon to produce 1,000,000 tons of manganese in 1944, was looked to as an alternative source for bauxite from which aluminium is made. Production commenced in 1941, when a total of 14,000 tons was mined ; but when a projected production of 70,000 tons for 1942 was altered to a projected production of 400,000 tons planned for 1944, the great task of working another deposit had to be undertaken.

Europe's Wartime Capitals in 1946

THE HAGUE
by P. S. GERBRANDY

FOREIGNERS generally call The Hague the capital of the Netherlands. Dutchmen call The Hague "de residentie," the residence ; for the Queen "resides" in The Hague. The commercial capital of the Netherlands is Amsterdam. The Hague is not only the residence of the Queen. There you find the seat of the Government, the Houses of Parliament. Many political people and civil servants have to reside there. It is the residence for ambassadors and ministers. It is a town in which many retired officials from all parts of the Kingdom of the Netherlands (which includes the Netherlands East Indies and the Netherlands West Indies) have found a home.

Dr. P. S. GERBRANDY
from the portrait by Cornelis Visser.

Those facts determine to a large extent the character of The Hague. In the centre you find the beautiful, old, historical part, where the political life of the Netherlands from the time of the foundation of the Republic of the Seven Provinces has been centred. Near to this small centre with its Houses of Parliament and other typical old buildings and the attractive "Hofvijver," are charming squares and avenues. The rest of the town lacks distinction—some parts remind one more of a village than of a town, many parts are ugly. But among all that ugliness there was formerly one great attractiveness : the verdure of woods. The Hague is the town of "Het Haagsche Bosch" (The Wood of The Hague) of "de Scheveningsche Boschjes" (the little woods of Scheveningen), of old country seats, of small parks and thickets spread all over the town. It is the town of dunes, beach and sea.

Sites and Dumps of V1s and V2s

During the years of Occupation it was the seat of the German Administration, the German Civil (and partly military) Service. The scars it bears are hideous, for the War as well as the Occupation has maimed this town in a horrible way. The Germans transformed The Hague into a hedgehog-position. It was made a formidable fortress in the West Wall defence belt ; safe, they thought, against every attack from the sea or over land. All through the large town from the dunes in the west to the suburbs of the north-east was dug a tank-ditch many miles long, partly interrupted by a heavy tank-wall of ferro-concrete. Large quarters with thousands of houses were completely broken down in order to offer to the defenders a free field of fire ; the centuries-old "Haagsche Bosch" was cut down.

The pleasant beach of Scheveningen was planted with piles and stakes to make it unapproachable for aircraft, the boulevard was covered all over its length with a wall of concrete, heaps of heavy bunkers were spread along the defence line. In short, the Germans showed that they could and would ruin this town, so dear to all Dutchmen. They carried out this catastrophic act, indeed, with the expressed idea that they would teach the proud Dutch how the Germans had the right and the intention to reshape the fine country (admiration for which they could not hide) into a barracks and a wilderness. The greater part of what

PROFESSOR of Law

PROFESSOR of Law in the Free University of Amsterdam, 1930-1939, and Minister of Justice in Jonkheer de Geer's Government at the time of the German invasion of the Low Countries, Dr. Gerbrandy was Prime Minister of the Netherlands Government in London from September 1940 to May 1945.

was charming disappeared, the greater part of what was ugly remained.

The Allied bombardment of March 3, 1945, aimed at the sites and dumps of the V1s and V2s, demolished a large quarter in the north, reducing an area of 150 acres to a heap of rubble. The inhabitants of The Hague themselves took away from the "Scheveningsche Boschjes" all the trees left by the Germans, and removed wood from ruined houses, in order to have warmth and means of cooking the small rations in the winter of 1944-1945, when cold, hunger and starvation reigned everywhere (see facing page). Ninety per cent of the historical part of The Hague was spared ; otherwise it would have been unrecognizable to one who left it in 1940 and returned in 1945.

Sacrificed to the Fortress-Plan

Some figures will demonstrate the physical changes The Hague has suffered. Five hundred acres of woods, plantations and parks have been destroyed. The people of The Hague took and burnt 60,000 trees, among them 20,000 from plantations and streets. More than 20,000 houses have been demolished or damaged, among them more than 8,000 of which no trace has been left. The Hague had a population of about 500,000.

Nearly all the transport, indispensable in this town that is the size of Paris, was requisitioned or stolen by the Germans. Many bridges were sacrificed to the fortress-plan. Twelve million bricks and paving stones were taken out of the streets to be used for the building of aerodromes, many public buildings were destroyed or severely damaged ; fine manor houses were ruined. Moreover, the Germans requisitioned or stole furniture, clothing, and valuables. When in May 1945 I saw The Hague and Scheveningen again for the first time after the war, I received the impression of a dead town.

The suffering of the population has been in proportion to the material destruction. Nearly 100,000 (about one-fifth) of the inhabitants, who could find no refuge in the crowded remaining buildings, had to move to neighbouring towns and villages, often to the east of the Netherlands. People of The Hague were amongst the tens of thousands of townsmen who daily passed the cross-roads in the Wieringermeer, about 80 miles north of The Hague, in order to find food in the countryside for their families.

In the first half of 1945, according to official statistics, 2,135 people in The Hague died from hunger, and that figure does not include those who died from disease and could not recover because of weakness. The death-rate grew and grew. Diphtheria and tuberculosis rose threateningly. Months after the liberation the consequences of this suffering were visible. Naturally, after the liberation, on May 5, 1945, normal life in The Hague did not return automatically. But the food situation improved immediately. The unforgettable dropping of food by aircraft and the splendidly prepared supply of food and medicines sent in by the Allies

and the Netherlands military government was a complete success. But exhaustion had gone too far ; disorganization had become too complete. For months after liberation the people looked listless and weary.

Notwithstanding all this, progress was made. Already during the Occupation leading men in the local administration had prepared plans for as speedy a restoration as possible. Although the means available were poor, work started immediately after May 5, 1945. Within a few months the dirt had gone ; many streets had been repaired (since September 1945 about 1,000 houses a month, beginning with those least damaged, have been restored), the desert of sand dunes, once the fine "Scheveningsche Boschjes," had been planted with young trees. Even the horrible wall of concrete and the tank-ditch had been tackled. A new design of the whole town is in the making.

BEHIND this activity lies a social fact of great importance. The work that had to be done needed skilled and unskilled labourers. It proved possible to adapt the execution of the work to the physical condition of the workers. You should not blame people who have been living for a long time under a reign of terror, who have gone through a horrible famine, if they show deviations from normal life, shortcomings in energy. The lead given by the local administration has contributed largely to paving the way back to normal life. There is hardly any unemployment.

The actual standard of living is difficult to define. The officials have received a general increase in salary of 15 per cent at least. In private firms there is a tendency towards paying high wages for skilled labour ; the same shows itself in some branches of the civil service. The food situation is not bad. There is a shortage of fat, meat, sometimes of vegetables ; the quantity of calories for one individual is 1,900. In the long run that must be insufficient ; but now the people are satisfied—after a time of privation.

The rationed foodstuffs, cigars, cigarettes, tobacco and furniture, also rationed, and obtainable because of its scarcity by very few, are almost the only things you can buy. Textiles are out of the question. A woman expressed the situation in the following words : "I applied for a skirt and got an allocation, I walked for one hour and a half from my home to the shop, and waited for four hours in a large queue, where my coat was torn, only to find that I could get nothing." Except for their windows, most of the shops are nearly empty.

Very Slowly the Scars are Healing

The result is that every family first of all provides itself with all the rationed articles, the sweets (more than in England) included. A worker's family earning not more than £3 10s. a week can buy all these things and have a small surplus. What to do with that surplus ? The problem of economic and social family life in The Hague, as in the whole Netherlands, will not be solved until sufficient goods are available. It will take time before The Hague gets back to the life of 1940.

Nevertheless, on the way it certainly is. The faces of the people have lost the weariness they showed. Clubs, hotels, restaurants have restarted on a moderate scale, the ministries are working full-swing in well-furnished offices. The Queen is back in her country house in the dunes, the States-General meet in the Houses of Parliament, Ministers and Ambassadors give their receptions, the new Permanent Court of International Justice has been inaugurated. But in our century the scars will not disappear.

After Years of German Occupation: The Hague

SEAT OF THE NETHERLANDS GOVERNMENT, The Hague, 14 miles north-west of Rotterdam, suffered severely at the hands of the Germans from May 1940 onwards. A devastated area (1), where debris has been piled for future use. The town's largest departmental store (2), one of the few modern buildings to escape damage. A recent view of Scheveningen woods (3), whence hard-pressed citizens took fuel for their fires in the winter of 1944-45. Ruins of the English Church, St. John and St. Philip (4). See also facing page.

Photos, Keystone, Jansen, Hague Tourist Organization PAGE 149

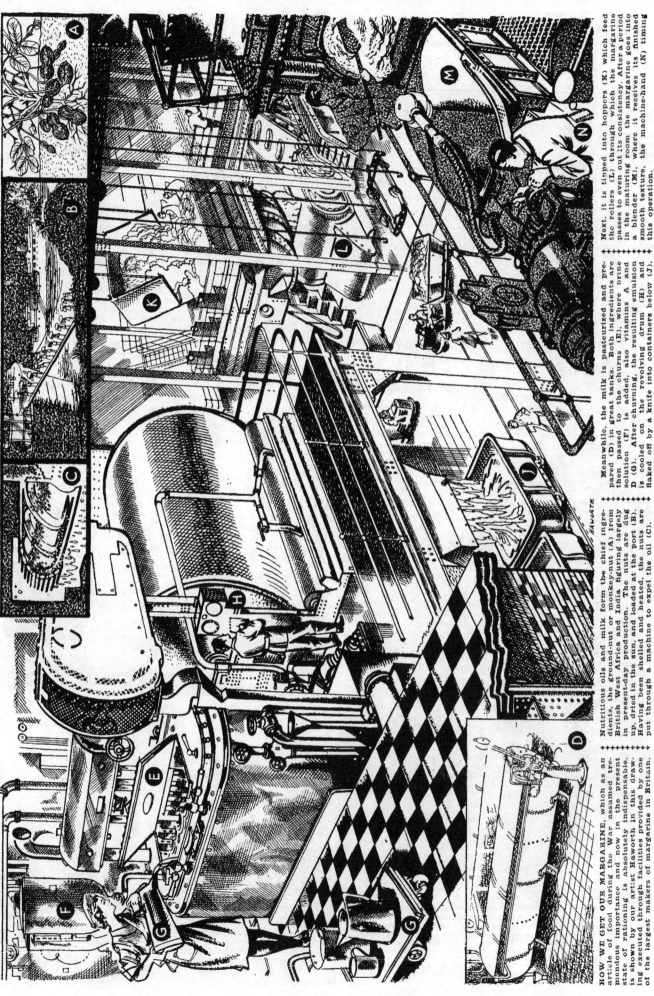

HOW WE GET OUR MARGARINE, which as an article of food during the War assumed tremendous importance and now in the present state of rationing is absolutely indispensable, is shown by our artist Haworth in this drawing executed through facilities provided by one of the largest makers of margarine in Britain.

Nutritious oils and milk form the chief ingredients, the ground-nut or monkey-nut (A) from British West Africa and India figuring largely in present-day production. The nuts are dug up, dried in the sun, and loaded at the port (B). Having been shelled and heated, the nuts are put through a machine to expel the oil (C).

Meanwhile, the milk is pasteurized and prepared (D) in great tanks. Both ingredients are then passed to the churns (E), where brine solution (F) is added, also vitamins A and D (G). After churning, the resulting emulsion is cooled on the revolving drum (H) and flaked off by a knife into containers below (J).

Next, it is tipped into hoppers (K) which feed the rollers (L) through which the margarine passes to even out its consistency. After a period in the maturing room the margarine goes into a blender (M), where it receives its finished smooth texture, the machine-hand (N) timing this operation.

Our War Leaders in Peacetime
SLIM

Famous leader of the 14th Army, General Sir William Slim, K.C.B., C.B.E., D.S.O., was the last of the war-generals to make the headlines. He abhors personal publicity. The latter fact is illustrated by his refusal to divulge the pen-name under which he writes, by way of recreation, in the newspapers and magazines.

On returning from India in December 1945, he found his family a house in Trevor Street, Knightsbridge, where he lives with his wife and their 15-year-old daughter Una. Knightsbridge is the fashionable quarter of London, but the Slims have no leaning towards a "fashionable" life. They like the theatres, "Because we've been starved of plays for so long."

Above all, Slim's interests are in his children. Una is still at school and is "insisting on becoming a vet.—she loves animals, you know." John, aged 18, entered the Army a few months ago, and "The lad is already an inch taller than I am!" John's father did not start life in the Army. General Slim, now 55, left King Edward's Grammar School, Birmingham, to be a junior clerk—"In other words," he says, "an office boy." Then he became an elementary schoolmaster, and next, before he joined up in 1914, foreman of a testing gang in an engineering works and a junior N.C.O. in the Territorials.

From those early days Slim has developed three main hobbies—soldiering, tinkering with machinery, and literature. And he likes writing. In fact, he has always wanted to be a journalist, and his magazine articles show a decided flair for that profession. But he does not always find it easy to say what he wants to say in the forceful way he wants to say it, without first roughing out a draft; and he has been known to tell his friends that in his experience it is easier to be a good general than a good journalist.

His articles are not the only things Slim signs anonymously—the 14th Army's famous "flash" came from his pencil. He submitted the drawing anonymously in a competition open to all ranks, and won the £5 prize offered for the winning design.

Both Sir William and Lady Slim like the peace and quiet of the country, and on returning from India one of the first things they did was to leave London for a district where, as Lady Slim said, "We can just sit." Slim himself likes to punctuate his "sitting" with sharp walks, and possibly a little shooting: he is reputed to be a good shot. Sometimes they take Una to see William Slim's 94-year-old mother in Birmingham. She has seen little of her grand-daughter during the last seven or so years, and less of her son.

Such is the home life of the man who drove the Japs out of Burma. When he is in uniform you know at once that here is a leader among men. But when he sits in his study writing, with thin-framed spectacles halfway down his nose, his appearance is more that of a kindly school-master than a soldier whose name has gained world renown.

BURMA MEMENTO, a Japanese hara-kiri knife, is shown by the General to his daughter Una (top), who handles it with the respect it deserves. The 14th Army, under Sir William's astute leadership, popularized the use of this weapon, by the enemy, in the age-old art of self-killing.

POLISHING SILVER in his London home at Knightsbridge (centre) should be second nature to the General, whose early training in the Army no doubt held him in good stead for the job here happily shared by his wife and daughter. An adept with the pen, Sir William settles down to write (left) while Lady Slim industriously gets on with her knitting, and Una, comfortably curled up on the settee, pores over a book.

Photos, Associated Press

The Roll of Honour
1939—1946

Readers of THE WAR ILLUSTRATED who wish to submit photographs for inclusion in our Roll of Honour must fill in the coupon which appeared in No. 230. No portraits can be considered that are not accompanied by this coupon.

Dvr. A. ANDERSON
Royal Army Service Corps.
Action: St. Valery. 12.6.40.
Age 24.   (Perth)

Stwd. N. A. BROWN
Royal Navy.
North Atlantic. 26.9.42.
Age 22.   (Stockton-on-Tees)

Gnr. A. C. BAXTER
Royal Artillery.
In action : Libya.   8.5.43.
Age 22.   (Forest Gate)

Cpl. C. J. BEER
Rifle Brigade.
In action : Barum. 17.4.45.
Age 31.   (Ewell)

Pte. R. BELL
Gordon Highlanders.
D. of wounds: Italy. 1.9.44.
Age 20.   (Tynemouth)

Sgt. L. BARRACLOUGH
78th Field Regt. R.A.
Action: R. Sangro. 27.11.43.
Age 25.   (Stocksbridge)

Pte. G. BUCKINGHAM
Royal Fusiliers.
Died of wounds. 31.10.43.
Age 28.   (London)

Sgt. M. COHEN
R.A.F.V.R.
Action : Finingley. 3.10.43.
Age 21.   (Bolton)

Tpr. S. COOK
Royal Armoured Corps.
In action : Italy. 18.6.44.
Age 24.   (Muswell Hill)

Pte. D. A. CRUMP
Oxford & Bucks L.I.
Died of wounds.   6.3.45.
Age 20.   (London)

Sgt. J. A. DARAGON
Royal Air Force.
Düsseldorf.   Jan. 1943.
Age 19.   (Streatham)

Pte. N. J. DODMAN
Essex Regiment.
Died of wounds. 25.3.45.
Age 19.   (Hutton)

Sgt. R. DOUCH
B.73 Anti-Tank Regt.,R.A.
Sidi-Rezegh.   7.12.41.
Age 27.   (Finchley)

Sgt. T. J. EVANS
Royal Air Force.
East Kirchen.   24.3.44.
Age 20.   (Lampeter)

L/Sgt. W. FREEMAN
York and Lancaster Regt.
N.W. Europe.   20.8.44.
Age 24.   (Sheffield)

L/Cpl. D. GASCOYNE
7th Cameronians.
Action : Rheine.   4.4.45.
Age 20.   (Leamington Spa)

Sgt. J. HALEY
460 Sqdn. R.A.F.
Action: Cologne. 31.10.44.
Age 24.   (Bradford)

Pte. W. S. HANSFORD
Worcestershire Regt.
D. of wds. : France. 1.8.44.
Age 19.   (Portsmouth)

Pte. W. HARLAND
1st Bn. London Scottish.
In action : Italy. 12.1.44.
Age 25.   (Manchester)

Pte. T. HOGGARD
7th Bn. Green Howards.
In action :   Nijmegen.
Age 23.   (Bridlington)

Sgt. D. HOPKINS
Royal Air Force.
Over Germany.   4.9.43.
Age 25.   (Porth)

Flt/Sgt. R. J. HUDSON
Pathfinder, R.A.F.
In action : Berlin. 2.1.44.
Age 20.   (Seaton Burn)

Cpl. A. G. LAND
12th Royal Tank Regt.
In action : Italy.   2.9.44.
Age 20.   (Bradford)

Flt/Sgt. S. MASON
356 Sqdn. R.A.F.
Action : Burma. 16.9.44.
Age 23.   (Wingate)

Pte. H. PARKINSON
York and Lancaster Regt.
N.W. Europe.   23.8.44.
Age 26.   (Gomersal)

Sgt. N. R. PIKE
Bomber Command R.A.F.
Action: Germany. 23.5.44.
Age 27.   (Pontypridd)

Flt/Sgt. H. J. A. ROGERS
70 Sqdn. R.A.F.
Over Rumania.   Aug. 44.
Age 22.   (Birmingham)

Pte. P. R. RUMMING
7th Somerset L.I.
In action : Goch. 17.2.45.
Age 19.   (Devizes)

Sgt. J. RYAN
2nd Border Regt.
Action : Burma. 18.3.44.
Age 24.   (Birkenhead)

L/Smn. B. SULLIVAN
Royal Navy.
Action : Java Sea. 8.3.42.
Age 21.   (Scilly Isles)

L/Cpl. H. SWINDALL
Royal Ulster Rifles.
Action : Bremen. 13.4.45.
Age 19.   (Woodville)

Pte. S. THOMAS
Royal Engineers.
Action : Dunkirk. 1.6.40.
Age 22.   (Clevedon)

Sapper G. F. TURNER
Royal Engineers.
On the Lancastria. 17.6.40.
Age 23.   (Birmingham)

Flt/Sgt. K. H. TURNER
Bomber Command R.A.F.
Action: Homburg. 20.11.44.
Age 22.   (Little Sutton)

Sgt. K. V. TURNER
Bomber Command R.A.F.
Action: Denmark. 13.8.40.
Age 20.   (Birmingham)

Pte. G. F. WEBB
Essex Regiment.
In action : Tunisia. 6.5.43.
Age 18.   (Woodford)

A/Cpl. E. S. WHITE
R.A.F. Regiment.
In action : Burma. 15.5.45.
Age 23.   (Rotherham)

Pte. R. L. WILLIAMS
6th Bn. N. Staff. Regt.
In action : Caen.   9.7.44.
Age 25.   (Birmingham)

THE BATTLE OF BRITAIN

By Group-Captain Douglas Bader, D.S.O., D.F.C.

I HAVE been asked to write about September 15, 1940, which I regret to admit—although I am sure most of the Battle of Britain pilots will agree with me—does not stick in my memory more clearly than any of the other days. I must qualify that remark quickly before the reader snorts, "He's shooting a line." On September 16 we read in the newspapers (while we were sitting at "dispersal" at readiness) that the previous day's score was the all-time best.

That was how we received the news—the same way as everyone else, from the B.B.C. and from the daily newspapers. We knew only what the squadrons operating from the same aerodrome had done; occasionally when one of us had had to land at another aerodrome for refuelling and rearming we would hear early unconfirmed news.

Unless a pilot were foolish in those September days he would land and be replenished with everything at any of the southern aerodromes. Flying about England between the South Coast and London might often prove interesting and nothing was more irritating than to find a Hun—perhaps staggering back after being smartened up by someone else a quarter of an hour previously—fly up to him to collect an absolute sitter, press your gun-button and hear the mocking hiss of compressed air instead of the satisfying crackle of eight Brownings accompanied by the smell of burnt cordite which was music to the nose of the fighter pilot.

A Hell of a Bang in the Cockpit

Worse still to be dreaming along at about 5,000 feet, conscious of having no ammunition and not much petrol; thinking it had been a good party; wondering whether it would be worth while finishing your interrupted lunch or sending for an early tea; reflecting that the lunch coffee would be cold and you craved a hot drink; deciding that it did not matter anyhow, because just as the tea came you would be off again after some more of these cursed Huns; anyhow, what the hell! One seemed to be doomed to a life of half-eaten, interrupted meals and cold drinks that should be hot.

Then—suddenly you see the tracer coming past the side of the cockpit and automatically you jerk the stick back and to the right, a flick of rudder, into a violent right-hand climbing turn just as there's a hell of a bang in the cockpit and you nearly die of fright. As you come round in your turn and start diving you look up and see two or more Me 109s climbing away, having caught you literally napping; you think unprintable things about those lousy Huns, at the same time thanking your lucky stars that they were such bad shots.

When you land back at your aerodrome, your ground-crew find some holes in your Hurricane, one or two fairly near the cockpit from behind, three in the cockpit that struck parts of the dashboard and several rolling about inside your self-sealing tanks. Casually you mention that it was a good party, and ask how many are back already; you say nothing of being caught like a clot on the way home. The Southern English sky was not all-English, by any means.

That was what it was like during those August and September days of 1940—from dawn until dusk the fighters were ready; long hours, boring hours, exciting hours, absolute hell on the digestion.

SEPTEMBER 15 was memorable chiefly for the fact that the Germans lost the largest official total in any one day of 1940. So far as the fighter pilots themselves were concerned it was not necessarily the most tiring, mainly because the majority of us were experienced in this type of fighting—i.e. against fighter-escorted bombers; second, because it was divided into two distinct attacks against London, one in the late morning about 11.30 hours and the second at about 14.30 hours; third, because no new aircraft or tactics were employed by the Hun, and the tactics to which we were accustomed were particularly easy to counter although, as is known, we were considerably outnumbered; last, and most important of all, the Hun morale was by this time most noticeably on the ebb.

True the strain was becoming increasingly apparent among the weary pilots in Fighter Command, but at the same time we were becoming more and more savage at the sight of the Hun bombing indiscriminately. At the beginning there was no great personal feeling about it because the Hun was—so far as we could see—attempting to hit specific targets out of cloudless skies, or bombing from below cloud.

Several times, however, before September 15, the Hun formations had been bombing when they could not see the ground because of cloud-layers between them and the ground,

so that they were throwing out bombs indiscriminately over London. This had been particularly noticeable on September 9, when they flew over London in force, about 18.00 hours, at 21,000 feet. London was covered with broken cloud at 3,000 feet, and thick haze up to 9,000 feet, *so that it was not visible except through occasional small gaps from 21,000 feet.* One or two attacks like this had made us very bloodthirsty, so that one got one's sights on a Hun and did not let up until the flames appeared; we were not keen for crews to bale out.

Hit the Ground from 19,000 Feet

On September 15 a broken cloud-layer at 5,000 feet almost completely obscured London and the South, and the Hun formations flew in around 20,000 feet. I remember in the morning shambles seeing a Dornier 17 on fire and one of the crew bale out with his parachute alight, and as it opened the whole canopy went up in a sheet of flame. I recall my reaction, which was, "Good show! You rat, now you've got a little time to think about it, and there's no answer." They say you don't lose consciousness until you hit the ground, and he went down from 19,000 feet, because I looked at my altimeter!

I can imagine the reader saying, "How horrible; what an un-Christian thought!" Well, I thought it, and when I landed back I found three other pilots had also seen it and were highly delighted. Later on, I saw a German rear-gunner in a Dornier bale out and get his parachute entangled in the tail-plane, so that from 17,000 feet it crashed to the ground in a series of dives and zooms which took quite a long time.

I hoped that both those Huns had taken part in the bombing of Warsaw, or the barbarous destruction of the virtually unprotected city of Rotterdam, because they died an unpleasant death with no chance of doing anything about it, like the women and children they had wantonly destroyed.

Each Squadron Did Its Stuff

Such was the temper of the fighter pilots around September-15, 1940. I doubt if any squadron was in action more than twice on that now memorable day, because the Huns made two large and distinct attacks on London and two smaller attacks in the Portland-Southampton area. There were no big bags by individual squadrons, which was as it should be; everyone had a smack and each squadron did its stuff. No one thought it had been a special day, until we heard it on the news.

It was the day that a Dornier minus its tailplane crashed on top of a tobacconist's shop just outside Victoria Station. I remember seeing a remarkable photograph in one of the newspapers of this Dornier about 100 feet from the ground. We all speculated as to how that photograph was taken, and came to the conclusion that it was some chap who had been standing-by for weeks with his camera at the ready and finally had his reward.

Well, we were not to know it at the time, but the end of that day was to herald an easier time for the fighters, and although

German formations continued to make desultory attacks on our island they were easily repulsed with very heavy casualties. No mass attacks of a similar nature to those during the first two weeks of September were made against England subsequently.

Never again during the War was the Luftwaffe to be in such a dominating position against a Royal Air Force weakened and neglected below the danger mark by a succession of British Governments who utterly refused to see what every man in the street could see, and who, when the darkest hour arrived after Dunkirk, could think of one answer only—a negotiated peace with Hitler—until one man—God bless him !— literally kicked them into a determination to resist and spoke the will of the people in his memorable broadcast to the world after the French capitulation.

That was the spirit of the people which was so gloriously displayed firstly by the Londoners during August–September 1940, and subsequently by the inhabitants of every bombed English town.

Kaleidoscopic Pictures in My Mind

I cannot end without voicing the fighter pilots' admiration and appreciation of the chaps on the ground, the civilians, without whose courage and resistance nothing we did would have been any good. We could not stop them being bombed, previous politicians had seen to that, there were too few of us. We could only go on shooting down the Hun until we wore him out or he wore us out, and the chaps on the ground had the sticky time, not us. We were up in the air doing something about it, while they were having to "take it" on the ground, unable to have a go at the enemy 20,000 feet away.

September 15 for us is not the memory of a special day, but a day made important subsequently by its result. I must look in my flying log-book and read my own short account of the day's battles and then I recall the incidents of that day.

Rather does it mark a milestone between being permanently tired and starting to get normal again : a curtain behind which certain kaleidoscopic pictures will always stay in my mind . . .The heavy oil smoke from burning tanks at Thameshaven into which dives a yellow-nosed Messerschmitt 109 in flames with the pilot dead in the cockpit . . . Two of my Hurricanes converging on the same Ju 88—"Look out, chaps, you're going to collide !"—too late, one wing

184 PLUS THIS ONE made up the recorded total of German aircraft destroyed over southern England on that memorable day in the Battle of Britain, September 15, 1940. A Dornier, minus its tailplane, crashed on a tobacconist's shop just outside Victoria Station London, where troops, N.F.S. and police are seen inspecting and guarding the wreckage. *Photo, Fox*

drifts away in the air and a tailplane ; just for a second in the mêlée I watch, and think " Thank God, no flames !" Someone may bale out, one did . . . Starting to close in behind a Ju 88, I happen to look up and see a Spitfire coming down vertically, watch it dive straight into the 88 and both go down in a burning twisted mass—no parachutes. Wondered if it was deliberate on the part of the Spit pilot or didn't he see the 88 ? Pilots sometimes went haywire . . .

A 109 zooms up out of the haze over North Weald aerodrome ; I close to 150 yards and am just about to fire when a Hurricane zooms out of the haze on his tail, the 109 goes up in smoke and the pilot bales out— right in front of my nose ! I pull up alongside the Hurricane and recognize "Butch" in spite of his oxygen-mask — good old "Butch," it would be him !

That's what September 15, 1940, means to me.

a Corps Signals which had recently been mobilized, including some Light Wireless Sections equipped with sets with a reputed range of about 40 miles. One detachment was ordered to get into action at Aldershot and act as base, while another was to be sent across the Channel to try to join up with the Military Attaché. Just as these arrangements had been completed, the corporal in charge of the detachment for G.H.Q. rang up from Dover to say he was stuck there and nothing seemed to be going across.

"Movements" promised to do their best, and as a precaution diverted the Military Attaché's set via Cherbourg. How the N.C.O. in charge of it managed to drive his truck right up through France and find the Military Attaché amidst the general confusion of a great retreat is one of the mysteries which will never be solved. As an example of guts and determination it was outstanding. He came " on the air " in a remarkably short time, and remained in contact with Aldershot, for at least a few hours in the day, until the party had nearly reached Bordeaux, when the set was transmitting over several times its stated range.

The other detachment seemed to be dogged by ill-luck. I was assured by "Movements" that they had actually left Dover, and I breathed a sigh of relief, but a few hours later the voice of the corporal came again over the telephone :

"Corporal Shale speaking, sir. We're back in Dover."

"What on earth's happened ? " I gasped.

"We got to the other side, sir, and I went ashore, but they wouldn't let me land the equipment or the men."

Frantic telephoning resulted in another, and no more successful effort.

We of the Signals Helped at Dunkirk

Colonel T. B. Gravely, O.B.E., late Royal Signals, relates the story of the Dunkirk evacuation in 1940 from a new angle. His is the tale of one small but vitally important part of the general effort : the provision of the necessary Army communications. At the time the author was a Senior Staff Officer to the Deputy Director of Staff Duties (Signals). See also pages 2–4.

From the Signals point of view, the trouble began some time before the evacuation took place. It started with a message to the War Office from the Signal Officer-in-Chief, B.E.F., informing the Deputy Director of Staff Duties (Signals), as he was then called, that all was not well with the wireless set which had been used as a rear-link to the War Office. While they were attempting to move it by rail, the enemy had most inconsiderately dropped two bombs on the line, one in front and one behind the truck which was carrying it.

To make matters worse, the spot where the truck was marooned was three miles from the nearest metalled road, across fields reported to be impassable to heavy motor traffic, and the equipment weighed several tons. As one of the two senior staff officers to the D.D. Signals, I was instructed to find another wireless set and detachment, and to get them over to G.H.Q. with all speed.

As it happened, a detachment and complete equipment were available, and in a very short time the corporal in charge of the party was in my office "somewhere in England" receiving his instructions, which were simple enough : he was to get his outfit across the Channel and up to G.H.Q., wherever it was, as quickly as he possibly could. Special arrangements were made with "Movements" to speed the party, and the corporal left for Dover, full of determination to do or die.

I had just finished writing a message to the Signal Officer-in-Chief, telling him what had been done, when an agitated voice on the telephone informed me that the British Military Attaché in Paris was in trouble. He had just realized that, once he left the British Embassy, he would lose touch with London by telephone. Could I help ?

Luckily, the answer to that was fairly easy. There was, in the Aldershot district,

Col. T. B. GRAVELY

When the Luftwaffe Was Smashed Over England

THREE OF 'THE FEW' who helped to shatter the might of the German raiders over Britain exchanged experiences (1) after an operational flight in London skies, in September 1940. A wounded Nazi pilot (2), shot down over Kent, was carried away after receiving First Aid attention. The Tower Bridge and the Pool of London (3) swathed in swirling smoke and flame during the first mass daylight attack on the Capital. This photograph was not released for publication until the end of the War. PAGE 155

No. 609 (WEST RIDING) SQUADRON

FORMED in February 1936, No. 609 (West Riding) Auxiliary Squadron distinguished itself in many of the great air battles of the war. By their deeds over Britain and France its officers and men made Yorkshire's name in the air war no less famous than in that on land. When the War broke out, in September 1939, the squadron had already exchanged its obsolescent light bombers for Britain's latest fighter, the Spitfire. Brought south from Catterick, it gained its first success in February 1940 by shooting down a Heinkel III which had been attacking a convoy.

Three months later No. 609 went to the aid of the B.E.F. at Dunkirk, along with other squadrons, engaging enemy forces of overwhelming size. In the Battle of Britain it fought over the towns and villages of Hampshire and Dorset, taking on odds as high as 80 to six. In one month (August) alone it destroyed 46 enemy aircraft. In the next month it helped in the defence of London. On September 15, when the Luftwaffe suffered its heaviest defeat, the squadron brought down six and damaged several more of the raiders.

CONTINUING to operate over Southern England, No. 609 was the first Spitfire squadron to destroy 100 enemy aircraft. In later days it was to achieve similar distinction by being the first Typhoon squadron to score 50 Huns. After converting to Typhoons, it engaged raiders harassing South Coast towns. It then developed the new technique of long-range, low-level sweeps over Northern France, Belgium and Western Germany, wrecking enemy communications, later switching its activities to anti-shipping strikes.

Equipped with rockets, No. 609's Typhoons helped to smash the string of radar stations along the Normandy coast just before D-Day, and a few days after the invasion it was operating in close support of the Army. Later, it was prominent in attacks on enemy troop concentrations, tanks and vehicles in the Falaise Gap. Its Typhoons were still battering the enemy when his surrender came, by which time the squadron's total of German aircraft destroyed had nearly reached the 250 mark. No. 609 has now been reformed as a night fighter squadron, equipped with Mosquito XXXs, with headquarters at Church Fenton, Yorkshire

It was clear that nobody on the other side was taking much interest in him, so I ordered him to get a meal for himself and his men and stand by for further orders. A little later, after an anxious conference with "Movements," the attempt was abandoned, and he was sent back to the place he had started from. So far we still clung to the hope that something might be done to stem the German advance. But we were soon jolted out of our wishful thinking.

In company with another officer I was detailed to attend a very special conference which was, in fact, the start of "Operation Dynamo." It was held with great secrecy in a room in the basement of the War Office. The Chairman stated that we had to prepare a plan to evacuate the B.E.F.

A representative from the Admiralty told us about the projected fleet of "Little Ships,"

and gave the ports from which they would operate. It was the Army's chief task to clear these ports as quickly as possible, to prevent congestion and reduce the risk of casualties from the expected bombing. The crux of the plan was a main control at Redhill, Surrey, to which all trains would report, and whence they would be directed to dispersal centres in each of the Army Commands. The driver of a train leaving, say, Dover would not have the faintest idea where he would finish his journey.

If bombing were heavy, there might be a breakdown in communications between Dover and Redhill. Could I help to prevent this ? I could. I could provide a mobile wireless set at each place. What about telephone communications at the outer end of the network ? That was the province of my colleague, who assured the meeting that the necessary telephones would be available at all military centres. When the time came it was possible, on peak days, for a train to leave Dover for an unknown destination every fifteen minutes from 6 a.m. to noon.

The Navy asked for some mobile wireless links between various points on the French coast and the base at Dover, and it was decided to loan them one complete Light Wireless Section, of four detachments—one to remain at Dover, three to go over via Calais, which was still holding out. One detachment was to stay at Calais, while the others tried to reach Dunkirk and Ostend.

Links Engulfed by Advancing Huns

The Calais station came on the air and did valuable work, but nothing was ever heard of the other two, and it was presumed that they had failed to reach their objectives. Towards the end, the operators at the Dover station reported that the Calais set was being manned by Lieutenant Morrow (which is not his real name), the officer commanding the Section ; they recognized his touch on the key. It looked as though the rest of the detachment were casualties, and that it was only a matter of time before the station went off the air.

At about four o'clock in the afternoon our fears were realized, and nothing more was heard of the little party until about a fortnight later, when a messenger came into my office and said Morrow had arrived to report.

I recovered from my astonishment sufficiently to welcome him as he deserved and to listen to his story. While they were being marched away as prisoners from Calais, he and another officer chose a suitable

moment and dived through a hedge into a patch of swampy ground where they hid. When the way was clear they moved off in a south-westerly direction towards Boulogne, cutting any German field cables they found on the way. In the middle of the night they nearly walked into a German mobile wireless station. Luckily, the sound warned Morrow.

They went on down the coast until they met some French officers who were trying to repair an old motor-boat. Between them they got it going and it took them halfway across the Channel, when they were picked up by a British destroyer.

As I mentioned before, there were two senior staff officers to the D.D.Signals. I had the wireless, while my colleague dealt with the submarine cables. We each carried a piece of millboard to which was clipped a diagram showing how our own bit of the communications stood. The diagrams had to be redrawn several times a day, for we crossed off the links, one by one, as they were engulfed by the advancing Germans.

As the means of communication grew less and less, we of the Signals Staff found ourselves acting as telephone orderlies and passing messages from the Chief of the Imperial General Staff to the Commander-in-Chief. The last message which I personally passed over the one remaining cable was taken down by another Signal officer, who was lying on the floor of a villa in La Panne, having just been hit in the head by a bomb-splinter. It fell to my colleague to get off the actual message ordering the evacuation.

At about one o'clock in the morning, before Operation Dynamo was put into force, I received a visit from an officer of the Signals Division of the Admiralty. He brought with him the Flag-Lieutenant from Dover, who said that Admiral Ramsay was most concerned at the possibility that isolated bodies of troops might arrive at the beaches and find no craft to take them off and nobody to take any interest in them. Could the Army do anything to provide communication with the beaches, now that the original scheme—of Morrow's Section—had failed ?

After our previous experience it was obviously useless to try to send any more wireless sets across, so the only thing to do was to reinforce the surviving detachment of Morrow's Section, which was still at Dover, and try to get a message to the Signal Officer-in-Chief, B.E.F., giving him the frequencies and call-signs, so that any troops

BRITISH WIRELESS TRUCK AT CHERBOURG, housing an operator listening for messages which may have been vital to the success of " Operation Dynamo "—a hitherto unpublished photograph. How efforts were made to establish mobile wireless links between various parts of the French coast and the base at Dover in May 1940 is explained above.

coming down to the beaches could call up the stations in England, which were to be strung out along the cliffs.

We carefully wrote down all the details in the form of a Signal Instruction—and then we struck a snag. Fighting was still in progress, and the final order for evacuation had not yet been given, though it was expected at any moment. The whole operation was being handled with the utmost secrecy, to avoid premature dislosure, and I was hardly in a position to act ahead of the Chief of the Imperial General Staff and the War Cabinet.

On the other hand, we knew that if our scheme was to work at all it was vital that details should be in the hands of the B.E.F. Signals staff with the least possible delay. Finally, I went to an empty clerks' office, locked myself in, and in eerie solitude typed out the instructions. I then went in search of the Director of Military Operations, who had been on duty for many hours and looked tired and anxious. He immediately agreed to sign the Signal Instruction and thus relieve me of responsibility.

I think I can claim that that document is unique in Signal history. The next problem was how to get the instruction over to the other side of the Channel. Luckily, an officer from the War Office was going over in a motor-boat, and the precious papers were entrusted to him. We did not know, then, that orders would be issued for the destruction of all wireless equipment before it got to the beaches, but a few sets did remain in action, so our efforts were not wasted.

There was still work to be done, and it was not long before we received a demand for a rear-link wireless set for the forces holding out south of the Somme. The obvious answer was to send Corporal Shale, who was still standing by. This time he had to travel via Southampton and Cherbourg, and "Movements" gave him quite a big ship all to himself. He got half-way across—then was sent back by the Royal Navy !

Field-Marshal Viscount Montgomery has said that good communications are essential to the success of any military operation, and that much of the work of Signals in the War was of the slogging, unspectacular variety. The Field-Marshal was speaking of the War as a whole, but he might have been thinking of Dunkirk ; he was one of those who came back.

guessing on my part, however ; I had been there in the dark days of 1942.

We formed part of the 1st Battle Squadron. With us were the battle-cruiser Renown, the Valiant, of Matapan fame, the Queen Elizabeth and the carrier Unicorn. The Illustrious was the only unit that had seen previous war service with the Eastern Fleet. She had now returned to finish the job she began at Madagascar in 1942.

Trincomalee in 1944 was a far cry from Trincomalee in 1942. Then the Fleet had fallen back from Singapore, capable only of defensive measures. Now it was at Trinco to carry the war to the Japs' back-door, the East Indies. The initiative was to be ours. The time had come to prepare for the final blow, and the Fleet's job now was to strike the enemy where and whenever possible, to ascertain their strength and carry out decoy attacks to divert their attention from major operations in the Pacific.

Preparing for Battle at Sabang

As soon as we were moored in Trinco the Fleet Air Arm squadrons were disembarked. Lighters came alongside to take the ground crews, kit and equipment to the Naval Air Station at China Bay. Then came the announcement that shore leave would be granted, for the first time since leaving the Clyde on December 30, 1943. The first liberty boats off from the ship were packed. We all had the same idea, to use our two beer tickets as soon as possible and then to have a good look around. Those two beer tickets were to last a week ! The two cinemas were very crude affairs, and I came out of one after seeing a three-year-old film, with a firm resolve never to go again : palm-frond and bamboo seats are far from comfortable ! I turned my attention to the native village and was staggered by the nauseating smells.

After a lot of shore practice the Air Arm squadrons re-embarked and rumours ("buzzes") went round the ship like wildfire. But we were out of luck ; this was to

I Sailed With the Carrier Illustrious

M. C. Hyde, then a Leading Writer in the pay office of the Illustrious, watched the take-off from her flight deck of Corsair fighters and Avenger torpedo-bombers to blast Jap targets. He tells of operations of the Eastern Fleet in the Indian Ocean in 1944, prior to formation of the British Pacific Fleet.

I shall never forget the tension on board as on January 10, 1944, we passed through the area where exactly three years previously the Illustrious had been so terribly mauled by the Luftwaffe. Although the Mediterranean was no longer Mussolini's "Mare Nostrum," sailors are superstitious and we all breathed sighs of relief when January 11 came and we were still afloat.

For most of us the passage down the Suez was a novel and exciting experience. For the ship's Quartermaster it was a nightmare. Steering a 750-foot carrier, with a beam of 95 feet, through the narrow twists and turns of the Canal was no picnic, and he fully earned the bottle of beer conferred on him by the Captain. After the Red Sea and Aden came the trip across the Indian Ocean to our new base, Trincomalee. The majority of the ship's company had never been there before, so there was much speculation as to what it would be like. There was no need for

FAREWELL TO THE U.S.S. SARATOGA, as with her four attendant destroyers she left the Eastern Fleet and returned to the Pacific, after the Surabaya operation in March 1944, was a memorable occasion. The British Fleet steamed in line ahead, the decks of every ship—including the Illustrious (foreground), in which the author of this story was serving—packed with cheering matelots as the American aircraft carrier passed within 75 yards, her decks similarly crammed.

Photo, British Official

H.M. BATTLESHIP QUEEN ELIZABETH, some of whose company are sunning themselves on one of her 15-in. guns, was in 1944 attached to the 1st Battle Squadron of the Eastern Fleet, of which the aircraft carrier Illustrious also formed a part. Carrying the war to the Jap's back door in the East Indies, as related here, these two ships played a successful role in the opening of the final Allied naval offensive in the Pacific. *Photo, British Official*

be only a patrol job. The monotony was relieved by a Crossing-the-Line ceremony on February 24. Everyone was roped in, even those who had already been initiated into the mysteries of Neptune's Court. There were the usual bears, policemen and Officers of the Court, and, of course, a very slimy pool of water; it took hours of scrubbing to restore me to anything bordering on cleanliness.

After another sojourn in Trinco the ship left again, together with the rest of the Fleet. This time it was to be the real thing. Not until we had been at sea some time did the awaited "D'ye hear there! D'ye hear there!" come over the ship's broadcasting system, followed by the announcement that Sabang, at the northern tip of Sumatra, was the destination. The heat and boredom were soon forgotten in preparations for battle. Even though the actual combatants were to be limited to the aircrews, we all considered that this was also our show—the real beginning of our long-awaited sea offensive against the Japs.

THE principal targets, we were told, were harbour installations and oil dumps—and perhaps units of the Jap Fleet based on Singapore would accept the challenge. That they did not was a great disappointment to us. We had to be content with the achievements of our fighter and bomber squadrons, who did a grand job of work. More surprising than the absence of sea opposition was the absence of enemy aircraft.

During the "strike" I was closed-up at my Action Station in the lower magazine aft, with the most disgusted members of the ship's company. We stood-to for the best part of twelve hours with practically nothing to do: completely shut off from the rest of the ship, sweltering in a temperature of about 110 degrees, and nothing to vent our feelings on!

Even ventilation is disconnected when guns are firing. We managed to amuse ourselves at the expense of the newcomers to the magazine by knocking the electric shell fuses with a mallet. This was a harmless pastime, but not for those who did not know the fuses could not be detonated in that manner. The return to harbour was uneventful, and after the reading of accumulated mail the ship settled down to normal routine once more. The fuss of disembarking the squadrons was experienced all over again; whilst in harbour they had to go ashore to maintain their high standard of efficiency. The Marines were bundled off to the jungle for a spot of combat training to equip themselves for the possibility of a landing sortie.

Ldg./Wtr. M. C. HYDE

I ranked as a Leading Writer aboard ship. Apart from my normal office work I had to close up in the magazine whenever the ship was in action, and also had to keep regular four-hourly watches in the cipher office. My workplace, the pay office, was a hive of industry. There were only a few of us to look after the pay of 1,700 matelots, and looking after the pay of only one sailor is a job in itself. All sailors have the idea that they are being "seen off" and ours were quite resigned to the fact that we made a personal rake-off on their pay accounts. I consider my pay of seven shillings per day

well and truly earned; I worked twelve to sixteen hours a day, and for quite a long time was unable to sit down owing to prickly heat in a very tender spot—a common complaint on board. The heat between decks on an aircraft carrier in the tropics is terrific. We were sandwiched between the heat coming up from the boiler rooms and that given off from the sun blazing down on the steel flight deck. The mess-decks, wardrooms, offices, storerooms and workshops were like furnaces all through the day.

Target Areas Nicely Plastered

Before long the ship was at sea again, due for further operations. The target this time was the Nicobar Islands, to the north of Sabang and in the entrance of the Malacca Straits. Again we were disappointed by the absence of any sea opposition. Air opposition was negligible and the target areas were thoroughly plastered; in fact, the whole show was more like a practice than an important operation. We steamed peacefully back to Trinco, chuckling at Hirohito's disciples who had been caught with honourable kimonos well and truly below their knees.

The ensuing weeks passed with the usual deck landing practices and exercises. This time, however, a treat was in store for us. The buzzes that had been circulating for some months were about to materialize. We were going round to Colombo to pick up certain stores and to give us a change from the monotony that was Trincomalee. Colombo, though quite an unpretentious place, was a paradise to the whole of the Fleet. Colombo was civilized, it had modern streets, cinemas, hotels, canteens and so on. The first day ashore I spent in an orgy of eating. I just had time to buy some reasonably cheap jewelry and silk before the U.S. Carrier Saratoga arrived with four destroyers—and the same day prices soared as much as fifty per cent. My meagre pay having long since disappeared into the palms of a few very wily wogs, I decided to grace the manager of the Hongkong-Shanghai Bank with my financially embarrassed presence. I must have looked honest, for he honoured my cheque for a tenner without the slightest demur. I have never spent ten quid so quickly in the whole of my life.

A few days later we put to sea with the Saratoga, rendezvoused with the Fleet twenty-four hours later and headed for Australia. Not until we had refuelled at a lonely spot on the coast of Western Australia some twelve days later was our destination made known. The target was Surabaya, on the far side of the Javanese coast, the Japs' principal naval base in the East Indies area. The attack meant a flight of approximately 300 miles over enemy occupied territory, and it was known that the Japanese had several large airfields in the area.

Off Over the Javanese Mountains

About 4 a.m. on May 19, 1944, we were called to our Action Stations. Having already completed the middle watch (from midnight to 4 a.m.) in the cipher office I was brassed-off at the prospect of several more hours of alertness. But a little later I had the good fortune to go up to the island (the bridge structure) just in time to see the aircraft take off for the attack. Against the red of the rising tropic sun the Avengers and Corsairs circled over the Fleet, formed up and flew out over the snow-capped Javanese mountains on their mission. Before the take-off the aircraft were tightly ranged on the flight deck—the Corsair fighters aft and the Avenger torpedo-bombers for'ard. Because of their heavy bomb loads and the shortness of their run (due to being ranged for'ard) some of the Avengers were boosted off by the concealed catapult.

Thanks to the strafing of the neighbouring airfields and the complete surprise of the attack the operation was successfully completed. Several merchant ships and enemy naval units were destroyed or damaged, two floating dry-docks and port installations received heavy damage also. A nearby oil refinery and its power house were completely demolished. To round off the day, Corsair pilots strafed dispersed aircraft at Malang airfield, one of the largest in the East Indies, and destroyed most of them.

On the way back to our God-forsaken spot on the Australian coast to refuel, the Saratoga and her four attendant destroyers left the Fleet and returned to the Pacific. The parting was a memorable occasion. The British Fleet steamed in line ahead, with the decks of every ship packed with cheering matelots as the Saratoga passed within 75 yards, her decks similarly crammed.

We were all pleased to get back to Trinco. For the last few days of the trip we had lived on corned beef and rice. Most of us ended up existing on tinned fruit from the N.A.A.F.I. canteen. After the squadrons had disembarked and the ship re-stored some of us were packed off to a jungle rest camp, which had just been opened for the benefit of the Fleet at Nilaveli, about three miles out of Trincomalee. Our stay lasted three days— three days of blissful freedom from Naval routine and tradition.

A beach of pure golden sand ran for many miles in either direction. A mass of tall, graceful palms leant over to the azure blue of the Indian Ocean. The dense jungle revealed only an occasional cluster of bamboo huts. It was near here, in the officers' mess of an isolated company of the King's African Rifles, that I heard of the Normandy landings. The only way we had of celebrating that tremendous occasion was by a midnight bathing party in a complete state of undress. It was an exhilarating experience under the starry tropic sky—until one was bitten by some of the thousands of small crabs that abounded on the shore.

By Army lorry and landing craft we returned on June 7 to the daily grind. It was about this time that a large floating dock was sent down from Bombay, in three parts. Knowing the ship was due for minor repairs the advent of this dock was viewed with great disgust. It was doubtful if it would have taken us, but everyone had been hoping for a trip down to Durban. We later heard that when the Valiant docked there she managed partially to sink the floating dock and herself into the bargain.

Before this was to take place, however, the Fleet again had sailing orders. We were returning to Sabang, but this time it was to be a far bigger show. Accompanied by the Renown, Valiant, Queen Elizabeth, the French battleship Richelieu and the carrier Victorious we were to subject Sabang to a heavy bombardment. The call to Action Stations came soon after sunrise on July 25. The bombardment, supported by fighter aircraft, lasted 35 minutes. The harbour installations were almost completely destroyed, workshops, wharves and sheds were hit by at least 16 salvos of heavy shells and were left in flame and smoke.

The barracks received 10 salvos, half the area being devastated and the remaining buildings almost totally destroyed. At the wireless station all buildings were destroyed or heavily damaged. Prior to the bombardment neighbouring airstrips were strafed, causing damage to hangars, buildings and a radar station. Four aircraft were destroyed on the ground and two other Jap aircraft which attempted to approach the Fleet were shot down. Later in the day when the Fleet was returning to Trinco a formation of enemy aircraft attempted to attack us. Three were shot down, two damaged and the remainder driven off by our A.A. guns.

Soon after our return to Trincomalee we sailed for Durban, regarded with affection by all sailors in the East. Calling at Addu Atoll in the Maldive group of islands, southeast of Ceylon, I saw an old shipmate of mine on a landing craft. Addu Atoll is one of the most desolate islands in the world. Disease and filth are so rampant that men stationed there are allowed no contact whatever with the natives. Facilities for amusement are non-existent. This old shipmate was exceeding "chokker" (fed up) and when he heard our destination was Durban he nearly cried. He had another 18 months to do at Addu before returning to England!

The Maldives behind us, our next port of call was Diego Suarez, Madagascar, scene of bloodshed two years earlier. One of the most perfect and beautiful harbours in the world, it was here that the battleship Ramillies was torpedoed by a Japanese submarine in 1942. An unexpected alteration of plans was announced after leaving Madagascar. We were to go to Cape Town to disembark our squadrons before proceeding to Durban.

Most Beloved Dog in the World

One thing I missed in Cape Town, as did others who had been there previously, was Able Seaman Just Nuisance. A.B. Nuisance was not a seaman but a Great Dane. Nuisance used to be a habitué of the Cape Town-Simonstown railway line. Simonstown is a Naval base and every morning on the early trains hundreds of sailors used to stream back there. At the station before Simonstown, Nuisance used to walk right through the train and awaken all the sleeping sailors. Soldiers, airmen and civilians he treated with contempt, but he would never leave a matelot until he had thoroughly roused him. A.B. Just Nuisance was the most beloved dog in the world, and when he died—in a Royal Naval hospital after weeks of treatment—he was the most mourned dog ever. He was wrapped in a White Ensign and buried with full naval honours ; a volley was fired over his grave by a detachment of the Royal Marines. After his death many ships' Commanders had much cause to complain at the numbers of sailors adrift from leave !

After Cape Town, Durban, with its wide sweeping streets and glistening white buildings, its skyscrapers, Yankee cars and modern hotels making it look more like an American holiday resort than one of South Africa's main ports. Here in Durban I left the Illustrious, for a long sojourn in hospital, and then came the trek back to England, leaving me memories of plenty of hard times and privations but also many happy occasions.

NEW FACTS AND FIGURES

Approximately 1,050 Axis warships and merchant ships were sunk as a result of British minelaying during the War, and a further 540 damaged, the Admiralty announced in May 1946, with additional casualties in Eastern waters still to be analysed. British mines laid totalled 263,088, the majority in the large defensive mine-barrage ; in offensive fields, about 76,700. Of this total some 56,300 were laid by aircraft of all types.

Admiral Dönitz, on trial at Nuremberg, testified on May 9, 1946, on the methods of the German submarine campaign. Quoting an Allied figure of 2,472 ships sunk by German U-boats, he estimated that in the course of the War between 5,000 and 6,000 submarine actions had taken place. Out of a total U-boat force of 40,000 men, 30,000 had not returned. Only 5,000 of these were captured. German losses in submarines were nearly 700.

During the first half of the War (up to 1942) German decoy sites and dummy factories were very effective against bombing. A decoy of the Krupp works at Essen proved to be exceptionally successful. It consisted (according to the International Committee for the Study of European Questions) of a system of lights, some of which were stationary and represented streets and workshops, whilst moving lights, varying in colour and intensity, simulated processes such as tapping, rolling and welding. A lorry with trailer moved continually about the site of this dummy factory. By the end of 1943 the trick had been discovered by the Allies ; but until January 1943, of bombs dropped by Allied aircraft about 64 per cent of the high explosive and 74 per cent of the incendiaries fell on the dummy and not the real works.

In convoying weapons and materials to Russia (Mr. A. V. Alexander revealed on March 13, 1946) 19 British warships were sunk and 19 damaged ; of merchant ships, 30 were sunk and eight damaged ; about 2,055 naval officers and ratings were killed and 87 wounded ; and about 525 Merchant Navy personnel were killed.

Authorities dealing with quislings and traitors in the Drammen district of southern Norway (comments the Norwegian State Information Service) have made the interesting experiment of classifying a cross-section of traitors into six groups, with the result that 25 per cent were found in the mentally defective group. Sixteen per cent were politically indifferent ; 13 per cent were opportunists ; 33 per cent had been misled into joining the Quisling Party ; 25 per cent were political illiterates and defectives who had not the ability to assess the political situation ; 6 per cent were idealists ; 7 per cent were "forced" into the Nazi Party or joined it in order to keep their jobs.

From West Africa for London's V-Day March

Photo, Central Press

REPRESENTING THE 81st and 82nd WEST AFRICAN DIVISIONS were troops who had fought the Japs in the Burma campaign: historic landmarks were pointed out to them as their ship docked at Tilbury. Marching at the head of the Colonial Empire in the column which took nearly two hours to pass H.M. the King in the Mall, on June 8, 1946, they typified thousands of warriors of Nigeria, the Gold Coast, Sierra Leone and the Gambia. Also in the Victory Parade were detachments from East and Central Africa.

Printed in England and published every alternate Friday, by the Proprietors, The AMALGAMATED PRESS, LTD., The Fleetway House, Farringdon Street, London, E.C.4. Registered for transmission by Canadian Magazine Post. Sole Agents for Australia and New Zealand: Messrs. Gordon & Gotch, Ltd.; and for South Africa: Central News Agency, Ltd.—June 21, 1946.　　　S.S.　　　*Editorial Address:* JOHN CARPENTER HOUSE WHITEFRIARS, LONDON, E.C.4.

Vol 10 *The War Illustrated* N° 236

SIXPENCE

JULY 5, 1946

I WAS THERE

INDIA'S DETACHMENT IN THE VICTORY PARADE (seen nearest the camera) is following the Dominions troops along the Mall to the Saluting Base. Viewed from the top of Admiralty Arch, the impressive marching column presents a striking contrast to the days when the Empire was slowly gathering its might for the bitter struggle whose triumphant ending the celebrations of June 8, 1946, so fittingly marked. Flags of Britain, the Empire, the Allies and the Services flutter symbolically along this processional route.

Edited by Sir John Hammerton

NO. 237 WILL BE PUBLISHED FRIDAY, JULY 19

Our Royal Family: The Salute to Victory

AWAITING THE CLIMAX OF THE PARADE, THE MARCH PAST, Admiral Lord Louis Mountbatten, the King's cousin, exchanges a word with Queen Mary (1) at the Saluting Base in the Mall, where H.M. the King, between the Queen and his mother, Queen Mary, is seen taking the salute (2) of his victorious troops and Allies. Their Majesties, with the Princesses Elizabeth and Margaret, driving in a State landau, accompanied by a Captain's Escort of the Household Cavalry with Standard, pass through Parliament Square (3) on their way to the Mall.

Naval Contribution to the Mechanized Column

APPROACHING ITS RENDEZVOUS WITH THE MARCHING COLUMN in the Victory Parade, the mechanized division of the Royal Navy is seen passing through Parliament Square. Outstanding among London's decorations for the occasion was the multi-coloured arch (right foreground) opposite the entrance to the House of Commons. Bearing the flags of the 51 United Nations, it displayed on each side a sixteen-foot "Sword of Liberation" whose flames were illuminated at night. See also illus. page 192.

Photo, Sport & General

Allied Commanders and British Chiefs of Staff

General Joseph Koenig (left), heroic French Commander at the siege of Bir Hacheim in the Western Desert, June 1942.

Admiral H. K. Hewitt (centre) and General Joseph T. McNarney (right), with Brigadier General Franklin A. Hart, U.S. Marine Corps (left), representing the U.S.A.

BRITISH CHIEFS OF THE THREE SERVICES travelled together to the saluting base in the Mall, in the Chiefs of Staff procession which preceded the mechanized column. Left to right, smiling at the cheering crowds, Admiral of the Fleet Viscount Cunningham of Hyndhope, former First Sea Lord and C.-in-C. Mediterranean Fleet ; Field-Marshal Viscount Alanbrooke, until June 1946 Chief of the Imperial General Staff ; and Marshal of the R.A.F. Viscount Portal of Hungerford, Chief of the Air Staff from 1940 to Dec. 31, 1945. PAGE 164 *Photos, L.N.A., P.A.-Reuter*

Great British Commanders Riding the V-Route

Field-Marshal Viscount Alexander of Tunis, wartime Allied Supreme Commander Mediterranean, with Admiral Mountbatten, Allied Supreme Commander S.E.A.C.

Field-Marshal Viscount Montgomery of Alamein, appointed Chief of the Imperial General Staff in June 1946.

General Sir William Slim, Commander 14th Army, Burma (right), and General Sir Richard O'Connor, VIII Corps Commander. Note corps and divisional signs on cars.

Lt.-Gen. Sir Miles Dempsey, 2nd Army Commander (left) and Lt.-Gen. Sir Richard McCreery, last commander 8th Army

BRITISH COMMANDERS WHO LED US TO VICTORY followed immediately behind the Allied Commanders with whom they headed the mechanized column in the Parade. At the head of the Senior Service, Admiral Sir John Cunningham (on left in right hand photograph) was accompanied by Admiral Sir Geoffrey Layton, followed by the Army Commanders and those of the R.A.F., the latter led by Marshal of the R.A.F. Lord Tedder, now Chief of Air Staff (left-hand photograph).

Photos, L.N.A., P.A.-Reuter, Keystone, Central Press

After the Armour Marched the Allied Forces

IN THE ORDER OF MARCH, following the mechanized column, precedence was given to the Allied Forces, the place of honour at the head falling to the U.S.A., here (4) passing the Royal dais at the appointed time—approximately one minute after midday; unfamiliar American uniforms included that of the Marine Corps.

They were followed by China, France, Belgium, Brazil, Czechoslovakia, Denmark, Egypt, Ethiopia, and (1) Greece, with two Evzones romantically garbed in their traditional clogs, white kilts and braided waistcoats, escorting the Greek colours. Iran followed, and Iraq, Luxemburg, Mexico, Nepal and (3) the Netherlands. Then came the Norwegians (2), dipping their country's flag in salute to His Majesty the King, followed by Transjordan.

Photos, New York Times Photos, Associated Press, P.A.-Reuter

Royal Armoured Corps in Beflagged Whitehall

IN THEIR FAMILIAR BLACK BERETS, the R.A.C. contingent, in foreground, have passed the Horse Guards Parade (right) and are nearing the end of flag-decked Whitehall on either side of which spectators cluster fourteen deep. White and stately in the distance is the Cenotaph—joint symbol of remembrance for the dead of two wars, and one of the two points along the processional route at which "compliments" were paid : the other being the saluting base in the Mall. Centre background is the Victoria Tower of the House of Lords ; left, Big Ben Clock Tower.

Proud Civilians Had Their Hour of Triumph

CIVIL DEFENCE SERVICES, led by two of the rescue dogs employed after air raids to locate casualties, pass the saluting base (1). The Alsatian seen above is "Jet." (See New Facts and Figures, in page 190.) In the industrial workers section, coal-miners, their cap-lamps aglow, march stolidly past the Cenotaph (2). Workers of the transport services (3), representing railways, tramways, buses, road haulage, docks and canals, were headed by the band of the National Fire Service.

Photos, The Daily Mirror, Topical Press

Vehicles of the Armed and Auxiliary Forces

CARS OF THE ROYAL ARMOURED CORPS passing the Tower of London (1) were followed by latest types of cruiser tanks. Much of this armour was designed specially for European operations and came into use for the first time after the D-Day landings. In appreciation of their great services to the Indian troops and the 14th Army in Burma, two ambulances of the Volunteer American Field Service were included in the parade (2). Passing over London Bridge and following the Police in the Civilian Services section of the mechanized column came National Fire Services equipment (3). Airborne dinghies of the R.A.F. were on 60-foot-long aircraft transporters (4). The medley of equipment and vehicles would have confused onlookers had not identification cards been displayed. PAGE 169 *Photos, Sport & General, Barratt's, Topical*

MINEFIELD-CLEARANCE AND BRIDGING TANKS, seen passing over London Bridge, were striking examples of Britain's ingenuity in armour as displayed in the Victory Parade. The flail tanks (leading) did invaluable work in clearing enemy minefields in the forward path of our advancing troops, the hanging chains rotating and beating the ground—thus exploding buried mines (see illus. pages 139, 273, 466, Vol. 8). Bridging tanks (here following the flails) provided Allied armour in Germany and Burma with a right-of-way over watercourses, shell-craters and similar obstacles. They could be transported in landing craft to where beach-landings were to be made, going into action immediately, if necessary, with the assault troops. See also pages 229, 237, Vol. 9.

Photo, G.P.U.

THE MARCH PAST SEEN FROM THE FLY PAST, as columns of troops left the Mall—flanked with 103 flags of Britain, the Empire, the Allies and the Services—and swung round the Queen Victoria Memorial in front of Buckingham Palace (right foreground). In this photograph, taken from one of the R.A.F. aircraft which flew past H.M. the King (see pages 179 and 180), the fountains in St. James's Park can be seen in the left background. At the night the Park and the fountains were one of the major spectacles in London's illuminations. At the foot of the Memorial reserved stands were allotted to orphans of the War.

Photo, Barratt's

After-Dark Magic of Lavish Floodlighting

POWERFUL ILLUMINATION OF BUILDINGS AND FAMOUS SITES gave many a familiar scene a transforming touch by night during Victory Week (June 8-15). In Trafalgar Square (1) the fountains flung great jets of coloured water. In Plymouth, stark ruins of blitzed St. Andrew's Church, within whose roofless framework is now a quiet Garden of Remembrance (see illus. page 105) were softened by the light-glow (2). And the sombre greyness of Windsor Castle's ancient Round Tower was turned to stately white (3).

On the Night Before and the Morning After

DETERMINED TO SECURE GOOD VANTAGE POINTS from which to view the Parade thousands of visitors lined the route overnight. With the resourcefulness for which the Royal Navy is remarkable, two sailors slung their hammocks in the Mall (1). Improvised beds in Trafalgar Square (2), where the fountain basins provided early-morning toilet facilities (3). When the jovial tumult and the shouting died, overturned litter-baskets, duckboards and mud were prominent along the Mall. See also page 185.

Photos. Topical Press, P.A.-Reuter, The Daily Mirror, Keystone

The Victory Parade

WHATEVER difference of opinion may have existed concerning the expediency of celebrating Victory Day in the fullest measure and at the very heart of the main target of Germany's attack on civilization, there can be nothing but joy and thankfulness that this historic event passed off " without a hitch " as the B.B.C. recorded.

Above all, it was a superb example of the genius for organization which the British people possess almost beyond their own belief. It was that same genius that made the final and decisive assault on Hitler's " Fortress of Europe " possible and brought the vast edifice of Nazidom down to dust, with the obliteration of the evil men who had reared it. The same genius that built the British Empire and Commonwealth of Peoples, the might and resources of which were so admirably symbolized in the V-Day Parade of June 8, a day that the British people had lived for and suffered for.

And it was also characteristic of Britain to be reminded at the very height of its rejoicing that while our self-reliant democracy may be sure of itself it can never be sure of its climate. But that very climate has played its part in the making of this island race whose faith in themselves assures them that " behind the clouds is the sun still shining."

V-Day 1946 is a splendid reminder that the Sun of Britain is still shining ; that the clouds will lift again. The spirit of our race, which in these six years of War proved itself the spearhead of World Freedom, is the same that breathed in the heroic days of Elizabeth ; and it was a happy augury that two Royal Elizabeths were present at the saluting base when King George VI paid tribute to his people's prowess for their share in saving all free peoples of the world from the greatest menace to the democratic way of life that has ever arisen since the fall of Ancient Rome.

THE EDITOR

Triumphal Day

ENGLAND has seen many pageants and the nation has celebrated many victories, but for brilliance, variety and majesty none has equalled the magnificent triumphal parade which marched nine miles long through the streets of London on Saturday morning to celebrate the final victory won after six weary years of sacrifice and courage.

It was a day in which popular enthusiasm triumphed over the weather. It was especially significant for the impressive tribute of affection and respect paid to the King.

With the Queen by his side and accompanied by the two Princesses and Queen Mary, he stood for nearly two hours at the saluting base in the Mall, gravely and proudly acknowledging on behalf of his people the serried lines of marching men and women and the cavalcade of tanks and engines of war which poured past him to represent the British nation, the Empire and Allies.

In the exactitude of its marshalling, in its timing and in the perfection of the turn-out, the parade was a triumphant success. And, revelling in its pageantry, Londoners and visitors from all over the country forgot the hardships of overnight camping, of crowded restaurants and of congested travel.

Disregarding the rain, which started at 11.30 and continued till late afternoon, they cheered till they were hoarse and then gazed skywards, spellbound by the armada of battle aircraft which roared through the leaden skies almost at roof-top height.

Past the King, the leaders of the nation and representatives of Empire and Allied nations marched the manhood of the Alliance, men and women from nearly all parts of the world, with uniforms of every type; their chests bearing medals won on innumerable battlefields.

THE only disappointment was the weather, as fickle as the official forecast was inaccurate. Instead of the light winds and fine weather promised there was a heavy downpour which, as soon as the procession had passed, drove the crowds to any shelter they could find. Some, more optimistic than others, went to St. James's Park and Green Park, hoping that the elaborate programme of open-air dancing and band concerts might still take place. But those arrangements had to be cancelled. It was not until early evening that, their enthusiasm revived by more favourable conditions, the crowd started to surge back to the West End in high spirits for the big evening carnival programme. Traffic in the streets became jammed, and they soon became solid from pavement to pavement with vast throngs

making their way to the river. Others gathered at Marble Arch and Trafalgar Square to dance to music from loudspeakers.

Many at Saturday's parade recalled a similar day of rain on July 20, 27 years ago, when the heroes of the 1914-1918 war, led by Foch and Pershing, Haig and Beatty, were similarly honoured. Other leaders, equally brave, equally resourceful and equally determined, appeared in this second war to take their place.

Of them and of the gallant sailors, soldiers and airmen who so nobly served their country

EISENHOWER'S MESSAGE

" TODAY we commemorate the British people's magnificent achievements in the long and desperate struggle against the Axis attempt to enslave the world," said General Eisenhower, in New York, on June 7. " Though long exposed to the full fury of attack, the Empire, both when alone and when fighting alongside her allies, refused to flinch from danger or modify her defiance.

The British contribution to the final victory will always command the admiration, respect, and gratitude of all peoples devoted to the cause of freedom. I salute the British fighting forces and join them in reverent remembrance of their fallen comrades."

in an hour of crisis it may be truly said : "They have forced every sea and land to be the highway of their daring and everywhere they have left immortal monuments behind them."—*Douglas Williams*

I Rode With Them

DURING the War there were many spontaneous Victory parades as our advanced troops liberated European cities. As a writing, and not a fighting, man I involuntarily took a bow at three of the most memorable—in Rome, Athens, Amsterdam.

Emotional experience of welcomes seemed exhausted, but London's greeting was something different—endearing, enduring and typically English, even to the weather. In Rome it was wine and flowers ; in Athens torchlights and feux de joie ; in Amsterdam hysterical relief breaking through Dutch

phlegm. All left lasting memories of frantic enthusiasm and gratitude.

London millions massed along 18 miles of route showed some of those qualities which helped win the war—discipline, patience and endurance. Then as the parade passed restraint gave way to a sustained demonstration of thankfulness and affection that touched every man and woman taking part.

The mechanized column closely resembled those processions in which we correspondents used to find ourselves jammed day after day behind the fighting fronts. But this time the monstrous engines of war were covered with varnish instead of dust and mud and were labelled so that we did not have to argue among ourselves as to their various purposes. Even to us it was an education to realize that such things as an air transportable boot repair plant play their part in modern war.

IT was Highway Six, leading to Cassino, choked with guns, tanks and pontoon carriers that I thought of chiefly as we moved out of Regent's Park for the start of the parade. But the troops were now spruce and stiff to attention, not grim and yellow with dust, as they often were on the deadly road to Rome. In my jeep were two other correspondents, as in the war days. We passed into Euston Road and from the packed pavements and the hundreds of crowded windows above had our foretaste of London's welcome.

People had forgotten their reserve and all ages were cheering, clapping, shouting words of encouragement and flag-waving. As we passed Moorfields Eye Hospital I noticed the pathetic sight of a nurse at the open window describing the passing parade to a small patient, who was listening seriously. We swerved round three tanks that had to be abandoned as casualties. In Whitechapel I was reminded of the Italian woman who in her exuberance threw Chianti over us in Siena. This time it was a woman with a bottle of beer, restrained by a smiling policeman.

Enthusiasm reached an early peak in Kennington, where the schoolchildren had secured the finest display of Union Jacks up to that point, including curious composite flags comprising the Union Jack, the Stars and Stripes and the Hammer and Sickle. When we stopped by the Oval for 20 minutes a local resident, out of his small supplies, spared us cups of tea and talked about "his bomb." Children swarmed over the jeeps; spectators told us they had easily recognized "Good old Monty." There were curious variations in the density of the crowd. In some places people were packed almost to suffocation; in others, such as Aldgate, there was only a thin line. Closing

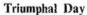

The Daily Telegraph
and Morning Post

LONDON MONDAY, JUNE 10 1946   Printed in LONDON and MANCHESTER

WE have chosen from The Daily Telegraph of June 10 the series of extracts which appear in these pages to present the various aspects of the Victory Parade as these were recorded by that newspaper, thus preserving something of the emotional reactions on the band of brilliant journalists who represented, on that uniquely grand occasion, the great newspaper, which, since the days of G. A. Sala, Sutherland Edwards, Sir Edwin Arnold, and Dr. E. J. Dillon, has been famed for its vivid descriptions of historic events.

Continued in page 179

At the Victory Parade Saluting Base in the Mall

The Southern Rhodesian Contingent in the Victory Celebrations, June 8, 1946, is passing the Royal dais where, on the right of Their Majesties, the Princesses and Queen Mary, are (l. to r. front row) Sir Hastings Ismay, Lord Louis Mountbatten, Lord Maitland Wilson, Lord Alexander, Lord Portal, Lord Alanbrooke, Lord Cunningham; on the left, Mr. Attlee, Mr. Churchill, Mr. Mackenzie King, Field-Marshal Smuts. In the second row, on the right of Their Majesties, are H.R.H. the Princess Royal, King George of Greece, the Crown Prince and Princess of Norway; on the left, H.R.H. the Duchess of Kent, Princess Alexandra, King Feisal of Iraq, the Regent of Iraq, the Princess Juliana of the Netherlands.

London's Memorable Day of Gay Pageantry

On the way to the saluting base a Royal Marines band is about to pass through Admiralty Arch and along the Mall towards Buckingham Palace in the distance. In this section of the marching column, Naval Forces were represented by seamen, engine-room department, band, miscellaneous branches and reserves, Royal Marines, followed by Queen Alexandra's R.N. Nursing Service and V.A.D.s, and Women's R.N. Service. Cheers echoed from dense crowds in Trafalgar Square.

Imposing Columns of 21,000 Men and Women

Unique in the history of the world was the triumphal procession of two spectacular columns, nine miles long, mechanized and on foot, comprising 21,000 representatives of our fighting, auxiliary and civilian services, with Allied and Empire contingents. At the saluting base flew the same Royal Standard which His Majesty the King had raised on the Normandy beaches ten days after D-Day. Above it, through heavy rain, streaked more than 300 R.A.F. aircraft in impressive fly-past.

Night Blaze of Fireworks Over London's River

Photo, P.A.-i

The glare of 80 searchlights and the thundering of maroons saluted Their Majesties aboard the Royal Barge which carried them to Westminster. From then on the Victory Night sky was alive with colour, rockets beyond counting soaring and flaring : this " cascade " was seen from the roof of Shell Mex House. In the immediate foreground is Charing Cross Railway Bridge, with a temporary wartime bridge beyond. On the right, the Houses of Parliament with Big Ben lighted-up.

178

350 PIPERS AND DRUMMERS OF SCOTTISH AND IRISH REGIMENTS marching and counter-marching in the Mall provided a stirring and colourful prelude to the arrival of the Parade. During this interlude H.M. the King chatted with his Service Chiefs : he is seen (left) with Field-Marshal Viscount Alexander of Tunis. On the dais are (left) Their Majesties the Queen and Queen Mary, and (right) the two Princesses. The Duchess of Kent in W.R.N.S. uniform, is seated on the extreme right, with her daughter Princess Alexandra. *Photo, Fox*

Continued from page 174

of approaches evidently prevented people from reaching less crowded vantage points.

In Parliament Square, where the mechanized and marching columns united, the first heavy raindrops did not abate the enthusiasm of the dense masses, tired with long waiting. Ambulances were busy and along the main processional route I saw eight fainting women carried off. At last we were bowling at a smart pace down the Mall, well spaced. Then, in accordance with instructions, we rose to attention or saluted or, if the vehicle did not permit, turned eyes left on passing the King.—*L. Marsland Gander*

Hours of Thrills

THE first big thrill came when massed pipers of Highland regiments, in kilts of many tartans, played their way, triumphantly, from Buckingham Palace to the Duke of York's steps. After that we welcomed the Chiefs of Staff. Then came the Dominions' Premiers or their representatives. There was a tremendous roar when the crowd saw the landau in which Mr. Attlee and Mr. Churchill were riding together.

The arrival of Queen Mary with her brother, the Earl of Athlone, brought more cheers, and then another prolonged cheer heralded the State landau bearing the King and Queen and the two Princesses. Near them in the Royal stand were seated Queen Mary, the Princess Royal, in A.T.S. khaki, the Duchess of Kent, in W.R.N.S. uniform, with her daughter, Princess Alexandra, who was next to the boy King Feisal of Iraq, Princess Juliana of the Netherlands with her husband, Prince Bernhard, in khaki, and the Crown Prince and Crown Princess of Norway.

Punctually at noon the head of the mechanized column reached the saluting base. Field-Marshal Viscount Montgomery of Alamein, who led the Army Commanders in the van of this procession, riding in a small Army car, was easily recognized and loudly cheered. Only a short break followed the immense parade of mechanized power. Then the "foot" procession came into view, the serried ranks

interspersed by bands playing lively tunes. There were special cheers for the "Desert Rats," the Airborne Troops, the Commandos, the Scots Regiments, the men of the Fleet, the Merchant Navy group and many others. Nor were the people sparing in their welcome for all those men and women of the civilian defence forces and of industry who served in the fight for victory. When, the last section was passing, there came the roar of more than 300 British aircraft.

The Fly-Past Men

VISIBILITY over London at mid-day was so bad that pilots taking part in the fly-past over the Victory Parade could hardly see the buildings below them. Sodium flares on the ground were of unexpected value in marking the run-in. Led by a single Hurricane, 307 aircraft streamed across the capital.

I flew from Graveley R.A.F. airfield, Huntingdonshire, in a Lancaster of No. 35 Squadron Bomber Command, part of the noted wartime Pathfinder Force. We took off at 30-second intervals and flew in the unaccustomed tight-packed formation which the bomber pilots have been practising for several weeks. Our course to join the converging stream of aircraft took us across Cambridge and round to the mouth of the Blackwater before we made for Fairlop, Essex, the beginning of the straight run-in. Slipstream from our compact formation

The Price of Victory

TOTAL casualties suffered during the war by the Armed Forces, Auxiliary Services and the civilian population of the U.K. were 950,794. Of these 357,116 were killed ; 369,267 wounded ; 178,332 prisoners of war or internees ; 46,079 missing. Those killed in the Services were— Royal Navy, 50,758 ; Army, 144,079 ; R.A.F., 69,606. Navy wounded, 14,663 ; Army 239,575 ; R.A.F., 22,839. Civilians killed, 60,595 ; wounded, 86,182 ; Merchant Navy and Fishing Fleets, killed, 30,248 ; wounded, 4,707 ; Women's Services, killed, 624 ; wounded, 744 ; Home Guard, killed, 1,206 ; wounded, 557.

would have had such a powerful effect on following planes that we were ordered to fly at 1,500 feet, 500 feet above all others, but bad weather forced us down to 1,300 feet. Even from that height London appeared shrouded in grey mist. St. Paul's loomed on our port side as I crouched at the bomb-aimer's window in a Lancaster.

Then in 20 seconds we flashed, at 180 miles an hour, down the length of the Mall, keeping 400 yards to its northern side to be seen easily from the saluting stand. We were over the stand a minute after Big Ben had chimed one o'clock and within five seconds of our appointed time. Over Buckingham Palace, and for a mile beyond, we kept our course, then swung to starboard for a circuit of London. Except that a squadron of Tempests was ordered slightly out of line, to avoid danger from jet-propelled Meteors coming up astern in low visibility, the "fly-over" was exactly as planned.

. . . and the Future ?

AS the last echoes of the rejoicing die the nations turn their thoughts to the future. There, victory has still to be won. The end of war has been celebrated before a background of world unrest. Absence from the processions of contingents from Russia, Poland and Yugoslavia, comrade nations with ourselves in the years that are past, is evidence enough that all is not yet well, and that the problems that war has left have still to be solved. Whether we look to Europe or to the East there is unrest and perplexity.

Not alone in the field of statesmanship have we to regain the unity of purpose that made possible the spectacles of Saturday last. To rescue the world from threatening famine, to restore the devastation that war caused, to bring back prosperity—all these call for a resolution and an endurance scarce less than was demanded in the six years of which we have just marked the end. Failure in these fields would be treason to the memory of those who fell and to the whole purpose for which the Allied nations entered battle.— *The Daily Telegraph Editorial*

R.A.F. and Naval Aircraft Skim Swiftly By

LED BY AN ANONYMOUS BATTLE OF BRITAIN PILOT in a Hurricane, R.A.F. and Naval Air Arm squadrons roaring through a rain-filled sky, and dipping in salute to the King, followed the conclusion of the March Past. In the Fly Past were Lancasters, our greatest bombers (I), Spitfires, passing over the Duke of York's column (2), Coastal Command Sunderland flying boats (3) and other famous aircraft. Meteor and Vampire jet-propelled fighters brought up the rear. See also pages 171 and 179.

Photos, G.P.U., The News Chronicle, Barratt's

Our Warships Ride at Anchor in the Thames

ILLUMINATED BY NIGHT AND BEFLAGGED BY DAY, representative craft of the Royal Navy were on show to London's visitors during Victory Week. Moored off Greenwich, the cruisers H.M.S. Diadem and Bellona after dark (1). A young sightseer inspects an Oerlikon gun on the Bellona (2). Four minesweepers were in the Upper Pool (3), below Tower Bridge. Four destroyers were at Woolwich, a sloop and a corvette at Deptford, and two submarines at Shadwell New Basin.
Photos, P.A.-Reuter, Planet News, G.P.U.

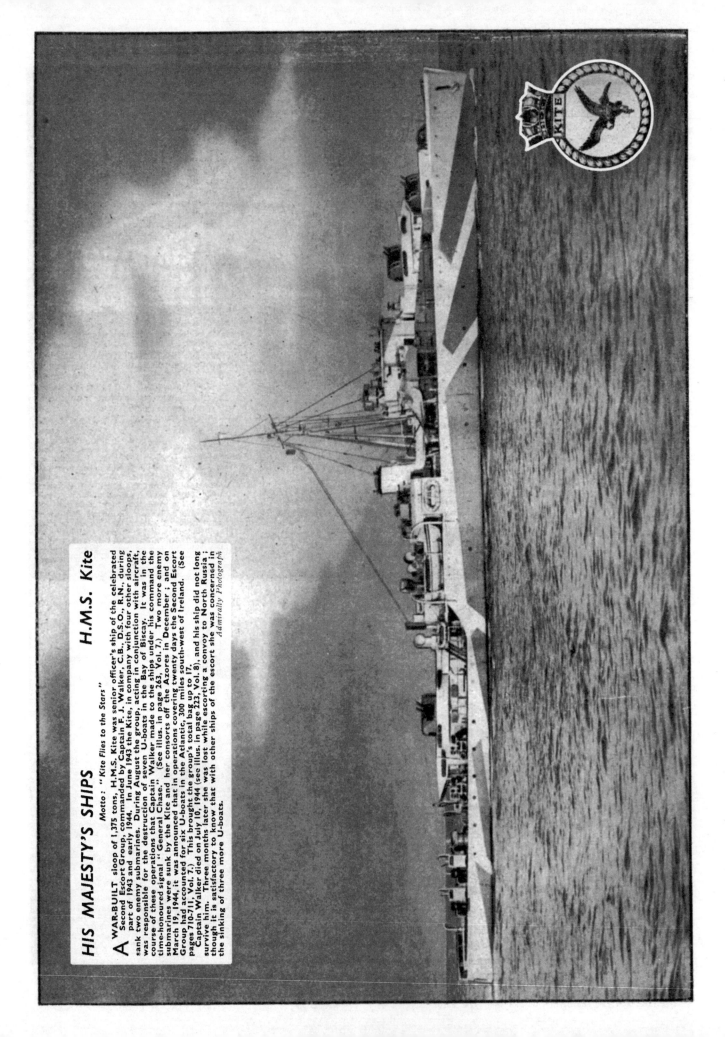

HIS MAJESTY'S SHIPS

H.M.S. Kite

Motto: "Kite Flies to the Stars"

A WAR-BUILT sloop of 1,375 tons, H.M.S. Kite was senior officer's ship of the celebrated Second Escort Group, commanded by Captain F. J. Walker, C.B., D.S.O., R.N., during part of 1943 and early 1944. In June 1943 the Kite, in company with four other sloops, sank two enemy submarines. During August the group, acting in conjunction with aircraft, was responsible for the destruction of seven U-boats in the Bay of Biscay. It was in the course of these operations that Captain Walker made to the ships under his command the time-honoured signal "General Chase." (See illus. in page 263, Vol. 7.) Two more enemy submarines were sunk by the Kite and her consorts off the Azores in December; and on March 19, 1944, it was announced that in operations covering twenty days the Second Escort Group had accounted for six U-boats in the Atlantic, 300 miles south-west of Ireland. (See pages 710-711, Vol. 7.) This brought the group's total bag up to 17.

Captain Walker died on July 10, 1944 (see illus. in page 223, Vol. 8), and his ship did not long survive him. Three months later she was lost while escorting a convoy to North Russia; though it is satisfactory to know that with other ships of the escort she was concerned in the sinking of three more U-boats.

Admiralty Photograph

HOW GIBRALTAR and MALTA WENT to WAR

By HARLEY V. USILL

THE strategic value of the British Colonies having been made clear, and a general picture presented of their wartime productive effort, the author now begins to deal with their individual contributions to victory. In the front line of battle were Gibraltar and Malta, which fittingly form the subject of the first of two articles on the Mediterranean colonies at war.

〜〜〜〜

IN the waging of total war individuals were called upon to play many different parts, and it is only by assessing the effort as a whole that the relative value of each contribution can be placed in its proper perspective. Each had a part to play in ensuring final victory. The same thing applies to the Colonies ; one was asked to contribute fighting manpower while another was required to increase food and raw materials, and one was subject to enemy invasion or intensive bombing while another suffered the inconvenience of an evacuation of its women and children to distant lands. The Mediterranean Colonies provide a picture in miniature of the Colonial war effort as a whole, as there was scarcely a war experience, except actual invasion, to which one or the other was not subjected.

There is a well-known legend that when the Barbary apes leave the Rock of Gibraltar the British will follow and their power in the Mediterranean be broken. Well, the Barbary apes are still there, but as an urgent war measure nearly 15,000 Gibraltarians were uprooted from their homes and sent away to strange lands. The men were left behind to carry on essential work in the docks, so that there was the double sacrifice of loss of home and the severing of family relations.

When it is remembered that Gibraltar, at its widest point, is only three-quarters of a mile across and its whole area covers just under two square miles, it is clear that there was no room for its normal population of about 20,000 plus the enormous influx of military personnel which the defence of the Rock demanded. This, then, was the major contribution of the people of Gibraltar to the war effort.

A Military Town Inside the Rock

The Rock cleared of the non-essential population, the colossal task began of ensuring its impregnability as a fortress. Expert Canadian and British tunnelling sections arrived and commenced the task of burrowing, like an army of ants. With modern mining and drilling equipment, miners, tunnellers and quarry workers from South Wales, the Midlands and Yorkshire, drilled and blasted new gun sites and emplacements, and drove intersecting defence tunnels and galleries to command every aspect of the Rock. They hewed out new reservoirs and food stores, and constructed underground dumps immune from bombing. In a very short time the inside of the Rock was transformed into a self-contained military town, with a road wide enough to take two lines of traffic and petrol stations by the roadside, a big hospital, troop quarters with equipment stores, sleeping and feeding accommodation for infantry battalions, and exit roads leading to various places on the outer face of the Rock.

The Admiralty harbour is 440 acres in extent, and there are three graving docks and one small dock besides equipment and fuel. Within the dock area, Gibraltarians, descendants of Italian and Spanish settlers, worked day and night to service the ships of the Royal Navy. The loyalty of the people of this British Colony, which was ceded to Britain in the Peace of Utrecht in 1713, is further exemplified by the fact that they contributed more than £35,000 in gifts or free-of-interest loans, a sum which exceeds thirty shillings per head of the population.

The George Cross Island Fortress

"To Great Britain, still unsubdued, these Islands are entrusted by the Powers of Europe at the wish of the Maltese themselves." Those words, in Latin, appear over the Main Guard at Palace Square, Valetta,

recording the freedom of choice which led this ancient people to become a part of the British Commonwealth and Empire. In 1798 Napoleon, on his way to Egypt, invaded Malta and occupied the island, but the Maltese revolted and drove the French troops within the fortified towns where, with the help of the British Fleet under Nelson, they held them closely blockaded for two years. In 1800 the French surrendered, and by popular consent the government of Malta passed to Great Britain under the Treaty of Paris in 1814.

Isolated by Air and Sea Blockade

The Colony of Malta consists of the two main islands of Malta and Gozo, separated by the Strait of Fleighi, the small island of Comino and a few islets, the whole occupying an area of 122 square miles, or about half that of the Isle of Man. For more than 40,000 years these islands have been part of the history of the Mediterranean, since they contain remains of both palaeolithic and neolithic ages. Invaded by successive conquerors, in 1530 Emperor Charles V of Aragon gave Malta to the Knights of St. John of Jerusalem, who held it until 1798. It was under the Knights that Malta was first called upon to play a vital part in the saving of civilization when, during the great siege of 1565, the Order of St. John resisted the attacks of the land and sea forces of Suliman the Magnificent, and saved Europe from the Turks.

In 1939 the total population of the Colony was estimated at 268,668. Italian propaganda tried to claim the Maltese as Italian by race, tradition and language, whereas they are of Semitic origin, and their language, although retaining some of the influence of the 9th-century Arab occupation, is believed to be probably the purest survival of the language of Phoenicia and Carthage. Miss Mabel Strickland, editor of The Times of Malta, a paper which never missed publication throughout the whole period of the siege, says of them :

" The island lies under perpetual sun, but the Maltese are strikingly different from their Latin neighbours. They possess the fine qualities of a seafaring race, in a degree only equalled by their Cornish brethren. They are traders rather than fighters, high-spirited but docile, and possessed of stubborn and dogged perseverance, which has kept their race distinct and famous." They are good colonizers, and large communities of Maltese are to be found in Australia, the United States and North Africa, among other parts of the world.

AT the beginning of the war the locally-raised forces in Malta consisted of the Royal Malta Artillery and the King's Own Malta Regiment, and later other new units were raised—the Malta Army Service Corps, Army Ordnance Corps and Army Pay Corps. Under siege conditions the Royal Malta Artillery was called upon to play the most active part, and its gunners manned both heavy and light anti-aircraft batteries. As British troops who had been sent to reinforce the defences of the island withdrew, however,

the King's Own Malta Regiment formed an increasingly large proportion of the infantry component of the garrison.

We have already dealt with the strategic value of Malta (see page 54), and now a few words about the actual siege. It began on June 11, 1940, with an attack from ten Italian bombers within less than seven hours of Italy's entry into the war. From then, until the lifting of the siege in November 1942, the island was under continual air attack by both Italian and German air forces, and was isolated by air and sea blockade. During this period the people of Malta, short of food, short of fuel, and often homeless, endured 3,215 air raids. Over 14,000 tons of bombs were dropped, 1,468 civilians were killed or died of injuries, and over 27,000 buildings were destroyed or damaged, many of them of priceless historical and sentimental value.

Malta is not and cannot be self-supporting in regard to food, and when it is remembered that during the last fourteen months of the siege only eleven ships reached the island, and two of these were sunk in harbour before they could be unloaded, some idea is gained of the sufferings of the people. Even the famous Malta goats had to be sacrificed, and in announcing this decision in July 1942 Lord Gort, the Governor, said :

" . . . Well, people always talk about Malta's goats and goat milk, but, unfortunately, the goats had to walk so far in trying to find anything to eat that the milk went very shy indeed, and that complicated my problem a bit, and I decided in the end that all we could do was to leave 20 per cent of the goat population behind. Then came the problem of eating the goats. They were remarkably tough, having walked so far . . . and people . . . complained that they could not get their teeth into it. Then our people who were handling it suddenly formed the idea of mincing it up and making a thing called ' veal loaf,' so the goat was issued out as veal loaf, and in that way it was consumed fairly easily ; short of that you could do nothing at all. That was the end of our dear friends the goats."

Deliverance by the Royal Navy

By October 1942 Malta was within two months of starvation, and then, on November 20, after running the gauntlet of the Mediterranean, the British Navy once again " delivered the goods," this time in the form of a convoy of four ships which entered the Grand Harbour. The blockade was raised. How did the people of Malta react to all this ? The reply is, in the same way as the people of Britain. Perhaps the best description was given in a broadcast in April 1942 by Commander Anthony Kimmins. He said :

" Never before in history have human beings endured or survived such an attack. Yet life goes on—schools are open, bands play amidst the rubble, and people listen in the sun : makeshift shops appear from the ruins. The daily papers make their regular appearance—they may be small, but nowadays there's little gossip or difference of opinion to swell the columns—the people are too united in one thought. And through it all, no sign of panic disfigures the dignity of Malta."

As was the case in Britain in similar danger, a Home Guard was formed and within three days 3,000 volunteers had registered ; similar response was accorded to the various Civil Defence services. On April 15, 1942, Malta was awarded the George Cross, the first time a decoration had been conferred on a part of the British Commonwealth. In making the award the King's message read : " To honour her brave people I award the George Cross to the island fortress of Malta to bear witness to a heroism and devotion that will long be famous in history." Thus for the second time in her history Malta had played a noble part in the saving of civilization; indeed a worthy prelude to self-government.

The NCOs & MEN Roll of Honour
1939—1946

O/S E. E. L. ALLWOOD
H.M.S. Jaguar.
Action : at sea. 26.3.42.
Age 19. (Reading)

Readers of THE WAR ILLUSTRATED who wish to submit photographs for inclusion in our Roll of Honour must fill in the coupon which appeared in No. 230. No portraits can be considered that are not accompanied by this coupon.

Tpr. H. A. AMBROSE
Queen's Bays.
D. of wds. : Tripoli. 4.2.42.
Age 31. (Cambridge)

 **Fus. W. F. BARRON**
Royal Scots Fusiliers.
In action : Goch. 22.2.45.
Age 31. (Bridlington)

 **Gnr. J. W. BALDWIN**
40/14th L.A.A. Regt.
Action : Tobruk. 14.9.41.
Age 22. (Kettering)

 **L/Cpl. A. BERRY**
13th Bn. King's Regt.
Action : Burma. 28.3.43.
Age 33. (Liverpool)

 **Sgt. J. A. BOWEN**
Pathfinder Force, R.A.F.V.R.
Over Kiel. Aug. 44.
Age 26. (Tipton)

 **A/B P. D. BRANSDEN**
H.M.S. Hood.
In action : 24.5.41.
Age 18. (Brighton)

 **L/Sig. J. A. BURNETT**
Royal Navy.
Home waters. 1.6.43.
Age 23. (Ruthin)

 **Cpl. J. CROUDY**
Royal Scots Fusiliers.
Action : Germany. 4.4.45.
Age 30. (Kingsbury)

 **Pte. G. FOWKES**
2/5 Leicestershire Regt.
Action : Tunisia. 9.4.43.
Age 27. (Leicester)

 **Gdsmn. W. GOLLIDGE**
Welsh Guards.
Action : Brussels. 8.9.44.
Age 24. (Ton Pentre)

 **Pte. A. HAHNER**
West Yorks. Regt.
Action : El Alamein. 5.6.42.
Age 27. (Kingsbury)

 **Stoker L. HEAD**
Royal Navy.
In action. 9.3.42.
Age 29. (Battersea)

 **A B R. W. KELLETT**
H.M.S. Loyalty.
Action : at sea. 22.8.44.
Age 19. (Leeds)

 **Gnr. J. H. LANE**
Royal Artillery.
D. of wounds: Italy 18.4.44.
Age 29. (London)

 **Cpl. C. W. McASSEY**
4th Hussars R.A.C.
Action : Sollum. 11.6.42.
Age 21. (Dagenham)

 **Sgt. K. M. McGREGOR**
Bomber Comd. R.A.F.V.R.
Over Bremen. July 42.
Age 21. (Worthing)

 **L/Sgt. J. McTIGHE**
2nd Northamptonshire R.
In action : Anzio. 3.5.44.
Age 30. (Chesterfield)

 **Sgt. J. C. MAYS**
35 Sqdn. Pathfinder Force.
Action : Cologne. 23.12.44.
Age 22. (Kenton)

 **Sgt. R. MANSBRIDGE**
Pathfinder Force R.A.F.
Action : France. 4.5.44.
Age 19. (Harrow)

 **Pte. R. F. MILL**
Royal Army Service Corps.
Action : Naples. 21.10.43.
Age 26. (Croydon)

 **Pte. R. MOODY**
1st East Riding Yeomanry.
Action : Normandy. 21.6.44.
Age 31. (Hull)

 **Sgt. W. MORGAN**
Royal Army Service Corps.
Died P.O.W. Siam. 27.10.43.
Age 23. (Auchtermuchty)

 **A B J. P. REID**
Royal Navy (Minesweeper).
Action : Dunkirk. 31.5.40.
Age 20. (Avoch)

 **L.A.C. R. RICHARDS**
78 Sqdn. R.A.F.
Action : Marseilles. 5.9.44.
Age 23. (Mansfield)

 **Driver J. A. ROWETT**
Royal Engineers.
Action: Pannerden. 18.6.45.
Age 24. (Boston)

 **Pte. R. SEABRIGHT**
5th Hampshire Regt.
Action : Salerno. 17.9.43.
Age 24. (Ringwood)

 **Sgt. S. B. SHAW**
150 Sqdn. R.A.F.
Market Rasen. 30.5.42.
Age 26. (London)

 **Sgt. C. E. SMITH**
Royal Air Force.
Action : Magdeburg. 21.1.44.
Age 33. (Wolverhampton)

 **Sgt. A/G. J. C. SMITH**
Royal Air Force.
Over Germany. 29.1.44.
Age 25. (London)

 **Driver H. SOWTER**
Royal Signals.
El Alamein. 9.7.42.
Age 22. (Lewes)

 **Stoker W. G. STOKES**
H.M.S. Daring.
Action: North Sea. 18.2.40.
Age 34. (Portsmouth)

 **Pte. A. E. TEASDALE**
York and Lancaster Regt.
Action : Khartoum. 20.5.40.
Age 27. (Malton)

 **Pte. G. WALKER**
King's Shropshire L.I.
Action : Germany. 10.4.45.
Age 19. (Rugby)

 **Flt./Sgt. A. J. WALLIS**
Royal Air Force.
In action : India. 28.1.44.
Age 21. (Portslade)

 **Pte. E. A. WILGROVE**
9th Durham Lgt. Infantry.
N.W. Europe. 17.7.44.
Age 21. (Rayleigh)

 **Flt. Sgt. J. H. ASPDEN**
Bomber Command R.A.F.
Over Germany. 16.4.43.
Age 28. (Pontnewynydd)

 **Sgt. A. B. S. G. BUGG**
Bomber Comd. R.A.F.V.R.
Action : Frankfurt. 10.4.43.
Age 20. (Tottenham)

HOW WE PAID TRIBUTE

By Hugh Massingham

IN the Mall the Parade ended with all heads turned skywards, hands and programmes shading eyes. The pilots in the fly-past no doubt could see the whole scene—the main streets, swarming, bee-deep, in crowds, the side streets drained dry of life, and the procession still nosing its way along the route, the motor-cyclists first, and then the odd jumble of total war—civilians as well as soldiers, rescue cars and tanks, coal-miners and commandos. And now the last of the pageant was here not on the ground but airborne.

Far away, all up Constitution Hill, Hyde Park Corner, and Park Lane, the crowds were still cheering, voices beat against the drumming of the aeroplanes. Over the firm lines of the Marble Arch flew tiny Hurricanes, heavy bus-like Sunderlands, Lancasters, Spitfires, Meteors, Tempests, bringing a fearful heave of the stomach as one remembered long August days in 1940 with the fighters crawling upwards, like flies on a window pane, or the burning entrails of a room, the jagged grin of a smashed window.

London bulged with people 24 hours before the day began. The normal was suspended, the mechanical life of a great city, with its people sucked into holes and then regurgitated at stated points, with the last drinkers being tipped out of pubs, a few hastening theatre-goers, and finally exhaustion, rest, sleep—these familiar things were either swamped by the millions of visitors or touched by the mad irresponsibility of sightseeing.

There was no sleep in the old way ; solitary lights burnt at three in the morning, and people crowded round coffee stalls, slept on benches, squeezed themselves into corners. The impression was of a city fighting off sleep, not patiently inviting it. The Mall was lined with people lying on ground-sheets or the wet ground. "This is the B.B.C. Home service..." The watchers stretched themselves out, cooling their feet, and the prim voice chattered away in the darkness under the trees. A little rain fell, the trees dripped water.

The crowds were awake just before dawn. So, too, were the soldiers in Hyde Park ; one imagined them swearing in their tents, hunting for the Silvo, the slimy button rag, entangled in stiff brown blankets. The watchers in the Mall stretched themselves and were still half asleep when they stood up. The day had begun.

Humanity hatched out of the side streets. Women armed against all weathers, carrying mackintoshes and blue parasols. Men walking delicately on new squeaking shoes. Swaggering men, happy in the comfort of tennis shoes, open cricket shirt, grey trousers. Mother and father with the children.

"I'll tell you," a man said to me. "I stood eight hours in the train. I took six hours looking at the sights. I've been up all night. How's that ?" "You like processions then ?" "What, me ! With my feet ? No, no. I just felt I was owed a holiday." It was the prevailing mood—no illusions, no wild hopes about the future, but a carefree gesture to the moment.

Approaching Climax to Long Vigil

The day revealed the crowds scattered about the pavements. Fantastic incongruities of the early morning—mussels, cockles, winkles, and ice-cream being sold at 3 a.m. A negro band playing in white trousers at the same hour. Families asleep under Union Jacks or grey blankets amidst the persistent coughing of gas rattles. A husband holding up a mirror for his wife—rough amenity of pavement life. A child, dead with sleep, wearing a huge red, white and blue rosette. A

man perched on a pillar-box, holding up a book to catch the first light. Between their ranks ran the empty, wet road ; the familiar mounted policeman pranced along on his horse. A motor-cyclist or two roared away—people with a purpose, they made even the haggard, sluggish morning seem important. In Trafalgar Square thousands of starlings were singing ; thousands of voices chirped on the ground, so that the birds seemed to be reflecting sound rather than making it.

At the grandstand in the Mall we were very nearly respectable—gentlemen appeared in top hats, grey waistcoats, shod in pointed shoes. Flags waved, and looking over the tops of the stands one had the illusion of country—enchanting glimpses of light and dark greens. Well-known figures wandered in—Mr. Greenwood, as tall as ever but frailer, whiter, than one remembers ; Mr. Ernest Bevin, in black hat, a flash of white from the handkerchief and collar ; Mr. Morrison with his cock's-comb of hair ; Sir Archibald Sinclair, gesticulating among friends. The great and glorious arrive—Alanbrooke, Portal, Cunningham, Alexander, Maitland Wilson, Mountbatten.

Again the cheering begins, and through Admiralty Arch comes an open Royal carriage, and there at the back is Mr. Attlee, unveiling the bald head, a conjurer performing expertly with a top hat ; and at his side the beaming old warrior himself, blessing the people with the "V" sign and episcopal gesture.

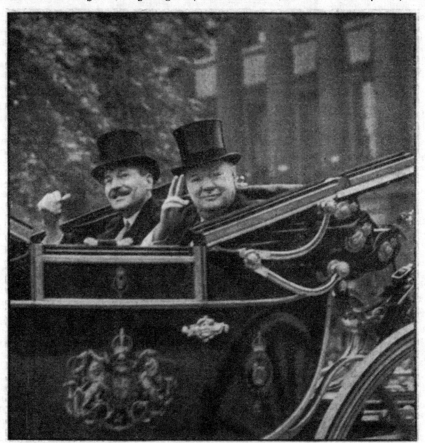

GIVING THE "V" SIGN, the Rt. Hon. Winston S. Churchill, together with his successor as Prime Minister, the Rt. Hon. Clement R. Attlee, rode from Downing Street in an open royal carriage driven by a scarlet-coated coachman through mightily cheering crowds to take up position at the saluting base.
PAGE 185   *Photo, New York Times' Photos*

"We shall fight on the beaches, we shall fight on the landing-grounds, we shall fight in the fields and in the streets, we shall fight in the hills, we shall never surrender." How his words to Parliament in the summer of 1940 come back ; the announcer's introduction, "The Prime Minister, the Right Hon. Winston Churchill," and then the familiar blurred voice. . . . *"We shall defend every village, every town, and every city. The vast mass of London itself, fought street by street, could easily devour an entire hostile army."* . . . *"The brutal Narzy power . . . the hated Jestapo. . ."* odd phrases, amusing intonations of voice. The chubby fingers mutely proclaiming victory—all these are a part of everybody's personal history, part of the war, of the fear, the tiredness, the All-Clears, the dawns, and sudden exhilarations. Their Majesties the King and Queen, too, are a part

of the history ; so, too, are the Princesses, who had obstinately stayed in my mind as children, and now seem, as if overnight, grown-up and serious. " God Save Our Gracious King," and the hats go off in the crowd, the people in the grandstand are on their feet. Are these the faces . . . This hundred-odd people in the stand, drawn from all over the world, but more particularly from Britain and the Empire, declared the war, organized and won it. One picks out the faces seen countless times at the movies or in the newspapers—faces which now have the familiarity of portraits in a family album.

On the King's right, Cunningham, with bright ribbons against the dark naval uniform ; Alanbrooke, embarrassed behind the glasses ; Portal, free of the strain at last and relaxed and happy ; Maitland Wilson, making Mountbatten look even slimmer than usual. On the other side of the dais Attlee and Churchill, both wearing a row of medals, and next to them Mackenzie King and the astonishing Smuts. Behind—turning the pages of the album—the little King Feisal, still a boy ; the Duchess of Kent in Wren's uniform, Prince Bernhard, and the politicians, the Ambassadors, even the Generals of other wars.

" THEY'RE coming . . ." Buzzing cyclists squeeze themselves through the Arch, roar and spread out into the gravel-stained road. Familiar faces again—Monty, by himself in an open car, rising repeatedly to the greatest cheer of the day, and after him each commander perched aloft in a scout car—one recognizes Slim's full features under a broad hat ; Vian of the Cossack and ignoble Altmark ; tough little Somerville ; Hugh Lloyd, one of the great defenders of Malta ; Saundby, able, charming Porthos of Bomber Command, complete to a black moustache.

The instruments of war followed ; for half an hour the fascinating mechanical monstrosities went by—the waddling amphibious jeeps, 10-ton tenders towing an aircraft refueller, troop carriers, with the men sitting on parade inside, a 22,000-lb. bomb, and interspersed among them homely robots—a trailer with eight shining sewing machines, mobile canteens, even a farm tractor or two.

The crowd had its own peculiar favourites —the air-sea rescue launch (a special cheer) ; coach filled with Waafs (loud whistles) ; the new fire engines and their silver ladders (enthusiasm) ; C.D. rescue service (more clapping) ; the land drainage excavator and land girls (pandemonium). The noise of the tanks swamped the cheering—the mouths moved but there was no sound. Ex-soldiers made these things human ; they talked of Knightsbridge and the fighting at Caen. Somewhere behind me a man began a careful and minute story of a friend who was trapped in a burning tank. The voice went on and on ; one caught odd phrases in between the clashing and roaring. " Well, they towed away the tank, of course. Funny how a tank becomes more important than a man." He might have been reflecting over a quiet game of golf, the putt on the 18th green.

Marching Infantry Steal the Show

The monster Cromwells, the light Chaffees, the Churchills (enthusiasm again), the humped Shermans had gone ; the 3·7 A.A. guns were being towed by, muzzles demurely pointing down, and one had a glimpse of one's own past—the morning dash through foot-high mist, the first uniform, puttees which wouldn't do up, awkward squad days of 1939. Important little jeeps, motor graders, aerial lighthouses, radar cars—what do these vital things mean to the civilian, ore wonders. And yet even the smallest, most unaggressive had played an essential part. Without the snowploughs the squadrons

would have been grounded, sometimes for days ; without the fire crash tenders thousands of pilots would have been burnt alive ; without the mobile canteens there would have been no hot treacle tea to warm one's suffering body. And there were surprises and sensations for those who looked for them—the secret flail tank, for instance, which thrashes out the enemy mines with chains.

After the weapons the men, the marching infantry who invariably steal the show. The day had been uncertain since the early morning, and a few drops of rain fell as the Americans went by, leading the procession. There was to be a lot of discussion all the morning as to which of the contingents

Colours : White and Red Rings interlinked on Black Background

BRITISH 36TH DIVISION

INCLUDING units experienced in the Madagascar campaign, the Division was formed in India, in December 1942, under the command of Maj.-Gen. F. E. Festing, D.S.O. It remained in general reserve, attached to XXXIII Indian Corps, Indian Expeditionary Force, until its first action in the later stages of the Arakan operations in Burma, in February-April 1944. Operating with Maj.-Gen. Wingate's Chindits the Division prevented the Japanese from cutting the Bawli-Razabil road, main communication of the 5th and 7th Indian Divisions. Successful assaults were carried out on the slopes of Maunghnama Pass, Hill 701, and Point 1301.

THE entire Division was flown from Ledo to Myitkyina in June 1944, and became the first British Division under U.S. orders in Northern Combat Area Command. In the battle of the Railway Corridor, early August 1944, the Division met sporadic enemy resistance, but Hill 60, Pinbaw (captured August 18), Hopin (captured November 2), Pinwe and Gyobin Chaung will be ever memorable to its men. The capture of Katha (December 10) and Indaw brought the Division to the west bank of the Irrawaddy, which it was the first British formation to cross.
Reaching the river Shweli, at Myitson, in February 1945, the 36th Division fought the fiercest battle of the campaign, overcoming flame-throwers and the heaviest artillery barrage yet experienced, and suffering severe casualties in making the crossing. Attaining its next objectives, Mongmit, capital of the Shan States, and Mogok (captured March 19), the Division reached the Lashio-Mandalay road, and striking for Maymyo linked up with the 14th Army. In the final stages of the Burma campaign the Division cleared the Japs from the jungle Coverhill country, north-east of Meiktila.

IN ten months the Division had marched more than 1,000 miles, through monsoon and heat, jungle and over mountain tracks, across desert scrub and plains. More than 6,600 feet of bridging had been built, including the Mountbatten Bridge over the Shweli river at Myitson, all from local material. In addition, over 6,000 miles of cable had been laid, in a campaign that was fought without the support of carriers, armoured cars, tanks or medium guns.
For nearly the whole time the Division was maintained by airborne supplies, and was a shining example of what British and Indian infantry can achieve with the support of field artillery only. The 36th Division was absorbed in the 2nd British Division in May 1946.

marched the best. My own favourites were the Ethiopians, or the little Chinese taking an extra-long step for good measure or the Egyptians in their red fezes.

This march-past of the Allies was delightful —bearded poilus, burnt-up Mexicans, bleached Danes and Norwegians, the ranks of khaki suddenly broken by Greek Evzones, irresistible in canoe-like clogs, white ballet kilts and braided waistcoats. Later, when the Empire was passing, I found each contingent invoked the name of a battle. Canada—Falaise. Australia—Alamein. New Zealand—Greece, Crete, Italy. They contributed more men and had heavier losses for their size than any other Dominion, and incidentally have the only double V.C.

With Fixed Bayonets the Navy Came

The fascinating variety of the Empire marched by—white faces, brown faces, black faces, bursting chests showing the ribbons of the Battle of Britain, Burma, and the Pacific. They had come from everywhere and gone everywhere—one was extraordinarily touched by these faces, so deadly serious, each man alone in his mind representing his country before the eyes of the world. They all had some of the warmest cheers of the day, but the crowd rightly picked out the Gurkhas, in white spats and blue turbans, the ferocious little men with the kukri knives, who won more V.C.s than anybody else and fought through Burma and the Western Desert and were with Wingate's Chindits.

Half-past twelve, and " Heart of Oak "— one had forgotten how well the Navy can march, remembering only the rolling walk which turns even a pavement into the bucking deck of a ship. Headed by three vice-admirals and a little major-general of Marines, perhaps this first sturdy contingent of the Navy, marching with fixed bayonets, had the loudest applause of the morning. They were drawn from ordinary seamen, leading seamen, chief and petty-officers of the R.N.V.R. After them came representatives of every arm of the Service—the engine-room, the submarines, the Wrens, the nurses—with a Marine band and a Marine contingent, and men from the Merchant Navy and fishing fleets, some in jerseys and civilian clothes. One was reminded suddenly of the vast anonymity of war, the men sweating below decks, the frozen convoys to Russia, the loneliness of lighthouses.

IT is 12.40 and one heaves up one's pancaked feet. For each of us this parade means something different—for some pure pageant, for others an evocation of memory. I found myself picking out units whose names I particularly remembered—the 11th Hussars who went through the Western Desert campaigns and were part of the 7th Armoured Division—first into Tripoli, first into Tunis, first into Berlin. The Germans, I remembered, stood in the Berlin rain to watch them—and cheer them, too. The Recce regiments, modern equivalent of the old scouts. The Guards—Dunkirk, Boulogne, one of the first V.C.s, Bou Akouz, 187 Hill. The Royal Norfolk Regiment, and a voice in the crowd talking of Burma. " There were flies as big as lobsters . . ." The Queens, who, like the 11th Hussars, were part of the 7th Armoured Division, and the Commandos in their green berets, marching brilliantly and for the last time.

And so to the Air Force—Bomber Command, Fighter Command, Coastal Command. Lancasters were flying in formation as they marched by, and the war years returned again with their slang—" A piece of cake," " A wizard prang," " Down in the drink "— worn words and phrases which bring back, unbearably clearly, bombers flying out in the evening.—*Reprinted from, and by arrangement with, The Observer*

A.T.S. Pattern of Victory on Constitution Hill

AUXILIARY TERRITORIAL SERVICE representatives, following the Home Guard, Queen Alexandra's Imperial Nursing Service and V.A.D., divided into a symbolic " V " at the foot of Constitution Hill, the marching column being too wide to pass through the Green Park Arch. Having passed the Arch the two divisions joined again, the same manoeuvre being necessarily adopted by other units. Admired for their smart bearing the A.T.S. deservedly featured in onlookers' discussions as to " which of the contingents marched best " (see facing page). *Photo, P.A.-Reuter*

FIREWORK AND SEARCHLIGHT AND WATER DISPLAY was watched at close range by spectators packed solidly along the length of Westminster Bridge (foreground), whilst Their Majesties shared the view from the terrace of the House of Commons (right). On Victory Night alone 20,000,000 gallons of water were flung into the air, as coloured fountains in controlled designs, from barges and N.F.S. boats during the Ministry of Works' " Operation Squirt," carried out between Westminster and Lambeth Bridges.
Photo, New York Times Photos

The Night of Our Year-Old Victory

As darkness closed in came the final event in London's giant programme of celebrations arranged for June 8, 1946. J. C. Trewin of The Observer tells the story of the Royal ceremony and the fireworks and floodlighting and searchlights that transformed the staid old Thames to something unreal yet thrillingly impressive to massed crowds along its banks.

AT 9 o'clock in the evening of Victory Day we wait at a window above the terrace of the House of Commons. It will be 25 minutes yet before the Royal barge comes down from Cadogan Pier at Chelsea, and the King and Queen pass by on London's oldest and noblest road, the processional way of the River Thames.

Meanwhile, the crowds are massing. Barges and fire-floats in mid-stream, moored opposite the Houses of Parliament and the Victoria Tower Gardens, hide from us some of the Albert Embankment, but we can see that it is lined by a dark, shifting frieze of spectators—a frieze repeated along those high grandstands, the bridges of Westminster and Lambeth, above the river's dull flood.

It is half-past nine : everywhere the crowd has grown, though on the Terrace itself there is room for many more. This is an umbrella and mackintosh-crowd. Cheerfully it defies the weather. Music has beguiled the wait ; there are spurts of community singing : and always there is plenty to watch—evolutions on this fire-float or that, the first trial jets, the flowering of lighted windows across

the water, the burdening of roof-top and balcony, the scampering of a launch.

What is this ? A cheering mass along the river bank. Away, up river, we can see the swift-moving lights of launches that precede the Royal barge. Then the barge itself threshes down in mid-stream, its Royal standard flying from the bow and its white ensign from the stern. We cannot see the King, the Queen, and the Princesses ; but we know that they are there, and cheering rolls like surf along the river banks. Then the barge has sped by us, foam frothing in its wake ; it is followed by the barge of the Commander-in-Chief at the Nore and by other attendant launches. They shoot Westminster Bridge and streak away down river to the turning point by H.M.S. Chrysanthemum, past Waterloo Bridge.

Stars tonight are lost behind a cloud-veil. Across the Thames the Surrey-side buildings of St. Thomas's Hospital are in deep shadow. Then, suddenly, the searchlights strike out their shafts. The Royal barge is coming towards the landing stage. Eighty search-

lights now thrust their fingers skywards, groping into the gloom. Inevitably they remind us of the stern years gone, of lights that raked the sky for another purpose.

This evening they dip in salute, a Royal salute, for the King (in the uniform of an Admiral of the Fleet) and the Queen (in pale blue) have landed beside the Houses of Parliament and are now leaving the barge to walk towards the Terrace. As they do so, followed by Princess Elizabeth and Princess Margaret, maroons are bursting overhead, each with a cracking, thrusting roar.

THEN trumpets sound, the National Anthem peals from the loudspeakers, the Royal Standard—caught in the lights—flutters from the Palace of Westminster, and everywhere people take up the words of the Anthem. They are singing it on the bridges and on the embankments and in the Gardens, and away back from the river where people can see nothing of the Thames, though they do see the fireworks that trace their fantasies across the dark.

For now, when Their Majesties—welcomed by the Lord Chancellor and the Speaker—have taken their places, the fireworks have begun in earnest. With a rending, swooping rush they soar up between Hungerford and Vauxhall bridges, and shower their cascading sparks, gold and cerise and violet, torrid reds, and helium blues. From the Terrace windows the colours

Motto: "I Strive Through Difficulties to the Sky."

No. 60 (FIGHTER-BOMBER) SQUADRON

ORIGINALLY formed on April 30, 1916, No. 60 went to France in May of that year equipped with two flights of Morane "Bullets" and one flight of Morane biplanes. A notable personality at that time with the squadron was Lieut. Albert Ball, who, while with the squadron, was awarded the D.S.O. and two Bars. (He later won the V.C.). By the summer of 1917, although suffering severe losses, No. 60 had built up a great reputation as a fighter formation. On August 11, 1917, Captain W. A. (Billy) Bishop was awarded the V.C. for an attack on an enemy airfield.

Between the wars No. 60 served in India and took part in the North-West Frontier operations in Waziristan, in 1928, when it acted as escort to the bomber transport flight which evacuated part of the civil population of Kabul. In 1941 the squadron was still serving in India, and in February they flew their Blenheims to Rangoon. After operating almost continuously for nearly a year in the face of great difficulties they were flown out to the Arakan and evacuated by sea to Lahore, where they re-equipped with Blenheim Mark IVs.

In May 1942 they were in operation again, their principal targets being airfields, supply dumps and ports used by the Japanese. In the early part of 1943 the squadron was re-equipped with Hurricane Mark IICs.

WITH the encirclement of the Allied forces at Imphal in March 1944, No. 60 Squadron moved to Silchar, west of the Naga Hills, and provided close support to the defenders of the Imphal Plain. With the advance of the 14th Army down the Tiddim Road No. 60 moved into an airfield on the Imphal Plain for fighter-bomber operations, which were continued at an intensive rate throughout the battle of Burma. They moved into Mingaladon on May 18, 1945, their mobility in such difficult country being a notable feat of organization.

The squadron moved to Thedaw, in June 1945, and to Southern India to re-equip with Thunderbolt aircraft in preparation for the assault on the Malayan coast. This task was not fulfilled owing to the Japanese surrender, but they moved into Malaya as a component of the Forces of Occupation, and in October 1945 moved again, to Java, where they took part in operations in connexion with the Indonesian disturbances.

seem to be flame and citron and rose, and a fresh madrigal-green, all reflected and repeated in the frothing Thames. Each barge burns on the water like a burnished throne. Wherever we look are coloured cataracts of a new water-world, and through the noise of the falling water, the hissing and the swirling and the seething, drifts the sound of Handel's Water and Firework music, written for the first Georges of the royal line.

It is 10.30, time for the sustained rocket-salvo. All at once they streak into the air, and the sky is showered with stars, looped and trailed with ribbons of light. All the while the crowd is cheering. After each flight or salvo of rockets there is a deep indrawing of the breath. This is a strange, unreal world; the Thames is aflame, the sky is aflame. The buildings of the Palace of Westminster around us shine in the wild witch-light. By now it is 10.45, and there are more search-

lights, here twisting and flashing, there shooting up to form a vast aurora. At the same time the fire-floats are spraying out a radiance of fire foam. A bomber is flying overhead. It is coned in the web of searchlights. And when it has passed over—more aircraft will come later—the barges opposite the Terrace and the Victoria Tower Gardens fire into a series of set-pieces, beginning with portraits in colour of the King and Queen and Princess Elizabeth. Other fireworks spring from the temporary bridges beyond Westminster and Lambeth. Everywhere one

looks is a polychrome of colour and spray. It is now past 11.30. The last scenes are coming. Under the lustrous sky, and among the rainbowing cascades and the rockets that break in filaments of fire, 50 magnesium shells fill the sky with light of 40,000 candles. Again the National Anthem sounds through the amplifiers. It is nearly midnight. Whilst smoke still mists the Thames, the Royal party drives away, the Terrace empties, crowds press towards the stations and home, and a last searchlight still sweeps London's now peaceful sky.

I Went Back to the Normandy Beaches

Whilst London was preparing to celebrate with a spectacular Victory March, a war correspondent who landed on the beaches on D-Day (June 6, 1944)—Richard McMillan of The Evening Standard—was paying a return visit and hearing from Frenchmen their own stories of the "finest show any man ever saw in his life." See also illus. pages 143-146.

"WHEN we went to bed the bay was a dreary waste of emptiness, with the Wehrmacht on guard. When we awoke the sea was filled with a vast Armada. The British were ashore and the Wehrmacht were in flight—on the first lap back to Berlin and destruction."

Shaking with glee at the recollection, Mayor Henry Jaquot, of the little village of Ver-sur-Mer, who claims he welcomed the first of Britain's D-Day men on the Normandy beaches, stood before his patched-up pharmacy facing the sea. On the wooden door to his garden is a slogan in blue paint: "Duck repair depot—keep out."

"The Navy did that," said M. Jaquot, "and it's going to stay for ever as a memento." His body heaved with mirth. "We have other mementoes. That hole up in the roof —the Navy did that, too. Only we had to

repair that to keep out the rain. Do you know there are some people living in the invasion area who sleep with umbrellas up at night to shelter from the wet? They have not been able to get repairs done yet."

Between the pharmacy and the sea two men were working. "That's my son," said the Mayor. "He's back from a P.O.W. camp in Germany. The man with him is a German P.O.W., picking up mines Rommel laid. Poetic justice, eh?"

With the Mayor I walked along the beaches. One thing is certain—men of the D-Day Armada who come back to try to identify the place where they landed will find it difficult. Tremendous gales during last winter wiped out landmarks. At the point where I landed with the Desert Rats— on Jig Red, adjoining King Red—I found the road running parallel with the sea had

COMMEMORATING THE ALLIED LANDINGS in Normandy two years ago, beach-head services were held on June 6, 1946, in the presence of British and U.S. airborne forces. At Courseulles (above), where the Canadians stormed ashore on D-Day, the French Minister of the Interior, M. Le Trocquer, is speaking after unveiling the plaque on the right. PAGE 189 *Photo Keystone*

13th LANCASHIRE PARACHUTE BATTALION RETURNED TO RANVILLE, first French village to be liberated on D-Day (June 6, 1944), to celebrate the second anniversary of its freedom. Before a commemorative plaque—the inhabitants' tribute to them—members of the battalion were presented with flowers by a young villager in native costume. *Photo, Keystone*

disappeared. Telegraph poles stuck up through the sands of the seashore.

"The Germans were in a feverish hurry to try to complete their so-called Atlantic Wall," said Mayor Jaquot, "but they did not succeed. They had four pill-boxes about a kilometre apart between Ver and Meuvaines. Look, you can see them now, smashed by your guns and now turned topsy-turvy by the storms.

"Between Ver and Courseulles, to the east, they had six more, also about a kilometre apart. A mile back they had bigger forts, but not enough of them, and some of them were not even ready. There is no doubt about it—your general staff had marvellous intelligence. They could not have picked a finer spot to invade. That's brains for you. And, all the time, the Wehrmacht officers and men were strutting and boasting you would never land. We could see their morale wilt as the end drew near."

DESCRIBING how the German forts opened out when the British Armada began to appear in the first light of dawn, Monsieur Jaquot said : "It would be just before 5 a.m. All the Nazi cannon burst to life like demon tongues shooting from the hillsides. They were firing at the big ships—the Nelson, the Rodney, Warspite and Orion. The British ships were silent. Then they replied.

"The whole coastline shook under the blast of their broadsides. A tornado of shell fell upon the German batteries. The big Nazi guns at Mare Fontaine were silenced. The accuracy of the British fire was astounding. Many of the vast minefields sown under Rommel's orders went up, too."

Like everyone else under the fire of the British barrage, Monsieur Jaquot and his family took refuge in the trenches. "We could hear the machine-gun rat-tat-tat grow closer. Then up out of the fog of the battle on the beaches came a captain of the Commandos. 'A Frenchman!' he cried to me. 'Here we are at last on the soil of France!'"

Mayor Jaquot continued : "The captain of Commandos was like a—how you say it ?—school kid. So joyous. He told me : 'You wondered why we were so long. Well, we wanted to make sure. Now go down to the beaches and you will see.' Later, I understood what he meant. We had never believed such a mighty force could be assembled. It was miraculous to see it coming ashore—tanks and guns and ducks and artillery and cars and jeeps, and all kinds of tractored machines, rolling through our little village, which was already half in ruins from Allied and enemy shelling.

It rolled on and on. Up over the hills toward Bayeux and to the battlefields of Caen and Tilly and Villers Bocage. The captain of Commandos ? He went on to fight in the battle of Caen. But he came back to visit us afterwards. And another boy we welcomed was Bernard Gregory of Manchester, who is now with the R.E. in Scotland. He has kept up correspondence with my daughter—a romance begun under the bursting shells of the invasion."

After leaving Ver-sur-Mer, with its board extolling the names of all the units which took part in the landing here, I passed along to Courseulles. Here the Canadians, with British elements, disembarked. Offshore, some sunken ships. "Those vessels were sunk to form a breakwater for the landing craft," a native of Courseulles told me. "We call it our 'little Mulberry.'"

A fisherman was idly repairing his net in his boat in the harbour. "Were you here when we landed ?" I asked him. His sunburned face wrinkled. He nodded his head. "The Germans, in a panic, came to me about two a.m. and ordered me ' Open the floodgates and sink the British.' They thought if we opened the locks we could inundate the countryside. We looked at them—and went out to watch the finest show any man ever saw in his life."

In the Town Hall of Courseulles I spoke to Monsieur Louis Meriel, one of the leading citizens. "What interested me about the invasion ?" he said. "The amazing accuracy of the British fire, the exactness of British intelligence and—this above all—the lighthearted coolness of the fighting men."

"Yes," said a buxom Norman woman. "I saw an admiral come ashore with his men. He asked me : 'Where can I get a nice juicy steak and fried potatoes ?'—that's English phlegm for you !"

ᘒᘒᘒᘒᘒᘒ NEW FACTS AND FIGURES ᘒᘒᘒᘒᘒᘒ

THOUSANDS of animals and birds who played their part in the War were represented in London's Victory March, on June 8, 1946, by the Alsatians Jet and Irma. (See illus. in page 168.) These two Civil Defence Rescue Dogs, who wear the Dickin Medal—the Animals V.C.—for rescue work in air raids, are members of the Allied Forces Mascot Club of the People's Dispensary for Sick Animals. This club was formed to obtain lasting recognition for all the animals who, besides actual war work, contributed so much in maintaining morale and giving companionship to men and women of the Allied Forces.

THE Allied Forces Mascot Club, as well as compiling records for the Imperial War Museum of the wartime work of transport animals, guard and rescue dogs and homing pigeons, wishes to commemorate in a practical manner those who lost their lives. An Animals' War Memorial is to take the form of Caravan Dispensaries to bring relief to sick and suffering animals. Used throughout the War as rescue vehicles for thousands of animal raid victims, many such caravans were damaged or worn out, and the P.D.S.A. hopes to replace them by means of the Memorial funds which are now being raised by public subscription.

OF the 996 commissioned U-boats (German, Italian and Japanese) destroyed by the Allies throughout all the oceans of the world (said Mr. A. V. Alexander on March 7, 1946) over 300, or nearly one-third, were within 500 miles of the U.K.—this showing the intensity of the U-boats' concentration against the British Isles.

THE two outstanding months of the war were the U-boat were May 1943, when 46 U-boats were sunk, and April 1945, when the Germans were evacuating the Baltic ports and 65 U-boats were sent down. The month of May proved the turning-point of the war at sea : losses of Allied and neutral shipping, which averaged well over 20,000 tons daily in 1942 and over 14,000 tons daily in March-May 1943, fell by June-August to under 7,000 tons, and subsequently even lower.

IN the whole course of the war (it was stated on March 7, 1946) nearly 51,000 officers and men of the Royal Navy, including the Navies of the Dominions, and of the Royal Marines, were killed or were still missing. This number exceeded by over 20,000 the numbers killed between 1914-1918. Up to the end of 1945 nearly 15,000 awards had been made to officers and men of the Royal Navy, including the Dominion Navies, Royal Marines and Reserves ; these included 23 V.Cs and 29 G.Cs.

FROM the beginning of the war to August 31, 1945, H.M. ships and craft lost amounted to 3,282. The figure included three battleships and two battle cruisers, or one-third of our capital ship strength at the outbreak of the war ; five fleet carriers ; 23 cruisers ; 134 destroyers ; 77 submarines.

PEACE stamps, to commemorate the Victory celebrations, were on sale at British post-offices on June 11, 1946, when it was expected that the special issue of 264,000,000 would be exhausted in about two months. The total cash value of £2,800,000 is made up of 240,000,000 of the 2½d. denomination and 24,000,000 of the 3d. They are not available in book form, their size being double that of the ordinary stamp. The 2½d. one is blue, its design emphasizing peace through victory and reconstruction at home. The 3d. stamp, deep violet, symbolizes peace abroad. His Majesty the King made the final selection of the designs. See illus. below.

Our War Leaders in Peacetime
CHURCHILL

BORN at Blenheim Palace, Woodstock, Oxfordshire, in 1874, the eldest son of Lord Randolph Churchill (third son of the 7th Duke of Marlborough), the Rt. Hon. Winston Leonard Spencer Churchill, O.M., C.H., Leader of the Opposition in His Majesty's Government, has spent a lifetime in politics. Only four days after entering Parliament for Oldham in 1901 he made his first speech in the House. Since then he has consistently followed the tactics he adopted when a fencing champion at Harrow, and as Home Secretary at the siege of Sidney Street (January 3, 1911)—careful defence and direct attack.

He started talking politics to Lloyd George in the vestry at St. Margaret's, Westminster, after his marriage in 1908 to Clementine Hozier, daughter of a Guards colonel. For 38 years she has been his constant companion, accompanying him on many of his travels. With their youngest daughter, Mary, they returned to Chartwell, their Westerham home in the heart of the Kent hop country, in July 1945, from No. 10 Downing Street where, for five years, "Winnie" had reigned as Prime Minister, First Lord of the Treasury and Minister of Defence.

THEIR 35-years-old son, Randolph, is a major and former M.P. Diana, the eldest daughter, aged 36, is the wife of Duncan Sandys, Minister of Works under Churchill during 1944-45. Sarah, aged 31, is an actress. The youngest of the family, 23-year-old Mary, was recently (April 1946) demobilized from the A.T.S., in which she was a Junior Commander. Mr. and Mrs. Winston Churchill have four grandchildren.

As a young man polo, shooting, cricket, fencing and travelling were his favourite pastimes, and he admits he finds pleasure in public speaking. When, in February 1946, he made his ninth trip to the United States, New York newspapers recalled that Mark Twain presided at his first lecture there. He shares the practised actor's ability to memorize his "lines" easily. But into the preparation of every major speech goes hours o work, preferably in the quiet of the night, constantly polishing and altering until he is completely satisfied with the phraseology.

Churchill thinks the spoken word should be no less well chosen than the written word ; and for fifty years, since he earned his first five guineas as a free-lance war correspondent in Cuba, writing has been among his hobbies. Also, he reads at an amazing pace, assimilating a book from cover to cover, his reading ranging from war strategy and parliamentary history to the Classics.

Although an amazingly energetic man, Winston Churchill has a great capacity for complete relaxation—so long as he has a cigar. Painting, he says, takes away his tiredness in a very short time. No mean artist, he paints purely for pleasure and refuses to admit his canvases are worth hanging in his home ; all but the best are bundled away in a boxroom. Indeed, he is much more proud of the garden wall he built at Chartwell (with a Bricklayers' Union card in his pocket !) than he is of many of the products of his brush.

OUR WARTIME PREMIER received warm greetings on the occasion of his 71st birthday (November 30, 1945) from notabilities all over the world, but none was more welcome than those of his grandson, Winston junior, son of Mr. Randolph Churchill. Grandparents and grandson were photographed together (1) on the great occasion, before the Leader of the Opposition left for the House of Commons.

Taking a rest from politics, accompanied by Mrs. Churchill he travelled to the United States early in 1946 to enjoy a three months holiday, the first in six years ; staying at Miami, Florida, he is seen in his studio there (2) indulging in one of his favourite hobbies, the painting of seascape and landscape subjects. In the study at his home at Westerham (3).

Photos, Keystone, Topical Press, Associated Press PAGE 191

Navy 'Ducks' Invade London's East End

TWO ABREAST ALONG 'THE HACKNEY ROAD, their crews standing stiffly to attention, rumbled famous invasion craft of D-Day and earlier campaigns—the Royal Navy DUKWs, a loudly cheered feature of the Victory Day parade. The word DUKW ("Duck" for convenience) is made up of the factory serial letters : D for the boat, U the lorry body, KW the lorry chassis. The Navy sent also amphibious jeeps, weasels, mobile wireless telegraphy units, aircraft refuellers and mobile sick bays. See illus. page 163.

Photo P.A. Reuter

Printed in England and published every alternate Friday by the Proprietors, THE AMALGAMATED PRESS, LTD., The Fleetway House, Farringdon Street, London, E.C.4. Registered for transmission by Canadian Magazine Post. Sole Agents for Australia and New Zealand : Messrs. Gordon & Gotch, Ltd. ; and for South Africa : Central News Agency, Ltd.—July 5, 1946. S.S *Editorial Address :* JOHN CARPENTER HOUSE, WHITEFRIARS, LONDON, E.C.4.

Vol 10 *The War Illustrated* N° 237

SIXPENCE

I WAS THERE

JULY 19, 1946

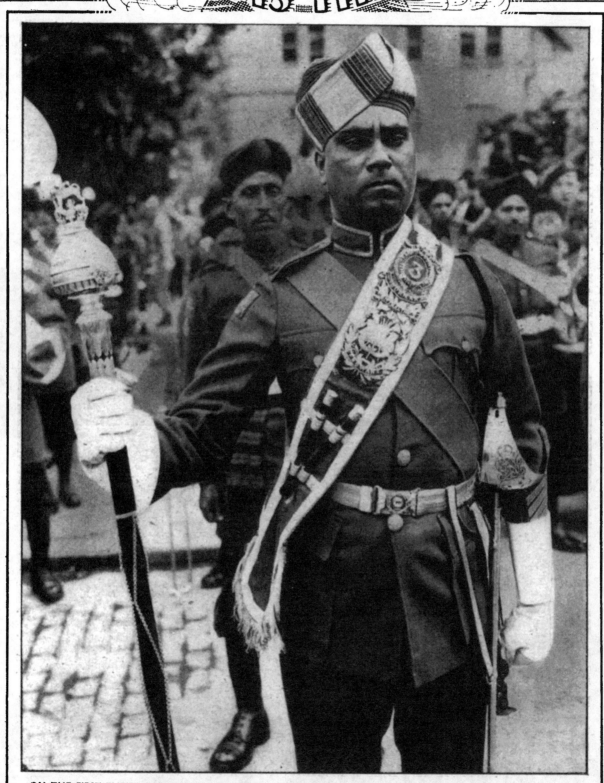

ON THE FIRST EMPIRE DAY SINCE THE DEFEAT OF JAPAN, Tokyo witnessed a ceremonial march past of British Commonwealth Naval, Military and Air Force contingents in the square in front of the Imperial Palace, twenty representatives of the Women's Services also taking part. May 24, 1946, was further enlivened by a public performance given in the floodlit Hibiya Park by Royal Navy and Royal Indian Air Force bands, at which this resplendent drum-major was present. See also illus. page 207.

Edited by Sir John Hammerton

NO. 238 WILL BE PUBLISHED FRIDAY, AUGUST 2

Fire Hastens the Doom of the Admiral Hipper

HEAVILY ARMED, the Admiral Hipper (1), one of the former German Navy's 10,000-ton cruisers, mounting eight 8-in., twelve 4·1-in. A.A. guns, and twelve torpedo tubes, had an undistinguished career from the time of her launching in 1937 until her destruction in June 1946.

Although she frequently had to seek refuge in the Channel and Baltic ports from Allied attentions, the Admiral Hipper was regarded as a potential danger to Allied shipping. She was engaged by the destroyer H.M.S. Glowworm in the North Sea, on April 8, 1940, an action for which the Glowworm's Captain. Lieut.-Cmdr. G. B. Roope, R.N., was posthumously awarded the V.C. (see page 236, Vol. 9).

STRANDED AT KIEL, the Admiral Hipper was found to be a complete loss by the Allies on the occupation of the port in May 1945. From her ripped deck-plates and battered superstructure (2), the result of R.A.F. bombing, hang strips of camouflage netting used, unsuccessfully, to harmonize with the environments of the port and render her unrecognizable from the air. While demolitions were being effected on board by the Royal Navy, in June 1946, fire broke out and swept the ship from bow to stern (3).

Photos, Planet News, New York Times Photos, Central Press

How Australia Was Saved from the Japs

By ROY MACARTNEY
Major, A.I.F.

It is now clear that many interlocking factors were jointly responsible for the failure of the Japanese invaders to violate Australian shores. Consider the position in Australia at mid-February 1942, when with the conquest of Koepang on Timor nearly every link in the island chain north of Australia lay in Japanese hands. The only Australian garrisons intact outside the mainland were in New Guinea, at Milne Bay and Port Moresby, each pitifully inadequate. The path to Australia lay wide open.

The best Australian troops were still in the Middle East or in transit on their way home. There were four Militia divisions in Australia, ill-trained and ill-equipped. Their ranks had been constantly denuded by enlistments in the overseas forces of the A.I.F. Much of what equipment had been in the country at the outbreak of war had been dispatched either to the Middle East or to the United Kingdom, following Dunkirk.

Although tens of thousands of airmen had been dispatched overseas, the Royal Australian Air Force did not possess a single modern fighter. Bombing strength was confined to a few squadrons of obsolete Ansons and Lockheed Hudsons. Four munition factories in the whole of Australia at the outbreak of war in September 1939 had increased only to eight by the time Japan entered the conflict. The aircraft industry was still in its blueprint stage, still waiting for jigs and dies ordered nearly two years before from the United Kingdom, which, so hard-pressed in Europe, had not yet been able to supply them.

Time the All-Important Factor

The Australian war effort had thus far been modelled on that of the 1914-18 war—she had played her part in the Empire defence scheme by supplying vast quantities of food and wool and by dispatching troops for service in the European and Middle East theatres. To do this she had had to rely on the Empire arsenal—the United Kingdom—for their equipment and armament. But Japan was no longer a benign ally as she had been in the last war. And in this conflict, war threatened in the Pacific. It was a dangerous policy for Australia to pursue, as was demonstrated when the attack on Pearl Harbour came with shattering suddenness. Not only were her troops dissipated all over the world, but she was also reliant upon the already desperately pressed United Kingdom for supplies of arms, not forthcoming at that crucial stage.

Australia's "phoney" war came to an abrupt end when her people were faced with invasion, just as did the United Kingdom's following Dunkirk. The Australian government, stung to desperate measures, threw the nation's whole strength into the struggle. They called for the return of the A.I.F. from the Middle East, mobilized the country's man and woman power, opened up hitherto unknown heavy industries in a drive for munitions, and prepared to build up the land, sea and air forces which would be required to repel the Japanese invader.

But while rifles and Bren guns, bullets and grenades could be expected in quick time, fighters and bombers would not be running off the assembly lines for many months to come. To America, Australia had to turn for aircraft for the coming struggle. In mid-February 1942 time was the all-important factor to Australia ; time to get her troops home from the Middle East ; time for the United States to ship across the vital supplies of aircraft, so that in the islands to the north of the continent the

Allies could fight yet another battle for time to allow Allied factories to bring their slow but ponderous superiority to bear.

Unexpectedly, the Japanese provided a heaven-sent breathing space. Through the remainder of February, through March and April, the enemy concentrated on the conquest of Burma and the consolidation of their already imposing bag of rich prizes down through the Indies. At the same time, in New Guinea and the Solomons, the Japs prepared advanced bases for resumption of their southern march. In early March they occupied Finschafen, Lae and Salamaua, and then, in the Solomons, established bases on Tulagi, Buka, Bougainville and Guadalcanal.

The first Australian division to return from the Middle East—the 7th—arrived in Australia in early March after a confused and dangerous voyage. Their ultimate destination had been the subject of lengthy and sometimes rather bitter communications between the United Kingdom and Australian governments. The former had requested that the returning troops should be diverted to Burma, where it was thought they might play an important part in halting the enemy drive into India. Apparently it was the view of the British that American protection and Australian militia would be enough to shield the country from invasion.

The Australian government held firm in their insistence that the Middle East forces must return to defend their homeland ; without them, they believed, the task might be beyond the untried Militia and what forces the United States could spare for the South Pacific theatre. Subsequent events

ONE OF MANY GRAVES at Darwin, Australia, in which unknown Japanese airmen were interred after a raid on the port, on April 4, 1942. All bear a similar inscription.
PAGE 195 *Photo, Keystone*

vindicated the judgement of the Australian government. Only troops with the esprit de corps of men of the 18th Australian Brigade, who had fought through the siege of Tobruk, could have adapted themselves so quickly to the jungle and outfought the Japanese in the latter's first bloody defeat in the savage battle of Milne Bay.

Through the two months' breathing-space, Generals MacArthur and Blamey disposed their meagre forces to meet the invader. Most of their troops were concentrated along the eastern seaboard, for it was obvious that was where the Japanese would try to establish their first foothold. Darwin and Western Australia, each garrisoned by a tiny force of only two brigades isolated at the end of inadequate lines of communication across two thousand miles of desert, would have been easy prizes for the enemy, but too far removed to be of much value in the conquest of the whole country.

The first Allied move was to dispatch the 7th Australian Division to reinforce the vital base of Port Moresby and a Militia Brigade to garrison Milne Bay. Australian and American engineers ripped airstrips out of the bush and jungle at Townsville, Iron Range, Horn Island, Port Moresby and Milne Bay. American aircraft coming forward in a mounting but still inadequate stream were quickly ferried forward, manned by both American and Australian airmen—Kittyhawks and Airacobras mainly to Port Moresby and Milne Bay, Fortresses and Liberators along the north-east Australian coast.

Enemy Headed for Port Moresby

In the South Pacific, Admiral Halsey, commanding most of the still seaworthy units of the United States Fleet, based his headquarters on Noumea, in New Caledonia. The Admiral was engaged in a grim race to prepare bases and build up sufficient strength to forestall the enemy drive down through the Solomons, which threatened to cut the lifeline between the States and Australia.

By early May the Japanese were ready to resume their southward drive. A large force of transports under heavy naval escort moved south into the Coral Sea, with Port Moresby their immediate goal. On May 4 a United States task force closed with the enemy in a battle which was to establish the pattern for subsequent naval engagements in the Pacific. In a series of engagements extending over four days and covering a wide area, few vessels of the opposing fleets sighted their opposite numbers. Instead, bombers and torpedo-carrying aircraft dominated the engagement, while from the mainland MacArthur's heavy and medium bombers also joined issue. At the end of the fourth day the enemy had had enough. Mauled and bleeding he turned and scurried back into less inhospitable waters, weaker for the loss of fifteen ships, including the aircraft carrier Ryukaku and three heavy cruisers. The American force had lost aircraft carrier Lexington, destroyer Sims, and tanker Neosho.

Shaken by their defeat, the Japanese High Command did not, however, abandon plans for their drive to the south but pigeon-holed them for the time being. The bulk of Japanese naval strength was temporarily withdrawn from South Pacific waters for a knock-out blow to be struck at Midway Island at the beginning of June. But the Americans knew they were coming, and northward from the Coral Sea raced the aircraft carriers Yorktown, Enterprise and Hornet to play a major part in the second naval defeat to be inflicted upon the enemy within a month.

Back in the South Seas the enemy sought to prepare the air bases to lend support to the Imperial Navy when it returned to resume the southward drive. Japanese troops landed at Gona in north-east New Guinea on July 23, and swiftly drove inland over the Kokoda trail, heading for the coveted base of Port Moresby. In the Solomons the Japanese had nearly completed an airfield on Guadalcanal. Consolidation of Guadalcanal as a base would have menaced the whole flimsy structure of defence which the United States Navy had prepared in the region. New Caledonia and New Hebrides would have become untenable, the way opened to New Zealand, thus severing the United States-Australia lifeline.

On August 7 Admiral Halsey struck with all the available force he could muster in a desperate gamble. Covered by American and Australian warships, an American Marine division stormed ashore on Guadalcanal to seize the nearly completed airfield. The enemy were quick to react, and soon the struggle for the island developed into the major engagement in the South Pacific, with the Marines fighting desperately with their backs to the sea to retain their slender foothold.

While the fate of Guadalcanal was in the balance, so, too, it was touch-and-go in New Guinea. The Japanese driving on Port Moresby encountered Australian troops astride their path at Kokoda. First elements of the veteran 21st Brigade A.I.F. arrived just in time to reinforce an untried green Militia battalion holding the airfield and the Gap. By August 12 Kokoda was in enemy hands. The Militia battalion broke in the first attack and the enemy were soon behind forward elements of the 21st Brigade, cutting it to shreds. In the long retreat over the heart-breaking 12,000-feet Owen Stanley mountain range which ensued, the Brigade was decimated and forced to fall back to Iorabaiwa Ridge, only thirty miles from Port Moresby, before its remnants, with the aid of their sister Brigade—the 25th—were able to halt the enemy.

Turning Point in the Jungle War

Meantime, between the fall of Kokoda and the halting of exhausted enemy patrols at Iorabaiwa, the climactic engagement of the holding battle in the South and South-West Pacific had been fought at Milne Bay. Precious months' respite afforded first by enemy dilatoriness and then by his defeat in the Coral Sea battle enabled MacArthur and Blamey to strengthen considerably the defences of Milne Bay. Kittyhawk and Airacobra fighters were moved in to cover the Militia brigade already there. Anticipating an early enemy move following the Coral Sea battle, the Allied Commanders slipped another brigade—the 18th, veterans of the siege of Tobruk—round to Milne Bay by sea. The last man to arrive disembarked less than a week before the enemy struck on August 26.

Picked Japanese Marines stormed ashore on the north of the bay and, despite incessant strafing from the Kittyhawks and stubborn resistance on the part of a Militia battalion which took the initial shock, succeeded in penetrating to the edge of the first airfield. The situation was precarious; guarded communiqués, preparing the public for yet another Allied reverse, were issued from General MacArthur's headquarters. And then the 18th Brigade, previously held in reserve, was thrown in to counter-attack.

One must think back to those early days of the Pacific war when the Jap, on the crest of his amazing wave of success, was regarded as a super-jungle fighter, to appreciate the task which confronted the men of the 18th Brigade as they entered battle. It was their first jungle encounter—they entered the unknown with confidence born of months of successful resistance in Tobruk, with familiarity in their weapons and discipline steeled by protracted desert patrolling.

For days a savage battle raged in the gloom of coconut groves and the oppressive jungle. No quarter was asked; none given. No prisoner was taken; none offered. It was with no bravado that each man ensured

AUSTRALIANS' PROUD BATTLE TROPHY, the standard of the Imperial Japanese Marines, captured during the enemy's assault on Milne Bay, New Guinea, August-September 1942. In this decisive battle the Japanese were " slashed to ribbons " by the Australian 18th Brigade, who exploded the myth of the enemy's invincibility as jungle fighters.　　　　　*Photo, Sport & General*

he was never without at least one grenade, in case he were wounded and perforce abandoned by his comrades in the jungle. Slowly the enemy were rolled back through the tangled undergrowth. On the night of August 30 a Japanese cruiser and eight destroyers landed substantial reinforcements. But they were not enough to hold the advance of the 18th Brigade. By September 2 the Japs' foothold was gone, their ranks slashed to ribbons and enemy warships were trying to evacuate the handful of survivors. It was a signal victory—the turning point in the jungle war. In that one action the 18th Brigade exploded the myth that the Jap was an invincible jungle fighter. Their success gave new heart to the American Marines struggling on Guadalcanal and encouraged General Blamey to prepare a full-scale push across the forbidding Kokoda trail.

It was still touch-and-go on Guadalcanal, which the Japanese were making a decisive trial of strength. Naval clashes were frequent, and had involved the near-disastrous loss to the Allies, on the night of August 8, of four heavy cruisers including H.M.A.S. Canberra, in the battle of Savo Island. Overhead, the air war approached its fortissimo. Merchant ships supplying the Marine division—there were barely sufficient for the job—were forced to run the gauntlet of heavy enemy bombing. Hellcats and Corsairs took a mounting toll of enemy aircraft, their successes soon reaching the amazing ratio of five to one. Fresh Japanese troops ferried down through the Solomons were thrown in, in ceaseless attacks; but the Marines held. The scales were slowly tipping in American favour when, towards the end of September, the Australians launched their offensive in New Guinea over the mountain trail from Port Moresby.

Spearheaded by the 16th Brigade, just back from the Middle East and Ceylon, the

Australians had little trouble in prising the enemy away from his precarious hold on Iorabaiwa Ridge. His small forces at the end of an incredibly difficult supply line were in no shape to fight a long holding battle. But the real test for the advancing troops was the most arduous crossing of the 12,000-feet Owen Stanley mountain range, toiling along in frequent tropical downpours and through inches of mud but ever alert for the next enemy ambush or small rearguard. It was also a test of Allied supply arrangements, but mounting Allied air strength eventually solved the problem, C47 transports daily dropping to the forces their meagre rations of bully and biscuits, also ammunition.

WITH the recapture of Myola and Kokoda, with their landing strips, supply problems were greatly reduced. Thereafter the tempo of advance quickened until the remnants of the Jap force were hemmed in around Buna and Gona, their backs to the sea, by early November. The American 32nd and 41st Divisions were brought round by sea to aid in the extermination of the last 8,000 Japs. But so well were their positions prepared with timbered bunkers bristling with machine-guns sweeping the swamps that not until early January 1943 was the last one prised from his foxhole on the point of a bayonet.

The Allies now had sufficient command of the air over New Guinea to fly in, complete, the 17th Australian Infantry Brigade, when the Japanese threatened Wau later in January. The Japs approached to within a few hundred yards of the airfield before the weight of the arriving Australian reinforcements told. It was the Jap's last offensive fling in New Guinea. Thereafter he was ever on the defensive.

The fierce battle for Guadalcanal swayed back and forth until the end of 1942. In October Japanese heavy units bombarded American positions on the island and landed further reinforcements which temporarily pierced the Marines' lines, but the breaches were soon sealed. Six important naval engagements were fought around the Solomons in four months. Evidence of their intensity was given in the most crucial engagement—the battle of Guadalcanal—fought November 13-15, when an American task force commanded by Rear Admiral Lee, including some of the latest recently arrived battleships, closed with the enemy. The battle cost the Japanese two battleships, eight cruisers, six destroyers and eight troop transports.

AGAIN and again the Jap came back for punishment, and on the night of Nov. 30 he made what proved to be his last effort to land reinforcements. In a sharp action—the Battle of Lunga Point—six enemy destroyers were sunk. By the end of January 1943 the last Jap on Guadalcanal had been wiped out. In six months Guadalcanal cost the enemy nearly 800 aircraft shot out of the sky—in all, something like 50,000 troops. Figures of enemy aerial losses over New Guinea ran into hundreds, and 15,000 troops was the total thus far sacrificed there.

By the end of January 1943 the holding war was at an end. The Australian and American servicemen had won their battle for time. Allied air, land and sea power in the South Pacific was thenceforth to be in the ascendancy and all threat to Australia of Japanese invasion was removed.

With the B.A.O.R. in Our Zones in Germany

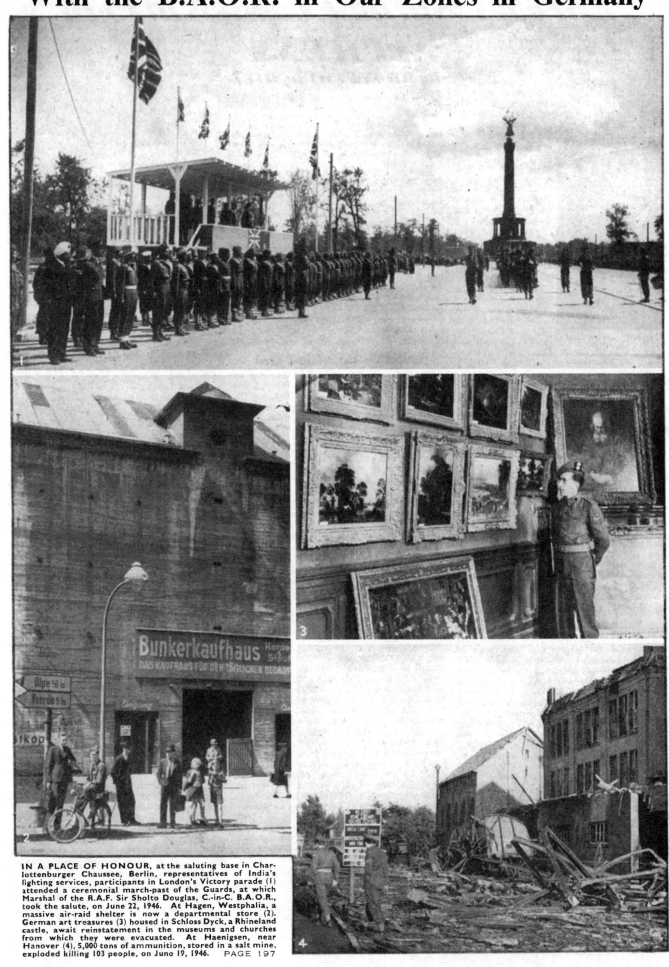

IN A PLACE OF HONOUR, at the saluting base in Charlottenburger Chaussee, Berlin, representatives of India's fighting services, participants in London's Victory parade (1) attended a ceremonial march-past of the Guards, at which Marshal of the R.A.F. Sir Sholto Douglas, C.-in-C. B.A.O.R., took the salute, on June 22, 1946. At Hagen, Westphalia, a massive air-raid shelter is now a departmental store (2). German art treasures (3) housed in Schloss Dyck, a Rhineland castle, await reinstatement in the museums and churches from which they were evacuated. At Haenigsen, near Hanover (4), 5,000 tons of ammunition, stored in a salt mine, exploded killing 103 people, on June 19, 1946.   PAGE 197

Europe's Wartime Capitals in 1946

ATHENS

By RHONA CHURCHILL

THE best way to go to Athens today is to travel by air with the Very Important Persons, drop into the large airport some ten miles from the city, be picked up by a relatively inexpensive Greek taxi and driven to the once luxurious Hotel Grande Bretagne. The worst way is to travel overland from Istanbul, which was the way I went early this year.

Before the war you could jump into the fast Orient Express at Istanbul and after a cosy night in a clean *wagonlit* be in Athens in a matter of hours, with hot meals en route.

RHONA CHURCHILL
Photo, Fayer

Last February when I told the Greek Consul in Istanbul that I proposed travelling overland to his home town he shook his head gravely, saying, " But, Mademoiselle, that is a thing altogether impossible ! Oh, yes, the trains run . . . sometimes . . . but one simply does not travel on them unless one must. Maybe it takes you three days to Salonika, maybe three weeks, who knows ! But after that there are no trains at all." The alternative was to fly via Cairo on an air service choked with priorities, or to board the once-fortnightly Russian-controlled Rumanian steamer that plies between Smyrna and the port of Athens.

I knew what that Greek Consul meant as soon as I got into my *wagonlit* for the first stage of the journey, and was assailed from all sides by a highly aggressive collection of crawling creatures who lingered with me till I reached the marble baths of Athens. I was lucky, for the Chief of the Greek Railways happened to be a fellow-traveller and had a special six-seater petrol-driven railcar waiting for him at the frontier. He invited me to occupy the vacant seat, and on this thirteen-hour drive to Salonika I gained a vivid impression of life in the Greek countryside as opposed to life in Athens.

Inflation and the Black Market

Greece is a hilly, rocky, barren land, and its railways are strung over thousands of bridges. Literally hundreds of small bridges, some only six feet long, link the single track line from the Turkish border to Salonika. Hundreds more link Salonika with Athens. The retreating Germans systematically ran every movable engine and wagon over the Bulgarian border, then blew every bridge, leaving Greece with only one-third of her railway track intact and virtually no rolling stock. They also removed or wrecked all road transport. That is why, though in the rest of Europe city dwellers starve while peasants grow fat, in Greece the peasants are often sick from malnutrition while the inhabitants of Athens and Salonika for the most part find enough to eat.

Thanks to the thoroughness of German requisitioning of livestock and seed, and to the Greeks' own civil war, Greece has, during the past year, had to import nearly every item of foodstuff in her national diet, the chief exception being olives, which she still grows in abundance, but which her farmers conceal and sell on the black market, if at all. It doesn't really pay you to sell anything in Greece today, for inflation is such that the price you get one day is only half of what you might get if you waited another week.

FOREIGN correspondent for a National daily newspaper, Rhona Churchill was in Greece for three weeks prior to the elections (March 31, 1946), and after interviewing leading political figures and ordinary citizens in the capital she drove extensively through the country with her own interpreter in an army jeep.

Bank of England experts have done their best to stabilize the drachma, and last February were patting themselves on the back after pegging it at its current black market rates of 20,000 to the pound sterling and 138,000 to the gold pound. " She seems to have stuck this time, old man," you could overhear the financiers congratulate each other over the Grande Bretagne bar. But only they believed the drachma had " stuck for good." For whose good ? As the financiers repeg the drachma, so the shopkeepers reprice their goods, so the farmers ask more for their olives, so the cost of living rises, so wages are raised—but never together. Cost of living is now 85 times pre-war level, but wages only 55 times.

Strikes Were at Epidemic Level

The man who owns a house or flat in Athens is in the best position. Rentals are demanded in terms of gold pounds and the gold pound rate is always sky-high, rocketing and bouncing in the clouds at from six to sixty times the rate of the pound sterling. Dissatisfaction over pay packets and indecision over prices play havoc with the country's industrial life. Factory owners, who must base their quotations on current and anticipated costs plus government controls, frequently waste months arguing. Workers' strikes were at epidemic level when I was there, neither side achieving anything, and the whole hard-hit country suffering greatly from these extra self-inflicted blows.

This is what impresses the visitor to Greece most forcibly today. While in other countries, notably Czechoslovakia and Belgium, you find a strong collective will to rebuild and recover, in Greece you find the reverse. Reconstruction, except where achieved by British pressure, is almost non-existent. Industrial capacity is 64 per cent of pre-war, but industrial output is only 28 per cent.

In Athens the Greek spends his working day either doing the minimum of work needed to draw his pay, or lounging in his dingy café arguing politics. He capitalizes on a German-introduced law which prohibits his employer from dismissing him, no matter how bad his work or how serious his absenteeism. He would rather knife the man next door, who is of another political faith, than join hands with him in rebuilding the bridge by the railway yard or tiling the roof of a nearby cotton factory. He would rather let the U.N.R.R.A. blankets rot in the warehouses, as they have done, than go to the children of old Economidus who talks a different brand of politics all day in another café. During winter I saw scores of rheumaticky Greek children lying on chilly mud floors without a single blanket solely because their fathers belonged to a different political party from that of the chairman of the local U.N.R.R.A. distribution committee.

Another thing that astonishes the visitor to Athens is the abundance of luscious chocolate éclairs and cream cakes in the patisseries, stacks of rich and fancy chocolates in the confectioners, and pyramids of U.N.R.R.A.'s corned beef and tinned salmon

everywhere. " Greece starving ? " scoffs the newly-arrived British soldier. " Why, she's better off than the folks at home ! " He soon learns differently.

It is no crime to sell your U.N.R.R.A. rations on the open market in Greece. Even U.N.R.R.A. doesn't mind, though to the visiting Briton, who risked police trouble if he sold the trotters off his back-garden pig, it seems immoral. U.N.R.R.A. foodstuffs are distributed fairly equitably at nominal prices. Rural Greeks, who number nine-tenths of the population, don't like tinned salmon any more than British housewives liked spam, so they sell it for what they do like, which is more bread to eat with their private hoard of olives. Their official diet now is the starvation level of 900 calories.

Income From U.N.R.R.A. Rations

Yet here you have the incongruous spectacle of Greek " white marketeers " following the U.N.R.R.A. food lorries round the rough-roaded countryside, watching the unloading, and offering immediate exchange of unwanted tinned meat and fish for the more welcome wheat and rye flour, and bringing the tins back a hundred and more miles to Athens, to sell openly in the street markets and shops at ten times the price quoted by U.N.R.R.A. The sugar finds its way into cream cakes and sweets, only generally it is sold for cash by poorer Greeks, who find their U.N.R.R.A. rations a welcome source of income.

Do not blame U.N.R.R.A. for what may seem to British eyes an unsatisfactory state of affairs. The Greek Government, of which there have been nine in fifteen months, is responsible for what happens to U.N.R.R.A. goods after they reach Greek ports. U.N.R.R.A. can do no more than advise after that. And no Greek Government could enforce a law compelling the Greeks to consume, not sell their rations.

The Athenians, because they often eat the rations that cannot be transported to the remoter villages, and because they are both prosperous enough and sufficiently cosmopolitan to eat tinned beef and salmon, look comparatively healthy and well fed. They will tell you mournfully that they are suffering severely, that poor Athens suffered terribly under the Germans. This is no doubt true. Tuberculosis is rampant among adults, and many children are dwarfed from past undernourishment. But it is also true that structurally, during their civil war, the Athenians hit their own lovely city far harder than ever the Germans hit her.

THE civil war has left much bitterness behind it. There is still isolated vendetta warfare. The eleven Athens newspapers, each representing a different trend of thought, scream abuse at each other. But if you do not read them and do not visit the prisons, you get the impression that Athens is carefree. Her shop-windows are decked with clothes that compare favourably with those in Britain, though prices are beyond the means of most Greeks. Her *tavernas* are filled with the young and the middle-aged making merry on the local ouzo and rizina. Her new grey-uniformed gendarmes keep order in the streets. In the heart of the city the national flag flies happily over the King's Palace, outside which the picturesque white-kilted troops stand guard.

And beyond all this, high up on the Acropolis Hill, still proudly stands the massive marble Parthenon. To this monument each sunrise and sunset come British soldiers, seeking and finding the peace, inspiration and stability that are utterly lacking in the city streets below.

Outward Peace of Athens Flatters to Deceive

EMERGING FROM YEARS OF OCCUPATION and months of civil strife, the Greek capital still retains its architectural grandeur. In Constitution Square (1) and in the narrow streets of the old quarters (2), apparently carefree Athenians go about their daily tasks. But the outward serenity of the capital, viewed from Acropolis Hill (3), does not reflect the true mood of the country beset with problems of black market, industrial malpractices and bitterly divergent political views. See article in facing page. PAGE 199 *Photos, Associated Press*

Italy's Monarchy Dies and a Republic is Born

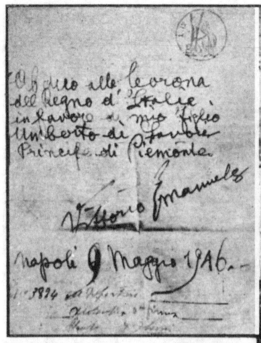

OF THE ITALIAN PEOPLE'S OWN CHOOSING, the Monarchy was dissolved in favour of a Republic by a majority of two million votes in the combined Parliamentary elections and referendum on the Monarchy held throughout Italy, June 2–3, 1946. Preceding the referendum, King Victor Emmanuel's Declaration of Abdication (above), signed on May 9, 1946, brought his forty-six years' reign to a close and nominated his son Prince Umberto as successor. Questioning the legality of the referendum, King Umberto II threatened to create a Constitutional crisis, but he departed for Portugal on June 13. Orderly crowds queued outside a polling station in Rome (1) in the first free election for 25 years. Giuseppe Romita, Minister of Interior (2, centre) broadcast the referendum results. Ex-King Umberto waved farewell from his plane at a Rome airfield (3). PAGE 200

2

3

France Remembers De Gaulle's Call to Fight On

SIX YEARS AFTER the surrender of France to Germany, ceremonies were held in Paris on June 18, 1946, commemorating General de Gaulle's spirited broadcast from London in 1940, calling on Frenchmen not to lay down their arms. The military parade passes M. Felix Gouin (1—right foreground) at the Invalides. Another ceremony was held the same day at Mont Valérien, on the outskirts of Paris, by members of the Order of Liberation; here the flame of remembrance was lit by General de Gaulle (3) at the grave of former Resistance leaders. In background are Gen. de Lattre de Tassigny, Gen. Catroux and—on right—Adm. d'Argenlieu.

Refusing the Government's invitation to attend the first Victory anniversary celebrations in Paris, on May 12, 1946 (see illus. page 101), General de Gaulle visited the grave of Georges Clemenceau at Mauchamps, Vendée (2). In Bayeux on June 16, for the unveiling of a monument marking his arrival in the Normandy beach-head, the General was warmly welcomed (4).

Photos, A.F.P., France

PAGE 201

HIS MAJESTY'S SHIPS   H.M.S. Renown

Motto : "Guardian of Ancient Renown"

A SHIP of 32,000 tons, launched on the Clyde in 1916, the Renown is the only remaining battle cruiser in the Royal Navy. She has a main armament of six 15-inch guns. From 1920 to 1922 the Renown was employed on special service, taking the Prince of Wales on official visits to the United States, Australia, New Zealand, India and Japan. Five years later our present King and Queen, then Duke and Duchess of York, went to Australia in her.

In 1936-39 the ship was completely rebuilt and re-engined at a cost of over £3,000,000, equal to the original expense of construction. Her first action after recommissioning was with the German battleship Scharnhorst and cruiser Admiral Hipper, off Northern Norway, in April 1940. After the Scharnhorst had been hit the enemy vessels managed to break off the engagement under cover of heavy weather. Not long afterwards the Renown became the flagship of Sir James Somerville in the Western Mediterranean. After engaging two Italian battleships at long range off Sardinia, she took part in the bombardment of Genoa. (See pages 219 and 309, Vol. 4.) In May 1941 she was one of the ships engaged in rounding up the German battleship Bismarck.

It was in the Renown that Mr. Churchill returned from the United States in 1943. A little later she joined the Eastern Fleet, but was back in home waters in 1945. The first meeting with German naval representatives to arrange for the surrender of enemy forces in Norway was held in the Renown at Rosyth on May 7, 1945; and on August 2 following, the King received President Truman on board her at Plymouth. (See page 267, Vol. 9.) Few ships have had had so many associations with distinguished personages.

Photo, P. A. Vicary

The Duke of Cornwall's Light Infantry

By L. S. SNELL

WHEN war broke out in 1939 the 1st Battalion D.C.L.I. was stationed in India, where it remained until 1941, when it moved to Libya by way of Iraq to take part in the defence of Egypt. The Battalion arrived in the firing line at a time when the British forces were reeling back under one of Rommel's attacks, and the story of the disaster which overtook them can best be told by a quotation from the official pamphlet entitled The Tiger Kills: "The Duke of Cornwall's Light Infantry was given the task of blocking lanes through the minefields which came out near Bir el Harmat. The Battalion arrived piecemeal during the afternoon of June 5, company by company, with newly issued anti-tank guns. As the Cornishmen arrived at Bir el Harmat they were attacked by strong formations from the south and destroyed in detail after a hopeless and gallant resistance. It was a sad end to a very fine Battalion which was only then completing its long march from Baghdad." This Battalion was replaced in 1942 by absorbing the small band of survivors from the action into the existing 6th Battalion and changing that Battalion's designation to the 1st.

Struggle for Cassino Stronghold

One of the first units to go abroad in 1939 was the 2nd Battalion, which proceeded to France in October and served with the British Expeditionary Force in the Maginot Line and in Belgium until the evacuation from Dunkirk in 1940. After a period of very hard training in England this Battalion proceeded to Tunisia, in March 1943, and within a few weeks of landing was fully engaged in fighting. It also served in Italy, with both the 5th and 8th Armies.

It played a conspicuous part in General Alexander's offensive against the Gustav Line which opened on May 12, 1944, and, in particular, was mentioned for its gallant all-day attack upon Point 63, a piece of high ground which occupied a commanding position overlooking the river Rapido. As a result of its capture of this fortified feature the British bridge-head across the river was finally consolidated and the success of the whole operation ensured. The Battalion also took part in the struggle for the famous stronghold of Cassino.

In June 1944 the 2nd Battalion saw heavy fighting in the region of Cassamaggiore, and on July 1 it occupied Petrignano. Despite counter-attacks by strong enemy armoured forces it pushed ahead and cleared Monte-varchi, on July 18, and afterwards continued its attack northwards against stubborn opposition. On August 8, 1944, the Battalion made a successful attack upon the Incontro Monastery, south-east of Florence. It is at the present time stationed in Greece.

AMONG the regiments named on March 26, 1945, as taking part in the great Rhine offensive was the D.C.L.I. The honour of sharing in this last attack upon the German homeland fell to the 5th Battalion, one of the Territorial Army Battalions of the Regiment. The 5th landed in Normandy with the 43rd (Wessex) Division on June 23, 1944, and four days later was engaged in a sharp action south of Cheux which helped to push the British salient beyond Grain-ville. The Battalion remained in action in this salient, which cut the road from Caen to Villers Bocage, and captured the villages

RAISED in 1702, the Regimental Colour of the D.C.L.I. bears a long list of Battle Honours, such as the capture of Gibraltar in 1704, First and Second Peninsular Wars, Waterloo, Indian Mutiny, Egyptian War of 1882, and the South African War. The style of "Light Infantry" was granted to the Regiment in 1858 by Queen Victoria "in consideration of the enduring gallantry displayed in the defence of Lucknow." During the 1914-18 war 57 honours were won, ten of which are displayed on the King's Colour.

Gen. Sir WALTER K. VENNING, G.C.B., C.M.G., M.C., Colonel Commandant of the D.C.L.I. since June 1935. He was commissioned in the Regiment in 1901. *Photo, G.P.U.*

of Verson and Fontaine Etoupefour on July 4, and recaptured them four days later after the enemy had temporarily re-occupied the positions. A military observer said :

"Throughout the campaign the men of the D.C.L.I. fought with great distinction.

No regiment of the British Liberation Army has fought with more dash and courage. Between the bitter struggle on Hill 112, when the D.C.L.I. did so much to break the cream of the German Army, and the Seine crossing, they fought a brilliant surprise action at Le Plessis Grimault on August 7, and were constantly in the forefront pinning and mauling the Germans while the famous American outflanking movement was in course of preparation."

The 5th Battalion fought a major action on August 25, 1944, when it took part in the assault crossing of the Seine with other West Country units. They extended their bridge-heads after severe fighting, and so weakened enemy opposition that by 4 p.m. on August 26 it was possible to bridge the river. Then the Cornishmen fought their way into Pressagny and afterwards cleared some woods of the enemy to give safe passage to the British armour now beginning to drive into Belgium and Holland. In September 1944 it was necessary to send infantry with stores to the relief of the 1st Airborne Division which was cut off at Arnhem, and the 5th D.C.L.I. were selected for the task.

Relief Column's Thrilling Dash

Riding on Sherman tanks they made a dash at 30 miles an hour through ten miles of enemy occupied territory. The tanks became separated from the Bren carriers which accompanied them, and found themselves followed by six German Tiger tanks. The officer in charge of the relief column placed PIAT guns in the ditches and set booby traps, and managed to knock out four of the Tigers. The advance went on, and the river was reached, but it was found to be impossible to send stores across to the Airborne Division as the "ducks" slipped from the dyke road into the ditch. Though they did not get through, the D.C.L.I. had made as thrilling and spectacular a dash as has ever been undertaken by British infantry. During the Anglo-American offensive of November 18, 1944, the 5th battalion captured

D.C.L.I. GUARD OF HONOUR AT ALLIED H.Q., ALGIERS, was inspected on February 1, 1944, by General Giraud and (behind him) General Sir Henry Maitland Wilson, who was then C.-in-C. Mediterranean. In the North African campaigns battalions of the Regiment participated in early disasters in Libya and in the final Allied triumph in Tunisia. PAGE 203 *Photo, British Official*

D.C.L.I. in the 1944 Advance Through Italy

THROUGH SHATTERED AND DESERTED MONTEVARCHI, north of Siena, whilst it was still being shelled by the Germans, passed a patrol (1) of the Duke of Cornwall's Light Infantry ; the town was cleared by July 18, 1944. Continuing their advance on Florence, men of the Regiment waited in slit trenches (3) before moving up in their Bren carriers to take the Incontro Monastery which, as shown by No. 2 of these hitherto unpublished photographs, was reached by a track bearing a warning sign. The monastery was captured on August 8. PAGE 204 *Photos, British Official*

In the Sudan and at a Crossroads in Normandy

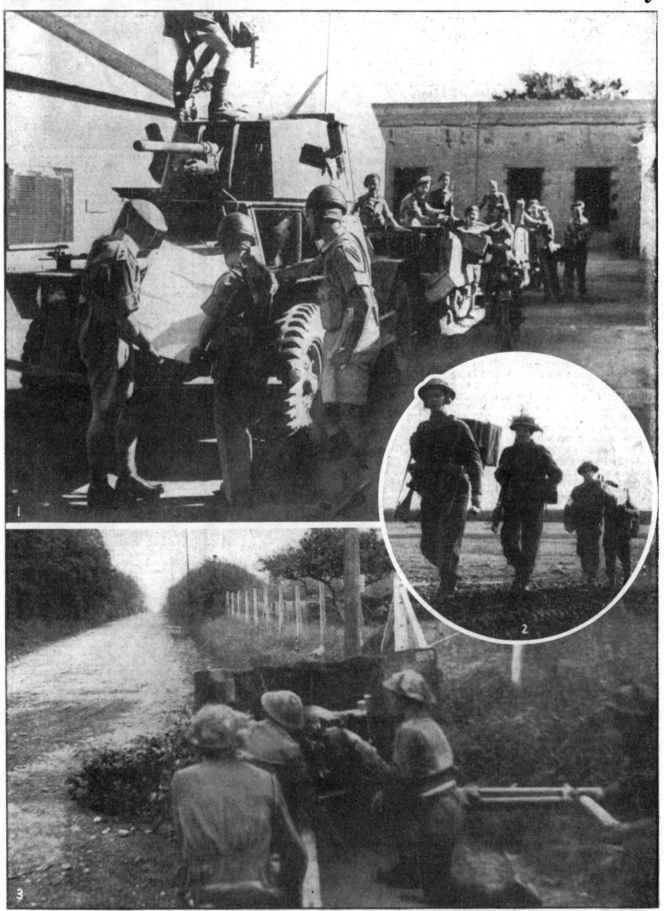

THE 5th BATTALION DUKE OF CORNWALL'S LIGHT INFANTRY, when it returned to France with the Allied Armies in June 1944, amply avenged the 2nd Battalion's retreat to Dunkirk four years previously. An anti-tank detachment manning a six-pounder gun at a crossroads in Normandy (3, hitherto unpublished). Moving forward in the Geilenkirchen sector (2) during the first British offensive on German soil, November 1944. An officer of a D.C.L.I. patrol in the Sudan (1, previously unpublished) checks the route with a dispatch rider. PAGE 205 *Photos, British Official*

the village of Hochheid, cut the main escape route of the Germans in Geilenkirchen and pushed two-thirds of the way through the thick wood stretching north-east from Hochheid. The Battalion held on there for four days, shelled incessantly by heavy guns, fighting and living under the most appalling conditions, in trenches half-full of water. At the extreme tip of this wood, on rising ground, lay the village of Hoven, which was strongly held by the enemy ; and across the narrow valley, and overlooked from Hoven, stood Wurms, a vital objective for the Americans attacking from the south-west. The British Commander saw that the task of the Americans in attacking Wurms would be made much easier if Hoven could be captured first, so he gave orders for the D.C.L.I. to attack the village.

THE 5th Battalion's attack upon Hoven started at 2 o'clock on November 22, in pouring rain. The supply of ammunition and other stores was a major problem, as all had to be man-handled through the woods and wounded had to be brought in on the backs of the stretcher-bearers. The first company to advance came under fire from spandaus, mortars and 88s from both flanks and was practically wiped out. The next company managed to fight its way forward to a position from which it was possible to neutralize the enemy fire with PIATS, mortars and Brens.

At 3 o'clock another part of the Battalion worked round the flank and fought its way into the village of Hoven at the point of the bayonet. Darkness descended, and orders were received that the village must be held until 12 noon on the following day. During the night some food and a number of boxes of ammunition were brought up, but all attempts at reinforcement failed.

At daybreak the Germans threw everything they could muster into the attack but were driven off, until finally the garrison had no more ammunition. At 12 noon they

wirelessed to the British headquarters for all available artillery to be brought to bear on the village in the hopes of killing the Germans who were in the open, the D.C.L.I. having taken shelter in the trenches and cellars. When the artillery fire ceased, seven of the D.C.L.I.—all that remained—crept back to the Battalion lines. The 5th had endured the heaviest shelling from the Siegfried line for 24 hours, and had thus enabled the Americans to push forward.

When the Cease Fire Order Came

When the Corps Commander visited the Battalion on the following day he thanked the officers and men for their gallantry. He said that he had almost every type of regiment in the Army under his command, including Guards, but he had never, in all his service, met such a magnificent fighting Battalion as that of the Duke of Cornwall's Light Infantry.

The 5th Battalion, with the 43rd (Wessex) Division, took part in the capture of Cleve, in February 1945, and a few weeks later in the capture of Xanten, vital hinge of the Wesel defence line, which Hitler had ordered to be defended at all costs. The Battalion's last real fight against the Germans took place on the night of April 13-14, near the important town of Kloppenburg, when the D.C.L.I., crossing the river by a bridge which the enemy had failed to destroy, broke up German attempts to re-form their scattered forces. It took part in the clearing of Bremen on April 26-27, 1945, and of the difficult, boggy country on the road to Bremerhaven and Cuxhaven on April 29-30. When the order to Cease Fire came, on the evening of May 4, the 5th was holding the village of Badenstedt, some 15 miles north-east of the port of Bremen.

Brief mention must be made of the two military bands of the Regular Army Battalions. At the beginning of the War the Band of the 1st Battalion D.C.L.I. was stationed in India, and in 1941 in Iraq. In

Colours : Yellow Dragon on Dark Blue

43RD (WESSEX) DIVISION

RE-FORMED before the war, the Division opened its fighting record within a few days of landing in the Normandy beach-head, on June 26, 1944, accounting for five enemy tanks south of Cheux. During July, after crossing the river Odon, the 43rd engaged the enemy in some of the bitterest fighting. Between August 5-8 the assault on Mont Pinçon was successfully carried out, an action notable for the gallantry of the C.O. of the Wiltshire Regiment, who was killed urging his men on by flourishing a walking-stick.

The Division continued to harry the enemy until the Falaise Gap was closed, August 14. By August 25, having covered 120 miles in two days, the 43rd forced the first British crossing of the Seine, at Vernon, and a month later, September 22, it was attempting a similar, but unsuccessful, feat across the river Lek, in Holland, in support of the Airborne forces at Arnhem. Here 250 men of the Division were ferried across the river ; 161 officers and men failed to return.

ON November 18 the 43rd cut the enemy escape routes out of Geilenkirchen, for the Americans to take the town the next day. In the offensive towards the Rhine, Cleve was entered on February 9, 1945, and the escarpment flanking the Cleve-Goch road was successfully attacked. Brought into the battle of the Rhine bridge head at Rees, the Division captured Mechelen (March 28) and Millengen, after crossing the rivers Ijssel and Aa. This re-entry into Holland brought further successes ; Hengelo and Borne were taken (April 3), Haselunne (April 9), and Loningen (April 11).

The capture of Hengelo severed one of the main V2 supply routes. Later, Bremen was reached, and by April 27 the city's area commander, Gen. Silber, and Lieut.-Gen. Becker were taken prisoner. At the time of the German surrender in the West (May 5) the Division had reached Cuxhaven Peninsula, and in the words of Lieut.-Gen. Horrocks, XXX Corps Commander, the men " had done more than their share of the fighting."

BAND OF THE D.C.L.I. accompanied the musical chairs event at the 33rd Armoured Brigade Victory Gymkhana, held near Lüneburg, Germany, on Aug. 30, 1945. The bands of the 1st and 2nd Battalions travelled widely—from India throughout the Middle East, to the Channel Islands (see illus. in page 77, Vol. 9), and with the B.L.A. on the Continent. PAGE 206 *Photo, British Official*

1942 this band proceeded on an extensive tour which took them through Kurdistan and Persia, Egypt, Palestine, Lebanon, Africa, Trans-Jordan and the Sinai Desert. In April 1943 they embarked for Tripoli, where they had the honour of playing for His Majesty King George VI, Generals Alexander and Montgomery, and the famous 8th Army. After two months in Tripoli the band returned to Egypt, where, in February 1944, they played for a review of the 10th Armoured Division by General Maitland-Wilson, and then returned to England to refit. This band was also chosen to accompany the British forces sent to the Channel Islands in May 1945 to receive the German submission. The Band of the 2nd Battalion proceeded to join the British Liberation Army in the summer of 1944, playing to troops in forward areas in France, Belgium, Holland and Germany.

Photos,
Associated Press, Keystone

Empire Forces Celebrate Empire Day in Tokyo

Recreation and information centre for British troops in Tokyo was officially opened on May 24, 1946, when Lieut.-Gen.
John Northcott, C.-in-C. the British Commonwealth Occupation Force, cut a ribbon strung across the door (1). Featured
also was a B.C.O.F. Empire Day parade ; the reviewing stand (3), with Gen. Northcott at the microphone. On May 8
troops paraded (2) to mark the arrival of units of the 66th and 67th Infantry of the Australian Occupation Force.

Our Largest and Fastest Carrier Comes Home

The last of the Fleet aircraft carriers of the British Pacific Fleet to return from service in the Far East, H.M.S. Implacable (1), our biggest and speediest, arrived at Devonport on June 3, 1946, from Australia, bringing 10,000 gift-cases of food from the Dominion. In just over a year she had covered 90,000 miles. Our latest carrier, H.M.S. Triumph (2) reached Southampton the same month; a relic of Mulberry Harbour on the foreshore there is doing excellent peacetime service.

B

H.M.S. Theseus With Her Seafires Visits Norway

In Bergen Harbour recently, the light Fleet carrier H.M.S. Theseus, with a long line of Seafires on her flight deck (3), quickly established cordial relations with the Norwegians. An innovation warmly acclaimed by the rank and file of the Theseus had its try-out : an electric scrubber (4), which may soon be a standard part of all Naval ships' cleaning equipment. One of her Seafires made an unhappy deck-landing (5), but the pilot escaped injury. See also illus. page 224.

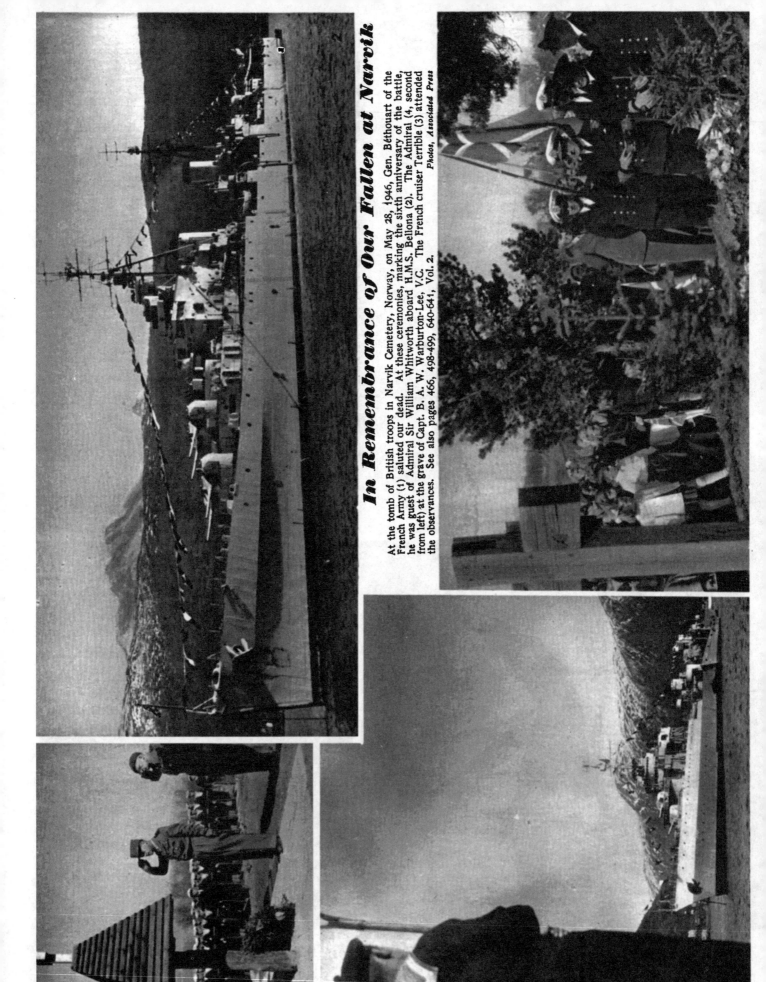

In Remembrance of Our Fallen at Narvik

At the tomb of British troops in Narvik Cemetery, Norway, on May 28, 1946, Gen. Bethouart of the French Army (1) saluted our dead. At these ceremonies, marking the sixth anniversary of the battle, he was guest of Admiral Sir William Whitworth aboard H.M.S. Bellona (2). The Admiral (4, second from left) at the grave of Capt. B. A. W. Warburton-Lee, V.C. The French cruiser Terrible (3) attended the observances. See also pages 466, 498-499, 640-641, Vol. 2.

Photos, Associated Press

General Eisenhower Sums Up

QUESTION 1.—*Generally, did Field-Marshal Viscount Montgomery, as Gen. Eisenhower's "Battle-Line Commander" in the Battle of Normandy, successfully implement the operational plan as it had been originally drawn up?*

Yes. The original "Cossac" plan of attack, as revised by Montgomery and finally approved by Eisenhower himself " . . . involved a D-Day assault on a five-divisional front on the beach-head between Ouistreham and Varreville, with the immediate purpose of establishing beach-heads to accommodate the follow-up troops. The initial objectives of the attack included the capture of Caen, Bayeux, Isigny and Carentan, with the airfields in their vicinity, and the essential port of Cherbourg. Thereafter our forces were to advance on Brittany with the object of capturing the ports southwards to Nantes. Our next and main aim was to drive east on the line of the Loire in the general direction of Paris, and north across the Seine, with the purpose of destroying as many as possible of the German forces in this area of the west.

"Because it was ultimately intended to supply the United States forces engaged in Europe directly from American ports, American troops were to take Cherbourg and the Brittany ports as supply bases, while the British, driving east and north along the coast, were to seize the Channel ports, as far north as Antwerp, through which they were to be supplied directly from England."

From the beginning, therefore, it was clearly Eisenhower's intention, no less than Montgomery's, that the American First Army should make the initial break-out from the beach-head on the Allied right. Moreover, the Allies had made their first crossing of the Seine by D plus 75—that is, 15 days ahead of schedule.

QUESTION 2.—*In particular, was 21st Army Group's progress in the Caen-Falaise fighting unjustifiably slow?*

No. During the days following D-Day " . . . exploiting the success achieved on D-Day, they (the British 3rd and Canadian 3rd Divisions) pushed southward, and despite heavy casualties, succeeded in reaching points some two or three miles north and north-west of the city (Caen). . . . . The struggle which took place during this period of the establishment of the lodgement area took the form of a hard slugging match on the British sector, with Caen as its focal point.

"Here the enemy concentrated the bulk of his strength, while the men of the United States First Army fought their way up the Cherbourg Peninsula to capture the port in preparation for what was to prove the decisive breakthrough at the end of July.

" . . . Our strategy, in the light of the German reactions, was to hit hard in the east in order to contain the main enemy strength there while consolidating our position in the west. The resulting struggle around Caen, which seemed to cost so much blood for such small territorial gains, was thus an essential factor in ensuring our ultimate success. As I told the Press correspondents at the end of August, every foot of ground the enemy lost at Caen was like losing 10 miles anywhere else. . . .

"Montgomery's tactical handling of this situation was masterly. . . . On August 17 Falaise was finally occupied. From our landings in June until that day the enemy's resistance in this sector had exacted more Allied bloodshed for the ground yielded than in any part of the campaign. Without the great sacrifices made here by the Anglo-Canadian armies in the brutal slugging battles, first for Caen and then for Falaise, the spectacular

THE Supreme Commander's report to the Combined Chiefs of Staff on the operations in Europe of the Allied Expeditionary Force from June 6, 1944, to May 8, 1945, published (H.M. Stationery Office, 2s. 6d.) in June 1946, runs to 149 pages. Lieut.-Gen. H. G. Martin, The Daily Telegraph Military Correspondent, has selected certain controversial questions of outstanding interest, appending thereto Gen. Eisenhower's answers extracted from the Report : a condensation from The Daily Telegraph is given here.

〜〜〜〜

advances made elsewhere by the Allied forces could never have come about."

QUESTION 3.—*What were the basic causes of the German failure in the Battle of Normandy?*

The primary cause was the losing by the Luftwaffe of the Battle of the Air. " . . . Without the overwhelming mastery in the air which we attained by D-Day our assault against the Continent would have been a most hazardous if not impossible undertaking. . . . The communications chaos thus produced had a fatal effect upon the enemy's attempts at reinforcement of the threatened areas after our landing."

Next I should put tactical surprise :

" . . . The enemy had concluded that any cross-Channel expedition was impossible while the seas ran so high and, with his radar installations rendered ineffective as the result of our air attacks, his consequent unpreparedness at our arrival more than offset the difficulties which we experienced. . . . In point of fact, we attacked shortly after low tide when the moon was full ; we landed away from large harbours and at some points below sheer cliffs ; and the waters through which we approached the shore were so strewn with reef and subjected to strong currents that the German naval experts had declared it would be impossible for landing craft. . . . We achieved a degree of tactical surprise for which we had hardly dared to hope."

QUESTION 4.—*During the advance from the Seine why did Eisenhower decide to put the full weight of his blow behind 21st Army Group's thrust to the north-east at the expense of the Third U.S. Army thrust eastward?*

" . . . It was our plan to attack north-eastward in the greatest possible strength. This direction had been chosen for a variety of reasons. First, the great bulk of the German Army was located there. Secondly, there was the great desirability of capturing the flying bomb area. A third reason for the north-eastward attack was our imperative need for the large port of Antwerp. Fourthly, we wanted the airfields in Belgium.

"Finally, and most important, I felt that during the late summer and early autumn months the lower Rhine offered the best avenue for an advance into Germany, and it seemed probable that, through rapidity of exploitation, both the Siegfried Line and the Rhine River might be crossed and strong bridge-heads established before the enemy recovered sufficiently to make a definite stand in the Arnhem area."

QUESTION 5.—*Were 21st Army Group operations to clear the Scheldt Estuary unduly delayed and unduly protracted, contrary to the Supreme Commander's wishes?*

Certainly not. To make the earliest possible use of the Port of Antwerp was a fundamental feature of Montgomery's original plan. Gen. Eisenhower gives the facts:

"My decision to concentrate our efforts on this attempt (the Arnhem operation) to thrust into the heart of Germany before the enemy could consolidate his defences along

the Rhine had resulted in a delay in opening Antwerp and in making the port available as our main supply base. I took the full responsibility for this, and I believe that the possible and actual results warranted the calculated risk involved."

QUESTION 6.—*Did Gen. Eisenhower and the Combined Chiefs of Staff hold a divergent view about the 1945 plan of campaign?*

Yes. The British Chiefs of Staff, certainly, would have preferred a single, powerful thrust into North Germany to any dissipation of effort. Gen. Eisenhower's views are :

" . . . When the Combined Chiefs of Staff expressed doubts as to our ability to maintain two thrusts—north of the Ruhr and in the Mainz-Frankfort areas—with the forces at my disposal, it was pointed out that such, indeed, would be the case if we did not clear to the Rhine before embarking on a major offensive to the east of that river. . . . Together with their suggestion that I should concentrate on a single heavy drive in the north, the Combined Chiefs of Staff submitted for my consideration a proposal by the British Chiefs of Staff that a single ground commander for the whole front north of Luxemburg be appointed to exercise, under me, operational control and co-ordination of all ground forces involved in the Rhine offensive.

"This suggestion was based on the assumption that all the remainder of the front would remain on the defensive, contrary to my plans. I pointed out that, under these plans, the Ruhr marked the logical division of Command zones and that Field-Marshal Montgomery would be in charge of all the forces there—the Canadian Army, British Army and United States Ninth Army."

QUESTION 7.—*Was the envelopment of the Ruhr brought about by the initiative of the Commanders of the United States First and Ninth Armies going beyond, or contrary to, Eisenhower's and Montgomery's intention?*

Certainly not. Gen. Eisenhower states :

" . . . Before operations deep into the German interior could safely be undertaken, the Allies had, following the Rhine crossings, to complete the encirclement of the Ruhr. . . . With this vast armoury in Allied hands and the Russians in control of its Silesian counterpart, Germany's power of continuing to wage war would be destroyed even were her armies to be preserved intact. . . . I determined, therefore, to carry out the policy originally envisaged by converging thrusts from Wesel and Frankfort."

QUESTION 8.—*Did the British Chiefs of Staff and Gen. Eisenhower hold divergent views on the plan of operation to follow the envelopment of the Ruhr?*

"The decision to concentrate first upon a major thrust in the centre nevertheless gave rise to some misgivings," says Gen. Eisenhower. "The desirability of bringing the U-boat war to an end, of opening supply lines through the north German ports, of acquiring the use of Swedish shipping, of relieving the Dutch and of occupying Denmark and Norway, and the political and psychological effects of an early entry into Berlin were all advanced in favour of an operation in the 21st Army Group sector.

"Our reply pointed out that we had not forgotten the important advantages to be gained by the conquest of North Germany. It was merely a question of timing that was at issue. It was vital that we should concentrate for each effort in turn rather than allow our power to be dispersed by attempting too many projects at once. . . . Berlin, I was now certain, no longer represented a military objective of major importance."

PRODUCTION OF WHALE OIL, vitally important now to help maintain our margarine and cooking fats ration, fell (by reason of adverse weather conditions) during the last whaling season, the catch figures being: Britain 37,000 tons; Norway 80,000 tons; Argentina 17,000 tons. Allocation of whale oil to the U.K. for 1946 by the Combined Food Board at Washington is 62,400 tons. This drawing shows the 21,000-tons Southern Venturer, one of Britain's new whaling-factory ships, back in port after operations in the Antarctic lasting from December 1945 to March 1946. By courtesy of her owners, Chr. Salvesen and Co. of Leith, our artist, Haworth, made his sketches aboard the vessel—here presenting the general idea of whale oil production.

A modern whale-catcher (A), 8 or 10 of which are attached to every factory-ship, is bringing in its catch; after refuelling it will resume its hunt. Devices such as Asdic detectors (B) enable the harpoon gunner to judge in which direction the whale has turned after "blowing." The harpooned whale is dragged (C) by 40-ton winches up a slipway at the stern of the factory-ship to the flensing deck (D), where the blubber, rich in oil, is cut away and put into eight Kvaerners (E), which revolve slowly whilst extracting the oil, which runs into settling tanks. The liver is minced (F), and its oil, containing Vitamins A and D, is extracted below decks. Mechanical saws (G) cut up the bones, which are cooked in pressure kettles (H) and the oil extracted. The residue is carried away on a conveyor belt (J).

The whalo meat is cut up by electrically driven machines (K), and later turned into meat meal (L), which is packed into 14-stone bags in the hold. Separators (M), remove water and other impurities from the oil before storage; this vessel has a capacity of nearly 20,000 tons. In the blacksmith's shop (N) harpoons and flensing knives are fashioned and repaired. The Ship's carpenter (O) is fully employed. The Captain's and officers' quarters and the navigating bridge (P). Specialized equipment includes radar for guiding the catchers back through fog to the factory-ship, locating "flagged" whales and avoiding icebergs.

Our War Leaders in Peacetime
WAVELL

As Viceroy of India, Field-Marshal Viscount Wavell, G.C.B., G.C.S.I., has little time for home life, and the loss to him must be a considerable one. But family anniversaries are duly honoured in turn—the day Archibald Percival Wavell married Eugenie Marie Quirk, in 1915; the birthdays of Pamela, aged 26, and married four years ago; of Felicity, aged 23; Joan, 21; and John, 30 years old and a major in the Black Watch, which was also his father's original regiment.

Shy and reserved, Wavell does not shine in glittering company. It is said to be a devastating experience for a lady to sit next to him at official dinners, for he "just sits." But friends who enter his home circle in New Delhi know him as a charming man and excellent company; to them he is "Archie."

The son of a soldier (Major-General A. G. Wavell, C.B., whose father was also a Major-General), educated at Winchester and Sandhurst, he is more interested in soldiering than anything else; and after-dinner conversation as often as not finds a level in military topics, the study of strategy and tactics being one of the Viceroy's hobbies. Another is the study of languages, of which he speaks several, including Russian, which he learned in 1910 when he applied for special leave to spend a year with a Russian family in Moscow. Today he is polishing up his Indian languages.

Even with the pressing problems of India on his shoulders he still finds time to settle down with Gibbon and the Stoics, and occasionally to add to his own already considerable literary output. He frequently quotes from the Classics and, a religious man, from the Bible. His wife shares his views and outdoor interests : married for 31 years now, the Wavells are inseparable.

A fine horseman at 63 he can still give many a younger man a good run, and he takes a particular delight in jumping. A judge of horseflesh, he goes to race meetings less to bet than to see the horses in the paddock. The Italians were caught napping when, as C.-in-C. Middle East, Wavell launched his first attack into Cyrenaica, in December 1940; for on the very afternoon of the attack Italian secret agents saw him enjoying himself at the Cairo races! Wavell's temperament is of that kind: calm and unperturbed.

ANNOYANCE he expresses by slowly removing his eyeglass and replacing it in his blind eye—he lost the sight of his right eye in the First Great War. But poor sight does not interfere with his shooting, neither has it spoiled his golf, which he improved during his Command in North Africa, when ski-ing—another of his favourite sports—was denied him. Now Wavell is playing his part in designing the future of 350 million Indians.

FIELD-MARSHAL VISCOUNT WAVELL'S daughter Hon. Felicity, in the gardens at Viceregal House, New Delhi (1). Accompanied by Lady Wavell and Felicity (2) he sets out from England to take up his duties as India's Viceroy in October 1943. In the ornate and luxuriant Mogul gardens, Wavell, with his wife (3), finds relaxation from work, much of which confines him to his desk in the study (4).

Photos, British Official, P.N.A., Illustrated

CYPRUS, PALESTINE AND TRANS-JORDAN

By HARLEY V. USILL

THE island of Cyprus lies in the Eastern Mediterranean, some 240 miles north of Egypt, 60 miles west of Syria and 40 miles south of Turkey. Its area is 3,584 square miles, slightly more than Norfolk and Suffolk together, and its population of approximately 410,000 consists of about one-fifth Moslems, almost all of them Ottoman Turks, while the remaining four-fifths are Orthodox Greek Christian, with a sprinkling of Armenians, Latin Catholics and Maronites. The great majority of the people live in the rural areas, and are most of them farmers and agricultural workers.

Throughout the long history of the Mediterranean, Cyprus has been occupied and colonized by successive waves of conquerors of the area. In A.D. 45 the island was converted to Christianity by Paul and Barnabas, the latter himself a Cypriot. In 1191 Richard Coeur de Lion conquered Cyprus, and there he married Berengaria of Navarre and crowned her Queen of the English, but within a year had sold the island to the Knights Templars. In 1571 it was conquered by the Turks, and although it was subsequently occupied by the British by virtue of a Convention signed with the Turks in 1878 it remained technically Ottoman territory until it was annexed in 1914, on the entry of Turkey into war against Britain. In 1925 it was made a British Crown Colony.

Cypriots' Great Work at Cassino

Cyprus has the distinction of being the first British Colony to send troops for service overseas. In the early months of 1939 it was decided to raise Cypriot units of Royal Engineers, Royal Army Service Corps, and other services, and when war broke out nearly 500 Cypriots were straightway enlisted into Cypriot R.A.S.C. Mule Transport Companies. The Cypriot Muleteers arrived in France in January 1940, and immediately proved their value. These men, about 700 of them, were successfully evacuated from Dunkirk, having destroyed their mules under protest. Throughout 1940 General Transport and Pioneer Companies were drafted to Egypt, and by the end of the year ten Pioneer Companies and one General Transport Company were in training.

Cypriot troops next saw action in the Middle East, where a number of Cypriot companies were the only Colonial troops in the hard fighting early in 1941 around Keren in Eritrea. Cypriot units were also sent to Greece, and when that country was overrun by the Germans, in April 1941, they were evacuated to Crete. In these two operations they lost nearly 3,000 men, mainly as prisoners. By the end of 1944 there were over 10,000 Cypricts in the Army, of whom 8,500 were in the Cyprus Regiment and 1,800 in the Cyprus Volunteer Force. Although this latter force was primarily a Home Guard, volunteers were accepted for overseas service, and some 300 of them served with the Cyprus Regiment in Italy.

It was at Cassino that the Cyprus Regiment did its most spectacular work. Five Cyprus Regiment Pack Transport Companies were serving with the Poles at Cassino in May 1944, three having been moved from Syria and two from Iraq. General Anders, commanding two Polish Corps, gave them high praise for the way they brought supplies up to the line under fire from the German positions around the Cassino Monastery. After the Monastery's capture, the Cypriots were employed in the Gothic Line fighting and remained in action until the end of the year. Without the Cypriot Pack Transport Group many of the operations of the 8th Army would have been impossible in the North Italy mountains; the Cypriots and

IN this second article on the Mediterranean colonies' war effort the author deals with the island of Cyprus—first British colony to send troops for service overseas—and with the mandated territories of Palestine and Trans-Jordan, whence Arabs and Jews were recruited to serve with the Allied armies on many fronts.

~~~~~

their mules reached places which were unapproachable by normal means. Cypriots also served in the United Kingdom, and by July 1941 some 2,500 had volunteered; a very worthy record of military service.

AT home, Cyprus did not suffer to anything like the same extent as Malta, although at one stage of the war it appeared that the island would become a main objective of enemy attack. Cyprus's first air-raid alarm came in June 1940, shortly after Italy had entered the war, but the first serious raid did not take place until June 1941; this was followed by haphazard attacks during July and August, and by the middle of the latter month there had been twenty-seven raids. Hostilities in Russia, and the British occupation of Syria, stabilized the situation in the Mediterranean, and the immediate threat to Cyprus lessened.

In 1942, however, the Middle East was again threatened, and Cyprus became important as a forward base against the enemy forces in Greece, Crete and Rhodes. The reinforcement of the small pre-war garrison of British troops, new fortifications, building of airfields and improvements to Famagusta harbour, increased Cyprus's strength considerably, and its defences were further augmented by the fact that R.A.F. fighter aircraft stationed in Syria, about 150 miles away, could operate over the island.

In common with the other British Colonies, Cyprus played her part in the supply of essential materials for the war machine. Since Cyprus is mainly agricultural, and in view of the extreme difficulties in regard to transport, this effort was on a relatively small scale; but, even so, there were a number of items which are of especial interest. Nearly 500,000 cubic feet of sawn and 86,000 cubic feet of round timber were exported for military use in the Middle East and for the manufacture of matches on the mainland. To the end of 1944 nearly 4,000 mules were exported for military purposes and 2,000 for agricultural and transport work.

The people of Cyprus gave about £30,000 to various war funds and subscribed over £1,500,000 to public loans.

Successes of the Arab Legion

By the Treaty of Peace signed at Lausanne on July 24, 1923, Turkey renounced all rights over Palestine and Trans-Jordan, and the Principal Allied Powers had previously selected His Britannic Majesty as Mandatory at San Remo on April 25, 1920. The terms of the Mandate were approved by the Council of the League of Nations on July 24, 1922, and the Mandate came into operation on September 29, 1923. A treaty between His Majesty's Government and the Government of Trans-Jordan, signed in London on March 22, 1946, marked the end of the mandatory regime and the emergence of Trans-Jordan as a sovereign independent state.

At the beginning of the Second Great War the full-time military forces in Palestine and Trans-Jordan were the Trans-Jordan Frontier Force and the Arab Legion. The former of these forces was recruited more or less

equally from Palestine and Trans-Jordan; the latter practically from Trans-Jordan alone.

Both were, and are, almost entirely Arab. When war came it was agreed by the Amir of Trans-Jordan that the Arab Legion should be brought up to full military strength and made available to the British Government for the duration. The personality of its Commander, Brigadier Glubb, a second Lawrence, undoubtedly contributed to the success of the Legion.

Its first major operation was in early 1941, when it was given the task of guiding a British mechanized column 500 miles through desert country to the Euphrates. This being successfully accomplished, the Legion then led a detachment from the main body to the north to cut the Mosul Road and then descend along the Tigris to Baghdad. A little later, in June 1941, the Legion was again used to guide British troops across desert country; this time the task was to lead a column to attack Palmyra in the Syria operations. The Legionaries again accomplished their work successfully and had a victorious action of their own with a Vichy French mechanized unit en route.

Palestinian Pioneers and Infantry

In addition to enlistment into United Kingdom units a number of locally raised forces were recruited in Palestine, the most important of which were companies of the Auxiliary Military Pioneer Corps and the Palestine Infantry Companies attached to the Buffs. The first company of the Pioneer Corps went to France in February 1940, shortly after the Cypriot troops had already arrived, and were therefore among the first Colonial troops to play an active part in the war. After the Dunkirk evacuation they were sent to Egypt, and in 1941 were part of the British forces which went to Greece, where over 1,000 of them were taken prisoner. At the beginning of August 1941 the strength was about 2,800 Jews and 1,200 Arabs.

Following our reverses in North Africa in 1942, it was decided that a Palestine Regiment of the British Army should be created, consisting of the separate Jewish infantry battalions and comprising the Palestinian (Jewish and Arab) Companies of the Buffs. The role of this new Regiment was to defend vulnerable points and to act as a mobile reserve, and by 1944 it had been spread widely over the Middle East. The infantry consisted at that time of three Jewish and an Arab battalion; of these, the first Jewish battalion was on prisoner-of-war guard duty in Egypt, the second Jewish battalion on internal security work in Cyrenaica, and the third Jewish battalion, like the Arab battalion, in Palestine itself. The transport units were also doing useful work, especially those in Italy, where transport was short because many such units had been sent to the United Kingdom for the Normandy landings.

The final development was the creation of a Jewish Brigade Group to take part in active operations. The Infantry Brigade was to be based on the Jewish battalions of the Palestine Regiment, and further recruitment was limited to the United Kingdom, Palestine and Mauritius where there were a number of Jewish refugees. The Brigade was engaged in active operations in the Italian campaign from March to May 1945, having gone in to the line in the area south of Alfonsine under the command of the 8th Indian Division. On April 10 it was employed in an attack across the Senio River and helped to secure a bridge-head one mile east of Riolo, from which it made advances on the following days. During its time in the line the Brigade had about 200 casualties.

Calm and Unrest in Middle Eastern Neighbours

IN TROUBLED PALESTINE Terrorist attacks led the authorities to take drastic action against the Hagana (Jewish National Army) and Palmach, its mobilized nucleus. In Tel Aviv the 4th Parachute Regt. (1) man obstacles in Allenby Road. Boarding a barge of the Palestine Potash Company (2) in search of arms.

ENTHRONEMENT OF KING ABDULLAH I OF TRANS-JORDAN at 'Amman, capital of the State, on May 26, 1946, marked the emergence of Trans-Jordan as a fully independent Hashimite kingdom after being administered under British Mandate since 1923. After the ceremony the new King (3, left), accompanied by Abdul Illah, Regent of Iraq, drove to a R.A.F. airfield near 'Amman to inspect all branches of the Arab Legion. Heading the parade was the Guard of the Camel Corps (4).

Photos, Associated Press, New York Times Photos

Cpl. R. AINSWORTH
8001 A.M.E.S. R.A.F.
Action : Corsica. 30.9.43.
Age 22. (Norwich)

Readers of THE WAR ILLUSTRATED *who wish to submit photographs for inclusion in our Roll of Honour must fill in the coupon which appeared in No. 230. No portraits can be considered that are not accompanied by this coupon.*

Sgt. F. V. G. ALLOWAY
Royal Air Force
Dortmund. 24.5.43.
Age 21. (Ross-on-Wye)

L/Cpl. A. R. ASHTON
Royal Tank Regiment.
El Alamein. 29.10.42.
Age 23. (Liverpool)

Cpl. R. BICKERTON
R. Signals (Airborne).
Normandy. 6.6.44.
Age 22. (Croydon)

Cpl. T. E. BIRCH
Royal Army Medical Corps.
Died of wounds. 13.9.44.
Age 24. (Walsall)

Stkr. W. A. BOWDEN
Royal Navy.
In action : at sea. 12.2.44.
Age 20. (Harefield)

Pte. W. BRANSON
6th Airborne Division.
Caen. 10.6.44.
Age 31. (Brentford)

Pte. W. BROWN
Worcestershire Regt.
Action : Burma. 28.2.45.
Age 29. (Halesowen)

Sgt. F. W. BURTON
Royal Air Force.
Mailly. 3.5.44.
Age 22. (Dagenham)

Stkr. J. E. BUTTERY
H.M.S. Minster.
Off Normandy. 8.6.44.
Age 40. (Leicester)

L/Bdr. V. H. CATTLE
57th Lt. A.A. Regt. R.A.
Action : Libya. 6.6.42.
Age 27. (Parkstone)

Pte. T. J. COLES
31st Suffolk Regiment.
Died of wounds. 8.2.44.
Age 19. (Northampton)

Ord. Sig. J. COOKSON
H.M.S. Achates.
Convoy to Russia. 31.12.42.
Age 20. (Leeds)

L/S R. COWTAN
Royal Navy.
Action: on Li Wo. Feb. 42.
Age 28. (Sutton, Surrey)

Pte. T. CROSS
K.O.Y.L.I.
Action : Burma. 2.5.42.
Age 22. (Huddersfield)

Pte. R. J. DALLOW
South Lancs. Regiment.
Normandy. 6.6.44.
Age 21. (Liverpool)

Pte. R. P. DARVILL
Cameron Highlanders
Ardennes. 11.1.45.
Age 24. (Willesden)

Cpl. W. R. DAY
R.A.O.C.
Action : Crete. 20.4.41.
Age 4L. (Gt. Yarmouth)

L/Sgt. F. DENT
88th Field Regt. R.A.
Died P.O.W.: Siam. 28.11.43.
Age 23. (Preston)

S/Sgt. B. DRUREY
Glider Pilot Regiment.
Arnhem. 24.9.44.
Age 21. (Wakefield)

Sgt. J. G. DURHAM
625 Sqn. R.A.F.
Over Essen. 23.10.44.
Age 22. (Seahouses)

Pte. J. F. EASON
Queen's Royal Regiment.
Action : Italy. 15.10.43.
Age 20. (Northampton)

Sgt. F. J. EDWARDS
106 Sqn. R.A.F.V.R.
Over Essen. 13.1.43.
Age 20. (W. Molesey)

L/Cpl. E. FINCH
Grenadier Guards.
Pont-a-Marcq. 3.9.44.
Age 19. (Hornchurch)

Pte. G. A. FRASER
Border Regt. (Airborne).
Sicily. 9.7.43.
Age 20. (Darlington)

Pte. R. GOOCH
Northamptonshire Regt.
Action : Burma. 25.2.45.
Age 20. (Bacton)

Spr. A. H. GREGG
Royal Engineers.
D. wds. Normandy. 8.7.44.
Age 22. (Brynmawr)

Pte. G. H. GRIFFITHS
Wiltshire Regiment.
D. of wds. Burma. 22.4.44.
Age 33. (Buckley)

Sgt. A G W. J. JARVIS
Pathfinder Force, R.A.F.
Over Hamburg. 10.11.42.
Age 21. (Cirencester)

Sgt. J. H. JEFFERIES
Royal Air Force.
Mediterranean. 28.11.40.
Age 20. (Downend)

L/Cpl. D. JONES
Parachute Regiment.
Southern France. 17.8.44.
Age 21. (Llangammarch)

Tpr. S. LUCAS
1st Reconnaissance Regt.
Action : Anzio. 3.6.44.
Age 23. (Felling)

Sgt. A. A. MIDDLETON
Coastal Command R.A.F.
Action: N. Ireland. 18.2 42.
Age 23. (Camberwell)

Sgt. R. MORLEY
218 (Gold Coast) Sqn. R.A.F.
Germany. 31.12.44.
Age 19. (Dagenham)

Seaman D. PENMAN
H.M.S. Fiji.
Action : Crete. 22.5.41.
Age 17. (Murton Colliery)

J. J. RIMMER
Ldg. W/M Royal Navy.
Off Normandy. 25.6.44.
Age 20. (Liverpool)

Pte. A. YOUNG
Royal West Kent Regt.
Action : France. 12.5.40.
Age 28. (London)

Pte. A. G. YOUNG
Hampshire Regt.
D. of wds. Italy. 3.11.44.
Age 28. (London)

I Saw the Mighty Thrust for Arnhem

The desperate gamble of our airborne landings in Holland was witnessed, from the point of view of the ground troops, by Lieut. J. L. Taylor. He relates how they struggled against impossible odds during the fateful week Sept. 17-24, 1944, first to reinforce and then to rescue the airborne men.

ON September 17, 1944, I was in Brussels in the position of Personal Assistant to the Senior Officer of the Reconnaissance Corps R.A.C. We had just arrived from England. Our establishment was one jeep, two Sten guns and two revolvers. Our mission was to visit the Reconnaissance Regiments then in action on this front.

Lieut. J. L. TAYLOR

Sunday the 17th was a notable date in the history of the war. A fortnight had gone by since the fall of the Belgian capital. Our forward troops had for some days been engaged at the canal crossings to the north. It had become apparent that the use of Antwerp, vital to the Quartermaster General, was to be denied as strenuously as the Channel ports. For lack of petrol, rations and ammunition, the momentum of our broad advance had already begun to slow down against the gathering German defence.

Attempt to End the War by Winter

How would the Allied High Command deal with this situation ? Sunday the 17th provided the answer. On that day rose from the airfields of England an armada of transport planes, many towing gliders, packed with men and equipment for a military gamble to end the war by winter. The terms of the gamble were these. If the Allies could seize from the air the three bridges in Holland over the Maas and the Rhine, at Grave, Nijmegen and Arnhem ; reach the airborne spearhead with a strong armoured shaft ; push to the high ground above Arnhem and launch quickly a drive due east to outflank the Ruhr—then there was a chance of victory in a matter of weeks.

Most of the forward ground troops were on the move. We set our jeep among them, and within thirty-six hours we were ahead of all the Reconnaissance Regiments. The guards at the Dutch frontier were still dutifully examining the papers of a civilian cyclist. Beyond the customs house stretched the road into Holland—straight, flat, deserted. Behind us there was a big hold-up of traffic at Beeringen. Somewhere in front were the Guards Armoured Division. It was the afternoon of Tuesday, September 19. There was nothing to notice on this highway that tomorrow would be the most talked-of road in the world. The countryside lay still on either hand, and the road quite empty before us. Of war there was no sign.

We came to Elst. It fell to Elst to provide Holland's official welcome to the Army of Liberation. It is a small town south of Eindhoven, and no one who was there on

that day is likely to forget it. When we arrived, the swirling stream of national costumes, flowers, fruit and flags had swamped in the street the tail-end of the convoy we had been speeding to catch. Thereafter to Eindhoven the way was thick with transport of the Guards Armoured Division. In Eindhoven, heading against the traffic, appeared a Press jeep bearing Mr. Frank Gillard with his dispatch—still far from a B.B.C. microphone : how he ever got back to one is his own secret.

Eindhoven, too, had an atmosphere of carnival. A few hours later the town of rejoicing was bombed. At dusk German tanks cut the road to Nijmegen.

Nijmegen lies low on the south bank of the Waal. In 1936 its fine road bridge over the river had been opened by Queen Wilhelmina. On May 10, 1940, the Dutch Army, retreating through Nijmegen, blew the bridge in face of the oncoming Germans. The latter rebuilt it, and now it stood again as a military objective, with dynamite charges once more underneath. The position on the morning

of September 20, when we caught up with the headquarters of the Guards Armoured Division temporarily established in a field just across the Grave bridge, was that fighting was still in progress for Nijmegen, and the bridge was intact.

At mid-day we moved with Divisional Headquarters eastward along a side road which brought us out on the main highway which runs due south of Nijmegen into Germany. A new Battle H.Q. was established in a patch of scrub beyond the few cultivated fields to the east of the road, by the village of Malden. A mile or so to the north was proceeding the struggle for possession of the town and the bridge. At a less distance to the south, a small party of the 82nd American Airborne Division, weary and bearded in their fourth day of fighting, were engaged in the village of Mook.

THE sound of war cracked and thundered about the little caravan town of command vehicles, armoured cars, 3-tonners, parked on the sandy grass among bushes and trees. Here quiet English voices gave instructions over the air, cursed mildly at someone's ineptitude, arranged administrative details and, in a spare moment, speculated on the turn of events. The betting was heavily on the side of Berlin by Christmas. For those

SPEEDING THROUGH GRAVE, ten miles south of Nijmegen, the Guards Armoured Division on its way to consolidate the Netherlands river crossings during the Arnhem operations, September 17-24, 1943, received an enthusiastic welcome from the inhabitants. Here, for a time, was the Division's H.Q., and dropping area for the U.S. 82nd and 101st Airborne Divisions. PAGE 217

ACROSS THE GREAT NIJMEGEN ROAD-BRIDGE streamed tanks of the British 2nd Army in an endeavour to reinforce our airborne troops cut off at Arnhem. Capture of this bridge, intact, by the Guards Armoured Division and the U.S. 82nd Airborne Division, in one of the fiercest actions of the war, gave rise to optimism—it was thought then that the Arnhem operation would indeed be successful. But efforts were defeated by impassable roads and bad weather on the "island" beyond Nijmegen.
Photo, British Newspaper Pool

able to come in from supervision of a battle which held the breathless attention of the world, tea that afternoon in the mess tent was served as usual.

After tea, down the road in Nijmegen, culminated the struggle for the bridge. The Germans, when they came to blow it, found the charges removed, which was not the first instance of their disadvantage in fighting in a country long tuned to underground resistance. They had, nevertheless, established a strong position on the roundabout where five roads meet a hundred yards from the south end of the bridge.

Against this strong point the Guards' tanks, supported by American airborne infantry, had been butting in vain and at cost in casualties. Finally the Americans got across the railway bridge, a few hundred yards downstream. Their wireless signal of

success was interpreted as relating to the road bridge. In a last charge, which brooked no denial, the Guards broke through the roundabout position and over the bridge, leaving corpses scattered along its length. The way was open, or so it seemed, to Arnhem and the next stage of the plan.

At the outset of the four days which followed, feeling as we caught it in the Nijmegen salient still sounded the exhilarated note of the start of the adventure.

It was unthinkable that the Arnhem garrison should not be relieved, now Nijmegen bridge was intact in our hands. So certain was authority on this point, and on the successful conclusion of the next stage of the gamble, that troops were unable to change Belgian for Dutch money on the ruling that they would not be likely to stay sufficiently long in Holland to need it.

The vital area of operations was now that stretch of country ten miles across from Nijmegen to Arnhem, which later was to become known as "The Island" and was to preserve its sinister reputation to the end of the war, since only then did we altogether turn the Germans out. It lies so low that the roads have to be supported on dykes. There are two main roads to Arnhem, which join just south of it and also become a single road at Nijmegen bridge. Otherwise, the roads on the map are lanes—tortuous and slippery and not the tank driver's dream.

Very quickly Nijmegen bridge was ranged, and one rarely crossed it without the accompaniment of an ominous whistle as a shell went by on one side or the other One landed on the town end of the bridge and made a hole the size of a jeep. But this could be negotiated. The Sappers made

ENEMY ATTACKS ON THE EINDHOVEN-NIJMEGEN ROAD, Allied supply route for the Nijmegen salient, succeeded in cutting the road and causing serious shortage in the salient on more than one occasion. American infantry (left) move forward past halted British lorries. Under heavy shelling by German self-propelled guns another British supply column on the road was temporarily stopped (right), two ammunition trucks being hit, whilst our tanks and Typhoons broke up the attack and cleared the way. PAGE 218 *Photos, British Official, British Newspaper Pool*

room for more than one stream of traffic by blowing the roadblock at the north end. On the "island" the main roads were so well covered by the enemy as to be impassable. Off the main roads going was extremely difficult in the bad weather which began to add to Allied troubles.

The Household Cavalry reconnoitred to the west for the Guards and, when the 43rd Division came up to take over on September 22, they fought to link up with the Polish Parachute Brigade which had by now dropped at Driel, on the south bank of the Neder Rijn to the west of Arnhem. The Poles, originally, had been intended for the south end of Arnhem bridge; their zone was now moved to where they would be in a better position to contact and aid the larger part of the airborne force penned in the suburb of Oosterbeek. Intelligence from the vital sector became confused. One factor which must have influenced operations at this crucial time was the uncertainty of the supply route back to Eindhoven. On the way up we had spent a precarious night isolated in a house at Zeeland, when the road from Eindhoven had been first cut by German tanks. Later, we had stood on the road at Malden and seen the soft supply vehicles arrive with jagged tears in their hoods, smashed windscreens and other signs of having run the gauntlet. So serious had been the threat then that a force of Guards' tanks had to be spared to go back and clear the road. On the wireless had come Hitler's personal prediction that all troops cut off at the tip of the corridor were about to be thrown into the river.

Food Dump Marked by Dense Smoke

A shortage of rations was at this time manifest in the Nijmegen salient and led, so far as we were concerned, to one incident typical of the shifting security of that district. A German military food dump of fabulous size had been captured at Oss, some few miles away to the west. With an hour to spare, and with a disposition to verify the source of tins of honey and tubes of cheese, we set off in that direction. Well on the road we overtook a troop of tanks and learned that our jeep was the vanguard of a force detailed to meet several hundred German infantry approaching Oss from the south. As we withdrew the battle started and the food dump was marked by billows of smoke.

In those days our duty took us over most of the area from which was being launched the rescue attempt that had started as an effort to reinforce the garrison for victory. We felt the atmosphere in the Nijmegen pocket change from a mood of exhilaration, that saw Berlin in our hands by Christmas, to a grim determination that the men of Arnhem must get help quickly.

THE men of the 43rd Division were inspired with their mission. River-crossing equipment rolled through the streets of Nijmegen and its purpose was clear. The fate of the rescue teams, pursued by Tigers along the treacherous lanes of the island, trying desperately to get into the water down the steep bank of the Neder Rijn against the German harassing fire, was known, and created the wave of determination that did at last, through the great gallantry and perseverance principally of the Dorsets, succeed in the rescue of the airborne troops.

Arnhem was being pinpointed by the fleets of supply planes and gliders coming up from the south-west, from the airfields of England. As they sowed their coloured parachutes away to the north, it was not difficult to imagine the besieged garrison waiting for its life-blood of food and ammunition. Among the pilots of these planes were examples of the greatest gallantry, making fine contribution to the morale and

WAITING TO COLLECT THEIR LIFE-BLOOD OF FOOD AND AMMUNITION, our hard-pressed airborne troops in Holland displayed extended parachutes to guide pilots of the fleets of supply planes, flying through intense A.A. fire, from England, to the dropping zones. Coloured parachutes are seen descending (background) away to the north. *Photo, British Official*

sense of urgency in the salient. They flew over, slow and ponderous, with fighter cover. Sometimes the Luftwaffe came up, notably on the afternoon of the 21st, when the sky might have been that over Kent in the days of the Battle of Britain. But most generally it was Ack Ack and even small arms fire that brought down the huge, vulnerable targets as their pilots aimed stubbornly on for the stricken area of Arnhem.

Because of the extent to which the thrust for Arnhem was an airborne operation, the battlefield had a romantic and colourful appearance. Along the Corridor, the dropping zones still showed the gliders, settled crazily in their first positions of arrival. And, going on all the time, were the drops and the supply drops. American reinforcements were promised and we went to see them come in at the dropping zone south-west of Grave. Most of the planes and gliders landed safely on the flat area of fields intersected by small ditches and dominated by a windmill—a picture which might have been designed to welcome the

newcomers straight to the conventional Holland of their imagination. Some machines tipped on their noses. In a matter of minutes the lane skirting the dropping zone was alive with a marching column of superbly equipped American Airborne troops. We sat on a gate and watched them go by. It was a tonic to see them.

But they were too late to make any difference. That was the Sunday, September 24. By the evening we heard that the rescue of the battered garrison at Oosterbeek had begun. It was a heartbreaking end to the high hopes launched exactly a week before from the departure airfields in England and from the Belgian start-line of the Guards Armoured Division. What history will say about that week history has still to decide. The impression of one who saw the Nijmegen side of the battle remains that the gamble failed nowhere through the tenacity and courage of those asked to accomplish the task in the air and on the ground. The odds, some of them necessarily unknown at the outset, in the end were too heavy.

My Charmed Life in H.M. Submarines

Risks of being blown out of the water, being depth-charged to pieces, or becoming stuck in the sea-bed are among the accepted hazards of undersea warfare. The tense excitement of that life of constant uncertainty is conveyed in these reminiscences by H. F. Piggott, Stoker 1st Class, R.N

I WAS called to the Colours on July 31, 1939, as a Reservist, and was detailed to Submarine H 49, which proceeded on exercises until the outbreak of the War, and then was sent to Portland on Asdic training for destroyers and other ships. One destroyer which trained with us was the Kelly, at that time commanded by Lord Louis Mountbatten.

In the summer of 1940 we were detailed to patrol near Flushing, Holland, which was an E-boat base. One night we were about to surface to charge batteries when the captain, at the periscope, saw that we were surrounded by E-boats exercising. We dived at once, and lay on the sea bed, and were silent until the E-boats returned to harbour; then we prepared to surface. You can imagine our horror when we found we were held fast by shingle! As we lay still the shingle had been gradually washing over us, so burying us. Cautiously we went ahead on the motors, then astern, and so on, until at last, after about two hours of careful manoeuvring, we were able to free ourselves.

After this patrol we were detailed (during the "invasion scare") to proceed to Dover, where we left at 1 a.m. for Calais looking for enemy transports, returning to Dover at 7 a.m. the following morning. We did this for some time, and then I was taken sick with lumbago, and when we reached Dover I was transferred to Chatham Hospital. That was the last I saw of H 49, for she was posted missing shortly afterwards.

My next submarine was the Thunderbolt, formerly Thetis, commanded by Lieut. Crouch, and then lying in dock at Cammel Lairds' yard. When she was ready we did our trials, and were ordered to proceed to Dunoon, Scotland, where the parent ship Forth was lying. On our first patrol, December 15, 1940, we were ordered to the Gironde River in France, to intercept and sink Italian submarines. We eventually saw one, escorted by three armed French trawlers. The depth of water here was only 60 feet. Lieut. Crouch gave the order "Blow up six fish" (give air to torpedoes), and when he got his bearing, the speed of the U-boat, and other details, we fired all

Motto: "Guardian of the Sea and Air."

NO. 240 (G.R.) SQUADRON

FEW squadrons during the six years of war fulfilled more roles or operated over more territory than No. 240. Formed in 1918, at Calshot, Hampshire, from seaplane and flying boat units, it was disbanded in 1919 and reform.d at Calshot as a General Reconnaissance squadron in March 1937. In the early days of the war it operated from Scotland over northern waters, and later, equipped with Catalinas, took part in the Battle of the Atlantic from Loch Erne, Ireland, and helped to maintain communications with Russia.

The squadron moved to Gibraltar, and was employed on anti-submarine operations in the Mediterranean until July 1942, when it went on to Madras. Where it remained until the end of the war with the Japanese. For the first two years of its service in India the squadron flew normal patrols and convoy escorts over the Bay of Bengal and, operating from a forward base at Addu Atoll (see page 268, Vol. 9), patrolled our sea lanes south of the Equator.

THEN, with the threat of Japanese seaborne operations in the Bay of Bengal and adjacent waters decreasing, No. 240 was detailed to carry out the first special duty operation involving a moonlight landing on the sea off the Isthmus of Kra.

In the months that followed, a special duties flight of three aircraft carried out an intensive programme of operations which included the parachuting of men and supplies into Jap-held territory. By August 1945 the flight had flown 85 sorties, of which 93 per cent were successful.

During the last months of the war No. 240 squadron (except the S.D. Flight) and No. 212 Air/Sea Rescue Squadron were merged in a new 240 squadron re-equipped with Sunderland V aircraft. During the war No. 240 flew a total of 35,340 hours, of which 28,180 were operational.

six torpedoes fanwise. There was a terrific explosion, and we knew we had scored. The captain took a quick look and saw a cloud of smoke : the U-boat was missing, and must have been blown to pieces.

We waited for the escorting trawlers to drop depth-charges, and they weren't long about it. They were, however, some distance from us, as the "fish" had been fired from the extreme range of about two miles, and they thought we were nearer. They dropped about 15 depth-charges, which didn't worry us, and then returned to harbour. We went up-river, and at night surfaced in order to charge our batteries.

We dived again at dawn, and Lieut. Crouch told us we were to proceed to the spot where we had sunk the U-boat. I'm afraid we did not exactly relish the prospect. We were doing about three knots submerged when Lieut. Crouch said to the Asdic rating,

"Can you hear anything, Asdics ?" The reply came back, "Nothing, sir." Lieut. Crouch gave the order "Up periscope !" and then, almost in the same breath, "Take her down—we're being rammed !"

We went down like a stone, shut off everything, and there was silence in the boat ; but not outside, for we heard a ship's screws passing overhead. Then there were explosions and it seemed hell had broken loose. Nobody knew what was happening, and after about five minutes all was quiet again. We eventually went slow ahead, and at night surfaced, when an inspection was made of damage. We found plenty. Half the upper deck casing was missing, and the jumping wire was hanging over the side as though it had been cut with a hacksaw. But at least we were clear of the enemy and we proceeded back to harbour at Dunoon.

Stkr. H. F. PIGGOTT

When we were going alongside Forth there was cheering coming from the ship's company, and Captain of Medway came from Forth to congratulate us. When he slipped off the gangway into the water more than one laugh went up. But he took everything in good part and came aboard us and congratulated Lieut. Crouch.

We Hit the Big Ship in the Stern

Soon after this we proceeded to Halifax, Nova Scotia, and on one occasion were returning from an Atlantic convoy when Lieut. Crouch saw a big liner approaching us. He at once looked in the silhouette book, but could not see a ship resembling her. "I believe she's a raider," he said. "Prepare three torpedoes. Stand by, guns' crew !" When we were within lamp range he told the signalman to give her the challenge, which he did—and she replied with a salvo of shells. We could hear the shrapnel falling on our ship's side. We quickly dived, and Lieut. Crouch said, "I'll give her five minutes to send out a signal." She did so, and this was it : "Admiralty emergency. Have engaged enemy submarine, believe sunk. Canton P. & O." That was certainly a near one for us !

I left Thunderbolt at Halifax and was detailed to the submarine Talisman in August 1941. While on patrol with her we were sent to "get" a 15,000-ton supply ship, or transport. We saw her after about four days out, escorted by six destroyers, and we prepared six torpedoes. Lieut. Wilmott, the captain, got his attack all ready and gave the orders, "Up Periscope" and "Fire ! Take her down." We heard one of the escorting destroyers go over the top of us. As soon as she had passed over the captain said, "Up periscope, fire 1, 2, 3. Down periscope. Shut off for depth-charge attack !"

We hit the big ship in the stern, and this was later reported by Italy. We dived deep, then about every quarter-hour they came dropping charges and would not leave us. Lieut. Wilmott told the First Lieutenant to tell the crew how we stood. "Well, men," he said, "we have just enough in the batteries to allow us to surface, and if the Italians are still up there we will abandon ship and blow up the sub !" We surfaced and, to our joy, the Italians destoyers had left us, having dropped in all 84 depth-charges, doing us no damage but giving us a very nasty shaking.

I left Talisman and went to the 64th Hospital, and after getting well was detailed to Medway, the submarine parent ship. On June 30, 1942, Medway left Alexandria for Haifa, Palestine, to open a submarine base, as Rommel was then getting too close. We left at about 8 p.m., escorted by destroyers and cruisers, and also, for a time, by aircraft. We had ideal weather, and Commander "Tiger" Marsh was on the bridge when hands fell in for work the following day. I was on the upper deck, wearing nothing but shoes and shorts, when "Tiger" saw me, and sang out, "That man there—put your lifebelt on !" I hurried below, put on my lifebelt, and was just getting some cigarettes and matches from my locker when there were terrific explosions. I was thrown on my back by the concussion, and lockers and everything movable toppled over around me. I at once blew up my lifebelt and proceeded to the upper deck.

BY this time, only about three minutes after being hit on the starboard side, Medway had a bad list, and I felt in my pockets for anything I could throw away to lighten myself. It sounds silly now, but it didn't seem so then—I threw away my cigarettes and matches ! Also I kicked off my shoes and waited for the order to abandon ship. Then someone gave the order for everything that would float to be thrown over the side, and presently rafts, Carley floats, spars, doors and stools were floating past us. The Commander gave the order "Abandon ship, every man for himself !"

The deck on the starboard side was now under water. I found a rope and slid down, cutting myself badly on barnacles on the ship's bottom. As soon as I was in the water I started swimming towards H.M.S. Hero, but seeing so many doing the same I went in the direction of another escorting destroyer, the Zulu. I was swimming for hours, it seemed, before I came to Zulu, and I was all-in when I was hoisted to her deck, but a cup of tea soon revived me. There were no boats lowered, as Medway went down too quickly—twelve minutes only from the time of being hit by four torpedoes to disappearing. (See facing page.)

We carried with us, taking passage, besides ratings and officers, three Wren officers evacuating Alexandria ; one of these was picked up by Zulu and was later decorated for giving her lifebelt to a drowning sailor. When all survivors were picked up Hero proceeded to Port Said and Zulu to Haifa. Depth-charges were dropped now and again when enemy submarines were detected, but the U-boat that sank Medway got away—no depth-charges then being dropped because of so many men swimming in the sea. On arrival at Haifa we were transported to an army camp in Palestine, where we stayed before being drafted.

The King Shook Hands With Me

I seem to have had a charmed life. At Weymouth, in September 1939, I was detailed whilst on H 49 to proceed to the aircraft-carrier Courageous for inspection by the King, myself representing the boat. All hands fell in on the flight deck, and the King inspected us. With him was Admiral Max Horton, then in charge of all submarines, and he recognized me as serving with him in K-boats (submarines with funnels and boilers). He asked my name, and passed it on to the King, who shook hands with me and asked how I liked being back in the Service. The Courageous was sunk by enemy action a few days later. The second boat I left that went down was H 49, then Talisman, Thunderbolt and Medway. My sixth was the minelayer, H.M.S. Abdiel, in which I took passage from Malta to Gibraltar, on January 26, 1943, and which was sunk in October of the same year.

Mediterranean Death-Plunge of H.M.S. Medway

" ABANDON SHIP, every man for himself," was the dread order given by the commander of the submarine depot ship Medway after she had been struck by four torpedoes when she was on her way to Haifa to open a submarine base, in the summer of 1942. There was no time to lower the boats, and in a matter of twelve minutes after being hit the Medway had vanished below the surface.

Listing heavily, with ropes dangling down the side (1), she gave little hope of life to her crew—seen scrambling for the water from the ropes. With a hiss and a roar, Medway takes the final plunge (2), her immediate neighbourhood dotted with the bobbing heads of men swimming amidst fragments of wreckage (3) in the direction of escorting destroyers H.M.S. Zulu and Hero. See story in facing page.

We Navigated the African Bush

Although the Battle of the Atlantic was raging, the War seemed a long way from the 6,000-ton oil-burning meat ship Viking Star on that sunny afternoon of August 25, 1942. What happened after the first "fish" smacked home is told by Clifford Maw then her 16-year-old deck-boy.

CLIFFORD MAW

WE had left Buenos Aires with a full cargo of frozen beef, and some of us were sunning ourselves on deck in the first dog-watch and talking about "fish"—torpedoes—their construction and method of firing them. Two or three were in bathing costumes; there was Kelly the donkeyman in overalls and a beret, and myself wearing only a pair of rope-soled shoes and grey shorts hitched by a sixpenny belt. The lamp-trimmer in his birthday suit was splashing happily in a canvas bath on the after well-deck.

I had just opened my mouth to say something when there came the muffled sound of an explosion. A couple of seconds later a louder explosion came from somewhere deep under the galley, near to which some of us were sitting. It was a real case of "talk of the devil." Two torpedoes had struck the ship like thunderbolts out of the blue; no periscope was visible in the wide circle of ocean and no bubbling tracks of the "fish" had given warning of the attack. At that second blow the Viking Star lurched violently to starboard till the side-rails were almost awash.

Two engineers, five firemen and a naval gunlayer were killed instantly. Two men on deck were blown into the air, and one of them, the third engineer, was never seen again; the other, an A.B., crashed down on a splintered hatch with a broken leg. The lamp-trimmer leaped out of his canvas bath on hearing the explosions and when the ship listed took a remarkable dive over the starboard rail into the sea. My recollection of the event is of lying in the scuppers looking dazedly into a smoke-filled sky, and

finding myself with a sprained ankle on attempting to scramble up.

We took to the lifeboats, on the captain's orders, and bellowed abuse when a U-boat appeared a cable's length away and smashed a third torpedo into the sinking ship. The seventy-third voyage of the old Viking Star was ending in the deep Atlantic, and by some freakish convulsion she rose in two halves with the bow pointing at one angle and the stern with stopped propellers at another. It looked like a gigantic V, symbol of Victory, as if, in her dying, the British veteran had made a last majestic gesture of defiance. So the Viking Star went down at 17.45 G.M.T., her position at the time of the attack being latitude 6 degrees North, and longitude 14 degrees West.

We were on tenterhooks lest the U-boat should start machine-gunning us, but it sheered off and we set course for the distant coast of West Africa. We felt fairly confident that a naval or air patrol from Freetown would find us, but it did not work out that way, and some of the rafts never reached land. Circumstances made it necessary for lifeboats and rafts to part company, and I will not dwell unduly on a voyage in an open boat crowded with thirty-six men in a space meant for twenty-six.

SHORT commons, seasickness, work, dangerous moments, spells of boredom, hopes raised only to be shattered—such formed our lot over four days and nights on the ocean. Time and again someone jumped up to point out "a sail" that proved to be no more than a wisp of cloud on the horizon or a shadow on the sea. So when Kelly yelled out one drizzly night, "Look! There's land, fellows!" he was told brusquely to "Pipe down and stop rocking the boat!"

But he was right, and we raised a hoarse cheer when doubts were dispelled. None of us was feeling too strong and I had taken my belt in to the last notch. But we kept rowing against the ebb-tide until caught by the heel in a breaking crest of sea. The first mate ordered "Ship the oars!" and

the boat rushed forward amid surf with foam creaming over the stern and gunwales.

Another giant roller struck us and our boat was hurled up and over, flinging us all into the sea. It looked like "curtains" for me. My kapok life-jacket had been soaked frequently and had lost its buoyancy. Instead of keeping me afloat it dragged me down, and I was lucky to find myself lying on the beach and Chippy, the carpenter, who had rescued me, bending over and applying first-aid with ham-fisted vigour. The other chaps were ashore and had hitched the sea-anchor to a thorny bush to hold the overturned lifeboat fast, then rigged a sail for a windbreak, and we all waited in this rough shelter for the dawn.

Savage Chief With Pearly Spats

At first light, a solitary figure was seen, motionless as a bronze statue, near a palm tree. He proved to be a negro, wearing a loin-cloth and armed with a spear. When he saw us looking at him he vanished, and presently returned with a score of full-blooded negroes armed with spears and knives, and led by their chieftain and a nondescript native of paler hue who had been educated at a mission school and could "speak de Inglees bery good, yes mistah," and kept on saying so.

They gathered in a half-circle round our improvised tent over which the spindrift was blowing from the crests of the Atlantic surf. The first mate had slept less than any of us in the boat, and was catching up with some of it when he was awakened to deal with these visitors. None of us had ever seen anything quite like these natives, particularly the chief, who looked as if he might have stepped straight out of a Hollywood film. His ebony face was decorated with scars in spiral design, his parted lips revealed a white half-moon of teeth in a fixed grin. Barter had provided him with fine raiment and doubtless much prestige, for not every savage chieftain could sport, as he did, an Arab burnous, a grey topper of the kind once popular at Ascot, a pair of spats with pearl buttons, and a golf umbrella of red, blue, green and yellow—with a couple of broken ribs to give it a quainter look.

They reminded me of all I had read about cannibals. But that topper, the spats and gamp were reassuring; and they had brought bamboo litters, which suggested the desire

LAST VOYAGE OF A MERCHANTMAN which, according to the German description accompanying these photographs (received in London through a neutral source), was torpedoed and sunk by a U-boat in tropical waters. The stern of the unnamed merchantman is still visible (left). Members of the crew who managed to get away in a lifeboat (right) witnessed one of the saddest sights that seamen can endure—the last moments of a gallant craft which had become as a second "home" to them.

Photos, Associated Press

THE VIKING STAR AT LONDON BRIDGE WHARF, unloading in 1935. **Seven years later, on her seventy-third voyage, this big meat ship was to meet her fate at the hands of the Germans on a sunny afternoon in the broad Atlantic, as told here by her deck boy.** *Photo, Associated Press*

to be helpful. The first mate held palaver with the mission-educated native, and discovered that we had made a landfall in French Guinea, which was territory under Vichy control at the time and therefore hostile to the Allies. We had landed, it appeared, a full 100 miles north of Freetown, Sierra Leone. It also appeared that these natives had heard something about a war being in progress, but had only the foggiest notion as to whom it was between and what it was all about.

The negroes stood watching us in silent curiosity, but presently some of them went to the cultivated patches near their village and returned with something to gladden the heart and stomach—green coconuts, bananas, oranges, limes and mangoes. This was just what the doctor would have ordered after our boat voyage on scant rations, during which I had taken in my belt to the last notch. In return for the hospitality, the first mate told the chief that he could have the lifeboat, which was no longer of use to us anyway. This further warmed the cockles of the chieftain's heart and we were taken to the village, some of the chaps carried on litters, and installed in thatched kraals, where we slept soundly.

Mysterious Code of the Wilds

Our portable radio set had been lost when the lifeboat had overturned, but these natives had their own broadcasting system—the signal drums which, from time immemorial, had relayed messages from tribe to tribe over vast stretches of African bush and swamp. So the tom-toms beat out the news of our rescue in the mysterious code of the wilds and, later on, throbbing drumbeats from the distance brought a response. Incidentally, what that gift of the lifeboat meant to these simple savages can be judged by the fact that they celebrated by song and dance for hours until even the strongest of them were exhausted.

When food and rest had refreshed us, the dusky chief suggested through the mission-schooled interpreter that we should go to another village nearer an outpost where two French missionaries were established. This was agreed to, and the chief arrayed himself in all his glory and announced he would act as our guide. Not to be outdone in courtesy, the whole tribe—with the exception of a few old crones, and mothers with babies—volunteered for escort and brought out the bamboo litters in case any of us castaways should fall by the wayside during our journey through the bush. A strange procession set off on the trail. The chief in his Hollywood rig-out went ahead, using his furled golfing gamp for a walking-stick. The half-naked negroes followed, chanting weirdly, and we of the lost Viking Star marched among them in our odds-and-ends of attire or bathing costumes. I padded along in the rear, badly sun-blistered, and barefooted because I had lost my shoes in the surf, my personal escort a bunch of pot-bellied, naked piccaninnies who were obviously enjoying the adventure to the full.

We snaked into the African bush. The air was humid, the heat stifling. Strange birds and gaily-coloured butterflies winged among the trees, shimmering in the shafts of sunlight that pierced the forest gloom. Myriads of mosquitoes swarmed over our sweating parade, and tormented those of us not used to such devilish attack. Thorns and ticks seared all who were bare-legged, and the pace slackened as some of the sailors began to limp and straggle.

What looked like a tarred path crossed a game-trail farther on. The chief uttered a warning shout, patted his grey topper firmly over his crinkly hair and made a ponderous leap. The other natives jabbered and gestured excitedly. That "path," which was moving like a sluggish stream of pitch, consisted of millions of stinging black ants. The agile negroes leaped clear, but many of us had to seize tough strands of creeper that dangled from the trees and swing over that formidable army of ants.

Worse going lay ahead. Beyond the bush was a swamp through which the grown-ups waded above the knees and the piccaninnies wallowed happily. A big snake slithered from under a mass of fetid vegetation, and so startled one of our chaps that he lost his balance and squelched full-length in the mire. This made everyone (with one exception) more cheery. Without serious mishap we arrived at a village on a broad, muddy river, a place much larger than the one we had left. Here we were treated by another tribe with equal hospitality, and a runner departed at top speed to tell the missionaries of our arrival.

A FEAST was prepared—and I dream of it now. Chicken was the main dish. The head of each fowl was removed and the feathered body plastered thickly with mud and laid over a brushwood fire. With fine judgement the native cook removed it when done to a turn, scraped off the mud and feathers, gutted the bird and carved it in satisfying chunks. There was enough and to spare, for the village seemed to be positively overrun by fowls.

One night, after the Hollywood chief and his tribe had departed with due ceremony, we sat round the fires and watched a dance by the village belles, whose scar-decorated faces shone as if with black boot-polish. The high spot of this pagan dance came when the girls went leaping gracefully into the bush, caught fireflies in their hands and came whirling back with their jet-black hair spangled with living sparks. Several days later the French missionaries came in an ancient motor-launch and took us to a trading post down-river. A message brought a patrol vessel of the Royal Navy into the estuary, and soon we were taken in fair comfort to Freetown, Sierra Leone.

⌐⌐⌐⌐⌐⌐⌐ NEW FACTS AND FIGURES ⌐⌐⌐⌐⌐⌐⌐

ABOUT 4,700 goods wagons, more than 425 passenger cars, and 200 engines were repaired in the British zone of Germany during April 1946. During the same month nine material collecting trains recovered 500 tons of scrap-iron and 400 tons of spare parts from more than 100 completely destroyed wagons and other debris. This result was achieved by a special department of the Hamburg Reichsbahn direction which has a staff of 2,800, mostly experienced engineers, artisans and railway workers. Thirty repair and material collecting trains, equipped with special workshops and sleeping-quarters, are employed by this department which assists the ten railway repair centres in the British zone. In the Hamburg area more than 3,500 damaged goods wagons are still in need of repair, and there are about 500 beyond repair, from which valuable spare parts can be collected.

AFTER the first major R.A.F. attack on Hamm—famous railway centre in the Ruhr—it required eight days to get the marshalling yards working. By the end of the War trains were moving again after 24 hours. Under the 60-year-old station-master, Herr Lohe, 1,000 Wehrmacht men and slave labourers worked to repair the damage. It is estimated (says the British Zone Review) that 2,500 tons of H.E. and 10,000 incendiaries were dropped on Hamm, damaging 100 locomotives, 144 passenger coaches and 3,473 goods wagons.

ONE thousand or more people are believed to have been killed in the Hamm raids. The death roll would have been higher if the town had not had one of the best air raid shelter systems in Germany. Nine of these, with walls six to nine feet thick, each capable of accommodating 5,000 to 6,000 people, are still standing. The shelters are divided into hundreds of separate rooms, which now provide sleeping accommodation for persons passing through the ruined town.

RAID casualties among German factory workers were much lower than Allied experts had thought. The International Committee for the Study of European Questions estimates that only about two in 1,000 were killed by air bombardment, on account of the discipline maintained in the excellent shelters. Of 160,000 employees at the Krupp Works in Essen, for instance, only 170 lost their lives.

THE above low casualty figure, however, does not imply failure of the Allied bombing policy. Towards the end of 1944, or early in 1945, most of the 50 German cities on the "priority list" had been crippled from an industrial point of view. Essen had lost 60 per cent of its production, Hanover 70 per cent, Kassel 75 per cent, and Düsseldorf 79 per cent. In Berlin not less than 326 big factories had come to a standstill as the result of air bombardment.

Good Companions Aboard Our Carrier Theseus

See also illus. pages 208-209. Photo, Keystone

A GREAT ADVENTURE CAME INTO THE LIVES of these two young representatives of Southern Norway when the light Fleet carrier H.M.S. Theseus put into Bergen Harbour for a short and friendly visit. Given the proud privilege of going aboard, they were received with open arms by one of the ship's company and, dressed for the occasion in their Sunday-best, were " snapped " against the background of the carrier's aircraft. Theseus returned to British waters on June 14, 1946. See also illus. pages 208-209.

Photo, Keystone

Printed in England and published every alternate Friday, by the Proprietors, The AMALGAMATED PRESS, LTD., The Fleetway House, Farringdon Street, London, E.C.4. Registered for transmission by Canadian Magazine Post. Sole Agents for Australia and New Zealand: Messrs. Gordon & Gotch, Ltd.; and for South Africa: Central News Agency, Ltd.—July 19, 1946.   S.S.   *Editorial Address:*   JOHN CARPENTER HOUSE, WHITEFRIARS, LONDON, E.C.4.

Vol 10 *The War Illustrated* Nº 238

SIXPENCE

AUGUST 2. 1946

I WAS THERE

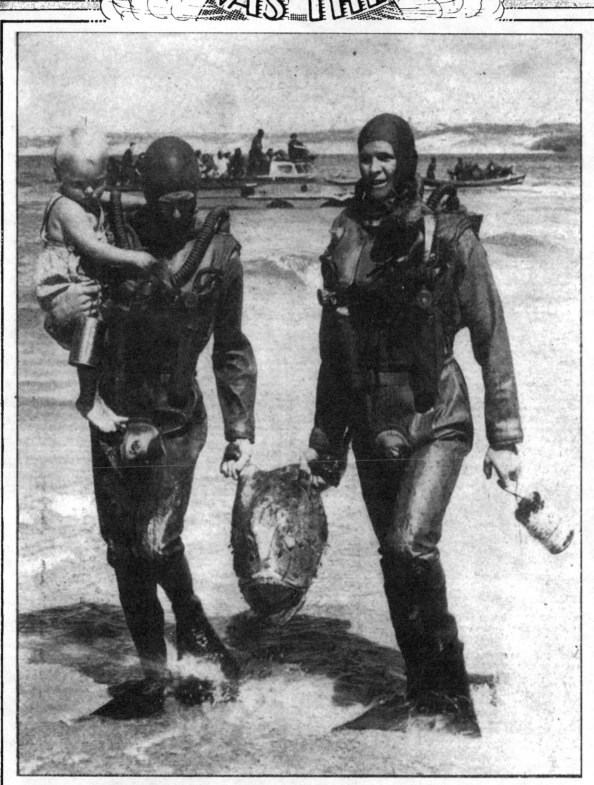

FROG MEN EMERGING FROM THE SEA AT ST. IVES, Cornwall, provided an exciting distraction for holiday-makers—the youngest of whom eagerly accepted a "lift." Bearing a finned trophy encountered on their undersea route, they were taking part in a demonstration by a Landing Craft Obstruction Unit in aid of the Commando Benevolent Fund. Their gallant work in connection with the Normandy landings on D-Day will long be remembered. See also pages 353 and 361, Vol. 9. *Photo, Mirror Features*

Edited by Sir John Hammerton

NO. 239 WILL BE PUBLISHED FRIDAY, AUGUST 16

Britain's Rising Exports Presage Better Times

FOR THE FIRST TIME SINCE THE WAR figures showed that Britain's monthly export volume had, in May 1946, exceeded that of the corresponding period in 1938, by eleven per cent. This followed an upward trend since January 1946, when only 74 per cent had been attained. February showed 87 per cent, March 90 per cent, and April 100 per cent. Principal contributors responsible for the May increase were machinery and transport industries, such as this locomotive works at Glasgow (1), where an engine for export to India is being lifted into testing position. India's order for £1,000,000 of road-making machines included steam-rollers, the rollers of which are protectively packed ready for shipment (2). Outstanding exports for the period included 5,622 cars against 3,677 in 1938; many went to Singapore, for unloading at Collyer's Quay (3). Other export figures for May compared with those of the same month in 1938 (in parenthesis) were: commercial vehicles and chassis 4,886 (1,190); rail wagons and trucks 17,749 tons (3,025); electrical generators 2,156 tons (858); and machine tools 3,927 tons (2,010).

Photos. British Official, Topical, and Central Press

The Invasion of Normandy

By GORDON HOLMAN

From the headquarters ship H.M.S. Hilary the author, a war correspondent who was twice mentioned in dispatches, saw the troops go into attack on June 6, 1944.

IN the spring of 1943, when the war's end seemed even farther away than it was, Britain's Prime Minister, Mr. Winston Churchill, went to Washington to meet another great war-time leader of free men, President Roosevelt. With their Chiefs of Staff they discussed the final shape of the amphibious operation that alone could place the Allied armies back in western Europe. Among the select and brilliant band of planners, the word "Overlord" rose up like a star. For those who thought mainly of the sea there was another word that both guided and inspired them, "Neptune."

"Overlord" covered the whole operation of invasion, "Neptune" its naval phase. Following these two bright stars, which held the destinies of many peoples, men laboured day and night for fourteen months. They overcame immense difficulties ; no problem was too great, no consideration too small. Then, in the first week of June 1944, with more at stake than thousands, of men's lives, they put the results of their long and arduous labours to the test.

Few of those who took part in the main attack on Hitler's stronghold knew more than the shape of their own tiny piece in the great jig-saw. In fitting that in, they were prepared to strive to the utmost, but "Overlord" and "Neptune"—the whole puzzle—remained as remote as the stars to them. They did not know the answers, and some of them never will.

How Could We Hope For Surprise ?

At the beginning of that fateful year there were rehearsals off our shores which the Germans were able to approach closely enough to sink at least two L.S.T.s. They did it with E boats. It was but an incident of the preparation, but men who had known such incidents naturally wondered what would be the outcome of "the real thing." How could we hope for surprise ? How could we get on to beaches thickly strewn with obstacles and mines ? How could we hope to maintain supplies without a major port in our hands ? The queries, if one thought for a little while, were endless.

Today it is possible to answer many of those questions. Neither the answers nor the smooth success with which our plans were carried through detract one iota from the magnificent achievement of D and its plus days. Here we are considering action rather than planning ; and first credit, perhaps, should go to those intrepid men who walked the Normandy beaches while watchful Germans still manned their front line in full strength. In small boats and by night they pulled on to the soft sands, scrambled ashore and made careful investigation of the first obstacles the invasion armies would have to overcome.

Their reports added detail to the information obtained by daring R.A.F. reconnaissance flights. The flyers brought back photographs, taken only a few feet above the beaches, which revealed clearly the explosive charges fixed to the tops of the angular metal obstructions ; before D-Day we knew that many of them were French shells adapted for a new defensive purpose. It was impossible to hide from the enemy—indeed, little attempt was made in those latter days—the fact that invasion was coming. Security, therefore, was chiefly concerned with the two vital secrets of time and place.

SOUTHERN and western England were steadily built up into one vast camp of armed men, with guns tanks and vehicles almost beyond number. There can be little doubt now that security was maintained to an amazing degree. Field-Marshal von Rundstedt has said "We could not tell where the landing would come." That we more than planned for success on D-Day is revealed by his further admission that should always give satisfaction to the men who carried out the pre-invasion air offensive against the enemy. "Our reserves were not so dispersed that I could not have met the D-Day landing, even though it surprised us, except for the fact that we had no mobility, and could not bring up our reserves," the Field-Marshal, as a prisoner of war, said. "Between Paris and Rouen there was not a single bridge across the Seine."

A river held up the Germans. Four years earlier, the narrow straits between England and France had proved an unsurmountable barrier although the defences on our shores were of the flimsiest character. In the face of long preparations and a knowledge gained in grim and deadly battles, we had to cross eighty to a hundred miles of sea to deliver our assault. Fortunately for us history has proved that land power and sea power are two entirely different things. But they can be made to function together. The damaging raids of our Special Service troops had left no doubt of this in Hitler's mind. But the sea and its ways cannot be mastered through text books, and even the thoroughness of the Wehrmacht applied to the German Navy could not give that understanding of the sea which is a natural asset of an island people.

For the invasion, it had to be interpreted into the handling of ships. There were leaders of unrivalled knowledge, such as the late Admiral Sir Bertram Ramsay, C.-in-C. of our naval invasion forces, to carry on our naval tradition. But by far the greater number of those who handled the 5,143 vessels that engaged in the great assault were men from civilian life. Bank clerks and butchers, schoolmasters and stockbrokers, bus drivers and garage hands took the little ships in. And, by some instinct, they had a sounder conception of sea power than the German generals who disposed the forces waiting on the farther shore.

Strong Tide a Natural Obstacle

The strong tide flowing up and down the English channel was a natural obstacle to the invasion. It created many and varied problems. What would suit at one state of the tide was quite useless at another. To the last, the Germans probably believed that we could only overcome those difficulties by capturing a port. And, as we saw later in Cherbourg and elsewhere, they made quite certain that any port we did succeed in capturing would be useless for some time.

Between the ports along the gently sloping beaches of the Bay of the Seine they put down their mines—contact mines, drag mines, magnetic mines and other varieties. Behind those they had their steel and wooden stakes and their long scaffolding of steel tubes. On the beaches were buried mines, and then came sunken concrete sentry boxes, pillboxes, gun emplacements, barbed wire, mined fields and roads and siege guns.

To assault this massive barrier the planners built up five Task Forces. The three to the east of the assault area were British and, for "Operation Neptune," came under the direct command of Vice-Admiral Sir Philip Vian.

BEACH OBSTACLES were still being erected by Germans along the French coast as an anti-invasion measure in the first days of June 1944. Spotted by a R.A.F. reconnaissance aircraft, a working-party is seen scattering for cover.

Photo, British Official

The two to the west were American and came under the command of Rear-Admiral Alan G. Kirk, U.S.N.

The first problem was to get these forces safely, and at the same time, into the assault area. Considering the vessels in three classes alone, the warships had two or three times the speed of the big transports, and the transports had a similar advantage over the L.S.T.s. Broadly, the major problem in co-ordination was overcome in this way: five channels were swept from a point 13 miles out to sea from the Isle of Wight and then, half-way to France, each channel was divided into two. This permitted the faster ships that had started later to overtake the slower units and fit into their appointed positions. Minesweepers headed the whole procession, and with them went the dan-buoy laying craft which marked the channels like so many streets.

Five British regiments and three American units handled these strange fighting monsters on D-Day. The British regiments were the 4/7th Dragoon Guards, the 13/18th Hussars, the Nottinghamshire Yeomanry, the 1st Canadian Hussars and the Fort Garry Horse. The Germans were dumbfounded by the D.D.s (Duplex Drive) and readily surrendered to them.

Novelties in the Great Build-Up

Their discarded "skirts" were to be seen in the squares and streets of such beach towns as Courseulles and Bernières, and days after the assault I heard French villagers arguing as to what they were. The general view was that they were some kind of collapsible boat, and a diligent search went on for the "bottoms" that would have filled the large holes which were, in fact, the size and shape of the tank hulls. Of four hundred

fire from the L.C.T.s that brought them in While the minesweepers went rapidly to work out in the wide anchorage, demolition teams operated on shore. Their task was one of the most unpleasant in the whole invasion. Going in with the first wave, they had to work against time to clear the beaches for the strong support forces coming just behind. While the initial battle still raged, they had to deal with mined stakes and dispose of the live French shells. This meant that, far from taking cover, they had to climb on to the exposed stakes and even on to each others' shoulders. Charges had tò be fixed to explode the German mines. In this they were greatly hampered by the choppy sea conditions.

There were many brilliant novelties in the great build-up which went on throughout D-Day and the anxious days that followed. Among these were the rhino ferries, which proved invaluable. Huge, self-propelling landing stages, the rhinos carried stores or became landing jetties. They could be loaded with immense quantities, and it was quite common to see the "skipper" of one of these craft, perched high on a mass of cases, passing his instructions by hand signal to the two coxswains handling the outboard motors in the stern. (See illus. on left.)

Ducks (D.U.K.W.s) swarmed about the invasion fleet, often handled by American coloured troops. They provided an endless belt on which supplies flowed unfailingly from ship to shore. Loaded at the side of a ship perhaps a mile or more out, they made their way in under their own power, grounded and then dragged themselves up on to the metal webbing put down on the sands. Without stopping, they checked through a control point and trundled down the

GOING ASHORE ON THE NORMANDY BEACH-HEAD, after the Allied landings on June 6, 1944, is a self-propelled, heavily laden Rhino Ferry, specially designed for "Operation Overlord." These craft were adapted as pontoons between landing ships and beach, or as wharf or dry dock, or (as above) for conveying trucks and ambulances. See also illus. in page 102, Vol. 8.
Photo, British Newspaper Pool

Before the invasion armada sailed, it was recognized that the congestion of vessels in the assault area would be very great. One secret weapon which had been tested and found successful was ruled out because of this. It was known as the L.C.G.(T). and was a heavily armoured gun-tower mounted on twin pontoons driven by Diesel power. The L.C.G.(T)s were to head the invasion and carry out a close-up bombardment with howitzers. When they were a thousand yards or less from the shore these bombardment towers were to "scuttle" themselves. Sitting firmly on the sea bottom with only the armoured casements showing above water, it was intended. that they should keep up a constant fire on the enemy during the assault. When they had fulfilled their function, powerful compressors were to blow the water out of the pontoons in preparation for the return trip to England.

A NOTHER secret weapon that *was* used—the "D.D."—had the advantage of mobility over the L.C.G.(T). It was a floating tank which the War Office gave Mr. Nicholas Straussler encouragement to experiment on as early as 1941. A collapsible screen was fitted to the hull of the tank, and this, when erected, enabled the tank to float. Power came from propellers at the rear operated by the main driving shaft. Within a few seconds of getting ashore the D.D.s could shake off their canvas "skirts" and fight as land craft.

"swimming" tanks used by the Allies on D-Day only one was sunk, it has since been stated. (See illus in pages 400–401, Vol. 9.)

Both tank bridges and ramp tanks were used successfully by the Royal Armoured Corps and the Royal Engineers on the Normandy beaches and farther inland. Sea-front walls and specially built anti-tank walls were mounted by these vehicles which were designed to overcome deep ditches and cratered roads. Developed by a team of Army officers, civilian scientists and technical experts, they included a scissors type bridge carried folded on top of a Valentine tank which was automatically unfolded by a mechanism operated from inside the tank; a Churchill bridge-layer, which consisted of a 30-foot span steel trackway mounted on top of the tank hull which was raised by a pivot arm and carried forward and lowered across the gap; two trackways made up of hornbeam sections of the small box-girder bridge, fixed together to form a bridge which was projected in front of the tank and a Churchill tank with the turret removed and track-ways on the top. In the last type, additional track-ways projected in front and behind the tank. The tank was driven directly into the gap and the ramps lowered to enable vehicles to pass right over it. (See illus. in page 237, Vol. 9.) In the assault, many of the tanks became amphibious in another sense. Their guns provided concentrated

narrow French roads to ammunition and store dumps. Empty, they went back by another route to the sea, plunged into the water and headed out for another load. They were successful beyond all expectations, and the tonnages put ashore by them in the early stages were triumphantly chalked up on beach headquarters notice boards as a source of inspiration to any who might doubt our ability to sustain the thousands flocking ashore. (See illus. in page 301, Vol. 7.)

L ATER, the Gooseberries were formed by sinking a number of old ships stem to stern close in-shore. Inside these artificial shelters many small craft assembled. There were converted barges with fully equipped work-shop-lorries secured in their depths, water carriers, floating cookhouses (L.C.K.s) and vessels that answered other problems of the great invasion. To move among them was to be in a busy, floating township; and it was almost impossible to believe that, not so many hours before, the Germans had looked out over its site on to a deserted seascape.

The Mulberries (see pages 430–434, Vol. 8), were built up even later, and although one of these amazing pre-fabricated ports was not destined to survive the unexpected frenzy of the storm that descended on the anchorage a fortnight later, they remained, perhaps, the most remarkable monument to the ingenuity of men who were determined to land armies from the sea in a way never known before.

Batavia Memorial to British Commonwealth Dead

19 46

TO THE GLORY OF GOD AND IN PROUD THANKSGIVING FOR THOSE OF THE BRITISH COMMONWEALTH OF NATIONS WHO GAVE THEIR LIVES WHEN FIRST THE TIDE OF JAPANESE AGGRESSION CAME TO THIS LAND, FOR THOSE WHO DIED AS PRISONERS OF WAR DURING THE JAPANESE OCCUPATION, AND FOR THOSE OFFICERS AND MEN WHO FELL IN ACTION IN THE OPERATIONS FOR THE ESTABLISHMENT OF PEACE AND JUSTICE IN THESE ISLANDS—

IN THE ENGLISH CHURCH AT BATAVIA, Netherlands East Indies, a memorial to British Commonwealth men and women killed in Java during 1942-1946 was un-veiled (2) by Lieut.-Gen. Sir Montagu Stopford, G.O.C. Allied Land Forces South-East Asia, in July 1946. Attending the ceremony (1) were Dr. Van Mook, Governor-General, and British and Dutch servicemen. Bearing the insignia of the XVth Indian Corps, 5th, 23rd 26th Indian Divisions, 15th Indian Task Brigade and the 5th Paratroop Brigade, the plaque (3) was designed by Corporal R. Roberts, R.A.S.C., and subscribed for by Service personnel.

Photos, British Official

More War Crimes Trials Run Their Tragic Course

GENERAL MIHAILOVICH, YUGOSLAV GUERILLA LEADER and former War Minister (1) as he was in 1941, and how he appeared in June 1946 (2) when, arraigned for war crimes, he faced the Yugoslav Military Tribunal at Belgrade. Purporting to have led the Chetniks, Yugoslavia Army of the Homeland, in the interests of his country and of the Allies, it was alleged at the trial that Gen. Mihailovich had, instead, collaborated with the enemy and co-operated with the quisling government of Serbia. Representations by the Allies on his behalf for clemency were rejected; he was sentenced to death on July 15, 1946, and shot two days later. Thirty-one members of the French Gestapo, which operated against partisans during the German Occupation of France, were brought to trial at Paris, on June 19, 1946; chief of the Organization, Charles Detmar, stands in the dock (3) among the accused. In Tokyo on June 4, 1946, the trial of the former Japanese premier Tojo and other Ministers opened. Ex-Premier Tojo, sixth from left in front row of dock (4), listens while Major Blaking, U.S. Army (standing in front, left), asks the court for adjournment to enable counsel for the accused to prepare their cases. Former Foreign Minister Matsuoka, also charged, was absent from the court, through illness, and died in hospital on June 27, 1946. PAGE 230 *Photos, G.P.U., Associated Press, Keystone*

Demonstrators Demand Trieste for Yugoslavia

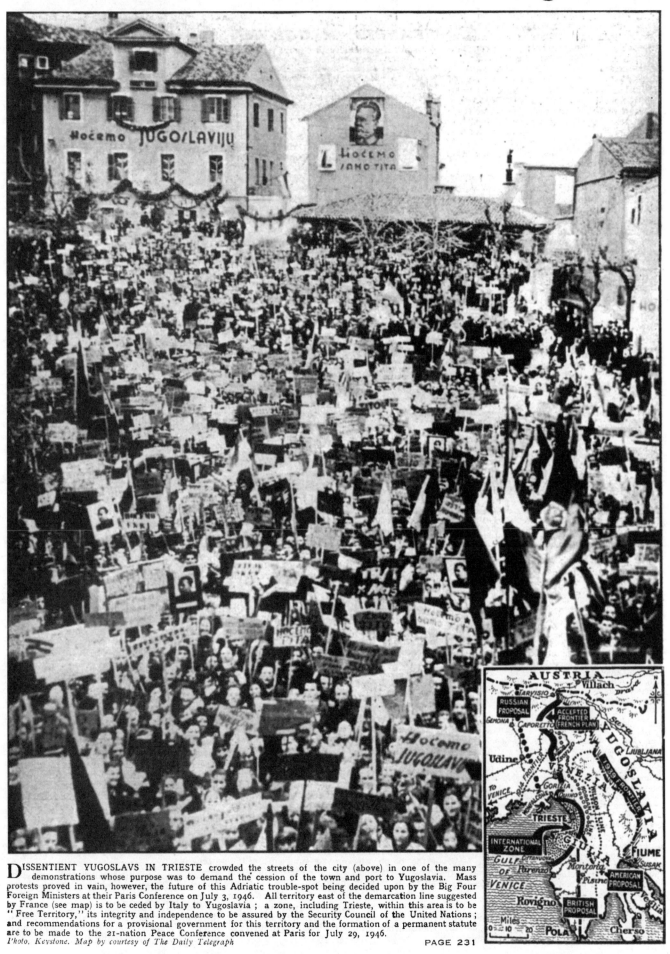

DISSENTIENT YUGOSLAVS IN TRIESTE crowded the streets of the city (above) in one of the many demonstrations whose purpose was to demand the cession of the town and port to Yugoslavia. Mass protests proved in vain, however, the future of this Adriatic trouble-spot being decided upon by the Big Four Foreign Ministers at their Paris Conference on July 3, 1946. All territory east of the demarcation line suggested by France (see map) is to be ceded by Italy to Yugoslavia; a zone, including Trieste, within this area is to be " Free Territory," its integrity and independence to be assured by the Security Council of the United Nations; and recommendations for a provisional government for this territory and the formation of a permanent statute are to be made to the 21-nation Peace Conference convened at Paris for July 29, 1946.

Photo, Keystone. Map by courtesy of The Daily Telegraph

Bikini Atom Bomb and the Future

By FRANCIS McMURTRIE

O N July 1, 1946 (Pacific time), an atom bomb was exploded in the air immediately above a collection of battleships, aircraft carriers, cruisers, destroyers, submarines and auxiliary warships in the lagoon of Bikini atoll. Publication of the news was the cue for a certain type of enthusiast, found in every country, to interpret the event in whatever fashion best agreed with his particular theory of the future trend of warfare. Some were eager to suggest that it foreshadowed the end of navies as we now know them. Others argued that so few ships had been sunk that the power of the atom bomb was obviously exaggerated.

Both, of course, are extreme views, which the known facts fail to support. Actually, far too few details have been released to enable a reasoned verdict to be given on such definite lines. Probably Admiral Sir John Cunningham, First Sea Lord of the Admiralty, was voicing the consensus of naval opinion in his advice to newspaper editors on July 2:

N AVAL experts of all countries are paying close attention to the effects of atomic bombs as demonstrated by the American experiments at Bikini (see facing page.) Already suggestions are being put forward for modifications in warship design necessitated by this new weapon, of which the reactions are not yet fully known.

the bomb dropped on Nagasaki than to its predecessor that descended on Hiroshima. Some time ago President Truman compared its power to that of 20,000 tons of T.N.T., while the U.S. Army Air Force admits that no aircraft smaller than a B-29 Super-Fortress was capable of carrying the load. From this it has been deduced that its weight may be in the region of four tons, though this is admittedly guesswork. Certainly its size and shape must be unusual. According to the Japanese, previous atom bombs were dropped

refit in a Navy dockyard, others rather less ; indeed, the damage to the old battleship Pennsylvania was within the scope of the floating repair ships' facilities.

It was emphasized that the first bomb was intended mainly as a test against superstructure and deck equipment.

Plans have been made for a second atom bomb to be dropped so as to explode below the surface of the sea at a limited depth, variously reported as from 18 to 50 feet. The maximum depth of the Bikini lagoon is 180 feet. Date of this test will depend upon the weather, as a day suitable for photography must be chosen. The target ships will be arranged as in the first test, except that the submarines will be submerged instead of remaining on the surface. A third test, in which a bomb will be set to explode in very deep water, is to be made by the American naval authorities in the spring of 1947.

Admiral Pierre Barjot, of the French Navy, has some interesting observations to make on the second Bikini experiment in an article appearing in France Illustration. He regards the underwater explosion as much the more important test, since the pressure exerted against the underwater sections of the ships' hulls will be beyond anything hitherto recorded. He envisages an enormous column of water being thrown into the air, and speculates concerning the distance at which the effect of the submarine explosion may be felt.

Revolution in Ship Construction

In the case of the submarine earthquake in the Aleutian Islands on April 1, a tidal wave was thrown up with an estimated velocity of over 200 miles per hour. A secondary wave, starting at the rate of 90 miles an hour, reached as far as the coast of Chile, at the other end of the Pacific. Such convulsions of nature make the efforts of the man-made atom bomb appear a comparatively trivial affair.

It may be assumed that more ships will be sunk by the underwater explosion than the four or five which succumbed to the overhead one. Subsequently they will no doubt be refloated, and the damage studied in order that its effect on different parts of the structure may be fully appreciated. On the report of the experts who undertake this examination the system of construction of future warships will doubtless depend (see illustration). Final conclusions will necessarily be withheld until the issue of the deep-water explosion next year can be taken into consideration.

A DMIRAL BARJOT suggests that it may be found necessary to increase the thickness of the horizontal armour of large warships, with superstructure reduced to a minimum, as in a submarine. A streamlined conning tower or bridge structure protected by thick armour will be essential. Aircraft carriers may assume the profile of a tortoise, with hangars insulated against fire. Battleships and cruisers will need more than ever to augment their anti-aircraft armaments, for in the destruction of the attacking bomber lies the best form of defence against the atom bomb.

Whether or not the submarine will prove the type of warship best able to resist this form of attack must depend on the results of the further tests. It will almost certainly be necessary to add greatly to her hull strength.

That other war uses will in due course be found for the atom explosion can hardly be doubted. Atom shells and torpedoes may be dreams of the future, but already, in spite of the difficulties hinted at in the Press by Sir James Chadwick, experiments are being planned for atom-carrying rockets.

TO MEET THE THREAT OF ATOMIC WARFARE, this hypothetical anti-aircraft cruiser of French design is driven by denaturized uranium engines. Her watertight superstructure, modelled like a whale, is designed to withstand tidal and radio-active waves. Powerful radar-directed A.A. guns would be capable of destroying aerial weapons whether radio-controlled or rocket-propelled.

" I would sound a note of caution against drawing too hasty conclusions from the results of the Bikini experiments, which we hope will soon be published, before they have been confirmed and tested. Because an atom bomb—or if an atom bomb—has had great success against battleships anchored in a tropical lagoon for three or four months, and pinpointed to an exactitude of a few inches for the attacking bomber, do not let us think that it has solved the problem. If we were to try out a new rifle on an old cow tethered in the middle of a field, it does not necessarily follow that it was the right kind of bullet to use against a wounded tiger in a thick jungle. I should be frightfully averse to stalking a West African buffalo with only a humane killer, although that is an excellent thing for a tethered cow."

" I think the effect of which we are most conscious is that the advent of the atom bomb increases the necessity for the dispersion of bases and repair facilities and all supplies. That is the first lesson of Hiroshima. As regards its effect on ships, we have a considerable experience from anti-submarine work of how close to a ship you have to put a large explosion, when in deep water, in order to achieve the desired result. Atomic explosions are greater than anything before, but it may be—I do not say it will be—that the safest place in the next war will be on board a ship.

" You must remember that the atom bomb as we know it at present has still got to be carried to its target and dropped by an aircraft ; and in the problems of interception and attack of aircraft all three Services have attained a considerable degree of proficiency. I do not think that proficiency is likely to decrease—rather the reverse."

Outside a very limited circle, no one has a precise idea of the weight or explosive force of the atom bomb, though it has been stated officially that it bears a closer relationship to

with the aid of some form of parachute, probably for steadying purposes, as in the case of magnetic mines.

An important factor to be considered is the high cost of this novel weapon. In the case of those so far used it is calculated to have averaged about £5,000,000 each, taking into account the cost of preparatory work and other attendant expenses. Only a first-class Power could therefore be in a position to make use of the atom bomb under the conditions at present prevailing.

Full and exact information is lacking on such essential points as the distance of each ship from the centre of the explosion, and the nature and extent of the damage suffered. Whether in fact personnel engaged below or behind armour would have been put out of action by the bomb is by no means clear.

On July 4, Vice-Admiral W. H. P. Blandy, U.S.N., expressed the following views, based on the results of the first explosion at Bikini :

(a) The explosion of an atom bomb overhead at an elevation of 200 feet would destroy any vessel afloat.

(b) In every one of the heavily damaged ships in the recent test, the destructive power of the bomb was proved sufficient to kill almost every man in an exposed position had the ships been manned.

(c) Of the heavily damaged vessels (other than those that sank), every one could be repaired if needed. The small aircraft carrier Independence would need nine months for

The First Post-War Atom Bomb Explodes

AGAINST WARSHIPS moored in the Bikini atoll lagoon, in the Pacific, an experimental atom bomb was dropped on July 1, 1946. To test the effects against naval craft a fleet of captured Japanese and German and a number of redundant United States warships (1), "manned" by animals treated with anti radio-active ointments was disposed as shown in the official plan (2). The smoke from the explosion rose to some 35,000 feet (3). Many of the animals survived, including the tethered goat (4), which appeared to be quite unaffected by the ordeal.

Drawing by courtesy of The Illustrated London News

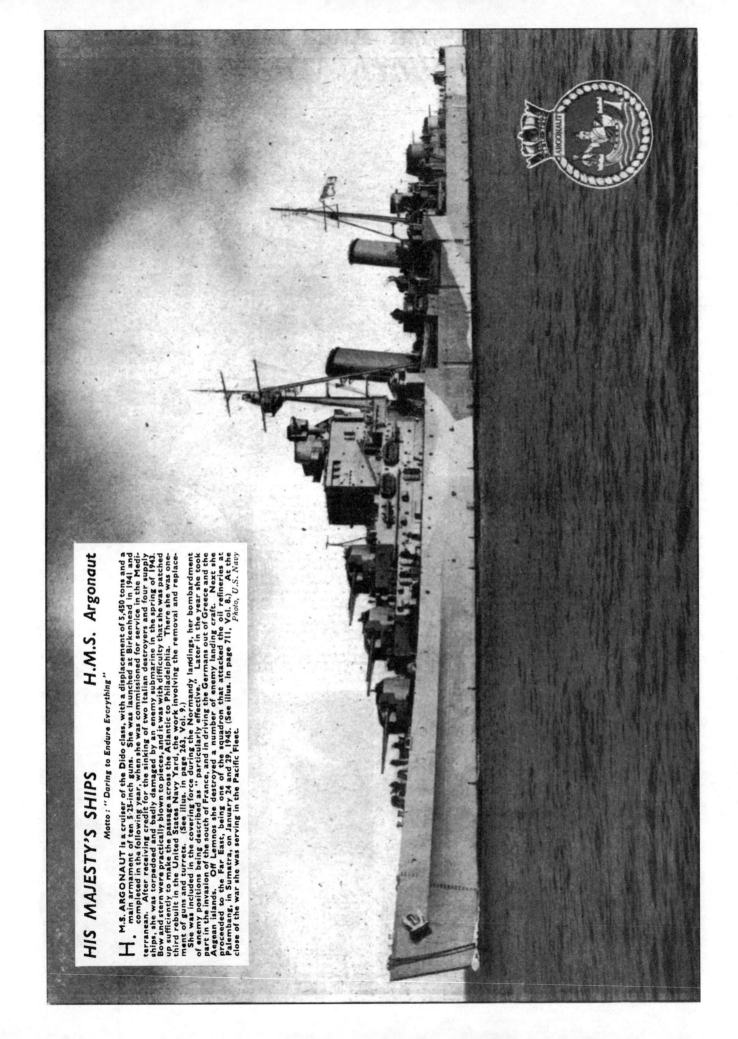

HIS MAJESTY'S SHIPS   H.M.S. Argonaut

Motto: "Daring to Endure Everything"

H.M.S. ARGONAUT is a cruiser of the Dido class, with a displacement of 5,450 tons and a main armament of ten 5·25-inch guns. She was launched at Birkenhead in 1941 and completed in the following year, when she was commissioned for service in the Mediterranean. After receiving credit for the sinking of two Italian destroyers and four supply ships, she was torpedoed and badly damaged by an enemy submarine in the spring of 1943. Bow and stern were practically blown to pieces, and it was with difficulty that she was patched up sufficiently to make the passage across the Atlantic to Philadelphia. There she was one-third rebuilt in the United States Navy Yard, the work involving the removal and replacement of guns and turrets. (See illus. in page 263, Vol. 9.)

She was included in the covering force during the Normandy landings, her bombardment of enemy positions being described as "particularly effective." Later in the year she took part in the invasion of the south of France, and in driving the Germans out of Greece and the Aegean islands. Off Lemnos she destroyed a number of enemy landing craft. Next she proceeded to the Far East, being one of the squadron that attacked the oil refineries at Palembang, in Sumatra, on January 24 and 29, 1945. (See illus. in page 711, Vol. 8.) At the close of the war she was serving in the Pacific Fleet.

Photo, U.S. Navy

The Black Watch

By Lieut.-Colonel
A. V. HOLT, D.S.O., O.B.E.

On the outbreak of war the Regiment consisted of six Battalions—two Regular (1st and 2nd) and four Territorial, to which was shortly added the 1st Battalion The Tyneside Scottish at Newcastle, formerly a duplicate battalion of the Durham Light Infantry. The 1st Battalion was stationed at Dover, the 2nd in Palestine, while the others were located within the Regimental recruiting area of Perthshire, Fife and Angus. After being inspected by H.M. The Queen, Colonel-in-Chief of the Regiment, the 1st Battalion embarked for France on October 5, 1939, with the 4th Division. Active operations were experienced during the period December 15-31, in the "ligne de contact" on the Saar front, when the unit was never in reserve and experienced extremely severe weather conditions.

A spell on the Belgian frontier then followed, until March 1940, when the Battalion joined the 51st (Highland) Division and in April was again on the British Brigade sector of the Saar; shortly afterwards the whole Division took up positions in that area, where much night fighting and skirmishes with advanced German units were encountered.

With the break-through of the Germans into the Low Countries, the Division was rushed across France to relieve the French on a long front opposing the enemy, who had already established two bridge-heads over the Somme, at St. Valery-sur-Somme and opposite Abbeville. By June 11 it had been necessary to retire to St. Valery-en-Caux,

THE record of the Black Watch began at Fontenoy in 1745. The Highlanders were to the fore in Egypt in 1800-1, and at Corunna, served through the Peninsular War, and were at Quatre Bras and Waterloo. They were in the Highland Brigade in the Crimea, and fought hard during the Indian Mutiny; later they served at Ashanti, and stormed the entrenchments at Tel-el-Kebir. During the First Great War many Battalions of the Regiment served, in addition to the two Regular Battalions.

When the position of the remaining Brigades became known, this Battalion was evacuated from Le Havre. The 6th Battalion had arrived in France with the same Division in January, but was transferred two months later to the 4th Division in place of the 1st Battalion. It distinguished itself in severe fighting in Belgium against much superior forces, particularly on the Comines Canal, and was eventually embarked at Dunkirk.

On May 20, the 1st Battalion The Tyneside Scottish was the

first British unit to take the shock of the German advance through the Ardennes— meeting, unsupported by any other arm, the attack of an armoured and a motorized division. This sacrifice (which, after five hours' fighting, resulted in twenty per cent of those engaged giving up their lives and the remainder spending

five years in captivity) had its unseen reward in appreciably delaying the enemy advance on Calais and beyond. From the collapse of the armies in the West, the Regiment was called upon to endure many severe tests in Africa and the Mediterranean: Italy had declared war on June 10, 1940, and the 2nd Battalion The Black Watch was detailed to provide a fighting rearguard in the evacuation of British Somaliland. In this action one Company especially distinguished itself by holding up the advance on Berbera against overwhelming odds. In 1941 the Battalion moved to Crete, and on May 21 faced the onslaught of hordes of fanatical parachutists dropped on the airfield at Heraklion by an enemy who had complete mastery of the air. Despite the enormous odds the Battalion held fast until May 28, when orders were received for a general withdrawal to the south coast, where the troops, after an arduous night's march, were taken off by the Royal Navy. During that time not one German had succeeded in landing within the airfield perimeter, and certainly hundreds had been killed in their attempts to do so.

After several weeks in Egypt the Battalion took part in the occupation of Syria and in October 1941 sailed for the beleaguered port of Tobruk. After a month spent in raids and patrols to obtain information about the enemy strongpoints, orders were given on November 20 to break out at dawn the next morning in an attempt to join up with the 8th Army. With pipes playing, the advance was made through withering machine-gun fire and the objectives captured. Then for three weeks the position on the "Corridor" was held until the main forces fought their way through. Heavy casualties had been sustained and special mention of the men's courage and discipline was made.

The Highlanders at El Alamein

Though the original 1st Battalion had met such a grievous fate at St. Valery no time had been lost in forming a new Battalion, and after two years of the most intensive training in the North of Scotland it sailed for the Middle East in the summer of 1942 with the

where the main part of the Division, including the entire 1st Battalion The Black Watch, with no ammunition or food and no prospect of evacuation, was obliged to lay down its arms the following day.

Thus a large proportion of the Regiment's Regular officers and other ranks went into eclipse . . . true to Highland tradition they and their comrades in the Division remained to the last with the remnants of our French Allies, although it would have been possible to have withdrawn earlier and embark at Le Havre. That this immense sacrifice had not been in vain may be judged from the fact that it had drawn on to St. Valery the German IV Corps of four Divisions, a Panzer and a Motor Division, in all six Divisions, and thereby diverted this force from harassing the withdrawal of other British troops from Le Havre and Cherbourg.

Meanwhile, the 4th Battalion, also in the 51st (H) Division, had been detailed, on June 9, as part of "Ark Force," a Brigade force undertaking the defence of Le Havre.

MEN OF THE 1st BATTALION THE BLACK WATCH are seen, in these hitherto unpublished photographs, outside their H.Q. at Henin-Lietard (left) shortly after arriving in France in October 1939, and along the river Bresle (above) June 1940. After this action the Battalion was forced to surrender at St. Valery-en-Caux, June 12. See also illus. page 248. PAGE 235 *Photos, British Official*

BACK FROM DUNKIRK, men of the 6th Battalion training in the Isle of Wight, August 1940, were equipped with bicycles (as in above unpublished photograph) ready for quick dispatch to threatened areas had the German invasion materialized. " Grundy," bull-terrier mascot of the Regiment, in Gibraltar in November 1941, stands guard over a defence post in the Rock. (left).
Photo, British Official

reconstituted 51st Division, which also included two other Black Watch Battalions, the 5th and 7th. Few of the men had been in action, but all were imbued both from the regimental and divisional point of view with a strong sense of duty to avenge their comrades in the Stalags of Germany and Poland.

Their opportunity came on the night of October 23, when under bright moonlight and supported by an unprecedented artillery barrage the Battalions went into action at El Alamein, their pipers proudly leading the advance. The epic success of this battle was but the prelude to the series of victories by which the 8th Army swept across North Africa to Tunisia, where the surrender of all Axis forces in Africa took place the following May : such battles are household words in this country and in each one the Black Watch troops displayed those qualities of discipline, fighting efficiency and sacrifice for which

this Regiment has been celebrated during the last two centuries.

The principal engagements were Mersa Brega, Wadi Zem-zem, Homs, Tripoli, Mareth Line, Gabès, Wadi Akarit and Enfidaville. The successful operations of the Regiment in this theatre of war ended with the invasion of Sicily, and towards the end of 1943 the Division returned to England.

In March 1943 the 6th Battalion landed in North Africa with the 4th Division to join Lt.-Gen. Anderson's 1st Army, and were soon engaged in a number of fierce mountain battles, culminating in the destruction of the main German armies at Mejez-el-Bab and the pursuit to Cape Bon. In April 1944 it took part in the battle for Cassino, and then commenced the protracted task of pushing the enemy right out of Italy. As the Battalion moved northwards, heavy rearguard opposition was encountered in many parts and, as the country was becoming more mountainous, the problems of supply and evacuation of casualties were extremely difficult ones. After the Germans had been pushed back beyond Florence, the Battalion was pulled out for a rest. At about this time it provided a guard of honour for H.M. The King.

With Wingate's Chindits in Burma

While the victors of the North African campaign were sailing home hoping to spend Christmas with their families, the 2nd Battalion, by this time in India, was undergoing a five-months' period of jungle training as part of the late Major-General Wingate's Chindits. Much of the training was entirely new—for example, making the men animal-conscious (it being necessary to take a large number of mules), teaching the men to locate targets in jungle growth, and so on. In March 1944 the Battalion moved to an assembly area in Assam and were then flown in Dakotas hundreds of miles behind the Japanese lines.

Here for the next twenty weeks the troops experienced the most severe conditions of fighting, climate, and terrain ; much of the country was so hilly and so thickly covered in jungle that an advance of two miles in eight hours was often considered good progress. Two major engagements were fought and many profitable ambushes carried out, but fortunately casualties were comparatively light. At the end of this part of the campaign, the Battalion was flown out to a rest camp in India.

No fewer than four Black Watch Battalions embarked for Normandy with 21st Army Group—the 1st, 5th and 7th, still with 51st (H) Division, and the 1st Battalion The Tyneside Scottish. The last-mentioned Battalion was soon engaged in the severest fighting, and on July 1 inflicted very heavy casualties on the enemy. Unfortunately it was found necessary several weeks later to split up this fine unit among other Scottish Battalions.

THE first task of the 51st Division was to hold the bridge-head immediately east of the Orne, in conjunction with the 6th Airborne Division. Soon after, when the Americans overran the Cherbourg peninsula, the whole Division moved to near Bourgebus, to come under the 1st Canadian Army for operations south of Caen, to link up with the Americans and the British 2nd Army.

Novel tactics were employed, involving the carrying of the infantry in dismantled Priests

MUSICAL PRELUDE to the invasion of Sicily : a Black Watch piper played while waiting to embark, in North Africa, in July 1943.

SHARING POLICE DUTIES in Sicily was one of the tasks of the Black Watch. This corporal accompanied a civilian policeman in Noto.

Pride of the Kilt in North African Deserts

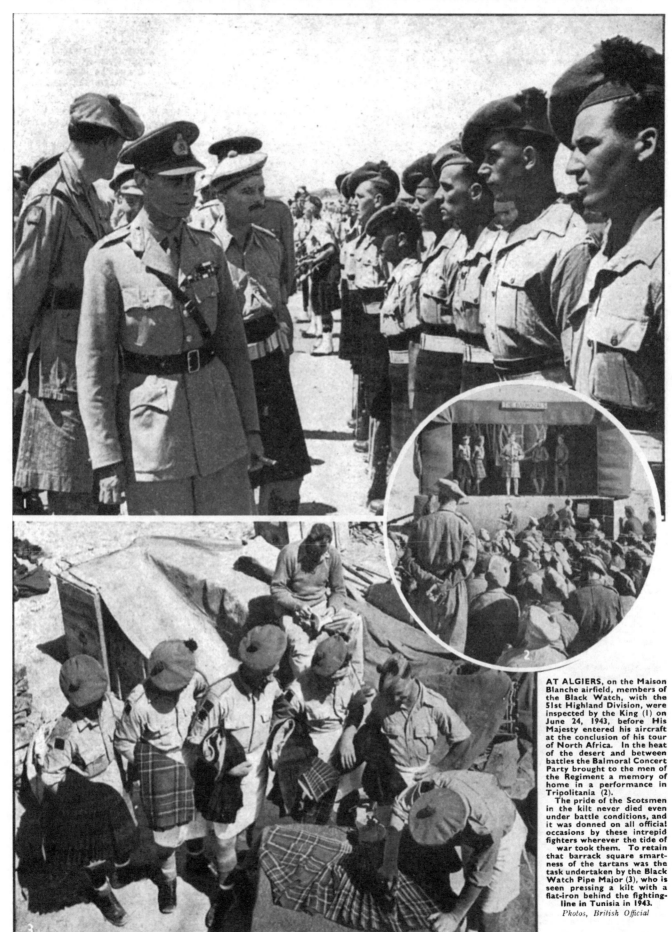

AT ALGIERS, on the Maison Blanche airfield, members of the Black Watch, with the 51st Highland Division, were inspected by the King (1) on June 24, 1943, before His Majesty entered his aircraft at the conclusion of his tour of North Africa. In the heat of the desert and between battles the Balmoral Concert Party brought to the men of the Regiment a memory of home in a performance in Tripolitania (2).

The pride of the Scotsmen in the kilt never died even under battle conditions, and it was donned on all official occasions by these intrepid fighters wherever the tide of war took them. To retain that barrack square smartness of the tartans was the task undertaken by the Black Watch Pipe Major (3), who is seen pressing a kilt with a flat-iron behind the fighting-line in Tunisia in 1943.

Photos, British Official

MOVING UP FOR THE BREAK-THROUGH south of Caen, August 7-8, 1944, troops of the 1st Battalion The Black Watch, with the 51st Division, are seen on the outskirts of Cormelles. Transported in specially adapted carriers, they debussed within a few yards of the enemy's forward positions to play a major part in the Battle of France. *Photo, British Official*

ABOUT TO ENJOY A RESPITE FROM THE LINE, men of the 7th Battalion in this hitherto unpublished photograph are entering billets at Hotton, Belgium, in January 1945. With the 51st Division, as the reserve of the American armies, the Battalion had recently joined up with the Americans across the enemy salient in the Ardennes. *Photo, British Official*

IN THE CEMETERY AT ST. VALERY-EN-CAUX, December 12, 1944, Lieut.-Col. Bradford, D.S.O., M.B.E., M.C., of the 5th Battalion (left), accompanied by the mayor, paid tribute to those of his Regiment and the 51st Division killed in the town in June 1940. St. Valery was liberated by the 51st Division in September 1944. See also page 248. PAGE 238 *Photo, British Official*

and white scout cars, and the attack commenced on the night of August 7-8. For the next fifteen days, in its advance from Tilly to Lisieux, the Division, fighting continuously in its most intensive period of operations up to that time, played a major part in the Battle of France. Over 1,600 prisoners of war were taken, and the troops were congratulated on their fine work by the Canadian Army Commander.

At the end of August the Division crossed the Seine at Rouen and was directed upon St. Valery. To all ranks, the entry into St. Valery was a source of deep pride, particularly to several senior officers who had been captured there in 1940 and had escaped while en route for Germany. The graves of many Black Watch men were found, and all had been well cared-for by the French; at the entrance to the cemetery at St. Pierre-le-Viger there was a notice, "Honour to The Black Watch who fought here with courage in 1940." To mark this proud day the massed pipes and drums—nearly 200 men—played "Retreat" on the site of the old Division's Headquarters in 1940 at Cailleville.

After the occupation of Le Havre which was taken with very light casualties, 154th Brigade, containing the 1st and 7th Battalions, was directed to Dunkirk to contain an enemy force estimated at about 10,000. During this investment one of the rare truces was arranged, for 36 hours, to permit the evacuation of 19,000 civilians. On October 8 this Brigade rejoined the Division in Holland; on the anniversary of Alamein a full-scale attack was launched to clear the Germans from Southern Holland northwards as far as the River Maas. So successful were the operations that by November 7 the Division, by its thrust from Schijndel to Gertrudenburg, had cleared some 300 square miles. Sincere congratulations on this achievement were received from the commander of the 2nd Army. By December the Division had reached a position north of Nijmegen.

They Led the Mass Rhine Crossing

With Rundstedt's Ardennes offensive, the Division became the reserve of the American Armies, and on January 8 took part in the drive across the enemy salient to link up with our Allies pushing north through Bastogne. In this operation the 1st Black Watch had the satisfaction of clearing the important road centre of Goch in appalling weather conditions. By February 8 the task of clearing the enemy between the Maas and the Rhine, south of Nijmegen and down to Wesel, had begun; and before these tasks had been completed nineteen days of the most strenuous fighting were experienced, both the 1st and 7th Battalions The Black Watch taking part in five major attacks, in addition to a number of minor clashes.

To the famous 51st Division was given the honour of being the first Division to make the assault crossing of the Rhine, and at 21.00 hours on March 23 the 5th and 7th Battalions led the attack, the main objectives being Rees and Esserden, which were captured the next day after grim and exhausting combat. The 1st Battalion also met stiff opposition in following through the initial attack. The crossing of this historic river, however, witnessed the death of the Divisional Commander, Maj-Gen. T. G. Rennie, C.B., D.S.O., a Black Watch officer who had served with great distinction and was extremely popular with all ranks.

Active operations concluded on May 3 with the news of the German capitulation, and the occasion was marked by an impressive march past on May 12 before the Corps Commander, in which a composite guard of honour from the three Black Watch Battalions took part. Thus ended six historic years in which all Battalions added new lustre to the traditions of this Royal Highland Regiment.

Gallant Malta Rebuilds her Shattered Streets

Photo, Illustrated

With the same indomitable courage which they displayed throughout the siege of their island, from June 1940 to November 1942, Malta's erstwhile defenders are now facing the problem of repairing the ravages of war. The task of rebuilding the bomb-shattered towns, of which this corner in Valetta is but a small part, is already under way. Towards Malta's reconstruction the British Colonial Secretary on July 9, 1946, announced the allocation of a further grant of £20,000,000 from United Kingdom funds to supplement the free gift of £10,000,000 made in 1942.

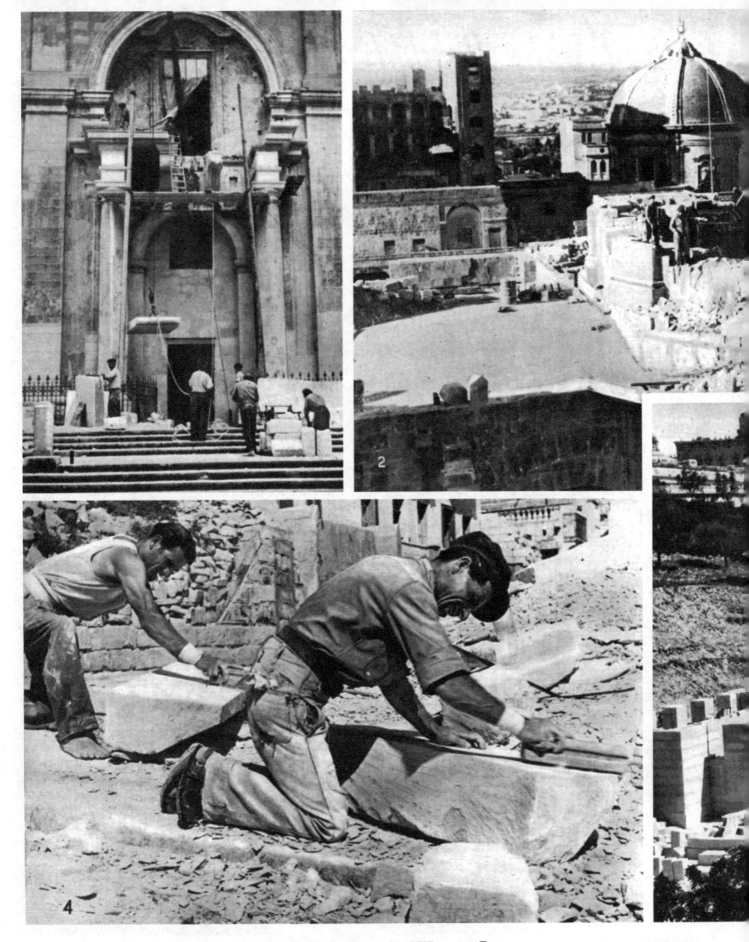

Healing Malta's Architectural Wounds—

Huge blocks of stone from the island's quarries are hoisted by primitive means to the portico of the famous Cathedral of
St. John of Jerusalem (1) at Valetta.   In the suburbs of the capital work is in progress on the cupola of St. Publius' church
(2), almost completely destroyed by a stick of bombs.   The dome seen in this photograph is that of the Sarria, a church of
the Maltese Order, built in 1678 ; immediately to its right is the Wesleyan Church.

Topic

—With Stone from Her Ancient Quarries

In a quarry at Luca (3), slabs of rock for reconstruction are hewn out of the solid mass by hand. But not all is newly hewn, much of the rubble from the ruins being planed down for re-use (4). The King George V Hospital at Valetta, destroyed in 1942, is being rebuilt (5) largely from funds subscribed by the Red Cross, especially the Scottish branch. The new building will incorporate a stone from London's bomb-damaged House of Commons.

R.A.S.C. Dumps Jap Ammunition in the Pacific

Photos, British Offi.

Destroying 40,000 tons of Japanese ammunition, found at Singapore, was a task recently allotted to 56 Water Transport Unit, R.A.S.C. Utilizing Japanese P.O.W. labour, the ammunition was loaded on DUKWs (1) by means of a gravity conveyor band. The dangerous cargo was then ferried (2) out to a L.C.T., into which it was stacked (3). Over deep waters of the Pacific the L.C.T. discharged the boxes of ammunition (4). Captain Richards, R.A.S.C. (5), directed operations.

FIRST BATTLES OF THE WEST AFRICANS

By HARLEY V. USILL

As a complete contrast to the Mediterranean, with its history of civilizations dating back to the pre-Christian era, we will return to West Africa (see pages 104 and 147). Before dealing with the military feats of its famous regiments, however, it may be helpful to background the environment from which they were recruited.

British West Africa is not one but four territories—the Gambia, Sierra Leone, the Gold Coast and Nigeria. From the Gambia to Nigeria is as far as from London to Gibraltar, and the four territories have a total area of 500,000 square miles. Nigeria, with the Mandated Cameroons, is the largest with 372,000 square miles ; it is bigger than any European country except Russia, and nearly four times as big as the United Kingdom. Twenty-six million people live in the four territories, over 20 million, of whom are in Nigeria. The great majority are Negroes and they speak about forty different principal languages. Of the 26 million, Christians number between one and two millions, and Moslems about eight millions. The rest are usually described as " pagans."

Nucleus of the Frontier Force

In British West Africa there is a bewildering complexity of race, tribe, tongue, religion, costume, custom, occupation and outlook. There is a highly sophisticated minority of intellectuals, many of whom have received the best education which Great Britain or America can give. There is the vast majority whose emergence from the days when each tribe lived for itself alone, and warred spasmodically with its neighbours, and when slaveraiding was the favourite commercial occupation and human sacrifice a common religious practice, is still in the process of achievement under our colonial administration.

As early as 400 years B.C. Hanno, the Carthaginian navigator, sailed along the coast of West Africa, but it was not until the Portuguese followed suit some 500 years ago that Europe began to receive accounts of some of the mysteries of the then unknown continent. The opening up of the New World led to an insatiable demand for cheap labour to work on the plantations, and the big profits in the handling of " black ivory " attracted competitors to the Portuguese, including merchant adventurers of England and Denmark. This slave trade prospered for 150 years, until, in fact, the humanitarian movement in Britain became strong enough to demand its abolition. At the Berlin Conference of 1884 the general basis of what came to be known as the " Partition of Africa " was laid down, the result of which was the acknowledgement of the claims of Britain to the four territories of British West Africa. By 1900 the frontiers had become stabilized, and the British have had only a matter of about fifty years in which to gain the loyalty and co-operation of these 26 million people.

The real nucleus of the force named the West African Frontier Force came into existence in Nigeria, where Lord Lugard was sent in 1897 to raise a local military force. Its function was to maintain internal security among the then warring tribes, and to defend the frontiers of British West African dependencies. With these ends in view, trained men and arms were sent from Nigeria to the Gold Coast and became the beginnings of the Gold Coast Regiment. Later a battalion was assembled for similar purposes in Sierra Leone and, later again, a company was formed in the Gambia. No one then thought that these small forces would develop into great fighting machines and that these fighting machines would play a vital part

REPRESENTATIVES of the twenty-six million inhabitants of the four territories of British West Africa, men of the Nigeria Regiment and the Gold Coast Regiment travelled across their continent in 1940 to play a magnificent part in the rolling-up of Mussolini's East African Empire.

11th AFRICAN DIV.   12th AFRICAN DIV.

in the war for survival in the next century. In 1901 the name West African Frontier Force came into being, the " Royal " being bestowed in 1928. By furthering the establishment of law and order, this force has greatly assisted the progress of civilization.

In view of the uncertainty regarding the attitude of Italy prior to the Second Great War it was appreciated that East Africa might become the object of enemy attack. Therefore, in 1937 and 1938 the African Colonial Forces were reorganized to provide the greatest measure of defence for the African Dependencies in general, and in particular to permit as large a force as practicable being instantly available for the defence of East Africa, for which latter purpose a proportion of the West African troops would be transferred. In the event, however, it was not until May 1940 that six West African battalions, three from Nigeria and three from the Gold Coast, amounting to over 10,000 troops, left for East Africa.

In a description of the Nigeria Regiment, which is typical of the rest, the recruits are portrayed as follows : " . . . they came from the forests and swamps of the Delta and the South ; artisans from the Yorubas ; pioneers from the Ibos ; transport drivers from everywhere : they came from the wide plains of Hausaland, from the granite hills of the Plateau, from the mountains of the Cameroons, from the blistered deserts of Bornu and Chad. Educated and illiterate, they came freely of their own wills to ensure that freedom shall not die from the world."

West Africans in East Africa

The spectacular events in the later stages of the War have largely erased from our minds those stirring events of 1940 and 1941, when the rolling-up of Mussolini's *ersatz* empire was laying the foundation for final victory. By the time that the 1st West African Brigade from Nigeria and the 2nd West African Brigade from the Gold Coast had arrived in East Africa, the Italians had invaded British Somaliland, and the British had been compelled to withdraw. Plans for the Abyssinian campaign then took shape, and consisted of a gigantic pincer movement ; the northern arm based on the Sudan under General Sir William Platt, the southern arm based on Kenya under General Sir Alan Cunningham. Simultaneously with the closing of the pincer, Emperor Haile Selassie was to enter Abyssinia across the Sudan frontier.

The Italians had reached the border of Kenya, and the first stage of the counter-offensive began when on December 16, 1940, Gold Coast troops with the South Africans made a most successful raid on the frontier post of El Wak, near the Kenya-Italian Somaliland border. By now the strength of the East and West Africans had been brought up to two divisions—the 11th and

12th African Divisions, and these were concerned solely with the southern operations.

General Cunningham arrived in Kenya on November 1, 1940, and on April 5, 1941, Addis Ababa was entered. The story of that 2,000 miles advance is the story of the southern of the two attacks. The drive began with an advance by both African Divisions to the Juba, which they reached in the middle of February 1941. After the Juba had been forced, the African troops split, the 12th Division advancing up the Juba and into the southern part of Abyssinia, while the 11th Division, consisting now of one East African, one West African and one South African Brigade, advanced along the coast to Mogadishu, which was reached on February 25. They then turned north, and at an astonishing pace reached Jijigga on March 17, when they were 744 miles from the starting point. Three weeks later the Brigade was in Addis Ababa itself.

The Nigerian troops led the great advance of over 1,000 miles in thirty days, from the Juba River to Harar, capturing the city of Mogadishu on the way. Supported by South African gunners they fought the decisive battle of the Marda Pass. Later the Brigade distinguished itself in the battles of the Rivers Omo and Didessa. General Cunningham paid this tribute to their work :

" . . . The final 65 miles into Harar entailed an advance through the most difficult country in face of opposition from three strong positions, yet the distance was covered in three and a half days. The Nigerian soldier, unaccustomed to cold and damp, fought his way from the hot and dusty bush to the wet and cold highlands of Abyssinia, where he maintained his cheerfulness and courage in spite of strange conditions and the strenuous operations made necessary by the terrain."

The Gold Coast Brigade had an equally impressive record. In addition to its brilliant raid at El Wak, it was among the first of the troops to enter Italian Somaliland. Against heavy odds it fought a series of successful engagements on the Juba River, thus paving the way for the Nigerian Brigade's spectacular advance. Later, by their persistent assaults on the Italians at Wadara, they gained a victory that had a decisive effect on the campaign in southern Abyssinia. Their commander, Major-General Godwin Austen, paid this magnificent tribute to the men of the Gold Coast : " In every situation they have distinguished themselves. Their spirit, their efficiency, their burning patriotism, and their high courage are admired and envied by all." Great praise must also be given to the British officers and senior N.C.O.s whose courage and leadership inspired all the troops under their command.

Work of African Pioneer Corps

So ended General Cunningham's campaign in which over 30 Italian generals and an army of 170,000 men had been put out of action by a force not one-third as numerous. The task in East Africa having been completed, and Vichy France having become a potential menace to the security of West Africa, the West African troops returned home. They did not know then that they would be called upon to wage another campaign in more distant lands, but this will form the subject of another story.

Mention must be made of the work of the West African Pioneers in the Middle East who, by May 1945, had reached a figure of over 16,000. The first West African companies arrived in April 1943, and they helped with the construction of base installations and aerodromes. As a reward for their extremely valuable work the original title of African Auxiliary Pioneer Corps was changed to African Pioneer Corps.

Why Bread Rationing Came to Our Country

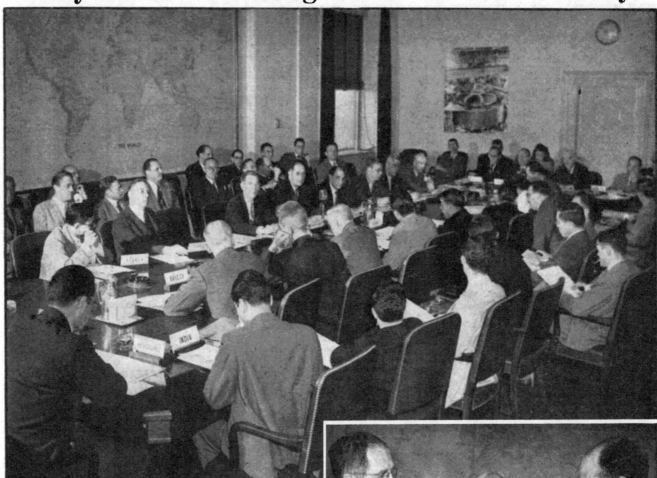

Dᴇᴛᴇʀɪᴏʀᴀᴛɪᴏɴ IN THE WORLD FOOD SITUATION, and need to control the distribution of many foods with a view to preventing widespread suffering and starvation, led the Food and Agricultural Organization of the United Nations to convene a special meeting in Washington on May 20, 1946. Delegates of 17 governments and five international organizations attended, and recommendations regarding the formation of an International Emergency Food Council (to replace the Combined Food Board) were submitted to the governments concerned. On June 20, representatives of 19 countries approved the establishment of this Council, which held its inaugural session in Washington the same day, as seen above. A central committee of nine was elected, consisting of the three Combined Food Board countries (Britain, U.S.A. and Canada) and Australia, India, China, Argentina, France and Denmark. Attending the meeting were (l. to r. at right) Mr. Clinton P. Anderson (U.S. Secretary of Agriculture), Sir John Boyd Orr, M.P. (for U.N. Food and Agriculture Organization), and Mr. John Strachey, M.P. (British Minister of Food).

BEGINNING ON JULY 21, 1946, rationing of bread, flour, and flour confectionery in Britain was announced by the Minister of Food in the House of Commons on June 27. Mr. Strachey stated that the Government had reached this decision because they were convinced that to fail to ration bread and flour would be to take an unjustifiable risk with the basic foodstuff of the British people. In the subsequent Parliamentary debates, Mr. Strachey disclosed that there was no great reserve store of wheat lying idle in the country; there was only the stock going through the "pipe-line" from ships to shops. It was estimated that at the end of August there would be some eight weeks' supply of bread and flour in hand—sufficient to satisfy with certainty the bread supply of the country if a system of rationing were introduced, but not without it. Rationing enabled the authorities to work with a considerably smaller amount in the pipe-line. The basic adult ration is 9 oz. a day, with graduated amounts for children and extra allowances for manual workers; the special bread card for the latter is shown (left). The bread unit coupons are interchangeable with ordinary "points" coupons to meet individual differences in the way of consumption

Photos, Associated Press, P.A.-Reuter

Britain's Food: Production of Our Precious Tea

FROM A FLOWERING EVERGREEN PLANT, Thea Sinensis, which flourishes in the moist, warm climates of India, Ceylon, the Netherlands East Indies and China, comes our tea ration. Pre-war, 450 million pounds of this commodity came into Britain from India and Ceylon, representing an annual consumption of nearly ten pounds per head—or 2,000 cups. Even now we are consuming tea at the rate of 89 per cent of pre-war consumption, stated the Minister of Food on July 17, 1946, and world production is not sufficiently recovered to justify abandoning rationing. This drawing, by our artist Haworth, has been compiled with the assistance of the Tea Centre, opened in London specifically to help people to make the most of their ration.

Stages in the growth of tea include the preparation of jungle ground (1). Seedlings, when strong enough, are transplanted, 2,000 to 4,000 per acre. Under natural conditions they would grow to a height of twenty feet, so heavy pruning is required to promote a maximum of leafy shoots. The young shoots are plucked by skilled women (2) about every ten days during the "flushing season," only

the terminal bud and top two leaves being taken. About 30,000 shoots a day are thus gathered, representing the equivalent of ten pounds of manufactured tea.

Tea contains tannin, caffein and an aromatic oil, and to make these soluble in water the picked leaves are processed at the factory. Spread on racks, the leaves are first withered (3), hot air passing through, evaporating moisture and concentrating the oil. Next, they are rolled (4) to break open the cells and release the natural juices, this being followed by oxidization (5), which preserves the juices on the leaf-surface and secures a coppery colour and pungent flavour. To check this at the required pitch, leaves are dried or fired (6) on a travelling belt which passes through increasing temperatures, the colour changing to the familiar black. Finally the tea is sifted (7) and graded. Weighed and packed into wooden chests (8) it is then transported by bullock-drawn carts or lorries to the docks (9), where it is loaded from barges on to a ship. Native workers are housed on the tea garden (10).

PAGE 245

D.E.M.S. Commemorated in H.M.S. President

ON THE MAIN DECK of H.M.S. President, the plaque (seen on right) is embossed with the D.E.M.S., gun-layer's badge, the figures 1939-1946, and bears the inscription "H.M.S. President and H.M.S. Chrysanthemum, Thames Area Headquarters. In Honour of Personnel of the Royal Navy who sailed from the area in Defensively Equipped Merchant Ships." Admiral Sir Martin Dunbar - Nasmith, V.C., who conducted the ceremony, stands to the right. During the war about 70,000 D.E.M.S. personnel underwent training aboard the two ships President and Chrysanthemum.

GOING ABOARD H.M.S. President, before the commemorative ceremony on June 28, 1946, Admiral Sir Martin Dunbar - Nasmith inspected the Guard of Honour drawn up on the landing stage. Forming it were ten D.E.M.S. ratings of the sixteen who, with one officer, were chosen from H.M.S. Chrysanthemum to represent the D.E.M.S. Section of the Royal Navy in London's Victory Parade on June 8, 1946.

Photos, P.A.-Reuter

PAGE 246

1939   1946

H·M·S PRESIDENT AND H·M·S CHRYSANTHEMUM THAMES AREA HEADQUARTERS

IN HONOUR OF PERSONNEL OF THE ROYAL NAVY WHO SAILED FROM THE AREA IN DEFENSIVELY EQUIPPED MERCHANT SHIPS

Q

DEMS

AS A TRIBUTE to the wartime record of the training and depot ships H.M.S. President and H.M.S. Chrysanthemum, moored off Victoria Embankment, London, a plaque was unveiled in the President on June 28, 1946, by Admiral Sir Martin Dunbar-Nasmith, V.C., K.C.B., late Flag Officer-in - Charge, London. Dedicated to the naval ratings who sailed from this area in Defensively Equipped Merchant Ships, the unveiling revealed the impressive record of the D.E.M.S. personnel as a whole : 27,680 officers and ratings passed gunnery and defensive equipment courses, the latter qualifying for the badge (inset). D.E.M.S. personnel, an integral part of the Royal Navy, ranged in numbers from two in the smallest to 100 in the largest transports. They fought off aircraft, submarine, mine and surface attacks, to carry supplies to Services and civilians and were present at every Allied landing.

Their record, analysed in part in the Naval Estimates 1944, and quoted by the First Lord of the Admiralty, Mr. A. V. Alexander, stated : " D.E.M.S. ratings and their defensive equipment saved not less than 100 independently routed ships a year, apart from those which were saved by their D.E.M.S. in convoy." This represented the saving of some 1,250,000 tons of shipping per year, but the sacrifices were heavy, 2,713 D.E.M.S. being killed or missing ; 841 earned awards, including 263 D.S.M.s, 110 B.E.M.s, 21 Lloyd's Medals for gallantry at sea, and one George Medal.

The Roll of Honour
NCO's & MEN
1939—1946

L/Sgt. R. BOYNTON
Coldstream Guards.
Action: Normandy. 1.7.44.
Age 33. (Hull)

Readers of THE WAR ILLUSTRATED who wish to submit photographs for inclusion in our Roll of Honour must fill in the coupon which appeared in No. 230. No portraits can be considered that are not accompanied by this coupon

L/Cpl. B. BUSHEN
R.E.M.E.
Died of wounds 10.8.44.
Age 21. (London)

Pte. W. CARTWRIGHT
2/5 Queen's Royal Regt.
Action: Italy 9.9.44.
Age 20. (Stafford)

Sgt. G. CHALLINOR
R.A.F.V.R.
Died of wounds. 5.11.44.
Age 22. (Pontesbury)

L/Cpl. L. H. CHUBB
6th Airborne Division.
Action: Normandy. 7.6.44.
Age 29. (Barking)

Gdsm. L. DAVIES
Grenadier Guards.
Action: Tunisia. 17.3.43.
Age 23. (Harrow)

Gnr. W. J. R. DUDLEY
534/191 Field Regt. R.A.
Action: France. 1.9.44.
Age 20. (Cheadle)

F/Sgt. F. H. ERDWIN
Bomber Command R.A.F.
Action: Eira. 16.4.41.
Age 19. (London)

Pte. H. N. GRIFFITHS
2/5 Leicestershire Regt.
Action: Italy. 12.10.43.
Age 26. (Walsall)

W. G. HAMBLIN
L/Stkr. H.M.S. Dunedin.
Action: Atlantic. 25.11.41.
Age 32. (Reading)

Pte. J. V. HAWKES
1st Middlesex Regt.
Died of wounds. 13.10.44.
Age 24. (Kentish Town)

Gnr. H. L. HIGLETT
70th Field Regt. R.A.
Action: Salerno. 23.9.43.
Age 31. (Hounslow)

Pte. W. C. HILL
1st Green Howards.
Action: Italy. 31.5.44.
Age 22. (Lanchester)

Sgt. A/G E. HOBBS
Royal Air Force.
Action: Norway. 21.12.44.
Age 22. (East Dulwich)

A/B J. T. HOWELL
H.M.S. Anking.
Action: Far East. 4.3.42.
Age 19. (Putney)

A/B I. E. JONES
H.M.S. Kite.
Convoy to Russia. 21.8.44.
Age 20. (Port Talbot)

Flt./Sgt. J. LIDDLE
R.A.F.V.R.
Middle East. 3.6.43.
Age 25. (Newcastle/Tyne)

Pte. R. MacPHERSON
4th Cameron Hdrs.
Action: Abbeville. 4.6.40.
Age 21. (Inverness)

Cpl. H. T. MELHUISH
Royal Engineers.
Action: Anzio. 10.2.44.
Age 28. (Birmingham)

Sgt. L. OXLEY
226 Sqn. R.A.F.
Over Germany. 27.7.42.
Age 21. (Ditton Priors)

Rfm. D. R. PLUMB
2nd Cameronians,
Action: Sicily. 1.8.43.
Age 21. (Wellingborough)

W/O C. G. POLKEY
184 Sqn. R.A.F.
Action: France. 25.5.44.
Age 22. (Warsop)

Sgt. G. J. POWELL
R.A.F.V.R.
Over Essen. 5.3.43.
Age 19. (Abergavenny)

Sgt. T. PRICE
35 Sqn. R.A.F.
Over Essen. 25.7.43.
Age 21. (Kimberley)

S/Sgt. G. A. L. REEVES
Glider Pilot Regt.
Action: Sicily. 9.7.43.
Age 29. (Acton Green)

L/Cpl. R. REILLY
Somerset Light Infantry.
Action: Caen. 17.8.44.
Age 30. (London)

Gnr. F. RICHARDS
Royal Navy.
Action: at sea. 12.1.42.
Age 21. (Swansea)

Flt./Sgt. E. B. RILEY
Pathfinder Force, R.A.F.
Action: France. 24.6.44.
Age 20. (Leicester)

Pte. J. ROBERTS
Royal Welch Fusiliers.
Died of wounds. 5.1.45.
Age 19. (Atherton)

Tpr. J. RYAN
Royal Tank Regiment.
Action: Tilly. 8.8.44.
Age 26. (Clydach)

Sgt. D. B. SACH
R.A.F.V.R.
Action: Rotterdam. 13.5.43.
Age 20. (Romford)

Tpr. K. J. SAYELL
Royal Tank Regiment.
Western Europe. 19.7.44.
Age 20. (Leighton Buzzard)

Gnr. J. SEMAINE
Royal Artillery.
Action: Italy. 5.9.44.
Age 42. (London)

Tel. L. J. SHEVILLS
H.M.S. Lawford.
Action: Channel. 8.6.44.
Age 21. (London)

Pte. F. SLINGER
Royal Engineers.
Action: at sea. 7.1.43.
Age 20. (Burnley)

Pte. A. SMITH
Somerset Light Infantry.
Action: Italy. 5.5.45.
Age 34. (Kensington)

Tpr. J. S. SMITH
2nd Dragoons.
Adelheide. 19.4.45.
Age 25. (London)

Flt./Sgt. R. Q. STEVENS
10 Sqn. R.A.F.
Over Germany. 1.10.42.
Age 24. (St. Ives)

ARRIVING TO COMMEMORATE BRITAIN'S LAST STAND ON FRENCH SOIL IN 1940, (these pipes and drums of 62 Gordon Highlanders, Seaforths, and Cameronians marched through St. Valery-en-Caux on July 7, 1946. Representing the 51st Highland Division (badge, lower right), they paid tribute, the following day, at the graves of 120 of their Division in the military cemetery, killed in or near the town in June 1940. Also attending were the Marquis and Marchioness of Huntly, and the Civic Chiefs of Inverness, Aberdeen and Elgin, towns which have helped in the reconstruction of St. Valery. See also illustration in page 238.

Photo, G.P.U.

I WAS THERE!
THE HUMAN STORY OF 1939-1946

A Week in the Twin Knobs Foxholes

Major (then Lieut.-Col.) J. R. C. Crosslé, 1st Battalion the Royal Inniskilling Fusiliers, lightheartedly relates experiences enjoyed while holding a hill in the Mayu Ridge. This was in February 1943, during the abortive British drive into the Arakan, along the west coast of Burma.

WHEN I reached the top of Twin Knobs I thought how worn and haggard the British officers of the 1/7th Rajput Regiment were looking. The Indian soldiers looked, as always, merely resigned. We were due to take over Twin Knobs from the Indian battalion on the morrow, and I had come on ahead to look around.

After I had been given the inevitable cup of tea the Rajput's C.O. said, "It's all right by day, and of course the view is marvellous. But the nights are pretty sticky, and we do most of our sleeping by day." Coupled with the fact that I had met two stretchers being borne down, I thought his remarks seemed somewhat ominous.

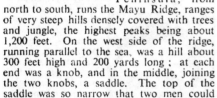

MAJOR J. R. C. CROSSLÉ

Down the Mayu Peninsula, from north to south, runs the Mayu Ridge, ranges of very steep hills densely covered with trees and jungle, the highest peaks being about 1,200 feet. On the west side of the ridge, running parallel to the sea, was a hill about 300 feet high and 200 yards long ; at each end was a knob, and in the middle, joining the two knobs, a saddle. The top of the saddle was so narrow that two men could not walk abreast on it, and the sides so steep that one could not climb it without pulling oneself up by the bushes. That was Twin Knobs. It was covered with trees, thickets of bamboo and jungle scrub.

At the south end the slope was quite gentle, and there was a Jap foxhole about 50 yards away. All round the top, except at the Jap end, where there was a sort of blockhouse, were double rows of two-man foxholes, the top row ten feet above the lower. In these sat rather dirty and jaded-looking Indian soldiers. One of the odd things about Twin Knobs as a position was that it stuck out into the Jap front line.

LOOKING west, one stared straight down on the Jap main position, Donbaik Chaung. Unfortunately the Japs never came out by day, so there were few opportunities of sniping them. We found out later that they were deep underground, in the most beautifully made bunkers. Looking east, away from the sea, there was a very steep ravine, solid with jungle, then rose another range, 300 feet higher than Twin Knobs, also densely covered with vegetation. On top of this ridge were Japs, with machine-guns and mortars, which they let off at intervals.

"They can look down on us but they can't see us, as we are hidden in the bushes. And we can never locate them for the same reason," observed the C.O., thoughtfully, as two mortar bombs landed with a bang. Thanks to the narrowness of the top, both fell well below the foxholes, one short, one over. The more I saw of Twin Knobs the less I liked the look of it.

Next morning we moved up, my carefully compiled programme of taking-over being ruined by a Jap sniper with a L.M.G. somewhere up in the hills. He commanded a bit of the path up, and let fly at everyone who came along. By hacking out a new path and blocking the old one we eventually took over with no casualties. Battalion H.Q., A and D Companies, assisted by oddments of H.Q. Company, held the fort on top. The other two Companies were in positions down below, and some way back.

Pandemonium and Spouting Flame

Tea and stew came up. The feeding and water problem was rather sticky, as the Administrative Area was about a mile away. But thanks to the Second-in-Command and the Quartermaster, this worked admirably all the time. The rations and water came as far as possible on mules, and were then man-handled the rest of the way. With dusk fell silence, with everyone in his foxhole.

Suddenly it is pitch dark. The next foxhole is at least a mile off. Rustle. A tree shakes, some leaves come pattering down. Was that a Jap ? I wish I could see. Dead silence again. The moon is due at 11 o'clock. Surely it ought to be coming up now ? I look at my watch. It is only 8.30. That silly song of Dorothy Lamour's—" Moon Over Burma "—comes into my head. Suddenly, rattle-rattle-rattle goes a tommy-gun somewhere below. Up starts a Bren, followed by more and more, and joined by all the rifles in the world. The noise rises, and after a quarter of an hour dies away. It is two of the battalions down below having a bit of a panic. Thank God we didn't join in.

Dead silence again for what seems a year or so. Bang goes a Bren on top of Twin Knobs. Is it A or D Company ? More and more join in, till Twin Knobs is spouting flame. Pandemonium is raging. I ring up

MULE TRANSPORTS FORDING A RIVER IN BURMA (right) were the means by which supplies reached the Royal Inniskilling Fusiliers holding Twin Knobs in February 1943. Faced with almost impenetrable country, in the last stages along the route this mode of transport gave way to man-handling methods. General Sir Archibald Wavell, C.-in-C. India (now Field-Marshal Lord Wavell, Viceroy of India), confers with British Staff Officers (left), at an advanced outpost on India's N.E. frontier in preparation for the Arakan drive early in 1943. PAGE 249 *Photos, British Official*

Colours: Sherwood Forest Oak with Brown Trunk and Green Foliage, outlined in White on Black Background.

46TH (NORTH MIDLAND) DIVISION

ORIGINALLY a Midland Territorial Division in the war of 1914-18, the 46th maintained its reputation if not its structure in the Second Great War.

Newly re-formed and drafted to France early in 1940 for Line of Communication duties, the Division's tasks resolved into front line actions, covering the southern flank of the B.E.F., and in defence of the Dunkirk perimeter, May-June. The Division was one of the last units to be evacuated from the beaches.

After two years of Coastal Defence in England, the 46th sailed for N. Africa in January 1943, where individual units fought brilliantly with the British 1st Army. Sidi Nsir, Kebel Kerrine and Sejenane were noteworthy actions. On September 9 the Division, under the command of the U.S. 5th Army, landed at Salerno, Italy, and captured the town on the following day. Forcing the road to Nocera, the Division opened the way to the capture of Naples by Allied armour on October 1. Two weeks later the Division forced and controlled the crossings of the Volturno river. Before being withdrawn to the Middle East its successes had assisted the Allies in gaining mastery of the approaches to the German Winter Line along the Garigliano River.

RETURNING to Italy in July 1944, the 46th breached the Gothic Line on August 25. In the attack on Monte Gridolfo, Lieut. G. Norton, a South African with the Hampshire Regiment, won the V.C. (portrait in page 478, Vol. 8).

In November one brigade was flown, in its entirety, to Greece where it helped to solve the problem of civil war; the remainder of the Division followed in February 1945. Back to Italy for the third time, in April, the Division helped the British 8th Army in the final phases of the campaign. After the German surrender in May the 46th assumed an Occupational role in Austria.

A Company. "What on earth is up?" I demand. "Don't worry," I'm told, "someone thought he heard a Jap creeping up." The noise gradually dies away, until silence is again shattered by a din down below. A few Very lights go up, but nothing happens. Here is the moon at last. I look at my watch for the millionth time. It is only just 11.0. I doze off.

Another nerve-shattering commotion wakens me, and grenades shower down on top of the hill. Off go the Brens again. I ring up A Company when the noise subsides and am told "Jap grenades and crackers. I think a Jap patrol slipped up the side and let fly. I don't think there is any damage, and I believe we bagged at least one."

This goes on all night, with intervals of dead silence. At long, long last dawn breaks,

and we come out of our holes and have an inspection. Two are dead. We bury them where they are, in their own foxholes. Breakfast appears. More ammunition is brought up. Guns and rifles are cleaned and oiled. Most of the men manage to clean themselves up a bit.

The day drags through, accompanied by odd mortar bombs and bullets from above. Every now and then, with a loud swish, a shell from a Jap 75 millimetre whizzes past,

apparently just scraping the tops of the trees, bound for our Artillery Gun Lines or Brigade H.Q. On one occasion one *did* hit the top of a tree above Battalion H.Q., but no damage resulted.

After a week of this nightmare existence we were relieved by another Indian battalion and though we knew we were to take a prominent part in an attack a few days later we did not allow that to interfere with our relief at seeing the last of Twin Knobs!

We Stormed the Walcheren Batteries

With the Royal Marine Commandos when they landed on the Westkapelle Dyke in Walcheren on November 1, 1944, Major W. R. Sendall tells the story of the heroic duel of the support squadron with the German batteries and of the battle on the Dyke that finally silenced them.

As dawn broke we sighted on the skyline the slender lighthouse tower of Westkapelle, sticking up alone, apparently straight out of the sea. This unmistakable landmark indicated the spot where, a month before, R.A.F. Lancasters with earthquake bombs had torn a breach in the famous dyke that for five centuries had kept the sea out of Walcheren, flooding the whole saucer-like centre of the island.

Our force of support-craft and landing-craft, carrying three Royal Marine Commandos with supporting troops, and shepherded by that grand old fighting lady H.M.S. Warspite with the monitors Erebus and Roberts, closed slowly in towards the shore. Everything seemed very quiet and still, even the sullen sea, which for two days before had been lashed by a gale. It was an anxious time. For more than a month Walcheren had been battered by our heavy bombers, but we knew that it had been fortified as the very corner-stone of the Nazi Atlantic Wall and bristled with heavy batteries that it was our duty to destroy so that our ships could use the great port of Antwerp.

Warspite's Mighty Broadside

The searoad to Antwerp was up the Scheldt estuary and the Walcheren batteries barred the way. So far they had been silent, but already they must have been aware of our approach. Another thing we knew. Late on the previous night the R.A.F. weather experts had stated that weather would prohibit a really big air effort. Admiral Sir Bertram Ramsay had left to our Commander, imperturbable Brigadier "Jumbo" Leicester, D.S.O., R.M., and Captain A. F. Pugsley, D.S.O., R.N., the Naval Commander, the decision whether or not to launch the assault. After an anxious conference they decided to go in, and at midnight our force slipped silently out of Ostend harbour.

Now the thin line of sand-dunes along the great dyke could be seen on the horizon, but still no sign from the enemy. Then there was a flash and a roar from one of the monitors, a big cloud of brown cordite smoke bellied out, hung in the air and slowly turned yellow. Seconds later the detonation thudded on my eardrums. Above the distant line of dunes a feather of black smoke leaped into the air. A few minutes later Warspite hurled her mighty broadside at the enemy. The enemy batteries still stayed silent.

Between us and the shore lay the support squadron, unarmoured landing-craft mounting a variety of guns. They were deploying to engage the big batteries north and south of the gap in the dyke; to the north the Domburg and Westkapelle batteries, known to us as W 17 and W 15, to the south two others called W 13 and W 11. All these had big guns up to 8·7-in., set in concrete emplacements and supported by a mass of smaller weapons. About this time we saw Domburg firing, but in the direction of Flushing, not at

us. This told us that our comrades of No. 4 Commando and the Lowland Division had launched their attack from the south across the river on Flushing.

We hadn't long to wait. The first of our ships to be fired on was ML. 902. Then the Germans opened on the support-craft. They replied, but the range was 10,000 yards and both sides ceased, waiting for it to close. Gradually the range shortened to about 4,000 yards. H-Hour—9.45 a.m.—was approaching. Then W 13 and W 15 opened up again on the support squadron with deadly accuracy, the little ships replying with everything they had got.

THERE began then one of the most amazing gun duels of the War. Time and time again the little unarmoured ships closed into the shore to pump their shells into the heavy concrete fortifications, despite a terrible fire of all calibres from the Germans. The biggest of the support-craft—the L.C.G.s—hung on to the main batteries like bulldogs, taking heavy punishment. The smaller craft engaged the subsidiary positions.

Just before H-Hour, rocket-craft let go their salvos with roar after roar of smoke and flame, and as a climax two medium-sized craft beached north and south of the gap, engaging enemy pillboxes literally at point-blank range. One of these craft burst into flames soon after beaching; the other kept up a rapid fire for twenty minutes till both turrets were out of action. Then it unbeached and sank immediately.

All the fury of the enemy was drawn to the support squadron, so that the landing craft were able to pass through to beach with comparatively slight losses. We were both proud of and grateful to our fellow Marines who manned their guns, keeping them firing though protected only by a light gunshield. The Germans flinched before they did. From one pillbox several men ran out in a panic and were cut down by machine-gun fire in the open.

Our first flight, drawn from 41 R.M. Commando, beached on the dyke itself just north of the gap. They landed on foot, and their first objective was a pillbox spraying bullets along the dyke. The leading craft was hit just before touching down and the section officer was killed. Sergeant Leslie Musgrove took charge. He went straight for the pillbox without a moment's hesitation with his tommy-gun blazing, pausing only to throw grenades. Single-handed he took the

Major W. R. SENDALL

Royal Marine Commandos at Ruined Westkapelle

ON WALCHEREN island, in the Scheldt Estuary, Westkapelle (1) was almost razed to the ground during a month of R.A.F. bombing which preceded the Royal Marine Commandos' landings on November 1, 1944. The operation was designed to silence the enemy batteries on the island which were preventing the use by the Allies of the approaches to Antwerp, already in Allied hands. In support of the landings, converted landing craft of the support squadrons suffered severely whilst heroically engaging the heavier guns on the shores. One of the craft, a L.C.G., shell-ridden and sinking, defies the attempts of her crew to save her (2). At the beach-head, Royal Marine Commandos drive their fighting vehicles off the landing craft (3). By dusk, Westkapelle, Domburg, Flushing and three of the four batteries had been captured.

Photos, British Official

pillbox, killing or capturing its occupants. Major Peter Wood, commanding the first flight, quickly and coolly directed his men into positions covering the village of Westkapelle, now a pathetic mass of wreckage, half-flooded, with only the lighthouse towering above the ruins.

The subsequent flights all landed in amphibians, which roared ashore among the maze of bomb and shell craters, shattered steel obstacles and huge, grotesque lumps of concrete. Beyond the gap the floods spread out over the flat, low fields, a scene of unutterable desolation. The twisted girders of a big radar station on top of the dunes south of the gap completed the fantastic picture, like a landscape of the moon.

Saving the Lives of the Wounded

North of the gap 41 R.M. Commando, under Lieut.-Col. Eric Palmer, quickly completed the clearance of Westkapelle and engaged the big battery W 15. South of the gap 48 R.M. Commando, under Lieut.-Col. Jim Moulton, cleared the enemy from the ruins of the radar station and advanced on W 13. Not until a firm footing had been won on both shoulders of the breach did the big guns shift from the support squadron and concentrate on the land force.

The so-called beaches were only tiny areas on each side of the gap. The enemy had the range taped, and for more than an hour they poured shells into these areas. Many amphibians loaded with ammunition were set on fire. Ammunition exploded in all directions ; fierce flames roared up. The big vehicles could not manoeuvre because of the bomb craters, mines and other obstacles. Many brave deeds were done, not only by Marines but by the Canadian medical personnel, the Assault Engineers and the Pioneers supporting them.

A shell struck the armoured front of one amphibian just before it disembarked from a landing craft. It caught fire and nearly 100,000 rounds of ammunition, together with other explosives, were threatened by the flames. Marine Donald Nicholson stayed in the hold of the amphibian with small arms ammunition exploding around him, throwing out explosives and inflammable material, saving the lives of men wounded by the shellburst. The craft retracted from the beach, only to strike a mine that blew several wounded into the sea. Nicholson, ignoring enemy fire, jumped in after them and succeeded in bringing several to the beach.

Into the midst of this inferno the second wave of the assault, 47 R.M. Commando to the south and an Allied Commando to the north, beached and roared ashore. One of the first of 47 Commando's craft took a direct hit, which set the amphibians loaded with ammunition and explosive ablaze. Many were killed and wounded, and there were several violent explosions, one man being blown into the sea with a broken leg.

Though not a strong swimmer, Marine F. W. Lanyon dived in after him and dragged him 200 yards to the beach. Lanyon was exhausted and had swallowed a lot of water. The Canadians took him to their beach dressing-station where their doctors were doing heroic work, and put him to bed. When he came round he got up at once and went off to rejoin his comrades—dressed only in a blanket. Having been fitted out with clothes from a casualty, he then joined in the battle again.

By this time a dashing attack by 41 Commando, led by Captain Peter Haydon, D.S.O., broke into W 15 battery and silenced it for good. Haydon found a way round the flank of the defences between the dyke and the floods and, covered by smoke and mortar fire, led his men in to storm. After half an hour's fighting the garrison of 120 surrendered. W 17 at Domburg was also silenced by Warspite, aided by a sortie of Typhoons taking advantage of a slight improvement in flying conditions.

48 Commando tried to rush W 13, but the Germans met them resolutely, bringing down heavy mortar fire that killed Major Derek de Stacpoole, leading the attack, and many others. The attack had to be broken off. Here there was no way round the flank, the space between sea and floods being too narrow. It was like trying to fight on the rim of a saucer.

Lieut.-Col. Moulton organized a heavy bombardment, H.M.S. Roberts pounded the defences, and a great concentration of artillery, firing from far away across the Scheldt near Breskens, fell with astonishing accuracy on the German redoubts. Then a squadron of Typhoons put in one of their shattering, pin-point attacks, the mortars opened up, and Captain Edwin Dunn led the Marines in again. Slipping and slithering in the soft sand, Dunn and his men pushed resolutely on. Lieut.-Col. Moulton was right forward, bareheaded among the bullets and shell-bursts, urging on the attack. At last the defences were penetrated, and by nightfall only one small position at the south end of the battery held out. This the Germans evacuated under cover of night.

During the late afternoon 41 Commando followed up their success at Westkapelle by storming along the dyke into Domburg. They drove the enemy, shaken by the heavy pounding from the battleship and Typhoons, from the battery and entered the little town by the lurid glare of the great fires started by Warspite's 15-in. shells. Peter Wood led a patrol to pursue the flying Germans to the edge of the thick woods north of Domburg. Thus at the close of this astonishing D-Day three of the four great batteries were in our hands. Flushing had been taken by No. 4 Commando and the Lowland Division. Only W 11 remained, the big southern battery close to a second gap that the R.A.F. had blown in the dyke just north of Flushing.

Nightmare Advance in Sandstorm

Early next morning 48 Commando pushed up and drove the Germans out of Zouteland, a little village between W 13 and W 11. Zouteland was badly knocked about but had escaped the utter ruin that had fallen on Westkapelle. Here the Dutch girls came out to greet our men. At Zouteland 47 Commando took over the battle from 48 and pushed on till they reached a broad anti-tank ditch and outer ring of minefields covering W 11. Lieut.-Col. C. F. Phillips, D.S.O., who had led this unit in the brilliant assault on Port-en-Bessin in Normandy, planned a double attack. The dry land between sea and floods was wider here. One thrust aimed to cross the anti-tank ditch and capture a German position at Klein Valkenisse in the low-lying ground ; the other was directed along the crest of the sand dunes against the battery.

Major J. T. E. Vincent led the first attack, which got across the ditch, but his force came under concentrated mortar fire in the open and suffered severely. Vincent himself being wounded. The attack along the dunes was commanded by Captain Dick Flower, who led his men for nearly a mile across the soft, steep sandhills covered with thick belts of wire and minefields. They were under heavy machine-gun and mortar fire the whole way, and many fell. Dick Flower walked about among his men, urging them on with a casual disregard for the fire, though he was in full view of the enemy. That advance was a nightmare. A strong, cold wind was blowing, whipping up a blinding spray of sand—so soft and loose that it was like struggling through newly fallen

81 (Fighter) Squadron

Motto : " Not For Us Alone."

Formed at Leconfield, Yorks, in July 1941, No. 81 Squadron won battle honours in Britain, Russia, North Africa, Sicily, Italy and Burma. Flying Hurricanes from a base near Murmansk in September and October 1941, it escorted Russian bombers and carried out sweeps and interceptions, claiming 13 enemy aircraft destroyed, with seven probables. Re-equipped with Spitfires, it started operations from Hornchurch, Essex, in May 1942, on escorts, sweeps and shipping strikes and helped give air cover over the Dieppe landings.

The squadron then moved to a base near Algiers, the first Spitfires in North Africa. On the day of arrival it took on 30-plus Ju 88s and destroyed eleven. It moved forward in support of the Army and by the end of the campaign had accounted for 90 enemy aircraft destroyed.

From North Africa No. 81 moved to Sicily and then on to Italy. By October 1943 the squadron had reached Foggia. Next month it was transferred to India where, early in December, it became operational in defence of Calcutta.

In February 1944, No. 81 joined in the battle for air supremacy over Burma, operating first from the Arakan then from the Imphal Valley. In March, six of the squadron's Spitfires were detached to the jungle airfield "Broadway," 200 miles behind the Jap lines, which was being used as a supply base for Wingate's Special Force.

In August 1944 the squadron was withdrawn, and after garrison duties in Ceylon returned to India, where its personnel was dispersed and its number plate transferred to a R.A.F. Thunderbolt squadron. With the end of the Jap war the squadron flew first to Malaya and then on to Batavia as part of the Occupation Forces.

snow in the teeth of a blizzard, except that the sand clogged automatic weapons, gritted between the teeth and blinded the eyes.

Within thirty yards of the first line of defences Dick Flower was wounded in the arm and chest, but under close fire of all kinds he rushed the first German weapon pit and killed the three men in it. Bitter hand-to-hand fighting followed. The two Troops following up suffered many casualties, both Troop commanders, Captains M. G. Y. Dobson and J. D. Moys, being hit. The Germans counter-attacked and drove Flower and his men back. That indomitable leader was hit again, but he continued to inspire his Marines with his courage and cheerfulness.

Despite this gallantry it proved impossible to break into the battery. Night was falling and all the Troop commanders had been wounded. Ammunition among these forward troops was running short. Signallers and their wireless sets were casualties, so that communication broke down. The Adjutant, Captain Paul Spencer, made his way forward in the darkness and reorganized them. Food, water, ammunition were all manhandled up over the steep dunes, and the wounded carried back. The position was organized in time to beat off a strong night attack.

The enemy came in just after midnight, calling our men to surrender, a request that was answered with laughter and a fierce burst of fire that stopped them dead. The ground won at such cost was held, to make a firm base close up to the defences for a renewed attack next day. In the morning, Lieut.-Col. Phillips asked for and obtained a most shattering concentration of artillery fire. The whole weight of the massed artillery from Breskens fell upon W 11. The Forward Observation Officers, from the high dunes, could see the flash of their guns across the broad estuary, the bursts upon the German bunkers and the Marines advancing to the final assault across the bare slopes of sand.

The Germans fought desperately, and again succeeded in checking the attack with a withering fire from their machine-guns. Then Paul Spencer led a bayonet charge, in the old style, up a steep sand slope, to break into one of the main positions. Having gained a foothold, Spencer pushed on through a maze of communication trenches and underground passages, driving the enemy before him. He was splendidly supported by Sgt.-Major J. P. England. Under fire from a trench and a concrete pillbox called "The Umbrella," England blinded the machine-gunners in the pillbox with a smoke grenade while he attacked the trench. Killing or capturing the defenders, he pushed on boldly into the network of trenches and tunnels.

Sweeping Irresistibly Forward

In face of this terrific attack and dazed by the shelling—many of the prisoners were half-crazed, the pupils of their eyes dilated till the whites were invisible—the German resistance cracked at last. They began to surrender in batches, and the advance swept irresistibly forward till the Marines reached the edge of the second gap. As dusk was falling they saw on the other side the green berets of No. 4 Commando, who had fought their way up from Flushing. Though there was more fighting to be done up in the north beyond Domburg before the island was finally cleared, the battle was won.

I shall never forget the first visible proof of our victory. I was standing next morning at the top of the radar tower near the Westkapelle gap when I saw a row of dark smudges out to sea, moving into the estuary. There was a sailor of the Naval Beach Party by my side. " What are those ?" I asked, pointing. "Minesweepers," he replied promptly. They were going in straight away to sweep the great sea highway up to Antwerp.

were lucky. Four hours on and four off was the regulation watch, but very often it was sixteen hours on. We sailed very slowly so as to reach Sidi Barrani by the following midday. Then, with engines full ahead, we would enter Bomb Alley. From that moment I was always scared, wondering what Jerry would manage this time.

The attacks generally came so suddenly that we hardly ever had time to put on our lifebelts or tin hats —but without these we had greater freedom of movement. We often opened fire with our pom-poms without orders ; to have waited those seconds would have spelt disaster. The Stukas seemed to come down from all directions, but that was because the skipper changed course so frequently. Some came so low they nearly took the mast off, and even so they missed us with their bombs. I used to fire bursts of

A/B C. LAWRENCE

about five to a plane, and then start on another one, because if we had let one have the lot the other—or others—would have done just what they liked.

After an action the gun pits were full of empty cases, and we reloaded the guns and ready-use lockers, praying for night and a little more safety. If we shot any down or damaged any, only the German air force could tell us. Our fighters didn't do so badly when they were with us, in spite of being outnumbered about four to one. They were mostly South Africans and they came to see us at Mersa Matruh whenever they could manage it.

At night we could see the German-held coast, and if they heard our powerful engines their ack-ack promptly opened up. The engines made so much noise that a dozen Hurricanes might pass over us without our hearing them. Just as dawn was breaking we would be headed through the boom at Tobruk, and Bardia Bill would begin to bark. That long-range German gun earned its nickname by reason of the fact that it was

We Ran the Gauntlet of Bardia Bill

Taking supplies from Mersa Matruh to Tobruk, during the period May-October 1941, was the job of destroyers and L.C.T.s, the latter known then as A Lighters. Adventure in plenty came to the lighters' crews, as told by Able Seaman C. Lawrence, who acted as gunner-helmsman-cook as required. See also story by Lieut. Gilbert Smith in page 61.

W E had 20 of these A Lighters, the first to be built. After Tobruk was relieved there were only four left, and I believe they are still afloat today. Each crew consisted of two officers, two motor mechanics, two stokers, one signalman, a coxswain and six seamen. H.M.S. Stag K, later known as H.M.S. Saunder, was our base, controlling operations.

About six A Lighters worked from Mersa Matruh at a time—two at Tobruk, two on the way and two loading at Mersa Matruh. If the German air force had done its job, none would have got past Sidi Barrani. I do not like to think of what would have happened if, instead of using Stukas and bombs, they had used fighters armed with cannons. We carried 4,500 gallons of 87 octane in our tanks, and a shell could have passed right through one and into the other. Once one of his fighters came down and gave us a burst, but only cut our Carley float adrift.

In Mersa Matruh we made as much noise as we pleased, but as we set sail on the 33-hour outward trip nobody would speak except in course of duty. The double journey occupied, all told, about 98 hours, and if in that time we had 13 hours rest we

CELEBRATING CHRISTMAS 1941 AT TOBRUK, the spirit appropriate to the season is evident in the bearing of the crew of Lighter A.9 (left). Seated, front row, are the two officers of the lighter. The author (Able Seaman C. Lawrence, portrait at top of page) of this story stands at the left in the back row. Used for conveying petrol, this A Lighter, Mark I (right), was one of the original twenty, of which no more than four survived, working from H.M.S. Stag K, base ship which controlled operations.

GERMAN GUNNERS AT BARDIA, after the first occupation of the town by Rommel's forces in April 1941. From that side of the Tobruk perimeter the German long-range gun nicknamed Bardia Bill shelled A lighters conveying supplies to the beleaguered garrison of Tobruk during the enemy investment of April-November 1941. *Photo, Sport & General*

on the Bardia side of the Tobruk perimeter ; somehow it managed to survive not only Allied air attacks but a Naval bombardment. The shelling would start as we reached the boom entrance—the gunners knew our time-table as well as we did—and sometimes we had to make a dash through the shells to the shelter of a wreck, of which there were plenty. If the shells happened to concentrate on the wreck we had chosen to anchor the lighter behind it wasn't so pleasant.

Troops would be waiting at Tobruk with camouflage nets to cover us from the sight of the Stukas, and they would unload us at night. Grand fellows they were, too—back from the perimeter for a rest. And what a rest ! Unloaded, by the following nightfall we would be on our way back to Mersa Matruh ; but unless we were due for a refit our return to base simply meant reloading and another trip.

Later, when we carried tanks to Tobruk, we felt a little more secure, for we had the tank crews to help us ward off air attacks with their machine-guns. They used to say they would rather fight their way back overland than return with us. We preferred sailing back to taking a chance by land in a tank !

Death Lurked in the Wake of Battle

A gunner officer, John Fortinbras, who took part in " Operation Clean-up " in the West Rhine area in March 1945—the greatest single clearance scheme of the N.W. European conflict—instances the perils and immense labour involved in work on the battlefields after the fighting had passed on.

ON the morning of January 24, 1945, during a period when vapour trails of Flying Fortresses on their way to bomb Germany etched white patterns in the blue overhead, at Nieuport on the Belgian coast a section of R.E.s was clearing beach obstructions in front of heavy A.A. guns engaged in firing practices. I was watching our bursts in the sky. Suddenly there was an explosion far different in tone from the 3·7's crackling *woosh*. Into the sky, from the beach in front of the gun park, a dirty brown column of smoke spiralled. Gunners at once ran to the tarmac's edge—the limit

DEMOLISHING HITLER'S WEST WALL FORTIFICATIONS was one of the tasks of battlefield clearance that came with the end of the War—many of them fraught with hidden perils, as told here. A Belgian demolition expert, with pneumatic drill and donkey-engine, tackles a large portion of reinforced concrete emplacement near Ostend. PAGE 254

of safety. Before them, amid the sand dunes, they saw the dismembered portions of a sapper who had been hard at work a few moments previously. A live minefield lay in front of him. "I was watching him," said a comrade, "and I thought he seemed a bit cool, hacking away at mines with his shovel."

Holzminen (wooden mines), forerunners of the deadly *Schuminen* (shoe-mines) lay thick in the sand, in some places shelved one above the other and displaced from their original positions by tidal forces, and because of the temperature, 30 deg. F., the ground was slightly frozen. This particular detachment of sappers, the R.E. sergeant in charge told me, had lifted 20,000 of them. As so often happened in tragedies of this sort the man who lost his life had been one of the ablest operators. Fifteen minutes later, a sapper who had been only five yards in rear of his pal at the time of the explosion was again at work, feeling, probing, locating, neutralizing and shovelling out

Booby-traps in Seaside Chalets

At the West Wall, between Nieuport and Ostend, Belgian demolition experts, blue overalled and smiling, toiled with pneumatic drills, donkey-engines and other devices, knocking down the massive, deeply embedded emplacements, disguised for the most part as kiosks; cafés and chalets by Hitler's camouflage artists. They could afford to be cheerful, for there was little risk. The danger lurked in adjacent sand dunes and waste tracts beside semi-derelict buildings, especially those enclosed by barbed wire fences, which had little bits of wire, looking like loose ends, projecting upright from the tops of odd posts—the Nazis' private sign for denoting the presence of live minefields.

Here and there you could read notices displaying the gruesome skull and cross-bones with the warning "Vorsicht ! Lebensgefahr. Minen. (Beware ! Danger to life. Mines)" repeated on the same board in French and Flemish. Houses in the locality were unsafe, too, especially those round Middelkirke, for in anticipation of our landings the Nazis booby-trapped very thoroughly these once popular seaside boarding-houses and lidos, including the tiny chalets of the Lac aux Dames. They failed in their purpose, as the Allied attack in this region eventually came from the landward side.

In France it was estimated that Allied Forces had recovered more than 40,000,000 of the 50,000,000 mines sown under Nazi orders, chiefly in coastal areas. It was, however, the odd thousands which engendered the greatest danger. Skilled, too, as engineer mine-lifters became, with their sixth sense of danger and their experience of counter-lifting devices, it was not possible for the work to be completed without fatal casualties. Often enough, as part of their harassing tactics to impede pursuit, the Nazis scattered grenades haphazardly in their wake, leaving them primed and with the safety devices removed ; but this practice seldom deceived our recce parties.

Liberation Marred by Tragedy

At Giel, in Normandy, during the time of the Falaise Gap, before anyone could give any thought to battlefield clearance, the joy of this little village at liberation was darkened by a tragedy. A grief-stricken mother told me the story. Her three children, a boy aged eight, and two girls, aged five and six, were playing in a lane immediately after we had liberated the village, when one picked up an abandoned stick grenade. It exploded instantly. All three children were killed. It is discarded missiles like these stick grenades and egg grenades, or anti-personnel mines, like picric acid "bottles" and wooden shoe-mines, which, left lying around, claim

USING GERMAN EXPLOSIVES, two Royal Canadian engineers prepare a detonator at the entrance of a concrete bunker at Wilhelmshaven, before demolishing the fortifications shielding the entrance to the U-boat base.
Photo, Associated Press

many innocent lives long after the tide of battle has rolled by.

But that is not the only reason for battlefield clearance. The greatest single clearance scheme of the N.W. European struggle, "Operation Clean-up" in the West Rhine area, following immediately after the Rhine crossing on March 24, 1945, had tactical urgency behind it. Prodigious quantities of ammunition had been accumulated for the supporting artillery fire plan, but with the crossing of the great water-barrier more easily forced than had been expected only a small percentage was used.

Ready-made Rhineland Supply Base

Hence, with the enemy in flight, largely a disorganized rabble, and with guns rumbling after him ready to soften any point of resistance obstructing our armour, this Rhineland area of swiftly evacuated sites, each left with stacks of ammunition beside empty pits, became a supply base ready-made. From here, supplies could obviously be ferried forward to our pursuing troops far more swiftly than if the ammunition convoys had to trek all the way back to Antwerp.

Accordingly, a gigantic scheme was "laid on." I took part in it. Two months of hard work, involving 5,000 to 7,000 men, were needed to clear the area. One difficulty was to convince gunners who considered

themselves veterans of the bridge-head that here was a task as important as dropping shells on the enemy, because everyone yearned to be in at the kill. However, the men peeled off their coats and humped every type of shell, from 40 mm. Bofors to 5·5 and even 9·2 super-heavies.

It amazed many to see how thick the ammunition lay on the ground—proof enough of immense artillery preparations. In one area alone close on 2,000 tons of 25-pounder shells had been left, and at least 10,000 unexpended smoke shells. Every piece was shifted. The job was not without its humours or hazards. In one instance a recce party in a 15-cwt. wireless truck, whilst prospecting for a German minefield on the edge of a gun area, took a sudden toss into a deep ditch with three feet of stale water at the bottom. They had fallen into an anti-tank trap cunningly concealed beneath brushwood.

The Search for Hidden Arms

Again, the officer in command of the enemy ammunition dump established near Xanten received one day a curt message which said, "Discovered German girl occupying farm building with Mausers stacked inside : your disposal instructions awaited." Back went the reply, "Girl is your baby : we'll take her arms." This was at a period when sabotage was still thought likely, and intensive house-to-house combings for concealed weapons were ordered.

Not an agreeable job ! More than once when searching those wretched, half-ruined Rhineland farmhouses and outbuildings, which were crammed tight with refugees, sometimes two families occupying a single room, you had to turn ailing, wounded and infirm people out of their beds, and probe their bolsters and pillows (if any) for rifles, pistols and anything else that was dangerous. But as a result the farmers could till their holdings with little danger of encountering infernal objects, and—even more important —what was virtually a huge arsenal was denied to roaming gangs of terrorists which later infested the countryside.

NEW FACTS AND FIGURES

THE "security" cloak which covered formational signs during the War has now been lifted and in his recently published book, Heraldry in War : Formation Badges 1939-1945 (Gale & Polden, 12s. 6d.), Lieut.-Col. Howard N. Cole gives details and illustrations of over 300 badges of the British and Allied armies. These, with brief histories of the formations which wore them, are confined to Brigade level and upwards, but even so the author does not claim that his record is complete.

A FEW formations in the British Army reassumed their 1914-18 badge in the Second Great War : the Guards Armoured Division bore the "eye" of the former Guards Division ; the 51st (Highland) Division retained its famous "HD," and the 55th the red rose of Lancaster. The signs became widely used, beyond the original intention of distinguishing personnel and vehicles. Routes allotted to formations were often signposted by means of a directional arrow and a stencilled badge on a board, billets and captured equipment were similarly marked. After the end of the War the famous boar of XXX Corps appeared on the sign of more than one German inn, and it is perpetuated by a statue at Nienburg (see illustration in page 609, Vol. 9).

ON June 18, 1945, releases from the Services commenced ; at first modestly, at the rate of 30,000 a week, gradually increasing to 60,000 a week in August. With the sudden cessation of hostilities in the Far East in August 1945, there was quick acceleration of the release rate ; by the end of December 95,000 men were passing

through the Civilian Clothing Depots every week. In January 1946 the figure reached 100,000. An average of 500 tons of clothing was moved weekly—during the busiest time as much as 780 tons in one week, to keep the distributing centres supplied. No less than 96 per cent of the items required were issued to the men at the Civilian Clothing Depots on the day of their release.

DURING the first year of demobilization 3,150,000 outfits, or 31,500,000 separate items, were issued, embracing a multiplicity of sizes (40, later increased to 60), colours and styles. This is probably the largest single undertaking in the history of the clothing industry.

NEARLY 300,000 men and women were specially trained during the War, for the armed forces and industry, in institutes controlled by Local Government authorities. Ministry of Education figures are : for radio, 59,815 men and 2,145 women ; Army tradesmen, 86,302 men ; naval artificers, 7,969 men ; cookery, 3,667 women ; A.T.S. clerical, 8,480 women ; intensive engineering, 3,707 men. Further education was also provided for 5,749 mining entrants.

ON June 22, 1946 (the fifth anniversary of the opening of Hitler's onslaught on Russia), it was announced that mines had been cleared from all formerly invaded Soviet territory. More than 70,000,000 mines, shells and bombs were detected and disposed of in two-and-a-half years. Helping in this work of clearance were tens of thousands of volunteers from the Civil Defence organizations.

The New Uniform for All Ranks of Our Army

Printed in England and published every alternate Friday, by the Proprietors, THE AMALGAMATED PRESS, LTD., The Fleetway House, Farringdon Street, London, E.C.4. Registered for transmission by Canadian Magazine Post. Sole Agents for Australia and New Zealand: Messrs. Gordon & Gotch, Ltd.; and for South Africa: Central News Agency, Ltd.—August 2, 1946.

DEMONSTRATION OF OUR NEW 'No. I ARMY DRESS' took place before H.M. the King, in the grounds of Buckingham Palace, on June 25, 1946. In indigo blue the uniform, for all ranks, bears a regimental colour stripe down the trousers, and similar coloured piping along the tunic epaulets. The dark blue beret worn when "walking out" is replaced by a forage cap on ceremonial occasions. Certain regiments will retain uniforms in traditional colours, and Scottish regiments their distinctive headdress, kilts and trews. Some modifications in detail may yet be made.

Printed in England and published every alternate Friday, by the Proprietors, THE AMALGAMATED PRESS, LTD., The Fleetway House, Farringdon Street, London, E.C.4. Registered for transmission by Canadian Magazine Post. Sole Agents for Australia and New Zealand: Messrs. Gordon & Gotch, Ltd.; and for South Africa: Central News Agency, Ltd.—August 2, 1946. S.S. *Editorial Address*: JOHN CARPENTER HOUSE, WHITEFRIARS, LONDON. E.C.4

Vol 10 *The War Illustrated* N° 239

SIXPENCE

I WAS THERE

AUGUST 16, 1946

ONE OF BRITAIN'S WARTIME SECRETS was this device for bridging tank obstacles with the aid of rocket propulsion. Called the Great Eastern Tank Ramp it consists of a Churchill tank to the front of which is hinged a ramp, itself centrally hinged. When propelled from the rear by rockets the ramp rested as an inverted " V " over the obstacle to be crossed ; the Churchill could then be detached, or retained as additional support. Twelve were constructed for the invasion of Europe. *Photo, G.P.U.*

Edited by Sir John Hammerton

No. 240 WILL BE PUBLISHED **FRIDAY**, AUGUST 30

Four-Power Allied Control Council in Germany

MEETING IN BERLIN on July 10, 1946, for the bi-monthly conference, delegates to the Four-Power Allied Control Council are seen in session (above). Facing camera is the delegation of the United States, with those of Great Britain on the left, U.S.S.R. on the right, and France in the foreground. Heading their respective delegations were the four Allied military governors of Germany: bottom, left to right, Marshal of the R.A.F. Sir Sholto Douglas, General Joseph T. McNarney (U.S.A.), General Joseph Koenig (France), General Vasily Sokolovsky (U.S.S.R.).

FORMING PART of the machinery of control in Germany, after her unconditional surrender on May 8, 1945, the Allied Control Council assumed supreme authority on June 5, 1945. Its function is, mainly, to ensure uniformity of action in the four Allied Zones of Occupation, and Germany's compliance with the surrender terms. Headed by the Commanders-in-Chief of the four zones, the Council has as its advisors a co-ordinating committee and a Control staff. The duties of these sub-sections entail the putting into effect of the Council's decisions, transmitting them to the appropriate German organizations and controlling the activities of the latter.

Why the "Cease Fire!" Sounded at Singapore

By PETER HUME

"FINALLY, the defenders of Malaya realized that they were stranded and doomed," wrote Chin Kee On, in his book Malaya Upside Down. "There was no fighting chance to retrieve what was lost, once they were bottled up in Singapore. The Japanese bombed the city just as they liked. They conducted land operations from observation planes and, towards the end, it mattered little whether air-raid sirens sounded or not. There was no meaning in sacrificing more lives both of the military and the civilian population. There was no meaning in seeing the besieged city of Singapore battered and reduced to ashes. That was why Singapore surrendered unconditionally. It was a military necessity. It was a humane necessity."

The author of those words is a Chinese who lived through the invasion, subjugation, occupation and reconquest of Singapore. Bitter about many things in the Malayan campaign of 1941-42 which preceded the surrender, he represents the feeling of a million civilians who had the same experience.

In his acceptance of the inevitability of total defeat in Malaya once the Japanese had reached Singapore island the only echoes Mr. Churchill, who on January 27, 1942— nearly a fortnight before the first enemy soldier set foot on the island—warned the House of Commons to expect "worse news" from that theatre of war. The statement was taken by all of Singapore's cosmopolitan population who heard and understood it to foreshadow their doom.

Admiral Phillips's Three Choices

As France's fall in 1940 enabled the Japanese to advance their bases to the borders of Siam and within 300 miles of the north-eastern shores of Malaya the needs of Singapore became greater, as well as more urgent, than was dreamed of by the original planners of the naval base and its chain of guardian airfields. Garrisons had always been maintained in Malaya and the possibility of attack from the North had been considered. But hitherto it had always been a question of a seaborne invasion from bases 1,500 miles away. Now new measures and new facilities were called for. They had to be demanded from a Government engaged in desperate war for survival on its own doorstep by a colony whose entry into the fighting line was problematical.

Britain did, though, spare two great ships, H.M.S. Prince of Wales and Repulse. They came to Singapore less than a week before the Japanese attacked in Malaya on December 7, 1941, and in defiance of all normal wartime rules of security their arrival was publicized as heralding the stationing of a British Fleet in Eastern waters. But Prince of Wales and Repulse were last hopes. The announcement of their presence gives the key to that. They came as part of the propaganda drive directed against Japan—the idea of Singapore's invincibility which should have deterred the Japanese from ever attacking.

But the enemy were not deceived, and when they did attack they were lucky to sink the two ships at one stroke on December 10. Even had they not done so it is hard to see what useful role Prince of Wales and Repulse could have played in the campaign. After his much-heralded arrival, Admiral Phillips had the three choices : of running away again, of remaining off Singapore inactive under constant threat of enemy bombing, or of making a desperate bid to strike at least one blow at the Japanese. He chose the third.

who was in Singapore in 1942 as Assistant to The Director of News, Malaya Broadcasting Corporation, established a reserve radio service from Batavia, and returned to Singapore in 1945 on the Staff of S.E.A.C.

So Singapore was a great naval base without the ships to use it. Equally, the chain of airfields built up for counter-attack were without the aircraft for which they were provided. It is a major tragedy of the Malayan campaign that the troops originally placed to guard these airfields so that they could be used for our bombers to move against the enemy had in the event to fight for them solely in order that the Japanese should not use them for attacks on Singapore and on Allied shipping bringing reinforcements and supplies to the so-called citadel.

IT was a delaying action, no more, that British troops had to fight from December 8, when their advance units went forward from the border only to find already well-organized opposition until, exhausted, they streamed back across the Johore Causeway in the last days of January. The enemy had airfields at Singora and Patani in Southern Siam ready and waiting, with petrol stocks available from the moment his troops moved forward. He had landing barges all ready to be transported across country and launched in the Malacca Straits. He had thousands of "tourists" in Siam and, in Malaya, suborned agents, experts who under free British rule had been surveying the tracks and jungle paths for years past. He had tanks which he could land on the friendly shore of Siam. Especially he had aircraft, good aircraft, which could be flown in to back up his troops and smash the puny British air power before it could even go into action.

Not many Japanese troops were used in Malaya, not many aircraft by modern standards, not a great fleet. But they were enough, and they were the best Japan could put out. All her other campaigns held their major fire while this great objective was reached. So all attention for two

IN THE LAST DAYS in Singapore civilians sought safety from the crumbling ruins and Japanese bombing which preceded the invasion.
PAGE 259   *Photo, Keystone*

months was on Malaya and on Singapore. That, as much as anything, is why the British defeat there seemed monstrous. Elsewhere the Chinese, the Americans, the Dutch were holding. Here we were pulling back, here we had surrendered. Why ?

The answer lies in the situation at the time of the first Japanese attack—in Britain's global strategic stringency, in Japan's concentrated determination. To look in detail at the campaign is to discover only whether the deployment and use of the scanty British forces available was such as to win the maximum of what was the Allies' dearest commodity—time.

The brunt of the first month's fighting was born by a single Division, the 11th Indian, which from the first sorties of its forward units into Siam, on December 8, fought a series of rearguard actions over something like 15,000 square miles of country. Faced with tanks, air mastery and enemy ability to land almost at will on the coast behind its lines, that single division at the cost of its own near-destruction and complete exhaustion kept an enemy force at least three times its own strength off Singapore's immediate approaches for a month.

During the greater part of the battle not only Singapore itself but its dangerous sea approaches had been mainly free from air attack ; for nearly a month the lightly protected convoys had sailed in safely and had found labour to unload their cargoes of defence unterrorized and unhampered by bombing. So it was in unjustifiably good heart that Singapore's people finally bore the news of the end of this first phase, of the establishment of a new front little over 100 miles north of the island itself.

Desperate News of 45th Brigade

I think there was no doubt in any mind then, in mid-January 1942, that the battle about to begin was the battle of Singapore. It was joined by our fresh forces—Major-General Gordon-Bennett's tough-trained Australian Brigades—on January 15, near Gemas, a railway junction in the centre of our forward line. And it opened with a local victory. At last we were hitting back.

But the Japanese still had cards up their sleeves, and we had weaknesses. The day after the Australians' success, trouble struck at the western end of the British line. This sector, the lower reaches of the Muar River, was held by 45th Indian Brigade which, after partial training in desert country at home, had been destined for the Middle East. The troops were raw in combat ; they were strange to the humid swamp and jungle in which they found themselves ; the training they had received had been for a wholly different type of warfare.

By a particular stroke of misfortune almost all their senior officers were killed in the first two days of fighting. The Indians were bewildered, some wandering aimlessly, some throwing away their lives in suicidally gallant and unco-ordinated attempts to get at the usually unseen enemy. That enemy, landed from the sea and launched across the river, was the Imperial Guards Division, a name which means as much for discipline and training in the Japanese Army as the Guards in Britain.

The breaking of the 45th Brigade was desperate news. From Muar, where they had been engaged—the town fell on January 19—a road ran south and inland to the main trunk road. A Japanese force coming down here could cut off the communications of our forward troops in the centre. Two Australian battalions were hurried west, but it was too late. The Japanese were all around them almost before they had reached the positions which it was vital to defend. In the words of The Times correspondent, "The bleak fact remained that the Johore line had gone. In the minds of many observers (including myself) there was now nothing on earth that could save Singapore" (Ian Morrison: Malayan Postscript). It was in such an atmosphere that on January 31 the Causeway was blown up (in so far as a massively solid concrete structure can be blown up) and we in Singapore were told:

" The battle of Malaya has come to an end and the battle of Singapore has started. For nearly two months our troops have fought an enemy on the mainland who has had the advantage of great air superiority and considerable freedom of movement by sea. Our task has been to impose losses on the enemy and gain time to enable the forces of the Allies to be concentrated for this struggle in the Far East."

So spoke General Percival in an Order of the Day, though he must himself have known already that this was but the prelude to the Order he would have to issue only sixteen days later:

" It has become necessary to give up the struggle. . . . The forward troops continue to hold their ground, but the essentials of war have run short. In a few days we shall have neither food nor petrol, and many types of ammunition are short, and the water supply upon which the vast civilian population and many of the fighting forces are dependent, threatens to fail. . . . Without the necessities of war we cannot carry on. I thank all ranks for their efforts throughout."

And in those intervening sixteen days, in the battle for Singapore which had in fact been lost before the battle was joined, there was much for which to offer thanks—at least as much as there was to blame. The important thing, impossible to realize at the time, is that praise and blame alike relate to no great strategic issue, but to a particular local engagement which might have been carried on for a few days longer, or abandoned a few days earlier. The fall of Singapore, on the most optimistic analysis, might have been prevented had Germany not defeated France and continued in action against Britain; it might have been delayed for a month or two longer than it was by a wiser disposition of forces (both by the planners in London and the Commanders on the spot) before Japan attacked; it might have been delayed for a week or two by a different strategy in the peninsula fighting. But once the enemy reached those narrow Johore Straits the counting had to be in days.

YET there were more than 70,000 British, Indian and Australian troops on the island. At least the enemy could not bring up that number; he hardly had so many in Malaya. There were massed artillery, ammunition, transport. There was food, there was water, though the main supply had had to be sacrificed when the pipes which brought it down from Johore to the island went up with the Causeway.

But who were those 70,000 troops, spread along 40 miles of immediately-vulnerable coastline with provision, too, for the sea side to the south? There were two sorts of soldier, apart from the top-heavy jumble of staffs and camp-followers jammed up in Singapore by the compression of our Forces.

There were the men who had hardly slept for two months while they held off the steady Japanese advance. And there were the men who had just stepped out of troopships, men to whom the noises of the tropics at night were themselves strange and fearsome. For all this they had eight days—in which their little remaining air support was finally driven away by shelling of three Singapore airfields and continuous bombing of the fourth, eight days in which they themselves were with growing intensity shelled and mortared across those narrow Straits—

JAPANESE REPAIRING THE JOHORE CAUSEWAY connecting the Malayan mainland to Singapore, after the latter's surrender. The Causeway was blown up by our Forces in a vain attempt to stem the Japanese advance and invasion of the island.

eight days in which to dig themselves some sort of shelter in the waterlogged ground.

The first shock came against the Australians guarding the mangrove swamps of the western coast. For a night and a day they huddled in their shallow, wet, slit-trenches while a barrage from every sort of gun poured on their positions. Then in the late evening of February 8 the Japanese began to come across. In rubber boats, in iron barges, in every sort of craft the mass assault was launched under cover of the guns. Sir Keith Murdoch, an Australian newspaper editor with access to the facts, writes: "We were overwhelmed in our forward positions, particularly where the 19th Australian battalion with its 60 per cent of new reinforcements stood . . . Singapore was lost in the first day's fighting."

That is not to say there was not some gallant action after that first day. But the Japanese, on one narrow sector, had put ashore two determined divisions. They had shot out our beach defences; their aircraft controlled the battlefield. Counter-attacks mounted by British units often made good progress but were swallowed up in the advancing mass. And some troops, thrown

into this maelstrom where even the climate was a positive enemy, could not stand the pace. Cut off from effective command they became stragglers.

The Japanese Divisions pushed across the northern sector of the island, taking in flank the units which were still watching the un-invaded beaches. They secured the southern end of the Causeway, threw bridging material across the gaps and brought over a third Division with tanks. Worst of all, they converged on Singapore's main dumps of food, fuel and ammunition, placed around Bukit Timah, the commanding hill in the centre of the island. Two days after the enemy landing General Sir Archibald Wavell, then in supreme command in the South-West Pacific, visited the battlefield and before returning to his Headquarters in Java issued an Order recalling Russian, Chinese and American feats of arms and saying, "It will be disgraceful if we yield our boasted fortress of Singapore to inferior enemy forces. There must be no thought of sparing the troops or civilian population and no mercy must be shown to weakness in any shape or form." In circulating this Order to the units under his command, General Percival, who remained on the Island, added the rider: "There must be no further withdrawals without orders."

Last Concerted Attempt

On the day after the Supreme Commander left Singapore for the last time, the final concerted attempt was made. Every available unit was mustered along the island's Central North-South road with orders to push west towards the original Japanese landing area, to split the enemy from his bridge-head on the Singapore side of the Causeway. In some cases these troops did reach their first objectives. But Japanese tanks were careering down the road in their rear, and in one case the Japs were optimistically mistaken by an anti-tank unit for "some of our own." As before, the counter-attackers were swallowed up in the Japanese flood.

The Japanese were closing in on the million civilians in the city. The last big battle was fought around the reservoirs on its northern outskirts. It was largely an academic battle, since the shortage of water which on February 15 finally determined the Command to surrender was caused not by enemy withholding at source, but by shells and bombs breaking so many mains that the supply from the reservoirs was running away faster than it could be pumped under Japanese or any other auspices.

ON Feb. 13, according to General Gordon-Bennett (the only person in authority who has yet been able to give a public account) he attended a conference of commanders at which "we agreed unanimously that the situation was completely hopeless." Two days more, and General Gordon-Bennett was hazardously taking back to Australia the news of Japanese power and skill; General Percival was arranging details of capitulation with General Yamashita. The troops who had fought the battles were stacking their arms. A million Asiatic civilians were hoping that the noise had stopped for good and that the thousand-odd of their number daily sacrificed in the past fortnight was sacrifice enough.

Rendezvous at Metz : Churchill Meets Giraud

ON THE ANNIVERSARY of Bastille Day, July 14, 1946, Mr. Churchill visited Metz, to receive the freedom of this French town and keep an appointment made at the time of the Allied landings in North Africa, November 1942, with General Giraud, then C.-in-C. French Forces. The General's telegraphed invitation to Britain's wartime Prime Minister to lunch with him in his native town as soon after the war as possible received the laconic reply, "Rendezvous at Metz," where Mr. Churchill is seen (1), with General Giraud (second from left), acknowledging the crowds.

At a banquet at the Town Hall (2) Mr. Churchill urged Anglo-French unity; M. Schuman, French Minister (seated) represented his Government and earlier accompanied Mr. Churchill at an inspection of French troops (3). On the airfield girls in national costume welcomed their guest with flowers (4). The following day Mr. Churchill was made an Honorary Citizen of the City of Luxemburg, where in Hamme cemetery (5), with his daughter Mary (right), he laid a wreath on the grave of General George S. Patton, late commander of the U.S. 3rd Army, who died on December 9, 1945.

'Operation Nipoff' Sends Japs Home from Burma

REPATRIATION of 35,000 Japanese prisoners of war, interned in Rangoon, is being effected by S.E.A.C. Headquarters. Under the direction of Allied H.Q., Burma, "Operation Nipoff" is administered by the Japanese themselves, who have reformed their old Army H.Q. in Burma for the purpose. The prisoners, some of whom are housed in this transit camp (1), leave for Japan in Liberty ships specially detailed by General MacArthur.

BEFORE EMBARKING prisoners take a bath (2) in petrol drums filled with water treated with disinfectant. The first of the Liberty ships, each with accommodation for 3,700, arrived at Rangoon on June 1, 1946. Repatriates are ferried out to the transport in landing craft (3). Of the total of 72,000 Jap prisoners in Burma 37,000 are to be retained for reconstruction work in the country. See illus. in page 271. PAGE 262

Triumphs of Royal Engineers in Malaya and Siam

THE KLANG BRIDGE, standing the test of a heavy locomotive (1) on June 24, 1946, restored the last link in the railway connecting Kuala Lumpur and Port Swettenham in Malaya. Starting work on the bombed structure in the previous September, the Royal Engineers, with skilled Japanese labour, raised the two centre spans from the river bed, overcoming lack of tools by the exercise of ingenuity and the shortage of steel by repairing the damaged girders. Side-view, completed (2).

At Bangkok, British and Indian Engineers replaced, temporarily, the wrecked bridge over the River Menan by a wagon ferry and piers. Accommodating two wagons, the ferry made fast at the pier (3). Crossing the fast-flowing river (4), it is used for transporting rice to the famine-threatened area in South-East Asia, between 30 and 40 wagons crossing daily.
Photos, British Official

Returning to the Egyptians the Cairo Citadel

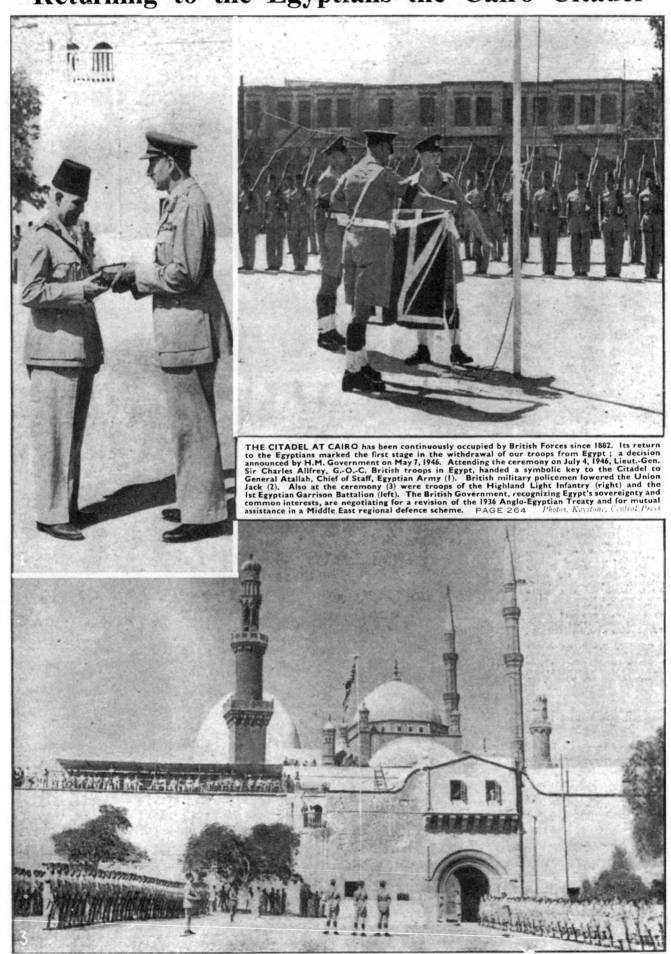

THE CITADEL AT CAIRO has been continuously occupied by British Forces since 1882. Its return to the Egyptians marked the first stage in the withdrawal of our troops from Egypt ; a decision announced by H.M. Government on May 7, 1946. Attending the ceremony on July 4, 1946, Lieut.-Gen. Sir Charles Allfrey, G.-O.-C. British troops in Egypt, handed a symbolic key to the Citadel to General Atallah, Chief of Staff, Egyptian Army (1). British military policemen lowered the Union Jack (2). Also at the ceremony (3) were troops of the Highland Light Infantry (right) and the 1st Egyptian Garrison Battalion (left). The British Government, recognizing Egypt's sovereignty and common interests, are negotiating for a revision of the 1936 Anglo-Egyptian Treaty and for mutual assistance in a Middle East regional defence scheme.   PAGE 264   *Photos. Keystone, Central Press*

Lancasters on Good Will Mission to America

N⁰. 35 BOMBER SQUADRON Lancasters stationed at Graveley, Huntingdonshire, took off from St. Mawgan airfield, Newquay, Cornwall, on a good will mission to the United States on July 8–9, 1946. Aircraft and crews were inspected on July 3 by Air Marshal Sir Norman Bottomley, K.C.B. (1), accompanied by the squadron commander, Wing Commander, A. J. L. Craig, D.S.O., D.F.C. Taking off in two groups, the sixteen Lancasters crossed the Atlantic via the Azores, arriving at Gander Airfield, Newfoundland, on July 11, where they were met by Mr. John Winant, former U.S. Ambassador in London. Continuing the flight to Mitchel Field, New York City, the aircraft passed over the East River, landing on July 17, (2). Lieut.-General G. E. Stratemeyer, commanding U.S. Air Defence Command (3—second from right), greeted Wing Commander Craig on arrival. Later, the squadron made a mock attack on New York. At St Louis, on their way to take part in the U.S.A.A.F. Day celebrations at Los Angeles on August 1, No. 35 Squadron received this greeting : "These aviators are the representatives of the loyal and intrepid band which stood between the West and the Nazi hordes before the weight of Russia and the U.S.A. was cast into the balance. It is difficult to over-estimate the importance of that heroic defence of Britain. So hats off to those few to whom the many owe so much."

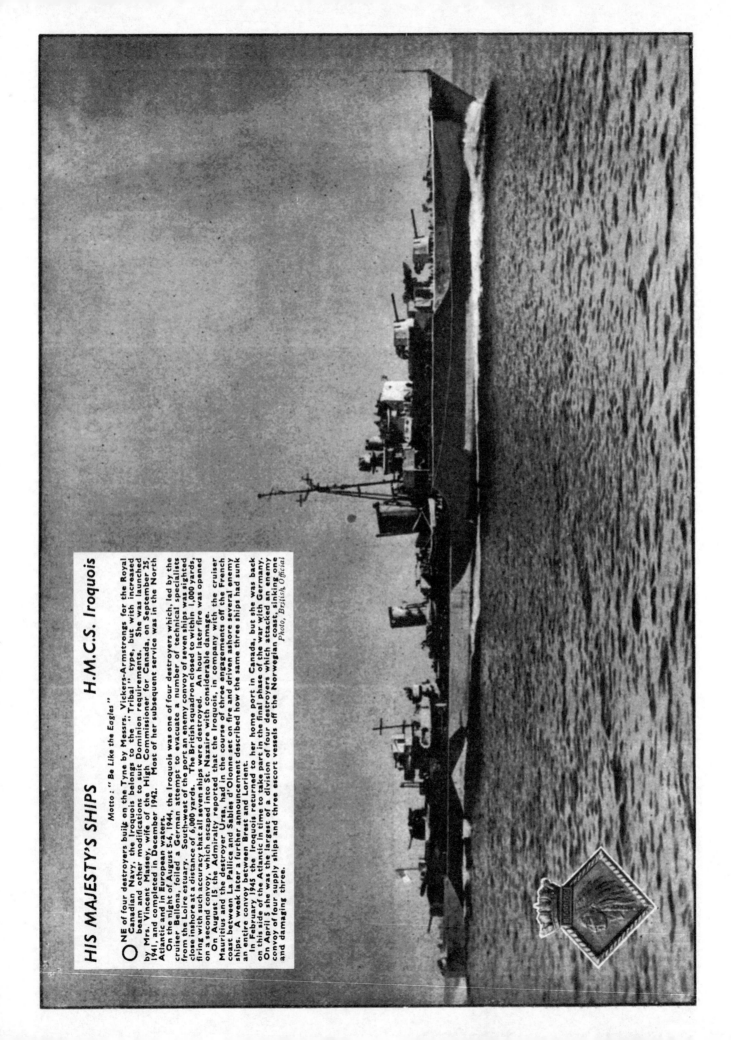

HIS MAJESTY'S SHIPS

H.M.C.S. Iroquois

Motto: " Be Like the Eagles "

ONE of four destroyers built on the Tyne by Messrs. Vickers-Armstrongs for the Royal Canadian Navy, the Iroquois belongs to the " Tribal " type, but with increased beam and other modifications to suit Dominion requirements. She was launched by Mrs. Vincent Massey, wife of the High Commissioner for Canada, on September 25, 1941, and completed in December 1942. Most of her subsequent service was in the North Atlantic and in European waters.

On the night of August 5-6, 1944, the Iroquois was one of four destroyers which, led by the cruiser Bellona, foiled a German attempt to evacuate a number of technical specialists from the Loire estuary. Southwest of the port an enemy convoy of seven ships was sighted close inshore at a distance of 6,000 yards. The British squadron closed to within 1,000 yards, firing with such accuracy that all seven ships were destroyed. An hour later fire was opened on a second convoy, which escaped into St. Nazaire with considerable damage.

On August 15 the Admiralty reported that the Iroquois, in company with the cruiser Mauritius and the destroyer Ursa, had in the course of three engagements off the French coast between La Pallice and Sables d'Olonne set on fire and driven ashore several enemy ships. A week later a further announcement described how the same three ships had sunk an entire convoy between Brest and Lorient.

In February 1945 the Iroquois returned to her home port in Canada, but she was back on this side of the Atlantic in time to take part in the final phase of the war with Germany. On April 5 she was the largest of a division of four destroyers which attacked an enemy convoy of four supply ships and three escort vessels off the Norwegian coast, sinking one and damaging three.

Photo, British Official

The Gloucestershire Regiment

By Lieut.-Col. R. M. GRAZEBROOK

THE Gloucester-shire Regiment was unfortunate in losing in 1938 two of its three territorial battalions, the 4th City of Bristol Battalion having become the 66th Searchlight Regiment R.A., and the 6th Battalion the 44th Battalion R.T.C. On the outbreak of the war, therefore, there remained only the 1st Battalion, serving at Rangoon in Burma, the 2nd Battalion at Plymouth and the 5th T.A. Battalion with its headquarters at Gloucester. Five other battalions were formed during the War but the majority of these remained training units. Actually only the above-mentioned three battalions and the 10th Battalion saw active service, and of these the 5th Battalion became the 43rd Battalion Reconnaissance Corps in 1941. It was therefore left to these few battalions to continue the gallantry and traditions of The Gloucestershire Regiment of other days.

The 2nd Battalion (the old 61st Foot) were the first to proceed overseas—in the 3rd Division. They formed part of the original B.E.F. and were employed in North-West Europe during the first winter of the war. In the Ligne de Contact in the Saar they gained invaluable experience in touch with the enemy, and also their first Military Cross. In January 1940 the 5th Battalion, in the 48th Division (the first T.A. Division to go over-seas), crossed over to France, and soon after, on a reorganization of divisions the 2nd Battalion were trans-ferred to the 48th Division. From then on the story of the two battalions was, therefore, much the same. The 5th Battalion were selected to represent their division in the Maginot Line.

Completely Cut Off at Zutpeen

On May 10, 1940, when the British Army was rushed northwards across Belgium to help stem the sudden German assault on the Low Countries, the 48th Division was held in reserve and it was not until May 14 that they were on the move. Reaching the vicinity of Brussels, the two battalions were in position on the British right near the field of Waterloo. Neither was really engaged, however, before the withdrawal began on the 17th. Then followed days of marching, the territorial battalion during one spell covering 80 miles on foot in 72 hours. Rearguard actions took place at the river crossings, notably at Jollain Merlin and Bruyelle on the Escaut Canal. From here the division fell back to Cassel at the south-east corner of the Dunkirk salient, and was ordered to take up defensive positions facing south to help cover the withdrawal of the other units farther to the north.

ON May 25 the 2nd Battalion were allotted the defence of the western portion of the town of Cassel, whilst the 5th Battalion after sundry moves occupied the villages of Ledringhem and Arneke a little to the north-west. Two days later the German assault commenced, first from the south-west. One company of the 2nd Battalion was com-pletely cut off at Zutpeen, at the foot of Cassel Hill, and after a most gallant stand at company headquarters the handful of survivors were forced to surrender. Cassel itself was from then onwards under heavy mortar and artillery fire from the enemy and was soon in flames.

On the 29th a fresh enemy attack developed and German columns were seen crossing the Cassel-Dunkirk road to the north. It had been ordered by Division to withdraw the gallant defenders during the night of May

IN 1831 the old 28th and 61st Regiments of Foot were formed into the Gloucestershire Regiment. It was the 28th who won the well-known "Back Badge" of the Gloucesters by their gallantry at the Battle of Alexandria in 1801, when they repulsed the French attacks on the front and rear of their key position. The Regiment prior to the Second Great War bore more battle honours on their Colours than any other regiment in the British Army. In the First Great War they had 24 battalions serving and were engaged in almost every campaign from Mons to the final defeat of the enemy.

〰〰〰

28-29, but the dispatch rider carrying the orders unfortunately lost his way and arrived too late. A withdrawal eastwards was there-fore planned for the following night, and after holding all attacks during the day companies and platoons began to pull out at about 10 o'clock in the evening. Other troops were, of course, also retiring in the vicinity and it soon became clear that neither by fighting nor by making use of the limited cover was it possible to get clear of the enemy. Eventu-ally the 2nd Battalion were encircled, and only one officer and nine men succeeded in reaching Dunkirk.

Bayonet Attack in Main Street

The 5th Battalion were more fortunate. They also were strongly attacked, and made a most valiant stand at Ledringhem, time and again counter-attacking with the bayonet down the main street. At about midnight on May 28/29 they succeeded in extracting themselves and reached Dunkirk where, on the 30th, they evacuated some two-thirds of the unit back to England.

The cadre of both battalions formed in Herefordshire and, slowly, new fighting units were built up. But in November 1941 the 5th Battalion was reconstituted as the 43rd Battalion Reconnaissance Corps and became lost to the Regiment. They eventually took part in the Normandy landing, but their ship struck a mine after the severe storm of June 24,

1944, and some 300 men became casualties. They were, however, the first British unit to reach the Seine, and after the dash through Belgium were engaged in the Nijmegen area and remained in action until the European War ended.

The 2nd Battalion were eventually posted to the 56th Independent Brigade and took part in the D-Day offensive, operating with the Canadian Army in the vicinity of Bayeux. After heavy fighting at Villers Bocage, Thury-Harcourt and Epaigne, they were largely responsible for the capture of Le Havre in August, and took as their prisoners the German Commander, his C.R.A. and also the Naval Commander. After the bridge-head fighting on the Turnhout-Antwerp Canal they were, in November, in the flooded Nijmegen area, spending an extremely un-comfortable winter there. [Typical scenes of British troops' experiences in this district are illustrated in pages 559 and 697, Vol 8.

First British Troops Into Arnhem

Early on April 13, 1945, crossing the Issel in buffaloes and an assortment of landing craft, the 61st had the honour of being the first British troops to enter Arnhem. The Battalion was now in the 49th Division and for the rest of the war were occupied with the Canadians in North-West Holland. They eventually had the task of disarming the 346th German Infantry Division who had been opposite them since the early days in Normandy and more lately at Arnhem. In May the Battalion entered Germany near Osnabrück, and commenced their roles as occupying troops with their usual tact, firmness, and sense of humour.

We now turn to the 1st Battalion, the old 28th Foot. When war broke out the Batta-lion was at Mingaladon, near Rangoon. They were kept there as the only British Infantry unit in Southern Burma on security duties until Japan declared war in December 1941. Needless to say they had not been idle, but training and duties had been made difficult by a large number of the more experienced officers and men of the Battalion being drafted home as instructors and as nuclei for new units. Nevertheless, the remainder of them were fighting fit and in good heart when the testing-time came.

COLONEL-IN-CHIEF OF THE REGIMENT, H.R.H. the Duke of Gloucester, now Governor-General of Australia, during a tour of Northern Ireland in 1941 visited the Gloucestershire Regi-ment at Victoria Park, Belfast, and chatted to a junior N.C.O. during the inspection. Accom-panying the Duke is Brigadier (now Maj.-Gen.) G. F. Watson, D.S.O.

COVERING THE EVACUATION OF RANGOON and the withdrawal of the H.Q. of the Army in Burma, in March 1942, mobile mortar detachments of the 1st Battalion The Gloucestershire Regiment fired into enemy positions in the Toungoo area (top). Others of the Battalion were deployed across the track to defend the railway (above). *Photos, British Paramount News*

The first Japanese air raid on Rangoon took place on December 23, 1941, and after that date the 28th were called upon to carry out almost every conceivable duty in the city. Besides keeping law and order amongst the demoralized population they were dealing with refugees and looters, running trains, milking cows, burying the dead, and by example and discipline reducing something of the panic in the threatened city, for by this time the enemy were overrunning all southern Burma and were approaching the capital itself from the south-east.

On March 7, 1942, orders were received to evacuate Rangoon, and the Battalion were soon called upon to help open the Prome road at a point some 21 miles north of the city, where the Japanese had established a road block and were holding up the withdrawal of the H.Q. of the Army in Burma and of the British and Indian troops who had escaped from the earlier battle on the Sittang front to the east.

The first engagement of the 28th was therefore at Taukkyan. Unfortunately only headquarters and one company were available, as the remaining companies were still detached covering the evacuation and destruction of the Syriam oil refineries and the Rangoon docks. After several gallant attempts and with considerable casualties they were unable to force a way through that evening, but on the following morning the road was cleared and for the next 24 days the Battalion was engaged in fighting one of

the most desperate and valiant rearguard actions of their long history.

Almost unaided they were responsible for covering the rear of the withdrawing Burma Army up the 140-mile road to Prome. Thanks to their far-seeing commanding officer, the Battalion had, during the latter months in Rangoon, equipped themselves by one means or another with a fleet of motor vehicles and with additional weapons. They had also carried out strenuous spells of intensive training. At Letpadan, after a couple of days of lying in wait, the 28th surprised and very roughly handled the Japanese advanced troops following up the Prome road. For this the C.-in-C. congratulated the unit. It was, in fact, the first real success the British had scored in the campaign.

Colours : White on Black

49TH (WEST RIDING) DIVISION

RECRUITED in the East and West Ridings of Yorkshire, the Division first saw action with the North-West Expeditionary Force in Norway, April - May 1940. After the Allied withdrawal from that theatre the "Fighting 49th" returned to England en route for Iceland, where it formed the main part of the garrison. It was there that the original Divisional sign, the white rose of Yorkshire, carried during the First Great War and after, was replaced by the Polar Bear.

Back in the U.K. again, in 1943, the Division trained for the Normandy invasion and was one of the formations to land early on the beach-head, June 1944. Its first success was the capture of Rauray. Not until after being heavily engaged in the Bocage country did the Division launch its first major assault—against Fontenay - le - Pesnil, which secured the road to Tilly and Juvigny, the former being captured on June 19.

THRUSTING east from the Falaise Gap, in August, the 49th crossed the Seine and rapidly covered the last fifty miles to take a prominent part in the assault on Le Havre, captured on September 12. Moving into Holland, Roosendal was taken, and on September 29 Cpl. J. W. Harper, of the Hallamshire Battalion of the York and Lancaster Regiment, was awarded a posthumous V.C. (see illus. in page 24, Vol. 9). Transferred to the Venlo sector, the Division cleared the enemy from the west bank of the river Maas. From November until March 1945, the 49th defended the "island" in the Nijmegen salient, the sole Allied bridge-head over the Rhine at the time. Here at Zetten, in January, a five-day battle was fought in floods and snowstorms.

After weeks of patrolling this flooded area in amphibious craft the Division took part in the Allied break-out and fought in the battle for Arnhem, captured on April 15. North of the town the Division continued to clean up isolated pockets of resistance until VE Day, May 8.

On the Western Front with the Gloucester Boys

LENDING A HAND to the local farmers in France was a welcome diversion (1) for men of the Gloucestershire Regiment in interludes of training and Front-Line duties during the quiet spell on the Western Front in 1939 ; they are gathering in the beet crop. Important task which fell to the Regiment was the training of the first of Britain's conscripted youths to become an active Field Force unit ; attached to the 5th Battalion, these underwent field training (2) at Thumeries, France, in January 1940. Salvaging the contents of a wine merchant's van, which skidded off a road near Péronne, in the Lille area, in October 1939, was well rewarded (3). The 5th Battalion was later evacuated—from Dunkirk, but the 2nd—the other Battalion in France — was encircled before reaching the coast.

Photos (previously unpublished), British Official

PAGE 269

advance up the Chindwin River, which was threatening the left flank of the Army as it withdrew over the mountains into India. Sharp but successful actions were fought at Monywa and Budalin before they fell back to Ye-u, whence began the 100-mile trek across country to the Chindwin once again. Crossing at Kalewa, the Battalion entered India by way of the Tamu Pass on May 11.

Regimental Treasures Were Looted

After resting and being slowly re-equipped in Assam the Battalion spent eighteen months on the frontier, when they were sent to Calcutta and given an Internal Security role, always an unpleasant one in India. Here they remained until 1945, when they started jungle warfare training once more with a view to getting their own back with the Japanese. However, the war was won before they received their chance. One big disaster suffered by the 28th during this first campaign in Burma was the loss of all their regimental and private possessions. The regimental plate, though carried almost to the River Chindwin, had to be buried in the jungle as a last resource, and later was found to have been looted and all the priceless old treasures are no more.

The only other Battalion to see active service, the 10th, also served in Burma. Raised at Bristol in 1940, after a spell of coast defence duty the Battalion, in 1942, was converted into a tank unit and as such proceeded to India. On January 1, 1943, they reverted to the infantry role and with the British 36th Division embarked for Calcutta, in February 1944, for the Arakan front. Here they were soon in action and helped very considerably to break up the stalemate situation thereabouts. In May they were withdrawn and after a short rest near Shillong in Assam moved to Ledo, the Indian terminus of the new Burma Road.

From there, in July, the Battalion was flown to Myitkyina in Northern Burma to take part in the operations with the American trained Chinese troops (the Northern Combat Area Command). They landed on the Myitkyina airfield, still unpleasantly near to the Japanese, and with their division pressed south-west along the railway through appalling country, under water on either side of the line, with elephant grass six feet high, and infested with mosquitoes and leeches.

ON RECONNAISSANCE in the Nijmegen area, Holland, during the winter of 1944-45, a patrol of the 2nd Battalion The Gloucestershire Regiment found the going very heavy. Lieut.-Col. R. A. Biddle of this Battalion received the D.S.O. from Field-Marshal (then General) Montgomery (left) on July 17, 1944, for gallantry shortly after the D-Day landings in Normandy. *Photos, British Official*

With companies covering enormous frontages the Battalion continued to keep the Japanese some 30 miles south of the Army, and this in spite of the difficult and enclosed country so suitable to the Japanese methods of infiltration and encirclement. At Paungde and at Shwedaung on the Irrawaddy they had another enemy column to deal with, one which had crossed the river from the west and had not as yet learnt their lesson at the hands of the Gloucesters. Fierce fighting ensued and the casualties were heavy, but the main column was enabled to slip away without undue interference.

The Battalion was now reduced to two companies but was employed protecting the demolition parties at work in the Burman oilfields about Yennangyaung. They then withdrew via Mandalay to Shwebo. Later they were called upon to help check the Jap

PASSING through the Chinese at Mogaung, after capturing Taungi, the 10th pushed on to Pinbaw. Against Japanese "suicide" posts the advance was continued some five to seven miles a day, and with the monsoon conditions the going was of the hardest. After a pause the Battalion were in action, in October, against an exceptionally strong position astride the Gobyin Chaung (stream), and after a battle which swayed wildly to and fro for five days the enemy were finally driven out with heavy losses. Casualties in the Battalion were also severe.

The railway town of Katha was reached on Christmas Day, and in January 1945 the Battalion, crossing to the east bank of the Irrawaddy, advanced up the Shweli River to Myitson, whence they pushed up the difficult and mountainous country to Mongmit and Mogok, the latter being the site of the world's largest ruby mines. After months of living in uninhabited jungles, being supplied entirely from the air and with practically no transport, the division linked up with the Chinese troops on the old Burma Road near Kyaukme. Then followed the final stages of the war in Burma in the vicinity of Maymyo. When the enemy finally surrendered, the Battalion had completed over ten months in continuous contact with the Japanese, fighting and marching over 1,000 miles in indescribable country largely in the monsoon season. No mean effort !

MANNING A BREN GUN CARRIER AT NISPER, Holland, on October 27, 1944, these men of the Regiment, positioned by the corner of a wrecked house, acted as observers. At the time, this town near the Dutch-Belgian frontier, entered during the Allied advance north of Antwerp, was under heavy mortar fire.
Photo, British Official

Moulmein's Pagoda is Moving Downhill

Bombed by the Japanese before they entered on January 20, 1942, and subsequently by the British, Moulmein was still beyond the farthest advance of our troops from Rangoon when the war in Burma ended, in August 1945. About 100 miles from Rangoon across the Gulf of Martaban, and near the mouth of the Salween River, this second seaport of Burma is familiar to readers of Kipling in the line " By the old Moulmein Pagoda, looking lazy at the sea." Now, affected by frequent landslides, the old pagoda is gradually slipping from its eminence (1), causing damage to nearby houses in its path. Japanese are working, not too hurriedly (2), to save it. Acting as patient builders' mates, elephants move great planks wherever required (3). There is no lack of timber: Moulmein in pre-war days was noted for its exports of teak, and the industry is getting under way again, felled trees being floated down-river from the jungle to the mills. Effects of Moulmein bombing (4) will not soon be erased.

Photos, British Official

'Millionaires' Beach' on an Adriatic Shore—

The famous bathing resort of Lido, claimed by Italians to be the best in the world, and in pre-war days exclusive to the very wealthy, is now thronged by British troops on leave. The Churchill-Roosevelt Club (1), formerly the Municipal Casino, a few yards from the seafront, is at their disposal. Its spacious lounge, once the baccarat room, has become a dining hall. Italian waitresses are seen serving light refreshments (2). On the sunny sands (3) relaxation is the order of the day.

—Now for the Relaxation of Our 'Other Ranks'

A splash in the sea just here (4) is for men only : Service girls have their own beach a little farther along. Leave accommodation is provided at the sumptuous Hotel Excelsior, in whose ornate entrance hall (5) sailors are checking-in. Afternoon tea, taken in bathing costumes, is an irresistible attraction (6). Eventually this pleasant site will be handed back to the Italian authorities ; but whilst British forces have still to be maintained in the area it will remain theirs exclusively.

Atom Bomb Aftermath in Hiroshima

Under the direction of the Chiefs of Staff, a British Mission visited Hiroshima and Nagasaki to study the damage done by the two atomic bombs which were dropped on August 6 and 9, 1945. In their report, published on June 30, 1946, it is revealed that in Hiroshima the bomb destroyed over four square miles of wooden houses, first by blast, then by fire. Buildings of reinforced concrete mostly resisted the blast but were burnt out. Light, single-storey concrete buildings were wrecked at about a mile from the centre of damage. When the bomb fell, approximately 80,000 were killed of the 320,000 in this Japanese city which was wiped out to end a war. A sailor of H.M.I.S. Sutlej surveys the Hiroshima scene (above), including (right foreground) the gutted ruin of what was an important newspaper office. The road which once led to the great Mitsubishi chemical works now trails away to nothing in the rubble. But signs of life are returning: here and there a rough shack has been built (left), and a few young shoots push up from the base of shattered trees.

Photos, Indian Official, Illustrated

FIRST BATTLES OF THE EAST AFRICANS

By HARLEY V. USILL

THE spirit which dominated the war efforts of Kenya, Uganda, Tanganyika, Northern Rhodesia, Zanzibar and British Somaliland can be summed up in the motto of the Northern Rhodesia Regiment, " Diversi Genere Fide Pares " (Different in Race, Equal in Fidelity). It is this comradeship of different races fighting a common battle against a common foe which permeates the story of East Africa at war.

Unlike West Africa, which is essentially the black man's country with only a handful of white officials and traders, East Africa has attracted white settlers, and other emigrant races, such as Indians, in considerable numbers. With few exceptions, the East Africans have not developed such highly organized tribal government as in West Africa. Thus the white administrator and settler play a much more varied part in affairs.

For centuries Arabs were visiting the coast in search of slaves, but the interior was totally unexplored. The Portuguese had been early in the field, but it was not until the early part of the 19th century that British explorers and missionaries took a serious interest in the area. Names such as Livingstone, Mackenzie, Speke, Grant and Baker, and Cecil Rhodes appear among the early pioneers, but it was only during the 1880's and 1890's that the British Government could be persuaded to consolidate the work of these men by establishing Protectorates.

All the Demands of War Were Met

When war came to East Africa for a second time within living memory, the upsurge of loyalty speaks well for the work of British administration, even with its defects, during the past fifty or sixty years. The task which the advent of war thrust upon British officials and settlers has been described by the Governor of Northern Rhodesia in regard to his Colony, but what he says is equally applicable to all the rest :

" The Civil Service of Northern Rhodesia released proportionately more men for the fighting services than any other African Colony. Most of our outstations had to be manned by one European alone. The war effort of these officers, in terms of loneliness and overwork, was as great as that of any other community in the Territory, although less spectacular. They were the men who were largely responsible for recruiting an army many times the size of the country's peacetime establishment, besides a Labour Corps, and many labour gangs to work on aerodromes, military roads and camps, and other war works. The multitudinous domestic affairs of the soldiers away at the front, the leave drafts with their pay, ration and transport arrangements, the administration of the many control measures, all fell largely on the shoulders of a seriously depleted staff of District Officers. Big schemes were undertaken by an almost skeleton staff, but the war made them necessary. . . . It is little realized what a strain the war put upon the country's food resources and how great were the efforts needed to boost production, to buy food and to control distribution. . . . There are few officials whose duties were not doubled. In spite of all this, all the demands of war were met."

Again, typical of the rest, the Governor of Kenya says of the women of that Colony :

" The figures of European woman-power make triumphant reading. Out of a total of 5,838 registered European women, 58 per cent have been in full-time employment during the years of the war ; 31 per cent have been tied to their homes on account of young families, and practically all of these have undertaken some form of voluntary war work in their spare time. . . . A word of praise must be given to the woman farmer, the wife of the young soldier-settler, the over-age or physically handicapped man. They may run not only their own farm but those of their fighting neighbours as well."

The British civilian population in East Africa may well feel proud of their part in the victory, for without their devotion to duty

AFTER covering the withdrawal of our troops from British Somaliland in the dark days of 1940, the East Africans shared the triumphs of West and South Africans in Italian Somaliland and Abyssinia. Then, taking part in the occupation of Madagascar, they helped to remove the last threat to the security of their shores.

much of the effort which we are now surveying would have been impossible.

In his foreward to the book, The Infantry of the East Africa Command, General Sir William Platt, General Officer Commanding-in-Chief, East Africa Command, says :

" To the infantry in East Africa have come men from every county in the United Kingdom and from every territory between the Gulf of Aden and Limpopo. . . . In comradeship they have mastered the novelty and complexity of the weapons with which the infantry soldier is now equipped. . . . Let us not forget that the tens of thousands of African infantry soldiers serving in this War came with only the haziest knowledge of the issues at stake and that, in all cases they came as volunteers. For the past five years these men have marched and stood sentinel over vast distances of the African continent and, in two campaigns where the major part of the East Africa forces were involved were infantry, they won notable successes.'

In addition to the King's African Rifles (which comprised battalions from Kenya, Uganda, Somaliland, Nyasaland and Tanganyika Territory), and the Northern Rhodesia Regiment, there was a large number of other units such as the E.A. Corps of Signals and E.A. Army Medical Corps. The Kenya Regiment was established in June 1937, its primary role to provide a reservoir of trained European leaders to cope with the anticipated expansion of the King's African Rifles and ancillary services in time of war. Out of over 2,900 men enlisted into the Regiment over 1,100 have been commissioned. The East African Scouts came into being in April 1942, and were recruited mainly from Southern Tanganyika and Kenya tribes, to whom bushcraft is second nature.

Held the Gap for Six Vital Days

The Northern Rhodesia Regiment was one of the first East African units to go into action. The entry of Italy into the war exposed the undefended border of British Somaliland to attack from Abyssinia. Heavily committed elsewhere in those dark days of 1940, and with few trained troops to spare, Britain decided on an orderly evacuation of British Somaliland. The total British forces available to effect this withdrawal to the port of Berbera consisted of the 1st Battalion of the Northern Rhodesia Regiment, the 2nd King's African Rifles, the Somaliland Camel Corps, two companies of Punjabis, the 1st East African Light Battery and a battalion of the Black Watch held in reserve to cover the final embarkation on August 17–18.

Tug Argan Gap, main gateway from the interior to Berbera, was the vital spot, and the 1st Northern Rhodesia Regiment with the East Africa Light Battery and a Machine-gun Company of the Camel Corps were given the task of delaying the Italians long enough to enable the main evacuation to take place. The official account of the action states :

" The enemy attacked on Sunday, August 11, 1940. Outnumbered ten to one, practically without air support, out-gunned by six to one, facing 100 armoured fighting vehicles . . . the men of Northern Rhodesia stood firm and fought viciously back. Under severe bombardment, heavy shelling and frequent massed infantry attacks, the Africans of Northern Rhodesia, under their leaders from the mines, the farms, the Government service and the towns of this Territory, held the gap for six vital days before receiving the order to withdraw during the night. . . ."

To Africans, five Distinguished Conduct Medals and 20 East Africa Force Badges were awarded for this action ; to Europeans, two Military Crosses, a Distinguished Conduct Medal, a British Empire Medal and an East Africa Force Badge.

After their success in British Somaliland it is difficult to understand subsequent Italian strategy. They had driven a King's African Rifle Company out of Moyale and advanced on Buna, but made no further progress into Kenya. It is true, of course, that the vast stretches of desert country between the Kenya Northern Frontier and the settled parts of the country proved a natural obstacle, but even so their overwhelming numbers might have enabled them to make dangerous inroads into Kenya.

The Breaking of the Juba Line

The major offensive against the Italians was originally timed for June 1941, after the rains, but the success of the El Wak operation (Dec. 16, 1940) had shown the superior morale and fighting qualities of the British. It was decided then to attack earlier, and in January the offensive began, with the 22nd East African Brigade leading the 12th Division to its first objective, Kismayu. The breaking of the Juba Line was a magnificent performance, and the most decisive action fought by East African forces in the whole campaign. In the final advance on Addis Ababa, the channel of the Awash provided the last of the great natural obstacles.

BY the time that the King's African Rifles arrived the Italians had destroyed the steel railway bridge at the point where the river runs through a deep gorge. Nothing daunted, the Africans flung themselves into the river, crossed it at two points and then charged the Italians on the opposite bank. The way was now open to Addis Ababa. With the capture of the capital on April 5, 1941, the fighting, however, was not yet over —the Battle of the Lakes had still to be fought. The 22nd Brigade and the 21st King's African Rifles Brigade played a prominent part in these very difficult operations, culminating in the fall of Gondar, last Italian stronghold, on November 27.

With the defeat of the Italians in Abyssinia the main danger to the security of East Africa had been removed, but there was still uncertainty while Madagascar remained under the control of Vichy France. The Abyssinian campaign had to be launched, but that against Madagascar had to be landed and launched. The 22nd East African Brigade landed at Majunga on September 10, 1942, and after the town had been cleared by British troops advanced rapidly to reach Antananarivo. Since the fall of the capital did not end resistance the East Africans continued to advance south, and when the Vichy Governor obtained an armistice, in November 1942, they had reached Ambalavao. In his booklet, Into Madagascar, the late Gandar Dower gives this description of the African Askari :

" During this period it was a pleasant sight to see the broad white grins, the broad black boots, and the newly acquired tin hats of the Askaris as they moved about Majunga. . . . They had learned a lot of strange things recently : that great hotels can suddenly put to sea, that ships do not run on rails, that sea-water is good to bathe in but not to drink, that this queer uneasy lake ran all the way to England, that improbable Paradise where white men live in their thousands and thousands, presumably kept alive by the unsung local equivalents of the Kikuyu and the Wakamba."

Both the East Africans and their brothers in West Africa had still many strange wartime experiences before them, but these must form the subject of another article.

Our War Leaders in Peacetime
TEDDER

MARSHAL of the Royal Air Force Lord Tedder, G.C.B., showed no symptoms of military genius as a young man. At Whitgift School he excelled at drawing; and from Cambridge, where he won the Prince Consort Prize, he entered professional football, before going to Fiji in the Civil Service, in 1914.

Tedder has the build of a Rugby "outside," being on the small side and lean. With a fondness for good literature and art, he looks more like a scholar than a dynamic war leader; and whenever possible he discards his uniform for "civvies," preferably a blazer in summer.

Born at Glenguin, Stirlingshire, in 1890, the son of Sir Arthur John Tedder, his military career began in 1914 when he joined the Dorset Regiment, serving in France. Two years later he was seconded to the Royal Flying Corps, and in 1919, transferred to the R.A.F., he laid the foundations of his career.

By then, Tedder had been married four years to the Australian girl he met in Fiji, Miss Rosalinde Maclardy. And already he was beginning to be recognized for his military as well as his academic qualities; his first book, The Navy and the Restoration, confirmed his University reputation. And within five years of his transfer to the R.A.F. he was given command of No. 2 Flying Training School.

His Bird-Pets at the London Zoo

Tedder's advancement was steady but unspectacular, until he succeeded to the Middle East Command in 1941. He has no time for orthodoxy, and once snapped " To hell with history—what's your *problem*? " But he is not normally given to sudden outbursts. A softly spoken, taciturn Scot, he likes the quiet things of life—among them, wild birds. The London Zoo has on exhibition several of the pets he brought home from Africa and Europe.

At 56 he likes cricket more than football. And, a good crayon artist, seldom without a sketching pad in his pocket, he finds contentment in sketching. At the Athenaeum and Royal Air Force Clubs Lord Tedder is known for his lightning head-and-shoulder sketches, for a fondness for argument, and a quick—and sometimes biting—wit. He has a habit of slouching in an easy chair with a pipe and a half-amused but scrutinizing and sometimes baffling expression.

TEDDER has a penetrating mind. From it sprang the "Tedder carpet" pattern bombing that helped to blast the Axis out of North Africa. As Deputy Supreme Allied Commander he was responsible for the Anglo-American air operations against Germany; and it was he who conceived the tank-busting Hurricanes which he named " can-openers."

The war brought its share of sorrow to Tedder. In it he lost a son (a bomber pilot), and his first wife was killed in an air crash near Cairo. He has a second son still at school, and a daughter who served in the W.A.A.F. In October 1943 Tedder married Mrs. Marie De Seton Black, and a son was born on May 23, 1946. The man who started life as a professional footballer and became Chief of Air Staff and Senior Member of the Air Council now lives at Corner Croft, Kingston Hill, Surrey, near to where he had his official residence as Deputy to Eisenhower.

THE MAN WHO CONCEIVED THE CARPET PATTERN BOMBING which so mightily disconcerted the Axis forces in North Africa watched with keen enjoyment the final in the shooting for the King's Cup on the Surrey rifle range at Bisley (1) in June 1946. His second wife, Lady Tedder, in their Surrey home at Kingston Hill (2). Thinking maybe of his own professional football days, he kicked off (3) at a match in North Africa, Christmas 1944. At his office (4) in the Air Ministry, London.

Photos, Keystone, British Official, G.P.U.

Glory of the Garden in a London Blitzed Street

PLANTED BY FIRE-WATCHERS during interludes of duties in the blitz days, lupins and other garden plants have prospered among the rubble at this flattened corner of Gresham Street and Foster Lane in the City of London. In the background is the tower of the gutted St. Alban's Church in Wood Street. Nature herself has covered with a prodigality of wild flowers much of the trail of the Luftwaffe over England—through the agency of seeds wind-borne or dropped by birds. See also page 286, Vol. 8.

Europe's Wartime Capitals in 1946

TIRANA

By D. R. OAKLEY-HILL

INSPECTOR of the Albanian Gendarmerie from 1929 to 1938, Major Oakley-Hill started Albanian resistance to the Axis in 1941 as Liaison Officer. In 1945 he returned to Albania as chief of U.N.R.R.A.'s mission to help with the country's restoration.

ALBANIA'S independence dates from 1912, but Tirana was established as the capital of the new State only after the National Congress had met at Lushnja in 1920. There were several historic towns that might have been chosen, but by their choice of Tirana the Albanians demonstrated their determination to make a new start, after the interruption of the First Great War, unhampered by local jealousies.

Tirana, before 1920, was a sleepy little town at the end of a 25-mile carriage-way from the seaport of Durres (Durazzo). It was a village by western standards, basking in a basin at the foot of the stark 5,000-ft. mountain ridge of Daiti, and ringed by green hills. There were ample gently-sloping fields for development. So the seat of government was set up there and building of a town began.

The old bazaar, or market quarter, was left untouched, a maze of cobbled alleys lined with single-storeyed stalls and workshops. There was Blacksmiths' Street, with the copper beaters at one end, an alley, which rang from dawn to dusk, six days a week, with the creative music of hammering, and where you could buy a horseshoe, a ploughshare, brass bells for your sheep, an iron gate wrought to your own design, or a copper tray with exquisite Oriental tracery. There were Cobblers' Street, Quilt-makers' Street, Grain Square, and Cooks' (or Eating-House) Street where the merchants and craftsmen, who never slept at their place of work, could get a mid-day meal or order for themselves and their customers the indispensable small cups of Turkish coffee. All this is still there; the same life goes on. But round it has grown up a new city.

Relics of Italian Empire's Day

Between 1920 and 1939 development was rapid; those were harvest days for the local merchant and landowner. Officials poured into the capital, and houses had to be run up as fast as possible. With the houses came the shops to cater for growing and changing needs; men who had been to foreign universities wanted other things than homespun wool and copper pans. So arose the Tirana of today. Streets of modern houses and shops grew out of the fields; there were no rules, the style depending on the pocket and the imagination, or the background, of the builder. The shopping streets looked ragged because the new shops were all of different height and style. Dwelling-houses were of every kind. Some were on the simplest plan; Albanians would jokingly remark of some friend, "He has a magnificent house, two rooms below and two above!" No bathroom, no plumbing, yet a home; a home for yourself, your wife, perhaps two or three parents, a maiden aunt, and several children; your castle, unless you gave a friend or stranger a pass into its privacy, and an Albanian loves nothing better than to ask either to share all he has.

Other houses were more elaborate, built on modern lines by architects who had learnt their trade in Vienna or Milan; complete with baths and taps, waiting for the day, now come, when water should run instead of being laboriously drawn from wells. The new civic centre, Skanderbeg Square, was a sunken garden surrounded by the two-storeyed offices of the Government Departments and the City Council, their austerity relieved by the beautiful minaret and dome of the old mosque, mercifully not sacrificed to modernity. Two boulevards, with a centre walk between flowering trees, made the evening saunter pleasant. They were named after Zog, the King, and

Mussolini, the rich neighbour who lent the money with an eye to the future.

From 10,000 the population grew to 30,000, and the mayor bewailed the difficulty of bringing roads and services to all the houses that arose under the scattered and capricious system of development. In the long run this haphazard tendency has increased the city's charm. It is an airy, spacious town. You never feel shut in by the streets and there is everywhere a width of sky. Today, standing on a hill to the south, you see the whole place straggling across its green basin, the roof-lines cut by the minarets of some twelve mosques and the traditional clock-tower; half veiled in summer by a wealth of trees, and sheltered by the great mountain barrier stretching away, past historic Kruya, to the north. No capital in Europe could present a more pleasing prospect.

Flying over Tirana, you notice first the white minarets, then the long straight arteries of the boulevards cutting through the acres of brown-tiled roofs, and then the group of big white buildings which are the relics of the Italian Empire's brief day. After the Italians invaded Albania, in April 1939, they concentrated on the Fascist façade. Great structures faced with white marble rose quickly along a new and very wide boulevard which slopes away to the south of Skanderbeg Square. This avenue, named then the Boulevard of Empire, is now the Boulevard of the National Martyrs. At the foot, and set against a hill, was built the Fascist Party's centre; today this is the home of Brash, the Union of Anti-Fascist Albanian Youth (see facing page).

NEARBY, the Stadium, with its attendant snowy buildings, where blackshirted youths once gave their mass demonstrations of the new *dynamisme*, is now the scene of the physical exploits of the boys and girls of another dispensation. Opposite is the long, classical-looking Congress House, the home also of the Praesidium or Supreme Council. Beyond are the offices of the Prime Minister and State Police; and farther up the hill is Tirana's finest hotel, the Daiti. It is State-owned, a building of airy and spacious marble halls and bedrooms as modern as could be desired. Each room facing the boulevard on all three upper floors has its own private balcony, separated from its neighbours by straight walls, so that the whole façade looks like a gigantic white mouth-organ. To the west of this avenue lies New Tirana, an area of private houses of the best type, the capital's Garden City.

This great boulevard has fallen naturally into use as a parade-ground. Military parades, State funerals, demonstrations of victory and of national pleasure or indignation, confident columns of children with model tanks and rifles, move along its wide, paved roadway. But it is the things unseen that really matter, and only the elected rulers of the new Republic can decide whether they have chosen the path really leading to the happiness of the people.

For this is an era of youth in Albania. The leaders of the State are largely young, and they have concentrated on the youth. In Albanian the words for new and young are the same, so that New Albania is Young Albania. The enthusiasm of the rising generation is obvious. Boys and girls claim and take an equal share in the new-found self-confidence of youth. The old people are a little bewildered. Parental discipline and family ties have always been strong, but now the colts have broken loose. However, they are working. They have their serious meetings and discussions, their music and their art, and in the holidays they go out in lorry-loads to camp in the mountains and dig new roads.

THE Italians brought water to Tirana. The Tirana river was dammed where it leaves the gorge beside Daiti mountain, and now almost the whole town has its supply. Main drainage, electric light and telephones date from pre-Italian days. But the war has swelled the population to about 80,000 and accommodation and services are strained. Many villages and towns in the south were destroyed either by the Germans or in the course of the Greek-Italian war. Refugees swarmed northwards, and Tirana received the lion's share; all are being cared for by the authorities.

Everything in Albania is organized by the State. The food problem would have been acute but for the supplies brought in by U.N.R.R.A. Bread, both maize and wheat, is the principal item in the Albanian's diet; it is rationed, and an efficient coupon system operates for both townsman and peasant. Bread queues, even in crowded Tirana, are normally unnecessary because each baker has his registered customers; others bake for those on the free list, which comprises the aged and families without a breadwinner. Work is found for almost all manual workers, who are organized in trade unions, but there is some unemployment amongst ex-officials. Orphans, especially those left by men killed in the war, are cared for in a State orphanage, and they were recently delighted to receive toys sent by the people of a London parish.

No Disorder and Hardly Any Crime

On the whole Tirana escaped from the war lightly, except for the airport buildings which were thoroughly razed by Allied bombing. But a number of shops in the centre of the town were destroyed in the last fighting with the retreating Nazis in November 1944, including the interesting old mosque of Suleyman Pasha.

The atmosphere of the place has changed since before the War. It is more crowded; too many small shops and stalls have been allowed to clutter up some of the central streets. The people are not well clothed, though Tirana is better off than other parts of the country and there are still goods of many kinds in the shops, the remains of stocks imported in Italian days. There is no disorder and hardly any crime; Albanians are traditionally honest, and sanctions are severe. To the horse-drawn carriages, which ply the streets for hire, have now been added bus services. Bicycles are legion. The uniformed police are polite but firm, and direct the traffic adequately from pedestals. There are all the trappings of a European city. There is more bustle than before, and less serenity. Perhaps that could be equally said of London and many another capital; the War has left its inevitable restlessness. All that the people want is peace and security. Let us pray that these may be granted them.

New Era of Youth in Albania's Young Capital

TIRANA ESCAPED SEVERE DAMAGE during the war, and some of its many fine buildings of modern design were erected during the Italian Occupation. Looking across the town (1) the Stadium (right) once resounded to Mussolini's marching Fascist legions ; in the left foreground is Congress House, seat of the Supreme Council. A military parade (2) passing the saluting base in front of the state-owned Daiti Hotel, named after the mountain ridge which dominates the town. With the revival of the Republic on January 11, 1946, after eighteen years sovereign rule by King Zog I, stress has been laid on the development of the Nation's youth. A physical culture demonstration staged in the Stadium (3), members of the Brash, the Union of Anti-Fascist Albanian Youth, taking part. The Headquarters of the Union occupy the former Italian Fascist Party centre, in the Boulevard of National Martyrs ; during the second Youth Congress, the H.Q. was floodlit and a portrait of General Enver Hoxha, head of the Constituent Assembly, was prominently displayed (4).

PAGE 279

The Roll of Honour

NCO's & MEN

1939—1946

Cpl. L. R. ALLAN
K.O. Scottish Borderers.
Caen. 1.7.44.
Age 36. (Perth)

So great has been the response of readers to our invitation to submit portraits for our Roll of Honour that no more can now be accepted. But we have every hope of being able to publish all those so far received.

Air Mech. E. C. ALTON
Royal Air Force.
Action : Notts. 28.7.42.
Age 20. (Brentwood)

Sig. R. BROWN
H.M.S. Rawalpindi.
Off Iceland. 23.11.39.
Age 19. (Acton)

Sig. G. CARTLEDGE
Royal Signals.
In action : Goch. 7.3.45.
Age 23. (Skeffling)

L/Cpl. D. H. CREASEY
Q.O.R. West Kent Regt.
Action : Termoli. 4.10.43.
Age 21. (Oxted)

Pte. W. J. FRASER
Royal Norfolk Regiment.
Action : Sangro. 18.5.43.
Age 29. (London)

Pte. G. T. GARMAN
2nd Royal Sussex Regt.
Action : Alamein. 28.10.42
Age 22. (Newhaven)

L/Cpl. W. GOURLEY
K.O. Scottish Borderers
Died of wounds. 16.7.44.
Age 27. (Edinburgh)

Sergeant R. C. HALL
Royal Air Force.
Action : Berlin. Feb., 44.
Age 22. (Handsworth)

Coder A. JACKSON
Royal Navy.
In action. 29.4.45.
Age 20. (Wakefield)

Pte. C. J. JOHN
2nd Border Regiment.
South France. 3.12.45.
Age 21. (Cardiff)

L/Cpl. J. JOHNSON
K.O. Scottish Borderers.
St. Odenrode. 27.9.44.
Age 24. (Willington)

Sgt. W. KILLIN
Royal Scots Greys.
Action : Belgium. 6.9.44.
Age 26. (Lanarkshire)

Pte. L. S. KNIGHT
2nd East Yorks Regiment.
Action : Holland. 16.10.44.
Age 20. (Plaistow)

L/Cpl. L. LANG
Royal Engineers.
Action : France. 12.8.44.
Age 29. (Cardiff)

Pte. E. W. LANGFORD
1st Suffolk Regiment.
Action : France. 14.8.44.
Age 19. (Reading)

Pte. R. McCALLUM
2nd Gordon Highlanders.
Action : Caen. 26.6.44.
Age 23. (Kilwinning)

Sgt./Plt. B. J. McGINN
Bomber Command. R.A.F.
Action : Cologne. Apr., 42.
Age 21. (Machynlleth)

Gnr. D. MACKENZIE
251/84th Med. Regt. R.A.
Action : Nijmegen. 28.9.44.
Age 24. (Glasgow)

A/B G. P. McKINLAY
Royal Navy.
Off Tobruk. 24.6.41
Age 23. (Prestonpans)

Marine C. H. NIBLETT
Royal Marines.
H.M.S. Royal Oak. 1939.
Age 21. (Portsmouth)

Bdr. L. J. NUNN
11 Regt. Hon. Artillery Coy.
Knightsbridge. 13.6.42.
Age 27. (Halstead)

Sgt./Obs. J. T. PARK
Royal Air Force.
Mediterranean. 20.1.42.
Age 26. (Leeds)

A/B J. A. PRITCHARD
H.M.S. Gallant.
Died of wounds. 12.1.41.
Age 26. (Birmingham)

L/Sgt. E. W. PYE
2/7th Queen's Royal Regt.
Action : Italy. 6.10.44.
Age 35. (Buckhurst Hill)

Pte. A. ROBINSON
2nd Lincolnshire Regt.
Action : Normandy. 20.7.44
Age 20. (Helpringham)

Gunner D. ROSIE
Royal Artillery.
Died of wounds. 26.10.42.
Age 41. (Glasgow)

Guardsman A. RULE
4th Bn. Grenadier Guards.
In action : Goch. 27.2.45.
Age 19. (Farnworth)

Pte. P. RUNCIEMAN
Gordon Highlanders.
Action : Rhine. 26.3.45.
Age 21. (S. Perrott)

Private J. RYAN
Worcestershire Regt.
Action : Burma. 8.3.45.
Age 28. (Manchester)

Tpr. G. A. SAMPSON
2nd Lothian Border Horse.
Died of wounds. 9.5.43.
Age 25. (Leith)

Pte. J. SHANKS
Royal Artillery.
Action : Salerno. 27.9.43
Age 25. (Alva)

L/Cpl. P. SINFIELD
4th Bn. Welch Regiment.
Action : Germany. 12.2.45.
Age 21. (Northampton)

Sto. P/O. W. B. STREET
H.M.S. Naiad.
Mediterranean. 11.3.42.
Age 29. (Edinburgh)

L/Sig. SUTHERLAND
H.M.S. Somali.
At sea. 24.9.42.
Age 21. (Forfar)

Pte. J. H. TILSON
Royal Irish Fusiliers.
Action : N. Africa. 25.4.43.
Age 22. (Nuneaton)

Sergeant J. WADE
Royal Air Force.
Action : N. Sea. 29.1.43.
Age 22. (London)

S.P.O. G. WEBB
H.M.S. Duchess.
Action : N. Sea. 13.12.39.
Age 33. (Caterham)

Eight Hundred Drowned This Night

The first British capital ship to be lost in the War, H.M.S. Royal Oak was torpedoed in Home waters in October 1939. The experiences of one of the 380 survivors are vividly conveyed by Surgeon Lieut.-Commander E. D. Caldwell, R.N. (portrait in page 728, Vol. 9). See also page 646, Vol. 9.

THE night it happened I had been listening to gramophone records with two fellows I was never to see again. At half-past twelve I picked my way carefully along the darkened quarter-deck to the hatchway leading to my cabin, undressed, and climbed on to my bunk.

We were in harbour—if such a term can be used to describe the wide, bleak waters of Scapa Flow—after a not unadventurous spell at sea, and with no thoughts of impending disaster in any one's mind, when at ten past one a muffled explosion shook the ship. "Lord !" I exclaimed to myself, and as I jumped down from my bunk I found my heart thumping more than a little. I locked into the next cabin and saw my neighbour pulling on a pair of trousers, and out in the cabin flat five or six officers were already discussing how and where the explosion could have occurred. (One must remember the vast number of compartments and storing places in a ship of this size.)

Eight minutes had passed. No alarms had been sounded and the general opinion seemed to be that whatever it was it was something inside the ship—it was later learned that many were not even awakened by this first torpedo. It was cold, and one or two men drifted back to their cabins. Just as I decided to do the same, another explosion occurred and the ship took a list to starboard. I heard the tinkling of glass falling from shelves and pictures in what seemed to be the awe-stricken silence that followed ; a

silence that was suddenly shattered by a third explosion. All lights went out, the list increased, and it was obvious we were for it.

I reached deck in my pyjamas, monkey jacket and one bedroom slipper—I dropped the other and remember deciding not to retrieve it. A fourth torpedo struck us, and the mighty bulk of the battleship shuddered again and settled deeper into the water. These last three blows had occurred in three minutes—and it was now every man for himself in a sinking ship with the cold, black water all around us. The rest of the Fleet was out at sea on this particular night, and apart from a tender some distance away and the Royal Oak's own drifter (a pre-war herring boat) which was tied up alongside us, we were all alone in the Flow, a huge sitting target for the U-boat.

"This Can't Be Happening to Me!"

I was certainly shocked, but, curiously, not frightened, as we stood on the sloping deck in the darkness, wisps of smoke eddyng round us. One heard shouts of reassurance, even of humour ; and sudden splashes as men clambered over the guard rails and dived twenty or thirty feet into the water below. The speed with which the Royal Oak was sinking, the list of the ship, and the intense darkness excluded the possibility of our boats being lowered. One was got into the water but was swamped by weight of numbers and sank. The drifter had to make feverish efforts to cut herself adrift, and immediately

she was clear she did magnificent work, picking up a full load of those who had jumped into the sea.

I had no plan. My mind was curiously blank with regard to my personal safety, although I can most vividly recall every thought and impression that passed through my brain—my new and rather expensive tennis racket, a book I had borrowed and promised to return, three pounds in the bottom of my drawer. A ship of this size must surely take a long time to sink, I thought: (six minutes later it was out of sight). Above all, the surprising thought, " This can't be happening to me ; you read about it in books; you see it on the flicks, but it *can't* be happening to me !" During this weird period I bumped into and talked to one or two people, but can't remember much what we said to each other, except a remark, "We'll take hours to sink. Stop the men from jumping into the drink !"

THE ship increased her list more and more rapidly. We were now on the ship's side and as she slid over, turning turtle, I lost my footing, fell, tried frantically to scramble up and dive clear, and was thrown headlong into the sea. ("I'll be sucked down—that's what they say happens—what a fool I was not to jump sooner !") I seemed to go down and down, and started fighting for breath. As I came to the surface, the stern and propeller soared above me then slipped slowly into the water and disappeared. A rush of water swept me head over heels, it seemed, and I went under again and came up in thick, black oil. I gulped it and retched at the filthy taste. My eyes smarted with it.

I swam and floundered about, hoping to find some form of support in the darkness. None of us had lifebelts. Normally, in

H.M.S. ROYAL OAK in the wide, bleak waters of Scapa Flow, the land-locked anchorage in the Orkney Islands, shortly before she was sunk by the enemy on October 14, 1939. Apparently immune from attack, the 29,000-ton battleship succumbed to torpedoes from a U-boat which defied the vigilance of patrol craft and penetrated the defences of nets, booms and block-ships. Announcing the loss, in the House of Commons, Mr. Churchill described Royal Oak as " a ship which, although very old, was of undoubted military value." PAGE 281 *Photo, Fox*

But I have no recollection whatever of finally succeeding . . . I found myself sitting on a hot grating in the engine-room, shivering uncontrollably from the cold, which I had not previously noticed. I stood up and vomited oil and salt water all over somebody sitting at my feet. I did this three times and apologized each time. He didn't appear to worry much, anyway.

WE were taken to the Pegasus and given hot drinks and helped into hot baths, and splashed and scrubbed. They were very grand to us, and we began to talk and recognize people and shake hands and try not to notice that friends were missing. About 380 of us had been very lucky. Over 800 had been drowned that night.

Of the happenings during the following days before we disembarked and were sent south I retain vivid memories. The air raids, the shattering noise, a German pilot lazily parachuting down silhouetted against a bright blue sky, while his plane, broken up by gunfire, crashed in flames on the hillside; the sinister whistle of bombs from the raiders; the marvellous kindness shown to

peacetime, lifebelts are never even thought of in warships, and we had not yet been issued with them. I heard cries around me, saw black heads bobbing, and I swam frenziedly again. I tried to wriggle out of my jacket, but found it heavy and slimy with oil. I repeatedly went under, until quite suddenly I gave it up and thought, quite dispassionately, "I'm going to drown. I'm going to drown now." Then, suddenly, I saw a group of heads not far off and tried to thresh my way towards them.

Somebody swam strongly past me and I caught his leg and tried to hold it. He kicked me clear. I saw an upturned boat ahead. How far was it? Or how near? Then I touched the freeboard—touched it and held on. I thought it was a pity one couldn't thank inanimate things, I was so grateful for that support.

I tried to wipe the oil out of my eyes with my free hand, and then with my sleeve, and realized how stupid that was. My mind flashed back to an old silent film of Buster Keaton as a diver drying his hands on a towel at the bottom of the sea. I said "Hallo!" to the indistinguishable face beside me, and it said, "Oh, this oil!"

THERE were about a dozen of us, I think, hanging on around a boat which kept steady as long as we did; but every now and then someone would try to improve his position or make himself more secure by clambering on to the upturned keel. Then, slowly but inevitably, our support would begin to roll over and back we would slip into the water, clawing frantically for a finger-hold on the smooth surface, shouting at each other till the movement ceased and we were supported once more. This happened many, many times, and every time meant a mouthful of oil and a thumping heart.

Time dragged on with no sign of our being picked up. We strained our eyes in the darkness for some glimmer of light, but none came. We sang "Daisy, Daisy, give me your answer do!" Daisy was the name of the drifter attached to the Royal Oak. At last we saw a mast-head light which grew brighter, and then the blacker darkness of a boat moving slowly towards us. We shouted again and again.

When she was within twenty yards of us we left our upturned boat and struck out in her direction. She had ropes hanging down, up which we tried to climb. I remember falling back into the sea twice. My hands were numb. I thought, "Mustn't lose now! Come on, mustn't lose now!"

us by the Thurso folk; the sense of relief we felt in the train taking us south (a relief broken almost comically by a train collision); the gradual acquisition of strange clothing, of odd meals and drinks, and so on, until at last—London, to find normality almost unreal after our chaotic experiences.

The World's Most Secret Garrison

Important in the planning of an Allied offensive on Jap positions, the Cocos Islands—remote in the Indian Ocean—were to form the most advanced of all S.E.A.C. bases. How the occupation was carried out, in 1945, and a fighter strip established is narrated by Flight-Lieut. Sydney Moorhouse who, as Public Relations Officer with No. 222 Group of the R.A.F., was responsible for reporting R.A.F. coastal warfare in the East.

TOWARDS the end of March 1945 I boarded a ship in Colombo Harbour to travel to the Cocos Islands, a little group of coral atolls midway between Ceylon and Australia and some 700 miles south-west of the Japanese-occupied island of Java. On board were men of the R.A.F. Regiment, part of No. 136 Spitfire squadron, which had fought with distinction on both the Arakan and Imphal fronts, Royal Engineers, and men of the Indian Engineers and R.I.A.S.C. Only a few knew that in a few days' time they would be forming the most forward of all S.E.A.C. bases.

On the second day out the Air Officer in charge, Air Commodore A. W. Hunt, told us the destination for which we were bound.

"We are going there," he said, "to build

an airstrip. There might be slight enemy resistance." Why, one might ask, build an airstrip on a place so remote as the Cocos? A glance at a map of the Indian Ocean shows the strategical importance of these islands in the planning of an offensive on the Jap positions in the Netherlands East Indies. The Cocos Islands were the farthest east of any land then remaining in Allied hands, for although they had taken possession of lonely Christmas Island, 100 miles or so west of Java, the Japanese had only carried out somewhat half-hearted air raids on the Cocos Islands. Perhaps it may seem that a little group of islands growing only coconut trees and housing but 250 Indonesians and Malays was hardly worth the trouble of occupying, and the enemy thought that regular reconnaissance flights would be quite

How Cocos Islands Became an Allied Air Base

TEN DAYS' HUSTLE BY BRITISH AND INDIAN FORCES transformed Cocos Islands jungle-ground into the nucleus of a formidable air base for use against the Japs, in April 1945. Published for the first time, these photographs show Indian Army engineers making a roadway (1), members of a R.A.F. maintenance squad beside a partly stripped Spitfire (2), one of the first aircraft to land, and R.A.F. personnel who helped to lay metal landing-strips preparing their quarters (3) for the night. See accompanying story.

Photos, British Official

sufficient to keep the place under observation. In any event, it would seem that the Japanese never appreciated just what was happening there; for long before the War a cable and wireless station had been set up on one of the outlying islands, and although the wireless station closed down in 1942 the cable link remained open throughout the whole war and maintained the only link of its kind between Australia and the rest of the world.

Throughout the War, too, we kept a small garrison here so that in the event of a Japanese attempt at invasion the signals station could be destroyed swiftly. Once or twice it looked as though the Japs had some idea of what was going on, and in the autumn of 1943 they raided the place, killing some naval ratings and several natives, but fortunately the raids ceased as suddenly as they had begun.

**Flight-Lieut.
S. MOORHOUSE**

For nearly three years the Cocos Islands remained the "top secret islands of the East." They were never referred to by name in official communications; they were even deleted from all maps and charts showing the disposition of Allied troops. Occasionally a Catalina put down in the lagoon on its way to or from Australia. From time to time some ship anchored off the group to land or take up some mysterious personage. In the early weeks of 1945 the number of mysterious personages visiting the Cocos increased, and so the islands were surveyed and all plans for the occupation by a larger body of troops made under a cloak of secrecy. It seems incredible that we should be able to sail, unescorted, right through the Indian Ocean without the slightest interference. I can not say that either Japanese intelligence was not so good as many imagined, or that the enemy was too fully occupied elsewhere to be able to divert either aircraft or shipping to interfere with a project that he knew must inevitably bring disaster to his forces in the Netherlands East Indies.

Land-Crabs and Rats for Company

On April 3, 1945, the fifth day out of Colombo, my attention was drawn to a slice of flat land on the horizon. Alongside me was the Civil Affairs Officer, who informed me that this was North Keeling Island, off which lay the remains of the German raider Emden sunk by the cruiser Sydney in the 1914-18 conflict. Soon the Cocos themselves were in sight, and at noon we were offshore. A Malay came on board and proceeded to pilot a way through the submerged coral reefs into the placid waters of the lagoon. Two other ships were there already, one laden with equipment, the other with more drafts of personnel.

Disembarkation began almost immediately. Although we had been unmolested throughout the voyage there was always the danger of Jap aircraft coming over the horizon. Landing barges came alongside and soon we were on the five-mile journey to the shore. The ships were a sitting target for any aircraft that turned up, and there was no protection for the barges. Shoals of sharks gathered around us made the prospect of an attack even less alluring.

UNTIL dusk a constant procession of barges plied between the ships and the shore. Wide-eyed natives gathered in their queer canoes. The presence of so many men must have filled them with bewilderment. However, even if there had been quislings among them —and I never heard of a Cocos islander being otherwise than loyal to the Empire—they had no means of getting messages away.

If the invasion was bloodless it was also comfortless. When I stepped out of the barge and went on to the island I wondered how the Cocos could ever be turned into an air base. There was hardly a tent space without some coconut tree, and the scrub was as thick as any Burmese jungle. Huge landcrabs scuttled about, and there was an abundance of rats.

Under such conditions the invaders settled down for the first night on shore. Black-out regulations were of the strictest and there was neither tent nor hut available for the majority. Some stretched out hammocks, others slept on the ground, covered with mosquito nets which offered no protection against the crawling and biting insects. All night long one heard rats and crabs scuttling about. And in the morning I listened to various hair-raising stories of men having their toes nibbled while they tried to sleep.

Bulldozers in the Undergrowth

Next day and succeeding days offered no chance of making living conditions any more comfortable. Ever-present was the threat of a Japanese raid. Anti-aircraft pits were made and guns, manned by Indian gunners and the R.A.F. Regiment, were mounted at strategic positions. A radar station quickly came into operation and searched the skies far beyond the range of the visible horizon; but the cathode-ray tube which would have given warning of any aircraft's approach remained clear.

Meanwhile, the barges were still crossing that blue lagoon and men were unloading and assembling plant. Soon bulldozers were crashing through the undergrowth and coconut trees were toppling down like ninepins. When at length sufficient space had been cleared, a landing strip of powdered coral and metal plates was laid, and within ten days of the landing of our expedition, some of the first Spitfires were flying overhead. The fighter strip was but the prelude to greater things. More trees were felled and scrub cleared away until at last a strip long enough to take a bomb-loaded Liberator was ready. The Liberators came, and personnel of a Dutch squadron carried out initial raids on Jap ships off Java. Then plans were made to extend the range to cover Batavia and Singapore—and at the same time the Jap capitulation was announced. The bombs were unloaded and Red Cross and medical supplies took their place.

Thousands of Allied prisoners made their first real contact with their countrymen through aircraft flying from what a few months earlier had been a few coral atolls, a cable station, and the home of the world's most secret garrison.

TOUCHING DOWN on the metal landing-strip laid in the Cocos Islands, the bomb-loaded Liberator in this hitherto unpublished photograph landed with one engine "dead." From here air raids were carried out on Jap ships off Java and, after the Japanese capitulation, supplies were flown to Allied P.O.W.
Photo, British Official

My Escape Bid in German Uniform

From Stalag 383, during the summer of 1943, L/Sgt. H. V. Suggit, 5th Royal Inniskilling Dragoons, together with Sgt. Beeson, R.A.O.C., made a well-planned and lively break. With somewhat grim humour is presented here the story (illustrated with the author's own vivid sketches) of incidents which caused it to become a circular tour.

THE Nürnberg - Stuttgart Express was roaring through the night packed with German and Austrian troops, possibly on their way to Italy—and bearing my companion, Sgt. Beeson, R.A.O.C., and myself nearer to freedom. Such was the lack of accommodation that we had had to squeeze ourselves into the junction between two carriages, one of which was first-class and for officers only, the other filled to overflowing with men, arms and baggage.

Beeson had slithered to the floor and I was leaning against the metal trellis of the connecting link, congratulating ourselves on our good luck so far, when a figure appeared and demanded our papers. Scrutinizing these in the light of the first-class compartment, he plied us with questions. We answered that we were from Breslau and were going to Stuttgart, to work in an aircraft factory, and would live with friends who were going to meet us. And so on. He was not satisfied, however, and pulling out a gun frisked us for arms and marched us down the corridor to the police compartment. Thus ended the most hectic twenty-four hours of freedom I had in nearly five years of escape activities in Germany.

Complete With Campaign Ribbons

About a fortnight previously I had been approached by Sgt. Beeson to forge him some " papers " for a " break " he had planned to make with a pal, using homemade German uniforms as a means of exit from the camp. Although I had previously given up the idea of further attempts at escape I agreed to make him the necessary " papers "—two Unteroffiziers' Passes and two Civilian Identity Cards. The former were copied from originals loaned by a friendly Alsatian guard, and the civilian cards were made on the pattern of the best specimens in the camp Escape Committee's hands at the time. Several days later, when the papers were ready, Beeson confided to me that his partner-to-be had changed his mind and asked me if I would care to go with him ; to which proposition I readily agreed, forgetting my resolution.

To make the uniforms we obtained, through the Escape Committee, two Australian tunics and two pairs of battle-dress slacks which we altered and dyed green in the cookhouse with dyes procured from the camp theatre. Whilst they were drying on the grass at the back of my companion's hut one of the camp Unteroffiziers came hanging around, so we took him in and entertained him to a cup of coffee !

From an old khaki shirt, and with the aid of a bit of cardboard and some wire, I made a peaked cap which I painted grey-green with water-colours. The peak was polished with boot polish, as was also the chin-strap, and silver paper-covered pieces of cardboard in the shape of badges at the front and buttons at the side completed the effect. Belts and holsters were made in the same way ; a touch of Indian ink on the buckles supplied the " emblem " and " Gott mit uns." White paper wrapped around tin and coloured with red and black ink served as campaign ribbons. Our genuine tunic buttons were supplied by our friend the Alsatian.

We had fixed the date at August 26, 1943, when we got wind of an attempt at the wire timed for the previous day. We immediately advanced the date to the 25th and redoubled our efforts to be ready in time. It was necessary to try to get away before the other escapees made their effort, otherwise, of course, we would be confronted by greatly increased difficulty.

At last our uniforms were complete, and at about 7.45 p.m. we started dressing up. We donned the camp-made civvy suits and tied string around parts that were liable to bulge. On top of these we put our " uniforms," which were still damp from the dyeing. Our belts and holsters, lacking real buckles, had to be sewn on. Friends were keeping watch outside the hut in case of intruders, English or German. Our pockets were filled with chocolate, New Zealand iron rations, cleaning kit, and maps and money. Sandwiches we carefully packed away in the holsters.

Searchlights Blazed On Our Road

We were just on the point of leaving when a friend I had " tipped off " appeared with his camera and snapped us. Immediately after this we left the hut and, taking advantage of the half-light—the time by now being about 9.30 p.m.—we walked leisurely towards the first gate, a distance of about 400 yards. To lend effect to our disguises, my companion called out " verdunkeln " (blackouts) once or twice.

At the first gate, so effective was our get-up in the poor light that the guard, after inspecting our passes, let us through without any bother and we continued our walk past the cookhouse and the German Camp Office to the main gate — where were brilliant lights and sharp eyes of the perimeter guards. But we made it !

We were no sooner out of the main gate when the lights surrounding the camp were put out and searchlights immediately came into operation, covering the wire and the road up which we had to walk in the direction of the

LOOKING THE PART in their home-made German uniforms, the author (left) and his companion, Sergt. Beeson, paused to be "snapped" by a friend before making their escape from Stalag 383. PAGE 285

Motto : " Everywhere Unbounded"

No. 8 SQUADRON

FORMED at Brooklands, Surrey, in the first months of the 1914-1918 War and reformed in 1920, No. 8 Squadron was principally engaged during the latter part of the Second Great War in dropping supplies to our agents in Burma, Siam and French Indo-China. The true value of this work was not revealed until months later when Rangoon fell, Burma was liberated and the full story was told of the achievement of our agents.

For some time the squadron was engaged with many others in dropping propaganda leaflets, medical supplies and food to Allied prisoners of war and internees. September 1945 arrived before the squadron's work was completed, and it was finally disbanded two months later.

AT Brooklands in 1915, this squadron was equipped with B.E.2 c. aircraft and fought in the battles of the Somme and Arras, building up an excellent reputation for co-operation with the Tank Corps. At the battle of Amiens, one of the pilots received the V.C. Disbanded on January 20, 1920, and re-formed on October 18, No. 8 moved to Mesopotamia in 1921, where it engaged in operations against local tribes. No. 8 participated in every operation there until the middle of 1927, when it moved to Aden, which continued to be its base until May 15, 1945. It operated as a ground reconnaissance squadron with Wellington aircraft carrying out anti-submarine patrols and convoy escorts. On May 15, when the ground reconnaissance force in the Indian Ocean was curtailed, No. 8 was disbanded again, but its famous number plate was transferred to No. 200 Liberator Squadron. So No. 8 Squadron continued its career to the end of the War.

German barracks and guards' quarters. We carried on speaking to each other in German and gesticulating in the German manner. Passing these buildings, we saw the guards hurrying out, buckling on equipment as they ran to fall-in by the road. In spite of our own precarious position we could not help thinking of our friends who were at that moment making strenuous efforts to get out through the wire, and every shot we heard set us praying that it had not found its mark. (On our eventual return to the camp the Germans, thinking we had escaped in that way, showed us two bullet-ridden dummies which had been used in the attempt, the latter being unsuccessful although no one was either injured or caught.)

Another minute or so and we should have been caught at the gate by the Camp Security Section. But here we now were, free and on the main road from Hohenfels to Parsberg. Our camp, Stalag 383, was on high ground in

we arrive at 1st Gate and are nearly "sunk" by some orderlies
asking us to take them to the Hospital! With "NIX" "MUSS WARTEN"...

...meeting some
"signals" laying a telephone, who shine light on us "but
say nothing...

very hilly country (Hohenfels means " high rocks "), and our course lay along the main road to Parsberg, the nearest small town and on the main line from Regensburg to Nürnberg, a distance of about 14 miles. On our way we had to pass the large military camp, from the canteen of which came the sounds of a piano and tinkling glasses.

Farther along we passed troops laying a field telephone, but beyond shining a light on us they paid no attention. After an hour's walk we transferred the contents of our holsters to our pockets and destroyed the holsters, as we were now out of the military area and obviously off duty and hardly likely to be carrying arms. Parsberg we reached at about 2 a.m., when we rested in a near-by wood to wait for our train due to arrive at 6.30. Before setting out for the station we took off and buried our uniforms.

The walk to the station was uneventful, as was the purchase of two tickets to Nürnberg. But whilst on the station my companion spotted a Gestapo agent who had previously been thrown out of his hut in the camp, and so we hurriedly boarded the first train that came in, though it was going in the reverse direction ! Half an hour later we alighted at Regensburg and boarded the Nürnberg train after a short wait. All went well until we had nearly reached Parsberg, when we were asked for our tickets. We had tickets from Parsberg to Nürnberg and were on the Regensburg-Nürnberg train, having to pass through Parsberg on the way. If we were asked for tickets after

Parsberg all would be O.K., but here we were, one stop still short of Parsberg.

To explain how we came to have tickets from a station we had not yet reached was the problem, but somehow my companion managed it. (He never really knew how.) At Parsberg the conductress checked up on our tickets at the booking office and then left us alone. We arrived in Nürnberg at 9 a.m. and Beeson went to buy tickets for Crailsheim whilst I dodged about the station trying to look inconspicuous. When he

[map: BADEN, HEILBRONN, DOMBÜHL, HEILSBRONN, NÜRNBERG, WICKLESGREUTH, HOHENFELS, Stalag 383, PARSBERG, WÜRTTEMBERG, BAVARIA, REGENSBURG, STUTTGART, NÖRDLINGEN. Miles 0 10 20 40. Roads, Railways]

returned with the tickets did we go hot and cold ! They were the wrong ones ! The similarity of some of the place names and my companion's accent were to blame, I suppose. Reference to the wall time-tables and maps decided us to change our plans and go via Heilbronn, to which place there was a train at 2.15 p.m. Realizing the danger of waiting in the station, we went to fill up the time at a cinema in the city.

After passing several picture-houses and seeing the queues, with police about, we thought better of it and went for a walk. We arrived back in the station just after one o'clock and went into the restaurant to while away more time. Here we had a drink—food required ration cards. An old man in uniform came along and sold us tickets in the National Lottery, but we weren't lucky, he said, after tearing them open ; it was all the same to us !

At our table were a German soldier and a civilian, the former writing a letter and the latter shelling a hard-boiled egg (he must have been in the black market). We dare not eat our sandwiches in full view or suspicions would have been aroused. They were of " bully" and bread, enclosed in lettuce leaves and wrapped in paper. The normal German snack was a hunk of bread eaten with a pocket-knife!

We boarded our train, and because of the congestion and to keep away from prying eyes we rode on the veranda. All went well for about half an hour, when the train pulled into a little country station called Heilsbronn. A look at our tickets showed us that this was the place we had booked for ; but something was wrong, for the town we wanted was near Stuttgart and several hours' journey from Nürnberg ! There was nothing we could do but get off. Surrendering our tickets, we inquired of the collector the time of the next train for Stuttgart. " You've just got off it," was his reply, to which we

love
bit of trouble re-tickets with conductress, but
get away with it!

...a nice little
pub offers itself to us so we
enter...

Once again we are Belgians with success and after
buying more tickets to Dombühl for fine...

said, "We've made a mistake. Will you give us tickets for Stuttgart ?"

There wasn't time, however, as the train was just about to leave, and so, not risking further trouble, we made ourselves scarce. Making our way along roads and cart-tracks close to the line, we arrived at Wicklesgreuth, in a hot and grimy state, after two hours' walk in the sun. At the rear of the station we found a pump and put it to good use,

after which we entered the station and studied the wall-maps. Our error was explained by the discovery that there were two places called Heilbronn and Heilsbronn, with only the letter "s" to mark the difference between them. The former was a town near Stuttgart, while Heilsbron was a village 20 or 30 kilometres from Nürnberg.

FINDING there was a train to Stuttgart due at 4.30 we bought tickets, which were of the hand-written type, and went for a drink in the little café. It was empty except for a couple of girl attendants, so we settled down to read the papers we had bought in Nürnberg and listen to the wireless. My companion amused me with his remarks of "schön" (nice) to the Italian singer who was doing his best for the Fuehrer and Duce over the radio. The entrance of a couple of railway policemen induced us to hurry out, to spend the rest of our wait on the platform bench. In due course the train arrived and we boarded it, to find seats in a compartment among several women. At Dombühl we had to get off, as this appeared to be the terminus, but the sight of so many police and officials panicked us into boarding the very next train we saw. That led us into more trouble. We were now on a branch line on the way to Nordlingen and, naturally, the conductress was puzzled with our excuses for having no

tickets. At Nordlingen she took us to the station-master, who delayed the train while we were questioned. We were Belgian volunteer workers and quite unused to German railways, we explained. In due course we were issued with tickets for the return journey to Dombühl, fined for our offence, put on the right train and handed over to the conductress of it. So we arrived back at the scene of our panic and were taken to the station office, there to be given a Stuttgart ticket (ours were made out for only one person, which we didn't know until the fact was pointed out to us !) to go with the odd one we had, and told the time of arrival of that train.

After a while the night express arrived and we scrambled aboard to find it was full of troops, and the only vacant space seemed to be one of the connecting links between coaches. Close on midnight, when we were only a few miles from Stuttgart, we had our

ONE OF THE PASSES (left) identical to those used by the camp staff, forged by the author of this story.

trouble with the Gestapo and, as already mentioned, we were " wheeled in." On the way down the corridor, realizing the game was up, we announced our identity for the special benefit of the troops who were taking quite an interest in our bit of bother. From the station we were conveyed to the gaol, and after being searched, questioned and finger-printed, we were slung into separate cells already full, for the most part, of French conscript labourers who wouldn't labour. After two or three days, during which time there was trouble with the guards because we would not stand to attention to them like the rest of the prisoners, we were transferred to a prisoner of war camp at Ludwigsburg.

There, at Stalag VA, we were in very mixed company, mostly Dutch Marines. On Queen Wilhelmina's birthday a party was held, our share in the concert being a stirring rendering of the National Anthem, in which we were assisted by a New Zealander escapee from Lamsdorf, Stalag VIII B. A few days later we were back in Stalag 383, and after another thirty days were free to try again, my pal to reach Paris a year later, myself to beat the Hun by a matter of days, by hiding and evading the march, along with 200 others, when Jerry cleared the camps that were in the line of the Allied Armies.

NEW FACTS AND FIGURES

THE bill for the Victory celebrations of June 8, 1946, which was presented to Parliament on June 28, amounted to £289.000. The saluting base and various works in the Royal parks and on the route of the parade cost £70,000 : decorations and floodlighting, £50.000 ; river and fireworks displays, £27,000 ; children's entertainments, including transport costs, £18,000.

TRANSPORT and accommodation of home and overseas civilian contingents to the Victory celebrations cost £22.000 ; hospitality and entertainment of official guests and Dominion, Colonial, Indian and Allied contingents, £80.000 ; miscellaneous expenses amounted to £22.000. A sum of £6.500 was recovered from the sale of official programmes and from other sources.

RADAR, according to evidence given by Admiral Dönitz at Nuremberg, was, next to the atom bomb, the most decisive weapon of the war. It was radar which brought about the collapse of U-boat warfare. U-boats had to stay under water, as the aircraft with radar could see them so many miles off ; there were even difficulties about surfacing for the purpose of recharging batteries. It takes at least 60 seconds for a submarine crew to descend through the conning-tower ; in that 60 seconds a plane could swoop in from about 20,000 feet to attack.

IN Poland war has left one million orphans, 800,000 invalids, one million people affected in health by incarceration in German concentration camps, and about four million unemployed. These figures were announced in July 1946 by M. Jan Stanczyk, Polish Minister of Labour and Public Assistance.

FROM August 1, 1946, cruiser squadrons and destroyer flotillas of the Royal Navy are reverting as nearly as possible to their pre-war numbering. This is being done in order to preserve the long-standing associations which individual squadrons and flotillas have formed with local British communities in various parts of the world, and also because the large majority of Fleet trophies and mementoes are inscribed with these numbers.

THUS, in the Home Fleet, 10th cruiser squadron becomes 2nd cruiser squadron ; 2nd destroyer flotilla becomes 4th destroyer flotilla ; 17th destroyer flotilla becomes 5th. In the Mediterranean Fleet, 15th cruiser squadron becomes 1st cruiser squadron ; 14th destroyer flotilla becomes 1st destroyer flotilla. In the East Indies Fleet, 5th cruiser squadron becomes 4th cruiser squadron. In the British Pacific Fleet 2nd and 4th cruiser squadrons become 5th cruiser squadron. On the South Atlantic Station cruisers become 6th cruiser squadron; on the America and West Indies Station cruisers become 8th cruiser squadron.

Red Caps in Venice Patrol the Grand Canal

Printed in England and published every alternate Friday by the Proprietors, THE AMALGAMATED PRESS, LTD., The Fleetway House, Farringdon Street, London, E.C.4. Registered for transmission by Canadian Magazine Post.

Photo, Keystone

POLICING THE WATERWAYS of Venice constitutes a novelty not to be found elsewhere by the British Military Policeman, whose duties are so often carried out on foot. In this Italian Adriatic city of some 150 waterways, patrols of one officer and four or five men proceed in motor launches, one of which is seen on the Grand Canal. Two major tasks of these Red Caps are maintenance of the many warning signs and the control of military and civilian craft. See also illus. pages 272-273.

Printed in England and published every alternate Friday by the Proprietors, THE AMALGAMATED PRESS, LTD., The Fleetway House, Farringdon Street, London, E.C.4. Registered for transmission by Canadian Magazine Post. Sole Agents for Australia and New Zealand: Messrs. Gordon & Gotch, Ltd.; and for South Africa: Central News Agency, Ltd.—August 16, 1946. S.S. *Editorial Address:* JOHN CARPENTER HOUSE, WHITEFRIARS, LONDON, E.C.4.

Vol 10 *The War Illustrated* N° 240

SIXPENCE

AUGUST 30, 1946

I WAS THERE

BRITAIN'S PRIME MINISTER ADDRESSING THE PARIS PEACE CONFERENCE which opened on July 29, 1946. Seated above the Rt. Hon. Clement R. Attlee (deputizing for our Foreign Minister during the Rt. Hon. Ernest Bevin's indisposition) is M. Bidault. Criticism of the deliberations, Mr. Attlee warned, should be tempered with consideration for "the nations who did the fighting (and that includes all those in this hall) are very tired." See also pages 303-306 and 313. *Photo, Associated Press*

Edited by Sir John Hammerton

NO. 241 WILL BE PUBLISHED FRIDAY, SEPTEMBER 13

In Japan a Year After the Two Atom Bombs Fell

A TOWN OF HUTS, known as "Palace Heights," has arisen in Tokyo's centre (1), for the accommodation of U.S. Occupation Forces' dependents, the first batch of whom arrived and were comfortably installed there in the spring of 1946. In the centre of this well-planned settlement is the main dining-hall; in the backgrond is the tower of the Diet (Japanese Government Assembly) building.

Visiting the graves of war dead in the Capital are (2) the younger brother of the Emperor and his wife, Prince and Princess Takamatsu.

Shortage of foodstuffs is being countered in diverse ways—primary schools are now "keeping" goats to supplement the milk ration. As part of the routine curriculum the children receive lessons (3) from their teachers in the care of these animals and the rearing of their kids. Goat's milk is somewhat richer in fat than cow's milk and is less liable to be infected with tuberculosis.

WHERE PARTS FOR JAP AIRCRAFT WERE MADE pots and pans are now being manufactured. Warrant Officer Robson (5) is supervising a worker in the Teijin Seiki Co.'s factory at Iwakuni, where more Spitfires recently arrived to reinforce the Air Component of the B.C.O.F. Cowlings are removed (4) before the Spitfires are hoisted ashore.

Photos, Keystone, New York Times Photos, British Official

The Tragedy of H.M.S. Glorious

By
FRANCIS E. McMURTRIE

Motto: " The Name
Explains Itself "

IN view of the important role played by aircraft carriers in the Second Great War, it is a deplorable fact that, almost to the last, the Royal Navy found itself shorter of these ships than of those of any other category. Yet at the start it possessed five large carriers, H.M.S. Ark Royal, Furious, Courageous, Glorious and Eagle. Though only the first was really modern, all with the exception of the last-named had a speed of 30 knots or more. Unfortunately, the Courageous was lost while on anti-submarine patrol in the Western Approaches, a fortnight after war had been declared. (See pages 115—117, Vol. 1.) It is the view of many naval air specialists that this was a case of an exceptionally valuable ship being thrown away through being assigned to duty for which she was not suitable.

It might have been imagined that after this the utmost care would have been taken to provide adequate escort for any other large carrier likely to be exposed to unusual risk. Yet in June 1940 the Navy learned with surprise and dismay that H.M.S. Glorious, sister ship of the Courageous, had been intercepted by a superior enemy force while returning from Norway practically unescorted. (See Admiralty announcement, page 676, Vol. 2.) For six years the facts of the case remained obscure ; but in May 1946 an official report was circulated to Parliament which for the first time gave details of this most unfortunate in-

cident. In the first four weeks of the Norwegian campaign almost the whole of our naval strength in home waters was engaged in escorting and carrying troops to and from Norway. With such efficiency was this work done that not a single soldier out of the thousands transported lost his life as the result of submarine or surface ship attack, and very few from air attack at sea. But with the invasion of France on May 10, and the heavy demands on the Navy for help to that country, Belgium and the Netherlands, a sharp change came over the situation. With the evacuation of the British Army from Boulogne and Dunkirk, an exceptional strain was imposed on naval material, the majority of the available destroyers being

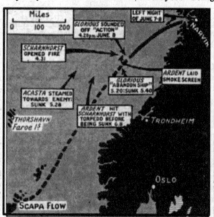

either sunk or put out of action in these operations. Obviously, too, the threat of an enemy invasion attempt could not be ignored, imposing a further burden.

It was in these circumstances that plans had to be prepared for the evacuation of Northern Norway. It was arranged that the forces should sail in four groups, aggregating 13 large transports and a number of storeships. To escort these, the cruisers Southampton and Coventry, six destroyers, the repair ship Vindictive, a sloop and a number of trawlers were assigned. The Commander-in-Chief, Home Fleet, Admiral of the Fleet Sir Charles Forbes, was asked by the Flag Officer, Narvik, Admiral of the Fleet the Earl of Cork and Orrery, if a covering force could be provided to escort the first group of six large ships. This was to assemble at a rendezvous some 210 miles to the west of Harstad, Norway, under the escort of the old Vindictive, and would be met by the battleship Valiant, which would escort it as far as the latitude of the Shetlands. The Valiant was to leave Scapa Flow at 21.00 on June 6, while the convoy would sail from Narvik very early the following day.

Glorious Sailed Independently

There were only four British capital ships in northern waters at this time, the battleships Rodney and Valiant and the battle cruisers Renown and Repulse. The Rodney, flagship of the C.-in-C., was at Scapa, while the Renown and Repulse were at sea, having been ordered on June 7 to Iceland to guard against a possible German landing there. Shortly after midnight on June 7-8 the C.-in-C. was instructed by the Admiralty to have two capital ships available to proceed south in case of invasion, whereupon the Renown was ordered to return to Scapa.

H.M.S. GLORIOUS was built in 1915 under emergency war programme as a shallow-draught cruiser, with a view to Baltic operations. Converted into an aircraft-carrier in 1930 at a cost of over £2,000,000, she displaced 22,500 tons on a length of 786 feet, and had a speed of 30·5 knots. She carried 48 aircraft and was armed with sixteen 4·7-in. guns and four 3-pounders. The map shows the route of her last voyage and action with the Scharnhorst and Gneisenau.

Photo, Wright and Logan, map by courtesy of " The Daily Telegraph "

Evacuation of the Narvik area was mainly carried out in two groups; but owing to the variety of vessels employed, it proved impossible to concentrate them all in a single body on either occasion, some ships having therefore to rely mainly on diversive routeing for their security. Despite these difficulties, the whole military force of 24,000 arrived safely in this country.

The aircraft carriers Ark Royal and Glorious had been sent to Narvik from Scapa on May 31, the former to provide fighter protection during the evacuation and the latter to bring back from North Norway much-needed Gladiator and Hurricane aircraft of the R.A.F. There seems to have been a misplaced assumption that the Germans

Motto: " Through Fire and Water "

lacked enterprise, presumably because for some months previously carriers and other heavy ships had been crossing the North Sea independently without incident. For this reason the Glorious was not allowed to accompany the second large group of ships returning, as her consort the Ark Royal did, but sailed independently. This unfortunate decision is understood to have been made on the grounds that otherwise the Glorious would not have had enough fuel left to get home.

Thus at 03.00 on June 8 the Glorious parted from the Ark Royal, which wore the flag of the Admiral (Air), in a position 17 degrees N. by 14 degrees 10 minutes E. She was accompanied by the destroyers Acasta and Ardent as an anti-submarine escort. Unfortunately she was sent right into the jaws of the enemy.

No Reconnaissance Aircraft Up

An enemy squadron, comprising the battleships Scharnhorst and Gneisenau, ships of nearly 32,000 tons each, armed with nine 11-in. guns, and the cruiser Admiral Hipper, of nearly 15,000 tons with eight 8-in. guns, had left Kiel on June 4 and passed Bergen at midnight on June 5–6. Their orders were to attack British convoys proceeding from the Narvik area. No suspicion of their presence seems to have been entertained by British Naval Intelligence; at any rate, neither the Flag Officer, Narvik, nor the C.-in-C., Home Fleet, was aware of it.

At 8 on the morning of June 8 the Admiral Hipper encountered the tanker Oil Pioneer, which she sank, rescuing 11 survivors. A

H.M.S. ARDENT, sister-ship of the Acasta (see below), was sunk with her and the aircraft carrier Glorious on June 8, 1940, after an engagement with Scharnhorst and Gneisenau. The two destroyers laid a smoke-screen in an endeavour to assist the Glorious to escape and later fired their torpedoes at the German battleships.
Photo, Wright and Logan

little later she did the same with the empty transport Orama and the trawler Juniper, picking up 112 from these ships. Though the British hospital ship Atlantis saw the Orama being shelled, the Geneva Convention precluded her reporting the fact by wireless. It may be doubted if our enemies would have acted so scrupulously in such a case.

Soon after 16.00 on the same day the Glorious sighted the two German battleships, the Admiral Hipper having put into Trondheim. No reconnaissance aircraft were up, nor had any been flown off since parting from the Ark Royal, or the encounter might have been avoided. As it was, the Glorious did her best to escape to the southward under cover of a smoke-screen laid by the two destroyers. Though this caused the enemy to cease fire for a time, the forward upper hangar had already been hit, destroying the Hurricane aircraft and preventing any torpedoes being got out before the fire curtains were lowered. About an hour after the enemy ships had first been sighted, a salvo hit the bridge of the Glorious, and further heavy hits were sustained about 15 minutes later. Soon after this the order was given to abandon ship, and she sank with a heavy list to starboard about 17.40. The carrier's armament of 4·7-in. guns was, of course, quite useless against two such powerful adversaries.

Both the destroyers were sunk, the Acasta about 17.28 and the Ardent at 18.08. They had duly fired torpedoes, one from the Ardent hitting the Scharnhorst abreast of

her after 11-in. turret, inflicting severe damage. As the result of this, the Scharnhorst made for Trondheim under escort of her sister ship, their cruise being abandoned. They took with them an officer and four ratings from the Glorious and one man from the Ardent as prisoners of war.

No intelligible report of the action was received by any British ship, though at 17.20 the cruiser Devonshire nearly 100 miles to the westward picked up the beginning of a wireless signal addressed to the Vice-Admiral (Air) from the Glorious; it must have been made as the ship was being abandoned. Unfortunately, with the exception of the Ark Royal, Southampton and Coventry, other ships in the North Sea were keeping wireless watch on a different wave frequency. This applied to the Valiant, which was then about 470 miles to the south-westward. On the morning of the following day that battleship made contact with the hospital ship Atlantis, which reported having seen a transport being attacked by the battleships Scharnhorst and Gneisenau, and the heavy cruiser Hipper.

This information was at once passed to the Commander-in-Chief at Scapa, who sailed with the Rodney, Renown and six destroyers to cover the convoys. First news of the end of the Glorious came from an enemy broadcast on June 9. Though diligent search was made for survivors, aircraft from the Ark Royal actually passed close over a number of men on rafts without seeing them. Owing to the heavy sea, which capsized the Acasta's boats, and the extreme cold, men soon perished, the total death roll in the three ships amount-

Motto: " Remember your Ancestors "

ing to 94 officers and 1,380 ratings, besides 41 R.A.F. personnel. The few who did survive were picked up by the little Norwegian steamer Borgund (341 tons gross), which landed them at Thorshavn, in the Faroe Islands (see map in page 291).

Apart from the fact that aircraft carriers were extremely precious, the loss of the Glorious must be accounted a sad waste of the lives of brave men, most of them of high professional qualifications, not easily replaced. In the absence of any official statement on the subject, it must be left to future historians of the War, who presumably will have full access to all relevant documents, to award the blame, for the disaster, if any is due.

H.M.S. ACASTA, 1,350-tons destroyer, gave her name to a very successful class, all of which exceeded the designed speed of 35 knots. Armament consisted of four 4·7-in. and six smaller guns, and eight 21-in. torpedo tubes on quadruple mounts—these being the first destroyers in which tubes were thus mounted.
Photo, Wright and Logan

Our Carrier Colossus Loaned to French Navy

THE 17,200-TON AIRCRAFT CARRIER COLOSSUS, launched in 1944, has been lent for five years to the French Navy by the Admiralty. Formally handed over at Portsmouth on August 6, 1946, she was manned by a French crew of 1,500 officers and men brought there on board the battleship Richelieu. The Prime Minister, the Rt. Hon. Clement R. Attlee, on behalf of the British Government, spoke at the ceremony (1). After the raising of the Tricolour on the carrier's flight deck (3) bluejackets removed the White Ensign (2). The Richelieu is in the background. Replying to Mr. Attlee, M. Michelet, French Minister for Armed Forces, said that his Government was grateful to Great Britain for the loan of this carrier because, owing to the destruction of their shipyards, they could not yet build ships of her type.

Photos, Keystone, Fox, G.P.U.

Arabs Welcome Jewish Ex-Servicemen Settlers

IN PALESTINE, midway between the River Jordan and the Nazareth—Jenin highway in the lower Galilee foothills where they merge into the Vale of Jezreel, Arab elders attended a ceremony of welcome to Jewish ex-soldier settlers when these founded the village of Kfar-Kisch, to start a new life and wrest a living from the land.

Typical of those which other energetic Jewish settlers have made into flourishing agricultural communities, the new village is named after the late Brigadier F. H. Kisch, C.B., C.B.E., D.S.O., Chief Engineer of the 8th Army, who was killed in action near Sousse in Tunisia.

At the founding ceremony Ibrahim Al-Tayb, leader of the neighbouring Arab village of Mader, said, " I have searched our history and failed to find any cause for enmity between the sons of Ishmael and of Isaac, of both of whom Abraham was the father. Only intriguers seek to sow discord between the two peoples."

LAYING the FOUNDATION of the village of Kfar-Kisch, where no habitation had been before : huts and houses under construction (1) on the first day ; in the background is historic Mount Tabor, legendary scene of the Transfiguration. After only eight hours' work (2) considerable progress had been made ; the sign in Hebrew at the planned entrance to the village reads, " And they shall beat their swords into ploughshares, and their spears into pruning-hooks." Ibrahim Al-Tayb (3, left) arrives for the ceremony ; prominently displayed is a portrait of the late Brigadier Kisch—the inspiration of the settlers' labours. Arab elders from Mader assembled (4) to welcome the new Jewish neighbours and offer all encouragement.

Photos, New York Times Photos

Jerusalem Bomb Outrage by Fanatical Zionists

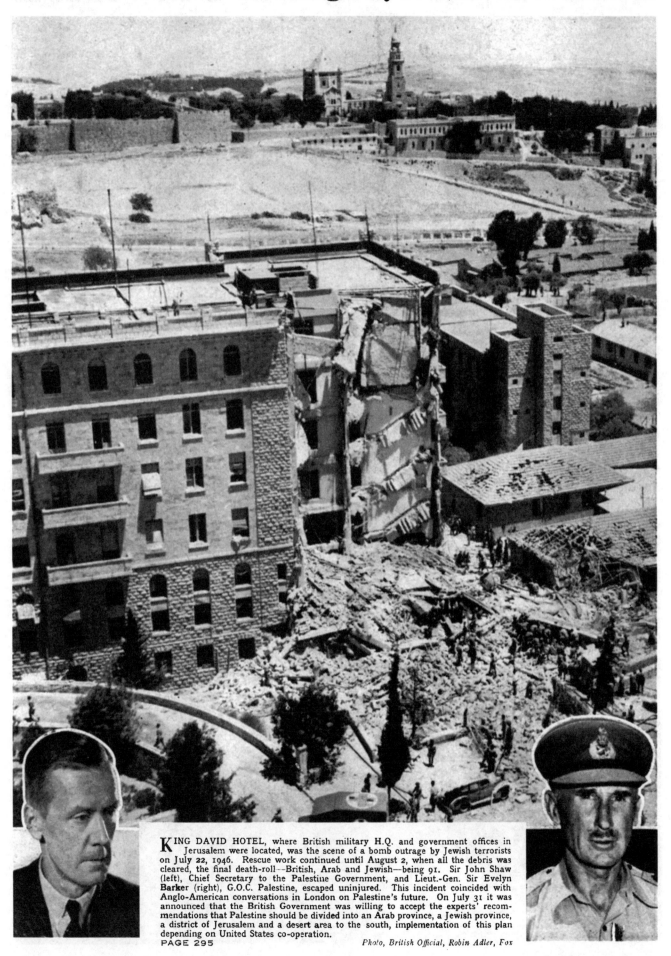

KING DAVID HOTEL, where British military H.Q. and government offices in Jerusalem were located, was the scene of a bomb outrage by Jewish terrorists on July 22, 1946. Rescue work continued until August 2, when all the debris was cleared, the final death-roll—British, Arab and Jewish—being 91. Sir John Shaw (left), Chief Secretary to the Palestine Government, and Lieut.-Gen. Sir Evelyn Barker (right), G.O.C. Palestine, escaped uninjured. This incident coincided with Anglo-American conversations in London on Palestine's future. On July 31 it was announced that the British Government was willing to accept the experts' recommendations that Palestine should be divided into an Arab province, a Jewish province, a district of Jerusalem and a desert area to the south, implementation of this plan depending on United States co-operation.

Photo, British Official, Robin Adler, Fox

British War Graves Adopted by Dutch Civilians

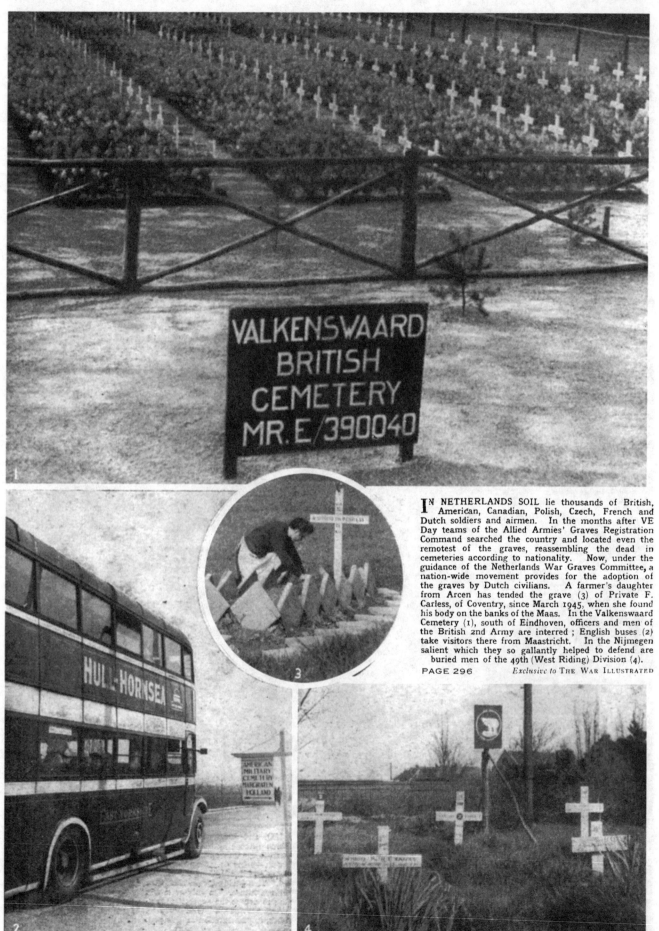

VALKENSWAARD BRITISH CEMETERY MR. E/390040

HULL-HORNSEA

AMERICAN MILITARY CEMETERY MARGRATEN HOLLAND

IN NETHERLANDS SOIL lie thousands of British, American, Canadian, Polish, Czech, French and Dutch soldiers and airmen. In the months after VE Day teams of the Allied Armies' Graves Registration Command searched the country and located even the remotest of the graves, reassembling the dead in cemeteries according to nationality. Now, under the guidance of the Netherlands War Graves Committee, a nation-wide movement provides for the adoption of the graves by Dutch civilians. A farmer's daughter from Arcen has tended the grave (3) of Private F. Carless, of Coventry, since March 1945, when she found his body on the banks of the Maas. In the Valkenswaard Cemetery (1), south of Eindhoven, officers and men of the British 2nd Army are interred ; English buses (2) take visitors there from Maastricht. In the Nijmegen salient which they so gallantly helped to defend are buried men of the 49th (West Riding) Division (4).

Exclusive to THE WAR ILLUSTRATED

Gift-Horses from Holland for Our King and Army

COMMEMORATING THE LIBERATION OF THE NETHERLANDS and the part played therein by Britain's Household Cavalry, thirty-two Dutch horses, gift of the Netherlands Government, were presented by Queen Wilhelmina to King George, in the forecourt of Buckingham Palace, on July 31, 1946. His Majesty, with Queen Wilhelmina, is seen (1) inspecting them. Two will form a valuable addition to the famous "Windsor Greys" which draw the Royal carriage ; Holland has always specialized in this particular breed. Queen Elizabeth, accompanied by Princess Margaret, makes friends with one of the Greys (2). The other 30 horses are blacks, from the provinces of Friesland, Groningen and Gelderland, individually chosen by the Remount Officer of the Royal Netherlands Household and destined for our Household Cavalry (see page 299), for whom Friesland horses were purchased before the war. Leaving after the presentation ceremony (3) the magnificent blacks are already accustomed to traffic but need parade training. Four more Greys, when these are out of quarantine, will complete the gift.   *Photos, Planet News, Fox*

PAGE 297

HIS MAJESTY'S SHIPS   H.M.S. Iron Duke

Motto : "Fortune is the Companion of Valour"

H.M.S. IRON DUKE was a battleship of 21,250 tons, launched at Portsmouth on October 12, 1912. She wore the flag of Admiral Sir George Callaghan from March to August 1914; that of Sir John Jellicoe in the Grand Fleet from August 1914 to November 1916 and of Sir David Beatty from November 1916 to February 1917. Thenceforward she was a private ship in the Battle Squadron until July 1919, when she hoisted the flag of Sir John de Robeck, Commander-in-Chief in the Mediterranean.

It was on the bridge of the Iron Duke at Jutland that Admiral Jellicoe made his instant decision to deploy the Grand Fleet to port on sighting the German fleet through the mist. This had the effect of placing the enemy at a disadvantage which soon compelled a retreat.

During the years 1919-28 the Iron Duke was flagship in the Mediterranean and Atlantic Fleets of a succession of distinguished admirals, including Sir Osmond Brock, Sir Michael Hodges and Sir Roger Backhouse. Unfortunately the ship had to be demilitarized under the London Naval Treaty of 1930, but she continued to be used for training purposes until the outbreak of the late war. Her next service was as base ship at Scapa Flow, a duty she performed from 1939 to 1945. Not till the end of the war did it become generally known that in a German air raid on Scapa in October 1939 the Iron Duke was so badly damaged that she had to be beached in shallow water. Thus, with the conclusion of hostilities, the grand old ship had to be sold for scrap after a record of service in two wars which has seldom been equalled.

Photo, Fox

FIRST HOUSEHOLD CAVALRY REGIMENT
by Capt. C. G. M. Gordon

The Household Cavalry

Few people would have guessed, in those first confusing days of the war, that the 1st Household Cavalry Regiment was destined to see action on three continents, travel through thirteen countries, or spend over five years abroad. Its first task was to complete the A.R.P. arrangements at Windsor Castle, and fatigue parties were busy in the Castle forecourt when the historic hour struck and the long war began. Shortly afterwards, His Majesty the King inspected the newly formed regiments; and a few weeks later they had moved up to Newark to join the 1st Cavalry Division. The cold mid-winter of 1939 soon passed in the Midlands, and in February 1940 the journey to Palestine began. The rigours of that journey with the horses has still not faded from memory; nor has the arrival at Tulkarm, the muddy weeks of the Palestine spring, or the hot dusty months of the summer. Nathanya, Azzib, Tiberias, Beisan, these towns and many others saw the tall men and their black horses from Whitehall.

A Few Brave Men in Morris Trucks

The part played by the 1st Household Cavalry Regiment in the Iraq and Syrian campaigns in 1941 is now part of history. The forced march across the Syrian Desert of the 9th Armoured Brigade under Brigadier Kingston, the actions of that tiny force at Ramadi, Falujah and Kadermain, were one of Wavell's most brilliant and successful gambles. Then came the Syrian campaign, Abu Kamal, and the march on Palmyra, which threatened Homs and the French left flank. These desert days were great ones in the history of the Regiment; the running fights with the mechanized outlaw Fawzi Bey, the mad charges with "Glubb's Girls," the investing of the pipe-line forts and the grim days outside Palmyra.

The men who fought those battles had only three weeks' mechanized training. They were equipped with obsolete Hotchkiss machine-guns, one taken from the museum at Hythe, and Mr. Churchill's allusion in Parliament to the "ring of steel around Palmyra" referred not to tanks or armoured cars but to a few brave men in Morris trucks. The Household Cavalry were now fighting the French Foreign Legion for the first time in history. The enemy were under no delusion about our strength or our air cover. Their aerodrome was one mile away and our lines of communication stretched for 700 miles. For ten days the ruins of Zenobia's palaces looked down on this tragic struggle between French and English. Then the enemy cracked and the column was once more on the move up the road to Homs, Hama and Aleppo.

Troops were now being massed for the conquest of Persia, and the Household Cavalry recrossed the desert, paused in peaceful Baghdad and moved north to the oil-fields of Khanaquin. Entering Iran south of the Piatak Pass, they entered Kerminshah and the short campaign ended. For the third time in six months they received the order to cease fire. After a short time garrisoning Senna and Shahabad, they advanced to occupy the capital and entered Teheran simultaneously with the Russians. Three weeks' rest and celebration followed with our new Allies, and parades and exchange of hospitalities became the order of the day. Then, with winter approaching, came the long march back to Jerusalem and, later, one memorable October afternoon, the battle-scarred trucks climbed their last

In September 1939 the Life Guards and Royal Horse Guards, horsed cavalry regiments, stationed in London and Windsor respectively, amalgamated to form the 1st Household Cavalry Regiment and the Household Cavalry Training Regiment. With the threat of invasion after the Battle of France the War Office decided there was no room in this country for horsed soldiers, and with the need for new units the 2nd Household Cavalry Regiment was formed.

〜〜〜

hill, the Mount of Olives, and coasted down into the Holy City.

The spring of 1942 found the Regiment in Cyprus for six months' garrison duty. These were the dark days before Alamein, and invasion was expected daily. Famagusta, Nicosia, Athalassa, waving seas of bearded barley, white villages and blue vine clad hills: in twos and threes our magnificent new "steeds," the Marmon Harrington Armoured Cars, began to arrive, and were driven gaily over the dusty stubbles in the heat of July afternoons. It takes two years to train a unit from nothing in this complicated role, but in August the Regiment was re-equipping at Kassassin, and a few weeks later drove through Cairo to take its place in the 8th Army. Not everyone was strange to the desert, for all that summer there had been a squadron of Household Cavalrymen in dummy tanks; and on one occasion, at the Rotunda Signals, they had bluffed the Italians into a hasty retreat.

The story of El Alamein is well known. The Regiment was in the south throughout, in the 44th Division, and was under the command of 7th Armoured in their first attack before they were switched to the north. The Quattara depression, Himeimat, the January, February and Avon minefields: these were the scenes of the Regiment's numerous actions, as the battle continued day after day. The Marmon Harringtons appeared still stranger sights with various captured weapons — Solothurns, Bredas, Spandaus—mounted on the turrets. Then one glorious morning they broke through the

Avon minefield to find the enemy in full flight. After four hectic days they found themselves driving across virgin sand with the defeated Italian army behind them and only a few gazelle in front. The ebb-tide of the war had passed.

Raqqa, a little Syrian town on the Euphrates near the Syrian border, was the next home of the 1st Household Cavalry Regiment. For 15 months they were destined to garrison the Middle East, train and wait for their next period of active service. The Marmons gave place to Humbers, Humbers to Daimlers. Staghounds appeared. Equipment improved, establishments changed as the 8th Army left the desert behind. The Regiment summered in the heights of Slennfe in Syria, and wintered in the tent town of Tahag. They trained in the little-known deserts south of Suez, made more than one visit to the Lebanon to quell Greek or French troubles, and spent six weeks in Alexandria waiting to sail for Italy.

Red Shield on Their Battle-dress

For the six months they were in Italy during the summer of 1944 the Regiment was almost constantly employed. Soon after landing at Naples they were re-equipped and sent round to join V Corps on the Adriatic Sector. The battle of Cassino had yet to be fought and the snow-clad Majella massif lay in the hands of the Germans. Leaving their cars behind them the squadrons moved forward on foot, and, based on the little monastery towns of Lama and Paiena, patrolled against the enemy. It was a strenuous affair of mules, carrier pigeons and special Alpine equipment.

With the fall of Rome the whole front crumbled, and after a spell of rest the next role was a mounted one in the Fabriano Scheggia sector, where at one time the Regiment held over 25 miles of front. Sassoferato and the ancient town of Gubbio fell after numerous small actions. The next move was to the Arno Valley, when the Regiment was in 6th Armoured Division and fought in the foothills of the Prato Magna. Then followed a long spell in the Line with the

PALESTINE HEADQUARTERS of the 1st Household Cavalry Regiment during the spring and summer of 1940 was in this ancient town of Tulkarm. Taken in the October, the previously unpublished photograph shows a sentry on guard at the entrance to the fort, while others parade in front of one of the old stone buildings.

Photo, British Official

CONFERRING IN THE WESTERN DESERT in November 1942, during the rout of the Axis forces, Colonel (then Major) R. E. S. Gooch is seen in the centre. With him are the Adjutant, Captain I. A. Henderson (left), and Major W. H. Gerard Leigh.

Polcorps during the advance to and the battle of the Gothic Line which culminated in the capture of Fano and Pesaro. To commemorate these actions the Regiment was decorated with the Sirenya Warsawa, and all ranks now wear the red shield of the Siren of Warsaw on their battle-dress. To fight alongside the Poles is to know the real meaning of the word bravery and to wear their badge is an enviable distinction. Two more periods in the line followed : one at Anghiara and the other at Monte St. Angelo. Advances were made as far as Carpegua and St. Leo before the Regiment was withdrawn. A month later they reached Liverpool and were soon installed at Aldershot.

Rattled Over the Rhine Pontoons

However, this was not quite the end of the story. After four months' resting and re-equipping, the Regiment crossed from Tilbury to Ostend and was soon in the Line again, on the Maas front under 1st Corps. Italian partisans had been exchanged for Dutch, the winding hill roads of Italy for cobbled highways of Holland. Then, one afternoon in April 1945 the cars rattled over the pontoons that spanned the Rhine and a week later were in action in the Munster Forest. Finally, they came under command of the Guards Armoured Division which was directed on Cuxhaven. Fighting alongside the sister regiment, the 2nd Household Cavalry Regiment, they captured Stade and after an exhilarating week crossed the Oste at Hechthausen. The historic signal was received in May and the heavy guns sounded the cease fire.

It is tempting to wax sentimental over this long odyssey. Let us simply be thankful that nearly three hundred men lived through

it all and that the Guard is mounted in Whitehall once again as it used to be to give pleasure to the people and do honour to their King.

SECOND HOUSEHOLD CAVALRY REGIMENT
by Major A. J. R. Collins

IT might be thought that the fast moving pattern of modern war holds no place for the cavalry soldier ; yet the role of the Armoured Car Regiment is very much that of the horsed soldier of old. Scouting ahead of the Armoured Division, seeing without being seen, reporting back the vital information to higher Headquarters, filling the sudden gap, watching the open flank, acting as the Commander's highly mobile reserve, such were the tasks of the old Divisional Cavalry, and such indeed were the tasks given to the armoured cars in the highly mobile battle.

As already stated, with the need for new units the Second Household Cavalry Regiment was formed. This Regiment was initially trained as a Motor Battalion, but in 1941, when the Guards Armoured Division was formed, the 2nd H.C.R. assumed its traditional role of cavalry or what now corresponds to cavalry, of armoured cars. There followed long months of training in this country, of gunnery, of driving and maintenance and of wireless, for everything had to be learned from scratch. Innumerable exercises on small and large scale made it seem at times that the Regiment would never fire a shot in anger against the Hun. Nevertheless, when after D-Day and the opportunities came there was not one officer or man who was not thankful for the most thorough

Colours : Red T's on Dark Blue Ground
50TH (NORTHUMBRIAN) DIVISION

AN old Territorial formation steeped in First Great War tradition, the 50th, mainly composed of North-Country infantry regiments, took on a more national appearance as the toll of casualties mounted during the Second Great War. In May 1940 its greatness was apparent at Arras and Ypres, where by hard-won successes the envelopment of the B.E.F. was averted. The intervention of G.H.Q. prevented a "fight to the last man" stand, and the Division embarked from Dunkirk.

Re-formed in England, the 50th arrived in the Western Desert, via Cyprus, in time for Rommel's offensive in June 1942. Defensive actions were fought along the Gazala Line, at Mersa Matruh and at Alamein, until Montgomery's final offensive from the last named in October 1942. Not engaged in the early phases of that offensive, the Division later took part in the pursuit of the Afrika Korps, attacked the Mareth Line in March 1943, and spread-eagled the Wadi Akarit defence line. Its final success in the Tunisian campaign was at Enfidaville on April 20.

IN Sicily the Division outfought enemy parachute troops at Primo Sola bridge on July 10. Catania was captured on August 5, Acireale on August 8, and Taormina on August 15, before the Division was withdrawn to England for the invasion in the West. Landing north of Bayeux on June 6, 1944, La Rosière was taken within a few hours and Bayeux was entered the following day. Costly engagements followed at Lingèvres, Tilly, Onchy, and Hottot in July. In the Bocage country, in August, the 50th captured Lictot, Amaye, Villers Bocage, Plessis-Grimoult and St. Pierre, cleared the Forest of Breteuil on August 23, and elements were over the Seine by August 27. Entering Belgium on September 4, the Division assisted in the liberation of Brussels (entered on September 3). In Holland the Division fought its last battle along the Eindhoven-Nijmegen road, September-October, and was withdrawn to England in December 1944.

SYRIA-BOUND AFTER ALAMEIN, in 1942, to take up Middle East garrison duties, squadrons of armoured cars created an impressive sight as they left the Egyptian Desert for the small town of Raqqa, on the Syrian border. When stationed in Syria, for fifteen months, the Regiment took advantage of the little-known deserts and the improved equipment coming to hand to train for its next period of active service, in Italy, where it campaigned for six months in 1944.

First Household Cavalry in Cyprus and Persia

NEW EQUIPMENT INSTRUCTION was an important part of the training of the First Household Cavalry Regiment when stationed on the island of Cyprus in 1942. Troops learning to drive a Bren gun carrier (1) on the sun-baked plains. Occasional rest from these exertions was enjoyed on the beaches (2).

LINK UP OF IST HOUSEHOLD CAVALRY Regiment and of Russian forces in August 1941, at Teheran, capital of Persia, brought to a close the Allied campaign directed against a threatened Nazi coup d'etat in that country. An officer of " C " squadron of the Cavalry is seen (3, right) with a Russian officer and an interpreter, extreme left, after the occupation of the city. Following three weeks rest and exchange of hospitalities with their Russian Allies, the Household Cavalry commenced their long march back to Jerusalem, after having been engaged in Iraq and Syria on missions similar to that which took the regiment into Persia.

After arriving at the camp at Jerusalem, in October, troops displayed their trophy, the German flag (4). Remaining in Jerusalem for the 1941-42 winter the Regiment was transferred to Cyprus in the spring of 1942, for garrison duties ; it was here that the obsolete Hotchkiss machine-guns and old light trucks with which the Regiment had fought its recent campaigns began to give way to modern armoured vehicles and armament, and training for the Alamein Battle was begun.

STAGHOUND ARMOURED cars, replacing other types "mounted" by the Regiment when in North Africa, were taken to Italy, where one is seen (left) on a patrol, July 1944.

training he had received. All ranks in the armoured car regiments were supremely confident in the vehicles and weapons with which they were to fight.

Owing to the confined nature of the Normandy bridge-head and consequent lack of space for wide-ranging armoured cars, it was not till 38 days after D-Day, on July 14, 1944, that the 2nd H.C.R. landed in France. However, almost immediately on arrival part of the Regiment was held in readiness to take part in the hoped-for break-through at the Caen battle. No break-through came, and it was almost reminiscent of the 1914-1918 war that the cavalry should be held up waiting for such an event. The 2nd H.C.R. had not long to wait, for it was immediately switched to the extreme right of 2nd Army front; under command of the famous 11th Armoured Division it took part in the thrust which carried a spearhead into the enemy lines towards Vire and Tinchebray and was simultaneous with the start of the big American offensive which carried them to the Loire and to Brittany.

The 2nd H.C.R. was truly blooded in this battle and the capture of a vital bridge at Le Beny Bocage, and many other exploits augured well for the future. This first experience was of vital importance to the Regiment, because after a week spent as infantry it made a quick move to XXX Corps who were by then blocking the south of the Falaise pocket and preparing for an assault across the Seine. The whole German line was crumbling; the hunt would start at any moment, and the cavalry were required to lead the way.

IN the event, the break came very suddenly and the result was that for the 2nd H.C.R. the pace was fast and distances long. The Regiment, after the Seine was crossed, was under the command of the Guards Armoured Division which was on the right of XXX Corps. The route followed was across the Seine at Vernon to the Somme at Villers Bretonneux via Beauvais, thence to Arras and Douai, and then on that most memorable Sunday (September 3) to Brussels. On one day 78 miles were covered, but on the day of the liberation of Brussels the distance was 95 miles. Each day there took place innumerable brushes with the enemy, fights to hold vital bridges and all the other varied incidents which unexpectedly fall to the lot of reconnaissance troops.

The entry to Brussels was unforgettable and more like a dream than a battle, but the respite given to the 2nd H.C.R. was short. The next day the advance continued to the Dyle bridges at Louvain, and together with the Grenadier Guards a stiff fight with S.S. troops took place before these bridges were secured intact.

Within the next fortnight the Albert Canal was crossed, and the Dutch frontier reached, and on September 17 came the start of the famous operation "Market Garden," ending with the glorious exploits of the 1st British Airborne Division at Arnhem. The 2nd H.C.R. was in the van of the 2nd Army, pushing forward to reach the successive parties of airborne troops, and as the reports came through that each successive bridge and waterway was crossed optimism reigned. However, despite the gallant capture of Nijmegen Bridge, progress could not be made over the last 12 miles to Arnhem. It was, indeed, two troops of Household Cavalry armoured cars who slipped through the German screen one morning in the mist and made first physical contact between the ground forces of the 2nd Army and the beleaguered airborne troops.

Throughout the action and the early winter of 1944-45 less spectacular jobs were the lot of the 2nd H.C.R. A long period

CHANGING OF THE GUARD in Whitehall, on October 5, 1945, by the Household Cavalry revived one of London's most popular spectacles. See also illus. page 425, Vol. 9.

watching the line of the Meuse in the mud and damp of Holland, a sudden dash to another part of the Meuse, this time in Belgium between Liége and Namur, at the time of the Ardennes scare, and later very little action for the Regiment in the battle to clear the country in the Reichswald, and between the rivers. Then came the crossing of the Rhine, and the vivid hope that the Regiment would take part in another gallop, this time on German soil.

In fact, XXX Corps was on the left of the British forces ranged against what remained of the German paratroops who were fighting in a country as if of their own choosing; an enclosed country of dykes and soft ground which made armoured warfare against a determined enemy almost impossible and progress very slow. Every wood and village was defended, and in consequence the work of the armoured cars was harder and less spectacular. Nevertheless, with the rapid progress of the right flank of the 2nd Army, advances were made despite heavy fighting, and by the time of the German collapse the 2nd H.C.R.—who during the last fortnight of the war had fought side by side with the First Household Cavalry Regiment recently arrived from Italy—had reached the North Sea at Cuxhaven.

"Splice the Mainbrace" Ordered

Such are the bare bones of the story; the descriptions which follow are those of some of the more spectacular incidents among the everyday happenings to armoured car troops. One lucky troop officer, at the beginning of the campaign, having kept a vital bridge in enemy territory under observation for 48 hours, went out on patrol the following day; his car was blown up by a mine. Changing cars, he met a Tiger tank which was immobile through track trouble. The officer tried to stalk the crew, and was himself wounded and taken prisoner. The German tank commander ordered him to remove his boots and sent him off, whereupon he regained his own lines and was evacuated wounded to England after 72 hours of war. A troop of armoured cars watching the Rhine engaged and beached a tug flying the swastika flag and towing two barges. On the result of the action being wirelessed to higher headquarters the command to "splice the mainbrace" was immediately given.

A single car with an officer and driver making a reconnaissance down six miles of straight Continental road ran into enemy country. He met a Panther tank, turned about, and by driving at racing speed regained his own lines carrying vital information, even though enemy infantry with an anti-tank gun were by then on the road between him and our territory.

All true cavalry work carried out in the spirit and tradition of the Household Cavalry. Though the glamour and the sparkle of the Household Cavalryman of old has departed, his successors in The Life Guards and "Blues" have proved as brave and as resourceful in modern war as their forbears —whose duty it was to protect the person of the King in battle.

Paris Peace Conference: Opening Scenes

To lead the British delegation at the Peace Conference, the Rt. Hon. Clement R. Attlee (1) flew from Northolt Aerodrome, Middlesex, on July 28, 1946; the Prime Minister was accompanied to the York aircraft by Mrs. Attlee, and was met at Le Bourget airport by the British Ambassador, Mr. Duff Cooper (2, left). On the following day arrived the U.S. Secretary of State, Mr. James Byrnes (3) and his wife, in readiness for the inaugural session in the flag-draped Luxembourg Palace (4).

" *Five Peace Conferences in One* "

REPUBLIQUE FRANÇAIS
10F
POSTE
CONFERENCE DE
PARIS 1946

WELCOMING the delegates to the Conference at the Luxembourg Palace (1), the French Premier and Foreign Minister, M. Bidault (2, extreme right), said, on July 29, " For the second time in less than thirty years France is the seat of the international convocations where the nations that have emerged victorious from terrible wars are striving to establish peace. The association of peace-loving nations who are inspired by a common ideal forms the basis of the United Nations Organization, the foundations whose corporate life were established last year at San Francisco . . . This same association . . . is now being called upon by the council of Foreign Ministers to take part in the working-out of the peace settlement." He recalled to mind " the meetings of the Council of Foreign Ministers in London in September 1945, in Paris in May, and again in June ; those were the meetings at which the drafts submitted to you today were prepared."

That this Conference would have to " accomplish the tasks of five peace conferences " was emphasized by Mr. Molotov when he greeted the assembly on behalf of the Soviet Union, at the plenary session on July 31. " It will have to express its opinion and offer recommendations on drafts of peace treaties for Italy, Rumania, Bulgaria, Hungary and Finland . . . five countries which entered the war as Germany's allies, as Hitler's satellites, but in the course of the war with Germany overthrew their Fascist rulers and, in general, came out actively on the side of the democratic countries in the war for victory over Hitlerite Germany."

In smiling mood the British Premier (4) climbed the main staircase in the Palace—passing resplendent Cuirassiers of the Garde Republicaine stationed at every few paces—en route to the Salle des Séances, to urge upon the delegates " the simple object of moving from the heart of the common people in all lands the brooding fear of another war and of enabling them to live together good citizens not only of their own States but of Europe and the world." Specially designed to commemorate the occasion were these two postage stamps (3) issued by the French Post Office. *Photos, Keystone, Associated Press*

RÉPUBLIQUE FRANÇAISE

3F

ONFÉRENCE DE PARIS 1946

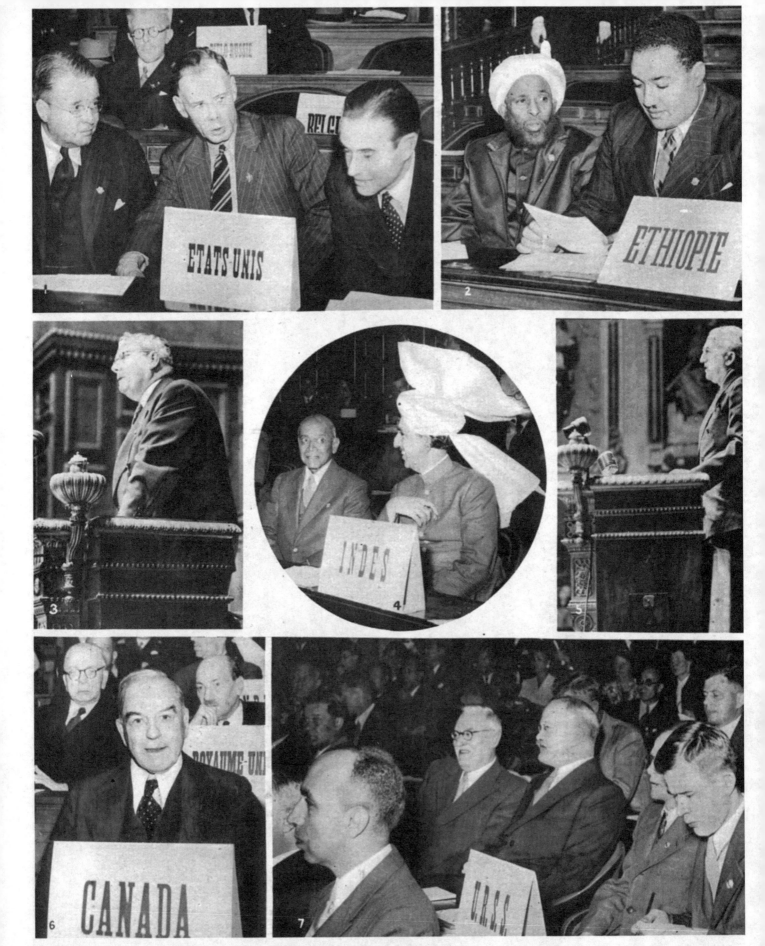

Representing Seven of the Peace-Seeking Peoples

Photos, G.P.U., Planet News, Keystone

1. U.S. delegates, Mr. Freeman Matthews, Lt.-Gen. W. Bedell Smith and Mr. Averell Harriman. 2. Ethiopian delegate Aklilu Abt Wolde (left) who remained unseated until placards which bore the name of Abyssinia were replaced by new, hastily printed labels. 3. Dr. H. V. Evatt, leader of the Australians. 4. Sir J. Bhor and Sir Khizar Hayat Khan Tiwana of India. 5. Mr. J. F. Byrnes, U.S. State Secretary. 6. Mr. Mackenzie King of Canada, and (behind) Mr. A. V. Alexander and Mr. Attlee. 7. Mr. Molotov and Mr. Vyshinsky of the U.S.S.R. See also pages 289 and 313.

SUDAN and OTHER AFRICAN TERRITORIES

By HARLEY V. USILL

"I F the Anglo-Egyptian Sudan had gone, the supply lines to the Middle East up to the Red Sea and across Africa from Takoradi to Khartoum would have gone, too. Egypt itself would have become untenable. There could have been, in fact, no front in the Middle East. . . . They (the Sudanese) deserve in the Battle of Africa the same tribute as the Prime Minister paid to the fighter pilots of the Royal Air Force in the Battle of Britain ; for rarely has so much been owed by so many to so few." This quotation comes from the official publication, The Abyssinian Campaigns.

The Sudan comprises a million square miles and contains about six million inhabitants, and has been under Anglo-Egyptian condominium since 1899. Geographically and culturally the country falls into two parts—the great North African-Arabian Desert, inhabited by Hamitic and Arabic-speaking Muslims ; and to the south, the Sudan proper, inhabited by negroid peoples yet linked by tradition and the Nile to the riverain Arabs of the Northern area.

When Italy declared war she had immediately available about 100,000 men, with powerful artillery support, for use on the Sudan frontier. Facing her, had she but known it, were 7,000 British and Sudanese. The 1,200 miles of frontier bordering Italian territory was thinly covered by the Sudan Defence Force consisting of only about 4,500 men. Three British battalions, less than 2,500 men, were all the other troops available for the defence of Khartoum, Port Sudan and such other vital spots as the Atbara railway junction. The "supporting" air force consisted of seven antiquated machines.

Supplement to British Battalions

A realization that *their* country was in danger, however, led a number of local sheikhs and chiefs to raise irregular forces from among the frontier inhabitants, and these were constantly in action against the enemy and proved an invaluable supplement to the British battalions and the Sudan Defence Force. In the region of the Upper Blue Nile, the Blue Nile Province Police, a civil force, assisted by a band of irregulars, took the first offensive action of the war by crossing the Akabo River, on June 21, 1940, into enemy territory and evicting the occupants of an Italian post.

They then held the frontier successfully until the King's African Rifles arrived to consolidate the position. On paper, of course, the general situation appeared hopeless, but there was no fifth column in the Sudan, and Major-General Platt and his men, few but good, succeeded in bluffing the Italians into thinking that our forces were far stronger than in fact they were. If, however, he had not been able to rely upon the absolute loyalty of the people of the Sudan no such bluff would have been possible.

The generosity of the people of Sudan was displayed in many ways. Nearly £100,000 was subscribed to the Red Cross, the Sudan Warplanes Fund and other Allied funds. The Rizeigat tribe, famous horsemen, presented the Army with the cream of their stock for remounts ; and the Meidob, the most primitive of North African peoples, drove a flock of sheep for 450 miles across the desert as a gift to the Commissariat. And so we could go on giving details of gifts great and small, but enough has been said to indicate something of the nature of Sudan's contribution to victory, and to justify the unconstitutional inclusion of this territory in the present survey.

The High Commission Territories are " in " South Africa but do not form part

CONSTITUTIONALLY, the Anglo-Egyptian Sudan and the three High Commission Territories of Basutoland, the Bechuanaland Protectorate and Swaziland have no place in a series of articles on the British Colonial Empire. Nevertheless, we feel justified in dealing with the considerable war effort of these territories in conjunction with those of our African colonies.

of the Union, being Protectorates governed directly from Britain. The agent for the discharge of these responsibilities is His Majesty's High Commissioner for Basutoland, Bechuanaland and Swaziland, who is also the High Commissioner for the United Kingdom in the Union of South Africa. The three territories are very diverse in character. Basutoland and Swaziland are smaller than Wales, whereas the Bechuanaland Protectorate is nearly two and a half times the size of the whole of Great Britain. Populations, however, bear no relation to the size of area, since Basutoland has a population of 600,000, Bechuanaland 280,000 and Swaziland 180,000.

BASUTOLAND is primarily an agricultural country with over a million acres under the plough. Here there are nearly twice as many human beings as cattle ; whereas in the Bechuanaland Protectorate the reverse occurs, there being more than twice as many cattle as human beings. In Swaziland the natives are mainly on a cattle economy, and the great bulk of the agricultural production is undertaken by Europeans on European-owned farms. The contribution of the three territories to the total war effort falls within the following categories, and to assess its relative value regard must be given to the comparative smallness of the populations.

As we have seen, all three territories are agricultural and pastoral, and throughout the War great efforts were made to increase food production. In Basutoland practically all the available land was ploughed and sown. In Swaziland the cultivated acreage was increased by 25 per cent. during 1940-41, and in the Bechuanaland Protectorate the additional lands cultivated were known as

" war lands." In addition to producing Kaffir corn, mealies, maize and wheat, the Territories exported quantities of livestock, hides and skins, wool, mohair and dairy products.

During 1942 alone, 33,000 head of slaughter cattle were exported from the Bechuanaland Protectorate to Johannesburg and the Rhodesias, and nearly 1,000 tons of chilled beef to the United Kingdom. The importance of this, and all other production drives in East Africa, is best seen against the background of two important roles which the whole of East Africa, Southern Rhodesia and the Union of South Africa were called upon to play quite apart from direct military contributions. It was essential that the whole area should become self-sufficient in regard to its own food requirements at the same time as it was developed into a supply base.

How Industrial Demands Were Met

Next in importance in the drive for supplies was the supply of manpower for the mines. A certain amount of labour is absorbed in Swaziland, where the most abundant mineral is asbestos, but the majority of the natives work in the gold and diamond mines on the Rand and in the coal mines of the Union. The great shortage of labour in the Union during the war added considerably to the value of the supply of labour from the three Territories. Industrial diamonds, for instance, were vital to the whole war effort, and a regular supply enabled South Africa to service its own production of machine tools.

In June 1941 units of the African Auxiliary Pioneer Corps were formed for service with the British forces. Since then over 32,000 have been recruited, roughly 20,000 from Basutoland, 8,000 from the Bechuanaland Protectorate and 4,000 from Swaziland. All these men were volunteers, and companies of the African Auxiliary Pioneer Corps formed from the High Commission Territories served throughout the Middle East campaign from Syria to Tunis. These troops took part in the advance from El Alamein to Tunisia, handling supplies at Tobruk and Tripoli. Basuto "diluted" units accompanied the 8th Army to Sicily and Italy, and in Sicily they were joined by units from Bechuanaland.

SWAZI TROOPS of the African Pioneer Corps, with men from Basutoland and Bechuanaland, served throughout the Middle East campaign from Syria to Tunis. Volunteers recruited with the co-operation of their paramount chief Sobhuiza II, they helped particularly in maintaining supplies ; those above are breaking-up salvaged enemy aircraft from North African battlefields, to provide material for other purposes. PAGE 307 *Photo, British Official*

K.O.Y.L.I. Celebrate Minden Victory in Minden

IN HONOUR of the men of the Regiment who fought, fell and vanquished the French Armies at the Battle of Minden 187 years ago, a battalion of the King's Own Yorkshire Light Infantry for the first time in Regimental history held its annual Minden Day parade in that German city, on August 1, 1946. In accordance with tradition, the 1st Battalion, with white roses in their khaki berets, doubled on to parade on the sounding of the "Advance." The Regimental Colour Party (above), consisting of Lieut. Derbyshire, C.S.M. A. Patterson, C.Q.M.S. Lane and C.Q.M.S. Tatchell, then took post in the centre of the Battalion, General Sir Charles Deedes, Colonel of the Regiment, whose son had fought with it during the Second Great War as a major, carried out his inspection of the parade (right) and the Colour Party returned to the saluting base in readiness for the march past.

Addressing the Battalion, the General said : "The Queen, Colonel-in-Chief of your Regiment, has asked me to convey her best wishes to you," and referred to the proud traditions established by the 51st of Foot (as it was then known) at the Battle of Minden on August 1, 1759. Accompanying General Deedes at the saluting base was Major-General G. P. B. Roberts, C.B., D.S.O., M.C., commander of the famous 7th Armoured Division (Desert Rats), to which the 1st Battalion the King's Own Yorkshire Light Infantry now belongs. The Battalion, which moved to its present station by way of France, Norway, Scotland, Ireland, England, India, Iraq, Iran, the Suez Canal Zone, Syria, Sicily, Italy, Palestine, Belgium and Germany, is engaged upon very heavy guard duties in the Minden area.

Photos, British Official

Britain's Food: Our Meat Ration from Overseas

ENSURING THE APPEARANCE OF THE FAMILY MEAT RATIONS in the butchers' shops ready for sale each week is a complicated task. Our artist Haworth was given facilities by the Ministry of Food to make this drawing, which shows some of the varied activities which go on behind the scenes when a refrigerated meat ship sails into port from Australia, New Zealand or elsewhere. The meat, which may be boneless beef, fore or hind quarters with bone, telescoped mutton carcasses, or individual joints packed in cardboard containers, all of which may add up to five or six thousand tons, is stowed away in the shelter deck, the 'tween decks and lower holds.

The temperature of these cargo spaces has been maintained at 14 to 16 degrees Fahr. during the voyage, by means of air-conditioning plant consisting of two fans driven by electric motor (A). The lower fan draws in air from the bottom of the hold (B). This is then passed through a series of chilled pipes (C), the upper fan forcing

it through a wooden trunk (D), which distributes the freshly chilled air around the top of the hold, whence it passes down through the cargo and is taken in again and reconditioned. The chilling of the pipes is shown inset; carbon dioxide is compressed at (X), condensed at (Y), passing through the evaporators (Z). Each hold has its own set of fans and pipes, and by means of a central control panel the temperatures of the many cargo spaces are regulated.

To facilitate dispatch, unloading of the meat is carried out by barges (E) for delivery to riverside cold storage depots, via transit sheds (F) to refrigerated railway trucks (G) for transport to inland cold storage depots. During the railway journey temperature is adjusted by means of a chemical compound called cardice, which is seen being stowed at (H). The remainder of the ship's cargo is put into cold storage depot at the dockside, there to await motor transport (J) by road to retailers in surrounding areas.

Europe's Wartime Capitals in 1946
PARIS
By
GEORGES GOMBAULT

a French journalist who, opposed to the Pétain armistice, came to London in June 1940 and became the editor of the French newspaper, France.

Conditions of existence in Paris are beginning to improve and intellectual, artistic, and social life resumed with intensity, but there are still great difficulties. The housing crisis is extremely serious. It is almost impossible to find an unfurnished flat, and it is hardly less difficult to discover a furnished one. This shortage is due less to destruction, which was not very extensive in the capital, than to inadequate building since 1930 and to the large number of refugees from up and down the country.

The number of persons who have a right to priority—refugees, big families, officials—is 135,000, and only some 30,000 have been assigned quarters ; the rest have been taken in by friends or are living in furnished apartments or in hotels. "When a jug of water is full to the top," the director of the Office du Logement (Housing Department) said to me, "not another drop of water can be got into it." The housing crisis will continue until a vast building plan can be put into operation, and for this, alas ! material and coal are lacking.

The Harassments of Shopping

The food supply still leaves much to be desired. Meat rations are small, fats entirely insufficient ; milk is still reserved for young children and old people ; fish is scarce. But during the summer fruits and vegetables have been abundant and sold without restriction. Potatoes were short for a time, but have reappeared and are now being sold without restriction. Many Parisians have families or friends in the country and receive parcels from them. Outside the official distribution there is, of course, the black market ; but there have been prosecutions, and results have been achieved in regard to sugar, thanks to which the official distribution has been resumed. The sugar ration is not large, and in most of the cafés, restaurants and hotels saccharin is given. Thus the food situation has not returned to normal. But housewives are no longer obsessed by the difficulty of finding the indispensable minimum on which their family can live.

Clothing is still subjected to the severest restrictions. Neither suits nor boots nor underclothing can be bought freely. There are hats to be had, but the fashion of going bareheaded is steadily spreading. However, manufacture has been resumed, and every month sees a growing quantity of ready-made clothes, shirts or footwear purchasable, of course for coupons. The seamstresses and milliners of the Rue de la Paix are busy on exports ; Paris fashions have kept their prestige and recovered all their vogue.

Men who hanker after elegance continue to go to their tailor and shirtmaker and shoemaker, but only a tiny minority can afford this luxury. Most Parisians are using up their pre-war stock of clothes and are renewing it only where absolutely necessary. Owing to the great shortage of stocks the big stores are no longer as frequented as in the past ; nevertheless, a comparison between this summer of 1946 and the morrow of liberation shows a certain progress in the field of shopping.

In transport the improvement is more decided. In September 1944 the only means of communication was the Underground (Métro), which ran only five days a week and only up to eleven o'clock at night ; many stations were closed. Now the Métro is running every day up to 1 a.m., and almost all the stations are open. Motor buses have been brought back into service, and about 1,500 are now on the road as compared with 3,500 before the war. Taxis have made their appearance ; there are 6,000 at present and there will soon be 8,000, compared with 14,000 before the war. After being reduced for so long to the Métro, the cycle, or walking, Parisians greatly appreciate the progress already made.

The number of private cars has also increased, but to no great extent. The great French works are making cars, though not on the same scale as they are manufacturing lorries ; but the greater part of the production is reserved for export. A proportion has been assigned for use within the country, but to buy a car it is necessary to possess a certificate supplied by a Ministry, and the categories entitled to such certificates are narrowly limited and defined—physicians, industrialists, journalists, and so on.

According to recent statements of the Ministry of the Interior, 400,000 cars (including taxis) are in use, compared with 60,000 at the time of liberation ; 500,000 cars are still laid up. In this field, too, progress is slow, due to the limited quantities of tires and of motor spirit available. Motor spirit has to be imported, and the French are compelled to go cautiously with their foreign exchange.

Fuel of all kinds presents one of the chief problems. The recovery of industry, and therefore of trade, depends on coal, and in spite of the effort made by the French miners, whose production now exceeds that of 1938, there is still a shortage. The French extraction of coal has always been inadequate for the country's needs. Parisians had no heating at all during the winter of 1944-45, and very little in that of 1945-46. They are wondering if they will suffer from cold next winter as much as in the past. The Minister of Public Works has recently stated that if the imports allowed to France are not increased, domestic heating will have to be sacrificed to the needs of industry. At least it is possible to hope that electricity will not be cut off for several hours every day as in the two past winters ; the reservoirs of the hydro-electric stations, which were empty, have been refilled by the abundant rain.

Thus life in Paris is far from easy, but every day it is becoming a little less difficult. Living is expensive, entailing especial hardship for all those with fixed incomes or salaries. The high prices have produced demands for wage increases. But social agitation has not so far assumed grave forms ; the working class is following the advice of its trade unions and is well aware that the parties that represent it have their share of power.

Intellectual and artistic life has been revived. In spite of the great shortage of paper, new books are now appearing. The French Academy and the Académie Goncourt are distributing prizes in conformity with their tradition and their statutes. The literary public is reading novels and historical works and accounts of the life of deported workers and prisoners. It is interested in the verse of Eluard, Pierre-Emmanuel, Aragon, and other poets who became widely known for their part in the Resistance.

The Théâtre Français, which has recently been reorganized and to which the Odéon is now subordinated, continues to produce outstanding dramatic works, and the public remains faithful to it. Great actors and original producers like Jouvet, Copeau, Dullin and Baty continue their pioneering work, and there has been a rush to one of the boulevard theatres to see the new interpretation of L'Ecole des Femmes by Jouvet, a Molière enthusiast.

Art exhibitions are multiplying and the cinema is flourishing, for it is within the means of all, of worker and bourgeois, of intellectual and ignoramus. The public is as hungry as ever for new productions, but it has enjoyed a revival of Chaplin films. Cinemas are nowadays more frequented than cafés, for restrictions interfere with the amenities of the latter. Real coffee and tea are rare ; there is no sugar ; and very often by the middle of the day there is neither wine nor beer nor cider left, and the customer must resign himself to simple fruit juices.

Among the young, football and athletics are having a great vogue. Swimming is increasing in popularity in the baths in the Seine, the Marne and the Oise. Horseracing has all its old attraction : the days of the Drags and the Grand Prix attract the same crowds as before the War.

The Old Fascination Unchanged

Except for a few buildings, Paris has remained intact : the Louvre, Notre-Dame, the Sainte-Chapelle, the Invalides, the Sorbonne, the Collège de France, the Arc de Triomphe, the Concorde, the Place des Vosges, and the old houses of the Ile Saint-Louis, are still there ; the splendid perspectives of the Champs-Elysées and the Champ de Mars remain. The tourist can still mount to the third storey of the Eiffel Tower, climb the Butte Montmartre or make the journey to Montparnasse. He can visit the museums and the libraries or stroll along the banks of the Seine and search the boxes of the secondhand booksellers for bargains. The background, the wonderful setting, the fascination of it all, have not changed.

But deeper observation reveals that Paris has been profoundly affected by the oppression she underwent through four years. She has not forgotten her moral sufferings or her privations. How could she forget them when so many of her own have not returned and so many essential things are still missing ? But Paris, still quivering at the reconquest of her freedom, does not despair : she is putting forth her energies to become once more what she always was in the eyes of the world. No one has any doubt that Paris will recover completely.

THE ARC DE TRIOMPHE now features a cab-rank for horse-drawn carriages (right), one result of shortage of modern transport in Paris.   PAGE 310   *Photo, Keystone*

Slow Progress of Paris to Peacetime Plenty

BOULEVARD DES ITALIENS on a fine Sunday afternoon is thick with promenaders (I) all outwardly well-dressed in spite of the severest restrictions to which the sale of clothing in France is still subjected.

QUEUE FOR MEN ONLY is attended by seekers after cotton shirts and underclothing (2), now less scarce than formerly and purchasable—when one is lucky—in exchange for the inevitable coupons.

PREPARING FOR LUNCH by the side of the Seine this wanderer (3) has his own method of dealing with the food situation. The derisively named Marché aux Puces (Flea Market) offers bargains in secondhand clothing and other goods (4). Boarding a bus on the Place de l'Opéra (5) in the absence of a regulated queue entails the skilful use of elbows and pushfulness. Only about 1,500 motor-buses are now on the Paris roads as compared with 3,500 before the War. See facing page.

Exclusive to THE WAR ILLUSTRATED

The Roll of Honour
1939—1946

Sgt. R. ADDIS
Royal Air Force.
Mediterranean.   7.5.44.
Age 20.   (Cinderford)

So great has been the response of readers to our invitation to submit portraits for our Roll of Honour that no more can now be accepted. But we have every hope of being able to publish all those so far received.

Flt./Sgt. H. ADDIS
Royal Air Force.
In action: 3.12.43.
Age 21.   (Cinderford)

Stkr. F. C. ANSELL
H.M.S. Penzance.
Action: Atlantic. 24.8.40.
Age 23.   (Erith)

Cpl. J. AMOS
Argyll & Sutherlands.
Action: Italy.   21.4.45.
Age 23.   (Stoke-on-Trent)

Pte. J. BAKER
Q.O. Cameron Highl'd'rs.
North Africa. March, '43.
Age 33.   (Birmingham)

Dvr. S. BEIGHTON
Royal Army Service Corps.
Action: at sea. 2.3.44.
Age 32.   (Sheffield)

Pte. F. BILLINGHURST
6th Airborne Division.
Action: Belgium. 24.3.45.
Age 29.   (Greenwich)

L/Cpl. K. BRAMLEY
130 Field Amb. R.A.M.C.
Action: Norm'dy. 5.7.44.
Age 24.   (Halifax)

Pte. W. BROWN
R.A.M.C./48 R.M. Com'do
Westkapelle. 1.11.44.
Age 26.   (Aberdeen)

Pte. L. CARPENTER
Dorsetshire Regt.
Arromanches. 6.6.44.
Age 20.   (Birmingham)

Pte. J. CHISHAM
Royal Sussex Regiment.
Action: France. 12.5.40.
Age 21.   (Portsmouth)

Sgt. T. A. CLARKE
K.O. Scottish Borderers.
Action: Burma. 23.2.45.
Age 31.   (Bathgate)

Cook E. COLLINS
H.M.S. Glorious.
Off Norway. 9.6.40.
Age 26.   (Oldham)

Cpl. C. CUNNINGTON
Royal Engineers.
Died of wounds. 3.12.44.
Age 26.   (Lewes)

Cpl. A. DAVIES
3rd Monmouthshire Regt.
In action: Caen. 28.6.44.
Age 24.   (Ebbw Vale)

Pte. W. I. DENNIS
1st Bn. Loyal Regt.
Mediterranean. 3.6.44.
Age 20.   (Hadleigh)

Pte. L. A. DOBSON
Sherwood Foresters.
Action: Anzio. 30.1.44.
Age 32.   (Lincoln)

L/Cpl. G. DOWNING
8th Bn. Parachute Regt.
W. Europe. 28.3.45.
Age 20.   (Rushall)

Flt./Sgt. A. E. EDWARDS
Bomber Comd. R.A.F.V.R.
Action: Greece. 30.11.43.
Age 21.   (Finchley)

Cpl. E. E. EDWARDS
1st South Staffs Regt.
Action: Burma. 11.6.44.
Age 23.   (Madeley)

Sgt. A. G. G. FILLEUL
Royal Air Force.
Action: Hamburg. Aug. '43
Age 22.   (Gosport)

Pte. F. FENNELL
Sherwood Foresters.
Action: Inchville. 8.6.40.
Age 20.   (Chesterfield)

Flt./Sgt. FISHBOURNE
R.A.F.V.R., A.F.U.
Market Deeping. 15.4.45.
Age 24.   (Eyemouth)

Flt./Sgt. R. FRANKLIN
15 Bomber Sqn. R.A.F.
Action: Ruhr. 18.8.44.
Age 21.   (Gt. Yarmouth)

Pte. C. B. GOOCH
Oxford & Bucks L.I.
Normandy. 8.8.44.
Age 27.   (Oxford)

Gnr. H. GRIFFITHS
14th Bn. 5 S.L., R.A.
D. of wds. P.O.W. 18.6.43.
Age 32.   (Liverpool)

Pte. A. T. HARRIS
Royal West Kent Regt.
Action: Burma. 8.1.44.
Age 30.   (London)

Gnr. A. M. HARVELL
85th A.T. Regt. R.A.
Jap. P.O.W. 21.9.44.
Age 37.   (Parkstone)

L.A.C. E. G. HILLS
Royal Air Force.
Jap. P.O.W. 20.11.44.
Age 24.   (Kingsbury)

Cpl. F. HOLDSWORTH
West Yorkshire Regiment.
Burma. 16.9.44.
Age 25.   (Bradford)

Mne F. W. HUBBARD
11th Bn. Royal Marines.
Action: Tobruk. 13.9.42.
Age 20.   (Romford)

Cpl. S. G. LEE
1st Cambridgeshire Regt.
D. ex-P.O.W. 15.3.45.
Age 32.   (London)

Ft./Sgt. A. W. G. MEECH
Bomber Command R.A.F.
Wuppertal 29.5.43.
Age 22.   (London)

Pte. J. F. MILLINGTON
Northamptonshire Regt.
D. w'nds: Burma. 17.4.45.
Age 20.   (Birmingham)

Tpr. L. PAYNE
Royal Tank Regiment.
Action: Italy. 6.9.44.
Age 22.   (Effingham)

Sgt. H. G. ROYSTON
Bomber Command R.A.F.
In action: 10.2.44.
Age 20.   (London)

Fus. J. B. VEITCH
Royal Fusiliers.
In action: 15.12.43.
Age 27.   (Newcastle/Tyne)

Sgt. W. WINDEBANK
1/6 Queen's Royal Regt.
Action: France. 29.8.44.
Age 32.   (Romsey)

21 Nations Meet to Make Peace

At four o'clock on the afternoon of July 29, 1946, the Peace Conference opened its formal proceedings in the Luxembourg Palace, Paris. Hundreds of unarmed police kept the way clear for the arrival of the delegates, and at the palace portals cavalrymen in magnificent uniforms and with drawn swords provided the sole military touch. The proceedings are described by A. J. Cummings of The News Chronicle. See illus. pages 289 and 303-306.

WHEN I reached the high gallery reserved for the Press, the lower galleries were already filled with members of the Diplomatic Corps and other privileged visitors. Delegates were beginning to assemble in the places reserved for them in the well of the Chamber, facing a tribune from which many years ago Briand delivered one of the most eloquent of all his speeches.

The sunshine barely filtered through the geometric glass roof and at first it was hard in that dim atmosphere to identify more than a few of the new arrivals. Only the photographers with their flashing lights brightened the general air of gloom. It was an afternoon of subdued calm—nobody can say yet whether it was the calm which sometimes precedes a storm, or whether it was a felicitous forecast of a new and common incentive. There was little conversation as the national representatives took their seats, arranged according to nationality alphabet.

The heads of delegations, led by Mr. Byrnes, entered from behind the President's chair on the spacious platform. Mr. Molotov and Mr. Vishinsky came next; and the British Prime Minister, looking a trifle bewildered as he gazed around in search of his colleagues, was almost the last to emerge. A modest cheer greeted the appearance of M. Bidault, the French Premier, who took the President's chair. Then followed a pause while the Assembly sorted itself out and the

horde of photographers, spasmodically and reluctantly, ceased from shooting.

M. Bidault read his speech of welcome in clear but unemotional tones, pitching his voice low. It was a brief utterance, rigor-

ously free from controversial matter. The nearest approach to controversy was his assertion that the basic cause of the failure of the peace settlement after the First Great War rested on the fact that " the two Great Powers whose arms had each in turn held the decisive military balance " remained outside the settlement. Now that defection has been made good and " all the Democratic Powers " are together in the task of making peace.

He pleaded for patience and tolerance in the difficult and complex enterprise ahead and insisted hopefully that it would be

possible to find solutions " which, if not perfect, will be at least reasonable and not contrary to justice or to honour."

For the rest M. Bidault was unanimously elected temporary chairman of the Conference ; Mr. Lie, U.N.O.'s Secretary-General, was welcomed as an honoured guest and observer for U.N.O. ; and a committee was set up to consider rules of procedure on the basis of unofficial recommendations made by the Big Four.

At that point Dr. Evatt, pugnacious leader of the Australian delegation, charged the academic atmosphere with a streak of lightning. Stepping briskly on to the tribune, he protested, as a champion of the little nations, that the decisions of the Procedure Committee would profoundly affect the entire organization, perhaps the very fate, of the Conference ; and it should therefore begin its work at once and not at the same time as the plenary session, so that heads of delegations might be in attendance. " My country," he asserted with a challenging air, " has as much right to participate fully in the making of peace as the Big Four." No one rose to gainsay this axiomatic declaration and his proposal was accepted.

Thus ended the opening ceremonial of a conference at which, I am pretty sure, the little nations are determined to make their voices heard and their influence felt.

LEADER OF THE BRITISH DELEGATION at the Paris Peace Conference, Mr. Attlee chatted with Mr. A. V. Alexander, First Lord of the Admiralty (above, left) and Australia's Dr. Evatt (right). An honoured guest was Mr. Trygve Lie, General Secretary of the United Nations (top, right), in conversation with Mr. Averell Harriman, an American delegate.

THE COMMITTEE OF PROCEDURE AT THE PARIS PEACE CONFERENCE held its first meeting at the Luxembourg Palace on July 30, 1946. The controversy on whether to adopt the two-thirds majority rule proposed by the Council of Foreign Ministers or the simple majority rule favoured by many of the smaller states was settled here by a British amendment on August 7, whereby all recommendations, whether passed by a simple or a two-thirds majority, would be forwarded to the Foreign Ministers Council. See story in page 313.
Photo, G.P.U.

I Crash-landed on Burma's Broadway

Air liaison officer to a Gurkha column, Squadron-Leader (then Flight-Lieut.) Leonard Hart flew with the glider-borne troops who formed the spearhead of the Chindits' landing behind Japanese lines in Burma. He tells how in March 1944 they held the jungle clearing of Broadway and helped to prepare an airstrip for the landing of the main body.

I WAS seated with a small party of British and Gurkha troops beneath the wing of a glider at Lalaghat, in Assam, on the evening of March 5, 1944. Throughout the day the giant airfield had been a scene of feverish activity. Scores of huge American and R.A.F. transport aircraft had been arriving and were lined up on either side of the airstrip, and troops had been loading mules and equipment into the gliders now dispersed in pairs at the head of the grass runway. All around us sat similar groups of men laughing and joking, smoking and grumbling. They were chiefly men of the 1st Battalion of the King's (Liverpool) Regiment, forming the spearhead of General Orde Wingate's Chindits.

Our task was to crash-land that night in an open stretch of grassland surrounded by dense jungle, behind the Japanese lines in Burma, and hold it against any opposition whilst American engineers constructed an airstrip to enable the rest of the Brigade to be flown in in Dakotas.

The airstrip was to be known as Broadway, and the original plan was to carry out two such landings; but only a few hours before, the other proposed landing area was found to have been blocked by felled trees, so the plan had to be hastily altered. At that time the nearest Allied troops were three divisions of Chinese under General Stilwell who were advancing southwards down the Hukawng valley towards Mogaung and Myitkyina, about 150 miles north of Broadway.

Each Dakota was to tow two gliders, and as the sun went down the first aircraft taxied up to where the gliders were standing. The nylon tow-ropes of the first two were hitched to the aircraft, which roared and lumbered off down the runway. The tow-ropes leapt off the ground like giant snakes until they were taut, drawing the gliders forward until they were airborne. The operation had begun. The first gliders contained the Battalion Commander, Lieut.-Col. W. P. Scott, M.C., and Col. Alison, U.S.A.A.F., and a few of his staff who were to build the airstrip. Soon after them went the Brigade

PAGE 314

Commander himself, Brigadier ("Mad Mike") Calvert, D.S.O.

Just before midnight I checked over my party and our glider was pushed into position. The men were silent as we took our seats, strapped ourselves in and eyed the flimsy construction nervously. The two in front of us took off, and it was our turn at last. As we moved, I began to wish I was in the tow-ship, but before we realized it we had left the ground and set course eastwards towards the Chin Hills which towered ahead of us. I had been used to powered aircraft, and it now felt very strange without the noise of engines. It was bumpy and the men sat quietly opposite one another in the darkness,

Squadron-Leader
LEONARD HART

chewing gum to prevent air sickness—though one or two were sick. I climbed forward at the invitation of the pilot, an American sergeant. He was having a bit of difficulty with the controls, for the other glider attached to our aircraft was swaying across our path, and it was a hard job to avoid the tow-ship's slipstream. Several times a crash appeared inevitable when the other glider threatened to foul our tow-rope, and I held my breath and closed my eyes and felt supremely thankful that I had not the pilot's responsibility. Suddenly

Chindits' Jungle Airstrip Behind Enemy Lines

BY AIR TO BROADWAY, in the heart of Japanese-held Burma, went Wingate's Chindits in the Anglo-American operation of March 5, 1944. Glider-borne troops who were the first to land cleared the jungle airstrip (1) for the Dakota troop-carriers. British and U.S. troops (2) fought off Japanese snipers and held the hastily prepared runway. British, West Africans and Gurkhas, included among the airborne Chindits, waiting to enter transport aircraft (3) at their base in Assam. See accompanying story.

PAGE 315   *Photos, New York Times Photos, U.S. and British Official*

BURMA'S " PICCADILLY " LANDING GROUND, one of the two airstrips intended for landing Chindits behind the enemy lines in March 1944, as it appeared from a R.A.F. reconnaissance plane—strewn with trees felled by the Japanese to render it inoperative. But operations went forward, from the other strip, called " Broadway."
Photo, Planet News

it swung towards us, and our pilot said a rude word and hauled the stick back as the cause of our trouble disappeared from sight beneath us and I breathed freely again. That was the last we saw of it, and I heard some days later that its pilot had cut off and landed in a field.

AFTER about an hour we crossed the Chindwin River, altered course and were sailing smoothly on at 12,000 feet, and I began to wonder how the first arrivals were faring at Broadway. As we neared our destination I kept a good lookout, but failed to locate anything that looked like our landing area. Suddenly we turned, and ahead of us I could see the tail lights of circling aircraft. We went down and joined them, and could distinguish the rough form of a flare path set out. There were no signs of fires or anything resembling enemy action,

and an Aldis lamp was flashing its green signal from the ground.

The pilot gave orders to prepare to land, and we came round in a perfect circle, but just as we were about to touch down the pilot observed that the airspeed indicator was reading 120 m.p.h., so he decided to go round again. The tow-ship screamed blue flames as it climbed round once more, but we were still going too fast and the pilot did not cut off. The third time we had no choice, because the pilot of the aircraft cut us off himself by using his emergency release.

We swept down towards the ground at a horrifying speed. In the clear moonlight I could see faces peering at us, and right in front of us was another glider—it would be a miracle if we could avoid it. I said a short prayer as the pilot tried to keep us airborne,

and as we seemed to come down right on the other glider he made a superhuman effort and wrenched the stick back with all the force he could command to clear the obstacle. He all but achieved it. The tail caught, there was a terrific jar, and I was thrown through the window with half a dozen fellows on top of me. I was dazed and breathless, but when we disentangled ourselves I found I was unhurt except for a few cuts and bruises. We had got off lightly— one man had a broken forearm, and another did not discover until the next morning that one of his ribs was broken.

When I looked around I found that the glider we had hit had landed fairly in the centre of the flare path, but its wheels had caught in a timber drag and it had turned over. Four or five others had done the same thing. Some were badly smashed up, and there was a good deal of blood around. A first-aid post had been set up and was dealing very efficiently with the casualties. The Brigadier had established a Command Post, and patrols had gone out, but no contact had as yet been made with the enemy. Gangs of men were working to get the crashed gliders out of the way and other gliders were coming in fast, spilling men, mules and equipment out in tumbled masses.

30 Were Killed and 60 Injured

One or two came in from the wrong direction, which added to the confusion. We tried to signal some of the gliders to wait, or go back ; but the trouble was that the aircraft had insufficient petrol to tow the gliders back to India, so they had to cast off. I saw two gliders come down in the tree-tops. Another, carrying a bulldozer, crashed into a tree and the bulldozer flew right over the head of the pilot, who was unhurt. "I guess that's just the way I planned it !" he remarked nonchalantly.

We were in wireless touch, and it had been arranged that if things were going badly we would wireless "Soya Links" and if all was well, "Pork Sausages." At about 4 a.m. on March 6, in view of the number of crashes and the fact that some of the gliders were missing in flight the Brigadier decided to send "Soya Links." However, when dawn came the situation looked rather better. Our casualties had been about 30 killed and 60 injured, and had the Brigade walked in from India we could hardly have lost less men. Complete surprise had been achieved, and the American engineers calculated that they had sufficient equipment to build a Dakota strip in twelve hours, so "Pork Sausages" was sent.

THE strip had been cleared, and work was begun at once. Every man who could be spared was employed to assist the engineers, and we toiled all day with spades and entrenching tools, pausing for only a few minutes to drink a hurried cup of tea or partake of a meal from our K-rations. Once we heard a plane overhead and knew it was not one of ours, but we were unmolested ; another time we heard rifle fire in the distance, which was never explained. At about 5 p.m. a strip 1,200 yards long was almost ready for the Dakotas, and during the day a squadron of American light aircraft flew in from India, under Captain Rebori, and evacuated all our casualties.

Soon after dusk the first aircraft landed, piloted by Brigadier Old, U.S.A.A.F., and was received with rousing cheers. Then, hour after hour, they came in a steady stream until nearly 100 sorties were recorded the first night. During the next few nights many thousands of men, mules and equipment were flown in without mishap—to attack the Japanese lines of communication in their most vital spots and thus clear the way for the recapture of Burma.

Rebirth of Walcheren as an Island

Strangest of all battlefields of the war is this island off the coast of Holland. Though parts of the village of Westkapelle lie buried for ever under the sand, the land is being restored to its people by the use of portions of Mulberry Harbour, as explained by The Evening Standard reporter Richard McMillan, lately returned from a visit.   See also pages 250-253.

IT happened to be a Dutch treat, and the town band from Flushing were balanced precariously on the little ferry boat pitching under the North Sea wind. The band played now sad and now glad airs as we ploughed across the Scheldt from Breskens to the island of Walcheren.

I was in the wake of the invaders—those gallant Britons who on November 1, 1944, made this same journey in the dark under the fire of the Germans on the Dykegirt, the Dutch island which defends the mouth of the River Scheldt. I was going back to see an historical and engineering novelty—the rebirth of Walcheren as an island, thanks to the concrete towers towed over from the now abandoned Mulberry Port at Arromanches. (See pages 144-145, Vol. 9).

THE occasion should have been a glad one, but as I drove across the desolation of the reborn island there was nothing to see but sadness. This is the strangest of all battlefields of the war. It is a Never-Never Land. Over miles and miles there is hardly a tree to be seen. And what are supposed to be farmlands and pastures look what they really are—weedy soil snatched from under the sea.

Some villages were under water for as long as a year. You pass through a village without knowing it. You come to an array of tombs. "What's that?" you ask. "That's the village cemetery," you are told. The rest of the village does not exist. Over

the billiard-table land you see the outline of an ocean-going barge stranded high and dry miles from the North Sea. It was sailing on the waters over the land until Mulberry came along and blocked up the gap in the dykes at Westkapelle, where the biggest breach was made.

Barges Converted Into Snug Homes

You see many of these stranded boats and barges. They look unused and derelict but they are not. The islanders who were driven from their homes when the R.A.F. turned Walcheren into a huge salt sea used everything at hand to help rebuild their lives. So the local version of a prefabricated home is one of these barges, daintily arranged with lace curtains for the windows and with wooden steps leading up to the door neatly cut into the hull.

"The R.A.F. blasted the dykes holding back the sea before the invasion of 1944 and now Mulberry has come to restore the island to us," the people of Westkapelle told me. Two of the concrete caissons refloated from Normandy and towed to Walcheren were placed in the big gap and then blown up to fill in the hole. Other blocks were afterwards sunk to form a breakwater to give double protection to the repaired breach.

On the sandy beach these blocks stand out like watch towers, a landmark for miles along the coast. While we were sinking the Mulberry blocks, Dutch workmen were

Motto : " Deeds Not Words."

NO. 20 SQUADRON

SEPTEMBER 1915 saw the formation, at Netheravon, Wilts, of No. 20 Squadron. It played a distinguished part in operations on the Western Front during the First Great War, and in May 1919 proceeded to India. Equipped with Hurricane 11Ds (armed with 40-mm. cannons) in 1943, No. 20 extended its role of tactical reconnaissance to close support of XV Corps in Burma.

In April 1944 the squadron sent a detachment to Imphal to provide the besieged garrison commander with a tank-busting weapon and some excellent results were obtained against the armour which the Japanese had brought to the perimeter of the Imphal Plain. In December the squadron went to Sapam for 14th Army support, and during the advance over the Chin Hills to the Chindwin Valley it provided indispensable aid to the ground forces.

BUT it was later, when the 14th Army debouched upon the plains of Central Burma, that 20 Squadron really came into its own, supporting the 19th Division's crossing of the Irrawaddy north of Mandalay, near Singu, and the 20th Division's bridge-head west of Mandalay, near Myinmu. In March the squadron was re-equipped with Hurricane IV R.P.s, which did good work against Fort Dufferin at Mandalay.

When the 14th Army leapt forward in the race for Rangoon against the approaching monsoon No. 20 went with them, first to Thedaw then to Toungoo, creating havoc amongst enemy rivercraft, dumps and transport. After the fall of Rangoon, No. 20 moved to Southern India. Required as part of the Occupational Forces for Siam, Spitfire VIIIs were allocated to the squadron, with which aircraft they moved into Bangkok during October 1945. The following month they re-equipped with Spitfires Mark XIV.

TO SEAL THE BREACHES AND DRAIN THE WATER from flooded Walcheren Island, Dutch workmen have been toiling day and night. One of the concrete caissons of Mulberry Harbour (used for the landings on the Normandy beach-head) is being positioned in the fourth and final gap in the sea-wall.   *Photo, Associated Press*

rebuilding the demolished dykes over the remains of the first two Mulberry caissons. This work is now finished and the land inside the restored dyke has been almost completely drained of the water that covered it.

"We shall never be able to restore the village of Westkapelle," a peasant woman told me. "The church and the mill and a few streets and houses are now buried for ever under the sand." She went down to the shore with me and pointed out under the sea the remains of some of the village. A German pillbox mounted on part of the old dyke is still visible above the waves.

"It is proposed to put up a memorial on the restored dykes close to the concrete caissons from Arromanches," said the villagers. "It will bear the words 'Destroyed by British bombing. Restored thanks to the British port of Mulberry.' Not only Walcheren but all Holland is grateful to

Mulberry and to Britain for what they enthusiastically call ' A last good deed.' "

They told me this story of the invasion. The Germans either drowned or swam to safety when the dykes burst. Those who survived came back in boats to reoccupy the pillboxes which remained above sea level. The defenders were in poor shape to meet the invasion when it came. Seven of them were posted to keep watch in the lighthouse at Westkapelle. They remained there too long. When the British landed they were trapped. Others tried to escape in boats, but they were soldiers not sailors. One after another the boats either capsized, ran aground, or fell victim to the Dutch Maquis. The ever-vigilant Maquis, well-prepared for their task, travelled in boats—the only naval Maquis in Europe.

" A number of civilian lives were lost when the dykes went," said the people of Walcheren, " but that is forgotten now, for it was realized that it was part of the price to be paid for liberation by Holland."

The Hounds of Okegem Betrayed Us

Clever use by the Germans of highly-trained, four-legged spies, to reveal British positions during the Dunkirk campaign passed generally unsuspected—until General Montgomery, G.O.C. the 3rd Division, ordered them to be shot on sight. How this spy system was operated is revealed by ex-Grenadier Guardsman A. A. Shuttlewood, then serving with the 7th Guards Brigade (portrait in page 760, Vol. 9).

BIG, wolfish creatures they were, with shaggy manes and, as we soon discovered, magnificently trained. To us they seemed tame, lovable creatures, as they brushed against our legs and made friends with everyone. I had my first glimpse of one at Okegem, a small town south of Louvain, where our Battalion H.Q. was situated in a large chateau, with extensive grounds sweeping down to the forest in the rear. I was patrolling these grounds, on sentry-go, on the morning of May 15, 1940, when a dog bounded over a hedge, paused for a few moments to snuffle at my boots, then leapt towards the outhouse which we used as an improvised cook-house.

The cook on duty, a lanky guardsman, proffered it a bone, which the dog sniffed and then ignored ; obviously it was well-fed. It was soon the centre of attention, scampering about, and friendly with all. During the morning three of them were roaming the streets, thoroughly " at home." In the afternoon they disappeared, and we concluded that they had gone to find their owners, probably Belgian folk who had evacuated the district that morning.

After dark, a German sniper suddenly commenced firing from the wood behind the château, and our R.S.M. was his victim—with a nasty wound in the stomach. Throughout that night the Battalion was attacked persistently by heavily-armed German patrols, but these were beaten back and a number of their dead littered the surrounding countryside the following morning. I suppose we found some sort of satisfaction in burying them and placing small wooden crosses on the mounds. A friend of mine, who had fought with No. 4 Company during these attacks, told me that he had seen the silhouettes of two dogs thrown into relief by the crimson arcs of tracer bullets. I thought no more about his casual remark until later on in the campaign.

Obeying orders from " higher up," our Battalion evacuated the area during the morning and marched off towards Brussels. The beautiful city was bathed in evening sunshine as we passed through its wide, tree-lined streets. Fountains played, shops displayed their wares, and it seemed that we had left Hell behind us and were now entering Paradise. The Royal Palace loomed over all, the Belgian flag fluttering above it. Little did we imagine that, a few days hence, the emblem would be hauled down in capitulation to the Nazi war lords. Although the people of Brussels must have realized, painfully enough, that we were retreating, they gave us a hearty welcome.

We stayed on the outskirts of the city overnight, and at dawn proceeded to Helchin, about 15 kilometres south of Brussels. During the march a dog appeared, and tagged on to our rear section. Again, no one was suspicious. Indeed, the animal, which somehow seemed lonely and in need of company, was welcomed as a diversion as we slogged along. We breasted a rise, our marching feet sending clouds of dust into the air. The sun had risen, and only a few kilometres separated us from our destination.

Enemy O.P.s spotted the dust, the artillery under their control opened up on our column, and we took cover on the farther side of the

LIVING UP TO THEIR MOTTO ' I STRUGGLE AND EMERGE,' the people of Walcheren, Holland, are erasing the signs of war with vigorous action. In the village of Oudendijk, which with the rest of the island was partly destroyed as the result of the smashing of the dykes by the Allies to drive the Germans out of the flooded land, workmen utilize old bricks and new for rebuilding now the flood-waters have receded. See story " Rebirth of Walcheren as an Island."

Photo, New York Times Photos

"SHOOT THEM ON SIGHT" was General Montgomery's order when, in 1940, German-trained Alsatian dogs were found to be "spying" on our troop movements. Tasks of other specially-trained dogs included work with German stretcher-bearers (left).
Photos, New York Times Photos, Keystone

We were all awake and alert ; the dog —again with us— was asleep in a barn. Early the following morning it was discovered that he had loped off, and he was not seen throughout that comparatively quiet morning.

At noon, B.H.Q. received a message, via Brigade H.Q., from Gen. Montgomery, G.O.C. the 3rd Division, of which our Battalion was a part. I was operating the Battalion telephone switchboard at the time and the message contained a description of the dogs, and the order "Shoot them on sight. They are highly dangerous animals and are being employed in large numbers by the enemy."

DURING the day the dogs returned. It galled us to have to shoot them : they had been such friendly creatures. But, as they jeopardized our safety and aided the foe considerably in his efforts to locate us, we made the best of an unpleasant job. That evening, on a radio left by a Belgian civilian, we heard two items of news. Belgium had "thrown in the towel," and, according to Lord Haw-Haw, "the 7th Guards Brigade, cream of the British Expeditionary Force, had been totally annihilated." We grimaced at the former item and grinned at the latter. We were the 7th Guards Brigade—and by no means "totally annihilated." Once more we moved, vacating Helchin the same night after burying the dead dogs.

hill, with a winding track leading down to a small village. I saw trees torn up by their roots. Roofs of cottages sagged. The spire of an old church buckled as shells scored direct hits. The shelling became fiendishly accurate, and we lost several men in a few hectic minutes. I subconsciously noted that a dog was standing on the top of the hill, calmly ignoring the whine of shells soaring a few feet above him.

Vital Message from Brigade H.Q.

The firing stopped. We formed up, in single file, and marched off down the earthen track. As we neared the village the Hun battery opened up again. We dropped flat on our stomachs, and fortunately no one was hit. Again we advanced, a dog trailing behind. I saw that the church had been hit yet again ; the top half of the steeple had completely collapsed.

When at last we reached Helchin, as yet unravaged by war, we discovered it to be a fair-sized town ; an agricultural one, judging by the fields of unripe wheat which ringed it, and livestock was plentiful. Here our B.H.Q. was in a large, rambling farmhouse. All civilians were ordered to leave the town by 4 p.m. The Intelligence Officer found it a difficult task to persuade some of the stolid peasantry that a mass evacuation was essential to their safety, and that the Germans, with their fast, mobile units, were not so very far in rear of us. It seemed, however, that our fears on the people's behalf were groundless; for no attack was launched that night.

NEW FACTS AND FIGURES

THE British Mission which recently investigated the effects of the atomic bombs on Hiroshima and Nagasaki (see illus. page 274) has estimated that in a similar explosion British houses would be demolished to a distance of 1,000 yards from the centre of damage ; damaged beyond repair to a distance of one mile ; uninhabitable without extensive repair to a distance of 1½ miles ; uninhabitable without first-aid repairs to a distance of 2-2½ miles. From the casualty figures in Japan, in the largest British cities with a density of population of roughly 45 per acre the number of people expected to be killed by one atomic bomb is estimated to be nearly 50,000. Risk of death is approximately 70 per cent at half-a-mile from the centre of damage and 20 per cent at one mile.

THUS in one of the larger British urban areas, for one atomic bomb of the power and exploded at the height of those in Japan, approximately 30,000 houses would be demolished or damaged beyond repair ; approximately 35,000 would need major repairs ; 50,000-100,000 would be uninhabitable until first-aid repairs had been carried out. A total of roughly 400,000 people, therefore, might be rendered temporarily homeless, of whom about one-half could return to their houses after lesser repairs. Of the remaining 200,000, about 50,000 would be dead or would die within eight weeks, and a comparable number would require extended hospital treatment, leaving about 100,000 non-casualties to be rehoused. These figures make a reasonable allowance for better housing, fire and rescue services than existed in Japan.

ALTHOUGH Japanese shelters were much below British standards, all survived except the very poorest earth-covered shelters within a few hundred yards of the centre of damage in Nagasaki. The standard British shelters (Anderson, Morrison and reinforced surface) would therefore have remained safe from collapse, even at the centre of damage. Deep shelters such as the London Underground would have given complete protection.

AT Wesel, in the British Zone of Germany, municipal art treasures worth millions of marks have been discovered in a grave in the cemetery. Gravediggers in November 1944 watched the mysterious interment of an "unknown soldier" which was attended by two prominent Nazis and some town officials. When their long-dormant suspicions were recently revealed to the authorities, the grave was opened and the coffin was found to contain valuable trinkets, jewels, money, and two vases, one-time gift of Antwerp to the town of Wesel.

THE Inquiries and Casualty Department of the Colonial Office, which has now closed down, was created in December 1941 to deal with inquiries about persons believed to be in Hongkong and Malaya at the time of the Japanese invasion. Altogether, inquiries concerning 20,000 persons were dealt with : some were subsequently found not to have been in the danger areas, or to have got away to safety before the Japanese arrived. More than 10,000 were interned or made prisoners of war, and 2,000 were reported to have died. Since the Japanese surrender some 6,000 have been repatriated. Some 5,000 persons are still reported missing.

Home from the Far East is H.M.S. Anson

Printed in England and published every alternate Friday by the Proprietors, THE AMALGAMATED PRESS, LTD., The Fleetway House, Farringdon Street, London, E.C.4. Registered for transmission by Canadian Magazine Post. Sole Agents for Australia and New Zealand: Messrs. Gordon & Gotch, Ltd.; and for South Africa: Central News Agency, Ltd.—August 30, 1946.   S.S.   *Editorial Address:* JOHN CARPENTER HOUSE, WHITEFRIARS, LONDON, E.C.4.

Photo, G.P.U.

ARRIVED AT PORTSMOUTH DOCKYARD on July 29, 1946, the £10,000,000 battleship Anson (the seventh of that name) was due for paying off and then becoming a training ship at Portland. Flying the flag of Vice-Admiral Edelsten, she was commanded by Captain F. S. Bell, who was captain of H.M.S. Exeter in the action with the German heavy cruiser Admiral Graf Spee in December 1939. Anson was "adopted" by the City of London in 1942. See also pages 366-367, Vol. 6.

Vol 10 *The War Illustrated* N° 241

SIXPENCE

SEPTEMBER 13, 1946

I WAS THERE

AS LORD WARDEN OF THE CINQUE PORTS, MR. CHURCHILL was formally installed in office, at Dover, on August 14, 1946. He had accepted the honour of this post—which has endured for nearly 1,000 years and of which he is the 158th holder—in September 1941. Dr. Fisher, Archbishop of Canterbury, alluded to Mr. Churchill as " one who in the years of our greatest peril and need kept watch and ward over England, over the Empire, and over freedom." See also illus. page 328. *Photo, Keystone*

Edited by Sir John Hammerton

NO. 242 WILL BE PUBLISHED FRIDAY. SEPTEMBER 27

Our Roving Camera Greets Battle-Famed Iron Duke

H.M.S. IRON DUKE, 34-year-old British battleship (right), was towed through the Firth of Clyde, Scotland, on August 19, 1946, en route to be broken up. Famous flagship of Admiral Jellicoe at the battle of Jutland in 1916, the Iron Duke was later used for training purposes and was bombed in an air raid on Scapa in October 1939. See also illus. page 298.

GERMAN POLICE on duty at the entrance to an Aldershot, Hants, internment camp (below) for German P.O.W. Themselves prisoners of war, they speak English fluently, and wear British battle-dress, but retain their Wehrmacht caps. Their duty is to keep a watchful eye on those leaving and entering the camp.

PLASTIC COINS in denominations of one penny and a halfpenny are now issued to the British Occupation forces in Germany, cashable only at military stores and canteens. A War Office idea, the coins supplement the ordinary currency of low denominations, and overcome the shortage of metal. Made not by the Royal Mint but by a private firm in England, they are stamped out in semi-liquid brown plastic material, hardened, and sent to Germany—to implement the two-fold purpose "emergency" currency.

Photos, P.A.-Reuter, R.Worth, Sport & General, Planet News, G.P.U.

MAGNETIC MINE, the first to be laid by the Germans in our home waters, was included in an exhibition of mines held at the South Kensington, London, Science Museum in August 1946. It was recovered in dramatic circumstances from the Thames Estuary in November 1939. See story in page 124, Vol. 7.

U.S AIRCRAFT CARRIER Franklin Delano Roosevelt (left, background), on its first visit to European waters anchored in the river Tagus after arriving at Lisbon, Portugal, in August 1946. En route for the Mediterranean, the 45,000-ton ship formed part of the 12th U.S. Navy Squadron, under orders of Admiral H. K. Hewitt, Commander-in-Chief U.S. Naval Forces in Europe.

The Airborne Crossing of the Rhine

ARNHEM is deservedly extolled as the finest exploit of British airborne troops, but I doubt whether the men of the 1st Airborne Division felt any more excited, tense and apprehensive than we who waited behind barbed wire for an unspecified operation in March 1945. We glider types were held *incommunicado* at a camp known as Mushroom Farm—a small town of Nissen huts somewhere near Braintree in Essex.

Merely to mention the name of that camp revives in me the sense of sickening foreboding I felt as, wearing a new red beret conferred by the courtesy of Major-General Eric Bols, the Divisional Commander, I passed through the gates to what I felt convinced was certain doom. Even the magnificent bearing and camaraderie of the trained sky-troops could not entirely banish my depression.

All that we knew about the coming operation, at that time, was that it would be the biggest of the war, with two complete divisions taking part—one British and one American—in close co-ordination. There were rumours that we were going to Denmark; even that we were going to beat the Russians to it by seizing Berlin itself. On the whole, however, it seemed most probable that we were destined to establish a Rhine bridgehead to open the way for the 2nd Army into the heart of Germany.

General Bols Unfolds His Plan

The men of the 6th Airborne, many of them heroes of D-Day drops, spent their time in preparation and occasional revelry. On these social occasions they liked to roar out their swashbuckling, blood-freezing choruses. One which ran to the tune of John Brown's Body had as its theme :

" Glory, glory, what a helluva way to die
'Cause we ain't going to live no more ! "

Another, sung to Red River Valley, concluded with :

" So come stand by your glasses so ready
Here's a toast to the men of the sky.
Let us drink to the men dead already
And here's to the next man to die ! "

Despite this fatalism the air-troopers were in fine fettle, and if they had any fears they concealed them beneath a nonchalant, good-humoured, bantering manner.

We were each served out with equipment which seemed to anticipate every possible form of violent or lingering death. First, a Mae West lifejacket in case we fell in the sea. Then a little red light (with battery) to insure against falling in at night, and a great slab of stuff to colour the sea yellow lest we should fall in in daylight. We were given emergency rations and shell-dressings, domed steel helmets, vests like fishing nets, and camouflage jackets. The one thing we were not given was parachutes, for the theory was that in gliders either you all landed together or you did not land at all. We war correspondents, of whom there were six with the 6th Airborne, took an increasingly dim view of it all.

One morning General Bols, slim, fair, debonair, supremely confident, unfolded his plans to us. We hardly knew whether to feel relieved or disappointed when he said that, after all, the operation—known by the code name of Varsity—might not come off if the weather did not suit. Sure enough, it was to be the Rhine crossing. But the airborne show, comprising ourselves and the 17th U.S. Division, under Major-General

By L. MARSLAND GANDER

who, as The Daily Telegraph War Correspondent, on March 24, 1945, glided across the Rhine with the 6th (British) Airborne Division.

M. B. Ridgway, commanding 18th U.S. Corps (Airborne), was merely a " bonus " to the land attack.

Applying the hard-learnt lessons of Arnhem it was intended that our landing, north of Wesel, should be supported from the start by the medium artillery of 21st Army Group. This meant that we should drop only a mile or two ahead of the land forces, which should be able to make a junction in a matter of hours, instead of days or weeks. If all went well, overnight a Commando brigade would have stormed into Wesel in the van of XXX Corps which was to cross the Rhine on a wide front. Then, with any kind of luck, we should be linking up with 15th Scottish Division shortly after landing.

This was a wise plan. The airborne boys were being used to widen and deepen a hole already made in German resistance. They were not to be left isolated for days or weeks in an island attacked by an ever-increasing weight of heavy weapons that could not be brought by air. So far so good. But the Germans, it seemed, were extremely well informed of our plans. Despite continuous defeat and collapsing morale they showed every intention of giving us a warm reception. This knowledge, plus the fact that the London newspapers, a day or two before our operation was due, began to discuss its possibilities openly, made farcical the elaborate pretence of a security black-out.

WE knew that the enemy had packed the probable dropping zone with small combat groups of parachute and S.S. troops trained to tackle glider troops and parachutists before these had had time to organize. He had also massed light flak for our reception. We were reassured, however, by intelligence officers, who said that the R.A.F. were putting on " the biggest blitz ever, a terrific stonk " which would wipe out every flak gun long

before we arrived. The only omission on the enemy's part was that, probably through lack of time, he had not studded the fields with anti-glider poles and wires or put down minefields in the likely dropping zones.

Greeted With a Torrent of Fire

I was invited to study an aerial photo of the field, on the fringes of Diersfordter Wald, where my particular glider was supposed to land. Noticing some white marks in the ditches I asked, innocently, what they were supposed to be. " Oh don't worry about that ! " said my cheerful adviser. " Those are German machine guns, but the R.A.F. will take care of them." Though I am the last to disparage the R.A.F. I am bound to say that on this occasion all the rosy optimism at Mushroom Farm was unjustified. Somehow the flak batteries eluded the scouring Typhoons, and when on the morning of March 24 our air armada arrived it was greeted with such a torrent of fire that only 88 out of 416 gliders landed undamaged. But I am racing somewhat ahead of my story.

AT THE POINT OF A STEN GUN a German prisoner is marched away by a British air-trooper who, jumping with the Allied airborne forces across the Rhine in March 1945, landed in the American dropping zone. To the right (near his helmet and rifle) lies a wounded German. *Photo, Keystone*

I had been assigned to a Horsa glider carrying men of the Divisional Headquarters defence company. The weather held good, and on a calm, sunny, Saturday morning I climbed into the glider at Shepherd's Grove airfield with 18 stalwart infantrymen, a Colonel of the Royal Engineers, and the Senior Chaplain as fellow passengers. We sat opposite each other on benches, trussed-up with equipment and strapped in. You could not see much through the small portholes. Somebody likened it to travelling in a tube. Half-sick and taut with nervous excitement which each hoped was not apparent to his neighbours, we felt ourselves, after an eternity of waiting, pulled off into the air. I was able to move from time to time into the pilot's cockpit, from where I could see the blue bowl of sky swarming with the silver " flying fish." High above sparkled the shoals of fighter minnows, paradoxically protecting the bigger fish below ; just ahead of our glider wallowed the whale of our bomber tug, a long sagging cable in between.

The eye could hardly take in the spectacle. Tugs, gliders, parachute aircraft everywhere ; the landscape rolling sluggishly below. We

Passed over the field of Waterloo. Then, at 10.20, fifteen minutes before we were due to land, I saw a wonderful, exhilarating spectacle—the stream of American tugs, with gliders towed two by two, joining us. More than 3,000 aircraft, carrying about 16,000 airborne troops, filled the sky while Allied troops below (whom we could not see) waved their hats, thrilled with awe and pride. It was the crowning achievement of the war, the aerial transport fleet of two nations stretching 75 miles from van to tail.

Foggy World Peopled by Spectres

I expected to see the Rhine, but straining over the pilot's shoulder I discerned instead a drifting black cloud of smoke obscuring everything beneath. The pilot shouted back, " Casting off. Strap yourselves in ! " Then for a few hectic minutes we were banking, twisting and plunging, the " unneutralized " flak bursting all around. Mercifully hidden was the sight of Wellington tugs and gliders dissolving in flames and rocketing to earth.

Then, with a bump we hit the earth. Our landing flaps did not work, and the shock broke off our tail. We prayed that those German machine-guns had been " dealt with," little knowing that on this field where gliders were crashing, gambolling and bursting into flames, some gallant U.S. parachutists of 513 Parachute Regiment, dropped by mistake, were already beginning to do our job of cleaning-up and capturing Kipenliof Farm as Divisonal Headquarters. Most of the gliders, lost in the unexpected fog— apparently caused by our smoke-screen and gunfire—landed far from their intended place. But we were not 100 yards from the right spot, and the only casualties were two or three men in the tail with broken bones.

No individual sees much of a modern battle, least of all the kind of diffused affair of small parties that follows an air drop. I saw men running about with tommy-guns and heard a few bullets whining over. Then, flat on my belly, I saw dozens of submissive prisoners lining the distant hedge, hands above their heads. Frankly, in this dangerous, foggy world, peopled by wild spectres, I had no idea which way to turn for safety. But, guided by the Colonel, I at last found my cautious way to the farm.

Contrary to the reports published at the time there was no effective link-up between 6th Airborne and the 15th Scottish for at least 24 hours, during which time the situation was extremely mixed and hazardous. Snipers were busy all round us in the Diersfordter Wald ; a German company almost stumbled into our headquarters by mistake during the night and I was rushed into a trench, unarmed non-combatant though I was, to help repel them. General Ridgway himself, who visited our headquarters during the night on his way back to his command post, drove into a party of Germans moving east. In the mad, confused mêlée which ensued he was slightly wounded in the shoulder, but he shot one German dead.

The most heroic exploit of that memorable day was accomplished by 6th Air Landing Brigade, whose headlong assault on the Issel bridges and the key village of Haminkeln was a modern Balaclava. While their comrades of the 3rd and 5th Parachute Brigades, rallied by hunting horns, were clearing the flanks, and in some cases dropping among the German batteries and receiving terrified submission, the 6th Air Landing Brigade made good its objectives but at the expense of heavy losses.

Gliders carrying *coup de main* parties of the Royal Ulster Rifles and the Oxfordshire and Bucks Light Infantry landed near enough to their objectives to secure them within an hour. But a number of gliders carrying the Oxfordshire and Bucks men were set in flames by light flak, the funeral pyres burning throughout the action. That night we had a message that a German counter-attack had been launched against the 6th Air Landing Brigade, headed by a Tiger tank which was " brewing-up " gliders on the ground. The counter-attack, though it necessitated blowing up one of the captured bridges, petered out. In 24 hours the link-up with 15th Scottish was firm and the Red Devils had begun to swan towards Bocholt.

German Flak Exacted High Price

Battle casualties in the 6th Airborne Division on that first day totalled 108 officers and 1,300 men killed, wounded, and missing out of a divisional strength of 8,000, and although some of the missing have since turned up, it was a high price. The Germans, admittedly, were not fighting with the discipline and fanatical resolution of 1940-44. Nevertheless they wrought terrible execution with their flak, and in places resisted with the courage of despair.

As Montgomery's armour flooded through the hole torn in Germany's last defences, on the victory tide, the British public tended to forget the part played by our airborne boys. A picture comes to my mind of a figure lying dead, his half-opened parachute lying beside him where he fell. His body was complete, apparently uninjured, yet every bone must have been broken, and on the hard earth was an exact impression, two inches deep, of a human form.

STIRLING BOMBERS AND HORSA GLIDERS crossing the Rhine, just before the gliders' tow-ropes were cast off. These were among the 3,000 aircraft taking part in the greatest of all airborne operations : the combined landing, behind the east bank of the Rhine and in advance of our land forces, of the 6th British and the 17th U.S. Airborne Divisions on March 24, 1945. All flew from 26 British and Continental bases. See also illus. pages 776-777 and 786, Vol. 8.

Photo, British Official

Demonstration Drop from Latest Air Transport

DEVELOPMENT IN TROOP-CARRYING AIR-CRAFT has as its latest example the twin-engine and twin-boom Fairchild C-82, or Packet, now a standard transport in the U.S.A.A.F. From it, parachute troops can be discharged in almost half the time customary during the War, as demonstrated at Beaulieu, in Hampshire, on August 9, 1946, when British and U.S. troops descended together (1). A 25-pounder gun, with tractor, is seen (2) emerging from the aircraft. Seating arrangement is shown at (3), a feature of the Packet being that troops can jump from both sides of the box-shaped fuselage.

Designed originally for military purposes, the Fairchild C-82, powered by a pair of 18-cylinder 2,100 h.p. engines, is now being developed as a cargo carrier on U.S. commerical air routes; it can carry a 9-ton payload at 200 m.p.h. In contrast, the famous Dakota was designed for commercial purposes and adopted by the Allies as a troop-carrying aircraft.   *Photos, Central Press*

Paris Peace Delegates Take Their Brief Ease

AT THE OPERA HOUSE, PARIS, on August 1, 1946, for a special performance of ballet were M. Molotov, U.S.S.R. (1, left) and his daughter, joined by Mr. James Byrnes, U.S.A., also seen (4) with his wife (left) in their box; M. Georges Bidault, French Premier, and his wife (3); Admiral Lemonnier, France (6, left), Mr. Mackenzie King, Canada (centre), and Mr. A. V. Alexander, Britain.

At M. Bidault's reception for the Peace delegates, Maj.-Gen. François Theron, South Africa (2, right) conversed with M. Edouard Kardelj, Yugoslavia (centre), through an interpreter (left). On the Political and Economic Committees on Italy, Dr. Herbert Evatt, Australia (5, right) is in discussion with M. Sava Kosanovic (left) and Dr. Leontic (centre), Yugoslav ministers to Washington and London respectively. PAGE 326

Ex-Enemy Countries Present Peace Treaty Pleas

Signor de GASPERI
Prime Minister of Italy

M. TATARESCU
Rumanian Foreign Minister

M. GYONGYOSSI
Hungarian Foreign Minister

VOICING THEIR OBJECTIONS to the draft Peace Treaties, delegates of the ex-enemy countries—Italy, Rumania, Hungary, Bulgaria, and Finland—presented their cases at the Paris Peace Conference. Signor de Gasperi, Prime Minister of Italy, on August 10, 1946, condemned the proposed modified French Line dividing Italy and the new Free Territory of Venezia Giulia as a "line of political expediency," and warned that "a clash between ethnic groups within the city of Trieste may well lead to an international conflict." Urging the Conference "not to fall into an irreparable mistake," he asked that the Trieste decision be postponed. Having to renounce all reparation claims against Germany, and at the same time to pay Allied Occupational expenses after October 1943 (when she became an Allied co-belligerent) together with Italy's own reparation payments "in their full and crude meaning" would be "beyond her capacity to fulfil."

M. Tatarescu (Rumania) speaking on August 13, considered the economic demands of his country's peace terms likely to jeopardize the restoration of her economy. He asserted that claims against Hungary and Germany should have been permitted, and appealed for the retention of arms by Rumania's military forces.

M. Gyongyossi, Hungarian Foreign Minister, on August 14 made "certain modest claims" including the return of part of Transylvania and hoped that the Conference would permit Hungary to meet her obligations and avoid complete economic collapse.

On the same day M. Kulichev (Bulgaria), requested the cession to his country of Western Thrace as an outlet to the Aegean Sea; this was opposed by M. Isaldaris, Greek Premier. He also stated that the economic clauses of the treaty would worsen the precarious state of Bulgaria's finances, and concluded by asking support for his country's request to enter the United Nations.

M. Karl Enckell on August 15 put forward Finland's case, asking for alleviations of the territorial concessions and the economic clauses in the treaty.

Photos Keystone, Associated Press, Planet

M. Karl ENCKELL
Finnish Foreign Minister

M. KULICHEV
Bulgarian Foreign Minister

Hell-Fire Corner Acclaims Winston Churchill

VISITING BRITAIN'S OLDEST SEAPORT on August 14, 1946, for ancient ceremonies attending his installation as Lord Warden and Admiral of the Cinque Ports, Mr. Churchill drove through Dover's streets (top) to a spacious marquee in the grounds of St. Martin's Priory (Dover College), where he addressed (bottom) the meeting of the Grand Court of Shepway—Mayors and officials of the Cinque Ports (Hastings, Sandwich, Dover, New Romney and Hythe) and other towns. See also illus. page 321.

Photos, Topical, P.A.-Reuter

Honouring Canadians Who Fell at Pourville

MEMORIES OF THE ALLIED RAID ON DIEPPE in 1942 were stirred afresh when on its fourth anniversary, August 19, 1946, Mr. Mackenzie King, Prime Minister of Canada, unveiled a memorial to the men of Canada's 2nd Division who were killed at Pourville during these operations (see pages 196-199, Vol 6). In a three-day pilgrimage Mr. Mackenzie King visited neighbouring areas associated with the raid, and graves of Canadians in Dieppe cemetery, and received the Freedom of the town.

Photo, Canadian Official

HIS MAJESTY'S SHIPS   H.M.S. Moonstone

THOUGH trawlers are a class of naval vessel which seldom becomes conspicuous, owing to so many of them being assigned to unspectacular duties, the Moonstone was decidedly "in the news" in 1940.

An Italian submarine of 880 tons, with a surface speed of 18 knots, the Galileo Galilei (named after the astronomer), was operating in the Red Sea when Italy entered the war. On her first cruise after hostilities began she was sighted by a British destroyer, which dropped depth charges near her. Slight leakage resulted, but much more serious was the dislocation of the air conditioning plant. So humid did the air become that ultimately the submarine was forced to break surface at frequent intervals. On one of these occasions she was spotted by aircraft, and the Moonstone, an anti-submarine trawler based on Aden, was detailed to deal with her. Depth charges induced the Galilei to break surface, and perceiving the small size and light armament of the trawler, the Italian captain made the decision to fight it out on the surface. Mr. William Moorman, Boatswain, R.N., in command of the Moonstone, opened fire almost simultaneously with the submarine, but with better aim. Her captain killed, the Galilei surrendered, and was brought proudly into Aden with the White Ensign flying over the Italian colours. This was the first enemy submarine captured in the War.

Not only was the submarine a bigger and faster ship, but she mounted two modern 3·9-in. guns against the trawler's single old 4-in. Mr. Moorman was awarded the D.S.C. and ordered to take a course to qualify for commissioned rank. The Moonstone is here seen in Aden harbour. In May 1941 the Moonstone took part in the operations around Crete.

The Royal Signals

By
Col. T. B. GRAVELY, O.B.E.

WHEN the Second Great War started the importance of communications as a vital factor in winning battles was not realized as fully as it was later, after experience gained in campaigns in the Western Desert. From then onwards, demands for men and equipment became so great that it was difficult to keep pace with them. In 1939 the proportion of Signals to the rest of the B.E.F. was 3·22 per cent. By the autumn of 1942 the proportion in the Middle East had risen to 6·22·per cent, and in 1945 the figure for India and Burma was 6·99 per cent. At the opening of the battle of El Alamein for every 1,000 men of the Royal Armoured Corps, Royal Artillery or Infantry engaged, there were about 130 men of the Royal Signals.

Concurrently with this expansion in numbers went a big change in technical design, and anyone who was acquainted with the normal equipment and scales of issue in 1939 would hardly have recognized the same units in 1945. Great improvements were made in performance and reliability and, wherever possible, in size and weight.

At the beginning of the war, wireless was regarded by commanders and staffs with a certain amount of suspicion and it was looked upon as a secondary means of communication. In the mobile conditions of warfare in the Western Desert the chief characteristic of wireless—its flexibility—made it indispensable to officers who needed to talk together without knowing each others' exact whereabouts, and the demand for wireless increased by leaps and bounds ; everybody wanted to be able to talk to everybody else. The extent of the increase is shown by the fact that the number of sets in an Infantry Division rose from approximately 75 to just under 1,000.

During the battle of Cassino, and the crossing of the Rapido in July 1944, wireless sets to the number of 4,000 were in use in the area. The fighting lasted for six days, and the fact that little trouble was experienced in the way of mutual interference speaks well for the standard of training and the quality of the equipment then in use.

DURING the period 1939–1945 there was no spot on the Earth's surface containing members of the Navy, Army or Air Force which did not also contain its quota of men of the Royal Signals : for these have work to do for all three Services. Some worked in mixed units of the Indian and African Signal Corps, others alongside Signal units from all over the British Empire and from the United States. The Corps was formed in 1920 from the Royal Engineers Signal Services, and its very appropriate motto is "Swift and Sure."

Unfortunately, military wireless sets are subject to the same troubles as civilian ones. Communication is liable to be lost through atmospherics or fading, the latter being particularly bad at night in certain parts of the world. There is also the big problem of battery charging, which often presents considerable difficulties, particularly in forward areas.

A noteworthy example of the risk of fading occurred in the Western Desert in February 1942, when H.Q. XIII Corps suddenly lost all communication with one of its divisions. The reason was "night fading," and although the division was only 30 miles away, nothing could be done. Luckily, the signals travelled 1,200 miles to Whitehall, where they were picked up and relayed back on another frequency, thereby saving what might have been a critical situation.

Cables Often Cut by Shell Fire

In spite of all technical improvements the greatest drawback to wireless as a means of communication—its lack of secrecy—was never fully overcome, and it was often necessary for troops to move in "wireless silence." An early instance of this was at the battle of El Alamein, where it was of the utmost importance that the movements of our armour should not be prematurely disclosed to the enemy. At the same time, it was necessary to co-ordinate the movements of the armoured striking force to concentration areas beyond the enemy minefields. The problem was solved by Royal Signals detachments moving forward with the Royal Engineers, whose job it was to clear gaps in the minefields ; the detachments laid cable as they went, and manned the telephones on the ends.

One detachment, in its jeep, went clean over an uncharted minefield and was only stopped by coming up against a tank, which was busily engaged in fighting a battle. At that stage, the officer in charge of the party thought it better to drop the end of the cable and wait for Brigade Headquarters to come up ! The cable subsequently proved to be of the utmost value. The cables through the gaps in the minefield were repeatedly cut by shell fire and picked up by the tracks of advancing tanks, but as often as they were cut they were repaired. It was dangerous and costly work ; nevertheless the advance went on according to plan.

Royal Signals are responsible for signal security, and for the composition and issue of codes and ciphers, also for operating the ciphers at the headquarters where they are used. "Policing" the air, in order to detect and correct breaches of security, was a never-ending task. Special units were employed on this, and others on gleaning all possible information from lapses on the part of the enemy. The distribution of ciphers was responsible for some anxious moments, as when

an aircraft crashed in the Burma jungle with ciphers on board, and ships carrying reserve copies failed to arrive at their distant ports. Everybody is familiar with the telegraph and telephone lines running beside roads and railways, and many will have seen linemen of Royal Signals or other arms laying field cables, but few realize what an important part line communications play in war, or the high-lights of achievement or depths of anxiety of those who are responsible for them.

An example of achievement in the face of great difficulties occurred during the rapid advance of the 8th Army after the battle of El Alamein. Owing to the difficulty of digging in the hard ground the obvious thing was to repair the existing enemy overhead route, particularly as the advance was so rapid that it was almost impossible to keep up. The enemy had cut down telegraph poles and laid mines round the stumps. Where lines were still standing maintenance had been poor, and some hundred joints had to be found, cut out, rejointed and soldered, in every mile.

NEARLY 600 tons of copper wire, 4,000 lb. of solder and 1,500 telegraph poles had to be brought up by road or by sea. But in spite of all these difficulties, on December 12, 1942, eleven days after 8th Army H.Q. had been established at Benghazi, the H.Q. was through to Cairo by telegraph and telephone. On January 30, 1943, the Chief Signal Officer, 8th Army, was able to telephone from Tripoli to Baghdad—more than 2,500 miles.

At the other end of the scale may be counted the experience of an officer of a Canadian Brigade Signals who toiled for three hours clambering across the twisted metal of a demolished railway bridge, 400 yards long, which spanned the Rhine, towing a cable behind him and followed by three line men making the cable safe. Just as he reached the east bank a shell blew a wide gap in the cable in the centre of the crossing !

It was the aim of Signals to build up line communications, by means of cable and overhead routes, as far forward as possible. Thus, for the crossing of the Rhine by XII Corps on March 24, 1945, 200 miles of cable were buried in an elaborate network up to the river bank, to provide a jumping-off point.

After the actual crossing of the Rhine the further advance by VIII Corps was so rapid

H.R.H. THE PRINCESS ROYAL, their Colonel-in-Chief, inspected a guard of honour of Royal Signals during her visit to a Northern Command depot in September 1943. *Photo, Photopress*

LINE MEN WITH THE B.E.F. in France in October 1939 utilized existing poles to lay Army telephone wires at Berneville, this communication system then taking priority over wireless.

Colours : Red on Blue

51ST (HIGHLAND) DIVISION

COMPOSED of Territorial battalions of all the Highland Regiments, the 51st Division retained the badge worn by its predecessors in the First Great War. It joined the B.E.F. in France in 1940, and in June of that year two battalions, cut off at St. Valery-en-Caux, fought heroically until forced to capitulate. Re-formed in the U.K., the Division was sent to the Middle East in 1942, where it built up a great reputation in desert warfare; from Alamein, in October, it fought with the 8th Army through Cyrenaica, Tripolitania and in Tunisia, where the storming of the Wadi Akarit, on April 6, 1943, was one of the finest achievements of the War. After taking part in the invasion of Sicily in July, and Italy in September, the 51st was withdrawn to England for the invasion of France.

Landing in Normandy with 21 Army Group, on June 6, 1944, the Division gained all its objectives in " Operation Totalize," the Allied breakthrough south of Caen, on August 7. Lisieux was entered on August 22, after bitter hand-to-hand fighting. The Seine was crossed at Elbeuf the same week, and the 51st advanced to capture St. Valery-en-Caux, September 2 (see illus. page 248).

WITH the 49th Division it attacked Le Havre, on September 10. By October 23 the clearance of southwest Holland brought the Division to St. Michelgestel, Boxtel and Hertogenbosch. After a short period in the Nijmegen salient in November-December, the 51st, under command of XXX Corps, took over the Hotton sector to help check the enemy's Ardennes offensive in January 1945. In February the Division sustained severe losses in the Reichswald Forest battle, and a fierce engagement was fought at Goch, entered on Feb. 15.

As an assault Division it crossed the Rhine on March 23, and the advance continued to Rees, where losses were again high. A hard battle ensued at Ganderkesee, April 21-22. Crossing the Weser, south of Bremen, the 51st fought towards Bremerhaven until the surrender of the German forces on May 5.

LAYING CABLE TO THE GUNS on the 8th Army front in Italy whilst the gunners were in action was accomplished by the Royal Signals as part of their recognized duties. Devising and maintaining intercommunication systems, here as elsewhere, presented endless problems for those whose motto was (and is) " Swift and Sure."   *Photo, British Official*

Reconditioning demolished routes was a big task on all fronts, and it was a great day when they were found to be in good enough condition to be workable. After the landing at Salerno, in September 1943, it was found that the lines to Naples were still intact. After putting in some feverish repair work on a dismantled switchboard it was possible to ring up Naples; and a British Intelligence officer, who spoke perfect Italian, called up the Italian admiral commanding the port and asked for the latest information regarding the German troops. The admiral gave information every four hours for the next three days, but he then became suspicious!

In common with the other methods communications by line has its limitations, chief among which are the fact that once lines are constructed the headquarters they serve must remain somewhere near them, and there is

that all communications had to be by wireless, supplemented by such civilian telephone routes as could be repaired in the time available. The Corps covered the 250 miles from the Rhine to the Elbe in 26 days, March 27—April 21, 1945, and Corps H.Q. made 13 moves, over an average distance of 20 miles each. Owing to the speed of movement, and difficulty of getting up materials, no building of lines was possible on the axis of advance, and lateral routes were impossible as the country on either flank was seldom clear of the enemy.

At each move, Corps Signals usually reached a new site only a few hours after it had been in the hands of the enemy. Brushes with the enemy were frequent, the largest bag of prisoners, numbering 32, being made by a Line Squadron reconnaissance party moving into a new Corps H.Q.

ARMY SIGNALS OFFICE IN BURMA was set up in an old building quickly adapted to the purpose. Owing to the nature of the country over which the Allies fought, communication was effected mainly by radio. Mobile wireless trucks (centre photograph) backed on to one another formed a compact Signal centre.   PAGE 332   *Photos, British Official*

Royal Signals' Devices in the Western Desert

IN A CAMOUFLAGED CATACOMB (1) used as a Signals post in North Africa in May 1941 signalmen escaped enemy attentions, and received their meals at the end of a rope. Dispatching messages by carrier pigeon was adopted (2) when other systems of communication were ruled out by the prevailing circumstances. Telephone cables had sometimes to be buried in hard desert sand by the use of a tractor-drawn plough (3), line men following with a reel of cable and laying it in the shallow trench.

Photos, British Official

WITH HIS PORTABLE WIRELESS SET this signalman was dropped with the Allied airborne forces at Arnhem in September 1944. Regarded at the beginning of the war as a secondary means of communication, wireless made great strides and with improved equipment and technique played an ever greater part in the British Army's campaigns. *Photo, British Official*

considerable risk of damage to the routes. Lines suffer more damage from our own vehicles than from enemy action. One enterprising officer serving in Italy took the trouble to analyse the cause of faults in his area and found that only 16 per cent were due to enemy action alone.

The motor-cycle dispatch rider who has for so long been a feature of the Army communication system is still a most important link, particularly for carrying such things as marked maps and documents the transmission of which by other means would be both difficult and slow. But he is liable to become a casualty, either through enemy action or mechanical breakdown, and there is, therefore, uncertainty as to whether he had delivered his package or not, when his times of arrival and departure cannot be reported by telegraph or telephone. The motor-cycle has often been replaced by a jeep, light aeroplane or motor-boat.

Special Units for R.A.F. and R.N.

Visual signalling, or "flag wagging" as it is popularly called, is now seldom employed except in unusual circumstances, or in special operations, such as a beach landing. Lamp signalling is sometimes used in forward areas or for communicating with aircraft. Pigeons, which are one of the oldest means of communication known to man, were extensively used for certain purposes, particularly in the organization of the Defence of Britain ; with airborne troops, and in the Far East. The great merit of pigeons is that they can traverse short distances over ground which may be impassable to any form of transport at a speed which is rather better than that of a dispatch rider travelling on good roads. Their chief drawbacks are their inability to fly with any certainty at night, and the difficulty of obtaining two-way communication.

Each formation, and certain units in the Royal Armoured Corps and Royal Artillery, have their own Signal unit specially designed to meet their particular needs. To satisfy the requirements of the Royal Air Force special units exist called Air Formation Signals, each one of which is able to provide line communications for about 15 squadrons. The problem of providing communications on the lines of communication and in base areas, not to mention the links from the headquarters of each theatre back to the War Office, and the requirements of the Royal Navy called for a number of special units, operating elaborate equipment over long distances.

Long-range wireless links, some of them capable of high-speed work, had to be maintained between the War Office and the Headquarters of all overseas commands. Many of these links carried all types of concession telegrams in addition to official traffic. A big problem was provided by communications across the English Channel, particularly as the Army was responsible for meeting a great many of the needs of the Royal Navy and Royal Air Force. During the period before the Tactical Air Force crossed over, instant communication had to be available for passing calls for air support.

The original submarine cables which had linked England with France and Belgium had all been cut in 1940, and it was decided that it would be quicker to lay new ones to meet immediate requirements. As laying cables would take time, all traffic would have to be handled by wireless during the early stages of the Normandy invasion. The wireless problem was dealt with in two portions : (a) Rear links required by the Royal Navy, Army, and Royal Air Force ; (b) rear links of lower power from the assault beaches.

A total of 65 transmitters was allotted to cover the needs of all three Services, these being distributed in huts at three sites along the South Coast. For working to the assault beaches smaller and more mobile sets were used, which for security reasons could not be in position until the night before the landing took place. Five mobile sets were landed on the beaches, and four came into action.

The first submarine cable was laid on D-Day + 3, but ended in an uncleared land minefield. It was not through until D + 5. A second cable was laid on D + 6, but the ship was damaged, and the end of the cable was dropped ten miles from the far shore. It was picked up and finished on D+11. By D+13, six telephone and up to 14 teleprinter circuits were working, using both cables, but a north-easterly gale sprang up and both cables were damaged by drifting wrecks a few miles off the French shore. Despite the gale, a cable ship put out and repaired one cable on D + 17, but repairs to both were not completed until D + 22. In all, ten Channel cables were laid and seven repaired.

Signals Became Motor-Minded

At this stage the latest technical invention, the Wireless Set No.10, came into its own. This apparatus was originally designed for bridging a gap in a telephone route, and was capable of providing eight telephone channels working simultaneously. Some of these sets were used to supply extra links across the Channel, and subsequently to keep Field-Marshal Montgomery's Tactical Headquarters in touch with the base and the War Office, during rapid moves when there was no time to lay lines (see page 556, Vol. 9). The B.B.C. broadcasts, heard by so many listeners, were relayed over the cross-Channel circuits provided by the Royal Signals.

The problems of different theatres, particularly those of the Far East, called for special treatment though not for any radical change in basic training. The main point of difference between the Far East and other theatres arose from different methods of transport. In the period of highly mobile warfare in the Middle East, the system of staff officers and their Royal Signals operators working together as a team inside a special command vehicle, which was sometimes armoured, had become highly developed, and Royal Signals had become motor-minded.

In the far East wheeled traffic was often limited to the jeep, and man or pack animal became the principal means of transport in forward areas. This meant that equipment had to be redesigned for pack transport and that officers and men had to learn how to load and handle pack animals and look after them. One of the biggest factors in the Far East was air transport. All equipment had to be redesigned, if necessary, to make it "air-portable" and units had to be ready to be "lifted" by air at short notice. Cable and batteries were supplied by air, the cable being made up in specially designed coils.

In the words of Field-Marshal Montgomery, " Much of Signals work was of the unspectacular slogging variety which the provision of a vast network of communications involves. The constant aim of Signals was to build up the solid cable head as far forward as possible, to prcvide reliable jumping-off places for communications in the battle area." Although the Field-Marshal was referring to operations in North-Western Europe, the same holds true of all theatres of war. Signals' part in every operation consisted of the build-up before the battle, using every means of communication available, intense activity to maintain essential links during the actual operation, and another build-up during the period of reorganization, so as to make sure that no failure of communications should delay the prompt arrival of reinforcements and supplies. Other troops might rest after their labours, but the work of Royal Signals went on continuously.

SIGNALS DISPATCH RIDER confronted with a churned-up road must make the passage as though potholes and mud were non-existent.
Photo, British Official

Where Eisenhower Watched On D-Day

In the Naval Room in H.M.S. Dryad, at Southwick Park, Fareham, Hants, hangs a wall-map of tremendous memories. On it, as the main tactical "plot," were shown all Naval movements before, during and after the launching of the assault on the Normandy beaches—and progress of events on D-Day, thus shown, were watched by the Supreme Commander, General Dwight D. Eisenhower. The unveiling of the map (above) in its original position, and a commemorative plaque, on August 7, 1946, was accompanied by a thanksgiving ceremony for the success of those gigantic operations which commenced on June 6, 1944, and led to the liberation of Europe from German domination.

The unveiling ceremony was performed by (right, pointing) Rear-Admiral G. E. Creasy, C.B., C.B.E., D.S.O., R.N. On the extreme right is Capt. John Ide, U.S. Navy (Asst. Naval Attache, U.S. Embassy, London). Centre officer, holding white paper, is Commodore Robinson, U.S. Navy, Air Naval Attache at the U.S. Embassy.

Photos, Associated Press

Amazing Demonstration of Disruptive Genius—

The first post-war atomic bomb was dropped (1) from an aircraft on June 30, 1946 (B.S.T.), over Bikini atoll lagoon (see pages 232-233). The following month the same waters were violently erupted from below, for the benefit of observers of the U.S. Navy. For this second test, on July 24 (B.S.T.), a bomb suspended, at an undisclosed depth, from a landing craft was detonated, in the midst of a target fleet, by radio impulses from a distance of 15 miles.

—World's First Underwater Atomic Bomb Explosion

When the sea burst open (2), thousands of tons of water roared up to 2,000 feet (3), a moment later (4) extending to 5,000 feet and measuring more than 2,000 feet across at the base. Dense smoke surged to 8,000 feet and, suffering varying degrees of damage, target ships which still remained afloat tossed in the tumultuous waters discoloured for miles around by the disintegration of the lagoon's coral bed. The shoreline of Bikini atoll is seen in the foreground.

Dunkirk Port Reopened to Navigation at Last

First ship to enter Europe's most historic port since June 1940—when Dunkirk was a last point of resistance for British troops, and for the Germans five years later—the 3,000-ton Swedish coaster Jupiter (top), dressed with bunting from stem to stern, was towed by tugs past rusty wrecks and ruined quays. Bombed frequently by Allied aircraft, the reopening to sea-traffic on August 7, 1946, followed the completion of lock repairs and an all-clear announcement regarding mines.

MALAYA AND SINGAPORE SUMMING-UP

By HARLEY V. USILL

Most people can recall the spate of criticism, even abuse, of the conduct of British arms and administration in Malaya when in 1942 public opinion was shocked by the disasters in the Far East. Cooler reflection shows that this criticism was unfair to our soldiers, civilians and officials. The truth is that they played their part in difficult circumstances, victims of a catastrophe beyond their control. The peoples of Malaya have been charged with universal treachery, and the corollary has been drawn that we had failed to gain their loyalty and goodwill. That also is untrue.

To present the true facts about Malaya in their right perspective, it is necessary to give a fairly full picture of the country and its people. For more than 500 years prior to the entry of the first white man into Malaya, there was a big Buddhist Malay Kingdom in Sumatra with colonies in northern Malaya that levied tax and toll on trade. In 1511 the Portuguese conquered Malacca and perpetuated the system of monopoly in Eastern waters, only to be ousted by the Dutch in 1641. Britain acquired Malacca by treaty from the Dutch in 1824, and meanwhile had leased the island of Penang from the Sultan of Kedah in 1786. By the simple expedient of free trade this almost uninhabited island was turned into a flourishing port. By the same initiative, in 1811, Sir Stamford Raffles acquired a mangrove swamp from the Sultan of Johore, and from this unpromising beginning Singapore was developed into one of the world's largest ports. Penang, Malacca and Singapore made up the colony of the Straits Settlements.

Neither Trained Nor Armed for War

Britain had no desire to extend her responsibilities further but, following urgent requests, in 1874 Britain appointed advisers to help the Malay chiefs to administer Perak, part of Negri Sembilan and Selangor. In 1888 Pahang accepted a British President, and these four territories formed the Federated Malay States. By a treaty with Siam in 1909 that country transferred to Britain control over Kelantan, Tregganu and Perlis, and in 1914 the Sultan of Johore applied for a British General Adviser and British civil servants. These five states formed the Unfederated Malay States. During British administration slavery, torture and forced labour were abolished, civil wars and tropical diseases eliminated, and a system of social services introduced which were second to none in any other Colonial territory.

The three main races in Malaya are the 2,169,000 Malays, 2,114,000 Chinese and 755,000 Indians. The Malay is, typically, a small peasant, and although a few aspire to Government employment the majority are easy-going, preferring to leave to others the worries of business and wage-earning toil on estates and mines. In contrast the Chinese are energetic and easily adaptable and have played an important part in the life of Malaya; while the Indians, of whom half a million are Tamils from Southern India and Ceylon, worked mainly on the rubber plantations, but some became Government servants, railwaymen, schoolmasters and lawyers. These peoples, together with a small minority of Eurasians and British, made up the "five faces of Malaya," and in 1938 a report to the League of Nations stated that "Having an adequate revenue, the Government of Malaya has been able to develop health and education to a point unattained elsewhere in the East. . . ."

If the foregoing is true why, it may be asked, did the peoples of Malaya not put up a better show when the Japanese invaded?

The disaster which befell our Far Eastern Colonies of the Straits Settlements and Malay States in 1942 prevented their completing the part in the war effort which they had begun prior to the Japanese invasion. Credit is here paid to the behaviour of their peoples in the tragic circumstances which were beyond their control.

The answer is simple—they were neither trained nor armed for warfare. At a discussion of African territories in 1919, in Paris, British and Americans agreed that there was no moral justification for imposing military training on native populations. Britain extended this principle to the whole of her Colonial Empire, including Malaya.

The defence scheme was based on the assumption that Siam and Indo-China would remain in friendly hands; that Singapore was impregnable to attack from the sea; and that the U.S. Pacific Fleet would be available in a vital emergency involving Japanese aggression. In the event, the attack on Singapore came from the land, and a large part of the U.S. Fleet was at the bottom of Pearl Harbour. Added to all this, Great Britain was herself fighting on many fronts for her very existence and was thereby rendered incapable of affording effective assistance. The peoples of Malaya were responsible neither for the defensive scheme nor for the disaster which ensued.

The test of loyalty can first be made by reference to the attitude of Malaya prior to the Japanese invasion. Malaya fulfilled its prescribed production function by producing record quantities of rubber and tin. In a country like Malaya every European in time of war is a keyman and accordingly they were forbidden to come home to join up, as many wanted, but were retained to maintain the efficiency of Malaya's economy and government under the extra strain thrown on it by the war. There was hardly a woman who was not engaged in medical or other war work, and these Europeans formed the nucleus round which gathered thousands of Asiatics, men and women, who manned the various defence services. All classes and races of the population voluntarily gave £20,000,000 to the war effort—an amount representing two-thirds of the total contribution of the whole Colonial Empire.

At the beginning of the war the locally-raised forces consisted of one battalion of the Malay Regiment, the small Johore military forces, and a number of volunteer units in the Straits Settlements, Federated Malay States, and Johore, Kedah and Kelantan. At the time of the invasion the total strength of the volunteers was 10,500. Some of the volunteer units fought and retreated with the rest of our armies down the peninsula into Singapore, and about 3,000 were captured, many showing great bravery.

Help and Sympathy for Our Troops

What of the attitude of the civilian population after the invasion? In the extreme rapidity of Japanese advance some confusion was inevitable, and Penang was a story of an unexpected enemy break-through on the nearby mainland causing a badly-executed evacuation. But against this must be set innumerable examples of men and women

MALAY PEOPLE'S ANTI-JAPANESE ARMY, formed in January 1942 as an "underground" movement to fight the Japanese during their occupation of the Peninsula, was disbanded on December 1, 1945. The army's 4th Regiment of Guerillas marched past Brigadier J. J. Cully, British 2nd Division, at Johore Bahru, during the disbandment ceremony. *Photo, British Official*

of all races staying obstinately at their posts until cleared out by the military; while in Singapore the passive defence services functioned well until the eve of surrender. Bewildered and stunned though they were by events which belied our propaganda that the Japanese could not conquer Malaya, the bulk of the Asiatic population behaved remarkably well. The average Chinese was enthusiastically on our side.

Was there a Fifth Column? Quite frankly, there was, but on nothing like the scale suggested in some quarters. Most of the stories arose from the inability of British troops to distinguish Malays and Chinese from Japanese, a difficulty which was increased by the trick used by the Japanese troops of disguising themselves in native clothing. Then there was the natural silence of the Malays which was interpreted as antipathy by those unaccustomed to their habits.

Such Fifth Column as existed was almost entirely confined to Northern Malaya where there was a considerable mixture of Malays with Siamese, whose pro-Japanese sentiments had hitherto not been fully appreciated. It is significant to note, however, that there is no single recorded instance of our troops, when cut off by the enemy or seeking to escape capture, failing to receive help and sympathy from the local people.

Our War Leaders in Peacetime
SMUTS

THE career of Jan Christiaan Smuts is among the most colourful of those of the Empire's war leaders. From commander of a Boer "commando" he became, on May 24, 1941, a Field-Marshal of the British Army; from a bitter enemy of Britain he became a staunch supporter of the Empire and, as Prime Minister of South Africa, and Minister of Defence, one of its main pillars.

In his 77th year he can look back on a life as statesman, scholar, soldier, scientist, lawyer, philosopher and explorer. Yet Field-Marshal Smuts remains a man of simple tastes, living in an unpretentious house on the outskirts of Pretoria.

Born on May 24, 1870, in a village near Malmesbury, in Cape Province, his father was a prosperous Dutch farmer and his mother of French Huguenot stock. At school he met his two main political rivals—Hertzog and Malan—and at Stellenbosch Victoria College he met Sybella Krige, the girl he was to marry in 1897. Today he calls her "Isie," and their house is noisy with grand-children when the family, two sons and four daughters, comes home.

A brilliant scholar, at Cambridge he compressed a two-years' law course into one, became a Bencher of the Middle Temple and, when only 28, State Attorney for the South African Republic. The Boer War interrupted his political career; but it proved his ability as a strategist, and with its termination he once again plunged into politics—the Field-Marshal's first interest. At the other extreme he has a great love of Nature. He still tells his friends about the days when, as a child, he spent hours with a Hottentot shepherd on his father's farm, listening to tales of the veld.

Now he keeps a variety of animals in his private grounds, among them a pet crane, and a year or so ago he had a lion cub. Another of his interests is botany; that, and the study of prehistoric implements and settlements, Smuts says, gives a purpose to the long walks he loves.

When in London in 1943 he went for a ten-mile walk every week-end. But during the week his secretaries were at their desks at 7.30 a.m.—so was Smuts. He still rises at seven a.m. and, in a study lined with books on philosophy, strategy, politics, physics and photography, he works until midnight with only short breaks for meals. Those who handle his documents have no easy task : the Field-Marshal's handwriting is remarkably illegible, and the secretary who typed his book "Holism and Evolution" had constantly to refer to him.

The Smuts entertain little, but the Field-Marshal's friends know him as a brilliant and witty after-dinner speaker. He is a deep thinker, and photography, he declares, clears his mind for another of his hobbies—the study of philosophy.

FIELD-MARSHAL J. C. SMUTS, Prime Minister of South Africa and Minister of Defence, and a great lover of nature, enjoys the flowers in the gardens of Groote Schuur (1) official residence of South Africa's Prime Ministers, at Cape Town. Mrs. Smuts (2) busy knitting in the grounds of their country home at Irene, near Pretoria. Arriving at Le Bourget airfield, France (3), on August 19, 1946, to lead the Dominion's delegation at the Peace Conference ; with him is the daughter of Major-General Francois Theron, acting leader of the Delegation in the Field-Marshal's absence. In his Cape Town study (4).
Photos, Topical, Associated Press, Illustrated

Scope for Reconstruction in Hamburg on the Elbe

ONCE A GREAT CITY AND SEAPORT, Hamburg, in the British zone in Germany, faces a gigantic task of reconstruction. A war casualty surveys mounds of rubble still covering acres of the city (1). In the badly damaged docks Canadian wheat is discharged from a Liberty ship into a grain barge (2). Wharves and quays have been almost obliterated; barges are moored to posts (3). Demolishing the remains of a bombed building (4). From R.A.F. bombers alone the city received 22,580 tons of bombs between May 1940 and April 1945, the most devastating attacks being those of July and August 1943.

Photos, Topical Press

Europe's Wartime Capitals in 1946

HELSINKI

by REINO KOIVULA

THE capital of Finland, Helsinki, like most of the other capitals of Europe lives a feverish life today. When in November 1939 Finland found herself at war with Soviet Russia there was hard fighting for 100 days, and Helsinki especially suffered much damage in the general bombing. Defeat was inevitable, and the Finns made peace, the treaty being signed in Moscow in March 1940. By way of indemnity large areas of the country were handed over to Soviet Russia, and there followed months of distress. In the summer of 1941 there came a swift and surprising turn—the Finnish Army was again mobilized, this time on the side of Nazi Germany, though no sympathy was felt by the people for the Nazi philosophy.

Armistice with the U.S.S.R. and Great Britain was signed on September 19, 1944, and the German troops left in northern Finland devastated the country in their retreat to Norway. There was hardly a building left unburned after the Nazis had been thrown out by the small remnants of the Finnish army. Finland had sacrificed 80,000 men killed and hundreds of thousands wounded in Hitler's war.

New Factories Offer Employment

The fighting over, the nation of barely 4,000,000 was faced with manifold problems. There were big areas over which the war had swept, leaving only ruins. New homes had to be found for the inhabitants of the areas given to the Soviet Union ; the majority of these homeless—more than 400,000—had flocked to the towns in order to earn a living. To Helsinki also came thousands of Karelians (see illus. in page 165, Vol. 8) and people who had been evacuated from the Porkkala district, thus increasing the serious shortage of dwelling places.

Lacking other accommodation the homeless persons took up their abode in schools and public air-raid shelters, and day after day more swarmed into the city. The officials were powerless to alleviate this shortage and in consequence were unpopular. Demonstrations are frequent, the authorities receiving resolutions and protests almost incessantly. But now building is in progress in Helsinki, including a vast new hospital for children which is approaching completion.

The heavy war-indemnity—300,000,000 dollars (about £75,000,000) payable in commodities over a period of six years to the U.S.S.R.—has been the cause of much trouble, but, paradoxically, it is one of the chief reasons for the absence of unemployment in Finland today. Many new factories have been set up, new businesses have been started, all hands are eagerly at work, though strikes have caused the general effort to fall short of full productivity.

Perhaps the most difficult problem has been the question of raw materials for the Finnish industries, which work under high pressure in order to supply Soviet Russia with ships and machines according to the terms of the armistice. Finland was never rich in metals, and so the people looked to the western countries for help. And the hoped-for materials came ; first from Sweden, then from England and the U.S.A. But Finland had to produce more than the amount to be sent to Soviet Russia. The goods imported had to be paid for and there was only one way to cover all this—to work as hard as possible to get more products out of the forests of Finland than were needed, to meet the indemnity.

The working tempo had to be speeded up. The social conditions of the forest-workers and those labouring in the factories were improved and wages raised, the result being that production showed a remarkable increase, and now it seems that the " green gold " of Finland—the almost boundless forests, source of veneer and other products manufactured from wood—will lead the country out of its difficulties.

LACK of tonnage has been an obstacle to obtaining raw materials from abroad. The Finnish merchant navy was never very large, though before the war it was almost large enough to carry all the imports needed from overseas. At the outbreak of the war most of the Finnish merchantmen were at sea or in foreign ports, where they were interned or sunk. Deep, therefore, was the joy when the governments of Great Britain and the U.S.A. proclaimed their willingness to give Finnish ships back to their original owners. As Finland had to hand over to Soviet Russia many of its most up-to-date ships as war indemnity the generosity shown by the British and American governments is very greatly appreciated. American and British ships have brought to Finnish ports gift-parcels, cars, agricultural tractors, machinery, medicine, sugar and tobacco. Cars from the U.S.A. have proved of very great value, as also the tractors. Almost every vehicle had been worn out and the situation was desperate. With the arrival of ships from the western world the wheels are turning again. The railway situation is still very bad, but new locomotives and wagons are being made with the utmost speed to take the place of thousands handed over to Soviet Russia.

Route of the First Coffee Ship

The " common " Finns, less concerned than others with political strife, accustomed as they are to a simple life are, of course, worried about how to get sufficient money to buy food and clothes, for prices have soared. Though the food situation is far from easy there is no actual starvation in Finland. Food has been rationed since 1941, the monthly rates per person now being approximately : bread 19 lb. ; sugar 9 oz. ; butter 1 lb. ; meat 7 oz. ; fish 2 lb. ; and 120 cigarettes (American). The milk ration is one-third pint per day. Potatoes, vegetables and fruit are not rationed, but are very expensive. But the black market is legal, as in Soviet Russia, so that the rich are able to buy and eat more and better food than the poor. Textile goods are of very bad quality and difficult to obtain. Woollen cloth has not been seen in the shops of Helsinki since 1941. Housewives have to do a good deal of queueing, with the exception of expectant mothers who can obtain a special exemption card. While mothers shop, children can be left in the care of a nurse in one of the city's numerous parks.

When after six long years there came the first ship with coffee to Finland—the S.S. Herakles, carrying more than 3,000 tons of coffee from Brazil—there was almost a national feast. Many of the leading newspapers and the big shops displayed maps showing the route of the Herakles bringing the " golden drink " to the thirsty Finnish people. Every day the situation of the ship on the Atlantic was marked on the maps so that all could see how their favourite drink drew nearer to the Finnish coast.

IN THE STRUGGLE FOR POST-WAR EXISTENCE in Helsinki less vital needs are not forgotten ; cut flowers (left) are obtainable but costly. Agricultural tractors from Britain and America shipped to Finland are replacing those worn out through constant use and lack of maintenance during the war years : a consignment from Britain unloading at Helsinki (right). Export of products from the country's vast forests is booming, and helping to pay for these and other essential imports.

Exclusive to THE WAR ILLUSTRATED

Helsinki Sets the Pace for Finland's Recovery

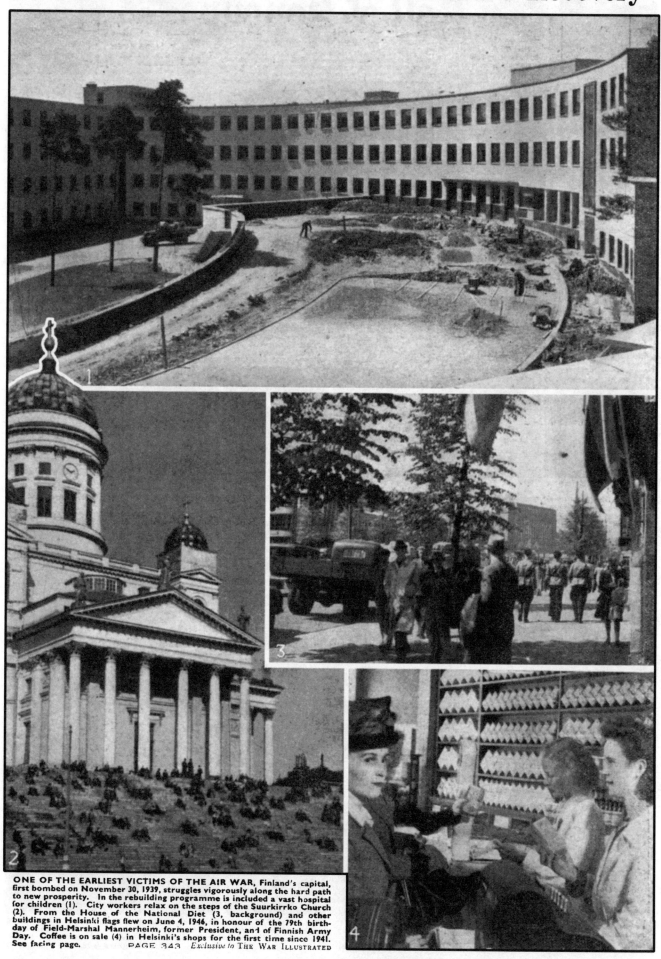

ONE OF THE EARLIEST VICTIMS OF THE AIR WAR, Finland's capital, first bombed on November 30, 1939, struggles vigorously along the hard path to new prosperity. In the rebuilding programme is included a vast hospital for children (1). City workers relax on the steps of the Suurkirrko Church (2). From the House of the National Diet (3, background) and other buildings in Helsinki flags flew on June 4, 1946, in honour of the 79th birthday of Field-Marshal Mannerheim, former President, and of Finnish Army Day. Coffee is on sale (4) in Helsinki's shops for the first time since 1941. See facing page.

The Roll of Honour
NCO's & MEN
1939—1946

Fus. T. ALFORD
R. Inniskilling Fusiliers.
In action : Italy. 19.1.44.
Age 24.   (Desertone)

So great has been the response of readers to our invitation to submit portraits for our Roll of Honour that no more can now be accepted. But we have every hope of being able to publish all those so far received.

Sgt. T. H. BAXTER
223 Coy. R.A.S.C.
Action : Arnhem. 23.9.44.
Age 36.   (Clipstone)

Cpl. H. BEECHING
4th Hussars.
Action : W. Desert. 1.6.42.
Age 35.   (Middle Stoke)

Cpl. S. W. BULL
Reconnaissance Corps.
Died of wounds. 25.5.44.
Age 23.   (Hackney)

Sgt. E. W. COX
51 Bomber Sqn., R.A.F.
Action : Hadamer. Apl. 43.
Age 22.   (Canterbury)

Spr. E. DARWENT
Royal Engineers.
Action : France. 11.6.44.
Age 26.   (Sheffield)

Rfn. W. EDGE
6th Airborne Division.
Died of wounds. 2.4.45.
Age 33.   (Nantwich)

Gdn. R. B. EDWARDS
Irish Guards.
Action : Tunisia. 30.4.43.
Age 28.   (Whitchurch)

Pte. S. FERDINANDO
Dorsetshire Regiment.
Died of wounds. 11.6.44.
Age 23.   (London)

Gr. W. FAIRBROTHER
422 S.L., Bty. R.A.
Died of wounds. 7.3.46.
Age 38.   (London)

Pte. T. D. FERRY
Argyll & Suth. Highlanders
Far East.   12.3.42.
Age 26.   (Sunderland)

Pte. A. GAMBLE
2nd Bn. West Yorks Regt.
Action : Burma. 14.1.44.
Age 22.   (Mansfield)

Chf. P.O. J. H. GREEN
H.M.S. Boadicea.
Action : At sea. 13.6.44.
Age 28.   (nr. Newmarket)

A/B W. GASKELL
Royal Navy.
Action : at sea.   2.2.43.
Age 21.   (Earlestown)

Spr. J. E. GUDGER
59th Field Coy., R. Engrs.
Action : Dixmude. 23.5.40.
Age 19.   (Atherstone)

Gnr. H. HARDSTAFF
1st Survey Regt., R.A.
D. of wounds: India. 13.2.45.
Age 30.   (Hucknall)

Pte. A. HEAL
Duke of Cornwall's L.I.
Action : Cassino. 12.5.44.
Age 28.   (E. Chinnock)

O/S H. D. HENWOOD
H.M.S. Galatea.
Mediterranean.   15.12.41.
Age 18.   (Newquay)

Bmdr. L. HURRELL
Royal Artillery.
In action : Java. 29.11.43.
Age 23.   (Dagenham)

Sgt. A/G. S. JARVIS
Royal Air Force.
Action : Antwerp. 22.5.44.
Age 19.   (Walthamstow)

Tpr. A. KENT
Royal Tank Regiment.
Action : Tobruk. 13.6.42.
Age 22.   (Liverpool)

L/Cpl. F. MAPLESTONE
Suffolk Regiment.
Jap. P.O.W.   20.9.43.
Age 40.   (Gloucester)

L/Bmdr. J. MARTIN
Royal Artillery.
In action : Caen. 25.8.44.
Age 29.   (Coseley)

L/A/C C. J. F. MORGAN
Royal Air Force.
India.   17.5.43.
Age 39.   (Salisbury)

Stoker. C. MORT
H.M.S. Galatea.
Mediterranean.   15.12.41.
Age 27.   (Ellesmere Port)

Y/Sig. A. G. NICHOLLS
H.M.S. Galatea.
Mediterranean.   15.12.41.
Age 28.   (Birmingham)

L/S. J. ROBERTSON
H.M.S. Charybdis.
Action : at sea.   23.10.43.
Age 30.   (Edinburgh)

Pte. H. G. PREVETT
Middlesex Regiment.
Action : at sea.   27.2.44.
Age 20.   (Ramsgate)

Sgt Plt. W. RAINE
610 Squadron, R.A.F.
Action : St. Omer. 21.8.41.
Age 22.   (Carlisle)

Lg/Str. A. RICHARDS
Royal Navy.
Mediterranean.   May, 40.
Age 22.   (Eastbourne)

Flt/Sgt. E. RIGBY
209 Squadron, R.A.F.
D/wds : Seychelles. 8.7.44.
Age 21.   (St. Helens)

A/B R. SHARP
H.M.S. Royal Oak.
Scapa Flow.   14.10.39.
Age 17.   (Grimston)

Sgt/Plt. L. G. SMITH
Bomber Command, R.A.F.
Action : Atlantic. 17.4.43.
Age 29.   (Taunton)

Gnr. T. R. SOWERBY
Royal Horse Artillery.
Action : Tobruk. Nov. 41.
Age 21.   (Sedbergh)

Gnr. R. TAYLOR
Royal Artillery.
Action : Greece. 21.4.41.
Age 26.   (Wakefield)

Dvr. A. H. STRONG
Royal Army Service Corps.
Action : Tobruk. 15.5.41.
Age 21.   (Ascot)

Flt/Sgt. A. THOMPSON
Royal Air Force.
Action : Berlin.   3.4.43.
Age 21.   (Middlesbrough)

Cpl. K. W. TOMPKINS
4th Bn. Somerset L.I.
D. of wds: Nor'dy. 11.7.44.
Age 28.   (Minehead)

I Was a Slave on a Japanese Railway

"You will go where no white men have ever been before, and you will work as white men have never worked before," said the Japs to their prisoners earmarked for labour on the Burma-Siam railway being constructed in 1942. J. A. M'Call, Telegraphist, R.N., telling the story here, endured the horrors of that prolonged toil. See also page 409, Vol. 9.

ON Friday, February 13, 1942, I was drafted from the Royal Naval Wireless Station at Singapore to H.M.S. Kuala, which was to evacuate Red Cross nurses and civilians to Batavia. Next morning we were discovered by Japanese bombers and were sunk, near the small island of Pulla-Pom-Pom. About half the people aboard us must have been killed or wounded. The remainder of us managed to reach the island, and found there was very little water there and no fruit of any kind.

Our rations worked out at one biscuit per person per day and one tin of sardines

between sixteen. After eight days we managed to get away, in three Chinese junks, to Sumatra; the women and nurses were given first transport to Padang, on the west coast, and most of them were then taken on to Colombo by British warships.

The remainder of us, with other Naval ratings, arrived there twenty-four hours after the last ship had sailed. We waited in the hope that another ship would come, but nothing did, and on March 16 the Dutch told us that the Japanese were to enter the town the following morning. And there, in Padang, I was taken prisoner along with about 900 other Britishers who had managed to get away from Singapore, or whose ships had been sunk off Sumatra.

About six weeks later 500 of us were sent to Mergui, Burma. There we were engaged in repairing an airfield, and though conditions were bad enough they were nothing to what we were to experience later on. Our next move was farther north, to a town called Tavoy, and again we were put to repairing an airfield. In both those towns the natives helped us all they could, especially the few Chinese, by giving us money and food. One woman was beaten to death for this, by the Japs, as an example to the rest.

Pouring Rain and Scorching Heat

Again we were moved, round about September 1942—crammed into a small coastal vessel in which there was so little room for us all that we were made to sit with our knees touching our chins. Two days and nights that awful journey lasted, and when we reached Moulmein we were put into the civil gaol for the night. The following morning we were packed, worse than cattle, into railway trucks and taken to the railhead, at a small town called Thanbyuzayat. Here we learned that we were to build a railway connecting Moulmein and Bangkok.

ROUTE OF THE RAILWAY (not drawn to scale) on which our men toiled for the Japanese, as narrated in these pages. PAGE 345

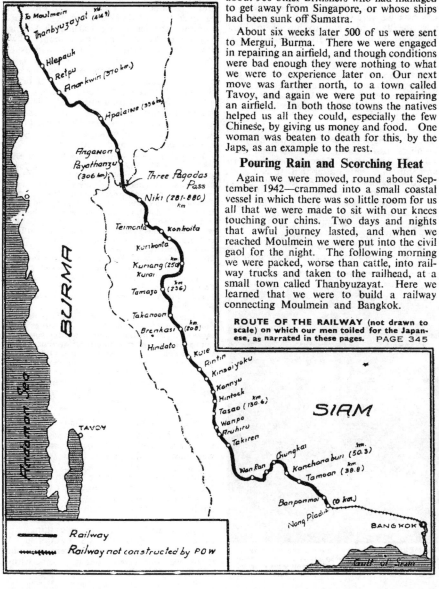

"Your lives have been spared," we were told, "through the generosity of the Emperor. You will go where no white men have ever been before, and you will work as white men have never worked before." For our labour we were to receive ten cents a day. Later this was increased to twenty-five cents, as prices soared from ten to fifty times pre-war rates. Other prisoners had been told that the railway would be built even if it had to be over their dead bodies. In the end over 16,000 prisoners died toiling on it.

We were to work on the Burma side, together with 10,000 Australian, American and Dutch prisoners, and drive forward and join up with the Siam side just over the Burma border at a place called Niki. Arrived at the camp, we were told our labours would include jungle clear-

Naval Telegraphist J. A. M'CALL

ing, making embankments, bridges and roads. We started at dawn and finished at dusk, working through pouring rain in the monsoon season or scorching heat in the dry season. As regards digging, the task started at one cubic metre per man per day, this gradually increasing until it reached two cubic metres. In the jungle we had to cut our way to the trees, fell them and haul them to the clearings where bullock wagons waited. Bridge building was considered the easiest job of all, though there were many casualties.

After a couple of months the bad food and the jungle began to take its toll of us. Our diet consisted mainly of rice, which was always full of maggots, weevils and dirt; during the dry season we could get no water with which to wash it. We had very little vegetable or meat, often just dry rice with a pinch of salt. Every day we gathered leaves from the trees and bushes, and boiled them to try to make soup. It was a case of trying anything. As a result we fell victims to diseases—practically everything known in the East, malaria, dysentery, cholera, beri-beri, ulcers and sores; and the Japs gave us very few medical supplies.

As men fell sick so the rations were cut, the Jap idea being that if a man is too sick to work he is too sick to eat. Inspection of the sick would usually be carried out by a Jap or Korean who knew as little about medicine as I knew about flying to the moon. Unless a man could show a gaping ulcer or was skin and bone and couldn't stand he was considered fit for work. At times I worked in the rain at night with nothing to wear except a loincloth, and once with a temperature of 103 degrees.

On this occasion I told the Jap engineer I had malaria, and he felt my forehead and told me to lie down on a pile of sleepers. I did so, but when a sentry came and asked what was wrong with me and I told him he promptly kicked me into a ditch. I crawled out, and received more blows on the face, and I had to go on working.

None of us had any clothing worth mentioning—just a few rags. Only one or two had footwear. Walking barefoot over stone ballast when you are laying rails is sheer torment. The huts we lived in were made of bamboo with a thatched roof, and we slept on bamboo raised about two feet from the ground. Many of us had collected old rice sacks, bits of canvas and odds and ends that would cover us at night. One day the Jap storeman took the lot, saying it all belonged to the Jap Army, so we went without bedding until we could steal more. We sometimes managed to light fires at night and sit round them because it was so cold and we had nothing to wear. The very few blankets were swarming with lice and the huts with bugs, so that if we did lie down we were in peril of being eaten alive.

Almost Everyone Had An Ailment

I saw two Americans punished for stealing some shorts from the Jap store. For three days and nights they had to stand to attention, without food. Only when one collapsed and the other was on the verge of it were they released. A Dutchman, for some small offence, had to kneel, with a stick behind his knees, and lean back facing the sun. This was kept up all day. If he moved only slightly one of the guards would kick or hit him. When released he had to be carried away ; he just couldn't walk. If we didn't bow or salute correctly we would be slapped and kicked, or made to hold a pick or shovel above our heads for an hour or two.

Work continued unceasingly although the number of prisoners was steadily decreasing. Men were dying every day. At each camp along the railway line there was a graveyard, sometimes containing six graves, sometimes over a hundred. Practically everyone had some ailment but still had to work, sometimes for 36-hour stretches, with a break of only four or five hours.

We had plenty of promises of better food, conditions, clothing, pay, anything to get more work out of us ; but the promises never materialized. Indeed, conditions steadily became worse. The Japs were rushing the railway through to get supplies to their front line on the India-Burma border, and we knew things weren't going well with our Forces. But often we heard R.A.F. planes passing overhead at night, on their way to Bangkok.

At last, after over a year of slavery and misery, the line was finished. But for several more months we were making railway sidings,

cutting trees for engine fuel, and repairing roads. When the labour was at an end we were given two days' rest. One was to be in mourning for the dead and the other for merrymaking. We held a service for the dead all right, but there was some doubt about the merrymaking. For the purpose of our "party" the Japs brought along six pigs, a bag of sugar, and some sweet potatoes —and informed us we were to pay for them.

They didn't know the meaning of generosity. For example, this was our menu for Christmas 1943 : breakfast, watery rice, with salt ; dinner, steamed rice with radish water ; supper, steamed rice, one tin of soup, a square inch of rice-cake and a spoonful of liquid sugar. The soup consisted of forty pounds of lentils, forty pounds of meat, and the radish tops left from dinner—this to be shared between 600 of us.

In March 1944 I left Burma for Siam and I was never so glad to leave anywhere in my life. We carried on through to Saigon, in French Indo-China, from where we were to go to Japan. But we stayed in Saigon. There I had dysentery, which remained with me for six months. The French people smuggled things into the camp, and altogether conditions were not so bad as in Burma. We even had a few blankets and some clothing. Also we were in fairly decent huts, with electric lights, but we were still tormented by lice and bugs. It was here that we received the first Red Cross parcels and got our first mail from Home, after very nearly three years. Each parcel was shared between six men. A few months before the war was over we were issued with boots and were told the Japs had had to buy them ; but they were British boots from the Red Cross.

Our prison camp was in the middle of a military target area, but though there were often raids on the town the camp itself was never touched. We didn't celebrate much when the war was over. We were too weary. Out of the original 500 men who had started out 147 had died.

We had the biggest air raid on Saigon on Jan. 12, 1945. It was carried out by dive-bombers from aircraft carriers, and considerable damage was done to enemy aircraft and shipping. Often after that we had raids by four-engined aircraft escorted by Lockheed Lightnings. In March, the French people were interned. This gave us much food for thought, but we still managed to keep in touch with them and they continued to give us news and money as before.

In August we heard something that really startled us. We were marching through the

FRANCAIS!
INDOCHINOIS!

LA guerre est terminée. Succombant sous les coups terribles qui lui ont été portés par les forces alliées terrestres navales et aériennes, le JAPON s'avoue vaincu et vient de se rendre sans condition. Partout les troupes japonaises ont reçu l'ordre de cesser le feu. De nouvelles destructions seront ainsi par bonheur, épargnées à l'Union Indochinoise et vous n'aurez pas à endurer les souffrances qu'aurait entraînées une libération par les armes ; vos villes et vos villages n'auront plus à subir de bombardement. Les forces alliées, comprenant des troupes françaises entourent déjà l'INDOCHINE, d'autres unités françaises sont en route.

Nos groupes d'action qui, depuis plusieurs mois, harcèlent les Japonais au cœur même de l'INDOCHINE, sont déjà sur place. Mais l'entrée en INDOCHINE des forces françaises et alliées pourra prendre quelque temps encore.

En attendant, les troupes japonaises ont reçu ordre de faciliter le fonctionnement des services essentiels du pays et de protéger vos vies et vos biens. Évitez avec eux toute querelle qui risquerait mettre inutilement en péril votre sécurité et celle de vos familles.

Venez en aide aux prisonniers alliés par tous les moyens en votre pouvoir.

Attendez les ordres qui vous seront donnés par les représentants du Gouvernement Français qui arriveront incessamment.

VIVE LA FRANCE,
VIVE L'UNION INDOCHINOISE!

LEAFLETS DROPPED BY ALLIED PLANES, printed in two languages, conveyed news of the end of the war to prisoners at Saigon, French Indo-China. See translation below.

streets to work when a passing Frenchman said, "Russia is in the war ! It will soon be over now, lads !" When we returned to camp that night we learned that other working parties had the same rumour. Two days later we learned that Japan had asked for peace. That seemed far too good to be true. But next day there were no working parties ordered out, and soon piles of boots, clothing, blankets, soap and tobacco came into the camp and food improved. Then an Allied aircraft came over and dropped leaflets and the Jap anti-aircraft opened fire on it. The leaflets, of which a French copy is reproduced above, read as follows :

The war is over. Succumbing to the terrible blows of the Allied land, sea and air forces, Japan admits that she is conquered and has just surrendered unconditionally. Japanese troops everywhere have received orders to cease fire. Further destruction will thus fortunately be spared to the Union of Indo-China and you will not have to endure the suffering which a liberation by fighting would have involved ; your towns and villages will no longer be subject to bombing. Allied forces, including French troops, surround Indo-China already, other French units are on the way.

Our guerilla troops, who for several months harassed the Japanese even in the centre of Indo-China, are already on the spot. But the entry of French and Allied forces into Indo-China will take some time.

While waiting the Japanese troops have received orders to facilitate the functioning of essential services in the country, and to protect your lives and your belongings. Avoid all argument with them, which will unnecessarily imperil the security of yourself and your families. Go to the help of Allied prisoners in every way you can.

Wait for orders which will be given to you by representatives of the French Government who will arrive without delay.

Long live France !

Long live the Union of Indo-China !

A few hours later one of the sentries told us that an armistice had been signed and we were moved to the French barracks to await the arrival of our own people. When two British officers arrived we began to believe the war really was going to end at last ! We sent letters home, and aircraft dropped us clothing and food. Finally aircraft came to take us away. We were flown to Rangoon, where we had the best of everything, and presently we left on the S.S. Ormonde. At Southampton arrangements were so slick that some of us were on our way home within two hours of landing.

GRAVES OF SOME OF THE 16,000 ALLIED PRISONERS who perished during the building of the Burma-Siam railway. This jungle clearing is at Kannyu. At each camp along the line these graves were dotted, in groups varying between six and 100. Of the original 500 men who started out with the author of this story 147 died.

The Bangkok-Moulmein Railway of Evil Memory

ONE OF MORE THAN 1,000 BRIDGES (1) which, spanning rivers and ravines, carry the 250 miles of railway joining Bangkok in Siam with Moulmein in Burma, constructed under merciless Japanese task-masters. Over towering hills, through winding valleys and previously unexplored jungle, Allied slave-gangs and more than 150,000 Asiatics toiled despairingly to complete this link with the Jap bases in Burma, as described in the accompanying story. See also illus. page 695, Vol. 9. *Photographs by Rev. J. A. E. Rutherford*

BAMBOO HUTS, flooded by monsoon rains and infested by mosquitoes, housed the exhausted labourers in their short periods of rest—as where the railway was being pushed out across a river (2) at Kanchanaburi (see map in page 345). Typical of a station scene (3), weapons and general stores for the Jap armies were dumped for removal in large quantities. The link-up between the two termini was completed by September 1943, and during 1944-45 the railway was in full use as the main Japanese supply line to their forces in Burma. Along unused stretches to-day the jungle is reclaiming its own, slowly but surely smothering the tracks in the laying of which so many thousands died through starvation, disease and deliberate ill-treatment.

When the Doodle-Bugs Came to London

Hitler's secret weapon, the VI—the flying bomb or doodle-bug—was first used against this country on June 13, 1944. The startling advent of these pilotless planes and some of the damage they caused is recalled by Chief Warder A. H. Cook, D.C.M., M.M., B.E.M., of His Majesty's Tower of London. See portrait and story in page 93.

WE at the Tower heard nothing much during the alerts on that first day, but two days later we realized that something very unusual was happening. The alert sounded at 11.38 p.m., and then commenced what to us was a night of mystery and guess-work. There were brief spells of liveliness—of rocket-guns, A.A. fire and very low flying aircraft—followed by long intervals of silence. At times it seemed impossible for some of the planes to clear the Tower.

We thought our fighters were doing a grand piece of work, as each time we saw something with a trail of flame behind it we concluded it was a piloted German plane in distress. The mysteries of the night were cleared up when Mr. Herbert Morrison stated on the wireless that pilotless planes were being used by the enemy on this country.

Amidst Awesome Flash and Roar

The din of the first four nights was terrific. It was impossible to make oneself heard above it. Under the shelter of the archways which the builders of seven centuries ago had provided we were able to look on, feeling safer than we really were. Shell cases from the rocket guns showered down. One unexploded rocket shell hit the ramparts and then burst, causing damage there and to the adjoining Salt and Well Towers. The flash and roar of these guns was awesome, and we rushed from one side of an archway to the other following with our eyes the path of the flying bombs which were covered by scores of searchlights.

A few minutes after 11 o'clock on Sunday morning, June 18, we were at parade service in St. Peter-ad-Vincula, when to our surprise (there had been no alert) the guns suddenly opened up on an approaching flying bomb which roared past over the Tower, uncomfortably close ; it fell, with calamitous results, on the Guards' Chapel at Wellington Barracks. That night the guns were silent and not another was fired in anger in the vicinity of the Tower during the remainder of the War. There were, I presume, good reasons for this ; civilian casualties were mounting daily from falling splinters and unexploded shells.

We had another narrow escape at 3.45 a.m. on June 26, when a flying bomb just scraped over the Tower and burst in Lower Thames Street, near the Customs House, damaging the western portions of the Tower and adjacent areas. On the following day General Eisenhower and his son were being conducted around the Tower by the Resident Governor (Lieut.-Col. Faviell, D.S.O.) at about 11 a.m. I had just unlocked the door leading into St. John's Chapel when a flying bomb fell near, slamming the door with a terrific bang. The General merely smiled, and continued his tour of inspection.

At 3.30 p.m. on July 3, I heard the approach of another and, foolishly, poked my head out of the window. I was met by a terrific blast which had beaten the sound of the explosion. This one fell in Billingsgate, and did us quite a lot of damage. Our nearest, up to this time, fell at 9 a.m. on July 12. The alert had sounded a quarter-hour previously, but nothing seemed to be happening, and I was leisurely putting on my collar and tie and gazing out towards Tower Bridge. Suddenly came a terrific blast of air, followed immediately by a deafening explosion. This one had glided in with its engine shut-off, thus giving no warning of its approach.

IT just missed the Bridge and fell on some barges. All buildings on the south side of the Tower suffered. Windows were out and most of the ceilings down. Our large double doors with their massive bars and locks which face the river were forced open and fractured. A large piece of one of the barges fell in the Tower near the Social Room, and other portions were scattered around. All temporary windows and some of the original ones in St. Peter's Chapel were blown out. We suffered no casualties, but it was reported that several men on the barges had been killed.

Motto : " *Unexpectedly* "

NO. 62 SQUADRON

FORMED at Filton, Glos., on August 8, 1916, the squadron moved to France in January 1918, took part in heavy fighting, went to Germany with the Army of Occupation on May 2, 1919, was disbanded there on July 31, and re-formed at Abingdon, Berks, on April 12, 1937, as No. 62 (Bomber) Squadron. Nothing is known of its earlier activities in the Second Great War, but it appears to have operated in the Far East and was in Sumatra during the debacle of 1942.

In June 1942, located at Dum Dum, near Calcutta, equipped with Hudsons, it moved to Cuttack for general reconnaissance activities and bombing raids, then to Dhubalia in January 1943, to Jessore in February, and assisted in the supply of the first Wingate Expedition of March and April. In July 1943 the squadron moved to Chaklala in the Punjab, for intensive training in dropping supplies and parachute troops.

THE first Dakota aircraft were received in September 1943, and they moved to Comilla in January 1944. When General Wingate's Third Indian Division was flown in to the North Burma jungle clearing 200 miles behind the Japanese lines (see story in page 314) No. 62 participated in the re-supply of this force. It moved to Agartala in July 1944 and supplied the now advancing XXXIII Corps, and on August 8 moved to Basal for rest.

No. 62 returned to Agartala in November and shortly afterwards to Comilla, whence it maintained support of the 14th Army, flying in reinforcement troops and evacuating casualties. In March the squadron moved to Akyab for supply duties to the IV Corps, and in September 1945 to Mingaladon, Rangoon. It was disbanded on March 15, 1946.

The next arrived on Sunday, July 30. It suddenly appeared over the top of Tower Bridge, and I could see it was diving to earth. I shouted to my wife and another warder having dinner with us, " Look out ! " then hurriedly withdrew to the centre of the room away from the window—and hoped for the best. Our only protection was a Tudor wall of plaster, four inches thick, but our luck held. My wife had crouched under the window, and although smothered with glass she escaped injury.

That one fell on the Children's Beach a few yards east of Traitor's Gate. A car on the wharf near-by was reduced to scrap-iron. Being Sunday all gates leading on to the wharf were closed and secured, and these ended up as matchwood. All crops in the warders' gardens were laid flat, and the dungeon walls of the Wakefield Tower were damaged. It appears the blast had got inside

VICTIMS OF A FLYING BOMB which, gliding in with engine shut-off, just missed the Tower Bridge and fell amidst craft on the Thames (story above), on July 12, 1944, included a tug (its bow just visible above water on the right) which was salvaged by Port of London Authority repair lighters. See also page 788, Vol 9. *Photo, Sport & General*

DURING THE ASSAULT BY FLYING BOMBS smoke towering above London's roof tops was a common sight, each cloud marking a scene of damage and, not infrequently, heavy casualties. The above incident occurred in the York Road, near Waterloo Station. In the distance are Big Ben, Westminster Abbey, and the dome of Central Hall, Westminster ; and, in the right centre, the new Waterloo Bridge. Adding new horrors to this indiscriminate aerial assault was the arrival of the first V2 (rocket bomb) in September 1944. See also page 715, Vol. 9.
Photo, The Star

the dungeon through the arrow slits and forced the wall outwards towards the bomb. To do this the blast had to come up from the beach, cross the wharf and moat, over the outer wall, and cross a road into the base of this Tower. This damage was all the more remarkable because the walls of the Wakefield Tower are about ten feet thick.

Fortunately there were no sentries on the wharf at the time. The storehouses under Tower Bridge Road had all their doors blown off, and the Well Tower, Cradle Tower and St. Thomas's Tower took the full blast but escaped complete destruction. Though from the outside they appeared undamaged, the interiors were in a frightful mess. Fire engines, police, rescue squads, ambulances, A.R.P. and C.D. cars were on the scene in minutes, but once again we had been spared casualties, only a few minor injuries having to be treated.

The night of August 3 was one of great activity. During a lull I lay down on the bed. Suddenly I heard a bomb approaching,

and I covered my head with a pillow. There was an awful crack, and the south side of the Tower had got it again. Debris was everywhere ; fresh scars were visible in all directions. The bomb had struck the gilded cross on top of the North Tower of Tower Bridge, removing about six feet of it, and then burst with a terrific roar in mid-air.

THESE were our nearest, but there were many others in the vicinity. From our windows we could often judge the nearness of an approaching bomb by watching the soldiers outside. Like traffic policemen they would wave the thing on, and as long as they waved we knew all was well. When they dived for cover we knew things were not so well. September saw the easing up of the flying bombs. Then came the V2 rockets. A direct hit from one of these might have proved disastrous in the Tower's weak and battered state. But fortunately for us our nearest ones, on October 30 and November 10, both fell about 1,000 yards away.

by force rather than choice. By fair means or foul they produced goods quite outside the reach of most Germans, but to every honest Pole there were a dozen whose sharp practices were brought to our notice.

We sold and exchanged things at a rate that depended on the district and the business acumen of those responsible for the negotiations. For instance, if one of us received ten eggs in exchange for twenty cigarettes and the word got round that somebody else had taken only eight for the same size packet of fags, eight would be the price from then onwards. That was in the days when parcels were coming through to us. Earlier—and again later—we were as anxious for a smoke as anything, and many were the treasured possessions sacrificed to that end. Watches, signet-rings, fountain-pens, and articles of clothing when many could least afford them, all were in demand and brought some kind of return either in food or cigarettes.

Searched by the Dreaded Gestapo

Of course, this trading with civilians, as with those in uniform, always entailed risks. Social contacts were strictly forbidden, as was the exchanging of articles, and penalties up to death were threatened.

As trading increased, searches became the order of the day. Working parties returning to camp would be halted in front of the guard-room and submitted to systematic scrutiny. Self-made poachers' pockets, slits in the linings of our greatcoats and such subterfuges were soon revealed, and we had to find new and better places of concealment. As we matched our wits with the Germans, it often became necessary for us to strip before they discovered the loaf distributed in slices about our person, the flour in bags under our armpits, or the eggs suspended in a bag between our legs !

Periodically we were submitted to barrack-room searchings, sometimes by the dreaded Gestapo, who would descend on us without warning. When these searches took place

Hat Trick in German P.O.W. Camp

A prisoner of war in German hands from May 1940 until April 1945, Charles J. Sadgrove, Royal Signals, speedily learned his way about when foraging was indicated. He relates how he acquired and developed a keen business capacity under the very noses of his watchful captors.

I SUPPOSE the first words I learned of the German language were "arbeit" and "essen." Often by doing the first ("work"), one could get the second ("food"). But as a prisoner I found that whereas the "arbeit" increased with the years the "essen" became less and less. I soon realized that to guarantee myself the right amount of calories for reasonable living I must increase my vocabulary. I then learned that "kaufen" meant to buy, "verkaufen" to sell and "umtauschen"—blessed word !—to exchange. Armed with these three verbs, and an almost negative knowledge of German grammar, I proceeded to take steps to augment my larder.

Of one thing I had failed to take account— the language of gesticulation. Without his hands and arms the average German would be dumb. And so I had to learn to show by gesture as much as by speech the thing I had to sell and that which I wanted in return. To say "brot" if I was in need of bread was not enough ; I had to show by sign language the extent of my requirements.

With demonstrations, then, and where possible the actual display of the goods in question, we prisoners developed commercial relations that were probably unparalleled in history. Our best customers for deals were the Poles, who spoke the German language

TOP-HATTED GERMAN CHIMNEY-SWEEP, at the right of the back row, smuggled into the camp the camera with which this photograph of himself and British prisoners of war was taken. Charles Sadgrove, author of the accompanying story, in which he pays tribute to the ingenious go-between, is at the left of the back row.

he had for sale, and in which he put those things we gave him in exchange. No conjurer's hat ever held a wider selection, and I stared unbelievingly the first time I saw it doffed for a deal and replaced almost in the one movement.

This sweep was a Pole by birth, but his German was so fluent that he passed for the genuine article. Had he been challenged his identity papers would have given him away, but his glib tongue and pleasing personality got him through many otherwise locked doors. After a friendly chat with our guards he would come into our part of the camp ostensibly to clean the chimneys, but really to have a cup of tea and a smoke with us and execute his business. When he left he would be the richer for English cigarettes and chocolate perhaps, and we for eggs, tooth-paste, or blacking.

Crowning Piece of Effrontery

We bought our camp amplifier from this man, and later convinced a high-ranking German officer that it had been sent out by the Red Cross to help gramophone reproduction. We bought watches from that adroit sweep, an alarm clock, a loud-speaker, and much else. His crowning piece of effrontery was committed on the day he smuggled a camera into the camp and persuaded a guard to be photographed in a group with us under the eyes of a particularly obnoxious S.S. officer who lived in the house adjoining our billet.

He was sharp, this sweep, but fair and honest. If in a deal he offered fifteen eggs for a packet of coffee and had no more than a dozen in his hat, the balance would not be forgotten. It might be a week or more before he could get to us again, but when he did arrive his first business would be the payment of outstanding debts !

cupboards were turned out and their contents strewn about the room, palliasses opened and their straw flung around, floorboards prised up and walls tested for sliding panels and secret recesses. And they would miss the secret map rolled up in the black-out blind and the new-laid eggs secreted in the hollowed-out base of the stove !

The people with whom we dealt were a mixed crowd, including our guards—and their officers for whom they acted as agents. We sometimes had things which they valued and which they had not seen for years, such as real coffee, cocoa and tea, and English

cigarettes of which there is no equal in the German's eyes. A business arrangement with someone in uniform within the camp saved a lot of complications and risks, and I have known even cleaners of chimneys who were past-masters in illegal trading with prisoners of war. One in particular comes to mind.

An expert at his trade, he wore the top-hat that signified this position in contrast with the junior, or apprentice, sweep whose headgear was a mere skull-cap. Indoors as well as out he wore that hat, but it was more than a sign of his calling—it was the receptacle in which he brought us the goods

LAST ACTION OF H.M.S. HEREWARD, sunk on May 29, 1941, during the evacuation from Crete, is depicted here. Two months earlier (March 31) this destroyer, on escort duty between Crete and Alexandria, picked up survivors of H.M.S. Bonaventure as narrated in the facing page. When last seen, Hereward was making slowly for Crete—every gun in action. PAGE 350 *From the water-colour by Lt.-Com. R. Langmaid, R.N., Official Fleet Artist*

How I Said Good-bye to Bonaventure

Early in the morning of March 31, 1941, H.M.S. Bonaventure, accompanied by the destroyer Hereward, was escorting two troopships from Crete to Alexandria, when she received two torpedoes in the starboard side aft. Royal Marine Musician H. T. Thompson took a hasty plunge overboard—and this is the mental picture he eventually brought ashore.

I HAD just been called for the morning watch, and was casually putting on my socks, when *wallop*. Seven seconds later came another crash, and the ship took a list of 45 degrees to starboard. I grabbed my lifebelt and proceeded cautiously to the upper deck—cautiously, because the second torpedo had put all lights out. I heard many voices in the water, some shouting "Come on, you up there, she's going !" and "Jump, if you don't want to go down with her !"

Realizing the ship would soon be gone from under my feet, unless I went first, I took one deep breath and slid down over the side, which took quite a few seconds owing to the list the Bonaventure now had. By the time I had swum well clear she had blown up and sank, seven minutes after the first hit. I was in the water almost an hour, though it seemed all night. It suddenly occurred to me that I was due for pension in a few months, and all other considerations apart I was determined not to be cheated out of that. Uppermost in my mind was the thought of my wife and son, and I decided that if I were to see them again—and draw my pension—I must keep calm and reserve my strength.

The Scrambling Net Was Out

The water did not seem in the least cold, at first, and as the accompanying destroyers had thrown overboard all the wood they could find—anything that would float, sugar boxes, tea chests, oars, bathroom grating boards, and so on—practically every man in the water had something to hang on to. Our boy bugler, Roy Marshall, aged 15½ and unable to swim, was as plucky as any. On being awakened by the first torpedo, he dressed just as if he were going on the parade ground : boots properly laced, tunic correctly buttoned, and with bugle slung. Over the side he went. Three or four of his

messmates took care of him and managed to get him safely on to a raft.

When I arrived alongside the Hereward she had the scrambling net hung and was picking up survivors. Attempting to clamber

up the oily net I was yanked off by someone behind, and it seemed to me I should stand a better chance if I lay off for a while and made another attempt a bit later. This I did, and on turning away from Hereward was horrified to feel—with my hands groping a couple of feet below the water—the bodies of men who, not having strength left to scramble up the net, had been drowned. However, my turn came, and some hours later I arrived safely in Alexandria, thank God, and thank you, Hereward !

H.M.S. BONAVENTURE was one of Britain's latest warships of her class at the time of her sinking in 1941. A 5,500-ton cruiser, she blew up and vanished beneath the Mediterranean waters seven minutes after the first torpedo struck her. Survivors were picked up by H.M.S. Hereward, depicted in facing page during her last action. *Photo, British Official*

MUSICIAN H. T. THOMPSON, Royal Marines, who was in the water for an hour after Bonaventure went down.

NEW FACTS AND FIGURES

IN the Aachen district teachers are cycling from village school to village school to counteract the shortage of teachers. The most that one teacher can cover is three schools, which means children cannot receive instruction every day. Moreover, lack of school buildings and of footwear, as well as transport difficulties, prevent 8,792 children of school age in the North Rhine region from obtaining any schooling whatever. Despite the many difficulties, however, 76,310 children are receiving either full-time or part-time education in the Aachen district, where 391 elementary schools have been opened. A further 1,118 attend intermediate schools and 3,505 the secondary.

OVER 2,000,000 Germans have been exchanged between the British and Russian Zones under " Operation Honeybee " since October 1945. During the war hundreds of thousands of people were evacuated from Hamburg and the Ruhr eastwards, and others fled from Berlin to country districts of the British Zone. The voluntary return of these evacuees to their own districts by special trains has resulted in a little over 500,000 moving into the Russian from the British Zone, and approximately 1,700,000 from the Russian to ours.

MORE people were evacuated from the Ruhr than from any other area, as it was the most heavily bombed in Germany. They have been settled as near to their old homes as possible, but unless they are miners few can return to the towns and houses they left in the Ruhr—they are no longer there.

" PACIFIC packs," designed originally as food supplies for British and Indian fighting troops in the Pacific theatre, have provided 1,638,000 meals for German children in the North Rhine Province since February 1946. Five hundred thousand packs were originally authorized for children

between three and six years : later the number was increased to 620,000 and the upper age limit raised to 17 years.

AMONG the contents of a typical pack are (in compressed form) meat and beef, ham and eggs, four oatmeal blocks, nine biscuits, meat biscuit, two cheese blocks, sugar, salt, three packets of boiled sweets, two chocolate bars and two sweet bars. The wooden cases containing the packs are made into children's furniture and the metal inner packing into feeding bowls.

VERY few British war orphans will emigrate to Australia. The Australian Minister for Immigration stated in July 1946 that it had been originally proposed to bring 50,000 British children to Australia. Happily, it had been found that only 3,000 to 4,000 children were orphaned by the London blitz or by submarine warfare, and these the United Kingdom Government wishes to keep in their own country.

THE Australian war memorial at Villers-Bretonneux, near Amiens, which commemorates the deeds of the Australian Imperial Force in the First Great War, was extensively damaged during the Second Great War. Towards the cost of reconstruction of the memorial (which covers ten acres and was unveiled on August 8, 1938) the Australian Government is to provide £15,000, the remainder of the cost being borne by the Imperial War Graves Commission.

URGENT need for labour to carry out reconstruction tasks in Vienna prompted Austrian authorities to take drastic measures in July 1946. The latest regulation makes it necessary for all able-bodied males between the ages of 16 and 60 to produce evidence of employment before they are issued with ration cards. In the case of students a certificate must be obtained from the academic authorities.

Extracting Death from Dorset's Studland Bay

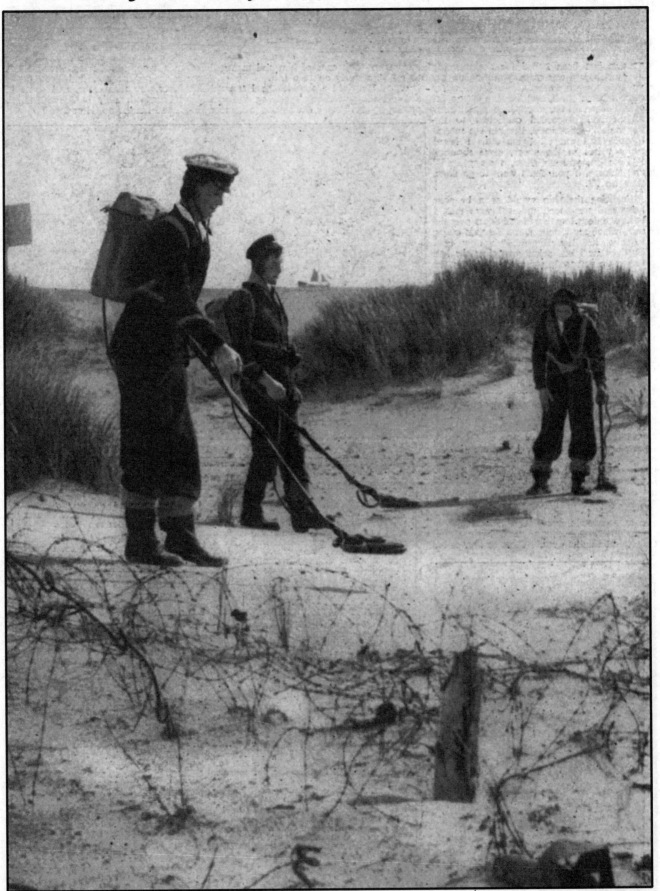

Photo, P.A.-Reuter

MINE DETECTING AND CLEARANCE at Studland Bay is being carried out by men from H.M.S. Purbeck, with the assistance of 100 Polish naval ratings. In the foreground are remains of two projectiles. In this former wartime training area and, in 1942, scene of a full-scale rehearsal of the Normandy invasion, 22,000 unexploded missiles have so far been accounted for in the 24 square miles. It is expected that operations will have rendered these beaches safe by the spring of 1947.
Photo, P.A.-Reuter

Printed in England and published every alternate Friday by the Proprietors, THE AMALGAMATED PRESS, LTD., The Fleetway House, Farringdon Street, London, E.C.4. Registered for transmission by Canadian Magazine Post. Sole Agents for Australia and New Zealand: Messrs. Gordon & Gotch, Ltd.; and for South Africa, Central News Agency, Ltd.—September 13, 1946.   S.S.   *Editorial Address:* JOHN CARPENTER HOUSE WHITEFRIARS, LONDON, E.C.4.

Vol 10 *The War Illustrated* N° 242

SIXPENCE

I WAS THERE

SEPTEMBER 27. 1946

LANCASTER BOMBERS OF No. 35 SQUADRON OVER ST. PAUL'S, London, on August 29, 1946, were returning to Gravely, Huntingdonshire, from a good will mission to the United States, where they had carried out a 15,000-mile tour. Welcoming the airmen at their base Sir Norman Bottomley, A.O.C.-in-C. Bomber Command, paid tribute to their discipline and flying, to the success of their mission, and to the efficiency of British equipment and heavy aircraft industry. See also illus. page 265.

Edited by Sir John Hammerton

NO. 243 WILL BE PUBLISHED FRIDAY, OCTOBER 11

Farewell to Remnants of the Late German Navy

UNSERVICEABLE SHIPS remaining after the usable units of the German Fleet had been divided among Britain, Russia and America were scuttled by the Allies in accordance with the decision of the Berlin Conference held in July 1945. The 6,000-ton cruiser Leipzig (1) is seen at sea for the last time. She foundered within four minutes of being blasted by explosions (2) in the North Sea, off Wilhelmshaven, in July 1946. In the previous April destroyers were dealt with in similar manner; one of the Narvik class settles on her side before going down (3). See also page 73, Vol. 9.

UNCOMPLETED U-BOATS in the Blohm and Voss shipyards at Hamburg were included in the Allied elimination plan. One is seen (4) after Royal Navy demolition parties had commenced to reduce the hull to scrap. A German landing craft (5) has been converted into a floating cinema for British naval personnel stationed at Kiel. See also pages 552, 584, Vol. 9.

Photos, British Official

The Truth About Lidice

By JOHN FORTINBRAS

who obtained from the Czech delegation at the Nuremberg trial information which enabled him to record the full account of this terrible Nazi crime of 1942.

ONCE a sizeable, peaceful Czech village in Bohemia, Lidice belongs now to history. It is not a village any more—nothing but a flat, sightless memorial to a nation's shame. Never, so long as written record endures, will the darkness associated with its name be forgotten. On May 26, 1942, the Deputy Reich Protector, S.S. Obergruppenfuehrer, Reinhard Heydrich, "Butcher Heydrich," as he was more deservedly known because of his regime of murder, was waylaid by Czech patriots. Theirs was a long-premeditated plot to rid their country of this evil man. As they fired at him Heydrich slumped forward in his car, struck by a revolver bullet in the chest ; a grenade splinter also hit him. Mortally wounded, he died eight days later.

Immediately following this assassination of one of their Party leaders, the Nazis launched a great cry for vengeance. Hitler, in a personal telephone call to Dr. Karl Hermann Frank, State Secretary to the Reich, Protector of Bohemia and Moravia, demanded at once the execution of 30,000 to 40,000 Czech citizens ; and since they were to be disposed of through the "Standgerichte," law courts only in name, Hitler's order was tantamount to condemning them to death without trial.

How Lidice Caught the Nazis' Eye

Frank, since executed by a Czech war crimes court, testified that he, by a personal interview with Hitler, had this order withdrawn. But other measures, scarcely less horrifying, were introduced and pursued with Nazi thoroughness. Ordinances were published condemning to death not simply the patriots responsible but all who might shelter them, might harbour knowledge of their whereabouts or hold any clue whatsoever to their identity or existence. Moreover, the entire families of such "accomplices" would, it was ordered, suffer a like punishment. Immense rewards were offered to informers.

But, thanks to Czech loyalty and the common hatred of their oppressors, no trace of the perpetrators was disclosed ; not the tiniest clue, though very many people, especially in Prague, knew their secrets.

Fanatically, the Gestapo hunted for evidence, finally for scapegoats. Then, fortuitously, its agents intercepted a postcard in the Czech civil post, in which the writer suggested that perhaps in Lidice was a man who could tell a thing or two about the Heydrich case. Not more than that. A mere "perhaps." And, as later evidence showed, this suggestion was utterly unfounded, a remark put down in innocence and without any malice. But Lidice thus caught the Nazis' eye.

One further reason added to this unwelcome prominence. The Nazis, according to their secret lists of Czech resistance members, knew that three members of a family in Lidice had escaped to England, and were serving, in our country, with the Czech Armoured Brigade. It was enough. Through the direction of Dr. K. H. Frank a fearful retaliation was ordered. Lidice was to be razed to the ground and its male inhabitants exterminated. That was the order. And swiftly was it executed ruthlessly and in appalling manner.

ON June 9, 1942, six days after Heydrich's death, the reprisal plan was launched. S.S. men, filling ten large Wehrmacht lorries, arrived from Slany. At once they threw a cordon round the village. All inhabitants had to stand fast in their homes. No one must leave the village. Peasants with work to do there were passed through the cordon, and their return prevented.

Rumours, terrible rumours, passed from mouth to mouth inside the village. They merged quickly enough into realities. A woman tried to break the cordon. As she ran, an S.S. man hit her with a bullet in her back. Some weeks later, during harvest time, neighbouring villagers found her body in a cornfield. A 12-year-old boy also bolted. He too was shot dead as he fled.

Then, with the cordon secure, and all means of communication with the outer world denied, the Gestapo acted. They locked the women and children in the village school. They locked and guarded the male inhabitants in the cellars, barns and stables of the Horak farm. They searched every house, but found not even a scrap of incriminating evidence. In the Horak farm, a remarkable atmosphere of spiritual calm prevailed. Each man, some of them boys, knew he was going to die. And perhaps not die easily. In their midst moved a patriarchal figure, the 73-year-old Priest Sternbeck. All night he prayed for the souls of these humble and innocent villagers. They knelt with him, a doomed defenceless company. Morning came—the morning of June 10, 1942—the last day in the life of Lidice. A firing squad, 30 strong, of Ordnungspolizei reported from Prague at 03.30 hours. Shortly after it was daybreak they began their foul task. S.S. Hauptsturmfuehrer Weismann first addressed them. "It is the will of the Fuehrer which you are about to execute," he said. They were warned under peril of death not to disclose the fate of any human being at Lidice, not to disclose that they themselves had ever heard of the village. Among these executioners may have been some who felt a spark of pity, but they gave no sign of it.

In tens the men of the village were led out from the Horak farm to the garden behind the barn. Here, their executioners waited for them. The killings went on intermittently until 4 p.m. At one period Dr. K. H. Frank arrived in full uniform, just to see how smoothly his orders were being carried out. According to evidence given at his trial four years later, he expressed the desire that "corn should grow where Lidice stood."

Photographed Beside the Bodies

As the light was clear—it was a serene June afternoon—and several Germans had cameras, the executioners let themselves be photographed in groups beside the bodies of their victims. Some, but not all, were proud to be snapped in these circumstances. From these prints, some of which have passed into the possession of the Czech Government, two facts emerge. One, the extreme youth of several members of the execution squad. One or two could not have been over 16 years. Secondly, the pictures testify to careful preliminary arrangements, such as the stacking

ARRAIGNED before the People's Court at Prague, Czechoslovakia, Dr. Karl Hermann Frank (centre) stood trial in 1946 accused of the Lidice massacre in which thousands of Czechs were involved. Found guilty, he was hanged before 5,000 people on May 22, 1946. *Photo, Keystone*

of large piles of straw against the barn wall to prevent bullets rebounding or ricochetting.

Next day Jewish slave labourers from Terezin came to bury the massacred. They dug a large communal pit near the execution scene, piled the bodies into it, some indiscriminately, others head to toe, poured quicklime over them, and finally covered the pit with boarding. Altogether this grave, designed to be unknown and unrecorded, all Christian rites being deliberately denied it, received 172 men and boys aged 16 and upwards.

Those inhabitants with the seeming good luck to be working outside Lidice on these terrible days did not escape. From the collieries at Kladno, an adjacent mining village, the Gestapo seized another 19 male members of Lidice families, drove them to Prague, and there executed them. Seven Lidice women perished with them.

Germans Filmed the Obliteration

A fate different, though in some respects more horrible, befell the remaining women and children of Lidice. The 195 women and girls herded into the schoolroom were deported to Ravensbruck Concentration Camp, a Vernichtungslager or death camp. There, 42 of them died from ill treatment and misuse ; seven others were gassed and three declared missing. Four of these women, being expectant mothers, were first sent to a maternity home at Prague. It is believed that their children were murdered. The mothers, later removed to Ravensbruck, never saw them after birth. Two or three other Lidice women bore children in Ravensbruck KL (Konzentrationlager). Those children, it is certain, were murdered almost immediately after their birth.

Then the children proper of Lidice were all torn from their mothers—90 to go to Lodz in Poland, after which they were transferred to Gneisenau KL in Wartheland. Other Lidice children, the very youngest of those shut up in the schoolroom, were sent for special examination by " racial physicians " to the German children's hospital in Prague. Their blood was evidently deemed good, of " Herrenvolk " quality. They were then deported to Germany, renamed with German names. Only the merest handful of these children have been traced since the end of the war.

It was not enough, for Nazi conceptions of vengeance, to kill and scatter the people. The village itself had to be erased. Already, whilst the massacre was continuing, Lidice began burning. Systematically, beginning with the home of the family Hlim, situated on the road to Hestoun, the Nazis placed canisters of oil and other inflammable materials, straw in the case of farm-houses, inside shops and simple peasant dwellings, and fired them, until the whole main street was ablaze.

As Lidice blazed and smoked, a German film unit, commanded by Dr. Franz Treml, photographed each phase of the obliteration. I saw his film, a testament in itself of crime, at the Nuremberg Courthouse, when the Russian Prosecution presented it as evidence of Nazi mass destruction of villages. It is a vivid documentary, and in contrast to burning village shops, with black oil-smoke sprouting from their windows, crumbling and erupting walls, destroyed implements and dead animals one sees groups of smartly dressed S.S. officers, studying the ruins with their field glasses, and joking together, as the village collapses in smoke and flame.

Pitiful Field of Hidden Skulls

Still the destruction went on. On June 12, explosive charges were sunk beside the foundations of St. Martin's, the village's ancient little church. Once again the Gestapo drove in from Kladno to observe their policy of obliteration in action. Under their eyes the church was shattered. The whole village lay mute, shattered, a single heap of rubble. Todt labour squads, nearly all their personnel conscripted natives, carted away the rubble for road making. The village became a waste, a field of hidden skulls.

Although many other villages in Eastern Europe, including hundreds of Soviet villages, shared the scorched earth fate of Lidice, their inhabitants in some cases being submitted to worse penalties, there is only one Lidice, only one name in Europe to symbolize mass murder of an entire community.

BESIDE THE COMMUNAL GRAVE AT LIDICE crowds gathered on June 9, 1946, to pay homage and to witness a moving ceremony on the fourth anniversary of the massacre of 1942. The grave and the cross, erected by the Russians, are all that remain to mark the scene where the mining village once stood ; many of its houses straddled the hill in the background. Whilst the male population were executed, women and children were deported to concentration camps, where many succumbed. See also illus. page 184, Vol. 9. PAGE 356 *Photo, Associated Press*

Airmen Heroes at Honoured Peace in Denmark

AT SHARRILD IN WEST JUTLAND, on August 27, 1946, a memorial stone was unveiled to seven R.A.F. men—members of the crew of a Lancaster bomber shot down by German fighters on August 27, 1944. Near to one of the airscrews (top) of the crashed Lancaster, the memorial stone set in the wall (bottom) is inscribed in English "To seven British Fliers who gave their lives for their country and for us. May they rest in Peace." Among those attending the ceremony were relatives from Great Britain and Canada. PAGE 357 *Photos, Keyston:*

British Schoolchildren at Scene of Arnhem Epic

VISITING HOLLAND for a two-weeks' stay, under the auspices of the World Friendship Association, 250 schoolchildren from London were officially welcomed by the Mayor of Arnhem on July 29, 1946, and attended a ceremony in the airborne troops' cemetery the following day. A wreath bearing the inscription " For those who died for Freedom " was laid by a boy and girl at the foot of the flagstaff (1). A tour of the battlefield, still bearing traces of the Allied airborne forces' struggle in September 1944, included a visit to Wolfheze, where a dump of wrecked gliders was inspected (2). Overlooking the Rhine, the children were shown where remnants of the airborne troops succeeded in withdrawing across the river (3).

On September 17, 1946, second anniversary of the landings, relatives of British troops who fell in the battle and officers and men who fought in it made the first official pilgrimage to the town and cemetery. See also pages 461-466, Vol. 9.

Photos, Associated Press

World Food Conference Staged at Copenhagen

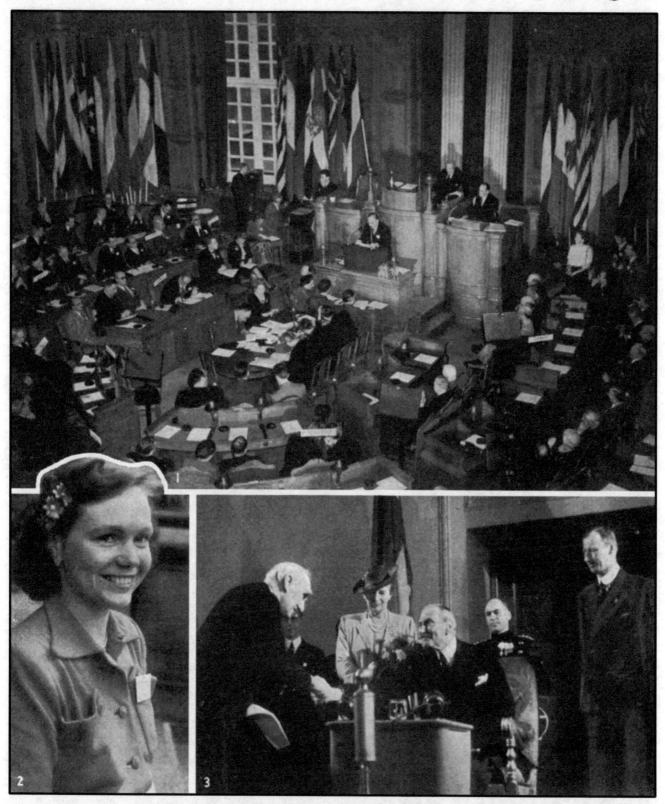

Photos, Associated Press, Keyston

IN THE CHRISTIANBORG PALACE, Copenhagen, seat of the Danish Government, on September 2, 1946, the World Food Conference of the United Nations' Food and Agriculture Organization (F.A.O.) was opened in the presence of members of the Danish Royal family and 700 delegates of the 42 member-nations of the F.A.O., the flags of which draped the hall in which the Conference is seen in session (1). To assist delegates to follow the discussions, carried out in multiple languages, interpreters were employed, each wearing a flower of a predetermined colour to denote a particular language : this interpreter (2) speaks French, English and Danish. Sir John Boyd Orr, Director-General of the F.A.O. (3, left), was received by King Christian of Denmark (seated) on whose right is Queen Alexandrine ; on King Christian's left is Prince Knud, their second son. This Conference, the second session of the F.A.O. (the first was at its inauguration in Quebec, in October 1945), is not concerned with the present world food situation, but mainly with proposals put forward by Sir John

Boyd Orr for a World Food Board designed to overcome existing difficulties, universally encountered, between food producers and consumers. The acceptance of the proposals will be tantamount to internationalizing finance for equitable supply of world agricultural produce ; the disposal of surpluses to the countries in special need ; the retaining of sufficient stocks to overcome crop failures ; and the stabilizing of agriculture prices.

At the first plenary session Herr Henrik Kauffmann, Danish Minister to Washington, was elected Chairman of the Conference. Of the non-member States applying for admission to the Organization, Portugal, Eire, Switzerland and Italy were elected, Spain being refused on technical grounds. Russia was not represented ; but, although a non-member, she can exercise right to admission without formal application by virtue of having taken an active part in the preliminary discussions at Hot Springs, U.S.A., in 1943.

De Gaulle at Ile de Seine to Keep a Promise

VISITING the Ile de Seine, off the Brittany coast, on August 31, 1946, General de Gaulle kept a promise, made in 1945 while touring Brittany, to a group of men from the island who had seen service with the Royal Navy during the Battle of the Atlantic. This gesture by the General was also an appreciation of the fortitude shown by the islanders during the German occupation from 1940 until 1945.

Receiving an enthusiastic welcome the General chatted with the children (1). A word or two with the sailors (2), all of whom had seen service in the Free French Navy, recalled that 130 able-bodied male inhabitants of the island rallied to the General's call to the French Nation to fight on—made from London after the surrender of France in 1940 (see illus. page 201). Sailing to England in fishing craft these men were absorbed into the Royal and Free French Navies. Touring the island General de Gaulle, led by the Mayor, M. Marzin (3, left), and followed by Mme. de Gaulle (right) passed under an arch of lobster pots and tackle.

Almost devoid of vegetation and mainly consisting of flat rock surface, the Ile de Seine is inhabited by Breton-speaking people whose sole industry is fishing. The island's telephone communication was severed by the Germans, who also destroyed the power-house, the only source of lighting, and of gas, as reprisal for the non-collaborationist attitude adopted by the people.

Photos, I.N.P., Associated Press

Royal Navy Lays Up Historic Flags at Portsmouth

FLOWN AT TWO FAMOUS SURRENDERS, a white ensign and a Vice-Admiral's flag were ceremoniously laid up by Vice-Admiral L. V. Morgan, at St. Ann's Church, Portsmouth, on September 1, 1946. The white ensign was flown at St. Germain-en-Laye, headquarters of Admiral Sir Harold Burrough, Allied Naval Commander, when the German forces surrendered on May 7, 1945. The flag of Vice-Admiral (now Admiral) Sir A. Willis was flown at the surrender of the Italian Fleet in September 1943, and again at the signing of Armistice terms at Malta. *Photo, G.P.U.*

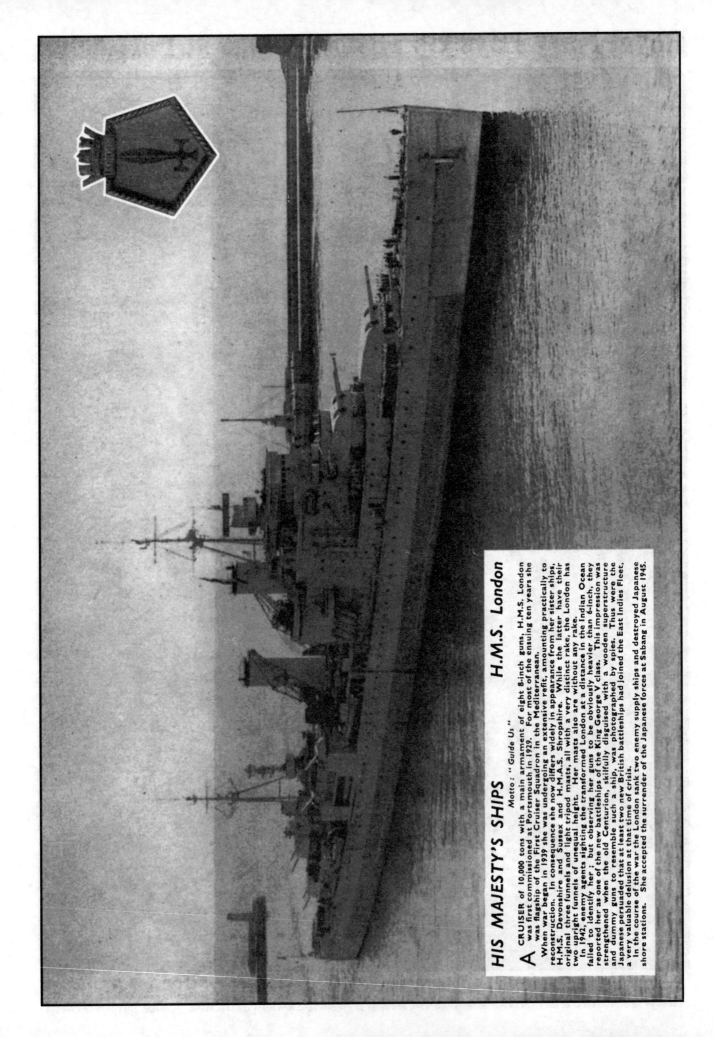

HIS MAJESTY'S SHIPS   H.M.S. London

Motto: "Guide Us"

A CRUISER of 10,000 tons with a main armament of eight 8-inch guns, H.M.S. London was first commissioned at Portsmouth in 1929. For most of the ensuing ten years she was flagship of the First Cruiser Squadron in the Mediterranean.

When war began in 1939 she was undergoing an extensive refit, amounting practically to reconstruction. In consequence she now differs widely in appearance from her sister ships, H.M.S. Devonshire and Sussex and H.M.A.S. Shropshire. While the latter have their original three funnels and light tripod masts, all with a very distinct rake, the London has two upright funnels of unequal height. Her masts also are without any rake.

In 1942, enemy agents sighting the transformed London at a distance in the Indian Ocean failed to identify her; but observing her guns to be obviously heavier than 6-inch, they reported her as one of the new battleships of the King George V. class. This impression was strengthened when the old Centurion, skilfully disguised with a wooden superstructure and dummy guns to resemble such a ship, was photographed by spies. Thus were the Japanese persuaded that at least two new British battleships had joined the East Indies Fleet, a very valuable delusion at that time of crisis.

In the course of the war the London sank two enemy supply ships and destroyed Japanese shore stations. She accepted the surrender of the Japanese forces at Sabang in August 1945.

The Irish Guards

By Major
D. J. L. FITZGERALD, M.C.

I N September 1939 His Majesty's Fourth Regiment of Irish Footguards—the " Micks "—consisted of two Battalions, the 1st, which had not long returned from service in Egypt and Palestine, and the 2nd, which had only just been re-formed. The 2nd Battalion had been raised during the First Great War, and then disbanded after a short, glorious and bloody career. All ranks were, of course, volunteers, the great majority of them Irishmen, with a valuable leavening of Englishmen. Volunteers from Eire continued to flow in steadily ; but as the war years and the casualty lists grew longer more and more Englishmen were drafted into the Regiment. These men, who came mainly from London, Liverpool and Lancashire, made fine fighting Irish Guardsmen.

On April 9, 1940, the Germans invaded Norway. Within a week the 1st Battalion, equipped for an Arctic campaign, landed in Northern Norway. The Norwegian Expedition was doomed from the start. The Germans had overwhelming superiority in troops, guns and tanks Most important of all they had complete air supremacy, which, as there was no real darkness, they were able to exploit all twenty-four hours of the day. The Battalion slowly closed in on the Germans in Narvik, trudging through the snow, or sailing from fjord to fjord in fishing boats—always being bombed. The Allied evacuation of Southern Norway left the road to the North unguarded, so the Battalion embarked on the liner H. M. T. Chobry to take up a defensive position 200 miles south.

At midnight on May 14-15, 1940, the Chobry was bombed. Direct hits killed or wounded all the senior officers and set the ship on fire. The Companies filed up from the troop decks and paraded on the promenade deck. On a sinking ship, loaded with tons of ammunition, burning in the Arctic Ocean, they waited quietly for the escort vessels, H.M.S. Wolverine and H.M.S. Stork. " There has been nothing like it since the Birkenhead," said the naval Commodore. The Battalion refitted as best they could and were again shipped south, to fight a delaying action against a German mountain division. At the beginning of June they were evacuated from Norway to England.

M EANWHILE, the 2nd Battalion had made two week-end trips on the Continent. The first was to the Hook of Holland, where they covered the evacuation of Queen Wilhelmina and the Netherlands Government. The second was in the last stages of the Battle of France, when the Germans were closing in on the Channel ports. The 2nd Battalion, with the 2nd Battalion Welsh Guards, was shipped to Boulogne, to hold the town as long as possible. The Battalion marched up through a sorry stream of stragglers and dug in round the outskirts of Boulogne. The German tanks could have driven straight on to the quays. The Battalion had no anti-tank mines, and the bullets from the anti-tank rifles bounced off the armour, but they shot any unwary tank commanders.

The Germans hesitated and then brought up their infantry to clear the town. During the night and following day the Battalion beat off a series of attacks. The perimeter, however, was gradually tightening, as first one company and another was ordered to close on the harbour. Finally, when the docks had been destroyed and every possible man evacuated, the Battalion itself embarked. In the following years the 2nd Battalion

R AISED in 1900 to commemorate the bravery shown by the Irish Regiments in the South African War, Irish Guards Mounted Infantry fought in the last years of that campaign, 1901 and 1902. The Irish Guards stood as a battalion for the first time in the line of battle on August 23, 1914, occupying trenches between Mons and Binche ; two days later they were street-fighting at Landrecies. The Regiment continued to distinguish itself throughout the First Great War.

〜〜〜〜〜

changed over to armour and a 3rd Battalion was raised. Both these were in the Guards Armoured Division, the 2nd in the Armoured and the 3rd in the Infantry Brigade.

FIELD-MARSHAL THE EARL OF CAVAN, late Colonel of the Regiment (died August 28, 1946), talked to a sergeant of the 2nd Armoured Battalion, at Fonthill Gifford, Wiltshire, on May 12, 1942. *Photo, British Official*

The 1st Battalion remained in the 24th Guards Brigade, and landed in North Africa early in March 1943. They went straight into the line by Medjez-el-Bab. After a month of fighting and small advances from hill to hill all was ready for the final blow. The Djebel Bou Aoukas—the " Bou "—dominated the approaches to Tunis. It was essential that this feature should be taken and held, so that the massed Armoured Divisions could break through to the sea. The 1st Battalion attacked Points 212 and 214 on the Bou. The Divisional Commander wrote, " The relentless courage, the cheerful sacrifices and the great tenacity of the 24th Guards Brigade was outstanding, and indeed without it the victory of the 1st Army would never have been achieved. I think that the story of the Irish Guards on Hill 212 will always stand in red letters on the pages of that glorious Regiment's history."

The Battalion had to move up to the start line in broad daylight in full view of the enemy. They crossed a flat plain in open order, waist-deep in grass and wild flowers. Every German gun and mortar for miles around opened fire. All over the plain new sinister plants sprang up—rifles stuck in the ground with helmets on them, to mark the dead or wounded. The Battalion pressed on steadily. " We did not think anyone could cross that plain alive," said a German prisoner. " Thank God for drill ! " said a

Guardsman. By nightfall the hill was taken, and on it were gathered the remnants of four companies, 120 men. Next day came the inevitable counter-attack. The Battalion halted it and finished it off by a charge. They sprang from their shallow holes in the rocks and, shouting " Up the Micks ! " swept the Germans back down the hill. For three days the rapidly decreasing handful of men held the hill, beating off five major counter-attacks supported by tanks and armoured cars. They were isolated and often surrounded. Short of food, short of ammunition, very short of water, deprived of sleep, continually shelled and mortared, machine-gunned and sniped from all sides, with no aid for the wounded and no burial for the dead, these Irish Guardsmen showed a fixed determination to hold their position, for ever if need be. It is an honour to have served with such men.

O N this hill L/Cpl. J. P. Keneally won the V.C. for breaking up an enemy attack single-handed (portrait in page 286, Vol. 7). Lieut. Kennard won the D.S.O., and Sgt. Lynch, Sgt. Ashton and Guardsman Nicholson the D.C.M. " Your magnificent fight," wrote General Alexander, " has not only added fresh laurels to the name of the Regiment but has been of the utmost importance to our whole battle. I am immensely proud of you all."

In January 1944 the 1st Battalion landed at Anzio. The Germans reacted promptly ; they massed divisions and every gun they could lay their hands on. Guns of every kind, age and nationality concentrated on the forward Battalions at Carroceto. In one day the 1st Battalion had 90 casualties by shelling alone. In a night attack up the main Anzio-Albano road the Battalion fought their way through massed machine-guns and formed a narrow salient beyond the " Factory." They found their objective occupied by German tanks. Lieut. Bartlet played hide-and-seek with a Tiger tank beneath a railway bridge, sliding Hawkins grenades beneath its tracks almost as if he were dealing cards.

Fighting Strength Fell to 150

During the night of February 3-4, 1944, the Germans counter-attacked ; they flung three battalions against the company on the left flank. Brens and machine-guns caught the enemy silhouetted against burning farms and shot them down in swathes, but the Germans pressed on. By dawn the left flank company no longer existed and the two forward companies and Battalion H.Q. were cut off. The reserve company attacked forward and extricated its comrades. Part of Battalion H.Q. was actually captured, but, led by Capt. S. Combe, M.C., killed their captors and fought their way back. L/Cpl. Cross, usually a peaceful orderly room clerk, won the M.M. for his gallant and ferocious conduct. The Battalion was then plunged into a welter of bitter hand-to-hand fighting. The Germans continually shovelled in fresh troops to maintain the pressure on the beach-head.

For weeks the Battalion fought in caves, in open muddy fields and in waterlogged gullies. It was a savage, primitive, troglodyte existence. Exhausted men were crippled by exposure ; asleep in their slit trenches they did not notice the water seeping in. The fighting strength of the Battalion fell to about 150. Just as it was about to be relieved the Battalion was ordered to take over from a full-strength American battalion. They held a network of gullies in an open plain, isolated by day and dependent for supplies on fatigue parties by night. Every evening the message came up, " You must hold on." And not only did the Guards hold on, but they went over to the offensive.

They turned the gullies into a murderous maze in which men like Major Kennedy, M.C., Sgt. Gundel, D.C.M., Guardsman Montgomery, D.C.M., and Guardsman Adamson, D.C.M., hunted down Germans. The Battalion was eventually withdrawn from the beach-head, its fighting strength reduced to 80. Unlucky shells during the final hand-over killed two of the Regiment's finest soldiers, Sgt. Wylie, D.C.M., and L/Cpl. Moriarity, D.C.M. The 1st Battalion returned to England and, as a battalion, saw no more action, but most of the individual members went out as reinforcements to the 3rd Battalion in France and Holland.

Tank Warfare in the Choking Dust

The 2nd and 3rd Battalions landed in Normandy with the Guards Armoured Division. With two other Armoured Divisions they made the first attempt to break out of the bridge-head. Instead of the German ordnance workshops and mobile bath units they had been told to expect, they ran into a strong defensive screen supported by heavy tank battalions. It was a day of confused tank warfare, fought in the choking dust and waving corn round Cagny. Well-concealed 88s "brewed up" the Shermans as they came over the crest.

Lieut. Gorman, M.C., trundling up a lane, rounded a corner and found four German tanks having a conference. The leader, a Tiger, slowly traversed its massive gun. "Lead on!" shouted Lieut. Gorman to his driver, L/Cpl. Baron, M.M., and they rammed the Tiger. Both crews baled out,

shaking their fists at each other. Lieut. Gorman went back for a 17-pounder. He found one, its commander headless, its crew stunned, and with it finished off the Tiger.

The Guards Armoured Division then moved to Caumont and attacked south to intercept the Germans moving westward. The two Battalions fought their way separately through the "Bocage"—a country of small fields, banks, high hedges, sunken lanes and marshy streams. The Germans switched their best Panzer forces and struck savagely at the exposed flanks of the Division. They cut in behind the 2nd Battalion at La Marvindière, so that for days the trucks bringing up petrol and ammunition and evacuating the wounded had to run the gauntlet. At Sourdevalles the 3rd Battalion attacked down an exposed forward slope to cut the German's main lateral road. Spandaus on both flanks decimated the leading companies ; mortar bombs turned the fields of ripe corn into a swirl of flame and smoke ; but the Battalion pressed forward.

AFTER the rout of the Germans in Normandy the Battalions crossed the Seine and began their spectacular advance. Through cheering French crowds they raced to Brussels, which they entered just after dark. Deliriously happy Belgians crowded the streets to welcome their liberators. Men and women, old and young, showered flowers and fruit and kisses on the Guardsmen; swarms of them clambered on to the tanks, laughing and crying at once, and pouring champagne, brandy and ice cream all together into the outstretched mess-tins. The

Colours : White on Pale Blue with Black Border.

52nd (LOWLAND) DIVISION

RECRUITED from the Lowlands of Scotland, the 52nd Division, a Territorial Army formation, retained the White Cross of St. Andrew in a modified version of the sign worn by the Division in the First Great War ; the word "Mountain" was adopted after the Division had been assigned this special role. Drafted to France in June 1940, after Dunkirk, the Division provided a covering force for the remnants of the B.E.F., most of it returning from Cherbourg on June 18. After long training in Scotland for mountain warfare—earmarked for the prospective Allied re-entry into Norway—much of the Division's active service was, ironically, confined to the flat lands of the Low Countries.

On October 26, 1944, under command of the 1st Canadian Army, the 52nd landed at South Beveland, Holland, for Allied operations on Walcheren Island to clear the Scheldt Estuary and the approaches to Antwerp. Baarland was captured the same day, and Eleewoutsdijk on October 28. Oostelde, Litt, and St. Georges fell to the Division in its advance on Flushing, assaulted, with the 4 Commando, on November 1 and, after severe street fighting, captured on November 3.

RIDING on Buffaloes of the Royal Tank Regiment, men of the 52nd assisted in the capture of Middelburg, November 7. In January 1945 the Division's advance east of the Maas brought further successes ; Hongen was taken on January 18. Waldeucht on January 21, Leffeld on January 22 and Heinsberg two days later. At this juncture the 52nd had penetrated farther east than any other British unit and was the first British Division to set up a H.Q. on German soil.

In late February the Division was engaged in clearing the area between the Maas and the Rhine. Crossing the latter after the major Allied assault on March 23, a heavy engagement was fought north-east of the Dortmund-Ems Canal, and in early April the defences at Ibbenburen were penetrated. Bremen was the final objective of the Division, now in the British 2nd Army. By April 27 most of the city had fallen, and all resistance had ceased on April 28. After the German surrender, on May 5, the 52nd became an Occupational Force.

CAPTURED BY THE 1st BATTALION of The Irish Guards on Hill 212, in North Africa, German prisoners (above) are led from the British First Army's Medjez sector, April 29, 1943. In a hitherto unpublished photo (below) the same Battalion is parading with the British First Infantry Division at Hammamet, Tunisia, before marching past General Eisenhower on September 4, 1943.

Photos, British Official

The 'Micks' in Germany near their Journey's End

ENTRENCHED along the Hamburg-Bremen autobahn in April 1945 an Irish Guardsman (1, left), made full use of the natural facilities to effect a good camouflage; almost equally well concealed is one of the battalion's tanks (right background). A short time later the Regiment reached the Baltic coast, whence across the narrow waters lay Norway —scene of the 1st Battalion's landing five years earlier, to take part in the Allies' abortive campaign of 1940.

FREED on April 4, 1945, in Germany, men of the 2nd Battalion The Irish Guards who had been captured by the Germans exchanged handshakes with their liberators—bereted members of the 1st Battalion The Coldstream Guards (2). The 2nd Battalion of "the Micks" covered the evacuation of Queen Wilhelmina from the Hook of Holland in 1940, and took part in the defence of Boulogne. With the Guards Armoured Division it landed in Normandy, June 1944. Troops of the same Battalion in this hitherto unpublished photograph (3) enjoy a cigarette while brewing tea during a halt in their advance into Germany, April 8, 1945.

Photos, British Official

BAND OF THE IRISH GUARDS playing at Piedmonte, Italy, on April 29, 1944, celebrated its 150th performance given to Allied units while on tour of the 5th Army front. On this occasion the band, conducted by its leader Captain G. H. Wilcocks, M.B.E., entertained an appreciative audience of U.S. infantry and A.A. personnel. *Photo, British Official*

Germans made desperate efforts to establish a new line along one of the great water barriers. The two Battalions now working together as one " battle group " led the advance. They found the Escaut Canal strongly held but with one bridge still standing. Lieut. Lampard's troop and Lieut. Stanley-Clarke's platoon rushed the bridge, and in one wild gallop secured the bridgehead. From now on the bridge was known as " Joe's Bridge," after the C.O. of the 3rd Battalion, Lieut.-Col. J. O. E. Vandeleur.

Flat-Out up the Road to the Rhine

The Division lined up for " the greatest break-out in the history of warfare "—the Armoured Drive to link up with the airborne landings at Nijmegen and Arnhem. The country was flat, wooded and marshy, impossible going for tanks but ideal for defence. The Irish Guards Group led the break-out. Preceded by a rolling barrage and supported by rocket-firing Typhoons, they drove flat-out up the straight concrete road. " The enemy was in considerably greater strength than had been anticipated," says the official report, " and but for the magnificent fighting qualities of the breaking-out troops the junction with the airborne troops might well have been delayed for a number of days."

The first nine tanks were " brewed up " one after the other, but the 3rd Battalion infantry, riding on the following tanks, dismounted and eliminated the 88s. With the Irish and Grenadiers leading alternately, the Division reached the Lower Rhine opposite Arnhem. Their lifeline, the one road, was continually cut by German counter-attacks. For days they lived on rations drawn from a German dump as they fought to the front, both flanks and the rear. " That's right. Have a nice rest ! " shouted an airborne soldier from the truck carrying him back to safety. An Irish Guardsman looked up from a ditch at the man who was being evacuated down the road that Guardsmen had captured and were keeping open. " Get out of it," he replied. " We've been fighting since D-Day, not since last Friday ! "

The Irish Guards went on fighting till V Day. It was a wet, cold, dreary winter, with hard fighting at Hommersum, Goch and Cleves. In the spring they crossed the Rhine and battered their way through Hanover to cut off Bremen and Hamburg. (In this last advance Guardsman E. Charlton of the 2nd Battalion won another V.C. for the Regiment.) When an Irish Guardsman stood on the shores of the Baltic the Regiment had made a full circle : across the narrow sea lay Norway.

PURSUING THE ENEMY FROM THE CAEN SECTOR, on the Western Front, in July 1944, Irish Guards in this hitherto unpublished photograph (left) protected their eyes with goggles and their mouths with handkerchiefs against blinding and choking clouds of dust raised by the columns of vehicles. Advancing south of Caumont with the Guards Armoured Division, a " Mick " prepares to engage enemy tanks with his Piat (right) near St. Martin-des-Besaces, August 1, 1944. *Photos, British Official*

Venice as a News Centre for Our Troops

News-Hungry Servicemen Kept Abreast of Events

Staffed by various Servicemen whose jobs in civil life fitted them for the responsibility, Union Jack became the official First Army newspaper in March 1943. The Editor (1) at work in his office in Venice, where the paper is now produced for circulation to all the remaining troops in Italy, North Africa and Austria, is assisted by the Sports Editor (2) and Chief Sub-Editor (3). The Army signalman (4) displays one day's batch of news "tapes" in the radio room.

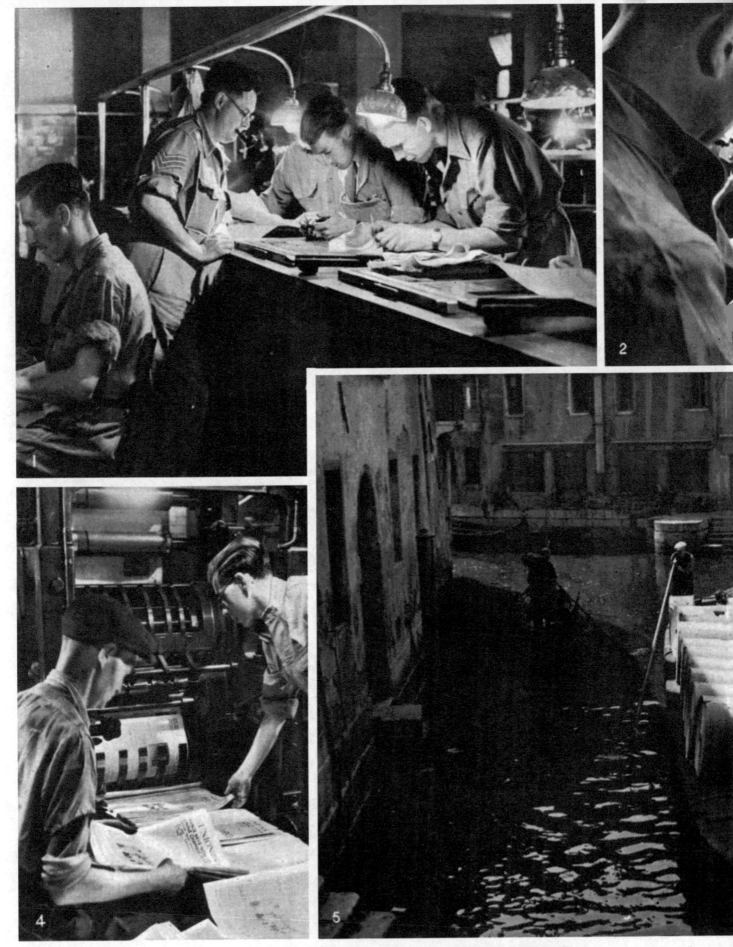

Here the Latest News Becomes the Printed Word—

Where the Germans once produced their services newspaper Nord Front, by the banks of the Grand Canal, Union Jack's offices hum with activity.   The Chief Sub-Editor (1, left) watches work on a set-up page, to form part of the printing-cylinder seen at (3), whilst a soldier linotype operator taps away in the bottom left corner.   Machine-setting type (2) is another soldier.
The printing-cylinder (3) is given finishing touches by an Italian under the supervision of a soldier machine-minder.

—On Paper Barge-Borne Down the Grand Canal

The rotary presses, capable of turning out 30,000 copies an hour, are throbbing. The minder checks Union Jacks as they come off the machine (4), his Italian assistant removing them for bundling and packing. Loaded with newsprint for the next edition, a barge is poled down the Grand Canal (5) to the offices, where Italians are waiting to roll the huge reels (6) into the warehouse in the building which Union Jack shares with the Venetian newspaper Il Gazzetino.

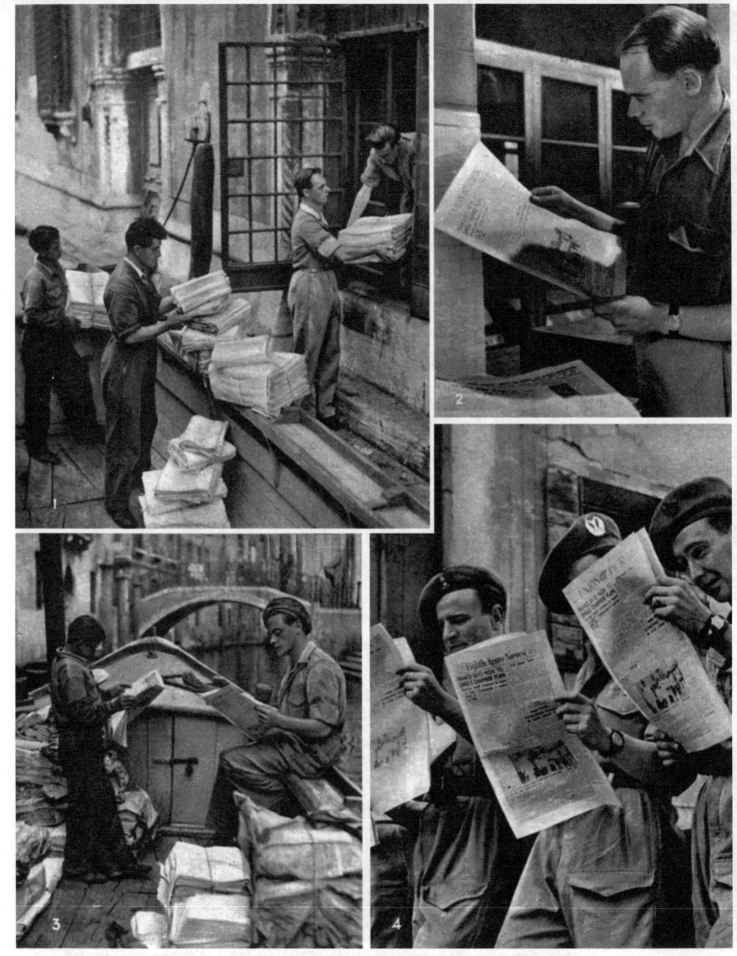

Over an Italy-Wide Network 'U.J.' Starts Out

Bundles of Union Jacks are passed out to a barge (1). The circulation officer (2) casts an appraising eye over the editorial and production department's efforts. In charge of distribution, a soldier (3) accompanies a consignment up the Grand Canal; the young Italian will sell copies, at four lire each, in Venice. Obviously it's good tidings today (4). Eighth Army News, which the boys have received with their Union Jacks, ceased publication in June 1946 after a run of nearly five years.

Montgomery's Strategy of Victory

THE Field-Marshal writes his report as a subordinate commander in an Allied team. In consequence, he studiously refrains from any expression of personal views which might be at variance with those already expressed by his Supreme Commander (see page 211). Properly, he limits himself to a bald and factual account During the period June 6 to September 1, 1944, while he was overall land force commander, his account deals with the Anglo-United States operation as a whole. After Sept. 1 he limits himself almost wholly to the doings of 21 Army Group. Certain passages stand out as of absorbing interest. For instance, if further proof were needed of the complete success with which Field-Marshal Montgomery discharged his responsibilities as overall land force commander in the beachhead, we should find that proof here :

"Once ashore and firmly established, my plan was to threaten to break out on the eastern flank—that is, in the Caen sector ; by this threat to draw the main enemy reserves into that sector, to fight them there and keep them there, using the British and Canadian armies for the purpose. Having got the main enemy reserves committed on the eastern flank, my plan was to make the break-out on the western flank, using for this task the American armies under Gen. Bradley, and pivoting on Caen ; this attack was to be delivered southwards down to the Loire and then to proceed eastwards in a wide sweep up to the Seine about Paris.

Operations Developed as Planned

"This general plan was given out by me to the general officers of the field armies in London on April 7, 1944. The operations developed in June, July and August, exactly as planned ; I had given D+90 as a target date for being lined up on the Seine ; actually the first crossing of the river was made on D+75. While I had in my mind the necessity to reach the Seine and the Loire by D+90, the interim estimates of progress could not, I felt, have any degree of reality. The predictions were particularly complicated by two major divergent requirements. On the one hand the general strategic plan was to make the break-out on the western flank, pivoting the front on to the Caen area, where the bulk of enemy reserves were to be engaged ; on the other hand, the Air Force insisted on the importance of capturing quickly the good airfield country south-east of Caen.

"Though I have never failed in my operations to exert my utmost endeavour to meet the requirements of the Air Forces in planning these operations, the overriding requirement was to gain territory in the west. In planning to break out from the bridge-head on the western flank, a prerequisite was the retention of the main enemy strength on the eastern flank. The extent to which this was achieved is well illustrated in the following table, which shows the estimated enemy strength opposing us in the eastern and western areas of our front during June and July."

FIELD-MARSHAL Viscount Montgomery's official account of the operations in North-West Europe from the Normandy landings to the unconditional surrender of Germany was published on September 4, 1946, as a supplement to the London Gazette. His record covers the period from June 6, 1944, to May 5, 1945. Lieut.-Gen. H. G. Martin, Military Correspondent of The Daily Telegraph (from which this condensation is given), comments on outstanding passages in the Report.

20, 1944, Gen. Eisenhower, the Supreme Commander, had put Field-Marshal Montgomery in command of the United States First and Ninth Armies north of the German salient. Field-Marshal Montgomery explains :

"On the 19th I ordered Gen. Dempsey to move XXX Corps west of the Meuse to a general line from Liége to Louvain, with patrols forward along the western bank of the river between Liége itself and Dinant. This corps was thus suitably placed to prevent the enemy crossing the river, and could cover the routes from the south-east leading into Brussels.

"It subsequently became necessary in connexion with the regrouping of American First Army to send some British divisions east of the Meuse. But throughout the battle I was anxious to avoid committing British forces more than was necessary. Had they become involved in large numbers an acute administrative problem would have resulted from their lines of communication crossing the axis of the two American armies. The battle of the Ardennes was won primarily by the staunch fighting qualities of the American soldier."

The dispatch serves also to rebut those who decry Field-Marshal Montgomery's carefully-staged crossing of the Rhine on the ground that this ponderous operation had already been preceded by improvised crossings on the United States First and Third Army fronts. Field-Marshal Montgomery had to cross that sector of the Rhine which gave direct access to Germany's vitals. Therefore he had to be prepared for maximal resistance. So he had started to plan his crossing six months before and had begun his actual preparations as early as December 1944. In consequence, on March 23 :

"Twenty-first Army Group launched the operation for crossing the Rhine a fortnight after completion of the battle of the Rhineland." The crossing succeeded. "We were now in a position to drive into the plains of Northern Germany. It was a matter of great satisfaction to see how plans which had been maturing back on the Seine were reaching their fulfilment."

That the Americans had been able to establish crossings on less vital fronts some days earlier was due to their dash and initiative in exploiting gross German errors.

It is the "Review and Comments" with which Field-Marshal Montgomery concludes his dispatch that is perhaps its most individual feature. Justly, he gives pride of place to administration, which is ever the foundation of our military success. Of the Normandy landing he says : "The task was a formidable one, and in plain terms, meant the export overseas of a community the size of the population of

Birmingham. Over 287,000 men and 37,000 vehicles were pre-loaded into ships and landing craft prior to the assault, and in the first 30 days 1,100,000 British and American troops were put ashore."

Next, he describes the administrative problem presented by the break-out across the Seine, which stretched his lines of communication 400 miles from Bayeux to Antwerp :

"This meant eating into the reserves built up in the Rear Maintenance Area, and it became a matter of urgency to get bases farther forward and shorten the lines of communication."

There were engineer tanks that could place or project charges to blow up sea walls ; there were other tanks that could launch bridges for the crossing of anti-tank ditches ; there were mat-laying tanks, amphibious tanks to lead the assault, flail tanks for mine-clearing, flame-throwing tanks, which were "outstandingly successful," and "saved us many lives." There were amphibious assault craft, too, for carrying infantry and light vehicles ; these made operations practicable over the flooded areas between Maas and Rhine. There were also armoured infantry carriers, "Kangaroos," which "enabled infantry to be transported across bullet-swept zones to arrive fresh at the vital part of the battlefield." Of more normal combat tanks Field-Marshal Montgomery has this to say :

"The capital tank must be a weapon of universal application, suitable not only for working with the infantry in the attack and in the dog-fight battle, but also capable of operating in the spearheads of the armoured division in pursuit. I am convinced, as a result of experience from Alamein to the Baltic, that it is fundamentally unsound to aim at producing one type of tank for co-operation with the infantry and another for the armoured division. We require one tank which will do both jobs."

Great Burden Borne by Infantry

That Field-Marshal Montgomery has here propounded an admirable ideal none will question. But there will be few users ready to agree that this ideal was attained by our "capital" tanks, Shermans and Cromwells, of the late war. Of the gunners Field-Marshal Montgomery has this to say :

"I doubt if the artillery has ever been so efficient as it is today. It has been found that a large number of small shells over a given time produces a greater effect on the enemy than the same weight of larger shells." Of the infantry, the Field-Marshal tells us :

". . . Although the infantryman may motor into battle, his training must keep him hard and tough, a point which must never be overlooked in these days of troop-carrying transport. It has again been the infantry who suffered the heaviest casualties. I cannot praise too highly the stamina and persistence displayed in the campaign."

The doctors, we learn, were ready to lay 15 to 1 against the death of any man who had got into their hands, no matter what his injury might be. Only one man died out of every three wounded in the stomach, as opposed to two out of three in 1914-18. Field-Marshal Montgomery concludes with this remark on morale :

"Without high morale no success can be achieved. . . . And the surest way to obtain it [morale] is by success in battle." In other words, morale spells success ; success spells morale.

Let us thank Providence, then, for a Montgomery who knew so well how to achieve morale and how to win success. But let us also pay a tribute to those whose high morale preserved us in the days before success had yet alighted on the Allied banners.

	Estimated Enemy Strength Opposite Caumont-Cotentin Sectors.			Estimated Enemy Strength Opposite Caumont-Caen Sectors.		
	Panzer Divisions.	Tanks.	Infantry Battalions.	Panzer Divisions.	Tanks.	Infantry Battalions.
June 15 ...	—	70	63	4	520	43
June 25 ...	1	190	87	5	530	49
June 30 ...	½	140	63	7½	725	64
July 5 ...	½	215	63	7½	690	64
July 10 ...	2	190	72	6	610	65
July 15 ...	2	190	78	6	630	68
July 20 ...	3	190	82	5	560	71
July 25 ...	2	190	85	6	645	92

Again, we have a complete answer to the criticism that, during Rundstedt's Ardennes offensive, 21 Army Group stood by when they should have played an active part. On Dec.

Europe's Wartime Capitals in 1946

LUXEMBURG

By HENRY BAERLEIN

After traversing the Belgian Ardennes, with their pine-clad heights, their rivers winding through the greenest of pastures and the ruins of Rundstedt's final offensive—now in course of repair—your train crosses the frontier into the Grand Duchy of Luxemburg. It stops for ten minutes at Kleinbettingen, not in order to trouble passengers with an examination of their luggage and passports—in my case this was performed by a smiling official who hurriedly walked through the train—but so that one may visit the refreshment room and drink a few glasses of corn brandy or of the more potent *quetch*, the national concoction of prunes and alcohol.

Before you have lost the feeling of exhilaration thus engendered you are in Luxemburg city, the Grand Duchy's capital. Walking from the station up the broad, tree-lined boulevard towards the centre of the town you may be overtaken by one of the two " toy " trains that, with a good deal of smoke and ringing of bells, go on their way to Echternach and to the spa of Monsdorf. These little trains are known as Jeangly and Charley—the names of the Heir-Apparent and of his younger brother being Jean and Charles respectively. Prince Jean, by the way, was educated at Ampleforth College, Yorkshire, and served in the ranks of the Irish Guards before he obtained his commission.

Complete Destruction Was Averted

You would be fascinated by the shop windows of Luxemburg, with their wonderful displays at quite reasonable prices. The numerous confectioners have a variety of cakes to offer, the establishments dealing in leather goods are most attractive, and those which specialize in female adornment would soon be depleted by British women. Most lavish, too, are the grocers' windows. And the people in the streets have a very comfortable appearance.

" But," you will ask, " are there no signs of war in the city ? This little country was for more than four years in German hands ! " Well, we have reached the viaduct which, at a great height, crosses the abyss separating the newer from the more ancient parts of the city which crown the rocks and the formidable ramparts of the fortress that was demilitarized by international agreement in 1867. This viaduct, whose main arch of stone is the largest in Europe, was spared by the Nazis, but not because it is known as the Adolph Bridge (in honour of the Grand Duke who reigned from 1897 to 1905).

If Rundstedt's troops could have regained the capital from which they had—temporarily, as they thought—retired, it would no doubt have been as thoroughly destroyed as many of the other towns and villages of the Grand Duchy. But General Patton ordered the cooks and other non-combatants of his American 3rd Army to hold out at Echternach, some twenty miles away, and thus the capital was saved. Whereas Echternach's famous old church of St. Willibrord (who arrived there from Britain twelve centuries ago) is now so utterly ruined that the dancing processon of Whitsuntide will not, alas, be celebrated again for many years.

With two exceptions, no building in the capital was demolished by the Germans, because the Gauleiter, after promising to respect the State's independence, proclaimed its annexation to Germany. " You have the honour," he announced, " to defend this part of Germany's western border." The two exceptions were the synagogue, a beautiful building of which all Luxemburgers were proud, and the monument to those young men who in the First Great War fought in the Allied (mostly the French and the Belgian) armies. Nothing remains of this monument but a pile of stones, and there they will stay as an example of German " kultur."

The cheerfulness that one sees on the faces of the Luxemburgers does not mean that they are altogether happy. Of a total population of 300,000, one man in every ten was deported to labour in the mines or on the farms of Silesia, some to serve in the German army ; and if anyone deserted from the Wehrmacht his entire family would be deported. Many a man was concealed by the farmers at great risk to themselves, many slept for months in the forests or the vineyards of the Moselle. The windows of a corner house in the city are covered with photographs, each attached to a form with details of the man's life. These are the young men whose fate is not known, unlike that of the steel-workers of the south (Luxemburg is the seventh most important steel-producing country in the world), for on the day following the annexation these men went on strike, and many were shot.

The Society which endeavours to trace the young men who have disappeared is called Ons Jongen, which in the Luxemburg dialect means " Our Young Men." Before the war the two official languages were French and German ; now they are French and the dialect, which is the same as that spoken in Lorraine and the south-east of Belgium. One newspaper is printed exclusively in French, the others in a mixture of the two languages: They print the speeches in the Chamber as they are delivered, a deputy perhaps putting a question in the dialect and the Minister replying in French, or vice versa. (The tendency nowadays is to spell the name of the country Luxembourg, the form without the " o " having a German flavour.)

Before the war the Luxemburgers had, so to speak, their hearts turned to France and their reasoning to Belgium, because of the economic union. The war made them vividly conscious of their own individuality. This is personified by them in the dynasty. No house, no shop, no café is without a portrait of the Grand Duchess, of Prince Felix, her Consort, and of the Heir-Apparent. All the political parties, including the Communists, are equally attached to the royal

family. The story is told of a German who derisively pointed, during the Occupation, to a portrait of the Grand Duchess on the wall of a certain café. " That woman has fled to England," he said. " She is here," retorted the Luxemburger. " What nonsense you talk ! " scoffed the Nazi. " Will you bet ? " asked the Luxemburger. " A million to one," laughed the German. " You have lost," said the Luxemburger. " She is here, in all our hearts ! "

When she and her family returned with the victorious Allies she visited every town and village of the Grand Duchy. Everywhere she was received with the wildest enthusiasm. The B.B.C. had given her the opportunity to speak to her people from London, where she inaugurated the programme in the Luxemburg dialect ; and if an important speech was expected from her or from one of the five ministers who were with her in exile, the Germans would cut off the electric current so that only people with battery sets could listen-in. To counter this, the B.B.C. would change the time of the broadcast.

Luxury of Two Eggs for Breakfast

Two sentries in British battle-dress were to be seen in front of the Grand Ducal Palace, a not very beautiful building in 16th-century Spanish style, with many balconies and oriel windows. It stands right on the street, and on one of its walls is an ordinary name-plate which tells you that this is the Street of the Vegetable Market. What could be more democratic ? As a rule the Grand Duchess is driven about the country by one of her daughters in a simple two-seater, with no other car in attendance. Such is the democracy of Luxemburg that when it was arranged that every man should be entitled to 200 cigarettes a month and every woman to half as many, no exception was made where the nuns were concerned. If they, as is probable, are non-smokers, they are at liberty to dispose of their cigarettes as they may wish.

It would be difficult to find any other town of comparable size with such dignity as Luxemburg. Everything is done in the best of taste—as at the cathedral, where a modern choir was audaciously and successfully added to the Gothic nave. The confessionals in that church do not resound with stories of smuggling, as this industry is left to foreigners. Prices of textiles are higher in France than in the Grand Duchy, but the Luxemburgers do not possess the smuggling spirit. They are preoccupied in rebuilding their country.

Apart from the capital, hotels in the country have suffered greatly; but everything is done to attract the tourist. A foreigner has merely to sign a paper and give his passport number ; then he can have two eggs for his breakfast and meat at every meal.

In Rundstedt's 1944 offensive a third of the Grand Duchy was destroyed ; and Mr. Bech, the Foreign Minister, told me that his Government has put in a claim for the cession of a strip of Germany, not because this small strip, inhabited by only 10,000 persons, belonged to Luxemburg before it was ceded to Prussia by the Congress of Vienna in 1815, but as reparation. It will cause the rivers on Luxemburg's eastern frontier to be in her hands instead of being partly German.

" You will have the privilege to be Germans for evermore ! " said the Gauleiter in 1942. " We want to stay what we are," say the words of an old Luxemburg song. " You have the honour to defend this part of Germany's western border." The wheel has turned full circle, for now the enlarged Luxemburg army is participating in the Occupation of Germany.

FIRST POST-WAR GRAPE HARVEST is loaded alongside a Luxemburg vineyard, one of many in which citizens concealed themselves to escape deportation to Germany.
By courtesy of the Luxemburg Government

Luxemburg Recovering from Long Nazi Occupation

OLD AND NEW TOWNS built on the sides of two valleys form the city of Luxemburg, capital of the Grand Duchy and home of the Grand Duchess. Looking along the main street (1) leading to the Grand Ducal Palace, in the old town, the absence of war damage belies the ravages of war which swept a third of the country into devastation during Rundstedt's Ardennes offensive in December 1944. Luxemburg Cathedral (2, right), dedicated to the patron saint St. Consolatrix, is viewed from the new town across the Petrisse valley ; one of its twin towers damaged in the War is now repaired. Spanning the Alzette valley is Adolph Bridge, as it appears from the public gardens in the old town (3). The bridge is named in honour of the Grand Duke who reigned 1897 to 1905. See facing page.

Photos by courtesy of the Luxemburg Government

Housing the Homeless: New Types for the U.K.

ADOPTING THE "MONOLITHIC CONCRETE SYSTEM" on the London County Council Minerva estate, Bethnal Green, will mean completion of 233 flats in eight four-storied blocks by April 1947, eight months sooner than if orthodox methods had been used: an unfinished balcony side of one of the blocks (1). Imported from Sweden, wooden Houses (2) erected at Clydach, Breconshire, incorporate latest developments in labour-saving devices. Aluminium prefabricated houses, made at a converted aircraft factory, are transported in four sections to an estate at Cheltenham, Gloucestershire, where a kitchen section (3) is seen arriving; one of these houses was assembled in half an hour.

Photos, Topical Press, Fox

Britain's Food: Securing Our Vital Milk Supply

THE FLOW OF MILK FROM COW TO CONSUMER is shown in this drawing prepared by our artist Haworth with the assistance of the Milk Marketing Board. On up-to-date dairy farms the cows are milked by machinery (A), the yield from each animal being automatically recorded; data thus gained enables the farmer to select the best cows for breeding. The milk passes to the farm dairy (B) for cooling; if the farmer is one of the 60,000 producer-retailers he will bottle it and call on his customers (C). Otherwise it is taken in churns to the main road to await the Milk Marketing Board lorry which calls at the churn stand (D) to collect it for delivery to the creamery. On arrival at the modern creamery, which may be owned by the Board or by one of the distributing companies, the milk is tested for condition and weighed (E), then pumped to the pasteurization machine (F), where the temperature is raised to 162 degrees F. and maintained so for 15 seconds to eliminate bacteria and assist keeping-qualities. If not required immediately the milk is stored in a stainless steel insulated tank (G). The bottling machine (H) can fill and cap 1,500 bottles an hour, these being supplied to it automatically by the washing machine (J), which cleanses them thoroughly then discharges them on to the conveyor. Dried milk powder is made by "feeding" milk on to steam-heated rollers (K) moving in opposite directions; a fixed knife cuts the dried powder, which is then conveyed to a sifter and packed. Milk churns are sterilized by inversion over jets of steam (L).

The Roll of Honour
1939—1946

Pte. F. ADAMS
Royal Marines Band.
H.M.S. Hood.   24.5.41.
Age 23.   (Gillingham)

So great has been the response of readers to our invitation to submit portraits for our Roll of Honour that no more can now be accepted. But we have every hope of being able to publish all those so far received.

Pte. J. A. ALEXANDER
Cameron Highlanders.
Action : Tunisia.   6.4.43.
Age 23.   (Liverpool)

A/B R. E. ALLEN
Royal Navy.
Action : S.W. Burma. 13.7.45.
Age 20.   (Cardiff)

A/B. P. BAILEY
H.M.S. Lapwing.
Action : Arctic.   20.3.45.
Age 22.   (Londonderry)

Sgt. A. F. DAVIS
Duke of Cornwall's L.I.
Action : Arakan. 11.2..44.
Age 29.   (Bristol)

Cpl. H. N. DAVIS
Reconnaissance Corps.
In action : Caen. 28.7.44.
Age 20.   (Darwen)

A.C.I. F. DIXON
Royal Air Force.
H.M.S. Glorious.   8.6.40.
Age 19.   (Middleton)

P/O Eng. J. B. ELLIS
H.M.S. Gairsay.
In action : at sea. 3.8.44.
Age 26.   (Mirfield)

Marine J P. FARGHER
46th R.M. Commando
Action : Normandy. 25.8.44
Age 23. (Dalton-in-Furness)

Pte. H. FLOUNDERS
Durham Light Infantry.
In action : Italy. 5.1.44.
Age 28.   (W. Hartlepool)

Pte. J. E. FENNER
R.E.M.E.
D. w'ds : Sumatra. 1.3.42.
Age 22.   (Chelmsford)

Pte. S. GILBEY
2nd Cambridgeshire Regt.
Action : Malaya. 19.1.42.
Age 28.   (Soham)

Mus. E. GOYMER
R.N. School of Music.
Mediterranean.   31.3.41.
Age 19.   (Gosport)

Spr. I. W. GREEN
Bomb Disposal.
Nottingham.   14.7.41.
Age 26.   (Keswick)

Pte. T. J. GREEN
Dorsetshire Regiment.
Action : Normandy. 4.7.44
Age 33.   (London)

Pte. J. R. GUNTRIP
Queen's Royal Regiment.
Action : Berlicum. 22.10.44.
Age 19.   (London)

Flt/Sgt. E. A. HAWES
R.A.F.V.R.
S. Rhodesia.   9.6.45.
Age 21.   (Southend-on-Sea)

Pte. C. HUTCHISON
King's Own Royal Regt.
Action : Burma. 14.5.44.
Age 24.   (Herstmonceux)

Sgt. J. W. HYDE
Royal Air Force.
Action : Rutland. 4.12.42.
Age 20.   (London)

L/Cpl. F. IRELAND
Royal Welch Fusiliers
Action : Kohima. 6.5.44
Age 24.   (Haresfield)

L/Cpl. E. R. N. KENNY
3rd Bn. Irish Guards.
Action : Holland. Oct. '44.
Age 19.   (Clonaslee)

Pte. R. D. JONES
South Lancashire Regt.
Action : Holland. 2.1.45.
Age 18.   (Manchester)

A. A B W. LAX
H.M.S. Blean.
At sea.   11.12.42.
Age 31.   (Leeds)

Ppr. W. MACDONALD
5th Bn. Seaforth Hghldrs.
Action : Tripoli. 21.1.43.
Age 28.   (Thurso)

Pte. T. ODELL
1st Bn. London Scottish.
Action : Italy. 5.9.44.
Age 21.   (Hanwell)

Spr. D. OLDHAM
Royal Engineers.
Action : Tripoli. 2.3.43.
Age 23.   (Long Eaton)

Gdsmn. A. SCOTT
Grenadier Guards.
In action : Caen. 5.8.44.
Age 32.   (Oldham)

Dvr. F. H. RUSHTON
686 A.W. Coy. R.E.
Action : N. Africa. 25.2.44.
Age 32.   (Bucknall)

Pte. G. SAINSBURY
N. Staffordshire Regt.
Action : Anzio. 22.1.44.
Age 30.   (London)

A/B W. SEDDON
H.M.S. Orchis.
Off France.   21.8.44.
Age 20.   (Liverpool)

Pte. R. C. STANDING
2nd Bn. Devonshire Regt.
West Europe. 25.1.45.
Age 21.   (Horsham)

Pte. P. H. TAYLOR
Royal Warwickshire Regt.
Action : Normandy. 18.7.44.
Age 22.   (Stockton)

Cpl. J. H. A. WHEELER
2nd Special Air Service.
Bulford. 15.2.46.
Age 21.   (London)

Pte W. J. WHEELDON
7/9 The Royal Scots.
Action : Holland. 3.11.44.
Age 21.   (Coventry)

Tpr. A. W. WAIGHT
Royal Armoured Corps.
Action : W. Des. 28.11.41.
Age 28.   (Trowbridge)

Pte. A. WHITE
Pioneer Corps.
Action : Dunkirk. June'40.
Age 35.   (Kettering)

Sgt. J. C. WOODCOCK
59 Squadron, R.A.F.
Action : Lorient. 23.11.40.
Age 20.   (W. Ealing)

Cpl. J. WILSON
Argyll & S. Highlanders.
Action : Egypt. 10.12.40.
Age 24.   (Barnard Castle)

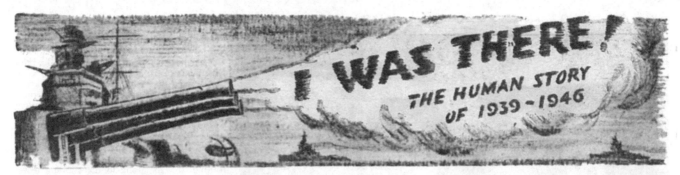

We Travelled to Malta by Submarine

For a short time when the siege of Malta was at its peak in 1941, surface craft were unable to reach the George Cross island with vital supplies. On what was believed to be the first occasion that a body of British soldiers was transported by submarine, H.M.S. Rorqual carried about 20 men to the island from Alexandria. Here George Arkell, formerly of the Royal Artillery, gives his impressions of this strange voyage.

ON Wednesday, June 4, 1941, I was at a Transit Camp at Amiraya, Egypt, when orders came through that we were on the move once again ; twenty of us had been picked for this and we were told that we were going to Malta by destroyer. After a roll-call parade and the usual hand-shakes to the boys who we believed would follow on, we boarded the wagons and headed for Alexandria, where we were taken by motor launch to a ship surrounded by five or six submarines. This was H.M.S. Medway (see page 221), parent ship to British submarines operating from Alexandria. From the sailors aboard we soon learned to our horror that we were to travel to Malta by submarine, and the craft—H.M.S. Rorqual—was pointed out to us. Looking at her, I felt thankful for one thing, anyway—seen beside the other submarines, the Rorqual loomed up like the Queen Mary does against a medium-sized merchant ship ! Thank goodness we weren't going in one of those small subs, I thought ; going in the Rorqual seemed bad enough. We had plenty of questions to fire at the under-water heroes, and after getting all the answers from the men of the Rorqual we finally settled down feeling a bit easier about the whole business. They told us pig-iron had been taken aboard for ballast, and the Rorqual had been out on a trial run.

After sleeping as well as we could that night—there was an air raid part of the time—we rose next morning to do a spot of work. More pig-iron was being loaded on board the Rorqual, as on her trial run out it was found that she could not dive quickly enough. We had the job of loading the pig-iron down the conning tower and laying it around wherever room could be found for it.

We Dive Into the Deep-Sea World

It was around 5 p.m. on the Thursday that hatches were closed, and we sailed out of the port of Alexandria. Unfortunately, from where I was below deck, I did not see Egypt from the after end of a ship, a sight many a Serviceman has enjoyed ! Excitement ran too high to think about that, and an officer of the ship came and gave us the gen of the trip. First of all we had to change our night into day, which meant that while we were submerged during the hours of daylight we had to sleep. This was, I imagined, to save as much oxygen as possible. We weren't to move to any part of the ship together in large groups, for reasons which we soon guessed. We were to make ourselves as comfortable as possible and sleep where we could. This most of us did in the torpedo-room with four torpedoes to keep us company and to use for pillows if we wanted.

It wasn't long after leaving port that I had my first scare. We were sitting around chatting among ourselves when suddenly a klaxon horn wailed, and across a speaker came the words, "Diving stations—Diving stations." Sailors were soon hopping to it, and we soldiers waited breathlessly to submerge into the deep-sea world.

GEORGE ARKELL

In the torpedo-room was a large depth meter, and my eyes watched it fixedly, while I wondered how deep we could go down. Slowly the indicator made its way down— 5 feet, 10 feet—until it reached 30 feet, and there it stayed. When the dive was over, the first thing that struck me was how easy going it was. There were no vibrations or rolling, and it was hard to realize we were moving. We were, but at only three knots. If this was how it felt to be submerged it wasn't so bad.

H.M. SUBMARINE RORQUAL RETURNS TO HER MALTA BASE, where she is seen (centre) entering the harbour at Sliema Creek after carrying out patrol duties. As told here, the Rorqual was used for shipping men and materials to Malta during the siege of the island in 1941. Now to be scrapped, the Rorqual is the only survivor of a minelaying class of submarine whose war losses included Porpoise and Seal. Launched in 1936, she had a displacement of 1,520 tons and a complement of 55. See also page 133.

Photo, British Official

COMMANDER OF THE RORQUAL since 1941, Lieut.-Commander L. W. Napier, D.S.C., R.N. (centre), in his quarters aboard the submarine, attends to formalities with a Customs officer (left) on arrival at Portsmouth after eighteen months' service in the Mediterranean, in December 1943. On the right is Lieut. I. M. Stoops, R.N., the commander's first lieutenant. *Photo, British Official*

When night fell we surfaced again, and then the steadiness and quiet were broken by slight rolling and the noise of the engines. Everything seemed to come to life as we broke surface, and when the conning tower hatch opened we all felt a ping in our ears which—we were told—always happens on surfacing.

Now was the time to explore our good ship Rorqual. Everything was compact and looked to me just a mass of levers, and clock or meter dials. Walking along the narrow passage-way I passed the storeroom, the P.O. quarters, where we ate, and the Commander's quarters. In the passage I had to squeeze past the cook who was busy preparing a meal. To me he was a miracle man after what I saw of his little galley and the lovely meals he served. Farther along, in a little corner, sat a petty officer whom I later found was named Johnny. We became great friends and I sat talking with him many an hour, while he described the working of the submarine, how she submerged, and how she laid mines.

AFTER passing Johnny at his job I came to the control-room, which is what they call the part of the submarine directly below the conning tower. Here there was a little more room than elsewhere in the ship, but even so the available space was well packed. In one corner sat a sailor, in front of him a big clock, and in his hands what I called the steering wheel. At correct intervals, this chap said through a microphone : "Five minutes, Sir," which I gathered had some bearing on the business of altering course. Behind him and to his right in a little recess, an officer was plotting a chart by means of which we followed our progress towards Malta.

Eventually I came to the engine-room. Walking along the narrow railed gangway, on either side of which there were rows of big pistons turning, the noise was deafening. Through another narrow passage, past more cabins, I reached the crew's quarters. Throughout my tour of the ship I found everything spotlessly clean, and nearly every other sailor appeared to carry an oily rag ready to wipe away any dirt that he saw.

That was my first look over the Rorqual before settling down for an eight-day passage. On this trip there were packed on the upper casing, where the mines are usually stored, gallons of aviation spirit, and I noticed that we were also carrying mail for the troops at Malta. The petrol, of course, was for the Hurricanes operating from Malta. We certainly seemed well and truly stocked.

In the torpedo-room, which for the journey remained our billets, I noticed above my head the crest and motto of the Rorqual, "Nec Temere, Nec Timide," meaning " Neither Rashly, nor Timidly"—a most appropriate motto for such a grand ship. Hanging proudly near the motto were several objects shaped like horseshoes on which were stamped names. It appeared that these were a kind of safety device which is taken from a torpedo before it is fired, and the ones hanging by the submarine's bridge were stamped with the names of enemy ships which had fallen to the Rorqual. The idea was similar to that of a soldier notching his rifle for every enemy life he took. I tried to secure one of them for a souvenir, but to those torpedo men they were worth their weight in gold. They would have given me a torpedo gladly, but not one of those proud treasures ! I wonder how many more there are hanging up there now ?

As the days went by we pestered the crew with questions, but they were a grand set of chaps and answered us willingly. We learned much about the Rorqual, especially the tricky business of getting those massive torpedoes down into their places below and how they were moved into position and into the torpedo tubes. Although the time passed slowly it wasn't for lack of interest.

At nights, after we had surfaced, it was our routine to walk along to the conning tower and stand beneath it for a good breath of fresh air. This was grand ; until then I had never realized just how lovely pure, clean air really is. Looking up, I could see that the sky was full of stars with a bright moon shining. Indeed, the nights we had on that journey were the kind that submarine crews do not like, as they were as bright as daylight.

Valetta's Grand Harbour in Sight

Most of our trip was very smooth, with but little rolling, until the last night just off Malta, where I thought we were boring a spiral course towards the island. It seemed as if we were turning somersaults. Cups, plates, and tins of rations crashed to the floor and rolled around crazily. But this bothered the lads of the Rorqual not at all. They were far too busy preparing themselves for a spot of shore leave at Malta ; dazzling white uniforms came out as if by magic, and from their scanty work clothes they soon emerged looking spick and span. I felt in the same mind myself, but all I wanted was to see some daylight for a change and to put my feet on firm ground and go for a nice long walk.

At daybreak on Thursday, June 12, we saw from the chart that we were heading for the Grand Harbour at Valetta. Orders came for all us soldiers to go up and stand on the upper deck. Sailors dashed around preparing to make fast. Passing H.M.S. St. Angelo there were the usual formalities of the Naval Salute. Down below all hatches separating each compartment of the submarine were closed tight, and we were told that this was a precaution against mines which Jerry had been making a practice of dropping into the Grand Harbour by aircraft.

At last our submarine pulled alongside the quay and was soon secured, and the operation of unloading our kits was begun forthwith. We bade a hearty goodbye to H.M.S. Rorqual and her grand crew, feeling that we had learned much and had had an unforgettable experience. At the same time, we all felt remarkably relieved to be back on dry land and congratulated ourselves on being in the Army and not having to go down to the sea in a submarine.

The Beacon That Went to Battle

From Margate and back again by way of North Africa, Italy and the Dalmatian Islands the Belisha Beacon went, marvelled at, admired and given great honour, the outstanding milestones in its three-year wanderings being duly inscribed on its globe. The astonishing story of this much-travelled veteran of the Second Great War is specially told for "The War Illustrated" by Capt. C. B. Turner, 567 (Indep) Field S/L Battery, R.A.

ON Xmas Eve 1942—the fourth wartime Christmas—I, with my usual luck, was Duty Officer, doing the routine rounds of billets, cook-houses, and so on. Somehow there seemed an extra festive air about this particular occasion. Our training during the last summer in the deserted seaside town of Margate was well behind us, and it was common knowledge that we should shortly be pushing off somewhere. Perhaps it was because of the need at such a time to cloak one's personal feelings that every officer, N.C.O. and man in the Battery was determined to make this a Christmas-de-luxe.

As I continued on my rounds the conversation was of nothing but parties—Troop A was entertaining Troop B, Troops C and D were entertaining certain officers and sergeants : in fact, everybody was party-minded, and with the latitude allowed in the Army at Christmas time I found that in the course of my duties I had joined in several of the gatherings before Xmas Day finally dawned.

Xmas Day itself had a not too happy beginning. The entire unit was to muster, and march to a Church parade in the centre of the town, and it was apparent that many of the personnel would have been happier in bed. Nevertheless, the training of years coming to our aid, we marched off. As the column approached a part of the front where stands a statue of a lifeboatman gazing out to sea, a titter started to run through the ranks ; and no wonder, for the familiar figure was wearing the most unfamiliar garb of denims, anti-gas cape and a tin helmet ! As attention was focused on this fantastic and amusing sight, the absence of the orange globe on a Belisha beacon opposite the statue went unnoticed. Church parade over, the unit settled down to the celebrations.

A few days afterwards the equipment and transport left Margate and the unit entrained for the North and thence to a destination (then) unknown. It is not necessary here to go into the details or the rigours of troop transportation and troopships ; they are only too well known to all who campaigned abroad. Let it suffice to say that it was with great relief we crept at dusk, about a fortnight later, into our most forward held port of Bône in Algeria, North Africa. We disembarked, and marched what seemed an interminable distance to the transit camp. Here we awaited news regarding the arrival of our equipment and for further orders. Eventually we learned that the greater part of our equipment had been sunk, and we were to await replacements.

Unsolved Mystery of the Borrower

Of our original transport all that survived were four S-L lorries, the jeeps and motor cycles. With these the unit was to move to the neighbouring port of Philippeville, and I went off in advance with the C.O. to the little Italian-peopled fishing village of Stora to see if I could successfully employ my one or two words of schoolboy French to assist in requisitioning billets for our Battery H.Q.

We were received with great ceremony by the Mayor of the village, and the C.O. quickly decided on his layout for the H.Q. offices, stores, etc. There was no

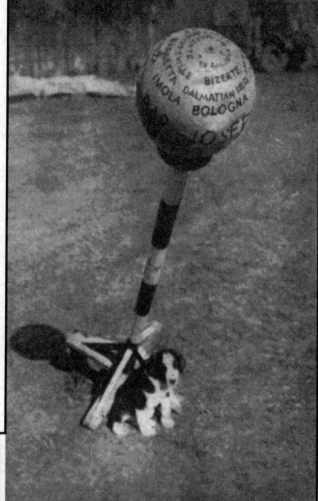

VETERAN of campaigns, the beacon is erected in a prominent position on the Monfalcone-Trieste road where one of the Battery's numerous mascots mounts guard over it.

garage space available, and our workshops were to be set up in the centre of the village square. Moving in started next day, and whilst I was struggling with the intricacies of requisition forms—and the Mayor—in two languages, he politely interrupted me to ask the significance, "s'il vous plaît," of the Regimental standard.

Puzzled, I followed him on to the balcony —and was amazed to see the familiar insignia of a Belisha beacon being placed at the entrance to the workshops. Here, then, was another piece of "equipment" that had survived ! The beacon remained outside the workshops, daily surprising newcomers as the Battery

mustered to full strength. Our efforts to trace how the beacon came to leave Margate and the U.K. at first met with no success, but as its fame and importance grew many were the claimants to the honour of being its keeper. Actually, the identity of the original "borrower" remained a mystery to the end.

The rest of our equipment arrived, we returned to Bône, and our Belisha beacon, in pride of position outside the workshops near the airfield, became almost as familiar a sign as the landing beacon. It seemed that it had become the special standard of the workshops, and the Battery painter took upon himself the task of recording on it the names of the places where the Battery had been established since leaving England.

Our next move was to Bizerta, and as this was a Yank garrison town our beacon did not have its usual number of surprised admirers, apart from the Wogs. As is the way in the Army, we were not at Bizerta for long. We were to return in convoy to Bône and embark for a new theatre of war. The beacon was constantly on view during the journey, as it was fixed to the bonnet of the Battery repair truck which patrolled up and down the convoy.

Back to the transit camp at Bône once more, the place where we entered and left the North African theatre. Again we parted company with the equipment, which went on slow ships, whilst the personnel enjoyed a short but pleasant voyage in faster craft to Naples, and then across Southern Italy by train to Bari on the East Coast. Here we learned that our next destination was to be the Dalmatian Islands, and after hurried refitting and assembling of emergency stores

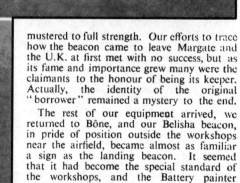

DISPLAYED BY THE MAYOR OF MARGATE, Alderman F. J. Cornford, the beacon that went to battle has been mounted and placed in a prominent position in the local library. Its silver plate bears the inscription : "A bit of old England. Mascot of 567 Searchlight Battery, R.A., from 1943 to 1946. Borrowed from Margate."

Photo, Fox

MEMBERS OF THE BATTERY AND THEIR BEACON MASCOT, photographed in Italy shortly before the beacon was dispatched to England. Seated extreme right is the author who with the C.O. of the battery, Major W. W. Thom, seated, centre, decided that their mascot be returned to its native town, Margate, whence it was taken mysteriously overseas in 1943.

the advance party set off for the island of Otok Vis, the H.Q. at that time of Tito. The island turned out to be a rockbound, waterless, barren stronghold with only one road, and the Recce groups were hard put to it to find accommodation and sites. But these difficulties were quickly overcome, and all was in readiness for the main part of the Battery which joined us a few days later.

The island was just off the mainland of Yugoslavia, then in enemy hands, and the Germans' frequent aerial visits necessitated careful camouflage of our equipment. You can imagine my amusement when, on entering B.H.Q. one day, I observed a personal camouflage net—which had obviously been considered part of the emergency stores— being draped with great care over our beacon, the ceremony being closely watched by a large crowd of heavily armed Partisans, who were obviously puzzled as to the function of this particular piece of our equipment. At this stage nobody's knowledge of the complicated Yugoslav language was adequate to furnishing the lengthy explanation of the significance which the beacon held for us.

IT soon became a familiar sight to the Commandos and Royal Marines and other units on the Island ; and I am told that it was once saved in the nick of time from being reborrowed to be used as a good-luck mascot on one of the many raids these troops carried out from Otok Vis. Fortunately it *was* saved, the would-be borrowers taking a jeep in its place. After a few months' sojourn on Vis and other islands, Tito entered Yugoslavia and, at the head of his Partisan armies, continued the campaign, so our work was over and we returned once more to Bari, there to refit, receiving orders eventually to proceed to the 8th Army front.

The beacon's first resting-place in the forward areas was outside Forli—then the most forward held town, where it was greatly appreciated by our troops and the Canadians and Kiwis, but it quite mystified the Poles. When Faenza fell, in December 1944, our Battery went in support of the Second Polish

Corps, and during that ghastly winter in the hills outside Faenza our beacon had many narrow escapes but, fortunately, survived the most intensive " stonkings."

One of the Toasts of V Night

In April 1945 the 8th Army, held up during the winter at the river Senio, launched its final offensive and our beacon started its hectic journey with the spearhead of the assault. It was cheered by uncomprehending but welcoming Italians as it made triumphant entry into Castel Bolognese—to Imola—on to Castel San Pietro—and finally to Bologna. Here the Battery went into reserve to enjoy a well-earned rest, and a few days afterwards came the long-awaited news. The Italian campaign was over—the Germans had surrendered unconditionally, and that night our beacon, lit by the rosy glare of bonfires and fireworks, was one of the toasts of that never-to-be-forgotten V Night.

However, our rest was not of long duration. We were ordered to join XIII Corps and the Kiwis in the Trieste area where differences were being smoothed out, and our beacon, in its usual place on the repair truck, safely shepherded the Battery convoy through Ferrara, over the Po—Mestre—the outskirts of Trieste—to end up at Monfalcone. After Field-Marshal Alexander's conference with the Yugoslavs the trouble was smoothed out. The workshops found most palatial billets, and our beacon was given an elegant black-and-white post and established in pride of place on the main Monfalcone-Trieste road (see illus. in page 379). The battle over, the unit settled down to police duties, searchlight tattoos, L.I.A.P., etc.

Demobilization gradually reduced the unit and we started training Italians, to whom our equipment was eventually to be handed over. Finally, only three officers and a few senior N.C.O.s remained to wind up the unit's disbandment, but the C.O. (Major W. W. Thom, R.A.) and I decided that our beacon could *not* be handed over with the

equipment. It should journey back to its home town, Margate, in the charge of a gunner from the unit—two returning war-scarred veterans together. He was instructed to hand back the beacon to the Mayor of Margate, with this letter from the C.O.

567 (Indep.) Field S/Light Bty., R.A., C.M.F.
My Dear Lord Mayor,   February 20, 1946.

In the autumn of 1942 my Unit enjoyed the amenities and hospitality of Margate and made many friendships which endured throughout the course of the War. In North Africa, the Dalmatian Islands, Italy and for a short period in Austria we often recalled the glorious days of mobilization and our experiences of parties at Dreamland, the Ruby Lounge, and, of course, " Uncles "—to mention only a few. But all this is beside the point and merely by way of mitigation for the " crime " to which I am about to confess.

Early in February 1943 we arrived at Bône, in N. Africa, and in due course moved to Philippeville, where, on a bright and sunny morning, there appeared in front of the Unit Workshops a Belisha Beacon. The familiar yellow globe and black-and-white post contrasted strangely with the assorted garments of the local " Wogs," who were gazing upon the latest piece of equipment with awe and respect.

A few discreet inquiries established the fact that at Christmastime this Belisha Beacon had supported a member of the Sergeants' Mess—it might have been the B.S.M. himself—and the N.C.O. concerned was adamant that the Beacon had expressed a wish to travel abroad. In any event, the Beacon arrived in North Africa, and commenced its overseas service. It was displayed at Philippeville, Bône, and Bizerta, and in 1944 appeared on the Dalmatian Islands at Otok Vis, where Tito's Partisans assisted in the unveiling ceremony, once again outside the unit workshops.

Throughout the length and breadth of Italy the Belisha Beacon was carefully tended, and after each move the placename of its recent abode was inscribed on the globe. It was commented upon at Bari, came under shellfire at Faenza, and with Polish support appeared in Imola in the drive for Bologna. Since hostilities ceased it has been prominent on the main Monfalcone-Trieste road, and after a gallant and distinguished career is being returned to you by a member of this Unit.

I wish to apologise sincerely to you, my Lord Mayor, and at the same time thank you and the Aldermen of Margate for the facilities granted to my Unit in 1942.—Yours very sincerely,
W. W. Thom, Major

Before its return to the U.K. the beacon was photographed with the remaining members of the unit. It arrived safely in the U.K. and was duly demobbed, and the C.O. received the following letter from the Mayor of Margate.

Dear Major Thom,   March 7, 1946.

I have received with much interest and appreciation your letter dated February 20, and in thanking you for writing to me I should like to say also how much I am looking forward to the return of the trophy, which has had such a glorious career during the late War.

I think it will have to be exalted, when it is returned, to a prominent position in our local collection at the Library, as I think its intelligence in expressing such a strong desire to travel to the particular member of your Sergeants' Mess makes it highly desirable that such enterprise on the part of a mere Belisha Beacon should deserve something more than to be replaced at an ordinary street crossing.

I can assure you that when the member of your unit arrives with this most delectable trophy he will receive a warm welcome ; in fact if either yourself or any members of your unit are visiting Margate during the coming season I should very much like to have the pleasure of meeting them here.

I am happy to note that when you were here in the autumn of 1942 you established friendships which have lasted, but although we were badly hit in Margate by war conditions it was always our endeavour to extend whatever hospitality we could to those gallant men who were occupying the town in place of the usual holiday visitors.

With every good wish, I am,
Yours very sincerely,
F. J. Cornford, Mayor

I Was Rounded-Up by Gestapo Gunmen

The day after she learned that she had been awarded the George Cross for her courage in remaining silent under torture by the Gestapo (August 21, 1946), Mrs. O. M. C. Sansom told her story to The Daily Express staff reporter John Murphy. She was betrayed to the Germans when she was working as a British secret agent in Occupied France.

I WAS given the name of Lise when the War Office sent me to a school for training agents. That became my war name and my contact name. That was the name they sent to the French underground movement. I had to get used to it. They used to wake me in the middle of the night at the training school outside London and take me to a classroom. There would be M.I.5 men and police officers dressed as German army officers and Gestapo men. They would interrogate me, using the name Lise — the way the Germans would if ever they caught me.

I would be asked what I had done the day before. I was supposed to think quickly and give them a full account — but it had to be different from what I had really been doing. At the school they taught me the usual things — how to carry messages, how to bluff my way, how to carry dangerous parcels under the noses of the Germans, how to read maps. Sometimes we had to trail M.I.5 men themselves, and put in a full report of what they had done.

Some of the people at the school were given the job of visiting places like Bristol or the rail works at Swindon. They had to snoop around and ask as many questions as they could about the war work that was going on. Perhaps the people in those places who had strangers arrested for snooping and asking questions will understand now why they never came before a court. Each of us carried an envelope explaining who we were. But our instructions were never to produce it unless we got into serious trouble.

Sometimes at the school I thought I would fail. I was torn between the desire to help win the war and to remain a mother. My colonel, Colonel Maurice Buckmaster, used to put my mind at rest. He would tell me what was already in my own mind, of the thousands of other children who had no parents, because they had either been killed in the war, or been sent to concentration camps, or were away in Germany working for the Germans.

The German Colonel Was a Fool

I told myself that my family were only three children among so many affected by the war, that they were being looked after in a safe place and in a comfortable home. During my training I made up my mind I was doing the right thing. But, even then, when my training was over, I went to my C.O. and told him frankly I did not think I was clever enough to go through with it. He looked at me and said : "You will succeed. I am counting on you."

I was taken to Gibraltar and went aboard a fishing vessel. I was wearing slacks and tried to disguise myself as a fisherman. Before I reached Marseilles I really did look like a fisherman. Up to then I had not met the man who was to be my C.O. in France. We had a rendezvous in Cannes, in what was known as "a safe house." I travelled all over France, by train and by car. I would

sleep in "safe houses," in farms, in hotels. Once I was taking some reports in a car and they were needed urgently in London. A French gendarme stopped me and asked me what I was doing out after curfew. I pretended to cry and said I had a son in Cannes. I had suddenly heard he was ill, and I had to get to him quickly. I looked at him and said : "You understand a mother's feelings." He let me go.

AWARDED THE GEORGE CROSS, the third woman to be thus decorated, Mrs. Odette Sansom displayed "courage, endurance and self-sacrifice of the highest possible order" during her two years in enemy hands. French-born wife of an Englishman, she is seen here with her daughters Marianne, Lilli and Françoise.

Another time I was taking a suitcase containing a radio transmitting set from Marseilles to Toulouse. When I got to the station I decided to travel first class because I was wearing very smart clothes. High-ranking German officers used to travel first-class. I got into one of their compartments. The suitcase was too heavy for me to lift up to the luggage rack, so I left it at my feet. A German colonel — he was about 60 — offered to put it on the rack for me. I thought it was all up then, because only a fool would not have been suspicious of a young, well-dressed woman carrying such a small case which was so heavy. He was a fool, and he put it on the rack for me. I smiled and thanked him.

I was kept very busy all the time, but during any free moments I had I lived just like an ordinary Frenchwoman (I was born in the Somme). I used to queue up at the shops, go to the cinema, visit a dressmaker. But my C.O. was working night and day and would not give anybody very much rest.

In April 1943 I was "sold" by a Frenchman. He was a double agent and was working for both sides. It was in my hotel, at night. The Gestapo came into my room when I was packing. That was a rule of ours — always to pack and leave everything ready. There were four of them. One stuck a revolver in my back. Another asked me where my commanding officer was. I said : "He is not here," but I knew it was no use pretending any more.

One of them held out his hand to me. He said : "Lise, you have played your cards very well. It is no fault of yours if you have lost." I did not take his hand. I took them to my C.O.'s room. I had two reasons. I knew he had a lot of papers and I wanted to help to get rid of them ; and I wanted to get together with him so that we could prepare our stories.

The Gestapo searched him and the room. I managed to get hold of his wallet. I slipped it up my sleeve. They took us to a car. As we were getting in, I pretended my dress was caught in the seat. That gave me a chance to push the wallet under the seat unnoticed.

I did not know what would happen to it. I was thinking that perhaps it would be some hours before it would be found, and by that time everybody mentioned in the documents would have heard of our arrest and would have managed to make their escape. And I was thinking that perhaps someone might need the large sum of money in the wallet and keep quiet about it. That was what happened. By posing as man and wife, my C.O. [Capt. Peter Morland Churchill, D.S.O., M.C.] and I travelled together when we were being taken from prison to prison. It gave us a chance to make up our story. We both stuck to it to the end.

They starved me in prison. They kept me in solitary confinement for almost two years. But what I did was nothing — I feel this honour is too much for what I have done. I have never been very strong, nor very brave. I am just an ordinary sort of woman who is very pleased to be back with her children.

How They Surrendered in S.E. Asia

For some time after VJ Day it was in the balance whether the Japanese in South-East Asia would comply with their Emperor's surrender order of August 14, 1945, or would oppose our long-planned Malaya landings. Coder S. D. Harper describes the Royal Navy's operations in September off Malaya as seen from the destroyer Petard.

MY ship, the Petard, lay for hours in the blistering heat of Trinkat Chomplong Bay, in Japanese occupied Great Nicobar Island, slipping out at intervals on some lone anti-submarine patrol or to relieve another destroyer escorting the heavier ships which had to stay at sea.

At night in the bay sentries patrolled the upper deck and smoking was not allowed, as a precaution against the local inhabitants, who were said to be enthusiastic head-hunters and expert marksmen with poisoned

darts. By day the only movement visible ashore was the surf on the untrodden beach and steam for ever rising from the dense green of the jungle.

The crews of the numerous ships of the Royal Navy, lying in the bay, ranging in size from minelayers to destroyers, had just finished their mid-day meal of "dog" and dehydrated potatoes when the yellow warning was received for the second time that day. Quickly the "buzz" passed from the wireless office to the mess decks, and hardly had it made the rounds when the bells clanged out

H.M.S. PETARD, the destroyer on which Coder S. D. Harper served and from which he witnessed the reactions of the enemy in the Nicobar Islands region after the unconditional surrender of Japan in August 1945. Petard's displacement is 1,540 tons. *Photo, British Official*

S. D. HARPER

action stations. All was activity in a moment. On each ship there was the orderly rush to stations. Pom-poms, oerlikons, and the four-inch guns of the destroyers pointed skywards. A minelayer was under way with turret elevated and pendants flying . . . VJ Day (August 15, 1945) had been celebrated exactly a week before.

At their action stations the crews awaited anything that might come. The East Indies Fleet had been at sea in the area of the Nicobars for several days. It seemed that the Japs in South-East Asia might not obey their Emperor's order to surrender. Singapore radio still declared the Japanese Army to be supreme, and threatened attacks on the

British Fleet in the Nicobars area. Two hundred miles from that quiet bay lay the bases of the Japanese "kamikaze" (suicide) aircraft and speedboats guarding the entrance to the Malacca Straits.

Rendezvous With Minesweepers

The "raiders passed" was signalled after twenty minutes, and the crews relaxed. It was only a Jap reconnaissance plane which raced homewards when Fleet Air Arm aircraft took off from the carrier force patrolling nearby. So the days passed, and it was a relief when eventually we left our hospitable bay and headed for the Malacca Straits at the head of a small detached force. Within an

hour of entering the Straits we sank a drifting mine with rifle fire as it was carried by the heavy swell across our bows.

For another two days we lay among splendid island scenery, near Penang, before moving to a rendezvous with the minesweeping force which was to clear a channel through the minefields to Singapore. The sweep began at 09.00 on September 2, 1945. The sweepers were fanned out ahead of us and we proceeded slowly through a marked channel with the cruiser Cleopatra, the flagship of the C.-in-C. East Indies. Everything was in readiness in case we hit a mine. Scuttles, hatches and some of the water-tight doors were closed, boats were swung outboard on the davits, the whole of the ship's company (with the exception of engine room and wireless staff watch-keepers) were on the upper deck and all wore inflated lifebelts.

It was a weary day, and the crackling rifle fire directed at drifting mines bobbing in the sea added to the monotony. Then, in the middle of the afternoon, a smudge of smoke was spotted far ahead. This smoke presently took the form of a strange-looking vessel of war. Excitement gripped our ship when, under orders from the Cleopatra, she left the swept channel and raced to overhaul the enemy. As we approached we saw a large

JAPANESE ENVOY ABOARD H.M.S. NELSON, the British battleship, operating with the East Indies Fleet off Penang, salutes the ship's commander on arrival for preliminary surrender talks, August 29, 1945. Following arrangements made at this meeting, a British minesweeping force, as related here, cleared a channel for the safe passage of "a vast armada of shipping of all types and sizes" through the Malacca Straits. On September 10 the Fleet made its victorious entry into Singapore Harbour. *Photo, British Official*

Motto: " Arise, Night is at Hand "

NO. 215 SQUADRON

FORMED at Coudekerque, near Dunkirk, on March 10, 1918, as No. 15 Squadron, R.N.A.S., it became No. 215 Squadron, R.A.F., on April 1, 1918, and on April 23 returned to England to be brought up to full strength. It returned to France on July 4 equipped with ten Handley Page O/400 twin-engined bombers. Returning to England in February 1919, it was disbanded on October 18 of the same year, and re-formed at Worthy Down, Hants, on October 7, 1935, as No. 215 (Bomber) Squadron.

What No. 215 did in the early years of the Second Great War is not known. It arrived in India on April 11, 1942, equipped with Wellington ICs, and operations commenced on April 24, dropping supplies to the British army in Burma. On October 2 it moved to Chaklala in the Punjab for airborne training with the Army; in March 1943 to Jessore, Bengal, and night-bombing of targets in Burma commenced on the 16-17th.

SEPTEMBER 1943 saw the squadron re-equipped with Wellington X's. On January 20, 1944, 4,000-lb. bombs were carried for the first time by special modified aircraft and used against Japanese Headquarters, supply dumps and troop concentrations. At the end of June 1944 all squadron crews were detached to Kolar in Southern India for conversion to Liberator aircraft.

The entire squadron moved to Digri, and in January 1945 chief targets were the Burma-Siam railway and supply areas in Southern Burma and Siam. In April it was selected for conversion to Dakotas, and in May was supplying the victorious 14th Army from Tulihal. The squadron was at Singapore in December 1945, and was renumbered 48 Squadron in February 1946.

white ensign above a small rising sun ensign. The enemy was the Japanese destroyer Kamikaze, and a more ineffective looking man-o'-war we had never seen.

Its decks seemed deserted, save for an officer in spotless whites making his way for'ard to the bridge and carrying a leather dispatch-case. As the Jap destroyer hove to scores of little men in green uniforms, with soft peaked caps, appeared on the fo'c'sle. They panicked for a few moments at the report when we fired a heaving line across her bows, and afterwards stood holding the heaving line, looking at it blankly. The fo'c'sles of the two ships were crowded, and as victor glared at vanquished a murmur began from the British ranks but was quickly silenced by the captain on the bridge. A laugh broke out as the upturned faces on the Petard saw the grin of sheer happiness on Jimmy the One's face as he stood and surveyed the surrendered enemy ship.

JAPANESE DESTROYER KAMIKAZE as viewed by the author of this story from H.M.S. Petard, which accompanied H.M.S. Cleopatra to investigate a " strange looking vessel of war " which appeared during minesweeping operations near Penang on September 2, 1945. The 1,270-ton Kamikaze flew a large white ensign above a small rising sun ensign.

On the Jap bridge the officer in whites lifted a megaphone to his lips and said in perfect English that he was sending over charts and two envelopes, one containing a receipt which he wished to be signed and returned. He got no receipt. The charts and envelopes were transferred to the Cleopatra, and we took up our position as before.

At the end of the minefield we anchored for the night while the Cleopatra and the sweepers proceeded to Singapore. Next day we retraced our way through the swept channel and anchored at the outer end of it. So we remained for five days and nights, a floating buoy, watching the convoys pass through, and scrounging what food we could from bigger ships to help out our depleted larder.

On the evening of September 8 we took the hook up and proceeded to a new rendezvous. During the night our searchlights picked out a narrow swept channel, through which we led a vast armada of shipping of all types and sizes. The lights stretched as far as we could see—one long file of ships. It was good to see the bright lights, for up to a few days earlier operations were strictly on a war footing.

September 9 would have seen an Allied invasion force in these waters even if the atomic bombs had not blasted the Japs into surrender. It was the long-planned D-Day for the Malaya Invasion, and the plan "Operation Zipper" was still going ahead. At first it was thought there might be some small opposition, but at dawn the ships were all in position off the beaches just above Port Swettenham, with the crews at action stations as the assault craft went in, fighter aircraft circling above them. The landings were unopposed and troops quickly moved inland, taking over airfields and imprisoning Japs.

TOWARDS evening that day we sailed past the impressive fleet, which stretched for miles, to join a force, including the Nelson and Richelieu, and we sailed into the harbour of Singapore next day. Longingly we gazed at the buildings, looking forward to a good run ashore. But orders came for sailing, and at dusk we returned up the Straits, on our way back to Trincomalee.

NEW FACTS AND FIGURES

IN addition to the many thousands of bottles of whole blood and plasma which went to the Fighting Services in 1945, and the large quantities used for civilian patients at home, about 4,000 bottles of dried plasma were sent to Holland after its liberation for the medical treatment of people suffering from the effects of starvation. There were over 400,000 blood donors on panels in England and Wales in 1945 (states the Ministry of Health) and the total number of blood donations was 393,677, of which 230,149 were taken by mobile teams.

UNDER an agreement signed in London on June 27, 1946, the Norwegian Government will purchase equipment in Britain for the Norwegian fighting forces, including 18 vessels for the Norwegian Navy, most of them ships which were on loan from Britain during the War. The agreement also confirms a previous contract for the purchase of aircraft sufficient for three fighter wings and two Mosquito wings.

OF the 140,000 civilian non-enemy foreigners in Norway on May 8, 1945, only 1,130 were left by July 1946, according to a statement by the Norwegian Ministry of Social Affairs. Of these, 970 were Poles who did not wish to return to Poland. But Norway also has her own displaced persons—Norwegians who were deported by the Germans from the northern province of Finmark. It was hoped to send 12,000–15,000 of them back to Finmark during the summer of 1946, but about 10,000 will have to stay in southern Norway for another winter, owing to lack of accommodation.

TO teach Germans the way in which democracy works, teams of experts from England are to hold three-day courses of lectures and discussions in towns and centres throughout the British zone. Germans, both men and women, taking the course will include district councillors, representatives of the main political parties, trade union officials and students. Subjects to be dealt with are the relationship between salaried officials and elected representatives, committee and council procedure, and co-operation of political parties in local government. The students will be allowed free discussion of all subjects.

OF the 600,000 men and women in the Australian services in August 1945, approximately 500,000 had been demobilized by July 1946. In announcing this, the Australian Minister for Post-War Reconstruction added that of a total of 900,000 men and women who served in the fighting services during the war 800,000 had been demobilized—a result which had not been equalled in any Allied country.

THE Royal Naval Dockyard at Chatham, where fighting ships have been built for more than 300 years, is to make dustbins, water-tanks, wheelbarrows, pillar-boxes and street-lamps. meat safes, prefabricated house carcasses, greenhouses and garden furniture. To prevent mass unemployment, the Admiralty decided in August 1946 to make the Royal naval dockyards available for manufacturing articles for civilian use. Other places affected are Sheerness, Portsmouth, Devonport and Rosyth.

German Prisoners Assist Our Harvest Home

AT THEIR OWN REQUEST, former high-ranking German officers at Island Farm Camp, Bridgend, Glamorganshire, assisted local farmers with the 1946 wheat harvest. Providing this welcome supplement to our shortage of field labour and relieving their own boredom engendered by idleness are, left to right, General Eisenbeck, Admiral Brauning and General von Boltenstern. Under the terms of the Geneva Convention officer P.O.W. cannot be compelled to do work other than daily routine tasks in connexion with the maintenance of their camp quarters.

Photo, G.P.U.

Printed in England and published every alternate Friday by the Proprietors, THE AMALGAMATED PRESS. LTD., The Fleetway House, Farringdon Street, London, E.C.4. Registered for transmission by Canadian Magazine Post Sole Agents for Australia and New Zealand : Messrs. Gordon & Gotch, Ltd. ; and for the South Africa : Central News Agency, Ltd.—September 27, 1946. S.S. *Editorial Address :* JOHN CARPENTER HOUSE. WHITEFRIARS. LONDON. E.C.4.

Vol 10 The War Illustrated Nº 243

SIXPENCE

I WAS THERE

OCTOBER 11, 1946

FIELD-MARSHAL VISCOUNT MONTGOMERY OF ALAMEIN GREETED BY GENERAL EISENHOWER at the National airport, Washington, when he arrived by air from Quebec on Sept. 10, 1946. Others meeting our Chief of the Imperial General Staff were General Omar Bradley and Field-Marshal Baron Wilson of Libya. Viscount Montgomery's nine-day visit to the U.S., primarily to inspect Army installations, included a call on President Truman. He reviewed cadets at the Military Academy, West Point, and placed a wreath on the grave of the Unknown Soldier in the Arlington National Cemetery.

Edited by Sir John Hammerton

NO. 244 WILL BE PUBLISHED FRIDAY, OCTOBER 25

Our Roving Camera Sees New Air Developments

THE ORBIT METER'S function is the ground control of air-liners in their final approach to land. This modern development of radio equipment was demonstrated at the R.A.F. station, Bassingbourne, Herts, on Sept. 13, 1946, to delegates of 50 nations attending the London conference of the P.I.C.A.O.

METEOR JET PLANE (below) was on show on Horse Guards Parade, London, on Sept. 11, 1946. The type is similar to that in which Group Capt. E. M. Donaldson, R.A.F., set up a new world's air speed record of 616 m.p.h. on a measured course between Worthing and Littlehampton, Sussex, on September 8.

B.O.A.C. BALMORAL, new Constellation air-liner, arrived at Prestwick, Ayrshire, Sept. 11, 1946, a ceremony marking this inauguration of first direct commercial air service between Scotland and U.S.A. Passengers were played off the aircraft by a Scottish pipe band.

LIKE A FLYING BULLET, Britain's latest jet plane (left) is the Supermarine E.10/44. Public saw it for first time at the Society of British Aircraft Constructors' display at Radlett, Herts., Sept. 13, 1946.

THE HASTINGS, R.A.F.'s most modern transport aircraft, was christened at the Handley Page works at Radlett, Sept. 4, 1946 ; the ceremony was performed by the Mayor of Hastings (on dais with Sir F. Handley Page).

Photos, Assoc. Press, News Chronicle, Planet News, C. E. Brown, I.N.P.

Australian Commando Raids on Singapore

By LEN BARKER

THESE details of a secret raid carried out by Australian and British commandos on Japanese shipping in Singapore harbour did not become available until August 1946—three years after the event. The commandos travelled more than 150 miles by canoe, and their magnificently daring attack resulted in the sinking of seven vessels totalling 37,000 tons.

By the middle of 1943 the Australian and American campaign to recapture Lae, Salamaua and Finschafen in New Guinea had commenced. Disorganization of Japanese shipping to the South-West Pacific was essential to Allied strategy. On September 3 of that year 14 British and Australian Servicemen set sail from Exmouth Gulf, Western Australia, in the motor vessel Krait, a former Japanese fishing ship. With a length of 70 feet and a beam of 11 feet, she was powered by diesel engines, was capable of a speed of 6½ knots and had a range of 8,000 miles. Tucked away in the Krait were two-man rubber canoes which contained space for limpet mines, and one month's supply of food and water.

Under the command of the late Lieut.-Colonel (then Major) Ivor Lyon, M.B.E., D.S.O., of the Gordon Highlanders, and a son of Brig.-Gen. Lyon, were Lieut. D. N. Davidson, D.S.O., R.N.V.R. (later killed), Lieut. H. E. Carse, R.A.N.V.R. (navigator), Lieut. R. Page, D.S.O., A.I.F. (later killed), Ldg. Seaman K. P. Cain, R.A.N., Ldg. Stoker P. McDowell, R.N., Ldg. Telegraphist H. Young, R.A.N., Cpl. R. G. Morris, M.M., R.A.M.C., Cpl. A. Crilly, M.M., A.I.F., A.B. B. A. Falls, D.S.M., R.N. (later killed), A.B. A. W. Jones, D.S.M., R.A.N. (later killed), A.B. A. W. Huston, D.S.M., R.A.N. (later killed), A.B. F. W. Marsh, M.I.D., R.A.N. (later killed), and A.B. M. Berryman, R.A.N. Their destination was Durian Island, some 30 miles distant from Singapore.

Scrutinized by Japanese Patrols

On September 9, when the Krait was approaching Lombok Strait into the Java Sea, Bali was only 11 miles to port and Lombok seven miles to starboard. The commandos had hoped to negotiate this hazardous five-miles passage within an hour, but a strong current was running and four nerve-racking hours had passed before the Krait had reached open water. At this stage the vessel had not met any Japanese sea or air patrols, but as such a meeting was inevitable the men stained their skins brown and wore cotton sarongs to give themselves the appearance of native fishermen. In addition, the Krait was flying the flag of a Japanese merchant vessel.

After drifting during the night the men of the Krait were startled at dawn to find they were surrounded by native fishing boats of all kinds. However, none of these displayed any interest in the Krait—a testimony to the effectiveness of her disguise—which led Major Lyon to decide that they should sail quite openly for the rest of their journey. For seven days the Krait threaded her way around the numerous islands which stud the Java Sea. Several times she was scrutinized by Japanese patrols, which always sheered off, apparently satisfied that she was just another fishing boat.

When the Krait approached Durian Island, which had been chosen as the canoeists'

base, a party of natives was seen ashore, so the commandos were forced to put back to sea. To kill time, Major Lyon's party sailed north until they approached Galang Island. When two miles from shore the crew spotted a Japanese observation tower. Unchallenged, they cautiously changed course to give the impression that the vessel had come from Sumatra and was proceeding to Singapore. To maintain this illusion she was

MAJOR IVOR LYON, commanding officer of the six commandos, viewed Jap shipping in Singapore roads and harbour from his hide-out on Dongas Island, some eight miles distant. A piece of cord secured his telescope to a sapling. *Photo, Australian Official*

kept to her new course, which eventually took her along the western side of Panjang Island.

As Panjang appeared to be uninhabited, Major Lyon decided to use it as a base rather than risk returning to Durian. A suitable anchorage was found, and by 5 a.m. on September 17 the canoes, with their cargoes of limpet mines, and food and water for one month, had been landed. Leaving Major Lyon, Lieut. Davidson, Lieut. Page, and A.B.s Huston, Falls and Jones to man the canoes, the Krait sailed for Borneo with instructions to rendezvous at Pompong Island between dusk and dawn on the night of October 1.

When dawn broke on Panjang Island the raiders found that they were only a quarter-mile from a native village. However, there

were no tracks indicating that the natives used this particular beach so a camp was made beside a water-hole in the jungle a few yards from the cove. After resting for two days, during which many enemy planes passed low overhead, they set out in the three canoes for another island 10 miles away at the entrance to the Bulan Strait leading to the target, Singapore.

The raiders rested for a day at this island which, while being secluded enough to allow them to swim, also gave them a full view of shipping moving in and out of the Strait. For several nights they jumped from one island to another, each one a stepping stone to Singapore. At times detection seemed inevitable. The spot where they landed and camped on one island turned out to be only 300 yards from a village.

In the early hours of September 23 the raiders went ashore at Dongas Island, which Major Lyon had chosen as their forward operation base. The high ground on the north side of Dongas provided an excellent view of Singapore, which was eight miles away. For some time the raiders watched shipping activity in Singapore, jubilant at the fact that there was not less than 100,000 tons of shipping in the roads and port.

At eight o'clock on the night of September 24 the six raiders set off to attack. They paddled hard for five hours to make way against a heavy tide, but were forced to put back at Dongas at 1 a.m. To use the tide to advantage the raiders decided to move that night to Subar, a small, bracken-covered island overlooking Singapore's examination anchorage. The following afternoon targets were chosen and allotted.

ON the night of September 26 the attack was launched, with Major Lyon and A.B. Huston in one canoe, Lieut. Davidson and A.B. Falls in another, and Lieut. Page and A.B. Jones in the third. As they moved silently towards the boom defence guarding Singapore, searchlights from the shore sprang into life and swept across the water near the canoes. However, the men managed to avoid the beams of the lights and continued on their way. Near the boom

OTTER BAY, PANJANG ISLAND, where the Krait dropped the six commandos for their attack on shipping at Singapore, 21 miles distant. They landed on the beach at night, and when daylight came they discovered there was a native village only a quarter-mile away ; but they escaped detection and resumed their journey by canoe. PAGE 387 *Photo, Australian Official*

the canoes parted company. Davidson and Falls entered the harbour in search of their targets and casually drifted along the well-lighted wharves, past armed sentries. On inspection they found the vessels to be unworthy of attack, so they paddled over the boom again into the roads where they selected three large freighters and on them placed limpet mines.

Meanwhile, Lyon and Huston selected a tanker as the object of their attack. While Major Lyon was attaching his mines to the engine room and the propeller shaft of the tanker, Huston drew Lyon's attention to a man who was intently watching them from a porthole about 10 feet above. They decided to ignore him and continued with their work. The watcher did not shift his gaze until they paddled away, when he withdrew his head and lit a lamp. Lyon and Huston then set off for Dongas, 12 miles away.

Page and Jones, in the third canoe, went to the Palau Bukum wharves, where they calmly watched men working. After attaching mines to three freighters, they headed for Dongas, which they reached half an hour before the first explosion.

Seven explosions in all were heard by the raiders and, shortly after, sea and air patrols were seen searching for the attackers. Ships attacked in Singapore by the six Commandos included one 4,000-ton freighter (either the Yamagata Maru or Nagano Maru) sunk ; five freighters, totalling 23,000

IN THE HIDE-OUT ON DONGAS ISLAND one of the commandos prepares a meal. A rubber canoe is drawn up. *Australian Official*

tons, probably sunk ; and one 10,000-ton tanker, damaged and burning. Names of ships attacked were Taisyo Maru, Nasusan Maru, Tone Maru, Samarang Maru, Yamagata Maru and Nagano Maru (freighters), and Sinkoku Maru (tanker).

The three canoes set out separately for the rendezvous with the Krait at Pompong 50 miles away. They were seen several times on the journey by native boats, but reached Pompong safely on October 1 ; next day they contacted the mother vessel, which immediately set sail south for home. When they made Lombok Strait they found a Japanese patrol vessel guarding the narrows. It was too late to turn back, so they kept going. Strangely enough the patrol boat let them pass, and the reached their home port, Exmouth Gulf, on October 19, with the grand total of 37,000 tons of vital Japanese shipping to their credit.

Ten Were Captured and Beheaded

In 1944 a second expedition left Australia in a submarine. It landed 23 men on Merapas Island in the Rhio group, south of Singapore. Included in the expedition were the six original raiders and Lieut. H. R. Ross (U.K. Army) and Major R. N. Ingleton, Royal Marines. Information recently gained from Japanese records reveals that the 23 men captured a junk. While they were approaching Singapore a Japanese patrol boat opened fire on them.

In the ensuing fight the raiders killed the patrol's crew of five and then blew up their junk after taking to rubber canoes. They retreated from island to island, fighting Japanese all the way. Colonel Lyon was killed on Sole Island in the Rhio archipelago after killing single-handed a Japanese officer and seriously wounding several men. Ten other members of the party were killed during similar fighting, the last of them on Timor. A.B. Marsh died of illness while a prisoner of war. The remaining ten were captured by the Japanese and beheaded after four months of captivity. These included Ingleton, Falls and Page.

Shortly after the executions, which were carried out in July 1945, a Japanese major-general lecturing to the Japanese General Staff in Singapore declared that unless the Japanese Army could emulate the courage and patriotism of these British and Australian enemies they could not hope to win the war !

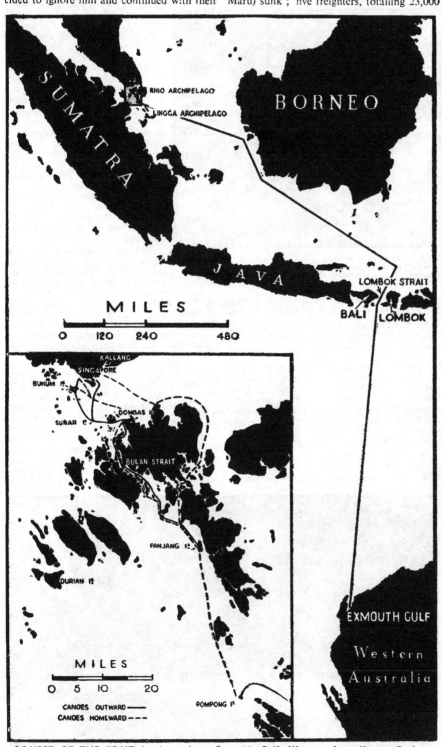

COURSE OF THE KRAIT is shown from Exmouth Gulf, Western Australia, to Panjang Island, in the Rhio Archipelago. There she dropped the canoes in which the British and Australian commandos sailed for the attack in Singapore Harbour. Their route is inset, on larger scale. The Krait returned to her home port on October 19, 1943. PAGE 388 *Australian Official*

Prelude to Destruction in Singapore Harbour

MOTHER-SHIP for six British and Australian commandos who, from canoes, destroyed 37,000 tons of Jap shipping in Singapore harbour in 1943 (see facing page), the 70-foot Krait (1), former fishing vessel, was seized from its Japanese owner at Singapore in February 1942, and later rescued more than 1,100 refugees off Sumatra. Two of the raiding party carry one of the canoes (2) used in the harbour attack. Five of the commandos (3) swimming at Bulat Island were keeping under observation Jap shipping in the Bulan Strait; all of these men were killed after a second raid in 1944 *Photos, Australian Official.* PAGE 389

The Dutch in Their Pride of Our Skymen—

ARNHEM GALLANTRY OF THE BRITISH 1st AIRBORNE DIVISION was commemorated on September 17, 1946, at the scene of the landings in Holland. Built from relics of the battle, a memorial (1) is inscribed "On the 17th September 1944, about 1 o'clock in the afternoon, the First Airborne Division landed on the heath around this point and began from here its grand operations." In the nearby Airborne Cemetery (3) schoolchildren of Oosterbeek stood with flowers beside some of the white crosses marking 1,600 graves of Allied parachute troops (see also illus. page 358). Simultaneously with the Dutch ceremonies Arnhem veterans paid their tribute at the Cenotaph in Whitehall, London (2). PAGE 390

—Honour Those Who Died in Arnhem Battle

PEOPLE OF OOSTERBEEK RAISED £2,500 to erect this impressive memorial to the skymen from Britain. Of yellow brick, it is more than 50 feet high and later will be surmounted by a symbolic figure, probably the Pegasus symbol of the Airborne Divisions. Four stone panels at its base were carved by the well-known Dutch sculptor, Jacob Maris. It stands in front of the Hartestein Hotel, Major-General R. E. Urquhart's H.Q. after the landings; the wreath was placed there by Queen Wilhelmina of the Netherlands on Sept. 17, 1946.   PAGE 391   *Photo, Planet News*

New Colours Presented to 1st Battalion H.L.I.

CEREMONY of CONSECRATION AND PRESENTATION of new Colours to the 1st Battalion The Highland Light Infantry took place on August 27, 1946, at Suez. The new King's and Regimental Colours were uncovered and placed over the drums (1) of the pipe band, and the Rev. N. McLean M.B.E., conducted a short service of consecration. The Colours were then formally presented to two lieutenants (2) by General Sir Miles Dempsey, K.C.B., K.B.E., D.S.O., M.C., C.-in-C. Middle East Land Forces, who later shook hands with Regimental Sergeant-Major Greenwell (4).

Close-up of the Colours (3); the King's Colour is on the left.

Photos, British Official

Physical Jerks on Training Ship H.M.S. Howe

NEW DEVELOPMENT IN TRAINING METHODS FOR R.N. RECRUITS is instituted by the Training Battleship Squadron based at Portland, Dorset, the squadron consisting of H.M.S. Howe (above), Anson and Nelson. Easing the accommodation position ashore and at the same time keeping these modern ships in commission without having to use full complements of trained personnel, elementary instruction is given in seamanship, gunnery and torpedoes for Special Service ratings. Each battleship has about 450 recruits during each 16 week course.   PAGE 393   *Photo, Keystone*

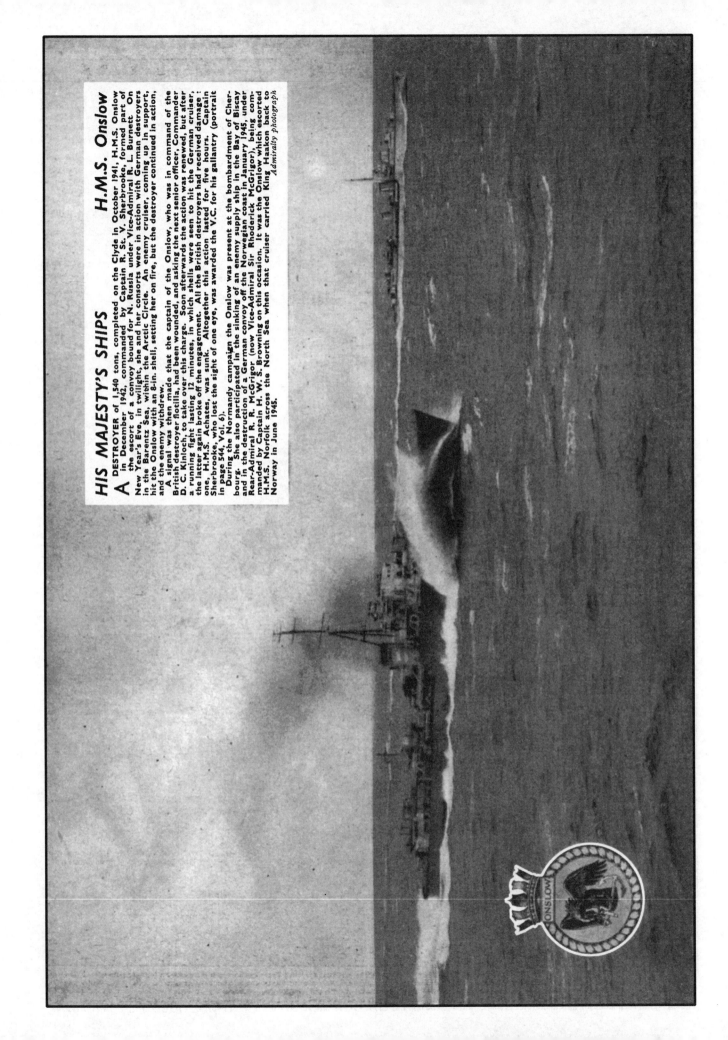

HIS MAJESTY'S SHIPS   H.M.S. Onslow

A DESTROYER of 1,540 tons, completed on the Clyde in October 1941, H.M.S. Onslow in December 1942, commanded by Captain R. St. V. Sherbrooke, formed part of the escort of a convoy bound for N. Russia under Vice-Admiral R. L. Burnett. On New Year's Eve, in twilight, she and her consorts were in action with German destroyers in the Barentz Sea, within the Arctic Circle. An enemy cruiser, coming up in support, hit the Onslow with an 8-in. shell, setting her on fire, but the destroyer continued in action, and the enemy withdrew.

A signal was then made that the captain of the Onslow, who was in command of the British destroyer flotilla, had been wounded, and asking the next senior officer, Commander D. C. Kinloch, to take over this charge. Soon afterwards the action was renewed, but after a running fight lasting 12 minutes, in which shells were seen to hit the German cruiser, the latter again broke off the engagement. All the British destroyers had received damage : one, H.M.S. Achates, was sunk. Altogether this action lasted for five hours. Captain Sherbrooke, who lost the sight of one eye, was awarded the V.C. for his gallantry (portrait in page 544, Vol. 6).

During the Normandy campaign the Onslow was present at the bombardment of Cherbourg. She also participated in the sinking of an enemy supply ship in the Bay of Biscay and in the destruction of a German convoy off the Norwegian coast in January 1945, under Rear-Admiral R. R. McGrigor (now Vice-Admiral Sir Rhoderick McGrigor), being commanded by Captain H. W. S. Browning on this occasion. It was the Onslow which escorted H.M.S. Norfolk across the North Sea when that cruiser carried King Haakon back to Norway in June 1945.

Admiralty photograph

The Honourable Artillery Company

By Major
G. GOOLD WALKER, D.S.O., M.C.

A T the outbreak of war, in 1939, the Honourable Artillery Company consisted of four batteries of R.H.A., a regiment of Heavy Anti-Aircraft Artillery and the Infantry Battalion. There were also two Home Defence Companies (Infantry). The R.H.A. batteries immediately went into training. Early in 1940 they threw off two new batteries, A, B and E forming the 11th (H.A.C.) Regiment, R.H.A. and C, D and F Batteries constituting the 12th (H.A.C.) Regiment, R.H.A. Later in the year another regiment was formed—the 13th (H.A.C.) Regiment, R.H.A., consisting of G, H and I Batteries. The 86th (H.A.C.) H.A.A. Regiment, R.A., went at once into battle stations in or near London, and in the next year threw off two new batteries—383 (H.A.C.) H.A.A. Battery, R.A., and 446 (H.A.C.) H.A.A. Battery, R.A.

The Infantry Battalion had undertaken an officer-producing role and formed 162 (H.A.C.) O.C.T.U. at Bulford, Wiltshire, from which practically all its pre-war personnel passed out as officers, and which then continued its officer-producing role until absorbed into the R.A.C. O.C.T.U. at Sandhurst in 1942. The two Home Defence companies were attached to the 13th Battalion The Royal Fusiliers and took over guard duties at vulnerable points in London. During the whole of the blitz they were stationed at the London Docks, and also provided the Bank of England Guard. This unit was finally disbanded towards the end of 1942.

After sending away almost all their original members for commissions, the 11th H.A.C. went overseas in September 1941, landing in Egypt as part of the 1st Armoured Division. They were at once sent forward into the fighting line and were heavily engaged near El Agheila, in January 1942, when Rommel staged an unexpected advance. All batteries suffered casualties in men and guns and were several times surrounded but managed to make a fighting withdrawal. On several occasions guns were fought to the last man, and two officers were killed and others wounded while acting as gunners.

T HE H.A.C.'s origin can be traced back to some time prior to 1537, in which year Henry VIII gave a Charter to an existing body of citizen archers, directing them to maintain the science of shooting for the better defence of the Realm, under the title of "Fraternitie or Guylde of Artillary of Longbowes, Crosbowes and Handegonnes." This became shortened to "The Artillery Company," but the word "artillery" was used in its original sense, meaning any missile weapon ; artillery in the modern sense was not added to the original infantry unit until 1781. The Company has been in possession of its present ground since 1641. Prior to 1914 the H.A.C. consisted of two batteries of Horse Artillery and a battalion of infantry, but in the First Great War five batteries and two battalions served in France, Egypt, Palestine and Italy.

After refitting, the Regiment was split up and attached to various "Jock" columns—small mobile parties of all arms used as raiding detachments, so named after Brigadier Jock Campbell, V.C. (a member of the H.A.C. in the First Great War), who initiated the system (portrait in page 512, Vol. 5). A troop of E Battery attached to the Free French was overrun by the German tanks near Bir Hacheim, but all ranks fought to the last, one gunner being afterwards found dead with a rifle in his hand and expended cartridges beside him.

The 11th H.A.C. were again heavily engaged at Knightsbridge, covered the retreat of the 50th and South African Divisions, and finally retreated down the precipitous Acroma Ridge with enemy tanks at their heels. They were again surrounded near Mersa Matruh, but broke out with heavy losses. Their casualties at Knightsbridge and in the subsequent retreat were 9 officers and 70 O.R.s dead, 7 officers and 158 other ranks wounded, 10 officers and 201 other ranks prisoners and 31 other ranks missing. Over 40 of these men were later drowned as prisoners of war while crossing to Italy.

The remnants of the Regiment fought as a composite battery in the six-day engagement which stopped Rommel's army at El Alamein.

They were then withdrawn to refit and were selected as the first R.H.A. unit to be armed with the new Priest self-propelled guns. After training with these they went into the battle of El Alamein, where their brigade (which included the Queen's Bays, 9th Lancers and 10th Hussars) eventually broke the line and followed up the retreating Germans after ten days of fierce fighting. The Regiment's losses at Alamein were one officer and 12 men killed, 8 officers and 87 other ranks wounded. The comparatively light losses compared to those suffered in previous actions were due to the great protection afforded by the armoured Priests.

Their next important action was when their brigade (2nd Armoured) made the

FIRST OF THE TERRITORIALS to be accorded the honour of mounting guard at Buckingham Palace, the H.A.C. sentry takes over from a Regular, on July 6, 1938.
Photo, Topical

famous moonlight attack at El Hammah, which turned the Mareth Line. After following up the German retreat, the 11th were passed over to the 1st Army and took part with the 6th Armoured Division in the capture of Tunis, the storming of the lines of Hamman Lif and the subsequent German collapse. An officer of the 11th was the first man of the 1st Army to make contact with the 8th Army near Enfidaville.

Fierce Fighting on Gothic Line

Immediately afterwards they were attached to the 51st Highland Division to prepare for the landing in Sicily. Theirs were the first guns to land in the invasion of Europe, on July 10, 1943, at Pachino, on the southern tip of Sicily. After fighting throughout the Sicilian campaign and adding the actions of Palazzolo, Vizzini, Catania, Gerbini, Catenanuovo, Centuripe, Adrano, Bronte, and Maletto to their list of battle honours, the 11th, suffering heavily from malaria, were withdrawn to rest in Algeria where they rejoined their Division.

After prolonged training they moved to Italy in May 1944, and took part in the fierce fighting on the Gothic Line in September. The 1st Armoured Division was ordered to pass through a gap broken by the Infantry and advance northward. Arriving at the starting point somewhat tired by a week of

FLYING A COMPANY'S FLAG at Tmimi, in the Western Desert, where the 11th H.A.C. with the British First Armoured Division spent much of the winter of 1942-43, after fighting at El Alamein. Leaving here in February 1943 the Regiment travelled 1,000 miles in two weeks, going direct into the battle for the Mareth Line near Medinine.

forced marches, the 2nd Armoured Brigade carried out an all-night march along tortuous hill tracks, crossed the Conca river and attacked. The German line, however, was far from broken and the tanks could only penetrate the outer defences and were then held up by concentrated artillery fire. The Division fought its way slowly forward through San Clemente, San Savino and Croce.

T HEN, in an attack on the commanding ridge of Point 153 near San Marino, The Bays encountered stiff resistance and lost 24 tanks, the Forward Observation Officer of the 11th and all his detachment being killed. The 1st Armoured Division was later disbanded, but the 2nd Armoured remained together as an independent armoured brigade.

The 11th were again heavily engaged at the crossing of the Ronco and Montone rivers, the Cosina Canal and the Senio river, and in the capture of Merzeno, Pideura, Celle and Faenza. After a relatively quiet period attached to the 1st Canadian Division, the 8th Indian Division, the Palestine Brigade and the Cremona Group of Italian troops, the Regiment was attached to the 78th Division. They were in action at the crossing of the Senio and Santerno rivers, and their brigade forced the Argenta Gap, an action which brought about the general retreat of the German armies across the Po and led to the final surrender on April 29, 1945.

The 12th (H.A.C.) Regiment, R.H.A., landed in North Africa in November 1942, as part of the 6th Armoured Division, and were in action at Tebourba and Mateur in the December. They helped to "plug the line" at Bou Arada and Robaa early in 1943, and F Battery fought a particularly gallant action at Thala, where for a night and a day they were part of the front line and repulsed several German tank attacks; three M.C.s, one D.C.M. and two M.M.s were awarded to the Battery for this action. The 12th also stopped the rot in the Fondouk Pass in April and then advanced towards Tunis. In the final battle for that town, fighting side by side with the 11th H.A.C., they attacked with the 6th Armoured Division and, after the capture of the town, helped to force the fortified lines of Hamman Lif, which compelled the final surrender. The losses of the 12th in North Africa had included three officers and 34 other ranks killed.

500 Miles' Fighting in Six Months

After a period of rest and training, the 12th went with their division to Italy and were heavily engaged near Cassino, up the Liri Valley, through the Gustav and Aquino lines, and then on to Perugia. In July and August 1944 they were in action round Arezzo and Florence. September and October saw the 12th engaged in difficult mountain fighting. The line became static;

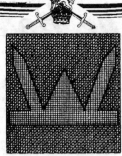

Colours : Red on Khaki

53RD (WELSH) DIVISION

C OMPOSED of Territorial battalions of the Welsh Regiment, the Royal Welch Fusiliers, the K.S.L.I., and Territorial regiments of Monmouthshire and Herefordshire, the Division was formed in 1939. Its badge is reputed to be symbolic of the offensive : the horizontal being the base of attack, the peak of the "W" the spearhead, and the side-members flanking movements, the "W" standing for Wales.

Moved to N. Ireland in 1940, it returned to England in 1942, and later joined 21 Army Group for the invasion of Europe, 1944. Concentrated south-west of Bayeux, after landing with the British 2nd Army in the Normandy beach-head on June 27, 1944, the Division, in the words of its Army Commander, Lieut.-General Sir Miles Dempsey, "Went straight into the tough and difficult fighting on the Odon against seasoned German troops." Hard struggles ensued at Evrecy, Le Caheir and Hill 112. Heavy destruction was wrought near Necy on August 17, in the Falaise Gap operations.

A CROSS the Seine by the end of August the Division was one of the first units to enter Antwerp after the Liberation. In September, the 53rd successfully defended the left flank of the Allied Airborne troops at Arnhem. A brief spell on the "island" in the Nijmegen salient was a prelude to the capture of Hertogenbosch, in November. Against the German Ardennes offensive, in December, the 53rd defended Brussels. From the start of the Reichswald Forest battle, February 8, 1945, the Division encountered bitter fighting, but without respite advanced 40 miles, to near Aplon and within four miles of the Rhine. Its last battles were fought over the Rhine at Rethem and Verden, and its unopposed occupation of Hamburg completed a record in which, to quote the XII Corps Commander, Lieut.-General Ritchie, the troops had "never failed . . . to carry through . . . any task which has fallen to their lot."

but in a pursuit lasting six months the Regiment had covered 500 miles, fighting all the way. After a winter spent in training, with frequent moves, the 12th H.A.C. again went into action, in April 1945, and took part in the crossing of the Senio, Santerno and Sillaro rivers, the capture of Traghetto and onwards towards Ferrara in the hard fighting which forced the Germans over the Po.

The 13th (H.A.C.) Regiment, R.H.A., after a prolonged period of training in England, landed in Normandy on June 15, 1944, as part of the 11th Armoured Division and was almost continuously in action from the crossing of the Odon until the closing of the Falaise Gap. After crossing the Seine, their Division formed part of the tremendous armoured thrust which broke through to Amiens, seizing the crossings of the Somme, and then on to Antwerp, which they entered,

PASSING THROUGH PALAZZOLO on July 12, 1943, two days after landing in Sicily, these self-propelled Priests of the 11th H.A.C. were the first Allied guns to land in Europe during this preliminary stage of the invasion. The Palazzolo action added yet another battle honour to the Regiment's impressive record.

Photo, British Official

11th H.A.C. Regiment in N. Africa with 8th Army

AFTER HELPING TO HALT ROMMEL'S FORCES AT ALAMEIN, in July 1942, the 11th H.A.C. Regiment (R.H.A.) was equipped with Priest self-propelled 105-mm. howitzers (1). One of the Regiment's 25-pdr. field guns which received a direct hit (2) was left derelict at Knightsbridge, where the 11th covered the withdrawal of the British 50th and South African Divisions in face of Rommel's June offensive. As 8th Army Commander, General Sir Claude Auchinleck spoke to officers of the Regiment from the roof of his car (3). The remnants of the 11th Regiment were then formed into one composite battery and went straight back into battle.   PAGE 397

CHRISTMAS GREETINGS (left) were received by the author of this article in 1943 at the Regimental H.Q. at Armoury House, London. The airgraph was sent by the 12th H.A.C. Regiment from N. Africa.

On March 28, 1945, the Regiment crossed the Rhine and again took part in the forward rush of 11th Armoured which crossed the Ems-Dortmund Canal, fought a heavy engagement at Tecklenburg and forced the Aller bridge-head. They reached the Elbe on April 18 and their last engagement was fought near Lubeck against German naval contingents, in which the Regiment captured many hundreds of prisoners, including the commander and entire crew of a U-boat.

The 86th (H.A.C.) H.A.A. Regiment, R.A., after sharing prominently in the defence of London during the aerial bombardments of 1940 and 1941, assumed a mobile role. After prolonged training they landed in Normandy on D-Day and for the first few weeks protected the beach-heads, shooting down a number of enemy bombers. Their guns then went into action in a field role to stiffen the barrages, and on the German retreat they took part in the capture of Havre. The 86th was then sent to protect Antwerp, in which capacity they shot down 78 flying bombs. Since 1941 the 86th had consisted of three batteries, 273, 274 and 383 (H.A.C.). H.A.A Batteries, R.A.

Magnificent Output of Officers

275 (H.A.C.) H.A.A. Battery, R.A. (one of the original Regiment) left the 86th in 1941 to act as an instructional battery and was later attached to another regiment. It landed in Normandy, took part in many actions there in a field role and, after the advance into Holland, was heavily engaged in the Nijmegen corridor, where its gunners fought as infantry when surrounded by the German counter-attack.

446 (H.A.C.) H.A.A. Battery, R.A., was permanently engaged in a home defence role and was in action in or near London up to the spring of 1944, when it was sent to the Orkneys and was later disbanded.

Perhaps the most important contribution of the Honourable Artillery Company to the war effort was the provision of some 4,000 commissioned officers to all arms and services. Almost all the Company's pre-war members received commissions, as did many of its reservists and former members. They were to be found in almost every unit of the Army and on every front. Many of them rose to the command of units, including regular batteries of R.H.A. and infantry battalions. The roll of members at the end of the war included five Brigadiers, eight Colonels and 152 Lieut.-Colonels, all of whom had originally served in the ranks of the Company.

Thus the ancient role of the Honourable Artillery Company, which for centuries provided and trained officers for the Trained Bands of London, and sent over 4,000 of its members to commissions in the war of 1914-18, has been fully maintained.

among the foremost troops, on September 4. Later they fought on the Albert Canal and in Holland, and then endured the rigours of the winter in that water-logged country.

KIEL CELEBRATIONS ON THE KING'S OFFICIAL BIRTHDAY, June 2, 1945, included a parade and march past of British armed forces. Hitherto unpublished, this photograph shows self-propelled guns of the 13th H.A.C. Regiment R.H.A. passing the saluting base at the head of the 11th Armoured Division. Taking the salute was Lieut.-General E. A. Barker, C.B., C.B.E., D.S.O., M.C., G.-O.-C VIII Corps, accompanied by Vice-Admiral M. T. Baillie-Grohman, C.B., D.S.O., O.B.E., R.N., Flag Officer-in-C. of this German port.

Photo, British Official

Britain Pays Tribute to 'The Few'

IN COMMEMORATION of the sixth anniversary of the Battle of Britain there took place over London on September 14, 1946, massed formation flights of more than 30 squadrons from the R.A.F., one squadron of the Fleet Air Arm, seven squadrons of Polish aircraft serving with the R.A.F., and three fighter squadrons of the U.S. Army Air Force from Germany. It had been planned to make this the first occasion on which the Battle had been commemorated by massed flights over the whole of the area in which it was fought, but bad weather caused the cancellation of this arrangement over some parts of Southern England. Twelve Lancaster bombers were the first of the many to pass over, at 2,000 feet, in salute to "The Few" who won the Battle fought in 1940. Then, massed fighters came in from the east over St. Paul's Cathedral (above). In two great columns a mile apart 300 aircraft patterned the overcast sky, and in five minutes had roared away, bound for their several dispersal points.

Because the clouds were low and grey over London, a yellow guide-flare burned (right) on the roof of the Air Ministry in King Charles Street, where a group of Air Marshals gathered to watch the modern types which have supplanted those of earlier fame—whose total number for combat duty six years ago no more than approximated to that of the force which on this day paid tribute on Britain's behalf to "The Few." *Photos, P.A.-Reuter, G.P.U.*

399

Remembering the Fallen in the Battle of Britain—

Lord Portal (1), with Lady Tedder, arriving for the Thanksgiving Service at Westminster Abbey, London, on September 15, 1946. Reopened with a special commemoration service on the same day, St. George's Memorial Chapel at Biggin Hill (Kent) now contains, behind the altar, six panels on which are inscribed in gold leaf names of pilots of the Biggin Hill Sector who were killed; prayers were conducted (2) by S./Ldr. the Rev. Cecil King, padre of No. 11 Group, Fighter Command.

Photos, T

—'Hinge on Which Our Lives and Future Turned'

Pilots who participated in the air battles six years ago relived their poignant memories when mock battles took place over Biggin Hill aerodrome : rushing for their aircraft (3), this time for the benefit of television audiences.   An anniversary dinner held at the Belfry, West Halkin Street, London, was attended by (4, left to right) Air Chief Marshal Sir Keith Park, Air Chief Marshal Lord Dowding, Air Marshal Sir John Robb and Group Captain Douglas Bader.

To the Honour and Glory of Our Air Forces

Marshals of the R.A.F. Lord Trenchard (1, left) and Lord Tedder arriving for the unveiling of a new inscription on the R.A.F. Memorial on the Victoria Embankment, London, on September 15, 1946. It reads, " This inscription is added in remembrance of those men and women of the Air Forces ῤ every part of the British Commonwealth and Empire who gave their lives 1939–45." Lord Trenchard taking the salute (2) as W.A.A.F. march past. Sounding the Last Post (3).

Dowding's Air Defence of Britain

LONG before the Battle of Britain began Lord Dowding was anxious about the forces likely to be available. On September 16, 1939, he wrote to the Air Ministry pointing out that the Air Staff's estimate of the number of fighter squadrons required for the defence of the country was 52 ; although on the outbreak of war he had only the equivalent of 34. He wanted 12 new squadrons and asked that eight should be raised immediately. The Air Ministry regretted that the most they could do was to form two new squadrons and two operational training units. After further correspondence they reconsidered their policy and ordered the formation of 10 new fighter squadrons, four of which were for Coastal Command.

On February 2 and 4, 1940, Lord Dowding wrote asking for an extension of airfield facilities, intelligence cover and communications. His proposals were not approved until May. He writes : " This delay was presumably unavoidable, but the result was that the organization and development of the defences of the South and West of England were incomplete when they were called upon to withstand the attacks which the German occupation of France made possible."

In July 1940 Lord Dowding had 59 squadrons " in various stages of efficiency." But Germany's occupation of airfields in France, Norway and the Low Countries enabled her to launch a far more formidable attack than any envisaged when the original Air Staff estimate of 52 squadrons was first made. Many of these squadrons " were still suffering from the effects of fighting in Holland and Flanders, at Dunkirk, and during the subsequent operations in France."

He was apprehensive about the wastage of Hurricanes in France, where, between May 8 and 18, 1940, 250 were lost. He writes :

" Hitherto, I had succeeded generally in keeping the Spitfire squadrons out of the Continental fighting. When the Dunkirk fighting began, however, I could no longer maintain this policy, and the Spitfires had to take their share in the fighting. I was responsible for the air defence of Great Britain, and I saw my resources slipping away like sand in an hour glass. The pressure for more and more assistance for France was relentless and inexorable. In the latter part of May 1940 I sought and obtained permission to appear in person before the War Cabinet and to state my case.

A Great Turning Point of the War

" I was accorded a courteous and sympathetic hearing, and, to my inexpressible relief, my arguments prevailed and it was decided to send no more fighter reinforcements to France, except to cover the final evacuation. I know what it must have cost the Cabinet to reach this decision, but I am profoundly convinced that this was one of the great turning points in the war."

After the Dunkirk evacuation the pressure on Fighter Command became less intense. But the Battle of Britain followed on without any appreciable opportunity to re-form the squadrons which had borne the brunt.

The battle, according to Lord Dowding, may be said to have divided itself into four phases : The attack on our convoys and coastal objectives, such as ports, coastal airfields and radiolocation stations. The attack on inland fighter airfields. The attack on London. The fighter-bomber stage, when the target was of subsidiary importance to the main objective of drawing our fighters into the air and engaging them in circumstances as disadvantageous as possible.

The most critical stage was the third phase. On September 15 the Germans delivered their maximum effort, when our

THE first R.A.F. wartime dispatch to be made public, that of Air Chief Marshal Sir Hugh Dowding (now Lord Dowding), Air Officer C.-in-C., Fighter Command R.A.F., dated Aug. 20, 1941, was published on Sept. 10, 1946 (as a supplement to the London Gazette). It thus became available in a week which marked the sixth anniversary of the critical stage of the Battle of Britain. The period covered is July 10, 1940, until Nov. 1940, when Lord Dowding relinquished his command. We give here a condensation from the commentary by Air Commodore L. G. S. Payne, The Daily Telegraph Air Correspondent.

THE LAST OF THE FEW

ONE episode should have a place in our history books for as long as we remain a nation. When the long-drawn-out battle still hung in the balance, Mr. Churchill went to Air Vice-Marshal Park's headquarters. On the radar screen he watched the advance of the German bombers.

As each wave approached, Air Vice-Marshal Park gave his orders to put in the British fighter squadrons. The Air Vice-Marshal was calm and businesslike. Mr. Churchill's nerves were taut, but underneath, his emotions were surging.

Each attack was successfully repelled, but to the waves of German bombers there seemed to be no end. At last, unable to control himself, Mr. Churchill turned to Park, " How many more have you got ? " he asked abruptly. Quietly the Air Vice-Marshal replied, " I am putting in my last."

Their eyes fixed on the screen, the two men waited for the next German wave. It never came. The Germans, too, had put in their last. With tears in his eyes, Mr. Churchill got into his car. It was on his way back to London that he composed the immortal phrase of the debt that so many owed to so few.
—*The Sunday Times*

guns and fighters together accounted for 185 aircraft. By the end of the month it became apparent that the Germans could no longer face the bomber wastage and the operations entered upon their fourth phase. Lord Dowding says : " Serious as were our difficulties, those of the enemy were worse and, by the end of October, the Germans abandoned their attempt to wear down Fighter Command, and the country was delivered from the threat of invasion."

He singles out Air Vice-Marshal (now Air Chief Marshal) Sir Keith Park, A.O.C., No. 11 Group, defenders of London and the Home Counties, for praise " for the way in which he adjusted his tactics and interception methods to meet each new development as it occurred."

Lord Dowding takes exception to two statements in the Air Ministry's published account entitled " The Battle of Britain," although he says there is very little in it he would have wished to alter if circumstances had allowed him to see it before it was published—he was in America at the time. First, he considers the speed of the Hurricane is seriously overrated at 335 m.p.h. The speed of the Hurricane was, he says, 305 m.p.h.

Situation Was Extremely Critical

Secondly, and he considers this of greater importance, he objects to the paragraph on page 33 which reads, " What the Luftwaffe failed to do was to destroy the fighter squadrons of the Royal Air Force, which were, indeed, stronger at the end of the battle than at the beginning." He says :

" This statement, even if intended only for popular consumption, tends to lead to an attitude of complacency which may be very dangerous in future. Whatever the study of paper returns may have shown, the fact is that the situation was critical in the extreme. Pilots had to be withdrawn from the Bomber and Coastal Commands and from the Fleet Air Arm and flung into the battle after hasty preparation. The majority of the squadrons had been reduced to the status of training units, and were fit only for operations against unescorted bombers. The remainder were battling against heavy odds."

At a later stage in his dispatch he mentions how Mr. Churchill " spoke with affectionate raillery of me and my ' Chicks.' " He adds, " He could have said nothing to make me more proud ; every Chick was needed before the end."

He gives high praise to the Royal Observer Corps, and states that " their work throughout was quite invaluable." Writing of the barrage balloons, he says :

" It is true that their material results, in terms of enemy aircraft destroyed, were not impressive ; they suffered staggering casualties in electric storms, and had brought down a number of our aircraft. On the other hand, they exercised a very salutary effect upon the Germans and, to a great extent, protected vital objectives against low altitude attacks and dive-bombing."

FORMER EAGLE SQUADRON PILOTS RETURNED for the Battle of Britain's sixth anniversary. Composed of U.S. volunteers the " Eagle " operated as a R.A.F. squadron in 1940. Here the pilots are seen at Odiham airfield. whence they took off for the great fly-past on September 14, 1946. See also pages 399-402.
Photo, Planet News

Europe's Wartime Capitals in 1946

OSLO

By O. F. KNUDSEN

NORWAY'S capital is her principal centre of trade and industry and shipping, the seat of the King, the Government, Parliament and the University. The population of the city, with its suburbs, now numbers about 400,000. Geographically, Oslo is unique. It is the most northerly city of its size in the world. It lies on the same parallel of latitude as Greenland, but thanks to the mildness of the Gulf Stream it enjoys an ideal climate, warm in summer and invigorating in winter. Situated at the head of the Oslo Fjord, the city is surrounded by wooded hills with magnificent views of mountain and forest. It has some imposing buildings, including the National Theatre, the Royal Palace, and the University Buildings, which all centre around the main boulevard Karl Johan—the "Piccadilly" of Oslo—and more modern structures such as the new Broadcasting House and the magnificent Town Hall which dominates the harbour scene. As few bombs fell on Oslo all these features of the city remain.

A visit to Oslo today is a heartening experience to anyone who knew the city some eighteen months ago. The progress made since the liberation in May 1945 is evident in every direction. As Oslo is the principal port of Scandinavia, the dock-area is perhaps the best place to go for a picture of the changed fortunes of the Norwegian capital. At the beginning of 1945 the harbour was a dead place, with only a few troopships departing for Germany. Now the available quays—some were destroyed as a result of the war—are bustling with activity. Warehouses are crammed with many goods that Norwegians never saw throughout the war.

Food Queues are Non-Existent

The shipyards are equally busy. Not only is every slipway occupied with new ships being built for the Norwegian merchant marine, but older ships are literally lining-up to be overhauled and repaired after five years' neglect and war service. Ships that were sabotaged and sunk during the war are being salvaged, quays and warehouses that were blown up are being rebuilt.

The food position, too, has greatly improved. At the beginning of 1945 the citizens of Oslo were subsisting on about 1,400 calories a day. Now, thanks to large shipments from abroad, their rations give them at least the 2,400 calories which dieticians claim are the minimum essential for health. The rationed commodities are much the same as in Britain—bread and flour, fats, sugar, coffee, meat, milk and eggs—and the quantities are also much the same. During the German occupation even the meagre rations then allowed were not always obtainable, but now everyone is assured of his fair share.

As a result queues are non-existent, except when some special seasonal delicacy is on the market. Indeed, the only queue of any permanence is the one in front of the Government Liquor Stores ; both spirits and cigarettes are off the ration now, a concession much appreciated by Norwegians. The absence of any black market on a large scale is a remarkable feature. In an occupied city, black market dealings are almost indispensable if the inhabitants are to live at all ; and Oslo was no exception. The people are proud of the fact that peace has ended their particular black market and a fair distribution of goods to rich and poor has been assured.

Another respect in which the attitude of Oslo people has changed is in regard to work. During the German occupation it was patriotic to do as little work as possible and to do it as badly as possible. For example, in the Oslo shipyards the construction of a vessel ordered by the Germans would be delayed year after year, tools would be lost, machinery would break down, materials would fail to turn up. Inevitably, this kind of slacking and deliberate inefficiency left an impression on the workers which could not be eradicated in a day or two. There were, also, so many occasions and pretexts for celebration after the liberation.

THE return of King, Crown Prince, and Government ; Independence Day and Allied Forces' Day ; the King's birthday and the end of the war with Japan ; all these, and many more, made the months following liberation a time of continuous gaiety. Allied troops in Oslo—including the famous 1st Airborne Division—found themselves amongst a people far different from the stolid, stodgy folk they had imagined. Indeed, Allied troops were inclined to criticize them occasionally for their over-exuberance. But now the people are working hard. The registered number of unemployed is the lowest ever recorded ; indeed, actual unemployment is practically non-existent. It is realized by everyone that peace is not a bed of roses, and that a return to pre-war prosperity means more and more production. Industry after industry is reporting a rise in output, often attaining the pre-war level.

All this might lead to a boom and slump but for the fact that everything, including prices and wages, is kept well under control by the authorities. But the rising production does not mean that Oslo citizens are yet enjoying a pre-war standard of living. It has to be remembered that, as in Britain, much has to be exported. For example, although enough paper is being produced to enable Oslo newspapers to print as many pages as they like, the number of pages is still restricted—so that paper can be exported. Also, as in Britain, the neglect and deprivation of the war years have to be made good.

Clothes are an example. It will be some considerable time before Oslo's depleted

PEOPLE'S HOUSE AND THEATRE, one of many imposing buildings in Norway's capital, is also the centre of most of the Labour organizations.

Photo, Royal Norwegian Government

PAGE 404

wardrobes can be renewed, for during the war practically no clothes could be bought. Clothing and footwear are, far more than food, a problem for Oslo people today. At present the clothes in the shops are, on the whole, of poor quality and high priced. Stocks have to be built up, and materials, labour and manufacturing facilities are short. It is not possible to import ready-made clothes or materials on a large scale ; foreign currency stringencies just will not allow it.

A Thousand Flats are Going Up

Even more serious is the acute lack of houses. About 20,000 people were on the waiting-list for houses in Oslo in May 1946. In relation to population, this would correspond to about 400,000 persons in a city such as London. When Oslo folk talk of "houses" they usually mean flats, for the majority of them live in blocks of apartments, many municipally owned. Before the war about 3,000 new homes were built in Oslo each year. As building was at a standstill during the war, there was a deficit of 15,000 homes when peace came. But in spite of shortage of labour and materials a good deal of building is in progress. Under the direction of the Oslo housing authority construction has started on over 1,000 flats which it is hoped to finish during the year, and in 1947 the output of homes will be back to the peace level. Nearly all flats now being built or planned are of the family type. When ready, large families, now overcrowded, will move in, thus making small flats available for single persons and childless couples.

Heating, a very serious problem, threatens to be no easier this winter than last. Except up in Spitsbergen, where the mining plant was destroyed during the war, Norway produces no coal of her own. The coal imported is all reserved for industrial purposes, and as far as domestic heating is concerned the capital is obliged to rely on wood. This is not really satisfactory, as the wood is needed for the manufacture of pulp and paper and other products, but there is no alternative. Last winter huge stacks of logs could be seen in Oslo, and the citizens are now being warned that this winter, too, they must build up their stocks of timber. Although Norway produces great quantities of electricity it is expected that this also will have to be rationed to domestic consumers during the winter.

OVERCROWDING, and lack of warmth, food and clothing during the war, naturally affected the health of people, particularly the children. Fortunately, the liberation came before really widespread and permanent deterioration of health could occur. The Swedes helped by supplying a great many of the children with so-called "Swedish soup" every day. Now they are to carry on the good work by building a special children's hospital in Oslo ; it will be one of the finest of its kind in the world. It is a sign of the times that it has been possible for the school authorities to restore the free daily service of the world-famous "Oslo breakfast" consisting of rye-bread, butter, fresh vegetables, fruit and milk.

Perhaps Oslo has been more fortunate than most of the occupied capitals of Europe. It appears a little grey and worn after five years of occupation, but as the two-month resistance against the Germans in 1940 was fought out elsewhere in Norway, the capital was not reduced to rubble and ashes like Warsaw, Rotterdam or Belgrade. There were occasional air raids, and a great deal of sabotage, but the marks which these left are rapidly being erased. Though the citizens lack many of the things which they enjoyed before the war they know that many other people are faring far worse.

Oslo's Revival After Five Years of Oppression

IN THE CAPITAL OF NORWAY AND PRINCIPAL PORT OF SCANDINAVIA there are today no food queues : people shop comfortably and at leisure in the open-air market (1). Boulevard Karl Johan, leading to the Royal Palace (3, centre), was on May 17, 1946, thronged with citizens celebrating National Day, revived after the five years' Occupation. Few bombs fell on Oslo, but 20,000 people were on the waiting list for houses on National Day : many flats are being built, and in the suburbs wooden villas (2) are easing the situation. *Photos, Royal Norwegian Government*

New Milestones of Victory Through France

FIRST OF THE COMMEMORATIVE STONES erected along the U.S. 3rd Army's " Liberation Route " from Avranches to Metz was unveiled at St. Symphorien, France, on August 26, 1946. Attending the ceremony (1) were American troops (left), and French armoured forces (right). A young French girl unveiled the stone (2). One of ten memorials (3) to the U.S. First Infantry Division, along the same route, was unveiled on September 2, 1946, at Havay, on the Franco-Belgian Frontier, where the first U.S. soldier was killed on Belgian soil in the Second Great War.   PAGE 406

Pluto Comes Back from the Sea-bed as Salvage

PIPE LINE UNDER THE OCEAN—Pluto for short—which conveyed petrol across the bed of the English Channel to Allied Armies on the Continent, is now providing valuable materials, notably lead, required for (among other purposes) the construction of British houses. A length of the pipe line is being wound in (1) by the S.S. Empire Ridley, and one of the marker buoys (2) is taken aboard. Operations are watched by Mr. A. C. Hartley (3), who developed cable used in the laying. Pipe line on board the Empire Ridley (4), temporarily renamed H.M.S. Latimer when she assisted in the laying operations. See also pages 120 and 533, Vol. 9. PAGE 407

The Roll of Honour
1939—1946

NCO's &MEN

Pte. D. J. ADAMS
East Lancashire Regt.
Action : Eystrup. 14.4.45.
Age 19.   (Cranborne)

So great has been the response of readers to our invitation to submit portraits for our Roll of Honour that no more can now be accepted. But we have every hope of being able to publish all those so far received.

Cpl. F. G. AVERALL
Gordon Highlanders.
Action : Italy.   29.9.44.
Age 29. (Sutton Coldfield)

Cpl. A. L. BLOCK
Rifle Brigade.
Action : Cassino. 17.5.44.
Age 27.   (London)

Gnr. H. BONFIELD
K.O. Scottish Borderers.
Act'n : Nijmegen. 23.10.44.
Age 23.   (Twickenham)

S.B.A. H. J. COLLEY
R.N.V.R.
Indian Ocean.   12.2.44.
Age 20.   (Bristol)

Sgt./Plt. R. CURNOW
R.A.F.V.R.
Action : Wales. 17.11.43.
Age 21.   (Redruth)

Sgt./Nav. S. CRACKNELL
Air/Sea Rescue R.A.F.
Fresian Isles.   8.10.44.
Age 21.   (Tottenham)

Chf./Yeo. CONSTANT
H.M.S. Harvester.
North Atlantic.   11.3.43
Age 29.   (London)

Sgt. C. H. CURTIS
Royal Engineers.
Action : C.M.F.   9.9.44.
Age 25.   (Oxford)

Pte. G. DODDS
16th Durham L.I.
Died of wounds. 12.6.43.
Age 32.   (Newbiggin/Sea)

Flt./Sgt. A. DOBSON
Royal Air Force.
Over Kiel Canal. 27.8.44.
Age 21.   (Alnwick)

Sgt. K. W. EDWARDS
Highland Light Infantry.
Siegfried Line.   25.2.45.
Age 26.   (Shirley)

Dvr. R. E. HATHERLY
12th Royal Signals.
D/wds. W. Europe. 2.5.45.
Age 23.   (Colyton)

Sgt. Flt./Eng. JEFFERIES
640 Sqn. R.A.F.V.R.
Action : E. Yorks. 2.2.45.
Age 19.   (Bedford)

Rfn. W. JOHNSTON
R. Ulster R., Airborne.
Action : N'mandy.19.6.44.
Age 22.   (Newtownards)

Sgt./Gnr. C. C. KINVIG
Royal Air Force.
Over Normandy.   2.7.44.
Age 21.   (Douglas)

Sgt. R. LEWIS
49 A.P.C. Regt. R.A.C.
Action : Goch.   18.2.45.
Age 34.   (Battersea)

Rfn. C. LINSEY
5th Commandos.
Action : Burma. 23.3.44.
Age 19.   (Whetstone)

Sgt. G. S. LOVE
Royal Air Force.
Act'n : Middelfart. 10.3.43.
Age 22.   (Norbury)

Sgt. R. NORMAN
Royal Air Force.
Market Harboro. 11.3.44.
Age 22.   (Wellingborough)

C.S.M. S. OAKLEY
1st Green Howards.
Action : Anzio. 11.3.44.
Age 36.   (Bedlington)

Tpr. C. C. OLDING
142 Regiment R.A.C.
D/wnds.: Tunisia. 23.4.43.
Age 29.   (Eastleigh)

Sgt./Plt. G. F. PECK
10 Bomber Sqn. R.A.F.
Yorkshire.   10.3.43.
Age 21.   (Isleworth)

Marine M. F. PINN
H.M.S. Southampton.
Mediterranean.   10.1.41.
Age 32.   (Faversham)

Pte. T. E. C. PICK
Lincolnshire Regiment.
Action : Venray. 3.11.44.
Age 20.   (Boston)

Flt./Sgt. C. PLATT
R.A.F.V.R.
Over Aegean.   30.9.43.
Age 32.   (Springhead)

L/Smn. W. POPHAM
H.M. Submarine Sterlet.
Action : at sea. April, '40.
Age 24.   (Andover)

Pte. F. RESTELL
Devonshire Regiment.
Action : W. Europe. 3.9.44.
Age 26.   (Dagenham)

L/Sgt. J. SMITH
2nd Battn. The Buffs.
Action : Burma. Feb. '45.
Age 25.   (Oxted)

Pte. D. STEELE
K.O. Scottish Borderers.
Action : Goch.   27.2.45.
Age 20.   (Shepherd's Bush)

L/Cpl. A. J. STEGGLES
R. Army Service Corps.
North Africa.   14.3.44.
Age 30.   (Thornton Heath)

Flt./Sgt. J. THOMPSON
57 Bomber Sqn. R.A.F.
Over Harburg. Mar., '45.
Age 22.   (Chester)

Sgt. C. TAYLOR
139 (B) Squadron R.A.F.
Action : Belgium. 12.5.40.
Age 23.   (Birmingham)

Sgt. H. TRUSCOTT
Royal Air Force.
Action : Berlin. 22.11.43.
Age 21.   (Chatham)

Spr. L. WALKER
Royal Engineers.
Act'n : St.Nazaire. 22.6.40.
Age 25.   (Burnham)

Elec. Artif. J. WATKIN
H.M. Submarine Grampus
At sea.   29.6.40.
Age 31.   (Illogan)

L/Cpl. S. S. WOODLEY
Grenadier Guards.
Action : Belgium. 30.5.40.
Age 20.   (Winchester)

Pte. W. R. YATES
R. Army Ordnance Corps.
Died of wounds.   2.4.43.
Age 23.   (Hednesford)

At Action Stations off Salerno

To be in a lower magazine with all hatches firmly clamped down, with the ship turning violently to avoid torpedoes and bombs, is unpleasant, to say the least. Such was the opinion of M. C. Hyde (portrait in page 158), who describes his experiences on the aircraft carrier Illustrious at the battle of the Salerno beaches, in September 1943.

WHEN news came through that the 8th Army had forced its way across the Straits of Messina to land on the beaches of Reggio we knew our turn for action would come soon—and we put to sea from Malta, our Mediterranean operational base, a few days later, on September 8, 1943. That the Fleet was going to cover another landing farther up the Italian coast most of us had correctly surmised, but the announcement of our Captain that same night came as a surprise.

After the familiar "D'ye hear there ! D'ye hear there ! This is the Captain speaking," had come over the ship's broadcasting system, we were told the Italians had formally surrendered earlier in the day, but the landings were to proceed, as arranged, on Salerno beaches, south of Naples, and our vigil was not to be relaxed on account of this last-minute surrender, as the Germans were expected to put up a stiff opposition. Salerno being not only the most suitable but also the most obvious place for an Allied landing, it was apparent the enemy would have it well protected.

After the clearing of minefields the first destroyers touched down on the landing beaches at 4 a.m. on the morning of September 9. Concurrently with this main landing at Salerno two other landings took place to the west with the object of seizing important military objectives. For some time before the actual landings took place we had been closed up at our various action stations on the Illustrious, standing by to ward off any surprise attack should the Germans have located us in the night.

Seamen and Royal Marines had to man the heavy dual-purpose 4·5-in. guns, the smaller oerlikons and multi-barrelled pom-poms ("Chicago Pianos") as well as maintaining look-out and gun direction positions. Stokers, apart from their normal duties in the engine, boiler and dynamo rooms, made up the damage control and aircraft fuelling parties. Telegraphists, signalmen, coders and radar operators had their own specialized duties to perform, whilst writers, supply assistants, cooks and stewards composed —as decreed by custom—the first-aid parties and worked in the magazines, hoists and ammunition conveyor-belt flats.

Waves of Enemy Aircraft Swept In

As a writer, I had my battle station in a lower magazine aft, two decks below the wardroom, and reached through two narrow hatchways which, in action, were kept firmly screwed down. In one corner of the magazine was the hoist, consisting of buckets attached to a continually moving belt, and our job was to supply a shell for at least every two buckets, but our motto was "one bucket, one shell," which meant we had to work at what seemed lightning speed.

We lay off the actual landing beach, giving it sea and air protection with the battleships Nelson, Rodney, Warspite, Valiant, King George V and our sister carrier Formidable. Together with these ships, and the cruisers Aurora, Penelope, Sirius and Dido, we formed Force "H," under the command of Vice-Admiral Sir A. U. Willis. Warspite, Valiant, King George V and the four cruisers left us a few days later to pick up the various units of the surrendered Italian Fleet.

NOR until that night did the enemy switch part of their attack to us. Spotting aircraft had been over earlier in the day, but with nightfall waves of bombers and torpedo-bombers came in to attack, and until the moon set our guns were continually in action. The enemy swept in wave after wave, their principal targets being, of course, the aircraft carriers, for could they sink or badly cripple them our aircraft would not have been able to give their vital support to the landing forces.

Down in the magazine we worked hard to supply all the ammunition our guns needed. Our crew supplied the heavy 4·5-in. guns, for which the shells weigh 56 lb. The main racks were soon emptied and the auxiliary magazines had to be drawn upon. Because of the heat we wore shorts only, and these had to be taken off and wrung out during any short lull in the firing. With the air supply disconnected to prevent back-flash from the guns entering the magazine by way of the ventilation tubes, temperature soon rose to nearly 110 degrees. Working in that

AFTER THE SALERNO OPERATION the aircraft carrier Illustrious (foreground) returned to her Mediterranean operational base at Malta—where this photograph was taken from her bows, showing H.M.S. Warspite (background) also returning to base. Besides giving protection to the landings with her fighter aircraft (a Seafire is visible on the flight deck), Illustrious had expended 4·5-in. shells to the total of 1,475 and 16,500 rounds of pom-pom ammunition off Salerno, and although the target of heavy German air attacks came through unscathed. PAGE 409 *Photo, British Official*

NIGHT ATTACK AT SALERNO, where the British aircraft carriers Illustrious and Formidable, covering Allied landings, were priority targets of determined but vain efforts by German bombers. A.A. tracer shells from one of the carriers illumine the dark sky in this photograph taken from H.M.S. Warspite, whose rigging is dimly visible (bottom right). *Photo, British Official*

awful heat and with no fresh air, by the time the first major lull came most of us were ready to faint. But because of the likelihood of further attacks no one was allowed out of the magazine for sleep; we snatched what we could on the steel deck, with shells as pillows. By way of refreshment we had some vile lime-juice and ship's biscuits, plus our action ration packs, containing vitamin tablets, chewing gum and sweets.

Throughout the following morning and afternoon we were allowed out of the magazine only for brief spells and had to take our meals in shifts, but even five minutes on a weather deck was a great tonic after the previous night's ordeal. During the day we replenished the empty shell racks and laid a good supply on the deck ready for instant use, but with nightfall came further heavy attacks and these shells were tossed about the deck every time the ship manoeuvred to avoid bombs and torpedoes, hampering our hard-pressed efforts. At times the ship lurched so violently that some of us were thrown right across the magazine; once I was pitched off my feet whilst holding a shell and came down with a resounding thud on top of it.

Our only communication with the rest of the ship was by a somewhat indistinct voice pipe, and occasionally we received reports from the bridge, by way of Commander (S) E. L. Tottenham, O.B.E., R.N., as to the progress of the action. The ship seemed to be eternally twisting and turning and the laconic injunctions of Commander Tottenham as to the many near misses did nothing to relieve our peace of mind.

ON one occasion twelve German torpedo-bombers made a concentrated attack on Illustrious, but as the Captain (Capt. R. L. B. Cunliffe) cheerfully remarked, we combed our way through them. We knew that if the ship had been hit aft there would probably have been no way of escape. Fire in the flat above us would have meant our hatches would have stayed clamped down: no chances could be taken with a magazine exploding on a crippled ship.

The following day, with the shell racks replenished, we were allowed on deck again for a few minutes at a time. The third night of action saw the enemy attacks not quite so intense, and towards early morning we were given permission to sleep near the magazine during lulls, which meant at least a camp bed and cleaner air. But we barely managed to get to sleep before the call to

battle stations would blare over the loud speakers, and a frantic quarter of an hour ensued: a mad rush to get down into the magazine, and an even madder rush to maintain a constant flow of shells up to the guns before we wearily made our way once more to our camp beds. During some of the lulls I assisted the leader of our magazine in producing Beacon, the ship's weekly humour-paper. How we managed to inculcate any humour into its pages I don't know, but at least we were successful in getting it out on time.

Middle Watch in Cipher Office

With Monte Corvino airfield firmly in our hands and the carriers' fighter protection no longer needed we returned to Malta. In all, Illustrious used 1,495 4·5-in. shells and 16,500 rounds of pom-pom ammunition in the Salerno operations. On an average our magazine had used most shells and before the final attack was launched we had been sent to another magazine as our ammunition had been expended. We had lived up to our motto of "one bucket, one shell," much to the consternation of the chaps on the receiving end of our hoist, who, of course, had to work at top pressure to avoid the shells jamming. Our only damage was shrapnel and machine-gun bullets on the flight deck, no casualties being suffered apart from the few fellows who had gone down with battle fatigue. Considering the number of very heavy attacks made by the Germans it was amazing the Illustrious had come through unscathed.

I was wrong in imagining that on our return to Malta I would have the opportunity to make up for lost sleep. That same night I found I had the middle watch (midnight to 4 a.m.) in the cipher office, where I had to assist in deciphering and typing the various messages received. Whilst on duty I was surprised when a signal came through

recalling the battleships and escorts to the assault area as things were not going so well and the landing forces needed further support. But the recall did not affect us, so we carried on to Malta with a destroyer escort. At this time the Italian Battle Fleet was surrendering and we saw large formations of them in and around Malta.

Motto: "It Shall be Done"

NO. 117 SQUADRON

NOTHING is known of the squadron's early activities in the war, but in June 1943 they were at Castel Benito in Tripolitania operating with Dakota transport aircraft throughout North Africa. In July 1943, during the Sicilian campaign, they flew supplies into that island, evacuating casualties on return trips, and did valuable work during the fierce battles for Catania, flying in supplies and evacuating some 2,749 casualties.

On October 25 the entire squadron moved to Cairo, where they received a glowing tribute from Air Chief Marshal Sir Sholto Douglas, A.O.C.-in-C. Middle East. The squadron settled in at Dhamial (Punjab) on November 1, and from that date until February 1944 were engaged in intensive training—paratroop and supply dropping—in conjunction with General Wingate's Special Force.

ON February 16 the move to Lalmai (Bengal) was commenced and the first supply dropping operations were carried out on the 24th. A few aircraft flew each day to Lalaghat to be fitted with mule stalls and to practise glider tugs in preparation for Wingate's airborne invasion of North Burma, and on March 4 aircraft were detached to Tulihal (Imphal) Valley. On October 31, 1944, No. 117 moved to Risalpur in the N.W. Frontier Province for rest, later to Bikram for training in glider towing, and in December to Hathazari near Chittagong. In January 1945 the Arakan offensive was—as far as air supply was concerned—sustained by 117 Squadron alone.

It moved to Kyaukpyu (Ramree Island) in May, back to Chittagong in August, and to Hmawbi in Southern Burma in September to prepare for the occupation by airborne forces of Bangkok and Saigon and the evacuation of Allied prisoners.

I Was King of an Island in the Aegean

German garrisons manning the Aegean islands in 1943 and 1944 were kept very much on the alert by raiding parties of British and Greek Commandos. On Symi, north-west of Rhodes, the British occupying force consisted for some months of one man—Coy. Sgt.-Major G. J. Roberts—who tells how, as "Lord High Everything," he administered that island.

AFTER the Germans and Italians had been driven out of North Africa in the summer of 1943 volunteers were wanted for the special intelligence service known as Force 133. I had served in the

R.A.S.C. from Alamein to Cape Bon, and previously had gained some sea experience sailing in small craft during short leaves, which stood me in good stead when I applied for transfer. From Cape Bon I was sent to Haifa in Palestine. From Haifa I was

On Symi Island With Commandos of Force 133

LANDING IN SEPTEMBER 1944 on Symi, an island of 22 square miles in the Aegean north-west of Rhodes, Force 133 Commandos were joyfully welcomed by the inhabitants (1). After setting up a radio station (2) to maintain contact with their H.Q., the British raiders (3) returned to the Santa Claus, leaving behind Coy. Sergeant-Major Roberts (see facing page). It was on Symi that all the German forces in the Dodecanese and Aegean, totalling over 20,000 men, surrendered to Brig. J. Moffat in May 1945.   PAGE 411

SANTA CLAUS, as the British members of her crew called the Greek caique Ios Nicolas, was the small but well-armed vessel in which "Force 133" raided enemy-occupied islands in the Eastern Mediterranean. On her arrival at Symi (above) on September 26, 1944, Greeks were taken aboard for interrogation; most of them co-operated wholeheartedly with the British "invaders."

given passage in an Arab schooner to Cyprus. There I was interviewed by Major Chapman, in command of the Famagusta base, who gave me a chance to back out without any of the stigma which attaches to an eleventh hour withdrawal.

"Force 133 is an entirely voluntary service," he emphasized. "It is fair to tell you that if you go through with this you will be engaged on highly secret and dangerous work." There was no need to "think it over," as he advised. My mind was made up. I had come hundreds of miles in search of something novel and exciting and had no intention of going back to the R.A.S.C. with my tail ignominiously down.

Company Sgt.-Major
G. J. ROBERTS

The decision was made then and there, for good or ill. Major Chapman took me down to the docks and introduced me to Regimental Sergeant-Major John Clayton, a young bearded buccaneer who might have been a direct descendant of Sir Francis Drake. Clayton was skipper of a Greek caique Ios Nicolas, which in English means Santa Claus, and I was appointed as mate. The Santa Claus became my floating home. She had a length of only 32 feet, but was 13 feet of beam and could accommodate a crew of seven in one cabin amidships and another for'ard. She was well-armed for her job of roaming and raiding in the enemy-occupied area of the Eastern Mediterranean.

For two days we were busy taking aboard stores and ammunition and making everything shipshape for a voyage. Then we sailed under sealed orders, and that excursion over blue sparkling sea into the Unknown thrilled me more than any of the former exploits in the dusty African desert. Beside the crew—six of us British and one Greek patriot—we had two passengers, both Greek agents in the pay of the British Intelligence Service. To all outward appearance the Santa Claus was a harmless caique manned by Greek fishermen, for Army uniforms had been replaced by attire in keeping with our role.

According to instructions our skipper Clayton opened the sealed orders when we were clear of Cyprus, and we learnt that our destination was Andros, an island in the Aegean Sea. This was no healthy spot, being near the mainland of Greece ; in fact, less than 50 miles from Athens as the crow flies. Our job was to land the two Greek agents there, and take off two others who, presumably, would have military information to impart to our Staff at Famagusta. Further instructions were to obtain photographs, if possible, waylay any Greek fishermen who might have contacted the Germans, and learn whatever we could of enemy defences, ship movements and so forth. Beside ammunition for our guns we took "ammo" of another variety—stacks of gold sovereigns and gallons of a native drink called mastica for the purpose of "sweetening" Greeks who might prove useful to the Allied cause.

To Collect the German Commandant

Thus began a three months' voyage through the maze of Aegean islands, some of them heavily fortified and garrisoned by the Germans. One ticklish bit of navigation was through the mined channel between Rhodes and the Turkish coast in the darkness of night. All nerves were on edge during this tricky passage. But though we steered well clear of Rhodes, the caique was seen and the German shore batteries gave us a bad quarter-hour as we ran under harassing shell-fire. In spite of German vigilance in the Aegean we accomplished the mission to Andros successfully, and afterwards made another more-or-less uneventful voyage.

The third exploit in which I took part was of a different kind. Our destination was Melos, and the order was to raid the strong German garrison and, if possible, capture the Commandant of the island. We arrived in darkness, shortly after midnight, and anchored in a small cove on what appeared to be a lonely part of the coast. I went ashore with the raiding party, consisting of four Englishmen and several Greeks, commanded by a Greek officer specially appointed to lead the attack. We crept ashore among the rocks, each man armed with a tommy-gun, automatic pistol and several hand-grenades. Unluckily, an alert German sentry must have seen movement and reported to headquarters by telephone, for within a few minutes a hot fire was directed on the cove by quick-firing 88-mm. guns.

No recall signal was made from the Santa Claus, and we pushed on inland for half-a-mile. The danger that the Germans might descend from their strongholds and cut off our retreat to the caique had to be

accepted—we became used to living dangerously in Force 133. For a time we returned the fire from scattered positions, and hoped thereby to give the impression that we were a really formidable raiding company.

The bold policy, aided by luck, paid handsome dividends. We reached a wide track and, hearing a motor vehicle coming our way, lay in ambush among the rocks and scrub. A German Staff car came along and drew sharply to a halt on our first burst of fire. The three occupants were the Commandant and two aides who had been hurrying across the island to discover what all the "liveliness" was about. But this was not the Commandant we had come to collect ; this was a new man recently arrived at Melos, and (as we discovered subsequently) a dyed-in-the-wool member of the Nazi Party.

The trio alighted, and our Greek officer called in German to demand their instant surrender. Response came in a burst of fire from the Commandant's automatic, and the two others began blazing away. Bullets whanged and ricochetted around us, and small-arms' fire from the hills was directed toward the track. There was only one thing to do, and we did it. An answering stream of bullets spat from our tommy-guns, and the three Germans slumped to the ground.

A hurried search was made of their bodies and the car ; then we wrecked the vehicle with hand-grenades and scurried back to the cove through the fire-torn night, taking with

REG. SGT.-MAJOR JOHN CLAYTON, skipper of the Ios Nicolas, "a young bearded buccaneer who might have been a direct descendant of Sir Francis Drake."

us the valuable military papers we had secured. We encountered no German patrols, but how we got the Santa Claus to sea under shell-fire without casualties was little short of a miracle. The caique herself was spattered with steel fragments from near-misses.

Life in Force 133 was a series of strange, nerve-testing adventures often under circumstances of acute discomfort, alternating with brief periods of "high life" in the only luxury hotel in Famagusta. We even landed on Rhodes, attacked a German convoy of ships on our way out, and ran for cover to Aplothika in Turkey. Then, en route to the small island of Symi, we were intercepted by heavily-armed R-boats which flashed signals to discover our identity. Luckily for us we had the German code, and were able to reply satisfactorily. But it was some time before our heart-beats settled to normal tempo.

We discovered by reconnaissance that the Germans had left Symi temporarily, and the shell-fire we encountered on approaching the place was from Greek patriots who imagined our craft was bringing some of them back. Having landed there, we hauled down the swastika flag still over the Government Building and hoisted a Blue Ensign.

"You must stay here in charge, Roberts," our skipper ordered. "I'll come back for you in a fortnight." But he did not return for three months, being busy with the capture of Santorin, which was garrisoned by no fewer than 90 Germans. So, for that period, I was sole British representative and administrator of Symi, virtually the king of the island. I heard later that Clayton requested the Royal Navy to send a detachment to occupy the place, but this was turned down. The reason given was that it was too near the island of Rhodes, strongly-held by the enemy, and that one man on Symi could be "as useful as a hundred."

By this time—September 1944—I could speak Greek fairly well. Another advantage was the co-operation of a large majority of Greeks who were overjoyed at their liberation. They acclaimed me wholeheartedly as their ruler, which meant that when I got cracking on the job I found myself enacting the role of Pooh Bah. At twenty-seven years of age, with no previous training for the multiple posts I had to fill (I was a commercial traveller before joining the Army), reliance had to be placed mainly on commonsense combined with an impressively authoritative manner.

My first concern was to organize a protective military force for the island and arm the Greeks enrolled with rifles discovered in a German armoury. About 3,500 islanders had to be fed, and it became necessary to train fishermen in the art of raiding. By intercepting and attacking German-manned caiques the food problem was prevented from becoming a serious menace, though this method of securing rations was risky in the extreme.

I appointed myself Chief Constable and formed a police force, opened a hospital and placed Symi's only doctor in charge. Then I restarted the schools, in my capacity as Superintendent of Education. As Clerk of the Peace I inaugurated licensing hours for the sale of liquor, based on the British system, with "Time, gentlemen!" at 10 p.m. sharp. And as Lord High Chancellor I confiscated certain surplus local funds, and distributed largess among the poor to enable them to buy the necessities of life. Later I sent the town crier round to collect money from the better-off inhabitants to buy food from Turkey. A rare collection was obtained for this purpose, consisting mainly of gold sovereigns, American ten-dollar pieces and Turkish gold pounds.

But life on Symi was rather like living on the brink of a volcano where a fatal eruption might occur at any time. Sentries were posted day and night, and twice I was hauled out of bed to lead in repelling German raiders who arrived in armed caiques under cover of darkness. On each occasion we beat them off, and I learnt later than the Jerries believed a strong British force had taken possession of the place. There is no reason to suppose that, until the end of the war, they had any idea that our occupying force consisted only of one British soldier !

As Lord Chief Justice, I had some cases to adjudicate that would have tested the ingenuity of Solomon himself. One was a complicated dispute among the shepherds with regard to certain grazing rights, which matter I contrived to settle harmoniously by holding a public auction—and distributing most of the proceeds afterwards to the unsuccessful bidders.

Another not-so-easy case related to a band of young zealots who were so incensed at the behaviour of thirteen Greek girls, who were alleged to have fraternized with the Germans, that they shaved the unfortunate girls' heads. In that undignified condition—shorn completely of their locks—they trooped angrily into court, unitedly shrilling their complaint at me.

The occurrence was not without humour, and it was difficult to restrain a smile at their quaint appearance. But it was a headache for me, right enough, and I was puzzled at the right step to take. At last, in view of the evidence submitted by the equally angry defenders, I imposed moderate fines, which the young zealots duly but grudgingly paid. I was careful enough to take measures to prevent a recurrence of any such regrettable display of patriotic indignation.

When at last Skipper Clayton and his buccaneers returned in the Santa Claus, the Greeks pressed gifts on me and urged that I might be appointed as permanent Governor of their island. This was out of the question, of course, and after a great celebration I took an affectionate leave of them. My hope is that one day I may return to that quaint island in the Eastern Mediterranean where, for a brief spell in wartime, I reigned as Lord-High-Everything.

Captured by the Admiral Graf Spee

The 8,000-ton Tairoa, a coal-burning cargo-carrier of the Shaw, Savill and Albion Line, under the command of Capt. W. B. S. Starr, sailed from Durban, homeward bound, on November 27, 1939, and ran foul of the notorious German pocket-battleship and raider, Admiral Graf Spee. The adventures of her survivors, taken aboard the enemy ship, are narrated by James Keating, a fireman of the S.S. Tairoa.

We heard the S O S sent out by the Blue Star liner Doric Star when, on December 2, 1939, she was being attacked by the Graf Spee. At once the old Tairoa altered course to get to safer quarters, and nothing befell us till the following morning, when we were sighted by the raider. Then things happened swiftly.

Captain Starr ordered our radio officer to send out S O S calls, whereupon shells came screaming over. No less than 50 of them hit the Tairoa in the vicinity of the bridge. In the oily heat below, we firemen of the duty watch just slogged away at our job of keeping the ship moving—hoping there would be no hit below the water-line to release high-pressure steam that could kill us as easily as shells or bullets.

Courage is a fine virtue when you have at least a dog's chance of pulling through, but live men may still be an asset to their country in the long run. That, I suppose, is how Captain Starr figured it when he hove-to and surrendered. Engineers and firemen were ordered on deck. We of the Black Squad climbed the warm ladders, sweat mingled with coal-dust on our faces and arms. We saw the awful damage done by the Graf Spee's shells, and saw the Captain calmly dump the Tairoa's log and secret papers overboard in a weighted bag.

The raider moved in and we were boarded by a German officer and marines, who

SCUTTLED ON HITLER'S ORDERS, the battleship Admiral Graf Spee was blown up off Montevideo on December 17, 1939, four days after her defeat in the Battle of the River Plate (see pages 505 and 526, Vol. I). The lives of some 1,000 of her crew were saved ; they were taken to Buenos Aires and interned. On December 20 her commander, Captain Hans Langsdorff (top), described in the accompanying story as a chivalrous foe, was found dead, in the naval arsenal at Buenos Aires, shot by his own hand.

Photos, Associated Press, Keystone

S.S. TAIROA, 8,000-ton coal-burning cargo-carrier of the Shaw, Savill and Albion Line, was on the homeward run from South Africa when she encountered the Admiral Graf Spee on December 3, 1939. The accompanying story tells of her sinking, with time-bombs and gunfire, and the subsequent adventures of her survivors.

Photo, Nautical Photo Agency

brought instructions that we were to follow their ship. But we had sustained so much damage that this was found to be impossible, so we survivors were sent aboard the Graf Spee—whilst the boarding-parties placed time bombs in the Tairoa's holds and engine-room. Most of us were a bit dazed by now, and it was not until we were actually on our way in motor-boats that we realized exactly what this fateful encounter meant to us.

The Germans slung rope-ladders over the Graf Spee's side so that we could climb aboard, and there on the quarter-deck of the pocket-battleship we saw the man whose name was destined to make world news.

Captain Hans Langsdorff was a fine-looking figure in his naval uniform of white with black-and-gold shoulder-straps and many decorations; and he addressed us in excellent English. We heard later that he had lived in the Isle of Wight before the war, and his English wife and daughters were still there; but he had been recalled to Germany as he was on the German Naval Reserve. Here is what he said to us, so far as I can remember:

J. KEATING

"I am very sorry to have to do this, but we are at war. Of all the ships I have caught, I have not left any members of the crews stranded. I have always fetched them on board and, when convenient, turned many of them over to my supply ship. You will be transferred to an oil-tanker. While you are here, you can have a fair share of what rations I have in my ship."

WHILE the captain of the Graf Spee was talking, our wounded shipmates were being taken to the sick bay for surgical treatment. Then some of the German crew gathered round, and one of them said to those of us who were grimy with coal-dust, "Come down and have a bath, and then you can have something to eat if you want it."

I was below decks when explosions tore the plates out of the Tairoa, and so was spared the sight of her final destruction. Because the bombs they had planted aboard her did not sink her at once, the Germans finished her off with gunfire, then the Graf Spee got under way. After a hot bath I joined some of my mates and was given tea with plenty of milk and sugar, white bread and cake. There was, it seemed, plenty of tea on board because the raider had taken 500 cases out of the Huntsman, another of her victims.

Men of the Doric Star were on board with us. A refrigerated meat-carrier of 10,000 tons, bound from New Zealand, she had a full cargo when encountered, and her master, Captain Stubbs, flooded the engine-room and refrigerated chambers when he knew himself to be trapped, and thus denied the Graf Spee a useful haul of supplies.

The Germans had not allowed us to bring extra gear away, and all I now owned was an old flannel vest, a pair of dungaree trousers and a well-worn pair of boots, but I was lucky to have a few cigarettes in my pocket. During the day, as the Graf Spee steamed westward at high speed, we were allowed on deck, although constantly under guard. The weather was perfect and the Jerries were in high spirits, especially the many youngsters in the crew—but then they didn't know what was coming to them off the coast of South America!

Cigarette-end for Adolf Hitler

We prisoners paced up and down and speculated vainly on what the future might hold for us. While so doing, we were astonished to see three of the Germans come along the deck carrying a 4-in. gun and casemate complete. But what seemed a Herculean feat proved not so very remarkable when we realized that this chunk of "armament" consisted only of grey-painted wood and canvas. To give the Graf Spee a more ferocious appearance they positioned several of these fakes in prominent places.

Another thing that took our attention and caused comment was the presence of an aircraft on board with equipment for catapulting. This was a monoplane and looked genuine, although we were not allowed near enough for any careful examination. The cause of most speculation about this machine was the curious fact that painted on the wings were the red, white and blue roundels of the Royal Air Force.

Later in the day we were issued with hammocks and shown where to sling them. To reach our sleeping flat forward we had to pass through a mess-deck of the German crew, and noticed that photographs of Adolf Hitler in various poses were stuck liberally over the bulkheads. On returning through this portrait gallery we fixed a cigarette stub to Hitler's mouth on a prominent picture. Directly the "decoration" was discovered the Nazi seamen came surging round us, gesticulating with their fists and giving tongue vociferously, but they were a highly disciplined company and the incident passed with nothing worse than threats.

OUR treatment as prisoners in the Graf Spee was very tolerant, and the food and accommodation beyond reproach. A typical dinner was roast pork, vegetables and currant pudding. The warship held a westerly course at speed, avoiding the normal trade routes, obviously to meet the oil-tanker to which Captain Langsdorff had referred.

After four days aboard we were ordered to assemble on the quarter-deck. The Graf Spee hove-to, and we saw another ship on the starboard beam. This was a sizeable tanker with single funnel aft and painted grey overall—and most of us were destined to know her only too well in due course as the notorious prison-ship Altmark.

Some of the more seriously wounded among us were kept on board the raider and later landed in the River Plate. Two masters, Captain Starr and Captain Brown, being over sixty years of age, were to be transferred with us seamen and firemen to the German supply ship. On December 7, 1939, Captain Langsdorff made a pointed reference to Captain Dau of the Altmark. Telling us we were to be transferred, he added:

"I warn you that your treatment in future may not be as good as you have received so far. The master of that ship was interned in the last war and he has no use for British people. Although he is one of my countrymen, I tell you plainly he is no good. All I can do is to wish you the best of luck."

Well, Captain Hans Langsdorff is dead and his grave is in the soil of a foreign land. In my opinion he was a "white man," and I base that opinion on his treatment of us chaps in the Graf Spee, and the fact that when he sought refuge in a neutral harbour he conformed to international law by releasing the British officers who were still on board.

(Continued in No. 244.)

Dover's Ordeal in the 49th Month

In this vivid sketch Frank Illingworth remembers the high-lights of the last month of bombardment of Dover by Calais and Boulogne long-range guns. In those tremendous days and nights the Germans were getting rid of as much ammunition—including 14-in. armour-piercing and shrapnel shells—as they could before the 1st Canadian Army overran Gris Nez.

DAY after day, night after night, from the week-end of September 1, 1944, to September 28, when the German radio said, "The last remaining long-range gun at Calais has fallen," my home-town shuddered to the roar of enemy artillery fire, with the Hun using contact shells first, then shrapnel, and finally, as from the cliff tops I watched the smoke of the Canadian advance surging across Cap Gris Nez, armour-piercing shells tore into the foundations of Dover's buildings.

The streets were empty of civilians except for police and wardens sheltering in doorways. The military were in their shelters. The whiplash crack of German shells and the deeper roar of our "Boche Busters" on the cliffs flanking Dover mingled with the

clang of fire bells. The night of September 1, 1944, was typical of those of the forty-ninth month of shellfire.

On that evening London newspapers hinted that the Calais guns might well have fired their last rounds; and Company-Officer George Muddle flung himself on his bed at the Fire Station and said to me, "Perhaps we can get some sleep." Barely had he spoken when one of our noisiest and most spectacular nights began. Dover had been shelled and bombed more or less at once; and we knew what it was like to be bombed and cannon-gunned simultaneously; but this night was to see us attacked by flying-bombs and long-range artillery.

The sky flickered and reverberated with A.A. fire, the roar of long-range (Royal Marine Siege Regiment) guns on the cliff-tops, and the explosion of German shells and flying-bombs. The telephone was shrilling when we entered the Fire Station Control Room. It carried news that a shell had killed Fireman Dowell, and of yet more destruction. For several hours the " Castle Look-out Wallah " was to be kept busy.

From 2 a.m. the Control log book recorded his words: " Shower of shrapnel shells over Dour Street. . . . Three shells —one at Dour Street, one at Tower Hamlets, one at the Tanyard." Then the A.A. guns opened up, and through the barrage I heard the buzz of a doodle-bug. Tracers ripped the night, and then the roar of a V1 shook the old town and from the Castle look-out came the news, "Flying-bomb destroyed over the Harbour. . . . Two shells in the Harbour. . . . Flying-bomb approaching. . . ."

Once again A.A. guns mingled with the crack of German artillery fire. A cone of green and red tracer converged on the red tail of the doodle-bug and, sweeping across the town, pointed out its route until a shell found its mark and the flying-bomb disintegrated in mid-air. George muttered, "First bombs, then shells, then shells *and* bombs ; now shells and doodle-bugs. What next, I wonder ?" The answer was, "More shells —by the salvo." Carefully the telephonist jotted them into the Station log-book: " Shells near Lord Warden Hotel, seafront, Clarence Lawn. . . . Three shells at St. Margarets. . . . Eastabrook Place blocked by fallen house. . . . Shells in fire station garden. . . . Union Road. . . . Odo Road."

Fire Was Getting the Upper Hand

There was a flash-back to the Odo Road incident. A begrimed messenger tumbled into Central with news that Leading-Fireman Ghilks was buried by debris there. Then the phones shrilled again. Fire—Leney's Brewery—get cracking ! Bells clanged as shells crashed into nearby Astor Avenue and the fire engines head for Leney's. Next came calls from the Prince of Wales' Pier. The 200-ton minesweeper H.M.S. Loise had been hit, and Company-Officer Crawshaw was ordered to take a crew on to the dangerous, cratered roads.

The heavens were reverberating. Brick-dust soared over Woolworths, over the Docks, the seafront, and over Clarence Lawn. Back at the Fire Station there was another "Call." An old couple at Clarence Lawn were trapped in a house reported to be burning. Send a crew ! The "smoke" proved to be a column of brick-dust following a direct hit, but if there was no fire to extinguish there was the old couple to rescue.

At 4.21 a.m. another German battery at Calais joined those already in action ; and fire bells clanged again as another fire crew took to the road, this time towards Chitty's Flour Mill. A lorry in the yard had been hit by a shell and set on fire. At first we thought that one fire-pump would be sufficient for the job of putting out the flames. But shortly a messenger hastened back to Central with news that the fire was getting the upper hand. More crews turned out as further German salvos crashed into the town.

This part of the town suffered badly during the 49th month. When the front of butcher Gore's shop was torn out George Muddle arrived at the scene to find Mrs. Gore still standing in front of her sink, "washing" plates and dishes in a pudding-like mixture of water and plaster. Typical of the fire incidents during this month, when German gunners between Boulogne and Gris Nez were "getting rid of their ammo.," was that behind the Castle. Column-Officer Percy Baynton, in control at Central, tried to get through to the Castle look-out when, from the entrance to the Station, I reported a flickering red glow behind the Castle ; as the telephone lines had been cut by shells he ordered George Muddle to investigate.

DOVER'S CAVES GAVE SHELTER to many inhabitants of the town during bombardment from long-range guns in September 1944. This 49th month under shellfire, of which one typical night is described in these pages, ended with the welcome announcement from the German radio that " the last remaining long-range gun at Calais has fallen." *Photo, Planet News*

I piled into the car with George. Shells exploding directly in front of us among the trees and houses in Park Avenue brought a tree down across the road, and we almost crashed into it in the dark. Reversing, George turned down Frith Street, raced up Waterworks Hill towards the blaze, and a salvo smacked into a house on Castle Hill as I helped him ease the car around a crater in the middle of the road. On rounding the bend we saw flames licking a military motor depot which had suffered a near miss.

A soldier rushed up, shouting, "I can't drive—you'll have to get the vehicles out !" A tall order, for several vehicles were a mass of flames and the burning roof was sagging over petrol-carriers. But at least we could try, and George clambered into a lorry as a burning rafter crashed in front of it. Meanwhile, our coastal guns had taken up the German challenge. The roar of artillery mingled with the pops of bursting tires and exploding petrol tanks. Time and again we emerged from the fire at the wheel of a lorry. Particularly did we appreciate that the burning lorries had to be got out when a soldier shouted : "It's not what's *in* the garage that worries us but what's *under* it—petrol stores!"

By the time Percy Baynton arrived with a fire engine we had driven or shoved some twenty cars and lorries into the open. Then jets of water were thrown into the cabins of vehicles which were too hot to touch, and these were hauled into the open by an officer in a Bren-gun carrier. In subsequent Orders issued by the South-Eastern Command the Fire Brigade was congratulated for its efficiency, and an army corporal and a civilian who helped to get the vehicles from the flames were commended.

When the night's bombardment came to an end I have no idea. . . . And so it went on, until the 28th when, during a spell of silence, I watched folk emerging uncertainly from their shelters. They did not know it at the time, but their ordeal was over.

NEW FACTS AND FIGURES

WHEN the Nuremberg War Crimes Tribunal adjourned on August 31, 1946, the longest trial in history came to an end. The court had sat on 217 days, held 403 open sessions, totalling approximately 2,400 hours. Five million words had been spoken in four languages, the transcript making a pile 30 feet high. Filed in the prosecution's library were over three million documents—as well as 4,000 double-sided discs of sound recordings made in court and 80,000 feet of film used as evidence.

WORK of the Red Army service and ordnance corps, communications and engineering troops and medical units, was commemorated in August 1946 by an Order of the Day to these " rear establishments." During the War more than 43,750 miles of railway track and over 10,000 bridges were restored in areas of the Soviet Union from which the enemy had been expelled. Some 6,250 miles of log road and 3,000 miles of gravel road were laid. Railway trucks transported a daily average of 400,000 tons of freight. On four occasions the entire Red Army was equipped with new outfits of summer or winter clothing.

ABOUT 7,000 British Servicemen in Germany have sought permission for wives and children to join them. They are distributed in the Services as follows : Army 4,000 ; Control Commission 2,100 ; R.A.F. over 500 ; Navy over 100. The proportion of children to wives is about two to one in groups receiving early passages, and about equal in subsequent groups—the reason being that most of the families with higher priorities are those of older Servicemen.

PLANS are being made (according to a War Office statement of September 3, 1946) to provide accommodation in Japan for wives and children of British Commonwealth Servicemen. In southern Japan 38,000 troops—British, Indian, Australian and New Zealand—control some of the largest industrial centres, including the naval base at Kure. The atom-bombed city of Hiroshima is also in the British occupation zone.

THE demobilization programme of the United States Navy was completed on August 31, 1946. Since the Japanese surrender (September 2, 1945) 3,070,581 officers and men have been discharged, leaving 644,857 on the strength.

SIXTEEN public holidays have been selected for the British Commonwealth Occupation Force in Japan, announced the War Office on September 2, 1946. These will be New Year's Day ; Australia Day (January 26) ; Good Friday ; Easter Saturday ; Easter Monday ; Anzac Day (April 25) ; VE Day (May 8) ; Empire Day (May 24) ; the King's Birthday (June 10) ; August Bank Holiday ; VJ Day (August 14) ; Trafalgar Day (October 21) ; Armistice Day (November 11) ; Christmas Day ; Boxing Day ; and a day to commemorate the Battle of Britain. Indian and Jewish troops will also celebrate their special religious festivals.

Forces Canteen at Waterloo Keeps a Birthday

SHARING A SEVEN-CANDLES BIRTHDAY CAKE WITH THE ROYAL NAVY on September 10, 1946, was a ceremony conducted by Lady Blane, O.B.E., and the lady helpers who have voluntarily staffed the Y.M.C.A. Forces Canteen on Waterloo Station, London, since its inception seven years ago. Millions of serving men and women passing through the Capital have had a snack at the canteen, and many still find it a congenial spot for rest and refreshment to help them on their way. Lady Blane's husband was killed at the Battle of Jutland in the First Great War.

Printed in England and published every alternate Friday by the Proprietors, THE AMALGAMATED PRESS, LTD., The Fleetway House, Farringdon Street, London, E.C.4. Registered for transmission by Canadian Magazine Post. Sole Agents for Australia and New Zealand: Messrs. Gordon & Gotch, Ltd.; and for South Africa: Central News Agency, Ltd.—October 11, 1946.   S.S.   *Editorial Address:* JOHN CARPENTER HOUSE, WHITEFRIARS, LONDON, E.C.4.

Vol 10 *The War Illustrated* N° 244

I WAS THERE

SIXPENCE

OCTOBER 25, 1946

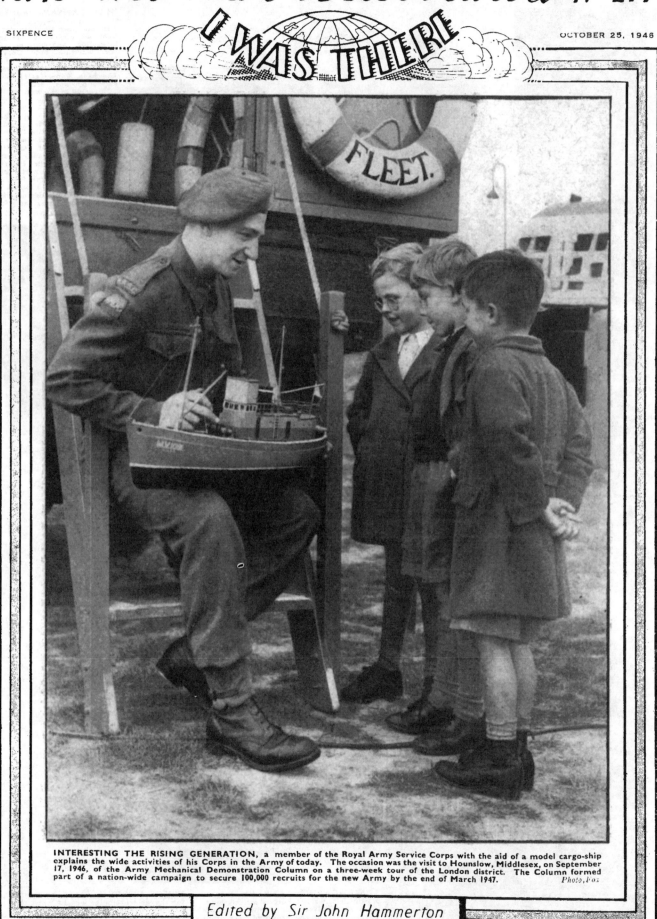

INTERESTING THE RISING GENERATION, a member of the Royal Army Service Corps with the aid of a model cargo-ship explains the wide activities of his Corps in the Army of today. The occasion was the visit to Hounslow, Middlesex, on September 17, 1946, of the Army Mechanical Demonstration Column on a three-week tour of the London district. The Column formed part of a nation-wide campaign to secure 100,000 recruits for the new Army by the end of March 1947. *Photo, Fox*

Edited by Sir John Hammerton

NO. 245 WILL BE PUBLISHED FRIDAY, NOVEMBER 8

Our Roving Camera on the Waterfronts

IN LINE AHEAD formation these minesweepers (left) were en route to Sheerness, Kent, after recently leaving Lowestoft, Suffolk, one of our wartime East Coast Naval bases, now in the process of being closed down. The base, known as H.M.S. Martello, was established early in the war.

PRESENTATION of the Ensign from H.M. aircraft carrier Indefatigable to the London Borough of Holborn took place on Sept. 19, 1946, ship's officers and men marching with the Ensign (below) to the Town Hall by way of Lincoln's Inn Fields. The Borough "adopted" the Indefatigable during the War—hence this valued gift.

INVASION CRAFT are broken up (above) at a Thameside salvage yard at Mortlake, Surrey, the sound timber to be used in house construction.

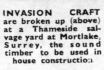

LANDING SHIP TANK the Empire Baltic (left) was at Rotterdam, Holland, on Sept. 12, 1946, after completing successful trials on the proposed ferry route between Tilbury and the Dutch port.

WRECK DISPOSAL FLEET, responsible for the destruction of wrecks when they become dangerous to shipping, takes soundings (above) in the Thames Estuary near a partly sunk U.S. merchant ship.

Photos, Planet News, Associated Press, Fox, Topical

The Amazing Facts about Pearl Harbour

By A. D. DIVINE, D.S.M.
Author of
'Dunkirk'; 'Destroyers' War'

As the preparatory signal for the ceremony of " Colours " was being hoisted at 8 a.m. on the Sunday morning of December 7, 1941, Japanese dive-bombers broke through the scattered cloud above the main base of the American Pacific Fleet at Pearl Harbour, on Oahu Island, Hawaii, to begin one of the greatest acts of treachery in the history of war. Five seconds later a telegraph boy fell off his bicycle on the road between Honolulu and Fort Shafter with, in his pocket, a warning telegram that might have made just that fractional difference between disaster and victory. Between these two things lies a chain of circumstance and mishap, of prevision and ill-judgement, probably unparalleled in modern history.

The report of the Joint Congressional Committee on the investigation of the Pearl Harbour attack, which has recently been made available, enables for the first time the full story of Pearl Harbour to be told. Starting points are always interesting. There are several for Pearl Harbour. My own, for choice, would be the morning early in January of 1941 when Admiral Isoroku Yamamoto, Commander-in-Chief of the combined Japanese Navy, ordered Admiral Onishi, Chief of Staff of the Eleventh Air Fleet, to prepare plans for an attack on Pearl Harbour. Admiral Yamamoto stated then, " If we have war with the United States we will have no hope of winning unless the United States Fleet in Hawaiian waters can be destroyed."

Jap Top Secret Operation Order

In the latter part of August matters moved a considerable step further when all Japanese Fleet commanders and key staff members were ordered to Tokyo for war games prior to the formulation of final operation plans against Pearl Harbour. On September 13 the outline of basic operation orders was issued, and by November 5 the detailed plans were complete and promulgated. On November 7 Admiral Yamamoto issued a top secret operation order which contained the words, " First preparations for war. Y-day will be December 8 " (December 7, Honolulu time). On November 14 units of the Pearl Harbour attack force began to assemble in Hitokappu Bay in the Kurile Islands.

At 9 a.m. on November 26 the Fleet left Hitokappu Bay under absolute wireless silence, while the Japanese ambassadors talked and talked with a suave tortuousness in Washington. On December 2 Admiral Yamamoto sent from his flagship, the Yamato, the message " Niita Kayama Nobore," which, translated, means " Climb Mount Niitaka," the code phrase which stood for " proceed with attack."

It is interesting to examine the state of the American Service mind during this period. For dates there we must go back as far as January 24, 1941, when the Secretary of the Navy addressed a communication to the Secretary of War (with copies to the Commander-in-Chief of the Pacific Fleet and the Commandant of the Fourteenth Naval District) stating, amongst other things, " If war eventuates with Japan, it is believed easily possible that hostilities would be initiated by a surprise attack upon the Fleet or the Naval Base at Pearl Harbour." The communication ordered the taking of all necessary steps to prepare for, and to guard against, such a possibility. Those steps were taken. From the end of January there was a progressive increase in the preparations for the attack, in the training of the forces for the attack, and in the assembly of matériel to enable such an attack to be held.

The most amazing feature of the whole American side of the preliminary period is beyond all question what is known as the Martin-Bellinger report. Admiral Bellinger, Commander of the Naval Base Defence Air Force, and General Martin, commanding the Hawaiian Air Force, prepared a joint estimate covering army and navy air action in the event of a sudden attack. Recognizing that relations were strained, the report said that Japan in the past " has never preceded hostile actions by a declaration of war." From that it went on to say that a fast raiding force might arrive in Hawaiian waters without prior warning from Intelligence.

That attack, it suggested, would take place at dawn from one or more carriers which would probably approach inside of 300 miles. It might be preceded by a surprise submarine attack, and a single submarine might well indicate the presence of an enemy surface force. In further discussion General Martin estimated that the Japanese could probably employ a maximum of six carriers against Pearl Harbour ; that the enemy would be more concerned with delivering a successful attack than with escaping and would be willing to accept considerable losses. It worked out in detail the probable points from which the attack would be launched. The Martin-Bellinger report is a masterpiece of clear thinking and proper appreciation of the mind of the enemy. In almost every single particular it was justified on the day of the attack. On the basis of the report, exercises were carried out and all preparations for the defence of the area were made. On November 27, following a long succession of messages, signals and letters giving the course of negotiations with Japan and events in general—which included a warning that the Axis powers moved for choice on Saturdays, Sundays and public holidays—a dispatch was sent to Admiral Kimmel which began with the words, " This dispatch is to be considered a war warning."

Organization 'Magic' at Work

It is not possible here to examine in detail the flow of events in Washington. American information to responsible officers, and in some degree American policy, was conditioned by the existence of a crypto-analytic organization which was able to " break " all Japanese codes in use, and which kept a very small group of responsible officers, politicians and the President, informed of all messages sent by Japanese diplomatic and consular officials, and a good deal of the material transmitted to the Fleet. The organization was known as " Magic."

Through Magic it was learnt on November 16 that, after various hesitations, the deadline time for negotiations was set for November 29. From then on the hints at an operation, secret, vital, urgent, were numerous. The American system for the checking of units of the Japanese Fleet had lost touch with the First and Second Japanese Aircraft carrier Divisions. The tension mounted intolerably as days and then hours went by.

By Saturday, December 6, it was almost at fever-heat in Washington, and on that day the first of a series of vital messages began. This, known as the " Pilot message," informed the ambassadors that a message of fourteen points, outlining the Japanese case, was arriving. At this stage of the proceedings it seemed possible that this was a virtual ultimatum. The first thirteen points, which came as one message, in a measure confirmed this. President Roosevelt, on reading them, said, " This means war ! " The " Pilot

AS VIEWED FROM AN ENEMY AIRCRAFT—Japan's attack at Pearl Harbour on Dec. 7, 1941, when " dive bombers broke through the scattered cloud to begin one of the greatest acts of treachery in the history of war." As the bombs dropped, columns of water rose high above some of the 86 U.S. warships moored off Ford Island in the harbour. The military dictators of Japan committed this act, said President Roosevelt in a broadcast, " under the very shadow of the flag of peace borne by their special envoys in our midst." PAGE 419   *Photo, New York Times Photos*

message," however, also stated that the document was not to be presented until a time fixed by Tokyo. The fourteenth paragraph arrived without containing any actual declaration of war, and the tension concentrated on the hour of delivery. There were mishaps this night in Washington. The army chiefs were at a dinner party. Admiral Stark was at the opera. But these things were of small importance—the time was not yet fixed.

At 4.37 a.m. (Washington time) on December 7 a message was picked up by a naval monitoring station which was decrypted and available in the Navy Department at 7 a.m. (It is important here to remember the difference in times—7 a.m. in Washington would be 1.30 a.m. in Honolulu.) And here begins the first of the final fantastic series of mishaps. There was no Japanese interpreter on duty in the Navy Department at that hour and it had to be sent to the army for translation. This was not available until approximately nine o'clock.

Chain of Tragic Misadventures

It was not seen by a responsible officer until Captain Kramer of the Translation Division returned to his office at 10.30. It was delivered by him to the Chief of Naval Operations and within ten minutes to Secretary Hull, and ten minutes later to the White House. The message stated that the fourteen points were to be delivered to the Secretary of State by the Japanese ambassadors at precisely one o'clock. In the course of the deliveries someone said that 1 a.m. Washington was "about dawn at Honolulu." This was the Navy Department side.

Within the Army Department the message was delivered rather earlier, but General George Marshall, the Chief of Staff, was riding in the country and could not be contacted for some hours. At 11.30 he eventually saw the fourteen-part memorandum and finally the "One o'clock message." He immediately assumed that there was a definite significance attached to this time and wrote at once the draft of a warning message to the Philippines, Hawaii, Panama and the Western Defence Commands. So impressed was he with the urgency of the situation that he asked how long it would take to dispatch the message. He was informed that it would be in the hands of the recipients within thirty minutes. But . . .

The army was out of touch by radio with Honolulu, owing to atmospheric conditions. Owing to the general lack of co-operation between the Services, which manifested itself at many points in the Hawaiian affair, the army was not prepared to use the more powerful naval transmitters. It therefore decided to send the message by commerical

means. There was teletype connexion between Washington and Western Union in San Francisco, and the army was informed that San Francisco was in touch with Honolulu. San Francisco had the message by 12.17 p.m. Perhaps it would be easier here to switch to Hawaiian time, for in Pearl Harbour the last of the grains of sand were running out; 12.17 p.m. would be almost a quarter to seven in the morning at Hawaii. It took three-quarters of an hour to get the message to Honolulu from San Francisco (7.33 a.m. Hawaiian time).

Normally there was a teleprinter between the office in Honolulu and the military headquarters at Fort Shafter, but this was early on a Sunday morning and the teleprinters were not in operation. The message was given to a telegraph boy and, as has been said, he fell off his bicycle as the first bombs fell.

For, even as the Martin-Bellinger report had prophesied, the Japanese Fleet had come in to the point of the compass that the experts had expected, to the distance they had prognosticated and in the strength they had estimated. Even the submarine attack had taken place "according to plan." And in a whirl of dive-bombers and torpedo planes, high-level bombing and ground strafing, the American Pacific Fleet was destroyed in 50 minutes; and with it the air defence of the island and, for all practical purposes, the possibility of immediate retaliation.

Four battleships were sunk, one heavily damaged, three others damaged. Two cruisers were heavily damaged and one damaged, four destroyers, a repair ship, a minelayer, a seaplane tender and an auxiliary ship were all out of action; 188 planes had been destroyed, and the U.S. forces lost 2,280 killed and more than 1,000 wounded. The Japanese lost five midget submarines, no ships, 29 aircraft and less than 100 men.

How had these things happened? In its findings the Committee states that the Hawaiian commanders had failed to discharge their responsibilities in the light of warnings and information, had failed to co-ordinate and integrate their facilities for defence, to effect proper liaison between the Services, to maintain effective reconnaissance and to employ the facilities, matériel and personnel at their command. But considering all the evidence, it had decided that "errors made by the Hawaiian commands were errors of judgement and not derelictions of duty."

Broadly speaking, these errors of judgement can be put down to one thing. Despite the Martin-Bellinger estimate and the consequent thinking and planning in connexion with the defence of Hawaii, despite the "disappearance" of the Japanese carriers

and the belief that a surprise attack of some sort was imminent, Admiral Kimmel and General Short, naval and military commander respectively, were convinced that the attack would be either against the Philippines or southward towards the Kra Peninsula and Malaya. They believed that the greatest danger Hawaii had to face was that of sabotage from Japanese sympathizers amongst Honolulu's large Japanese population.

To that basic error can be added the accumulation of small errors that were due to the lack of co-operation between the U.S. Army and the Navy that showed itself in war for the first time on this grim December morning. The Japanese in their planning had allowed for the loss of at least two carriers and a number of surface vessels. That they lost nothing was primarily due to precisely this circumstance of non-co-operation.

Speculation about Pearl Harbour has been endless and will so continue, but to my mind there are two channels that are more than ordinarily filled with fascination. How would the Pacific war have developed if the Pearl Harbour attack had been followed immediately with a landing to exploit the temporary destruction of American sea power and the establishment of Japanese air domination in the Hawaiian region? I found few people in the Pacific who did not think that such an attack should have succeeded. How would the Pacific war have been fought with America shorn of Pearl Harbour?

U.S. Fleet Inferior to the Jap

My second channel of speculation is as to what would have happened if Pearl Harbour had *not* been attacked. In the opinion of the Admirals the American Fleet in the Pacific in December was inferior to the Japanese Fleet to a degree that precluded all possibility of major hostile operations. But if the Japanese had contented themselves with attacking the Philippines, and if General MacArthur had, by his defence, sufficiently inflamed American public opinion, is there not a possibility that political expediency might have forced the over-ruling of the Service chiefs and sent the Fleet with reinforcements for Bataan?

What would have happened then? It may be that Japan, with the apparent victory of Pearl Harbour, the victory that more than any other thing served to unite the immeasurable force of the American nation in war, denied herself the possibility of defeating the American Fleet at sea, where it could not have been saved, and destroying an army of reinforcement. A sea battle with odds utterly in favour of Japan in the deep waters off the Philippines might have changed the whole outcome of the Pacific war.

AT THE HEIGHT OF THE ATTACK by the Japanese on Pearl Harbour sticks of bombs straddled the stricken warships, and oil storage tanks ashore burned furiously. In a whirl of dive-bombers and torpedo-carrying aircraft, high-level bombing and ground strafing, the American Pacific Fleet was destroyed in 50 minutes. American planes to the total of 188 had been destroyed and the U.S. forces lost 2,280 killed and more than 1,000 wounded. The Japanese lost no ships, 29 aircraft and less than 100 men.

Photo, New York Times Photos

Tribute to Warrior Birds Who Gave Their Lives

IN THE GARDEN OF ALL HALLOWS-BY-THE-TOWER, London, this memorial to carrier-pigeons who died on active service, 1939-1945, was unveiled on Oct. 4, 1946, by Miss Nancy Price, who had collected funds for its erection, and a short service of dedication was conducted by the vicar of All Hallows. On the rowan tree branches, set in two pools of water in the stone base, are troughs for crumbs, and birds carved in wood by the Sussex craftsman, George Mann, seen above.

Photo, Associated Press

Ingeniously Switching War Efforts to Peace—

ACHIEVEMENTS in our industrial sphere so soon after the cessation of hostilities were brilliantly displayed at the Britain Can Make It Exhibition at the Victoria and Albert Museum, London, sponsored by the Council of Industrial Design and opened by H.M. The King on Sept. 24, 1946. " Let us today set out," he said, " to make British design a hall-mark of pre-eminence in the eyes of the world, as British materials and workmanship have long been." A crashed aircraft staged against a background of bombed London indicates (1) how salvaged material is used in the production of household articles. Development in house planning includes the all-electric kitchen (2) adjacent to the dining-room. Ultra-modern are the enclosed electric sewing-machine (3) and the air-conditioned bed (4) the temperature of which is automatically controlled. Originality is the keynote of new toys (5).

Photos, G.P.U., P.A.-Reuter,
The News Chronicle

PAGE 422

THE AIR-CONDITIONED BED

—We Show the World that Britain Can Make It

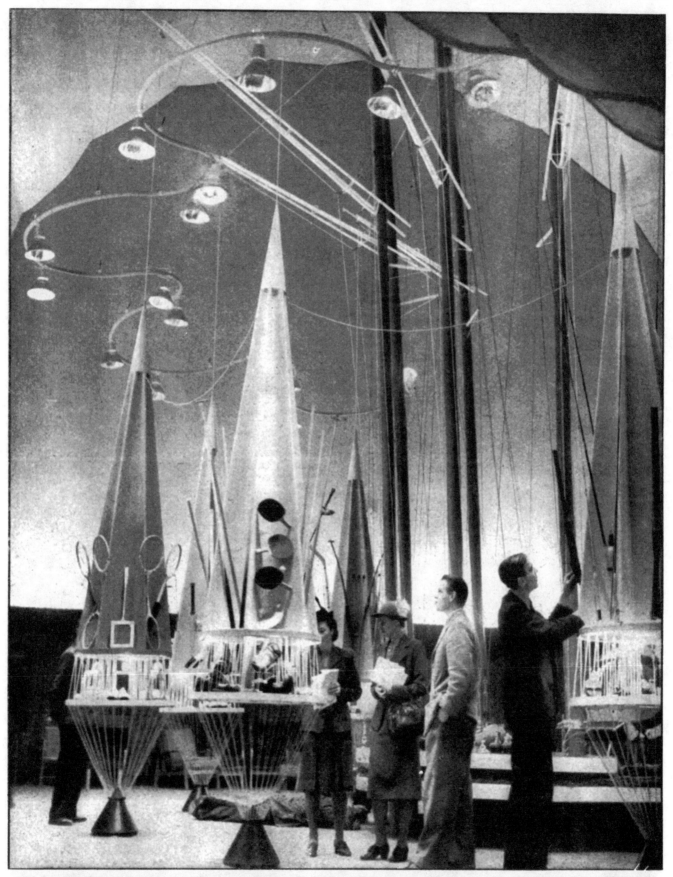

THE ART OF SHOWMANSHIP finds full expression in this display of equipment in the Sports Room of the Exhibition : first-class goods presented attractively to catch the eye and fire the imagination of buyers for the Overseas and Home markets. So remote from the atmosphere of war, this section contributed fully to (as H.M. the King expressed it) "evidence of our power of recovery in the face of all difficulties, and of our continued leadership in the arts of peace." His Majesty was amused to note that the two golf balls on view were firmly fixed in their places! The exhibition as a whole contained nearly 6,000 exhibits, coming from more than 1,300 firms, and chosen from 18,000 items put up for the consideration of the Council of Industrial Design. Of the goods shown, 36 per cent were reported by their makers as already available for the Home market (though not necessarily in quantities adequate to meet the demand). A further 14½ per cent would be ready by the end of the year, so that just over half the goods displayed would be available, to some extent, by 1947.

Photo, The News Chronicle

Berlin Remembrance Day for Victims of Nazism

DEN TOTEN ZU EHREN   DEN LEBENDEN ZUR PFLICHT

24 Pf. DEUTSCHE POST

WIR

LUX

CROWDED IN THE LUSTGARTEN on September 25, 1946, Berliners watched the Mayor place a wreath at the flag-draped former museum (1), now a memorial to victims of Nazism. At Weezen, near Hanover, voters did their duty (2) in the Municipal elections on September 15, 1946. B.A.O.R. family goes shopping in a N.A.A.F.I. canteen at Hamburg (3). Another memorial to Nazi victims (4) at Itzehoe in the British zone. Inset: new German stamp for use in the British, U.S., and Soviet zones. PAGE 424   *Photos. Planet News, New York Times Photos, Topical Press, Associated Press.*

New Memorials and One That Will Not be Built

SYMBOLIC OF THE CO-OPERATION between British armed forces in the war, and dedicated to all ranks of the Commandos, the submarine section of the Royal Navy, the Airborne Forces and the Special Air Service, a group of three sculptures by Mr. Gilbert Ledward, R.A., is to be erected in the cloister of Westminster Abbey, London. Clay models of two of the figures have been completed : the Commando (1) and the Parachutist (2). The third will be that of a submarine sailor. The group, in bronze, will be backed by panels each bearing a typical feature of the Service ; behind the Parachutist will appear a winged horse, emblem of the Airborne Forces.

At Le Havre, France, a memorial was unveiled (3) to commemorate 3,675,000 U.S. military personnel who passed through the port between September 1944 and August 1946. At Narvik, in Norway, King Haakon, in naval uniform (4), gazes at a memorial dedicated to the French who fell there in 1940. One never to be erected is that planned by Hitler for Berlin to commemorate victory after the fall of France in 1940 : its granite blocks (5) remain at Bovallsand, Sweden.

Photos, Topical, Keystone, Associated Press

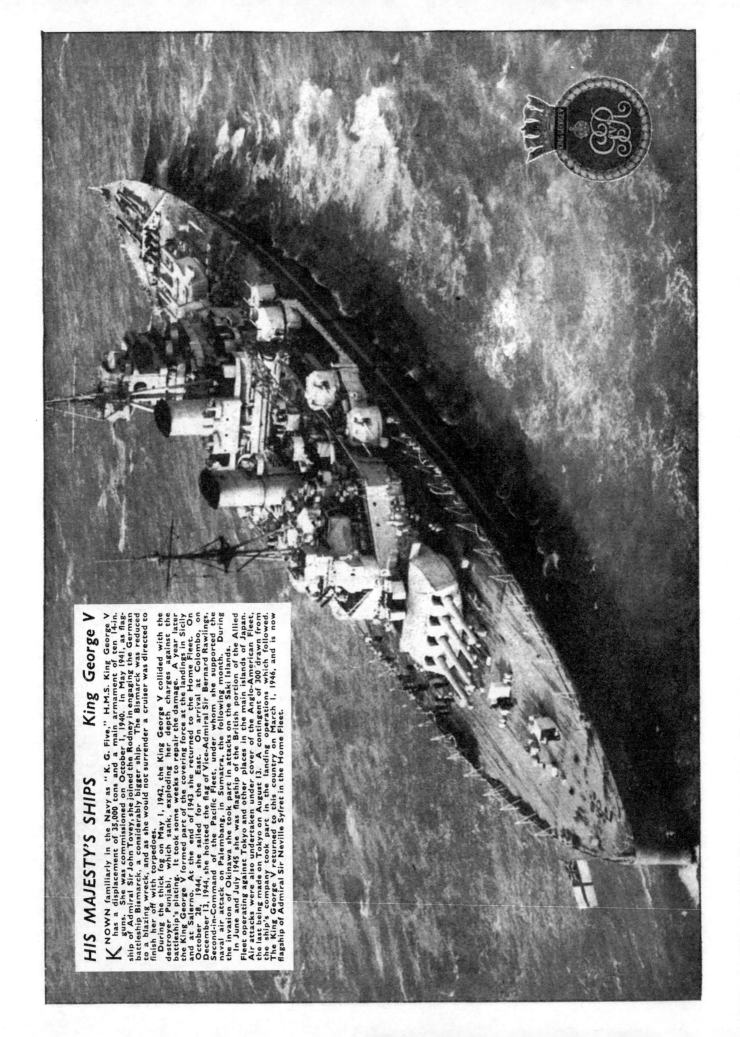

HIS MAJESTY'S SHIPS   King George V

KNOWN familiarly in the Navy as "K. G. Five," H.M.S. King George V has a displacement of 35,000 tons and a main armament of ten 14-in. guns. She was commissioned on October 1, 1940. In May 1941, as flagship of Admiral Sir John Tovey, she joined the Rodney in engaging the German battleship Bismarck, a considerably bigger ship. The Bismarck was reduced to a blazing wreck, and as she would not surrender a cruiser was directed to finish her off with torpedoes.

During the thick fog on May 1, 1942, the King George V collided with the destroyer Punjabi, which sank, exploding her depth charges against the battleship's plating. It took some weeks to repair the damage. A year later the King George V formed part of the covering force at the landings in Sicily and at Salerno. At the end of 1943 she returned to the Home Fleet. On October 28, 1944, she sailed for the East. On arrival at Colombo, on December 13, 1944, she hoisted the flag of Vice-Admiral Sir Bernard Rawlings, Second-in-Command of the Pacific Fleet, under whom she supported the naval air attack on Palembang, in Sumatra, the following month. During the invasion of Okinawa she took part in attacks on the Saki Islands.

In June and July 1945 she was flagship of the British portion of the Allied Fleet operating against Tokyo and other places in the main islands of Japan. Air attacks were also undertaken under cover of the Anglo-American Fleet, the last being made on Tokyo on August 13. A contingent of 300 drawn from the ship's company took part in the landing operations which followed. The King George V returned to this country on March 1, 1946, and is now flagship of Admiral Sir Neville Syfret in the Home Fleet.

The Durham Light Infantry

By Captain E. W. SHORT

THE many battalions of the D.L.I. which fought in the Second Great War added to the Regiment's heritage a wealth of valour and gallantry and proved once more its claim to the title "Faithful" which it gained over 150 years ago. Three weeks after the declaration of war, in 1939, the 2nd Battalion (one of the two regular battalions) arrived in France, twenty-five years after the same battalion had landed to fight in the First Great War.

In January 1940 they were followed by the 6th, 8th and 9th Battalions—three Territorial Battalions which formed the 151st (Durham) Brigade in the 50th (Northumbrian) Division—and then by the 10th and 11th, two second-line Territorial Battalions. There were thus six battalions of the Regiment in France before the storm broke in May 1940. During the waiting period between September and May it was feared that the enemy would attack through Belgium rather than make a frontal attack on the Maginot defences. Accordingly, most of this period was spent in strenuous preparation of defences along the Belgian frontier. Plan "D" adopted by the High Command was for the Allied forces to move into Belgium as soon as the attack started and take up positions along the River Dyle, which lay behind the Belgian positions along the German frontier. The B.E.F. were to occupy the line from Louvain to Wavre.

On May 10, 1940, the enemy started his attack, aided by good weather. By May 12 the Dyle defence had been manned exactly as planned. The 2nd Battalion reached its position around La Tombe in about 10 hours. The 9th Battalion undertook part of the Movement Control work during the move into Belgium. It was near La Tombe, on the River Dyle, that Second-Lieutenant R. W. Annand gained the first V.C. to be awarded to a member of the Regiment in the Second Great War (portrait in page 250, Vol. 3). His platoon was astride a blown bridge. During the night of May 15–16 they beat off a strong attack. Next morning the enemy had pushed forward a bridging party along the sunken bed of the river.

Enemy Headed for Channel Ports

Lieut. Annand attacked the party, ran over open ground himself and, reaching the top of the bridge, drove out the enemy with hand grenades. After having his wounds dressed he carried on in command. In the evening another attack was launched. Lieut. Annand again went forward and attacked with hand grenades. He withdrew his platoon when the order to do so was received, but on the way back he learned that his batman was wounded and was left behind. He returned at once to the forward position and carried him back in a wheelbarrow, before himself losing consciousness as a result of his wounds.

By this time news was received that the enemy had broken through the French lines on the right and ten Armoured Divisions were pouring through France towards the Channel Ports. This movement seriously endangered our right flank, and Lord Gort realized that he must establish a defensive position to the south of the B.E.F. The 50th Division was sent to take up a position along the canal running north-west from Douai. It was obvious that if the Armies in the north were to be saved an attack must be made towards the south to cut off the

THOUGH not all are borne on the King's Colour and the Regimental Colour of The Durham Light Infantry, the Regiment had 76 Battle Honours to its credit up to the outbreak of the Second Great War, these ranging from "Salamanca, 1812" to "Archangel, 1918-19." Its record, dating from 1756, was enhanced when the call came in 1914 and no fewer than 37 battalions of the D.L.I. fought and were sustained from the County. Its outstanding achievements in the greatest of all wars are now outlined.

LIEUT.-GENERAL SIR M. E. FRANKLYN, K.C.B., D.S.O., M.C., in Flanders in 1940 commanded the British 50th Division, of which three battalions of the D.L.I. formed a part.
Photo, British Official

enemy streaming towards the Channel. Accordingly, the 5th and 50th Divisions under Major-General Franklyn made one of the few successful attacks in the battle of Flanders in the Vimy area. The 151st Brigade took an outstanding part in this attack. But support promised by the French on the left was, unfortunately, not forth-coming and the force had to be withdrawn. By May 30 the whole B.E.F. was withdrawn to the Dunkirk perimeter. After three weeks of constant rear-guard fighting with a disintegrating ally on either flank nobody lost heart. The remnants of the D.L.I. battalions reached Dunkirk with the rest, returning considerably depleted but not knocked out. The 2nd Battalion, less than 150 strong, came back under Captain and Quartermaster O. H. Pearson, one of the best-known figures in the Regiment. The following months were spent in re-organization, re-equipment and the raising of new battalions—among them a Young Soldiers' Battalion.

The summer and autumn of 1940 were anxious days for England. The threat of invasion hung like a dark cloud on the horizon. The Government decided to raise armed bands throughout the land, as they had done in Napoleon's days. In May 1940 the L.D.V. was formed throughout the county, and Durham men drilled and trained and stood on guard in hastily improvised defences with the barest minimum of equipment and weapons. The spirit of the Old Armed Legions was alive again. At first the L.D.V. had no connexion with the Regiment except that many of its members were old Durham Light Infantry members.

From China to the Middle East

Later in the year, however, as the movement developed, it came under the control of the County T.A. Association, and in August 1940 the volunteers started to wear the badge of The Durham Light Infantry. The name was changed to Home Guard, new units were formed, and a definite organization began to evolve. The County force became over a score of battalions strong, all well-trained and well-equipped and proud to wear the badge of the Regiment.

The 1st Battalion (the other regular battalion) had returned from China to the Middle East at the outbreak of war and saw much fighting in the areas of Fort Capuzzo and Halfaya Pass in the early months of 1941. On one occasion the Battalion captured Fort Capuzzo but had to withdraw, with heavy casualties, because of lack

ANTI-TANK RIFLE INSTRUCTION given to men of the 2nd Battalion Durham Light Infantry during the lull on the Western Front in February 1940. One of the two regular battalions of the Regiment (the other being the 1st), it arrived in France within three weeks of war being declared in September 1939.
Photo, British Official

Colours : Black Cat on Red

56TH (LONDON) DIVISION

FORMERLY the 1st City of London Territorial Division, the 56th Division's associations with London were embodied in its Divisional sign "Dick Whittington's Cat." Sent overseas in 1942, after a spell in the Home Forces, the Division was employed on garrison duties in Palestine, Syria, and Iraq, before being committed to its first action, at Enfidaville, in 1943, during the Tunisian campaign.

The 56th took part in the Italian invasion, landing at Salerno on September 9. Heavy casualties were sustained at Battipaglia, finally taken on September 18. Baronissi was captured on September 27, and Nola early in October. At the Salerno landings the Division's first V.C. was awarded to C.S.M. Peter Wright, Coldstream Guards (portrait in page 478, Vol. 8). The Division was across the Volturno by mid-October. In January 1944, fierce battles were fought along the Garigliano river and on Monte Damiano; at the latter the second V.C. was awarded, posthumously, to Pte. G. A. Mitchell, London Scottish, on January 24-25 (portrait in page 376, Vol. 8).

SWITCHED to the Anzio beach-head in February the Division extricated a beleaguered Allied force. Following a comparatively quiet period, the 56th faced the task of penetrating the enemy's Adriatic defences, including the Gothic Line, and within two weeks of starting operations, on September 1, had crossed the Morano river, taken Montifiore, and reached the Croce area, where in an epic struggle the Gemmano feature was captured.

Assisting in the clearance of the approaches to the Senio river, early in January 1945, the Division seized positions over the river on February 23. An amphibious assault was undertaken on Lake Comacchio, in April, and File was captured on April 16. Ten days later the Po was reached. By April 30 the Division had advanced beyond Venice, at which juncture the Italian campaign was brought to a close.

MEALTIME IN CYPRUS was an alfresco affair for the 9th Battalion D.L.I. men in this photograph (hitherto unpublished) taken in August 1941. They went on, with the 151st Brigade, to take part in much of the most bitter fighting in Egypt and North Africa, including the battles of El Alamein and the Mareth Line. *War Office Photograph*

of reinforcements. In June the Battalion was sent to Syria, where the supporters of the Vichy regime were resisting the Allied occupation of the country.

Eventually they arrived at Aleppo and did garrison duties until August 1941, when they were sent to relieve the Australians at Tobruk. For five months the Battalion endured constant bombing and shelling by the German and Italian forces outside the perimeter. Most of the time was spent in patrolling and outpost duty. By January of 1942 they were in Malta, where they spent the greater part of the year, helping in the defence of the island bastion against almost incessant attack from the air. Most of the supplies had to come in by air or submarine, and for some months food was very scarce.

Meanwhile, the 151st Brigade had reached the Middle East, in April 1941. These battalions after a period in Cyprus and Iraq took part in much of the most bitter fighting in the desert, including the break-through at Gazala and the assaults at El Alamein and the Mareth Line. One great deed must be mentioned. On June 27, 1942, one of our two-pounder guns at Mersa Matruh had a short-range duel with an enemy light gun. All the crew of the two-pounder became casualties. One, however, Private A. H. Wakenshaw, who belonged to the 9th Battalion, crawled back to the gun although his left arm was blown off.

He managed to load it and fired five more rounds, which damaged the enemy gun and fired its tractor. A near miss then killed the gun aimer and blew Wakenshaw away from the gun. In spite of further severe wounds he dragged himself back, and was preparing to fire again when a direct hit killed him. He was posthumously awarded the V.C. (portrait in page 284, Vol. 6). The two-pounder now occupies an honoured place at the Depot at Brancepeth, Durham.

SHAVING TIME was any time for this member of the D.L.I., whose battalion was covering the withdrawal of Allied units from the Tobruk area in June 1942. A patrol of the 6th Battalion in the photograph on the right (published for the first time) was skirmishing on the outskirts of the Mareth Line in March 1943. *War Office Photograph*

Distinguished Actions of The D.L.I. in Sicily

THIS STEPPED WALL (1) formed a convenient observation post for a major of the 8th Battalion Durham Light Infantry in the course of a three days' battle on the Gornalunga river in July 1943. In Acireale on the German escape route to Messina, in August, troops of the 9th Battalion are seen, in this hitherto unpublished photograph (2), clearing the town of the enemy. Destruction of the bridge across the Simeto river did not hinder the advance on Catania; crossing by boat (3) these were among the first Allied troops to enter the town. Catania, in fact, fell to an officer of the D.L.I., and the documents of surrender are now in the Regimental Museum.

War Office photographs

had embarked at Syracuse for the United Kingdom, where they started their six months' arduous training for the final mighty assault on Hitler's European fortress. The 16th Battalion continued to fight its way north with the armies in Italy.

Fighting in the Cos Island Hills

In September 1943 the 1st Battalion, which by this time was back in Syria, was sent to the Island of Cos, off the coast of Turkey. They spent a few weeks in the construction of air-fields, but on October 2 the Germans made sea and air landings on the salt flats of the island. The defenders withdrew to the hills and from then on received no supplies, living off the land. Eventually, after a fortnight's bitter fighting without air support, about 100 men from the Battalion escaped to Egypt, via Turkey and Cyprus, where they were re-formed. In March 1944 they sailed for Italy and joined the 10th Indian Division near Ortona.

The 2nd Battalion by April 1942 had embarked for the Far East. At the end of February 1943 they were in the line in the Arakan Peninsula and remained there until the end of May. In the early months of 1944 the Japs had attacked at Imphal and the Battalion was sent to Kohima, where it suffered severe casualties. Kohima was captured, and the Battalion was leading the column which met the troops who had broken out of Imphal. Later, after resting for some time, the 2nd Battalion was again in action south of Mandalay.

MEANWHILE, preparations for the European invasion were proceeding, and on June 6, 1944, the great attack was launched. The regiment was represented by the 6th, 8th, 9th, 10th and 11th Battalions. These fought their way from the Normandy beaches and by the end of 1944 were back in Belgium, from which they had been driven four years earlier. Deep into the heart of Germany they went, playing their part in achieving the final and unconditional surrender of the German armed forces on May 8, 1945.

The 9th Battalion formed part of the Occupation Force in Berlin for a time, and the 16th Battalion in Vienna. Another battalion also served with the British Forces in Greece. It is also gratifying to know that the 2nd Battalion took an outstanding part in the Burma campaign, which was an important factor in forcing Japanese surrender only three months after the German collapse.

AS LIBERATORS the D.L.I. were among the first Allied troops to land in Normandy, on June 6, 1944. These previously unpublished photographs show (top) a D.L.I. sergeant, a week later, at Lingevres, lighting up after his head wound had been dressed at the Regimental Aid Post, and (bottom) men of the Regiment making good use of a captured German officer's horse.   *War Office Photographs*

Before the North African campaign had ended the 16th Battalion—one of the new battalions formed after Dunkirk—had landed with the 1st Army in Tunisia and played a costly part in achieving the final victory on the southern shore of the Mediterranean. On June 16, 1943, the 151st Brigade made its assault on the Sicilian coast, near Avola. In the conquest of the island the Brigade distinguished itself by capturing the Primo Sole Bridge before Catania and establishing the bridge-head which made the capture of the city possible. The city of Catania was actually surrendered to Lieutenant Gardiner, an officer of the Regiment. The documents of the surrender are now in the Regimental Museum. By October the three battalions

TROOPS OF THE 9th BATTALION in a Kangaroo at Weseke, Holland, on March 31, 1945, prepare to advance on a town near Stadtlohn not far from the Dutch-German frontier. With the British Seventh Armoured Division (the Desert Rats) this Battalion during the same month had advanced seventy miles beyond the Rhine in the Westphalian operations.   *War Office Photograph*

Justice Overtakes the Nazi Leaders

As the climax of the greatest trial in history drew near even Lord Justice Lawrence, President of the International Military Tribunal at Nuremberg, was requested to show his pass (1) before entering the courthouse and taking his place in the closely-guarded Judges' Room (2). Seated round the table in this room and considering their judgement (3) are (r. to l.) Lieut.-Col. Volchkov and Maj.-Gen. Nikitchenko (Russia), Mr. Justice Birkett, Lord Justice Lawrence (Gt. Britain), Mr. Francis Biddle and Judge J. J. Parker (U.S.A.), and Prof. Donnedieu de Vabres (France).

Hitler's 'Old Guard' on Trial for Their Lives—

On the afternoon of October 1, 1946, after a trial lasting 217 days and costing £5,000 a week and involving 300,000 affidavits, 200 witnesses and more than three million documents, sentences were pronounced on the 21 Nazi defendants in the dock at Nuremberg and on one other: Hitler's deputy, Martin Bormann, who, in his absence, was condemned to death. Of the 21 present, the hangman claims 11; seven face imprisonment for varying terms, three are freed.

Photo

— Hear the Verdicts the World Has Awaited

In the dock, front row l. to r., Goering, Hess, Ribbentrop, Keitel, Kaltenbrunner, Rosenberg, Frank, Frick, Streicher, Funk, Schacht. Behind them, l. to r., Doenitz, Raeder, Schirach, Sauckel, Jodl, Papen, Seyss-Inquart, Speer, Neurath, Fritzsche. The condemned were allowed four days in which to lodge appeals against the hanging to be carried out at Nuremberg on October 16, 1946. Those sentenced to imprisonment would go to a Berlin prison to be chosen by the four Allied Powers.

433

Surprises for Some on the Day of Reckoning

Photos, Associated Press, G.P.

" His guilt is unique in its enormity," said Lord Justice Lawrence of Goering (1), who listened hunched forward in his seat in the dock—guilty on all four counts. Streicher (2, centre) and Frick (left), to hang with Goering, could have had no feelings of astonishment : unlike Funk (right) who, expecting the death sentence, is to be imprisoned for life. Judged not guilty, surprise perhaps came in full measure to Fritzsche, Papen and Schacht (3, left to right, after their acquittal).

Judgement at Nuremberg

"**M**ANACLED and heavily guarded to prevent any attempts at suicide, the 11 Nazi war criminals sentenced to death by the International Military Tribunal were today (October 2, 1946) moved to the condemned cells in a special isolated block of the Nuremberg prison . . . Some of them may ask to be shot instead of hanged," reported The Daily Telegraph. "In another part of the prison, unattended and with their cell doors open, were Papen, Schacht and Fritzsche, who were acquitted ; with most of Germany demanding their retrial, the Allies did not consider it safe to free them completely until arrangements can be made to send them to their destinations." The seven who were sentenced to terms of imprisonment ranging from ten years to life awaited notification of the prison to which they would be transferred.

From the time when the first defendant, Goering, entered the dock on the afternoon of Oct. 1, 1946, it took only 42 minutes for the Tribunal to pass sentence on the 19 men found guilty. Goering listened to the level tones of Lord Justice Lawrence : "The evidence shows that after Hitler he was the most prominent man in the Nazi regime . . . He developed the Gestapo and created the first concentration camps . . . Goering persecuted the Jews not only in Germany but in the conquered territories as well. There is nothing to be said in mitigation . . . his own admissions are more than sufficient to be conclusive proof of his guilt."

Called for Guns Instead of Butter

Then it was the turn of Hess, of whom the Russian Judge said : "He became Hitler's closest friend and confidant, a relationship which lasted until Hess's flight to the British Isles. In September 1939 Hess was officially announced as successor-designate to the Fuehrer after Goering . . . He urged the people to sacrifice for armaments. He repeated the phrase, 'Guns instead of butter' . . . He blamed Britain and France for the war."

Delivering the Tribunal's verdict on Ribbentrop, Lord Justice Lawrence stated : "He played a particularly significant role in diplomatic activity which led up to the attack on Poland . . . participated in a meeting on June 6, 1944, in which it was agreed to start a programme under which Allied aviators carrying out machine-gun attacks on the civilian population should be lynched." Of Schacht, it was announced "He was active in organizing Germany's economy for war . . . The case against Schacht depends on the inference that he did, in fact, know of the Nazi aggressive plan . . . The Tribunal comes to the conclusion that this necessary inference has not been established beyond a reasonable doubt."

KEITEL had his plea that "he was a soldier and acted under superior orders" rejected on the ground that "Superior orders even given to a soldier cannot be considered in mitigation where crimes so extensive have been committed casually, ruthlessly, and without any military excuse or justification." Of Papen it was declared he could "be held guilty only if he was a party to the fostering of aggressive war . . . it is not established beyond reasonable doubt . . ." The third acquitted man, Fritzsche, was described as "best known as a radio commentator" who "sometimes made strong statements of a propagandist nature in his broadcasts, but one cannot hold they were intended to incite the people to commit atrocities on conquered peoples."

Kaltenbrunner as leader of the S.S. in Austria was active in the Nazi intrigue against that country, was aware of conditions in concentration camps and ordered the execution of prisoners therein. Head of an organization whose agents engaged in Nazi intrigues all over the world, Rosenberg knew of the brutal treatment meted out to Eastern Europeans. Responsibility for the ghettoes in Poland and the systematic extermination of Jews were among points brought home against Frank. Largely responsible for bringing the German nation under complete control of the National Socialist party, Frick was also in large part responsible for legislation to suppress the trade unions, the Press and the Jews.

Five Million Doomed to Slavery

Streicher's rabid anti-Semitism—incitement to murder and extermination—"constitutes a crime against humanity." Funk took part in the economic planning which preceded the attack on Russia and in the printing of roubles in Germany before the attack. U-boat crimes were proven against Doenitz. Against Raeder, who urged attack on Norway, the most serious charge was that "he carried out unrestricted naval warfare, including warfare on neutrals." Raeder admits that he passed the order to shoot Allied prisoners of war down through his chain of command and did not object to Hitler about it." Schirach, corruptor of German youth, although not the originator of "the policy of deporting Jews from Vienna, participated in this deportation, though he knew that the best they could hope for was a miserable existence in the ghettoes of the East." Of Sauckel it was said the evidence showed he "was in charge of a programme which involved deportation for slave labour of some 5 000,000 human beings, many of them under terrible conditions of cruelty and suffering."

Arch-planner of the war, Jodl "took part in all the conferences preceding the invasion of Russia, and signed the order to shoot commandos and prisoners of war." Seyss-Inquart's cruelties in three countries were established. Of Speer, it was recognized in mitigation that in the closing stages of the war "he was one of the few men who had the courage to tell Hitler that the war was lost." Neurath escaped the death sentence in that he "intervened with the security police and secret service for the release of many of the Czechoslovaks who had been arrested on September 1, 1939, and for the release of students arrested later in the autumn. In 1941 Von Neurath was summoned before Hitler, who complained that his regime had not been harsh enough."

Bormann, tried in his absence, "was extremely active in the persecution of Jews . . . If Bormann is not dead and is later apprehended, the Control Council for Germany may consider any facts in mitigation and alter or review his sentence if deemed proper."

When Lord Justice Lawrence and Mr. Justice Birkett returned to England, they commented on the bearing of the

HOW THEY FARED was the cause of this wild rush on newspaper sellers in the Nuremberg streets.
Photo, Planet News

THE VERDICTS AND SENTENCES

DEATH BY HANGING

Hermann Wilhelm Goering, 52, former Luftwaffe chief and successor-designate to Hitler. Guilty on all four counts, which were : 1. Common plan or conspiracy to wage aggressive war ; 2. Crimes against peace ; 3. War crimes ; [4. Crimes against humanity.

Joachim Ribbentrop, 53, Hitler's Foreign Minister and at one time Ambassador in London. Guilty on all counts.

Wilhelm Keitel, 63, former chief of the German High Command. Guilty on all counts.

Ernst Kaltenbrunner, 43, Himmler's Deputy and former chief of the security police and S.D. (Security Service.) Guilty on counts three and four.

Alfred Rosenberg, 53, head of the Nazi ideology department and former Minister for Occupied Eastern Territories. Guilty on all counts.

Hans Frank, 46, former Governor-General of Occupied Poland. Guilty on counts three and four.

Wilhelm Frick, 69, former Protector of Bohemia-Moravia and ex-Minister of the Interior. Guilty on counts two, three and four.

Julius Streicher, 61, owner and publisher of the anti-Jewish newspaper Der Stuermer and Gauleiter of Franconia. Guilty on count four.

Fritz Sauckel, 48, Director of Man-power under the Nazis. Guilty on counts three and four.

Alfred Jodl, 56, Chief of Staff 1942-45. Guilty on all counts.

Arthur Seyss-Inquart, 54, Governor of Austria after the anschluss and Commissioner for Occupied Holland 1940-45. Guilty on counts two, three and four.

Martin Bormann, 45, Hitler's former Deputy. Guilty on counts three and four.

IMPRISONMENT

Rudolf Hess, 52, Hitler's former Deputy. He flew to Scotland during the War to propose peace terms. Guilty on counts one and two. Life imprisonment.

Walter Funk, 56, Reichsbank President, 1939-45. Guilty on counts two, three and four. Life.

Erich Raeder, 70, C.-in-C. German Navy, 1928-43. Guilty on counts one, two and three. Life.

Baldur Schirach, 39, Hitler Youth leader and one-time Governor of Austria. Guilty on count four. Twenty years.

Albert Speer, 40, former Armaments Minister. Guilty on counts three and four. Twenty years.

Constantin Neurath, 72, Protector of Bohemia-Moravia, 1939-41, and former Ambassador in London. Guilty on all counts. Fifteen years.

Karl Doenitz, 55, C.-in-C. U-boats until 1943, when he succeeded Raeder as C.-in-C. German Navy, and Fuehrer from Hitler's death until Germany's surrender. Guilty on counts two and three. Ten years.

DISCHARGED

Hjalmar Schacht, 69, former Reichsbank President and Minister of Economics. Charged on counts one and two. Not guilty on both.

Franz von Papen, 66, diplomat and former Ambassador to Austria and Turkey. Charged on counts one and two. Not guilty.

Hans Fritzsche, 46, Goebbels' assistant at the Propaganda Ministry. Charged on counts one, three and four. Not guilty.

Nazis. Said Lord Justice Lawrence, "They behaved with great dignity and propriety throughout the whole trial," Mr. Justice Birkett adding, "Their behaviour in court was a model of dignity, and most impressive." . . . The first words of approval spoken for quite a long time—and almost certain to be the last.

Europe's Wartime Capitals in 1946

BRUSSELS

By EMILE CAMMAERTS

W E should never forget that Belgium has suffered two invasions and two occupations during the last thirty years. A casual observer is apt to overlook the bitterness caused among the older generation by the catastrophe which struck the country when it had only just begun to recover from the economic and financial crises which followed the First Great War. I have vivid memories of the triumphal entry into Brussels of King Albert, at the head of his troops, on November 22, 1918. Owing to the presence of the ministers of neutral Powers the Belgian capital had been spared the wholesale destruction which had been inflicted upon some neighbouring towns ; but the city, so clean and cheerful in former days, had nevertheless a dismal look. Neither the street-decorations, nor the music of the bands, nor the cheering of the crowds could prevent a careful observer from noticing the marks of suffering on the people's faces and the dilapidated look of the streets, where grass grew between the cobblestones.

But correspondents who accompany the triumphal march of armies do not always look below the surface. They were over-optimistic in November 1918—and they showed even greater optimism in September 1944 when, for the second time, the people of Brussels greeted their liberators. Newspapers then were filled with glowing accounts of the glorious reception given to the British troops, how their tanks were covered with flowers, how soldiers enjoyed the lavish hospitality of the citizens ; and the impression spread abroad that Brussels, and Belgium as a whole, had not suffered severely from the German occupation, that accounts of disease and starvation given during the previous years had been grossly exaggerated. It was some weeks before the British public realized that this first impression was entirely misleading and that the Belgians, in their reckless enthusiasm, had expended in a few days of celebration with their liberators whatever small stores of food they had managed so carefully to set aside.

Dangers of Inflation Avoided

The situation was, in fact, far worse than it had been 26 years earlier. This time the Belgians had not received any relief from abroad, because of the British blockade, during four and a half years of occupation, and they had been subjected to a material and moral oppression far more severe than on the previous occasion. Almost every family had suffered the loss of a relative through disease, execution, deportation or service in the army.

The wild enthusiasm of the autumn of 1944 was followed by a sad reaction as soon as it was realized that the war was going on, and that the needs of the Allied Armies had priority over stocks of food and all means of communication when these could be restored. The expulsion of the enemy from the greater part of the country did not mean that sufferings were over. People lacked fuel, clothes and adequate rations. In fact, the food situation became worse in the winter months of 1944-45 than it had ever been during the previous years of war.

The northern provinces were not cleared of the enemy until November 1944, and no sooner had plans been made by the Allies and the Belgian authorities to ensure better distribution of food and fuel, when Rundstedt launched his counter-offensive of December-January, bringing German tanks once more within sight of the Meuse. For a few days the country was on the verge of panic, which was avoided only through the prompt check imposed on the German advance by British

intervention and the timely arrival of American reinforcements.

During the period which followed, work of reconstruction which had been impeded by military operations could start in earnest. Within a year the daily production of coal rose from 23,000 tons to 80,000 tons. Activity was resumed not only in the metal industry but in the glass and textile industries where it had been brought to a standstill. The situation on the railways and in the port of Antwerp improved monthly. Unemployment practically disappeared, and food prices remained under control. Financial measures taken by the Pierlot Government bore fruit under M. Van Acker, the danger of inflation was avoided, and it is now generally agreed that Belgium occupies a privileged position among the liberated nations. The food and coal ration is as adequate in Brussels as in London, but the cost of living remains much higher compared with pre-war standards.

A N English visitor wandering through Brussels gazing at crowded shops and restaurants would no doubt gather the impression that life has become easier in Belgium than in England. But every home hides its own problems connected with the calamities of the past and the uncertainty of the future. Brussels is certainly alive, and in certain of its aspects this life may even appear cheerful ; but it lives from hand to mouth. In most cases reserves are exhausted and the country remains vulnerable to diplomatic and financial accidents. Inflation has been prevented only by drastic measures, and if these measures were to be relaxed, in order to satisfy a misguided public opinion, Belgium would once more be at the mercy of soaring prices and rising wages.

Many remember the bitter experiences of 1923 and 1929 and realize that even the wisest home policy would not preserve them from the consequences of an international depression. From this point of view, as from that of security, the future of Belgium, as of all smaller countries in Europe. really depends on the wisdom of the Big Powers who control the resources of the world and can either maintain order or provoke disorder.

Belgian patriots draw some comfort from the thought that economic improvement is beginning to exert a calming influence on the political struggle. For behind this super-

ENGLISH NEWSPAPERS and magazines are displayed, together with Continental ones, on this kiosk in a street in Brussels.

Photo, New York Times Photos

ficial aspect of contentment Brussels has passed, since the liberation, through a severe crisis which may be revived at any moment. The two parties which played a most important part in the resistance movement—Socialists and Communists on the one hand, Christian Democrats on the other—broke the close alliance they had maintained against the common enemy, as soon as the danger was removed. Divisions were embittered by privation and by vindictiveness felt towards those who had been guilty or suspected of collaboration.

The aftermath of war is made up not only of economic disorder but also of moral disintegration, and it is extremely difficult to persuade people who have made a virtue of hatred for many years to unite in a common effort of co-operation. Political tolerance is not fostered by oppression, and conflicts of opinion become dangerous when an opponent can be accused of disloyalty. This is what happened in every liberated country, and Belgium did not escape the contagion.

In order to understand future events it is necessary to remember that last year's economic progress was accomplished amidst a political tension of unprecedented violence, and that this tension was increased by the dynastic crisis which divided the country into two rival factions. Had King Leopold been in Brussels in September 1944 he would no doubt have resumed his constitutional power, in accordance with the declarations made by the members of the Pierlot Government when they were in London. His removal and imprisonment in Germany, on the morrow of D-Day, and the delay which preceded his liberation in May 1945, gave time to his opponents to marshal their strength.

The controversy which raged for three months through the country threatened the success of reconstruction. It was finally understood that the people themselves should decide the issue. If the Socialists and Communists who supported the Government were to win the election the King would be asked to abdicate ; if the Social Christians won the day they would proceed to settle the question by way of a referendum.

E LECTIONS which took place on Feb. 17, 1946, however, gave no single party an over-all majority in the Chamber. Administration since then has been in the hands of a Socialist-Liberal-Communist coalition headed first by M. Van Acker and then by the veteran statesman M. Camille Huysmans. The future is still uncertain, but such uncertainty should not blind us to the fact that the progress realized surpasses all expectations and prospects are far brighter than could have been expected a year ago. A certain sense of security has been restored and is reflected in the external aspect of the capital.

All the familiar landmarks and monuments escaped destruction during the war. The Gothic town hall still stands in the ancient market place. The classical " Quartier du Parc " has been preserved. The famous Renaissance glass windows of Saint Gudule's Church have been put back into place. There is one exception ; the modern Palace of Justice, which stands at the end of the Rue Royale, has suffered some damage. The Germans set fire to it before leaving the town, in order to destroy some of their archives, and one looks in vain for the familiar dome which crowned the temple erected in the last century to Law and Justice. Some gloomy prophets take this as a bad omen and declare that Justice herself has left the land. But Justice does not depend on stones, however venerable, or on the fear of criminals, however reckless.

Forgetting the Occupation in Post-War Brussels

FOOD SITUATION in the capital of Belgium—which occupies a privileged position among the liberated nations—is on a level with that in London: the shopping situation (1) appears to be easier. In the Old Market (2) a vendor plays an accordion to draw attention to his wares. Transport difficulties (3) have still to be eased. A British soldier on leave assists with a toy boat (4) on the pond before the Palais de la Nation. Businessmen outside the Bourse (5) throng the Boulevard Anspach. See facing page.
Photos, New York Times Photos

Our War Leaders in Peacetime
BEVIN

THE RT. HON. ERNEST BEVIN, M.P., P.C., became a Minister without graduating through the House of Commons. At the age of 59 he went straight from the polls into the key position of Minister of Labour and National Service, with a seat in Churchill's Cabinet and the job of gearing labour to the war effort. Today, as Foreign Secretary, he has a small flat near the Foreign Office in Whitehall, London, where he lives with his wife and their daughter.

His friends say that Mr. Bevin would not have achieved such eminence but for his wife. He has not always been as robust as he looks, and she has superintended his diet, persuaded him to go to bed early (he has always been an early riser) and in a dozen-and-one other ways looked after "Ernie" (her own name for him). She has travelled hundreds of thousands of miles with him, from Scotland to the United States. During the blitz Mrs. Bevin remained by her husband's side—in a hotel in Whitehall. The Bevins find no pleasure in social life. Their circle of friends is small and closely selected. He himself likes after-supper arguments, but his overriding interest is the Trade Union Movement, and particularly the Transport and General Workers Union, which he played a large part in forming.

Born in 1881 at the Somersetshire village of Winsford, his interest in politics began when, a lad of ten working on a Devon farm for 3s. 6d. a week, his job included reading the daily papers to a nearly blind employer. His parents died when he was a child, and his sister, who brought him up in Devon, wanted him to work on the land. But what he read fired his thoughts, and in his early teens he left for Bristol and worked in turn as an errand boy, page boy, seller of ginger beer and as a tram driver.

Remains a 'Working-Class' Man

It was in the latter capacity that he met his wife, a Bristol girl, thirty-odd years ago. Since then she has actively supported his fight for better conditions for labour. She remembers the day when Bevin joined the Trade Union movement and developed, in street-corner oratory, the booming voice heard at international conferences today: "Better wages!" and "Better conditions!" He quoted Burns, whose works he read by gaslight in his room: "The real tragedy of the working-class is the poverty of our views." In 1922, aged 40, Bevin became General Secretary of the Amalgamated Transport and General Workers Union,. People who remember him in those days say he has altered little. He has, indeed, remained a "working-class" man and never seems to tire of pointing out this fact.

HE had been General Secretary of the Transport and General Workers Union for 18 years when, in 1940, returned for Labour at Central Wandsworth, he entered the Cabinet as Minister of Labour. He did not cut adrift from his Trade Union work when appointed Foreign Secretary in 1945. He and his wife continue to work in the Labour movement. Given to ready, robust laughter, Bevin abhors class distinction : " If a boy can fly a Hurricane, he can also help to build the new world ! " He likes reading, largely on social topics, and Burns' works (partly because Burns, like himself, was a working man). And he likes writing, though less for pleasure than as a means of setting down his findings. In 1942 he published A Job to be Done. Now he is helping to direct the country's footsteps into the New World.

BRITAIN'S FOREIGN SECRETARY, the Rt. Hon. Ernest Bevin, and Mrs. Bevin, chatted to Mr. Byrnes, U.S. Secretary of State, at a reception (1) at the British Embassy in Paris in May, 1946. His official London residence (2) is in Carlton House Terrace. Arriving (3) at the Quai d'Orsay, Paris. After opening a Rest Home (4) at Tunbridge Wells. At his office desk (5).

Here Battle Flowed Fiercely Three Summers Ago

TOURING BATTLEFIELDS OF NORMANDY in September 1946, a party of pupils from British Public Schools viewed the devastation at Caen, captured by British and Canadian troops on July 9, 1944 ; the cathedral stands out in striking contrast. Arranged by the Franco-British Society and led by its Chairman, the Earl of Bessborough, the tour included a visit to Falaise, scene of the " pocket " trap of the German Armies in the West in July-August 1944. See also illus. page 145.

Photo. G.P.U.

The Roll of Honour
NCOs & MEN
1939—1946

Pte. G. ALLWOOD
Northamptonshire Regt.
Died of wounds. 4.5.44.
Age 31. (Nottingham)

So great has been the response of readers to our invitation to submit portraits for our Roll of Honour that no more can now be accepted. But we have every hope of being able to publish all those so far received.

Sgt. D. APPLEYARD
R.A.F.V.R.
Action: Holland. 29.12.43.
Age 20. (Romford)

Gnr. H. J. ARCHER
4th Med. Light R.A.
Action: Italy. 17.12.44.
Age 32. (Epping)

Sgt. J. L. ARTHUR
Royal Air Force.
Action: Swaffham. 11.11.41.
Age 27. (South Shields)

Sgt. H. BERRY
45 Squadron, R.A.F.
Action: Antwerp. 14.5.43.
Age 18. (Birmingham)

Gnr. A. E. BLUNDEN
Royal Marines.
In action: Crete. 1.6.41.
Age 23. (Fareham)

Sgt. J. BOOKER
Royal Air Force.
Action: Holland. 17.6.44.
Age 21. (Sidcup)

O/S. L. BOWERS
H.M.S. Hood.
Action: at sea. 1941.
Age 18. (Fareham)

A.C.I A. C. BROGAN
57 Squadron R.A.F.
On operations. May. 43.
Age 18. (Dagenham)

Marine W. J. CANHAM
Royal Marines.
Action: at sea. 23.7.42.
Age 43. (Southall)

Sgt. H. CHARLTON
Royal Air Force.
Died of wounds. 9.10.43.
Age 22. (South Godstone)

L/Cpl. E. W. G. COCKLE
R. Army Service Corps.
Died: Romney. 16.9.45.
Age 33. (Bishop's Waltham)

Sgt. H. W. COLLINS
No. 9 Pathfinder, R.A.F.
In action: Laon. April '44.
Age 19. (Maidenhead)

A/B R. K. COLLINS
Royal Navy.
Action: Anzio. 18.2.44
Age 43. (Lymington)

Sgt. N. P. COOK
422 Squadron, R.C.A.F.
In action. 20.11.43
Age 21. (Burnham)

W/T.Op. W. G. COOPER
H.M.S. Audacity.
Action: at sea. 22.12.41.
Age 27. (Portsmouth)

A/B D. DOGGETT
Royal Navy D.E.M.S.
Action: at sea. 26.11.42.
Age 21. (St. Margarets)

Stkr. P. EAMES
Royal Navy.
Action: at sea. 12.2.42.
Age 27. (London)

Cpl. G. A. ELLIOTT
R. Army Service Corps.
Died of wounds. 27.3.43.
Age 25. (Arnold)

Dvr. G. FRY
R. Army Service Corps.
Action: Dunkirk. 29.5.40.
Age 39. (Stockton/Tees)

L/Cpl. T. GAME
3rd Bn. Irish Guards
Action: Buhren. 12.4.45.
Age 19. (Hertford)

Cpl. F. W. GIBBINS
9th Bn. Durham L.I.
Temple Mars. 3.9.44.
Age 24. (South Norton)

Pte. A. GROOME
Queen's Bays.
Mediterranean. 5.10.43.
Age 23. (Eastbourne)

Offs. Std. T. HAINES
H.M.S. Welshman.
Action: at sea. 1.2.43.
Age 26. (Loughborough)

Pte. R. HALL
York & Lancaster Regt.
Action: Burma. 12.4.45.
Age 21. (Balby)

Gnr. H. KYLE
Royal Artillery.
P.O.W. Osaka. 14.3.44.
Age 29. (Clogher)

Stkr. J. McCOY
S.S. Amsterdam.
Action: Normandy. 6.6.44.
Age 21. (Bury)

Sgt. A. D. PENNYCORD
Royal Air Force.
Missing. 8.4.43.
Age 22. (Selsey)

Cpl. O. J. POUND
Worcestershire Regt.
In action: Caen. 4.8.44.
Age 31. (Malvern)

Flt/Sgt. H. C. RATTRAY
Bomber Command, R.A.F.
Over Nesle-Hodeng. 1.7.44.
Age 35. (Ickenham)

A/B R. J. SMITH
Royal Navy.
Action: Anzio. 18.2.44.
Age 20. (Beaconsfield)

Sgt. D. H. STEVENSON
48 R. Marine Commando
D. wnds. P'tmouth. 11.6.44.
Age 23. (Barnehurst)

Tpr. S. E. THORNE
3rd County of London Yeo.
Middle East. 14.6.42.
Age 26. (Bedford)

C.P.O. C. WILKINSON
Royal Navy.
North Sea. 13.2.44.
Age 27. (Southend/Sea)

Pte. S. E. WOOLLSEY
Queen Victoria Rifles.
Died of wounds. 26.5.40.
Age 21. (Knapton)

Tpr. R. WRIGHT
R. Gloucestershire Hussars
Action: El Alamein.15.7.42.
Age 21. (Crosby)

L/Cpl. G. A. YAXLEY
2nd Bn. R. Norfolk Regt.
Action: France. 27.5.40.
Age 35. (Irstead)

Cpl. H. W. YAXLEY
2nd Bn. R. Norfolk Regt.
Action: France. 23.5.40.
Age 29. (Irstead)

I WAS THERE!
THE HUMAN STORY OF 1939-1946

In Burma with 19th Indian Division

One of the major headaches of the Staff of the famous "Dagger" Division concerned rations. Many were the ingenious ways of dealing with this, as explained by Capt. R. R. G. Blackmore, 115th Field Regiment, R.A., who tells also of Burmese guerillas and their brilliant British organizers. See also portrait and story in page 58.

DURING Christmas 1944 I and my O.P. party of twelve men were supporting a battalion of the Frontier Force Rifles which had been sent off on a special job by itself somewhere between the Chindwin and the Irrawaddy. On Christmas Eve the track we were following suddenly ended in the middle of a teak forest and it was impossible to proceed any farther with jeeps. So we started to retrace our steps, and spent the night on a small rise of ground.

The job we were doing had been expected to end on the day before Christmas Eve, and we were short of rations. On Christmas morning we went back and took another track, which was not marked on the maps. At about 11 o'clock we bumped into some Japs who were evidently withdrawing, and a running battle commenced.

By three in the afternoon we were still advancing slowly, but we were of the opinion that the Jap force numbered not more than about twelve men, sniping, then withdrawing into the jungle to snipe again 100 yards farther on. At this time we found ourselves on a strategical rise, and, the C.O. calling a halt and ordering an all-round defensive position to be prepared, we dug ourselves in.

At about 4.30 the C.O. sent for me and told me that it was Christmas Day. I was sadly aware of the fact. He then said that as we were out of range of our guns and the enemy force was so small, he would like my men to be his guests for dinner. He called the Subadar Major and, explaining the situation to him, asked him to take command of the battalion while we kept the feast. There was in the battalion area a small nullah or dried-up river bed, in which a fire was prepared for cooking, and at about 6.30, after "stand-down," we made our way there.

The C.O. Worked a Jungle Miracle

The officers of the battalion, twelve in all, about half of them British, the others Indian, proceeded to serve Christmas dinner to my men. First came tinned soup, then a side of sheep and vegetables, then tinned fruit and condensed milk, followed by sweets and cigarettes. After which, the C.O. became the complete worker of miracles and produced a Christmas cake. The body of it was rich, like a wedding cake, with a thick layer of marzipan, the whole covered with real icing of intricate design and across the top "A Merry Christmas." I had seen nothing like it since the war started.

Think of it, in the middle of the jungle, away from our own unit, surrounded by about 700 Indians, none of whom were Christians, keeping a Christian feast which was provided by the officers of the battalion, and all around the odd rifle shot and grenade. When the men had been given the cake the C.O. sent them back to their holes with a bottle of rum, and I sat down with the officers of the battalion to the same meal, including another cake, similar to the first. I asked the C.O. how he came to have such food.

"It's simple," he explained. "The cook acquired the sheep this morning, the soup and vegetables and fruit came out of tins." That seemed simple enough, but, "The cakes?" I asked. "Oh, the cakes," he smiled. "I was in Bangalore last January and saw the cakes and had them sealed up in airtight tins. I think Christmas without a proper cake is very dull." Fortunately the battalion suffered no casualties that night, and the next morning we had a real Boxing Day shooting party, attacking the Japs with overwhelming success; I doubt if any lived to get away.

In the 19th Indian Division there were three British battalions and one British Field Regiment, one British A.T. Regiment, and the rest of the operational troops were Indian or Gurkha. The Gurkhas are not Indians. They come from Nepal, an independent State into which only a very few

INDICATING JAPANESE GUN POSITIONS to the British, this loyal Burman was following the example of many of his fellows. Their knowledge of local conditions and enemy movements frequently proved invaluable. Appreciation of the natives, and an account of some of the difficulties of campaigning in this country by Capt. Blackmore, appear in these pages. PAGE 441 *From a sketch by Capt. R. J. M. Dupont, Official S.E.A.C. artist*

THE DAGGER ARMS, the 19th Division's club at Maymyo, Burma— which these refreshed members are seen leaving (left)—was organized by Anglo-Burmese and attained tremendous popularity.
Photo, British Official

British go, and then only at the express invitation of the Maharajah of Nepal. So all recruiting of Gurkhas is done by Gurkhas. They are born soldiers, generally short of stature and with Mongolian features.

There is a story told about some of them who were training to be a parachute battalion. There was not available for training purposes the elaborate paraphernalia used for training parachute troops in the U.K., but they had practised jumping off moving lorries and off high walls and were ready for their first leap from an aircraft. The Company Commander called them together and told them that he would jump first, who would go next, and so on, the Subadar (the Gurkha second-in-command of the company) to jump last. He ended by saying that the jump would be in three days' time and that it would be from 1,000 feet. After this, parachutes were issued and the men were told how to fold them.

In the evening the Subadar asked for an interview with the Company Commander. "Sahib," he said, "this new training is very good. We shall be the first Gurkhas to jump from an aeroplane. We are all very proud to have this honour. We shall do our utmost to be the best company in the Division." The Company Commander replied, "Sahib, I know this Company will be the best. The men are all very keen; but I don't think you came here to tell me that. What is worrying you? What's wrong?"

"WELL, Sahib, the men are not keen to make their first jump from 1,000 feet. They would like it to be a jump from 500 feet," was the reply. The Company Commander thought for a moment, then said, "I am sorry, Sahib, but it will have to be from 1,000 feet. That will give more time for the parachutes to open. When we have jumped successfully from 1,000 feet, perhaps we shall try from 500 feet. The whole Division will jump from 1,000 feet and so we should lose no face by starting at a safe height."

"Oh, Sahib, we are to use parachutes? Well, that's all right then, Sahib! We will jump from 1,000 feet—or 2,000 feet if you wish, Sahib!" This story may sound absurd to anyone who does not know

Gurkhas, but I have told it to show that it takes a lot to shake their faith in anything that their officer might ask them to do even though to them it seems impossible.

The Indian troops of the Division consisted of Punjabi, Mussulmans, Pathans and Cuttacks, Sikhs, Jats, Dogras, Madrassis, and many other races. I have supported all these and have never been happier in battle than with them, but one of the difficulties the Staff had to face was rations. In any Army, rations are quite a problem; in the Indian Army it was a headache. When it comes to necessity the Indian troops will eat whatever there is, but prefer to stick to their religious observances. Thus a Mahomedan will not eat bacon or pig in any form. Neither Hindu nor Mahomedan will touch sheep, unless it has been killed according to the manner of their own beliefs. And goats and chickens are killed in a different manner for the adherents of each religion.

We Bartered Old Clothes for Food

Again, some Indians are rice-eaters and some are atta-eaters—atta being a coarse flour from which chapattis are made. Consequently, the R.I.A.S.C. tried to deliver goats on the hoof, and chickens, when available, alive, to the Indian troops. Others of them would not eat any meat or fish at all, but lived entirely on tinned peas, beans, and cheese; they all drink tea, but with more milk and sugar than is normal for Britishers.

The rations throughout the campaign were delivered daily by American and R.A.F. Dakotas, which flew over and dropped the stuff along with ammunition and supplies by parachute. As was only to be expected, the rations were not very exciting, but we were short only once, for a brief period, just before the capture of Shwebo (January 7, 1945). Then we were very hungry indeed, and we received permission to barter old clothes for local produce, if any. After about two days of living on a kind of porridge made from atta and water we found a village where eggs and chickens were plentiful and most people were able to acquire a good meal. After that, rations were satisfactory if monotonous; but we nearly always got bread (except in O.P. parties) and plenty of "M and V" and bully-beef and bacon.

When we entered Fort Dufferin, in Mandalay (March 20, 1945), there were a number of internees there, mostly Anglo-Burmese. They had been kept there by the Japs while we bombarded the fort with guns and air strikes, and they must have had a most unpleasant time. Although some of their number had been killed by our shells they did not hold that against us, and their welcome was so heartrending that I felt that all the sweat and toil involved in getting to Mandalay had been worth while. To

them, our arrival meant more than freedom and peace. It meant the end of humiliation, and the justification of their faith.

I was not at Maymyo when it was captured, on March 13, 1945, but I went there shortly after the fall of Mandalay. Maymyo, a lovely town in the hills, laid out with a beautiful cantonment and parkland and a lake (in peacetime it must have been very gay and romantic) had been the H.Q. of the Japanese Army in Burma. The Anglo-Burmese gave us a wonderful welcome and organized the running of our Divisional Club, "The Dagger Arms."

Dropped With a Wireless Operator

Throughout Burma there were many men of particular note, including Major Britten, who was killed about an hour after I last saw him. The men I have in mind—like Major Britten—were dropped, together with a wireless operator, by night into Jap-occupied territory. Britten spoke no Burmese, but he and his operator set about organizing the villagers under the very noses of the Japs. They found out who were loyal and who would help. They wirelessed back information and news to Calcutta, and later arms and ammunition were dropped to them. For months they lived alone, organizing groups of guerillas; Britten's group numbered nearly 3,000 men and boys, so that no Jap could move or enter a village in his area without Calcutta knowing, within an hour if necessary. The Japs knew, roughly, where such men were operating but not exactly where to look for them. A price was on their heads, but the Karens of the Hills and the Burmese of the Plains valued the hope these men brought more than all the rewards of Nippon.

To get some idea of the magnitude of their work, place yourself in their position. Your orders are: "You will be dropped in Japanese-occupied Burma by night. You cannot expect the British Army to reach you for six months. You are to organize a group of 2,000 villagers to bring you accurate information of Japanese movements and arms. You will have no authority over these villagers except that which your own personality commands. How you do the job is left to you. If you are captured you will probably be treated as a spy. You will receive no rations and only the barest medical supplies. You will take a radio set for passing on information." These teams, normally a major and a sergeant, were some of the greatest unsung heroes of the war.

THE first orders I heard Major Britten give to a patrol of ten who were to search a swamp for some Japs were, "If you find more than a hundred Japs, come back and tell me. If you find less than a hundred, kill them, and then come back and tell me. Any questions?" There were no questions; his men would do anything for him. His "Adjutant" was, I believe, a porter on the railway in peacetime, and could speak and read a little English. Britten was one of those gallant souls who cannot keep out of scrapping for long—a bullet found its resting place in a vital spot and he lies buried in Toungoo.

Their underground movement covered every village. No Jap could show himself without our knowing. The news travelled by bullock cart, by pony, by canoe, by runner, by women going to market, by children going to school; many and ingenious were the means employed, and the news always arrived hot and accurate. In the final "Battle of the Break-through," July 1945, the guerillas had their field-day. In the small area in which I was operating more than 1,000 Japs fell to the assorted small arms of the guerillas—some of them children of ten, armed with Sten guns.

They Snatched Us From a Hell-Ship

James Keating, a fireman in the S.S. Tairoa, told in the story which began in page 413 how the crew were captured by the Admiral Graf Spee in Dec. 1939, and warned by the latter's commander, Capt. Langsdorff, of the treatment they could expect in the notorious German tanker Altmark to which they were to be transferred. He concludes his narrative here.

AFTER Captain Langsdorff had made his farewell remarks to us we were ordered into motor-boats and taken across to the tanker. Armed guards of the tanker's crew took charge of us from the German marines, who returned to the Graf Spee, and during a short wait on deck we caught a glimpse of the man into whose hands we had been delivered. Captain Dau, master of the Altmark, was thick-set, weather-beaten and adorned with trim moustaches and beard that had earned him the nick-name of Old Natty-Whiskers among British Merchant Navymen already in the prison holds aboard. He wore a blue square-cut rig with gold braid on his cap and sleeves, and looked a tough sea-dog—as indeed he was. That he was a first-class navigator was proved by events; that he was a born bully of the Prussian type was indicated when he glared balefully at us and ordered the guards to take us below.

Forty-seven of us were stowed in a compartment forward, and other compartments on different decks were crowded with the rest of the merchant seamen to a total of roughly 300. It was close on noon by this time, and those of us newly-arrived from the Graf Spee were getting hungry. No dinner was brought to us and protests were ignored, but shortly before five o'clock in the afternoon one of the German guards who could speak broken English told four of my shipmates to "come and get it." What they got for us was a dixie of strong black tea, some black bread and ship's biscuits of the kind known as "hard tack." At eight o'clock next morning a similar meal was provided, and this fare became only too familiar on the ensuing voyage of two months and more.

Three Days on Bread and Water

That night we were kept below, cramped in our stuffy quarters with a steel watertight door securely fastened while the tanker remained hove-to with the pumps going to refuel the Graf Spee. The stifling heat affected several of my mates, who complained of illness when a young German doctor visited us next day. He seemed a decent sort, but his efforts to be helpful were strictly limited owing to Captain Dau's supervision and, as he himself explained, because there were no medical stores on board. However, he ordered the watertight door to be left open so that we might have more air, and advised us to drink a cup of seawater each day in lieu of medicine.

On the second day, after the tanker had parted company from the Graf Spee, Captain Dau came to inspect the prison decks with the doctor and the Master-at-Arms, whom he called the "prisoner-officer." This gave him the opportunity to deliver a lecture in English to those of us newly placed in his charge. Apparently, after initial successes in running the British blockade in the First Great War, he had been caught and interned at Donington Hall. His allegation was that he had been badly treated, and he said bluntly that he was going to treat us in like manner. If he were intercepted by the British Navy this time, on his way to Germany, he would drown us like rats. If he succeeded in getting us to Hamburg, he would march us from the docks with hands above our heads and then make us scrub the streets like the Jews.

"While you are aboard my ship," he concluded, "all you have to do is to behave yourselves and cause no trouble. But I do not forget that in the last war——" Here one of our deck-boys interrupted impatiently, "What's the good of talking to us about the last war?" That touched Natty-Whiskers on the raw. "Lie down, you English dog!" he roared. "You listen here!" the lad retorted. "If you were a prisoner of war in England you were well looked after—and you know it!"

This second interruption sent the Nazi captain into a violent rage—the first of the many we were to experience while in his hell-ship. What he said in German I couldn't understand, but it sounded none too good, and then he vented his spite by sentencing the boy to three days' solitary confinement on bread and water. Immediately, some of us volunteered to do it for him, as the lad was none too strong, but he took his punishment, although it left him sick and weak.

EACH day we were allowed out for half-an-hour's exercise, and one day a member of the German crew told us we were off the Georgia whaling station. Many of the Altmark's crew were youngsters of from eighteen to twenty-one years of age; these were the fanatical Nazis, and some of the older Germans told us they hated the sight of them. Possibly this was true; anyway, it was the older men who surreptitiously performed small acts of kindness. They had no chance of giving us the extra food we needed, but now and again they slipped us a few cigarettes and matches.

It is true that the Altmark had no heavy armament, but she was by no means the unarmed vessel that German propaganda tried to make the world believe. Pom-poms and machine-guns were concealed under the bridge, and there appeared to be a goodly supply of light firearms for the crew of 50 officers and men.

When the Graf Spee fell foul of the three British cruisers, Exeter, Achilles and Ajax, off the South American coast, the news that she was in battle became known aboard the prison-ship. "Then it's good-bye to your blinkin' pocket-battleship!" one of our chaps told the German guards. How right he was! But it was long before we knew definitely of the fate of the Graf Spee and her commander, Captain Hans Langsdorff.

After the first fortnight, Natty-Whiskers reduced our time in the open air to a quarter-hour each day. We gasped and sweated in close confinement in the tropics, and when the long voyage took us far to the north of Scotland we shivered and ached with cold. During all the time aboard we were given only one treat. That was at Christmas, and our celebration was made possible by the gift of some tins of cherries. One tin duly arrived in the cramped quarters of the Tairoa's seamen and firemen, and when the contents were shared we received the large helping of two cherries apiece.

Carpets From the Trapped Huntsman

Our hopes of rescue faded as time went on. The tanker had been repainted and her name altered six times, and we were inclined to bet long odds that she would run the gauntlet of the British naval patrols and bring up triumphantly in a German port.

Water from a leaking hydrant seeped down to some of the prison-decks, which were illuminated day and night by electricity, and numbers of us suffered from rheumatism and internal chills due to sitting and lying in the wet. Our complaints resulted in the Germans giving us carpets, of which they had a good stock, part of the pirated cargo of the Huntsman, which had been trapped by the Graf Spee while on route from Calcutta and Bombay. These carpets became wet through, but we hung up some of them to form partitions in our wretched quarters.

There was very little to do except sit around and talk during the daytime, but the chaps who had been weeks in the Altmark before our crew arrived were more than a little tired of talk. In desperate need of recreation some of them wrenched one or two iron plates from the ammunition racks and managed to chip them to form a pattern

IN JOESSING FJORD, NORWAY, in the cold darkness of a February night in 1940, H.M.S. Cossack (right) edged through the ice-floes towards the Altmark picked out in a searchlight's glare. With the rescue of about 300 merchant seamen there was about to be completed "one of the outstanding feats of the war." PAGE 443 *From the painting by Norman Wilkinson, O.B.E., P.R.I.*

of squares, and by using small nuts and bolts acquired here and there we were able to play draughts, the only game we had during the miserable voyage.

One day a boy from my ship got a notion, and asked the middle-aged German carpenter for a bit of solder. The German thought it was for a boat the lad was trying to make, and gave it to him. He had a penknife, and obtained some scraps of wood, and he had saved part of his ration of "butter," a rank concoction that looked and tasted like axle-grease. He used this "butter," with a wick made of soft string, to heat the solder and seal a quarter-lb. tobacco tin. Inside the tin was a note he had written: "We were caught by the Graf Spee and are in a German oil-tanker. Will you come to our help?" Next, by various ruses, he got hold of some paint, and coloured a rag in fair imitation of a Union Jack. This he fixed to the sealed tobacco tin, and slipped his handiwork into a bucket of refuse which he had to empty.

The Carpenter Went to the Cells

Whenever a prisoner had to throw refuse over the side an armed German guard stood watchfully by. However, the boy dumped the stuff in the sea without being detected, the tin with its little flag floating away on the surface and into the wake. By the worst of luck someone on the bridge happened to look over the side-screen and saw it, and reported to the Officer of the Watch, who instantly rang down on the engine-room telegraph for the ship to be stopped.

After that, Natty-Whiskers created more violently than ever, while the vessel put about and a search was made until the tin and flag were located and hauled aboard in a bucket attached to a rope. Meanwhile, the youngster had gone below and mixed-in with the crew of the Doric Star on the lowest deck. His hope of avoiding recognition, though, was doomed to disappointment, for eventually the German guard identified him and he was taken to face the angry captain, who demanded: "Where did you get the solder from?"

The lad prevaricated, unwilling to involve the ship's carpenter in trouble; and finally he was sentenced to six days' close confinement on bread and water. When the German carpenter heard of this he went straight to the captain to plead for the boy and to explain that he himself thought the solder was for a model boat. The upshot of it all was that Natty-Whiskers remitted the lad's sentence and sent the carpenter to the cells in his stead.

At last the tanker, the name Altmark painted in letters a foot high on her quarter, drew in unmolested towards the Norwegian coast. All lights were extinguished, and our state was even less enviable in the darkness. Hopes of rescue revived when one day the Second Officer of the Doric Star and the Fourth Officer of the Tairoa passed the word that they had seen Norwegian destroyers.

"We're all right now, boys," one of them assured us. "A Norwegian destroyer is coming alongside!" Norway was neutral, and the Altmark had steamed within the three-mile limit, so we expected to be taken out of the German ship and interned. That we should not fail to be discovered, one of our officers told us to shout as if we were at a football match when he gave the signal. In growing excitement we crowded round the companion ladders to be near the hatches, and when the signal was given we yelled, kicked and hammered on the bulkheads, blew the S O S on whistles, and generally raised pandemonium.

Natty-Whiskers immediately got the steam winches going to drown the noise, and then some of the German crew turned the hoses on us through the hatches and drenched us

to the skin. Norwegian naval officers came on board, and as they stayed half an hour they must have known there were prisoners in the ship (we shouted continuously), and that they were acting contrary to international law when they left without making any examination below decks. To say we felt dispirited when thus left to our fate is to put it very mildly.

This affair, as I know now, occurred off Bergen, and Captain Dau issued a typed notice in English, dated February 15, 1940, stating that on account of our behaviour all prisoners would get only bread and water next day and the "prisoner-officer" and doctor would no longer make their regular rounds, and "any severe case of sickness can be reported on the occasion of handing down the food. . . ." Incidentally, full diet often consisted only of bowls of boiled

Motto: " We Search Far "

NO. 230 SQUADRON

FORMED at Felixstowe in Sept. 1918, No. 230 Squadron remained there until May 1922, then moved to Calshot. In the following year it was disbanded and reformed at Pembroke Dock in Dec. 1934 as a flying boat squadron. In 1935 it went to Alexandria, and to Singapore in 1936. It seems that the squadron remained in the Far East until after the commencement of the Second Great War, when it moved back to Egypt.

It was based at Aboukir until Jan. 1943, when it moved to Dar-Es-Salaam in East Africa to participate in the coastal war in the Indian Ocean. Sunderland IIIs constituted the equipment. During 1943 it was engaged on anti U-boat patrols, air-sea rescue patrols and transit flights; and in Feb. 1944 it moved to Ceylon.

In June 1944 two of its Sunderlands were sent to an anchorage on the upper reaches of the Brahmaputra, whence by day and night they flew to Indawgyi Lake in North Burma to evacuate 500 casualties which otherwise would have been left to the mercy of the Japanese. These flights were extremely hazardous, since hills up to 10,000 feet had to be surmounted, and one of the Sunderlands was lost in a hurricane whilst at anchor. In July 1944 its aircraft were instrumental in the rescue of 230 survivors of a torpedoed ship. During Jan. and Feb. 1945 the squadron re-equipped with Sunderland Vs and commenced training in anticipation of anti-shipping operations in the Bay of Bengal; meanwhile, its aircraft transported stores from Calcutta to Kalewa on the Chindwin river in Central Burma. In April it moved to Akyab, to Rangoon in Sept. and later to Singapore. No. 230 was the first Sunderland squadron to operate in South-East Asia.

maize. A day or two later, three aircraft, wearing the roundels of the R.A.F., appeared, diving and zooming over the ship before vanishing again.

Our rescue was one of the outstanding feats of the war. Those R.A.F. scouts had reported what they had seen; moreover, they had given Captain Dau warning of what to expect, and he took the ship two-and-a-half miles up the Joessing Fjord on the small chance of lying doggo till conditions favoured a run down the coast to Germany.

THE prison-ship had been intercepted and identified by destroyers of Captain P. L. Vian's flotilla, we learnt, but no action was taken owing to the Altmark being within Norway's territorial waters. When Admiralty orders were received, Captain Vian's ship, H.M.S. Cossack, entered the fjord twice, the second time after dark when no satisfaction could be obtained from the Norwegian gunboats anchored there.

We could hardly breathe with excitement when a searchlight was focused on the Altmark and a destroyer drew alongside. An officer and some bluejackets leaped aboard and Captain Dau was roughly handled when he tried to give orders to the engine-room to go astern, apparently with the object of driving the warship aground.

The German crew were being rounded-up when one of the Nazis fired a shot—which was most unlucky for him and a few others. Some of the Altmark's crew jumped overboard and crossed the ice to the shore; one or two fell in the sea and were rescued by British officers. Those who reached land opened fire with rifles, the bluejackets replying with tommy-guns and dispersing them with casualties. But we unfortunate prisoners of course saw little of all this.

We Helped Ourselves to Vengeance

Hatches were presently opened and a voice shouted: "Are you all British seamen down there?" Even then we could hardly realize the turn events had taken, and someone replied: "Aye! Who are you?" The answer convinced us that our imprisonment in the German hell-ship was over: "All right, boys! The Navy is here!" And out we came, a dishevelled, scraggy crew, cheering ourselves hoarse.

"You need some decent rig-outs, lads," one of our officers exclaimed. "Go and help yourselves!" And we did! The Germans had done nothing to outfit us after our capture, and many of our clothes and other personal possessions were at the bottom of the Atlantic. Therefore we had no qualms about "borrowing" a few useful articles of attire and comfort from them. I was lucky to lay hands on a new civvy suit belonging to the Altmark's Chief Officer, plus two white blankets, two pairs of shoes, six pairs of socks and four silk shirts. After the weeks in the prison-ship, from December 7, 1939, to February 16, 1940, I had some hot feelings to work off. So I parked my "winnings" in a safe place and helped to smash up the wireless operator's room.

In the cold darkness of the February night, H.M.S. Cossack slid out of Joessing Fjord, homeward-bound with nearly 300 happy merchant seamen. We landed next day at Leith, where we had a rousing reception and washed some of the sea-salt out of our throats with British beer. Some of us, too, were lucky in travelling down to King's Cross in company with Elsie and Doris Waters, better known as Gert and Daisy, who treated us royally.

Two years later I was recuperating from the Huns' savagery when a bomb fell in a Rotherhithe street and postponed my recovery. But, praise be! I still have strength to raise a tankard in congenial company at the Merchant Navy Club.

'Altmark Overpowered by British Sea Pirates'

RESCUED BY THE ROYAL NAVY from the German hell-ship Altmark, nearly 300 joyous merchant seamen were landed (!) at Leith, Scotland, from H.M.S. Cossack in February 1940. Erected by the outwitted Germans, near the scene of this stirring rescue, the sign (2) is inscribed " On February 16, 1940, the Altmark was here overpowered by British Sea Pirates." In Jœssing Fjord, the Altmark's flag at half-mast (3). Story in facing page. PAGE 445 *Photos, G.P.U., Associated Press*

I Was a 'Guest' of the Japs in Tokyo

Together with about 70,000 other Imperial troops, Gunner H. W. Berry, 5th Field Regiment R.A., 9th Indian Division, was captured at Singapore, on February 15, 1942. After a spell in Changi P.O.W. Camp (see page 90) he found himself again on the move, heading for further adventure.

ANNOUNCEMENT OF VARIETY SHOW produced by the author of this story is evidence of the high morale maintained by prisoners in Tokyo's Omori Camp in May 1945.

ELEVEN hundred of us, mainly Artillery, were told we were being sent away from Singapore, and without delay we were carried in lorries, with such kit as we had, to the docks. We presumed we were going to Japan, and although we did not fancy the idea of moving farther East and away from the Allied forces we did think that, physically, we should be better off. "We will be better fed—probably European food," we told each other, "and we shall receive better medical attention." We knew also that Japan's climate was healthier than that of tropical Singapore.

H. W. BERRY

A shock came when we saw our "liner." It couldn't have been more than a 4,000-tonner — an old tramp steamer which the Japs had renamed "England Maru." We did not think it possible they could crowd us all on that small vessel, but they did—plus 1,100 Japs who were going home. Conditions were hellish. There were three holds, each with wooden partitions built in around the sides. The prisoners occupied the bottom of each hold and the Japs the upper "berths." We had been wise enough to bring along some of the Red Cross food which had reached us in Singapore a few days previously, otherwise we should have starved. There was a small amount of rice, and some greasy stew made with unfresh meat, issued three times a day. This diet naturally made us all very thirsty, and it was difficult to get water for drinking purposes; what we did get was salty.

It was not long before many of us became ill with dysentery. For ten days I had nothing except Japanese tea (no sugar or milk). Four men were buried at sea, and one of the senior British officers was tied to the mast and whipped because he objected to the terrible conditions. Finally the Japs began to get worried in case their own troops became infected, and wirelessed for advice. They were told to put in at Formosa, and were highly pleased about it.

"You have nothing more to worry about," they told the sick. "Directly you dock you will be taken away in ambulances to a nice hospital." The ambulances proved to be one Army lorry, and the "hospital" was our prison

camp. It was situated just outside Taihoku, the Formosan capital, and consisted of seven bamboo huts. Geography books tell us that Formosa has a mild climate, but none of us was ever so cold before as we were during that first winter of captivity. We were not allowed fires, and rations were just sufficient to keep us alive. At one time an epidemic of diphtheria struck the camp, and two or three prisoners were dying every week.

After three months in "hospital" (on reduced rations, because I was not earning my keep by working) I joined my fellow prisoners in making some kind of a park immediately outside the camp—digging holes, putting the soil in a bamboo basket and then dumping it about a hundred yards away. It was extremely monotonous and tiring, and we worked from seven in the morning to five or six in the evening. We all lost three or four stone in weight (I weighed 7 st. 12 lb.) and our ribs showed plainly.

He'd Get Us Safely to Japan!

However, with the approach of summer and the warmer weather we began to feel almost normal, and after our day's work was finished we set about organizing pastimes. A concert party began to function and despite the interference of the Japs morale began to soar. After a year of this existence they decided it was time to start splitting us up and interchanging us with prisoners in some of the other camps on the island. One day three of us were told to report to the Japanese Camp Commandant.

"You have been selected," he told us. "for a very special purpose. I cannot tell you what it is now, but you are going to the finest camp in the Japanese Empire. You have nothing more to worry about, You will be well treated and will receive a Red Cross parcel every day." We had heard similar promises before so we were not impressed, and I wondered what it was the

Japs had up their confounded sleeves. However, on the following day, November 4, 1943, we started on our journey. Before we left Formosa we picked up fifteen other P.O.W. from the half-dozen camps, and were then divided into two groups, one of ten and one of eight. The larger group, we were informed, were to be known as the technicians and the remainder as the "cultural group." We were put aboard a convoy (which had just arrived at Takao from Java), already full of Dutch prisoners going to Japan. Conditions were a little better than on the England Maru, although we were only allowed on deck for 15 minutes' exercise each day.

Before we set sail the Commandant said he would endeavour to get us safely to Japan, but if we disobeyed orders we would be severely punished. We reached the port of Moji, on November 14. Saying good-bye to the technicians we "culturals" embarked on a train for Tokyo. We understood now

CHRISTMAS PANTOMIME, 1944, in the temporarily transformed bathhouse at Omori, organized, run and thoroughly enjoyed by the P.O.W.—the majority of whom were astonishingly fit, largely because, working in railway yards and at docksides, "they managed to steal enough food to keep them going."

FIRST P.O.W. CAMP IN JAPAN TO BE FREED was this at Omori, Tokyo, over the roofs of which an aircraft is skimming low. " It was a tremendous thrill when the Flying Fortresses made their appearance "—and a greater thrill still when on August 29, 1945, U.S. Marines came ashore on the beach from the landing barges.
Photo, U.S. Navy

that we were included in this group because of the activity we had taken in camp entertainments. After a thirty-hour journey we reached Omori P.O.W. Camp, Tokyo. At first we were called " special prisoners " and were excused all work and fatigues, but this lasted for only three weeks. We were then interviewed by an English-speaking Jap officer who informed us that they wished to send us to a special propaganda camp where we could study Japanese culture. When I was asked, " What do you know about politics and economics ? " I answered, " Nothing ! " Thus I lost my chance of a Red Cross parcel every day.

On December 7 I started work again. I was amazed at the fitness of the majority of the prisoners in Omori Camp as compared with the comrades I had left in Formosa. They were strong, strapping fellows and full of life. This was because, working in railway yards and at docksides, they managed to steal enough food—even if it was sometimes only rice—to keep them going.

At first I was in no condition to do heavy work. I couldn't carry 70 lb. of rice, and when I saw men with 200-lb. sacks of beans on their backs, walking up and down planks in warehouses, I was in despair. Again the winter for me was a nightmare. I hadn't the strength to lift an empty shovel at times, and I couldn't sleep at night because of the cold. But the climate was far healthier than that of either Formosa or Singapore, and after I learned the art of stealing from the Japs I found things a little easier.

On some days quite a variety of foodstuffs was shunted into the railway yard, and despite the vigilance of the guards the vans were often looted by the prisoners. At times it became a battle of wits between the British and the Japs. A luxury such as sugar came in only on rare occasions, and knowing that the prisoners would make every effort to obtain some a special watch was kept. At the end of the day the Japs would be congratulating themselves on their successful vigilance,

whilst prisoners would be secreting socks stuffed with sugar beneath their working clothes. The same thing happened with rice, beans, fish and various tinned foods.

In order to fox the few Japs who knew a little English, slang words were used for different commodities. Sugar was " Tate and Lyle," rice was " white mice," fish was " tiddlers," and so on. Sometimes it was possible to bribe a Japanese foreman for a percentage of the " loot." They were usually quite willing. Despite a search before the ride back to camp it was seldom anyone was caught, and in spite of repeated warnings of " severe punishment " hardly a day went by without something being smuggled back.

Tokyo's Wooden Buildings Blazed

The expert looters lived almost as luxuriously as they would have done in wartime England. They were known as Barons, and could even afford to employ someone to make their beds of an evening and wash their dishes in exchange for a share of their surplus food. Once again I began to take a share in the camp entertainments. The Japs finally allowed me three days off from work in order to write, produce and rehearse a show—after I had convinced them that it couldn't possibly be done in a few minutes.

It was a tremendous thrill, of course, when the Flying Fortresses made their appearance. But also rather frightening. We weren't allowed to stop work during the day raids, and at night chaos was caused when thousands of Tokyo's little wooden buildings were set aflame. It was possible to read a book in the middle of the night by the light of those fires. Never believing in rumours it was a long while before I was really convinced that the Japanese had surrendered, on August 15, 1945. About a fortnight after this date the Jap Commandant paraded us and announced the end of hostilities. I took down his speech in shorthand. He had the cheek to say he hoped we would bear no malice, as he had always tried to do his best for us. He has now, I believe—and hope—been shot.

On August 29, at four o'clock in the afternoon, American Marines landed on the beach outside our camp, from three landing barges, and by four o'clock the next morning we had all been taken to a hospital ship. We lucky ones at Omori were the first prisoners to be released from a camp in Japan itself.

NEW FACTS AND FIGURES

THE last Tiger Moth had left the de Havilland factory (Hatfield, Herts), by September 1946. Now superseded, this trainer aircraft—on which nearly every R.A.F. pilot did his first solo flight—first flew in 1931, and was one of the only machines to fly throughout the Second Great War. The total number built was 8,962, in factories at Hatfield, Sydney, Toronto and Wellington, N.Z. Of these, 630 were Queen Bee pilotless aircraft, used for A.A. practice.

DURING the Battle of Britain Sir Geoffrey de Havilland designed a tiny bomb-rack to carry eight 20-lb. bombs under the wings of the Tiger Moth. Of these racks 1,500 were made, for use in case of invasion, but no Tiger Moth ever dropped a bomb. If they had been used the second seat would have had to be empty, for the little aircraft could not lift two passengers and 160 lb. of bombs.

WHITE Russia, according to Mr. Richard Scandrett, head of a U.N.R.R.A. mission, is the most devastated country in the world. A conservative estimate gives over 2,000,000 people killed by the Germans in the Vitebsk area, where there was a well-organized partisan movement. During their three-years' occupation the Germans removed all equipment from hospitals, wrecked factory machinery and destroyed nearly all the livestock.

THE U.N.R.R.A. relief programme allotted to White Russia was 61,000,000 dollars (about £15,250,000), half of which was represented by food, all of which has been received or shipped. The work of reconstruction is immense. Minsk, for

example, might take as long as 15 years to rebuild. White Russia's war orphans, who number 300,000, have priority in everything.

BY August 1946 (states Soviet News) the repatriation of people from White Russia who had been driven into German slavery had been virtually completed, over 300,000 having returned home. The Soviet Government assigned funds totalling over 3,500,000 roubles for financial assistance and resettlement of the repatriates. Clothing and footwear were provided and in the towns 9,000 flats were put at their disposal, and in rural regions 10,000 houses.

A FIVE-YEAR Plan for Japanese national rehabilitation was published in Tokyo on September 2, 1946, by the National Land Bureau of the Ministry of the Interior. A population estimated to reach 80,000,000 by 1950 is to be redistributed within the country's reduced territory. Of the estimated working population of 38,000,000, some 16,500,000 are to be engaged in agriculture and forestry : 600,000 in fishery ; 6,300,000 in industry (a reduction of 3,000,000 compared with the war years) ; 7,100,000 on building and road making ; and 5,000,000 in commerce. Japan's urban population is not to exceed 30,000,000 ; the remaining 50,000,000 are to be restricted to the farming, fishing and mining villages.

MORE than 50,000 German prisoners of war released from captivity in the Soviet Union had reached Frankfort-on-Oder by August 1946. Beginning to arrive in July, they came at first at the rate of about 1,200 a day, the number rising to between 3,000 and 5,000 a day.

Preparing for Our Third Post-War Harvest

Photo, Planet News

CHAMPIONS OF THE PLOUGH, eight-year-old Welsh Shire horses Jill and Judy, with ploughman Jack Uzzell, plodded a winning furrow at the Chertsey (Surrey) Agricultural Association's Show on Sept. 19, 1946, adding another first prize to a previous 30. On four occasions they have gained championships, and the trio—valiantly holding out against the increasingly persistent call for complete farm mechanization—here demonstrate the perfect team-work which will help the good earth to produce more food for Britain again next year.

Photo, Planet News

Printed in England and published every alternate Friday by the Proprietors, THE AMALGAMATED PRESS, LTD., The Fleetway House, Farringdon Street, London, E.C.4. Registered for transmission by Canadian Magazine Post. Sole Agents for Australia and New Zealand : Messrs. Gordon & Gotch, Ltd. and for South Africa : Central News Agency; Ltd.— October 25, 1946.   S.S.   *Editorial Offices :* JOHN CARPENTER HOUSE WHITEFRIARS, LONDON. E C 4.

Vol 10 · The War Illustrated · N° 245

SIXPENCE

NOVEMBER 8, 1946

I WAS THERE

VICE-ADMIRAL SIR PHILIP VIAN, K.C.B., K.B.E., D.S.O., seated at his desk, shortly after assuming his new appointment as a Lord Commissioner of the Admiralty and Fifth Sea Lord (Air), on September 23, 1946. In his appointment he will be responsible for the co-ordination of naval air services. Sir Philip is particularly remembered as commander of H.M.S. Cossack when she rescued British prisoners from the Altmark in February 1940 (see story in pages 443-445; and page 171, Vol. 2).

Edited by Sir John Hammerton

NO. 246 WILL BE PUBLISHED FRIDAY, NOVEMBER 22

Our Roving Camera: Poppies for Remembrance Day

FINISHING TOUCHES TO A CROSS OF POPPIES being deftly given by an ex-Serviceman in preparation for Remembrance Day, Nov. 10, 1946. Since 1921 at this time of year Flanders Poppies have been sold in aid of Earl Haig's British Legion Appeal Fund. See also New Facts and Figures page 479.

BLACK BILLY, 32-YEAR-OLD PIT PONY, worked down a Lanarkshire coal mine for over a quarter-century, until the National Equine (and Smaller Animals) Defence League obtained his release. Black Billy is now in retirement at the League's voluntarily endowed Home of Rest for Horses at Carlisle, and is noted for his passion for tea—in a basin. He was just one of the 23,000 ponies at work in British coal mines on whose behalf a petition, containing 50,000 signatures, was recently presented to Parliament by the League. A 23-year-old pony, named Dobbin, died a short while ago after almost a lifetime in the service of a Co. Durham colliery ; badly hurt by a runaway wagon, he had been brought up to ground-level and cared for—but it was too late.

GERMAN P.O.W. AS BOMB DISPOSERS are seen assisting a R.E. squad with equipment for removing a 3,000-lb. German bomb at Addiscombe, Surrey. Others, drafted from N. Italy and Belgium, will, after training, replace demobilized Royal Engineers in this work.

CAMPAIGN STARS awarded for service in the Second Great War are now being struck by the Royal Mint, in conjunction with Woolwich Arsenal—where rings are seen being attached to the 1939-45 Star. Seven other Stars—the Africa, Italy, Burma, Pacific, France and Germany, Atlantic, and Air Crew Europe—complete the eight campaigns for which decorations have been awarded. It will take about two years to complete the 10,000,000 required.

H.M. THE KING'S DUTCH HORSES, magnificent blacks presented by Queen Wilhelmina, are now being trained in London, for ceremonial occasions, by our Household Cavalry, here seen exercising them in Rotten Row. See also illus. page 297.

Photos, Keystone, The Cumberland News, Planet, Central Press

'The Bismarck has been Sunk'

By FRANCIS E. McMURTRIE

WHEN Mr. Churchill made the brief announcement in Parliament on May 27, 1941: "The Bismarck has been sunk," he rang down the curtain on a sea drama as thrilling as any recorded in history.

In that month the Battle of the Atlantic had entered on its third phase. Though shipping losses had subsided somewhat from the high figures of July-December 1940, a total of 41 vessels of over 250,000 tons gross had been sunk during April 1941 through U-boat attack. During February and March the battleships Scharnhorst and Gneisenau were also raiding commerce in the Atlantic, aided by the heavy cruiser Admiral Hipper. Between them they sank or captured 27 ships, but late in March the two former ships were driven into Brest for recuperation. There they continued to represent a menace to Atlantic convoys should they emerge without interception.

ON May 22 it became known to the Commander-in-Chief of the Home Fleet (Adm. Sir John Tovey) that the big new battleship Bismarck had sailed from Bergen, where she had been located a short time before. This momentous news was obtained by Commander G. A. Rotherham, R.N., of H.M.S. Sparrowhawk, a naval air station in the north of Scotland, who made a personal reconnaissance in very adverse weather conditions to satisfy himself whether or not the ship was still in port.

As a result of the dispositions immediately ordered by Admiral Tovey, the Bismarck, accompanied by the heavy cruiser Prinz Eugen, was sighted on the evening of May 23 in the Denmark Strait, between Iceland and Greenland. The ships which sighted her were the cruisers Norfolk (Captain A. J. L. Phillips) and Suffolk (Captain R. M. Ellis), the former wearing the flag of Rear-Admiral W. F. Wake-Walker. Both enemy ships were proceeding at high speed to the south-westward, and it was difficult to keep them in view through storms of snow and sleet and patches of mist, which at times reduced visibility to no more than a mile. In spite of these obstacles, the enemy continued to be shadowed by the British cruisers throughout the night.

Located by a Catalina Aircraft

Early in the morning of May 24, H.M.S. Hood (Captain Ralph Kerr) and Prince of Wales (Captain J. C. Leach) made contact with the enemy. The former ship, a battle cruiser dating from the First Great War, was wearing the flag of Vice-Admiral L. E. Holland, Second-in-Command Home Fleet.

Early in the engagement which immediately ensued the Hood received a hit in a magazine from one of the Bismarck's 15-inch salvos and blew up with the loss of practically everyone on board. Some time later the Prince of Wales received a hit which put her fire control system out of action for the time being. Nevertheless, she did not lose touch with the enemy, the Norfolk and Suffolk continuing their skilful shadowing. The Bismarck had not escaped without damage, one of the hits causing a fire to break out on board. On the evening of May 24, having effected temporary repairs, the Prince of Wales was able to renew the action for a short time. At this stage the German ships turned away to the westward, and then swung round on to a southerly course, still closely pursued by the British.

During the night a very gallant torpedo attack was carried out by naval aircraft from H.M.S. Victorious (Captain H. C. Bovell),

which had arrived in the vicinity. This attack was a hazardous enterprise, from which those engaged in it had little hope of returning, so bad were the weather conditions. In spite of this all got safely back to their carrier, after hitting the Bismarck with one torpedo. The intrepid leader of this operation, Lieutenant-Commander E. Esmonde, afterwards lost his life in an even more desperate affair—the attempt to torpedo the Scharnhorst and Gneisenau as they passed through the Strait of Dover in February of the following year (see pages 131-133).

SPLINTER-HOLE caused by a shell fired from the Bismarck almost joined up with a porthole of H.M.S. Sheffield, one of the ships engaged in shadowing the German battleship in May 1941.
Photo, British Official

Early on the 25th the weather became thicker, and touch with the enemy was unavoidably lost; she was then in a position about 350 miles S.S.E. of Cape Farewell, the southerly extremity of Greenland. A most anxious period of suspense followed. Not until 10.30 a.m. on May 26, nearly 32 hours later, was the Bismarck located by a Catalina aircraft of Coastal Command, about 550 miles west of Land's End. She was steaming at 22 knots and had parted company with the Prinz Eugen, which was ultimately found to have taken refuge in Brest.

ALTHOUGH driven off and damaged by the Bismarck's well-directed anti-aircraft fire, the Catalina got her report through, enabling the German battleship to be sighted again at 11.15 by naval aircraft from H.M.S. Ark Royal (Captain L. E. H. Maund), belonging to Force "H," based upon Gibraltar. During the afternoon a striking force of torpedo aircraft flew off from this carrier to attack the Bismarck, but did not reach her.

Shortly after 5.30 H.M.S. Sheffield (Captain C. A. A. Larcom), a cruiser which had been detached from Force "H" by Vice-Admiral Sir James Somerville, made contact with the Bismarck and proceeded to shadow her. Twenty minutes later a second striking force flown off from the Ark Royal pressed home its attack and achieved an important success, one torpedo hitting the Bismarck amidships and a second on the starboard quarter. The latter evidently damaged the steering gear, for immediately afterwards the great battleship was seen to make two

complete circles. Thenceforward her speed, already affected by the hit from the torpedo-bombers of the Victorious, was reduced to about 12 knots. A fresh gale from the north-west now forced the Bismarck, owing to the damage to her rudder, to head straight towards her pursuers.

Just before dark a destroyer force under Captain P. L. Vian, including H.M.S. Cossack, Zulu, Sikh and Maori, and the Polish ship Piorun (Commander E. Plawski), made contact with the enemy. They had been steaming all day at high speed in a heavy following sea, but maintained touch with the Bismarck all night under most difficult conditions. During the middle watch they attacked with torpedoes and obtained at least two hits. Though under heavy fire from the Bismarck, they sustained only a few minor casualties.

Bright Flame Showed in Bismarck

On the morning of May 27 the sun rose on a heavy sea with the north-westerly gale continuing. At times visibility was very good, about 15 miles, until reduced to three or four miles as heavy rain squalls swept across the water. In the British ships the hands had been at action stations all night, taking it in turns to doze off at their posts. In view of the speed with which situations develop in modern warfare it would not have been wise to allow them to go below for breakfast, so cocoa, soup, sandwiches, cake and ship's biscuits were issued.

At eight minutes past 8 the Norfolk reported that she was again in touch with the enemy. The necessary alterations of course were ordered by the Commander-in-Chief, and at 8.42 the Bismarck was sighted 15 miles away, some 500 miles west of Brest.

In the flagship King George V (Captain W. R. Patterson) the following message was given out to officers and men by Sir John Tovey : "The sinking of the Bismarck may have an effect on the war, as a whole, out of all proportion to the loss to the enemy of one battleship. May God be with you and grant you victory."

At 8.47 the battleship Rodney (Captain F. H. G. Dalrymple-Hamilton) opened fire, followed a minute later by the King George V, the range then being about 12 miles. The Bismarck opened an accurate fire at the Rodney at 8.50, narrowly missing her. The first of the King George V's hits was soon observed to enter the base of the Bismarck's forward superstructure, where a bright flame burned for some seconds. Splashes from the 16-inch guns of the Rodney and the 14-inch guns of the King George V rose as high as the enemy's foretop, while those from the 8-inch guns of the Norfolk, and later from those of the Dorsetshire, combined to keep the German battleship almost continuously surrounded by splashes. The enemy's cordite smoke hung heavily, flashes of his guns appearing through it as a dull orange glow.

SHORTLY after 9 the enemy shifted his fire to the King George V, where a whistling noise was heard over the bridge, after which splashes of heavy shell were some 400 yards over : but the nearest approach to a hit was a 5·9-inch shell which burst about 50 yards short of the conning tower. In the Rodney nothing worse than a near miss was experienced, a fragment of shell passing through the starboard side of the director controlling the anti-aircraft armament. It smashed the cease-fire bell, passed through a steel helmet hanging near, cut the trainer's telescope in half, hit the fire gong attached to the director and passed out to the rear, just grazing the trainer's wrist on the way.

By 9.20 the Bismarck, having been repeatedly hit, began to blow off steam, and a strong fire started amidships. Both her forward turrets appeared to be out of action, and the other two were firing intermittently and erratically. She had a heavy list to port, which at 9.25 became most noticeable. As the range decreased, the 5·25-inch batteries of the King George V were ordered to open fire, with devastating effect on the super-structure and upper deck of the enemy battleship. In both the King George V and Rodney the noise of gunfire was no longer noticed. Occasionally, when the turrets fired on extreme bearings, their blast rattled round the superstructure, causing discomfort to the personnel and minor damage. At 9.45 the Bismarck, which was yawing considerably, exposed her starboard side to view for the first time. Observers noticed at least three large fires amidships, and a gaping hole in the bows near the waterline. The few guns left intact were firing spasmodically. The range was now closed to 3,000 yards, and three hits in one salvo were clearly seen. Two entered the deck at the base of the superstructure, and one appeared to tear off the whole of the back from "B" turret, which was quickly enveloped in an enormous sheet of flame. Men were now seen jumping off the quarterdeck into the sea to escape from the intolerable heat. The whole ship had become a blazing wreck, so "Cease fire" was ordered at 10.21. There were no casualties or damage in the British ships, due to the skilful tactics of the commander-in-chief and the heavy fire poured into the enemy throughout the action.

Turned Turtle and Disappeared

Torpedoes were fired at the Bismarck by the Rodney (one of which hit, probably the only instance in history of one capital ship torpedoing another) in the closing stage of the action, and at 10.36 she sank with colours still flying after further torpedoes had been directed at her by H.M.S. Dorsetshire. She went down in about two minutes, turning turtle and then disappearing, the bows being the last part to submerge. The position as recorded at the time was Lat. 48.10 N., Long. 16.12 W., depth about 2,500 fathoms.

More than 100 officers and men were rescued and made prisoners of war, among them Lieut.-Commander Freiherr von Mullenheim, second gunnery officer, who had been Assistant Naval Attaché in London before the War. Submarines being reported in the vicinity, it was impossible to institute a thorough search for survivors. Two days later the Spanish cruiser Canarias, which was passing through the area, picked up a number of bodies which were later landed for burial.

How many torpedoes were absorbed by the Bismarck is uncertain, but it can hardly have been less than nine; three from naval aircraft, two or more from the destroyers, one from the Rodney and at least three from the Dorsetshire. It will be recalled that some six months later the Prince of Wales, a smaller ship, required a similar number to sink her. Being much better protected by armour than the Hood, the Bismarck's magazines remained intact throughout the action, illustra-

ting the remarkable progress made in naval design between 1916 and 1936.

When addressed by their commanding officer before the action, the ship's company of the Bismarck were assured that the Luftwaffe would be coming to their aid from French airfields. All that was seen of it was a single Focke-Wulf brought down by the King George V's 5·25-inch guns shortly before 4 p.m. on May 26. Still, the Luftwaffe arrived on the following day, a trifle late. As the destroyers Mashona and Tartar were on their way towards their base on the morning of May 28, they were attacked again and again by German aircraft, which continued to come over in waves until nearly midnight. H.M.S. Mashona was sunk with the loss of an officer and 35 ratings. This loss might well have been heavier but for the energy with which the Tartar set about the work of rescue. One stout fellow, a range-taker in the Mashona, took over a corresponding post in the Tartar and continued at his action station for the next 12 hours. When relieved he apologized for being tired out—yet he had been bombed, swum to safety and withstood further attacks during that time !

From German accounts it was learned that the Bismarck wore the flag of Vice-Admiral Luetjens, who perished with her. His last signal is said to have reported the ship to be incapable of manoeuvring, and avowed his intention of fighting to the finish. The destruction of this fine ship, with an exceptionally full complement (there are said to have been nearly 2,000 on board) must have been a bitter blow to the Germans, to whom she had been lauded as "unsinkable."

W HAT was the object of sending the Bismarck out into the Atlantic with nothing but the Prinz Eugen to support her ? It was certainly not a sound move from the strategical standpoint. Everything points to the fact that Hitler, impatient at the failure of his U-boats to maintain the rate of destruction achieved in the second half of 1940, sought to supplement it by surface raiding, even though an earlier effort with the "pocket battleship" Admiral Graf Spee had ended in her defeat by three British cruisers in the Battle of the River Plate. Her sister ship, the Admiral Scheer, when operating in the Atlantic between October, 1940, and April, 1941, had been fortunate in encountering nothing more formidable than the heroic Jervis Bay, and in the five months that she was at sea her total "bag" numbered only 16 ships. This tended further to depreciate the value of the "pocket battleship" for raiding purposes, so recourse was had to the faster and more powerful Scharnhorst and Gneisenau. These being immured in Brest

a substitute was provided in the Bismarck, which it was fondly hoped by the Germans would prove faster than any ship able to stand up to her, and powerful enough to overwhelm all other opponents.

Lengthy List of Decorations

Honours and awards to those concerned in the hunting down and destruction of the Bismarck included: Admiral Sir John Tovey (now Admiral of the Fleet Lord Tovey), the K.B.E.; Captain (now Vice-Admiral Sir Frederick) Dalrymple-Hamilton of the Rodney and Captain (now Vice-Admiral) Patterson of the King George V, the C.B.; Rear-Admiral (the late Admiral Sir Frederic) Wake-Walker; Commodore (now Vice-Admiral Sir Patrick) Brind, Admiral Tovey's Chief of Staff; Captain (now Rear-Admiral) Bovell of the Victorious; and Captain (now Rear-Admiral) Maund of the Ark Royal, each the C.B.E. Six officers received the O.B.E., and a petty officer in the Ark Royal was given the British Empire Medal. Captain (now Vice-Admiral Sir Philip) Vian obtained a second bar to his D.S.O., while those who were awarded the D.S.O. included Commander Rotherham of the Sparrowhawk, Lieut.-Commander (A) Esmonde of the Victorious, Lieut.-Commander T. P. Coode of the Ark Royal, the commanding officers of H.M.S. Sheffield, Prince of Wales, Dorsetshire, Norfolk and Suffolk; and the engineer officers of H.M.S. Rodney, Prince of Wales, Cossack, Suffolk, Norfolk and King George V. A bar to the D.S.C. was conferred on Commander (now Captain) H. T. Armstrong of H.M.S. Maori, and the decoration itself on the commanding officers of the Zulu and Sikh and 27 other officers. To 32 ratings the Distinguished Service Medal was awarded. The officers in charge of the Catalina aircraft which re-located the Bismarck on May 25, and of a Sunderland which shadowed the Bismarck on the night of May 23, each received the Distinguished Flying Cross.

For the guidance of readers who may not have the information at hand, the principal particulars of the various ships mentioned are given in the panel below.

NAZI NAVAL PRIDE reached its zenith in the battleship Bismarck which was launched, like her sister ship the Tirpitz, in the spring of 1939. Bismarck sank H.M.S. Hood and damaged H.M.S. Prince of Wales before being brought to bay and destroyed on May 27, 1941, after a six-day chase of 1,750 miles, from Bergen to Iceland and across the N. Atlantic. *Photo, Associated Press*

H.M. Ships	Tons	Knots	Guns
King George V (1939)	35,000	28	Ten 14-in.
Prince of Wales (1939) — —	35,000	28	Ten 14-in.
Rodney (1925) — —	33,900	23	Nine 16-in.
Hood (1918) — —	42,100	31	Eight 15-in.
Victorious (1939) —	23,000	31	Sixteen 4·5-in.
Ark Royal (1937) —	22,000	30·5	Sixteen 4·5-in.
Dorsetshire (1928) —	9,925	32	Eight 8-in.
Norfolk (1928) —	9,925	32	Eight 8-in.
Suffolk (1926)— —	10,000	31·5	Eight 8in.
Sheffield (1936) —	9,100	32	Twelve 6-in.
Maori Mashona Cossack Tartar Zulu Sikh } (1937)	1,870	36·5	Eight 4·7-in.
Polish Ship			
Piorun (1940) —	1,760	36	Six 4·7-in.
German Ships			
Bismarck (1939) —	41,700	30	Eight 15-in.
Gneisenau (1936) —	32,000	29	Nine 11-in.
Scharnhorst (1936) *	32,000	29	Nine 11-in.
Prinz Eugen (1938) —	15,000	32	Eight 8-in.
Adm. Scheer (1932) —	12,000	26	Six 11-in.
Adm. Graf Spee (1933) — —	12,000	26	Six 11-in.

Royal Navy Destroyers Handed Over to Norway

FULFILLING PART OF THE ANGLO-NORWEGIAN NAVAL AGREEMENT signed in June 1946, two British destroyers, H.M.S. Croziers and H.M.S. Crystal, renamed the Trondheim and Stavanger respectively, were handed over to representatives of the Royal Norwegian Navy, at Chatham, Kent, on October 10. The new nameplate on the Croziers was unveiled by Mme. Erik Colban (1) wife of the Norwegian Ambassador, who (2, centre), inspected the Norwegian crews. The destroyers, with crews (3).   PAGE 453   *Photos, Associated Press, P.A.-Reuter, Keystone*

Hamburgers Angered by Nuremberg Acquittals

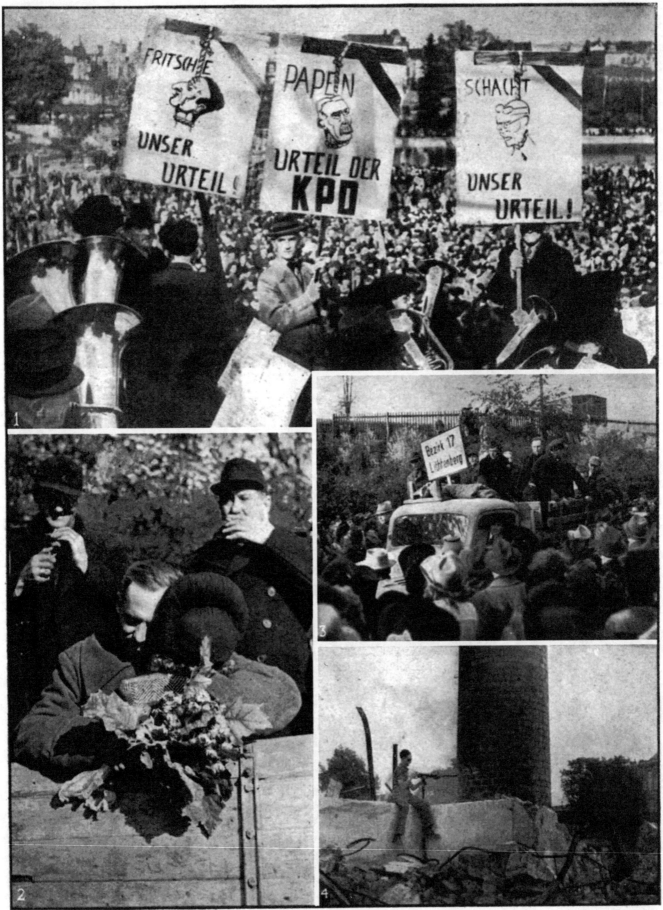

DISSENTIENT GERMAN VOICES WERE RAISED when the Nuremberg judgement (see pages 431-435) became known ; leaders of a Hamburg demonstration (1) carried banners which left their wishes regarding the three Nazis in no doubt. Repatriated from Britain, German P.O.W. recently arrived in Berlin—this one (2) to a wifely greeting. Returned prisoners were taken from Berlin stations to their home towns by motor transport (3). R.E.s fell a chimney (4) in Hamburg—" capital " of the British zone—in clearing a site for the erection of houses for British families.

Last Milestone in The Desert Rats' Long Trek

1939 **1945**

AFRICA
WESTERN DESERT
EL ALAMEIN TOBRUK BENGHAZI
TRIPOLI MARETH TUNIS

ITALY
SALERNO NAPLES VOLTURNO

FRANCE
NORMANDY THE SEINE ROUBAIX

BELGIUM
OUDENARDE GHENT MALINES

HOLLAND
EINDHOVEN TILBURG THE MAAS

GERMANY
THE RHINE AHAUS SOLINGEN
NIENBURG SOLTAU HAMBURG

BERLIN

IN THE HEART OF THE ENEMY'S CAPITAL, this stone memorial marks the termination of the 2,700 miles route from beginning to end of which the British 7th Armoured Division—the far-famed Desert Rats—fought and defeated their Axis opponents. Erected and unveiled without ceremony the memorial stands at the end of the Ruhr autobahn, and replaces the temporary wooden one set up when the Desert Rats entered Berlin in July 1945 (see page 244, Vol. 9). The memorial originated at Alamein, where in 1942 a crude wooden signpost read "To Berlin."

Death Brazenly Defied at Arms-Train Explosions

Scene of the two explosions

Ammunition trucks

AT SAVERNAKE, WILTSHIRE, on January 2, 1946, during the loading of an ammunition train an explosion occurred and fire rapidly spread to another ammunition train alongside. There were further explosions and extensive fires, causing the death of eight soldiers, injuries to others, and the destruction of 27 railway wagons and two lorries containing shells, mines and other explosives, out of a total of 96 loaded wagons in the sidings. Major K. A. Biggs, R.A.O.C., the officer in charge, arrived at the site soon after the first explosion and began to direct operations to prevent a major disaster, danger to the neighbouring town of Marlborough being very real. With complete disregard for their own safety, he and another officer uncoupled and pushed a burning wagon loaded with shells away from the fire and helped to extinguish it. He organized fire-breaks in the face of further cordite fires and explosions. His work in the midst of this inferno, in which more than 200 tons of explosives detonated, was largely instrumental in minimizing the disaster.

AFTER a third severe explosion, at about 4.30 p.m., when he was knocked down by blast, Major Biggs went forward and inspected the blazing area closely, refusing to permit anyone to accompany him. Having decided that further loss of life might occur if the fire-fighting was continued he ordered the evacuation of the rail-head, he himself being the last to leave. Major Biggs had the situation fully under control and had done everything reasonably possible. He was awarded the George Cross. Staff-Sergeant S. G. Rogerson, R.A.O.C., took command at the siding when the trucks were blazing furiously and further explosions were momentarily expected. On his own initiative he organized fire parties and commenced unloading ammunition from wagons threatened by the fire. He rescued injured men from under blazing

wagons and helped organize the removal of wounded from the danger area. For his cool appreciation of the situation before the arrival of a superior officer he was awarded the George Cross. Sergeant D. A. Kay, R.A.O.C., also displayed complete disregard for his own safety and was one of the first to assist Staff-Sergeant Rogerson in rescuing injured men. With other soldiers he partially emptied a wagon loaded with mines until he was driven away by the fire. He was awarded the George Medal.

SERGT J. H. MATTHEWS, Pioneer Corps, arrived at the siding with his tender and fire-fighting crew immediately after the first explosion. He initiated the removal of six threatened wagons to a place of safety and personally uncoupled them, although the end one was blazing, relaxing his efforts only when the water supply had been exhausted and he was ordered to withdraw. He was awarded the George Medal. Corporal A. J. Adams, R.A.O.C., also displayed great bravery and initiative, rescuing several of the injured, and was awarded the British Empire Medal. Driver A. J. Baker, R.A.S.C., drove away four three-ton lorries which were in close proximity to the exploding ammunition and burning wagons. His action cleared a way for the fire-tenders. He was awarded the British Empire Medal. Privates F. Barnett and D. Gallagher, of the R.A.O.C., ran to the engine driver and the shunter of another train in a subsidiary siding and, with them, endeavoured to move some twenty loaded wagons to safety. When that method was found to be impossible these two privates went along the track releasing the brakes, regardless of the exploding ammunition. Both were awarded the British Empire Medal. Sub-Conductor F. W. Godliman and Pte. J. W. Prendergast, R.A.O.C., were respectively awarded the M.B.E. and the B.E.M. for rescuing an injured man in great danger.

WRECKAGE at Savernake after the train blew up (1). This aerial view (2) of the railway shows trucks, containing 500 tons of ammunition, which escaped destruction. Award of the George Cross to Major K. A. Biggs (3), who was the officer in charge, and to Staff-Sergeant S. G. Rogerson (4, left) both of the R.A.O.C., was announced (with other awards detailed in this page) on October 11, 1946.

More Victoria Cross Awards to Empire Heroes

Jem. RAM SARUP SINGH
This Jemadar of the First Punjab Regiment, twice wounded, led a charge against a hill fortress in Burma on October 25, 1944.

Sqn.-Leader
L. H. TRENT, D.F.C.
Leading his squadron of eleven Venturas in an attack on the power station at Amsterdam, Holland, on May 3, 1943, Sqn.-Ldr. Trent (above), of the Royal New Zealand Air Force, succeeded in bombing the target after the other ten aircraft had been shot down. Eventually brought down himself, he was made prisoner.

C.S.M.
J. R. OSBORN
This Winnipeg Grenadier (right), knowingly sacrificed his life to save his comrades when he threw himself on an enemy grenade during an attack on Mount Butler, Hongkong, on December 19, 1941. Earlier he had covered the withdrawal of his men, exposing himself to intense fire, and holding overwhelming opposition for over eight hours.

Lieut.
R. H. GRAY, D.S.C.
Flying off the aircraft carrier H.M.S. Formidable, on August 9, 1945, in Onagawa Wan bay, Japan, this Royal Canadian Navy flier (above), pressed home his attack on an enemy destroyer to within fifty feet although his aircraft was repeatedly hit by A.A. fire. He gave his life but sank his victim.

Sqn.-Leader
A. S. K. SCARF
Seeing the remainder of his squadron destroyed by enemy bombers on the ground at Butterfield R.A.F. station, Malaya, this Blenheim pilot (left), on December 9, 1941, carried out the ordered sortie over Singora, Thailand. Completing his mission against overwhelming opposition, mortally wounded, he crash-landed at Alor Star without injuring his crew.

Major J. W. FOOTE
At Dieppe on August 19, 1942, this member of the Canadian Chaplains' Services exposed himself to withering enemy fire on the beaches for about eight hours, assisting the medical officers, ministering to the wounded, and helping in their evacuation. Ignoring opportunities to embark, he saved numerous lives.

P/O. C. MYNARSKI
In a Lancaster bomber over Cambrai, France, on June 12, 1944, this R.C.A.F. pilot officer, although aflame, made heroic but vain attempts to extricate the rear gunner cut off by fire. He stood to attention and saluted the rear gunner before descending with blazing parachute into France, where he died of his injuries.

Guardsman E. C. CHARLTON
Engaging a battalion of the 15 Panzer Grenadiers, single handed, with the Browning from his tank at Wistedt, Germany, on April 21, 1945, this Irish Guardsman, with one arm shattered, inflicted severe casualties on the enemy, and retrieved a desperate situation. He died, later, of his wounds in enemy hands.

Photos, Topical, British, Canadian and Indian Official, The News Chronicle, P.A.-Reuter, G.P.U.

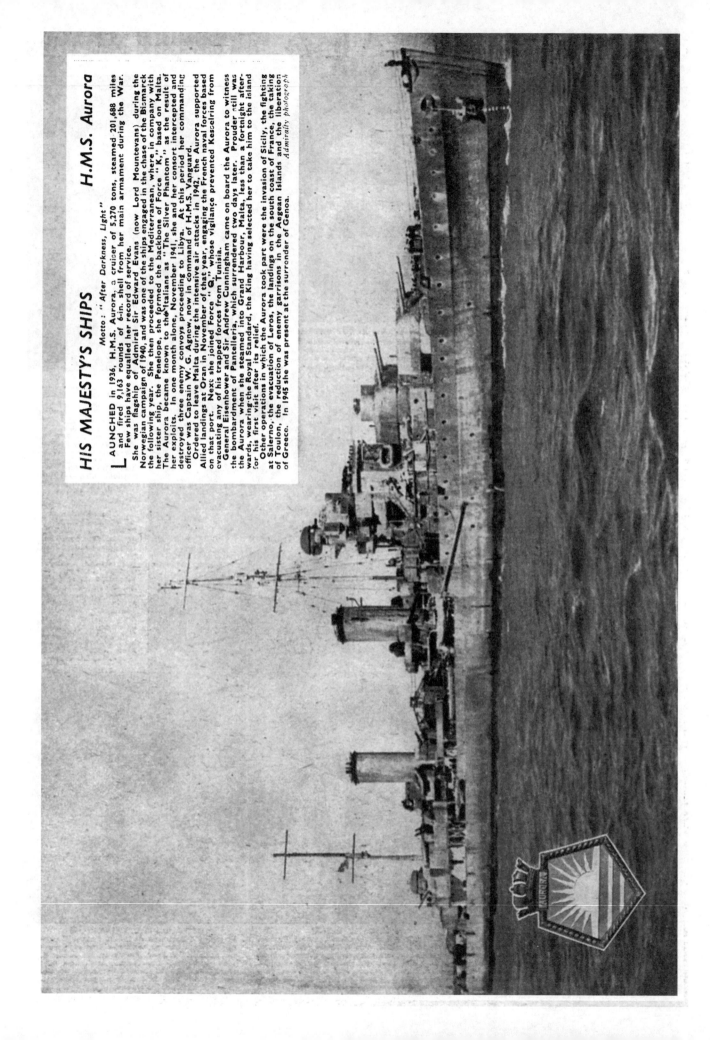

HIS MAJESTY'S SHIPS — H.M.S. Aurora

Motto: "After Darkness, Light"

LAUNCHED in 1936, H.M.S. Aurora, a cruiser of 5,270 tons, steamed 201,688 miles and fired 9,163 rounds of 6-in. shell from her main armament during the War. Few ships have equalled her record of service.

She was flagship of Admiral Sir Edward Evans (now Lord Mountevans) during the Norwegian campaign of 1940, and was one of the ships engaged in the chase of the Bismarck the following year. She then proceeded to the Mediterranean, where, in company with her sister ship, the Penelope, she formed the backbone of Force "K," based on Malta. The Aurora became known to the Italians as "The Silver Phantom," as the result of her exploits. In one month alone, November 1941, she and her consort intercepted and destroyed three enemy convoys proceeding to Libya. At this period her commanding officer was Captain W. G. Agnew, now in command of H.M.S. Vanguard.

Ordered to leave Malta during the intensive air attacks in 1942, the Aurora supported Allied landings at Oran in November of that year, engaging the French naval forces based on that port. Next she joined Force "Q," whose vigilance prevented Kesselring from evacuating any of his trapped forces from Tunisia.

General Eisenhower and Sir Andrew Cunningham came on board the Aurora to witness the bombardment of Pantelleria, which surrendered two days later. Prouder still was the Aurora when she steamed into Grand Harbour, Malta, less than a fortnight afterwards, wearing the Royal Standard, the King having selected her to take him to the Island for his first visit after its relief.

Other operations in which the Aurora took part were the invasion of Sicily, the fighting at Salerno, the evacuation of Leros, the landings on the south coast of France, the taking of Toulon, the reduction of enemy garrisons in the Aegean Islands and the liberation of Greece. In 1945 she was present at the surrender of Genoa.

Admiralty photograph

The Royal Inniskilling Fusiliers

By Major J. R. C. CROSSLÉ

At the beginning of the Second Great War, The Royal Inniskilling Fusiliers comprised two regular battalions: the 1st and 2nd. On September 3, 1939, the 1st Battalion was stationed at Wellington, S. India, and the 2nd at Catterick, Yorks. It was only in 1937 that the 2nd had come back into the Army, having been disbanded in 1922. During the period 1922–1937 the 1st Battalion was linked and formed one corps with the Royal Irish Fusiliers (Princess Victoria's), another one-battalion regiment. During the war of 1914–18 there were 13 battalions of Inniskillings. In the Second Great War only one extra "Active Service" Battalion was raised, the 6th, and it was finally disbanded in 1944, having blazed a path of glory for itself through Algeria, Tunis, Sicily and Italy.

Of the three battalions the unlucky one was, undoubtedly, the 1st. It was unlucky to be on the losing side twice, both times in Burma, and was not at the "kill" when all was going well. The 6th Battalion, having started late, was disbanded after it had passed Rome and was well on the way to the winning post. It was thus left to the 2nd Battalion to finish the race, which it did in Austria. One thing is greatly regretted by the Regiment, that no battalion of the Inniskillings took part in the D-Day operations, nor in the sweep across France, Belgium and Holland to the Rhine; many individuals were represented, but no battalion.

As previously stated, the 1st Battalion was at Wellington, S. India, when war broke out. There it remained until the end of 1941, when it moved to Meerut (U.P.), with one company at Delhi Fort. At last, in February 1942, when all thought they were going to miss the whole war, they mobilized, leaving Meerut for Calcutta, by train, in March. Things were now looking very black in Burma, and this Battalion had the distinction of being one of the very few to be ferried by air from India to Burma. On March 14 the Battalion was complete at Magwe, Central Burma.

Sad but Proud Record in Burma

Then began a dreadful series of battles, retreats and road blocks, the Japanese perpetually infiltrating, aided by Burmese fifth columnists. Prome was left behind; then, on April 17–19, came the battle of Yenangyaung, the oil town. By this time the Battalion had suffered terrible casualties, including two Commanding Officers killed. After Yenangyaung there began the long and weary trek through Upper Burma. The remnants of the Battalion reached Imphal, Assam, on May 19, 1942. Two months later it arrived at Jullundur, Punjab, and was immediately filled up by drafts from home. Little time was allowed for this almost new Battalion to get to know itself, and on September 30 it left, again for the East.

It joined the 14th Indian Division at Feni, East Bengal, and soon moved south to Chittagong. Christmas Day 1942 was spent in Maungdaw, on the Arakan coast. Directly afterwards, the Division moved south, aiming at Akyab, the Inniskillings in the van. The first clash with the Japs occurred at Donbaik, on the Mayu Peninsula. Here the Battalion alone hit the Japs, and thus gained the somewhat dubious honour of starting the Donbaik Front Line position, which, though attacked over and over again by British and Indian troops, held up the British advance

THE defence of the town of Inniskilling, in County Fermanagh, Northern Ireland, against the Irish and French troops of the deposed King James II in 1689 so signally proved the warlike ability of its defenders that King William III took a large portion of the garrison into his pay and ranked them as regiments of the British Army. Enniskillen, as it is called today, is still represented in the British Army by the 5th Royal Inniskilling Dragoon Guards and The Royal Inniskilling Fusiliers. From 1689 to 1751 the latter Regiment bore the name of The Inniskilling Regiment of Foot. From then until 1881 it was known as The 27th Inniskillings, and from 1881 to the present day the name has been The Royal Inniskilling Fusiliers. Its long list of battle honours includes Martinique 1762, St. Lucia 1796, The Peninsular War, Waterloo, Central India, Relief of Ladysmith, and The Great War 1914–18.

until, in April 1943, the Japs took the initiative, and recaptured the whole Mayu Peninsula and Maungdaw.

From Christmas 1942 until April 1943 the 1st Battalion fought the Japs continuously, on both sides of the Mayu Ridge, suffering grievous casualties. The reinforcements being from all parts of the U.K., the variety of accents became rather like the Tower of Babel. Ulster, Eire, Scotland, North Country, Midlands, West Country and Cockney were all represented.

The end came at the beginning of April, when the Japs cut round and isolated the whole 14th Indian Division and all other troops on the Mayu Peninsula. The remnants fought their way out. Fresh troops were brought in, and a line was stabilized 20 miles north of Maungdaw. The Battalion was again decimated, many of the survivors being riddled with malaria and dysentery. It was then posted to Cawnpore, and early

in 1945 to Dehra Dun, where it was on V.J. Day. A sad but proud record of rigorous service in two campaigns, in both of which the Japs were more numerous and better equipped for the jungle. Of the many deeds of valour and self-sacrifice there is not space to tell.

September 3, 1939, found the 2nd Battalion at Catterick Camp, Yorkshire, serving in the 5th Division. It went overseas immediately, fought in France and Belgium, and came back from Dunkirk. The most tragic happening in these operations was the loss, by capture, of Battalion H.Q. complete. The 2nd Battalion remained in the 5th Division until June 1944. After Dunkirk it was stationed in Scotland, Liverpool (during the blitz, with nights of fire-watching in Bootle), then Ireland, and finally Caterham, Surrey. The 5th Division sailed from Glasgow in March 1942 for an unknown destination.

With the 8th Army in Sicily

In May the 2nd battalion took a minor part in the first assault on Madagascar, and in the capture of Diego Suarez. Exactly a fortnight after the assault landing the Battalion boarded the transport again and set sail for India, coming to rest at Ahmednagar, near Poona. Then started a glorified Cook's Tour: in August to Iraq, then to Kermanshah, Persia, Qum, across the desert to Damascus, Tripoli (Lebanon), El Shatt (Egypt), and in July 1943 the landing in Sicily. It was shortly before the landing that the 5th Division joined the famous 8th Army.

From now on the 2nd Battalion was continuously in the front line—Syracuse, Augusta, the action at Lemon Bridge (in which two D.S.O.s, two M.C.s and an M.M. were earned in a few hours), Catania, Tremonti, the road to Messina. Then, early in September, the invasion of Italy, in which the Battalion was one of the spearheads. They had left Scotland in March 1942 and now

OUTWARD BOUND TO JOIN THE B.E.F., in September 1939, these members of the 2nd Battalion Royal Inniskilling Fusiliers, aboard the troopship Royal Sovereign whiled away the time by playing "Housey Housey." Of the three battalions of the Regiment the 2nd was the first to see action, in France in 1940, and the last to remain in the field, being in Austria on V E Day,

War Office Photograph

Colours : Yellow Battle-axe on Black

78TH (BRITISH) DIVISION

ALTHOUGH not formed until mid-summer 1942, the 78th had as its nucleus troops who had served in France with the B.E.F. in 1940. Within six months of its formation the Division landed in N. Africa with the British First Army, on November 8, 1942, and bore the brunt of the fighting early in the campaign. It cut off Algiers shortly after landing, and captured Bougie, November 11. Medjez el Bab was taken on November 27. Bitter fighting was experienced near Tebourba, and again, in January 1943, in the Oued Kebir and Ousseltia valleys, and at Bou Arada. Sedjenane was captured on March 30, and Cap Serrat reoccupied four days later. All but one slope of Longstop Hill fell on April 23 to the Division, which it is claimed was the first Allied infantry formation to enter Tunis, in the first week in May.

LATE in July, and now with the 8th Army, a landing was made in Sicily, where the Division captured Centuripe, on August 5, and Adrano a few hours later. The Simeto and Salso rivers were forced. Elements of the Division landed at Taranto for the Italian invasion in September, taking Foggia on September 27. Other units landed at Termoli early in October and quickly crossed the Bifferno and took Monecilfone. Costly struggles ensued in the subsequent stages of the campaign, notably along the Trigno, in October, and the Sangro, which by November 14 had been crossed and the powerfully defended line penetrated. During March and April 1944, the 78th distinguished itself in the battle for Cassino. It was prominent in the capture of Orvieto on June 14.

By June 25 the Pescia had been crossed and Castiglione reached. By September the Gothic Line had been penetrated. In the Allies' final Italian offensive in April 1945, in the battle of the Argenta Gap, the river Po was reached and crossed during the last week of the month. After the surrender of Germany the 78th became an Occupational Force in Austria, and was disbanded in September 1946.

RETURNING FROM THE BATTLE FOR TWO TREE HILL in Tunisia, in January 1943, these men of the 6th Battalion Royal Inniskilling Fusiliers found the going very heavy. Although occupying this prominent feature the enemy failed in his objective, the taking of Bou Arada. In particularly fierce exchanges the Inniskillings inflicted and sustained severe losses. *War Office Photograph*

landed on the mainland of Europe in September 1943, having encircled Africa and set foot in nine different countries.

A most gruelling 19 days followed the immediate landing in Italy, in which the 2nd Battalion advanced 240 miles, of which 100 miles were by sea in assault craft, 40 in M.T. (Mechanical Transport) and 100 on foot. The mountainous and rocky nature of the country made this an immense physical effort. Next came Isernia and Castel di Sangro. On January 7, 1944, the Battalion left the 8th Army, having served in it for just over six months, during which time it had been in action against one Italian and nine different German divisions. It joined the 5th Army, and in mid-January and early February came the battle of the Garigliano, which involved the 2nd in its bloodiest and most tragically glorious battle.

IN February came sinister Monte Damiano, and on March 11 the 2nd sailed for Anzio. After the break-out from Anzio the Battalion reached Rome in June 1944, then left the 5th Division, in which it had served so long, returning to Egypt, where it was made up with the personnel of the 6th Battalion, which also had come back to Egypt, to be disbanded. The Battalion now joined the

Irish Brigade, taking the place which had previously been held by the 6th Battalion. By way of Taranto, Mt. Spadura, Senio, the Argenta Gap and the Po, and still fighting all the way, it passed the winning post in May 1945, at Villach in Austria. A hard road and a long, long trek.

The 6th Battalion was formed at Holywood, Co. Down, on October 9, 1940, and was disbanded in Egypt in July 1944. During its short life it saw a tremendous amount of hard fighting, and suffered very heavy casualties during its triumphant sweep through North Africa, Sicily and Italy. After its formation it was stationed in various places in Ireland, including Belfast during the blitz, and in January 1942 it crossed to England. After a short time at Frinton-on-Sea, Essex, it moved to Shakers Wood in Norfolk, where it joined the Irish Brigade,

FROM IRELAND TO IRAN via Madagascar and India was the route taken by the 2nd Battalion Inniskillings before joining the 8th Army in N. Africa for the Sicilian invasion in July 1943. Above, a battalion officer briefs his C.S.M. when in the Iranian Desert. After Sicily the Battalion formed a spearhead for the assault on Italy in September 1943. *War Office Photograph*

2nd and 6th Inniskillings Campaign in Sicily

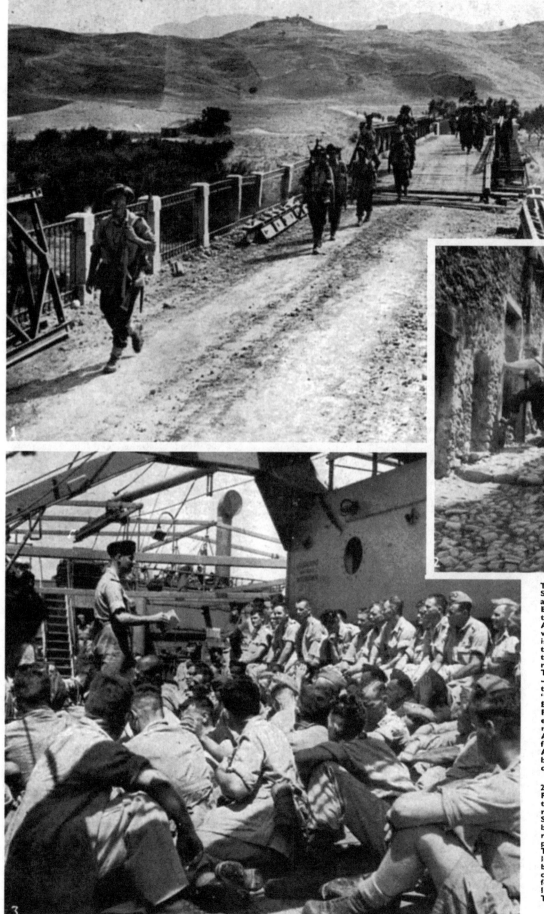

TAKING CENTURIPE, Sicily, was the outstanding achievement of the 6th Battalion Inniskillings in the Sicilian campaign in August 1943. Operating with the British 78th Division, troops of the Battalion are seen crossing a temporary bridge on the road leading to the town (1). The storming of Centuripe —"Cherry Ripe" to the troops—was a feat which "will live in the annals of British arms" declared F.-M. Viscount Montgomery of Alamein, then Commander of the British 8th Army. Desperately defended, the town fell on August 2, and then not before the Battalion had cleared the enemy house by house (2).

2nd BATTALION of the Regiment, aboard the troopship Dunera (3), en route to take part in the Sicilian invasion, is briefed by one of its officers in the role which the Battalion played in these operations. This involved many front line actions, including the battles for Catania, Syracuse and Augusta, to be followed by landings in Italy in September 1943. The Battalion had seen service in nine countries.

War Office Photographs

ST. PATRICK'S DAY IN THE ANZIO BEACH-HEAD, Italy, may have lacked traditional custom with which this Irish National holiday is usually celebrated, but the 2nd Battalion Inniskillings did not allow March 17, 1944, to go unnoticed. Some of them are here enjoying the extra rum ration sent to them by the C.O. for the occasion. *War Office photograph*

with which it served until its disbandment. The Irish Brigade soon moved to Scotland, whence it sailed in November 1942 for North Africa as part of the 1st Army. Algiers was reached on November 22, after an uneventful trip. The Battalion moved immediately up to the Goubellat area, where it had its first clashes with the Germans.

"A Triumph for the Inniskillings"

After a slight pause, in which both sides were sparring for an opening, the 6th Battalion were engaged in the most ferocious fighting in Goubellat Plain and Grandstand, in January and February 1943. During these actions very heavy casualties were inflicted and received. At this time the enemy were mainly from the Hermann Goering Jaeger Regiment, a tough crowd who asked for and gave no quarter. At the end of March the Brigade left the 6th Armoured Division in which it had served since leaving Scotland, and came under the command of an Infantry Division. Quickly there followed the storming of Djebel Mahdi and Tangoucha, in which actions the Irish Brigade particularly distinguished itself.

A newspaper account at that time said, "The taking of Tangoucha was a triumph for the Inniskillings. The capture took them three days. They were driven back twice, but refused to go from the hill. The Germans bowled grenades down at them, covered them with deadly machine-gun, shell and mortar fire, but the Inniskillings just wore down the enemy's resistance until he finally surrendered." About the same time Sir Stafford Cripps, speaking in Belfast, said, "The Irish Brigade did the hardest fighting and had the longest service in the whole of the First Army." Then came

the triumphant entry into Tunis and the end of the enemy in North Africa.

Now the story reaches out across the sea, to the landing in Sicily in July 1943. The outstanding achievement of the 6th Battalion in Sicily was the storming of Centuripe, on August 2—that town perched like an eagle's nest on the top of a precipice. For this action the Battalion received a D.S.O., three M.C.s, and a M.M. The account of the action, issued by the Ministry of Information, declared, "The taking of Centuripe, which forced the Germans to reorganize their entire line, was primarily a triumph for The Royal Inniskilling Fusiliers." The Brigadier wrote, "Centuripe was the 'Skin's' battle." And

the Army Commander, General Sir Bernard Montgomery, said, "The taking of Centuripe is a great feat, which will live in the annals of British arms."

The Irish Brigade reached Randazzo on Friday, August 13, the last of the fighting in Sicily. There followed five weeks' rest, a sea voyage to Taranto in Italy, then Barletta and another sea voyage to Termoli, where the Brigade had a very sharp clash with the Germans. It was then early October 1943. Now came a series of stiff engagements with the enemy, who was fighting as hard as he knew how to hold up the advance for as long as possible before withdrawing to a fresh prepared position. Such were the crossing of the River Trigno, the battles for San Salvo and Vasto, the crossing of the Sangro and the capture of San Vito, which the Germans had decided to hold as their "Winter Line."

Motoring Along the Road to Rome

By December 4 the 6th Battalion was on the line of the Moro River, having broken through the "Winter Line." The Irish Brigade was now relieved, the casualties since landing in Italy having been 36 officers and 823 O.R.s. In this last stage it had been in continuous action for seven days and nights without respite.

At Christmas 1943 the 6th Battalion moved up to Capracotta, a famous winter sports centre in peacetime. Snow fell heavily, and rations were short. Owing to snowdrifts on the roads a flight of Douglas Transports had to come to the rescue, and rations fell from the sky attached to gaily coloured parachutes. In March and April 1944 a hair-raising month was spent among the rocks, high up in the mountains just north of Cassino. May found the Battalion crashing its way through the Gustav Line, and June 8 saw it motoring along Highway 6— the Road to Rome. On June 12 a representative party was received by the Pope, in the Vatican, and the Irish Pipes played in front of St. Peter's.

Action came again near Lake Trasimeno, after the chase of a somewhat demoralized enemy. This was the last battle in which the 6th Battalion took part. The official reason given for the disbandment of the 6th, at the height of its fame, was the lack of Irish reinforcements. The Battalion travelled south to Taranto, and so to Egypt, to be greeted on the quay at Alexandria by the pipes of the 2nd Battalion.

A short time was spent in amalgamating the 6th Battalion with the 2nd—and the 6th Battalion The Royal Inniskilling Fusiliers had ceased to exist. The Regiment as a whole consoles itself with the thought that its distinguished career was brought to a close while it was still at the very pinnacle of its success.

THE Inniskillings who stormed the heights of St. Lucia in 1796, and who withstood the onslaughts of Napoleon's Armies at Waterloo in 1815, had every reason to welcome into Valhalla the young generation of Inniskillings who fought and died so bravely in Africa, Sicily, Italy and Burma. The great traditions of the Regiment had indeed been faithfully maintained.

GUARDING THE AUSTRO-YUGOSLAV FRONTIER in 1946, this Fusilier of the 2nd Battalion appears to have a lonely vigil. This frontier post was held by one officer and a small platoon only. PAGE 462 *War Office photograph*

Britain's Swift Change-Over to Peace Production

This scene at the Sheffield works of the English Steel Corporation, showing rear-axle casings for heavy road vehicles—so urgently needed in our trade push—being removed from the drop-forging department, typifies the rapid reconversion of our factories to post-war needs. During Battle of Britain days the drop-hammer here was the only one which could forge crankshafts for Spitfires; it was worked 16 hours a day and it produced ten crankshafts an hour.

463

Our Machines of War Now Hum to the Tune of—

Opening the "Britain Can Make It" Exhibition in London on Sept. 24, 1946—the first exhibition of Industrial Design to be organized after the gravest crisis in our history (see illus. pages 422-423)—H.M. the King reminded the world that "no country was more completely given over to war than ours." In the nation-wide change-over are included workers in a factory where containers for Service rations were made : now they stamp out (1) lids for tobacco and other tins.

—a Mighty Drive to Bring Back Prosperity

Machinery which pressed out parts for bomb-racks delivers components of electric cleaners (2). At a textile machinery foundry a hydraulic mangle (3) is for export to India—for finishing linen. A toy factory (4) becomes again the source of many things to delight the youthful heart. The plastics industry was of great account in war : now telephone instruments are moulded (5). Wellington bombers engaged the attention of workers who now assemble washing-machine cabinets (6).

Little Things That Mean So Much to All of Us

Grim austerity further fades with the production of tennis balls (1) at this factory which turned out Halifax bombers; there, too, bicycle valves (3) are vulcanized. Where brass fuse-caps came into being collar studs (2) are now processed. Emphasis is placed on new design and methods not only for the Home market but, in the words of H.M. the King, " The Overseas markets, upon which our prosperity, our solvency, and our standard of life must depend in years to come."

HONGKONG, BORNEO, FIJI AND TONGA

By HARLEY V. USILL

WITHIN less than a hundred years Hongkong, the British Colony off the south-east China coast, was built up from the headquarters of a few pirates and fishermen to a great centre of international trade. In the general strategic set-up of the Pacific the function of Hongkong was mainly that of a forward outpost ; but with the emergence of Japan as a strong naval and air power, and the development by the Japanese of Formosa, Hongkong was rendered unsuitable as an independent strategic point for defence. As events developed and the Japanese gained more and more offensive bases on the mainland, the fatal weakness of Hongkong's position became more apparent.

The loyalty of the Colony prior to the Japanese invasion was never in question. In addition to a gift of £200,000 towards the war effort from the Hongkong Government, private individuals of all classes subscribed £168,890 for the purchase of aircraft and £30,841 for war charities. The pre-war defence contribution of about £400,000 per annum towards the cost of the Imperial garrison in Hongkong, was also continued. The local factories contributed several million dollars' worth of war materials (chiefly rubber footwear, electric torches and textiles) which went to the Middle East. There was a Volunteer Defence Force, and over 15,000 of the inhabitants, with a substantial proportion of Chinese, manned the Civil Defence Services.

On December 7, 1941, Japan opened hostilities against the United States, and on the following day Japanese forces, estimated at one division, with a second division immediately in reserve, crossed the frontier of the Leased Territories on the mainland forming the hinterland of Hongkong. In spite of brave resistance, the mainland became untenable ; by midday on the 11th it was decided to commence a withdrawal, and by the 12-13th all troops were back on the Island of Hongkong. Operating from depth, the Japanese had the overwhelming advantage against the defenders of this small island—defenders who were denied adequate air or naval support. On December 25 the end came when the Military and Naval Commanders informed the Governor that no further resistance could be made. On the same day the Secretary of State for the Colonies sent this message to the Governor : "The defence of Hongkong will live in the story of the Empire, to which it adds yet another chapter of courage and endurance."

BORNEO, in the East Indian archipelago, is the third largest island in the world. At the time of the Japanese invasion, in December 1941, about two-thirds belonged to the Netherlands ; the remaining one-third, consisting of British North Borneo, Sarawak and Brunei, was under British protection. When invasion came, the two local forces, the Sarawak Volunteer Force and the Sarawak Rangers, did not stand a chance. Prior to the invasion, the contribution to the war effort lay in the valuable supplies of oil, rubber and timber, and the loyalty of the peoples was displayed in the generosity of their gifts to various war funds. In North Borneo and Sarawak private individuals donated £313,900, and in addition over £15,000 was contributed for the purchase of aircraft. Gifts from Brunei, equally generous, were included in those of British Malaya.

LIKE Malaya and Singapore, the colonies of Hongkong and Borneo suffered the fate of being overrun by the Japanese invasion of 1941. Other British possessions in the Far East were more fortunate, among them the Fiji and Tonga islands, which contributed in no small measure to the final Allied victory in the Pacific.

❧ ❧❧❧❧ ❧

Japanese propagandists attempted to present the war in the Pacific as a struggle of the coloured races trying to free themselves from an unbearable yoke of white oppression or, in the case of the British islands, from the intolerable grasp of British Imperialism. In the Pacific islands we find the lie direct given to the Japanese. The circumstances in which the war was fought in this area were such as to enable aggressive warfare to be waged against the Japanese by Colonial peoples. They played a great part, for instance, in the Guadalcanal campaign, which was to prove

VISITING BRITISH NORTH BORNEO, which was proclaimed a Crown Colony on July 15, 1946, the Governor-General of Malaya, Mr. Malcolm MacDonald, shook hands with an aged Dyak chief who claims to have 30 Japanese heads to his credit. *Photo, British Official*

a turning point of the Pacific war and the graveyard of Japanese dreams of Empire.

The British Colony of Fiji, situated in the Southern Pacific, midway between Tonga and New Caledonia, consists of about 250 islands of varying sizes covering an area of over 7,000 square miles. In 1942 the population was approximately 234,000, of whom 109,200 were Fijians, 105,500 East Indians, 4,900 Europeans and the rest Chinese. The presence of a large number of troops necessitated an intensive food production drive to meet requirements on the home front. In addition, during the year 1943, as an example, more than 10,000,000 lb. of fruit and vegetables were delivered to the United States, New Zealand and Fijian military forces. Financially, Fiji's all-round total contribution to the war in gifts up to the autumn of 1944 amounted to nearly £167,000.

Early in the war compulsory military training in the Fiji Local Defence Force for Europeans and part-Europeans was introduced, and in January 1942 all territorial defence forces were called up for full-time service. Europeans, Euronesians, Fijians, Indians, Rotumans and Solomon Islanders served together in the Fiji Home Guard. In December 1942 a "sample force" of Fijian Commandos went into action with the Americans at Guadalcanal, in the Solomons. In a very real sense they were "on approval," since on their behaviour depended the

decision as to whether or not Fijians were fit to play an active part in the war. They became "the finest jungle fighters in the world," and on Guadalcanal, although their own total of Japanese killed ran into three figures, did not suffer a single fatal casualty. They took many prisoners and destroyed quantities of enemy stores and equipment.

Later, the Commandos took part in the invasion of New Guinea, and their timely arrival on the Zenana beach-head prevented what might well have proved a disaster for the Americans, who were in danger of being outflanked and cut-off by the Japanese. The authorities were now convinced that the Fijians were first-class fighters, and in 1943 the Fiji Military Forces were reorganized as a Brigade. On April 13 the First Battalion of the Fiji Infantry Regiment left for Guadalcanal, and was later sent to Kolombangara to mop up the Japanese after their withdrawal. From here the Battalion went to the Empress Augusta Bay beach-head at Bougainville, where it made a deep penetration on reconnaissance and patrol into the enemy-held areas of the island.

The Battalion then set out on the Numa trail to establish an outpost at the small village of Ibu, from which position patrols could range over a wide area. After repelling repeated Japanese attacks it was decided to evacuate Ibu ; and, with one Fijian to 110 Japanese killed, the Fijians carried out a rearguard action which an Allied Commander described as "an action which I think will go into the records as a minor tactical classic."

On March 12, 1944, the Third Battalion, which had a smaller proportion of Europeans than any unit which had gone overseas before, joined the First Battalion in the Solomons. They were accompanied by the Fiji Dock Company, which had been recruited from the Fiji Labour Corps. This Battalion was detailed to carry out a series of seaborne raids behind the Japanese lines, and the Commander of the American Division wrote that they carried out "in a superior manner" one of the first important tasks entrusted to them. The culminating achievement of the Fijian forces came in November 1944 with the first award of the V.C. to a coloured Colonial soldier during the war. (See portrait of Cpl. Sukanaivalu in page 599, Vol. 8.) By January 1945 both Battalions of the Fiji Infantry Regiment were back in Fiji, having played a truly magnificent part.

The centenary of the Kingdom of Tonga, a group of about 150 islands, was celebrated on December 4, 1945. In September 1939, though there was no obligation for her to do so, the Queen Salote undertook to devote the whole resources of her Kingdom to the Allied cause. By early 1944 Tongans, who number about 32,000, had subscribed nearly £82,000 for defence or for war charities.

The Tongan Voluntary Defence Force was originally organized as a defensive measure, but their then second-in-command, Lieut. Henry Talaai, a full-blooded Tongan, was confident of their fighting qualities. "We were famous warriors in the old days," he said, "and were feared all over the Pacific Ocean ; we are a bit out of practice but we think we can pick it up again." Actually the Force was not called upon to play a part in the war as a separate unit, but a detachment was sent to Fiji and served with great credit alongside Fijian troops in the Solomons.

Europe's Wartime Capitals in 1946

SOFIA

By JOHN D. MACK, M.P.

ONLY sixty years ago Sofia, the capital of Bulgaria, was a village of less than 5,000 inhabitants. When the Russians liberated Bulgaria in 1878 and Sofia was established as a capital, it contained only three houses which had more than three rooms. One of these houses was converted into a " Palace." The second became Government House, with the Cabinet sitting in one room, the general staff in the second and all the other Ministries in the remaining room. The third " big house " was reserved for the foreign diplomats.

Sofia is now a city of three-quarters of a million people, and with a pre-war reputation of being the tidiest and cleanest capital in the Balkans. There are no fine, historic buildings, but the centre of the town, though badly knocked about by air raids during the War, is well planned and has large squares and beautiful boulevards. The largest square is in front of the Sobranie, the Bulgarian Parliament, where 150,000 people assembled recently to hear me speak about Britain. The great boulevard across that square, called Tsar Liberator, in honour of the Russian Tsar Alexander II who liberated the country, leads to a beautiful and well-kept park, known in the past as the Boris, but now, significantly, renamed National Park. (Boris was the last reigning king of Bulgaria, whose German dynasty has now been voted out of favour with the Bulgarians.)

Next to the Sobranie is the most interesting building in Sofia—the great cathedral Alexander Nevski, built by the Bulgarians before the 1914-18 war to mark their feeling of friendship towards Russia. In this magnificent building the most important religious ceremonies are held. The church is still very much honoured in Bulgaria and the priests wear colourful garments just as the Eastern Orthodox and Russian priests do. The religious service is sometimes held in old Slavonic, the common language of all Slavs 1,000 years ago.

Black Market Almost Non-Existent

On the other side of the city I visited some of the worst slums I have ever seen, sad relics of the past when the majority of Sofia's workers lived in wooden huts, usually built around the factories they worked in. Strangely enough, in the centre of this slum area the governments of the past had built a vast " central political prison," which had housed, in the last 20 years, most of Bulgaria's present Ministers and political leaders. The Prime Minister, Kimon Georgiev, had been in and out of it 22 times. His deputy-Premier, General Terpeshev, had been there for 18 years of his life, and survived it ! His War Minister, General Velchev, had been there for " only " six years. No wonder that the present Bulgarian leaders are reported to have nerves of iron.

Sofia is one of the very few cities in Europe where the black market is almost non-existent. There are, of course, traces of it, because of the lack of commodities, especially clothes and shoes. But the Bulgarians act mercilessly towards black marketeers, and an offence of hoarding can result in a death sentence. Whilst I was there two prominent Sofia business men were sentenced to penal servitude for life for hoarding large quantities of flour. The bread ration is about 1-lb. per head daily. The butter ration is twice as large as that in Britain. Milk is not rationed, and there are plenty of eggs—as many as 10 to 15 a week per person.

Almost all civil servants and workers eat in co-operative restaurants, run by their own Trade Union. The big restaurants in the centre of the city, where you can have food as good as can be obtained in any of the best hotels in London's West End, are frequented only by the diplomats, foreign correspondents, members of the Allied Missions and members of the few rich Bulgarian families. The common people love going out to the so-called coffee houses, where for the equivalent of 6d. you can have an ice-cream, or for the equivalent of ½d. a Turkish coffee. These houses are the meeting-places of politicians, journalists, actors, officers and so on. Many people will sit for hours quarrelling and gesticulating over a cup of coffee. You are usually offered this beverage even when you go to visit a civil servant in his office. One newspaperman told me that he drinks on the average about 40 coffees a day. In no capital in the world does one receive more hospitality and warmth of welcome. All Sofia looks forward earnestly to the closest contact and friendship with Great Britain.

Cultural Life is Flourishing

Bulgaria is the only country in Eastern Europe which has not fallen into the wild abyss of complete inflation. Prices are, on the average, four or five times higher than they were before the War. Salaries have increased only twice, and this puts all white-collar employees and workers into a disadvantageous position. The treasury has been obliged to vote huge credits for supplementary remuneration for the civil servants, but no substantial increases of the basic salaries will be made, I was told, until there are more goods on the market and the economic position is stabilized.

Reconstruction in the capital is very slow because of the general lack of building materials. Most of the new houses and shops now being erected are small wooden huts. Only a very few large Government buildings have been started. Road and railway construction and the building-up of bridges, however, appears to have made good progress. Though machinery and tools are very scarce, there is no unemployment, as the small Bulgarian industry is now able to work at full capacity ; indeed, there is lack of teachers, doctors, technicians and competent and well-trained civil servants.

One of the most extraordinary things concerning life in Sofia is the theatre. It is a National theatre, and all Bulgarian actors and directors are civil servants in so far as remuneration is concerned. There are National theatres in several of the towns, whilst touring companies visit the remotest parts of the country. In Sofia alone there are three National theatres performing what the Bulgarians call " drama," two theatres for opera and ballet and three for comedy and musical shows. In addition, there are four symphonic orchestras and over ten repertory theatres run by the State Dramatic Schools.

The stage can well compare with the very best in Europe. It is under the strong influence of the world-famous Moscow Arts Theatre, and Russian producers and actors are very popular. All theatres and concert-halls are absolutely packed, the most expensive ticket costing only a shilling or two. The whole theatre world there is under the general guidance of the Ministry of Information and Arts. I had a long talk with the Minister himself, Mr. Kazassov, a jovial and highly cultured little fellow with a white beard, by profession a journalist and playwright. He is helped by a "dramatic council" elected by the Association of Artists.

Incidentally, this Trade Union is one of the most influential in the country, and the Minister of Arts appoints the directors of the Sofia and provincial theatres only on the recommendation of the Union. When I was there they played Shakespeare, Shaw, Eugene O'Neill, Chekhov, Gorki and several Bulgarian writers. " The darlings of our State," Minister Kazassov told me, " are the writers, the actors and the producers. Some of them are real national figures, much more popular and influential than many politicians."

The beauty of Sofia is in its surroundings. A fifteen to twenty minutes' drive to the south-west will bring you to the foothills of the Vitosha mountain, covered with snow almost the whole year round as its height is well over 6,000 feet. During the winter almost everyone goes ski-ing there, and during the summer every Sunday nearly half of Sofia's population climbs the Vitosha by way of week-end fun. For not so enterprising tourists there is a motor road, which takes one as high as 5,000 feet.

City of Extraordinary Contrasts

During the War and the German occupation Vitosha was full of partisans, and you can now see many commemorative plaques which record that at such and such a date a heavy battle was fought in this beautiful and now quiet place, and that so many people lost their lives in it. Sofia suffered chiefly from air raids, and some fighting when the forces of the present Government coalition, known as the Fatherland Front, attacked it, fought their way into the centre, and promptly arrested all Ministers and leaders of the Fascist regime. That was on the night before September 9, 1944, and the date is now proclaimed a National holiday throughout the country—Liberation Day as they call it.

It is usually celebrated with a big parade, which continues for hours, and in which not only the army, the civil servants, the workers and the students take part but also practically the whole population of the city. As it continues for more than seven hours and everyone is thoroughly exhausted, the next day is usually a bank holiday in order that all who took part—including the Ministers and Generals who stood for hours on the rostrum—can enjoy a much-needed rest.

Thus Sofia today is a city of extraordinary things—of contrasts, of slums and of symphonic orchestras, of dingy coffee houses and beautiful mountains ; the capital of a small, lovable, warm-hearted and hard-working Slav people, conscious that now, for the first time in its history, it has taken its destiny, for better or for worse, into its own hands.

WATCHING THE PARADE in Sofia which marked the Republic's founding were the Premier, Col. Kimon Georgiev (right), and M. Georgi Dimitrov, leader of the Fatherland Front. PAGE 468 *Photo, I.N.P.*

Sofia's Citizens Welcome Their New Republic

CELEBRATIONS IN THE CAPITAL followed the proclamation of a Bulgarian People's Republic on September 15, 1946. By an overwhelming majority the plebiscite held on September 8 rejected the monarchy which had twice led the country into disastrous wars. Popular feeling is expressed in the cartoon (top) of Kings Ferdinand and Boris and the latter's son, the child Simeon (see illus. page 270, Vol. 7), whose Regents had finally discredited the monarchy. Above, young Bulgarians in national costume parade through Sofia's rejoicing streets. PAGE 469 *Photos, International News Photos*

Housing the Homeless: Aluminium and Concrete

TURNING THEIR BACKS ON TRADITIONAL METHODS, builders at Cheltenham, Glos., ran up an estate of 173 aluminium houses (1) in 11 months. At Greenwich, London, the "Orlit" type (2) consists largely of precast concrete. Near Hillingdon, Mdx, in the "Shutter" method (3) shutters are removed after concrete poured between them has set. Kitchen sections (4)

Tremendous Task of Clearing the Corinth Canal

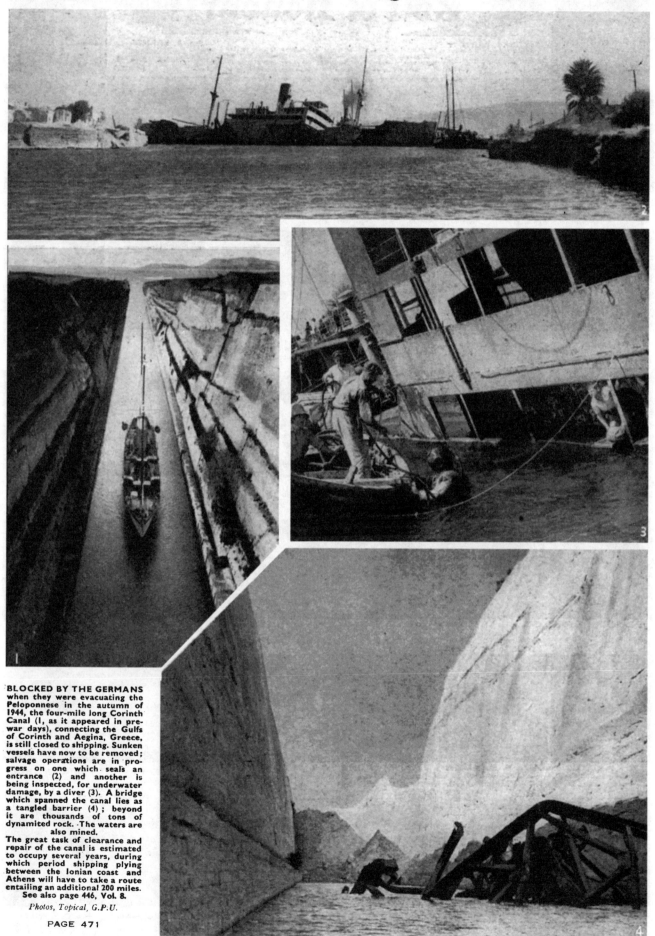

BLOCKED BY THE GERMANS when they were evacuating the Peloponnese in the autumn of 1944, the four-mile long Corinth Canal (1, as it appeared in pre-war days), connecting the Gulfs of Corinth and Aegina, Greece, is still closed to shipping. Sunken vessels have now to be removed; salvage operations are in progress on one which seals an entrance (2) and another is being inspected, for underwater damage, by a diver (3). A bridge which spanned the canal lies as a tangled barrier (4); beyond it are thousands of tons of dynamited rock. The waters are also mined.

The great task of clearance and repair of the canal is estimated to occupy several years, during which period shipping plying between the Ionian coast and Athens will have to take a route entailing an additional 200 miles.

See also page 446, Vol. 8.

Photos, Topical, G.P.U.

The Roll of Honour

NCOs & MEN

1939—1946

Sgt/Obv. J. BARTON
Coastal Cmd. R.A.F.V.R.
Action: Cheltenham. 31.3.43.
Age 21.   (Orrell)

So great has been the response of readers to our invitation to submit portraits for our Roll of Honour that no more can now be accepted. But we have every hope of being able to publish all those so far received.

Pte. A. BARNES
King's Reg. (Liverpool).
D. wnds: Kalewa. June '43.
Age 29.   (Preston)

L/Sgt. A. E. BAYLISS
Northamptonshire Yeo.
Action: Caen. 19.7.44.
Age 25.   (Northampton)

Gdsmn. R. BLACKBURN
1st Bn. Irish Guards.
Action: N. Africa. 28.4.43
Age 32.   (Garstang)

L/Cpl. A. K. BROAD
Oxford & Bucks. L.I.
Monastery Hill. 4.12.43.
Age 28.   (Brixton)

Cpl. J. H. BURDON
Royal Army Service Corps.
West Africa. 23.7.43.
Age 27.   (Wyken)

Sgt. G. CHARLESWORTH
Bomber Command, R.A.F.
Action: Düsseldorf. 16.9.42
Age 21.   (Barnsley)

Pte. J. CROWTHER
East Lancashire Regiment.
Action: N.W. E'pe. 27.6.44.
Age 19.   (Leeds)

Sgt. W. A. DIDLUCK
R.A.F.V.R.
Action: Italy. 18.1.44.
Age 21.   (Abergavenny)

Gdsmn. J. J. GEE
Grenadier Guards.
Died: P.O.W. 3.11.41.
Age 29.   (Manchester)

Cpl. W. HANAWAY
Royal Marines.
Action: Atlantic. March '42.
Age 34.   (Manchester)

L/Cpl. N. HARDY
King's Own Royal Regt.
Action: Leros. 16.12.43.
Age 21.   (Canvey Island)

L/Sgt. B. HENDERSON
Irish Guards.
Action: N. Africa. 29.4.43
Age 23.   (Belfast)

L/Sgt. G. HOWARTH
253/81 H.A.A., R.A.
Lost at sea. Nov. 43.
Age 25.   (Stockport)

Cpl. B. S. E. HUDDLE
2nd Monmouthshire Regt.
Action: Rethem. 11.4.45.
Age 34.   (Pinner)

L/Cpl. E. HOWELLS
South Wales Borderers.
Yugoslavia. 7.10.44.
Age 25.   (Swansea)

Pte. D. L. HUGHES
R. Army Ordnance Corps.
D. wnds. Tobruk. 2.12.41.
Age 27.   (Holyhead)

Gnr. T. INGHAM
88 Field Regt., R.A.
P.O.W. Siam. 29.7.43.
Age 23.   (Preston)

Gdsmn. J. JARDINE
1st Bn. Scots Guards.
Action: Tunisia. 21.4.43.
Age 31.   (Dumfries)

L/Cpl. W. J. JONES
Royal Engineers.
N.W. Europe. 12.9.44.
Age 35.   (Braunstone)

Sgt. R. M. JOHNSON
Royal Air Force.
Action: Stuttgart. 29.7.44.
Age 23.   (W. Molesev)

O/S. J. G. KITCHING
H.M.S. Nubian.
Action: at sea. 26.5.41.
Age 21.   (Esh Winning)

L/Cpl. W. LAURIE
Scots Guards.
Action: Caen. 30.7.44.
Age 27.   (Banknock)

Sgt. N. LEES
467 Sqn. R.A.A.F.
Action: Staffs. 3.1.45.
Age 19.   (Oldham)

Gnr. J. MABBUTT
Royal Artillery.
Action: Accroma. 16.6.42.
Age 32.   (Harrow)

Stkr. W. J. PAYNE
Royal Navy.
Action: N. Sea. 10.6.41.
Age 21.   (Kingston)

Dvr. H. PURKIS
Royal Army Service Corps.
Greece. 28.4.41.
Age 29.   (Selby)

Pte. J. G. REYNOLDS
Green Howards.
P.O.W. Tobruk. 7.6.42.
Age 26.   (Witton Gilbert)

Cpl. A. RICHMOND
Queen's Royal Regiment.
Action: Holland. 22.10.44.
Age 28.   (London)

Pte. R. ROBINSON
York & Lancaster Regt.
Action: Italy. 13.10.44.
Age 21.   (Shildon)

Tpr. J. RYAN
144 R.A.C.
Action: Caen. 7.8.44.
Age 26.   (Swansea)

C.P/O. C. V. SHORT
Royal Navy.
Missing. 17.1.42.
Age 44.   (Plymouth)

Tpr. A. M. SMITH
3rd Recce. Regt., R.N.F.
Action: Vire. 6.8.44.
Age 23.   (Corbridge)

Sgt/Nav. A. THOMSON
Royal Air Force.
Over Germany. 10.7.43.
Age 20.   (Buckhaven)

A.S.P/O. THORNTON
H.M.S. Gloucester.
Action: Crete. 22.5.41
Age 33.   (Widnes)

A/B. J. VURLEY
Royal Navy.
Action: Anzio. 29.1.44.
Age 35.   (Preston)

L.A.C. B. D. WICKHAM
Royal Air Force.
Canada. 15.3.42.
Age 20.   (Godstone)

Pte. C. E. WILES
7th Bn. Black Watch.
Action: N.W. E'pe. 16.8.44.
Age 19.   (Ilkeston)

'I Will Lead You Again!' Said Monty

With the last of our battle-wearied troops to leave the Dunkirk Beaches in June 1940, Grenadier Guardsman A. A. Shuttlewood took part in the nightmare withdrawal from Furnes—and lived to listen to a heartening prophecy made by Field-Marshal (then Major-General) Montgomery.

WE left Furnes, eight miles inland from the Belgian coast and 16 miles east of Dunkirk, after three days and nights of ceaseless bombing and shelling. It was there that we had lost our Commanding Officer, Lieut.-Colonel J. Lloyd, and two Company Commanders, victims of snipers' bullets. (See story in page 760, Vol. 9). Considering the enemy's fierce attempts to blast a way into Dunkirk itself, and the stiff resistance we put up to prevent him doing so, my battalion's losses were fairly light. But the other two battalions of the 7th Guards Brigade—the 1st Grenadier and 1st Coldstream Guards—suffered heavy casualties, mainly due to their heroic defence along the banks of the Albert Canal, north of Louvain, at the beginning of the campaign.

The road to Dunkirk was littered with fallen telegraph poles and wires, broken glass and shell craters; the sky was brilliantly lit by flares and gun-flashes. The leading elements of the battalion wore sacking tied beneath their boots to deaden the sound of approach to the beach zone; enemy infiltration had been rife, and we were taking no chances. We were dog-tired, for we had had little sleep for the past week. Arduous forced marches had been our lot since May 12; one of them had exceeded 30 miles, which, wearing full equipment, is no mean feat of endurance. This final trek to the beach seemed the worst of all—after three weeks of absolute hell on earth.

Dunkirk loomed well to our rear, its shell-wrecked buildings like jagged grey spectres in the half-light provided by incessant gunfire all around us. British naval guns belched tongues of flame from the Channel, to our right; their missiles screamed over our heads, to land amongst enemy concentrations with explosions which shook the sand beneath our feet. German batteries, inland, fired salvo after salvo into the beach area; here at last we were halted, and ordered to dig ourselves in.

On the Shell-Spattered Beach

The *crump* of shells was drawing closer, and it seemed that the deeper we dug the greater was the quantity of sand which trickled back into the holes. Fortunate ones amongst us possessed short-hafted entrenching tools. Others scooped out holes with their bare hands. However, we completed our slit-trenches and quickly took advantage of them. Suddenly the guns became silent. The first pale rays of dawn broke through the barrier of darkness, to glimmer wanly on the shell-spattered and bomb-cratered beach . . . It was dawn of June 2, 1940.

We could see the silhouettes of naval vessels offshore, thousands of them, it seemed, of all shapes and sizes, all having one set purpose : to rescue the living and the wounded remnants of the B.E.F. from the enemy's baffled fury. The coming of dawn heralded the reappearance of enemy planes, which zoomed down at us, unleashing their bomb-burdens and raking the beach with machine-gun fire. They came over at regular intervals of about ten minutes or so, and we blazed away with Bren-guns and rifles. Three lots came, and went. But they did slight damage.

Then followed a lull of about twenty minutes, and we were reassembled and trekked onward along the beach. Bodies lay sprawled in the sand, some covered with blankets and great-coats. Smashed vehicles were grouped between the dunes. Weapons of former evacuees (for this was the rearguard of an evacuation which had commenced several days before) were to be seen littering the water's edge.

With the turn of the tide the big ships nosed farther inland; boats were lowered, and drew nearer. Wounded men were the first to go aboard, many hands aiding them. When all the wounded were safely in the boats we were permitted to wade out to sea and to clamber on board. I am over six feet, yet the water lapped above my shoulders. Many of the smaller fellows were forced to swim for it. The boat I boarded, filled to capacity with its human cargo, headed out into the Channel and drew alongside a minesweeper, and we climbed the rope ladders. Soaked to the skin, we descended into the engine and boiler rooms, undressed, and enjoyed a brisk rub-down with towels which were readily provided by members of the crew out of their own kit.

Then, the bark of hundreds of guns sounded—ack-ack guns blaring away at Hun dive-bombers. In varying states of undress, we went up on deck to witness the fight. I saw a destroyer hit amidships, and small figures crowding on her deck. I saw seven of the dive-bombers receive direct hits ; four

ABANDONED BRITISH BOFORS GUNS on the Dunkirk beaches (above) still pointed defiance to the skies when the last of the B.E.F. had been evacuated in June 1940. Some of the rearguard (top) who had made arduous forced marches for three weeks, found time for much-needed foot treatment before embarking. *Photos, F. H. Brindley, Associated Press*

GRENADIER GUARDSMEN RETURNING FROM DUNKIRK in June 1940 had not failed to maintain the magnificent tradition of their Regiment. Here, heavy-eyed and weary, but still showing something of their parade-ground smartness, they are disembarking at Dover from the ship which had evacuated them from the deadly beaches. Only a few hours before, with the rearguard of the B.E.F., they had fought tenaciously to retain the slender hold on the soil of France. See accompanying story by Guardsman Shuttlewood, and pages 7-11. *Photo, The Times*

exploded before they reached the water. The planes sheered off, and the evacuation continued. The embattled array of our naval might, stretching for miles along the beach, was a stirring sight.

We set sail for Dover—and home. Words cannot describe the reception we were given at the quayside. Steaming cups of tea, cigarettes, cakes and biscuits were bestowed upon us ; and, most important and reassuring of all, smiles of welcome. When we reached our destination, after a hot meal the order of the day was "Sleep !" The orderlies of the huts allotted to us were instructed to "Let them sleep it out. Don't waken them." When I finally awoke I discovered that I had slept for 21 hours. There were men in the same hut still deep in blessed sleep.

My battalion reformed at Shaftesbury, Dorset, several days later. Here, Major-General Bernard Montgomery visited us, and congratulated the 7th Guards Brigade upon its splendid showing throughout the three weeks of the campaign. Incidentally Major-General Montgomery (as he was then) had commanded the 3rd Division in Belgium and France, of which our Brigade formed a part. He made this prophecy :

" We will return to France one day, you and I. We will rout the Hun—smash him and his beliefs. I will lead you again,—and you will follow me. And next time (God grant it be soon) we will be equipped with the very best : the very best weapons for the very best troops !" How magnificently that prophecy was fulfilled the world now knows.

and other devices, for the approach of hostile submarines or aircraft. All ships maintained doubled look-outs to scan sea and sky ; for this voyage was undertaken at the period before the British battles in Tunisia and Sicily had been fought and won, and no one but a blind optimist expected a Malta-bound convoy to go through without a tough fight. We proceeded westward on a zigzag course, thereby increasing the journey of 920 miles—a four-days' voyage at the convoy's speed—and approached the first zone of peak danger in the 150-miles-wide stretch of sea between Derna on the North Africa coast and the island of Crete.

TOWARD the close of the second day urgent warning was given and "Action Stations" sounded. Soon a wave of German bombers swept in at a great height toward the convoy like vultures to a feast, and the warships put up a terrific barrage. A few bombs raised columns of foam in the sea, then the Huns hurriedly took the sky-road for home. It was plain they had no stomach for infighting against the punching power of the Royal Navy. Our watchdogs—that formidable array of warships—made a comforting spectacle. After the Huns had beetled off, I turned to the storekeeper.

"Well, Charlie," I said, "we're as safe as houses on this trip." He relighted his pipe. "I hope you're right, Horace," he drawled. "But there's some houses near where I live at Birkenhead that haven't been so safe." All was plain sailing for the next thirty-six hours. Charlie and several others were inclined to bet we would get through safely. Hopes of avoiding serious trouble, however, were dampened by signals flashed from the cruiser flying the flag of the Senior Naval Officer.

"The Italian fleet is out !" That was the dramatic message which had been received in code over the radio by the S.N.O.'s ship and passed to all vessels in the convoy. Soon came orders from the Commander-in-Chief, and these in turn were communicated to the warships and four merchantmen. The next thing we saw was our escort threshing up to full speed on a northerly course on another hunt for Musso's phantom-like navy, and so we were left to fend entirely for ourselves. We had become mere pawns in a greater game, and whereas the Italians proved elusive as usual, it is noteworthy that only a few days later—on March 28—the Battle Fleet under Admiral Cunningham smashed

A Chief Steward in Battle Malta-Bound

When the S.S. Pampas was running the gauntlet in convoy to Malta in March 1942 the escort of eight cruisers and 20 destroyers was suddenly called away and the fully laden merchant ships were left to fend for themselves. The lively story is told by Chief Steward Horace Carswell, D.S.M., M.M., B.E.M. (See also portrait and story in page 27.)

I WAS at Montevideo in December 1940 when the German pocket-battleship Admiral Graf Spee slunk into port ; and I saw the funeral of her commander, Captain Langsdorff, after his crippled ship had been scuttled. On the homeward voyage of the Pampas from Buenos Aires to Tilbury our passengers included Captain Dove of the Africa Shell, and other British prisoners whom Captain Langsdorff had released when he knew his raiding days were over. (See story in pages 413 and 443.)

On reaching England I was transferred to another ship, which happened to be in dock at Liverpool during the German bombing raids that lasted for three nights. Two nights of the blitz were enough for our Negro cook, who departed down the gangway after exclaiming to me, "Aw, hell ! I ain't a-goin' to stay here, boss !" He took train for Manchester, where, by the irony of fate, his arrival coincided with the worst air raid on that city. So he came back next day to the ship at Liverpool, and on getting a cool reception from me, retorted warmly, " Aw, hell ! I ain't a-goin' to stay there, boss !"

About the time when the 8th Army was pushing Rommel's alleged "invincibles" out of Libya I was again Chief Steward in the Pampas, which was really a fast cargo-carrier, although we had previously conveyed

passengers on occasions. Our job was to take a vital cargo of tanks, speedboats and munitions to Port Said via the Cape, and we got through safely and discharged according to schedule. This done, we proceeded to Alexandria and loaded up again, with arms and general supplies for Malta, which was having a rough time from German and Italian bombers based across the narrows of the Mediterranean.

Dramatic Message Over the Radio

The Pampas left the Egyptian port on March 20, 1942, in convoy with three other fully laden merchant ships, to run the gauntlet through a zone where sea and sky were infested by the enemy. Malta's urgent need was known to us all, and the importance of our convoy was evident from the fact that no less than eight British cruisers and twenty destroyers gave us a protective screen. Only one alarm was sounded in the early part of the voyage, and a single German plane came over for a "look-see." The A.A. guns of the naval escorts loosed off a few rounds, and the scout departed at top speed. But the incident was disturbing, because we knew the convoy had been located.

Specialist ratings aboard the warships listened constantly, with the aid of the asdic

Rough Journey's End at Beleaguered Malta

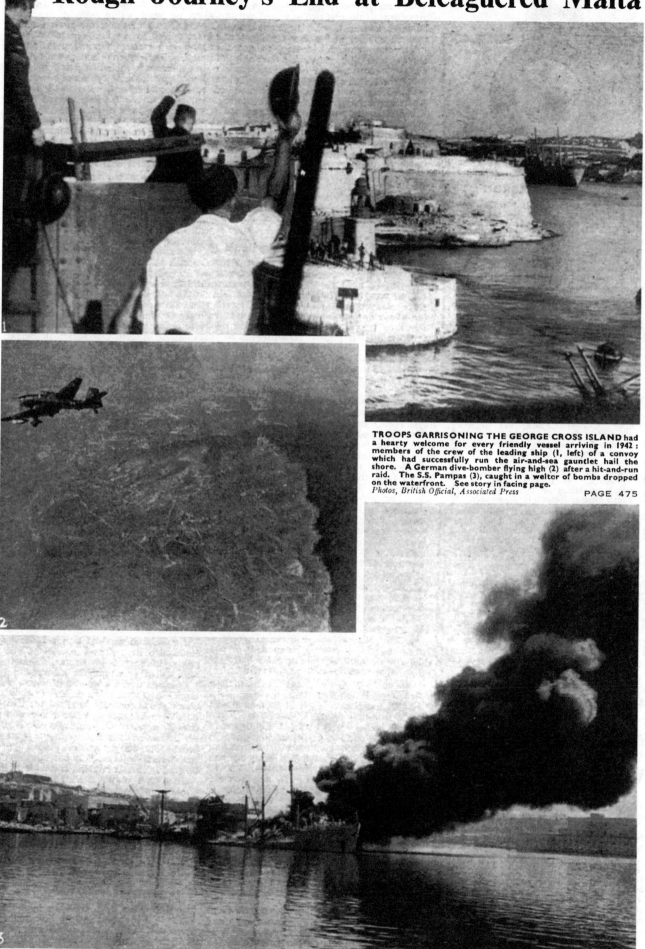

TROOPS GARRISONING THE GEORGE CROSS ISLAND had a hearty welcome for every friendly vessel arriving in 1942 : members of the crew of the leading ship (1, left) of a convoy which had successfully run the air-and-sea gauntlet hail the shore. A German dive-bomber flying high (2) after a hit-and-run raid. The S.S. Pampas (3), caught in a welter of bombs dropped on the waterfront. See story in facing page.
Photos, British Official, Associated Press

Motto : " We Act with One Accord "

NO. 35 SQUADRON

FORMED at Thetford, Norfolk, on February 1, 1916, the squadron flew to France in Jan. 1917, where it was allocated to the Cavalry Corps, association with which is perpetuated in the unit badge, which bears a horse's head " winged." It was reformed in Bomber Command in Nov. 1940, and on March 11, 1941, became operational, attacking docks at Le Havre and Hamburg.

On June 30 it undertook its first daylight operation, at Kiel, and in September three Halifaxes made the 1,700 miles round trip to Turin in Northern Italy. The year 1941 ended with a heavy daylight attack on the Scharnhorst and Gneisenau at Brest. On Feb. 12, 1942, six Halifaxes took part in " Operation Fuller," the attack on the Scharnhorst, Gneisenau and Prinz Eugen, in their escape up the Channel to North German ports. The Tirpitz, lying near Trondheim Fjord, was twice attacked in April, and on April 29-30 the squadron took part in the historic 1,000-bomber raid on Cologne.

USING the Pathfinder Force technique, 10 Halifaxes led an attack on Milan on Oct. 25, 1942. The Schneider locomotive and armament factory at Le Creusot was attacked on June 19-20, 1943, and on August 17 the German experimental station at Peenemunde (engaged on rocket projectile development) on the Baltic coast, and in September the rocket weapon sites in the Pas de Calais area.

No. 35 began to play its part in the landings in Normandy shortly after midnight on June 6, and in October it bombed the German gun batteries on Walcheren. On the cessation of hostilities, " Operation Exodus," the repatriation of Allied prisoners of war, was carried out by the Squadron. See also page 353.

two enemy squadrons in the night action off Matapan. which had a vital effect on subsequent operations in the Mediterranean.

WHILE the smoke of our escorts faded on the horizon, the Pampas and the other three cargo-carriers held a westerly course. With every turn of the propellers we cut the distance to Valetta—the port of Malta—and also to Sicily, stiff with bases of the enemy air forces. There was no surprise when the alarm bells rang. The Luftwaffe was in the air, and at the first threat our four merchant ships separated widely and made zigzag courses at the best speed possible. No longer able to rely on an intense naval barrage, they would have presented an easier target if bunched together. The combined armament of all four cargo-carriers making up the convoy was less than that of a single destroyer of the Royal Navy.

PAGE 476

The Pampas went into action in self-defence directly the first two or three German bombers appeared. We had one gun of medium calibre, and a few Oerlikons and Lewis guns—enough, anyway, to put the Huns off-aim a bit. The other three ships of our small convoy, one a Norwegian, made a brave show with their light armament while manoeuvring in the general direction of Malta and keeping in sight of one another. The first bombs that came screaming down did harm to nothing except the fish. But attacks developed apace. The Luftwaffe ran a shuttle service from Sicily, bent on preventing the ships and cargoes from winning through. Bombers came over two or three at a time, and presently by the dozen. They attacked from heights varying to close upon sea level, and occasionally Stukas came thundering down in power-dives that made the severest test on the nerves of our lads manning the guns.

Meals Were Served Amid the Battle

For hours that day the entire crews of the merchant ships were dealing with attack after attack until the light defensive guns became red-hot. The Pampas had her fair share of attention, and there was no time for officers or men to leave their posts to take meals in the ordinary way. One of my tasks—the most important perhaps—was to keep the crew fed well, as opportunity served, and thereby help maintain their strength and morale throughout the ordeal. My staff worked with a will, and I cannot speak too highly of the way they carried on with normal domestic duties amid the battle.

It was not part of my regular job to carry trays about, but extra help was needed. Taking food and beverages over the exposed decks to the bridge, gun positions, engine-room and stokeholds, was not without excitement as the Pampas shuddered and lurched from the effect of near-misses, and fragments of bomb casings spattered the hull. The job of Chief Steward tends to inculcate *sang froid*, or at least provide a veneer of this quality. When things go very wrong the geniality may be varied by the raising of an eyebrow in a slightly pained expression, which is about all the outward emotion the role of Chief Steward permits.

It pleases me to recall that this appearance of calm and sweet reasonableness was an asset in that grim battle on the Malta route. The sweating, grimy lads behind the gun-shields found comfort in my somewhat portly presence, and received a benediction with the hot food served to them. Perhaps they thought, "It can't be so bad, or old Horace wouldn't be ambling about," forgetful that appearances may be deceptive.

Suddenly a German aircraft burst into flames and spiralled into the sea. An exuberant signal by daylight flash-lamp was made from our bridge : "One to us !" To which another sorely harassed ship retorted : "That was our bird !"—thereby starting an argument which continued in a sporting spirit after another Hun had gone hurtling out of the blue like a fiery comet. Two of the merchant ships were hit, and suffered casualties. But the convoy steamed on. It is not possible to estimate the tonnage of bombs that came screaming down that day.

The most formidable attack developed when we were within sight of the Malta citadel, two of the cargo-carriers receiving direct hits in vital compartments. Both sank in a matter of minutes, their passing marked by columns of smoke while survivors in the lifeboats headed for port through a sea lashed into foam by cannon shells and machine-gun bullets. Luck and judgement combined to save the Pampas, and the other vessel manned by Norwegians, and we reached Valetta with comparatively slight damage. Meantime, the Malta batteries drove off the enemy, who suffered further losses from R.A.F. fighters in air-battles to the shores of Sicily.

What a welcome awaited us ! Crowds thronged every vantage point round the Grand Harbour as our two sorely scarred merchant ships moved to their berths at the quayside. Almost before the cheering had died away the winches were clattering and derricks discharging the precious cargo. Although the Pampas and her Norwegian consort had made port our ordeal was not over. German and Italian aircraft were still in strength within easy striking distance of the island, and Rommel's army had not yet been kicked out of North Africa. But the defences of Malta were stronger than heretofore, and the raiders were no longer having the easy ride of former days. On an average, one out of every five hostile planes failed to return to base. A red-and-white flag was hoisted when it became certain that raiders were on the way and Malta was the likely target. Orders were that we all had to leave our ships—crews and stevedores alike—and go to the dugouts and tunnels ashore. Those places were almost impregnable, but our nerves had a shaking one day when a bomb exploded directly on top of the dugout where I and several shipmates were sheltering.

We Had Lost All But Our Lives

One day the warning signal was followed by the most determined air raid for weeks. Eighty German bombers came over, accompanied by several Italians, and within a few minutes the dockside area was an inferno. We huddled in our shelters while bombs crashed on the battered waterfront and plane after plane dived upon the two merchant ships moored at the quay. In a short time the Norwegian was ablaze from stem to stern. Whilst the fire raged, a bomb fell plumb through the squat funnel and exploded in the engine-room—and that was the end of one stout ship.

The Pampas survived only a little longer. Hammered beyond hope of salvage, she lay partly submerged in wreckage when the raiders had gone and the smoke and dust still drifted over the oil-strewn waters of the Grand Harbour. We emerged from our dugouts and dazedly surveyed the destruction. We had lost all but our lives and the clothes we wore. Our employment was gone. As Distressed British Seamen, we were dependent now on the good offices of the Royal Navy to take us to our home-port in England. In due course the cruiser H.M.S. Aurora gave us passage, and I wasn't the only one who was heartily glad to leave the "hot-shop" now honoured by the title of "The George Cross Island."

Let's Give the Nazi Devil His Due

Wounded on the road to Dunkirk, Sergeant Charles J. Sadgrove, Royal Signals, was captured in a casualty clearing station at Krombec on May 30, 1940. Sent first to Stalag XXA, Thorn, and later to XXB, Marienburg, he describes some of the Germans he met in five years as a prisoner of war.

I SHALL never forget the camp commandant who brandished his revolver on every conceivable occasion, or the brutality of many of the guards on our enforced march across Germany. But many of the Nazis had themselves been prisoners in the First Great War and had some understanding of our plight. Others were considerate toward1 us because they had suffered under the Hitler regime. And there were those who

STALAG XXB, Marienburg, viewed from the main gates. Here the author of this story spent much of his time as a P.O.W.

RIVAL TEAM CAPTAINS (left), with referee, toss for choice of ends on Stalag XXB's football ground. *Photos, International Red Cross*

were soldiers only because they had to be and who tried to be helpful to us.

There was a feldwebel (our rank of sergeant) who had charge of us for a time in our camp in East Prussia. " Lon Chaney " we called him, because of the wounds that scarred and twisted his face. We had reason to know that his heart was in its proper place, for no man, of whatever nationality, could have argued more for prisoners' rights. We men wanted time off for Sunday work—he saw that we got it. The billet needed redecorating—he arranged for it to be done. Swimming facilities were asked for in the nearby river—he saw that we got them. Canteen stocks were low—he arranged regular shopping expeditions. Every day we ticked off on a list the various things he had done for us.

Our Rights as Prisoners of War

With him as a guard was a youngster from Saxony, whom we knew as Harry. A front-line soldier (he was wounded in Russia) he was never too tired to do us a kindness— it might be the arranging of a football match with a neighbouring camp, a railway journey into Stalag XXB, Marienburg, a local shopping expedition, or merely a trip to the post-office for parcels. Most ex-prisoners of war remember a Franz or a Willy or a Fritz who " forgot " to lock the billet at night, or who did something else equally praiseworthy in their eyes. Best of all were those guards who stuck by their " Englanders " on the march, foraged for food for them when they themselves were hungry, or shared with us their own dwindling smoke ration.

Although under strict military discipline, those of us out on working parties contacted not a few civilians. Many of these well earned the title " swines " with which they frequently chose to label us. But there were good as well as bad civilians ; among the best was the old carter who was often accused of sabotage for absenting himself from work in order to collect for us our Red Cross food parcels. Contact with womenfolk was especially forbidden. But circumstances made it impossible to avoid breaches of this regulation. Prisoners were made to work in the fields and factories alongside women and girls, some of them old, but many remarkably attractive. As leader of a working party, I came in daily contact with them.

First to my mind comes one whom we found in charge of the kitchen at our billet, and who watched our interests among the shopkeepers of the town. Her sales talk on our behalf left nothing to be desired. She would be told in one shop, perhaps, that potatoes were scarce ; therefore, the prisoners would have to go short until the civilians

had been supplied. But we didn't go short. The shopkeeper was reminded emphatically that we were prisoners of war, not criminals ; that we had certain rights which had to be upheld ; that if we went short of rations we would not work, and that in these circumstances he, the shopkeeper, would face a charge of sabotage against the German Reich. It was the same with the baker who tried to supply us with stale bread, the butcher who said that horse-flesh was good enough for " the English swine," the grocer who thought he could pass on to us jam of

CHARLES SADGROVE (left), leader of a P.O.W. working party, and a companion at Stalag XXA, Thorn, Germany, in 1941.

PAGE 477

an inferior quality, and all those who attempted in any way to sidetrack their obligations towards us.

My companions did not always see eye-to-eye with this woman. Their usual suspicions of the " Quarter-bloke " were now directed at her. She was " in the rackets," they said. If by that they meant that she was frequently to be seen smoking an English cigarette, they forgot her good works on our behalf, the number of eggs, white rolls, butter, first-quality jam and other commodities she risked her freedom to bring into the camp on an exchange basis.

It was the same with the woman in charge of the works' kitchen, to which, normally, we had no right of entry. The men suspected her of tampering with their rations. They forgot the times she left the vegetable cellar unlocked so that our cooks might help themselves, of the odds and ends with which she supplied us from time to time to improve our " Mittagessen," by which name we came to know our midday soup. A neighbour to whom most of us were endeared was the wife of the caretaker of our billet. Her poultry were fed on most of our kitchen scraps, and in return there wasn't a tool or pot of paint in her husband's workshop that was not ours for the asking. She even lent us her precious electric iron with which to put a crease in our Sunday suits.

We Bought " Under the Counter "

There was a girl of about twenty in the works' kitchen who bore us no animosity, despite the fact that her family had been killed and her home destroyed in an air raid. Very friendly, too, were the sisters whose dressmaking business in Berlin had been closed to them for ever ; many were the tailoring jobs they did for us in exchange for a little chocolate or a smoke. Generally speaking, the shopkeepers were most helpful, selling us everything that was in their power to sell, even at the risk of offending their civilian customers. One greengrocer always gave us preference, as did the woman in the local chemist's shop, while the manageress of a music shop in a nearby town had the " under the counter " system to a fine art as far as we were concerned. One staunch supporter was the proprietress of a local distillery where we bought lemonade for the canteen. A competitor lodged a complaint with the police regarding her excessive sales to us. Straightway she telephoned the authorities at Marienburg in protest. Their protection was granted, and authorization given for continued sales to us.

The enforced march gave us little opportunity to contact civilians, men or women, but I remember the help given to me by the married daughter of the burgomaster of a little town in the province of Mecklenburg-Schwerin where we rested for a few days. By interceding with her father she got for us extra things, such as potatoes and peas for our soup, and fuel for our kitchen fires. For me she collected dainties the like of which I had not seen for many a day. When I went to say good-bye there were tears in her eyes.

A final memory is coupled with sadness at the loss of a comrade. His death occurred a few days before the Americans arrived to liberate us, in April 1945. The privations had proved too much for him, and we buried him in a grave alongside others of our party who had succumbed to months of suffering

and hardship. We were without the usual guard; the commandant had not thought one necessary in view of the rapid approach of the Allied forces, and the womenfolk who had been interested sightseers of our simple ceremony plucked up sufficient courage to come and talk with us.

Their condolences for the dead quickly turned to practical consideration of the living: they ran to their respective homes to bring us, the one bread and cakes, another soup and meat, a third coffee and cigarettes. I should like to call these Germans typical of their race, but—well, in a land where bestiality and cruelty were commonplace it was indeed refreshing to find those in whom some spark of decency remained.

I Waited Six Years to Collect It

A jeep-ride from Central Germany to the Belgian coast and a train journey in fog-bound Eastern England form the background of these reminiscences by John Fortinbras, who in the autumn of 1945 travelled 1,000 miles to collect a Civvy Suit and be demobilized. His narrative will revive in many readers of "The War Illustrated" memories of their own Home-coming.

"SEE you in Civvy Street!" were my final words to those I left on service. Fellow B.A.O.R. officers, with their release groups recently frozen, looked rueful and shrugged their shoulders. But I was too elated with my own freedom to pay much heed to their problems . . . In the early hours I left the ruins of Hanover, bound for the port of Ostend. I dodged the rail journey, primarily because of affection for my jeep; in it, through many hazards, I had travelled without mishap 19,630 miles to date, and the urge to knock up the 20,000th mile was irresistible.

We raced over wet, slippery roads via Minden, thence by the Reichautobahn to the borders of Hamm of railway (or is it Bomber Command?) fame, and thereafter by route 240, over the Rhine at Xanten, into Holland, through Venlo and Roermond alongside the Maas and into Belgium by Maaseyck. It felt queer to travel through places like the villages close to Venlo which a year ago, as an artilleryman, I had stonked day and night. I gazed at a church, once a suspected enemy O.P., which we had sniped with heavy guns from 12,000 yards, and noted the rents we had torn in it.

We celebrated our 20,000th mile at a spot between Diest and Louvain, recalling former

narrow squeaks and humiliations there, including confinement for some crucial minutes, during the previous winter, in Dutch snow, from which we had been rescued by two big-limbed horses, and half a dozen Dutch yokels who shoved as hard as the horses pulled.

I stayed the night with friends—a Belgian notary and his wife—at Braine le Comte, receiving wonderful hospitality, and my driver was similarly feasted. My hostess deplored the heavy prices in the black market —2,000 francs for a cycle tire, 120 francs for a pound of butter, 90 francs for a pound of meat, and (most iniquitous of all) 2,600 francs for a pair of thin-soled shoes for her nine-year-old daughter. As 175 Belgian francs ran to the pound sterling, that last item put the price of a child's shoes at no less than £15 a pair.

Next day we travelled on via Soignies, the market centre for Belgium's great cart-horses, Alost, Ghent, and so to Ostend. I reached No. 1 Embarkation Release Camp at 1.30 p.m.—just 30 minutes too late; for 1.0 p.m. was zero hour for sailing arrangements. Instead, therefore, of sailing the next day I would have to wait until the day after. The lift in the Hotel Metropole in the Rue d'Eglise, where I was billeted, was placarded:

"Warning—Mines and Booby Traps—Read the Notice in your Bedroom!" I did, and refrained from prying too closely into houses on the Atlantic Wall, and the adjoining sand dunes: this certainly was no time to die!

I spent my spare day wandering through Bruges, the so-called Venice of the North, but I was not enraptured. The city was dirty, untidy, the canals scum-ridden and frowsty-smelling, the people very sombrely dressed, and I disliked the sight of so many dog-propelled carriers, although the dogs in most instances looked frisky enough in their harness. At last came the day of sailing. It opened with two pleasures, first a little card with Monty's signature on it, which I found on my breakfast plate, being a message of thanks and Godspeed, and second, the changing of foreign currency into sterling. English silver which never excited me before did so now—it symbolized the passage Home.

The Couldn't Care Less League

I now imagined myself free of all further military responsibility. But no. My name rang out over the ship's loud-hailer as the officer commanding the Oxford draft. This involved, I quickly discovered, some responsibility for personal documents and—a far heavier task—organization of a fatigue party to brush decks after the trip. By loud-hailer I called for two officers, who in turn called for two W.O.s, and eventually by resort to some luckless gunners and privates two sweeping parties were laid on. I fear all members belonged to the C.C.L. (Couldn't Care Less) League; but the job was done.

Our boat, the Prince Charles, manned by a Flemish crew, reached Dover at 5 p.m., and after a short delay we stood behind our kit and baggage in the Customs sheds. A ticklish moment. Especially for one officer with £70 in his pocket available for meeting his dues. But, by a complete mischance, someone unknown to him passed through the Customs his heaviest case, containing spirits and some Zeiss glasses, and with this lucky let-off he counted out a mere £5 of his wad. I found the officials most reluctant to levy charges. They didn't demand, "Have you any wines or liqueurs? Have you any scent?" They said, "You haven't a camera, have you?"—and so on.

At Dover a hot meal was served us—meat chunks and greasy globules. It tallied not at all with our Overseas standards. "First

TO CIVVY STREET BY EASY STAGES is the basis of the plan for demobilizing Servicemen due for release under the Age and Service Group system. queueing up to hand in their documents (left) at No. 12 Transit Camp, Tournai, Belgium. For the "birds of passage" the camp offers facilities and amenities calculated to charm the heart of officers and other ranks, not the least popular being a spacious and comfortably appointed reading-room (right). A permanent staff of British soldiers and Belgians gives first-class service.

Photos, British Official

EXCHANGING LOCAL CURRENCY FOR ENGLISH MONEY at No. 112 Transit Camp, Tournai (left), brings demobilization a step nearer. But much land and some water. has to be crossed before selection of the civilian outfit. At the clothing depot at Olympia, London, five who are making the great come-back (right) have donned the headwear of the man-in-the-street, and soon will be on the last lap Home with their newly acquired possessions in cardboard boxes. See also illus. page 619, Vol. 9.

Photos, British Official, Keystone

taste of Civvy Street, gentlemen!" grinned one of the party's live spirits. Then, at 7 p.m., we moved away by special train for Oxford, and we were soon enveloped in fog. It was well after midnight when we arrived at Oxford, thence a coach ride to Slade Disembarkation Camp. "Should have a V in place of the D," said a disgruntled, overweary M.O. as, beyond the illuminated sign, we saw the severe outlines of Nissen huts. "They ought to see my Continental chalet and keep up the standards," commented another pessimist.

We ate well here. After bedding down at 2 a.m., we breakfasted at 8.0, having had the usual 7.15 cup of tea, an Army custom mercifully sustained to the end. So began our final day. We handed in surplus kit and received notice of train timings to dispersal centres. I found it would be 3.0 p.m. before my train was due to leave for Northampton. I idled away the morning in Oxford, and thought how providential for England that our land-battles had been fought out elsewhere.

"Tha's Always Worse to Cum!"

Just before we boarded the Northampton train a tragedy befell one of us. He put down his suitcase in the yard of Oxford station and left it unattended for a few moments to fetch other baggage. Meanwhile, a lorry charged over it, and his wines and liqueurs, the prizes of his European campaign, so carefully packed and treasured, oozed out of the crumpled remains—a cracked, soggy, pathetic mess.

At Northampton, an Army lorry whisked us to Talavera Barracks. Documentation was quickly completed. I give the organization at all three centres—Ostend, Oxford and here—full marks for their efficiency, and an extra 10 per cent for unfailing politeness and courtesy. Then came the acquisition of the Civvy Suit. "You can get £18 for what they give you at the clothing centre!" whispered a man to me, confidentially. But I wasn't interested. I admired the quick service system, with a tailor at the entrance to take one's measurements, a girl clerk who wrote them down, and courteous direction to the clothing stalls whose wares tallied with the figures.

In no time, it seemed, I gathered up a blue suit, raincoat, pair of black shoes, shirt, hat, two collars, tie, two pairs of socks,

collar studs, and a pair of cuff links; the least promising of these possessions were, I thought, the socks which, conforming to the most spartan utility cut, couldn't possibly extend more than half-an-inch above the shin bone. And why, I wondered, no handkerchiefs? Not even one. I drew my eight weeks' ration of cigarettes, paid for at duty-free prices, and two weeks' sweets ration, ate a hasty but appetizing dinner in the Officers' Mess, and was dumped with all my belongings and the cardboard box of clothing at the Castle Station, well in time to catch the train to Peterborough, and from there the 11.0 p.m. connexion to my East Anglian home.

A more dismal conveyance than the Northampton to Peterborough train can hardly exist in Europe. It started twenty minutes late. It stopped at every station. It never hurried. The porters who served it called out the names of stations in accents more difficult to understand than two or three foreign languages . . . I reflected bitterly on the hundreds of comfortable railway installations which the War had des-

troyed. One of my companions, an R.A.S.C. officer, huddled miserably in a corner, having abandoned all hope of catching his 9.30 p.m. connexion to York, was mournfully philosophic. "Doan't mind if things be glum," he said, quoting the old Yorkshire tag. "Tha's always worse to cum!"

Our spirits brightened when a newly demobbed padre, an Irishman brimming over with cheerfulness, began pushing a porter's barrow laden with our baggage along the Peterborough platform. Cold and subdued, I finished my journey in his company, together with a colonel newly returned from West Africa and facing acclimitization to chill and foggy nights. I walked home, ate a supper thoughtfully laid out for me, looked at my watch—it indicated 3.0 a.m.—and crept into bed, without rousing anyone. It seemed the best way to begin one's civilian life by appearing suddenly, as it were, at breakfast. And then, in the morning, I lacked moral courage: I hesitated to don that Civvy Suit. The more I looked at it the more comfortable and familiar appeared my travel-stained old battle-dress.

⌐⌐⌐⌐⌐⌐ NEW FACTS AND FIGURES ⌐⌐⌐⌐⌐

AT the British Legion Poppy Factory at Richmond, Surrey—largest factory in the world employing only disabled labour—disabled men of the Second Great War are now working beside veterans of the First Great War. Numbered among the recent recruits are former Commandos and Airborne troops.

FOR this year's Poppy Day appeal (Nov. 9) 45,000,000 were made, of which 3,000,000 were shipped to 54 countries overseas, including supplies to the British forces in Germany, Italy and Japan. In the manufacture of poppies and wreaths this year the factory used 100 miles of material, 1,700 miles of wire and 17 tons of metal. A big warehouse staffed by ex-Servicemen is kept busy all the year round shipping the poppies to all parts of the world and preparing collecting boxes and trays for the annual appeal. See illus. in page 450.

CUNARD-WHITE Star liner Mauretania, arriving at Liverpool from Canada on September 1, 1946, was released from Government service. The work of completely refitting the ship will take about five months. During the years 1939-1946 the Mauretania steamed nearly 600,000 miles and carried more than 330,000 passengers and troops.

REPATRIATION of German P.O.W. from the United Kingdom began at the end of September 1946 at the initial rate of 15,000 per month. The scheme applies to all German prisoners in Britain except senior officers and those known to be strongly pro-Nazi. About 394,000 prisoners were eligible; of these, 158,000 were engaged on agricultural work; 50,000 were employed by the War Office on labour duties and 36,000 in camp duties; 35,000 by the Ministry of Works and 19,500 by the Air Ministry.

THE British and U.S. Military Governments on September 5, 1946, announced agreement on the economic merger of their zones in Germany. Five joint boards were set up: Food and Agriculture at Bad Kissingen (U.S. zone); Finance, at Frankfort-on-Main (U.S. zone); Economics, at Minden (British); Transport, at Bielefeld and Hamburg (British); and Communications.

MORE than 170,000 tons of food were imported into the British zone in Germany during August 1946. Among these were 59,000 tons of wheat from Britain, Canada and the U.S.A.; 95,982 tons of potatoes from Britain, Holland and Czechoslovakia; 17,853 tons of fresh vegetables from Britain and Norway; and 930 tons of meat from Britain.

U.S. 100-ton Tank That Never Went to War

Photo, Planet News

DESIGNED TO BATTER-THROUGH HITLER'S WEST WALL, this 100-ton tank, the U.S. Army's heaviest, was shown for the first time to the public at the recently held Twenty-eighth Annual Meeting of the U.S. Army Ordnance Association, at Aberdeen, Maryland. In addition to its size, the most notable feature is the 105-mm. gun, set in the hull as opposed to the usual turret mounting, and which well outstretches a jeep in length. The T-28 never fired a shot in the Second Great War, hostilities ending before this giant was ready for use.

Printed in England and published every alternate Friday by the Proprietors, THE AMALGAMATED PRESS, LTD., The Fleetway House, Farringdon Street, London, E.C.4. Registered for transmission by Canadian Magazine Post. Sole Agents for Australia and New Zealand : Messrs. Gordon & Gotch, Ltd. ; and for South Africa : Central News Agency, Ltd.—November 8, 1946.   S.S.   *Editorial Address :* JOHN CARPENTER HOUSE, WHITEFRIARS, LONDON, E.C.4.

Vol 10 *The War Illustrated* N° 246

SIXPENCE

NOVEMBER 22, 1946

I WAS THERE

ADMIRAL SIR WILLIAM HALSEY, PRESIDENT OF THE NAVY LEAGUE, placed a wreath on behalf of the League at the foot of Nelson's Column, in London's Trafalgar Square, on Oct. 21, 1946—the 141st anniversary of the Battle of Trafalgar. Representatives of the R.N. and Dominions and Colonies also paid tribute to the great little admiral. The League was founded in 1895 for the purpose of maintaining interest in the Royal Navy and keeping it strong and efficient.
Photo, P.A.-Reuter

Edited by Sir John Hammerton

NO. 247 WILL BE PUBLISHED FRIDAY, DECEMBER 6

Prize of Cassino and Part of Victory's Price

RUINED HILL-TOP MONASTERY AND POLISH CEMETERY are awesome reminders of the bitter and prolonged struggle for Monte Cassino. The ceremony of dedication of the Cemetery (top), where in serried ranks lie 1,000 Poles, took place in September 1945 : the entrance is flanked by two finely sculptured Polish eagles. From the aerial photograph the Monastery (bottom) would appear to have been completely destroyed ; but two chapels were left practically intact and much of the cloisters remained. See facing page.　　PAGE 482　　*Photos, The Times, Air Ministry*

Cassino : Ypres of the Second Great War

By L. MARSLAND GANDER

who as War Correspondent of The Daily Telegraph saw the capture of Monastery Hill and the town of Cassino in May 1944.

THE jagged, piled masonry of Cassino today poses one of the great mysteries of the war. Did the Germans occupy the massive Benedictine monastery which the Allies smashed with tons of bombs in the biggest, most concentrated air attack of the Italian campaign, in February 1944 ? It may seem shocking that such a question can be asked. Yet immediately after the attack the late Abbot Diamare, head of the fraternity, gave a broadcast denouncing the bombing and declaring that the Germans did not use the building. This statement, discounted at the time as German propaganda, has recently been confirmed by Don Martino, who was the Abbot's private secretary and who added that the Germans moved in after the place had been reduced to rubble. He describes it as "one of the mistakes of war."

I entered the ruins of the Monastery on May 18, 1944, the day on which it was captured by the Poles, and can affirm from personal observation that there were plentiful signs of German occupation—boxes of ammunition, grenades, Spandaus, empty tin cans, dirty blankets, and three wounded German N.C.O.s. But this is, apparently, agreed by the Abbot's secretary and throws no light on whether the 6th century Monastery had been used as a strongpoint before our air bombardments. There can be no doubt that the Allied high commanders were convinced that it had been used, at least as an artillery observation post, before they authorized the bombardment of February 15.

Dominating Direct Road to Rome

Consider the situation. Cassino was cited in Italian military text-books as the ideal defensive position. It was the central bastion of the German's winter defence line—the Gustav Line. Highway Six, the direct road to Rome, is dominated for miles by 1,700-foot Monte Cassino (otherwise Monastery Hill) and the Monastery, rebuilt in the 19th century, with walls like a fortress, perched on the top. How strong the building may be judged by the fact that even after thousands of bombs had been rained on it a substantial part of it still remained. I estimated that the shattered outer walls, which we reached finally by climbing a steep slope of dust and rubble on hands and knees,

were eight or ten feet thick. Piled up behind Monastery Hill were the still more forbidding slopes of 5,000-foot Monte Cairo.

It is interesting to recall that Cassino's military possibilities had been painfully impressed upon Hannibal in 217 B.C. After winning the battle of Lake Trasimene he had marched into Southern Italy hoping to rally the Samnites to his support, only to find himself approximately in the same position as the British in 1944, with the Romans

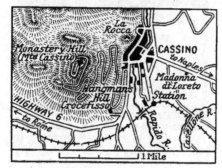

(instead of Germans) holding all the heights round him. Crucifying the guide who had misled him, he then diverted the Romans by tying lighted faggots to foxes' tails, thus making good his escape while the Romans investigated this phenomenon.

The Monastery, almost as solid as the rock on which it was built, seemed to grow out of the hill-side and to fit into its geographical features, just like the numerous grey stone buildings in Cassino itself. Whether the Germans entered it or not, they could always, to some extent, shelter behind it. Frankly, I do not know whether they did in fact occupy it before the bombardment; but there was always a strong likelihood that, sooner or later, they would. It is certain that they were using sangars in the vicinity of the Monastery

buildings. Sangars, which are shelters built of stone and timber on rocky hillsides where it is impossible to hack out trenches, were commonly used by both sides among the Italian mountains. It may be that the German sangars on Monastery Hill gave them adequate cover without taking over the Monastery itself. But the Germans had used monasteries before, so why not this one ?

Cassino stands out in the annals of a war of swift movement as almost the only example of prolonged, swaying battle round a fixed point. It was the Ypres of this war, though the fighting, with long intervals between offensives, lasted only five months compared with the years of bitter and bloody struggle round Ypres in the First Great War. Three previous attempts had been made to lever the Germans out of Cassino and open the road to Rome before, in May, the Allies gave up the disastrous policy of using men in "penny packets" and assembled an overwhelming force of men, tanks and guns. Briefly summarized the previous attempts were as follows.

First, that of General Ryder's American 34th Division in January. They forded the Rapido River, penetrated into the town from the north, and pushed boldly up Monastery Hill. Then we discovered how strongly the Germans had fortified themselves among the ruins. On Feb. 4, after a foggy, wintry week of desperate fighting, the attack died down.

Second, that of the 4th Indian and 2nd New Zealand Divisions, after an air bombardment. On February 14, Allied aircraft flew over the Abbey dropping leaflets warning the civilian occupants to leave the building. Three hundred aircraft next day bombed, or attempted to bomb, the Abbey, but it was considered that only one bomb of ten scored a direct hit. My colleague, Christopher Buckley, states that the greatest tragedy of the whole operation was that the infantry were not ready to go into action. They did not do so until two days later, after a five hours' bombardment which seems to have had little effect on the Germans' deep stone and concrete positions among the rubble. A few Gurkhas actually rushed the Abbey ruins but could not hold them. Their corpses were lying on the hillside, as grim evidence of their gallantry, three months later when I climbed

CLEARING THE TOWN OF CASSINO OF SNIPERS is the job of this patrol (left). In the distance is Monastery Hill crowned by the famous Monastery. Seized by Polish infantry on the same day that Cassino was captured by 8th Army troops, the road to Rome was opened to the Allies and the Gustav Line ceased to exist. On the right, British armour outside the town, with a slit trench under the barrel of a 17-pounder anti-tank gun. See also illus. page 727, Vol. 8.

those barren slopes of death. The New Zealanders, attacking across the waterlogged plain while the Indians stormed vainly up the mountains, fared little better. They gained some ground, bridged the chief tributary of the Rapido and captured Cassino station, only to lose it in a counter-attack next day.

Third, the attempt following a bigger and better air bombardment on March 15, this time by 500 aircraft, the entire bomber force of the Mediterranean air command, which dropped 1,400 tons of bombs. They were to have fallen on a single square mile of the town, reducing it and the hidden defenders to dust. In practice many of the bombs fell wide. One destroyed the caravan of General Leese, the 8th Army Commander, three miles away ; fortunately, he was not in it. One formation discharged all its high explosive on the Corps headquarters town of Venafro. Another intensive artillery bombardment followed. Then for eight cruel days the New Zealanders fought among the rubble with the fanatical German parachutists, the majority of whom had remained, undaunted and unharmed, in their cellars and pillboxes throughout all the bombing and shelling. Piles of shattered masonry in the streets of Cassino, caused by our own efforts, proved an insuperable obstacle to our own tanks. We were, once again, checked. General Freyberg, in his dispatch giving an account of the operations of the New Zealand Corps at Cassino, wrote : "Our plan was to reduce the second phase to a minimum by the violence of the initial air blow, but blitz bombing proved a double-edged weapon and produced obstacles which made the speedy deployment of our armour impossible."

That was the situation in April 1944, when I arrived on the Cassino front. We held approximately three-quarters of the town, including the spur of Castle Hill. The Germans had the western fringe of the town, including the formidable strongpoints of the Colosseum, the Baron's Palace, the Continental Hotel and the ancient amphitheatre. All our positions were overlooked by theirs, and during daylight the whole area had to be smothered with a smoke-screen for the safety of our troops.

"Wrench Out the Aching Tooth"

Field-Marshal Alexander was, meanwhile, at Caserta headquarters, working out the details of the master plan which was (in his own words) to "wrench out the aching tooth." This time there was to be no mistake. The 8th Army had been secretly and swiftly transferred from the Adriatic sector so that on the vital Cassino sector the attackers could have the three-to-one superiority they needed. Finally, fourteen Allied divisions were massed against five German divisions. This, by the way, was a purely local superiority.

The plan was to squeeze out Cassino by an enveloping movement by two Corps, the Polish Corps on the right and the British XIII Corps on the left. Late on the night of May 12 eleven hundred guns of the 8th Army began to pound the German positions with a fiendish volume of metal and explosive greater than any previously used in war. After 40 minutes of this violent bombardment the 8th Indian Division and the 4th British began their perilous crossing of the Rapido, while the Poles, as the other arm of the "pincer," began to fight uphill towards the distant Monastery. The Indians flung the first Bailey bridge across the river, and the Gurkhas in a ferocious kukri charge cleared the key village of San Angelo on the other bank. The Poles, working painfully against the mountain grain, began to make slow but steady progress. Victory had been shaped in the first 24 hours.

On May 18, British tanks had intersected Highway Six beyond Cassino, thus cutting the Germans' main escape route.; Guards mopping up in Cassino town could see through

ISSUED BY THE POLISH GOVERNMENT these stamps commemorate heroism at Cassino. Poles occupied the Monastery after the Germans, who were almost surrounded, had been forced to withdraw.

their field-glasses that the Polish flag was flying over the Monastery. The Germans, practically surrounded, had evacuated their monastic castle-fortress. It was an unforgettable day—exciting, momentous, tragic. For months we had been in the habit of jeeping down Highway Six to a point where the road swings left round a rugged hill and then runs dead straight for three miles into Cassino. It was death to proceed beyond that point in daylight, for the enemy had it under observation and fire. All traffic turned right to the smashed mountain village of Cervaro.

Looking down from the Cervaro heights on that deserted stretch of road one felt very near to the Pearly Gates. Suddenly on that day of victory the traffic no longer turned right but went straight on into Cassino, now that the Monastery was neutralized. Alas, two of my war correspondent colleagues, eagerly following the stream, were accidentally killed by our own mines—Roderick Macdonald, of The News Chronicle, and Cyril Bewley, of Kemsley Newspapers. I automatically turned right and, reaching Polish Corps headquarters, began a crazy trip up to the Monastery. Fifteen or twenty correspondents — mostly American — had arrived with the same intention. We started off in six or eight jeeps, with Polish conducting officers, raising clouds of dust that must have been visible for miles.

Where Every Tree Was Blasted

Eventually we found ourselves climbing the barren hillside in single file, odd mortar bombs lobbing down here and there. Our guides disappeared. Each man blindly followed the man in front, not quite sure where he was going. Those behind me bawled to me not to go so fast ; I shouted to those in front, but without any effect.

Everywhere were the corpses of Indians, Americans, Poles—the dreadful track of war. At one point we were mixed up with the mortar bomb barrage of a counter attack. Sometimes we were following white tapes indicating mine-free paths, sometimes we were blundering along regardless. It was a miracle that none of us was killed.

Running, creeping, cowering, falling flat on our faces from time to time, we finally made it, half-dead with fatigue. We staggered through a wood where every tree was blasted, and then clambered into the white jagged pile that had once been a noble monastery. The surprise was that so much of it remained. In places the crumbling walls were 30 or 40 feet high. Two chapels were practically intact. Much of the cloisters still remained. The crypt had survived, and anyone sheltering in it would have been unhurt.

The stench of burning timbers and rotting bodies is in my nostrils today. In my mind there is the ironic picture of a dove, carved out of stone, over one of the archways, with the Order's motto, "Pax," underneath it. The epitaph of Cassino itself was written by Allied Military Government : "No civil affairs officer will be appointed because there is nothing left to administer."

SUNLIGHT THROUGH THE HEAVY SMOKE-SCREEN over Cassino picks out a spur of Castle Hill. Under cover of this screen New Zealanders entered the town on March 15, 1944, and for eight days amidst the ruins they fought with German parachutists who had been living in cellars and strong-points during the shelling and bombing. PAGE 484 *Photo, Keystone*

Royal Marines 'Beating the Retreat' in Nauplia

UNITS OF THE MEDITERRANEAN FLEET visited Nauplia towards the end of September 1946, and the colourful ceremony (a parade for special occasions) of Beating the Retreat was performed in the main square by a band of the Royal Marines. The Hill of Palamidhi, surmounted by a Venetian fortress, dominates the town, capital of the department of Argolis in the Peloponnesus. The Fleet had been engaged in exercises and after a stay of several days split up in order to call individually at ports in the Aegean Sea.

Photo, G.P.U.

From Alamein to Reunion in London's Albert Hall

FIVE THOUSAND MEN who fought at El Alamein gathered at the Royal Albert Hall on Oct. 23, 1946, to celebrate the fourth anniversary of the opening of the battle. Addresses were delivered by Mr. Winston Churchill (1), who used the occasion to remind his audience and the B.B.C. listeners that "Up to Alamein we survived. After Alamein we conquered and never stopped conquering until the final victory was achieved," and by Field-Marshal Montgomery (2). At the concert that followed old comrades (3) sang "Roll Out the Barrel" and "Bless 'Em All," and "Lili Marlene," the song introduced into the desert by the Germans and which the 8th Army adopted as its own—and the years rolled back to desert days of sizzling heat, dust storms and nights of bitter cold, recalled to his men (4) by Monty. Some of the nursing sisters who staffed the hospitals not far behind the lines were also present (5).

Photos, Keystone, Associated Press, G.P.U.

First U.S. Warship to Visit the Port of London

ANCHORED IN THE THAMES, off Greenwich, the U.S. anti-aircraft cruiser Spokane (1), said to have a speed of over 40 knots, was on a four days' goodwill visit in October 1946. Her commander, Captain L. Edson Crist (2), unlike many Americans, prefers tea to coffee, which is being served by a Filipino steward. Many members of the crew are quite young (3), and a number of them have relatives in Great Britain. Admiral R. L. Conolly, commander of the U.S. Naval Forces in Europe and the 12th Fleet, addressed the crew when he officially took over the 6,000-ton cruiser as his flagship (4). "The People of Britain," he reminded them, "were in the War two years before us. These people over here are worthy of your respect and consideration. Remember that when you go ashore." The jeep being unloaded (5) from the Spokane will help to solve the transport problem ashore.

Photos, G.P.U., Planet News

HIS MAJESTY'S SHIPS   H.M.S. Illustrious

F IRST fleet aircraft carrier to be completed after the outbreak of war, H.M.S. Illustrious, of 23,000 tons, was launched at Barrow in 1939. Her outstanding achievement, as flagship of Rear-Admiral (now Admiral Sir Lumley) Lyster, was at Taranto on the night of November 11, 1940, when her Swordfish aircraft struck a crippling blow at the Italian fleet as it lay in harbour. The battleship Conte di Cavour sustained injuries from which she never recovered, and two other battleships were put out of action for some months. While helping to escort a convoy to Malta in January 1941, the Illustrious became the target for six air attacks, in one of which 40 German dive-bombers secured a number of hits. On fire fore and aft and with her steering gear out of control, the carrier fought her way through to Malta, where temporary repairs were effected in spite of further air attacks. Ultimately she reached Alexandria, and thence proceeded to the U.S.A. for refit.

Present during the occupation of Diego Suarez, Madagascar in 1942, and at the Salerno landings in 1943, the Illustrious went East again in 1944. She took part in a surprise raid on enemy airfields in Northern Sumatra in April of that year, and a month later was concerned in a similar raid on the naval base at Surabaya, Java. In June targets for her aircraft were at Port Blair, in the Andaman Islands, followed by a successful attack on the port of Sabang, Sumatra, on July 25. In the early months of 1945 she was one of the carriers whose aircraft wrecked oil refineries in Southern Sumatra; and in the attack on the Saki group of the Ryukyu Islands, south-west of Japan, she wore the flag of Vice-Admiral Sir Philip Vian. On this occasion she was narrowly missed by Japanese suicide aircraft.

Photo, Charles E. Brown

The Long-Drawn Battle of the Atlantic

GERMANY surrendered on May 7, 1945... Nearly 18 months later there has appeared an official account of the ceaseless struggle to defeat the U-boat campaign against seaborne commerce. Published by H.M. Stationery Office at the modest price of one shilling, it is described in the opening chapter as, "The abbreviated story of a few of the more important highlights in the several phases of a ruthless and protracted campaign which, but for the grace of God, might well have brought about not merely the defeat of Britain and the disruption of the British Empire but the eventual Axis domination of the world."

It will be generally agreed that the author, understood to be Captain Taprell Dorling, D.S.O., R.N., has done admirable work in this chronicle, titled The Battle of the Atlantic, more especially in view of the limited space afforded. The narrative is divided into eight phases, covering the respective periods, September 1939–June 1940; June 1940–March 1941; March to December 1941; January-July 1942; August 1942–May 1943; June-August 1943; September 1943-April 1944; and May 1944-May 1945.

"UNTIL the very end the German U-boat arm fought with discipline and efficiency.... Had the U-boat war continued for any appreciable period, it would have imposed an increased and severe strain upon Allied resources.... New and improved types were coming into operation."

During the first phase the enemy attack was held until, by the middle of March 1940, "the offensive had died away." This was due mainly to the prompt institution of the convoy system and the efficiency of the Asdic method of locating submarines under water. With the fall of France and the entry of Italy into the war the situation changed radically for the worse. "Air and U-boat bases were available to the enemy in Norway and the Biscayan ports of France. The capture of Asdic material supplied to the French may have helped the enemy to work out tactics to frustrate it...." Losses in escort craft during the evacuation of the British Army from France had been serious, and these forces had to be built up anew.

Worst Period for Shipping Losses

In the meantime the Germans reaped a heavy harvest, 152 merchant ships of 747,000 tons being sent to the bottom by submarine attack alone during June, July and August 1940. Moreover, the enemy had developed a new technique: using their U-boats as submersible surface torpedo boats at night, thus defeating the Asdic. In September, 59 ships of 295,000 tons were sunk; and in October, 63 of 352,000 tons. Partly owing to winter weather, things quieted down in the four ensuing months. In January 1941 one notable event was chronicled—the first unaided success of a Coastal Command aircraft. This was a Sunderland which caught the Italian submarine Marcello on the surface and destroyed her by depth charges.

In March 1941 the enemy's spring offensive opened. Most fortunately, British countermeasures, built up slowly and painfully as the result of the winter's experience, proved effective to the extent of sinking seven U-boats —the highest figure for any month since the war began. Among them were those commanded by the three most able German submarine captains—Prien, Schepke and Kretschmer. The two former were killed and the latter made prisoner.

Attempts to supplement the U-boat attack by surface raiding were scotched when the Scharnhorst and Gneisenau were driven into Brest; and the destruction of the Bismarck in May was a severe blow to the enemy. Yet

OFFICIAL account of the fight against the U-boats in the Atlantic by the British and Allied navies, air forces and merchant navies, 1939-45, is here reviewed by

FRANCIS E. McMURTRIE

the total British, Allied and neutral loss through all causes in the three months to the end of May totalled 412 ships of 1,691,499 tons, worse than any corresponding period of the war up to then. In June the first escort carrier, H.M.S. Audacity, was at sea. Losses were slightly less, while six enemy submarines were destroyed. In July and August there was further improvement; and the first instance of a German submarine surrendering was recorded. This was U-570, afterwards H.M.S. Graph (see illus. page 497, Vol. 8). A new type of net defence was fitted to a few ships about this time. By the end of the war 700 vessels had these nets.

Exceptionally bad weather was encountered in the Atlantic for the last three months of 1941, and losses fell accordingly. But December witnessed the entry of Japan into the war, bringing fresh encouragement to our enemies and placing a further strain upon our

KITE BALLOONS PROTECTING COASTAL CONVOYS against German dive-bombing and mast-high attacks were operated by a special section of the Royal Navy. Ocean-going shipping encountered more complex problems: and in this article the submarine aspect of the Battle of the Atlantic, which began in Sept. 1939, is dealt with.
Photo, Central Press

resources until the United States could bring its weight to bear. Still, the satisfactory number of nine U-boats were accounted for in that month, affording further evidence that counter-measures were gaining ground.

The period from mid-January to the end of July 1942 was the worst of the whole war as regards shipping losses, which totalled 495 vessels of over 2,500,000 tons, including 142 tankers. Enemy submarine losses numbered 42. Most of the sinkings were on the far side of the Atlantic, off the coast of the United States and in the Caribbean. The U.S. Navy was short of surface vessels and aircraft to patrol this vital area, though the Royal Navy sent 10 corvettes and 24 trawlers to assist. Not until May was a convoy system brought into force. Another anti-submarine weapon was brought into use during these months. This was the Hedgehog, a mortar which fired a salvo of 24 depth charges, each containing 32 lb. of explosive, ahead of a ship. Three years later it was to some extent superseded by the Squid, a three-barrelled mortar which fires a pattern of large charges ahead of a ship with great accuracy.

BY August 1942 new U-boats were coming from the builders faster than they could be destroyed. Attacks were now being made chiefly by "wolf packs" against the North Atlantic convoys, as the American seaboard had ceased to be the "U-boat paradise" which the Germans had at first found it.

Several grain ships and tankers were fitted with flight decks to carry aircraft for their defence; these became known as "Mac" ships (see illus. page 540, Vol. 9). Still more valuable were the escort carriers, of which by the end of 1942 the Royal Navy had six in commission. These were ultimately able to bridge the mid-ocean gap between the extreme ranges of land-based aircraft on either side of the Atlantic.

In spite of the successful landings in North Africa, November 1942 was the worst month of the war for mercantile losses, which totalled 134 ships of 800,000 tons. December and January were better; and though the improvement was not maintained in February, 20 U-boats were sunk. In March the submarine effort reached its peak, with 112 U-boats at sea; losses totalled 108 ships of 627,000 tons, against which U-boats disposed of numbered 15.

During April and May 1943 the offensive at sea passed to the Allies and was never again relinquished. For the first time some of the U-boat captains showed signs of losing heart. In addition to much stronger escorts they had to contend with independent support groups, which hunted the U-boats wherever they could be found. Most celebrated of these was the Second Escort Group under the late Captain F. J. Walker, which destroyed more U-boats than any other (see portrait in page 223, Vol. 8). Improved co-operation between ship and aircraft was one of the secrets of success against the U-boats.

THOUGH the Germans gained temporary successes by the use of fresh devices, such as the acoustic torpedo (homed on to its target by the noise of the propeller), or the "Schnorkel" breathing tube (see illus. page 681, Vol. 8), our own scientists contrived always to keep a move or two ahead of the enemy's. Fortunately we never had to face a full attack from the new submarines which were being assembled when the war ended. Able to travel under water at a speed of 25 knots, these would have been very difficult to defeat.

April 1944 saw the loss of only nine Allied merchantmen from submarine attack, the lowest figure for four years. This was particularly encouraging on the eve of the Normandy landings. During that operation the attempts of the U-boats to interfere met with disaster, notwithstanding the employment of the Schnorkel device by the enemy. In the first six months of 1944 the Germans lost 122 U-boats. By the end of the war Norwegian waters were practically the only area in which they could find any refuge from attacks. The final U-boat sinking of the war was achieved on May 7, 1945, by a Catalina of 210 Squadron in Danish waters.

Notable Travellers Seen by Our Roving Camera

AUSTRIAN CHILDREN from former concentration camps of Europe recently arrived in England (left) where new homes will be found for them. Most have lost their parents and are in the care of the Christian Executive Committee. Physically, they have recovered amazingly quickly from years of neglect and malnutrition.

FROM FRANCE children of former Resistance workers come to enjoy a holiday at Wren's Warren Camp, near Hartfield, Sussex, where they were visited by Mrs. Attlee, and M. Massigli, the French Ambassador (right). It was arranged that after the month's holiday the children would stay in British homes for a further eight weeks. The visit was organized by the Reception Committee for Young People of Occupied Countries, who have also brought parties of Dutch and Czech children to England.

MAJOR-GENERAL G. H. A. MAC-MILLAN will succeed Lieut.-General Sir Evelyn Barker as C.-in-C. of the British Forces in Palestine on Feb. 1, 1947. He has been Director of Weapons and Development at the War Office since May 1945.

GIFT FROM SOUTH AFRICA TO BRITAIN, a gold certificate worth £985,000, was handed to Mr. Clement Attlee at No. 10 Downing Street by Field-Marshal Smuts (left foreground) on Oct. 18, 1946, to be used for the benefit of the British. In addition there was a bank draft for £196,625 from Durban and the province of Natal.

GIRLS FROM THE BALTIC STATES arrived in England in October 1946 to take up domestic work in sanatoria—the first displaced persons to be permitted to leave their camps in the British zone of Germany to start a new life in Britain.

Photos, Topical, Planet News. P.A.-Reuter, I.N.P.

PAGE 490

SIDKY PASHA AND MR. BEVIN had discussions in London in October 1946 on the revision of the Anglo-Egyptian Treaty of 1936. The Egyptian Premier (left) hoped to return with fresh proposals regarding the Sudan

The Duke of Wellington's Regiment

By Major S. E. BAKER, T.D.

THE 1st Battalion was one of the first to land in France in 1939, followed by the 2/6th and 2/7th in the early spring of 1940. The 1st Battalion fought an heroic battle as part of the rearguard at Dunkirk, and suffered about 250 casualties during the evacuation. The 2/6th and 2/7th had been in action south of the Somme at that time, continued to fight valiantly with the French, suffered heavy casualties, and were eventually evacuated from St. Valery or farther south.

The heroism of the 2nd Battalion during the First Burma Campaign, 1942, has seldom been equalled. Without respite or relief or adequate sleep, and sometimes without food for as long as six days at a time, they were part of a force which, for over two months, held a Japanese force three times their size and regularly reinforced with fresh troops. Over and over again in the course of the fighting, often hand-to-hand, it seemed that the limit of human endurance had been reached, but they fought on, and the gallantry with which Rangoon was defended could not have been surpassed. When the inevitable withdrawal started the Dukes fought tooth and nail to keep open their lines of communication, and when the Sittang river was reached they constantly counter-attacked to maintain a bridge-head on the far side, to enable the whole force to get away. Their gallantry was unavailing, and on the morning of February 23, 1942, the bridge had to be blown up, with most of the Dukes on the wrong side of it, and then began, as one man described it, "a party which made even Dunkirk look like a picnic." The river was some 800 yards wide and very swift, and the men had to swim across, bombed, shelled, and machine-gunned from the air, under the blaze of a Burma sun. Those who could not swim improvised rafts and kicked their way across. Doors and rafts were launched, the wounded were gently lowered upon them and the men, acting as outboard motors, ferried them across the river; all this under a terrific hail of Japanese fire.

Mopping-Up in a Grove of Olives

The 1st Battalion, 1/4th Battalion (now the 58th Anti-Tank Regiment), and the 8th Battalion (now the 145th Regiment, R.A.C.), all fought magnificently throughout the North Africa campaign, 1943, with the 1st Army. The 1st Battalion was in the thick of it; amongst their notable engagements were those of Banana Ridge, Point 174 and Bou Aoukaz. The 145th Regt., R.A.C. (8th Battalion, Duke of Wellington's Regiment) landed in Africa on April 19, 1943, to join the 1st Army. During the remainder of the North Africa campaign they were constantly in action and won great honour in supporting the infantry; the Regiment did not go into action as a complete unit but Squadrons were detailed individually, and occasionally a Squadron found itself supporting its own 1st Battalion. It is impossible to give here details of all the actions in which the Regiment was engaged; the following, which is typical of them, occurred when C Squadron was supporting the attack on Banana Ridge on April 23, an action in which the 1st Battalion Duke of Wellington's Regiment were also heavily engaged.

The object of the attack was the capture of dominating high ground east of Grich-el-Oued and the exploitation and mopping-up of the village and olive grove to the north. At 10 a.m. the infantry advanced across very

THE Regiment was formed in 1881 by the linking of the 33rd and 76th Foot, with both of which the first Duke of Wellington had been intimately connected. The 33rd Foot, now the 1st Battalion, was raised in 1782, and in 1853 adopted the crest and motto of the late Duke of Wellington, the crest now being worn as a cap badge. The 76th Foot, now the 2nd Battalion, was raised in 1787, and for distinguished service in India was granted the badge of elephant with howdah and mahout, now worn as a collar badge. Immediately prior to the Second Great War second-line units of the four Territorial Battalions were formed; and after Dunkirk the 8th, 9th and 10th (raised during the 1914–18 war) were revived. During the late war some of the Battalions were converted into R.A.C., A.A. Units, Searchlights and Anti-Tank Regiments, but continued to wear the "Duke's" badges and red Regimental lanyard.

open ground, and the Squadron leader employed smoke to blind the enemy observation posts. The wire was gaped through the enemy positions and the tanks passed through while the infantry were ferreting out the trenches and dug-outs. The second-in-command gave very valuable assistance from the left flank throughout, shooting up an anti-tank gun and two machine-gun nests in the objective area. Some crews then dismounted and cleared enemy trenches on the left, while two tanks moved to position on the left to engage enemy groups who were trying to escape westward. No. 12 Troop on the right flank destroyed a 50-mm. anti-tank gun on the edge of the village and then supported an infantry platoon in mopping-up, covered by No. 13 Troop, who destroyed a machine-gun position and two mortar observation posts. The village was intensely mined and booby-trapped. Mopping-up in the olive grove was carried out by 12 and 13 Troops, with two or three infantry on each tank to mop up "the bushes." Considering the great severity of the action and the object attained the casual-

ties sustained were very light in what was the opening of the final assault on Tunis.

The 58th Anti-Tank Regt. R.A. (4th Battalion Duke of Wellington's Regt.) arrived in North Africa in the early days of 1943 and, like the 145th Regt. R.A.C., were in action throughout the campaign in their role of infantry support. Like the 145th they, too, were not normally used as a regiment but the individual batteries usually worked as a unit.

The 58th landed at Salerno on D-Day plus 5 and, except for one short break, were in action till the end of the European War and endured the misery of the Gothic Line during the winter of 1944-5 without losing an iota of its morale or offensive spirit.

THE 145th Regt. R.A.C. (8th Battalion Duke of Wellington's Regt.) arrived at Naples during the early days of April 1944 to take part in the Italian campaign and were, from that time, constantly in action till nearly the end of the war. Their role was similar to that in North Africa, though here they were often employed as a complete regiment. The crossing of the River Savio was due to commence on the night of October 21–22, 1944, with the Regiment in support of the Canadian Infantry Brigade. Infantry companies crossed, but were forced back for want of armour, and no bridge-head could be established to allow the bridging of the river for the tanks to get across. On the 24th information came through that the Germans had had enough and were pulling out. B Squadron were ordered to stand by, and after some delay crossed the river, about noon. Then the Squadron supported the infantry and, as each bound of the advance was reached, the tanks helped in the consolidation of it: hard slogging under bad conditions, with the object of keeping the Germans continually on the run and giving them as little time as possible to prepare their next defence position.

Anzio produce probably "the finest hour" of the 1s Battalion. Having indulged

MEN OF THE DUKE OF WELLINGTON'S REGIMENT support a light tank as it goes forward to reconnoitre a crossing at Clery, north-west of Peronne, France, in March 1940. The white tapes in this hitherto unpublished photograph outline a defence post that will be dug when the reconnaissance has been made.

War Office photograph

QUAINT SETTING FOR A CONCERT—but these members of the Duke of Wellington's Regiment, though on active service, have nothing more serious to contend with for the time being than exercises, many of which were undertaken in France in 1939-40. Even exercises have their spells of inactivity, best filled in with music and song. *War Office photograph*

in the bloodless occupation of Pantelleria, the 1st landed at Anzio with the leading troops and, after the brief lull following the landing, fought tooth and nail to retain the precarious occupation of the beach-head. When the perimeter of the beach-head was so small that landing craft were constantly under fire, the Dukes pushed out a " carbuncle " in the direction of Campoleone Station to a depth of three miles. The Germans attacked with great ferocity and nipped off the bulge and the Dukes had then to fight their bloody way back. This they did, but losses were heavy—approximately 300 casualties in this particular operation alone. During the operations at Anzio, Lieut.-Colonel B. W. Webb-Carter, the Commanding Officer of the Battalion, was awarded a bar to the D.S.O. he won during the campaign in North Africa.

For its work at Anzio the Battalion was given the honour of leading the victory march into Rome in June 1944, when General Mark Clark, 5th Army Commander, took the salute. Later, in the Gothic Line, the Battalion was engaged in bitter fighting, and it was during this time that Private R. H. Burton won the first Regimental V.C. of the War (portrait in page 664, Vol. 8).

The 6th and 7th Battalions, which after a period of service in Iceland had been undergoing strenuous training in various parts of this country, landed together in France shortly after D-Day. Both were heavily engaged during the early days, when the British and Canadian forces held the German attack round Caen while the Americans broke through on the right. The 6th Battalion, about 10 days after they landed, were called

Colours: Red triangle surrounded by three black ones

3RD (BRITISH) DIVISION

NAMED the ''Ironsides,'' in 1940, by Field-Marshal Viscount Montgomery of Alamein when in command of the Division, the 3rd, a Regular Army formation, is proud of three distinctions. It was the last (and only) unit to come out of France at Dunkirk as a division ; it was the first back, being the British 2nd Army's assault division on D-Day, June 6, 1944 ; and it is the only British infantry division which fought throughout from D-Day to VE-Day, May 8, 1945.

After taking the fiercely held Calvados beach in Normandy on D-Day, the 3rd linked up with the British Airborne troops at Benouville, and Bielville was reached on the same day. In the Château de Londe area they fought the battle of the ''bloodiest square mile,'' and were subjected to heavy shelling until the middle of July 1944. This vital role in the battle for Caen resulted in the town falling to the Division on July 12. Fighting in the Bocage country, the Division's first V.C. was gained by Cpl. S. Bates (portrait in page 599, Vol. 8), at Sourdville, on August 1.

RAPIDLY advancing through France and Belgium, in September Holland was entered and the towns of Weert and Helminde taken. At Graves an assault crossing of the Maas was successfully undertaken and U.S. Airborne troops relieved. In October the battles for Venray and Overloon were among the fiercest experienced by the Division. From November, the 3rd ''watched'' the Maas until February 1945, when, in Germany, engagements were fought at Hevenheim, Winnekendonk and Kervenheim. At the last-named the Division's second V.C. was gained by Pte. J. Stokes (portrait in page 216, Vol. 9). Crossing the Rhine after the major Allied assault on March 24 the 3rd advanced to Nordhorn, and to the Dortmund-Ems Canal at Lingen. Switched to a new sector, the Division cleared Wildeshausen, Brinkum, Stuhr and Arsten before entering Bremen, May 5, 1945.

WAITING TO SAIL FOR NORWAY in April 1940, a sergeant of the Duke's holds an inspection of anti-gas equipment. The troops are on board the Polish liner Sokieski, which was used as a troopship for some months during the early stages of the war and is here seen lying off Gourock, at the mouth of the Clyde. PAGE 492 *War Office photograph*

upon to bear the brunt of a furious German counter-attack in which they suffered severely. The Dukes were ordered to attack the Parc de Boislande, a big wooded area with a château in the centre. No air support was possible, owing to the weather, and the Germans offered very stiff resistance, especially by mortar and machine-gun fire. The attack was pressed home with great determination and the objective was taken in four hours. But the cost had been very heavy, including a large number of officers and senior N.C.O.s.

No immediate counter-attack was launched, but on the following morning, after a heavy barrage of mortar and medium gun fire, during which the 6th suffered more casualties, the German infantry came forward in overwhelming strength, supported by tanks.

The 'Dukes' Lead the Victory March Into Rome

FOR ITS WORK AT ANZIO the 1st Battalion The Duke of Wellington's Regiment was given the honour of leading the Victory March into Rome in June 1944, General Mark Clark, U.S. 5th Army Commander, taking the salute (top). At Ronta (below), in the Apennines, men of the Regiment began the long struggle to pierce the mountain range and gain the plain of Lombardy; the village was demolished by the Germans before they withdrew, leaving snipers and booby traps to impede the advance.

War Office photographs

NIGHT PATROL RETURNED FROM DUNKIRK reports to an officer : the 5th Battalion The Duke of Wellington's Regiment was present at the investment of the town, where more than 10,000 Germans offered stubborn resistance. Allied activity was confined to night patrols and harassing fire, and the garrison held out from Sept. 1944 until May 11, 1945.   *War Office photograph*

Gradually the Dukes, fighting every yard, were forced back. Many examples of collective and individual heroism are on record during this retirement, which helped to break the impetus of the German attack. The Battalion was nearly decimated, and, shortly after, was evacuated to this country to refit.

THE 7th Battalion was engaged throughout the campaign in north-west Europe and no adequate record of its achievements can be given here. Typical of the Battalion's work is the operation which saved the Nijmegen bridge-head on December 4, 1944. The 7th were holding the right flank of the bridge-head in close contact with the Boche. There was deep flooding of the fields in the area, and movement was impossible during the daytime owing to the vigilance of the enemy.

Patrolling on the night of December 3–4 found the Hun active and full of fight ; at about three in the morning heavy Spandau firing and mortaring was directed against the forward platoons of D and B Companies. The Commander of 18 Platoon, D Company, reported by phone that two of his sections had been overwhelmed by at least a platoon of Germans but that he, at the moment, had been by-passed.

A few minutes later he said that more than a company had gone through and more were following. Considerable casualties had been caused to the enemy by Platoon Headquarters and the section still in action. A minute later, communication with the platoon ceased ; it had been overrun by sheer weight of numbers on a narrow front. The situation

at Battalion Headquarters was now becoming very sticky ; the Germans had occupied some school buildings about 200 yards away and were endeavouring to push on.

The Boche swept down the road past 18 Platoon of D Company and came in contact with the reserve platoon of C Company, which opened fire, and the Boche toppled like ninepins. The Platoon Commander held the enemy all night, firing till his ammunition was exhausted.

The Battalion Commander realized that the gap in the bridge-head, in the vicinity of No. 18 Platoon, must be closed, and he ordered Major G. V. Fancourt, Officer Commanding C Company, to use one platoon and his section of carriers to regain the 18 Platoon position. This was speedily carried out by 15 Platoon under the command of Lieutenant D. R. Siddall and the position restored after sharp fighting. The Germans were still occupying much of the village, but at daybreak they started to withdraw. They had converted some houses into strong-points and were putting up fierce resistance, and in the attack on one house, defended by several Spandaus, a number of men had been killed.

Surrounded and Without Ammunition

After P.I.A.T.s had failed to penetrate the solid concrete of this house plans for bringing up an anti-tank gun and the wasp flame-throwing section were made, but their help was not required. A report arrived that the main force of the Boche had surrendered, and 60 prisoners under escort were seen marching through the village. The enemy in the house defended by Spandaus saw that the game was up and showed the white flag. When the ground, originally occupied by Lieutenant Evans of 18 Platoon, was regained it was found that he had succeeded in denying his Platoon Headquarters to the enemy, though he had been completely surrounded and had used up all his ammunition. At 11 o'clock Brigade was informed that the situation was back to normal ; the Nijmegen bridge was saved.

In the course of the operations the following decorations were won by the Battalion. Both Commanding Officers, Lieut.-Col. (now Brigadier) J. H. O. Wilsey and Lieut.-Col. C. D. Hamilton, were awarded the D.S.O. Fourteen officers gained the M.C., two Other Ranks won the D.C.M., one an M.M. and Bar, and 12 the M.M. Fifteen officers and men were mentioned in dispatches, and three won the French Croix-de-Guerre.

THE 5th Battalion Duke of Wellington's Regiment was converted into Searchlights, under a storm of protest, prior to the war. After being attached to the Royal Engineers they subsequently became the 143rd Regiment R.A., and finally the 500th Regiment R.A., but they have always considered themselves Dukes and they wear the regimental badges. They hope that they will be allowed to resume their role as an Infantry Battalion of the Dukes. The Regiment was on service in this country till the early part of 1945. Their role was not spectacular, but very essential, and many of the sites occupied by the section were in exposed places where amenities were extremely few. But the Regimental spirit prevailed, and later they went to B.L.A. as part of the Dunkirk Force which had the mopping-up of the Channel ports. The unit is now doing garrison duty in Germany and calls itself the 5th Battalion Duke of Wellington's Regiment.

The 9th Battalion were converted to the 146th Regiment R.A.C. (D.W.R.) in 1941, left for India in 1942, and saw service in Burma in 1944–45. The Regiment did not go into action as a whole, though various detachments saw service, generally in support of the 26th Indian Division.

RIDING INTO BATTLE ON TANKS, Yorkshiremen captured the town of Ede, west of Arnhem, on April 17, 1945. Units of the 49th (West Riding) Division, including the Dukes, carried out the attack, supported by tanks of the 5th Canadian Armoured Division. The 1st Canadian Army comprised several British formations.   PAGE 494   *War Office photograph*

'The Isles of Greece, the Isles of Greece! ...

THE Byronic dream of freedom for Greece (for which the poet gave his life at Missolonghi in 1824) became an actuality in 1829 when the country was declared an independent monarchy (see illus. page 1), though the Dodecanese (from the Greek for " twelve islands ") remained under Turkish rule. This group of islands in the Aegean Sea, clustered along the coast of Asia Minor, comprises Symi, Patmos, Leros, Cos, Niceros, Carpathos, Casos, Charki, Tilos, Astropalia, Lipso and Calimno ; Rhodes is usually included, making 13.   For six centuries their control had been disputed, many Powers casting envious eyes thereon, the people meanwhile remaining essentially Greek in language, mentality and traditions.

IN 1911 Italy occupied the Dodecanese, and these—of great strategic value —should have come into Allied hands during the Second Great War, after the Italian armistice with the Allies on September 8, 1943.   But the Italian garrison on Rhodes, the seat of Italian administration, surrendered to the Germans after the latter, incensed by the defection of their ally, had launched a dive-bombing attack. Small Allied forces were at once landed on Cos, Leros and Samos but were overwhelmed by German landings. Italian

garrisons of Patmos, Niceros and Lipso were likewise forced to capitulate. The islands continued to be bombed by Allied air forces and raided by Commandos until the surrender of German forces in the Aegean, which took place in May 1945 on Symi, where (1) a view of the harbour is seen. After the announcement on June 27, 1946, that the Conference of Foreign Ministers in Paris had unanimously decided that the Dodecanese should be ceded by Italy to Greece an aircraft from Athens dropped Greek flags on all the islands : Patmos flew hers from the top of the monastery belfry (2).   In meditative mood sits a woman of Leros in richly embroidered national costume (3).

Scenes in the Long-Lost Islands of Greece—

Glorious pages are enshrined in the long history of Rhodes, centre of culture in ancient times, and it made news headlines in the Second Great War. It had its share of bombing and shelling : inhabitants are clearing away the debris (1). In this street (2) is still preserved the atmosphere of a medieval city. Used by the Germans during the War, the large Italian-built aerodrome (3) was bombed consistently by the Allies. This hill-top shrine (4) shared in the damage.

THE W

— *That Have Now Been Restored to the Motherland*

Through many ground-strafing raids by the Germans on Cos, in September 1943, the guns of the R.A.F. Regiment were the
island's only defence against air attack (see page 310, Vol. 8). A view from Kephalos (5), on the south-west coast, where
a new spring has been brought into operation by U.N.R.R.A. Pottery making (6) is one of the crafts of Cos. Though
one of the most agriculturally developed of the Dodecanese, threshing (7) is still carried out with oxen.

Time and Mood for Joyous Living

The national dance (1) of the Dodecanese is performed lightheartedly once more in Emborio, village of Niceros. The lyre and guitar (2) are heard throughout Carpathos, where in the mountain village of Othoz (3) women toe the steps of a traditional dance, and overlooking the quiet bay (4) the Greek flag serenely flutters.

Exclusive to THE WAR ILLUSTRATED

Goering: Architect of Aggression

GOERING has died as he had lived, dramatically. His suicide in the condemned cell at Nuremberg—virtually on the threshold of the execution shed, under the eyes of his guard and, indeed, of the world—might have been devised by a master of melodrama. It was the final unexpected twist to a story of which the ending had seemed wholly inevitable and predictable, the last turn of the screw.

So he joined Hitler and Himmler, Goebbels and Ley in the company of those Nazi leaders who cheated judicial punishment. It was an ending pre-eminently in keeping with his leadership of the accused in the dock, with his last defiant oration in which he sought to perpetuate the hollow myths of his master. It was, in fact, an epitome of his stormy, adventurous career.

Founder of the Gestapo, creator and supreme commander of the Luftwaffe, successor-designate to the Fuehrer, he had been condemned by the Nuremberg Tribunal for guilt "unique in its enormity." Second only to Hitler, he was the motive-power of Nazi politics and German aggression.

HERMANN Wilhelm Goering was born on January 12, 1893, at Rosenheim, Bavaria. He was the son of a judge who had been appointed by Bismarck as the first Commissioner in what was then the German colony of South-West Africa.

In the war of 1914–18 he served first as an infantry officer on the Western Front. Soon he transferred to the air force, became an ace pilot and obtained the most coveted Prussian decoration, the Order Pour le Mérite. Ultimately he was selected by his brother officers as Richthofen's successor in command of the famous "Death Squadron." Republican Germany was little to his liking. On his own admission he never forgot the humiliation of having his ribbons and badges of rank torn from his uniform by revolutionaries. The bitter memory was to bear fruit, 15 years later, in his ruthless suppression of Socialists and Communists.

Four Years in Impoverished Exile

He went to Denmark. For a year he was adviser to a Danish civil aviation company, and from 1920 to 1921 he was director and chief pilot of the Swedish concern Svenska Lufttrafik. Returning to Germany, he became interested in the political programme of an obscure and derided agitator named Adolf Hitler. In 1922 he joined the National Socialist party. Backed by his reputation as a war ace, he rapidly gained prominence in the movement. His first major task was to organize the newly formed S.A., or Storm Troops. By the summer of 1923 he was commanding the picked body known as the Hitler Shock Troops.

In the Munich putsch of November 8 and 9, 1923, Goering marched with Hitler and Ludendorff in the front rank of the Nazi demonstrators. But their premature attempt at a *coup d'état* was frustrated. Goering, seriously wounded, escaped across the Austrian frontier to Innsbruck, recovered and went on to Italy. He was sentenced in his absence to five years' imprisonment. The next four years he spent in impoverished exile in Rome and Stockholm, working for a short time as a commercial traveller—apparently the only civilian post he held after leaving the Swedish company in 1921.

Meanwhile, Hitler had been released in December 1924 from the Landsberg fortress, having dictated "Mein Kampf" to his cellmate, Rudolf Hess. The Nazi movement was again in being. Hindenburg proclaimed a general amnesty for political offenders, and in 1927 Goering returned to Germany. He

RISE to power and final crash of the Nazi leader who cheated the hangman on October 15, 1946, as outlined in The Daily Telegraph by Hugh Sutherland. See also pages 431–435.

immediately rejoined Hitler. In May 1928 he was elected to the Reichstag as one of 12 Nazi deputies. As the Fuehrer was not himself a member, it fell to Goering to lead the group through the years of stress which preceded the collapse of the Weimar Republic.

Inexorably his power increased, for the times were propitious. By September 1930 the Nazis had 107 members and formed the second largest party in the Reich. By August 1932 he had become President of the Reichstag. On January 29, 1933, Hitler became Chancellor, the Nazis assumed power and, with the rest of them, Goering had arrived.

He became Cabinet Minister Without Portfolio, Reich Commissioner for Air,

FOUNDER OF THE GESTAPO—Goering in the uniform of a Field-Marshal of the Luftwaffe, shortly after his capture. He was deprived of his rank and decorations before his trial.
Photo, Associated Press

Prussian Minister of the Interior and presently Prussian Prime Minister. It is now established that, on the night of February 27, 1933, he contrived the Reichstag fire, pretext for outlawing the Communists and prelude to a trial in which he was badly bested by the defendant Dimitrov. A Dutch imbecile, Van der Lubbe, was beheaded as the scapegoat.

Appointing himself Chief of the Prussian Police, Goering founded the Gestapo, instigated the concentration camps and remorselessly "liquidated" the Fuehrer's opponents within and without the party. He played a lethal part in Hitler's great purge of June 30, 1934, known as the "Night of the Long Knives." Openly he boasted of his utter lack of scruple. Speaking at Dortmund, he said:

"A bullet fired from the barrel of a police pistol is my bullet. If you say that is murder, then I am the murderer. . . . I know two sorts of law because I know two sorts of men —those who are for us and those who are against us."

ALREADY, unknown to the world at large, he was secretly creating the Luftwaffe. In covert places, defying the Versailles Treaty, as he later declared, production went forward 24 hours a day. In March 1935 the air rearmament of Germany was openly announced by Hitler. In 1936, with the unequivocal slogan "Guns Before Butter," Goering launched Germany on the Four-Year Plan of

Self-Sufficiency. It was, in effect, a mobilization of the country's economy for total war. By 1938, shortly after Munich, he announced a five-fold expansion of the Luftwaffe.

Amid Europe's pre-war crises he was not idle. He played a part even more decisive than that of Hitler in the annexation of Austria in March 1938. On his own admission he inspired the crucial message from Seyss-Inquart, the Austrian Nazi quisling, calling for German troops. A year later Goering was threatening the destruction of Prague by bombing to force the surrender of Dr. Hacha, President of Czechoslovakia.

His "peace moves" on the eve of war were much publicised during the Nuremberg trial. The prosecution was able to show, however, that the terms offered by Hitler were tantamount to a new Munich, another bloodless victory for aggression. Goering was trying, in effect, to prevent Britain from keeping her pledge to Poland. On September 1, 1939, the day of the invasion of Poland, Hitler designated Goering as his successor. A few months later he was appointed Economic Dictator of the Reich, with a view to ensuring "strong and unified leadership in the economic war." Soon after the Nazis' rise to power he had been promoted at one step from captain to general. Five years later he was raised to field-marshal, and in July 1940 he was to become Marshal of the Reich, a rank of which he was the first and only holder.

Haunting the Ruins of the Reich

By that time the variety of his functions was surpassed only by the multiplicity of his uniforms and decorations, which became a stock jest even in Germany. He entertained lavishly amid the barbaric splendours of his Karinhall estate. He filled his house with old masters, *objets d'art* and curios of all kinds —including loot from the battlefronts.

His enormous energy was matched by his flamboyant confidence. He boasted that he would not permit the Ruhr to be the target of "one single bomb from hostile aircraft." By the summer of 1940 he stood at the pinnacle of his power. Nemesis followed swiftly. The Battle of Britain shattered the Luftwaffe's legend of invincibility. As the Allied attacks gained weight the prestige of Goering inevitably declined. It is possible that as early as 1941 he read the omens aright, for towards the end of that year he was planning to invest the enormous sum of £12,500,000 in United States industry—a plan disrupted by Pearl Harbour.

BY 1942 he was gradually fading out of the picture. By 1943, as the war passed its climacteric, his influence over Hitler waned. By D-Day he was in disgrace. Ignored by Hitler, thwarted by Bormann and despised by Himmler, he became a strange, Falstaffian ghost haunting the ruins of the Reich. As the darkness deepened he left Berlin, made his way to Berchtesgaden, and attempted a last-moment palace revolution. He was arrested on Hitler's orders and condemned to death, but a Luftwaffe party set him free.

He fled to Austria, there to be captured by United States troops. In form, as in substance, his power had vanished. The Fuehrer's last will and testament had dismissed him "for negotiating with the enemy and attempting to seize control of the State." Then there came the long wait for the trial in Nazism's own citadel of Nuremberg. In this he filled the role, as it were, of the chief prisoner, and among the fallen tyrants in the dock his was the dominating personality.

In the witness-box Goering made a hard and even an adroit fight for his life, but there was never a shadow of doubt about the guilt of this architect of aggression who in his prime knew neither mercy nor scruple

Europe's Wartime Capitals in 1946

WARSAW

By J. CANG

THE most ruined and devastated capital in Europe, for about six months, from the Warsaw Rising in August 1944 till the middle of January 1945, the Germans methodically dynamited and burned down almost every building in Poland's chief city. Only those the Germans themselves occupied were spared. Of about 25,000 dwelling-houses and offices on both sides of the Vistula—Warsaw proper and its suburb Praga—only 7,000 were habitable after the Germans left and the Russians entered in January 1945. There is not a street, not a lane, not a square in Warsaw without ruins.

It will take a generation at least to clear away the piles of bricks, lime, iron and dust. It is estimated that, in pre-war currency, the damage the Germans caused by the destruction of Warsaw is well over £400,000,000. But such is the attachment of the Polish people to this city that no obstacle would make them abandon the idea of making it again the capital of Poland. Although when liberated from the Germans there was not a single Polish civilian living in the place, there are now over 500,000 people working, living and enjoying life amidst these vast ruins. There are cinemas, cafés, theatres, shops and offices where life is normal, and in them one almost forgets, for the time being, that one is in a devastated city. There are even cafés and restaurants where the dancing and general gaiety are far livelier than in most capitals of Europe today.

Astonishing Stocks in the Shops

The first thing the Government did in order to make Warsaw a capital again was to move the seat of Government from Lublin to Warsaw immediately after its liberation, though there were not sufficient houses to shelter all the administration, which had, for a time, to remain in Praga, on the eastern bank of the Vistula. Now, however, all the Government offices are settled in repaired houses in Warsaw proper. Water, light and gas are available everywhere, and over 5,000 telephones are in use compared with 200 in 1945. Communication is almost normal; trolly buses came from Moscow, U.N.R.R.A. lorries from New York, and some 20 double-decker buses from London. These double-deckers scared people at first; many would

not board them; some would cross themselves in trepidation when forced to look for a seat upstairs. Taxis have recently reappeared, parked outside the Polonia Hotel, the centre of all Warsaw life, high and low.

This hotel was used by the Germans till the last moment of their stay, and so was saved from destruction. Now it houses some 15 of the 20 embassies and legations in Poland. It is a babel of languages, habits, parties and rumours; above all, rumours. There, over whisky, Polish vodka and Russian wine, the wildest rumours are born, denied and born

again. Gossip starting from the porter on the ground floor occasionally becomes a "serious document" by the time it reaches a diplomat's chancery on the sixth, or it turns into a bloodcurdling story in some correspondent's room on any floor of the Polonia.

WARSAW has an abundance of food. It would make any English housewife cry with envy to see the large stocks in the shops—little happy islands in a sea of ruins. You can get as much fish and meat as you like, and butter, eggs, cream, cheese, sugar—even lemons and grape fruit. You can order yourself as much turkey or chicken or steak or schnitzel in the restaurants as you wish. The only restriction is that you cannot have meat on three days in the week, but even then poultry and fish are available. The sale of cakes—some of the most luscious I have ever seen—is also restricted three days in the week, which is no great hardship.

But, whilst offering a foreign visitor the best food any capital in Europe can now offer, Warsaw also asks the highest prices. A luncheon consisting of soup, meat, dessert, beer and coffee will cost at the Polonia restaurant about 500 or 600 zlotys, which is about 30s. at the official rate. Breakfast of eggs and bacon (they always give you three eggs), coffee and rolls, will cost up to 10s. or more. Dinner, again in the Polonia, will cost about the same as lunch, and with drinks, including a couple of vodkas or cocktails, will reach the £2 figure. A room in the Polonia (if you can manage to secure one) costs about £1 per day.

For Poles there are two prices for everything. In the official market they are low, in the free market very high. A pound of butter, for example, costs about 1s. in the officially controlled market and over 5s. in the free market. Meat will be 6d. a pound in the official, and 1s. 6d. in the free, and the same with every other commodity. Workers, officials, and all those employed by the State, whether in factory or office, are entitled to purchase goods at the official price.

All others, such as businessmen, doctors, lawyers, manufacturers, writers working on their own account, must pay the prices in the free market. For instance, an official or worker pays £3 for a suit manufactured in the State-

owned factory. The tailor who is working for himself is compelled to make one or two suits a month at the price of £1 for an official, while to his ordinary customers he will charge £10 for making a similar suit. The same applies to shoes, furniture, carpets and so on.

Salaries and wages are low. The Prime Minister gets about 8,000 zlotys a month, which at the official rate is approximately £20. A post-office official gets just over £3 a month. How do they contrive to exist? Well, their standard of living is generally lower than that of their opposite numbers in Western Europe, and they manage somehow. Normally, the official or worker receives his rations (often hitherto supplied by U.N.R.R.A.), and with the little he is able to buy with his money can make a living. He is entitled to shelter and a meal a day in the place where he works. Even Cabinet Ministers receive their meals from the departmental kitchen. As Warsaw cannot and does not house all the half-million people who work there, many live in the less-damaged suburbs or in the countryside around. There they have vegetable gardens, often orchards, which help out their supplies.

Princes in Search of a Living

In spite of the ruins Warsaw has all the characteristics of a capital. It is full of movement and life. There is a constant rush of traffic, as busy outside the Polonia as in London's Piccadilly Circus. Cafés and restaurants are crowded; so are the streets—those that have been cleared. New shops are being opened every day, mainly provision shops and cafés. The dispossessed gentry, former princes and counts deprived of their large estates by the social revolution, have come to Warsaw in search of a living and small, tastefully arranged cafés and ice-cream shops run by noble ladies are a common feature in present-day Warsaw.

Over 1,000 architects, engineers, town-planners and other specialists are busy preparing details for the building of Poland's new capital. It is to be a model city, free from smoke and other evils of large towns. Warsaw is to be divided into five different sectors: a business centre with banks, shops, offices; an administrative centre, a kind of modern Whitehall; an educational, with the University, museums, libraries; an industrial, and a dwelling centre. There is also to be a separate district near the Royal Lazienki Park which will house all the foreign embassies and legations; here the British and Russian Embassies already have their offices.

It will take many years to clear Warsaw of her ruins, and many more to build a new capital. But the Polish people are determined to attempt it and are hastily laying the foundations for this gigantic task. They have cleared about 50 streets and are daily clearing more. Given years of peace and security they will accomplish their task.

WARSAW TRAFFIC is now almost back to normal. Fewer primitive carts (above) are seen and, an innovation, double-decker motor buses (right) are running. About 20 of the latter arrived from London, and at first people were too scared to board them. Trolly buses came from Moscow, and lorries from New York. Taxis have reappeared.

Amidst Warsaw Ruins a New Capital is Planned

PREPARING DETAILS for the building of Poland's new capital are more than 1,000 architects, engineers, town-planners and other specialists. Their target is a model city replacing the old Warsaw which the war largely destroyed. Essential services have been restored—water, light, gas, telephones; but a generation at least will be required to effect clearance of all the debris. The Poniatowski Bridge (1), which connects the city with the suburb of Praga on the east bank of the Vistula, has already been rebuilt.

The shell of the Prudential Insurance building (2) is included in the many structures that must be demolished to clear the way for reconstruction. The shattered tomb of Warsaw's Unknown Soldier (3) is being restored. Not a street, not a lane, is without ruins: but 50 streets have been cleared and the daily total is mounting. Students are giving their services one day a month for this vital work: some are seen (4) setting out for their labours in Jerozolimska Avenue—imbued with enthusiasm and undaunted by the magnitude of their task. (See also facing page.)

Photos, Associated Press, L.N.A.

FROM DRIFTER TO TABLE is a long and complex journey for the herring. From October until December large numbers of fishing vessels operate from East Coast ports: 42 million herrings were landed at Great Yarmouth in one week of November 1946. Our artist Haworth recently visited the port and his drawing was executed from sketches made at that time. The small inset (bottom, left) shows a drifter with its nets in position, the location of the nets

being marked by coloured buoys. Seventy nets form what is known as a "fleet," and may extend for more than a mile. As soon as a vessel comes alongside the quay the task of unloading the catch (A) is begun. Baskets of fish are swung overside and tipped into large wicker containers (B) called "swills." The latter are then loaded on to carts (C) for delivery to the purchaser. The buyers are able to gauge the value of the catch from the small sample

basket that is sent to the market as soon as the drifter comes alongside. The herrings may be sold fresh, quick-frozen or pickle-cured. In the Mediterranean countries prefer their fish pickled; in the Baltic countries there is a big demand for the "red" herring; the home market has a preference for kippers and bloaters. For kippering, the fish are placed in a gutting-machine and cleaned (D) before being washed (E). After being pickled in brine

for several hours (F) they are opened out, placed on racks (G) and carried into the smoking-kiln (H). Oak shavings supply the heat and smoke (J). After curing the fish are ready for packing. In the preparation of bloaters the fish are not opened but simply soaked in brine for a period, washed and threaded on long rods (K), hung on racks to drain and then placed in the smoke-house. See also facing page.

Britain's Food: from Fishing Grounds to Farm

MEN OF THE EAST COAST HERRING DRIFTERS are not deterred by rough weather ; leaving Yarmouth harbour (1) for the North Sea fishing grounds. The abundant herring ultimately becomes food in one form or another. Fish that would otherwise be wasted may enrich the farmlands as manure, or it may be converted into fish meal—conveyed by factory elevator (2) to a drying plant, the ground-up product being bagged (3) for sale as animal or poultry food. See also facing page.

Photos, Associated Press, Topical

The NCOs ROLL OF HONOUR & MEN
1939—1946

Sgt. N. W. S. ABBOTT
Royal Air Force.
Action: Germany. June 44.
Age 21. (Feltham)

So great has been the response of readers to our invitation to submit portraits for our Roll of Honour that no more can be accepted. But we have every hope of being able to publish all those so far received.

Dvr. H. E. S. ALCOCK
Royal Engineers.
Action: Walcheren. 1.11.44.
Age 19. (Guiseley)

L.A.C. H. ALLEN
Royal Air Force.
In action. 6.5.42.
Age 20. (Dresden)

Sgt. C. J. ALLWRIGHT
1st Hertfordshire Regt.
Action: Bologna. 11.11.44.
Age 28. (London)

Pte. B. ARLISS
1st Parachute Regt.
Action: E. Africa. 28.3.43.
Age 20. (Louth)

L/Cpl. F. ASHWORTH
Glasgow Highlanders.
D/wnds. Holland. 23.9.44.
Age 24. (Oldham)

Ldg/Smn. E. CHARMAN
510 L.C.A. Flotilla, R.N.
Action: Walcheren. 7.11.44.
Age 21. (Chelsea)

Pte. L. CHAPMAN
Gordon Highlanders.
Buchenwald Forest. 8.2.45
Age 32. (Harpenden)

Pte. C. C. CLARIDGE
4th Bn. Suffolk Regt.
Action: Singapore. 22.4.42.
Age 24. (Luton)

A.C.2 A. COLEMAN
Royal Air Force.
Accident: Sudan. 4.7.42.
Age 21. (S. Wigston)

Sgt. A. DENNIS
R. Warwickshire Regt.
Action: Dover. 26.9.44.
Age 32. (Birmingham)

Sgt. D. W. FRANCIS
R. Canadian Regt.
Action: Ortona. 20.12.43.
Age 23. (Toronto)

L/Cpl. A. FALLOWFIELD
R. Norfolk Regt.
Jap. P.O.W. 27.4.45.
Age 24. (Southend-on-Sea)

Pte. W. FALLOWFIELD
Suffolk Regiment.
Action: Burma. 14.4.44.
Age 19. (Southend-on-Sea)

Ldg/Stkr. R. GILTROW
Royal Navy.
Russian convoy. 29.3.42.
Age 45. (Exeter)

Gdsmn. L. C. F. GLEEN
Coldstream Guards.
Action: Italy. 7.8.44.
Age 24. (London)

Cpl. G. E. GOLDSMITH
Honourable Artillery Coy.
In action. April 41.
Age 27. (London)

Gnr. J. W. HARLEY
Royal Artillery.
Action: Cowes. 16.3.41.
Age 21. (Newport)

Sgt. W. F. HARRISON
Royal Air Force.
Action: Denmark. Apl. 44.
Age 31. (London)

Flt./Sgt. D. HARRISON
Pathfinder, R.A.F.
Action: Germany. Feb. 44.
Age 23. (London)

Tpr. A. HOWLETT
12th Bn. R. Tank Regt.
Action: Rimini. 19.10.44.
Age 22. (Burton-on-Trent)

Fus. J. HUGHES
R. Inniskilling Fusiliers.
Action: Italy. 12.10.43.
Age 27. (Widnes)

Pte. S. JENKINS
South Wales Borderers.
Action: Pinwe. 15.11.44.
Age 30. (Salford)

Seaman F. O. MUNDAY
R.N. Patrol Service.
Off Iceland. 3.3.45.
Age 38. (Dartford)

Sgt. D. NORMINGTON
Bomber Command R.A.F.
Action: Cologne. 30.5.42.
Age 23. (Richmond)

Marine H. OGDEN
Royal Marines.
Died of wounds. 15.7.43.
Age 30. (Rochdale)

Sgt. D. S. PHILLIPS
K.O. Scottish Borderers.
Action: W. Europe. 2.3.45.
Age 28. (Bala)

Pte. D. Y. POIGNAND
Hampshire Regiment.
Action: N. Africa. 8.4.43.
Age 24. (Jersey)

Dvr. A. POLLARD
R. Army Service Corps.
Action: Sirte. 13.1.42.
Age 21. (Hanging Heaton)

Pte. W. F. REID
Essex Regiment.
Died of wounds. 8.2.44.
Age 29. (Shoeburyness)

E/R.A. F. SANDFORD
Royal Navy.
Action: Europe. 15.6.44.
Age 21. (Runcorn)

Pte. W. SHAND
Gordon Highlanders.
Action: Italy. 14.12.44.
Age 21. (Aberdeen)

L/Cpl. T. R. SHAW
Royal Engineers.
Action: Tobruk. 16.12.41.
Age 21. (Long Eaton)

Sgt./Plt. R. F. SHIRLEY
Royal Air Force.
Northants. 15.7.42.
Age 19. (Dagenham)

Pte. J. W. WEST
Middlesex Regiment.
Action: Normandy. 21.7.44.
Age 20. (Sutterton)

Dvr. W. WHITE
Royal Signals.
P.O.W. Siam. 13.1.44.
Age 37. (Denton)

L/Cpl. J. S. WILLIAMS
Royal Welch Fusiliers.
Action: Burma. 1.3.45.
Age 31. (Carnarvon)

1st Cl. Boy R. WILLIAMS
Royal Navy.
Action: Malta. 15.2.42.
Age 18. (Normanton)

Wise Pootung Pete of Shanghai Camp

In charge of the health work in civilian internment camps "run" by the Japanese, R. Kenneth McAll, M.B., C.B., a medical missionary of the London Missionary Society, narrates how by means of drawings and posters done with brush and ink in Chinese style he helped through months of confinement to restore and maintain the morale of fellow internees.

ONE day in January 1939 news came to us of a skirmish about 10 miles away, in which twenty Chinese guerillas had been executed by the Japanese. The local populace, searching for loot, had found one of the guerillas still alive and had hidden him in a temple. He had been there ten days. We found him with a great sword gash extending from the back of his neck round to the corner of his mouth : he had refused to kneel down for the stroke and had been too tall for the little Jap to reach properly. We brought him in on a mule cart to hospital and sewed him up.

R. K. McALL

Three months later he asked, in English, for painting materials. He told us he was a graduate of the Peking College of Fine Arts who had been press-ganged into the Communist army. For two years he lived in our house, hiding from Japanese and Communists alike and painting birds and flowers—his speciality. For days he would think about his painting and the meaning he wanted to express, then with a few strokes of his brush would appear the finished product. From him I learned nearly all I know of Chinese art, a gift which has been invaluable to me in more ways than one.

Six of Us Lived in a Lift-Shaft

On March 11, 1943, we waited, cold and wondering, in the garden of Shanghai Cathedral. The Japanese had finally decided that the concentration of enemy aliens in Shanghai was not enough. Some 7,000 British, American and Dutch nationals were to be interned ; 500 of them, mostly men of some prominence, had already been taken without warning. Another 1,000 of us were to be taken up-country and divided between three camps. I and an old schoolfriend who also was a doctor had volunteered to go with our wives, one a doctor and the other a nurse, and our small girls, then 18 months old, to one of these up-country camps, as they were short of medical help there. So here we were with our daughters strapped on our backs, Korean fashion, to leave our hands free for luggage-carrying. We had been allowed to take one trunk each and as much as we could carry in our hands.

To our coat lapels were tied identity labels on which was written our camp, "Civil Assembly Centre B," and our number, 10/175. On the river steamer we were warmed up with small portions of curry and rice, the curry so hot that only the strongest could eat it. There was great excitement among

the guards as we disembarked from the steamer—two of the prisoners were missing. They counted and recounted. Finally someone pointed out the two little figures strapped to their fathers' backs, and all was well.

Our camp was in a mission school compound. We did our best to settle down cheerfully to our life of roll calls, food queues, water carrying and community living ; but for many these first days were very hard. Most of us had lost our homes and nearly all our worldly possessions. There were men whose families had evacuated earlier, and women whose men-folk had joined up, for whom there would be years of separation with a minimum of news. We had to change over suddenly from normal feeding to two helpings a day of soup with bits of vegetable and a few lumps of meat in it and rice of doubtful quality. Sanitary arrangements could be described as primitive, and we had to dig two wells ourselves.

I was put in charge of the public health work, so out came my Chinese brush and ink to produce health posters in Chinese style for the camp. I illustrated such topics as "Did you wash your hands ?" and "Swat that fly" and "Eat your potato skins." At the same time I began to keep a diary of camp life, also done with Chinese brush and ink on the only available paper—a toilet roll. By the end of the War there were 35 yards of drawings. The example of those who were out for the good of everyone gradually bore fruit. When a boy had an attack of acute appendicitis, the whole camp wanted to help. The carpenters prepared a table, the sanitary squad cleaned out a small room, the kitchen staff lit fires and boiled water. An anaesthetic mask was made out of a piece of wire, and the operation was quite successful. In September 1943 we were transferred to

MISSIONARIES' CHILDREN at Pootung improvised their own toys to while away the time in the compound whilst older playmates were in the camp school.

Shanghai, to a camp which had been running for several months for men only. It was an old tobacco factory in Pootung across the river from the city. Conditions here were much worse. Sixteen large rooms housed 1,100 people. Our two small girls were the only young children in the camp, so we were given the privilege of living together in a space half of which had once been the lift-shaft ! The lift was pulled up to the top floor, where another family lived on top of it, while the shaft was boarded over with two heavy doors to make the floor of our room. Our entire space measured 13 feet by 9 feet for the six of us, and through it ran the oily lift cable. However, we had a wooden partition between

AMUSEMENT COMBINED WITH EXHORTATION came from the brush of our contributor. Health posters, as on the left, were backed up with wisecracks about daily occurrences in the camp, in which Pootung Pete (right) figured as a kind of Asiatic "Chad"—unshaven, down-at-heel, but full of infinite wisdom. These drawings were kept going for close on two years.

LIFT-SHAFT HOME FOR SIX, including two small girls, was formed by boarding over the shaft with two heavy doors to form the floor of a room measuring 13 feet by 9 feet. The lift itself was pulled up to the top floor and another family lived on top of it. Sixteen rooms in the old Pootung tobacco factory across the river from Shanghai housed 1,100 people.

us and our neighbours, whereas the rest had nothing—or at best a curtain hung precariously on a piece of string.

There were 38 different nationalities living in the camp, including the crew, mostly "darky," of the S.S. President Harrison ; the leader of one of Shanghai's best dance bands ; a bishop ; and a few ex-convicts, missionaries, engineers and university professors. Once again I was put in charge of public health, and my Chinese pen and ink came into play. I soon found that mere "public health" posters were not enough. People realized very little the menace to our health from inadequate feeding, dirt, mosquitoes, rats and boredom. Something more had to be done, and quickly, to stimulate the thinking and morale of the camp.

One far-seeing man had already begun the publication of a daily paper in which figured Pootung Pete who made wisecracks about the events around us. He immediately came to life in my mind as a little unshaven man with much-worn clothes, and before long he was appearing in a new set of cartoon posters. Together we thought out the subjects for Pootung Pete's wisdom and managed to keep the drawings going for nearly two years. They appeared under the heading of "THINK," in the camp dining-hall.

Other people got busy with the entertainment side. An internee who for 25 years had been a military bandmaster turned a medley of "swing" artistes into a symphony orchestra. A nephew of the late Sir Walford Davies trained a choir and soloists and wrote music for variety shows. Experts of the Shanghai amateur dramatic club produced numerous plays. For period plays such as Shakespeare, artists drew pictures of the costumes they wanted, then wandered round the camp eyeing bedspreads, curtains and personal clothing till they found what they needed. They hardly ever met with a refusal to lend. At a show the front row of seats was always reserved for the Japanese commandant and his friends ; they would sit unmoved while the orchestra finished a programme with a carefully camouflaged version of "God Save the King."

FREE education was another prominent feature of camp life, and if one had time one could study anything from bio-chemistry to ship-designing. School was run for the older children and several sat for their Cambridge School Certificate examination behind a curtain in the dining-hall while the camp barbers, masseuses, lecturers and bridge-players carried on on the other side.

As medicals we had little spare time. There were clinics to be held, drains to be examined, rats to be caught and beds to be de-bugged. We realized the value of our medical experience under such conditions and spent six months making a complete analysis of the health record of the camp. This is now in the hands of experts along with other prison camp medical officers' reports. A long queue waited daily outside the dentists' room. The dentists, one a young missionary and the other an engineer, filled teeth, did extractions and repaired dentures, doing jobs which have since successfully passed the critical eye of dentists at home.

Hot Brick and a Cold " Darky "

The "family" feeling grew, and so did the family. Subdued cheers from the surrounding men's dormitories greeted the first wails of Michael, born at 2 a.m. on a bitter January night. He was under five pounds and we had no heating except for a small electric hot-plate, the use of which was officially forbidden. However, the nurses won the battle for Michael's life. Cases needing operation were allowed to go to the big hospital in Shanghai. Stretcher squads worked by rota to get an equal chance of a trip across the river. This was not all fun when the patient was heavy and the tide was low. Sampans are not the steadiest of crafts, but no patients ever had a ducking, thanks to the expert training and teamwork of their bearers. Over 100 people took the course and passed the tests for the St. John Ambulance badge. They were posted in different parts of the camp to act as dressers and assistants whenever an air raid threatened.

Every Saturday morning, when the fire brigade was practising, the camp was flooded with water ; the old factory hoses which they used squirted water not only at the business end but right along their length. The nearest thing to a fire happened when a cold "darky" decided to warm his bed with a brick from the kitchen fire. When he came to go to bed he found his brick had made its way through his mattress and was slowly burning its way through the floor. The Japanese left us alone most of the time ; roll-call twice a day served as a reminder of our position. We lined up on the playing field—a levelled-out portion of a bombed village—and for anyone whose feet were not together, whose arms were crossed or whose face had a smile on it, there would be a push or a slap and much talking.

THEY never quite decided what to do with us in air raids. For the earlier night raids we were herded out on to the playing field, and there we sat huddled on the ground listening to the distant drone of our own aircraft. As raids grew more frequent they left us in the building ; the upper floors were evacuated, as shrapnel, like the rain, came through the thin roof only too easily and we were surrounded by anti-aircraft guns.

When our last Christmas together came round I collected a team to work with me, and together we painted Christmas scenes on the walls and matting window-screens. For colouring we used powdered brick, white-wash and soot, mixed with rice paste. On one of the walls we painted an old English fireplace complete with Toby jugs, bed-warmers and a stag's head. The carpenters made a mantelpiece and a mock fire. Round this imitation piece of Home people gathered to smoke, chat or play games. On one of the window-screens was painted the camp coat-of-arms with the motto : *Te vince ut pacem fruare* " (Conquer yourself that you may enjoy peace). When the American relief mission visited the camp at the end of the War we heard that the Pootung area had been scheduled as the place of landing for the airborne troops in the invasion which was to have taken place two days after the date on which Japan surrendered.

We Were First Into Liberated Paris

Arriving in the forefront of the Allied armies after a night-drive without lights, Civil Affairs teams received a delirious welcome from the people of Paris on the triumphant morrow of the city's liberation, August 26, 1944. The story is told by Capt. L. E. Stone, R.A.S.C. Supply Officer, then attached to the 1st European Civil Affairs Regiment, U.S. Army.

A NUMBER of American Civil Affairs teams, of one of which I was a member, assembled on August 23, 1944, in the woods some 30 miles south-east of Paris. All along the route to our assembly point we had been greeted with the cry "Paris est libéré !" by excited inhabitants of villages and towns. Actually, its fall was imminent. The 2nd French Armoured Division had passed us a couple of days previously, and to them had been given the honour of being the first to enter Paris and co-operate with the F.F.I. in clearing the city of the Germans.

The Civil Affairs teams had been hurriedly withdrawn from rear areas and detailed to assist the Paris authorities in restoring the life of the city to something approaching normal. The teams were composed of American and British officers, each a specialist in some branch of civil life—law, banking, transport, public utilities, welfare, food supplies—with a long and thorough training in civil affairs work. Each team had its complement of enlisted men, all American—jeep-drivers, clerks, and so on. We were lectured at high pressure on the governmental set-up and all the known conditions existing in Paris, to enable us to get to work without delay. Finally each team was told the district (arrondissement) of Paris for

which it was to be responsible, and given a list of the last-known public officials it had to contact immediately on arrival.

We had arrived at the assembly point in the woods early in the evening. To make things more difficult it started to rain, and we had to delay pitching our tents to attend conferences. It was nearly midnight when word arrived that Paris was not yet free of the enemy, and we would not move until the following day. Then came the unpleasant business of bedding down in the darkness of the wood, and the rain so heavy that soon we were wet to the skin. All our kit was loaded on the jeep trailers and it was impossible to sort it out in the darkness, so we made ourselves as comfortable as possible in the jeeps and under them. No one slept for more than a few minutes at a time. Heavy armoured vehicles thundered along the road by the side of the wood. Small-arms fire kept us on the alert—parties of Germans cut off from their units were wandering about and sniping in the direction of any sound or light.

Early next morning, with the rain still falling heavily, a very sad, stiff and tired lot of Civil Affairs officers and men roused themselves to eat a breakfast of "K" rations. Fortunately my team had some petrol cookers and we were able to enjoy a cup of hot

coffee. All day we waited for news from Paris, attending lectures, drying our clothes, and making arrangements to stay another night. With suppressed excitement we speculated on the job before us—what would Paris be like after four years under the Germans ? What sort of reception would we get from the people ?

There was still no news on the evening of the 25th, and at 11 p.m. we bedded down, prepared to make a sudden move. At 11.30 the order came, and at midnight we started for Paris : a 30-mile journey, no lights, and some uncertainty as to which roads we would have to take. Each team had with it an unreliable 3-ton captured German lorry we had loaded with token food supplies, for we did not want to go in empty-handed. Sitting in the back of a jeep we peered intently into the darkness, trying to see road signs, to recognize villages we passed through and to read our maps with a pinpoint of light. Packed in as we were with our equipment movement was impossible, and acute discomfort gradually overcame the excitement we had felt at the start of the journey.

German Road-Block Dead Ahead

Suddenly the leading vehicles came to a stop. The motor cyclist guide came down the column telling drivers to turn around—we had run into a German road-block. With as little noise and as quickly as possible the convoy was turned in the narrow road. Another route, involving a detour of many miles, was mapped out, and we travelled to enter Paris from the south. Dawn was breaking as we entered the outlying suburbs,

AT VERDUN A CIVIL DEFENCE TEAM started work immediately after the liberation of the town on September 1, 1944. There was very little damage in Verdun itself, but there were many homeless in neighbouring districts, and for these food, clothing and shelter had to be provided in the manner described in this story. Four team members here are, left to right, Private Georgette Mercier, of Vire, France ; Capt. J. B. Bearman, of Stanmore, England ; Capt. Paul E. Middleton, of Indianapolis, U.S.A., and Private Evelyn Chambon, of Madagascar. PAGE 507 *Photo, U.S. Information Service*

NO. 10 SQUADRON

Motto: "To Hit the Mark."

DISBANDED after the First Great War the Squadron was reformed as a bomber formation at Upper Heyford, Oxfordshire, in 1928. In September 1939 it was stationed at Melbourne, Yorks, and took part in the leaflet raids over Berlin. Originally equipped with Whitley aircraft, it was later converted to a Halifax squadron. It went to France in November 1939 and operated security patrols over Borkum, Sylt and Heligoland.

During 1940 the targets were many and varied, including Berlin, the Ruhr and submarine bases. In 1941 the operational area was extended to include Frankfort, Rostock, Stuttgart and La Pallice, where the German battleship Scharnhorst was hiding. Up till 1944 the squadron was continuously engaged in the bombing of strategic targets in Germany, but is proudest of its work after D-Day.

IT helped to neutralize the heavy guns on the coast of Normandy. Caen was bombed before the final assault; keypoints on the French railways were destroyed; and Falaise was attacked. In the 11 months following D-Day the squadron operated on 149 nights and days, dropping 7,600 tons of bombs, in addition to 600 mines. Gelsenkirchen, Essen, Cologne and Chemnitz were heavily-defended targets attacked, and the squadron suffered severe casualties.

The visit to Chemnitz was made in support of the advancing Russian armies and involved a flight of nine hours. The remarkable expansion of the heavy bomber units of the R.A.F. is shown nowhere better than in the development of this squadron—"The Shining Tenth," as it calls itself. During its first few sorties only a handful of airmen were briefed; but in the latter part of 1944 an average of 20 Halifaxes went on each mission.

by which time the jeep seats seemed incredibly hard. It was now light enough to smoke, and with a cigarette came a renewal of excitement. What were we to find in Paris? The French Armoured Division was already in the city, but we were the first British and Americans to enter. The streets of the suburbs were deserted, except for one or two early workers who seemed not in the least interested in our historic arrival, and we felt somewhat disappointed.

On we went, signs of the recent fighting now becoming apparent: road-blocks, damaged buildings, abandoned light tanks, overturned cars, barricaded streets. Then the Eiffel Tower—every one of us had been watching for the first sight of it, to convince ourselves that this really was Paris. There were now more early workers in the streets, and one or two stared, then waved or gave the V-sign. At seven o'clock on the morning of August 26 we entered the Tuileries.

What a scene of devastation! The famous gardens were strewn with wreckage of the previous days' fighting between the last of the German rearguard and the F.F.I. and French Armoured Division. The Germans had loaded a number of trucks and buses with their equipment; these had been wrecked, and the contents lay scattered about. Tanks had been put out of action and set on fire. Parts of rifles and machine-guns, and spent ammunition, littered the roads. Clothing and personal belongings were strewn haphazard all over the place.

Tanks Operating 500 Yards Away

For three hours we waited in the Tuileries while our C.O., an American major, attended a conference with the other team C.O.s, under the direction of an American lieutenant-colonel. As we expected to move any minute we did not attempt to wash and shave, and despite the excitement of being here in the centre of Paris we felt very grimy, tired and hungry. Soap and water and a cup of coffee would have brightened our outlook considerably. A crowd of excited Parisians had collected, all eager to shake our hands and to say how grateful they were.

They told us about the horrors of life during the German Occupation, about the excellent work of the F.F.I., and that there were still thousands of the enemy holding out in the suburbs. They asked innumerable questions about the war, about England, America and Russia. Would Churchill come to Paris? they asked.

Our C.O. returned with orders that his team had to report at once to the officials of the arrondissement for which we were to be responsible. Our small convoy of three jeeps and the 3-ton lorry loaded with food was piloted through the city by an armed F.F.I. man. The streets were empty of traffic (there was no public transport) except for a number of F.F.I. cars which always travelled at an amazing speed, and bicycles. Never had I seen so many bicycles. The Germans had commandeered thousands, yet still the streets were almost impassable because of cyclists. People lined the pavements, cheering and giving the V-sign. This brought others to the windows of their apartments, and not a few ran into the street in pyjamas and dressing gowns to wave and shout in the utmost excitement, "Vive l'Amérique! Vive l'Angleterre!"

A grand display of flags, French, British, American and Russian, fluttered from every building. How, after four years of Occupation, had the French people managed to produce so many Allied flags? Closer examination revealed that they were mostly home-made. Later we heard how people had sat up all night dyeing sheets and sewing them into flags, patiently cutting out and fastening on the 48 stars of the American flag, puzzling about the correct stripes of the Union Jack, and the hammer-and-sickle of Russia; and of course their own flag was brought out of hiding to be flown triumphantly with those of the liberators.

We pulled up in the square outside the Town Hall where we had to report, and at once our vehicles were mobbed. In seconds the big square was packed with an excited crowd all pressing to get near us. We were pinned to the sides of the jeeps and the lorry. Men, women and children reached for our hands; we were kissed by hundreds of them, tears rolling down their faces as they tried to thank us for coming.

The F.F.I. boys, armed with rifles, automatics, hand grenades, and in civilian clothes, did their best to keep the crowd from suffocating us. At last they managed to get our C.O. in to see the Mayor and when they appeared on the balcony together the cheer that

went up was deafening. Almost at the same moment machine-gun fire came from the church tower in the square. Some F.F.I. men near us hurriedly explained that this suburb was not clear of the enemy, that we were the first military to arrive there, that the French Armoured Division was expected but had not yet arrived, and that German tanks were operating about 500 yards away. At the sound of the shots panic broke out,

Capt. L. E. STONE

and we urged the police and the F.F.I. to clear the square immediately. Being a Civil Affairs unit we were not, of course, equipped to deal with tanks, so we were ordered to return to the Tuileries. Back there at about midday we had our first meal — "K" rations, consisting of biscuits, tinned meat, sweets, coffee and cigarettes contained in a small box. The day was hot, and we sat in the shade of the trees. Scores of Parisians came and watched us, curious about our food. We gave sweets to the children, and cigarettes and packets of coffee to their parents—the first real coffee they had seen for four years. The cigarettes were most prized: the ration for civilians then was 80 French cigarettes per month, and American or English cigarettes reaching the black market were selling at anything up to 30s. for a packet of 20.

At about 2 o'clock we were ordered to return to the Town Hall to hand over our lorry of foodstuffs. We found the streets crowded. Laughing faces and pretty dresses were everywhere. The Parisiennes looked almost unchanged by the exigencies of war. Our reception this time was beyond anything we had imagined possible. Our three jeeps were literally besieged. Masses of people lining the boulevards, waving, shouting, ran into the road and stopped us. Fruit and bottles of wine were offered to us. Hundreds of hands sought to shake ours. We were embraced by old and young. We submitted to it all, speechless with emotion, and we arrived back in the Tuileries practically submerged by boys and girls; there were fifteen youngsters on my jeep.

Snipers Fired Into the Crowds

At 4 p.m. we had at last an opportunity to wash and shave. The gardens and neighbouring roads were a mass of people. General de Gaulle had just passed, after reviewing the French Armoured Division. Suddenly shots rang out. Snipers were firing into the crowds from the high buildings in the Rue de Rivoli. Pandemonium broke out: F.F.I. men returned the fire, and we saw men scrambling about on the roof-tops. A large volume of fire which seemed to come from a big apartment house was returned by heavy machine-guns mounted on the French tanks. Fear struck the people, and they threw themselves flat on the ground or took cover behind trees and vehicles.

When at last the firing died away Paris began to enjoy the first evening of actual freedom. Crowds wandered through the streets, gazing at burnt-out German tanks, shell holes in buildings, barricades and other material of war. Actually the centre of Paris had suffered very little damage during the war. As we walked to the hotel that had been reserved for us we were stopped time and time again for our hands to be shaken, and we were deafened with invitations to many homes. The next day we settled down to the serious business of Civil Affairs. Municipal government was working extremely well, and our main tasks resolved themselves into welfare work, supplies and transport.

I shall always remember the fortitude and high spirits of the British civilians in the internment camp at St. Denis, who would have starved to death but for the care given to the sick by the French in the prison hospital and the Red Cross parcels received from England.

I was greatly impressed by the results of the precision bombing of the R.A.F. They had wiped out big areas of marshalling yards and factories, bridges and junctions, with a minimum of damage to the surrounding non-military objectives. The centre of Paris was quite untouched by our bombs.

The shocking condition of German railway equipment and rolling stock amazed me, though I expected it to be pretty poor. Freight cars I saw were falling to pieces through lack of serviceing, and the inscriptions in Russian bore testimony to the great mileage these had run.

Although accustomed to the high quality of British and American food and packing I was surprised at the excellence of the German army food supplies abandoned in Paris. In the warehouses I had to inspect I found white flour, sugar, tinned milk, fancy cakes and biscuits, tinned meats, butter, jam, etc.—all of pre-war quality and packed in well-made, strong cases. Two things we never found—coffee or tea ; ersatz coffee in plenty, but not a grain of the real thing.

I spoke to many people about the difficulty of having the Boche in their midst for four years and not collaborating with them in business. One Frenchman, the director of a large firm of distributors, explained it this way. "We *had* to get along with them. None of us could run the risk of having our business ruined and employees left jobless by being awkward and hostile. Remember, until 1943 we could see no hope of liberation. You knew what was happening in the world ; we didn't. Then, again, the German wasn't such a fool as to goad us into being hostile—he needed our co-operation. Consequently he was not always unreasonable in his demands. We knew this and traded on it. Sometimes strange accidents happened: we always apologized profusely and set to work furiously to put things right—with our left hands.

"I was responsible to a high German officer for certain army supplies. He would come and sit in the chair you're sitting on now. We'd be alone. He couldn't speak French very well, and I can't speak German, so we'd talk in English, and very often about London as we both knew it. Five days ago he sat in that chair and said, 'Well, I have come to say goodbye. I shall be sorry to leave Paris, but I shall return before very long.' I said, 'Surely you don't expect to retake Paris ?' He smiled and said, 'Oh no ! When you send for us to discuss the Peace Treaty I shall come as a member of the trade commission !' He then put his hand in his pocket and brought out a bottle of port and placed it on the table. 'Here is a present for you,' he said. 'I want you to drink it with the first of your English friends to arrive in this office.'" There was a pause, then my friend went to a cupboard and brought out the German's bottle of port, still wrapped in the original soft brown tissue paper. We drank to De Gaulle and Churchill, Roosevelt and Stalin !

On the Trail of the Opium-Runners

Under the Japanese regime thousands of pounds' worth of opium reached Malaya by the sea route from the Netherlands Indies or along remote land trails from Siam. How this drug traffic was cleaned up by the British is told by Bernard T. Ridgway, then an Army Observer (Public Relations).

For months following the liberation of Malaya in September 1945 patrol craft and launches, manned by men of the Royal Army Service Corps, or scratch British crews, patrolled the lonely creeks and island-studded coastal waters by night and day, maintaining ceaseless watch for opium-runners. I went out on one of these anti-opium smuggling patrols in the Straits of Malacca with a British Customs officer and his three Malay assistants. We slipped our moorings at Port Swettenham and in the R.A.S.C. motor launch Peggy headed out into the Klang Straits.

Slowly the string of merchantmen fell away behind us, and we had the waters to ourselves but for a few odd junks and sampans. A shout from the bows directed our gaze to an idling sampan a short distance to starboard. The Customs officer pointed towards it, and the craft's nose was swung round in the required direction. An age-old sampan man and a youth shook their hands in the typical "I'm doing no wrong" manner of the East. But we decided to have a look, all the same.

Out went the boathook from the bows, and the two craft bumped gently and remained locked. Over into the sampan went one of our Malay investigators—and up came the floorboards and hands groped in the darkness for the sack or container that might contain a thousand pounds' worth of drugs. A quick look over the bows, stern and sides, and he returned to our vessel. "They often trail the stuff over the sides at the end of a piece of string," observed the Customs officer.

Our next intercept was a small junk lying at anchor. The crew were there to greet us as we came alongside, and the master waved his port clearance papers in our faces as we went aboard. Documents showed that he was bound for Penang with a mixed cargo. Living quarters and holds were minutely scanned by the search party. Nothing ! Grinning faces and obsequious bows greeted us as the papers were handed back and the master was told to proceed on his way.

A Catch off the Mangrove Swamps

We doubled on our tracks to catch up with our next customer. A hawk-eyed Malay on our launch had seen a fishing junk moored close in to the mangrove swamps. Three Chinese of varying ages stared vacantly down at us, and their inactivity drew forth muttered protests from one of our deck-hands whose mooring rope lay dangling across the bows. Two of the men eventually stirred themselves and made fast our ropes, and we clambered aboard over a pile of stinking fishing nets.

A shout from one of the Malays down in the living quarters took us all aft. From a wicker basket containing a weird and wonderful collection of junk he had extracted a largish pot. Unscrewing the top he sniffed

the contents. "Chandu!" (opium) was his comment. Then began an all-out search for further stocks and opium pipes. That boat was turned inside out but we found nothing more. We even searched through those odorous nets and the furled sail, but still without result. We took the pot of opium along with us, cast off and moved into the open sea. The first large trading junk we accosted was flapping along at a snail's pace. Handwaves and shouts greeted us. "We examined them the other day," said the Customs officer. "They are bound for Penang." He shouted to know why they had not yet set out on their journey. Pointing hands stretched to the sky and back to the tattered sails. When we caught up with a powered junk that at one time had been a mere speck on the skyline we were running in quite a swell, and it needed a sure foot and steady eye to jump from one see-sawing boat to the other. She was bound for the small port of Telok Anson with a mixed cargo of kerosene, tires and spices. We searched her from stem to stern, but found nothing.

Capt. B. T. RIDGWAY

We had one more call to make—a check-up for opium dens in a small fishing village on one of the islands. We cleared the choppy seas and ran into the comparative calm of backwaters. The outline of many masts drew my attention first, and gradually the outlines of the village came into focus. The coxswain shouted for half-speed, and we glided in towards a rickety-looking jetty.

Carved out of the mud swamps, the whole village was raised upon trestles above the level of the lapping waters.

Children paused in their play and men and women came hurrying to their waterfront doorways as we scrambled on to the landing stage. The search party set off up the jetty at a spanking pace, speed being essential if we were to catch-up on the opium den operators before they had time to hide their stocks. News travels fast in these parts, and already some man or child might be speeding ahead of us bearing tidings of our presence. The wooden "pavement" groaned and bent under our feet; through the joints I could see the oozing mud beneath.

From one small alley into another we chased, at times having to make a jump for it where broken timbers left gaping holes. The leading Malay shot into one shop, and the rest of us continued on and raced into an eating-house reeking of wood-smoke and cooking fats. In a small cubicle a recumbent Chinaman tossed and turned on his straw palliasse. Crouching near him was a wizened old man, who commenced protesting directly we appeared. One of the investigators combed baskets and containers under a table, a second made the old man open up a number of locked boxes.

The befuddled addict gave a groan and rolled over. We searched all around him, but drew a blank. Baffled, the Malay got to work on the floorboards. Shifting a board near a joist he thrust his hand into the cavity and drew out two tins. Both contained opium. But the old man was too cunning for us this time, for although a fine comb was drawn through that building not an opium pipe came to light. The man who had been checking up lower down the street strolled up swinging a long pipe in one hand and holding a small tin in the other. He had found his men before they had had time to take evasive action. As we headed back across the Straits the sun was setting and by the lights of blinking buoys we edged into the busy river traffic off Swettenham.

Battle of Britain From Underground

From the subterranean Operations Room at Headquarters, R.A.F. Fighter Command, from July to September 1940, A. J. Wilson watched the Battle of Britain being fought out "like a giant game of chess with coloured counters" and here describes his experiences. See also page 403.

WHEN in 1939 I first walked down the tree-flanked drive which leads to Bentley Priory, at Stanmore, Middlesex—Headquarters of R.A.F. Fighter Command and the control centre of Britain's air defence—I knew little about the strategy of air fighting. A few months later, however, I was able to follow, move by move, the great air battle which turned the course of the war and was a main factor in saving Britain from invasion by the Nazis. I saw the Battle of Britain not as most people in Southern England saw it—as the endless procession of German raiders against a shell-torn sky, the twisting and turning Spitfires and the horror of the bombing. I saw it as a giant game of chess played with coloured counters on the board of the Operations Room deep down beneath the gardens of the Priory.

Work on this subterranean headquarters had begun before the war and was hurriedly completed only a few weeks before Goering launched his first big air attacks. It was here that airmen and W.A.A.F. plotted the track and strength of every enemy raid

BENTLEY PRIORY, at Stanmore, Middlesex, as R.A.F. Fighter Command H.Q. was the control centre of Britain's air defence during the Second Great War. The "brain" of the Command worked in chambers beneath the gardens of the Priory. In the Operations Room information concerning hostile and friendly aircraft was plotted, presenting a picture of the air battle-front. This headquarters was completed only a few weeks before the commencement of the Battle of Britain, though work on it was started before the outbreak of the war. **PAGE 510** *Photo, Aerofilms*

from reports coming in from radiolocation stations and Observer Corps centres. It was here that Air Staff officers and representatives of all the other Services co-ordinated every method of defence against the raiders : fighter squadrons, anti-aircraft guns, Balloon Barrage and Civil Defence.

From the balcony of this Operations Room Air Chief Marshal Lord (then Sir Hugh) Dowding, Commander-in-Chief of Fighter Command, the genius behind this great organization, watched the progress of the battle for which he had planned so thoroughly, but with such slender resources.

For twelve weeks we who worked down " the Hole " rarely saw an aircraft—British or German—but we saw the pattern of the battle even more clearly than those who fought it in their Spitfires and Hurricanes.

In July and early August 1940 I watched the plotters round their table-map juggle with the counters over the English Channel. The convoys of ships battling their way through the Straits were having a grim time, but our fighters were there and shortly after each attack intelligence reports showed how badly the enemy had been mauled. I remember the thrill of learning one day that a single squadron—No. 145, under Squadron Leader " Johnny " Peel—had put 21 shipping raiders into the sea.

Vapour Trails of Sky Battles

By mid-August the counters had multiplied and were thrusting in over the coastline to our airfields at Manston, Hawkinge, Tangmere, then to Biggin Hill, Kenley and Croydon. This was to be the knock-out blow to Fighter Command, but the tactics which destroyed air resistance in France and other conquered countries failed. Reports poured in to us of cratered landing grounds and flaming hangars but the Spitfires still rose from their damaged aerodromes to give battle with the invader.

Then, throwing caution to the winds, the Luftwaffe struck at London. I was on duty in the Operations Room shortly after 4 o'clock on Saturday afternoon, September 7, when our radiolocation stations flashed the first warning of the approach of 150 German aircraft off Dungeness. A little later their plots were joined on the " ops " table by more counters, denoting a second raid of 250. In they came, heading straight for the capital. For an hour and a half London was

ringed with air battles and though a number of the enemy broke through and dropped their bombs on the banks of the Thames, they paid with the loss of 100 of their aircraft in their first big attack on the capital.

Like most other members of Fighter Command, the day I remember most vividly is Sunday, September 15, the anniversary of which is now celebrated all over the world as Battle of Britain Day. As I made my way to the Headquarters just before mid-day the sirens were wailing and later, from the garden terraces of the Priory, I could see the scribble of vapour trails in the sky over London and heard the noise of the battle as the immortal " Few " fought the enemy in their greatest clash.

DOWN the " Hole " there was no noise, no excitement, but the expressions on the faces of high-ranking operations officers and airmen alike were tense. Everyone felt that this was the big show. Only the soft buzz of muffled telephone bells and the clink of the metal counters as the plotters released them on to the table from their magnetic " wands " broke the silence. Air Chief Marshal Dowding himself was on the balcony, tall, stiff and unsmiling.

Since first light there had been " plots " over the Channel and coastal districts, but most of these were either reconnaissance or feint attacks. The first main thrust came when 200 raiders zig-zagged over the coast at 11.30 and then spread out for London. Scarcely had their tracks been removed from the operations table as our fighters chased the survivors back across the Channel, when a second wave of 300 arrived.

Again Fighter Command controllers worked to a smooth pre-arranged plan, its

execution a triumph of organization. As the enemy came in our fighters were ordered up to meet them over the coast, then more challenged them over Kent and Sussex, and others tackled them over London itself.

Teleprinters Kept the Scores

In a room along the corridor from the Operations Room I watched the teleprinters of the Intelligence branch tick out their messages like scores in a cricket match— 50 German aircraft destroyed for five of ours ; 100 for 8 ; 130 for 12 ; 160 for 22. Then came the individual squadron reports, often with the names of the men who had scored the victories. To me the names meant little then, but today they are very honoured names in Fighter Command and throughout the civilized world.

I remember reading in those signals that Stanford Tuck had shot down an Me.110 over Barking and was nearly killed a moment later when a bullet from another raider crashed through his windscreen a few inches from his head. The teleprinters stuttered out the news that Douglas Bader's wing were claiming 52, including a Dornier which the legless pilot had fired at, which went down with the rear gunner swinging from the tail by his parachute (see page 153). R. W. Oxspring had forced a Heinkel to land at a Kent airfield and then shot down a Dornier over Chatham. These were some of the " Few " who won the day.

Intelligence officers worked all night on these reports, checking and double-checking the pilots' claims. It was not until next morning that we heard the final figures— 185 German aircraft destroyed for 25 of ours, with 12 of our pilots safe. The climax was passed, and although the battle continued for another month victory was assured.

NEW FACTS AND FIGURES

POST OFFICE men and women gained over 870 military and civil awards during the war, for gallantry with the Forces or as civilians at home. These include 125 Distinguished Flying Cross ; 50 Distinguished Flying Medal ; 20 Military Cross ; 93 Military Medal ; nine D.S.C. ; 14 D.C.M. ; and 64 D.S.M. The British Empire Medal was awarded to 216, and the George Medal to 12. One member of the G.P.O. gained the George Cross. Among other decorations were seven American Bronze Star ; nine Croix de Guerre ; a Czechoslovak and a Norwegian Gallantry Medal ; and a Bronze Medal of Honour of the Royal Netherlands Navy. Over 74,000 Post Office men and women joined the Services, and the dead, missing, and prisoners of war still not accounted for exceed 4,000.

AT Rosyth on September 5, 1946, three British submarines—Votary, Viking and Venturer, of the U-class—were handed over to the Royal Norwegian Navy by Admiral Mansfield, Flag Officer, Submarines, on behalf of the Royal Navy ; Commodore Jacobsen, Norwegian Naval Attaché in London, accepted them on behalf of the Norwegian Navy. This was under an agreement reached in London in June, and further warships, including destroyers, have been transferred to Norway (see illus. page 453). An agreement has also been signed for the purchase of British aircraft and equipment for the Royal Norwegian Air Force, to the value of about £700,000.

OWING to lack of coal, reductions in the iron and steel production in the British Zone of Germany were to be made from September 30, 1946. Five steel works were closing entirely, and in eight others production was considerably reduced. The steel production programme for September was for a total of 272,000 tons of ingots and castings ; for each of the last months of the year production of 224,000 tons was planned.

IN September 1946 it was announced that German P.O.W. in Britain, in addition to sending a maximum of 5s. a week home

to their families, would be allowed to save money in a credit fund for conversion into Reichsmarks on their return home. Additional to their normal earnings, bonuses would be granted in certain circumstances which would bring total weekly earnings to about 15s. a week. Money which a prisoner did not wish to spend himself after sending 5s. home could be placed in the credit fund.

POLISH Displaced Persons to the number of about 335,000 were still in U.N.R.R.A. camps in the western zones of Germany in September 1946. To induce them to return home, the British, American and French Military Governments agreed to supply each returning Pole with 60 days' rations when he arrived in Poland, in addition to the ordinary Polish ration. Since May 1946, over 65,000 left Austria for their own country, but in September there were still 31,000 Poles.

A BRITISH military mission, consisting of representatives of the R.A.F. and the Army, has lately been making a thorough search of North Norway to find the remains of British aircraft and the graves of British Servicemen. The R.A.F. mission found the remains of 50 aircraft shot down by the Germans and 100 war graves, mostly in the area round Harstad. It was possible to identify the bodies, which were reburied in Norwegian soil with full military honours.

IN the British Zone of Germany by the end of August 1946 there were open 11,541 elementary and intermediate schools with 2,838,651 pupils ; 619 secondary schools with 261,468 pupils ; and 1,737 vocation schools and courses with 456,853 pupils. There were 296 approved schools and orphanages. Total number of teachers available was 59,023. Six universities and eight colleges were open in the Zone, with a prospective student membership for the winter term of 28,457. Adult educational facilities were being utilized by 79,218 students, while there were 10,546 youth groups with a total membership of 559,797.

A. J. WILSON, formerly of the R.A.F., contributes this story of the Battle of Britain as he saw it from a most unusual angle.

R.M. College Colours are Laid Up for Ever

Photo, G.P.U.

THE ROYAL MILITARY COLLEGE, SANDHURST, CEASED TO EXIST on Oct. 17, 1946, its buildings to reopen on Jan. 3, 1947, for the first term of the new R.M. Academy—combining the pre-war functions of the R.M. Academy, Woolwich, and the R.M. College, Sandhurst. Following the Trooping of the college Colours, these were laid up for ever in the Memorial Chapel. The Colour party is seen halted at the chancel steps, where the Commandant has taken the King's Colour in his right hand ; the Regimental Colour will next be handed over.

Printed in England and published every alternate Friday by the Proprietors, THE AMALGAMATED PRESS, LTD., The Fleetway House, Farringdon Street, London, E.C.4. Registered for transmission by Canadian Magazine Post. Sole Agents for Australia and New Zealand ; Messrs. Gordon & Gotch, Ltd. : and for South Africa, Central News Agency, Ltd.—November 22, 1946. S.S. *Editorial Address :* JOHN CARPENTER HOUSE, WHITEFRIARS, LONDON, E.C.4.

Vol 10 The War Illustrated N° 247

SIXPENCE

I WAS THERE

DECEMBER 6, 1946

IN NEW YORK, FOUR FOREIGN MINISTERS met at the Waldorf-Astoria Hotel on Nov. 4, 1946, for the purpose of reaching final agreement on the five peace treaties—with Italy, Rumania, Bulgaria, Hungary and Finland—which were debated by the Paris Conference (see illus. pages 303-306). In front of their national flags are (left to right) M. Couve de Murville (acting as deputy for M. Bidault, the French Foreign Minister), Mr. Bevin, Mr. Molotov and Mr. Byrnes.

Photo, Associated Press

Edited by Sir John Hammerton

NO. 248 WILL BE PUBLISHED FRIDAY, DECEMBER 20

Our Roving Camera at Military and Civil Events

BRITISH POLICE OFFICERS are training the new force that will maintain law and order in the Dodecanese. Inspector H. Hickinbotham of Birmingham, has assisted in the formation of the corps of 700 volunteers. (left)

ENGINES FOR CHINA'S railways are being exported from Britain. Above, two of them are awaiting shipment in the Royal Victoria Dock, London. A powerful searchlight is an obligatory fitting, for many Chinese railways are unfenced.

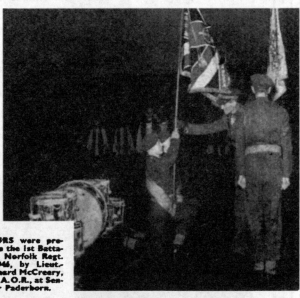

BULBS FOR MINERS have come from the Netherlands. Lord Citrine (extreme left) accepted the first token presentation at Chislet, Kent. The donors are giving 500,000 tulip bulbs, worth £10,000.

NEW COLOURS were presented (right) to the 1st Battalion The Royal Norfolk Regt. on Nov. 8, 1946, by Lieut.-General Sir Richard McCreery, G.O.C.-in-C., B.A.O.R., at Sennalager, near Paderborn.

GERMAN RAIDERS seriously damaged the ancient parish church (above) of Chilvers Coton, Warwickshire, on May 16, 1941. In 1946 it was being restored with the help of German P.O.W., the sculpture being the work of one.

NEW PLYMOUTH, N.Z., has been presented with the century-old bell of St. Michael's Church, Devonport. The Lord Mayor of Plymouth, Mr. Isaac Foot (right), tolled the bell at the handing-over ceremony in England.

Photos, G.P.U., Fox, Keystone, P.A.-Reuter

The Daring Raid on Rommel's H.Q.

By KENNETH HARE-SCOTT

IN 1940 and 1941 the plight of the Allies precluded any major offensive in Europe and caused the world to turn its gaze upon the British Empire's struggle in the Middle East. The campaigns in North Africa —initiated by Wavell and concluded gloriously by Alexander and Montgomery—destroyed the Italian Armies and were eventually to expel the Nazis from African soil, smarting under their first major defeat of the war. The fighting lasted many months, and as many heroic deeds are recorded in the annals of the soldiers of the Western Desert. None, however, is so worthy a story of British gallantry as the raid by the men of No. 11 Scottish Commando upon the residence and Headquarters of the General Officer Commanding the German Forces in North Africa, Field-Marshal Rommel.

Late in 1941 a large-scale advance by the 8th Army was planned with the object of relieving Tobruk, then besieged for many months, and rolling back the Axis army with such heavy losses in men and material that the security of Egypt and our Mediterranean bases would be assured. At that time Colonel (later Major-General) Robert Laycock was flown out, on the instructions of the Prime Minister, to organize the Commandos ; but on his arrival there remained only No. 11 Unit, commanded by Lieut.-Col. Geoffrey Keyes, son of the famous Admiral who was at that time Director of Combined Operations.

Laycock found Keyes engrossed upon a plan for raiding Rommel's Headquarters. He did not share Keyes' enthusiasm, expressing the opinion that " the chances of being evacuated after the operation were very slender, and the attack on General Rommel's house in particular appeared to be desperate in the extreme. This attack, even if initially successful, meant almost certain death for those who took part in it." But Keyes and his Commandos were not to be deterred. The elimination of Rommel might well crumple Axis resistance, and such a project 250 miles in the rear of the enemy, timed to coincide with the 8th Army's attack, was worth a gamble, however desperate the odds.

Exhausting Landings On the Beach

Accordingly, at 4 p.m. on Monday, November 10, 1941, two officers and 25 other ranks, under Keyes' command, embarked upon the submarine Torbay at Alexandria. Three days later—on the Thursday—they arrived off the selected beach and carried out a periscope reconnaissance of the surrounding area. The following day preparations were made for disembarkation, and at dusk the Torbay surfaced. The first seven rubber boats pulled away and after a few upsets soon reached the shore, where Senussi guides led the force to a cave. Owing to the increasing swell and the inexperience of some of the soldiers several of the remaining boats capsized many times.

Eventually, however, all were landed, after an exhausting experience. According to the Torbay's narrative, " Those of the crew who took part received a very severe buffeting while handling the boats alongside in the swell and nearly all of them were completely exhausted at the finish. No less splendid was the spirit of the soldiers under strange and even frightening conditions. They were quite undaunted by the setbacks experienced, and remained quietly determined to get on with the job."

During the landing the men had been soaked through, not only by their immersion in the sea but by heavy rain. A few hundred

LIEUT.-COL. GEOFFREY KEYES, V.C., M.C., led the raid on Rommel's H.Q. Warned that the attack meant almost certain death, he refused to be deterred. *From the painting by Sidney Kendrick, by kind permission of Lady Keyes*

yards from the beach a cave afforded good shelter, and with the aid of a fire, clothes were soon dried and spirits cheered. By 2 a.m. the landing was completed. Unfortunately, the second submarine with Col. Laycock's party had not been so successful in making the beach, and only a handful of men were landed to reinforce those from the first submarine. During the evening the men rested, dried their clothes and fed themselves while Keyes continued to supervise the landing of stores and equipment.

The morning of the 15th brought sunshine and an anxious moment. An enemy ambulance aircraft flew overhead at 800 feet, but failed to detect the party. As little more

than half the original force had been able to land the plan for the attack needed modification and, in consultation with Laycock, Keyes spent the morning doing this. In the afternoon the new plan was explained to the men, and the evening was spent in opening, repacking, and distributing ammunition, explosives, and rations. A local Arab shepherd had been enrolled as a guide to substitute for two Senussi from the Arab Battalion who had failed to land.

Inland March Over Rocky Tracks

During the latter part of the afternoon more rain had fallen and it was a damp and cheerless company of men who set off at 8 p.m. on their march into the interior. The difficulty of the conditions and the spirit of determination which prevailed are best disclosed in this personal record of Captain Robin Campbell who was at Keyes' elbow throughout the operation :

" That night we reached the top of the first escarpment (which is half a mile inland) at about 9.15 p.m., I imagine, after a fairly stiff climb, and all that night we marched inland over extremely difficult going, mostly rock-strewn sheep tracks. Our guide left us at about midnight, fearing to go any farther in our company. Geoffrey then had the difficult task of finding the way by the aid of an indifferent Italian map, his compass and an occasional sight of the stars. Just before light he led us to the top of a small hill, arranged for relays of sentries, and ordered the rest of the party to disperse among the scrub for sleep."

Drizzle and a scare ushered in the next morning. The sound of excited shouting brought a report from a Palestinian soldier, who was a member of the party, to the effect that the force was surrounded by armed Arabs. Rascally-looking Arabs brandishing short Italian rifles seemed everywhere, but they appeared neither particularly formidable nor implacably hostile, so Keyes gave the order for the chief to be brought to him for a talk. A few civilities were exchanged and, although a letter from the Chief of all the Senussi Tribes, instructing his subjects to co-operate, was unintelligible to a " Deputy Chief "

ROMMEL'S HEADQUARTERS AT SIDI RAFA was 250 miles behind the German lines. To get within striking distance the Commandos had to accomplish a three-day journey by submarine and a landing in rubber boats through a heavy swell. Where the man is standing in this photograph are the steps leading to the door by which the raiders entered. PAGE 515 *War Office photograph*

IN ROMMEL'S H.Q.: from the room with the open door (left) was fired the shot that killed the leader of the raiders, Lieut.-Col. Geoffrey Keyes. *War Office photograph*

who could not read, a promise was eventually made that at nightfall he would guide the force to a cave within a few hours' march of their objective. Meanwhile, a kid would be prepared for them to eat. Later an Arab boy, on instructions from his chief, produced cigarettes for Keyes' men ; he had run off and bought these from an Italian canteen while the meal was in progress !

WHEN darkness fell the march continued, and two and a half hours later the cave which the Arab had mentioned was reached. It was roomy, dry, and—apart from an appalling smell of goats—an ideal place to spend the rest of the night. At daybreak the party moved to a small wood, and here Keyes left Campbell in charge while he went off on a final reconnaissance with the Arab guide, Sergeant Terry, and Lieutenant Cook, who was to lead the party attacking a communications pylon near Rommel's Headquarters. The result is again best described in Campbell's own words :

"Geoffrey told me that he had been able to see in the distance the escarpment, about a mile from the summit of which lay Rommel's Headquarters and that he was going to try to prevail upon the Arab to send his boy to the village of Sidi Rafa (the Italian name for which is Beda Littoria) to spy out the lie of the Headquarters building and report on the number of troops he saw there, and so on, before making his final, detailed dispositions for the attack. The boy set off after receiving careful instructions from Geoffrey, who had promised him a big reward if he brought back the desired information. This proved a brilliant move, for when the boy returned a good many hours later Geoffrey was able to draw an excellent sketch map of the house and its surroundings, enabling him to make a detailed plan of attack and to give the men a good visual notion of our objective."

A thunderstorm and heavy rain which followed turned the countryside to mud before the eyes of the party ; and spirits sank at the prospect of a long, cold, wet and muddy march before reaching the starting point of a hazardous operation. The men passed the time eating, dozing, or collecting water from the dripping roof in empty bully-beef tins.

From the start the attack had been planned for midnight, November 17-18, 1941, to coincide with the launching of the big offensive in the Western Desert. In view of the state of the ground, Keyes decided to allow six hours to reach his objective. At 6 p.m. the company assembled with parade ground precision for the final stage of the operation, and at a whistle signal the march began. Rain continued and, ankle deep in mud, the men slipped and staggered through the night. Occasionally one would fall and the column would halt for his recovery. Another would lose touch with the man in front of him, and a reshuffle would mean further delay.

Grim Encounter at Close Quarters

At 10.30 p.m. the bottom of the escarpment was reached, and after a short rest the 250-foot climb of muddy turf with occasional protruding rocks was begun. A man slipped, and in striking his tommy-gun against a rock roused a watchdog. A stream of light came from the door of a hut as it was flung open, 100 yards away. The party crouched motionless. The dog received a rebuke, and presently the door closed and the march was resumed. At the summit Cook and his party detached themselves, and those who remained, about 30, continued along a path towards Rommel's Headquarters. At this point the guides could stand the strain no longer and fell back, having been promised that their reward would be forthcoming when they linked up with the returning body at the conclusion of the operation.

At 11.30 p.m. the outbuildings were reached, and Keyes with Sergeant Terry made the final reconnaissance of the building. Again a dog proved troublesome. His furious barking brought an Italian and an Arab from a hut, and it required Campbell's best German and his Palestinian interpreter's Italian to convince them that a "German" patrol did not like being interrogated ! When Keyes returned he led his men into the garden of the house and here again Campbell's own account can be taken up.

"We followed him around the building on to a gravel sweep before a flight of steps at the top of which were glass-topped doors. Geoffrey ran up the steps. He was carrying a tommy-gun for which he needed both hands and, as far as I remember, I opened the door for him. Just inside we were confronted by a German in steel helmet and overcoat. Geoffrey at once closed with him, covering him with his tommy-gun. The

man seized the muzzle of Geoffrey's gun and tried to wrest it from his grasp. Before I or Terry could get round behind him he retreated, still holding on to Geoffrey, to a position with his back to the wall and his either side protected by the first and second pair of doors at the entrance. Geoffrey could not draw a knife, and neither I nor Terry could get round Geoffrey as the doors were in the way, so I shot the man with my '38 revolver, which I knew would make less noise than Geoffrey's tommy-gun. Geoffrey then gave the order to use tommy-guns and grenades since we had to presume that my revolver shots had been heard.

"We found ourselves, when we had time to look round, in a large hall with a stone floor and stone stairway leading to the upper storeys and with a number of doors opening out of the hall. We heard a man in heavy boots clattering down the stairs, though we could not see him, or he us, as he was hidden by a right-angle turn in the stairway. As he came to the turn and his feet came in sight, Sergeant Terry fired a burst with his tommy-gun. The man fled away upstairs. Meanwhile, Geoffrey had opened one door and we looked in and saw it was empty. Geoffrey pointed to a light shining from the crack under the next door, and then flung it open. It opened towards him, and inside were about 10 Germans in steel helmets, some sitting and some standing. Geoffrey emptied his Colt '45 automatic, and I said, " Wait, I'll throw a grenade in." He slammed the door shut and held it while I got the pin out of a grenade. I said, ' Right ! ' and Geoffrey opened the door and I threw in the grenade which I saw roll in the middle of the floor.

Died As He Was Carried Outside

"Before Geoffrey could shut the door the Germans fired. A bullet struck Geoffrey just over the heart and he fell unconscious at the feet of myself and Sergeant Terry. I shut the door and immediately afterwards the grenade burst with a shattering explosion. This was followed by complete silence, and we could see that the light in the room had gone out. I decided Geoffrey had to be moved in case there was further fighting in the building, so between us Sergeant Terry and I carried him outside and laid him on the grass verge by the side of the steps leading up to the front door. He must have died as we were carrying him outside, for when I felt his heart it had ceased to beat."

The men's spirits fell when they heard of their Colonel's death—his inspiring leadership gone. Almost immediately afterwards Campbell was shot through the leg, and subsequently taken prisoner. Terry mustered the remainder of the party and began the long march back to join Laycock on the beach.

Rommel, by chance, was away from his Headquarters that night and so eluded the fate designed for him by the courageous Commandos. At Keyes' funeral, at Sidi Rafa, Rommel made an oration and pinned his own Iron Cross on the body of the dead hero. This token of admiration for the bravery of his personal antagonist by an enemy Commander-in-Chief must be unique in the history of chivalry.

When the official account of the raid could be made known Geoffrey Keyes was awarded a posthumous Victoria Cross, on June 19, 1942. A Memorial Service held in Westminster Abbey was attended by many Commandos who had shared with him the events of that week in November 1941.

IN BENGHAZI CEMETERY, the resting-place of many others who fought and died with the valorous 8th Army, is now the grave (left foreground) of Lieut.-Col. Keyes. He was awarded the V.C. posthumously on June 19, 1942. *War Office photograph*

Home Fleet on Its Biggest Post-War Exercises

"BATTLE" THRILLS were experienced for the first time by many young members of the crews when the Home Fleet carried out its autumn exercises during October and early November 1946, off the north of Scotland, in the Irish Sea and the English Channel.

Under cover of a smoke-screen (1) laid by destroyers, torpedo attacks were made on H.M.S. King George V, flagship of Admiral Sir Neville Syfret, the C.-in-C. who, in 1942, commanded the Naval Forces in the Madagascar operations (2). Light units steamed up the Channel in line ahead (3). H.M.S. St. James (4) formed part of the destroyer escort to the King George V, which Beaufighters (5) attempted to bomb.

Photos, Topical, P.A.-Reuter.

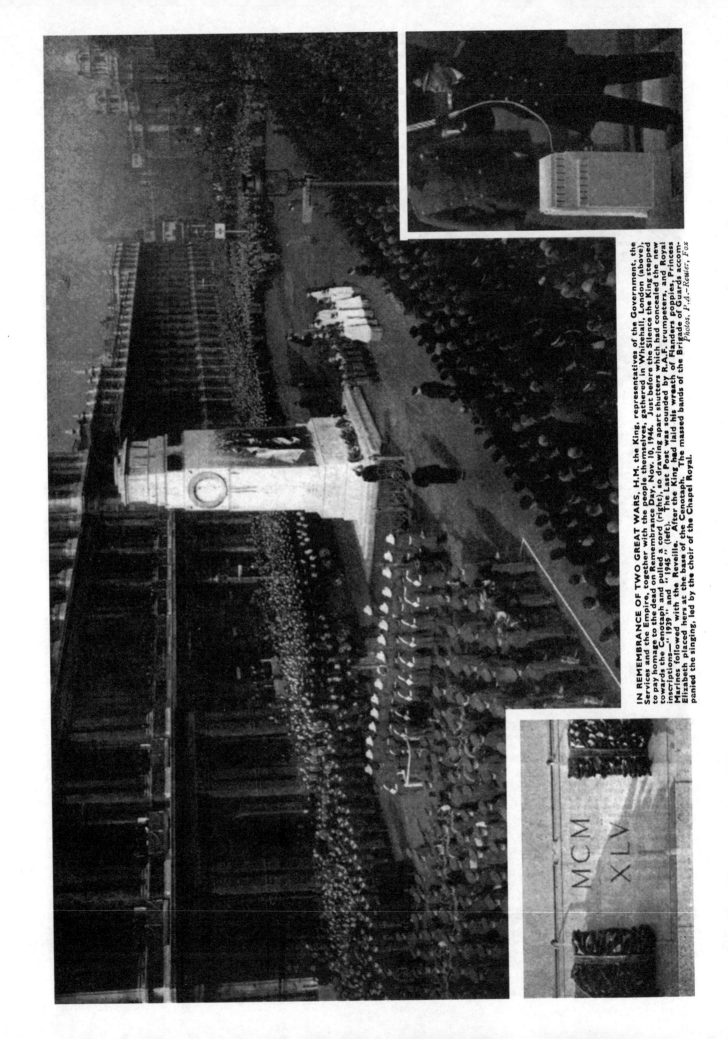

IN REMEMBRANCE OF TWO GREAT WARS, H.M. the King, representatives of the Government, the Services and the Empire, together with the people themselves, gathered in Whitehall, London (above), to pay homage to the dead on Remembrance Day, Nov. 10, 1946. Just before the Silence the King stepped towards the Cenotaph and pulled a cord (right), so drawing apart shutters which had concealed the new inscriptions—" 1939 " and " 1945 " (left). The Last Post was sounded by R.A.F. trumpeters, and Royal Marines followed with the Reveille. After the King had laid his wreath of Flanders poppies, Princess Elizabeth placed hers at the base of the Cenotaph. The massed bands of the Brigade of Guards accompanied the singing, led by the choir of the Chapel Royal.

Photos, P.A.–Reuter, Fox

PAGEANTRY AT THE STATE OPENING OF PARLIAMENT ON NOV. 12, 1946, was still somewhat dimmed by austerity. H.M. the King, in the uniform of Admiral of the Fleet, and H.M. the Queen, rode in the Irish State coach drawn by four Windsor Greys and accompanied by a Captain's Escort of the Household Cavalry. Troops of the Brigade of Guards lined the route, together with many regular and special constables. Unprecedented precautions were taken in view of threats made by Jewish terrorists. Among officers of State awaiting Their Majesties at the royal entrance was Field-Marshal Viscount Alanbrooke, bearing the Imperial Crown. As the King and Queen entered the Palace of Westminster the Union Jack on the Victoria Tower was lowered and the Royal Standard hoisted, and a salute of 41 guns fired in St. James's Park. *Photo, P.A.-Reuter*

In Palestine Where Peace Still Stands Aloof

TO HAIFA, in November 1946, came the refugee ship San Dimitrio, carrying about 1,300 illegal Jewish immigrants. Under British escort, the vessel arrived with a heavy list (1) and leaking badly. When Royal Marines boarded her to inspect the passengers they met with fierce resistance. After two British Army lorries had been mined on a road outside Jerusalem the village of Givath Saul was searched for concealed arms and explosives (2). Eight Jewish leaders, released from the Latrun detention camp, returned to Jerusalem on Nov. 5; they included (3, left to right) David Hacohen, Moshe Shertok and Dr. Bernard Joseph.

New Jewish settlements of prefabricated houses (4) are springing up in the desert wastes of southern Palestine. These new ventures were initiated in 1943. Palestine police (5) searched for victims after the suitcase-bomb outrage at Jerusalem station on October 30.

Photos, I.N.P., Planet News, Associated Press

New Badges for the Army and Royal Air Force

HIS MAJESTY has approved a new badge for the Royal Signals (right). It is a modification of the present design, which consists of the figure of Mercury poised on the Globe, enclosed in an oval band bearing the title of the Corps and surmounted by the Imperial Crown, but without the motto scroll. It will be the same for officers and other ranks, except that the badges of the former will be in silver and gilt and those of the latter white metal and brass. The pattern was approved in September 1946.

MANY NEW FLASHES appeared in the Army during the war; but the War Office waited for Peace before changing theirs. The new badge, which Field-Marshal Viscount Montgomery first wore when he went to Canada in September 1946, consists of the arms of the Board of Ordnance on a red and black background. The arms date back to the 15th century and are among the oldest in War Office records. The shield has always appeared on the flag of the Army Council and forms the centre of the R.A.O.C. badge.

VIKING'S HEAD is a fitting formation sign for the East Anglian District (Eastern Command). The District, which covers the nine counties north of the Thames, adopted the Viking's head (right) in white on a red background in October 1946. It was designed by Lt.-Col. W. S. Shepherd, who formerly commanded 15 Infantry Training Centre at Colchester. The new sign will be worn by all ranks within the district. The sign of the Eastern Command as a whole, is a white bulldog on a black background.

NEW RANK BADGES FOR R.A.F. AIRCREW were approved by the King in September 1946, and will be worn by aircrew below commissioned rank. The basic design is the R.A.F. eagle above a laurel wreath, the ranks being denoted as follows: (1) Master Aircrew; (2) Aircrew I; (3) Aircrew II; (4) Aircrew III; (5) Aircrew IV; (6) Aircrew cadet. The badges are embroidered in light blue on a Service blue background; and Master Aircrew insignia will be worn on the lower part of the sleeve, in the same position as a Warrant Officer's badge. *War Office and Air Ministry photographs*

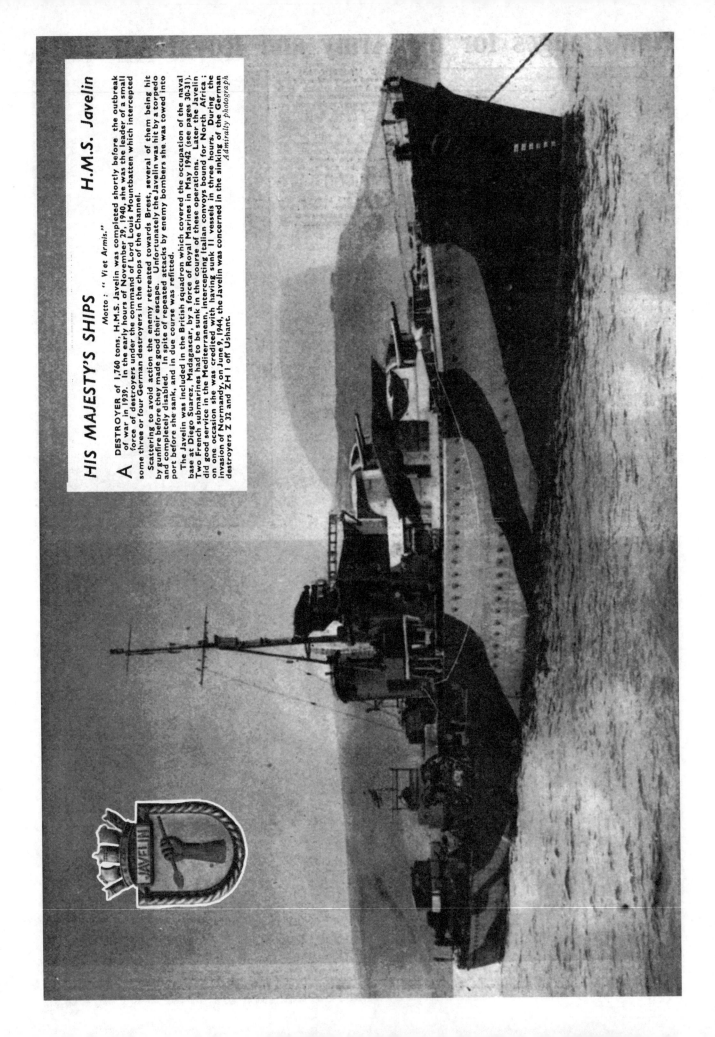

HIS MAJESTY'S SHIPS

H.M.S. Javelin

Motto : "Viet Armis."

A DESTROYER of 1,760 tons, H.M.S. Javelin was completed shortly before the outbreak of war in 1939. In the early hours of November 29, 1940, she was the leader of a small force of destroyers under the command of Lord Louis Mountbatten which intercepted some three or four German destroyers in the chops of the Channel.

Scattering to avoid action the enemy retreated towards Brest, several of them being hit by gunfire before they made good their escape. Unfortunately the Javelin was hit by a torpedo and completely disabled. In spite of repeated attacks by enemy bombers she was towed into port before she sank, and in due course was refitted.

The Javelin was included in the British squadron which covered the occupation of the naval base at Diego Suarez, Madagascar, by a force of Royal Marines in May 1942 (see pages 30-31). Two French submarines had to be sunk in the course of these operations. Later the Javelin did good service in the Mediterranean, intercepting Italian convoys bound for North Africa ; on one occasion she was credited with having sunk 11 vessels in three hours. During the invasion of Normandy, on June 9, 1944, the Javelin was concerned in the sinking of the German destroyers Z 32 and ZH 1 off Ushant.

Admiralty photograph

The Cameronians (Scottish Rifles)

On the outbreak of war in 1939 the 1st Battalion was stationed in India, where it stayed for over two years. A great deal of intensive training was carried out, but officers and men felt keenly a sense of frustration at being relegated to an Internal Security role, aggravated by constant news of the bombing of their homes, and a drastic process of "milking" for parachute battalions and other units which eventually reduced the strength to about 550. On Feb. 17, 1942, the Battalion embarked for Burma, arriving during the involved fighting on the Sittang River, then took part in the hard-fought battle of Pegu and in the long, weary withdrawal to Prome.

After the abortive counter-offensive on Paungde the 1st Battalion covered the withdrawal from Prome, which called for the utmost in mental and physical endurance, and on April 7 moved to Magwe, where it formed the nucleus of Magforce, an improvised independent Brigade which came under the command of the 1st Burma Division. The Battalion covered the withdrawal of this Division to the Pin Chaung and took a considerable part in the costly action of Yenangyaung, was involved in the loss and recapture of Monywa, and shared in the prolonged agony and heroism of the withdrawal into Assam. At the end of June the Battalion, now reduced to under 100 All Ranks, returned to Secunderabad to refit and absorb the large number of reinforcements awaiting it. In October it moved to Ranchi and joined the 50th Indian Tank Brigade, its role being that of Motor Battalion to the Brigade. In March 1943 the Brigade was broken up and the Battalion was selected to form part of a Long Range Penetration Brigade, to undertake operations similar to those of General Wingate's famous 77th Brigade. The 1st Battalion had been personally selected by General Sir William Slim for this role.

In the Heart of Northern Burma

The next 12 months were spent undergoing perhaps some of the toughest training any British troops were asked to carry out during the war. Such items as beds and leave were almost forgotten luxuries for this period of training in the Central Provinces of India during both the hot weather and the monsoon. On March 10, 1944, the Battalion was flown into the airstrip of Broadway, behind the Japanese lines in the heart of northern Burma. Names of the places where the 1st fought its innumerable actions are in many cases not even marked in an atlas. It took a major part in destroying Jap lines of communications in the Imphal area during the critical month of April; in the famous block known as Blackpool, established south of Mogaung in the Railway Corridor; and in the harassing tactics immediately south-west of Mogaung prior to the latter's capture by another brigade of Special Force.

Certain features of this campaign are worthy of note. For five months the 1st Battalion was fed and equipped by air, the greater part of the time all supply-drops taking place by night. All casualties were evacuated by air, in most cases from strips constructed by the men themselves in clearings of no more than 300 yards in the jungle. It was controlled and directed by wireless from India. It marched well over 800 miles, each officer and man carrying, on an average, 75 lb. All sick and wounded had to be carried by stretcher, mule or horse, until it was possible to construct an airstrip from

The Regiment was raised from the amnestied survivors of the Cameronian Covenanters to help William of Orange against James II. Enrolled in the Regular army as the 26th Regiment of the Line, they fought in Marlborough's great battles. The 2nd Battalion (the old 90th) was raised in 1794 and fought in Egypt and at Corunna, in the Crimea took part in the assault on the Redan, and in India marched to the relief of Lucknow. In 1881 the 26th Foot was linked with the 90th Perthshire Light Infantry and the name The Cameronians (Scottish Rifles) came into use. The Regiment fought in Abyssinia and Zululand and through the S. African war. The 1st and 2nd Battalions, the 5th and 6th Territorial Battalions and the Service Battalions gained considerable distinction in the First Great War.

~~~~~~~~~

which to evacuate them. The staple diet for the whole of this period was three "K" ration packets per day, supplemented by a luxury "drop" of bread and bully beef once every five days. Apart from the last three weeks, the whole of the period was spent behind the Japanese lines.

On July 29 the Battalion, some 115 men strong, was flown out from Burma to India, to recuperate and re-form at Dehra Dun. In May 1945 it joined the 36th Division, and soon after peace was declared in September became part of the 2nd Division and embarked for occupational duties in Malaya.

The 2nd Battalion, part of the 5th (British) Infantry Division, moved to France in September 1939, wintered in Comines and moved to Hal in Belgium, on May 10, then to Fresnes, Vimy Ridge, and the Ypres-Comines Canal to fight a great battle, with its famous bayonet charge, before withdrawal to Dunkirk. June 1940 till March 1942 was spent in England and Ireland, in intensive anti-invasion training. In March 1942 the 2nd Battalion sailed for India, but on the voyage became Reserve Battalion for the Madagascar landings. Fighting was brief there, and after three weeks, harassed by malaria, it re-embarked

for India and was stationed at Ahmednagar for a time to recuperate and train. A change of plan switched the 2nd Battalion in August 1942 to Persia where it spent a severe winter under canvas. Orders came in February 1943 to move to Syria for combined operation training. Then, with the 8th Army, it embarked at Suez on July 3 and landed in Sicily as follow-up battalion on July 10, capturing Floridia the same day. Swinging north through Augusta, Villesmundo and Lentini, it arrived at Simeto River before Catania and met the Germans in strength. A hard battle ensued; the Boche cracked and the Battalion pursued the enemy, with minor actions round Mount Etna, Sferro and Paterno, before the campaign ended on August 16.

Big Actions in Italian Campaign

In September 1943 the 2nd landed in Italy at Reggio, as an assault battalion, seizing Isernia in October. Winter was spent patrolling the snowbound Apennines, around Castiglione, until January 1944. The Battalion then moved to the 5th Army front and took part in the successful crossing of the Garigliano river, near Tufo. Embarking on March 11 for Anzio it quickly went into action, first at the celebrated "Fortress" sector. This proved the biggest action for the 2nd in the Italian campaign and a high sacrifice in lives was paid before it broke out of the beach-head, pursuing the Germans to Rome and reaching the Tiber on June 4. After refitting and training in Palestine it embarked in February 1945 for Italy, and thence, in great secrecy, to Belgium. With the Rhine forced, it followed up the German remnants to the Elbe, where at Bleckede it fought its last major battle of the war. Crossing the Elbe it went to Lubeck, accepting surrender of the German garrison there and taking proud part in the first divisional Victory Parade of the war.

The 6th (Lanarkshire) Battalion was mobilized at Hamilton on September 1, 1939, moved south to Hawick, and in April 1940 to Dorset. When the B.E.F. started to withdraw from Dunkirk the 6th received orders to the effect that the Division would move to France to reinforce the Line. On June 11 the Battalion disembarked at Brest. But France capitulated, and the 6th had to return to the U.K. as quickly as possible.

H.M. THE KING INSPECTED CAMERONIANS at Aldershot in June 1940 and spoke to many of the men, including a Company Sergeant-Major who had fought in the First Great War. The Regiment had three battalions in France in 1940, the 2nd, 6th and 7th; but only the 2nd, one of the Regular battalions, was heavily engaged.

Photo, New York Times Photos

Colours : White eye on blue with red border

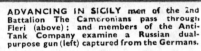

ADVANCING IN SICILY men of the 2nd Battalion The Cameronians pass through Fleri (above); and members of the Anti-Tank Company examine a Russian dual-purpose gun (left) captured from the Germans.

Re-equipped, it commenced intensive training in combined operations, mountain warfare, and as an air-transportable battalion. In September 1944 it joined the B.L.A. in Europe. From Terneuzen on the Scheldt, in its first operation against the enemy, the 6th made an assault landing on South Beveland in the early morning of September 25, and after five days of fighting the enemy withdrew from the island. The Battalion took the towns of Baarland, Sudeland and Drierwegan.

The Division's next task was to capture the island of Walcheren. The 155th Brigade had made an assault landing at Flushing, a Special Service Brigade had landed at West-kapelle, and the 157th Brigade were assaulting the causeway connecting Walcheren to South Beveland. The position was very sticky and the 6th was ordered to cross the Sloe in assault boats and attack the enemy flank. After a very hard struggle this was accomplished. After the Battalion disembarked it had to cross a mud flat three-quarters of a

GUARDS ARMOURED DIVISION

THIS formation was composed of regiments and battalions of the Household Brigade, the Household Cavalry forming the Reconnaissance Regiment ; and the badge worn by the Guards Division during the First Great War was reintroduced for use by the Armoured Division in the Second Great War. The Division was formed in September 1941, and Major-General A. H. S. Adair, C.B., D.S.O., M.C., assumed command in the following year. There followed more than two years of continuous training at home.

It constituted part of the 21st Army Group for the invasion of Europe ; with VIII Corps it landed in Normandy in June 1944, it was present at the struggle for Caen and helped to close the Falaise gap, where the bulk of the German 7th Army was destroyed. After leading the thrust of the British 2nd Army to seize the Seine crossings, the Division, now with XXX Corps, captured Arras on Sept. 1, and on Sept. 3 it liberated Brussels.

LATER in the same month it made a dash across the Netherlands to Nijmegen to secure the bridge already seized by American airborne forces, and made a desperate attempt to break through to the British 1st Airborne Division at Arnhem. In February and March 1945 the Division took part in the operations which cleared the area between the Meuse and the Rhine.

Crossing the Rhine under the command of XII Corps, it fought its way across Germany to Bremen and Cuxhaven, receiving the surrender of the latter port shortly before May 8. On June 10, 1945, the Division was converted into an infantry formation and redesignated the Guards Division, forming part of the British Army of the Rhine. On July 28, 1945 the Burgomaster of Brussels presented the Division with plaques and standards recording the citizens' gratitude for their liberation.

CAMERONIANS IN ITALY spent much of the winter of 1943-44 patrolling the Apennines : a Bren gun team in the hills on the Sangro front. The 2nd Battalion fought their heaviest action in Italy at Anzio when they broke out of the beach-head, pursuing the Germans to Rome. It formed a part of the British 5th Division. *War Office photograph*

mile wide before coming to grips with the enemy—a most treacherous journey, for at no time was the mud and slime less than three feet deep.

After the battle of Walcheren the 6th enjoyed a well-earned rest in the Goes area and later near Hertogenbosch ; then, on December 6 it took over part of the line at Hoschrid Wood, Geilenkirchen. This area was to become its home for a month. It was a desperate place, with companies in tight blobs about a mile apart, with not a building in sight, and patrols had to try to contact the enemy who was sitting behind a most formidable minefield. The next operation was " Blackcock," when the Division swept the enemy from Sittard through Heinsberg and across the Maas. The 6th were responsible for capturing Heilder, Hongden, Breberan, Nachbarhird, Busherhird, and assisted in the taking of Brunsrcrk. Then came

Cameronian Battalions Thrust Through Germany

WELL-NIGH UNBEARABLE conditions—snow, a bitter wind and deep mud—were encountered by the 6th Battalion who were fighting an obstinate and skilful enemy near Havert (1) in January 1945. The white-painted, supporting Bren carriers and tanks were bogged down time and again, leaving the unfortunate infantry to slog forward alone.

On the night of April 2, 1945, the 7th Battalion crossed the River Ems to seize the town of Rheine (2), which was held against several determined counter-attacks; this Battalion was then operating with the supporting infantry of the 7th Armoured Division (the Desert Rats) thrusting towards Bremen.

On April 18, Uelzen (3), 20 miles from Lüneburg, fell to the 9th Battalion, and by now the pace of the advance was becoming so hot that small packs and all unnecessary equipment were left behind, under guard, by the assaulting troops.

War Office photographs

PIPE BAND OF THE CAMERONIANS toured the Middle East towards the end of 1944, entertaining isolated outposts as well as large camps. Pipers and drummers had a wonderful record of service in France, Madagascar, India, Iraq, Persia, Sicily and Italy. First British battalion to reach the Tiber, Cameronians marched through Rome to the skirl of the pipes.

later moving to eastern England for training as airborne troops.

In the autumn of 1944 the 7th crossed to Belgium, participating in the South Beveland and Walcheren campaign, then moving to the Geilenkirchen area and holding a widely extended line on the northern edge of the German thrust in the Ardennes. Hogmanay found them facing several " Boche " attacks. On January 18, 1945, it moved to the Roer triangle, engaging in operations to crush enemy resistance west of the Roer. Next, to the River Maas, crossing at Mook and fighting in the right sector of the Reichswald Forest operation. The 7th moved then to Goch, attacked part of Alpen and occupied positions opposite Wesel, next taking part in the crossing of the Rhine and pushing through the bridge-head to relieve the 6th Air Landing Brigade. That accomplished, the Battalion advanced in support of the 7th Armoured Division.

Clearing the Bremen Dock Area

Next task of the 7th Battalion was the assault crossing of the River Ems. Here a bridge-head was quickly seized, and after bitter fighting in the streets and gardens the Battalion seized the town of Rheine and repelled several hot counter-attacks. This operation was barely completed when they were called on to force the Dortmund-Ems Canal, and after heavy losses established a bridge-head. The 7th then crossed the Weser, advanced through Baden and shared in the capture of Bremen, their last task being the clearing of the dock area, with considerable street fighting. Thereafter the Battalion remained in Bremen until after VE Day, when as a unit of the British Army of the Rhine it formed part of the garrison of Occupied Germany.

The 9th Battalion, though the youngest fighting battalion of the Regiment, was destined to suffer by far the heaviest casualties. With the famous 15th (Scottish) Division they were repeatedly in the forefront of battle. Their first action was " Scottish Corridor," followed by the Normandy slogging, where ground was held against the best German troops. The 9th led the Division in the Caumont attack, prelude to the break-through that formed the Falaise pocket and caused the total collapse of the Germans in Normandy.

Then came a period of pursuit, including the assault crossing of the Seine. Thereafter the battle of the canals was waged in the mud and floods of Belgium and Holland—at Avelghem, Larum, the Escaut and Wilhelmina Canals. The Battalion cleared and captured Best, was the first unit into Tilburg, then back to repel the German thrust through the Americans round Leisel, then the Deurne Canal and Helenaveen of wicked memory, with its well-sighted Spandaus and masses of deadly shoe mines. An intensely cold and unpleasant winter was spent in static defence on the Maas, but January 1945 saw a brief respite in Tilburg.

the battle of Alpen—last German strong-point west of the Rhine. This was a bitter struggle with high losses. C Coy was cut off and captured complete, while B Coy suffered 50 per cent casualties ; but despite these severe losses the Battalion emerged from the battle with honours.

The 6th then spent about 14 days on the banks of the Rhine, mostly in reorganizing. It had a grandstand view of the actual crossing of that river by the airborne troops and the 15th (Scottish) Division. In early April it followed up the assault divisions and rapid progress was made until it reached the Dortmund-Ems canal. It was in action again here, and after crossing the canal the Battalion captured Drierwalde and assisted in taking Hopsten. Then it made long advances in motor transport and eventually reached Verden and prepared for the attack on Bremen—its last action. In a comparatively

short time the city was in the hands of the 52nd (Lowland) Division. The casualties were surprisingly low, but the enemy suffered heavily. A week later the Battalion was sent to guard a concentration camp at Sandbostel, near Bremervörde, and while so employed it received word that all German resistance in N.W. Europe had ceased.

Busy Roles of the 7th Battalion

The 7th Battalion was mobilized at the outbreak of the war with the 52nd (Lowland) Division. During winter and spring of 1939-40 it trained in Lanarkshire and the Borders. In May 1940 it crossed to France, and after a few weeks there and some fighting it was evacuated from Cherbourg in June. After returning to this country the 52nd became a mountain division, and for the next two years the 7th Battalion was trained in the Scottish Highlands for that type of warfare,

THE 15th (Scottish) were the centre division for the assault on the Siegfried Line. The 9th Battalion penetrated the defences on the first day to a depth of 2,000 yards, taking all objectives. Most desperate fighting with fanatical paratroopers ensued in the forests towards Moyland. Spandaus and snipers were everywhere. Thick fog alternated with heavy rain, enemy shells, mortars and grenades—days and nights of heavy casualties, no sleep, and constant strain. A few weeks' respite was but prelude to the Rhine crossing, in which the 9th had its share, with four days of constant attacking on the far side. Then the drive to the Elbe started—the 9th's third assault crossing of a major river. Two days before VE Day a heavy counter-attack at dawn was successfully repelled. It proved to be the last struggle of a stricken enemy.

LAYING DOWN THEIR SWORDS, 37 Japanese officers formally surrendered at the command of Major-General C. G. G. Nicholson, C.B., C.B.E., D.S.O., M.C., at Johore Bahru, Malaya, on Feb. 25, 1946. The pipe and drum band of the Cameronians played the General Salute, while armoured cars covered the ranks of the defeated enemy. *War Office photographs*

Ambush in Khyber Pass

A hostile reception was accorded Pandit Jawaharlal Nehru, Vice-President of the Indian interim Government, when on Oct. 20, 1946, he visited the North-West Frontier. During a skirmish between his military escort and armed tribesmen just outside Landi Kotal in the Khyber Pass shots were fired and stones flung from the mountainside (1) and the windscreen and one side-window of his car were shattered: Nehru, who was unhurt, surveys the damage (2). On fortress-like lines, complete with observation towers, the only openings in the walls of this tribal village (3) in the Pass are slits from which rifles can be fired.

Photos, Associated Press

527

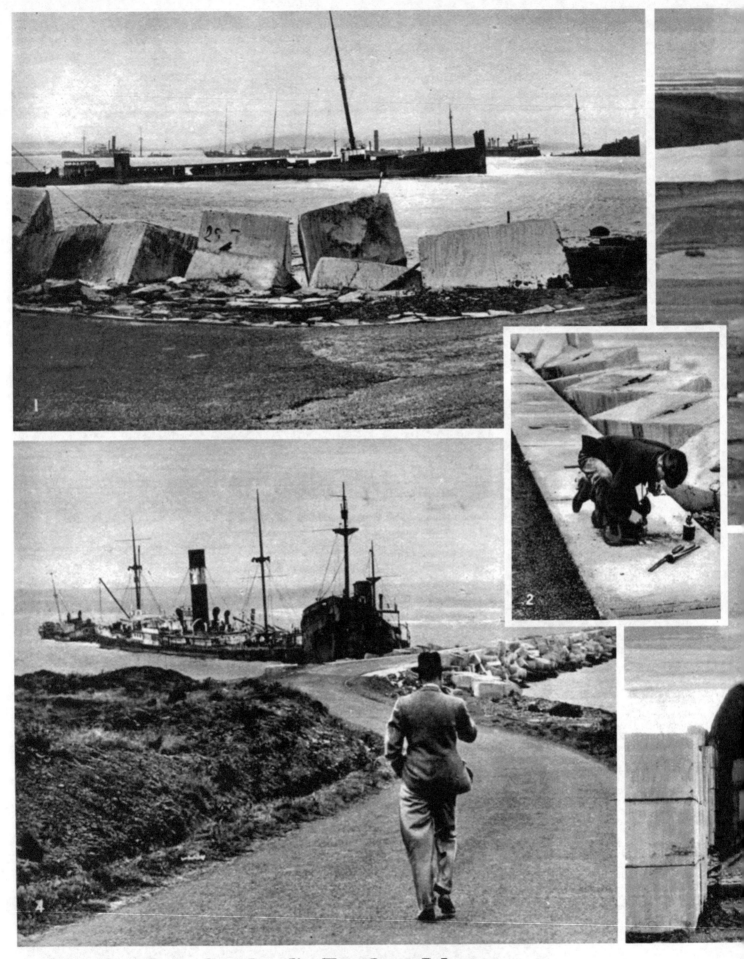

New Roads to Scotland's Farthest Isles—

Built early in the Second Great War to protect our naval base at Scapa Flow—anchorage in the Orkney Islands—against U-boat attacks such as that which sank H.M.S. Royal Oak (see page 281), causeways formed barriers closing the channels which also, as in the First Great War, were sealed by blockships (1). In 1943 these causeways were surfaced and a year later became the finest traffic roads in northernmost Scotland. Maintenance work in progress (2).

— That Grew Out of Threats to Scapa Flow

With the Fleet away the Flow is strangely peaceful: below this stretch (3) lies the 29,000-ton Royal Oak. Almost as lonely appears this causeway (4), constructed like the others of concrete blocks and other material placed in position by giant cranes (5). To the islanders this one (6) meant the end of sea-trips to the mainland of Orkney, and mail services were speeded up: but now the causeways are slowly sinking and the sea may close them in the end.

...*And Quiet Flows the Rhine!*

Photos, Associated Press, Planet News

No shadow of the Swastika is cast on this Dutch tug (1) passing the famous Siebengebirge, range of hills south-east of Bonn, overlooking the Rhine and giving glimpses of 12th-century castles.   At Remagen, French students view the collapsed Ludendorff Railway Bridge (2) which spanned the river.   Navigable again is the Dortmund-Ems Canal (3), linked with the Rhine.   Great river-port on the Rhine, Düsseldorf's travel office (4) is now a military information post.

Conquest of Enemy & Nature in Burma

THIS campaign was never one which was easy to explain to the British public—at least, within the bounds of a popular article. The battle fronts were too scattered and difficulties of the terrain too hard to understand at long range. Names of places, too, were unfamiliar, and in many cases their geographical situation was undiscoverable on the average atlas. Even after D-Day, when public interest in the Burma war increased enormously, it is doubtful whether the intricacies of the campaign were ever fully appreciated by the large majority of people. Written by Lieut.-Colonel Frank Owen, the book under review gives a complete and at the same time human account of the struggle in South-East Asia from start to finish.

An added virtue is that it tells the story not only from the point of view of the High Command but also from the point of view of the average sailor, soldier and airman. It contains maps of great clarity, and photographs which tell more than words could hope to do of the conditions under which the campaign was fought. The early chapters give a vivid and heartbreaking picture of gallant retreat by our outnumbered and ill-equipped forces. Every improvisation was tried, but nothing could cover that crippling basic lack of supporting arms, anti-aircraft guns, transport and air power. By the spring of 1942 Burma had fallen, and the Japanese, in the full flush of their victory, had isolated China from the rest of the world by land and sea and had brought their own forces right up to the jungle and mountain barrier which divides Burma from India.

On the other side of that barrier the pitifully small Allied forces were deployed, waiting for the Japanese to consolidate and possibly to leap forward again towards Assam, the Brahmaputra Valley and Calcutta. The Japanese had 80,000 troops in Burma, but Lord Wavell, then Allied Commander-in-Chief, had to divide his own scanty defence forces between the 700-mile Burma-India frontier and strategic points along India's 4,000-mile coast-line. "These," as Colonel Owen remarks, "were lean days."

But the Japanese did not attack, and in January 1943 Wavell tried to block the easiest approach to India by pushing the Japanese back along the Arakan coast strip and beyond the port of Akyab. He had only the 14th Indian Division to do this, and it was repulsed. The venture cost 2,500 battle casualties, malaria cost infinitely more, and morale was badly shaken. Characteristically, Wavell himself took the blame and said, "I set a small part of the Army a task beyond its training and capacity."

ABOUT this time there occurred one of the few things which could then be set on the credit side of the Allied ledger—the first Wingate expedition. This, too, suffered heavy casualties, but the exploits of the Chindits behind the enemy lines captured public imagination, and the morale of the theatre was raised by proof that the British soldier was more than a match for the Japanese—even in the jungle. These two offensives—one a failure and the other of no real strategic importance—nevertheless kept the Japanese busy during 1943, and perhaps prevented an all-out thrust on India which might have been difficult to parry.

At the end of 1943 Mountbatten came to Burma. The book records that his orders were to maintain and broaden our contacts with China—in other words, to safeguard the

WITH the title The Campaign in Burma a book has been prepared for South-East Asia Command by the Central Office of Information and published by H.M. Stationery Office, price two shillings. It is here reviewed

By CHARLES GARDNER

〜〜〜〜〜

air route over the Himalayas and to reopen the Burma Road. In that simple directive lies the key to the whole of the subsequent Burma war—and the book clearly develops this theme. The Stilwell campaign in the North and the Ledo-Road project can be seen as at one with Wingate's second (Airborne) expedition and the whole Northern offensive. Simultaneously the reader can see, as a coherent whole, the plan for liberating the remainder of Burma and for restoring the old Burma Road from Rangoon. Owen makes it seem as suddenly straightforward as a solved anagram. The bits of the jig-saw begin to fit—the need for a land campaign

JEEP RAILWAYS IN BURMA are helping to solve the problem of communications. Indian engineers have constructed such a line southwards from Myitkyina, and others are being built throughout the country as quickly as possible. See also illus. page 399, Vol. 8. *War Office photo*

because the promised amphibious equipment was needed "elsewhere"—the decision to base this land attack on air supply because there were no roads—the Arakan coastal offensive to obtain the necessary air supply ports and the need for absolute air supremacy to make the whole idea practicable.

Not Imagined in Previous Wars

These things become clear and, with them, we are given the plain tale of the man in the jungle, how he lived and fought on the mountain sides, and in the mud, and along the great rivers. Perhaps the most graphic chapters deal with the two Japanese offensives of 1944—both designed to break through to India, both defeated after bloody and sustained fighting. The epics of Kohima and Imphal are outstanding in the Burma story, not only because of their gallantry but because they were the turning points of the struggle. On the tide of victory the 14th Army chased the defeated Japanese from the Indian borders to Rangoon, and in so doing virtually destroyed the enemy armies and air forces in South-East Asia.

Although the great planning work of Mountbatten and Slim is unfolded by inference in this story of a fabulous campaign, the heroes are not the generals : they are the little men, the rank and file who fought the battles and crossed the rivers and flew the aircraft. "It depended on the soldier and how he bore himself . . . each fighter had to conquer his own heart," says the book, and only after reading it, and especially after seeing the pictures of the campaign ground, will full realization come of what this phrase implied in Burma Victory.

The tangled problem of supply and transport on a front which Mountbatten himself described as, "propounding the biggest logistical nightmare of the war," is dealt with. Field-Marshal Lord Wavell in one of his works wrote, "I have soldiered for more than 42 years, and the more I have seen of war the more I realize how it all depends upon administration and transportation." In South-East Asia this all-important battle of supply rose to a peak not imagined in previous wars. The operational area of the land forces gradually expanded until it was larger than that embraced by Eisenhower's armies in the west of Europe—a fact which is not generally appreciated. The different tastes, habits and religious customs of British, Americans, Gurkhas and Indian Moslems, Hindus and Sikhs, multiplied the difficulties of the ration problem.

The nature of the country, its climate and its lack of land communications has to be seen to be believed, yet half a million Allied troops marched and fought in South-East Asia for years. The 14th Army alone required 2,000 tons of food a day, and in the later stages of the campaign nearly all this was delivered by air. None the less, certain roads had to be built, most of them on grass tracks where human foot had hardly traced its print, and eventually a local labour force of coolies was employed totalling a quarter-million men. The railway problem was almost as great, for the track originally designed to carry a few tea-plantation trains was required to move 12,000 tons a day.

All these things were done, and at the same time the great air supply organization upon which the offensive depended was built up at the coastal airports. The British, Canadian and American Dakota squadrons of Combat Cargo Task Force operated a 24-hour, seven-day week service which, at its peak, carried 90,000 tons of supplies and equipment to the army. To help them land the stuff close to the front line and to supply them with air protection, something like 200 airfields were constructed in six months. Another vitally important matter which is dealt with comprehensively is that of the battle against sickness—a battle every bit as important as that against the Japanese, as it was one which, at one stage, was inflicting far more casualties on the Allies. The success of the Burma war was, in no small measure, due to the medical victory over malaria and other jungle scourges. At one time over a quarter-million of the Allies were malaria and dysentery victims, but by 1945 the sickness rate had come down to two per thousand.

Salute for the Life-Line Men

How all this was done—supplies secured and delivered, malaria conquered and the life-line maintained is, perhaps, not so exciting as stories of actual combat and jungle exploits. But it is obvious that without the "life-line men" there would have been very little jungle exploit and certainly no victory.

Colonel Owen's book gives the back area troops their full meed of praise. In so doing he will have the approval of all ranks who served out in the Far East, for no fighting army had learnt the lesson of supply more thoroughly than the 14th. Many of its veteran troops had seen Burma fall for lack of supplies, and they knew the recapture of Rangoon was not even feasible until the "life-line men" had conquered the jungle and the mountains, the rivers and the rains, the railways and the airfields.

Europe's Wartime Capitals in 1946
COPENHAGEN

By H. R. MADOL

As we approached the Danish shore—on board one of the giant planes accomplishing the journey from New York in less than 24 hours—we wondered how we should find Copenhagen after so many years. There used to be no country in the world where people had developed the joy of living into so fine an art, no better place than Copenhagen for hospitality, gaiety and pleasure. Was it not to be feared that years of bitter struggle would have taken the sheen off this finest jewel of the Baltic Seas, that bombs and guns would have made havoc of Copenhagen's streets and monuments and left the people hard and bitter ?

Circling over Copenhagen before landing at Kastrup airfield we found the city as beautiful as ever : lofty spires of churches, copper roofs of ancient castles, the quaint serpent spire of its Hanseatic stock exchange, the King's four palaces—all could be clearly seen. The blue waters of the Swedish straits, here and there touched with the whiteness of

We soon learned, however, that Copenhagen's finest quality has suffered no harm and the virtue of its hospitality is unimpaired. Friends offered us the necessary bed-linen (the absence of any at the hotel was apparently caused by a strike of laundrymen !) and invitations were forthcoming at an overwhelming rate. The Copenhageners are as eager to hear what is happening in the world as the returning stranger is to find his bearings in their midst.

I can think of no better way of doing this than to stroll in pleasant company from Kongens Nytorv along the Stroget, Copenhagen's main thoroughfare, towards the Raadhuuspladsen, the town-hall square, past the fashion shops (as elegant as ever, in spite of the scarcity of raw materials),

In Tivoli the great gay pleasure park, we admired the " Pantomime," lively and charming, a performance unique of its kind, with dancing and music, whilst around us crowds of young people were enjoying the attractions of a fairground—rifle-range and giant wheel, switchback and swing. The concert hall and other buildings were destroyed, together with the famous Lange Linie Pavilion of the Royal Yacht Club, when the Nazi invaders tried to frighten the Danes by counter-sabotage towards the end of the Occupation period and the resistance movement was at its height.

Flowers Where the Patriots Fell

But much has been repaired, and the sight of Tivoli with its hundreds of thousands of glowing lamps under the fine old trees is one to be remembered, though the music and gaiety did seem somewhat toned down. At the Royal Opera enormous torches adorned the roof. Young students were everywhere in evidence with their white caps ; in spite of the shortage there will always be enough material for these and for the country's flag. In the morning we walked around the fishmarket, one of the celebrated sights, where the stout fisher-women are as solid as ever and their wares as varied and appetizing as they used to be. And walking along the waterways we were happy to find again the charming bronze statue of the Little Mermaid, inspired by Hans Andersen's fairy tale.

Long promenades in Copenhagen streets followed ; we found that the Marble Church is still one of the finest buildings of the town ; Christiansborg, where Parliament is sitting, is as busy and Rosenborg and Berstorff gardens as peaceful as before the war. But here and there we see bomb-damaged houses, empty places with large, flower-crowned crosses, and remember that the Danish fight for freedom had its victims as numerous as elsewhere. Bunches of flowers mark spots on the streets where patriots were killed by the Germans. There is a big empty space where once was a school and where a great number of children were killed during a raid, when the headquarters of the Gestapo were blown up by the R.A.F.

BROADCASTING HOUSE AND CONCERT HALL, Copenhagen, combine to form an excellent example of modern architecture. Erection work began under the German Occupation, the project being entirely Danish, though the premises were used for a time by the German-controlled Danish Radio. The building was completed in 1946.   *Photo, T. R. Yerbury*

sails, the green parks—all were shining under the summer sun. It looked as if no shadow of the Swastika remained, as if the clouds of foreign rule had gone for ever. The white and red flag flying everywhere looked as gay as it had ever been.

Multitudes Stranded by the War

But, as we rode a little later in one of the few available taxis, we passed on the outskirts of Copenhagen a town we had never seen before—a town of drab wooden barracks, housing some of the hundreds of thousands of refugees, German and Baltic, whom the flood of war left stranded here : masses of humanity for whom the Danes (whether they want to or not) will have to care until the problem of refugees finds a world-wide settlement. It is indeed a heavy burden on the budget of a small country greatly impoverished by Nazi looting.

The elegance of the streets and squares of Copenhagen has given place to much austerity. Arriving at one of its best-known hotels you find there is no linen on the beds, no towel in the baronial bathroom, no response from the hot-water taps. And on the open-air terrace the waiters, once immaculately clad in white, have become a little shabby, and some of their once world-renowned politeness has gone. For years Denmark has had no cloth. It has no wood, no coal. It has not long woken up from the uneasy dream of war. The German nightmare has gone, but much clearance work and readjustment has yet to be done

sit on a terrace when evening comes and the Copenhageners swarm home on bicycles from work, when the nearby Tivoli, the pleasure ground of Scandinavia, comes to life and a few neon lights appear timidly on the background of a clear night sky which at the height of summer hardly darkens in this northern country.

The fare at the famous restaurants is as rich, varied and well prepared as ever and still not quite out of reach of the purse of the man of modest means. In this home-country of dairy-butter, breakfast bacon and fresh eggs, of great culinary traditions, of Tuborg and Carlsberg beer, of some of the world's richest fishing grounds (where the finest sole and the finest lobster and, in season, the most renowned oysters abound) there is no real need to curtail the menu.

Rationing is limited to butter and bread, and a man who takes his friends to lunch at a restaurant will have to deprive his wife of some of the butter-cards otherwise used at home. The most severe shortage, as already mentioned, is that of materials of all kinds, and people have to present a really serious case of hardship before they obtain a permit to buy any articles of clothing. Prices have gone up everywhere. The cost of living is at least 50 per cent higher than in pre-war days. On the other hand, there is practically no unemployment. In any case, being predominantly an agricultural country, Denmark has never had the unemployment commonly encountered in industrial countries.

Yes, Copenhagen has its scars of war, but it is speedily recovering. There are plenty of photos still on view in shop windows showing the city's decorations at the time of liberation, the magnificent welcome given to Field-Marshal Montgomery, the enthusiasm of the crowds surrounding King Christian at his first visit to the free Parliament. They leave in the beholder no doubt as to the Danish people's vitality, patriotism and national power of recovery.

When the first heavy German tanks arrived on Copenhagen's town-hall square, where for years summer-houses or boats were usually on show as high lottery prizes, a little Danish boy climbed up to a German soldier and asked : " How much are the tickets ? " When the first heavy guns appeared in the streets, Copenhageners thought of their small, defenceless country and wondered why cannon should be used against sparrows.

But two years of German " protection " taught them that their freedom and democratic achievements were at stake and their lives in danger every day—and they reacted violently. The Copenhagener, ordinarily so peaceful, became a fighter, a saboteur, an avenger. All that happened before Freedom was regained will not soon be forgotten. But the Copenhagener cannot help looking at the pleasant side of things and—given a chance of real peace—his town will again fully reflect his frame of mind.

Full-Fed Now and Busy in Beautiful Copenhagen

NO SCARCITY OF WORK troubles the people of Denmark's capital, many of whom cycle (1) to and from their places of employment. And there is little curtailment of menu, only butter and bread being rationed. Numerous open-air cafés (2) are patronized. Overlooking the harbour (3) is the tower of Christiansborg Palace, now housing the Parliament and Supreme Court; the twisted spire is that of the 300-years-old Bourse. One of the celebrated sights of Copenhagen is the fish-market, where white-bonneted saleswomen (4) have great abundance to offer. See also facing page.

Photos, New York Times Photos

PAGE 533

How the Front Line Battle News Reached Home

FROM FOREMOST AREAS of battle to the front pages of the world's daily newspapers the news of some of the greatest fighting of the war was transmitted by mobile wireless units of Cable and Wireless, Ltd. Members of the units shared the hardships and some of the dangers of the men whose achievements they communicated to an expectant public. In North Africa, Italy and the Far East these units, moving with the British Armies, dispatched correspondents' descriptions of the fighting and provided a link between the soldier in the field and his family at Home. The first of the "Telcom" units, which were known as Blue Trains, was sent to Algiers shortly after the Allied landings in French North Africa in November 1942, and went to Italy in January 1944. Naples was its first headquarters, and after the capture of Rome it moved forward to the capital, whence it made an eventful journey of 200 miles to Forli.

DURING the closing stages of the war the unit found itself in Padua, where the members, watching a procession of tanks, guns, lorries, jeeps, and staff cars stream through the city, realized that they had outstripped the British 8th Army, which was then advancing to deliver the knock-out blow. After the surrender of the German forces in Italy "Telcom" crossed the frontier into Austria and installed themselves in Vienna, where they established direct communication with London. A small mobile unit of the type used in the field is seen at (2) with an operator transmitting a message by wireless. In the Far East another mobile wireless unit landed near Rangoon immediately prior to its liberation in May 1945, and messages were being flashed to Colombo within 2½ hours of their arrival. At Colombo an infantry landing craft was converted into a Press ship (1). which followed the British fleet to Singapore in

September 1945. The ship provided facilities for wireless telegraphy and phototelegraphy and the staff dispatched 160,000 words of Press messages in the first few hours after their arrival ; within about a week they had transmitted 500,000 words.

THE story of the Liberation of Malaya and the surrender of the Japanese forces in South-East Asia was flashed to London by high-speed automatic transmitter (3). On arriving at Singapore the officer in charge of the unit went to the Cable and Wireless office in the port, where he had been employed before the war. Here he found a Japanese colonel sitting in his chair—and who left in great haste ! In addition to war correspondents' stories the Press ship dealt with thousands of free messages from liberated prisoners of war to their families at home. In 70 countries and on the High Seas a staff of 10,000 men and women of Cable and Wireless, Ltd., worked throughout the war to maintain the British and Allied lines of communication over the 355,000-mile Imperial cable and wireless network. The operators played their part in the defence of Malta and manned a score of other vital stations, such as Gibraltar, Aden and Cocos Islands. The cable ships often carried out their work in dangerous waters, cutting and diverting enemy cables and laying anti-submarine loops for the Admiralty. Cable stations were priority targets all over the world for enemy aircraft, and in the course of their duties operators were bombed, machine-gunned, shelled and torpedoed. "Time and again," says Charles Graves, telling the story of these achievements in his book The Thin Red Lines (Standard Art Book Co., 5s.) "the staff remained at their posts until the last minute in the best traditions of wireless operators in sinking ships."

Photos, British Official, D. J. Mackie

Our War Leaders in Peacetime
PORTAL

As chief of the wartime R.A.F., Charles Frederick Algernon Portal earned a name for determination, a quick-thinking brain and a deep interest in aviation matters. His juniors knew he had been a first-class cricketer : what they did not know was that their chief has been a student of flight ever since, as a boy of 16, at Winchester, he trained his first falcon.

He is the only top-ranking Allied war-leader to " fly hawks." Before the war, when he had time for falconry, near his Hungerford home, the 4,000-years-old sport was one of his relaxations. He is a foremost authority on this " sport of kings " and did not lose interest in it even during the war.

Marshal of the R.A.F. Viscount Portal of Hungerford, G.C.B., O.M., D.S.O., M.C., born at Pangbourne, Berks, in 1893, is of Huguenot stock ; his ancestors are said to have crossed the Channel hidden in empty casks among a shipment of wine. A swarthy young man with the " Huguenot nose," he married Joan Margaret, the daughter of Sir Charles Glynn Welby, in 1919, and if she did not ride a motor-cycle at breakneck speed (a craze of his) she has shared his other interests, over a wide field, for 27 years.

He's Never Still for a Moment

When an undergraduate he won the 1914 Inter-Varsity Motor Cycle Hill Climb, and he took up flying because it is faster than motor-cycling. By way of contrast, three years ago he bought a camera and became so interested that he embarked upon micro-photography. Long ago Portal added fishing and sailing to his other outdoor sports, and promptly Lady Portal and the two Portal girls, Rosemary Ann, born in 1923, and Mavis Elizabeth Alouette, born in 1926, became enthusiasts. A first-class shot, fisherman and cricketer, he has also proved himself handy with a boat.

He is not a family man in the generally accepted sense of the word—a stay-at-home ; but he likes to have his family with him when he goes sailing or swimming. He craves for activity : his wife declares he is never still for a moment. His recreations are not entirely restricted to outdoors. He likes reading and writing—largely on aeronautical matters and on his precious falconry. When at Winchester he contributed scholarly articles on hawking to The Field periodical.

On January 1, 1946, he resigned as Chief of Air Staff, and at the end of the month he was appointed head of an organization set up by the Ministry of Supply for the production of materials for atomic research.

BEFORE HIS RETIREMENT as Chief of Air Staff : Viscount Portal at his desk (3) in the Air Ministry, London. On June 26, 1946, Oxford University conferred upon him the honorary degree of D.C.L. (Doctor of Civil Law) ; wearing his academic robes (4) he is about to enter the Sheldonian Theatre, Oxford, for the ceremonial presentation.

Photos, New York Times Photos, Air Ministry, Fox,

Keystone

AT A RECEPTION held at the American Embassy in London, Viscount Portal of Hungerford is seen (1) in conversation with Lady Hartington, daughter of Mr. Joseph Kennedy, at one time U.S. ambassador to Great Britain. Lady Portal (2) presents a "Dig for Victory" trophy to the squadron-leader commanding a R.A.F. maintenance unit.

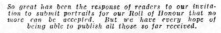

The Roll of Honour

NCOs & MEN

1939—1946

D/R. V. BAKER
Middlesex Regiment.
In action : Caen. 9.6.44.
Age 24 *(Tottenham)*

So great has been the response of readers to our invitation to submit portraits for our Roll of Honour that no more can be accepted. But we have every hope of being able to publish all those so far received.

Pte. E. BARNES
P.P. Canadian L.I.
Action : S. Italy. Oct. 43.
Age 23. *(Medora)*

L/Sea. D. BOOTH
H.M.S. Welshman.
Action : at sea. 1.2.43.
Age 21. *(Sevenoaks)*

L/Sea. L. J. CLAYFIELD
Royal Navy.
Action : at sea. 7.5.40.
Age 22. *(Nailsworth)*

A/B C. COE
H.M.S. Juno.
Action : Crete. 21.5.41.
Age 25. *(Bishop Auckland)*

Sgt. A. J. COURTMAN
Royal Norfolk Regiment.
Action : R. Orne. 8.8.44.
Age 31. *(King's Lynn)*

O/Sig. F. CRANAGE
Royal Navy.
Action : at sea. 26.1.45.
Age 18. *(Leeds)*

Sgt. H. COLLIN
Royal Air Force.
Over Germany. 21.3.45.
Age 23. *(Peterborough)*

L/Cpl. R. DOCHERTY
8th Bn. Royal Scots.
Action: Normandy. 3.7.44.
Age 22. *(Tranent)*

Gnr. J. DONALDSON
Royal Artillery.
D/wnds. : Italy. 13.9.44.
Age 25. *(Preston Pans)*

Gnr. G. O. DONOGHUE
Royal Navy.
Action : Atlantic. 1.3.44.
Age 18. *(Pontypool)*

O/S. F. EASTON
H.M.S. Royal Oak.
A'n : Scapa Flow. 14.10.39.
Age 18. *(Liverpool)*

A/B. R. ELDRIDGE
Royal Navy.
Action : at sea. 4.3.42.
Age 41. *(Nr. Southampton)*

Tpr. E. K. GILLVRAY
4th Recce Regt., R.A.C.
Action : Arezzo. 12.7.44.
Age 20. *(Doncaster)*

Pte. R. GOATLEY
5th Scottish Para. Regt.
Action : Italy. 13.12.43.
Age 23 *(Nottingham)*

Stkr. J. J. GRAINGER
Royal Navy.
Action : at sea. 24.12.41.
Age 20. *(Connah's Quay)*

Spr. J. R. GREEN
1st Field Pty., R.E.
D/wnds. : Italy. 1.6.45.
Age 35. *(Newhaven)*

O/S. S. HAIGH
H.M.S. Martin.
N. Africa landing. 10.11.42.
Age 19. *(Pudsey)*

Rfmn. J. W. HARRIS
London Irish Rifles.
Action : Faenza. 4.1.45.
Age 21. *(Osbournby)*

L/Cpl. A. HUDSON
Royal Engineers.
Action : Malaya. 26.1.42.
Age 22. *(Holywell Row)*

L/Sgt. G. JONES
Royal Engineers.
Act'n: W. Europe. 25.3.45.
Age 29. *(Rhyl)*

L/Sig R. W. LAMONT
Royal Navy.
Action : Red Sea. 18.3.41.
Age 20. *(Ipswich)*

A/B. J. LYNCH
H.M.S. Rawalpindi.
A'n : off Iceland. 23.11.39.
Age 19. *(Liverpool)*

L/Cp. S. E. MADDISON
R. Inniskilling Fusiliers.
Action : Italy. 13.4.45.
Age 20. *(Whitwick)*

Sgt. A. J. MATTHEWS
1st Gordon Highlanders.
Action : Rhine. 23.3.45.
Age 27. *(Thurlaston)*

Pte. J. PENTELOW
Lincolnshire Regiment.
Action : Italy. 10.11.43.
Age 24. *(Spalding)*

Cpl. J. W. PETERS
Welch Regiment.
Action : Holland. 1944.
Age 28. *(Spalding)*

Ldg. Stkr. R. A. PRATT
Royal Navy.
Action : Crete. 21.5.41.
Age 24. *(Kingston, Cambs.)*

Sgt./Plt. I. PRICE
Royal Air Force.
Over France. 12.7.41.
Age 24. *(Penmaenmawr)*

Stkr. P. R. SMITH
H.M. Submarine Porpoise.
Malacca Strait. 16.1.45.
Age 19. *(Wokingham)*

Tpr. M. P. STONE
1st Royal Tank Regt.
A'n: Normandy. July. '44.
Age 19. *(St. Erth)*

Pte. W. J. SILVESTER
Oxford and Bucks L.I.
Died of wounds. 9.6.44.
Age 23. *(Stoke-on-Trent)*

Pte. J. I. TWISS
K.O. Scottish Borderers.
Action : Caen. 2.7.44.
Age 20. *(Edinburgh)*

P/O. E. J. THORNHILL
H.M.S. Prince of Wales.
Action : Malaya. 10.12.41.
Age 21. *(Nottingham)*

Pte. H. TONGUE
13th Bn. Parachute Regt.
Act'n: Normandy. 19.8.44.
Age 21 *(Manchester)*

Pte. G. A. G. WILSON
East Surrey Regiment.
Action : Italy. 19.6.44.
Age 23. *(Egerton)*

A.C.1. W. WILSON
Royal Air Force.
Died of wounds. 17.11.41.
Age 36. *(Hull)*

Pte. C. WHITEFIELD
Hampshire Regiment.
Action : Italy. 15.9.44.
Age 22. *(Fareham)*

From the Philippines to Canada

Aircraft carriers of the British Pacific Fleet, specially converted to troopships, assisted in the repatriation of P.O.W. from the Far East in the autumn of 1945. The varied interests of one such voyage in H.M.S. Glory are described by Lieutenant J. L. Wells, R.N.V.R.

I HAD been a prisoner of war myself in Germany and now, as a repatriation staff officer, I was watching over 1,000 of our Far Eastern repatriates embark aboard H.M.S. Glory (Captain A. W. Buzzard, D.S.O., O.B.E., R.N.), a light Fleet carrier of 14,000 tons which had come up from Sydney to Manila to take them one more stage on their 15,000-mile journey home. Men of all Services climbed happily aboard—stretchers b r o u g h t others. They included Canadians ; for them the journey would be shorter. That evening we sailed from the Philippines for Esquimalt, Vancouver Island, via Pearl Harbour.

It was difficult for me to imagine all the reactions which these men must have felt on boarding this ship flying the white ensign. A sailor rarely talks of his flag, but it means a great deal to him ; on this occasion it must have meant as much to the passengers. I recalled my own joy of liberation in May 1945 and realized that in comparison theirs must be tenfold after the greater strain of a Japanese P.O.W. camp. I had already spoken to many of them and knew that until their arrival in Manila few had seen British uniforms, had read British magazines or had spoken to Britons from the " outside world." Their American liberators had been most hospitable to our prisoners returning ; but in captivity these had been starved not only of food but of contacts with the Homeland, and a man in this frame of mind naturally looks forward eagerly to living again in a completely British atmosphere. This they found in H.M.S. Glory.

AFTER leaving Manila I was soon able to get a composite idea of all that had been done to make the voyage pleasurable. The large hangar deck, formerly the busy aircraft maintenance depot, had been cleared to provide sleeping accommodation and restaurant space for about 1,000 men. Spare propellers and fuel tanks still bore witness to its earlier activity, and now colourful Empire posters lent a bright tone. After the filthy conditions of a Japanese prison, this was real comfort. A smaller section at the after end of this deck, separated from the main accommodation by administrative offices, was the improvised hospital where four naval nursing sisters, eight British nurses and ten Australian V.A.D.s attended the patients. A dispensary, offices and feeding facilities provided the staff with all requirements.

Owing to a temporary disability I spent three days in that hospital and quickly sensed the deep appreciation of the patients for the grand way in which these women carried out their task : untiring, working long hours, the nurses had a ready smile for all. They worked under the Senior Medical Officer of the ship, who was assisted by five other naval doctors. Conditions for the nurses were certainly not normal ; the illnesses were unusual. But they remained undeterred by the crowded ward, the double-decker beds, the steady Pacific swell, and the sulphur fumes which now and again blew down from the funnel. One nurse said to me, " It's impossible for us to understand what these men have been through. We can only guess ! I'm terribly glad I came."

One man died during the voyage, and was buried at sea. And despite their gay way of talking I knew the monotony which was endured below in the hospital. Three British Red Cross women did their utmost to relieve it. They seemed to be all over the ship, issuing cigarettes, clothing, sun-glasses and other aids to comfort. Naturally they paid particular attention to those in bed, writing letters for them and shopping at the canteen. Service payments were made, books, jig-saw puzzles and occupational therapy material were given out.

At each end of the hangar deck, lifts, formerly used for bringing up aircraft to the flight deck, were half raised. Windscoops solved the question of ventilation. Gangways led on to these lifts and thence on to the flight deck, where we used to sit and benefit from the tropical sun. The officer passengers were accommodated in cabins aft, made available by a reduction in Naval Air Arm personnel. Some were in operational rooms. My cabin was the Asdic office, with a bewildering array of knobs and dials. We slept in these rooms and lived in the wardroom, smoking and chatting about the last few years. I knew what an awful vacuum those years seemed in the lives of the passengers, who could scarcely credit the fact that I had been at home only two months previously. Lectures on the war and life at home co-operated with the ship's newspaper, Glory News, in making every one familiar with events, past and present.

No Lack of Helpers in the Galley

I spent part of one day watching the feeding organization up for'ard. Initial difficulties for the galley, involved by an increase of 800 men, were solved by the peacetime experience of one of the ship's officers. The familiar prisoners' cry of " Big eats ! " came true in this cafeteria restaurant. Strangely enough, they preferred their own aluminium utensils to the crockery put on board for their use.

I watched them all cheerfully helping the galley staff. They were as willing here as elsewhere, for the reduced ship's company could not do everything.

Passengers paraded each morning at 9.30, and each day the parade became smarter as a result of the struggle to regain self-respect—a struggle made more difficult by their not having their own Service uniforms. They had watched the Royal Marines drilling, they had seen the ship's company at Sunday divisions, we had all sensed the thrill of entering Pearl Harbour in true naval style, paraded and with band playing ; but I realized how difficult it was to be enthusiastic about mass organizations when all that they wanted was to become individuals again.

Lieutenant J. L. WELLS, R.N.V.R.

BOARDING H.M.S. GLORY AT MANILA, men of all Services saw the White Ensign for the first time after years in Jap camps. This was one stage in the long journey Home, with—for those needing it—skilled attention by British and Australian nursing sisters. Normally the Glory carried 39 to 44 aircraft. See illus. page 327, Vol. 9.

THE HANGAR DECK OF H.M.S. GLORY provided most of the sleeping accommodation (1) for the 1,000 repatriates, and the lift well (2) made an excellent stage. Those suffering from the effects of semi-starvation were cared for in the ship's hospital (3).

The bridge was a grand point of vantage for me to view the sporting activities on board, and I was amazed at the vigour displayed and the determination shown to get fit before arriving home. A wide choice lay open to the passengers : I watched them engaged in musical P.T., boxing, deck tennis, deck hockey, and various kinds of shooting.

We berthed at Pearl Harbour on October 20. The stay was of short duration, and liberty was confined to the dockyard. But the view of the beautiful countryside, the joy of seeing a fully-lit town again, and the great attraction of a Hula dance on the flight deck all added to the pleasure of the call at this big American naval base. A wooden stage was erected, and early that evening we watched a genuine Hula production, with grass skirts, garlands of flowers and all the mysteries of this exotic dance.

Consolation for Ship's Company

Many were the interests of this peaceful voyage. The dentist was responsibile for 206 stoppings, 90 extractions, 12 scalings and one fractured jaw reduced and immobilized. The officer responsible for the laundry might have been called the " Laundry Lieutenant," but he happened to be a peer, so we called him the " Dhobi Duke." It was strange to realize it was only three months since this ship was ploughing the ocean with the intention of war in the Pacific. Men who had been keeping watch on the bridge, searching the seas for enemy ships, torpedo tracks and periscopes, or scanning the sky for hostile aircraft, were now bent on avoiding rain squalls so that their guests could enjoy the fresh air of the flight deck !

One of the ship's officers gave me perhaps the best description of the feelings of the ship's company. He explained how H.M.S. Glory had come out here to join the Pacific Fleet. They had worked up for war and the war had ended, leaving them feeling flat and disconsolate, though naturally not disappointed at the cessation of hostilities . . . and this repatriation trip, he said, was the finest consolation prize they could have had. The end was in sight with Esquimalt—and a presentation of three silver bugles and a mace by the Brigadier to the ship. I have rarely witnessed such hospitality or seen such ready appreciation of it.

Entertainment was an integral part of the ship's routine. The Royal Marines band played each morning, and promenade concerts were given daily on records over the ship's radio. ITMA and Tommy Trinder were popular—and I found it pleasant to sit on the flight deck in the warmth of a tropical night and listen to the Intermezzo from Cavalleria Rusticana or to Elgar's Pomp and Circumstance while a phosphorescent wake faded away into the darkness. An Epilogue closed each day.

Further activities were provided for us by tombola, and a revue staged by repatriates and starring " The Two Twits " and " The Waiter, Blondie and Blimp."

We Found Himmler's Buried Secrets

Even in death the Gestapo chief defied the victors to recover his most precious secrets. A slip, and the search party, a Czechoslovakian mountain and the narrator of this story, L. S. B. Shapiro, European Correspondent of Maclean's Magazine, would have been blown to bits.

THERE were thirteen of us. Leroy, the diminutive southern private who drove the command car which led our little convoy through snow-covered Czech mountain passes, didn't like it—not one bit. He kept mumbling : " Hot dam—thirteen—'tain't good." I smiled uneasily at his superstition and looked for reassurance in the faces of my companions in the command car. Lieut. S. of the French Army's *Deuxième Bureau* looked ominously serious. Lieut. O. of the American Army Intelligence shrugged his shoulders and continued to pore over maps of southern Bohemia.

Yes, there were thirteen of us. I figured it again as we lurched and skidded over frozen roads. With Lieut. Wayne Leeman, St. Louis, a Signal Corps photographer, there were five of us in the command car. Two trucks and an air-compressor vehicle behind us each had a driver. That made eight. In the engineer carrier, which brought up the rear of the convoy, there were three engineers —Capt. Stephen Richards of Decatur, Georgia ; Sgt. Taylor Fulton of Kenosha, Wis., and Sgt. Philip Urquhart of Chicago. That made eleven, and in the cab of one of the trucks there were two more—Sgt. Vital of the French Army, guarding his prisoner, former S.S. Sgt. Gunther Achenbach, a tall, handsome, sad-eyed Nazi. On a deserted stretch of road the convoy halted and Capt. Richards summoned us into a huddle.

"I can't tell you what this is all about, men," he said quietly. "All I can say is that it's a secret mission and it may be dangerous. Don't talk to anyone, do what you're told and we'll come out of it O.K. We'll be stopping in Prague tonight, and tomorrow morning we'll tackle the job."

All Concerned Sworn to Secrecy

It was February 10, 1946—a curious time, I thought, to be going on dangerous missions. The war had been over nine months and Czechoslovakia was an eminently friendly country. But was the war really over ? No—not quite. We were still struggling to win, the peace. In the Security Council of the U.N.O. men were debating ways of peace with fire and eloquence. In Nuremberg the Allies sat in judgement on the sins of the Nazis. This, too, was an integral part of the struggle for peace : if light were shed on the horrible past we might be able to see ways of wisdom for the future.

Our little band was on a mission to shed light on the past. Somewhere in the wild Czech hills Heinrich Himmler, the Gestapo chief, had buried his most precious secrets—buried them so deep and protected them so lavishly that even in death he defied the victors to recover them and come away alive. Our job was to dig them out. The key lay in the hands of a S.S. prisoner whom none of us could trust.

As the convoy got under way again I climbed into the cab with Achenbach and heard from his lips the story that had dispatched us on this mysterious journey. In early April 1945 Hitler's Reich was crumbling fast. From Stettin to the Brenner the Nazi war machine was in chaos. But there was still discipline in the ranks of the engineer regiment of Das Reich S.S. Division on duty south of Prague. Achenbach's company was ordered to find an obscure place far from the prying eyes of the Czech population and there to construct a deep shaft which could be covered over and hidden—if need be, forever. For three days and three nights work proceeded feverishly, and in the darkness of early morning of the fourth day two S.S. trucks accompanied by a squad of Gestapo agents rolled into the area.

Thirty-two heavy cases were deposited in the shaft, each case being separately booby-trapped by Teller mines fitted with blasting caps. Then the S.S. engineers wired the entrance doors of the shaft with the most ambitious booby traps ever installed in so small an area. Fourteen hundred pounds of dynamite and half-a-ton of flame-thrower oil were attached to detonators so designed that movement of a quarter of an inch would explode and burn the contents of the shaft. Only two diagrams of the shaft were drawn. One went to *Reichsprotector* Karl Hermann Frank, the Nazi overlord in Prague, the other to Himmler himself. All the men who worked on the job were sworn to secrecy. S.S. officers guaranteed Himmler that his documents were safe forever from unauthorized eyes. Together with the remnants of his division, Achenbach fled westward from the oncoming Russians. In May 1945 General Leclerc's French Army, advancing along the line of the Swiss frontier, picked him up an exhausted straggler.

FOR months Achenbach lay in the wretched prison for S.S. officers and non-coms near Mulhouse. The French were severe with their prisoners. Remembering vividly the millions of starving Frenchmen in German prison camps, they hewed close to the minimum laid down by the Geneva Convention. For the hated S.S. their standards of treatment fell even lower. The French programme designed to break the spirit of these die-hard Nazis fell hard on Achenbach. He was twenty-four. He felt he hadn't yet lived, and he longed desperately to return to his home in Essen. For months he held firm—and then he broke. In November he asked to speak to the camp commandant. The latter heard his story and summoned the *Deuxième Bureau*, the famed French Intelligence service. After some weeks of intense questioning, Achenbach was brought to American Intelligence Headquarters at Frankfort, accompanied by his guard, Sgt. Vital, and Lieut. S. of the *Deuxième Bureau*.

Final arrangements were then made to send a secret mission into Czechoslovakia. Not even the Czechs were taken into the confidence of the French and Americans. It was felt that a flick of the finger by a loose Nazi or an undiscovered Czech collaborationist could destroy forever Himmler's last secrets. True, a technical violation of Czech sovereignty was involved, but diplomatic embarrassment had to be risked in order to ensure success of the mission. It was more important to bring light into the dark history of Nazi methods than to make obeisance to international protocol. Thus it was that the expedition set out from Nuremberg on February 10 with the highest degree of secrecy.

He Moved Like a Man in a Trance

Dawn was just breaking over Prague when our convoy rolled out of the sleeping city on February 11. We sped through the suburbs and along a magnificent highway hewn from the base of mountains on the west bank of the Moldau. A few farmers on the way to market eyed us curiously. Foreign military vehicles had been a strange sight in Czechoslovakia since December, when both the Russians and Americans withdrew their forces. Fifteen miles south of Prague we halted on the outskirts of a small resort town called Stechowice. Achenbach was transferred from a truck to the front seat of the command car. He was to be our guide. He bit his lips excitedly and directed the convoy across the Moldau bridge at Stechowice.

We churned along country roads for five miles, then turned off on to a muddy cowpath. Luckily snow hadn't fallen here, and our convoy could easily follow a path across the bare fields. For two miles we penetrated into the woods, our truck roaring and sputtering in heavy going. Suddenly there was no more road—only thick forest. Leaving the trucks behind in the charge of their drivers, Achenbach, Lieuts. S. and O., three engineers, Leeman and myself pushed through the woods on foot. For one hundred yards we made way through undergrowth so thick our faces and hands were scratched. Then we came upon a fast-running brook. We splashed up its bed for another fifty yards. Here Achenbach stopped and surveyed the side of the ravine

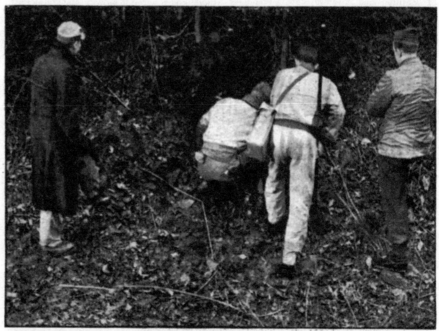

KNOWING A SLIP WOULD MEAN INSTANT DEATH, searchers probed the wild Czech hillside with mine-detecting apparatus whilst the former S.S. sergeant who had guided them to the spot looked on. The entrance of the shaft which they sought and each of the 32 heavy cases were elaborately booby-trapped

Photo, U.S. Army Signal Corps

Motto: *" Glory Is the End "*

No. 43 SQUADRON

DISBANDED after the First Great War, this squadron was re-formed in 1926, and at the outbreak of the Second Great War was stationed at Tangmere, Sussex. Hurricanes of No. 43 fought over the beaches at Dunkirk and destroyed 43 of the Luftwaffe during the Battle of Britain. The squadron made many moves before returning to Tangmere in June 1942, and while there it formed a part of the fighter cover during the raid on Dieppe on August 19. In the following November it accompanied the British 1st Army to French North Africa, and there the Hurricanes were replaced by Spitfires.

In June 1943 it moved to Malta, carrying out operational sweeps over southern Sicily. It covered the invasion of Sicily and the landings at Salerno and Anzio, moving to Italy and following in the wake of the U.S. 5th Army almost to Leghorn. In July 1944 the squadron was transferred to Corsica, in preparation for the invasion of southern France.

THEY harassed the retreating German armies and had advanced as far north as Lyons when they were ordered back to Italy in October. The squadron operated from Florence for some weeks, during which period it was converted to a Spitbomber unit. It gave constant close support to the 8th Army during the advance in the Po valley. Between December 1944 and March 1945 it attacked 57 gun positions and 59 railway and 11 road cuts were recorded.

No. 43 has a long history of ground-strafing behind it, because its predecessors introduced this form of aerial warfare in May 1917, when massed troops and transport were successfully attacked with machine-gun fire from the air.

rising steeply from the brook. He seemed lost. The rest of us looked at one another with doubtful eyes. It appeared impossible than an engineering operation could have taken place in this area where Nature was so completely undisturbed.

" I think it's here," Achenbach said, spreading his arms to encompass a six-foot area on the side of the ravine. He sounded far from positive. We made no move. Like a man in a trance he moved along the bed of the brook another twenty yards. Suddenly he fell on his knees in the water and turned over a large rock. "There!" he yelled excitedly. " See that mark ? "

We examined the rock and found a slight mark which might have been made by a drill. Achenbach stood up straight as though on the parade ground. With his toes touching the rock he leaned forward and grasped a small fir tree apparently growing on the side of the ravine. The tree came out of the ground, roots and all, and Achenbach held it up in triumph. " Yes ! Yes ! " he shouted, this time with genuine emotion, " I myself planted this tree as camouflage. Here is where we must dig." Grave doubts entered our minds as we looked upon the wild setting. There was nothing whatever here to indicate that human agencies had ever been at work.

"Please believe me !" Achenbach begged. " This is the place. It's under far—far under ! " We turned to Capt. Richards, stocky twenty-three-year-old former student at Georgia Tech. As ranking engineer, he was in charge from now on. He took a quick, querulous look at Achenbach, then peeled off his coat, picked up a shovel and began to dig. At the same time his assistants, Fulton and Urquhart, rigged up mine-detecting apparatus and probed the immediate area on the hillside. Achenbach grabbed another shovel and dug feverishly. Lieuts. S. and O. joined in the work ; then Leeman, then myself. In a few moments the place looked like a gold strike.

The Hand That Probed in Darkness

By noon we'd dug four feet into the side of the ravine without hitting anything but hard ground, and Richards called time for lunch. We retired to a clearing on the opposite side of the ravine to probe into our ration boxes, and we were halfway through before we noticed that Achenbach was down there alone, digging like a man possessed. Richards ordered him to stop and eat. The prisoner climbed wearily to the clearing, then sat down under a tree and fell to weeping bitterly. Prison life near Mulhouse must be tough, I thought, for any man to be anxious to be of service to his enemies.

At one-thirty Richards threw up his right hand. We all stopped digging. " I've hit something !" he yelled. Carefully he scooped away earth and slowly there came into view the entrance doors of a huge wooden shaft. For an hour we worked with extreme caution and finally we uncovered the whole of the entrance doors and a three-foot section of the roof of the shaft thrust deep into the mountainside. Achenbach was elated. But his elation turned to near panic when Richards decided to open the shaft from in front. The prisoner maintained it was impossible to move a single bolt or even a single board without blowing the whole party sky-high. He suggested that we dig a tunnel into the mountainside and open the shaft from the rear. Richards vetoed this plan on the ground that we didn't have the manpower or equipment for such an operation. We'd have to take a chance.

THE next three hours were the most tense and probably most dangerous any of us had known, even in war. A snowstorm blew up and swept along the ravine. Achenbach stood by, red-eyed and pale, as Richards, Fulton, and Urquhart probed the top of the shaft with mine detectors. The rest of us were helpless to do anything but watch.

Finally Richards made up his mind. " It's my birthday today," he said. " I've just got to be lucky." How he divined that the third board on the top of the shaft would be safe to remove I'll never know. When I asked him later he said it was part instinct, part luck and part knowledge of German booby trapping methods. In any case, he stepped up briskly, and while we watched breathlessly he wedged up the third board and made an opening just wide enough for his hand to reach into the darkness behind the entrance doors. As it turned out, the third board was the only one which could have been removed without blowing up the whole mountain.

But that was only the beginning of a perilous job. Richards now stretched, stomach down, on top of the shaft and with a small wire-cutter in hand probed blindly behind the entrance doors. Achenbach stood by, shivering. " A quarter of an inch," he kept murmuring. " If you move one of those wires a quarter of an inch we'll all die !" For fifteen minutes Richards' hand probed with the sensitiveness of a surgeon's. It seemed an endless time before it emerged from the darkness with a length of primer cord he had cut from the inside of the door.

That was only the first piece of primer cord. For two hours Richards lay almost motionless on the shaft and produced lengths of primer cord like a magician. At last he shook the snow from his back, climbed down, and said, " I think we can winch the doors off." The engineers' truck, with a winch on the front axle, was brought to the edge of the ravine, about 150 yards above the shaft. A long winching cable was attached to the entrance doors and we all hid behind sturdy trees. Richards gave the signal to the winch operator, the machine whirred and the door came crashing off without incident. Richards had effectively cut each one of seventeen separate primer cords which had been attached to the inside of the doors.

What we saw inside the shaft was almost terrifying. Boxes of wired TNT interspersed with tins of flame-thrower oil comprised the first layer. Behind this were thirty-two huge crates, each with the Gestapo seal. Wedged between the crates were Teller mines fitted with blasting caps which would explode on the slightest pressure. It was growing dark by this time and the party retired to nearby Stechowice for the night. Early next morning we were on the job again and peril was once more with us. Each crate weighed 800 lb. and had to be removed from a constricted space without disturbing the Teller mines.

Pursued by Czech Secret Police

Achenbach forgot he was a prisoner. The Intelligence officers forgot their special privileges. Even I rolled up my sleeves, and we all plunged to work. By nightfall the job was done. All thirty-two crates were safely stowed in our trucks. Himmler's last fortress had fallen and its secrets were in our hands. But the adventure wasn't over. As we raced through the night over snowy mountain passes towards the American zone of Occupation we didn't know that Czech secret police had been on our trail. They had discovered the empty shaft and were now pursuing us. We found out only next day that Richards, Fulton and Urquhart, who'd lingered behind, had been arrested and were being held incommunicado. We learned later that a first-class diplomatic storm had developed between the United States and Czechoslovakia over our expedition.

The remaining ten of us crossed the Czech frontier into Germany at four in the morning on February 13, and later that day delivered our precious crates to the American Intelligence Headquarters. There Czech observers were invited in and Himmler's secret boxes were opened. What we found far outweighed in importance any temporary embarrassment between the governments. The full record of Nazi Germany's merciless occupation of Czechoslovakia was at last revealed. We had S.S. and Gestapo files, including all the secret orders issued by Frank and "Butcher" Heydrich.

We had the names and addresses of all Czech collaborators, including those who had paved the way for Hitler's seizure of their country. We had the inside story of German administration of the little country between 1939 and 1945. It was all there—recovered from the bowels of the earth and brought into the blinding light which not only illuminated the past but would also clarify the future. Another battle for peace had been won—over Himmler's dead body.

Cracking Himmler's Secret Cache in the Hills

AFTER 17 CORDS THAT WOULD HAVE DETONATED explosive charges had been cut by Capt. Richards, a long winching cable was attached to the shaft doors (1) to wrench them off. To the right of men removing the first of the 32 cases (2) is dynamite. Each case was examined for traps (3). See story in facing page. PAGE 541 *Photos, U.S. Army Signal Corps*

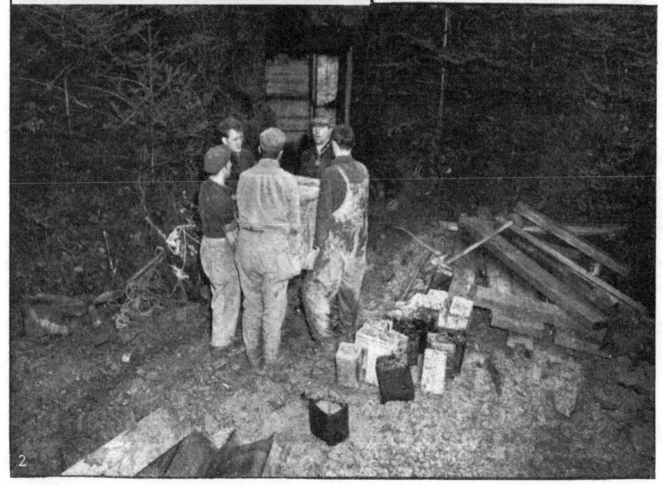

Through Fire and Flood in Walcheren

Mrs. Margaret Haverman, her Dutch husband and two children, were in
the thick of all that happened behind the shooting in Walcheren Island's
bitter ordeal. She presents the scene from 1940 to 1944—when she had
the honour of welcoming the liberating British troops on behalf of the
Dutch. See also page 317.

THE first shock came at four o'clock in
the morning of May 10, 1940, when
we were aroused by the thunder of
aero-engines. Herman (my husband) and
I hurried to the window. In the ghostly
light of many flares we could see the airfield
with farm-carts, ploughs, harrows and other
obstacles all over it, placed there to prevent
the landing of German transports. Bombers
marked with a black cross roared down from
the sky. The earth erupted in flame and
smoke. Shells and bullets lashed over the
aerodrome and around our house. We
looked mutely at each other, aware that our
own little domestic world of happiness was
being shattered in this new Nazi treachery.

Events moved swiftly. Next day many
Dutch planes rose into the air from a cleared
runway and winged across the North Sea to
England. Dutch ships slipped out of
harbour and sought sanctuary in British ports.
French troops crossed the Scheldt in ferries
and moved up through Walcheren. And
within a week of that first unprovoked
German attack on our pleasant island,
hordes of German troops poured in from
other parts of Holland. My husband spent
energetic days in Flushing trying to make
arrangements for getting us away. But it
was hopeless. All the ships and boats had
gone and we were trapped.

There was fierce fighting in some parts of
the island. In dreadful apprehension we saw
the French in disorderly retreat, leaving tanks,
guns, equipment and hundreds of horses
which they cut loose from their limbers and
transports. All Holland came under German
occupation. As the days went by our island
was transformed into a grim fortress. The
Germans constructed bunkers, emplacements
and even levelled the tops of the encircling
sand dunes, overlaying them with concrete
for their gun batteries. The whole place
bristled with guns and searchlights.

One of the first orders that the German
commandant issued to all Dutch residents
was for radio sets to be given up. If the
Nazis caught you with a radio after that
they would confiscate your house and furniture and send you to a concentration camp.

Herman and I decided to take a chance. We
laid our set flat under a bedroom floor.
Almost automatically this involved us in the
underground movement that developed in
Holland under the noses of the Nazis.
Having hidden the set, we proceeded to make
use of it. We listened-in regularly to

**WALCHEREN ISLAND, showing the position
of Koudekerke where the narrator of this
story lived, and the dikes bombed by the
R.A.F. before the assault on the island.**

broadcasts by the B.B.C. on military and
political subjects, made notes of salient
points and passed them on to other residents
to offset the subtle German propaganda.

Because they opposed the Nazi regime
many Dutch people became fugitives, and
we made ready to help anyone in danger.
There were two recesses under our attic
floor where we could hide fugitives before
passing them on under a system designed to
smuggle them out of the country. By early
1944 the Germans had erected a maze of
obstructions to prevent aerial invasion by
the Allies—mainly poles with barbed wire
strung between and explosive mines suspended,
and the sergeant in charge of their maintenance was Feldwebel Sanzenbacher, whom
we came to know only too well. Until

January 1944 we were uncommonly lucky in
having no German billeted on us, but then
came Sanzenbacher armed with an official
order that he was to have a room. The
household consisted of my husband, myself,
Ronnie aged five and my baby girl Rosalind
not yet two years old, and we had no more
association than necessary with our " guest "
and kept the children away from him.

On May 20, 1944, a young Dutchman
named Hillebrand, a friend of my husband,
came to the house. He was a Civil Servant,
a member of the underground movement,
and had received warning that he was on the
Germans' black list and about to be arrested.
We kept him for three weeks, feeding him
from our own scanty rations. The fact that
various friends were frequently visiting us
helped to keep from Sanzenbacher's mind
any suspicion that we were sheltering a
fugitive. It was still possible for us to
receive the B.B.C. broadcasts on our hidden
wireless set when the German was out of the
house, but impossible to keep the secret
from our children, and we were in dread that
they might let it slip out.

Cold Terror Behind Locked Doors

However, all went well enough until a day
in June, which lingers like a nightmare in my
memory. Hillebrand was in the bathroom,
the children playing about the house, and I
was at work in the kitchen when, without
ceremony, the back door was flung open and
three Gestapo strode in. It was a great
shock, but I managed to ask coldly what
they wanted. " Where is your husband ? "
one demanded. I said he was at the office
of the Evacuation Bureau at Middelburg,
and the spokesman gave a grunt and announced that he had orders to search the
house. I realized that something had
occurred to make the German authorities
suspicious. The " wanted " man, Hillebrand, was upstairs. Between a floor and
ceiling was the hidden wireless set ; there
were the two secret hide-outs under the
attic that obviously had been occupied,
and at that moment contained enough pamphlets and other documents to seal our fate.

The Gestapo locked the doors and set
about the search systematically. They
pulled everything out of drawers and cupboards, and generally turned the place upside-
down. From room to room they went,
tapping the walls and spreading disorder,
first on the ground floor and then upstairs.
All the time one or another kept a close
watch on me and fired questions, but I
managed to avoid the many traps. I
dreaded lest they should interrogate the
children, but to my unbounded relief the
Germans ignored them. The search occupied
fully two hours of almost unendurable strain.

FOR one short period they kept me in a
bedroom where they believed I could do
nothing to interfere, but this happened to
give me a chance. We had a next-door
neighbour and friend, Mynheer Mol, who
knew of Herman's connexion with the
underground movement. Our friend's wife
was at the back of her house and by gesticulating at the window in the direction of Middelburg I conveyed a hint she, having already
glimpsed the Gestapo men, was quick to
appreciate. She told her husband that
something was wrong, and he set off on a
bicycle intending to warn Herman.

Naturally I thought that Hillebrand would
be alive to the danger and would scurry into
one of the recesses : in either of the hide-
outs under the attic floor he might have
been safe. When these were closed there was
no indication of them, and the Gestapo
never discovered them nor the hidden radio
set, otherwise events would have taken an
even more tragic turn. And so I had no
qualms when the Germans flung open the

WHEN KOUDEKERKE WAS INUNDATED water rose to three or four feet in some of the
houses and numbers of the villagers were evacuated in horse-drawn boats. Their destination
was Middelburg, which escaped the sea-deluge that poured in through breached dikes after
R.A.F. bombings—part of the price of liberation.

Photo, Associated Press

bathroom door, but a moment later guttural voices announced the capture of the fugitive. Hillebrand had stayed there, fearful of being caught by making a move up to the attic. That brought the search to an end, and so far as myself and family were concerned it was fortunate he was found there rather than in one of the secret hide-outs where the incriminating documents were kept.

The young Dutchman was taken direct to gaol, first stage of a journey that ended with his death from malnutrition in a German concentration camp. Having got the prisoner off their hands, the three Gestapo men sped by car to the Evacuation Bureau in Middelburg where they arrived only a minute after Mynheer Mol on his bicycle, and before our neighbour could give my husband a hint of their visit to our home. Meantime, I was left with the task of putting the house straight, and worried as to what reprisals the Germans would most probably adopt toward us.

I learned later what happened at the office. My husband was quite in the dark about it all when the Gestapo came for him, and preserved our secrets in spite of being struck repeatedly in the face during a long grilling. The only definite charge they could make against him was that a Dutch fugitive had been found in the house, but they could not prove that he knew the young man was on the Germans' "wanted" list. That evening a priest who saw Herman in the Middelburg gaol smuggled out a note which informed me of his arrest. I saw and spoke to my husband when he and other prisoners were taken from the island, and for months after that I knew not where he had been taken, or whether he was alive or dead.

First Leaflets, Then the Bombs

Satisfied by the arrest of my husband and Hillebrand, the Germans allowed me to carry on unmolested with my household duties and care of the children. Worry about the fate of my man was combined with bitter hatred of Sanzenbacher, the German "guest," whom I learned had informed the Gestapo that we were anti-Nazis and had suggested the search. I did not know until long afterwards that Herman was kept at the notorious concentration camp at Amersfoort, from which many hundreds of Dutch people were sent to death or to slave labour. Three times he was led to believe he would be taken out and shot, left in suspense and then allowed to resume the usual grim camp routine.

He never was able to get news of me and the children, yet the Germans never broke his spirit. When they threw away a small radio set which they believed was beyond repair, Herman secretly put it in working order and listened-in to B.B.C. broadcasts to cheer his fellow prisoners, but was not discovered because after each secret use of the set he dismantled it and left it a seemingly useless wreck on the rubbish dump.

THRILLINGLY the tempo of the war quickened in 1944 after the D-Day invasion of Normandy. The victorious armies swept through Western Europe until Holland reverberated to the thunder of the guns. On October 3 the R.A.F. made a sweep over Walcheren and dropped leaflets warning the Dutch people. At 1 p.m. next day the bombers were over the coast dropping delayed action bombs that burst the dike near Westkapelle. The sea poured through and many Germans were killed—and many Dutch people, part of the price that had to be paid for liberation. A week later the R.A.F. came again. The

MRS. HAVERMAN AND HER CHILDREN, Ronnie and Linda, endured the German occupation of Walcheren, a rain of British bombs and shells and the floods that came. One of her anxieties was that the children might divulge their "illegal" wireless set.

island, which had become a German fortress, was not flooding fast enough. More dikes were breached. I saw bombs fall on the Nolle Dike, and later the fearful explosions that were to help lay the land in waste. From all directions the sea rushed in, sweeping over the fertile fields, through the villages and over the German bunkers and other defence works. Koudekerke was inundated. The sea surged into my house, rising three or four feet with each high tide. Sometimes I could not get downstairs, and the gas stove in the kitchen was under water. There were times when no fresh food was obtainable, and I and the two children had to stay in the upper rooms and make do with raw potatoes and carrots.

Not having seaboots or Wellingtons, I usually paddled about barelegged in the icy water when it was necessary to go outdoors to do my shopping. Very few Dutch people were left in the neighbourhood, and the Germans had abandoned their flooded defence works and were dug in on the dunes. November saw Walcheren still in the hands of Germans prepared to fight to the bitter end. On an unforgettable Sunday, two British warships cruised off the Scheldt

estuary and began shelling the island. The ordeal of fire and flood lasted intermittently from Sunday until the following Thursday morning. Time and again shells came screaming over my roof, and one house after another collapsed under direct hits.

All the windows of my house were broken by blast, the cupboard under the stairs was flooded, so that I could not put the children inside : when the guns came into action I sat with them on a ledge, and each time a shell screamed over, made them bob their heads under the stairs. Some former neighbours came from a house they occupied in a safer area and urged me to leave my home and join them, I agreed, but after making preparations I dared not venture out owing to renewed shelling. But late that night, during a lull, I piled blankets in a pram and perched Ronnie and Linda on top, well wrapped against the cold. Barefooted and wearing my long, fur coat, I set off along the road pushing the pram.

A strong tide brought the sea rushing in through the breach in the Nolle Dike, and the cold water swept round my ankles. On lower ground the sea swirled waist-high, and to the top of the pram, so that only the blankets and the children were above water. I had to get Ronnie and Linda to that distant dwelling where my Dutch friends were sheltering. There were times when I despaired. My fur coat became saturated, and its dragging weight added to my distress. Providentially, we reached our destination, and an hour or two afterwards my own house received a direct hit.

Liberation came at the end of November. Tank landing craft came through the Nolle Dike on the tide, and the Germans were cleared from the sand dunes after desperate fighting. British tanks rumbled over the island at low water, and as the only English-born woman there I welcomed the first troops on behalf of the Dutch. My husband was liberated in May 1945, and did we have a joyful reunion !

NEW FACTS AND FIGURES

THE battle for Walcheren Island, in the early days of November 1944, involving the breaching of dikes and flooding of the countryside, brought about the destruction of a million and a half trees. When, two years later, a fund was opened by the Dutch Government for the reafforestation of the district (at an approximate cost of 4s. 10d. per tree), contributors included personnel of the Royal Navy, and especially the Royal Marines, who played a major part in the capture of Walcheren. See story above.

THE United Nations War Crimes Commission has issued a further progress report of war crimes trials, up to September 30, 1946. It shows that in cases tried in Europe by the United States, Britain and France, out of a total of 1,018 accused, 392 received the death penalty, 438 were sentenced to various terms of imprisonment, and 188 were acquitted. In the Far East 1,120 war criminals had been charged by the United States, Britain and Australia ; of these, 326 were sentenced to death, 554 imprisoned and 240 acquitted.

IN August 1946, for the first time since the war, began the number of workers in Britain engaged on goods for the Home market was greater than in 1939—4,885,000 against 4,680,000. The corresponding figures for the export trade were 1,375,000 in 1946 as compared with an estimated 990,000 in 1939, an increase of 39 per cent.

THROUGH the agency of the German bureau of missing persons, known as the German Zonal Search Bureau, 81,000 Germans were reunited with their relatives in September 1946. The card index system of the Bureau comprises a total of four million names of missing people. Children too young to know their own names are photographed and their particulars recorded. A series of daily broadcasts giving names of children registered with the Bureau was the means of reuniting 370 children with their parents during September. It is estimated that in all four zones of Germany there are about 10 million Germans known to be searching for their relatives. Considerable progress has been made in linking up the work of the Bureau in Hamburg with other zones.

BETWEEN April and October 1946 over 7,000 civilians were interviewed, recruited and sent to Germany to replace released military personnel working with the Control Commission. These included men and women of all categories and qualifications. Many further candidates selected were still waiting in England, the chief cause of delay being difficulties arising over accommodation in the British zone. This is by far the most damaged part of Germany ; at the close of hostilities it was estimated that more than half the dwellings had suffered from bombing or shell-fire ; two million of the five-and-a-half million houses in the zone have been totally destroyed.

From Ceylon to Learn Our Farming Craft

Photo, Fox

BRITAIN'S FOOD-RAISING ACHIEVEMENTS DURING THE WAR have attracted Empire students to the Institute of Agriculture at Usk, in Monmouthshire, where these girls from Ceylon are gaining experience that will fit them to become instructors when they return home. Handling and maintenance of latest mechanical implements is an important part of the curriculum. Their tropical clothing, though bringing colour to British farm work, will of course give place to garments more suited to their occupation and our climate.

Photo, Fox

Printed in England and published every alternate Friday by the Proprietors, THE AMALGAMATED PRESS, LTD., The Fleetway House, Farringdon Street, London, E.C.4. Registered for transmission by Canadian Magazine Post. Sole Agents for Australia and New Zealand: Messrs. Gordon & Gotch, Ltd.; and for South Africa: Central News Agency, Ltd.—December 6, 1946.   S.S.   *Editorial Address:* JOHN CARPENTER HOUSE, WHITEFRIARS, LONDON, E.C.4.

PRIVATE WOZTEK OF THE POLISH ARMY is "on the strength" of the 22nd Artillery Supply Corps. He does not really approve of this bareback riding act ; but as the men have made a pet of him ever since they adopted him as a cub in Persia he allows them to take certain liberties. He went with the Polish troops through North Africa, Sicily and Italy and is now at Duns, Berwickshire. His favourite pastime is wrestling with his friends. *Photo, Mirror Features*

Edited by Sir John Hammerton

NO. 249 WILL BE PUBLISHED FRIDAY, JANUARY 3, 1947

With Our Roving Camera from Home to Bahamas

GENERAL VON MACKENSEN, charged with the responsibility for the massacre of 335 Italians in March 1944, was sentenced to be shot by a British War Crimes Court in Rome on Dec. 1, 1946. He is seated at the back of the court, behind defence counsel at the left of the table.

H.M.S. PUFFIN (on left), her bows damaged after ramming a midget U-boat in the North Sea, was laid up for scrapping at Shotley, near Harwich, with the remaining seven of the Duck class corvettes. She was one of the original patrol sloops.

MODEL OF ROOSEVELT STATUE, by Sir William Reid Dick. The London memorial will be ready for unveiling on April 12, 1948, the third anniversary of Mr. Franklin Roosevelt's death. See also illus. page 576. The project was suggested by Lord Derby, and the site in Grosvenor Square was made available by the Duke of Westminster.

METAL PARTS OF MULBERRY HARBOUR are being cut up at Southampton for scrap. Each of these sections weighs 5½ tons. Concrete caissons used in the great prefabricated port were employed to block the breaches in the dikes on Walcheren Island (see story in page 542).

AT NASSAU, BAHAMAS, is this memorial (right) to Allied airmen reported missing from flying operations in the Bahamas—Nassau being the westernmost Allied staging post on the southern Atlantic route. Sir William L. Murphy, the Governor, unveiled it. *Photos, I.N.P., P.A., Vicary, Keystone, Planet*

The First Attack by British Parachutists

By A.J. WILSON

O N February 10, 1941, a small band of determined men dropped by parachute from six R.A.F. aircraft through a starlit sky in Southern Italy. Their mission was to demolish an important aqueduct not far from Monte Vulture, a 4,000-foot peak in the lonely border country between the provinces of Campagna and Apulia. In the light of the great Allied airborne operations which were to follow, this small raid has been almost forgotten. But on this cold, clear winter's night, amid snow-capped mountains, these men made history—they were the first British airborne troops to go into action in the Second Great War.

The operation was only partly successful. The damage done to the aqueduct had a negligible effect on the course of the war in the Mediterranean, and the gallant parachutists finished up in prison camps. They did not, however, lose their liberty in vain. This first practical experiment in the employment of British parachute troops showed the extent to which the joint work of the Army and R.A.F. had developed within a few months, and it laid the foundations for that co-operation between the two Services which led to such epic events as the leap over the West Wall on D-Day, the Arnhem operation and the airborne landings on the east bank of the Rhine.

Only eight months before—on June 22, 1940—the Prime Minister, Mr. Churchill, had given instructions to his Chief of Staff for the training of "a corps of at least 5,000 parachute troops." Major J. F. Rock, Royal Engineers, was given charge of the military organization; and shortly afterwards the Central Landing Establishment, cradle of British airborne forces, was formed under the command of a R.A.F. officer, Group-Captain L. G. Harvey, to train men for this new type of warfare. Major Rock found ready co-operation among his Air Force colleagues, chief of whom were Wing-Commander L. A. Strange, D.S.O., M.C., D.F.C., and Wing-Commander Sir Nigel Norman, Bt., C.B.E.

What the Target Meant to Italy

All through the summer and autumn rigorous training went on. It was the R.A.F.'s task to produce the parachute equipment, to evolve the methods of dropping, and to teach the troops their air technique. Meanwhile, the Army studied the special organization for fighting on the ground and the weapons and tactical training of the parachutists. Shortly after Christmas 1940, a sufficient number of troops had been trained to high enough pitch to make a small-scale operation possible. Targets were considered,

FLYING-OFFICER A. WARBURTON, D.S.O., D.F.C. and Bar, flew in a Glen Martin and secured air photographs which revealed not one but two aqueducts. *Air Ministry photograph*

and it was decided that the blow should be against the Italian aqueduct near Monte Vulture—1,800 miles from Britain.

The strategic importance of the aqueduct to the Italians was considerable. A London firm of engineers had suggested the target and provided important relevant details. Its destruction was obviously a task for ground forces, as precision bombing had not then been sufficiently developed to give a reasonable chance of hitting it at its vital points. Spanning a small stream, the Tragino, the aqueduct carried the main water supply for the whole of the province of Apulia, with its thousands of industrial, dockyard and armament factory workers in Taranto, Brindisi, Foggia and Bari.

It must be remembered that at this time Mussolini was making his biggest military effort in North Africa and in Albania. If the operation behind the enemy's lines were successful, the people in the heel of Italy might well be deprived of their regular water supply for a month, and their work and war production be seriously dislocated. It was also calculated to have a considerable effect on the morale of the Italians, who at that

time never dreamed that the war would involve any fighting on their soil.

Such was the enthusiasm of the men of the Central Landing Establishment when they heard that the first "real show" was being planned that they rushed to volunteer. Seven officers and 31 other ranks were eventually selected. Major T. A. C. Pritchard was given command of the force, which was divided into two parties, one of engineers under the command of Captain G. F. K. Daly to carry out the actual demolition, and the other a covering party under Lieutenant A. J. Deane-Drummond, M.C. Malta was the obvious choice for a base, and on January 24, 1941, Lieutenant Deane-Drummond flew to the island in a Sunderland flying boat to make preparations, taking with him the equipment and maintenance staff.

Men "Spilled Out" at 400 Feet

Meanwhile, there were three weeks of rehearsals in England under the supervision of Major Rock and Wing-Commander Nigel Norman. Six Whitley aircraft were prepared for the transportation of the troops, and two more were detailed for a bombing diversion on the railway yards at Foggia. A large-scale landscape model of the area was built, and airmen and troops familiarized themselves with every feature.

To the parachutists the operation seemed from the start to be a "one way trip," but the plan did include provision for their re-embarkation. Demolition completed, the men were to endeavour to make their way on foot across country to the Gulf of Salerno, on the west coast where, at the mouth of the River Sele, H.M. Submarine Triumph would await five nights later to pick them up.

So, as daylight began to fade on February 7, the first stage of the journey was begun. The parachute troops filed into their places in the Whitleys, and the aircraft took off on the 1,600 miles flight to Malta. The R.A.F. pilots and crews did their job with characteristic accuracy and efficiency. Their route took them over hostile territory, and for long periods they flew in bad weather, navigating to pin-points, but they ran to schedule, and early next morning the party had landed safely in Malta.

Here, Lieutenant Deane-Drummond had everything prepared. Bad weather had prevented air photographs of the target being taken, but the day after the arrival of the main force Flying-Officer A. Warburton, D.S.O., D.F.C., flew over the area in a Glen Martin and secured some good pictures. These pin-pointed the target south-west of Monte Vulture and disclosed not one but two aqueducts. Outlined clearly against the snow-covered ground they showed up some 200 yards apart, the one to the east being the larger. It was decided to attack this one

The following night, February 10, the eight Whitleys took off again, six bound for Monte Vulture, with the parachutists on board, and two which were to continue to Foggia with bomb-racks full. In one of the latter was Wing-Commander Sir Nigel Norman,

OVER THE TRAGINO, this was the aqueduct (left) whose reinforced concrete pier was demolished, the waterway it supported breaking in two. *By courtesy of Engineering*

who was to have a ringside view of the operation he had helped to plan. It was a glorious night, with a full moon and stars above patches of white cloud. The sea was clear of mist, and as the Italian coast was approached the snow-capped ridges of the Apennines could be seen in the distance. As the Whitleys went in, the pilots and navigators could pick out every feature and landmark, looking exactly like the landscape model they had used in their training.

First aircraft over the target arrived at 9.42 p.m., and from 400 feet the first British skymen made their jumps, the containers, with the explosives and other equipment, floating down with them. The drop was a good one, the men landing from 50 to 250 yards from their objective. Four other Whitleys followed, spilling their load of men and containers in the area. Their aim was a little less accurate than the first, some of the men landing in a dry river bed, but the farthest was not more than three-quarters of a mile away, and very soon they had all made contact with Major Pritchard. Of the sixth Whitley there was no sign. This was a serious blow, for the missing aircraft contained Captain Daly and his party of skilled engineers who were to set the explosives.

Torrents of Water in the Ravine

Pritchard, meanwhile, gave the order for collecting the containers. They were fairly widely scattered and the lights on some of them had gone out. Pritchard decided that his men should have some assistance in their search, and the parachutists audaciously knocked up a nearby farmhouse and ordered its 12 inhabitants to help. Obediently these Italian peasants combed the fields under the watchful eyes of the British skymen. Two containers of explosives were missing, and it was found that these had failed to leave the aircraft owing to the severe icing conditions.

Still there was no sign of Daly's aircraft, and Pritchard ordered Second-Lieutenant G. W. Paterson and a few other engineers who were with him to prepare for the demolition, with Deane-Drummond and his men as cover. They crossed the Ginestra, a small tributary of the Tragino, over a rough bridge to the aqueduct, and here they had their second disappointment. The pier was not of masonry, as they had been led to believe, but of reinforced concrete, presenting a much more difficult proposition, particularly with two containers of explosives short.

Paterson decided to concentrate all his explosive against the western pier and its abutment. Six hundred and forty pounds were stacked against the pier and 160 pounds against the abutment. The charges were put into place by Lance-Corporal Watson, the Italian peasants were herded into some nearby farm buildings, and shortly after midnight all was ready. At 12.30 a.m. the main charge was fired. A great explosion shattered the countryside and reverberated through the mountains. A moment later the bridge over the stream also went up, large pieces being tossed on to the roof of the neighbouring farmhouse.

A FEW minutes later Pritchard and Paterson anxiously proceeded to the aqueduct to inspect the damage. They found that the pier had collapsed and the waterway it supported broken in two. Already the water was gushing over the debris and beginning to flood the ravine.

Ironically, the roar of the explosion reached the ears of Daly and his engineers in the next valley. Their aircraft had lost its way—and eventually arrived, three-quarters of an hour late and slightly off course. On hearing the explosion there was nothing for it but to start their trek for the coast—and the expected submarine.

Pritchard and his men now also turned their faces westwards towards the rendezvous, first throwing away their heavy equipment. In three parties they made their way up a mountain, skirting the snow-line to a wooded valley, where they hid all next day. Next night they located the River Sele and slipped across one of its bridges unobserved. They had planned to spend the daylight in what their maps showed to be a small wood on the summit of the Cresta di Gallo—the Cock's Comb. Higher and higher they pressed on up the mountain in search of the wood, until they found themselves trudging through the snow which capped the peak. They failed to find the wood, and at dawn they went to earth near the summit, some lying down to rest in the shelter of a cave, others huddling as best they could behind boulders and tree stumps.

Their tell-tale footprints in the snow led to their discovery. A farmer spotted the tracks and gave the alarm, and presently a large number of villagers were seen approaching. Women, children, peasants, dogs, all in an excited crowd, came stumbling up the mountainside. Behind them were troops and several of the local *carabinieri*. The parachutists were ready to fight it out with the little ammunition they had, but to do so would have endangered the women and children in the van of the advancing crowd. Pritchard had no choice —he surrendered.

Daly and his party retained their liberty for a little longer. By dawn on February 15 they were still 18 miles from the mouth of the River Sele, hungry and extremely tired. As the submarine was due to pick them up that night they would have to

FORTUNATO PICCHI, formerly of the Savoy Hotel (London) staff, who accompanied the British parachutists as interpreter, was taken prisoner by his countrymen and shot in Rome.

cover the remaining distance in daylight. They decided to make a dash for it; but at about midday they unfortunately ran into some soldiers, police and civilians.

Even then they tried to bluff their way out, declaring that they were German troops on special duty. They even demanded a car, saying they had to be in Naples by two o'clock. The local mayor was appealed to, but he asked Daly for papers to prove his words. The game was up. The parachutists were handcuffed, chained together and taken to Naples, where they were threatened with death. Eventually they were sent to a prison camp, with the exception of their anti-Fascist Italian interpreter, Picchi, who was later court-martialled and shot. Daly's men were not, after all, as near to escape as they thought. Even if they had reached the Sele there would have been no submarine to take them off. H.M.S. Triumph's orders had been countermanded at the last minute.

"We're a Surprise for the Duce!"

By a piece of cruel luck, one of the two Whitleys which had been detailed to bomb Foggia—not the one carrying Wing-Commander Nigel Norman—developed serious engine trouble. The pilot, who knew nothing about Triumph's intended part in the operation, sent out a wireless message saying that he was about to make a forced landing near the mouth of the Sele. It was obvious that his signal would be picked up by the enemy, and as a result the position of the Triumph would be seriously endangered. The High Command decided that the risk was too great in view of the very remote possibility of a successful re-embarkation, and the submarine was withdrawn.

The Italians managed to repair their aqueduct before its damage had any appreciable effect on the towns it supplied. The damage to Italian morale was, however, much greater. Alarm spread throughout the country. Over a wide area additional guards were posted at strategic points, air-raid precautions were tightened up, and the whole district around Monte Vulture was barred to neutrals.

Wing-Commander Nigel Norman, whose aircraft made a successful attack on the Foggia railway yards, paid a great tribute to the courage of the parachutists when he arrived back in England. "I shall always remember," he said, "the efficiency and wonderful spirit of the men we dropped and the way they got into their aircraft singing a song with rather special words, the refrain of which was 'Oh, we're a surprise for the Duce, the Duce'!" . . . . They certainly were—and by no means the last.

DROPPING ZONE for the demolition parties, showing areas of the successful landings at Hill 427 in the vicinity of the two aqueducts. Monte Vulture lies about nine miles to the north-east of Hill 427. PAGE 548

Commemoration of Coventry's Ordeal by Fire

IN THE RUINS OF COVENTRY CATHEDRAL on the evening of Nov. 14, 1946, representatives of all denominations attended a service commemorating the sixth anniversary of its destruction by German bombs. The service closed with an act of rededication in the Chapel of Unity, in which the Bishop joined. The simple cross is made of charred timber taken from the Cathedral on the night of Nov. 14-15, 1940. Gifts totalling nearly £95,000 had been received or promised for the restoration fund.

Photo, Topical

Hirohito is Now a 'Mixer' in the New Japan

HE RULED JAPAN AS THE SON OF HEAVEN, but since the Allied Occupation of his country emphasis has been placed upon the Emperor Hirohito's democratic qualities. In Western dress he drives in an open carriage with the Empress (1). Formerly she rarely appeared in public and he invariably used a closed vehicle. In November 1946 he visited grain-producing centres and was received by a local headman (2). People still bow to the royal train when it passes (3). Hirohito displayed considerable interest in an exhibit at the Chibaken Agricultural Experimental Institute (4), and watched farm-workers cultivating the paddy fields (5). PAGE 550

Homes and Activities in Our Zone in Germany

LIVING CONDITIONS of the civilian population of Düsseldorf were inspected, in October 1946, by Marshal of the Royal Air Force Sir Sholto Douglas (1, centre), C.-in-C. of the British zone in Germany; he is seen talking with a woman who for three years has lived in an underground bomb-shelter. The well-stocked N.A.A.F.I. at Iserlohn is appreciated by B.A.O.R. wives and families; shopping completed (2) glances are exchanged with a German boy leaning against the shopfront of concrete (the latter a necessary precaution against looting).

The body of a lorry (3) solves the housing problem for a native of Hamburg. British schoolchildren find fascination in a geography lesson (4) given by Army chaplain the Rev. S. B. Harris. The German Coastal and Fishing Services fleet, part of which can be seen (5) in the distance, was reviewed on November 11, 1946, by Air Vice-Marshal Hugh Vivian Champion de Crespigny, the Military Governor of Schleswig-Holstein.

Photos, Topical, G.P.U., Sport & General

From Active Service to Imperial War Museum

RELICS NOW DISPLAYED in the well-known building in the Lambeth Road, London—part of which was reopened to the public on Nov. 27, 1946, after having been closed since Oct. 9, 1940—include (1) front section of the fuselage of a Lancaster heavy bomber, and (2) a Spitfire Mark I that was flown in the defence of London during the whole of the Battle of Britain and destroyed five enemy raiders. On part of its launching ramp, ready to be dispatched, is a V1, or doodlebug (3). German one-man submarine (4), captured intact and used in extensive trials by the Royal Navy, as a result of which counter-measures were devised. Italian human torpedo (5), like those used against H.M.S. Queen Elizabeth and Valiant at Alexandria.

Under Repair in Australia's Captain Cook Dock

H.M.A.S. SHROPSHIRE, presented by the Royal Navy to the Royal Australian Navy in 1943 to replace the lost Canberra, was the first cruiser to enter the Captain Cook graving dock, Sydney (1), which was opened in 1945. Timber blocks (2) on which the Shropshire will rest whilst her stem is repaired. A huge caisson will seal the dock entrance (3) preparatory to the water being pumped out, leaving the cruiser standing high and dry (4). See also illus. page 72.
Exclusive to THE WAR ILLUSTRATED

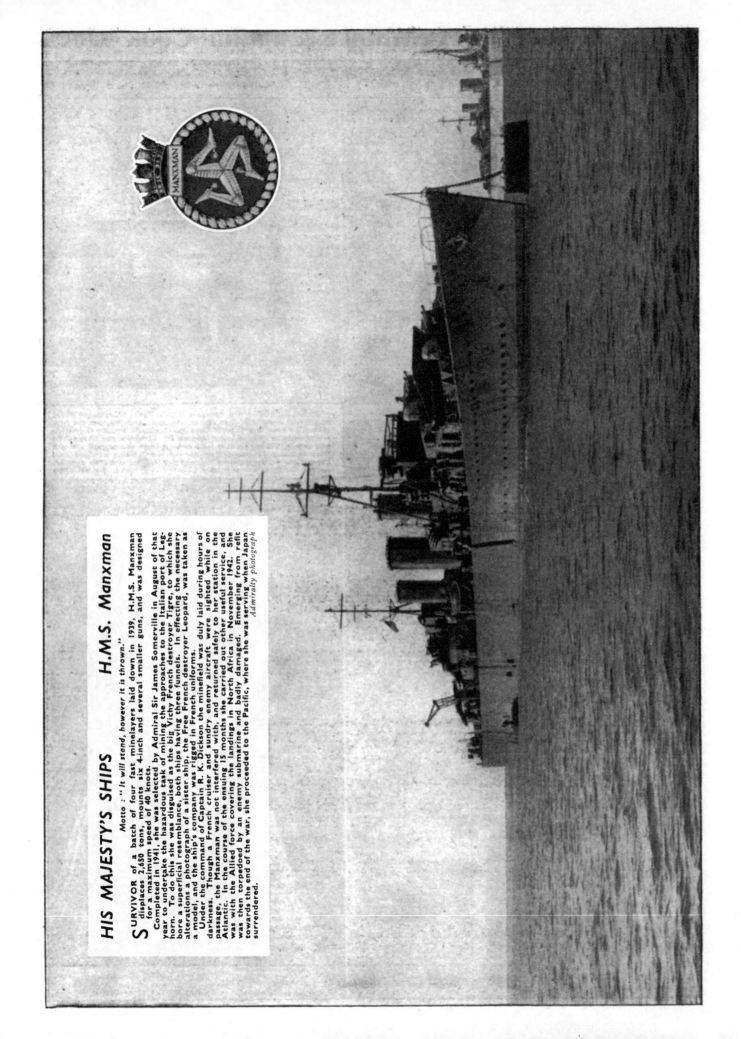

HIS MAJESTY'S SHIPS   H.M.S. Manxman

Motto : "It will stand, however it is thrown."

SURVIVOR of a batch of four fast minelayers laid down in 1939, H.M.S. Manxman displaces 2,650 tons, mounts six 4-inch and several smaller guns, and was designed for a maximum speed of 40 knots.

Completed in 1941, she was selected by Admiral Sir James Somerville in August of that year to undertake the hazardous task of mining the approaches to the Italian port of Leghorn. To do this she was disguised as the big Vichy French destroyer Tigre, to which she bore a superficial resemblance, both ships having three funnels. In effecting the necessary alterations a photograph of a sister ship, the Free French destroyer Leopard, was taken as a model, and the ship's company was rigged in French uniforms.

Under the command of Captain R. K. Dickson the minefield was duly laid during hours of darkness. Though a French cruiser and sundry enemy aircraft were sighted while on passage, the Manxman was not interfered with, and returned safely to her station in the Atlantic. In the course of the ensuing 15 months she carried out other useful service, and was with the Allied force covering the landings in North Africa in November 1942. She was then torpedoed by an enemy submarine and badly damaged. Emerging from refit towards the end of the war, she proceeded to the Pacific, where she was serving when Japan surrendered.

Admiralty photograph

The Buffs

By Authority of the Colonel of the Buffs, Major-General the Hon. P. G. SCARLETT. C.B., M.C.

IN Egypt, at Mersa Matruh, at the beginning of the war, the 1st Battalion returned to Palestine at the end of 1939. The 2nd was at Pembroke Dock and had been temporarily turned into a Pioneer Battalion. The one Territorial Battalion, the 4th/5th, had been expanded into two, the 4th and the 5th, in the summer of 1939. Dealing with the period 1939-40 first, the 2nd Battalion was one of the first to disembark in France, landing about the middle of September 1939. It was employed as Corps Troops with I Corps till April 1940, when it resumed its role as a Battalion of the Line and joined the 131st Infantry Brigade of the 44th Division.

The 4th Battalion left for France in November 1939 and was split up into separate companies employed on duties in connexion with the lines of communication. The 5th Battalion was sent to France in April 1940 with the object of helping to dig new defensive systems: it formed part of

IN 1572 the ancestors of the Buffs (The Royal East Kent Regiment) sailed from England to the Netherlands to assist the Prince of Orange in his struggle against the power of Spain ; composed of volunteers from the Trained Bands of London, they fought under the Dutch flag. In 1662, when Holland declared war on England, some of the descendants of those volunteers remained in the Dutch service ; others returned to this country and from them was formed a regiment eventually known as The Buffs. Originally the Holland Regiment, then Prince George of Denmark's Regiment, it received its present title—given on account of the uniform facings—in the 18th century. It saw much service in France and Flanders under William III and Marlborough, in the Peninsula under Wellington and in various theatres during the First Great War.

Given a wider sector to hold and with practically no artillery or anti-tank weapons to support it, the 5th was over-run and a large number of officers, including the C.O., and Other Ranks became casualties—killed, wounded or prisoners.

The 4th was hastily collected together from its lines of communication duties and moved up to assist the French in their efforts to stem the German break-through in its last stages. The Battalion fought gallantly, but suffered from lack of sufficient artillery support and from practically no air support. It found itself on the left of the 51st Division and narrowly escaped that Division's fate. It did, in fact, lose the best part of two of its Companies, but the remainder of the Battalion managed to withdraw to Cherbourg and was then evacuated to England. During its spell of active operations it had managed to collect the Quartermaster and 50 Other Ranks of the 5th battalion who had escaped when over-run.

AFTER Dunkirk the 2nd Battalion again formed part of 44th Division and was first in Lincolnshire, then in Sussex, and early in 1941, Kent. The 4th and 5th Battalions were reconstituted and trained, the 4th sailing for Malta at the end of October 1940, and remaining there until the end of the war. New battalions were raised : the 7th, 8th, 9th and 10th were formed and made a Buffs Brigade, stationed initially in Devonshire. An 11th Battalion was raised, and a little later a Young Soldiers' Battalion was formed and subsequently numbered the 70th Buffs.

In 1941 the 1st Battalion had its first experience of active service during the Second Great War. Forming part of a Guards Brigade it took part in the attempt to relieve Tobruk in June 1941, and captured Capuzzo. Its C.O. was killed ; otherwise it suffered few casualties and had the satisfaction of taking a number of prisoners. Later on in the year it joined the 5th Brigade of the 4th Indian Infantry and took part in General Auchinleck's offensive of November-December 1941.

After some successful actions, on December 14 the 1st Battalion was told to hold on at all costs to the position known as Point 204. The Germans, attacking heavily on that day, were held off, with the aid of magnificent support from the 31st Field Regt., R.A. and 12 tanks, but they attacked in greater strength, with considerable armoured forces and with support from dive-bombers, on the following day. The Gunners fought to the last round and the Regiment was loud in their praise, but they were unable to prevent the advance of the German armoured forces, and the 1st

VICTORS OF ALAMEIN: Buffs and a burntout Italian tank. The 2nd Battalion took part in the fighting with the 44th Division, which was disbanded shortly after the battle. The 1st Battalion also participated in routing the Axis forces, acting as a Support Battalion with several divisions, and they were among the first troops to re-enter Mersa Matruh.

the 12th Division which, together with the 23rd and 46th Divisions, went to France only partially trained and ill-equipped, the intention being to return them to the U.K. in a few months to complete training and equipment. The 6th, later renumbered as the 30th Battalion, was formed of old soldiers and was used for guarding vulnerable points.

WHEN Germany violated the neutrality of Holland and Belgium, the 2nd Battalion formed part of the B.E.F. which moved up into Belgium to assist the Belgian Army in holding back the German advance. It was heavily engaged on the River Escaut on May 20 and 21, losing 13 officers and 170 Other Ranks, and later took part in the withdrawal to Dunkirk. At and around Meteren on May 28-29, when the Battalion was on outposts, the orders for its withdrawal did not reach H.Q., and as a result the C.O. and others were cut off and became prisoners of war.

The 5th Battalion, partially trained and, as previously mentioned, inadequately equipped for active operations, found itself in the path of the German armoured drive towards the sea.

THE 2nd BATTALION IN FRANCE during the early part of 1940 quickly established friendly relations with local farm folk and took the opportunity to relieve the monotony of army rations. This Battalion suffered very heavy casualties during the fighting on the River Escaut and the withdrawal to Dunkirk.

War Office photographs

WELCOME OCCASION in a soldier's life is when he receives his N.A.A.F.I. rations of cigarettes, chocolate, and matches. In this hitherto unpublished photograph, taken in March 1943, these anxiously awaited supplies have reached some of the 5th Buffs in North Africa, where they served with the British 78th Division as part of the 36th Brigade. *War Office photograph*

Battalion was insufficiently equipped to do more that knock out some of the German tanks ; but the enemy infantry suffered very heavy casualties. Although the Battalion and its supporting Gunners were overrun and very few managed to get away, the Germans were unable to pursue their object of a break-through on account of their casualties.

The C.O. of the Regiment was wounded and taken prisoner, and of the 550 of all ranks who had started the battle only the Quartermaster and 38 Other Ranks answered Roll Call that evening ; but leave parties, officers and men temporarily attached to other units, and wounded who had been evacuated during the early stages of the battle, made up the number to over 100. The Battalion was then withdrawn into Egypt to be reconstituted and in 1942 became a Support Battalion of an Armoured Brigade.

The only other Battalion to see service during 1941 was the 4th, which was in Malta

throughout the siege. The 7th Battalion, during 1941, was selected for conversion into a unit of the R.A.C., but kept its connexion with the Regiment until the end of the war.

In 1942 the 2nd Battalion sailed with the 44th Division and landed in Egypt shortly after the retreat to El Alamein. It took part in the battle of Bare Ridge, when Rommel attacked ; the C.O. was wounded and there were other casualties. The 1st Battalion, in process of conversion to its new role as a support Battalion, had sent up some of its anti-tank guns to help in the initial withdrawal to El Alamein, and it fought with the 10th Armoured Division when we took the offensive.

After El Alamein had become a definite success the 1st Battalion followed up and were well to the fore throughout, first in one Division then in another. They were among the first to re-enter Mersa Matruh, served later in the 1st Armoured Division, and then again in the 7th Armoured Division. The

Colours : Pale blue Pegasus on maroon

1ST (AIRBORNE) DIVISION

THE badge of Bellerophon astride Pegasus is worn by all British airborne troops, there being no separate badges to distinguish between the units of the 1st and 6th Airborne Divisions. In Nov. 1941, Major-General F. A. M. Browning, C.B.E., D.S.O., M.C., was appointed G.O.C. of the Airborne Forces, which resulted in the formation of the 1st Parachute Brigade. This was the birth of the 1st Airborne Division, which first went into action in French North Africa in November 1942.

To support the landing of the British 1st Army the 1st Parachute Brigade was allotted the task of capturing and securing the aerodrome at Bône, which was successfully accomplished. A second landing was made at Souk el Arba ; and there was much confused fighting before the two forces linked up with the 1st Army.

AFTER fighting as infantry during the winter of 1942-43, preparations were made for the invasion of Sicily. Glider-borne troops landed on the island on July 9 and 10, and three days later parachute troops were dropped in the region of Syracuse. The Division also took part in the invasion of the Italian mainland, capturing Castellaneta and Foggia. The Division was relieved and returned to England at the end of 1943. Its next action was in the Netherlands.

The 1st Airborne Division won undying fame at Arnhem, between Sept. 17 and 25, when, under the command of Major-General R. E. Urquhart, C.B., D.S.O., it established a bridge-head north of the Waal in an attempt to seize the bridge over the river for the British 2nd Army, advancing from Nijmegen. The final objective was not achieved, but the efforts of the Division were not in vain. The survivors of this battle were withdrawn to England ; and in April 1945 the reformed Division landed in Norway as part of the British forces of liberation.

44th Division was withdrawn and subsequently disbanded, so the 2nd Battalion found itself out of the battle and moved back into Egypt and later into Iraq and Persia.

The 5th Battalion again went on active service. It formed part of the 36th Infantry Brigade of the 78th Division which took part in the original landing in North Africa in November 1942, and together with one other Infantry Brigade and an Armoured Brigade constituted what was then known as the 1st Army, in reality hardly a Division, engaged in the race for Tunis. The 5th Battalion with the 78th Division, and the 1st Battalion in the 1st and later the 7th Armoured Division, were thus fighting towards each other, the one in the 1st Army, the other in the 8th.

The 1st Battalion were among the first to enter Tripoli, then were pushed north and west of it, where they remained when all the celebrations took place in that city. They

U.S. AWARDS TO THE 7th BUFFS were presented by General Simpson, G.O.C. U.S. 9th Army, at Enkereind, Netherlands, on Jan. 3, 1945. The 7th became 141 R.A.C. and served in the 79th Armoured Division. Equipped with flame-throwing tanks, they went as squadrons to soften up enemy defences for assault troops of any division, corps or army. PAGE 556 *War Office photograph*

The Buffs: Feared in Italy, Admired in Malta

ALONG THE ROAD TO FLORENCE in July 1944 the 5th Battalion pursued the enemy; not always was progress as smooth as in this (top) hitherto unpublished photograph, for heavy demolitions and thickly sown mines were frequently encountered. The 4th Battalion was stationed in Malta throughout the siege: to mark the occasion of the King's birthday in 1943 the Battalion's drums and the pipes of the Royal Irish Fusiliers (bottom) carried out the time-honoured parade ceremony of "Beating Retreat." PAGE 557 *War Office photographs*

THE 2nd BATTALION The Buffs arrived in Burma early in 1945, its first action there being fought at Myitson (left) on the River Shweli.
War Office photograph

was involved in the very heavy fighting at Cassino. The 1st Battalion landed at Naples and was sent on to take part in the landing at Anzio and was there throughout the occupation of the bridge-head. Later, the 1st took part in the advance up central Italy and were among the first to cross the River Arno in the vicinity of Florence. The 78th Division was withdrawn from the Line for a short period of training in Syria and returned to the battle later in the year. The 1st Battalion was also withdrawn when the 1st Armoured Division, to which it then belonged, was disbanded.

At the end of 1944 and the beginning of 1945 the 1st Battalion returned to active operations in Italy as part of the 24th Guards Brigade. The 5th Battalion was still with the 78th Division and both Battalions took part in the hard and successful fighting which finished the Italian campaign.

After the enemy army group facing Field-Marshal Alexander had surrendered, the 5th Battalion, as part of the 78th Division, was moved into Austria and spent a hectic period trying to sort things—and people—out. The 1st Battalion was employed in the Trieste area, and later moved to Greece.

In 1944 the 2nd Battalion moved from Persia and Iraq to India, where it underwent intensive training in preparation for Burma. Early in 1945 the 2nd moved into Burma along the Ledo route and after a period of much hard marching in terribly difficult conditions had their first heavy fighting against the Japanese at the River Shweli. The 2nd succeeded in crossing the river and establishing a bridge-head, but it was not practicable to support the bridge-head properly and to expand it, and the troops who had crossed over were withdrawn after suffering heavy casualties. Later they recrossed successfully, and then followed the enemy southwards coming out on the plains of Meiktila. Subsequently the 2nd was withdrawn to India, and trained for the projected invasion of Malaya. The Japanese surrendered before this took place, and the Battalion was moved to Malaya and then to Java.

So ended the war as far as the Regiment was concerned ; two battalions in Italy and Austria, one in Malaya, but (unlike the First Great War) none in France or Flanders —except the 141 R.A.C. (formerly the 7th Buffs), which formed part of the 79th Armoured Division and, equipped with flame-throwing tanks, fought as separate squadrons with different formations with considerable success. The 8th Battalion had been converted into medium artillery in 1942 and subsequently served in N.W. Europe, but unfortunately it lost its identity as a battalion of the Buffs. The 11th became a Light Anti-Aircraft Regiment, fought on the Continent and managed to retain its connexion. So, although none of the battalions proper of the Regiment were represented in France, Flanders or Germany, the original 7th, 8th and 11th were all there. The 9th and 10th became Training Battalions and did not see active service.

---

continued to see much hard fighting in the advance of the 8th Army to Enfidaville, and were part of the force attached to the New Zealanders under General Freyberg when he carried out his famous turning movement of the Mareth position at El Hamma. The 5th was the battalion responsible for the final capture of Longstop Hill in the 1st Army's memorable campaign.

A new phase of the war had arrived with the clearing of North Africa. Malta was relieved and the task of the 4th Battalion came to an end. The 5th Battalion with the 78th Division did not take part in the initial landing in Sicily, but were landed later during that campaign and saw much hard and successful fighting, particularly at Centuripe. As part of the 78th Division they subsequently landed on the east coast of Italy and fought their way up to the River Sangro. The 1st Battalion saw no further action during 1943, but were withdrawn for training and re-equipment and became part of a Lorried Infantry Brigade

The 4th were sent on the ill-fated expedition to Leros in the late autumn of 1943, and on the voyage suffered grievous casualties : a vessel carrying one company was sunk and nearly all aboard were lost. When the Germans attacked the island the Battalion held its own, successfully counter-attacked, and having been rather isolated from events on the remainder of the island was somewhat astonished to hear it had been surrendered ! The few survivors were reformed in Egypt ; but in view of the very heavy casualties sustained it was decided not to reform the 4th Battalion, and so it was temporarily disbanded. The 2nd Battalion serving in Iraq was selected to form the British Guard of Honour at the Teheran Conference and was rushed there for the occasion.

Heavy Fighting at Shweli River

The year 1944 found the 5th Battalion fighting, still with the 78th Division, in Italy. It took part in many actions and suffered considerably, losing its C.O., killed. It

Present Day Scenes along Normandy's Invaded Coast

Main landing beach of British forces on June 6, 1944, Arromanches (1) has been renamed Port Winston, and the village (background) is on the way to resuming its status as a holiday resort. Eastwards, at Bernieres, the shell-damaged church steeple (2) is under repair, the main street is now known as Rue de Royal Berkshire Regiment, and beside a German gun villagers have erected a temporary memorial (3) to Col. Paul Mathieu, D.S.O., who led Canadians in the assault.

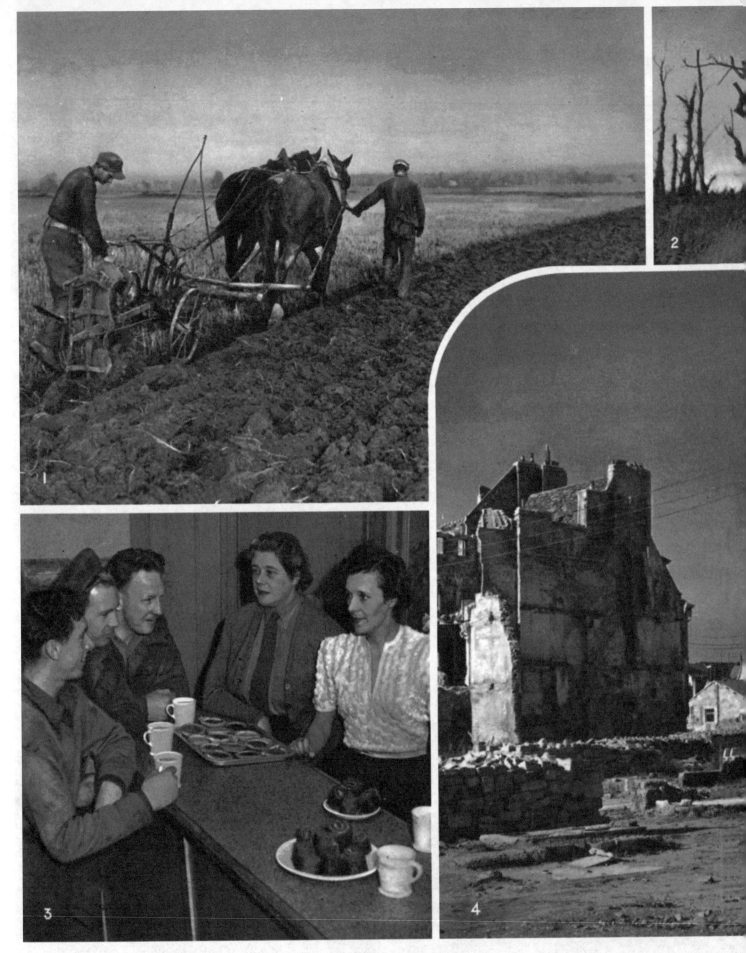

In the Footsteps of the Invasion Army—

With memories of the dread harvest of yester-year, German P.O.W. (1) plough rich Normandy land that their countrymen overran near Villers le Sec. As war left it in June 1944 remains Hill 122, near Esquay (2): smashed tanks of the Royal Scots Greys stand rusting. A still living link (3) with the invasion is the Bayeux Y.M.C.A., where locally stationed troops are yet served with tea by Hilda Colman (right) of Norwich, who supplied the D-Day soldiers.

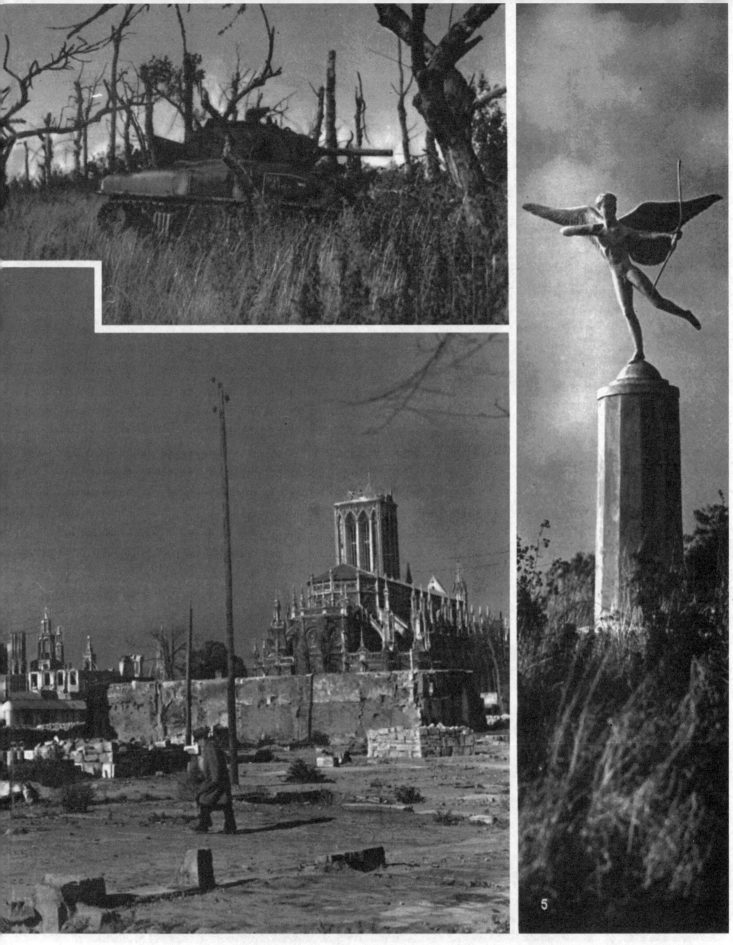

—Where Time has Stood Still in Normandy

Hinge of the great break-through, Caen (4) shows scant sign of recovery. Few shops are open and a little business is transacted in the ghostly streets (see also illus. page 146). A few miles from the beaches is a statue of Eros (5). Erected by No. 179 Special Field Coy., R.E., on August 23, 1944, at the junction of the roads to Bayeux, Tierceville and Caen, it remains to mark a spot which most troops passed while fighting in the bridge-head.

The Peace that Came at Last When Battle Passed

Photos, G.P.U

Eighteen miles from Caen, with Normandy's Bayeux Cathedral as background (1), white crosses are spaced in simple dignity. Here, on All Saints' Day (Nov. 1), comes in reverent homage a procession from the town to place flowers—on the last occasion to the value of over £2,000. Even the children " remember " the great sacrifice (2). Within sound of the sea which the Germans dared them to cross is the cemetery at Hermanville (3), where every grave has been adopted by a French citizen.

SOLOMONS AND OTHER PACIFIC ISLANDS

By HARLEY V. USILL

IT was in the Solomon Islands that so much of the crucial fighting against the Japanese took place. In fact, the largest Solomon Island of all, Guadalcanal, was the scene of the turning point in the Pacific War. The British Solomon Islands Protectorate consists of a double row of mountainous islands, extending from Bougainville Straits to Mitre Island, in the Santa Cruz Group, and north and south from the Ontong Java Group to Rennell Island. The population, mainly Melanesian, was estimated in 1937 to be 94,000. Before 1939 there were no military forces in the Solomons, although there was an armed Native Constabulary about 100 strong.

When Japanese invasion was threatened, the Resident Commissioner was told to evacuate all Government officers except such members of the District Administration as might volunteer to remain behind for coast-watching and intelligence work, and for the control of the native population. The officers who remained, with the few hundreds of Solomon Islanders under them, performed a service out of all proportion to their small numbers, and their work provides one of the outstanding epics of the war.

Each Administrative Officer was given commissioned rank in the Defence Force, and together they proceeded to organize a virtual resistance movement. The plans for coast-watching had been worked out before the war, but owing to the lack of wireless equipment it was not until early 1942, when a medium-powered transmitter and receiver was set up in Malaita, that station messages could be sent by District Officers operating small transmitters in the various islands of the Group.

The Japanese started to move into the Solomons at the beginning of May 1942, but in spite of their occupation of the more important parts of the Islands the coast-watchers kept up administration. They stimulated morale and taught the Islanders the technique of non-co-operation; they made preparations for their future activities by establishing food dumps and routes for sending messages, and so on, and their system proved so efficient that by the time the Americans landed at Guadalcanal, in August, they were able to give them accurate information of the movements of the Japanese ships and aircraft. Wherever the Americans moved they felt they were among friends, whereas the Japanese were constantly in fear of the hidden enemy.

Coast-Watching Radio Station

To these Administrative Officers—Bengough on Malaita, Forster on San Christoval, Wilson at Vanikoro, Clemens on Guadalcanal and Kennedy in the Western Solomons—a large share in the subsequent success of the campaign must be credited. When all did so well it is perhaps invidious to particularize, but the work of Kennedy and Clemens will serve as examples of the tasks performed by these District Officers and the loyal Solomon Islanders.

After the occupation of Tulagi and Guadalcanal by Japanese forces, Kennedy stationed himself behind the enemy lines on Vangunu Island, in the New Georgia Group, and set

BOUGAINVILLE and Guadalcanal in the Solomon Islands, Tarawa in the Gilberts, are memorable names in the war with Japan. Here the author deals with these and other Pacific islands, some of which were occupied by the Japanese for a time and recaptured one by one by the Allies as the tide began to turn.

up his coast-watching tele-radio station. When the Americans arrived in both these places he was able to give them regular warnings of the approach of enemy aircraft. He organized, and led personally, offensive patrols equipped with captured Japanese weapons at a time when it was impossible for him to obtain arms from Allied sources. It was Kennedy's information, in October 1942, that enabled the Americans to dive-

LOYAL SOLOMON ISLANDERS under Captain Clemens, Administrative Officer on Guadalcanal, during the Japanese Occupation carried out offensive patrols and did invaluable intelligence work in preparation for U.S. landings. Their service was out of all proportion to their numbers.

bomb the Japanese positions at Gizo, making them leave behind 92,000 gallons of aviation spirit. In December, information from the same source led to the destruction of a Japanese destroyer and three cargo vessels at Wickham Anchorage in South Vangunu. He and his men particularly distinguished themselves in jungle fighting, and many parties of Japanese were ambushed and killed through their efforts.

In a similar manner Clemens was operating on Guadalcanal. When the Americans landed, in August 1942, he organized a Services Battalion, and in New Georgia a Labour Corps was also formed and was entrusted with such tasks as the loading and discharge of cargo vessels, construction and maintenance of roads, clearing of camp sites, erection of telegraph lines and the operation of small auxiliary vessels carrying supplies to outlying areas.

Six natives of the Treasury Islands in the Bougainville Group, serving in the Solomon Islands Defence Force, went ashore with the first wave of New Zealanders when that Japanese outpost was attacked in October 1943. They were used as guides in subsequent operations, and also did a valuable job of work in maintaining liaison between New

Zealand Command and the native population of the islands. The services of these six volunteers won unique recognition—it was one of their number whom the New Zealand Brigadier chose for the honour of hoisting the Union Jack over the first Solomons territory reconquered by British troops.

Outposts on the Farthest Fringe

Another valuable contribution of the Solomon Islanders was the use they made of the native canoe—humble counterpart of the little ships of the Royal Navy. This canoe is of the dug-out type, with few refinements, but in the hands of the skilful Islanders the tiny craft brought wounded pilots safely back to their bases through Japanese-controlled waters, carried supplies to ground forces temporarily isolated by the enemy, and maintained a regular mail service to lonely outposts on the farthest fringe of this far-flung battle zone. These native mariners are proud that of the many hundreds of European personnel they carried aboard their canoes every man was delivered safely to his destination.

The Gilbert and Ellice Islands, in addition to Ocean, Christmas, Fanning and Washington Islands, consist of a rough triangle of three groups—the Gilbert, the Ellice and the Phoenix. The population, mainly of the Malayo-Polynesian race, numbers approximately 34,000. Circumstances prevented the Gilbert and Ellice Islanders from being given the same opportunities as the Fijians, Tongans and Solomon Islanders of meeting the Japanese in actual combat. Towards the end of 1943, a day or two after the Americans had liberated Tarawa in the Gilberts, a former Guards officer was sent to recruit and train a Gilbert and Ellice Islands Labour Corps. Almost immediately on landing he received news that the Americans were about to invade the neighbouring Marshall Islands and that they urgently needed labour with which to unload supply ships. By the end of February 1944 the Labour Force had a strength of 1,800, including men from every island in the Gilberts. The swift and tireless work of the Islanders certainly contributed much to the success of the Marshalls campaign. One company of the Gilbert and Ellice Corps served on Guadalcanal.

AT the outbreak of war the New Hebrides to which are attached the Banks and Torres Islands had no military forces at all, and no provision had been made for the raising of any defence units from among the population of approximately 40,000. When war with Japan threatened in 1941, it was decided to form a Garrison Company with non-native officers and N.C.O.s, and natives as privates, and a part-time militia unit of local non-natives. The first of these units became the New Hebrides Defence Force; the second, the Volunteer Defence Force, which was disbanded in 1943. When the Americans took over the Vila air base in the Solomons from the Royal Australian Air Force, the New Hebrides Defence Force helped as pioneers, and later in guarding the base.

Too small and too distant to have been much use from the belligerent point of view, the remote and tiny Colony of Pitcairn, midway between New Zealand and Peru (see page 14), played its part in demonstrating the Pacific Islanders' loyalty to the Allied cause.

Europe's Wartime Capitals in 1946

BELGRADE

By PAUL TABORI

In the days immediately preceding the German evacuation of Belgrade in October 1944, a young Serbian schoolteacher sat crouching in a garret overlooking the main Danube bridge. Day and night he watched. He saw Nazi sappers place the demolition charges. He saw machine-gun nests being set up to sweep the approaches of the bridge if anyone should attempt to tamper with them : the Germans wanted the bridge to remain intact to the very last moment so that they could withdraw their troops across it. Then, with Marshal Tito's Liberation Army approaching in a triumphant sweep, the young schoolteacher made his own great contribution to his country's victory. In a hail of machine-gun bullets he removed the explosive charges and, though severely wounded, saved the bridge.

Today this bridge is the salvation of Belgrade. Because of it supplies can flow into the Yugoslav capital from the rich black soil of the Voivodina, and U.N.R.R.A. help can pass freely into the mountain provinces where starvation is still just round the corner. This single bridge has had to take everything — pedestrians, buses, trams, cars, even trains. But now a second railway bridge is rising across the broad river, and within a few months the traffic problem will be much eased.

In 1941 the Luftwaffe attacked Belgrade for three days. It had been declared an open city, but that did not prevent the Nazis from bombing it with concentrated fury, killing tens of thousands of civilians. Many buildings were destroyed, yet more of the capital is standing than one would have expected. Belgrade has never been a beautiful city, and four years of war have left their mark on its buildings and streets. It is shabby, ill-paved. Even the Government centre is without dignity, and many ministries are housed in ugly blocks of flats. The parks, such as the famous Kalimegdan, have suffered heavily ; most of the trees were cut down to provide fuel, which is still very scarce.

The city's only skyscraper escaped damage — which, considering the complete lack of A.A. defences during the German attack, is almost a miracle. The Skuptchina, the stately parliament building, also looks unscathed ; and when in November 1945 the first federal parliament of the new democratic Yugoslavia assembled, Marshal Tito was able to address the gathering in the same chamber where many a stormy sitting had taken place and where the Croatian peasant leader Raditch was shot to death in 1928. Hard by, the large and impressive central post office also remained intact. Several hotels—the Srbski Kral among them—have been destroyed, but the Moskva and the Majestic are open and doing business and rooms in both are very hard to get.

Two features in post-war Belgrade struck me as remarkable. One was the fact that every public building, every hotel and restaurant, every apartment house in which anyone of the least importance lived, was heavily guarded day and night. Soldiers with fixed bayonets stood outside every alternate building or stamped their feet in the bitter cold just inside the front door. One explanation given me was that the partisan army had too little to do, could not be disbanded and therefore had to be kept somehow occupied. Another explanation maintained that the Tito regime was still worried about hostile elements. The first seemed to be nearer to the truth, as the regime is certainly firmly established and its enemies, if not annihilated, are largely driven underground.

The other special feature of Belgrade at the time of my visit was the incredible number of processions and parades taking place throughout the day and often at night. Men, women and children were marching, carrying flags and banners with slogans crudely painted on them, cheering Tito and singing the partisan songs. Sometimes half-a-dozen such processions weaved their way

RUSSIAN PROPAGANDA is plentiful in the shop windows of Belgrade and many Russian books are for sale, but nowhere did our contributor see English or French books. The Cyrillic lettering over this shop is Serb, the alphabet differing but little from the Russian.
Photo, Associated Press

through a narrow street, became entangled and had much difficulty in extricating themselves. Loudspeakers blared out marches and dance tunes ; almost every night there were fireworks, and people danced in the streets. Their high spirits were due to the removal of tension and fear which the German Occupation had brought. They were free, and confident of the future. The icy winds that swept the Danubian plain did not disturb them, nor lack of food and shelter.

Shops Surprisingly Well Stocked

As regards food, Belgrade is well provided — at least for the foreigner who can afford to pay. Since April 1945 U.N.R.R.A. help has been pouring into the country ; 600,000 tons of wheat alone were brought in between April and November of that year, and 10,000 trucks and cars—about 6,000 more than Yugoslavia ever possessed. But U.N.R.R.A. under its Russian head worked only in certain provinces : in Croatia, Bosnia-Herzegovina, Montenegro and Dalmatia. The Voivodina, with its rich black soil and comparatively undamaged towns, did not

need food, though clothes and footwear were problems even there. So the Voivodina supplied Belgrade with food.

In the famous restaurant Dva Ribara (The Two Fishermen) I enjoyed a five-course meal with a half-bottle of red wine for about £1 at the official rate of exchange. This was reasonable for the traveller in the Balkans, especially as such a meal consisted of at least half a pound of meat, a whole chicken or half a duck or one-third of a turkey, and included such long-forgotten delicacies as goose liver or whipped cream with chestnut purée. The local wine, too, was cheap, and a bottle of the famous *slivovitza*, the Serbian plum brandy, cost only about 12 shillings.

For the local inhabitants, however, such prices are quite prohibitive. Some of the lowest-paid workers earn no more than 1,800 dinars (about £9) a month, and Marshal Tito's monthly salary is only 6,000 dinars (less than £30). Though the shops are surprisingly well stocked, prices are high for most things ; but bread, strictly rationed, sells at about 3d. a pound. All the biggest shops in the main streets of Belgrade are labelled Na-Ma, signifying "National Store," for about three-quarters of the country's industries have been taken over by the State.

There were only a couple of newspapers in Belgrade and a handful of magazines when I was last there. The bookshops displayed chiefly Russian books, expensive-looking sets of the works of Stalin and Lenin. I saw no English or French books anywhere, and the only place where I saw portraits other than Stalin's and Tito's was the Park Restaurant which displayed Mr. Churchill and President Truman. Britain and America were not exactly popular in Belgrade, as one could see from caricatures and cartoons in the papers and even some posters in the streets. The Trieste dispute rankled with the Yugoslavs, and Russia was seen as their only true friend—in spite of all the help the Allies gave the partisans during the war.

The city is dotted with graves of Russian soldiers and Yugoslav partisans who fell during the final fighting—graves decorated with red flowers and rough marble or stone monuments. The principal monument to the Russians who gave their lives for the liberation of the capital is near the National Theatre. At this small theatre the ballet is especially excellent. I attended one performance and found the place packed. The members of the orchestra wore rather shabby lounge suits, but the stage costumes were brilliant and quite lavish, nor did the scenery evidence any lack of material. Theatre life is much encouraged by Marshal Tito, an inveterate playgoer. Cinemas do roaring business, showing mainly Russian films though now and then a very old American talkie turns up.

Life is not easy in Belgrade today, though it is in many ways easier than in Budapest, Vienna or Athens. A large-scale plan for rebuilding and beautifying the city has been prepared, but it will be several years before it can be started. Tito and his men believe in first things first ; and the capital will be shabby and badly heated until the more important economic and social problems have been solved. But the Yugoslavs feel that they can now build a capital worthy of a free and democratic federal Yugoslavia.

Gaunt Prospect Today in Yugoslavia's Capital

MARSHAL TITO, the virtual ruler of the Yugoslav Republic, has a huge audience when he addresses his people (1) in the Square of the Republic, which is overlooked by the only skyscraper in the capital. Ruins of an engine shed at the station (2) and a shattered bridge over the River Save (3) are reminders of the German onslaught in April 1941. Wages in Belgrade, and in the country generally, are low ; and the goods in a well-stocked confectionery shop such as this (4) are beyond the purses of most of the people. See also facing page.

Photo No. 4, Associated Press

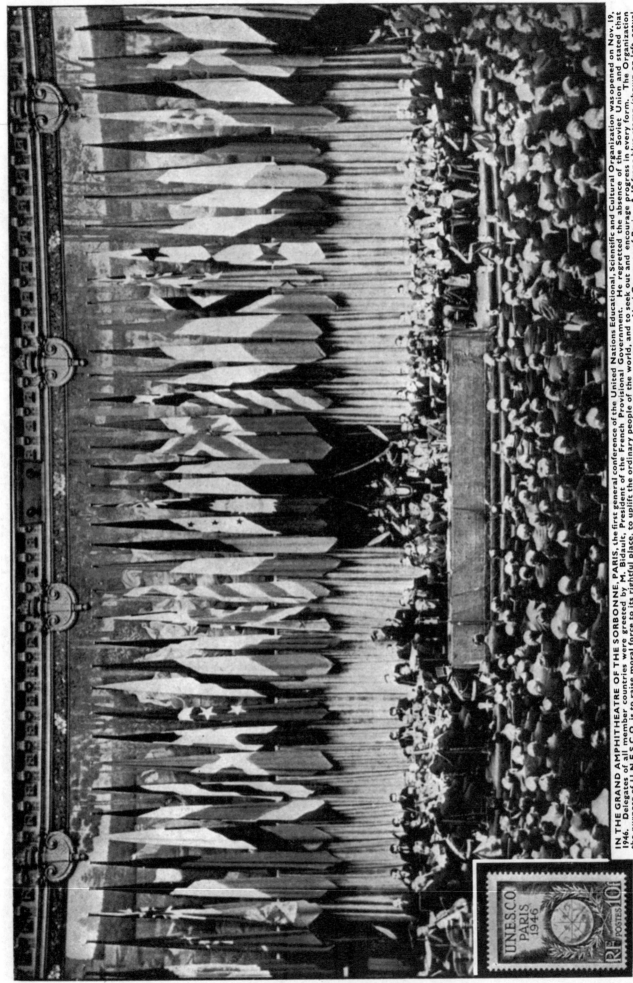

IN THE GRAND AMPHITHEATRE OF THE SORBONNE, PARIS, the first general conference of the United Nations Educational, Scientific and Cultural Organization was opened on Nov. 19, 1946. Delegates of all member countries were greeted by M. Bidault, President of the French Provisional Government. He regretted the absence of the Soviet Union and stated that the purpose of U.N.E.S.C.O. is to raise moral force to its rightful place, to uplift the ordinary people of the world, and to seek out and encourage progress in every form. The Organization has its offices at Unesco House in the Avenue Kleber, formerly the Hotel Majestic and the headquarters of General Stulpnagel when the latter was Nazi Governor of Paris. A 10 franc blue stamp (shown on left, actual size) has been issued in France to mark the meeting of the conference. On Dec. 6, M. Leon Blum, conference president, announced that by secret ballot Dr. Julian Huxley had been elected first director-general of U.N.E.S.C.O. for a two-years term. Dr. Huxley had been executive secretary of the preparatory commission since March, 1946.

Photo, International News Photos

Last Words on the 'Invasion' of 1940

IN July 1940 Hitler had outrun his immediate plans and was faced with the first major unexpected check to his strategy. If he was to avoid a prolonged war, with the danger that, if forced to a final reckoning with Russia, he would be involved in a war on two fronts, he had to find means of compelling Britain to abandon the struggle. The military situation resulting from the fall of France seems to have encouraged Hitler to believe that Britain would be ready to accept a compromise peace.

But concurrently with his efforts to obtain such a peace, he directed that planning for the invasion of the United Kingdom should be begun and pushed rapidly forward, both as a threat to supplement the peace offer, and as a practical alternative to be adopted if that offer should fail. Until then the Germans had undertaken no long-term planning for the invasion of this country, apart from certain purely naval plans which had been elaborated by the Naval Operations Division since November 1939. On May 21, 1940, Raeder discussed the subject with Hitler, and on July 2 Hitler ordered intelligence appreciations to be prepared and planning to begin for Operation Sealion (the invasion of England). The following is an extract from a directive issued by Hitler on July 16, 1940 :

Since England, in spite of her militarily hopeless situation, shows no signs of coming to terms, I have decided to prepare a landing operation against England and, if necessary, to carry it out . . . The preparations for the entire operation must be completed by mid-August.

The German Staffs were, therefore, given little over a month in which to make all preparations. It is clear that the General Staff of the German army were apprehensive of the proposed operation. The German advance to the Channel coast had been unexpectedly rapid, and no plans had been prepared for such an ambitious undertaking. Part of the Luftwaffe had already been redeployed elsewhere. Assault shipping was limited to barges and river boats to be brought from Germany or the Netherlands.

German Leaders' Several Doubts

These craft were incapable of standing up to anything but a calm sea, or of disembarking tanks or vehicles without elaborate conversion. The troops had no training in amphibious assaults, nor had the Staffs any experience in this unaccustomed technique. In the last resort, everything depended on the ability of the Navy and Air Force to transport and cover the invading forces.

According to Doenitz, subsequently Commander-in-Chief of the German navy, it was generally accepted by the German leaders that their navy would be no match for the Royal Navy, which they expected to be sacrificed to the last vessel and the last man to counter a landing. They thought it essential, therefore, that the German air force should accept the double role of both destroying the Royal Air Force and preventing the Royal Navy from attacking a landing force. Goering was confident that the German air force would be equal to both.

The German Naval High Command appear, however, to have taken the view, in spite of the confidence of Goering, that even if the Luftwaffe had succeeded in defeating the Royal Air Force in the Battle of Britain, it would still have been incapable of carrying out its second task—preventing the Royal Navy from attacking a seaborne landing force. In spite of the view of the German Naval Command, it is probable that if the Royal Air Force had been defeated the operation would have been launched.

The preparatory phase of the whole operation was to be an air offensive, whose

BASED on captured German documents and interrogation of German prisoners, this account of Hitler's plans for invading Britain was given by the Prime Minister, Mr. Attlee, on November 18, 1946. See also page 420, Vol. 9.

objectives were the destruction of the Royal Air Force in the air and on the ground, and the destruction of ports, communications, aircraft production plants and food storage depots in London. The air offensive was to begin on August 13, though, owing to naval factors, it would be impossible for the invasion itself to take place until September 15. A decision would be taken later, in the light of the success gained in the preparatory phase, whether the operation could take place at all that year.

This would depend on two factors : whether the German air force could neutralize the Royal Air Force and so obtain air mastery over the whole invasion area, and whether, given the inadequacy of the German navy, the German air force could provide protection for the invasion forces and prevent attacks by the British Navy. So far as it went, the general plan of Operation Sealion was for landings by two armies, with 25 divisions in all, between Folkestone and Worthing. Ten divisions were to land on the first four days to form the bridge-head.

Hitler's Weeks of Indecision

After about eight days an advance was to be made to the first objective, a line running from the Thames Estuary along the hills south of London to Portsmouth. The course of the battle would then depend on circumstances, but efforts were to be made to cut London off from the West as quickly as possible. Parachute troops were to be used only for the capture of Dover. A third army might possibly be employed for a landing in Lyme Regis Bay if necessary.

The orders issued subsequently showed that Hitler was most reluctant to take a decision on Operation Sealion. On August 16 an order was issued to the effect that a decision was still delayed, but that preparations should continue up to September 15. On August 27 orders were issued to prepare for embarkation at Rotterdam, Antwerp and Le Havre. On September 3 D-Day was fixed for September 21, but it was provided that all operations were liable to cancellation 24 hours before zero hour. On September 17 Hitler decided on the further postponement of the operation, and on September 19 orders were given to discontinue the strategic concentration of shipping and to disperse existing concentrations of craft in view of Allied air attacks.

ON October 12 the operation was called off until the spring, though deception measures were to continue. The result of the Battle of Britain had been that the Luftwaffe had failed to carry out the first of the tasks assigned to it, namely, the destruction of the Royal Air Force. As this essential preliminary to invasion had not been achieved, the whole operation was postponed. The deception measures mentioned above were maintained through the spring and early summer of 1941. In July of that year Hitler again postponed the operation until the spring of 1942, on the assumption that by that time "the Russian campaign would be completed." The project does not seem to have been seriously considered again.

It has been widely believed in this country that a German invasion attempt was actually launched in 1940 ; this belief is based partly on the fact that a number of German bodies were washed up on the South Coast of England in August and September 1940, and partly on the knowledge that the "in-

vasion imminent" signal was issued by General Headquarters, Home Forces, on Sept. 7, 1940. The facts are as stated in the following paragraphs.

In August 1940 the Germans were embarking their army in the barges in harbours along the French coast, but there is no evidence that they ever left harbour as a fleet to invade this country. Bombing raids on those harbours were carried out by Bomber Command, and some barges which put to sea, probably to escape the raids, were sunk either by bombing or on encountering bad weather. During the next six weeks bodies of German soldiers were washed up at scattered points along the coast between Cornwall and Yarmouth (amounting to about 36 over a period of a month). On September 7, 1940, the British Chiefs of Staff considered a report on possible German action against the United Kingdom. The main features of this report were :

The westerly and southerly movement of barges and small ships to ports between Ostend and Le Havre suggested a very early date for invasion, since such craft would not be moved unnecessarily early to ports so much exposed to bombing attacks. The striking strength of the German air force, disposed between Amsterdam and Brest, had been increased by the transfer of 160 long-range bomber aircraft from Norway ; and short-range dive-bomber units had been redeployed to forward aerodromes in the Pas de Calais area, presumably in preparation for employment against this country. Four Germans captured on landing from a rowing boat on the South-East Coast had confessed to being spies, and had said that they were to be ready at any time during the next fortnight to report the movement of British reserve formations in the area Oxford-Ipswich-London-Reading. Moon and tide conditions during the period September 8-10 were most favourable for a seaborne invasion on the South-East Coast.

This report indicated that German preparations for invasion were so advanced that it could be attempted at any time. Taking into account the German air attacks, which were at that time concentrated against aerodromes and aircraft factories, the Chiefs of Staff agreed that the possibility of invasion had become imminent, and that the defence forces should stand by at immediate notice. At General Headquarters, Home Forces, there was then no machinery by which the then existing eight hours' notice for readiness could be adjusted to a state of readiness for "immediate action" by intermediate stages.

Church Bells and the Home Guard

The code word "Cromwell" signifying "Invasion imminent" was therefore issued by General Headquarters, Home Forces, that evening (8 p.m., September 7) to the Eastern and Southern Commands implying "action stations" for the forward (coastal) division. It was also issued to air formations in the London area and to the 4th and 7th Corps in General Headquarters Reserve, implying a state of readiness at short notice. The code word was repeated for information to all other Commands in the United Kingdom.

In some parts of the country certain Home Guard Commanders, acting on their own initiative, called out the Home Guard by the ringing of church bells. This in turn gave rise to rumours that enemy parachutists were landing. There were also various reports, subsequently proved to be incorrect, that German E-boats were approaching the coast. On the following morning (September 8) General Headquarters, Home Forces, gave instructions that the Home Guard were not to be permanently called out on receipt of the code word "Cromwell," except for special tasks ; also that church bells were to be rung only by order of a Home Guard who had himself seen at least 25 parachutists landing, and not because other bells had been heard, or for any other reason.

The Roll of Honour
NCO's **& MEN**
1939—1946

Stkr. D. ANSELL
H.M. Submarine Thistle.
Action : Channel. 27.3.45.
Age 18. (Southa'l)

So great has been the response of readers to our invitation to submit portraits for our Roll of Honour that no more can now be accepted. But we have every hope of being able to publish all those so far received.

L/Bdr. L. G. BARNES
Royal Artillery.
Died of wounds. 27.5.44.
Age 23. (Street)

Stkr. R. BEECHAM
H.M. Submarine Thistle.
Action : N. Sea. Apr. '40.
Age 22. (Stansfield)

Sgt. F. BUTTERFIELD
Royal Air Force.
Meppen/Ems. May '43.
Age 19. (Bradford)

A/B. J. BIRD
H.M.S. Lightning.
Mediterranean. Mar. '43.
Age 20. (Leicester)

Sgt. A. T. CARTER
149 Sqn., Bomber Com.
Action : Turin. Nov. '42.
Age 35. (Shoreham-on-Sea)

Smn/Gr. L. CRESSWELL
Royal Navy.
At sea. 29.1.42.
Age 21. (Greenwich)

Sgt. F. C. DARE
Royal Army Service Corps.
Died of wounds. 18.7.44.
Age 27. (Cardiff)

Sgt. E. W. DICKMAN
Royal Air Force.
Over Germany. 20.12.43.
Age 23. (London)

Pte. T. DOIG
The Black Watch.
Action: Nr. Goch. 16.2.45.
Age 22. (Leven)

Sgt. W. J. EDGELEY
Royal Air Force.
Action : Oding. 2.6.42.
Age 27. (Clapham)

O/S. J. F. EDWARDS
H.M.S. Royal Oak.
Scapa Flow. 14.10.39.
Age 19. (Birmingham)

A/B H. R. GREENALL
H.M.S. Aurora.
Dodecanese. 30.10.42.
Age 20. (Evesham)

Sgt. B. ESCOTT
Coldstream Guards.
D/wnds. : France. 31.5.40.
Age 35. (Tredegar)

Sgt. C. HEYWORTH
Bomber Command R.A.F.
France. 25.11.43.
Age 26. (St. Annes-on-Sea)

Gdsmn. W. M. HAILL
Grenadier Guards.
Action : Italy. 2.1.45.
Age 21. (New Malden)

Flt/Sgt. H. HARWOOD
Pathfinder Force, R.A.F.
Action : Nuremb'g 8.3.42.
Age 26. (London)

Pte. C. LAMB
1st Parachute Regt.
Died of wounds. 1.1.46.
Age 30. (Knutsford)

Marine H. LAYCOCK
Royal Marines.
Ac. : H.M.S. Hood. 25.5.41
Age 35. (Liverpool)

Pte. R. LEYLAND
Suffolk Regt.
D/wnds.: Holland. 16.10.44.
Age 18. (Liverpool)

Tpr. E. R. C. MALLETT
Beds & Herts Regt.
Action : Sicily. 14.7.43.
Age 21. (Enfield)

Pte. L. MARSHALL
Royal Norfolk Regt.
Died of wounds : 18.2.42.
Age 22. (Blofield)

Pte. H. A. MINNS
Royal Norfolk Regt.
P.O.W., Siam. 13.7.43.
Age 28. (Wymondham)

Sgt. G. OSBORNE
R.A.F.V.R.
On ops. 17.12.43.
Age 20. (North Shields)

Flt/Sgt. J. W. PEARCE
494 Sqn., R.A.F.
Over Norway. 5.11.41.
Age 19. (Oxford)

A/B. H. L. PORRETT
H.M.S. Thracian.
Action: Hongkong. 25.12.41
Age 22. (Seven Kings)

Gdsmn. M. PRENTICE
Coldstream Guards.
Action : Mareth. Mar. '43.
Age 23. (Rotherham)

Tele. J. R. ROOKE
H.M.S. Grenville.
At sea. 19.1.40.
Age 23. (Brighton)

Spr. D. A. SHERLOCK
Royal Engineers.
Actn : Florence. Sep. '44.
Age 27. (Monasteraden)

Tpr. T. SMITH
Royal Scots Greys.
D/wnds: Bayeux. 15.7.44.
Age 37. (Rotherham)

Pte. H. SPEAKMAN
Gordon Highlanders.
Action : Lisieux. 23.8.44.
Age 18. (Boarshead)

Fus. H. H. SPICER
13th Bn. Royal Fusiliers.
London air raid. Apr. '41.
Age 42. (London)

Sgt. W. TINKLER
Hampshire Regt.
Died of wounds. 14.2.40.
Age 30. (Hallybourne)

Flt/Sgt. E. STEVENSON
151 Sqn., R.A.F.
Bay of Biscay. 11.4.44.
Age 20. (Nottingham)

Fus. G. W. WEBB
Royal Fusiliers.
Action : Italy. 29.8.44.
Age 28. (Enfield)

Pte. R. D. WILLARD
Hampshire Regt.
Action : Cessena. 9.10.44.
Age 26. (Lewes)

Spr. W. J. WILLARD
245 Royal Engineers.
Action : Salerno. 13.10.43.
Age 29. (Newhaven)

Sgt. L. E. WRIGHT
Oxford & Bucks L.I.
Mediterranean. 10.9.44.
Age 28. (Farringdon)

At a Place They Call El Alamein

Known first as the spot where Auchinleck's tired 8th Army halted Rommel's drive on Alexandria in June 1942, El Alamein won eternal fame as the point whence the same army—reinforced, re-equipped and under new command—set out on October 23 on the triumphant march which ended only at Tunis. John Kerr, of the Royal Artillery, tells this dramatic personal story of the opening of the great assault.

THERE is a queer feeling in the air, and if you walk around the camp at night you will see and hear little groups of soldiers discussing the coming attack. We have been engaged on a night training scheme for the past three weeks, but from the C.O. down to the sanitary man none of us knows just where or when it will come off. Word goes round that all senior N.C.O.s have to report to the Brigadier's lecture, and off we go, saying "Well, here it is at last !"

Picture a little group of men listening to the "Big Shot" telling them how they are going to throw the Hun out of Egypt. It is to be the night of October 23, and the place is the line out of which we have just come. And now we of the 51st (Highland) Division will have our revenge for Dunkirk and St. Valery ! We have good company on our right flank. Next to the sea will be the New Zealand Division, on our left flank the Aussies. Monty says it will be the finest fighting combination in the world. We are to be supported by eight hundred 25-pounder guns and they

will fire 500 rounds per gun. Zero hour will be 10.0 p.m., but counter-battery tasks will begin at 9.40 p.m.

On the day of the attack we move into positions dug behind our main line. Orders are that we shall keep as much underground as possible, the reason being that our whole division is confined in a battalion area and if the gunners of enemy aircraft spot us we'll be in a hot spot. Time is wearing on, and everyone becomes fidgety—with a queer sort of feeling inside. At 4 o'clock in the afternoon the 1st Battalion the Black Watch has its first casualties. One of the Pioneers and an R.E. are blown up while fitting a Bangalore torpedo (used for blowing gaps in the enemy wire entanglements). They were only 20 yards away from my detachment at the time.

The moon is rising, and it's getting on for 9 o'clock. Now we get a tot of rum, limber up the guns, shake hands all round, and off to— what ? Eternity ? At 9.40 a colossal barrage starts, and as far as the eye can see is one sheet of flickering flame. Twenty minutes

pass, and now it's zero hour. For three long years we have sweated and trained for this. "Can we do it ?" is the thought foremost in every mind. Nobody laughs now.

The signal is given, "Advance the Jocks !" Over the start-line dead on time. The guns are battering the first enemy defence positions. Some shells are dropping short, and a man on my left goes down. Is he dead ? Can't wait to see. Through our own minefield now, and on to the first enemy minefield.

At 10.20 B Company takes the first objective — and no prisoners. D Company advance through B and go into the inferno. The guns move on, each drawn by a Bren gun carrier loaded with reserve ammunition, and at 10.40 through the gap in the first enemy minefield they go in a long column. The Germans have spotted the gap and shells are tearing into our men. The stretcher-bearers

JOHN KERR

THUNDER OF BRITISH GUNS AT ALAMEIN on the night of Oct. 23–24, 1942, announced the breaking of the storm of steel and men that was to sweep the Germans and Italians out of Africa. Eight hundred 25-pounders took part in the opening barrage that blasted the enemy's positions. The German artillery was overwhelmed at first but soon opened up on gaps in the minefields that had been made by the Royal Engineers for the following guns and infantry. Streams of tracer marked the axes of advance and the flanks of units.   PAGE 569   *War Office photograph*

are already coming back in an endless stream with wounded. Strange, but the jokes have started again and most of the tenseness has disappeared. A man by the edge of the gap is lying with his legs blown off. He is going, and he knows it, but he shouts for us to "square it up" for him.

The column stops, and the Second-in-Command comes back shouting for a jeep as the one he had has been knocked out. I light a cigarette and am pleased to note that my hands are quite steady, but I keep wondering: If I get hit how will I behave? The mortars have got the range to a yard now. We move again, but at slower pace, the way being prepared by a mine-clearing tank. Twenty yards on, and a couple of shells register direct hits on a jeep and a carrier; confusion reigns for a second or two and when the smoke clears I get up and check that all is well with my crew. My carrier is second in line now. More of our wounded are coming back, but very few prisoners.

We are passing through A Company; they're lucky—they are digging in. Now about 200 Jerries come over, with their hands in the air. Barney Shaw comes along with his arms full of Lugers and grenades, and I scrounge some of them. A chap starts to give me a commentary on the battle to date as it has affected him. I remember one of his remarks: it was "It makes you laugh!" Whatever else *I* was doing, I wasn't laughing.

Another minefield—and a Hun with a machine-gun starts to plaster us with nickel-capped shot, but someone quickly settles his hash. I'm told a good pal of mine "got his" a little while ago; according to report he took half-a-dozen Italians and two Jerries with him. I'll remember to have a drink to him—if I get through.

In Their Hundreds Came the Tanks

Word comes along the column that we have to dig in where we are. Does my shovel move! I'm the grandfather of all moles. Lying in my slit trench I begin to dread the next move. It's the reaction. I feel almost dead inside. Casualties are high. Guns and carriers and a good few crews are knocked out. By 2.0 a.m. we are on the last objective. The tank sweeping for mines in front of us suddenly goes up, and I'm blown about ten yards by the blast. I pick myself up, and run to the carrier to check my crew. All safe, thank heaven!

Most of us were sort of half-witted and bomb-happy, but we took that last objective and held it against counter-attacks. We've blasted a gap for the tanks, and here they come in their hundreds. . . . But the tanks did not get through that first night, and it was only after ten days' fierce infantry and tank fighting that Jerry's last defences cracked and our armour swept through. In that ten days I saw courage indescribable: the lads we left at Alamein went out like champions.

LIEUT. J. HERBERT, R.N.V.R., with members of the crew of a 40-mm. twin Bofors which was "in" at the death of the E-boat.

'Twixt Riven Halves of a Flaming Hull

On patrol against E-boats seeking to penetrate the Anzio anchorage, the destroyer H.M.S. Grenville had her share of lively occasions: as on a night in March 1944 when there came the abrupt order "Stand by to ram!" Lieut. John Herbert, R.N.V.R., recalls the sudden rush of dramatic events.

OUR night patrols were arranged to give the greatest possible protection to merchantmen lying at anchor inshore. Most nights passed without any special diversion save for the investigation of some radar contact or other, which usually resulted in nothing more than one of our own small patrol craft which had strayed off the "beat" assigned to her. There were times, however, when we were rewarded by a real contact in the form of an E-boat trying to sneak through our guard and attack the anchorage. So it was on the night of March 24, 1944.

I turned in early that night, and the light had not long been out when the throb of the propeller shaft began to increase and the ship to heel over—always a sure sign that we were investigating something suspicious. Within five minutes the alarm bells were ringing, followed by the clatter of the watch below tumbling out of their hammocks

and, grabbing scarves, lifebelts and duffel coats, doubling up the ladders.

As I dashed forward along the upper deck a thin ribbon of tracer suddenly shot down the side of the ship and I wondered what was going to happen next.

On reaching the bridge, I found that we had intercepted an E-boat and were about to open fire with star shell. The first round burst out on the bow, then another and another—three balls of fire hanging in the sky and casting brilliant light on to the waters. The third star shell illuminated her perfectly, as she scurried ahead, buried in a smother of foam, zigzagging in an effort to escape us and hide herself in the darkness.

Orders were passed swiftly—the fire bell rang—then came a crash as all guns opened fire together. With only short pauses, necessary for reloading and corrections to be made to the instruments, the fire bell rang

every five seconds, the air filling again after each interval with cordite smoke and blast from the guns. Every now and then the E-boat managed to zigzag clear of the star shell's bright glow, but we could still see her through our glasses, surrounded by shell bursts and fountains of water.

To add to the inferno, the close-range weapons opened fire, sending red ribbons of tracer arcing towards the target; they were uncanny to watch, ending their flight in splashes of phosphorescence. The Oerlikon gunners were firing in long bursts, allowing a few seconds for smoke to clear away before they recommenced their staccato barking. With the telegraphs showing "full ahead together" the ship bounded through the water, and what with the wind and the noise of the guns we were well worked-up.

They Sat on the Safety Valves

Down below in the engine-room the Chief and his stokers were watching their gauges. The throttles had been opened wide and two hands instructed to sit on the safety valves to prevent them blowing off! Here below the waterline they were unaware of what exactly was taking place, but they were fully aware that a torpedo might suddenly shatter the ship's side and transform below-decks into a nightmare of escaping steam and rushing water. In the magazines and shell rooms the supply parties were sending up

H.M.S. GRENVILLE, E-BOAT RAMMER, in which the author of the accompanying story (portrait at top of page) was serving in March 1944, is here seen in the Bay of Naples after the action which he describes. A destroyer of 1,710 tons displacement and a designed speed of 34 knots, the Grenville sheered through her unlucky target with the greatest of ease. The main armament of 4·7-in. guns with which the enemy was first engaged off Anzio is clearly visible.

Admiralty photograph

8th Army Desert Warriors Advancing at Alamein

IT WAS THE INFANTRY, not the tanks, that broke through the Axis defences at El Alamein. There was little cover in the desert, except the hole that each man dug for himself; so even a wrecked enemy vehicle (1) gave some sense of protection. Light transport, carrying reserve ammunition, moved forward with the infantry (2). Shell fire did not deter 8th Army men (3) who flung back Rommel's troops after ten days' grim struggle. See story in facing page.　　　PAGE 571

TWIN BOFORS ON H.M.S. GRENVILLE, firing streams of tracer, helped to disable the German E-boat before the destroyer rammed. These dual-purpose guns are also part of the anti-aircraft armament, and their firing may be controlled by an officer on the bridge, who can see a target which is invisible from the gun position.

duffel coat and a life-jacket of the blow-up variety. In the afternoon we entrained for Southend, and arrived there during an air raid, with no one to meet us. The stationmaster would not let us leave our gear in the station, so a lance-corporal mounted guard over it whilst we found our own billets.

On March 14 my mate (K. Crowther, of Leeds) and I were told to embark from Southend Pier on to the 667-ton S.S. Eddystone. There were two Naval ratings on board in charge of a 12-lb. dual purpose gun which was situated aft. There were also two Lewis guns, which belonged to the Navy, fixed on the wings of the bridge. Amidships on the deck were two concrete sewer pipe mains as potential gun pits. There were already two soldiers of the King's Own on board, and between the two Army gun teams we had two Lewis guns, one in each pit.

the shells and cordite as fast as they could. On the bridge the noise was terrific and each officer had to bawl his orders at the top of his voice down his own particular phone to make himself heard above the roar.

It was in the midst of this frenzied scene that the wire rammer on "A" gun parted. The captain of the gun, a three-badger named Able-Seaman Walker, the oldest hand in the ship and one of those men on whom the Royal Navy relies so much, was equal to the occasion. Urging his crew to redouble their efforts and load by hand, he speedily spliced the severed strands in the darkness, thus enabling the gun to be loaded again in the correct manner.

Up on the bridge the gunnery officer and the officer in charge of the close-range weapons found themselves shouting their respective orders each down the other's phone ; they realized their mistake simultaneously, and for a moment glared at each other in baffled fury. Then each hurled the "unwanted" set of phones at the other and grabbed at his own, the exchange being effected to an accompaniment of much lively language.

After the chase had been going on for half an hour we saw that the enemy was slowing down, till eventually she lay stopped, just rocking in the short swell, her small mast leaning drunkenly to one side. Some of her crew began to wave their arms—and it was at this stage that our captain gave the order "Stand by to Ram !" and directed the

ship straight for the enemy. When our intention became clear to those on the E-boat some of the crew began to dive overboard, others simply stood there paralysed with fear, watching our sharp bows rushing towards them.

When we hit there was scarcely a bump. We might have been cutting through a pat of butter. There was an extremely tense moment down in the magazine, where the news of the captain's intention had not yet been received ; unaware of what was happening the men stood expectantly with a hand on the rung of the ladder—ready to move quickly ! As we rammed the E-boat's petrol tanks blew up, and for a few seconds we were silhouetted between the riven halves of her flaming hull, with great tongues of fire curling up our sides.

Mixed Bag of Shaken Survivors

Next moment we were through, and she lay astern of us, bows and stern pointing skywards, ablaze from end to end. By some miraculous chance one of her crew had managed to keep his feet when we hit and he now stood right out on the bows, his body outlined against the flames which crackled so closely behind him. By the time we had turned round the flames were dying down and we picked up a mixed bag of survivors—Germans and Italians, all very shaken and the worse for wear. When that had been completed we returned to our patrol line filled with the satisfaction of a job thoroughly well done.

We of the Army Served in D.E.M.S.

Defensively Equipped Merchant Ships carried Army as well as Navy gunners (see illus. page 246). The Army's part in this work is championed by A. J. Willcocks, who served on 16 different vessels, part of the time as a gunner in the Maritime Royal Artillery. Names of the latter who were killed in the Second Great War are inscribed in Sheerness Garrison Church, where a commemorative service took place in December 1945.

After four months' drill as a private in the Duke of Wellington's Regiment, at the barracks at Halifax, and two months' guarding a tunnel at Diggle on the frozen Yorkshire moors, a batch of about 50 of us were detailed for special service and sent to Hull. On March 9, 1941, we were billeted in St. Augustine's Convent, and a more varied representation of the British Army would have been hard to find. It was not without some misgiving that we

learned we were to help defend merchant ships against air attacks.

The next day we marched to the docks, and in the D.E.M.S. Naval School, Hull, received instruction on Lewis and Hotchkiss machine-guns from a Royal Marines sergeant. The following morning we were divided into pairs, as teams. Each team received a gun, a thousand rounds of ball and tracer, and spare parts, plus hammock and oilskins,

Motto : "I Change My Body but Not My Spirit"

NO. 57 SQUADRON

Disbanded in 1919, at the end of the First Great War, the Squadron was reformed at Netheravon, Wilts, on September 5, 1932, as No. 57 (Bomber) Squadron, and a month after the outbreak of the Second Great War it was in action in France, flying Blenheims. It continued to operate until May 19, 1940, when it moved to Boulogne and thence to Southampton. Flying again, two days later, from Wyton, Hunts, it then moved to Lossiemouth, Elginshire.

During the remainder of 1940 and in 1941 the Squadron carried out daylight sweeps over the North Sea and made attacks on Stavanger, in Norway. During the winter of 1941-42 it was re-equipped with Wellingtons, and among targets raided were Düsseldorf, Cologne, Mannheim, Hamburg, Duisburg and Bremen.

In 1942 the Squadron joined in the attacks on the German warships Gneisenau, Scharnhorst and Prinz Eugen, on February, 12, and in the following month bombed the Renault works at Paris. In the summer of 1942 it joined No. 5 Group, and with other squadrons breached the Moehne Dam and attacked the Tirpitz. By October 1942 the Squadron, converted to Lancasters, was in the forefront of the offensive against Germany.

During 1944 it was continually on operations, attacking German lines of communication and V-weapon sites after D-Day. It played its part in the successive attacks that breached the Dortmund-Ems and Mittelland canals, and helped to destroy the town of Wesel immediately before the 2nd Army crossed the Rhine on the night of March 23, 1945. The defences were so pulverized that Commandos were able to seize it with only 36 casualties, a feat praised by Field-Marshal Montgomery.

A. J. WILLCOCKS, author of this story (on left), manning a Lewis gun, and (top) in front of the concrete gun pit, after engaging enemy aircraft.

About four o'clock in the afternoon I was watching our air escort—a solitary Sunderland—when suddenly there appeared two planes in line astern of it. More air support, I thought. But the Captain knew better. "Those are Junkers 88s," he said, and as he spoke the two planes swung in towards the convoy astern of us and, with my heart in my mouth, I saw the bombs go down and geysers of water spout up. They missed their targets, fortunately, and managed to get away although the ships had opened fire on them. Our guns had a maximum range of only 400 yards.

The Captain told us that night would be the worst, as German E-boats would be waiting for the convoy at Sheringham Buoy; they even tied up there whilst awaiting convoys! I thought he was exaggerating—and he may have been about the tying up—but at about 1.30 p.m. a terrific explosion shook me awake. I dived out of the cabin and on to the deck, and saw flares coming slowly down and lighting up the ships. Some of the latter were shooting at flares and others firing dangerously across each other; a ship astern of us had been hit by a torpedo and was drifting. Between land and the convoy, and from seaward, E-boats replied for a short while to the fire of the convoy.

Ninety Bullets Just Bounced Off

I raced to the bridge—my mate was on the starboard Lewis and I manned the port one. The other two Army gunners went aft with the Navy on the 12-pounder. There was a sudden roar of aircraft engines, and the Navy signaller, who was standing outside the wheelhouse—which was situated between the two bridge guns—exclaimed, "It's one of ours—she has her lights on!" The next moment he had dived into the wheelhouse as streaks of fire cut the air behind him and myself.

I heard our Captain, a real tough nut, saying, "Not yet. Not yet . . . Now!" The roar of the aircraft almost drowned my mate's gun—I expected the plane to wheel and come in on my side and I was all tensed up, but I got just a hasty glimpse of it as it sped away. My mate had fired ninety-odd rounds at it, and the bullets simply bounced off its undercarriage. The aft end of the convoy was now receiving attention,

and soon we were back in station, shaken up but thankful to be afloat. After standing by for half an hour, the usual watches were resumed. That was the worst part of life at sea in those days: you may have just finished a four-hour watch, then up to action stations when the alarm bells rang, and by the time it was all over your four hours off had been knocked silly and you were back for another four.

Nearly Run Down by a Big Convoy

The Captain told us that the Yorkshire coast and the Peterhead were also dangerous spots. However, we reached Methil on March 18, for coaling. I noticed as we came up the coast that there were plenty of green buoys, denoting wrecks, also that the course at night inside our own minefields was denoted by buoys with varied flashes per minute. In bad weather the ships' officers spent many anxious moments trying to pick out the position of these buoys.

Our Captain came back from conference ashore and the next day we left Methil for Belfast. The weather worsened as we crossed the Moray Firth and entered the Pentland Firth. We were now in submarine waters and had still to be on our toes. On March 22 our ship left the convoy and headed out towards the Skerryvore lighthouse. We entered Belfast Lough two days later, and tried to get some pay, but for various reasons no Army unit would own us. This matter regarding both pay and gear wasn't settled for a long time—not until we of the Army were amalgamated into the Maritime Royal Artillery and had depots established in many parts of the world.

Crossing the Irish Sea in a bad fog we were nearly run down by a convoy of big ships going up north. On March 26 I saw the Clyde for the first time, and was amazed at the amount of shipping that was being turned out. As our ship was due to be taken over by the Navy we were sent back to Hull by train. When we arrived there we found that several of our party had failed to get through. Four of them had been lost on the S.S. Rothermere, several more on a tanker, and on a tug which had hit a mine at Southend.

Having had no leave since being called up, my mate and I were granted six days,

The Eddystone was made commodore, and as there were plenty of passenger cabins we had good quarters. We left Southend on the morning of March 15 and I had my first glimpse of the forest of masts of sunken ships which marked that once-dreaded run known as E-boat Alley. Owing to dense fog we had to return, and the Commodore himself transferred to the S.S. Royal Fusilier; he left one of his signallers on board the Eddystone and made us vice-commodore.

On the evening of March 16 we witnessed a big raid on the London area, then left in convoy bound for Methil in the Firth of Forth. We did four hours on duty and four hours off, alternately, on the bridge where the guns were fixed, and there I realized how exposed one could feel in such circumstances. I could look back for miles and see the two lines of ships following us. There were plenty of signal flags going up and down, and in later years I got to know some of those signals very well indeed. There were a few mines floating around, and the destroyer ahead signalled to warn the Commodore of their presence; message was then passed down the ships, the escort disposing of the mines by firing at them.

ROYAL NAVY AND ARMY PERSONNEL manned many of the guns of the Merchant Navy, and here a mixed squad is receiving instruction in the Oerlikon. The gunner is braced against two shoulder pieces by a strap passing around his back, to prevent vibration jerking him out of position when the gun is firing.
Photo, G.P.U.

! went home to Plymouth, which had been badly blitzed, and on returning to Hull I was met at the station and detailed to help clear up the ruins of the Shell Mex building, which had been shattered by a land-mine. Then my mate and I joined the S.S. City of Singapore and went to Alexandria. But to return to E-boat Alley; I did several more periods of service up and down it from May 5, 1942, until July 23, on the collier Dalewood. The escorts were now more numerous and the air cover was very good indeed, although Jerry was still busy. But still we had no Oerlikons, though we met-up with the 1914-1918 American aircraft machine-gun, the Marlin. If anything went wrong with the Marlin you had so many parts to sort out that you'd "had it."

From September 16 to October 3 I sailed up and down the Alley on the Knitsley collier; she was sunk just after I left her. The Alley was still lively but our people were now giving Jerry all he could take. After a long period of service in the Far East as ship's gunner I came to my last vessel, the Farrandock, a collier, running from Hull to Southampton. The only aircraft I saw then were ours—going over to blast the Germans. On my last run we left Southampton on May 8 1945, the day the Germans signed the unconditional surrender at Berlin—and a ship ahead of us struck a mine. When we neared Newcastle some ships were torpedoed in a convoy ahead. I was one of many disbanded into Woolwich Royal Artillery depot in July 1945.

When France Fell My Luck Went With It

Her terrier, Roy, was the reason for Eileen Desmond remaining at Nice after the fall of France in 1940 instead of leaving with other British nationals. She could not bear the thought of Roy being kept for months in quarantine if she returned to England. . . . And so was set going the flow of strange events and severe ordeals that almost overwhelmed her.

THE bitterest episodes of my life had their origin at Nice in the autumn of 1938, when I became friendly with a lady who claimed to be of Swedish nationality. Ruth, as she called herself, was the wife of a wealthy man whom I knew by his Christian name Charles and her abode was a luxury-flat off the famous Promenade des Anglais.

The features of the man were strangely familiar; I had met him before but could not think when or where. Then one day I recalled the circumstances. The place where I had seen him was the Casino, and he had been in conversation with Hermann Goering who had visited Nice the previous spring after a conference with Musso-lini in Italy. The recollection did not rouse my suspicion. The occasion was before the war, and in those days many people, themselves opposed to Hitlerism, had contact with Nazi leaders. Both Charles and his wife adopted a neutral attitude about the war.

EILEEN DESMOND

I became a frequent visitor to their flat, but saw little of Charles himself for he invariably retired to an adjoining room that he called his laboratory. I did not ask questions but presumed that he indulged in chemical experiments of some sort. One night —the war had then been on some months— I happened to be left alone in the lounge. Ruth had gone into the kitchen to prepare coffee, and Charles, bemused by over-indulgence in Burgundy, had retired to his laboratory and neglected to shut the door. My curiosity overcame me. I walked quietly across the room and peeped in, and what I saw caused a drastic change in my outlook. The man had uncovered a radio transmitter and now sat with code books open in front of him, laboriously sending a message.

Considerably shaken, I resumed my seat as Ruth entered the room. She gave me a keenly inquiring look. I tried to appear at ease, but that Casino meeting now appeared in a new light and I strongly suspected that Charles was a German, or at any rate in the Nazis' pay. And I felt fairly certain that information to Berlin was being transmitted from this luxury-flat. Subsequently, my "Swedish" friends proved to be Gestapo agents; but before I heard about this (very much later) I became convinced they were

Nazis by an incident that affected me personally. What happened, I feel sure, was due to Ruth suspecting that I had discovered the secret of the flat.

Unwisely I had neglected to provide myself with a carte d'identité from the Sûreté officials, though my passport and other papers were in order. And, indiscreetly, I had mentioned this to my friends, who surreptitiously reported the lapse. This occurred in the summer of 1940, when there was considerable anti-British feeling in Nice, a temporary *volte face* on the part of the French due to misunderstandings about the withdrawal of the British Army from Dunkirk.

First British Woman Gaoled There

The upshot was that a message was delivered informing me that "it would be to my advantage" to attend at police headquarters for an interview. Unaware of the treachery of the couple at the time, I arrived at headquarters, where I was taken before the Commissaire. He examined my passport and remarked in a curiously bantering tone, "Mon Dieu! Whatever have you been doing in all these different countries, ma chérie?" I explained that, being of independent means, I had stayed in those places because I liked travelling and the sunshine.

"Indeed?" the Commissaire said. "It appears to me that you have the air of an espionne, and obviously you have plenty of money. For being without the carte d'identité there may be a fine of 50,000 francs." That took me completely aback and, in a brusque tone, he ordered me to be taken into an adjoining room and searched. But the police found only seven francs and, fortunately, I was wearing no jewellery for them to confiscate.

In spite of my pleas I was arrested, and to my further alarm had my photograph and finger-prints taken like a common criminal. No charge was preferred against me, not even the minor one of neglecting to obtain an identity card; and without more ado I was bustled into a kind of Black Maria and taken off to the Women's Prison. I was quite distraught. My worry about clothes and jewellery left at the *pension* was less than for Roy, for I had made no arrangements for his care, expecting to return in an hour or two.

The other inmates of the prison were French, Poles, Italians, Hungarians or Czechs. A wardress told me that I was the first British woman to be gaoled there, and volunteered the shattering information that I would be tried for espionage and would probably get ten years. It seemed more like a dreadful nightmare than reality. I was confined in a filthy cell with a small window

fitted with iron bars. The cell had been occupied by two Arabs, so I was told, and had never been cleaned. My only view of the outside world was the yard where for half an hour each day I was taken for exercise.

The only food given to me was a thin lentil soup, black bread and water, and as the dreadful days passed I became so thin and ill that the prison doctor ordered me some milk. This extra diet, however, was frequently "forgotten" by the wardresses, whom I suspected of having it. I pleaded to be allowed to communicate with the British Consul, but was told curtly there was no such official in Nice. I reached the depths of despair when a wardress told me that it might be weeks, possibly months, before I was brought to trial.

Among my fellow-prisoners was a Madame Blanchard, with whom I sometimes had opportunities for talking when we were in the same section for our half-hour's exercise. One day she whispered to me that she was seeing Maître Garibaldi, her advocate, and promised to speak to him on my behalf.

When I look back on my ordeal in that Riviera prison I can scarcely credit that this lasted only fifteen days, for every one, in solitary confinement, seemed like a year. There was nothing to read, nothing to do except stare at the stone walls of the cell. The authorities never let me wash nor allowed me a comb for my hair. They had taken away my hat and handbag, and I should have had to sleep on my plank bed without any cover but that I happened to be wearing a tweed overcoat when arrested. The doctor visited me twice. He was an Italian and showed me the only kindness I received from any of the staff. In addition to the milk he prescribed sleeping tablets, but these were never given to me. Being a Roman Catholic I asked to see a priest, but this request, like others, was ignored by the authorities.

There came the day when I was taken into court, a heartfelt relief from suspense for which I had to thank Maître Garibaldi. I was charged simply with having no identity card, and sentenced to 15 days' imprisonment, a fine of 600 francs and expulsion from France on my release from gaol. As I had been held for a fortnight I had only one more day to serve, but the last quarter-hour of that day

ROY THE TERRIER, whose tragic end removed Eileen Desmond's sole reason for staying in Vichy France after her imprisonment and release in the summer of 1940.

CAPTAIN HANS LANGSDORFF, commander of the German battleship Admiral Graf Spee, is seen (left) with Dr. Martinez Thedy, the Uruguayan Minister, at Montevideo. He committed suicide in Buenos Aires, on Dec. 20, 1939, after his ship had been scuttled in the River Plate on Hitler's orders. His grave (right) in Chacarita Cemetery, Buenos Aires, was covered with wreaths from his shipmates and members of the German colony. These photographs further illustrate the story Captured by the Admiral Graf Spee in page 413.

spent in solitary confinement was the most nerve-racking of the whole period in prison.

On my release I found my belongings intact at the Cimiez *pension*, but was distraught when I learnt that Roy had disappeared. I inquired everywhere in the hope of tracing him, and finally obtained news that an officer of an Alpine regiment had found him starving in a market-place and taken him away. Further inquiries enabled me to locate the officer, and I made the long rail journey to Lyons, where Roy was returned to me, to our mutual happiness. Meanwhile, the French Government had moved to Vichy, and in the general confusion caused by the German Occupation nothing official had come through from Paris confirming the expulsion order. So I remained in Nice until flocks of German and Italian "tourists" brought influence to bear on the French authorities to expel British people from the Riviera. From a list of six towns in the provinces exhibited to those of us who remained, I chose Grenoble for future residence.

A STRONG pro-British feeling was evident among the people of Grenoble, whose living conditions gradually became worse than those prevailing in Nice. The staple ration was half-a-pound of bread a day, a cut of veal occasionally and a little olive oil once a month. No fats were obtainable even in the restaurants, and all food had to be cooked in water. Ordinary wine which used to be placed freely on the table or cost no more than 25 centimes was on sale only between 11 and 1 o'clock at 2.50 francs a glass. Owing to the lack of fats and green vegetables, there was an outbreak of scurvy in the town.

Each British refugee was provided with 1,000 francs per month by the local representative of the British Consul in Lyons. Out of this allowance I had to pay 35 francs a day for a room at the International Hotel, and my food had to be bought from money raised by the sale of my jewels and what I earned precariously by giving pianoforte recitals. Often I went hungry that Roy might have something to eat. The proprietor of the hotel was of German birth, but he was well-known in Grenoble and accepted by the French as one of themselves. He was always considerate and polite to me. I stayed at the hotel for several months, and began to run into debt. A day came when I could not pay for my room. Unfortunately,

the proprietor was away at the time, and I was turned out the same evening.

The weather was foul. I walked through the streets of Grenoble with Roy padding miserably at my heels, and strove in vain to find other accommodation. I spent that unforgettable night in wet clothes on an iron seat at the railway station. For two days and nights I was without shelter and had scarcely any food for myself or the dog. Then occurred another disaster—Roy was run over by a coal lorry and killed instantly ; and so my one reason for staying in Vichy France was removed. I reported to the authorities who added my name to the quota of British people wishing to be repatriated, and I was found temporary lodging and board till my turn came to leave the country.

At the Spanish frontier I was turned back to Perpignan because my visas were said to be out of date. These were renewed after days of delay and worry, and, almost pros-

trate, I boarded a train for Barcelona on what proved to be a nightmare journey. The train crawled, and stopped at every rural station ; the compartment was crowded to suffocation and many of the Spaniards were accompanied by live ducks, chickens and rabbits for sale at the market towns. Their treatment of me, a lone British woman, was vile. Insults and threats brought me to a state bordering on hysterics.

At last I reached Barcelona and, after a rest resumed the journey through Spain to Caldas da Rainha in Portugal, where I was provided with free accommodation by the authorities at the Hotel Rosa. It was like entering paradise. Dinner consisted of seven courses—the first satisfying meal I had eaten for months. The last stage of my journey to England, in July 1942, was made by air from Lisbon ; but I was allowed only one suitcase. All my other luggage was left behind and lost.

NEW FACTS AND FIGURES

THE opening, in October 1946, of two more holiday hotels for personnel of the British Commonwealth Occupation Force in Japan brought the total number of leave hotels to six, one of which is for officers. Widely dispersed throughout Japan, and offering a variety of scenery and attractions, live will take from 30 to 60 N.C.O.s and men each week. The six are the Lakeside Hotel, 90 miles north of Tokyo in one of Japan's National Parks ; the Jisoya Inn, in the heart of Kyoto, ancient capital of Japan : the Kokkasa Hotel, on the shores of Lake Biwa, 15 miles from Kyoto ; the Yannigaya Hotel, for 20 officers, also on Lake Biwa : the Maiko Hotel, on a hill overlooking the Inland Sea south of Kobe ; and the Hakuun Hotel at Beppu.

BEPPU, on the island of Kyushu, is one of the best-known thermal regions in Japan, and the leave hotel there is plentifully supplied with a constant flow of boiling water for its baths. It is reached by boat from Kure, the base of B.C.O.F., and the journey by sea to Beppu takes the holidaymakers through some of the most beautiful reaches of the Inland Sea, calling at various B.C.O.F. stations en route to take on more leave passengers. Beppu was once the holiday resort of Japanese millionaires whose magnificent homes were built among pine woods behind the town.

MORE than 1,700 collective farmer families from White Russia (states Soviet News) have been resettled in the region of Kaliningrad—new name of Königsberg in former East Prussia. The settlers were given cows, sheep, pigs, poultry and money, and provided with food and medical attention on the journey. They are granted big tax reliefs by the Soviet Government.

RELIEF supplies to be shipped from Britain for refugees in the British zone of Germany include 27,000 blankets, according to a Military Government statement. Other Government surplus stores to be sent to the zone include 150,000 metal A.R.P. stretchers for use as beds, 13,500 metal beds and 20,000 suits of battle-dress.

IT was announced on November 13, 1946, that the economic directorate of the Allied Control Commission for Germany had allocated as reparations 25,000 units of machine tools and general purpose equipment from German war plants. The value of the tools and equipment is 58 million reichsmarks (about £6,000,000). The tools are to be taken from the three western zones, and 25 per cent will go to Russia and Poland as laid down in the Potsdam Agreement. The remainder will be divided by the inter-Allied reparations agency in Brussels among 18 western Allies.

Tribute to 'A Man Who Loved the People'

THE ROOSEVELT MEMO

DONATIONS HERE

ALL CONTRIBUTIONS OF UNDER 5/- HERE

Photo, G.P.U.

DONATIONS FOR THE FRANKLIN D. ROOSEVELT MEMORIAL poured in so quickly at a collecting office in London's Trafalgar Square (above), and the response from all parts of Great Britain and Northern Ireland was so magnificent, that the appeal was closed on November 24, 1946. In six days some £40,000 had been donated, nearly all in amounts of five shillings. The monument, designed by Sir William Reid Dick, is to be erected in the garden of Grosvenor Square, London, which has long associations with the U.S.A. See also illus. in page 546.

Printed in England and published every alternate Friday by the Proprietors, THE AMALGAMATED PRESS, LTD., The Fleetway House, Farringdon Street, London, E.C.4. Registered for transmission by Canadian Magazine Post. Sole Agents for Australia and New Zealand : Messrs. Gordon & Gotch, Ltd. ; and for South Africa : Central News Agency, Ltd.—December 29, 1946.   S.S.   *Editorial Address :* JOHN CARPENTER HOUSE, WHITEFRIARS, LONDON, E.C.4.

NIGERIA'S NAMESAKE, H.M.S. NIGERIA recently paid a visit to Lagos, the capital of the West African Colony and Protectorate, where she is here seen in harbour. Of several official ceremonies marking the occasion the most important was a service at Christ Church Cathedral, at which the ship's company paraded behind the Royal Marines band. Cordial relations established by this visit were enhanced by facilities granted to the local inhabitants to inspect the warship. H.M.S. Nigeria is a cruiser of 8,000 tons displacement, with a main armament of twelve 6-in. guns and a designed speed of 33 knots. *Photo, Pictorial Press*

Edited by Sir John Hammerton

When Great Thunder of Battle Rolled Over Crete

IMPERIAL FORCES on the island of Crete, lacking air support, had to endure ceaseless bombing by the Luftwaffe and assaults by parachutists. During the evacuation all embarkation points were subjected to attack, among them the British naval base at Suda Bay (1). The decisive attack on the island opened on May 20, 1941, when Heraklion (2) was plastered by German aircraft. Airborne assault units were mostly Alpine regiments and were transported in Junkers three-engined troop-carriers and gliders (3). British, New Zealand and Greek troops took such heavy toll of their assailants that the Germans never again used airborne troops in force. See facing page.

Photos, War Office, N.Z. Govt.

Was the Defence of Crete a Turning-Point?

By Major-General
SIR CHARLES GWYNN,
K.C.B., D.S.O.

THE loss of Crete, following on the failure of our intervention in Greece and Rommel's counter-offensive in Libya, was a bitter blow. It is not surprising that at the time there was a tendency to believe that there had been lack of foresight in preparations for defence and of co-operation between the Services in meeting the attack.

Publication on July 3, 1946, of the dispatch written on September 5, 1941, by General Sir Archibald Wavell (as he then was) enables us now to judge more fairly. Primarily, it reveals the extent of our commitments in the Middle East and the lack of resources to meet them. Incidentally, it confirms the accuracy of the vivid unofficial account of the fighting in Crete compiled by the archivist of the 2nd New Zealand Expeditionary Force. These two records are summarized below.

Shortly after the Italian attack on Greece in October 1940, but before we intervened in that war, two battalions were sent to Crete to strengthen the defences of Suda Bay, which was a convenient refuelling port for the Navy. With the Greek Division then on the island this gave adequate protection against any Italian attack. But the Greek Division was soon transferred to the mainland, together with all available labour and mules, and when in February 1941 the Greeks appealed for assistance in view of the German threat, a third battalion was sent to the island and orders were given to prepare a base for a division and to press on with the construction of airfields. When, however, we became deeply involved in operations in Greece, Iraq and Libya, it became impracticable to reinforce the garrison, and airfield construction was hampered by lack of materials and labour. But since Suda Bay was increasingly used by the Royal Navy, the Mobile Naval Base Defence Organization (M.N.B.D.O.), under Major-General E. C. Weston, R.M., was sent to improve its defences.

Minus Equipment and Transport

That was the situation on the island when the evacuation from Greece took place at the end of April 1941. Some of the troops evacuated were sent direct to Egypt, but in order to have a shorter voyage and economize shipping about 27,000 were landed in Crete, pending shipping being available for their transfer to Egypt and for their relief by fresh troops. Some units were actually sent on, but owing to the situation in Iraq and Egypt it was impossible to replace the remainder by a fresh division until one could be brought back from Abyssinia.

It was therefore necessary to be prepared to meet the anticipated attack with the troops actually on the island, in spite of their having lost all their heavy equipment and transport, and of their exhausted and disorganized condition. Every effort was made to replace deficiencies, but Egypt had no large reserves and much was sunk en route; guns sent forward were mostly captured Italian weapons, and only nine infantry tanks could be supplied.

GENERAL SIR ARCHIBALD WAVELL as C.-in-C. Middle East, on a tour of inspection in the Suda Bay area (see map below) in Nov. 1940.

Seldom can troops have been so poorly equipped. Moreover, the island was singularly ill-adapted to defence against the form of attack which threatened. From east to west 160 miles long and 40 miles in depth at its widest, a high mountain chain skirts the southern coast, making communications from north to south very difficult. The main ports are all on the northern coast—from east to west, Heraklion (Candia), Retimo and Suda Bay—and on it there are also many beaches where landing by boat or aircraft is practicable. Roads in the interior are little more than mule tracks, and the only good road for lateral communication runs along the coast. As a result ground troops of the defences were widely dispersed.

The Navy, to give protection against landings, and to convoy ships carrying heavy stores, had to operate in waters exposed to air assault, and airfields, within easy range of superior forces on the mainland, were equally subject to attack. It was therefore apparent that when the enemy opened a full-scale air offensive the Navy would only be able to operate on the north coast under cover of darkness and at great risk, and that any attempt to station aircraft permanently on Crete would invite their complete destruction.

Discharge of Cargoes Difficult

The evacuation from Greece which began on the night of April 24-25 was practically completed by April 29, and on April 30 General Wavell appointed Major-General Bernard Freyberg, V.C., D.S.O., to take command in Crete. His troops were already distributed as follows:

At Heraklion, two British battalions (2nd Black Watch, 2nd Yorks and Lancs, later to be joined by the 2nd Leicesters from Egypt), three Greek battalions, a composite unit of 300 Australians and 250 Artillerymen armed as infantry. At Retimo, four Australian battalions, six Greek battalions. At Suda Bay and Canea, under command of General Weston, two improvised Australian battalions, 1,200 British infantry of various units, a regiment of R.H.A. armed as infantry, the M.N.B.D.O. and two Greek battalions. In the Maleme sector, the 4th N.Z. Brigade and 1st Welsh Regiment (in the area west of Canea); the 5th N.Z. at the Maleme Aerodrome (10 miles west of Canea); the 10th Infantry Brigade (consisting of the 20th N.Z. Battalion, a composite N.Z. battalion formed from various personnel, and two Greek battalions), with one unbrigaded Greek battalion was distributed in the Galatas area south-west of Canea.

Owing to the shortage of transport, Heraklion and Retimo were practically isolated and out of supporting distance from the Suda Bay group. The 4th N.Z. Brigade was in general reserve, not to be committed without orders from Headquarters. The main airfield was at Maleme, but there were also airstrips at Heraklion and Retimo.

THE immediate business was to reorganize these various units and construct defences. The former task included the withdrawal of men from units to man guns arriving from Egypt. For the latter little material was available, and there was an acute shortage of entrenching tools and native labour. From the first the island was subjected to frequent bombing attacks, but in the earlier stages these were mainly directed against the ports. A number of ships were sunk and discharge of cargoes was very difficult, but A.A. defences and the few aircraft still based on the island inflicted substantial losses on the

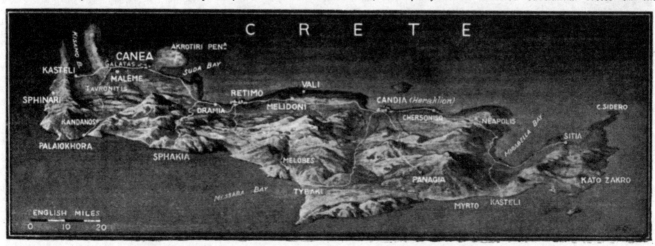

enemy. The troops in the cover of orange groves escaped serious casualties, and when they had recovered from exhaustion their morale was high.

But it was realized that the test would come when the enemy had completed his concentration of air power and preparation of additional airfields, at which he was known to be hard at work. It was also known that he was busily collecting craft for a seaborne landing. From May 13 onwards the scale of air attack increased, and it was evident that aircraft based on the island were in danger of being completely destroyed. It was therefore decided to withdraw what were left—four Hurricanes and three Gladiators—on May 19. On that day there was a brief respite; presumably knowing the coast was clear the enemy was preparing for decisive action.

Seaborne Landing Attempts Crushed

At 6.10 a.m. on May 20 this began with a heavy attack directed on the perimeter of the Maleme airfield, and shortly before 8.0 a.m. intensive bombing and ground strafing on an unprecedented scale developed over the whole area from Canea and the Akrotiri peninsula, which encloses Suda Bay, to the Tavronitis valley, south-west of Maleme. The attack was specially concentrated on the defences around the airfield, where it continued in full violence for 90 minutes leaving the troops crouched in their slit trenches dazed and stunned.

Then suddenly from the south-west, flying low over the foothills, came streams of Junkers 52s, and from them hundreds of parachutists dropped, reaching the ground quickly from a height of 300-500 feet. They met practically no A.A. fire, for the approach had been cleverly planned to escape the fire of guns which mainly faced north and whose crews were too stunned for quick action. Parachute troops who landed near the aerodrome had short lives. But all could not be located, and in particular those who dropped to the west in the dried-up river bed of the Tavronitis, met no defenders. There also, and on the western beaches,

gliders were able to land; and this success the enemy correctly concentrated on exploiting, together with another danger spot which developed in the Galatas area where a Greek battalion was surrounded and ran out of ammunition. Apart from these two danger spots the enemy had no lasting success, and group after group of parachutists was disposed of during the day. A gallant attempt to deal with the landing west of the airfield by a counter-attack supported by two tanks was held up when both broke down.

Retimo and Heraklion were also attacked during the afternoon, but only parties that landed out of range of the defences were able to secure a permanent foothold, and the sole success they achieved was to complete the isolation of the two detachments. Thereafter these attacks were not pressed, the enemy concentrating his efforts in the Maleme-Canea area.

By the end of the first day the N.Z. battalion on the west side of the airfield was in danger of being cut off, and another counter-attack having failed to relieve the situation it was withdrawn to the east. By midday on May 21 the defenders were forced off the aerodrome altogether, though it was still kept under fire, and in the late afternoon enemy troop-carriers began to land on it. They suffered desperate losses, but persisting in the attempt the enemy's strength steadily grew.

During the night a deliberate counter-attack was organized to recover the airfield, but it failed, in spite of a particularly gallant effort by the Maori battalion. But on that night the Navy disrupted an important part of the enemy's plans, for it met and completely destroyed an attempt at a seaborne landing. Early in the morning of the following night a similar attempt was also frustrated. But the enemy succeeded in withdrawing most of his force under a smoke-screen and, unfortunately, unable to get clear away before daylight, two of our cruisers and a destroyer were sunk by aircraft. Thereafter the Navy could not afford to operate effectively north of the island.

During May 22 airborne troops continued to pour in and pressure on the New Zealanders increased, the enemy working around the flank of the 5th Brigade and threatening to cut it off; consequently it began to withdraw to the Canea defences, and by the morning of the 23rd it was in its new position. By that time, however, the enemy's western and southern groups could co-operate and the situation grew even more serious. That night the 4th Brigade was brought in from reserve to relieve the 5th for rest and reorganization.

Severe March for Exhausted Troops

During the 24th the enemy, now in greatly superior strength, maintained heavy pressure but was evidently massing for a decisive attack. On the 25th it came, and a furious battle raged all day. The line substantially held, but the defenders, desperately depleted, had to fall back again during the night and the whole force in the Canea-Suda Bay area came under Major-General Weston's command. During the 26th it withdrew to a position just west of the village of Suda, where it was reinforced by two Commando battalions, under Brigadier Laycock, which disembarked from warships at Suda on the night of the 26th.

By now it was evident that the game was up. The greater part of the base area was in enemy hands, and Suda Bay could no longer be used. All troops were exhausted and had suffered under air attacks which, once positions of opposing troops could be located, had been intensified. Early in the morning of May 27 Major-General Freyberg asked and received permission to evacuate the island, and Major-General Weston's command started to withdraw across the mountains to the south coast. Unluckily, attempts to communicate orders to Retimo failed, and though the group held out till May 31 it was finally overwhelmed. The Heraklion force was, however, evacuated by cruiser and destroyer on the night 28th-29th, just in time to escape a heavy attack the enemy was preparing.

The retreat of the main force involved a severe march for exhausted troops, but it was successfully covered by rearguards and was not closely pursued. Embarkation from the south coast began on the night 28th-29th, but owing to heavy losses of ships in passage to and from Egypt it was decided that it must end on May 31—June 1. This necessitated leaving behind part of the rearguard, including most of Laycock's force and an Australian battalion, but out of 27,650 Imperial troops on the island at the beginning of the attack 14,580 were evacuated.

All through the struggle the troops had fought magnificently and had inflicted very heavy losses on the enemy, who in the end had landed over 30,000 men as well as possessing overwhelming air-power and superiority in armaments. The Navy also had had a desperate task, and never has it better earned the gratitude and admiration of the Army.

The enemy's success was due to his reckless exploitation of lives and material, and we now know how disastrously this affected his strategic plans. He had to postpone his attack on Russia by a month—the primary cause of his failure to take Moscow and his involvement in the winter campaign of 1941-42. He was also compelled to abandon his designs on Iraq and Syria, immensely relieving our dangerous situation in the Middle East.

General Wavell may well claim that the battle of Crete was not fought in vain. But it is certainly amazing that, writing while the situation in Russia was at its worst, he had the courage and foresight to prophecy that "the fighting in Crete may prove a turning point in the war."

STREAMS OF JUNKERS appeared over Crete on May 20, 1941, flying so low that the German parachutists were in the air for a very short time. The aircraft approached from an unexpected direction—the south-west—and many of the A.A. guns, being wrongly sited, were unable to engage the large, slow-flying targets.
War Office photograph

Trooping the Colour for First Time in Japan

BRITISH TRADITIONAL CEREMONY never before performed in Japan was carried out recently by the 2nd Battalion Royal Welch Fusiliers, outside the Imperial Palace at Tokyo. Headed by the Pioneer section wearing white leather aprons, the drum and fife band (1) played throughout the parade. In the march past (2) the Colour was saluted by Lieut.-General H. C. H. Robertson, C.B.E., D.S.O. (3, right), appointed C.-in-C. of the B.C.O.F. on April 15, 1946. Led by a drummer, the Regiment's goat mascot (4). See also illus. page 101.

The Army Stages Its Own Battlefronts Show

ON A BOMBED SITE IN OXFORD ST., London, in December 1946, the Army exhibited realistic jungle and mountain warfare scenes and war relics the latter including the two swords surrendered to Admiral the Viscount Mountbatten by Field-Marshal Count Terauchi, Supreme Commander of the Japanese Expeditionary Forces in the Southern Regions. The bullet-proof car used by Field-Marshal Goering was displayed—a Mercedes 20 feet long and weighing five tons, with an eight-cylinder, supercharged engine, armour plated and, as an additional protection against mines and grenades, with a specially fitted steel floor.

Authentic drawings of the Malayan campaign and of 3½ years of life in Japanese prison camps were made secretly, at risk of torture and death, by Mr. Leo Rawlings, late of the Royal Artillery. His brushes were made from human hair and the colours from blood, chalk, crushed stones, soap and oil. A special exhibit was the Union Jack which was flown outside Field-Marshal Montgomery's headquarters on Lüneburg Heath on May 4, 1945, when he received there the formal surrender of the German forces. A varied display of German medals and badges, and of German and Italian uniforms and equipment, called for attention. Arranged by Headquarters London District, the well-attended exhibition was in aid of The Army Benevolent Fund.

BRITISH ARMOURED STAFF CAR, one of two made but not used, has armour plating of 14 mm. and is fitted with wireless and an interior telephone. The glass in the windows is 2½ inches thick, yet affords perfectly clear vision.

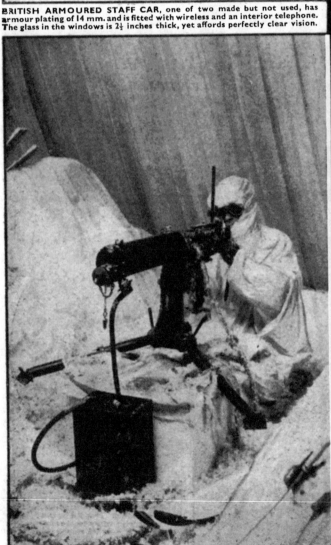

MOUNTAIN WARFARE under Arctic conditions demands specialized equipment ; and here Cpl. "Frost," wearing a white camouflage suit, is manning a Vickers machine-gun mounted on a Nansen battle sledge. Mountain troops wore string vests to conserve body heat. PAGE 582

IN THE JUNGLE REPLICA a British patrol is seen wading through one of the swamps so frequently met with in the Arakan. The sufferings and heroism of the armies that campaigned in Burma were realistically depicted in this special section.

Photos. THE WAR ILLUSTRATED *Planet News*

New Power for London's War-Battered Dockland

AT THE ROYAL ALBERT DOCK, NORTH WOOLWICH, replacement of wartime losses of cargo-handling equipment forges ahead : this scene on the south quay shows new cranes in course of erection. From the laying of the first German mine in 1939 to the last V2 fired in 1945 the blocking of the Port of London was one of Germany's primary objectives. Although the great Port was subjected to heavy bombing, a large part of our invasion forces sailed from the Thames in June 1944.

By courtesy of the Port of London Authority

How the Aluminium House is Erected in Minutes

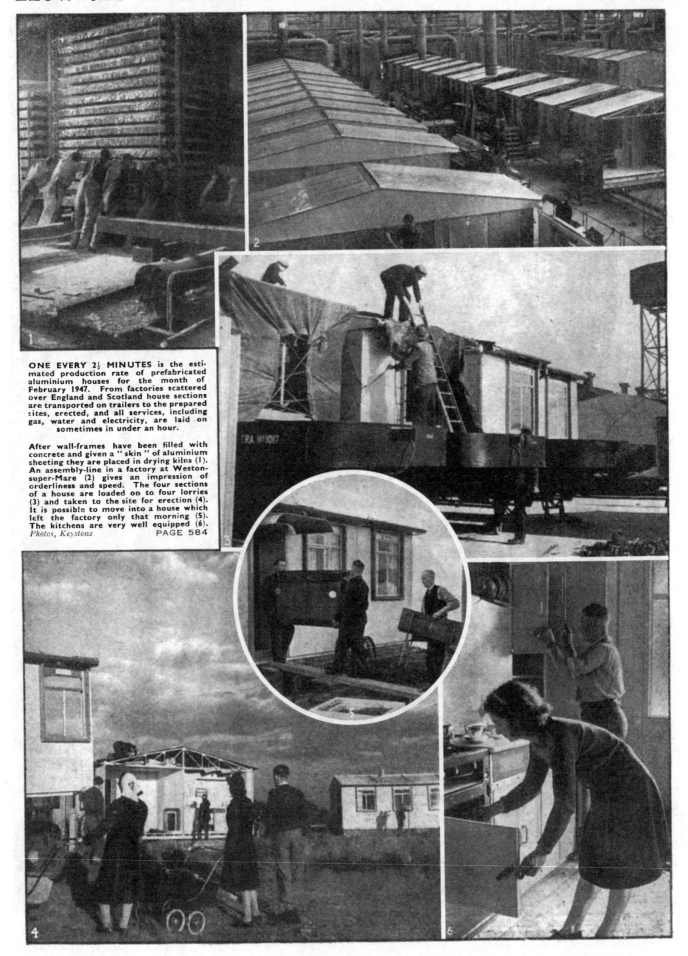

ONE EVERY 2½ MINUTES is the estimated production rate of prefabricated aluminium houses for the month of February 1947. From factories scattered over England and Scotland house sections are transported on trailers to the prepared sites, erected, and all services, including gas, water and electricity, are laid on sometimes in under an hour.

After wall-frames have been filled with concrete and given a " skin " of aluminium sheeting they are placed in drying kilns (1). An assembly-line in a factory at Weston-super-Mare (2) gives an impression of orderliness and speed. The four sections of a house are loaded on to four lorries (3) and taken to the site for erection (4). It is possible to move into a house which left the factory only that morning (5). The kitchens are very well equipped (6).

Photos, Keystone   PAGE 584

Fresh Visions of Hope for Leaderless Germany

THE VISIT TO ENGLAND OF DR. KURT SCHUMACHER, chairman of the German Social Democratic Party, and the statements he made represent a most heartening tonic to the Germans. At the invitation of the British Labour Party he arrived here (with a number of his colleagues) in November 1946 to speak for his people, describe frankly the existing state of affairs in that devastated and hungry land and to suggest remedies. Brushing aside certain adverse criticisms as to the nature and purpose of his visit, he said in London (Sunday Times, Dec. 8):

"We have made some frank criticisms in these talks, but nothing has been said which would justify the anxieties expressed in some parts of the world. Naturally, we understand the historic reasons for these anxieties, but we tell the world that we are ready to accept an invitation to any country which shows the same progressive international good will as has been shown to us here, and that we trust that in any such talks we could create an atmosphere of conciliation, whether those who meet us round a table are the Labour movements or other progressive forces. There has been much whispering about the purposes of our visit here, but there is nothing mysterious about it. The Labour Party has simply given us the chance to break the ice; that was our only purpose. Some people have slandered us as being instruments of the Labour Party or the Labour Government. We have come here as free and independent German Social Democrats and we return the same. A German party which would make itself the tool of any one of the occupation Powers would be lost—there are examples."

Dr. Schumacher's visit brought about the first constructive personal contact between devastated, chaotic Germany and the outside world, and combined with the zonal fusion agreement to raise British prestige among the German people.

DR. SCHUMACHER, one-armed leader of the German Social Democratic Party, who stated in London that the British people had so far made the biggest sacrifices in food and foreign exchange to help the Germans, paid a visit to the German P.O.W. "university" at Wilton Park, Beaconsfield, Bucks, where he spoke to his youthful compatriots about the future of their country (above and left).
Photos, Keystone, I.N.P.

MR. BEVIN, the British Foreign Minister, may have experienced a feeling of frustration at the United Nations Conference at Lake Success, New York (below), but he had the satisfaction of signing, on Dec. 2, 1946, the agreement for the economic fusion of the British and American Zones of Germany, to come into force on Jan. 1, 1947; France and the Soviet Union to be welcomed into the merger at any time they might wish to join. Mr. Bevin expressed the opinion that it was the beginning of the end of economic troubles so far as Germany was concerned. Great Britain and the United States would make equal financial contributions to put the combined area on a self-supporting basis, total joint expenditure over three years being estimated at £250,000,000.

Danger of Revival of National Socialist Party

Speaking in London on Dec. 3, Dr. Schumacher expressed his confidence that this plan to rehabilitate the joint zones could be made to work, and that this portion of Germany could become self-supporting in three years.

To ensure success, Dr. Schumacher advocated the cessation of the dismantling of factories in both zones and the granting of priority to the reconstruction of key plants. He suggested that German exports of electric power should be halved, to permit of a greater home consumption; and the big industries —coal, steel, chemicals, electricity, gas, water and building materials—subjected to socialization, but small and "middle" capitalists might be allowed reasonable margins of profit on goods for export, providing nothing were done to encourage monopolies. He stressed the fact that Big Business had supported the Nazi regime, and Big Business still existed in Germany today. While there was the possibility of the transference of its monetary power into political power, the danger of a revival of the National Socialist party would exist.

HIS MAJESTY'S SHIPS   H.M.S. Truant

ON the evening of April 9, 1940, H.M.S. Truant, a submarine of 1,090 tons, completed early in the war, torpedoed the German cruiser Karlsruhe off Kristiansand while that ship was engaged in covering the enemy invasion of Norway. Though hunted by destroyers for 4½ hours, she escaped with slight damage from depth charges. Not long afterwards, while on passage to Gibraltar, she intercepted and recaptured the Norwegian motor ship Tropic Sea, which the Germans had seized.

In the Mediterranean the Truant was active in operations against Italian convoys proceeding to Libya. In December 1940 she destroyed two supply ships and a tanker; and in March 1941 she entered the harbour of Buerat, in the Gulf of Sirte, to attack another tanker. While engaged in sinking an enemy ship in the Adriatic she was obliged to dive in 20 feet of water, with the result that her bows became embedded in the mud.

Later the Truant proceeded to the Far East. After the Battle of the Java Sea she was one of the last vessels to get away from Surabaya before the Japanese occupation. In December 1942 she returned to Britain for refit. She is here seen in Holy Loch on the Clyde after her 2½ years abroad. Recently she has been used for experimental work, and is expected to be scrapped in the near future. (See also illus. in page 600.)

Admiralty photograph

5th. Royal Inniskilling Dragoon Guards

AFTER completing mobilization the Regiment embarked for France and landed at St. Nazaire at the end of September 1939. A few days were spent unloading the vehicles and collecting stores, then the trek to Northern France began. The first stage was a train journey to Malincourt, near St. Pol, thence to the Lille area, in and around which the rest of the winter was spent training. Occasional increases in tension, which threatened the unreality of the "phoney" war, caused swift and usually midnight moves up to the Franco-Belgian frontier in the area of Roubaix.

May 10, 1940, found the Regiment in the outskirts of the town; an overnight air raid on Lille, and varying disquieting reports over the wireless, suggested interesting developments. Early in the morning news was received that the German army had invaded Belgium, and the British Government had pledged their support to the latter. At 4 p.m. the move into Belgium commenced, the Regiment being part of the 3rd Infantry Division, commanded by the then Major-General Montgomery. At dawn the following morning the 5th Royal Inniskilling Dragoon Guards were in the area of Louvain.

The next three weeks—up to the final evacuation from Dunkirk—was one long series of rearguard actions, the Regiment, as Divisional Cavalry, always covering the retirement of the infantry. During this period it worked with nearly every division

By permission of Lieut.-Col. R. P. HARDING, D.S.O.

THIS regiment was formed by the amalgamation in 1922 of the 5th Dragoon Guards and the Inniskilling Dragoons. The former were raised by James II. in 1685; the latter were raised in N. Ireland to oppose him after his dethronement. Both regiments saw their baptism of fire at the Battle of the Boyne in 1690. During Marlborough's campaigns both gained several battle honours in the Low Countries. The Inniskilling Dragoons at Waterloo in 1815 formed with the Royals amd Greys the Union Brigade which played a large part in the victory. In the Crimea both regiments took part in the charge of the Heavy Brigade, and both served in France throughout the First Great War.

in the B.E.F., ending up with covering the retirement of the 46th Division into Dunkirk from Bergue Canal. On the night of June 3-4 squadrons embarked independently on destroyers from the mole at Dunkirk and returned to England. The Regiment re-formed and mobilized shortly after, first as an anti-invasion force in lorries, and later as an armoured regiment. From 1940 until the summer of 1944 it formed part of the armoured reserve kept in England against the possibility of a German invasion, and went on training steadily with various types of armoured vehicles in preparation for the invasion of Western Europe.

The Regiment went to Normandy in the middle of July 1944, and joined the 7th Armoured Division immediately after the second battle of Caen, replacing the 4th County of London Yeomanry who had

suffered very heavy casualties in the fighting around Villers Bocage. Within two days of joining the division the Regiment went into action for the first time since Dunkirk. During all August it took part in continuous attempts all along the British line to engage the enemy armour and contain it while the Americans broke through on the right. The fighting, though without outstanding features, was continuous and hard, and the Regiment operated under both the Canadian 1st Army and British 2nd Army. By the end of the month the Falaise Gap had been closed and the German armies in France were on the point of retreat.

Tremendous Reception in Belgium

Next, the Regiment took a leading part in the memorable five days' pursuit through France, the 7th Armoured Division—the left-hand armoured division of the British Army—being directed on Ghent. The 250 miles from the River Seine to Ghent were covered in five exciting days, a mixture of sharp rearguard encounters with the Germans in retreat and a grand triumphal procession through the heart of Northern France. The Belgian frontier was crossed on September 4, late at night, amid scenes of great rejoicing from the Belgians; and Ghent, the final objective, was reached the following day. Once in position there the results of the pursuit came quickly and within 24 hours the Regiment had captured 1,500 prisoners.

It had a particularly warm reception in Belgium, as it soon became known that King Leopold was its Colonel-in-Chief, and many were the toasts drunk to the "Regiment du Roi." After a short rest it

IN CAMP AT FOLKESTONE, KENT, immediately prior to mobilization in 1939. The 5th Royal Inniskilling Dragoon Guards were in France before the end of September. Armed with light tanks and Bren gun carriers at the outbreak of war, they experienced many changes of armament before being equipped with the latest Comet tanks in 1945. The Regiment joined the 7th Armoured Division in Normandy in July 1944; the offensive of Jan. 1945, which brought them to the Roer River, was the first British winter offensive in which an armoured division had taken a major part.

IN NORMANDY the 5th Royal Inniskilling Dragoon Guards were engaged in very heavy fighting during July and August 1944. B Squadron is seen (left) formed up to attack across a cornfield. Crews rested on the road to Villers Bocage (lower left).

placed under the command of the 53rd (Welsh) Division. The initial attack lasted for four days and was a great success. The town was captured and the major part of two German divisions was destroyed.

Then the Regiment reverted to its own Division and took part in clearing the southern bank of the River Maas as far west as the Dutch Islands. After a short period of training in Belgium it again went into the line, just before Christmas, north of Sittard. It was then on the extreme right of the British line, with the American 9th Army as neighbours. Von Rundstedt's offensive against the Americans passed to the south and the Regiment was left unmolested.

The New Year brought with it a period of great cold and snow but, in spite of the weather, in the middle of January the Regiment took part in the limited British 2nd Army attack which cleared the Germans from the triangle formed by the rivers Maas and Roer and the British front line. Here, the Germans had had two months in which to lay minefields and construct anti-tank obstacles and it was realized that the advance would be slow. The attack was launched, and after 15 days' fighting, with the thermometer always showing 30 degrees of frost, the Regiment found itself on the banks of the river Roer, looking at the fixed defences of the vaunted Siegfried Line—and hearing therefrom at all too frequent intervals.

This was the first occasion that an armoured division had been asked to take a major part in a winter offensive, and the results had shown once more that the limitations by ground and weather are relative and not absolute in the employment of armour. The Regiment's tanks were impressive in their white paint as camouflage against snow

The weather broke at the end of January and the Regiment was lucky in being able to extricate all the tanks when the order came to hand over to the Americans and go once more out of the line and into Belgium

moved on again, and was soon in action to the west of Eindhoven at the start of the combined air and land offensive against Arnhem. The Regiment had the task here of clearing the main road between Eindhoven and Nijmegen after German counter-attacks had cut it. Here it first met and worked with elements of one of the American airborne divisions.

Great, however, as was the success gained, the final objective was never achieved. The bold plan having miscarried, it became necessary to build up the lines of communication and, particularly, to free Antwerp before the assault on Germany could be considered. The next major operation was the assault on 'S-Hertogenbosch. For this, the Regiment was

CROSSING THE SEINE the Regiment was engaged in the pursuit of the beaten German armies. With the 7th Armoured Division it covered the 250 miles from the river to Ghent in five days, crossing the Belgian frontier on Sept. 4, 1944. Having King Leopold as their Colonel-in-Chief, the Dragoons received a very warm welcome in Belgium and visited the mess of the 1st Guides, the Belgian Household Cavalry. After a brief rest they were again in action, this time in the Netherlands, clearing the Eindhoven-Nijmegen road after the Germans had cut it.   *War Office photograph*

Inniskilling Dragoon Guards: Normandy Memories

RUINED AUNAY-SUR-ODON lay under a pall of dust (1) when the 5th Royal Inniskilling Dragoon Guards advanced south-east of Caumont in August 1944. Tank crews will not quickly forget the blinding, choking dust of the Normandy roads; besides causing acute discomfort it betrayed their movements and increased the risk of shelling. German prisoners (2) were searched immediately to prevent the destruction of papers that might be of value to the Intelligence. Many German divisions had horse-drawn transport: at Bonneville troopers of the mechanized cavalry amused themselves with a captured cart (3).

UNDER FIRE, two of the 5th Royal Inniskilling Dragoon Guards plunge back through the mud to their tank near Gangelt, in the Netherlands. The Regiment participated, in conjunction with the 53rd Division, in the capture of 'S-Hertogenbosch, completed on Oct. 27, 1944.

War Office photograph

tremendous encircling movement in the Ruhr basin, were advancing rapidly against diminishing opposition, while on the Regiment's northern flank the Canadians and XXX Corps were fighting a hard but successful battle against a German paratroop army which was withdrawing slowly. The 5th Royal Inniskilling Dragoon Guards, in the middle, so far had been lucky, and though it would be incorrect to say that no opposition had been encountered, it had never been determined. The beginning of April, however, brought the Regiment two days of very heavy fighting to secure a road leading through the plateau to the north of the Dortmund-Ems canal. Fanatical resistance was met from the cadets and N.C.Os. of the Hanover Infantry School, and in a fierce two days' battle the ridge was secured.

Once this nest of opposition had been crushed, resistance became less determined, and the Regiment drove on north-eastwards towards the River Weser. With the leading elements of the Division on the Weser, the Regiment was directed north towards Bremen in order to cut the escape routes of the German parachute army retreating before the Canadians. This was achieved in two days, in spite of an unexpected night attack on Regimental Headquarters—on the last night before the Regiment was relieved of its position. It then went on again, eastwards, over the rivers Weser and Aller.

THE German Naval Headquarters at Buxtehude, on the Elbe, was captured, complete with its admiral and 400 German Wrens, who were far from pleased at finding that they were no longer considered to be of the Master Race. After much parley and discussion Hamburg surrendered and, with that surrender, to all intents and purposes the war in the British sector was over. Hamburg presented a spectacle that will be remembered for a long time by all who drove in that first day. The B.B.C.'s familiar announcement "Our aircraft bombed Hamburg last night" took on new significance on May 3—the ruins of Coventry, Southampton and London paled before the enormity of the damage over so wide an area.

The following day the Regiment marched to the Kiel Canal, where the news of the end of the war was heard on the wireless. It was lucky to finish up in a district of pleasant farmland completely unspoiled by war, where, apart from one short interlude, it has since remained. In the six years of war the Regiment earned five D.S.O.s, 11 M.C.s, seven D.C.M.s, 12 M.M.s, and two Croix-de-Guerre ; and at the end of hostilities it had supplied from its pre-war officers one Corps Commander, three Brigadiers, and seven Lieutenant-Colonels commanding armoured regiments. Equipment varied from Bren Gun Carriers and Light Tanks, in 1939, through Stuarts, Covenanters, Crusaders, Shermans, Cromwells to Comets in 1945.

While the Americans and the 1st Canadian Army set out to drive the Germans from the west bank of the Rhine the Regiment had a breathing space to clean up and prepare for the last offensive, which all were waiting for—the assault over the Rhine and the pursuit through Germany. After a period of tense waiting the Regiment saw the Airborne Divisions fly over one sunny morning and it knew that the final round had started. The Regiment crossed the Rhine some 70 hours after the initial assault, in the early morning of March 27.

THE 7th Armoured Division was the first armoured division to cross the river, and as leading regiment it was obvious that the 5th Royal Inniskilling Dragoon Guards were in for a busy time. With the exception of certain S.S. and paratroop formations it was not expected that the bulk of the German Army would be capable of any organized resistance, and a quick break-out would entirely prevent the German High Command from any effective control of the battlefield. After passing quickly through the dropping zones of the Airborne Divisions—an area covered with coloured parachutes, gliders and all the wreckage of battle—the Regiment passed through the leading elements of the 6th Airborne Division and took the lead.

An average of 12 miles a day was kept up for four days and nights of continuous fighting. Chief causes of delay were blown bridges and various isolated self-propelled guns and A.A. batteries that the Germans had not been able to withdraw. After an initial advance eastwards of some 25 miles the Regiment was directed north-east to reach the Dortmund-Ems canal in the area of Rheine. The latter was reached on the fourth day after crossing the Rhine, after many German self-propelled guns and more than 300 prisoners had been taken. This was the first phase of the final offensive, and the Regiment had been fighting its way forward over a distance of 80 miles continuously for four days and nights.

The general pattern of the Allied drive was now becoming clear. To the south of the British 2nd Army the Americans, after a

ON THE KAISER WILHELM CANAL, near Steenfeld, the Regiment seized three armed vessels in May 1945, one loaded with wireless sets looted by the Germans from Norway. Another "naval" engagement was the capture of the German Naval Headquarters at Buxtehude, on the Elbe, complete with 400 German Wrens, on April 22, 1945. PAGE 590 *War Office photograph*

(The Editor gratefully acknowledges assistance with photographs by the Marquess of Kildare.)

Our Last Display of Wartime Art

GERMAN SEARCHLIGHT ACROSS THE ENGLISH CHANNEL

Charles Pears

It is interesting to note that the Germans were very proud of this super-searchlight which threw its beam for a distance of 25 miles—from the French coast to the South Foreland. By its means they hoped to deter Allied shipping from passing through the Straits at night. But when they came to use it they discovered that its designers had neglected to take into account the earth's curvature and so, however low they depressed the beam, it struck the cliffs well above the height of any ships which slipped by in the dense shadow beneath.

FROM time to time, since they were first publicly exhibited at the National Gallery, London, and elsewhere, we have reproduced representative works of Britain's War Artists. Examples will be found on pp. 15–18 and 719–722, Vol. 7 ; and pp. 527–530, Vol. 9. Here we present a final selection from those displayed at the recently reopened Imperial War Museum. Among them are two paintings which, though executed during the war, are only now allowed to be seen. They are by Charles Pears (above) and Clive Upton (see p. 592).

NAVAL AND MARINE P.O.W. ON THE MARCH
Lieut. John Worsley

In John Worsley's painting (right), the column of P.O.W., marching ahead of the Allied advance in Germany between Bremen and Lübeck, is anxiously watching aircraft overhead to see if they are friend or foe ; eventually the P.O.W. produced a home-made Union Jack which they displayed prominently so that the Allied airmen might not bomb them. The artist, taken prisoner when his ship was torpedoed, is on the extreme left.

Crown Copyright throughout

LISTENING FOR TICKING

Clive Upton

RUNWAY CONSTRUCTION

ROCKET-FIRING TYPHOONS AT THE FALAISE GAP

FIELD-MARSHAL LORD WAVELL   Epstein   MAJOR J. W. RIDDELL   John Berry   GEN. SIR A. CUNNINGHAM   Epstein

A 'STICK' OF PARATROOPERS AT RINGWAY, 1945   W. Dring   SUBMARINE CONTROL ROOM DURING AN ATTACK   W. Dring

**WOMEN AT WORK
ON AN ERECTED TANK**
Ethel Gabain

**R.O.C. POST, COPYTHORNE, HANTS.
CHIEF OBSERVER. D. H. B. HARFIELD;
LEADING OBSERVER, J. O. ISSACS**
William Dring

**BURMA—14th ARMY. THE BATTLE OF THE SITTANG BEND.
MEN OF QUEEN'S OWN (R.W.K.) MAKE AN ARMED PATROL**
Capt. Leslie Cole

General Giffard's Claim to Fame

By Sir JAMES GRIGG

CONTEMPORARY reputations and judgements are chancy things, in no sphere more so than the military. The names of some generals very quickly become household words while others, who may have done as much as or more than the popular heroes, are never heard of. General Sir George Giffard made a great contribution to our victory, particularly in the Far East, yet he is perhaps the least known of all the British generals who held high command in the Second Great War.

I shall try to make clear what this contribution was, but I am afraid that for full justice Giffard will have to wait till the Official History appears, and by that time he will be beyond the reach of earthly praise.

11th ARMY GROUP

Giffard was commissioned in 1906. He spent more than half the time between then and 1939 with native troops in Africa. At the outbreak of war he was Military Secretary in the War Office, and to my knowledge an extremely good Military Secretary. A few months later he went to Palestine as G.O.C., and then, on the collapse of France, he was moved to West Africa. He knew more about Africa than any living soldier, and West Africa was now a vital staging area for our convoys round the Cape, and a source of indispensable raw materials.

Fighting the " Powers of Darkness "

The French and British colonies there were so intermingled that it could easily become a plague centre for Vichy, and therefore for German intrigues. It was an essential link in the air route to Egypt, and from it we could, if necessary, develop land routes across Africa. In it also we could raise both fighting and labour units to relieve our manpower stringency. How important this region was can be gathered from the fact that it was later judged necessary to appoint a Resident Cabinet Minister for it. Shortly after his appointment the Minister went out of his way to send to the War Office the warmest of tributes to Giffard's work.

The Mediterranean was reopened in the spring of 1943 and the strategic importance of Africa decreased accordingly. And so when Field-Marshal Wavell asked for Giffard's services in the Far East it was found possible to release him. His new task was to take charge of the land forces based on India for operations outside India, with first priority for the recovery of Burma.

Certain lessons had been learned from the disasters in Malaya and the retreat in Burma in 1942. It was plain that neither British nor Indian troops would cope successfully with the Japanese in the jungle until some grave initial disadvantages had been removed. The standard equipment was too heavy for use against a lightly furnished and highly mobile enemy.

THEN there was the jungle hoodoo, which the Japs fostered by employing all sorts of noises and ruses to rattle troops who disliked fighting against what seemed to be the powers of darkness. And, perhaps most important of all, our men had to rid themselves of the idea that, once the Japanese had infiltrated behind our positions, there was nothing to do but to get back helter-skelter to some position where they could form an orthodox defence system again.

To evolve a complete outfit of tropical equipment would take time. To overcome

---

THE Secretary of State for War 1942-45 reveals in this article reprinted from The Sunday Times the unpublicised achievements of " perhaps the least known of all the British generals who held high command in the Second Great War "—General Sir George Giffard, who left the Army on August 17, 1946, on retired pay.

〰〰〰

the hoodoo and to acquire a suitable jungle fighting technique meant new and concentrated training. After that it was necessary that the new equipment and the new technique should be successfully applied in battle before going all out for the reconquest of Burma and of the Malay Barrier. At the beginning of 1943 Wavell ordered certain minor-scale operations in Arakan. But they were not a success and more preparation was needed. Then it was that Wavell asked for Giffard.

ALL that summer the process of intensive training went on. Later in the year it was decided to set up a separate South-East Asia Command for all offensive operations based on India or Ceylon. It covered all three services and also the comparatively small American forces in the area whose role was to supply China, whether by air or by a reopened Burma Road. Lord Louis Mountbatten was appointed Supreme Commander, and the British Empire ground forces in his charge were formally constituted the 11th Army Group under Giffard.

The Group was to comprise initially the 14th Army under Slim for operations overland into Burma, and later another Army in addition for seaborne operations—probably against Rangoon in the first instance. S.E.A.C. Headquarters were at Kandy, the Army Group was in Delhi, while the 14th Army were near Calcutta. It was 1,500 miles from Kandy to Delhi, nearly 1,000 from Delhi to Calcutta and another 1,000 again by narrow-gauge railway or newly made mountain roads to the Assam-Burma frontier, where the troops were in contact with the Japanese.

The operations projected for the cold weather of 1943-44 consisted partly of a renewed southward thrust in Arakan, partly of a move over the mountains into and down the valley of the Chindwin, and partly of an airborne operation by Wingate's Long-Range Penetration troops behind the main Japanese positions. Complementary opera-

General Sir GEORGE GIFFARD, G.C.B., D.S.O., whose unspectacular work hastened the day of victory in the Far East.
From a sketch by Robin Guthrie   PAGE 595

---

tions were to be undertaken under the American General Stilwell aimed at the capture of Myitkyina.

At Kandy, particularly from the Americans there, there was a good deal of criticism of both the limited scope and the slow progress of the land operations, and all kinds of suggestions for more spectacular action were forthcoming. Giffard had to resist these, first, because they were not administratively practicable in that country and over those distances, and second, because he felt that it would be wrong to plan too large until it had been demonstrated in actual battle that the 14th Army could play the Japanese at their own game and beat them. Once this had been done the troops, British, Indian and African, would have unbounded confidence in themselves.

Anyhow, Giffard's caution turned out to be wise. The Japanese were masters of infiltration, and the country was ideally suited for such tactics. In the southern part of the thousand-mile front they got behind the British positions and isolated the 7th Indian Division. This division immediately organized itself for all-round defence and stood to its ground. When it was possible the troops were victualled from the air, and when it was not they went on short rations. In the end it was the enemy who caved in, leaving the bulk of the original penetrating force dead either in battle or of starvation.

Japanese Morale in Burma Broken

So far so good, but an even greater task was at hand. The Japanese determined to strike in considerable strength through the mountains at Kohima and Imphal on the Assam borders. They broke through far enough to invest both places. Both had to be supplied by air. Kohima was the key to Imphal, and if Imphal fell our communications with the whole of the long Burma front would be cut, while the Japanese would be free to make forays into Bengal. And invaluable as was air transport for rationing or moving troops in an emergency, it was out of the question to make it the regular and normal means of supply.

However, both places held, and what had happened with the 7th Division at the Ngakyedauk Pass happened here on a much larger scale. Thousands of Japanese were killed in battle, thousands more of them died of starvation on their retreat, and it was now the Japanese in Burma whose morale was broken, while it was the British Empire forces who had acquired an unbeatable spirit.

GIFFARD had vindicated himself, and the way was now clear to speed up operations, in the secure knowledge that the troops would answer any call made upon them. The campaign was continued throughout the monsoon, and it ended only with the capture of Mandalay and Rangoon. But Giffard was not there to see the crown of his work. At the crisis when Kohima and Imphal were in hazard, Mountbatten told him that he no longer had confidence in him. Giffard accepted the judgement without complaint or comment, and left as soon as his replacement arrived several months later. But he did not leave until it was established beyond doubt that he and his work had been triumphantly vindicated. The work was, until after he left, unspectacular.

Giffard was, and is, an unspectacular man, but he and Slim did for our armies in the Far East what Alexander and Montgomery had done in the Desert. The dog had a tin can tied on to its tail. He looked as unlike a mastiff as it is possible to imagine. The tin can was removed, and the mastiff stood forth in his full and unbeatable magnitude.

Europe's Wartime Capitals in 1946

MOSCOW

By J. CANG

IN 1947 the Russian people will celebrate the 800th anniversary of the founding of Moscow. From a mere collection of mud huts on the banks of the river Moskva in the 12th century it has become a great city and capital of the vast territory of the Soviets numbering 200 million people. Today Moscow is like a city reborn. Things that have not been seen there for years are beginning to appear in shop windows—crockery, samovars, toilet articles, toys, confectionery, wines and cigarettes—but at prices rarely within reach of the average man and woman.

What strikes the visitor most in Moscow now is the fact that the whole city seems to be dressing up ; streets and buildings are encased in scaffolding and workmen are patching up, painting, plastering and building—to make it smart for its anniversary. The gilded and painted cupolas of churches and palaces have been cleaned of the grey camouflage paint which coated them during the war and now glitter as of old on Moscow's skyline. The great walls and towers of the Kremlin are being restored, the first time since 1866 that major repairs have been undertaken. Modern bricks being unsuitable to replace the ancient fabric, 600,000 bricks of special type are being made according to an old formula. The great ruby-coloured five-pointed stars which adorn the Kremlin towers have been remounted and shine more brightly than ever.

Unlike those of Napoleon, Hitler's armies never entered Moscow ; although in 1941, while the bitter struggle raged almost outside its gates, preparations were made to burn the city to the ground—as the Muscovites did in 1812. Goering's bombers did get through and leave some marks, but compared with London bomb damage in the city was small and already it has been tidied up.

New building is going on at a great pace. Leading Russian architects have been assigned to plan the new Moscow and the blue-prints are prepared. Talk of the town is the striking model for the new "House of Books" designed by the famous Soviet architect Bovet to replace the historic 17th-century Pashkov Palace housing the Lenin library. Moscow will be the subject of another interesting experiment in Soviet town planning, a distinct feature of the new Russia. The town dwellers of the U.S.S.R. mostly live in flats, for small houses belong to a bygone era and are too reminiscent of the crowded, squalid villages of those days, and the severe climate of the northern cities makes large blocks of flats, centrally heated, a more practical type of home.

IN no country are so many cities being replanned and rebuilt as in the Soviet Union : Stalingrad, Smolensk, Kiev, Leningrad, Minsk, Odessa, Sebastopol, Voronezh, were either destroyed or severely damaged by the Germans. Even cities that were untouched by the war are being rebuilt in accordance with modern planning ideas. But it is on the new Moscow that Russian pride is particularly concentrated. Muscovites will tell you that their city will soon be the largest in Europe, bigger than London, and perhaps have skyscrapers like New York. To them the skyscraper is the symbol of the modern age and technical perfection. A 16-storey block of flats is being erected on the river embankment, to be topped by a 300-foot tower ; 18-storey blocks are envisaged.

The population of the city is estimated to be between four million and five million persons and expanding rapidly. It is believed it may double in the next ten years, for every day 300 children are born. In spite of the underground railway, street traffic is very congested. Moscow's trams are gradually being diverted from the centre of the city, where hundreds of new trolley-buses, painted sky-blue, have recently made their appearance. Also, a new traffic tunnel under the square before the railway station in Gorki Street—one of the busiest spots in Moscow—has recently been opened for the use of cars, trolley-buses and pedestrians (see facing page).

"PYGMALION" IN MOSCOW is played to crowded houses at the Maly Theatre. In addition to Shaw's play, productions of Shakespeare, Sheridan and Wilde, and a dramatization of The Pickwick Papers, are very popular. All the city's places of entertainment report record attendances, and new theatres are planned. *Photo, Planet News*

From a medieval, almost provincial, city in Tsarist days, Moscow has developed into a modern capital. Streets have been widened, straightened and paved ; spacious blocks of offices and flats, as in other European cities, have become common. So determined are the Russians to expand and beautify their capital that they allow nothing to stand in the way. Old houses are pulled down, new ones which do not fit into an assigned scheme are promptly removed. Some quite extraordinary undertakings have been carried out in the shifting of whole houses, fully furnished as they stand, even with the inhabitants inside.

Extraordinary House Removals

Every visitor to Moscow is taken to see Gorki Street ; when this was widened to fit into the new Moscow plan it was necessary to shift nine big buildings, one weighing over 25,000 tons. One of them, a hospital, had to be turned around 97 degrees, and this was accomplished. During the process nothing inside was disturbed and doctors were able to go on performing operations.

This lifting of buildings from place to place seems to give Russians almost a childish delight, particularly if the inhabitants are persuaded to remain within and carry on with their ordinary tasks. Plumbers and electricians fix things up so that all the services continue to function ;' while the house is on the move people can even take baths or use the telephone. The feat is performed by

inserting a steel plate on rollers between the foundation and the building. These rollers are placed on rails and the house moved at the rate of 18 yards an hour, propelled by electric levers.

Among things the visitor misses in Moscow are restaurants and public houses. The only restaurants (as such) are in the big hotels inhabited by foreign diplomats, journalists and occasionally high Russian officials. Their prices are very steep. The workers, of course, have their own canteens and eat in their own homes. In blocks of flats the communal kitchen is being introduced ; it is welcomed by Russian housewives, nearly all of whom work during the day in factories and offices. Food rationing is still in operation, but housewives supplement the family supplies wherever possible with goods bought from State shops and collective farm markets at the higher "commercial" prices.

Moscow is making plans to increase greatly its reputation as a cultural centre with new theatres, cinemas, a library, a picture gallery and a much enlarged university. More and more students flock to Moscow, attracted by the fame of its great scholars and scientists, so that the old university is almost bursting its sides. Always well patronized, Moscow's theatres have never known such overwhelming attendances as now. Every evening crowds besiege the box-offices in the slender hope of buying an odd ticket at the last moment. Plays by foreign authors now showing include Shaw's Pygmalion, Sheridan's The School for Scandal, Wilde's Ideal Husband, more than one Shakespearean production and a dramatization of The Pickwick Papers. Another very popular entertainment is the circus, where this winter audiences are welcoming back from the war survivors of a famous team of Don Cossack trick riders who joined up in the cavalry in 1941.

With the Pan-Slav ideal (the age-long Russian ambition to bring about a unity of all the Slav nations, such as Poles, Ukrainians, Czechoslovaks, Bulgars, and Yugoslavs under Russian patronage) becoming a reality, Moscow is something of a Mecca for the people of those countries. Here come their leaders for frequent consultation with Stalin in the Kremlin ; here come their academicians, scientists, and engineers, to exchange ideas and learn of the latest Russian achievements. To Moscow, too, comes the youth of the Slavonic nations, to study at the military academy which Russians boast is the most up to date in the world.

The people of Moscow cannot be said to be keeping pace with their city in smartness. They are eating much better than during the war, but they are still wofully lacking in clothing. In the summer, girls managed to make themselves look almost smart with odd pieces of cotton cloth made up into loose blouses and full peasant skirts. But as the leaves of autumn began to fall and the first winds swept through the streets, the drab, worn coats and cloaks of last year (and many years before) began to cover up the summer cottons. Muscovite women tell you, however, that under the new Five Year Plan the textile mills are pouring out woollen cloth and soon there will be new coats for all : and Moscow will have no cause to be ashamed of its citizens. Already the reopening of shoe-repair shops, laundries and dry-cleaners, is helping in the smartening-up process.

The Swiftly Changing Face of Post-War Moscow

TO EXPAND AND BEAUTIFY THE CAPITAL is one project on which Russia is concentrating. Some 20 years ago Gorki Street (1) was but a narrow, cobbled way. Now it is one of Moscow's busiest thoroughfares, and further architectural changes are planned ; on the right is the Moskva Hotel, Moscow's largest. Arbat Station (2), on the city's underground railway. The wartime camouflage of grey paint has been removed from the Bolshoi Theatre (3), home of opera and ballet. See also facing page.   PAGE 597   *Photos. Pictorial Press.*

The Roll of Honour
NCOS & MEN
1939—1946

Gnr. G. H. BAKER
No. 1 Commando, R.A.
Action : Burma. 31.1.45.
Age 23   (Kingston)

Since its inception on page 88 of this volume, our ROLL OF HONOUR has appeared regularly as a single page. In order to accommodate the large number of portraits accepted, this space will henceforward be increased to two pages in alternate issues.

Pte. W. BAMBER
The Loyal Regiment.
Action : Anzio. 19.2.44.
Age 19.   (Gt. Eccleston)

Pte. S. J. BALDWIN
Hampshire Regt.
Action : Italy.   4.12.44.
Age 21   (Cheriton)

O/S. W. BARLAS
H.M. submarine Triad.
Mediterranean.   Oct.40.
Age 21.   (Walton, Lancs)

Pte. I. BARSON
Pioneer Corps.
Action : N. Africa. 4.3.43.
Age 19.   (Halifax)

Gnr. S. J. BINES
7th Field Regiment, R.A.
Action : Caen.   8.8.44.
Age 23.   (Hastings)

Sgt. A/G. F. BOYLE
R.A.F.V.R.
Over Germany. Sept. 44.
Age 21.   (Manchester)

L/Cpl. K. BRANSTON
6th Airborne Division.
Over Normandy. 6.6.44.
Age 20.   (Scunthorpe)

Sgt. T. F. BURN
Coastal Comd. R.A.F.
Action : Brest.   8.1.42.
Age 20.   (Kirkoswald)

Pte. R. BREWIN
Suffolk Regiment.
P.O.W. : Siam. 11.11.43.
Age 27.   (Mansfield)

Tele. F. J. BURFORD
Royal Navy.
P.O.W. : Osaka. 16.10.42.
Age 22.   (Smethwick)

Cpl. F. BURKINSHAW
D. of Wellington's Regt.
Action : Dunkirk. 30.5.40.
Age 29.   (Sheffield)

Sgt. E. J. CLARK
40th Royal Tank Regt.
Action : Italy. 23.9.43.
Age 33·   (Hammersmith)

Gnr. G. BUTLER
20 Heavy A.A., R.A.
D./wnds.: Greece. 21.4.41.
Age 22.   (Langley)

L/Cpl. S. W. CLARK
1st Essex Regiment.
Action : Libya. 21.11.42.
Age 25.   (Leigh-on-Sea)

Sgt./Obs. A. COLLING
Royal Air Force.
Action : Belgium. 11.5.40.
Age 20.   (Darlington)

Sgt. B. COWELL
24th Lancers.
D/Wnds.: Caen. 12.6.44.
Age 28. (Saffron Walden)

O/S. R. H. COX
H.M.C.S. Fraser.
Action : Channel. 25.6.40.
Age 21.   (Swadlincote)

Fus. R. H. CROUCHLEY
Royal Welch Fusiliers.
Act'n.: N.W. E'pe. Aug. 44.
Age 24.   (Northwich)

Fus. S. W. DAWSON
R. Northumberland Fus.
Bonninghardt.   6.3.45.
Age 20. (Newcastle/Tyne)

Flt./Sgt. E. F. DEAN
78 Sqn. R.A.F.
Action: S. France. 5.9.45.
Age 20.   (Isleworth)

Gnr. S. J. DENSHAM
1st Field Depot, R.A.
D./wnds.: Italy. 23.10.44.
Age 36.   (Newton Abbot)

Dvr./M. F. T. DEXTER
107 Regt., R.H.A.
Action: Tobruk. 30.11.41.
Age 25.   (Bulwell)

Cook C. E. DOWLAND
H.M.S. Fiji.
Action : Crete. 23.5.41.
Age 24.   (Swanage)

A/B. R. I. GRABHAM
H.M.S. Tweed.
Action : Atlantic. 7.1.44.
Age 19. (Newcastle/Tyne)

Pte. F. GRAHAM
The Green Howards.
Action: N. Africa. 5.6.42.
Age 33.   (Langley Moor)

A/B. A. T. GULLESS
H.M.S. Jervis Bay.
Action : Atlantic. 5.11.40.
Age 24.   (Camberwell)

Tpr. A. GREENAWAY
142 Regt., R.A.C.
Action : Tunisia. 24.4.43.
Age 29.   (Northants)

Fus. J. HALL
R. Northumberland Fus.
D. wnds.: Tunisia. 25.4.43.
Age 30.   (Whitley Bay)

Sgt./Nav. A. HANDLEY
Bomber Cmd. R.A.F.
Over Hamburg.   9.11.42.
Age 21.   (Epsom)

Pte. R. HILL
Royal Army Medical Crps.
D./wnds.: India. · 5.10.41.
Age 25.   (Doncaster)

L/Bmdr. E. HAWKINS
Marine Section, R.A.
Action : at sea.   3.3.43.
Age 26.   (Bath)

Pte. A. W. HOLMES
Cambridgeshire Regt.
P.O.W. : Siam.   4.7.43.
Age 23.   (Wembley)

P/O. G. HINKINS
Royal Navy.
Action : Pacific.   9.5.45.
Age 33.   (Green Field)

L/Cpl. A. B. HOWSON
Royal Ulster Rifles.
Action : Holland. 2.10.44.
Age 19.   (Brighton)

Dvr. N. HUNT
Royal Army Service Crps.
P.O.W. : Malaya. 28.8.43.
Age 29.   (Silchester)

L./A.C. J. JACOBS
Royal Air Force.
H.M.S. Courageous. 17.9.39.
Age 24.   (Berwick-St. John)

Sgt./Obs. W. JACOBS
Royal Air Force.
Gloucester.   5.8.42.
Age 21. (Berwick-St. John)

The Roll of Honour
NCOs & MEN
1939—1946

L.A.C. A. KING
Royal Air Force.
Jap. transport. 8.11.44.
Age 23. (Norwich)

So great has been the response of readers to our invitation to submit portraits for our Roll of Honour that no more can now be accepted. But senders may rest assured that all those so far received will be published.

Cpl. W. LANCASTER
The Green Howards.
Middle East. 29.5.42.
Age 24. (Gargrave)

Tpr. K. LANE
23rd Hussars.
In action : Caen. 18.7.44.
Age 23. (Kettering)

Pte. J. D. LOCKWOOD
Duke of Cornwall's L.I.
Action : Florence. 8.8.44.
Age 21. (Warrington)

L.A.C. T. J. LOWRY
Royal Air Force.
Action : Holland. 13.5.40.
Age 17 & 11 m. (Chiswick)

Pte. M. MANNION
The Loyal Regiment.
Action : Italy. 22.12.44.
Age 27. (Widnes)

A.C.2 J. E. MARKEY
271 Sqn. R.A.F.V.R.
Action : Ampney. 25.3.44.
Age 18. (Crawshawbooth)

L/Str. L. A. V. NASH
Royal Navy.
Action : at sea. 9.6.40.
Age 38. (Southgate)

Pte. R. NAYLOR
Hampshire Regiment.
Action : Italy. 4.9.44.
Age 29. (Preston)

Sgt. A. OATES
Royal Artillery.
Action : France. 12.4.40.
Age 29. (Dawdon)

L/Sgt. A. POLLARD
Royal Artillery.
In action : Leros. 1943.
Age 25. (Bolsover)

Pte. J. REEDER
Royal Norfolk Regiment.
Action : Malaya. 27.1.42.
Age 28. (Lowestoft)

Gdsmn. D. REES
1st Bn. Welsh Guards.
Action : Caen. 11.8.44.
Age 27. (Neath)

Tpr. S. RILEY.
Royal Tank Regiment.
Action : Rimini. 20.9.44.
Age 23. (Horsforth)

A.C.I. T. J. ROBERTS
84 Sqn. R.A.F.
P.O.W.: Sumatra. 20.6.45.
Age 24. (Potters Bar)

Tpr. J. ROBERTS
Royal Tank Regt.
Action : Burma. 27.4.42.
Age 27. (Bridgford)

Sgt. S. H. ROOTS
10th Bn. Rifle Brigade.
Action : Italy. 1.9.44.
Age 31. (Wandsworth)

L/Cpl. J. H. RUDRAM
Queen's Royal Regiment.
Action : Burma. 27.5.45.
Age 21. (Mundesley-on-Sea)

L/Cpl. R. S. SANDERS
King's Royal Rifle Corps.
Action : Germany. 16.2.45.
Age 21. (Wembley)

Sgt. J. K. SHARP
Bomber Cmd. R.A.F.V.R.
Action : St. Trond. 2.4.42.
Age 30. (Hull)

Tpr. D. SANDERSON
Reconnaissance Corps.
Action : Anzio. 8.2.44.
Age 24. (Rotherham)

A/B. J. SHERWOOD
H.M.S. Isis.
Off Normandy. 20.7.44.
Age 19. (Melton Mowbray)

A/B. S. SLATER
H.M.S. Lawford.
Seine Estuary. 8.6.44.
Age 22. (Breaston)

Sgt. N. SMALLBONE
No. 2 Commando.
Died of wounds. 11.3.45.
Age 26. (London)

O/S R. E. SURRIDGE
H.M.S. Duchess.
Action : at sea. 12.12.39.
Age 19. (Edmonton)

Pte. G. SIMPSON
Royal Artillery.
D/wnds : Tunisia. 29.5.43.
Age 24. (Kelfield)

A/B. H. T. TALMAN
H.M.S. Pakenham.
Action : at sea. 16.3.43.
Age 20. (Camberwell)

Pte. G. H. THORNTON
East Lancashire Regt.
Action : Weetje. 1.3.45.
Age 18. (Alkborough)

Tpr. F. WADDINGTON
4th Reconnaissance Regt.
Action : Cassino. 30.4.44.
Age 20. (Mexborough)

Gnr. J. T. WARD
71 Anti-Tank Regt. R.A.
Action : Holland. 25.10.44
Age 24. (Norton-on-Tees)

A.C.2 J. WATERHOUSE
R.A.F.V.R.
P.O.W. : Macassar. 16.8.45
Age 23. (Wolverhampton)

Pte. B. G. WATKINS
Queen's Royal Regiment.
D/wnds : Italy. 21.9.44.
Age 31. (Enfield)

Spr. W. WEDDELL
Royal Engineers.
D/wnds. : Gazala. 7.4.42.
Age 22. (Newcastle/Tyne)

Sgt. B. C. J. WHITE.
R.A.F.V.R.
Over Stettin. Apl. 43.
Age 19. (Kilmington)

Marine G. WEBSTER
Royal Marines.
Ac. : W. Europe. 29.4.45.
Age 21. (Bethnal Green)

L/Cpl. T. G. WHITE.
Maritime Royal Artillery.
Action : at sea. 15.10.41.
Age 21. (Huddersfield)

Flt/Sgt. J. A. WILLIAMS
Royal Air Force.
Düsseldorf. 16.8.42.
Age 24. (Wrexham)

A.C.I. A. WOOD.
Royal Air Force.
Off Ostend. 7.11.44.
Age 20. (Huddersfield)

Our Roving Camera Sees War Reparations Arrive

QUEEN ELIZABETH IN LONDON emerged from her wartime retirement in December 1946 when workmen removed the last of the bricks from the statue over the porch of St. Dunstan's-in-the-West, Fleet Street. The wall was built early in the war to protect the figure from damage during air raids.

ST. GEORGE'S MEMORIAL CHAPEL at Biggin Hill, Kent, was burned out in the early hours of Dec. 3, 1946, only the commemoration tablet remaining intact. The Operations Headquarters at the aerodrome will now become the memorial chapel and will incorporate all the features of the original edifice. See illus. pages 400-401.

FIRST REPARATIONS FOR BRITAIN FROM GERMANY were landed at Tilbury Docks, Essex, in December 1946, consisting of secret drawing presses which enabled the Germans to substitute steel for brass in the manufacture of heavy cartridge cases. The machinery came from a Hamburg factory that escaped damage from the R.A.F.'s attacks during the war.

AT LILLE, FRANCE, a memorial was unveiled on Dec. 1, 1946, to Capt. Michael Trottobas, who as Capitaine Michel has become an almost legendary hero of the French Resistance movement, and to his men who also lost their lives. The cat's head was the badge of the group, which was known as W.O. (War Office).

H.M.S. TRUANT, one of the most famous submarines of the Royal Navy, broke adrift from a tug on Dec. 5, 1946, while being towed to South Wales for breaking up, and grounded on the rocks of the Cherbourg Peninsula on Dec. 10, where she was found by the R.A.F. and a naval frigate. See also page 586.

Photos, Keystone, John Topham, Topical Press, Planet

We Covered the Landings in Sicily

The invasion and capture of Sicily in August 1943 was acclaimed as the greatest combined amphibian attack carried out up to that date by any nation. The part of H.M.S. Mauritius in the initial and final assaults is outlined by ex-Petty Officer C. E. Curtis, then serving in that cruiser.

WE left Malta at 8.30 a.m. on July 9, 1943, for an unknown destination, in company with the cruisers Orion, Uganda, Aurora, and destroyer screens. Thirty minutes after sailing a broadcast speech by Captain W. E. Davis informed the ship's company of the impending operation and asked all hands to stand by for immediate action stations. Enormous convoys of tank and troop landing craft were steaming northeast in a smooth sea; we could just see the battle fleet, consisting of battleships and aircraft carriers.

At noon we took over a convoy of 20 transports and about 50 landing craft carrying two full divisions and equipment. Shortly afterwards we passed 60 large ships carrying

P/O C. E. CURTIS

two more full divisions and tanks. The whole convoy, now spread out over more than 1,000 miles of sea, made a very impressive sight. Towards evening the weather began to get rough, and the small troop transports and tank landing craft were making heavy going of it, but as Sicily came in sight, with Mount Etna prominent against the setting sun, we engaged in a last check-up on our guns and communications.

At 10.45 p.m. our glider towing planes passed overhead with the Airborne divisions —to drop behind the enemy lines, destroy communications and prevent the destruction of bridges that would be useful to us. They were soon detected, and an enormous amount of flak started going up from Italian positions round Syracuse, which our bombers were pounding to cover glider landings and smother gun-fire as the convoys approached.

ALL ships stopped two miles off Avalon beaches. Heavy bombs were falling over Syracuse, whole groups of houses appeared to be going up, and many oil fires were burning in the harbour area. The sky was a mass of coloured tracer as the Italians frantically tried to beat off our aircraft. But no one appeared to be looking our way yet—it seemed incredible that we should have some 4,000 ships only 500 yards off an enemy coast still undiscovered.

At 1.40 a.m. on July 10 the troops entered the barges, and soon the sea was black with boatloads making for the shore. They landed undetected. All enemy positions had apparently been put out of action by our Commandos, and our men moving off inland met only slight opposition. The Americans, however, seemed to be meeting with stiff resistance in their sector, to the south, for we

could hear a very heavy naval bombardment going on in that direction.

Two signals from shore at 4.55 indicated that our 1st and 2nd Brigade landings had been successful. As it began to get light we heard cries for help all round, and found many survivors from the airborne divisions whose gliders had fallen short into the sea. Destroyers and small craft now steamed in to bombard enemy guns which had begun shelling our landing craft taking in stores. These guns were firing from concealed positions above Syracuse, and many shells were falling among our beach areas. We opened fire with our 6-in. guns, and soon all our warships were bombarding. Shells could be seen bursting all along the road crowded with the retreating garrison from Syracuse, where, by 8 a.m., all organized resistance appeared to have ceased.

Hospital Ship Bombed and Sunk

Later that morning we had our first sight of enemy aircraft, when Stukas came into action. All ships opened up with full A.A. fire, and the bombs fell wide. Tip and run raids by single F.W. 190s and Ju 88s continued during the afternoon, and we had some near misses. In the evening we were subjected to continuous dive-bombing by groups of eight to ten F.W. 190s. From three very near misses with 500-pounders a hail of splinters hit us, and two ratings and one officer were slightly wounded.

We saw German dive-bombers attack the hospital ship Talamba, with wounded on board, although she was fully lit-up with

red crosses and the usual neutral markings. A direct hit was scored on the operation rooms and wards, and as the Talamba sank fast by the stern, her lights dimming, we could hear the cries of the drowning nurses and cot cases. She went down inside a quarter-hour. The air attacks on our shipping went on incessantly all night, and the ships' A.A. guns were in action from 10 p.m. till 4.30 a.m.

BY the early morning of July 11 all Syracuse and its surroundings were in Allied hands, and enemy airfields were being reconstructed for Allied use. In the afternoon, lying off the naval base of Augusta, we began a 6-in. gun bombardment of German shore batteries. Allied dive-bombers joined in, and large oil fires were started. That night, more airborne troops passed over to drop behind the German lines in gliders. In the morning the monitor Erebus began a 15-in. gun bombardment of German shore positions in the van of advancing 8th Army units. The enemy retaliated with dive-bomber attacks, but caused no damage, and Erebus continued to bombard at a range of 15 miles. An Italian submarine, after being depth-charged, surfaced and surrendered, and was towed away by a trawler to Syracuse.

At 7 in the evening a large transport of storm troops arrived, and destroyers closed range, bombarding gun batteries round the dock areas of Port Augusta in preparation for a landing. Beach parties were away an hour later, and were soon fighting in the streets. The town was captured intact that night, with the seaplane base, naval barracks and oil fuelling equipment.

The next morning, assisted by Erebus and the cruiser Uganda, we began to bombard Lentini, to dislodge Germans who were dug in on the hills. Four very heavy shells which straddled the Mauritius appeared to come from railway guns some 12 miles away. A signal

H.M.S. MAURITIUS, with main armament of twelve 6-in. guns, bombarded enemy positions near the Sicily beaches and later engaged targets farther inland to soften up the resistance. The author of this story was serving in this 8,000-ton cruiser when she was subjected to continuous bombing and shelled by railway guns.

Admiralty photograph

from shore at 11.25 a.m. announced that Lentini had been captured by 8th Army units, who were advancing on to Gerbini airfield and towards Catania. While we and the Newfoundland were bombarding the retreating German 15th Panzer Division on the coast road, another salvo of four heavy shells just missed my ship (I actually felt them pass our bridge), but we could not spot the guns.

On July 14 we and the Newfoundland proceeded to Malta for fuelling and ammunitioning. There, too, we had a visitation from enemy aircraft, in spite of a very heavy barrage, and Mauritius again had a couple of near misses. After two days we left Valetta Grand Harbour, and sighted part of the main battle fleet—Rodney, Nelson, Formidable, and a destroyer screen—returning from an unsuccessful search for the Italian battle fleet.

Ammunition Ship Torpello Blown Up

In the afternoon we closed range to two miles, when both our own lines and the enemy's were in plain sight. We began shelling the Hermann-Goering armoured division, our shells bursting neatly among the Germans. Many tanks were burning on the roads, and after an hour we ceased as the dust from our shells obscured the German lines. In the evening we bombarded a chemical works in the Catania dock area ; after four salvos the walls of the factory fell in and large explosions occurred. We then turned south and returned to Augusta, anchoring at 9 p.m. From midnight till 3.30 a.m. there were continuous heavy enemy bombing attacks. It was estimated that 200 enemy planes were over the area, and 15 were shot down. Meanwhile, the Warspite and other heavy ships bombarded Catania with 15-in. guns, causing enormous damage and starting big fires among enemy supply dumps.

By July 17 more than one-third of Sicily was in Allied hands, and the total number of prisoners (mostly Italians) amounted to more than 35,000. The Germans were still trying to bring in fresh troops across the Messina Straits under continual Allied air attack. During the night there were further German air attacks on Augusta and the harbour area, and our A.A. fire was kept up continuously. Enormous numbers of shells were used ; we fired 1,600 pom-pom, 6,000 Oerlikon and 314 4-in. shells. The next day two more transports arrived, one of them bringing 25 Greek nurses to serve in the front line.

At 4 a.m. on July 19 a dive-bomber attack made a direct hit on the ammunition ship Torpello. There was a tremendous explosion and shells and burning debris were thrown all over the harbour, the smoke rising to two miles. The few survivors picked up from the wreck were cared for in our sick-bay. That morning we and the Dutch sloop Flores proceeded out of Augusta towards Catania to assist our forward troops. Meanwhile, Flying Fortresses were bombing the German positions from four miles up. As we were being heavily shelled by German shore batteries and tanks (I counted up to 40 near misses), we closed range to one mile and opened up full 6-in. and 4-in. fire at the enemy gun flashes—and the Germans ceased firing. All the afternoon we bombarded selected targets as requested by the Army on shore, until 7.30 p.m., when we ceased fire and returned to Augusta to anchor.

That night there were heavy air attacks on the anchorage by bombers using groups of flares. Two direct hits were scored on an ammunition ship, which blew up, leaving no survivors. All our ships put up a full barrage, and not until the All Clear came at 4 a.m. did the guns' crews relax. Large reinforcements of heavy tanks had reached our troops. The Canadians closing in to the north-west were threatening to outflank the Germans in the Catania salient. More than half Sicily was now in Allied hands, the prisoners totalling 41,000, but crack units of the Hermann-Goering division were holding good positions all round the lower slopes of Mount Etna and appeared well supplied.

IN the morning of July 21, accompanied by destroyers, we left to attempt to spot concealed German guns which were shelling the harbour area. Heavy shells from these hidden guns fell round us but caused no damage. Large ammunition dumps were blowing up, where the Germans were apparently destroying all their heavy equipment. Unsuccessful in spotting and destroying the concealed guns, which were reported to be in railway tunnels, we returned to Augusta.

On July 22 we and the Newfoundland again left Sicily for Malta, for fuel, repairs and ammunition, and while there we heard the dramatic news of the resignation of Mussolini, on July 25. Returning to Augusta, we found the 8th Army slowly advancing against stiff opposition from crack German troops who were slowly being driven from every strong-point. The Erebus assisted by bombarding, with 15-in. turret guns, the enemy dug in on the lower slopes of Mount Etna. August 5 found large fires and explosions taking place in the German lines, where they appeared to be destroying their heavy dumps prior to withdrawing northwards to avoid a threatened Allied pincer movement. The coastal roads leading out of Catania were packed with masses of German tanks when we commenced a bombardment of the crossroads. During the morning reports showed that our troops were in Catania at last. Paterno, the

H.M.S. WARSPITE hurled shells from her 15-in. guns at German positions in the Catania area in July 1943, causing tremendous damage and destroying vast quantities of enemy supplies of all kinds.
Admiralty photograph
PAGE 602

6TH AIRBORNE DIVISION

Colours : Pale blue Pegasus on maroon

THE badge of this formation is the same as that of the 1st Airborne Division — Bellerophon astride Pegasus. The 6th Division was formed in May 1943 and placed under the command of Major-General R. N. Gale, D.S.O., O.B.E., M.C. It was trained and equipped to play an important part in the invasion of Europe, its task being to cover the left flank of the British Army on the Orne. The first landings, by gliders and parachute troops, were made in Normandy in the early hours of June 6, 1944, the bridges over the Orne and Orne Canal being speedily captured.

The swing-bridge at Bénouville has been renamed Pegasus Bridge in recognition of the gallantry of the airborne troops. Units which were to have relieved the Division became absorbed in the heavy fighting around Caen, and the 6th remained continuously engaged for more than two months. From August 17, 1944, onwards, it advanced steadily eastwards, finally reaching Honfleur.

IT was a seriously depleted formation that returned to England to rest and reorganize during the next few months. In December the Division was fighting in the Ardennes under the command of Major-General E. Bols, having been thrust into the western tip of the Ardennes salient. It returned to England early in the New Year, and was dropped east of the Rhine on March 24, 1945, landing with the U.S. 17th Airborne Division to seize the crossings of the River Issel and the important railway running from Wesel to Bocholt.

All the objectives had been taken by the following afternoon, and the next morning a firm junction was made with the British forces advancing from the Rhine. The Division then took part in the advance across Germany, reaching the Baltic Sea and having linked up with Russian troops at Wismar before the unconditional surrender of Germany. The formation remained in Germany until the autumn of 1945, when it was transferred to Palestine.

junction of the German supply lines from the north, was entered and occupied by the 51st (Highland) Division later in the day.

On the morning of August 7, proceeding north past Catania, we saw groups of German tanks jammed on the roads outside Riposto ; we opened a full 6-in. bombardment, and many blew up. Four shells from long-range 88-mm. guns just missed our stern. At noon a signal from our troops attacking Riposto said that their advance was held up by German mortar fire. The Mauritius accordingly bombarded the German mortar batteries from close range and destroyed them.

The enemy were still holding out on the lower slopes of Mount Etna on August 8, but observation was difficult owing to the rain of shells and bombs. That night and the following night ships in Augusta harbour were again the target of air raids by Ju 88s using chandelier flares, and all the A.A. guns were in continuous action. On August 10 we proceeded north with a destroyer screen to shoot up the Germans retreating towards Messina. Observing columns of motor transport moving along the road north of Riposto we opened fire. Later we closed in to bombard coastal forts and houses where the Germans were using concealed mortars.

During the next day or two we heard of Allied bomber raids on Milan and Turin, also that Rome had been declared an open city. On Sicily the Germans were retreating in disorder towards Messina, abandoning

large stores of equipment. Remnants of their forces were still trying to escape across the Straits. R.A.F. aircraft flying through intense A.A. fire were strafing and bombing barges and many hundreds of Germans were drowned. Our men made successful Commando raids on Reggio Calabria in the toe of Italy—our next objective. By August 16 Allied troops were entering the outskirts of Messina—last Sicilian port in German hands —and stragglers were being surrounded and mopped up. So the curtain fell on this most brilliant and successful 38-days campaign.

Our Badge Was the Venomous Scorpion

Among remarkable enterprises of the war were the formation and exploits in N. Africa of the Long Range Desert Group. Consisting of only about 200 hand-picked officers and men, all volunteers and some of them well-known explorers and scientists, the L.R.D.G. aided in brilliant 8th Army successes. Cpl. Arthur Biddle recalls experiences whilst serving with them.

I HAD no idea when I went to the Middle East as a member of the Royal Signals in 1940 that I was destined for nomadic desert adventures. The opportunity occurred when I volunteered for special duty and gained a transfer to the newly formed Long Range Desert Group, whose first commander was Lieut.-Col. Ralph A. Bagnold.

Primed with youthful confidence, it seemed a waste of time for me to have to take a few weeks' course in wireless telegraphy. But I found a lot more to learn for specialized desert work, including transmission and reception of messages on a radio set designed to cover 20 miles, and which in practice would have to be used up to 1,000 miles despite weird atmospheric

Cpl. A. BIDDLE

conditions. Signalling, it was considered, was the most important function of the desert patrols, for without regular contact the enterprise would fail in its main object—which was reconnaissance. Secondary objects of the newly formed force were hit-and-run raids on the Germans and Italians, the hampering of rail and road communications, capture of prisoners for interrogation, and conveyance of secret agents and other specialists to areas far behind the enemy lines.

It was "A Quartermaster's Hell"

The patrols consisted of Guards, New Zealanders, Rhodesians, Indians, and the Yeomanry. I was attached to the N.-Zedders throughout the campaign. Our means of transport were Chevrolets and jeeps mounted with machine-guns and Bofors, and equipped with sand-tires ten inches wide. Among our gear were sun-compasses and Log. Tables for navigation over the Libyan Desert (which is nearly as large as India), spades, sand-mats and perforated metal sand-channels for "unsticking" vehicles bogged in soft sand or the treacherous salt marshes of the Great Depression.

Our operations were over that vast area which General von Ravenstein declared was "a tactician's paradise and a quartermaster's hell." Supplies were a knotty problem, and often a few cars went into the blue on routine patrol over distances that would have necessitated the preparation of a major expedition in pre-war days. Our greatest peril was from enemy aircraft, and sometimes trucks were bombed into scrap-iron. There are grim records of L.R.D.G. men, deprived of transport, wandering in the scorching desert until overcome by heat and

thirst, and of others who survived by miraculous endurance after tramping incredible distances. Some of the escapes were due to a chain of supply dumps that gradually were installed in the desert at 25-mile intervals en route to the oases.

In summer we had to combat heat up to 120 degrees in the shade, and in winter a temperature that fell below freezing point at night. Our trucks regularly crossed the untrodden zones of the desert known as the Sand Seas—one with an area as large as Wales—where the sand was hundreds of feet deep and lay in waves beautiful to see in the dawn and early evening. But this part of the desert was almost as treacherous as the salt-marshes. Truck driving was a specialized art when the sun was high and there were no shadows to give warning of undulations. A sudden descent from a low dune, and wheels might become stuck in soft sand to the axles. Then we toiled, sweated and swore, while we adopted all the regulation devices for "unsticking." Occasionally, in particularly bad going, we could look back a couple of miles at supper-time and see the ration tins at the spot where we had breakfasted before setting out in the morning !

Our desert bases varied during the course of the North African campaign in relation to the ebb and flow of the main fighting. When Colonel (afterwards General) Leclerc, in command of the Free French Force from the Chad Province, seized Kufra in the south from the Italian garrison we used this oasis. At different times we were based on

other oases—Faiyum, Jalo, Zella, and Siwa where the best dates in Africa are grown. It was necessary to explore almost untraversed country for knowledge vital to future large-scale military operations. Perhaps the most important duty of all was the maintenance of the Road Watch, which was continued day and night for many months on end. The object was to obtain a census of all the enemy tanks, guns, supply lorries and troops passing to or from the enemy front lines.

A patrol would undertake this exacting duty for two or three weeks, then be relieved by another patrol. Trucks were parked, and two men would go forward under cover of darkness and lie among low scrub from 50 to 200 yards from the main coastal road, the Via Balbia. There they remained doggo all day until nightfall, hardly daring to move, except to jot down in a notebook an account of every single thing that passed by. Well I recall the occasion when on this Road Watch we were encamped near the Arc Philaenorum—familiar to our Army as the Marble Arch—engraved with the portrait and inscription in Latin of Benitus Mussolini. Our lorries were parked and camouflaged in a wadi, and two fellows crawled up as near to the road as was consistent with security. While some others played cards, I squatted beside my truck with headphones adjusted, transmitting information to Group Headquarters periodically and fingering the frequency dials while trying to decipher faint signals coming over the ether.

Our Men Prepared to Shoot It Out

We looked a rough lot. Some of the fellows were bearded, and stripped to the waist. Most of us wore the Arab headdress and Indian sandals which were part of our regulation kit. Around us was thorny scrub, and myriads of flies tormented us during that long, hot day in the late spring of 1942, months before the battle of Alamein was fought and won. Traffic along the road was not considerable. Presently, towards evening, a lone motor-car of the touring type came along, and to our dismay halted only a few yards from where our two watchers were lying. An Italian officer stood upright in it and began to survey the ground through field-glasses. Our men prepared to shoot it out, almost certain of discovery. Then along the coastal road came a great convoy of armoured cars, guns and trucks—300 of them. The Italian officer, unaware of our

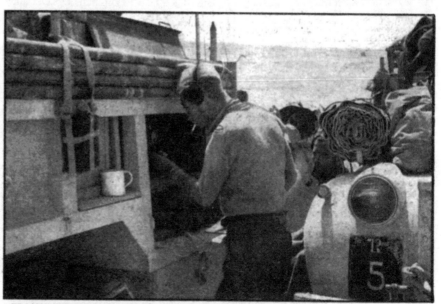

TRANSMITTED TO HEADQUARTERS BY WIRELESS, information secured by the Long Range Desert Group in their incursions deep into enemy territory could have been gathered in no other way ; though for fear of revealing a patrol's position the smallest possible use was made of the radio car. The author of this story is seen adjusting his set.

Motto : *"Thundering Through the Clear Air"*

NO. 61 SQUADRON

DISBANDED after the First Great War the squadron was re-formed on March 18, 1937, as No. 61 (Bomber) Squadron. In September 1939 it was stationed at Hemswell, Lincs, equipped with Hampdens, then at various aerodromes for short periods prior to November 1943 when it was at Skellingthorpe, Lincs.

In the summer of 1942 it went to Cornwall for a few weeks when the Battle of the Atlantic was at its height, and operated anti-submarine patrols. From the beginning of 1940 it carried out hundreds of mine-laying and bombing missions, targets including the warships Scharnhorst and Gneisenau; when the former vessel went to Kiel for repairs No. 61 gave it yet another pounding.

ON October 17, 1942, it penetrated deeply into France, without fighter escort, to attack the Schneider works at Le Creusot. On the 22nd it bombed Genoa, and Milan was the target on the following day. During 1943 the squadron was engaged in the battles of the Ruhr, Cologne and Hamburg, and raided Friedrichshafen and Spezia, the Lancasters re-fuelling in North Africa between the two raids. Berlin was attacked many times in the winter 1943-44.

From D-Day onwards No. 61 worked unceasingly, communications and V-weapon sites being priority targets during 1944. It successfully attacked the Dortmund-Ems and Mittelland canals, both waterways being drained, and took part in the destruction of Wesel on March 23, 1945, immediately before the British 2nd Army crossed the Rhine, thereby saving the assault troops hundreds of casualties. The squadron is justly proud of having shared in this attack, which received especial praise from Field-Marshal Montgomery.

Montgomery of the information collected and radioed of enemy numbers and movements when it came to making vital decisions of strategy and tactics.

By good luck I was at the Desert Group's most successful "beat-up" of the enemy—the raid on Barce, beyond Benghazi, 600 miles behind the lines. The raid took place more than a month before Alamein was fought, and the L.R.D.G. was then under the command of Lieut.-Col. G. L. Prendergast, D.S.O. There was a good deal of "hush-hush" about the preparations. All that the rank-and-file like myself could surmise was that there was something unusual in the wind when our patrol set out from our base at Kufra. Actually, we were

bound on a dare-devil mission to enter Barce in Cyrenaica and near the Mediterranean coast, and other mobile units were also engaged in crossing the great desert to rendezvous with us and take part in a brilliantly planned enterprise.

We learned this after crossing some hundreds of miles of sand. Afterwards, in the light of events, our deduction was that the secret must have leaked, with the consequence that 2,000 German troops reinforced the Italians in Barce shortly before our visit. Our lightly-armed trucks and jeeps moved up stealthily from the south and converged on the enemy-occupied town and airfield. The patrol with which I was serving halted within striking distance, but well out of sight of the objectives, and there ensued the inevitable nerve-racking waiting. Fortunately, no Arab nomads who saw the patrols recognized the nature of them, and when an Italian motorized unit happened to pass one patrol the hand-waving of our men was answered by an equally "friendly" greeting from the unsuspecting foe.

The sun dipped below the rim of the scrub spattered waste and the pink afterglow faded. Night brooded silently over the desert, and at nine o'clock we moved northward through the warm darkness, thankful that the waiting was over. Everyone detailed for the raid had been primed in his particular task, and we drove hard for Barce confident of catching the Italians on the hop. The late Major Jake Easonsmith, D.S.O., halted his car at a crossroads and from there dispatched the various patrols. My truck

---

stopped, as arranged, near the perimeter, and I opened fire with the Vickers .5 as the "party" started up full blast. The target was a number of Italians who had suddenly appeared and made a dash for cover, firing wildly as they went. Meantime, the commander of one patrol, Captain N. P. Wilder, D.S.O., led his New Zealanders for the attack on the airfield. He forced the gate open and the trucks roared in, the light guns flaming as some of the enemy ground staff made their appearance.

Lively Lone Wolf Act in a Jeep

Those of us, like myself, who had the job of covering the attack put in some shooting practice whenever targets appeared, and at intervals got off a few bursts at some of the buildings to deter any lurking enemies. The N.-Zedders roared over the airfield, their guns drilling incendiaries into the petrol tanks of the aircraft ranged on the ground. One after another the machines caught fire, and when a petrol lorry flared up the whole town was illuminated. Delayed action bombs were used to destroy aircraft which failed to blaze from the impact of the incendiaries. Grenades carried by some of our L.R.D.G. men were flung into mess buildings, sleeping quarters and hangars. While this was going on, the desert patrol of the Guards went charging through the town to assault the barracks and keep the Germans and Italians too busy there to intervene at the aerodrome. While the attack lasted, the brilliant Jake Easonsmith in his jeep performed a kind of lone wolf act among the Barce buildings, chasing any enemy troops he saw and generally creating confusion with his Mills bombs.

The job was done; then came the tricky task of extricating ourselves. As on almost every stunt in which the L.R.D.G. took part we were greatly outnumbered, and we did not get off scot-free. Some trucks were lost and several of our men were taken prisoner. But we picked up others who had no means of transport except their own legs, and also rescued the wounded where possible. There was a great hue-and-cry for us, and we were ambushed with some losses and later bombed from the air. We lost 14 vehicles in all. Our six wounded, who were rescued, recovered in time, and ten prisoners remained in enemy hands. I have never heard how many casualties the enemy suffered in that Barce raid, but it is known that we destroyed over 30 of their aircraft, which meant the saving of many British lives when it came to the great trial of strength at Alamein.

I Fought the Germans Underground

A Professor of English in Belgium when war broke out in 1939, Mr. G. P. O'Sullivan remained there throughout the long Occupation, uplifting the morale of the people and, at the ever-present risk of detection by the Gestapo, assisting in the anti-Nazi campaign by every means in his power.

---

presence, made a hand signal indicating that he had selected a suitable parking area for the night. Our nerves were on edge as those vehicles deployed from the road, surrounding us and cutting off the retreat from the wadi of the two L.R.D.G. watchers. For ten hours or more the situation was tense. Yet neither the trucks nor any of us were seen, and at first light the convoy departed without knowing that British troops had been lying within their encampment. Nor, perhaps, would they have credited that any British unit could have gained a position nearly 500 miles behind their own front lines without being intercepted.

Amazing though it may appear, neither the Germans nor Italians knew during the whole North African campaign that an almost continual watch was kept on their traffic along the Via Balbia. Little imagination is needed to realize the importance to General

---

ALWAYS in civilian clothes, the dreaded Gestapo followed immediately in the wake of the advancing German armies. Already the ground for their dastardly work had been prepared by members of the Flemish National Movement—anti-Ally and, in particular, anti-English. These had got to know many of the patriots during the " phoney " war period up to May 1940, and when the Gestapo began functioning in a commandeered private house in the Avenue de la Faille (a name we shuddered to hear) they had a list of names prepared by those members—many of whom, since the Liberation, I am glad to say have been condemned to death or sentenced to long terms of imprisonment.

The Germans employed hirelings to frequent cafés for the purpose of checking-up the pro-Ally customers and proprietors.

And though we were pretty keen at the same game it took us nearly two years to know for certain the patriotic cafés from the pro-German ones. As we identified more and more members of the Gestapo we passed on the information—always on our guard against the many " doubtful " ears.

At the Hour We Learned to Fear

The Gestapo system of arrest was as follows. A number of them would arrive by car at the house of a listed victim at three in the morning—an hour we learned to fear. They were fairly certain of finding the wanted one at home then, because of the curfew from 11 p.m. to 5 a.m. If no reply came to their bell-ringing or knocking they forced the door, and if the wanted person was there he or she was straightway bundled into the car and taken to the headquarters in the Avenue de la Faille for interrogation.

Watchers and Watched in the Western Desert

ALONG A DESERT ROAD in North Africa enemy transport moved (1) unaware of the close watch kept upon it by a two-man patrol (2) of the Long Range Desert Group — that hand-picked collection of specialists whose individual efforts meant so much to the valorous 8th Army. Equipped with all necessary paraphernalia, including field-glasses, notebooks, and photographs of enemy transport and armoured vehicles for recognition purposes, the road-watchers—past-masters in the art of camouflage and concealment—supplied British Intelligence with prompt data as to movements, numbers and types.

The road from Tripoli to Cyrenaica was the main German supply route by which tanks and reinforcements were dispatched to the Front, and the L.R.D.G. kept it under close observation. Sometimes their information would be secured and sent back from an area as much as 400 miles behind the enemy's lines. Once in hostile territory a patrol (3) depended for its continued existence on unflagging vigilance, maintaining a never-ceasing watch on the skies as well as the ground. See story in facing page.

War Office photographs

The questioning started on a polite note, with a promise of immediate release if guilt were admitted or the information (such as a list of friends) asked for were given. If that method of approach failed, the beast in the Gestapo make-up was let loose and the victim would be battered black and blue. Several I saw after their release (which was only temporary), and I still shudder when I think of what might have happened if the Gestapo had arrived in England. Often I heard the thugs gloating in anticipation of "getting at" the "Engelsche Schweinhunden," and my blood boiled.

If the victims gave no information (and many did not however terrible their ordeal) they were transported to a hell-camp at Breendonck, near Antwerp—a disused fort surrounded by water, where atrocities worse than those at Belsen or Dachau in Germany took place. Bodies were still being found at Breendonck in June 1946 of persons arrested by the Gestapo and never again heard of alive. There, patriots under interrogation were hung by an arm for hours. There was also an electric glove in which locked hands were thrust until, in unbearable agony, the helpless victims gave themselves (and others) away.

G. P. O'SULLIVAN

Our Secret Camp in the Ardennes

It sometimes happened that the Gestapo failed to find a victim at home. Other members of the family, or inmates of the house, would then be arrested and kept in prison for weeks. When we learned that the Gestapo had visited a certain house and found their intended victim not at home we immediately contacted him and smuggled him away to a patriotic camp at Bievres, in the heart of the thickly wooded Ardennes.

More than 40,000 "wanted" men were in hiding there, some of them for years. They slept on tarpaulins stolen from the railways, under tarpaulin roofs to guard against detection by German aircraft. They could not, with safety, have fires in winter, and their hardships could not be measured. To prevent treachery, no one was allowed to leave that secret camp once he had been admitted. We provided them with food obtained with our own coupons, or stolen ones (thousands of them were "lifted" every month for a patriotic end) or those which we printed ourselves.

The Germans suspected there were men hiding in the Ardennes, but they did not dream the camp was so well organized—and they did not take the risk of going into the forest to search for the missing. When the enemy was retreating in 1944 through the Ardennes to their "Heimat" (Homeland) these men, all well armed, attacked them in the rear and thus helped, with the utmost joy, to demoralize an army already sick of the war. Jews were hidden in Christian houses from 1942 onwards (to avoid deportation), but some were denounced by Belgian traitors. Then followed arrest and a beating-up, and the unlucky patriots concerned were thrown into prison.

Listening to B.B.C. broadcasts was a crime against the German Army, and hundreds of Belgians were arrested for it. But daily for four long years I listened-in and never once missed passing on the war communiqué to patriots, who spread the news far and wide "underground." One trick the civilian-garbed Gestapo had for the detection of patriots was in the offering of revolvers for sale (possession of arms was punishable by death). Posing as patriotic Belgians these devilish salesmen found many victims. Do you wonder we were careful of every word we uttered, that we learned to smell-out the Gestapo and their hirelings and hate their very shadows during those terror-years?

We Were Crippled 800 Miles From Land

In convoy one placid day early in 1942 the motor vessel G. S. Walden, 11,000-ton tanker, ran into big trouble. There came the unexpected " bolt from the blue " and her engine-room became an inferno of scalding steam. This recollection is by T. C. Skeats, one of the ship's officers.

MY watch over, I retired to my cabin for a read and smoke before turning in for the night. The weather had been calm and sunny, and I was in peaceful mood and unprepared for the sudden, ear-shattering explosion, which was followed almost immediately by another. The ship shook from stem to stern.

I leaped out of my bunk and flicked the electric light switch, with no result. In a twinkling I flung open the port, and was met by clouds of hissing steam and showers of sparks from the funnel. My brain registered swiftly, "We've been torpedoed in the engine-room !" There sounded the clattering feet of running men, and groping about in the darkness I managed to pull on some clothing. A fellow officer appeared, heavy with sleep and worrying about the gyro compass because the "juice" was off. "We've been bumped !" I told him and he dashed to his room for his gear with never another thought for the compass ! In a few lightning movements I was up on to the bridge, to check up on the situation.

I saw a succession of sputtering rockets and whizzing flares speeding into the night sky and lighting the scene with a wan and ghostly luminance. Orders were shouted, and the lifeboats were swung out for lowering, while all around ships careered in all directions as the convoy scattered, fanwise. Peering along aft, I could see that our stern was settling as the sea rapidly poured into the engine-room. Preparations for a trip in the boats went on apace, with each man, anxiously but efficiently, carrying out his duties. Several firemen, severely scalded by escaping steam, were receiving first-aid on the boat deck. The action of the bitterly cold night air on their overheated bodies caused their skin to peel off in huge pieces, and their suffering was indescribable.

A roll call revealed that three men were missing. A search was conducted and we found two of the absent members, badly injured but still fighting for life. The missing man was a young engineer, and our continued search for him was of no avail. Suddenly a dim shape out at sea appeared silhouetted against the light of a star shell. Snatching a torch I sent a signal in its direction, thinking it was a corvette. My signal was answered, and I felt relieved. A few seconds later I was astounded to see the black shape materialize into the sleek lines of a large enemy submarine. Our 6-inch gun was almost awash, but our gunners lost very little time in giving the arrival a taste of shot and shell. It soon disappeared into the darkness, and I believe it was badly damaged, if not sunk. About ten minutes later one of our corvettes loomed up and hove-to alongside us. We transferred our wounded to the care of the corvette surgeon and it was soon under way again.

IT was still bitterly cold, and an order was given for surplus warm clothing to be commandeered from the officers' quarters and issued to the firemen and greasers who were shivering in their vests and overalls. The stern portion of our ship had ceased to sink and it was considered that she would probably remain afloat. Meanwhile, all hands stood by ready to abandon ship if

T. C. SKEATS

MOTOR-VESSEL G. S. WALDEN, a helpless hulk of 11,000 tons, her engine-room smashed up, encountered further misfortune whilst being towed (left). The hawser parted and a new one had to be prepared. On arrival at St. John's, Newfoundland (right), examination by divers revealed extensive damage to the stern and confirmed that rudder and propeller were missing. Disaster was only narrowly averted on the final stage of her journey to Halifax, Nova Scotia, when again the tow-rope parted. Skill and luck combined eventually saved her.

the need should arise. Rockets and flares still cast their yellow light over the scene and it became apparent that the majority of the vessels that had been in the convoy had disappeared. There was another large tanker, crippled like ourselves and wallowing. A freighter, away in the distance, appeared to be on fire. I knew three other fine ships had gone to the bottom in as many minutes.

Our corvette friend steamed up again, and a quick decision was made to attempt towing our helpless mass—an inert 11,000 tons. The corvette commander told us that he had radioed for salvage tugs but they would take a while to arrive as we were about 800 miles from the nearest land, which was Newfoundland. The following morning the corvette, without warning, dropped the towing hawser and made off at full speed, dropping "cans of concentrated hell" (depth charges) as she went—action which obviously indicated the presence of a lurking submarine. But no attack was made on us and four hours later the corvette returned.

We spent days and nights just wallowing in a long swell, with the corvette attending us. The only food we had was tinned salmon and potatoes ; our storerooms and refrigerators were under water and the galley was completely wrecked. But our cooks did a wonderful job : fried salmon and chips, salmon and mashed potatoes, salmon and potato fish cakes. So the menu went on, for about ten days. I haven't eaten salmon since ! On the most miserable day of all, dawn brought swirling mists that shrouded the ship in a mantle of greyish gloom. We paced the bridge as usual, deriving cold comfort from Longfellow's "All things come round to him who will but wait."

At noon a Catalina flying boat passed over us—without seeing us, and we cursed the Newfoundland fog. But the Catalina proved to be the herald of our salvation. Late in the afternoon a dim shape emerged from the fog, and I recognized the familiar lines of a big salvage tug. A terrific cheer—amplified by the fog—greeted the new arrival, and almost immediately the difficult task of making a towing hawser fast was commenced. It took four weary hours of pulling, shouting, cursing and sweating before the job was executed. We calculated that about five more days should see us safely into the nearest port—a long and tedious voyage without heat, light or proper food. My thoughts turned to my dead shipmate down below. His watchmate had been extremely fortunate in escaping : the

terrific inrush of water into the gaping hole had washed him up from the very bottom of the engine-room and he was able to clamber through a skylight, totally oblivious of a broken wrist.

Our progress was very slow and the next day misfortune overtook us again—the tow-rope parted. By dint of much hard labour a new hawser was prepared and the tug once more began towing us. And so we continued through six long and cheerless days and nights, the sailors attempting to sleep on the open decks 'midships and the firemen and stewards in the officers' saloon, for their own accommodation was awash and entirely uninhabitable. At last the friendly, rugged coast of Newfoundland loomed up and in no time at all we were passing through the narrow entrance of St. John's harbour. Loud cheers rent the air and we were soon moored to a large buoy. The mainbrace was spliced then as it had never been spliced before !

Many days of official visits by shore authorities followed, and the ship's hull was examined by divers. This revealed extensive damage to our stern and confirmed our idea that the rudder and the propeller were missing. No trace was then found of the

dead engineer, and it was presumed his body had floated away through the hole in our hull. We lay six weeks in that anchorage and it was finally decided that we were to be moved to a suitable port for repairs. Eventually, with fresh stores aboard, we once more were taken in tow. After one day at sea the weather broke and we were subjected to a very trying time by the pounding of waves on our helpless hulk.

One of the engineers, rummaging about in the flooded engine-room, discovered the battered and decomposing body of his missing colleague. It came as a great shock to all hands after such a lapse of time. The unrecognizable remains were sewn in canvas and we covered it with the flag he had served—the red ensign. Two days later we reached Halifax, Nova Scotia, not without mishap. When nearing a dangerous shoal the tow-rope parted and only by the most amazing combination of skill and luck was disaster averted and the vessel safely moored. The next day officers and men attended the funeral of the engineer, his work done and his voyage o'er. Ours was, too, as far as saving the ship went. The important thing was that she "lived to fight another day."

NEW FACTS AND FIGURES

Replying to a question in the House of Commons on October 22, 1946, as to the number of carrier pigeons, dogs, horses and other animals used by the Army during the war, the Financial Secretary to the War Office stated that the peak total of carrier pigeons in use by Royal Signals was 157 lofts in all theatres of war, containing in all about 15,700 pigeons. The number of animals employed by the Army in all theatres during the war was approximately 40,000 horses, 120,000 mules, 6,000 bullocks, 16,000 camels, and 5,000 dogs. These, apart from the dogs, represented riding and transport animals.

On November 11, 1946, in the Allied war cemetery in Berlin the bodies of 70 Allied airmen were reburied. Killed in bombing raids, they had been laid in temporary graves on the outskirts of the city. The reburial service was attended by officers from the R.A.F. station at Gatow, and two Grenadier Guardsmen sounded the Last Post.

The bodies of 16 British airmen killed while attempting to bring aid to the Poles during the Warsaw rising of 1944 were reburied in the Polish military cemetery in Warsaw in November 1946. The ceremony

was attended by the air attaché at the British Embassy, and a company of Polish infantry mounted a guard of honour.

In recognition of help given by Australia, an ancient Corinthian urn, containing soil from the graves of Australian soldiers who died in Greece, has been presented to Mr. Chifley, Australian Prime Minister. The urn is believed to be 2,600 years old and had been a museum-piece in Greece for hundreds of years. In making the presentation in Australia, Mr. Stratigos, Vice-President of the Australian-Greek League in Athens, said it was the first time in Grecian history that soil had been presented to another country.

There were about 7,200,000 German prisoners in Allied hands when the European war ended, according to a statement from U.S. Army H.Q. in Frankfort. It was expected that all P.O.W. held by the United States in the European theatre would be discharged by July 1, 1947. In November 1946 these totalled 59,000 in the European theatre and 30,000 in the Mediterranean. Prisoners held by U.S. authorities in France would be returned to Germany by March 1947 ; those in Italy were being repatriated at the rate of 1,000 a week.

Photo, Central Press

NAIK KAMAL RAM, who won his V.C. as a 19-year-old sepoy with the 8th Punjab Regt. (8th Indian Div.) in Italy in 1944, came to England recently under a leave scheme enabling troops of the Indian Army in the Mediterranean and Middle East to see something of this country. A friendly policeman points out to him interesting features of Buckingham Palace architecture ; and Naik Kamal Ram will return home with proud memories of his glimpse of the royal residence in London. See also page 376, Vol. 8.

Printed in England and published every alternate Friday by the Proprietors, THE AMALGAMATED PRESS, LTD., The Fleetway House, Farringdon Street, London, E.C.4. Registered for transmission by Canadian Magazine Post. Sole Agents for Australia and New Zealand : Messrs. Gordon & Gotch, Ltd. ; and for South Africa : Central News Agency, Ltd.—January 3, 1947. S.3. *Editorial Address :* JOHN CARPENTER HOUSE, WHITEFRIARS, LONDON, E.C.4.

GUARDING THE IMPERIAL PALACE, TOKYO, in Dec. 1946, this Royal Navy sentry, at his post on one of the bridges spanning the Palace moat, is from H.M.S. Commonwealth, said to be one of the loneliest shore bases of the R.N.   It comprises a force of 350 officers and men stationed at Kure, former Japanese naval base near the atom-bombed city of Hiroshima.   Our seamen in Japan have earned for themselves unstinted admiration.   See also illus. page 615.   *Admiralty photograph*

Edited by Sir John Hammerton

NO. 251 WILL BE PUBLISHED FRIDAY, JANUARY 31

British 1st Army's Gruelling Task in Tunisia

TROOPS NEWLY ARRIVED AT BONE gazed at the wreckage of the port (1) in December 1942. On a hillside outside Mateur a sniper (2) watched for that sign of movement which would betray an unwary enemy. A six-pounder anti-tank gun in position in the hills outside Medjez-el-Bab (3), captured on Nov. 26, 1942. See also facing page.   PAGE 610   *War Office photographs*

Blade Force's Gallant Failure was Invaluable

By A. D. DIVINE, D.S.M.
Author of
' Road to Tunis.'

O N December 3, 1942, the spearhead of the British 1st Army—Blade Force, the 11th Brigade and a handful of American armour—was thrown back, fighting with superb gallantry from the little town of Djedeida on the Medjerda river, 12 miles from the outskirts of Tunis. On May 12, 1943, Colonel-General J. von Arnim, General Officer Commanding-in-Chief Army Group Afrika, surrendered in the areas north and south of Djedeida with his staff and more than a quarter-million men. Between these two things there is a direct connexion. The failure of Blade Force to reach the capital in the first rush of the race for Tunisia was one of the most valuable failures in the history of the British Army. It was, incidentally, one of the most gallant.

Why did we fail ? To form a just estimate of the cause of the retreat from Djedeida and Tebourba it is necessary to examine the French North African campaign as a whole and Operation Torch in particular. Even in this war of enormous distances the lines of communication for Operation Torch were exceptional. The port of Algiers is 1,782 miles from the Clyde. It is almost precisely 4,000 miles from New York. Everything that the Army used—tanks, guns, food, men, petrol, ammunition—had to be carried by sea. In the dire circumstances of the submarine war at the time it was obvious that there was an absolute limit to the amount of shipping available for the operaton.

General Anderson's Great Problem

The campaign was begun, therefore, with a fixed maximum of men. That maximum, because of the enormous distances involved in the area to be occupied, had to be split in three : the Casablanca landing force to capture the west coast and to cover the expedition against the possible intervention of Franco-Spain ; the Oran force to capture and hold the centre ; the Algiers force to occupy the most important port of North Africa and to form the springboard for the advance into Tunisia.

From this Algiers force—remember it was approximately a third only of the expedition —there had to be retained sufficient troops to handle the French, to garrison the area of Algiers and to provide lines of communication elements. The remainder was the army of Tunisia—an army working from a base

balanced precariously on the incessant threat of the submarine. And from that base the problem of distance arose in a completely new guise. Tunis is 560 miles from Algiers port—560 miles of the desolate passes of the high Atlas—560 miles with two roads only, roads never built for the passage of modern armies—560 miles with only one precarious, broken-down line of rail.

O N November 9, 1942, when Lieutenant-General K. A. N. Anderson landed on Maison Blanche aerodrome at Algiers he had to face the problem of those 560 miles and his inadequate transport. He had to face, too, a multitude of other problems. The first of these was the question of the French ; the second the question of the small ports to the east of Algiers. A single paragraph from General Anderson's dispatches admirably illustrates those things :

" I must state here that when in the planning stage it was decided that no assault landing should be made east of Algiers, then, in my opinion, my chance disappeared of reaching Tunis before the Germans, unless the French put up a stout resistance to Axis entry into Tunisia. In actual fact, the French resisted us in Algiers (feeble though their resistance was, yet its consequent repercussions caused delay and doubt) and did not resist the Axis in Tunisia. The first German landings at El Aouina airport on November 9 were not opposed."

There has been criticism of the failure to make landings simultaneously with the main invasion at the three small ports to eastward : Bougie, Djidjelli and Bône. The principal reason for that failure was the decision which placed the "bomb line"—the line inside which the powerful German-Italian air forces of Sardinia and Sicily could seriously challenge a shipborne invasion—a little to the east of Tunis itself. If the critics had seen, as I saw, the wrecked ships of Bougie—if they had crouched, as I crouched, under the incessant night raids on the harbour of Bône —it is possible that that criticism might have been less vocal. That was the first part of General Anderson's problem.

The second was that of the French. It was one of the strange illogicalities of the attitude

of Vichy that while after capitulation there was never any attempt to oppose the forces of the Axis (Indo-China, Tunisia and Southern France are the classical examples). French logic found it necessary to withstand her late allies with the utmost vigour, as in Syria, Madagascar, Dakar and Morocco. In considering General Anderson's problems it must be remembered always that the resistance put up by the French in North Africa was no mere token resistance.

Nearest Supply Base 2,000 Miles

The French fought hard against us in the first phase of Operation Torch. In Tunisia not only did they fail to offer the slightest opposition to Von Arnim's landing at El Aouina and at Bizerta, but from November 9, when that landing began, and up to the 19th, when General Barre, in command of the French Army of Tunisia, rejected Von Arnim's ultimatum, the considerable French forces that had withdrawn from the Tunisian littoral lay on the southern flank of General Anderson's advance as an obscure and sinister threat.

These things are the essentials of the race to Tunis : it sprang from an improvised base 2,000 miles from the nearest source of supply ; it had to be carried out by a handful of men from an invasion force already split in three ; it had to be driven almost 600 miles over lamentable land communications. And it had to challenge not only the threat of the German counter-invasion but, for ten dangerous days, the potential threat of the French themselves with all the possibilities of sabotage thrown in. The wonder is not that our splendid spearhead was thrown back from Djedeida, but that it ever succeeded in piercing so deep.

A GAINST these things must be balanced the possibilities that lay in Von Arnim's hands. Germany had expected an attack on Northern Africa—not, it is true, at the precise points at which we landed, but none the less in that quarter of the globe. She had in Italy a variety of forces. Most important of these was the extraordinarily powerful section of the Luftwaffe that operated from the island airfields of Sicily and Sardinia. In addition to these there were ancillary ground forces. There were formations training or being staged for the reinforcement of Rommel, and there was an adequate and

ON THE ROAD TO MEDJEZ-EL-BAB, TUNISIA, men of The Hampshire Regiment pass French troops guarding a bridge after the French adherence to the Allied cause on Nov. 19, 1942. The Hampshires greatly distinguished themselves at Sidi Nsir on Feb. 26, 1943, when they held one of the key positions of the Medjez-el-bab salient against assaults of German infantry and armour. As part of Blade Force the Regiment saw some of the severest fighting in North Africa and suffered very heavy casualties.

Photo, British Official

By November 22, Blade Force (17/21 Lancers Regimental Group) was concentrated at Souk-el-Arba. Farther south, American parachute troops of the 503rd U.S. Parachute Battalion had dropped at Youks-les-Bains. One medium American tank battalion, one light battalion and a handful of tank destroyers completed the force. General Anderson's plan comprised a two-pronged attack—one along the northern road to Mateur and Bizerta, one on the southern through Medjez-el-Bab to Tunis. Two brigades of infantry, a handful of tanks and armoured cars, a few parachutists and virtually no air support—all dangling at the end of 560 miles of atrocious mountain road—came within 12 miles of winning Tunis in their first onset.

indeed elaborate supply organization operating down the roads and railways—as yet undamaged—of Italy and across the short sea passage of the Sicilian Channel, 90 miles against our minimum of 2,000.

Flying, disembarking, walking unhampered into Tunisia, Von Arnim completed his build-up with remarkable speed. On November 26, when we established ourselves for the first time across the Medjerda river, General von Arnim had concentrated in Tunisia the Storm Regiment Koch, the Barenthin Regiment, the Marsch Battalions 17, 18, 20 and 21, the Parachute Engineer Battalion Witzig, the 190 Tank Battalion, advance elements of the 10 Armoured Division, and miscellaneous artillery and anti-tank units; there were also the Italian 10 Bersaglieri Regiment and elements of the Superga Division, including four infantry battalions.

Enormous German Reinforcements

Those troops operated on lines of communication seldom more than 12-20 miles from the two good ports of Tunis and Bizerta. They operated under complete air superiority from airfields unaffected in this period by the rain and mud which destroyed our mountain landing grounds.

Again the wonder is not that they pushed us back from Djedeida, but that scarcely 12 miles down the road that runs beside the meanders of the Medjerda we held them fiercely, courageously and enduringly outside Medjez-el-Bab. That holding, it may well be, sealed the fate of Von Arnim and a quarter-million men, for it gave us the advantage of the strategic position on the downward slope on the tangled outliers of the Atlas Mountains. We commanded the passes to the sea and we never lost that command.

But, on the other hand, it afforded the Germans

depth enough to give them grounds for hope—depth enough to encourage enormous reinforcements, to induce Hitler and the German General Staff to pour into North Africa a treasure in men, aircraft and equipment that was to affect considerably the grandiose schemes for the conquest of Russia, that was to overload, dangerously, the German production machine and was finally to break the heart of Italy.

What was the force that accomplished this triumph ? General Anderson, setting up his headquarters at Algiers on November 9, moved forward at once. By November 13 he had occupied Bougie, Djidjelli and Bône in an effort to reduce the precarious nature of his lines of communication. Bône was occupied by two companies of the 3rd Parachute Battalion and No. 6 Commando. Already the first elements of the infantry, "a small column of all arms from the 11th Infantry Brigade Group (known as Hart Force and made mobile by pooling all the available Brigade transport)," had gone off into the blue in the sublime confidence that Bône would be ready when they reached it. On November 15 the 36th Brigade—on assault scales—had passed Bône and occupied Tebarka. On November 16 the 1st Parachute Battalion dropped at Souk-el-Arba aerodrome, and by November 17 that enterprising force, commandeering local transport, had advanced far beyond Béja and made contact with the Germans.

What men could do, these men did. The Lancashire Fusiliers pinned in the bed of the Medjerda River under withering mortar fire, the East Surreys attempting to capture the Djebel Mourbea by moonlight, the Hampshires cut to pieces outside Tebourba, the 36th Brigade storming Djebel Abiod and the heights of Jefna, again and again, made for themselves an imperishable history. And their failure reaped a tremendous reward.

IT reaped a reward in other directions, beside the fantastic booty of the Tunis plain. In the tangled, difficult months that followed the American Army was "blooded." It learned the weaknesses of its material and of its training, and it learned the weaknesses of its psychological approach to war. The new American Army that was trained by the veterans of Tunisia was a fighting machine utterly different in impact, in strength, in fitness for war, from the troops which landed in Africa on November 8, 1942.

And there was still another prize, for in North Africa from the complexities of divided command, from the difficulties of liaison with the French when once they threw in their lots with ours, from the inevitable frictions, acerbities and failures of co-operation with the American Army, was forged the superb combined weapon that two years later smashed the Western Wall.

GERMAN A.A. GUN being dug in at Tebourba, whence men of the British 1st Army withdrew on Dec. 3, 1942, the 2nd Battalion The Royal Hampshire Regiment particularly distinguishing itself. The town finally fell to the Allies on May 8, 1943.

Photo, Keystone

Empire Outposts Now Provisioned From the Air

Photos, Indian Official

IN 700 FLYING HOURS half-a-dozen Dakotas accomplished in December 1946 a task that previously had employed 3,000 coolies over a period of six months. Maintenance of the Himalayan outposts has always been a matter of considerable difficulty, lying, as they do, in districts covered with dense jungle. They stretch from Balipara, just south of Tibet, to the north of the Naga Hills in Assam, and the Lohit Valley, south of Sikiang. The operation entailed the dropping of more than 300 tons of supplies, sufficient for six months, in narrow valleys shut in by mountains, there being no room for error of navigation or mechanical breakdown.

UP THE SIANG VALLEY, in the Himalayas, flies a Dakota (top) with supplies stacked in the doorway ready for dropping on an isolated British post. Inside, men of an air dispatch platoon are preparing to eject the cargo over the dropping zone; each wears a special harness to prevent his being dragged out of the aircraft (above). Items dropped included rice, butter, tea, potatoes, fish, biscuits, salt, soap, kerosene oil, cigarettes, matches and general medical necessities.

AT MOHANBARI, near Dibrugarh, on the Bengal-Assam railway, the aircraft are loaded with stores (left). The aerodrome has an all-weather surface of steel matting, because the vital operation of revictualling the outstations must not be delayed by bad weather. This system of air-supply was first used on a large scale by the late Major-General Wingate in 1943.

We Sweep Treacherous Corfu Channel Waters

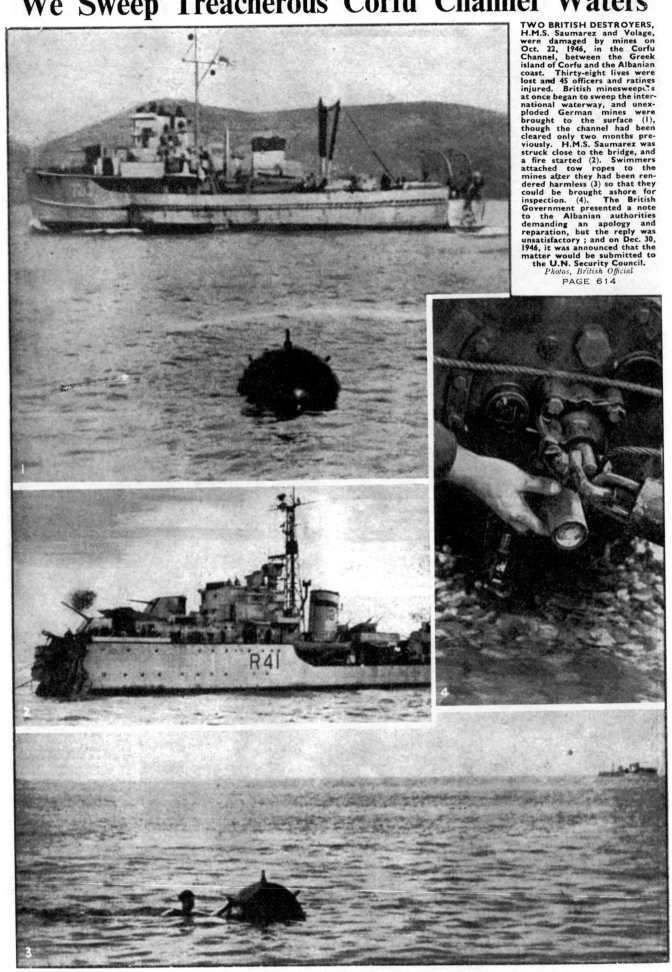

TWO BRITISH DESTROYERS, H.M.S. Saumarez and Volage, were damaged by mines on Oct. 22, 1946, in the Corfu Channel, between the Greek island of Corfu and the Albanian coast. Thirty-eight lives were lost and 45 officers and ratings injured. British minesweepers at once began to sweep the international waterway, and unexploded German mines were brought to the surface (1), though the channel had been cleared only two months previously. H.M.S. Saumarez was struck close to the bridge, and a fire started (2). Swimmers attached tow ropes to the mines after they had been rendered harmless (3) so that they could be brought ashore for inspection. (4). The British Government presented a note to the Albanian authorities demanding an apology and reparation, but the reply was unsatisfactory ; and on Dec. 30, 1946, it was announced that the matter would be submitted to the U.N. Security Council.

Photos, British Official

Shore Base of the Royal Navy in Occupied Japan

H.M.S. COMMONWEALTH at Kure, on the island of Honshu, is the British naval base that handles the supplies for the 40,000 men of the British Commonwealth Occupation Force in Japan. There was a ceremonial parade (1) in December 1946 when the station was visited by Vice-Admiral Sir Denis Boyd, K.C.B., K.B.E., D.S.C., Commander-in-Chief of the British Pacific Fleet. He inspected a guard of honour (2) and chatted with patients in the sick bay (3), which is in a specially constructed Nissen hut. See also illus. page 609.　　　　PAGE 615　　　　*Admiralty photographs*

Delhi Meeting Momentous for India's Leaders

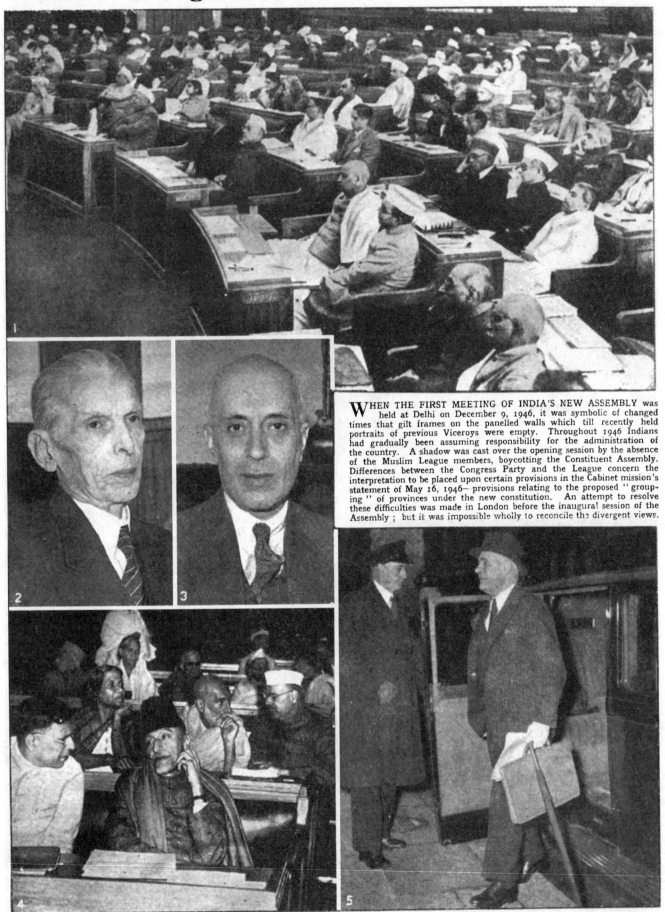

WHEN THE FIRST MEETING OF INDIA'S NEW ASSEMBLY was held at Delhi on December 9, 1946, it was symbolic of changed times that gilt frames on the panelled walls which till recently held portraits of previous Viceroys were empty. Throughout 1946 Indians had gradually been assuming responsibility for the administration of the country. A shadow was cast over the opening session by the absence of the Muslim League members, boycotting the Constituent Assembly. Differences between the Congress Party and the League concern the interpretation to be placed upon certain provisions in the Cabinet mission's statement of May 16, 1946— provisions relating to the proposed "grouping" of provinces under the new constitution. An attempt to resolve these difficulties was made in London before the inaugural session of the Assembly ; but it was impossible wholly to reconcile the divergent views.

In the Council House, New Delhi (1 and 4), members of India's Constituent Assembly sat in provincial *blocs*, attired in a wide variety of costumes. Mr. Jinnah (2), leader of the Muslim League, and Pandit Nehru (3), chief of the Congress Party, arrived in London on Dec. 3, 1946, to confer with Mr. Attlee about difficulties which threatened the breakdown of India's Interim Government. Viscount Wavell (5), Viceroy of India, returned to England to take part in the discussions. See also illus. page 527.

Photos, Keystone, Central Press, P.A.-Reuter, Associated Press

U.N. First General Assembly Concludes its Work

THE UNITED NATIONS First General Assembly opened its second meetings on Oct. 23, 1946, at Flushing Meadow, New York. Adjourned in London early in the year it should have been convened in early September, but protracted talks at the Paris Peace Conference caused further postponement. The session opened somewhat under a cloud but closed on a hopeful note, largely owing to the more conciliatory attitude of Mr. Molotov, leader of the Soviet delegation. The plenary sessions were held in the Assembly Hall at Flushing Meadow ; but the committees, in which the delegates spent most working hours, sat at Lake Success, 10 miles farther out of New York City. It was estimated that 450 meetings would be necessary to dispatch the 53 items on the agenda. The last act of the Assembly was to reject a proposal to hold the 1947 session in Europe. It was agreed to meet again in New York on Sept. 16, 1947.

FOUR-FOREIGN MINISTERS HELD DISCUSSIONS at the Waldorf-Astoria Hotel, New York, during November and December 1946 in an endeavour to reach agreement on the peace treaties with Italy, Rumania, Bulgaria, Hungary and Finland. Mr. Bevin is seated on the far side of the table, facing the camera ; M. Couve de Murville, the French representative, is the fifth figure on the British Foreign Minister's right hand ; Mr. Byrnes has his back to the camera ; Mr. Molotov is screened by one of his colleagues. The ministers decided on Dec. 11 that the treaties with the former satellite states should be signed in Paris on Feb. 10, 1947. At one of the debates Mr. Bevin asked Mr. Molotov for specific information of what was going on behind the " iron curtain," and stated that Great Britain favoured some form of federated Germany, reserving certain functions for a central authority. The Ministers agreed to the appointment of a commission of inquiry into the Italian colonies and their future; but no decision was reached upon the financial arrangements for the Free Territory of Trieste after the Allied Military Government had been replaced by a Governor.
PAGE 617

FLAGS OF 51 NATIONS flew outside the Assembly Hall, Flushing Meadow, New York (1), on Oct. 23, 1946, to greet the delegates. Sweden, Iceland and Afghanistan were admitted to membership, their representatives being (2, l to r. front row), Besten Unden, Thor Thors and Hosain Aziz. Assistant secretaries-general were sworn in (3). Mrs. Pandit (4) led the Indian delegation and was one of the most forceful speakers in the Assembly, championing the cause of the Indians in South Africa.

HIS MAJESTY'S SHIPS   H.M.A.S. Sydney

A CRUISER of 6,830 tons, launched in 1934, the Sydney bore one of the most famous names in the Royal Australian Navy. Her predecessor of the same name, also a cruiser, was responsible for sinking the notorious German commerce raider Emden in the Indian Ocean in the First Great War.

In 1940 the Sydney formed part of the First Cruiser Squadron, Mediterranean Fleet. She took part in various sweeps carried out by Admiral Sir Andrew Cunningham in the hope of bringing the Italian Navy to action, and greatly distinguished herself in the second month of these hostilities. On the morning of July 19, 1940, she intervened in a running fight off the coast of Crete between four British destroyers and two Italian cruisers, both very fast ships. One of these, the Bartolomeo Colleoni of 5,069 tons, was hit repeatedly by 6-inch shells from the Sydney, and ultimately stopped, with smoke and flames pouring from her. Leaving the destroyers to complete her destruction with torpedoes, the Sydney continued in chase of the second enemy cruiser, which was also hit a number of times but succeeded in escaping through superior speed.

After Japan entered the war the Sydney returned to her home waters. On November 20, 1941, she intercepted a disguised German armed merchant cruiser, the Kormoran. Though the latter was sunk, the Sydney seems to have ventured too close to her opponent to ensure that she should not escape. At any rate, the Australian cruiser was heavily damaged, and when last seen by those in the German ship was on fire from end to end. She may have been torpedoed, but no one from her survived to report what happened ; she simply disappeared.

Photo, Wright and Logan

The Green Howards

By
Major E. W. CLAY, M.B.E.

WHEN the call came in 1939 North-countrymen flocked to the Green Howards, to serve in battalions which were the descendants of Luttrell's infantry of many years ago. The two regular battalions (the 1st and 2nd) were swiftly reinforced by the four Territorial battalions—the 4th, 5th, 6th and 7th—and these then were ready to withstand the first shock of war. The 1st Battalion played a notable part in the difficult campaign in Norway, then moved in turn to Scotland, Wales, Ireland, England, India, Persia, Syria, Palestine and North Africa; thence it took part with the 6th and 7th Battalions in the landing on the east coast of Sicily, and fought doggedly northward in the van of the 8th Army. It won great distinction in the Anzio bridgehead, south of Rome, and ended the war in Europe on the Baltic coast of Germany.

There are certain experiences which stand out from the rest in the minds of those who fought with the 1st—the journey in motor transport across the Sinai Desert; prolonged and bloody fighting in the Plain of Catania, Sicily, in which Captain Hedley Verity was among those killed; the fast pursuit of the enemy up the west coast of Italy; winter patrols on the Sangro; casualties at the rate of 70 or 80 a week in the key "fortress" in the Anzio bridge-head; and the battle of Buchen Station in Germany, on May 1, 1945—the 1st Battalion's last action in their long war in many and varied theatres.

FORERUNNER of the Green Howards, the 19th Regiment of Foot was raised in 1688 by Colonel Francis Luttrell, of Dunster Castle, near Minehead, and the men were drawn almost entirely from Somerset. Nearly 200 years later, the 2nd Battalion was raised at Exeter. The Regiment received its present title 200 years ago, when regiments were known by the names of their colonels. In 1744 there were two units in the same campaign commanded by a Howard; to avoid confusion one became known as the Green Howards (from the colour of the facings on the uniforms) and the other as the Buff Howards: the latter are the Buffs of today (see page 555). Yorkshire and the Regiment first became officially associated in 1872. Twenty-four battalions who wore the badge of The Green Howards in the First Great War added substantially to the Regiment's long list of battle honours.

The other regular unit, the 2nd, was in India from the beginning of hostilities and saw service on the Frontier before taking part in the Burma campaign, including the Arakan landing. The 8th Battalion was formed of old soldiers soon after the war began. So quickly did its ranks swell that it was able to throw off a second battalion, and subsequently both were merged to form the 30th Battalion, which went to the Mediterranean theatre in 1943 to work on the lines of communication.

The 9th Battalion was converted into a Light A.A. Battery, and the 10th Battalion turned parachutist and dropped on the Germans near Caen on D-Day in 1944.

Another battalion which changed its name was the 12th—it became a Recce Regiment. The 11th Battalion remained in this country throughout the war.

One's mind now turns to the four Territorial battalions which fought with the famous 50th (Northumbrian) Division—that much-travelled and war-scarred infantry division which was fighting in the Western Desert of Egypt in the half-forgotten days before Typhoons and Shermans, when "Strafer" Gott and Jock Campbell and others of that gallant company were struggling to save the Middle East in the face of heavy odds. The disastrous battles of Gazala and Matruh, the triumphs of Alamein, Mareth and Akarit, and the assault on Sicily: the Division, with its Green Howards, sadly depleted after a desert disaster, experience! them all between 1942 and 1944 and was then brought home to be the spearhead of the assault in Normandy.

The story is too long to be told in all its rich detail of endurance and suffering, of setback and triumph. But there are some snapshots from the album of memory which throw the record into relief here and there. Let them serve, therefore, as a bird's-eye view of the war as seen by some of the Green Howards battalions, and as an indication of the contribution made not by individual persons or battalions but by the Regiment as a whole.

JUNE 1942—a month which the 8th Army of those days will never forget—is passing in a procession of fierce and sombre days. A tide of German armour and lorried infantry swirls against the Imperial positions in the Gazala Line. Like the tide, it comes on and then recedes, then advances again. Two battalions of Green Howards and a third battalion from Yorkshire, standing

TRAINING AT HOME IN THE LATE SUMMER OF 1940 the 7th Battalion The Green Howards took part in many anti-invasion exercises on the coasts of Britain; after Dunkirk the lessons so hardly learned on the battlefields of France had to be taught to young soldiers who were eventually to help to beat the Germans. The 7th was in the 50th (Northumbrian) Division, whose "T.T." formation sign (see page 300) denoted its principal recruiting grounds—the banks of the Tyne and Tees.

Photo, British Official

ON THE BARE HILLS OF CYPRUS Green Howards sweated and toiled in September 1941 during training in the mopping-up of parachute troops. The clear atmosphere and treeless, hilly country afforded excellent opportunities for the employment of visual signalling. The flag made a trustworthy substitute when the radio set went "dead." *Photo, British Official.*

Colours: Red Eagle on Black

4TH (INDIAN) DIVISION

THIS division, whose personnel was about two-thirds Indian or Gurkha and one-third British, concentrated in Egypt in the autumn of 1939 and was a part of the original desert force under General (later Field-Marshal) Wavell. When the offensive was launched against the Italians in December 1940 the 4th shared with the British 7th Armoured Division, the honours of the victory of Sidi Barrani.

It was then transferred to Eritrea, where it gained, with the 5th (Indian) Division, another victory over the Italians, at Keren. It was next sent to the Middle East, one brigade taking part in the operations against the Vichy French forces in Syria. Once more reunited, the Division participated in the action at Sollum, in June 1941, and was engaged in General Auchinleck's offensive in November 1941, the battle of the Omars, the relief of Tobruk, and the hard fighting in Cyrenaica.

IN March 1942 it was split up once again, one brigade going to Egypt, another to Palestine, and the third to Cyprus. The Division was with the 8th Army at Alamein; it assaulted the Mareth Line and won a great victory at Jebel Garci in April 1943. Then it was switched to the 1st Army front to take part in the final battle for Tunis and the capture of Gen. Von Arnim. In the following December it crossed to Italy, and in February and March 1944 took part in the bitter fighting at Cassino. In June the 4th was in action in the region of Lake Trasimene, and broke into the Gothic Line in August.

The Division then went to Greece, where the Germans were withdrawing, and remained there until the cessation of hostilities, embarking for India in February 1946, (see illus. in page 5). Military experts have adjudged the 4th to be one of the best divisions not only in the forces of the Empire but in the world. It won four V.C.s, and two George Crosses.

squarely in the path of a Rommel "schwerpunkt," are slowly strangled by encircling forces and finally go under in the heat and dust of the notorious "Cauldron." They were the 4th and 5th.

Farther north the 6th and 7th Battalions fight on, but the British gradually lose their grip on the Gazala positions. The 6th and 7th are surrounded in their turn. The 8th

Army withdraws. But the Green Howards cannot withdraw in the usual sense of the word, for the enemy are at their backs. Therefore, at night they break out westward, straight through the enemy's front, and drive in a great southward sweep through his rear areas, then eastward round his southern flank at Hacheim.

The enemy is startled and shaken as he

realizes that the troops he has been attacking and had thought to squeeze out of the battle are now attacking him. Some fight wildly, some run away. It is like a mad and lethal Guy Fawkes night as glowing tracer bullets and shells whiz in all directions through the darkness. Italians fight Germans. The Green Howards, in their battle-worn transport, drive through it all and on to Egypt, there to face about for the next round.

MARCH 1943, and the tide of battle has turned at Alamein, where the Green Howards inflicted severe punishment on the crack Italian Parachute Division, Folgore. The 6th and 7th Battalions have avenged the loss of their sister-units at Gazala by the capture of thousands of Italians and the General commanding the Brescia Infantry Division.

Now the 8th Army rumbles over the Libyan-Tunisian frontier and squares up to the Mareth Line. The main defences of this

TRANSPORT OVERHAUL was an urgent matter, tracked vehicles, such as Bren carriers, especially suffering from rough usage, after the 6th and 7th Battalions broke out westwards at night through the Axis positions in June 1942. From the Gazala Line the Green Howards turned south, then east to rejoin the retiring 8th Army. *Photo British Official*

Green Howards Will Not Be Forgotten in Italy

NEAR LANCIANO, in January 1944, the 1st Battalion The Green Howards marched through snow on their way to the front line, the Bofors gun (1) guarding the track against low-level attacks by German aircraft. In the following February the Battalion was occupying trenches between Minturno and Santa Maria ; one section in a reserve position amused themselves picking out tunes on a captured organ (2).

The Regiment won great distinction at Anzio, where this mortar team (3) bombed German positions in a wood. Even jeeps were unable to reach some of the forward positions near Forli, and men of the 1st Battalion, climbing a rock-strewn track, had to bring up their supplies on mules (4). In some places the country through which the 8th Army advanced to the Sangro River in November 1943, was inaccessible even to mules and everything had to be taken forward laboriously by hand.

Photos, British Official

THE 6th BATTALION IN SICILY, advancing from Mount Etna towards Messina, marched through dense thickets of bamboos, which made them wonder if they had not reached Burma by mistake (left). Front-line troops were often quite ignorant of the course of the war and even of events taking place only a mile or two away, so at the headquarters of the 7th Battalion in Normandy maps were displayed (right) showing Allied progress.

formidable Axis position are screened by outposts ; the Green Howards are charged with the task of obliterating them as a preliminary to the main assault. It is dark when " the Thugs " go forth. They are the special fighting patrol formed under the enthusiastic guidance of Lieut.-Col. D. A. Seagrim, C.O. of the 7th Battalion. They are tough and expert fighters who precede the Battalion to the objective. They lift a path through the minefields and pass silently on. Then there is a brief, hard fight with men of the Young Fascists' Division—and when the 7th Battalion arrives " the Thugs " are in complete control of the situation.

Later the main attack goes in. The Green Howards storm a flanking strong-point, and fight hand to hand through a tortured night with German infantry. Seagrim leads the attacks and kills many Germans. You understand the quality of his achievements that night when you know that they earned for him one of the three V.C.s gained by the Regiment during the war. He was killed later at the Battle of the Wadi Akarit, before he knew of the award (portrait in page 59, Vol. 7). The Green Howards move on, towards Tunis, then through Sicily.

H Hour, D-Day, 1944.—The Green Howards return to France. The men of these battalions have made the journey via Cyprus, Palestine, Persia, the Western Desert, Tunisia, and Sicily. It is cloudy, with a choppy sea. The 6th and 7th Battalions approach the beaches of Normandy. The 6th lead the way into Occupied Europe, with the 7th at their heels. Once ashore, the 6th Battalion goes as far and fast as any other leading unit. This day, Company Sergeant-Major S. E. Hollis wins the Regiment's second V.C. of the war—the first V.C. in the Army to be awarded for the fighting in Normandy (portrait in page 376, Vol. 8).

THE battalions with the 50th Division had a full share of the heavy fighting in Normandy in the late summer, and were among the first infantry to cross the frontier into Belgium and Holland. They finished their fighting in the Second Great War near Arnhem, at which point the 50th Division, by this time one of the Army's veteran formations, was brought back to England for a well-earned rest and to assist in the training of new infantry cadres. The Green Howards found themselves in the pleasant country near the Vale of Pickering, in their own county once more, and shortly after VE Day they marched, with other members of the 50th Division, to their own service of remembrance and thanksgiving in the stately cathedral at York.

The link between the Home Guard Battalions of the North Riding and the rest of the Regiment was a very close one and promised to remain so even after disbandment. Middlesbrough, Scarborough and Bridlington conferred upon the Regiment the honour of marching through their streets with bayonets fixed, Colours flying and bands playing. As a result of the 1st Battalion's exploits in Norway in 1940 His Majesty King Haakon VII was made Colonel-in-Chief, succeeding in that capacity a close relation in the late Queen Alexandra.

The old Parish Church of Richmond, Yorkshire, which is the home of the Regiment, contains the Regimental Memorial Chapel. Every day a recruit from the barracks is detailed to turn over one page of the book containing the Roll of Honour of the 1914-1918 War. This Chapel serves also to commemorate those of The Green Howards who fell in the Second Great War.

THE 2nd BATTALION IN BURMA experienced much hard fighting : here a patrol is being briefed by an officer in the Taungup area in April 1945 after taking part in the landings on the Arakan coast. The 2nd had been in action on the North-West Frontier of India before it was transferred to the Burma theatre.

War Office photographs

Lisbon's Story Can Now be Told

Throughout the war the Portuguese Government of Dr. Salazar maintained neutrality, in spite of the long-standing Anglo-Portuguese alliance and the pro-British feelings of the people. Though the country was virtually cut off from the rest of the European continent by the German conquests, a steady flow of ships and aircraft entered the port of Lisbon from the Americas and the East—and the capital is still busy. Foreign import and export trade is handled at the West Docks (1), and goods from the Portuguese colonies at the docks in Lisbon's East End: here (2) the cargo is melons. New British cars, just arrived, crowd the waterside (3).

Exclusive to THE WAR ILLUSTRATED

The Daily Round in Portugal's Capital

Though war brought increased trade to neutral Lisbon, where life continued in more or less peacetime conditions, privation began to be experienced, and in April 1944 bread rationing was introduced. Peace has been marked by rumours of revolt, and armed soldiers are seen on the streets : National Republican Guards change sentry (1) outside one of their headquarters in the city, whilst the busy kerb-side shoeblacks (2) continue their shining apparently without a care in the world.

Where Europe Gambled As Europe Bled

Diplomats and agents of belligérent and neutral countries entered and left Lisbon freely ; Estoril, ten miles from the capital, became the wartime rival of Monte Carlo and to the gaming tables of its Casino (3) flocked spies and wealthy refugees and business-men to gamble and conduct large-scale intrigues at the same time. Architectural splendour of Lisbon includes the imposing entrance to Rossio Railway Station (4), the National Theatre, Donna Maria II (5), and the Houses of Parliament (6).

Airport of Lisbon a Great World-Junction

Exclusive to THE WAR ILLUSTRAT

Twenty-three different air transport companies now use Lisbon's Airport, through which large numbers of refugees from Nazi persecution made their escape during the war. The first of its kind to arrive there, a Vickers Viking (1) of British European Airways was on a proving flight. Trans-Atlantic air-liners use it as a refuelling and passenger halt : in front of the entrance to the Airport building (2) the Avro York "Star Dale" (3) is outward bound from London to Buenos Aires.

CEYLON, MAURITIUS & THE SEYCHELLES

By HARLEY V. USILL

B Y the Peace of Amiens in 1802, Ceylon (formerly a Dutch possession) was ceded to Great Britain and constituted a separate Crown Colony. The inhabitants of Ceylon were then no more than a haphazard gathering of heterogeneous peoples, divided by race, religion, tradition and interests ; today she is fast becoming an integrated community and has a constitution which is well advanced towards control of her own affairs.

The population of Ceylon is approximately 6,650,000, of whom more than 3,300,000 are Sinhalese, descendants of invaders who came from Southern India in the 5th century B.C. They maintain a peasant tradition, whereas the bulk of the labour for the estates is drawn from the next largest group, the 1,500,000 or more Tamils. The remainder of the population is made up of about 325,000 Moorish descendants of Arabs who arrived centuries ago from the Malabar coast of India and have established themselves as traders ; the so-called Burghers (about 32,000) descendants of the old Portuguese and Dutch inhabitants ; a group of 15,000 Malays, who form the backbone of the native police force ; and some 10,000 Europeans.

It was clear, even before the rapidity of the Japanese advance in early 1942 hit the Pacific with such force, that Ceylon would be called upon to play a many-sided part in the war, and steps were taken to prepare for any eventuality, including the distinct possibility of invasion. An Essential Service Labour Corps, organized on semi-military lines, was recruited for all kinds of emergency work. Tasks allocated to this Corps included the construction of runways, clearance of fire gaps, loading and unloading of ammunition, laying of underground cables, the painting of ships, the police and guard duties. A.R.P. measures were modelled on similar lines to those in force in India, and 30,000 men and women, of whom 20,000 were unpaid, had been enrolled by July 1942.

The Ceylon Defence Force included the Ceylon Light Infantry, the Planters' Rifle Corps, Ceylon Engineers, Ceylon Garrison Artillery, Ceylon Medical Corps (which provided the entire staff of the Ceylonese military hospital), Ceylon Army Service Corps, and Ceylon Auxiliary Pioneer Battalion. There were also two Companies of the Ceylon A.T.S., and in June 1943 an Air Training Scheme was launched for Ceylonese young men. The Ceylon Defence Force passed to War Office control in October 1941, and by May 1945 was over 25,000 strong. One of the main difficulties encountered, as was the case in Malaya and elsewhere, was to establish the relative priority between civilian and military duties for the small number of Europeans who held key positions in almost every aspect of the Ceylon war effort. The general policy introduced was to the effect that any manpower which could be spared from non-essential industries should be employed in local defence rather than overseas.

Nevertheless, individuals served in various theatres. Volunteers from the Ceylon Planters' Rifle Corps served in Syria and Libya,

T HE point at which the Japanese westward drive was halted, the base from which S.E.A.C. planned the recapture of Burma, the island of Ceylon accomplished much in the war. The worthy efforts of other Indian Ocean islands—Mauritius and the Seychelles—are also dealt with.

◆

and others left for training in India. A unit of the Ceylon Garrison Artillery served overseas in the Seychelles and Cocos Islands, and several thousand Ceylonese saw overseas service in units of the British Army, mainly with the R.A.S.C. and the Royal Engineers. Members of the Ceylon R.A.F.V.R. completed their training in Britain preparatory to taking their places in R.A.F. squadrons.

I N the matter of contributions to various war funds, the Ceylonese of all classes displayed the utmost generosity. By September 1943 there were over 2,000 Savings Groups in the Island. Gifts for aircraft amounted to £375,000 from the Ceylon Government, and

PIONEERS FROM MAURITIUS put finishing touches to a water-point at Benghazi after the final capture of the port by the 8th Army on Nov. 20, 1942. The first Mauritian Pioneer Company arrived in the Middle East in January 1941 and was followed by several others. Their work was mainly constructional engineering.
Photo, British Official

£236,000 from private sources. Other gifts from private sources totalled £241,883.

The testing time for Ceylon's defences came in April 1942. With the Japanese established in Burma, Malaya and the East Indies, the position in the Andaman Islands off the coast of Burma became impossible to hold, and the British garrison was withdrawn on March 12. When the Japanese moved in to the Andamans, Ceylon was right in the front-line and had not long to wait before she was attacked. On Easter Sunday (April 5) a force of 75 aircraft operating from carriers based on the Andamans made a dive-bombing and low-flying attack on Colombo Harbour, and the airfield and railway works at Ratmalana, eight miles south of Colombo. Of this force, 27 were either destroyed or damaged. A few days later, on April 9, the Japanese made another attack on the Island, this time on the R.N. base at Trincomalee. Guns and fighters accounted for 37 aircraft almost certainly destroyed, and two damaged.

Admiral Lord Louis Mountbatten, Supreme Allied Commander in South-East Asia, transferred his headquarters from New Delhi to Ceylon in April 1944. Thus the island of Ceylon, which earlier had marked the point at which the Japanese advance to

the West was halted, now held the proud position as the centre from which the enemy was to be driven back to final destruction.

The island of Mauritius (see page 83) was annexed in 1715 by the French, who imported about 65,000 slaves from Africa to work on the sugar plantations. The British took possession of the island in 1810, and with the introduction of the Abolition of Slavery Act in 1833 the slaves were freed. Since many of them refused to continue to work on the plantations Indian immigration at the rate of 6,000 a year was introduced in 1842, and lasted until abolished in 1878. Thus, out of a population of about 420,000 there are 270,000 Indians. The rest of the population is made up of white Mauritians about 10,000, coloured Mauritians about 130,000, Chinese 10,000 and a few hundred British.

The whole of the agricultural life of Mauritius was bound up with the intensive cultivation of the sugar cane, the production of food for internal consumption being barely one-tenth of that required. And so, when war broke out, one of the most pressing problems facing Mauritius was to set about the task of increasing the production of food for the inhabitants.

The only local military unit in Mauritius then was the Mauritius Territorial Force. Later, it was decided to create a Mauritius Regiment with an overseas liability, and after training, in September 1943, the First Battalion was sent to Madagascar for garrison duties. The experiment was not a success, and in August 1944 the battalion was disbanded. Excellent service was performed, however, by Mauritians serving in pioneer units. The first Pioneer Company left for the Middle East in January 1941, and others followed until by May 1945 their strength totalled nearly 3,000. These units served with distinction not only in the Middle East but also in Malta, in Sicily and in Italy. A number of Mauritians served with the R.A.F. as aircrew and ground staff.

All classes of the community subscribed generously to various war funds. Altogether gifts and loans free of interest received through the Colonial Office totalled £534,378 by July 1943. Thus, by the saving of shipping space by restriction on imports and by a successful campaign to make the Colony less dependent on imported food supplies, by the maintenance of a steady supply of sugar to the U.K., by the recruitment of men to serve overseas and volunteers for the R.A.F., Mauritius showed up well.

P OPULATION of the Seychelles (see page 83) is about 30,000, and up to July 1943 the people and Government had given over £13,000 to the U.K. Government, in addition to an interest-free loan of £3,750. The Colony's part in war production was represented by the export of thousands of tons of copra. A small Defence Force was raised in 1939, but in view of the vital strategic importance of the Colony it was not considered advisable to rely upon this Force to take over from regular troops garrison duties or coastal defence. But the Seychelles Pioneers, like the Mauritians, served with distinction in the Middle East and Italy.

Europe's Wartime Capitals in 1947

BUCHAREST
By J. C. GORDON

It has often been said about the capital of Rumania that no city in Europe affords more striking and pitiful contrasts of wretched poverty and almost fabulous wealth, Oriental customs and Hollywood-like ways, Byzantine tradition and modern French culture. These strange contrasts truly reflect the various influences which superseded one another in the making of Bucharest.

Legend has it that in the 12th century a shepherd named Bucur built a church on the Dambovitza, a small river which flows into the Danube 30 miles to the south. In his honour the village, which in due course grew up around the church, was called Bucuresti, "esti" being the usual Rumanian ending for names of localities. Rumanians still call it Bucuresti (pronounced Boocooresht). Bucharest is the French way of spelling it. Under the Turks, who controlled the Rumanian Provinces from the 15th to the 19th century, the village grew and prospered as a trading centre. It eventually developed into a town marked by local colour and native beauty; picturesque white one-storey villas, the architecture of which was inspired by that of peasant houses, old Rumanian wooden churches with artistic carvings and Byzantine frescoes.

The real Westernization and moderniza-tion of Bucharest began as late as the last century, when Rumania had achieved her national independence. A palace was built for the King, luxurious villas for members of his court and prominent Government officials, greystone monumental buildings to house Government departments and national and municipal institutions. To commemor-ate final victory against the Turks which resulted in Rumania achieving her inde-pendence in 1878, Bucharest's main street was named Calea Victoriei, which means "The Victory Road."

Today Calea Victoriei, with its luxurious shops, café-terraces and concrete multi-storeyed blocks of flats and offices, looks much like a modern street in any up-to-date city. The central telephone exchange built by an American company on the pattern of a New York skyscraper looked rather out of place some 13 years ago, but since then similar blocks have mushroomed year after year along the Calea Victoriei and the big boule-vards in the city's centre. Now it is the few remaining little wooden huts and brick bungalows which strike a discordant note. In spite of this astounding progress achieved in less than three decades the suburbs remain very much what they were—narrow, dusty or muddy streets with small, dilapidated, primitive and unhygienic cottages, inhabited by desperately poor people.

Most conspicuous among them are the gipsies—barefooted girls in their colourful costumes balancing huge baskets of flowers on their heads, their mothers offering to tell your fortune from your hand, or from a greasy old pack of cards, or by putting a large sea-shell to their ears and listening intently to mysterious echoes; while their menfolk follow the more prosaic occupations of street corner traders, newsvendors and shoeblacks. Others make a living in cafés and bars, fiddling those haunting melodies for which the Rumanian gipsy is famous throughout the world.

Bucharest, which in 1939 had just short of 1,000,000 inhabitants, today has more than one and a half times that number. Thousands of refugees from the drought-stricken provinces and the war-ravaged towns and villages of Eastern Rumania, Poles who fled from the advancing Germans in 1939, and other international flotsam have made this one of the most overcrowded cities on the Continent. Phenomenal prices, even by London standards, are daily paid for leases of houses and as "key money" for flats. The housing situation was further worsened by war damage. Though Bucharest did not suffer much from air raids, one-tenth of its 102,559 buildings were completely destroyed by military operations and a rehousing drive launched in 1946 has yet to bear fruit.

There are things of which Bucharest is certainly not short: good restaurants, night clubs and places of amusement. The average Rumanian can seldom afford to take full advantage of them, but this does not seem to worry their proprietors unduly, for the restaurants are usually full. The mystery of their sources of supply remains to be solved by the authorities concerned with the re-pression of black market offences, for there is practically nothing one cannot order in a Bucharest restaurant. Nowhere in Europe is food so abundant and cheap.

Paved With Black Market Gold

Though first-class restaurants are not within the average person's reach, the black market is. Fear of starvation has become almost second nature to many Rumanians, who think nothing of storing half a pig and 50 pounds of cheese (if they can get it) in their larders. Food hoarding is, of course, a punishable offence, but Bucharest citizens are not afraid of breaking the law where food is concerned. Workers and civil servants, however, have their own sources of supply for scarce goods—the newly created "econo-mate" or co-operative shops which purvey to members, at official prices, a wide variety of commodities in short supply which are other-wise obtainable only at prohibitive prices.

GIPSY GIRLS SELLING NEWSPAPERS in Bucharest did brisk business on the night of Nov. 22, 1946, when the papers gave the news of the Government's victory at the elections.
Photo, Associated Press PAGE 628

Most precious and sought-after items (unobtainable even at the co-operative shop) are chocolate, coffee and tea. Officially, practically none of these has been imported since the end of the war, but provided you are willing to pay the price any amount will be promptly delivered to your home. Rumanians are said to have a sweet tooth, and in order to make their famous "placintae" (a kind of fluffy apple pastry) they have to supplement their meagre sugar ration on the sly. Leather shoe soles (which are rationed), razor blades and American cigarettes are other commodities in which there is a flourishing illegal trade.

The black market in foreign exchange has a street of its own. Situated between the National Bank and the Stock Exchange Building you can see there little knots of gesticulating men bargaining noisily in broad daylight. Suddenly word is passed around that a police raid is imminent. Everyone scatters and next day the newspapers pro-claim in two-inch headlines that "Bucharest streets were paved with gold." For some of the traders were forced to jettison their sovereigns, gold dollars and louis napoleons.

But Bucharest life is not all restaurants and black market. Since the war there has been a great cultural revival. Theatres and cinemas, art galleries and concert halls are thronged. New editions of Rumanian and foreign books are sold out within a few days. Rumanians, whom Goebbels had starved for six years of Anglo-Saxon drama and new works by English and American authors, are eagerly snapping up every new translation. Plays by Shakespeare, Oscar Wilde, J. B. Priestley and Eugene O'Neill are having record runs. Cinemas which showed such films as San Demetrio-London, Kipps, Fanny by Gaslight and Colonel Blimp were be-sieged by eager crowds.

The people of Bucharest are fond of fresh air and spend a good deal of their time out-of-doors. The most popular public park is the Cismigiu, beautifully laid out and situated in the centre of the city. Its wide alleys bordered by multi-coloured beds of flowers converge to a central lake featuring a big water-jet magnificently illuminated at night. There, sitting at a table on the terrace of the popular café called "Monte-Carlo," overlooking the lake, you can watch the soldiers on leave, young boys and romantic couples rowing or paddling in the summer and skating on the frozen lake in the winter. On Sundays most of the visitors to the Cismigiu are servant-girls, buxom, apple-cheeked country maidens wearing bright-coloured skirts and scarves. Hundreds crowd around the brass band to hear martial tunes and the latest popular songs.

The well-to-do spend summer evenings and often a good deal of the night at the open-air restaurants and cafés listening to gipsy music and drinking glass after glass of "spritz," which is white wine with iced soda-water. The most fashionable of these places are along the Kisseleff Chaussée, a wide tree-lined avenue with spacious lawns, parks and luxurious villas on either side, and described as the Champs Elysées of Bucharest. Club-houses such as the Country Club (golf, tennis, riding) frequented by foreign diplo-mats and big business men are also here, as well as the Kisseleff Strand, one of the largest and best equipped swimming pools in Europe. Fifty years ago the whole area was a marshy and wooded strip of land, infested by mos-quitoes and frequented by armed robbers. Now the swamps have been drained and the grounds turned into a beauty spot.

Crowded Hours in Modernized Old Bucharest

ACCLAIMING THEIR NEWLY-ELECTED LEADER, Premier Petru Groza, a great concourse assembled on Nov. 22, 1946, in 8th June Square (1). Railways are uncertain and passengers storm the trains at North Station (2). Trams provide the principal means of transportation and these too are usually besieged. New buildings in course of erection in Bratianu Boulevard (3), the Rumanian capital's main thoroughfare. See also facing page.   PAGE 629   *Photos, Associated Press*

Sight-Seeing in Europe with Our Roving Camera

A BRIDGE-MAKING FACTORY is in course of erection at Czernowitz, Russia. Parts of the plant are already in production and have supplied the ironwork for a new bridge over the Dniester River. Czernowitz, or Cernauti, is in N. Bukovina, finally ceded to Russia by Rumania in September 1944.

WAR-SCARRED BELL of H.M.S. Illustrious was exhibited at a naval exhibition in Paris during December 1946. This aircraft carrier had a distinguished war record. She was at Taranto and was severely damaged in January 1941 when she fought her way through to Malta with a convoy.

BRITISH D-DAY EQUIPMENT aroused great interest at an exhibition in Bratislava, Czechoslovakia. In the foreground is a model of a large tank-landing craft, and on the wall hang photographs of Mulberry Harbour. Included in the display were examples of all major weapons and devices used against the German coastal fortifications and in the Allied advance across Europe.

IN THE SAAR on Dec. 23, 1946, the French took the first step towards economic annexation of this region by placing 1,200 Customs officials along the German frontier. Two Customs men are seen erecting a sign at cross-roads near Homburg. Reason was to prevent extra food supplied to Saar miners passing into Germany.

HUNGARY'S DANUBE FLEET vanished with the retreating Germans in 1944 and was later found in the American zone in Austria. The U.S. authorities agreed to return the vessels, the first craft arriving at Budapest in December 1946. In the background (left) are ruins of the chain bridge destroyed by the Germans.

Deathless Honour for Such as These

Lieutenant THOMAS WILKINSON, V.C., R.N.R.

POSTHUMOUS AWARD OF THE V.C. in recognition of his heroism and self-sacrifice and of that of all who fought and died with him in a most gallant action on February 14, 1942, was announced on December 17, 1946. On the former date H.M.S. Li Wo, a patrol vessel of 1,000 tons and formerly a passenger steamer on the Upper Yangste River, was sailing from Singapore to Batavia. Her ship's company consisted of 84 officers and men, including one civilian. The crew were mainly survivors from others of His Majesty's ships, but a few were from units of the Army and R.A.F. The armament was one 4-inch gun, for which she had 13 practice rounds, and two machine-guns.

Since leaving Singapore the previous day four air attacks had been beaten off, and the vessel had suffered considerable damage. Late in the afternoon two enemy convoys were sighted, the larger of which was escorted by Japanese naval units, including a heavy cruiser and destroyers. Lieutenant Wilkinson (left) gathered together his ship's company and told them that rather than try to escape he had decided to engage the convoy and to fight to the last, in the hope of inflicting some damage on the enemy. In making this decision, which was heartily endorsed by the entire crew, he knew that his ship faced certain destruction and that his own chance of survival was small.

H.M.S. Li Wo hoisted her battle ensign and steamed towards the enemy. In the ensuing action her two machine-guns were used with effect upon the crews of all ships in range, and the crew of the one 4-inch gun set on fire one of the transports.

AFTER a little over an hour the Li Wo had been critically damaged and was sinking. Lieutenant Wilkinson then decided to ram a large transport that had been abandoned by her crew. It is known that this ship burnt fiercely throughout the night following the fight and was probably sunk. H.M.S. Li Wo's gallant fight ended when, her shells spent and under heavy fire from the enemy cruiser, Lieutenant Wilkinson gave the order "abandon ship." He himself remained on board and went down with her. There were only about ten survivors, who were later made prisoners of war.

Sub-Lieutenant Ronald G. G. Stanton, R.N.R., who was First Lieutenant of H.M.S. Li Wo and her only surviving officer, was appointed a Companion of the Distinguished Service Order on Dec. 17, 1946. The organization of the ship devolved on him; and during the action he served as a member of the volunteer crew of the 4-in. gun, which weapon was fought with steadfast courage in the face of overwhelming odds. Acting Petty-Officer Arthur William Thompson was awarded the Conspicuous Gallantry Medal for his outstanding conduct in such a brave company. He volunteered to serve as gun-layer to the 4-in. gun, carrying out his duties with great coolness and displaying the utmost skill, courage and resource throughout the action. Leading-Seaman Victor Spencer, who manned the port machine-gun, received the Distinguished Service Medal for his resolution and steadiness. Able Seaman Albert Spendlove, who was a member of the 4-in. gun crew, was also awarded the D.S.M.

Madame VIOLETTE SZABO, G.C.

AWARDED THE GEORGE CROSS posthumously on December 17, 1946, Madame Szabo, as a member of the Women's Transport Service (First Aid Nursing Yeomanry), had volunteered to undertake a particularly dangerous mission in France and was parachuted into that country in April 1944. In her execution of the researches entailed she showed great presence of mind and astuteness. She was twice arrested by the German security authorities, but managed to escape each time. Eventually, however, with other members of her group, she was surrounded by the Gestapo in a house in the south-west of France.

Resistance appeared hopeless, but Madame Szabo, seizing a Sten gun and as much ammunition as she could carry, barricaded herself in a part of the building and exchanging shot for shot with the enemy killed or wounded several of them. By constant movement she avoided being cornered and fought until she dropped exhausted. She was arrested and had to undergo solitary confinement. She was then continuously tortured, but never by word or deed did she give away any of her acquaintances or tell the enemy anything of value. She was ultimately executed. Madame Szabo gave a magnificent example of courage and steadfastness.

She was 24 years of age, and in 1940 married an officer of the French Foreign Legion (right), who was killed at Alamein in 1942. She joined the A.T.S. in 1941, and later was attached to the W.T.S., being employed on Intelligence work after her husband's death. She spoke perfect French, having been brought up partly in France and partly in England. She is survived by a four-year-old daughter. (see illus. page 640).

THE final story of the fate of this very brave woman was told at Hamburg on January 1, 1947, during the trial of 16 members of the staff of the notorious Ravensbruck concentration camp, where she was imprisoned with two other women agents—Lilian Rolfe and Denise Madeline Bloch. In a deposition read to the court, Johann Schwarzhuber, the deputy camp commandant, described how the three heroines were shot, without evincing the slightest sign of fear.

Lilian Rolfe was an Englishwoman, born in Paris, who joined the W.A.A.F. in 1943. Because of her fluent French she was voluntarily transferred to a section of the Army which was preparing to staff the Underground Movement on the Continent. In March 1944 she was parachuted into France, where she joined up with Denise Bloch. Both women worked as wireless operators, keeping in touch with Allied forces until their capture by the Gestapo in July 1944. They remained silent under six months of torture and questioning, their bravery evoking the admiration even of their persecutors.

Photos, Keystone, Topical

Shpwt. C. BADROCK
Royal Navy.
Action : France. 7.8.44.
Age 20. (Alpraham, Ches.)

So great has been the response of readers to our invitation to submit portraits for our Roll of Honour that no more can now be accepted. But senders may rest assured that all those so far received will be published.

Pte. F. BULLEN
Royal Norfolk Regt.
P.O.W. : Siam. 6.2.44.
Age 29. (Lowestoft)

L/Sgt. D. J. BAITUP
The Buffs.
D. wds. : N. Africa. 27.3.43.
Age 21. (Cranbrook)

L/Bdr. CHATTERTON
Royal Artillery.
Action : El Alamein. 2.7.42
Age 25. (Liverpool)

Flt./Sgt. H. CLARKE
Bomber Command R.A.F.
Wilhelmshaven. 16.10.44.
Age 25. (Birmingham)

L/Cpl. F. J. COE
City of London Yeomanry.
Action : Libya. 19.11.41.
Age 28. (London)

Flt./Sgt. S. COWLEY
Royal Air Force.
Over Germany. 4.11.43.
Age 21. (St. Helens)

Pte. J. L. COLLETT
Gloucestershire Regt.
Action : N'mandy. 12.8.44.
Age 18. (Bristol)

Dvr. CRUDGINGTON
R.A.S.C.
Action : Dunkirk. 1.6.40.
Age 37. (Nottingham)

Pte. T. CUNNINGHAM
Seaforth Highlanders.
Action : Somme. 4.6.40.
Age 19. (Wakefield)

A/B. E. DAY
H.M.S. Puckeridge.
Action : At sea. 6.9.43.
Age 19. (Sheffield)

L/Cpl. H. G. DEARDEN
No. 1 Commando.
Action : Burma. 31.1.45.
Age 27. (Swinton)

Pte. J. A. DEARDEN
The Green Howards.
D.wds.: M. East. 25.3.42.
Age 22. (Sheffield)

A/B. H. DEWHIRST
H.M.S. Repulse.
Action : At sea. Dec. 41.
Age 20. (Keighley)

Torp. F. T. FRENCH
H.M.S. Exeter.
Action : R. Plate. 13.12.39.
Age 19. (Plymouth)

Boy E. FRESHWATER
Royal Navy.
Action : Singapore. 16.2.42
Age 18. (Upper Dean)

Sgt. D. O. HENN
Staffs Yeomanry.
Action : Caen. 18.7.44.
Age 29. (Gnosall)

Cpl. R. JACKSON
London Irish Rifles.
Action : Italy. 15.5.44.
Age 21. (Carnmoney)

Pte. C. M. KENT
Beds. & Herts. Regt.
D.wds. Medit. 28.8.44.
Age 27. (Leek)

B.Q.M.S. C. LAHRA
Royal Malta Artillery.
Action : Rabat. 20.7.43.
Age 27. (Rabat)

Pte. G. LE MAITRE
East Lancashire Regt.
Action : Holland. Feb. 45.
Age 19. (Birmingham)

Sgt. P. McGINN
Royal Air Force.
Action. 23.4.44.
Age 20. (Durham)

Pte. R. MILLER
R. Northumberland Fus.
Action: M. East. 22.11.41.
Age 20. (Newcastle)

L.A.C. D. G. MOPPETT
R.A.F.V.R.
P.O.W. : Celebes. 6.1.45.
Age 24. (Lewes)

A.C. J. M. MORTON
Royal Air Force.
A/S. St. Mawgan. 21.10.44.
Age 22 (Leicester)

Sgt. H. OLIVER
Dorset Regiment.
Ac. : W. Europe. 29.4.45.
Age 26. (Croydon)

Cpl. R. W. PADFIELD
Somerset L.I.
Action : N'mandy. 21.7.44.
Age 23. (Holcombe)

Pte. J. RENSHAW
S. Staffs. Regt.
Action : Falaise. 12.8.44.
Age 19. (Leek)

A/B. A. ROLLIN
H.M.S. Campbeltown.
Ac². : St. Nazaire. 28.3.42.
Age 23. (Retford)

Cpl. A. E. SHAND
Scots Guards.
Action : Norway. 24.5.40.
Age 25. (Burnham)

Sto. S. F. SMITH
H.M.S. Charybdis.
Action : Channel. 23.10.43
Age 19. (Yiewsley)

Flt./Sgt. A. TAYLOR
R.A.F.V.R.
Action : Burma. 19.2.45.
Age 21. (Aberdeen)

L/Sgt. G. THURLEY
Suffolk Regiment.
Action : Italy. 26.11.43.
Age 30. (Bishop's Stortford)

L/Cpl. R. J. TOMS
Dorset Regiment.
Action : Burma. 1.5.44.
Age 26. (Salisbury)

Gnr. H. TURPIN
R.H.A.
Action : Italy. 7.7.44.
Age 32. (Bradford)

A/B. L. J. WALKER
Royal Navy.
Act. : Java Seas. March 42.
Age 21. (Eccles)

L/Sto. E. H. WATTS
H.M. submarine Orpheus.
Act.: Off Benghazi. 29.6.40
Age 25. (Yateley)

Dvr. A. C. YOUNGS
R.A.S.C.
Action : N. Africa. 1.11.44.
Age 27. (Salcott)

A Clerk Takes a Jump Into France

When the Great Invasion of 1944 was in full swing Private Roger Messent of the 2nd Parachute Brigade "dropped in." He presents a behind-the-scenes picture of the Allied landing in Southern France as seen by a soldier whose job was not fighting but clerical work.

AFTER many days of frantic preparation we arrived, on the evening of August 15, 1944, at an airfield near Rome. The sight of many huge American transport planes was awe-inspiring—as also was the fact that before long we would be leaping out of them over Occupied France. We had a meal, then lay down beneath the wings of our plane and tried to get a little sleep, as we had to emplane at 1.30 a.m. The time wore on, and presently we were donning our mass of equipment, struggling to fix parachute harness on top of everything. There was much perspiring and heaving of straps and buckles before we were ready, and I was so trussed up and weighted down that I had to be helped on board. Soon after 2 a.m. the planes were away. I marvelled how so many big machines, with only one runway, could get into the air so quickly.

ROGER MESSENT

So began our long flight. My harness was too tight, but it was so dark inside the plane that I dare not risk taking off my 'chute to adjust it. I tried to sleep, but was too uncomfortable. After some three hours our armada approached the French coast near St. Raphael. We had been told to expect heavy anti-aircraft fire, but we heard nothing. We stood up, waiting to jump. Suddenly the red light glowed, then changed to green. I was jumping number four, and remembered just in time that it was my job to pull the container-release switch. I had no time to shout "Containers away!" when the others started jumping; then I was at the door.

I leaped out into the dark night, the slip-stream hit me hard, and my 'chute opened. Before I had a chance to collect my wits I was lying on my back in an expanse of grape-vines. For a second or two I remained motionless, thinking "So this is France!" then wriggled out of my harness. My first sensation was one of loneliness, for I could neither see nor hear anyone or anything.

Above the Crowded Landing Zone

With rifle to the fore I started to walk, and after travelling about half a mile I heard someone calling "Number four plane!" Thankfully I joined the other fellows—and realized that I had left my pack behind. But it was too late to worry about that. What we had to do now was to find the hamlet in which we were to make our H.Q. Suddenly rifle shots sounded in the distance and we saw bursts of red tracer. Bullets whistled uncomfortably close, and we took cover in a ditch until all was quiet again, and we reached our appointed destination without having seen the originators of the firing.

Some of my colleagues had already arrived, and with the help of two members of the airborne Military Police had taken possession of a house for use as H.Q. Quickly we organized an office in the kitchen. There was not much work for us to do—just the handling of wireless messages; we carried only a small amount of office equipment when we dropped, but later we expected to get a typewriter and stationery, which would be delivered by glider.

As soon as we were settled in I was given permission to look for my pack, with the warning that there were snipers about. It was a fruitless journey, and just as I was about to return to H.Q. I heard the roar of aero-engines. Looking up, I saw a long stream of aircraft towing gliders; as they arrived overhead the gliders were released, and soon they were landing all around me. Many of them came down with a fearful crash, for the ground was not level, and in addition to trees dotted about there were poles which the Germans has stuck in the ground to prevent such a landing. One huge glider hit the ground with an awful smack, about 300 yards away, and I ran to it expecting to see carnage. I found the crew enjoying a handful of grapes. I told them the general situation, and made my way back to H.Q.

In the evening came more aircraft towing gliders. Soon the sky was full of them, turning and twisting as the pilots sought for a place to come down on the crowded landing zone. It was a terrific picture of Allied air might. Next morning planes dropped supplies by parachute; it was a beautiful sight as the sun's rays caught the hundreds of coloured 'chutes floating down. Among the dropped items was the war correspondent of a London newspaper. It was his first jump, and although all went well for him his precious typewriter, which was in a kitbag strapped to his leg, broke away and crashed to the ground a tangled mass.

TROOP TRANSPORT AIRCRAFT OF THE R.A.F. parked nose to tail on an airfield in southern France in August 1944. Twin-engined Dakotas were often used for parachuting operations as described in this story, and their pilots were usually expert at locating the dropping zone. Some of the author's comrades, however, were dropped in error 40 miles from the rendezvous, but joined up with the Maquis and added to the bewilderment of the enemy.

Air Ministry photograph

Motto: " By Force of Arms "

No. 65 SQUADRON

DISBANDED after the First Great War, the squadron was re-formed at Hornchurch, Essex, on July 10, 1934, was there at the outbreak of the Second Great War and was eventually equipped with Spitfires. At one time or another it had pilots from England, Northern Ireland, Iceland, Canada, Australia, Jamaica and Trinidad. Equipped and maintained by East India funds raised in 1940 for the British war services, it became known as No. 65 (East India) Squadron. It took no part in the campaign in Northern France, 1939-40.

For some time it operated with the U.S. 8th Army Air Force, accompanying the heavy bombers on a series of daylight raids to Berlin. Before D-Day it was converted to a Mustang squadron, and moved to France in June 1944, operating from an advanced airfield that was within range of the German guns. Forming part of a mobile wing that bombed and shot-up bridges, enemy armour, transport, troops, barges and trains, No. 65 was credited with having destroyed or damaged 1,000 armoured vehicles in two months.

ITS moves were rapid, and carried out at short notice. At one airfield the squadron was able to fly only one mission before it was on the road again ; on another occasiona the entire airfield was transferred a distance of 75 miles in 13 hours. During the German retreat across France and the Low Countries, the squadron's pilots stated that once they saw British and German convoys on the same road, separated by only 200 yards.

No. 65 was eventually based near Brussels and flew in support of the air landings at Arnhem. Returning to England it acted as escort to R.A.F. bombers on missions to Norway and Germany, as well as operating over Denmark.

Sitting down and trying to be a clerk when others were chasing Jerries struck me as dull, and I was glad when I had the chance of going after some captured transport. I managed a lift on a French vehicle to a large building, about a mile away, which had been a German H.Q. There were Germans everywhere, and our men were bundling them on to a big charabanc affair. I got hold of an onlooker and managed to convey to him that I wanted a car ; without a word he led me to a garage at the back of the house, showed me a smart-looking camouflaged Opel, and I drove back to H.Q. in great style.

More gliders came, until there were hundreds scattered about, some parked in a small clearing side by side like taxis. Parachutes were dotted wide over a large area. Some of our men were dropped, in error, as much as forty miles away ; but this,

instead of being a liability to our main forces, proved invaluable, as they joined with Maquis troops and created havoc among the enemy. I was impressed by the Maquis, some of them mere lads but armed to the teeth with weapons and ammunition dropped by the R.A.F. in months past.

We moved from our village house to the German H.Q. where I had obtained the car, and our office there would have done credit to Whitehall ; big desks, an excellent typewriter, a duplicator and a vast amount of assorted stationery, all supplied by Germany, Ltd. It was an enormous house and the original occupants, a French lady and her servants, were still living in part of it. The amount of German equipment lying about was unbelievable. They had left in too great a hurry to remove anything. Some of their souvenirs included pictures and crockery from the Star Hotel, Jersey.

So This Was the Invasion Coast

Again we moved, our next H.Q. being in a house high up in the hills, from which there was a wonderful view. Besides our brigade an American airborne division had been engaged, and with the capture of Fréjus and St. Raphael the remainder of the large task force streamed ashore. Our brigade was then withdrawn from action, and there was not much to do in the office so I decided to visit Cannes, which had just fallen. For transport I had to rely on my thumb, and it did not let me down. It enabled me to pick up a truck that was going in the direction I wanted. The road ran along the coast, which from a distance looked like a part of Cornwall, with bright-looking villas and hotels at the cliff edge.

But first appearances were deceptive, for this was the invasion coast, and on D-Day Allied warships and aircraft had shelled and bombed all the beach defences. The cliffs, beaches and woods were a mass of barbed wire, and 𝟏everywhere there were notices " Achtung—Minen." German equipment and clothing were strewn about, and for miles we did not see a soul. It seemed impossible that the desolate, war-battered region would ever again echo with the laughter of holiday-makers.𝟏

As we rounded a curve I saw across the water the white town of Cannes stretching down to the edge of the deep blue sea. Here the truck stopped, for the driver was turning inland. I got out, the lorry moved away, and I was left high and dry and lonely. After about a quarter of an hour a jeep appeared filled with fellows whom I knew. They managed to squeeze me in, making eight all told.

Narrowly missing running over a dead German in the middle of the road, we passed through a small village about four miles from Cannes, then came to a blown bridge with a mine-shattered jeep on the wreckage. We tried to cross a track at the side, but it was blocked by a smashed lorry. Another truck had stuck in the middle of the river, which was about two feet deep. As we were debating what to do, there was a terrific explosion and bits of metal fell around ; a half-track vehicle, trying to cross at a point five yards downstream, had exploded a mine at the water's edge and injured some onlookers.

The Concealed Visitors' Book

Certainly that river was not healthy, and we decided to take a track which looked as if it might lead over the mountains to Cannes. After a very bumpy two-mile trip the track ended at a house, whose occupants received us with open arms. On learning that we could not stay they pressed us to accept a bottle of wine. We reluctantly agreed that we could not make Cannes, and so started back along the coast road. At the half-way point we encountered an hotel that seemed to be not only undamaged but open. It was the Hotel St. Cristophe, and the proprietor, Monsieur Barbero, expressed himself as very pleased to see us. He explained that he had little food, but we gave him a couple of tins of Spam and he fixed us a salad. Before leaving he asked us to sign our names in the register.

I turned the pages, covered with names of people from all over the world. Across one page was scrawled "Liberation, Aug. 23 !" Then followed the names of a few Americans who had paused for a "quick one" as they chased the Germans towards Cannes only a couple of days before. Apparently the Germans had been only too eager to shoot anybody who professed friendship with the English, so Monsieur Barbero had hidden the book with its many English names, assuring them that it had been burned. He had agreed to keep his hotel open as a German officers' club, and so had been allowed to stay. When we bade good-bye to our genial host we had the utmost difficulty in persuading him to accept any money.

CHALKED faintly on a wall near the hotel were the words " J'ai perdu mon coeur a un sergent allemand ; je n'aime pas la France. Vive l'Allemagne." (I have lost my heart to a German sergeant. I do not like France. Long live Germany.) The girl who wrote the words was pointed out to me. Her hair had been shaved off.

I Swam For Life Through Black Oil

Of a crew of 59 only 11 survived when the tanker Tricula, of the Anglo-Saxon Petroleum Company, was destroyed by enemy action, in the Atlantic, on August 3, 1942. Third Officer J. R. Richardson gives a graphic account of his nightmare ordeal and escape.

TOWARD the end of July 1942 the motor-vessel Tricula left Curaçao, Netherlands West Indies, after loading a cargo consisting of 8,000 tons of fuel-oil : heavy, dark stuff, 8,000 metric tons of which is the equivalent of about 1,760,000 gallons. All that oil, and a good deal more, was needed urgently for our naval forces in the Mediterranean. We sailed in convoy, and parted company from the other ships on the morning of the third day of August.

The weather was fine and the sea smooth. Radio warnings of U-boats kept our look-outs on their toes ; so when a dark object was sighted, we made a hurried attempt to ram —and realized just in time that it was only a whale on the surface. When the attack on the Tricula was launched the time was 4.20 p.m., and Captain Oswald Sparrow was on the right wing of the bridge talking to Chief Officer K. J. Morris. Second Officer

N. H. P. Davies was in the chartroom writing up the log, and I was off-duty. It was customary for me to take a nap in the afternoon, and that day I stayed longer in my bunk meditating on questions for a projected quiz —until there came a thunderous din.

It seemed as if the bunk had been wrenched away bodily from under me. How the devil I came to be standing upright on the cabin deck when a split second before I had been lying flat, was quite incomprehensible at the time. I must have performed an involuntary somersault and alighted right way up, like a cat. Instinctively I grabbed the side of the bunk and my desk. All around me books and other loote articles which had been flung down slithered about from the effect of two more violent explosions. Then, as the deck began to list, I realized that the Tricula had been torpedoed—and I must get out of that cabin pronto. How many of our officers and crew below had been killed by the explosions will never be known. Some lost their lives by drowning, carried down by the ship, which sank within a minute of the first blow from the unseen U-boat.

My cabin was next to the Fifth Engineer's in the amidships accommodation, which also includes the navigation bridge, chartroom and radio office. Fortunately, I had sense enough to grab my "strangler"—the life-jacket—and turning to the open door saw two or three of my fellow officers hurrying past. I stumbled out, but the ship was now listed so badly that I had to scramble along the port alleyway with one foot on the deck and the other on the acutely sloping bulkhead. The tanker was rolling over slowly and horribly. I heard the First Radio Officer call out that the alleyway door was jammed. Yet this seemed the one chance of escape, and by a desperate effort I got that door open and dragged myself out. It was impossible to see farther than a few yards through the writhing smoke. I groped for the ladder leading to the lower bridge, and clawed my way up with the sea rushing at my heels. Not a dog's chance of getting a boat away— no second thought was needed about that. I managed to scramble into the life-jacket on reaching the bridge deck, and I remember getting a fleeting glimpse of the Second Mate on the starboard side. Any delay now and I knew I would be carried down as the ship turned turtle, so I dragged myself over the rail and plunged into the sea that was now swirling over the tank-deck.

J. R. RICHARDSON

Like Struggling Through Treacle

Instead of coming to the surface I was held down. Something that suggested the tentacle of an octopus fastened on my right leg— probably a rope attached to one of the rafts. My ears felt as if they would burst, and I gulped acrid brine. Strangely enough I lost all sense of fear. Absurd though it may seem, I had only a feeling of sadness that the wedding I had planned for my next leave could never take place! Yet I must have struggled fiercely, because suddenly my leg became free and I rose with extraordinary speed and shot half out of the water into a blaze of sunshine. The kapok life-jacket which had helped

me up supported me when I settled back in the sea. My eyes opened on a fantastic scene —and I wasn't aware then that my forehead had been cut open and my right eyelid slit in halves by something during the underwater struggle. The tanker had gone. Rolling smoke obliterated part of the tropical sky. All round me the sea was black, and the floating wreckage was black. The fuel-oil had burst from the shattered tanks and the ocean surface was covered thickly with it over a wide area.

I didn't know it, but in addition to seawater I had already swallowed enough fuel-oil to render me an invalid for months. All my mind and remaining strength became devoted to reaching some kind of solid support, and the best chance appeared to be a black raft some distance away with what looked like two Negroes crouched on it. The ensuing swim for life was the sort of ordeal one might have in a nightmare. It was like struggling through treacle. The thousands of gallons of fuel-oil that would have been a priceless boon to the Mediterranean Fleet had become a deadly menace to the lives of those members of the Tricula's company who, like myself, had survived the torpedo explosions. The sea was covered two or three inches thick with the stuff. My arms and legs threshed desperately. My body seemed to be encased in elastic bands that impeded all efforts.

Glimpses of the raft on which three figures were now to be seen dispelled a tendency to despair. A couple of black objects near to hand proved to be water-breakers which must have been blown out of one of the ship's lifeboats, and I tried to push them forward with the idea that water might become a vital need in the future. But a shout came from the direction of the raft: "Come on! Come on! Leave those ruddy things!"

I reached the raft and was dragged on it by Second Officer Davies, who recognized me only by my voice—because I was as black with oil as himself and the others. For a time I could only lie flat, too ill and weak to stir a finger. Whistles and voices came from various directions in that wide area of oil-polluted sea. We couldn't see anyone; but eventually we were approached by another raft, and these blackened survivors proved to be Chief Officer Morris, one of the passengers and a Chinese quartermaster. Two others also reached us, making eight in all on the rafts; and later three more, who weren't seen by us, were picked up. Among the lost was our gallant master, Captain Sparrow, believed to have gone down with his ship.

Some of us had severe spells of sickness due to the oil swallowed. Our eyelids were gummed up and we had to unstick them at

intervals with our fingers. Our bodies were coated with the awful stuff, and we slithered about helplessly on the oily rafts. When I sat up, blood dripped on my right shoulder; but I didn't know how severely I had been injured and no one could tell me because of the oil smeared over my face. I had lost my shorts in the sea and now wore nothing except the soggy life-jacket over my chest and back.

Amazing Sight in the Dark Night

Presently the rafts drifted through a clear channel, and I picked up a clean splinter of wood and tried to scrape the oil from my face, but without much success. We knew roughly the position where the Tricula had been "bumped," and reckoned we were about 175 miles from the nearest point of the West Indies. By drifting, with due allowance for tides and current, we thought we might make a landfall in about seven or eight days. But our main hope of rescue was pinned on the chance of a passing ship or aircraft.

No one had a watch, and we could only guess the time by sunset, the rising of the moon and position of the stars. The paddles weren't much good for getting along; they were smothered with the slippery oil and we had no means of removing the stuff as our hands and everything else were oily. The rafts, which we had managed to moor together, were equipped with water kegs and emergency rations, but most of us were too sick to worry about meals. A heavy shower during the night added to our discomfort. For long periods the silence was broken only by the creaking of the rafts and lapping of water, and (I was told afterwards) by my weird ejaculations during spells of delirium.

Suddenly one of the Chinese roused us: "Light! Can see light!" We unstuck our eyelids and looked with amazement at a blaze of lights—a fully-lighted neutral steamship! Chief Officer Morris yelled for us to get out the flares, but we couldn't unscrew the caps —our oily fingers slipped round them—and we cursed in our fear that the ship would pass without sighting us. At last someone jabbed one open with a knife, and the red flame attracted the notice of the liner's look-outs. Soon we were taken aboard the Rio San Juan, an Argentine vessel bound for Pernambuco.

Our rescuers mistook us for Negroes, and it took lashings of kerosene, hot water and soap before we regained our natural colour. My injured eye was operated on by a German doctor who was a passenger in the ship, and he made a good job of it. For months afterwards I had spells of sickness owing to the oil that had got into my system, and everything I ate or drank had a nauseating flavour.

MOTOR-VESSEL TRICULA, of the Anglo-Saxon Petroleum Company, was carrying 8,000 tons (about 1,760,000 gallons) of fuel-oil intended for our forces in the Mediterranean when the incidents described by Third Officer J. R. Richardson occurred. The terror of swimming when the stricken Tricula's cargo poured out in a sticky flood and covered the surface of the sea he shared with ten others from the crew of 59 on that memorable day in August 1942—and as a result of his experiences was an invalid for months.

First to Meet the Japanese in Malaya

When the enemy struck their first blow at Malaya in December 1941,
British gunners of the 5th Field Regiment, R.A., fought to hold the airfield
at Kota Bharu. Their unavailing struggle and the start of the fighting
retreat which ended at Singapore are described by Gunner H. W. Berry.
See also portrait and story in page 446.

WE arrived at Kota Bharu on the night of December 5, 1941. After the bright lights of Ipoh, on the opposite side of the Malay Peninsula, where we had been stationed for the past month, our new camp did not impress us. We were about 30 miles outside the town, our "barracks" being wooden huts in the middle of a rubber plantation. Everyone was heartily fed up with rubber plantations, and we were to get even more tired of them during the next few months. The most popular song among the isolated British troops was a parody, "I hope that I shall never see another blinkin' rubber tree!"

In the middle of our first night there we were called on parade and informed that a Jap convoy had been sighted heading towards Malaya and it looked as if they meant business. We "rookies" from England were confident that it was a false alarm. After weeks of standing-to on the British coast at the beginning of the same year prepared for the oft-threatened German attack we were inclined to be sceptical. But this time we were wrong, and on the night of December 7-8 the blow fell. The Japs had commenced landing operations at Kota Bharu and we were officially at war.

Our unit was the 73rd Field Battery of the 5th Field Regiment, R.A., and we were the only British troops of the 9th Indian Division, which had the job of defending the whole of the north-east corner of Malaya. The rest were Indians, mainly Hyderabad State Troops. We climbed into our vehicles and in convoy formation rolled off towards the battle-front. Dawn was breaking when we arrived at our rendezvous. The vehicles were parked and camouflaged and we waited further orders. Except for occasional explosions in the distance and the faint hum of aircraft it seemed fairly quiet. Excitement rose when, early in the afternoon, a dispatch rider who had accompanied some officers to the front returned with what we took to be authentic news.

"You'll be back in your camp by this time tomorrow, boys!" he told us. "The Air Force has sunk hundreds of landing-barges and the Japs have been beaten off!" We congratulated each other, gave silent thanks to the Air Force and began to look forward to relaxing in our camp bunks. Our optimism was short-lived. A few hours later we were ordered to advance and go into action. The Japs had returned at a different part of the coast and had already been successful in establishing a beach-head.

Our Confidence Rudely Shattered

A half-hour's journey brought us to the aerodrome on the other side of the town. We pushed our guns into position, well-hidden by the trees surrounding the airport, dug trenches, and waited for the order to fire. Nothing startling happened, so we commenced making ourselves "at home." We brewed tea and the cooks prepared a bully-beef stew. There was not much activity on the airport, but we knew that sooner or later the Japs were bound to come and bomb either us or the nearby hangars. With grand fatalism we refused to let that worry us. The immediate consideration was rest—and something to eat and drink. The future would look after itself . . . Suddenly a shout went up.

"Take cover! Here they come!" The faint hum of approaching aircraft grew louder, and presently we saw them. There were five, and they confirmed the impression we then held of the Jap Air Force. They were all single-cockpit biplanes, and as they sailed slowly over our position we couldn't help chuckling. "Wait till the Spits and Hurricanes get on their track," we told each other. "It will be sheer slaughter!"

BUT as they passed right overhead we gave gasps of astonishment. They weren't Japs. They had the circular red, white and blue on their wing-tips! Someone suggested they were our training planes getting away whilst the going was good, and it seemed the only reasonable explanation . . . It was a long time before we realized that we had very few aircraft in Malaya and that they were nearly all out of date. Neither did we appreciate at the time the splendid fight our pilots put up in their 100-m.p.h. crates against the superior Jap craft.

Our confidence was again shattered when, a few minutes later, we saw a squadron of low-winged monoplanes approaching from the north. "At last!" we said. "Here come the Spitfires!" We stood out in the open and cheered, but rushed for cover when they started dive-bombing and machine-gunning the drome. This time it *was* the Japs. Before we went into action that night we saw most of the hangars on fire and all the aircraft on the ground destroyed. Our air arm had ceased to function.

As soon as night fell we received the order to fire. I was a signaller, and grew more miserable as the night wore on, trying to

LANDINGS AT KOTA BHARU opened the Japanese offensive against the British forces in Malaya in Dec. 1941. Assault troops came ashore in landing barges under cover of fire from a fleet of warships. Lightly equipped, very mobile and well-trained in jungle warfare, the Japanese threatened to overwhelm the scanty British force in the north-east corner of the country. If the landing at one point was checked another would be made at a different place, probably miles behind the British front line.
From the drawing by Leo Rawlings

CIVILIANS EVACUATING KOTA BHARU streamed out to escape the Japanese invaders on the night of Dec. 7-8, 1941. Smoke from burning oil-dumps rises thickly in the background. *From the drawing by L. Rawlings*

and the railway remained the only way open to the south and safety. One by one, whilst still firing, the guns were withdrawn and hauled to the station. All night we worked loading guns, vehicles, ammunition and other war material on to the open railway trucks, and as dawn broke we pulled out en route for Kuala Lumpur, some 200 miles to the south-west, and to what we thought would be a rest, with time to overhaul our equipment and strengthen our defences. Strange how optimism refuses to die, even when one knows the odds are piled heavily in the enemy's favour.

But such was the speed of the Jap advance that within a few days we were once again in the front line. By January 11, Kuala Lumpur and its aerodrome had to be abandoned. And so the sad story continued until February 15, 1942, when at Singapore we received the order to cease fire—and we commenced our weary three and a half years as prisoners of war.

get messages through on a faulty line, and to hear and make myself heard above the continuous noise of the howitzers only ten yards away. Then it started raining ; and indeed it knows how to rain in Malaya. I had orders to try to repair the cable leading to our other troop of guns. Having no torch I had to grope my way through the undergrowth, and when I reached " Eddy " Troop I found they had ceased fire and were preparing to move. I dashed as fast as I could in the darkness back to my own lines and with more luck than judgement managed to find my vehicle.

Knew Not What Was Happening

The main route from Kota Bharu that night looked like the London-Brighton Road on a Bank Holiday. Hundreds of vehicles were trailing each other with headlights full on. If the Jap Air Force had thought to come our way then all would have been lost. And so for the next fortnight the battle raged along the 50 miles to Kuala Krai. Days and nights had little meaning for us. We slept and ate when we could. It was impossible to stay in one position for longer than 24 hours, as the Jap pilots would spot us. So we would go into action for as long as possible, beat a hasty retreat, find a " hide " a few miles farther down the road, then go into action again. So it went on, a queer nightmare without beginning or end.

None of us knew exactly what was happening. We didn't even realize that the war was going badly for us and that on the other side of the Peninsula the Japs were making a far speedier advance. Having a knowledge of shorthand, it became my job (when we weren't in action), to tune-in to the B.B.C. every night and take down the news. We felt quite proud when the announcer stated that British troops in the north-east of Malaya had made contacts with the enemy. It often struck us as quaint that people in London, 5,000 miles away, knew more of what was going on out here than we did !

Although we thought we were putting up quite a good show we realized it couldn't last. Losses among the Indian infantry were enormous, and we were always in danger of being cut off by the enemy thrust through Penang. Eventually we were finally driven back to Kuala Krai, where the road ended

STREET FIGHTING DEVELOPED AT KUALA LUMPUR as the Japanese followed hard on the heels of the close-pressed and greatly outnumbered British forces. Though each road-crossing (upper) was hotly contested the enemy worked through the town, as these Japanese photographs show, covering the main advance with light automatic weapons (lower).

Chased by a Radio-Controlled Bomb

Searching for U-boats off the coast of Spain, on August 27, 1943, H.M.S. Grenville made the uncomfortably close acquaintance of an eerie secret weapon—dubbed "Chase-Me-Charlie" by the Royal Navy. What happened is told by Lieut. John Herbert, R.N.V.R. (portrait in page 570).

THE war seemed very far away. A few miles distant lay the coast, its azure blue mountains dimly visible in the sweltering heat. Officer of the Watch, signalmen and look-outs had discarded their shirts, and their brown backs were evidence of the days we had spent in the Bay of Biscay under the heat of the sun. We were off the north-west corner of Spain—Cape Ortegal—with the sloop Egret, the frigates Rother and Jed and the Canadian destroyer Athabaskan, searching for U-boats which were in the habit of returning to their hide-outs in French ports by creeping round this corner of Spain and then up the coast.

It was about 1 o'clock when the alarm sounded. Everyone in the wardroom made a dive for the door, and on reaching the bridge we found we were being attacked by about 20 JU 88s which had come in very high but were now flying at about 3,000 feet, circling around us. All ships had broken formation and were now manoeuvring at high speed. Over towards Spain I saw a long line of splashes where a stick of bombs had fallen quite near to one of the frigates.

The Captain ordered "Open fire," and the Grenville shuddered at the first salvo. For 20 minutes we were firing while the ship heeled under full helm and the increase of speed. We shifted target continually, in order to engage as many aircraft as possible. The little frigates were armed only with 3-inch guns and contributed little to the barrage we had to put up to keep the Germans at bay. Presently we noticed that several aircraft were flying parallel to each ship's course and not attempting to make the usual bombing attack. That was ominous, for the day before we had received a signal from another ship that had been attacked by aircraft armed with a new secret weapon.

Suddenly an object, looking rather like a paravane—a small body with short wings set in the middle—darted out from underneath the fuselage of the aircraft nearest to us. The bomb, which was emitting quantities of smoke from its tail where there seemed to be some kind of rocket propulsion, started off in the opposite direction to that in which we were going. When it was about 300 yards in front of the parent aircraft it started to turn towards us.

Searching for Egret's Survivors

The captain altered course—and the bomb changed direction with us ; it was approaching us fast now and everyone's gaze was fixed on this uncanny horror. The close-range weapons—the Oerlikons and Bofors guns—beat out a rapid tattoo, but the thing was moving very swiftly and the gunners found it difficult to assess the deflection. "Hard a'starboard full ahead together !" ordered the Captain, looking over his shoulder at the fast-approaching bomb.

"Thank God ! " most of us muttered, for now we were swinging under full rudder faster than the bomb could turn, and as it plunged into our wake we heaved sighs of relief. We had been so preoccupied that we had had little time to see how the other ships were faring. Now we saw that the Egret had been hit. We spotted her through a huge mushroom-shaped pillar of smoke

STRUCK BY A SECRET WEAPON, H.M.S. EGRET appeared as a huge pillar of smoke and flame (top), then was seen sinking (above), off the coast of Spain in August 1943. Completed in 1938, the Egret's displacement was 1,200 tons and designed speed 19·25 knots; main armament, eight 4-in. A.A. guns. The author of this story, who served in H.M.S. Grenville, which narrowly escaped the Egret's fate, recounts the uncanny experience of pursuit by one of these secret weapons—a radio-controlled bomb.

Admiralty photographs

GERMAN RADIO-CONTROLLED BOMB, directed towards a large Allied convoy by the pilot of the parent aircraft, swoops down upon its selected target. Though this secret weapon was at first very successful against merchant shipping, its premature use in attacks on warships permitted counter-measures to be developed before the losses had assumed serious proportions.

just after her magazines had blown up, exploding hundreds of rounds of Oerlikon and Bofors shells. Through the smoke and flame we saw her roll slowly over.

We had another bomb directed at us, but now we knew what to look out for. It was towards the end of the attack that the Athabaskan was hit. A bomb struck her just below the bridge and started a fire on B gun deck. She was immediately enveloped in clouds of cordite smoke, but she fired on ; through the smoke we saw four of her six guns belching. The Germans had now used up all their bombs and departed to the east. Keeping a good look-out for any more aircraft that might be lurking around, we set about searching for survivors of the Egret, whose bows were still visible. Wreckage was strewn over a large area and over it all the thick sickly smell of fuel-oil. The latter was inches thick on the water, and it saturated the hammocks, fenders and general flotsam. We saw a few small groups of survivors, trying to keep together, every now and again giving a shout, and we must have seemed agonizingly slow in our approach to them.

Amazing Underwater Experience

The three ships lay stopped and were lowering boats as quickly as they could. These were soon hard at work, returning to us every few minutes, their human cargo so exhausted that they lay in the positions they had assumed when they were dragged over the side. As each man was received aboard he was taken away to the bathrooms, stripped, and washed with shale oil. Between the three ships about half of the Egret's company was picked up—including her doctor, who had had an amazing experience.

The bomb had, apparently, hit the Egret's depth charges, which accounted for the tremendous explosion, and the shock had stunned him. When he recovered his senses the ship was on her side and every-

thing was in darkness. There was only one small patch of light, and he realized that it must be the surface of the sea : he had somehow got into an air pocket and would have to dive down under the ship if he were

to get out ! This he did, and was now cheerfully engaged in telling us about it—dressed in borrowed clothes and drinking tea.

There came the shrill squeal of the bos'n's call and the cry of " Clear lower deck—up first and second motor boats—up whaler !" and in a few minutes we were once more on patrol. Much to our regret we had to leave the Athabaskan to make her own way back, crippled as she was. The Commander-in-Chief, Plymouth, signalled us that, owing to the pitch which the U-boat warfare had reached, every ship available had to be launched into the fight and we could not be spared to escort the Athabaskan back to England. It was with heavy hearts that we steamed away from her and left her to limp home alone, at the mercy of any JU 88 that might sight her. That night the Germans claimed to have sunk her, but five days later we heard that she had arrived safely in Plymouth harbour.

Sinkings Might Have Been Doubled

From that day, these weapons that had sunk the Egret, damaged the Athabaskan and frightened the wits out of us, were known to the Navy as Chase-me-Charlies. We claim that it was one of the Grenville's able seamen who thought of the name and abbreviated it to C.M.C. They were rocket propelled, and radio-controlled by the pilot in the parent aircraft, who conned the bomb on to his target. The Luftwaffe eventually sank a large number of Allied ships with these bombs, and if they had used them more judiciously they would have doubled their sinkings. Instead of launching their first attacks on a large Atlantic or Mediterranean convoy, or at a beach-head congested with shipping, the first and second attacks were against a small and relatively unimportant naval force that could manoeuvre with far more flexibility than any slow-moving convoy ; and the result was that a detailed description of the secret weapon and the tactics to be used when avoiding it was soon circulated to the Allied fleets.

ᔕᔕᔕᔕᔕᔕᔕ NEW FACTS AND FIGURES ᔕᔕᔕᔕᔕᔕᔕ

ALL over East Africa branches of the British Legion are springing up, members being mainly coloured ex-Servicemen who volunteered during the war and served in many parts of the world. In Kenya, Tanganyika, Uganda and Nyasaland there are now nearly 40,000 Legionaries, and a special badge has been produced for native members : about the size of a sixpence, made of an alloy that will not deteriorate in hot climates, it has a ring and safety-pin for attaching to native clothing.

THE first of two ships carrying 955,000 pairs of footwear for men, women and children in the British zone of Germany docked at Hamburg in November 1946. German production of footwear is rising, but even with this British consignment it is possible to provide only every third person in the zone with a pair of boots or shoes.

HAMBURG at the end of 1946 was still the most badly damaged port of North-West Europe. At the time of the German surrender (May 1945) 75 per cent of the installations had been destroyed. The amount in working order has been increased to 40 per cent, but the cargo turnover in 1946 was no more than 4,000,000 tons, compared with 25,000,000 tons in 1938.

BREMEN, next biggest German port, and its sister ports of Blumenthal and Bremerhaven, also lost 75 per cent of their installations. With 50 per cent again in operation they handled some 3,800,000 tons in 1946 against 6,000,000 before the war.

RELEASES from British forces and auxiliary and nursing services in October 1946 totalled 117,960. The number of men and

women released and discharged from June 18, 1945, when demobilization began, to the end of October 1946 was 4,109,730 ; the target was 4,098,420.

IN the British zone of Germany 48 factories worked to produce a Christmas allocation of sweets for German children up to 18 years of age. More than 1,625 tons of sugar, besides other ingredients, were required to produce the ration of just under nine ounces for each child. No sweets are normally available for German children.

THE last contingent of British and Indian soldiers left Batavia on November 29, 1946. Their 14 months in the Netherlands East Indies from September 1945 had cost the British Army 63 killed, 153 wounded and 23 missing ; the R.A.F. 22 killed, 22 wounded and one missing ; and the British Indian forces 528 killed, 1,239 wounded and 297 missing. Our forces, including the Royal Navy, evacuated 125,000 people, among them 84,000 prisoners of war and civilian internees ; the R.A.F. alone flew 30,000 people out of the islands. Our troops disarmed and repatriated 300,000 Japanese and collected huge quantities of arms and ammunition ; landed 700,000 tons of supplies ; rehabilitated docks and restored essential services.

PLANS are being made for the return home of some 50,000 of the 200,000 German refugees in Denmark. The British zone is receiving 12,000 ; Russian military authorities announced in November 1946 that they would accept 15,000 Germans who before their evacuation were resident in the Russian zone ; the French and American zones are to take 12,000 each.

Daughter of One Faithful Unto Death

Photo, G.P.U.

HER MOTHER'S GEORGE CROSS will be four-year-old Tania Szabo's most treasured possession in the years to come. On Dec. 17, 1946, it was announced that Violette Szabo, the English widow of a French officer, had been awarded the George Cross nearly two years after she had been shot by the Germans for her work with the Maquis : the story is in page 631. According to her grandfather, Mr Charles Bushell, of Brixton, London, Tania is the image of her mother and a great tomboy.

Printed in England and published every alternate Friday by the Proprietors, THE AMALGAMATED PRESS, LTD. The Fleetway House, Farringdon Street, London, E.C.4. Registered for transmission by Canadian Magazine Post. Sole Agents for Australia and New Zealand : Messrs. Gordon & Gotch, Ltd. ; and for South Africa : Central News Agency, Ltd.—January 17, 1947.   S.S.   *Editorial Address :* JOHN CARPENTER HOUSE, WHITEFRIARS, LONDON, E.C.4.

Vol 10 *The War Illustrated* Nº 251

SIXPENCE

I WAS THERE

JANUARY 31, 1947

PIPE MAJOR OF THE 5th BATTALION THE 1st PUNJAB REGIMENT led his pipers and drummers in the grounds of the Imperial Palace, Tokyo, in December 1946, when Punjabis and a company of the 27th Regiment of the U.S. Army mounted a joint Palace guard. Several Indian and Gurkha regiments have a similar band, of which they are immensely proud. The Indian units with the British Commonwealth Occupation Force have created an excellent impression in Japan. (See also page 646.)

Edited by Sir John Hammerton

Sicilian Adventure : Prelude to Italy's Fall

PART OF THE VAST INVASION FLEET that transported Allied forces to Sicily in July 1943 is seen (top) anchored offshore to land troops, tanks, guns, ammunition, food and all stores required by an army in the field. Tactical loading ensured that what would have to be unloaded first was loaded last and that each unit was accompanied by its equipment. New types of invasion craft were used. Prisoners marching along the beach (bottom) gazed in amazement. See story in facing page, also page 601.

Photos, British Official

How the Marines Went In at Sicily

By Major
W. R. SENDALL, R.M.

At dawn one day in the last weeks of June 1943 a powerful military force landed on the beaches between Troon and Irvine on the west coast of Scotland, advanced a little distance inland and then turned around, marched back to the harbour, re-embarked and disappeared.

I have often wondered if the good citizens of Troon, who watched those troops—men of the 1st Canadian Division and of the Royal Marine Commandos—march singing through the rain back to their ships realized that this brief incursion was the last rehearsal of one piece of the invasion of Sicily, the landing of the left-flank division of the 8th Army. The beaches between Troon and Irvine had been selected for their similarity to another beach on the west of the Pachino peninsula, at that time being anxiously patrolled by disillusioned soldiers of an Italian coast defence division, who little realized the nature of the thunderbolt being prepared so far away for their annihilation.

Certainly we ourselves knew little enough of our destination. But we did know that we were training to attack coast defences somewhere on that long coastline from Narvik to Salonika, that our part involved landing before the main force, scaling a cliff to take the defences in the rear, and clearing the way for a dawn landing by the Canadians. Every move in this action, which needed speed and perfect timing for success, had been worked out precisely. Each Troop knew the distance from the landing point to its objective, the order in which attacks were to be made, and the relationship of their task to that of other Troops of the Commando. Where the blow would fall, however, we had no idea.

The Troon exercise was the last "dummy" run. The whole complex machinery of an amphibious assault was tried out between midnight and first light, the staff watching the dress rehearsal anxiously to apply the last drops of oil that would ensure a smooth performance on the day.

The veil was lifted a few days later when we were at sea in our fine transport, the Durban Castle. The great ships of the convoy ploughed zealously forward, constantly altering course and station, weaving in and out like grand ladies in some intricate, progressive dance that was not to end till they dropped anchor again after more than 2,000 miles. After 36 hours of this, the ships' companies were told to assemble near the loudspeakers, and with mounting excitement they heard the secret revealed by Admiral Vian. Well I remember his words : "We are sailing to take part in the greatest combined operation in history, the invasion of Italy through Sicily."

Through Waters Rich in History

Following this announcement the sealed parcels of maps and air photographs were torn open and the final stage of battle-briefing began. Our Marines were shown on map, air photograph and scale model just where the manoeuvres they had practised so sedulously would fit on the actual ground, just who were the enemy against whose imaginary presence they had fired thousands of rounds of ammunition during the past months of training. After a general outline of the plan by our commander, Lieut.-Col. "Bertie" Lumsden, R.M., each Troop Commander went over it in the minutest detail with each man individually. So painstaking was this briefing that one Troop Commander made a scale model of a building it was his task to capture, basing it on air photos, indicating to each man the point for which he would make.

We were attacking the defences on and west of a narrow promontory, the Punta di Castellazzo ; after scaling the cliffs we would reach a footpath running between the cliff-top and a shallow salt lake inland. This path gave us direction to reach the various strongpoints, which included a fortified villa—the Casa della Marza—that commanded the only exit from the beach where the Seaforth Highlanders of Canada were landing. Having destroyed these strongpoints we would move inland to help hold the left flank of the beach perimeter while the Canadians landed their heavy weapons.

So the time passed, and Gibraltar slipped by in the night. On July 9 we were sailing between Cap Bon and Sicily, through waters richer in history than the North Sea with herring. Quite suddenly one of those startling Mediterranean gales blew up, one of those outbreaks of ill-tempered violence such as plagued Odysseus and St. Paul. We were all alarmed lest the plan which had been nourished so carefully should have to be changed or abandoned. The Hilary, Admiral Vian's headquarter ship, butted her way through the waves, and from her yard-arm hung a black ball. In the late afternoon every eye in the convoy was directed at that ball, which would be dropped to give us a time signal whereby to synchronize watches. If the ball dropped we should know that the show was on.

It fell at 17.00 hours precisely. Tomorrow was D-Day. One might have said, like Caesar at the Rubicon, "The die is cast." But personally I said nothing of the kind. Like most of the Marines, I went to bed.

I woke at nine, had a shower and went down to supper. Then back to dress for the show, a really elaborate process. First a good pair of socks—a pair once washed and without darns ; then one's best boots, well broken-in by long marches across the Scottish hills and dubbined till they were soft as gloves. We knew well that a soldier in battle is just as good as his feet. Long drill slacks would give protection against mosquitoes ; short puttees and a bush shirt completed the rig. Then we climbed, amid great hilarity, into our bulky equipment, loaded with ammunition, grenades, rations, with ropes and climbing irons for the leaders. Personal possessions—photographs of wives and sweethearts, watches, fountain pens—were waterproofed by any and every kind of ingenious, improvised means.

CAPTAIN OF A LANDING CRAFT addresses his company and the soldiers who will help storm the beaches, prior to the invasion of Sicily on July 10, 1943. The success of this amphibious operation largely depended on the skill and courage of the commanders of these little vessels, who had to beach their craft at the right spot at the correct moment. PAGE 643 *Photo, British Official*

WADING ASHORE FROM LANDING CRAFT, British troops found the opposition unexpectedly light : the Sicilian shore defences collapsing under the initial assault. Months of training and planning down to the smallest detail preceded the operation, in which Britons, Canadians and Americans participated, Royal Marine Commandos forming our spearhead.   *Photo, British Official*

Then the last touch : to wipe the oil from rifles, Bren guns and pistols, for oil would pick up sand and clog the action. We had just finished when we were aware that the vibration of the ship's engines, continuous accompaniment of every moment, day and night, since we left the Clyde, had stopped. It was midnight. A sudden quietness fell. Then the ship's loudspeakers crackled, and the voice of the Senior Naval Officer controlling the landing was heard.

"Can you hear me ? Can you hear me ? Control calling all Naval personnel and Royal Marine Commando. To operation stations—to operation stations." The Marines hitched up their heavy packs and tramped quietly along the dim-lit corridors and up the brass-bound ladders to the boat-deck. The gale had dropped as suddenly as it arose. The stars were brilliant, but they were dimmed by the long line of flares with which the R.A.F. illuminated the coastline of Sicily. An endless roar of bombers and the distant, shuddering thump of bombs filled the night air.

Instructed by the voice over the loud-speaker we packed ourselves in our assault craft, swinging from the davits. I quenched an irresistible desire for a smoke by sucking a boiled sweet. After a tense few minutes, Control ordered : "Davits numbers 1—3—5—7—9, lower awa-ay." The falls whined

and the little craft swung down the cliff-side of the ship, till we were heaving and tossing on a sea still disturbed by the recent storm.

We cruised around for what seemed endless time while blue signal lamps flashed, then fell into formation and set off at top speed for the coast. Soon, but for the loom of a protecting flakship, the little flotilla was alone. The dim mass of Sicily lay on the starboard bow as we ran diagonally inshore. The swell was heavy, crashing on the blunt ramps of our craft. Presently I noticed a trickle of cold sea-water running round my boots. In a few moments it rose above my ankles, then half-way to my knees. We were shipping an uncomfortable amount of water and called for the pump, but so tightly were we packed that there was not enough room to work the hand-pump. I heaved myself out of the well-deck and lay flat on the coconut matting of the flat top of the engine-room aft. Others followed, lying beside me and on the flat gunwales, leaving room for the rest to pump and bale with their steel helmets. But the water still rose and we were forced to reduce speed, dropping out of place in the formation.

The land was close now. Startlingly, a searchlight stabbed a bright finger out to sea and swept the tumbled surface. Just as we thought it must illuminate us, it snapped off.

In another minute a gun fired close at hand. I flattened on the deck instinctively, but it was an anti-aircraft gun engaging bombers overhead. The whole flotilla then altered course directly inshore and changed formation into line abreast for the run-in. The engines revved up, and we raced into the shadowy arms of a cove.

From the left a machine-gun opened fire, stuttering a few bursts. The bullets shrieked overhead. The beach was narrower than we expected, with long, rocky shelves running out, between which the craft had to feel their way slowly. Our craft grounded quietly, the ramps went down and we leapt from the cold water of the well-deck into the lukewarm surf, ploughing in to the beach.

The Machine-Guns Fired No More

We were surprised to find there was no cliff, only a long shelf of limestone, across which it was not difficult to scramble, but it was several minutes before we realized it was the wrong beach. The machine-guns were mercifully silent, but as we crossed this shelf they opened up again, catching some of our men in their deadly swathe. We took shelter to reorganize in a shallow depression in the sand-hills, where the bullets kicked up the sand on the banks around us and whined harmlessly overhead. It took a little time to pick up landmarks in the darkness, but scouts reconnoitring forward located the footpath, and after that the Troops moved off confidently for their objectives.

As I moved forward, crouching low over the rough grass of the sand-dunes, to join headquarters, I heard shrieks and shouts in Italian from the left, the burst of a grenade, followed by silence. Then a stream of red tracer shot out towards the little headland whence the machine-gun post had been firing. The machine-guns fired no more. Further bursts of red tracer marked for us at head-quarters the progress of other Troops as they made their way along the cliffs from strong-point to strongpoint, towards the Punta di Castellazzo and the Casa.

Quite quickly, it seemed, the sun came up and flooded the scene with brilliant light. As I made my way up the cliff path to find out the position on the Punta I saw a large batch of Italians with their hands above their heads making their way back to the beach, escorted by a single Marine. On the edge of the cliff I passed a machine-gun nest, its defenders dead at their guns, surrounded by thousands of rounds of unfired ammuni-tion. The rising sun illuminated the white Casa in its dominating position, and a stream of tracer rose high towards one of its upper windows as the Marines put paid to a sniper.

When I reached the top of the headland the battle was ended. I looked down over the main beaches, and in the great bay the big ships lay close inshore, while streams of small craft and DUKWS, like water-beetles, plied busily to and fro. The Canadians were ashore and already pushing up the dusty road to meet us. A big monitor pumped its shells regularly at some target far inland, and three Spitfires were the sole tenants of the intensely blue immensity of the sky. There seemed no sign of opposition anywhere, though a few shots could be heard from the left where our men were rounding up stragglers and snipers.

At the Casa della Marza I found a dilapi-dated bicycle, which I commandeered and rode down the rough, narrow road to meet the Canadians coming up. The men I spoke to told me they had only one casualty. It seemed almost an anti-climax, after our months of planning and training, to succeed with such ease, but it was because of that meticulous care that the operation had indeed gone "according to plan."

Secrets of our Motorized Submersible Canoes

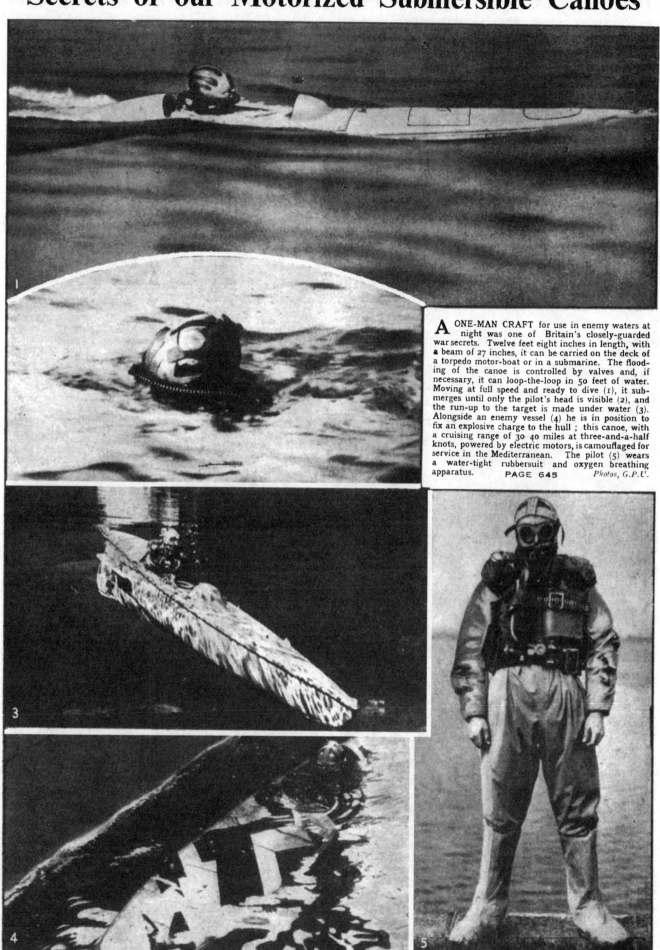

A ONE-MAN CRAFT for use in enemy waters at night was one of Britain's closely-guarded war secrets. Twelve feet eight inches in length, with a beam of 27 inches, it can be carried on the deck of a torpedo motor-boat or in a submarine. The flooding of the canoe is controlled by valves and, if necessary, it can loop-the-loop in 50 feet of water. Moving at full speed and ready to dive (1), it submerges until only the pilot's head is visible (2), and the run-up to the target is made under water (3). Alongside an enemy vessel (4) he is in position to fix an explosive charge to the hull ; this canoe, with a cruising range of 30–40 miles at three-and-a-half knots, powered by electric motors, is camouflaged for service in the Mediterranean. The pilot (5) wears a water-tight rubbersuit and oxygen breathing apparatus.　PAGE 645　　*Photos, G.P.U.*

Indian Troops Share Tokyo Guard with Americans

UNITED at a joint guard-mounting parade at Tokyo in December 1946, with the band of the 5th Battalion The 1st Punjab Regiment on the left and the Indian guard on the right (1), the American contingent being in the centre, troops were drawn up for inspection by Brig.-Gen. R. E. Starr of the U.S. Army (3). Owing to their uncut hair being coiled on the tops of their heads, Sikhs of the Punjab Regiment are unable to wear steel helmets. Indian regiments delight in "spit-and-polish," so it seemed quite natural to the buglers that they should dust one another's boots at the last moment (2). At the parade were Jemadar Singh and Capt. Dale, both of the 5th Battalion, and Technical-Sgt. E. Lacoutorf of the 27th Regiment U.S. Army (4). See also illus. page 641.

Photos, Planet News

Jap-Held Drum of Royal Scots Coming Home

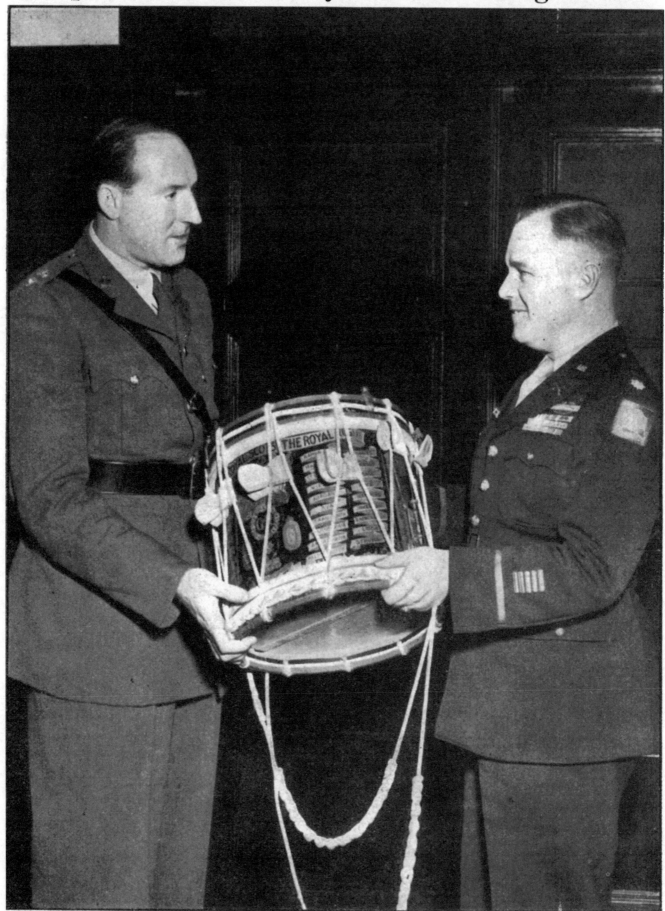

FOUND IN THE MILITARY MUSEUM, TOKYO, this drum of the 2nd Battalion The Royal Scots was handed over to Lieut.-Col. G. Figgess (left), of the U.K. Liaison Mission in Japan, by Lieut.-Col. F. R. Sibbert, of the U.S. Army, in Tokyo in November 1946, for transmission to its original owners. When the Japanese overran Hongkong in December 1941 they captured also the Regimental Colour; this was recovered in Singapore and is now at The Royal Scots Depot, Glencorse, Midlothian.

Photo, Planet News

Stern Toil for Berliners in Winter's Keen Grip

DAILY TASK OF THOUSANDS in Germany's capital is sorting millions of useable bricks recovered from bomb-shattered buildings. Well-wrapped against the biting cold—in January 1947 the thermometer recorded 24 degrees of frost—a woman (right) chips mortar from salvaged bricks while others at the dump are securing another load. Only materials readily available for the immense work of reconstruction are those retrieved from the ruins.

COMMUNICATIONS are slowly being restored : overhead cables of the tramway along the Kurfuerstendamm receive attention (below). Debris has been cleared from the main thoroughfares and shops are reopening along this street which was formerly a fashionable shopping centre. With their few possessions on a handcart a woman and her husband (lower right) set out for another dwelling. The centre of the city is a vast waste, though streets have been cleared and the ruins tidied-up. Conditions are better in the little-damaged suburbs, notably Frohnau and Zeylandorf, to the north-west and south-west of the city.

Photos, Associated Press

PAGE 648

Royal Daffodil of Great Renown is 'Demobbed'

PLEASURE STEAMER KNOWN TO THOUSANDS of cross-Channel passengers before the war, Royal Daffodil was released by the Royal Navy in January 1947 and returned to her berth at Deptford, London, to refit. Requisitioned at the beginning of the war, she carried 2½ million troops. Now she will "work" the London-Ostend route. Members of her crew before and during the war : J. Benham and S. Bell (top left) ; Capt. A. Patterson, D.S.O., and G. Smith (top right). See also pages 458-459, Vol. 9.

Photos, John Topham

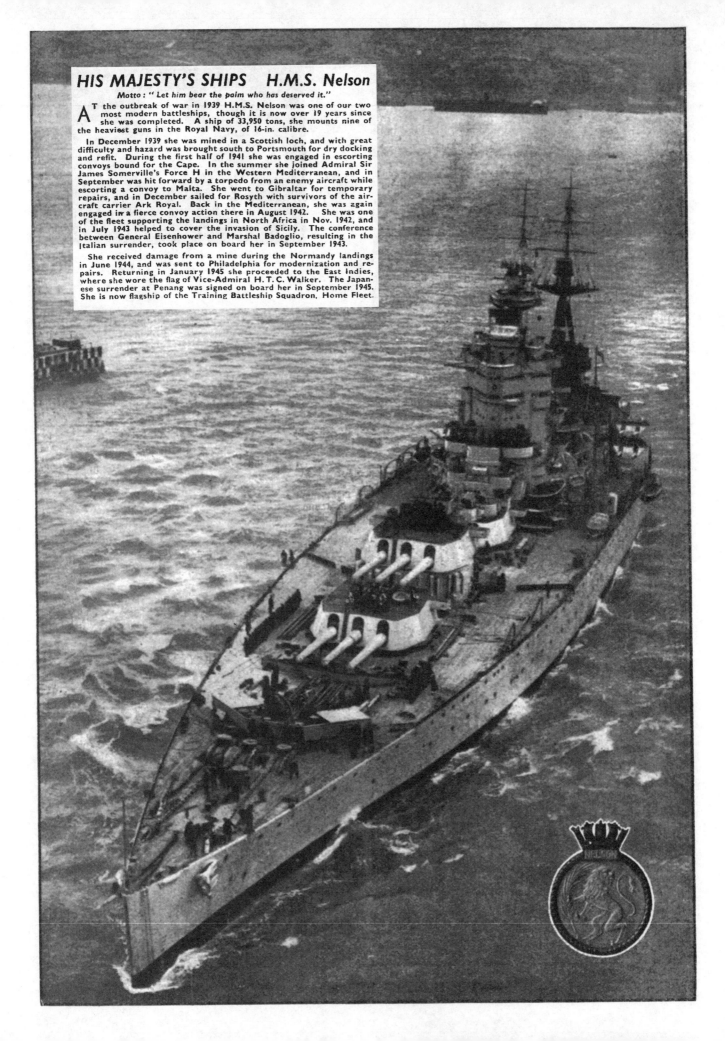

HIS MAJESTY'S SHIPS H.M.S. Nelson

Motto : " Let him bear the palm who has deserved it."

AT the outbreak of war in 1939 H.M.S. Nelson was one of our two most modern battleships, though it is now over 19 years since she was completed.   A ship of 33,950 tons, she mounts nine of the heaviest guns in the Royal Navy, of 16-in. calibre.

In December 1939 she was mined in a Scottish loch, and with great difficulty and hazard was brought south to Portsmouth for dry docking and refit.   During the first half of 1941 she was engaged in escorting convoys bound for the Cape.   In the summer she joined Admiral Sir James Somerville's Force H in the Western Mediterranean, and in September was hit forward by a torpedo from an enemy aircraft while escorting a convoy to Malta.   She went to Gibraltar for temporary repairs, and in December sailed for Rosyth with survivors of the aircraft carrier Ark Royal.   Back in the Mediterranean, she was again engaged in a fierce convoy action there in August 1942.   She was one of the fleet supporting the landings in North Africa in Nov. 1942, and in July 1943 helped to cover the invasion of Sicily.   The conference between General Eisenhower and Marshal Badoglio, resulting in the Italian surrender, took place on board her in September 1943.

She received damage from a mine during the Normandy landings in June 1944, and was sent to Philadelphia for modernization and repairs.   Returning in January 1945 she proceeded to the East Indies, where she wore the flag of Vice-Admiral H.T.C. Walker.   The Japanese surrender at Penang was signed on board her in September 1945. She is now flagship of the Training Battleship Squadron, Home Fleet.

The Highland Light Infantry

By Major-General Sir Andrew McCulloch, K.B.E.

The national tradition of producing too small and ill-prepared an army for its initial task results in hard knocks for those early in the field. So, early in the Second Great War, the 1st Battalion (like others) had to stand up to the Wehrmacht in its prime and overwhelming superiority in tanks and aircraft. In Belgium in 1940 the 1st was attacked by a Panzer Regiment which it repulsed with skill and courage. Lieut.-Colonel J. D. Russell and others were decorated for their fine work ; but withdrawal to Dunkirk was inevitable, and au revoir was said to Europe till 1944. It then joined in the defeat of the Germans in Normandy, and won high praise for many successes in the Low Countries.

The 2nd Battalion joined with an Indian Force in chasing the Italian troops out of the Sudan and Eritrea in the spring of 1941, from Abu Hamed and Barentu, and also in the epic battle of Keren. During one of the actions, the company of Captain Mark Hollis was ordered to take an important hill. It came under heavy machine-gun fire from a flank. But Hollis pressed on, and reached the top of the hill with some 13 men. Meanwhile, he had been wounded. Once on the hill the small band came under heavy gun and mortar fire.

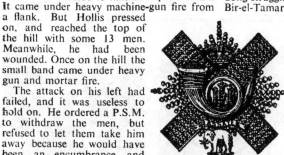

The attack on his left had failed, and it was useless to hold on. He ordered a P.S.M. to withdraw the men, but refused to let them take him away because he would have been an encumbrance and would have prevented them getting clear in time. He knew that as soon as the enemy reoccupied the hill the British Artillery would come down on it. It did, and Mark Hollis was killed ; but he set a magnificent example of self-sacrifice and heroism. Some time later the Italian general concerned was captured.

The Regiment was formed by the union of the 71st Highland Light Infantry and 74th Highlanders in 1881. These regiments were raised after the Jacobite Rising of 1745, and contained many sons of the Jacobite Highlanders. Discounting the memories of the harsh treatment meted out to their fathers after Culloden, they went to fight alongside their old foes the Sassenach. The Regiment has taken part in Britain's most memorable battles from Vimiero in 1808 until the final defeat of the Nazis in 1945.

He asked to see the Commanding Officer and told him he had been astounded at the bravery of the Highlanders at Barentu.

In the Western Desert campaigns the 2nd Battalion earned fame in that ferocious ding-dong struggle. On June 5, 1942, after taking Bir-el-Tamar it was counter-attacked by tanks and infantry from lorries. One company was overrun, but the rest held up the enemy. Casualties were severe and the Commanding Officer, Lieut.-Col. Thorburn, was wounded. An independent witness tells of a fine example of devotion to duty by the hard-pressed troops at this juncture. A battery of 25-pounders escorted by a Bren gun and six men of the Highland Light Infantry was ordered to cover a gap in a minefield till some of our columns had passed. Desperately assailed, the guns fired over open sights against the attacking Germans, and after one had been knocked out the Captain gave the order to withdraw. There was a sudden lull in the firing, and in the dusk of the evening six ghostly figures advanced calmly and deliberately against overwhelming odds — moving and firing steadily as though on the parade ground. Taken by surprise, possibly by the sheer boldness of the Highlanders' action, the Germans halted—long enough for the guns to get away.

In the fighting retreat to El Alamein the 2nd Battalion was so roughly handled that it was withdrawn to reorganize, and took no further part until Tunisia was won. At the landing in Sicily Lieut.-Col. Thorburn was killed by a sniper—a sad loss. Thereafter the Battalion fought in Italy and on the Dalmatian coast islands. Later on it was given the unenviable task of repressing the E.L.A.S. faction in Athens.

During the first year of the war the 12th (Home Defence) Battalion was raised from men who were too old or unfit for general service abroad. Many men were veterans of the First Great War, and some of the war in South Africa. This Battalion did much useful work in watching the coast and guarding factories and docks in Scotland.

Three Territorial Battalions, the 5th, 6th and 1st Glasgow Highlanders, H.L.I., went to France in 1940 and were used in a fruitless attempt to support the French Army. From a variety of causes the French Divisions no longer had the intention of fighting. By the skin of their teeth, and after losses in men and transport, the Battalions made good their withdrawal to Cherbourg and re-embarkation. They did not see Europe again until 1944, when the 5th and 1st Glasgow Highlanders Battalions, H.L.I., took a leading part in freeing Antwerp and the mouth of the Scheldt.

As a preparation for the capture of Walcheren Island, which was essential for the command of the Scheldt, the 5th Battalion had to seize the village of Molenberg. Thereafter, it had a difficult task in landing on the Island. But this it carried out in spite of muddy shores and enemy shelling.

H.L.I. BATTALIONS WERE IN BOTH FRANCE AND NORTH AFRICA in 1940. The stretcher bearers (left) at Conges, on the Seine front, in June 1940, were members of the Band and, as such, entitled to wear kilts. Three Territorial battalions went to France with the 52nd (Lowland) Division to support the disintegrating French army, but had to re-embark at Cherbourg. The 2nd Battalion helped to strengthen the defences of Mersa Matruh (right) in the same year, and later distinguished itself in the North African campaign.

Photos, British Official

SKIRL OF THE PIPES in the Libyan Desert heartened comrades who had been living and fighting there for two years. In June 1942 the 2nd Battalion H.L.I. suffered in contact with enemy armour and had severe casualties during the withdrawal to Alamein.

The final assault on Walcheren was to take place with 155 Brigade landing and capturing the Port of Flushing, while the 157 (H.L.I.) Brigade was to cross the narrow causeway between South Beveland and the Island—an embankment some 1,200 yards long and 40 yards wide. A Canadian regiment (The Regiment Maison Neuve) had gained most of the crossing but were unable to advance beyond the west end thereof.

THE 1st Glasgow Highlanders (H.L.I.) were ordered to relieve the Canadians, but did not get more than two-thirds of the way across. However, this enabled the Canadians to withdraw. A forward movement was well-nigh impossible. The Germans realized the importance of the causeway, and the place was under heavy fire from Spandaus, mortars and artillery. A, B and D Companies lay all day in this stricken area, warding off

a series of counter-attacks at dusk and during the night. Under cover of darkness C Company brought up food and ammunition, carrying back the wounded to the medical post which had been established at the east end of the causeway.

ON the following day (November 3, 1944) the Air Force came to help, and the Highlanders were encouraged by Typhoon attacks on the enemy defences. Then a landing to the south by the 156th Brigade distracted the German defenders, and after dusk the men were able to gain a small bridge-head west of the causeway. C Company further widened the bridge-head on November 4 by seizing Gronenberg. Owing to the large number of German wounded there Arnemuiden was evacuated by the enemy and occupied by us on November 5. By the 9th, Walcheren was in Allied hands. During the operation the 1st Glasgow Highlanders had captured about nine hundred prisoners. It was a hard task, courageously carried out.

The winter in Holland was enlivened by raids, and at 6 a.m. on December 30, 1944, the enemy launched an attack on the village of Tripsrath held by the 2nd Glasgow Highlanders (H.L.I.). Desperate hand-to-hand

WINSTON CHURCHILL was cheered by the 10th Battalion H.L.I. near Otley, Yorks, in March 1944. The Battalion was with VIII Corps, which was to be the British striking force at the invasion of Normandy. It was a period of intensive training and careful preparation, rigours of the exercises being at times only too realistic.

struggles went on all morning, Captain J. W. Brown and C.S.M. J. Boyd ably defending Company H.Q. by using every type of weapon and grenade available, while the anti-tank detachments fired at the buildings holding the enemy. The Germans in an ultimatum to Captain Brown threatened to shoot prisoners, who included our Carrier and Signals Officer. The answer he returned was that if any British prisoner was shot, German prisoners would be similarly dealt with. Just then the tide of battle turned. No. 8 Platoon of A Coy., led by Lieut. J. Renwick, along with a troop of the Sherwood Rangers, counter-attacked. The enemy were driven back and all our prisoners released. Meanwhile, on the other side of the road down which the enemy was trying to drive towards Geilenkirchen, a company and a half were overrun. Our company, however, gallantly held firm until A Company of the 6th Highland Light Infantry came up and relieved it.

The 6th Battalion arrived independently of the rest of the 157 H.L.I. Brigade and fought in the Nijmegen salient, the Leopold Canal, and in the Sittard offensive, where it

TO AID TITO'S PARTISANS the 2nd Battalion went to the Dalmatian island of Vis in August 1944. Here they became mountaineers, negotiating rocky tracks and scaling cliffs. The sister battalions in the 52nd (Lowland) Division had months of training in mountain warfare before assaulting Walcheren Island, one of the lowest ports of Europe. *Photos, British Official*

Maintaining Proud Traditions of the H.L.I.

ARMOUR AND INFANTRY, which included the H.L.I., advanced together east of Echt (1), in the Southern Netherlands, during the battle to clear the Germans from the west bank of the Maas in November and December 1944. Snow covered the battle-front in January 1945, and patrols of the 1st Battalion Glasgow Highlanders—a Territorial battalion of the Highland Light Infantry—were issued with white camouflage cloaks (2). Sten guns also had white covers. In April 1945, while a patrol from the 5th H.L.I. was reconnoitring on the east bank of the Dortmund-Ems canal near Rheine, Germany, several members were injured by booby traps; as the nearby bridge had been destroyed, wounded were ferried across in a rowing boat (3). The 10th Battalion assaulted Best, near Eindhoven, on Sept. 22, 1944, and took a number of prisoners (4) after Typhoons and the artillery had bombarded enemy positions in a wood.

Photos, British Official

brought off two well-planned and successful attacks on the towns of Bocket and Aphoven.

The 10th H.L.I., 13 days after the landing on the Normandy coast, were in the battle which won the crossings on the River Odon. The attack was furiously opposed by the enemy, who knew it was essential for us to enlarge our bridge-head on the coast. Rundstedt later admitted that their chance of ultimate Nazi victory went as soon as our grip on Normandy was unshakeable. They counter-attacked with tanks, and four infiltrated into a farm close to Battalion H.Q. Captain Scott, without thought of his personal safety, brought two of his anti-tank guns into action at 100 yards range and knocked out all four tanks. For this he won the Military Cross and Lance-Sergeant Oldale the Military Medal.

The 2nd Glasgow Highlanders, H.L.I., were in the same division, the famous 15th, and took a notable part in the battle. Both Battalions were in the operations leading to the crossing of the Seine. Later, the 2nd Glasgow Highlanders had severe struggles in the Ghent area. On September 10, 1944, a platoon made a memorable assault on a

factory and captured two officers and 198 other ranks. Another platoon was vigorously counter-attacked. Private Albert Evans was ordered to cover two roads with his Bren gun while the platoon withdrew. Evans was wounded by Spandau fire, but declined to be removed. He kept his gun in action and died at his post. He had covered the escape of his comrades, killed ten Germans and wounded others.

THE 10th Battalion had a "front seat" at the crossing of the Rhine north of Wesel, with 21st Army Group on March 23, 1945. They crossed in Buffaloes and landed without difficulty, but shortly afterwards became involved with a complete Parachute Battalion in fierce and close fighting. Even Battalion H.Q. was partly surrounded, for the Germans were struggling fanatically. But the Jocks, fighting like demons in close work, with grenades and Sten guns, were not to be denied. After three hours, and as it was getting light, they mastered the Nazis and were able to advance again. Casualties in this action were severe—eight officers and 45 other ranks.

The 10th Battalion also took part along with Scots Guards' tanks in the capture of Uelzen in April, defeating a German plan to hinge their defence of the Lower Elbe on this town. Our advance had been continually held up by German rearguards, which cratered the roads on our direct line of advance. So a bold plan was adopted. The H.L.I. and Scots Guards were directed to make a detour and find an alternative route through a forest in the dark. With men of the H.L.I. mounted on Scots Guards' tanks

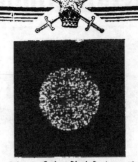

Colours: Red on Black Background

5TH (INDIAN) DIVISION

THE Division was formed in 1939 by Major-General L. Heath, C.B., D.S.O., M.C., who commanded it until April 10, 1941. It left India in September 1940, its first action being against the Italians on the Sudan frontier at Gallabat. It assisted in the capture of Kassala, and at Keren, and received the surrender of the Duke of Aosta at Amba Alagi on May 15, 1941.

From Abyssinia the 5th moved to Iraq and Cyprus, joining the 8th Army in the Western Desert in March 1942. When Rommel attacked in May 1942 the Division fought a rearguard action eastwards from the Gazala line. It suffered heavy losses at Knightsbridge and during the retreat to Mersa Matruh, but gained a notable victory at Ruweisat Ridge on July 16, 1942.

IT then moved to Iraq and Persia, returning to India in June 1943. By the following November it was in action against the Japanese in the Arakan, and relieved the encircled 7th (Indian) Division in February 1944. The 5th took part in the defence of Imphal and Kohima and the reoccupation of Tiddim. After a period of rest in Assam it returned to Burma in March 1945 to participate in the final operations of the 14th Army, fighting its way southwards towards Rangoon.

It held the line of the Sittang River against a stream of Japanese, who probed for lightly-held crossings and endeavoured to make a way across the river to relative safety in the east and south-east. After landing at Singapore on Sept. 5, 1945, the Division was transferred to Java to disarm the Japanese garrison and rescue prisoners of war and internees. There it was engaged in many minor actions against the Indonesian Republican forces. One of the most important was the clearing of Surabaya in November 1945. The city was occupied by a force of 15,000 to 18,000 Indonesians, supported by guns and tanks. The fighting lasted 19 days, the extremists offering fanatical resistance.

the column rumbled on through the night, past villages where German soldiers were sleeping.

Turning a corner as Uelzen was reached, the tanks found themselves "double-banking" a German column, with bewildered Nazis caught on their way to breakfast. Alarm flares set the German garrison of the place in motion and a spirited action took place. The timely arrival of a reinforcing squadron of tanks swung the combat in our favour, but most of our tanks were down to their last round before success was assured.

When the war drew to its close in the dying struggles of the Nazi, all seven battalions of the Regiment which were abroad were well to the fore. At Hamburg, at Bremen and in Italy, they were in at the death when the hour of German doom struck. One may claim that our men in this great struggle maintained the proud tradition of their Regiment. They paid to posterity the debt they owed to the past.

FROM A BEACH IN SOUTHERN ITALY (lower) the 2nd Battalion H.L.I. entered upon the long campaign which opened with the breaching of Germany's European fortress on Sept. 3, 1943. The landing was virtually unopposed. Signallers operating a wireless set (upper) at Cudiolo in March 1945 are Privates W. Gallaghan of Glasgow (right), and J. Gee of Derby.

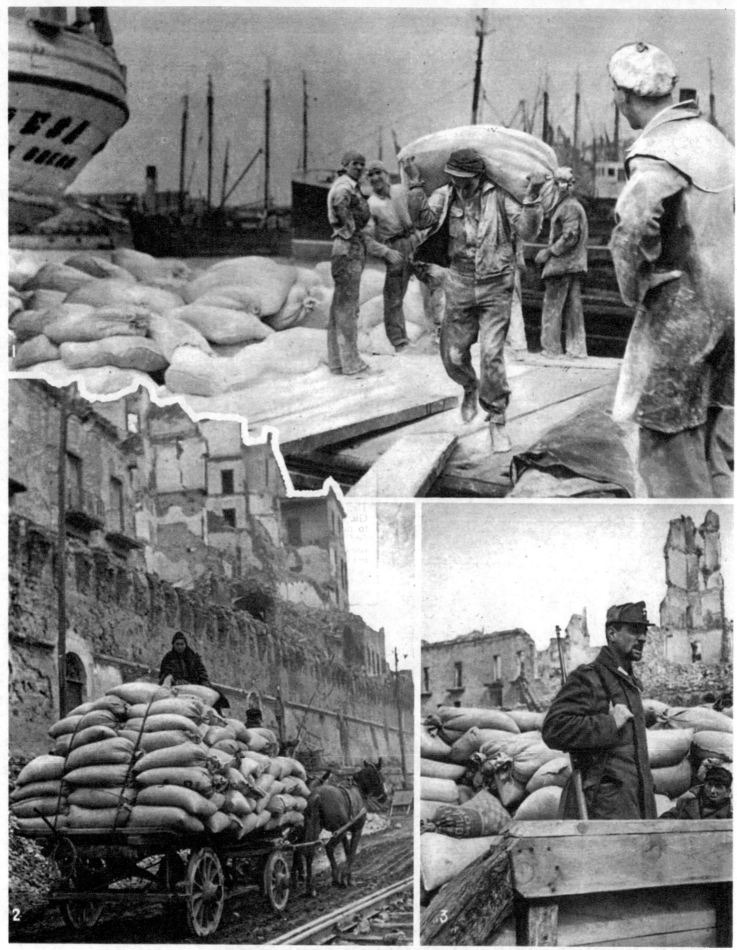

Relieving the Bread Line in Hungry Italy

Shipments of flour are unloaded at bomb-shattered Civitavecchia (1), port of Rome. Sacks of grain are taken by horse-drawn drays (2) to the railway sidings. Armed watch is kept (3) by day and night at the docks; earlier shipments were pilfered, to appear on the black market at extortionate prices. Italy had received 1,844,000 tons of food through U.N.R.R.A. up to December 31, 1946, when, except for the fulfilling of outstanding contracts, that organization ceased to function.

Mechanical Working of Britain's Coal Fields—

On January 1, 1947, our 1,500 British coal mines, acquired by the State, were vested in the National Coal Board (see page 664). Immediate aim is to increase output and improve working conditions by bringing backward mines into line with such as Whitehill Colliery, in Scotland, whose methods are here seen in operation. Unlocking his canister, the shot-firer (1) will extract an explosive " shot " to be placed in a machine-bored hole (2), and 30 tons of coal will be brought down.

Exclus
THE WAR I

—To Meet the Urgent Needs of Vital Industry

An electrically operated cutter (3) penetrates to a depth of about six feet, saving considerable pick work. Loaded into a rubber-tired shuttle-car (4) powered by electric batteries and driven by a Bevin boy, the coal is transferred to a conveyor belt (5) which moves it to trucks on the main pit road. At the mid-shift break (6) the miners, thanks to the mechanical aids, are still comparatively clean—and in good heart to renew efforts to speed the flow of " black diamonds."

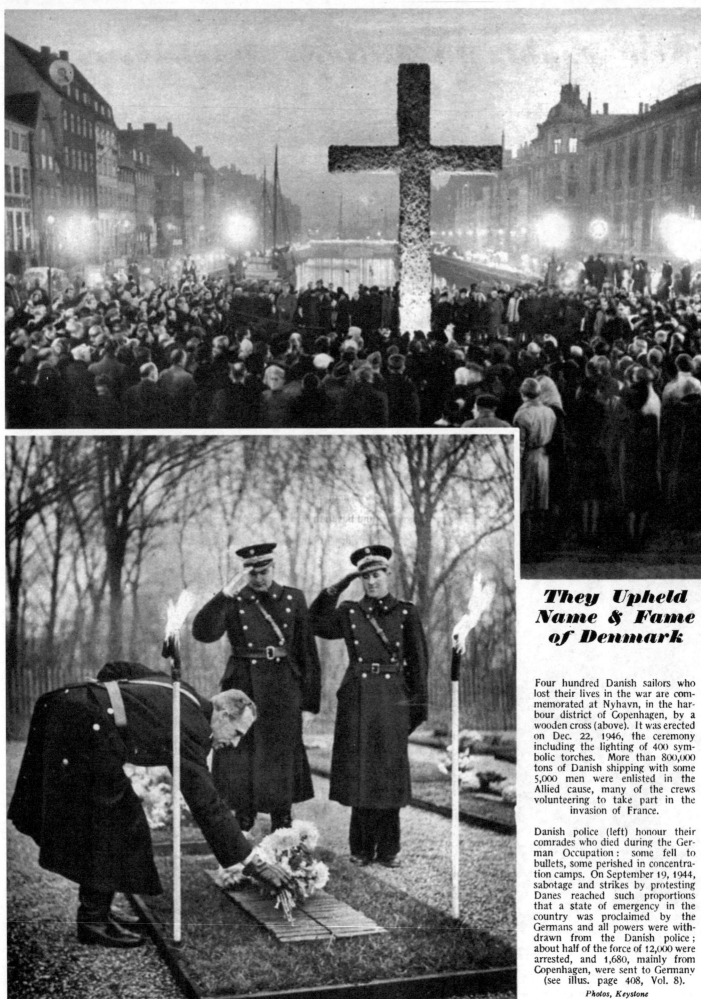

They Upheld Name & Fame of Denmark

Four hundred Danish sailors who lost their lives in the war are commemorated at Nyhavn, in the harbour district of Copenhagen, by a wooden cross (above). It was erected on Dec. 22, 1946, the ceremony including the lighting of 400 symbolic torches. More than 800,000 tons of Danish shipping with some 5,000 men were enlisted in the Allied cause, many of the crews volunteering to take part in the invasion of France.

Danish police (left) honour their comrades who died during the German Occupation: some fell to bullets, some perished in concentration camps. On September 19, 1944, sabotage and strikes by protesting Danes reached such proportions that a state of emergency in the country was proclaimed by the Germans and all powers were withdrawn from the Danish police; about half of the force of 12,000 were arrested, and 1,680, mainly from Copenhagen, were sent to Germany (see illus. page 408, Vol. 8).

Photos, Keystone

New Light On Hitler's Dark Career

SINCE the dust subsided in Germany and the darkness has receded, many secrets have come to light. We have learned much of the origins of the war and many details of its course; what have we learned of the personality of its author? He was a genius, of course; a revolutionary genius—it is useless to deny that, for no ordinary man could have achieved such a masterpiece of destruction.

But wherein did his genius lie? In what respects was he outside human categories, in what within them? Some people have suggested that he was himself an unimportant man, a mere symptom, a pawn, moved by big business, heavy industry, the army, the Junkers. This is an impossible doctrine. For a time all these interests thought they could manage Hitler. They helped him to power. In the end he ruled and ruined all.

IT was in his last days that his absolute personal power was exhibited most clearly. Then he had no army, no Gestapo, no propaganda. Failure of his mission was obvious. He had ruined Germany. Yet such was the compelling power of his personality that his orders were still implicitly obeyed. Deputy Fuehrer Martin Bormann and many others wished to escape from Berlin before it was surrounded. But Hitler refused to move, and they stayed. They even stayed for more than twenty-four hours after his death in order to carry out his orders and burn his body. In consequence their escape was impossible and most of them perished in Berlin. Only one man tried to make a secret escape in those days—Hitler's own brother-in-law. Hitler ordered him to be found and shot, and again he was obeyed.

How can we explain this extraordinary power? The habit of obedience no doubt confirmed it, but what caused it? Apart from political reasons, Hitler certainly had an extraordinary personal magnetism. His eyes had hypnotic effect, a dim intensity which subdued the beholder. One of the ablest of his court admitted that Hitler's mere presence left him exhausted and void. Hitler was a sorcerer who convinced a nation that he alone understood the mystery of politics. He even convinced himself, believing to the end that he was a German messiah who alone had the will-power to carry Germany through to victory; and it was partly for this reason that he lived in fear of assassination, hiding night and day in deep underground bunkers. In other respects, too, he can be compared with a sorcerer. Both he and Himmler kept astrologers and consulted their horoscopes on important occasions.

One of the Scourges of Mankind

But Hitler was never a constructive genius. At the bottom of his heart, behind the meaningless phrases of peaceful intentions and the defence of Western civilization, he wished only to destroy. When he thought of himself as a great historical figure, it wasn't as any of the great builders of civilization; it was as one of the scourges of mankind—Alaric, Attila, Genghis Khan. In his early philosophy this nihilism was obvious to all who examined it. In his middle years it was obscured by the vested interests which rode on the Nazi tide. At the end Nazism resumed its original character. The appeal to the Werewolves was an appeal for universal destruction; Germany was to go down in a Wagnerian twilight of the gods.

Though Hitler was physically afraid of blood, the thought of it excited and intoxicated him. Nor did he mind whose blood it was that he shed. An officer once began to explain apologetically that German losses had been severe. Hitler cut him short.

THE mystery that surrounded Hitler in death as in life has been partly dispelled by captured records and the testimony of some of his associates, and it is now possible to draw a more detailed portrait of him. This psychological study is by Maj. H. R. TREVOR-ROPER, British Intelligence Officer in charge of investigations into Hitler's last hours in Berlin. See also pages 522-523, Vol. 9.

See also pages 522-523, Vol. 9.

"Losses can never be too high," he exclaimed eagerly, "they sow the seed of future greatness!"

Hitler always thought of himself as an artist and of politics as a form of art. Before the war he lived an "artistic life." He kept irregular hours (his working day was from noon till 4.30 in the morning), worked erratically, played truant from his office, went picnicking in the hills, and surrounded himself with people from the screen and studio. Both Eva Braun and his physician, Dr. Morell, entered his circle in this way.

He came from the lower middle class; and though in his politics and his ideas he was a demonic figure, in taste and in his private life he always remained the petty bourgeois. In some ways it was useful to him to do so; for the German workman, the German common soldier and the German black-coated worker, never felt estranged from Hitler. He was always one of them. He lived simply and had his meals regularly, when Eva Braun was away, with his secretaries and his vegetarian cook. Nevertheless, there is a somewhat macabre contrast between the revolutionary nihilism of his doctrines, with his unlimited plans of conquest and the background of cosiness and triviality from which they proceeded: tea-cups and cream-buns, cuckoo clocks and Bavarian bric-à-brac.

THE most significant evidence of these petty-bourgeois standards is to be found in his relations with Eva Braun. She was not a conventional tyrant's mistress. Though attractive, she was not glamorous. She had no exotic tastes, no love of power. A photographer's assistant, she came from the same class as himself; and for that reason Hitler preferred her above all the blowzy

EVA BRAUN (upper) shared death with Hitler the day after their marriage. He had a fondness for being photographed with children (lower). PAGE 659 Photo, Planet News

Nordic actresses whom Goebbels introduced to the chancellery. She never interfered in politics, but attended quietly to the details of bourgeois life. She kept the politicians away when he wanted rest, saw that his social receptions (at 2.30 a.m.) were not disturbed by business, and supplied him with a private world. When everyone else seemed to be deserting him, he retained his complete confidence in her.

The exact position of Eva Braun in Hitler's household will probably always be an enigma. Hitler described it as "true friendship," and so that base considerations of cash should not disturb it he made her independent. For about fifteen years she was neither wife nor acknowledged mistress. Even her existence was a secret outside the court. Since Hitler certainly loved her, his unwillingness to give her any definite status for so long requires explanation. The easiest explanation is that their relations were platonic or at least were so represented. The status of either wife or mistress would have been inconsistent with such relations. Ultimately her status had to be established if she was to share in the ritual death of the Fuehrer. Hence the last-minute symbolic marriage.

His Physical and Mental Collapse

But no character remains static, especially in such a giddy position. In Hitler's last year the failure of hope and the corruption of power emphasized other characteristics. His Cabinet had become a despotic court of toadies and flatterers in which he heard only the echo of his own megalomania. Under the pressure of defeat he gave up all relaxations, all "artistic" activity and irregularity and became a weary hack. Quite suddenly, from looking younger than his age, he became an old man. His hands trembled, his body stooped; he was obstinate and morose. Two causes hastened his physical and mental collapse: his physician and the generals' plot.

His relations with his physician are as extraordinary as anything in that extraordinary history. Dr. Morell was a mere quack. As court physician he used his position to obtain lucrative monopolies for his own proprietary medicines, and in nine years he made a large fortune. All this time he was treating Hitler with an endless series of drugs and injections upon which, in the end, his patient became dependent. Three other doctors discovered the facts and warned Hitler that he was being slowly poisoned. For their reward they were all dismissed and one of them later sentenced to death. For the last six months of his life Hitler's health was in the sole charge of Dr. Morell. By this time, though he suffered no organic complaint and had a very strong constitution, he was a physical wreck.

MEANWHILE, the generals' plot of July 20, 1944, also had its influence. From the physical effects of that attack Hitler soon recovered; from the mental effects, never. Thenceforth the fear of treachery obsessed him; he saw it everywhere and especially in the army. "Everyone has lied to me!" he would scream. "The armed forces have deceived me; even the S.S. has left me in the lurch!" As defeat followed defeat, he became more hysterical in his denunciations, and Martin Bormann, eager to eliminate all rivals for the succession, fanned his suspicions into flame.

The last news from the outside world informed him of Himmler's treachery. That was the end. It was "a shattering blow." The faithful Heinrich had betrayed him. He decided to postpone his death no longer. Like Caesar, Hitler died with an "Et tu, Brute!" (You too, Brutus) on his lips.

Europe's Wartime Capitals in 1947

PRAGUE

By EUGENE ERDELY

THE visitor landing on Czechoslovakia's only international airfield, at Ruzyn, is given a hearty welcome by the passport and Customs officials, and a similar friendly atmosphere prevails throughout his stay in the country. In Prague, the capital, your first impression is of being in a city of young people. In the trams (so crowded that, especially at peak hours, passengers need the energy of youth to manage to cling to the platform !) you see many young men carrying attaché cases with an important air.

It would appear from this that the entire population is either studying at the University —in fact, there are some 53,000 students—or employed in Government offices on negotiations in which the fate of the country will be decided for the next thousand years. Later you learn that attaché cases are, so to speak, a part of the national costume : they contain mostly a substantial snack or a good lunch.

In Comparison London is Quiet

Even in the offices of Government departments youth prevails. The average age in important positions in the State administration is about 40. This administration naturally has its own little defects. For instance, in Parliament one day the Minister of Industry declared that he could not do much in the way of increasing production because of the 106 holidays the country had been enjoying since its liberation. Half of these were Sundays, the others mostly celebrations of the country's release from six years of German rule. Of the eight days following October 27, 1946, four were public holidays. At last Parliament had to intervene, and now a Government order has reduced the number of annual holidays to ten.

Two more early impressions of Prague are the noise in the streets and the great fatigue felt after a period of walking. The cause of the noise is that the roadways are paved with great cobblestones and the wheels of vehicles are not provided with rubber tires (due to wartime economy). These, and the very heavy tram-cars, make a rumble in comparison with which the City of London is quiet. Add to all this the constant hooting and shouting—chauffeurs use their horns with utmost freedom and coachmen their mouths to overcome the difficulties of traffic —and the result is indescribable. The fatigue of the visitor is increased by the small stones with which the pavements of Prague are paved and which make one immensely tired unless one wears shoes with soles about an inch thick.

PRAGUE suffered very little from the war in comparison with London. In the city you see only about a dozen houses demolished —by English and American bombers in the last phases of the war, or by the Germans in the last four days when they vented the last of their spleen upon the Czechs. In the country districts the situation is worse. Moravia especially suffered—its capital city, Brno, has more ruins than buildings—but the people are making the greatest efforts to restore their industries and raise the country's trade to its pre-war level. Many obstacles have yet to be overcome ; factories must be rebuilt, skilled workers replaced by a process of slow training.

The country has resolved to achieve industrial rehabilitation in a Two Years' Plan. Everyone is speaking enthusiastically of the Plan and the particular task his own factory, office, shop or field has to contribute to it. Officially, the Two Years' Plan was to have been put in operation on January 1, 1947, but the ambitious Czechs and Slovaks started it on October 29, 1946. If things turn out in accordance with the Government scheme, in 1949 Czechoslovakia will have not only as much of everything as there was before 1938 but even more.

This desire to restore things to as they were before the Germans arrived, and to improve upon them, is characteristic of Czechoslovakia. Every relaxation of food rationing is hailed by the population as an important step towards this aim, and today the food situation is nearly back to normal, although ration cards are needed for a meal in a restaurant. Milk and cheese are among unrationed items.

Sugar is an important export commodity —Czechoslovakia buys fats in exchange for it—but the Czechs are allotted three pounds of it every month, and four and a half pounds of beef, pork or veal. Mutton, poultry and game are unrationed, and jam has recently been placed on the "free" list. A good middle-class lunch or dinner costs twenty to thirty crowns in the restaurants (from two to three shillings) and consists of soup, meat, vegetables, a sweet, and a glass of good beer, service included.

Better Dressed Than in England

This winter Czechs are eating goose with sauerkraut . the "old times" will be fully restored when the goose is replaced generally by pork, because pork with sauerkraut is the national dish and nowadays only the richer people can buy it. More than half the pigs in Czechoslovakia in 1937 were removed by the Germans, and even before the war fat pigs were imported for the production of the ham which made Prague world-famous.

Prague is a city of ancient monuments and modern suburbs. The foreigner naturally stays in the centre of the city, and is fascinated by the busy life of the Václavské Námesti, where the monument of the famous "Good King Wenceslas" stands before the National Museum, another pride of Prague. Such magnificent buildings as Prasná Brána next to the Obecní Dúm (the City Hall) and the St. Nicolas Church in the Malá Strana on the other side of the river Vltava are enchanting. Looking down from the Hrad-

TRAFFIC POLICE in Prague are smart, well trained, and carry arms—and the great noise of traffic in the cobbled streets is one of the visitor's first impressions. *Photo, Keystone*
PAGE 660

sanin, the castle hill where the President's palace is situated, together with the embassies of foreign powers and the ministries, you have a marvellous view.

Descending to the streets of Prague, to the many crowded market-places with their tents crammed with everything that can be bought without coupons, you are again in the midst of the daily life of this town of a million inhabitants. Here, curiously enough, there are no evening papers, newsvendors continuing to sell the morning newspapers until late at night. It is reported, however, that one Government evening newspaper will be permitted to appear.

PEOPLE in the streets are better dressed than their counterparts in England, although the materials to be obtained by the general public are of very poor quality. Perhaps the garments one sees date from before the war, though Czechs began eagerly to buy new clothes when the Russians freed Stalingrad ; or they may be from the black market. Clothing is the only field in which black marketeers (who are faced with severe penalties) are operating with success.

In Prague cinemas the visitor may now see English and American films which were shown in London four or five years ago. During the war the Czechs had to rely upon their own, German-controlled films, or Berlin films. In one recent week there were shown eight Soviet, seven American, 25 British, nine French, 21 Czech and two Swedish pictures. There is an excellent film studio at Barrandov, near Prague—the largest in Europe, and the Germans finished building it just before they left Prague for ever ; its facilities are available to anyone who can pay for them, and some British companies may go to Prague to try them out. The Czechs themselves are producing high quality puppet films and cartoons ; their other films are rather sentimental and patriotic, as is understandable in a nation which suffered so much during the Occupation.

Every Opportunity for Amusement

A recent exhibition on loan from the Tate Gallery (London) of war pictures and scenes from daily life in Britain was studied with interest. But to the younger Czech painters English art does not particularly appeal. For generations they have studied in Paris, regarding French art as leading the world. Now, however, they are inclined to turn towards Russian art and forms of expression.

An English theatrical company recently visited Prague. Posters announcing performances of Candida, They Came to a City, and Macbeth, were seen everywhere in the town and all seats were sold in advance. The 15 theatres are at this time showing, among other foreign writers, Bernard Shaw, Eugene O'Neill, Terence Rattigan and J. B. Priestley. The National Theatre has presented a fine new production of Tchaikovsky's opera Eugen Onegin, and Faust, and the concert-halls are packed.

After the day's toil the people of the capital still have time to amuse themselves. There is a place called *U Fleku* where you may find representatives of middle-class Prague in the evening. It is a brewery, producing one of the finest local beers ; and because it is not suited to transport or bottling, the beer (much too sweet for the English palate) is served only on the premises of *U Fleku*. There are night clubs where you may be admitted without being a member and where you may pay up to 300 crowns for a bottle of wine—which is a high price in Prague, but in pounds sterling does not amount to more than 30 shillings.

Czechoslovakia's Capital Almost Untouched by War

GROCERS' SHOPS are well-stocked (1) and there are no queues, the food situation being far better than in Britain. There is only one bomb-damaged building in St. Wenceslas Square (2), and scarcely more than a dozen throughout the city. Charles's Bridge (3), spanning the Vltava River, is overlooked, in the distance, by the President's palace. Václavské Námesti, or St. Wenceslas Square (4), is the "Piccadilly Circus" of Prague; in it stands the statue of the "Good King" of the Christmas carol. *Photos, New York Times Photos, Keystone, March of Time*

The ROLL OF HONOUR

NCOs & MEN

1939—1946

Pte. G. AISBITT
The Black Watch.
Action : N. Africa. 6.4.43.
Age 24. (W. Hartlepool)

From its inception on page 88 of this volume up to page 568, our ROLL OF HONOUR appeared regularly as a single page. In order to accommodate the large number of portraits accepted, this space has now been increased to two pages in alternate issues.

Pte. D. H. ARCHIBALD
Lothian and Border Yeo.
Action : N. Africa. 21.2.43.
Age 26. (Edinburgh)

L/Cpl. T. H. ALLEN
Essex Regiment.
Action : Sfax. 6.5.43.
Age 26. (Highams Park)

Dvr. C. W. BAILEY
Royal Army Service Corps.
N.W. Europe. 25.11.44.
Age 25. (London)

Sgt. A. E. BARNETT
Royal Artillery.
Act'n : N. Africa. 16.11.42.
Age 23. (Fulham)

P/O. J. R. G. BARRITT
H.M.S. Prince of Wales,
Off Malaya. 10.12.41.
Age 21. (N. Shields)

F/Eng. J. E. BEAUMONT
R.A.F. Bomber Command
Act. : Oxfordshire. 28.12.42
Age 20. (Fulham)

Marine J. BERRY
Royal Marines.
H.M.S. Barham. 25.11.41.
Age 22. (Gilford)

Sto. J. H. BLACKWELL
H.M.S. Glowworm.
Action : Norway. 8.4.40
Age 22. (Billingham)

A/B W. BRINDLE
Royal Navy.
Action : Messina. 8.9.43.
Age 20. (Preston)

Sig. C. BROSTER
Royal Navy.
Action : At Sea. 5.2.42.
Age 30. (Derby)

Mne. A. BREMNER
Royal Marines.
Action : Italy. 11.4.45.
Age 22. (Erith)

Pte. R. BUTLER
Rifle Brigade.
Action : Anzio. 10.5.44.
Age 20. (Ipswich)

Sapper S. COWEN
Royal Engineers.
Tobruk. 28.6.41.
Age 21. (Sheffie'd)

Pte. J. DAVAGE
Monmouthshire Regt.
Action : Caen. 19.7.44.
Age 20. (Pontywain)

Pte. C. DUNN
South Staffs Regt.
Action : Burma. 17.3.44.
Age 27. (Sneyd Green)

L.A.C. J. T. DYSON
Royal Air Force.
P.O.W. : Far East 29.9.44.
Age 34. (Sheffield)

O/S A. H. ELLIOTT
H.M.S. Janus.
Action : Nettuno. 23.1.44.
Age 19. (Dagenham)

Cpl. P. EVINS
Royal Sussex Regiment.
Action : Italy. 12.7.44.
Age 20. (Dorney Common)

Pte. H. EVANS
Seaforth Highlanders.
Action : Havre. 11.9.44.
Age 26. (Armadale)

Sgt. J. FINCH
Royal Air Force.
Actn.: Magdeb'rg. 20.1.44.
Age 19. (Barnet)

Sgt. E. C. FOX
Royal Air Force.
Actn.: Hamburg. 29.7.43.
Age 19. (Plumstead)

L/Sgt. J. FOXLEY
Grenadier Guards.
Actn.: N. Africa. 18.3.43.
Age 35. (Liverpool)

Pte. B. FRANKLIN
Queen's Royal Regiment.
Action : Italy. 12.8.44.
Age 19. (W. Bromwich)

Sgt. T. E. GIBBS
Royal Artillery.
Action : Tunisia. 9.5.43.
Age 34. (Eltham)

P/O W. GORDON
Royal Navy.
Actn.: Atlantic. 15.11.42.
Age 26. (Glasgow)

Pte. V. HALLETT
Reconnaissance Regt.
Action : Italy. 28.7.43.
Age 23. (Treharris)

Pte. A. B. HARTLEY
Seaforth Highlanders.
Actn. : Holland. 31.10.44.
Age 19. (Manchester)

Gnr. C. L. HOLT
Royal Artillery.
D/wnds. : Athens. 16.12.44.
Age 31. (Yeovil)

F/Sgt. F. HUMAN
R.A.F.V.R.
Actn.: Wiesbaden 3.2.45.
Age 21. (Keighley)

Sgt. W. IDDON
Royal Air Force.
In action. 15.2.44.
Age 20. (Banks)

L/Sgt. H. JARMAN
Coldstream Guards.
Action : Salerno. 9.9.43.
Age 23. (Leeds)

Pte. J. JARVIS
West Yorkshire Regt.
Action : Burma. 12.3.44.
Age 32. (Nottingham)

Dvr. E. JONES
Royal Artillery.
D/wnds. 6.11.42.
Age 26. (Birmingham)

Sgt. H. JONES
No. 1 Commando.
Action : Burma. 31.1.45.
Age 25. (Swansea)

Sgt. W. KENNEDY
Royal Air Force.
Accident.: Glos. 17.12.44.
Age 23. (Newcastle)

Fmn. J. R. KENNEDY
Merchant Navy.
Action : Channel. 20.8.44.
Age 19. (Newcastle)

F/Sgt. R. KENNEDY
Royal Air Force.
Accident.: Glos. 19.5.44.
Age 21. (Newcastle)

Pte. L. LENNARD
3rd Parachute Bde.
Action : Rhine. 24.3.45.
Age 34. (Radcliffe)

So great has been the response of readers to our invitation to submit portraits for our Roll of Honour that no more can now be accepted. But senders may rest assured that all those so far received will be published.

Gnr. L. LINDSEY
315 S.L. Battery.
P.O.W. : Siam. 3.9.43.
Age 35. (Birmingham)

Sgt. E. LUMLEY
Royal Engineers.
D. wds. Egypt. 7.2.45.
Age 37. (Selby)

Pte. R. McDUELL
Royal Fusiliers.
Action : Italy. 28.11.43.
Age 26. (London)

A/B T. P. MURTAGH
H.M.S. Dorsetshire.
Action : Indian O. 5.4.42.
Age 19. (Manchester)

Pte. F. C. PARKINSON
Loyal Regiment.
P.O.W. : Far East. 21.9.44.
Age 21. (Preston)

Sgt. E. J. POOLE
Middlesex Regiment.
Action : Caen. 15.6.44.
Age 27. (Plumstead)

Sgt. R. W. PAYZE
Royal Air Force.
Action : Bremen. 25.6.42.
Age 22. (Ilkeston)

Pte. A. G. POTTER
Royal Berkshire Regt.
Action : Burma. 2.4.43.
Age 24. (Willesden)

Pte. S. A. PRONGER
Oxford & Bucks L.I.
Action : Germany. 13.4.45.
Age 18. (Godmanchester)

Mechn. W. RADFORD
H.M.S. Dorsetshire.
Action : Indian O. 5.4.42.
Age 29. (Calstock)

Sgt. W. G. REED
R.A.F.V.R.
Action : Germany. 14.6.43.
Age 20. (Putney)

Fus. G. ROBERTS
Royal Welch Fusiliers.
Drowned off India. 19.11.43.
Age 24. (Holyhead)

Dvr. S. J. RADLEY
Royal Horse Artillery.
Action : Mid. East. 29.6.42.
Age 21. (Witham)

Cpl. J. ROBINSON
No. 3 Commando.
Action : France. 13.8.44.
Age 28. (Sidcup)

A/B G. H. SCOTT
H.M.S. Fratton.
Action : off N'dy. 18.8.44.
Age 29. (Haywards Heath)

L/Sto. H. C. SHORT
Royal Navy.
Action : Medit. 8.1.43.
Age 23. (Albourne)

Gnr. W. STOKES
Royal Artillery.
Action : Alamein. 27.6.42.
Age 27. (Beeston)

F/Sgt. J. T. SIMPSON
Royal Air Force.
Action : Hanover. 27.9.43.
Age 26. (Horden)

F/Sgt. L. SLATER
Royal Air Force.
Died of wounds. 25.11.43.
Age 30. (Acton)

Gdsmn. R. G. TAYLOR
Grenadier Guards.
Action : Overloon. 13.10.44.
Age 26. (Woodbridge)

F/Sgt. D. TAYLOR
R.A.F. Bomber Command.
Action : Pforzheim. 23.2.45.
Age 22. (Methley, Leeds)

L/Cpl. L. TAYLOR
Royal Engineers
At sea : 17.6.43.
Age 35. (Darlington)

Sapper. A. THOMAS
Royal Engineers.
Action : Alamein. 23.10.42
Age 27. (Windhill)

Smn. G. THOMSON
Royal Navy.
Action : Atlantic. 24.2.41.
Age 21. (Dundee)

Asst./Std. A. K. TODD
Hospital Ship St. David.
Action : off Anzio. 24.1.44.
Age 32. (Rosslare Hbr.)

L/Cpl. W. VIRGO
Royal Marines.
Action : Burma. 24.4.42.
Age 21. (Waldridge Fell)

F/Sgt. T. WADDELL
Royal Air Force.
Action : England. 6.5.44.
Age 22. (Dunoon)

Pte. G. H. WALTON
Durham Light Infantry.
P.O.W. Tobruk. 7.7.42.
Age 29. (Leeds)

Sgt. S. J. WEBSTER
Royal Air Force.
Action : Bremen. 24.6.42.
Age 26. (London)

Sgt. WESTMORLAND
Royal Tank Regiment.
Action : Italy. 19.4.45.
Age 29. (Hull)

A/B W. WILLIAMS
H.M.S. Acasta.
Action : Narvik. 8.6.40.
Age 40. (Portland)

Sgt. C. G. WILSON
Royal Air Force.
Action: Trondheim. 20.6.40.
Age 24. (Elgin)

Pte. F. S. WILTSHIRE
Wiltshire Regiment.
Action : Caen. 22.7.44.
Age 23. (Chippenham)

Sapper H. K. WOOD
Royal Engineers
Action : N'dy. 11.6.44.
Age 22. (Wilmslow)

Sgt. A. WOODALL
Royal Artillery.
Action : Mid. East. 6.6.42.
Age 25. (Wigan)

Cpl. N. WRAITH
Royal Army Service Corps.
Died : Egypt. 4.10.41.
Age 39. (Leeds)

Pte. F. W. YARDLEY
Highland L.I.
Action : W. Europe. 5.4.45.
Age 22. (Smethwick)

N.C.B. Unfurls Its Flag Over Britain's Mines

NATIONAL COAL BOARD celebrating the taking over by the State of all British coal mines, formerly belonging to 800 separate companies, had its white-initialled blue flag flown on Jan. 1, 1947: as at William-thorpe Colliery, Derby-shire (1). At Garngoch Colliery, near Swansea, miners held a meeting on New Year's morning beneath the notice announcing the change of ownership (2). Uniform of the Board's messengers is dark blue, with patch pockets, white metal buttons and "NCB" on the lapels (3). At the informal vesting ceremony (4) in London, Mr. Shinwell, Minister of Fuel and Power, addressed his colleagues. Mr. Attlee is seated on Mr. Shinwell's left; other Cabinet ministers are seen. See also illus. pages 656-657.

PAGE 664

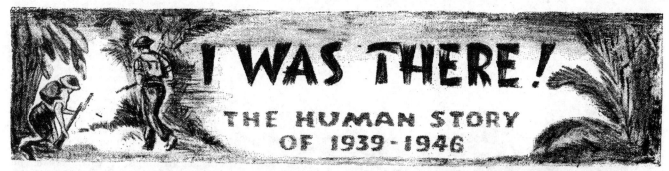
On the Road From Assam to Rangoon

Vital factors in the 14th Army's final push towards Mandalay and Rangoon were the Ordnance Field Parks. The arduous southward journey of one of these "ordnance depots on wheels" is described by Major L. L. Bearman, R.A.O.C., who commanded an ordnance sub-park of the 19th Indian Division.

WE were at Golaghat, in Assam, for rest and refitting, and having a really grand time among the tea plantations, when orders came to move to Dimapur as quickly as possible, first filling up with as many stores as we could carry. As to the function of an Ordnance Field Park, it is a unit peculiar to war, some 60 vehicles carrying stores comprising M.T., wireless and signals, artillery, engineering, small-arms—the complete equipments and spares for them. It amounts, in fact, to an Ordnance Depot on wheels. It can go anywhere at very short notice with an army, corps, division; or a small section can go with a brigade. The job is to issue stores on the spot to replace those lost in battle. Some of the transport is fitted with steel bins divided by shelves and small partitions for carrying the smaller items; the others are General Service lorries used for carrying bulk. Then there are jeeps for delivery service, a battery charger, battery carrier and a breakdown. The number of spare parts carried would often be near the 8,000 mark, so it was a most important matter that everything should be kept in its proper place.

Major L. L. BEARMAN

Awful Yellow Dust Three Feet Deep

We were off on December 19, 1944. The big push was on. The stretch from Golaghat to Dimapur was covered not without mishap; in the 50 odd miles along a flat road we had three vehicle casualties, one of them serious, overturned into the rice fields, and the other two with broken radiators. Our unit workshops, therefore, arrived many hours after the main body. We received a message saying we were required much more urgently than was at first anticipated, and we were to go to Moreh, which is just inside Burma, close to Tamu. After two days in Dimapur, collecting many tons of stores, which were to be needed so badly in the weeks to come, we took the road again.

Leaving early in the morning of December 21 we started the long climb back to where we had come from two months previously—up 8,000 feet to Kohima first. It was bitterly cold when, at about 7 p.m., the first half of us arrived at Konglatongby, where we were to stage for the night. My chief clerk stayed with me on the road to guide the remainder in to the site: and were we frozen! This cold was a completely new thing to us. By morning there were still ten vehicles missing, and it was decided that a day on

maintenance, and a search for the remainder, would be the best course to adopt.

It proved a good plan, enabling us, next morning, to pull out all together, every vehicle in perfect running order. So it was good-bye to Imphal, on to Palel, then another climb to Moreh. The dust was awful —two to three feet deep, and yellow. It clung to us from head to foot and filled every eye, ear, nose and throat. It was impossible to see more than one yard in front of the lorries, and a mistake meant a "drop" of thousands of feet. Many unfortunates did go down that precipice, but none of our lads came to harm. It was 6 p.m. when we started to pull in, and what with the darkness and the dust we couldn't see a thing.

Moreh was the first place for us to open up shop, and I cannot think of a worse spot

in the world—barren, devoid of all life. But we settled in, our workshops section arriving some 24 hours later. What a sorry sight our vehicles were: battered and broken, some needing new springs, or centre bolts, or grills, or radiators. It seemed that another ten miles would finish them off completely. But a few days (including Christmas) in Moreh, altered all that, and once again the vehicles were in tip-top condition. This was a magnificent feat by the drivers, who worked hard with never a grumble.

NEXT stop was Taukian, no great distance, but with a big hill to negotiate. It was night when we started, and when, after covering about ten miles, I pulled up, to my amazement I discovered there were only five other vehicles with me. I turned and raced back, and found that one driver had missed the road and had turned off, the remainder of the convoy following him. He could not be blamed; the dust was the cause of it. We managed to stop about four lorries from going the wrong way, and then raced after the rest of them. After going about four miles

BURMESE GIRLS AT TOUNGOO welcomed a little assistance with their work from the Indian soldiers when the latter had any time to spare. In the race to Rangoon the Ordnance Field Park (story above) was well to the fore—and was greeted with machine-gun fire when it arrived at Toungoo on April 26, 1945, four days after our leading troops.

BRITISH CONVOY HALTED AT PYAWBWE, with smoke from demolitions carried out by the retreating Japanese rising in the distance. A road and rail junction about 300 miles north of Rangoon, Pyawbwe was reluctantly evacuated by the Japanese in April 1945.

arriving on January 18, when we had been on the march about a month.

In the early afternoon of February 1 a frantic message came for us to move that night. A lot of hard work was done : there were tents to strike, messes to be packed up, food to be prepared for the journey. By 9 p.m. all the vehicles were lined up, and we left an hour later. Looking back on it, the trials and tribulations encountered on that trip were enough to turn one grey. Dust, hills, shocking gradients, rivers, chaungs (dried-up river beds, all sand), crashes, and Japs all hindered us. We had to stage at a place called Tillin : it was dark when we arrived, and our biggest job was to get the Sepoys, dead-tired and just about all-in, to put up their mosquito nets. Next day we learned that there were 200 Japs only half a mile from us, and we decided to move off at once and keep going until our destination was reached.

Our Overflowing Cup of Woe!

So we came to Sinthe on February 3, by which time our vehicles were just about fit for the breakdown park—or so it seemed. Each one had at least three or four things wrong with it. Our cup of woe was filled to overflowing by a message from Corps H.Q. —"Urgent ! Send 20 three-tonners back to Kan. Pick up XXX Brigade and take to Pakokku. Operational."

We had only 28 vehicles in, so far, and 14 of these were off the road for major repairs. The others needed considerable attention before they could be used again. Another eight came in during the day, and by taking out the steel bins from 10 of them we were able to have 18 ready by nightfall to send back along that treacherous road. The Brigade was put into action over the Irrawaddy, and there was secured another bridge-head opening up the way into Central Burma. After more than a week our 18 three-tonners came back to the unit lines. They were battered and broken, and it looked like the very end, yet within three weeks all but one were ready again, and that one needed a new engine—in fact, it practically needed remaking.

On March 4, I went on a recce to Myitche, our new site by the bridge-head, found a good spot, and sent an advance party off in

the "road" became a mere bullock-cart track, and I could neither pass the tail of the convoy nor turn around. Another officer with me got out of the jeep and ran to catch up with the leading vehicle. He managed it, and also found a dry field to turn in.

THEN they started coming back, and as they came I could see more trouble. How were they to pass the oncoming vehicles ? It took us three hours to get out of that mess. I shall never know to whom most thanks should have gone, the Unit Transport Officer or my excellent Jemadar Sahib. To cap it all, one vehicle towing a 25-pounder gun ran into a bad patch, covered with steel wire which wrapped itself around the wheels and hubs —which meant a long job with hacksaws. Eventually the convoy joined up once more and we were on our way.

We arrived at Taukian on January 5, 1945. There I went out shooting duck one evening, and in a village found all the natives very drunk on rice wine. An old Indian told me the celebrations were because the Japs had been driven out of the village, and they —the villagers—were so glad to see the British back once more. Twelve days later we left for Kan. It was a good trip, and our vehicles behaved extremely well. Though we had to drive through many rivers, fast running and up to the axles, there were no casualties, and we arrived at 6 p.m. Now the distance from base was too great for us to be supplied by road, so it had to be air supply, the first

"KEEP THE WHEELS TURNING," was a constant cry once the British drive into Burma had begun ; and here Corporal W. H. Carpenter, of Battersea, London, is repairing a jeep engine in the Pinwe area, northern Burma. Indian Electrical and Mechanical Engineers worked night and day to keep vehicles under their care on the road.　　PAGE 666　　*War Office photographs*

quick time to "sit" on it. More trouble was encountered, this time burned-out clutch plates ; there were so many chaungs to cross, some over half a mile wide. Most of the vehicles had to be winched over them. But all came in safe to Myitche on the 6th. From now on, once over the river, there would be proper roads right down to Rangoon. At least, so we were told, and we were foolish enough to believe it.

The next blow came when we were told to move to Meiktila, 80 miles south of Mandalay. Just at that time an East African Brigade had been flown out and had handed all their vehicles into our R.V.P. (Returned Vehicle Park). All of these we had to move with our own on the next hop. The establishment for the R.V.P. was 12 drivers, and now there were over 120 vehicles to move ! Well, there was only one way. Havaldar clerks to drive, all officers, W.O.s and sergeants to drive, even the sweepers if only we could train them in time. A lot of new drivers were born in the next few days ! So on to Meiktila.

Burying Japs All One Afternoon

Leaving on April 2 we covered that 100-odd miles of desert waste, staging the night at Taungtha : not because we wanted to stage but because there were large numbers of Japs about, cutting the road and in other places shelling it. Convoys were split up into blocks of about 200, sub-divided into 50s and again into sixes, each six to be self-maintained in the case of trouble. We had eight heavy armoured cars from the R.V.P. with us, and these we spread out through the convoy, and our destination was reached with only minor incidents.

Another nightmare came upon us. The men had driven thousands of miles on that long and arduous trek and were accustomed to the gradients, the bends, the dust, sand and mud. They were *not* used to good roads ! So broken grills and radiators were the order of the day. Getting into the site at 2.30 p.m., it took us all the rest of the day burying Japs. Snipers were still busy, hiding in bombed buildings and pagodas.

From then onwards it was rather different, racing down to Rangoon and with everybody's tail well up. Leaving Meiktila on April 25, we halted for the night at Lewe, 15

STEAM FRIGATE H.M.S. BICKERTON was torpedoed by a German submarine off the coast of Norway on Aug. 22, 1944, when she was with a force escorting two aircraft-carriers (story below). Of 1,500 tons, she had a main armament of three 3-inch guns and a designed speed of 23 knots.

miles south of Pyinmina ; next day we arrived at Toungoo, at 1 a.m., amid lots of small arms and machine-gun fire. On May 8 we left for Pegu. At milestone 91 on the Rangoon-Mandalay road a bridge was down, but our vehicles managed to cross at intervals throughout the night and we arrived in Pegu with the first part of the convoy at 3 a.m. Sad to say, we were just beaten on the post. We were only 50 miles from Rangoon when we heard that the town had fallen to seaborne and airborne forces.

We felt it rather keenly ; but drivers of my unit had the satisfaction of having covered all those thousands of miles over mountain tracks with their four-by-twos : and not a vehicle lost. With the fall of Rangoon, and nearly all of Burma back in our hands, the end soon came, as also did the end of our trek. To the Indian "other ranks," to every officer, warrant officer and sergeant who served under me in the Ordnance Field Park, my sincere thanks for the splendid job they all did—the best bunch of boys ever collected together.

A Frigate in Search of the Tirpitz

Participating in one of the Fleet Air Arm attacks on the notorious German battleship Tirpitz, in August 1944, the escort carrier Nabob and the frigate Bickerton were torpedoed off the North Cape, Norway. The story is told by P. H. Martin, a survivor from the Bickerton, who served for four years in the Royal Navy as a telegraphist. See also page 218, Vol. 9.

The dawn of August 16, 1944, saw us in company with a great array of ships of the Home Fleet raising steam in that windswept expanse known as Scapa Flow. By 10 a.m., at the head of our frigate group, we were hurrying to station ourselves around our charges—two aircraft carriers. Sealed orders were opened and it was revealed that our mission was to screen the two carriers forming part of our forces meant to deliver a crippling attack on the Tirpitz in its lair in Alten Fjord, Norway (see illus. page 477, Vol. 8).

On we steamed through foul weather. Away to the north of us lay the main force of carriers, cruisers and destroyers led by the mighty Duke of York. August 22 dawned—a fine day. The rocky Norwegian coast lay to our west, stretching away in a white haze as far as the eye could see. By twelve o'clock my busy morning was over—away for a little while from the perpetual buzzing of monotonous wireless signals, the humdrum of the Bickerton's radio room. I joined my friends on the torpedo deck and we clustered around the guard rails eager with expectation. Signal lamps were wink-

ing, orders were being flashed to the Fleet and as one ship the destroyers manoeuvred into stations astern while the aircraft carriers turned into the wind.

Hulls down to our east, the big carriers of the main force sent up their aircraft : Corsairs, Seafires and Barracudas ; and in squadrons these bore in over the enemy's coast and in a moment were lost to view. A lull followed, with everyone keyed up, waiting for results. Winking lamps recalled destroyers and restationing began.

Steaming Amongst the Wreckage

The afternoon dragged on, the weather began to deteriorate, and we were wallowing in a murky sea when the air armada returned in groups of twos and threes. It became evident that a second strike was in the offing. The next few hours I remember as though it were yesterday. Tea-time came and passed and I left, armed with my lifebelt, for the little wireless office, ready for what I thought would be another two hours of strained listening. I became very busy, phones over my head, pencil-pushing, having not an

inkling of what was happening outside. The Petty Officer in charge was doing his best to deal with the large inflow of messages in his usual competent way.

It must have been about five o'clock when shouts came from the upper deck, sounding to me like "Carrier Nabob has been hit astern of us !" In a matter of seconds "action stations" was sounded, orders were barked, the radio telephone crackled as emergency orders were passed to the rest of our screening force. I heard the Captain telling the quarterdeck crew to set "depth charge pattern D for Dog." We turned violently and then came a thud and we shuddered from stem to stern. Books, chairs and tables cascaded about, cordite smoke poured in through the vents and we became aware of the stark fact that we were torpedoed. Speedily we dragged ourselves out of the wireless office.

P. H. MARTIN

We had been hit in the after-part of the ship and were slowly listing to starboard ; a fire was burning and a pall of smoke hung over us. In a few seconds I was in the water, striking out through the oil to a Carley float. I clawed desperately to get in, helped by two others. The Fleet had retired across the horizon, leaving in its wake a battered carrier two or three miles astern of us and our little ship in a doomed condition. A few frigates patrolled in the distance.

Bickerton remained afloat, stern under water, and all that could be heard were men's voices. It was bitterly cold, and we hastened to scramble back aboard the ship, to await the arrival of our rescuers. The wounded were cared for, and cigarettes were passed around. Patiently we sat on the forecastle, whilst the list grew and our bows were poised perilously in the air. It all seemed so utterly unreal, sitting there idly, and I am convinced that a number of us were temporarily beyond caring what might or might not happen next.

After a while it became safe for one of the patrolling frigates to relax vigilance, and she steamed in amongst the wreckage to within a half-mile of us. Hastily, monkey nets and ladders were slung over the sides, improvised stretchers were made from rafts and floats for the wounded, and they were lifted down from the torpedo deck to the starboard side ready for the painful process of being lowered into the approaching boat. Then, with the best discipline possible in such circumstances, we queued to take our turn for final abandonment of our ship. The Captain stood in a wrecked gun position, calmly directing the operation. The whaler came alongside, heaving awkwardly in the heavy swell, handled in an expert manner by a sublieutenant of the R.N.V.R.

My turn came at last, and I slithered over the side and down the net ; hands grabbed me, and they pushed off, hampered by a boat crowded to capacity. The gulf between us and our rescuing ship H.M.S. Kempthorne narrowed slowly and soon we were heaving alongside her and climbing her nets. How grand it was to feel the deck beneath our feet ! A tot of rum from "Jack Dusty's" store, and I stood with most of our survivors to watch the final proceedings which were to end the career of my ship. Signal lamps were busy, and while the frigates maintained their vigil a twin-stack destroyer dashed by astern of us and, closing the Bickerton, unleashed a torpedo. With a muffled explosion the Bickerton reared, then slowly slid below the surface. Bubbles and more wreckage appeared—and she was gone.

We Sang the Marseillaise in Prison

Captain in an infantry regiment of the French 8th Army, Raymond Borie was captured during confused fighting in the Vosges in June 1940. He relates incidents of his five years' incarceration in German prison-camps, ending in his release by the British in May 1945.

AFTER eight months of digging trenches, planting nets of barbed wire, felling trees, constructing dug-outs and strong-points of concrete, we received the order, on June 13, 1940, to quit the Line. Leaving a minimum of soldiers there we moved back some eight miles to a forest.

A nerve-racking period followed, with alternating rumours of good and bad news. At last we entrained, but the line had been blocked and we did not go far. Our destination was changed three times in two days. Eventually we were ordered to a point near a pass in the Vosges, which we were to defend against great odds and in almost impossible conditions.

Our Government had already asked for an armistice, and everyone knew it. Apparently Alsace had been abandoned without fighting—and two-thirds of my men were Alsatians. A hundred-odd, we had now to defend a front of about a mile, steep and hilly, and covered with trees which prevented us from seeing more than two or three yards in front. Nevertheless, we held the ground for three days. And then, on June 22, running short of ammunition, entirely surrounded by the enemy, who occupied heights from which he could fire at us, we had to surrender.

Then came a two-days' march to Strasbourg. The Germans gave us nothing to eat, but happily for us we were in Alsace. In spite of strict orders, and of our captors' threats and blows and inevitable reprisals (I saw an elderly woman struck because she had put out for us a pail of fresh water) the people flocked to give us food and shout encouragement. As we entered Strasbourg someone in our ranks began to sing a well-known French song, affirming the loyalty to France of Alsace and Lorraine. We drew ourselves up, marched like soldiers again, throwing that song defiantly in our captors' faces ; and the onlookers sang it, too, in spite of all German efforts to silence them.

Devising Ways to " Go on a Trip "

My first prison camp was at Edelbach, in Austria. It had a picturesque background of fir woods, mountain ranges and splendid sunsets. But inside the camp there was no tree whatsoever—no shade. Grass withered under our tramping feet. There was dust in summer, snow in winter and spring, mud in autumn, wind all the time—and the eternal barbed wire around us. No news came through to us at the beginning. Food was bad and very scarce. Most of us were still mentally stunned, unable to grasp the situation, now hoping for a quick release and the resurgence of our country, now dreading years of separation and captivity.

My own chief anxiety while a prisoner was for my family in France ; and, as I learned later, my concern as to their fate was not unfounded. (Five close relations, two of them women, for their part in the Resistance movement were sent to German concentration camps, where two died and two others barely survived.) A great strain for me, too, was the enforced crowding of camp-life . . . never alone even for a few minutes, whether sleeping, waking, dressing, washing, eating or working. Small wonder some of us lost our reason. But as the days went by we recovered our spirits to some extent and organized our life. Lectures were arranged and, later, courses in all kinds of subjects. One man set up as a teacher of Chinese, and not until his pupils had had three lessons did they discover that he knew not a word of the language !

AT my next camp, Colditz, I met British, Belgian, Dutch, Polish and even four Serbian officers. The atmosphere there was lively ; the prisoners dreamed of nothing but escaping, of devising ways to "go on a trip" as they called it. Our place of confinement, an old castle perched on a hill overlooking a river, looked picturesque from outside. Inside it was a real prison, with heavy doors, thick walls, and a very small yard for exercise. The number of escape-tunnels begun here by prisoners was amazing, considering the thickness of the walls and the rocky nature of the ground.

On New Year's Eve 1941 the beginning of the Russian victorious winter offensive shattered German hopes and sent ours soaring. At midnight we French officers left our rooms to wish one another a Happy New Year. Other prisoners joined in, and soon the yard, white with snow, was filled with shouting figures. The German officer on duty asked us to return to our rooms. When he gave the order to a prisoner, the latter had to move towards his quarters ; but after a few steps, when the German was trying to persuade someone else, the first man stopped, turned back and went to another part of the yard. The German naturally became angry.

Suddenly an enthusiastic Marseillaise broke out, taken up by prisoners of all nationalities in the yard and at the windows. The ancient walls vibrated to the sound. The German officer wavered, stopped, and froze to attention. The Marseillaise ended. The German hurried forward ; but God Save the King began, and he stopped again. The Belgian, the Dutch, the Polish and Serbian national anthems were sung before we returned to our quarters.

Savage Threats Were Implemented

Towards the end of May 1942 I was sent to Lübeck, where I was to remain for three years. The officer commanding the camp "welcomed" us in a speech in which he denounced us as Communists, Jews, freemasons, capitalists, and believers in the victory of England (the last accusation at least was true). He threatened us with all manner of dire penalties, and warned us not to expect a quick release after victory (a German victory, of course). His threats of rigorous treatment were not idle : a few days later a Polish officer was wounded because he closed his shutters a few seconds after the signal ; another was shot dead because he went out of his hut before the signal—he was in pyjamas and it was obvious he had no intention of escaping ; a Frenchman lost an eye from a shot because he stood on the threshold of his hut during an air-raid alarm ; and many of us only escaped death thanks to the unskilful shooting of the old soldiers who guarded us.

Attempts at escape were numerous in this camp. One tunnel was discovered at night just as two officers who had been working in it were about to go back to their room. Asked by the guard whether anybody else was below, they said no, although another officer was still crouching at the far end of the hole. The German, doubtful, sent in his dog. The Frenchman saw the beast coming,

FRENCH P.O.W. IN MAUBEUGE, north-east France, close to the Belgian frontier, in the summer of 1940, eagerly accepted a drink from a countrywoman. Weary and disheartened, they received as little consideration from the Germans as prisoners elsewhere. At Colditz, as this story tells, prisoners chanted their defiance on New Year's Eve 1941. └ PAGE 668 *Photo, Associated Press*

COMMANDER OF THE 7th ARMOURED DIVISION, Major-General G. L. Verney received a great reception when he entered Ghent in his Staghound armoured car on Sept. 8, 1944. British troops reached the southern outskirts of the town on Sept. 5, but the Germans were still resisting strongly in the northern section on Sept. 9; the last enemy opposition was overcome the following day, though positions along the Zeebrugge-Ghent canal were not taken until two days later. The part of an R.A.S.C. Troop Carrying Company in the confused fighting is told below.

called to it softly in German "Here, boy!" patted it, and sent it back! Its master, reassured, thereupon left the way clear for the officer in the tunnel to regain his quarters.

Everything was done to daunt us and prevent us from trying to escape, and everything failed until in 1944 all escaped prisoners, when recaptured, were handed over to the Gestapo. Some were killed, and only their ashes were returned to the camp; others disappeared without trace. The chance of being killed became a certainty, and our friends had to desist from their endeavours. But what daring they had shown! Three had passed the gate disguised as a fatigue party led by a "German" N.C.O. Another got out as a member of the Gestapo, hundreds of whom had come to search the camp. Three successful tunnels had been dug. One of these was in the parade ground: all work on this had to be done during roll-call. Sometimes prisoners entered the tunnel during morning roll-call and remained there until the evening one. Escapes were made through that tunnel on four different

occasions, and although we were counted twice a day we always succeeded in preventing the Germans from ascertaining—sometimes for a considerable period—that prisoners were missing.

In May 1945 came the blessed day of release. The Germans were still in their watch-towers round the camp. From time to time we heard shots in Lübeck. On the motor-road that ran beside the camp nothing moved for hours. Dressed in our Sunday best we crowded into strategic spots from which to see the fighting, if any. We had to wait a very long time. Far away we heard a few guns, and we saw the smoke of a few scattered fires. Then silence again, and waiting. At last, in the distance, some armoured cars appeared on the road. We still were not sure whose they were. Then came a wild, deafening shout, a savage rush, pandemonium. We yelled and hugged one another, and climbed the barbed wire to get closer to the English cars as they passed. We were no longer prisoners. The long nightmare was over.

Near dawn the shelling suddenly stopped, arousing suspicion that this might have been a self-propelled gun trying out its armament. Breakfast, consumed under the hungry gaze of the civilians, was scarcely finished when a messenger arrived to say that two of our trucks had been knocked out during the night and replacements were required at once. Having detailed reserves, the Platoon Commander and I sped off to Battalion Tactical Headquarters—a Bren carrier standing on a bridge spanning the canal close to the factory area and in radio contact with all the sub-units.

In the Beaten Zone of Shells

We were informed that in addition to the shelling, which made it difficult to move along the water-front, there was also the risk of being sniped at. If the infantry were under fire, so were our drivers. Besides, we had the latest mail delivery with us. Deciding that the risk was justifiable we dashed along the deserted quayside in the 15 cwt. truck, expecting each moment to hear the crack of a rifle and feeling that the eyes of the whole German army were on us. But nothing happened. Apparently we were considered too insignificant for the enemy to worry about.

The German guns were lobbing their stuff from about 700 yards, the majority of it crashing into the open between the factory buildings occupied by the infantry. Beyond splinter danger it seemed quite ineffective. Inside the building the foot-sloggers were resting or sleeping; the drivers were "brewing up." Everything was O.K. now, though it had been a bit lively during the night. The two trucks were a write-off as they had both received direct hits: and at the moment they were not available for inspection—they were in the beaten zone of the shells, and no one dreamed of trespassing there.

Suddenly loud cries of "Fire!" were raised. Looking through the open doors we saw one of the parked troop-carriers well alight. Hastily formed fire-parties dashed sand and sacks over the flames and pumped extinguishers frantically. Fragments of shell-casing whistled through the air as successive rounds crumped down near by. The conflagration out, we returned to the shelter of

In Ghent With R.A.S.C. Troop-Carriers

Liberated by the British 2nd Army in a record dash north from the Seine in September 1944, the city of Ghent lies on the Scheldt midway between Brussels and Ostend. Scenes in the final mopping-up of the German defenders are recalled by ex-Sergeant Sidney W. Sharp, R.A.S.C.

VISITORS to the cathedral of Ghent, in Belgium, will find in it a plaque to the memory of the officers and men of 131 Brigade, 7th Armoured Division (The Desert Rats), who fell during the liberation of the city. It was placed there by the appreciative townspeople as a mark of their gratitude and respect.

Ghent was the Divisional objective in the 2nd Army's race to capture the port of Antwerp, and we reached it in the early days of September 1944. No. 507 Company, R.A.S.C., performed troop-carrying duties for the Queen's Infantry Brigade, B Platoon, of which I was transport sergeant, being assigned to the 1/6th Battalion "for all purposes." During the preliminary operations in the city this battalion had the task of clearing the Germans from the factory area where, strongly ensconced in a chemical

works, they were making themselves a general nuisance with mortar and artillery fire.

As was the custom, the Platoon's vehicles and drivers, six to a rifle company, were retained with their sub-units in the fire zone, whilst our Platoon H.Q., with its officer and myself, gratefully retired to Battalion-H.Q. A2 Echelon, located in the comparative quiet of Frère Orban, a magnificent boulevard.

At eleven o'clock on the night following the entry, the Germans put down an annoying stonk which ranged all over the town, but with only superficial damage. One o'clock was signalized by a thunderous explosion as a battalion truck loaded with ammunition detonated under a direct hit, bringing down the house against which it stood but injuring no one. The front axle travelled over four streets before finally landing!

Motto : " Swift "

NO. 72 SQUADRON

SOON after the end of the First Great War this squadron was disbanded in Baghdad, and reformed at Tangmere, Sussex, in February 1937. It was equipped with Gloster Gladiators, but was converted to a Spitfire squadron at the outbreak of the Second Great War. The first few months were spent in assisting in the defence of the Humber estuary and the Firth of Forth, and early in 1940 it was protecting north-east England.

It helped to cover the evacuation at Dunkirk, was engaged in the Battle of Britain, and later made many sorties on defence patrols and convoy protection. No. 72 went to North Africa with the British 1st Army in November 1942 and gained 53 combat victories in less than six months. It participated in the Sicilian campaign, being based on Malta, and helped with air cover for the Salerno landings.

TRANSFERRED to Italy, the squadron moved up the west coast in the wake of the Allied armies, and by Sept. 16, 1943, its score had mounted to 200. Bomber escorts, fighter sweeps and the shooting-up of enemy transport were amongst its tasks. From Corsica, No. 72 patrolled the Allied beach-head in the south of France on Aug. 15, 1944, moving into France five days later. In the following October it returned to Italy, going to Rimini in November to be equipped with Spitbombers.

Until the end of the war it was engaged in bombing and strafing close-support targets, cutting roads and railways, and attacking transport, many congratulatory messages being received from the 8th Army. The squadron is one of the R.A.F.'s named units and, generous contributions to the Empire's war effort having linked it with the people of Basutoland, it has the title of No. 72 (Basutoland) Squadron.

the factory building. The whole place shook when "strays" crashed against the walls, which were, however, too thick to be much damaged by those missiles.

Word came that the replacement lorries were now running the gauntlet of the canal bank. This should be interesting, was the general thought. They could be seen trundling down the approach road and had almost reached the main gate when a burst on the pavé halted them. One came on again, but the other was obviously in trouble. Nobody was keen, but there was a driver in the cab. Volunteers ran to the derelict and hauled him down—he was our smallest chap, incidentally—whilst the first vehicle, appraised of the situation, backed down on to the damaged one, hooked up and drew it into the factory yard. The one burst had been enough. Both vehicles' tires were riddled, one driver was a casualty with shrapnel in

the stomach, and the deficiency position was as before. A dispatch rider was sent back to Company Headquarters to draw a reserve from the "pool," whilst I and the Platoon Officer made another frantic dash along the quayside, again unmolested.

At about two o'clock Typhoons, called by radio, commenced softening-up the German gun positions. Enthusiastic crowds, unmindful of stray shells, cheered frantically as the "Tiffies" peeled off and swept low over the enemy sites. The thunder of impacting rockets went on for nearly ten minutes. Then the Typhoons circled lazily over the area, blanketed with oily smoke. Thanks to them the guns were silent.

Road Erupted in Smoke and Flame

Back at Frère Orban we were thrown into another flap at three o'clock by Brigade, who had given instructions for the Battalion to unload all our vehicles and return them to the Platoon, as they would be required to pick up a Brigade of the 15th (Scottish) Division, delegated to assist the Queens'. Just as the complete convoy was assembled we were given the map reference, quite near to the city, and were away. The loading-up was completed in good time.

Standing in the main square by the Cathedral I waited for the vehicles to pass. As the first lorries arrived the road erupted in smoke and flame. The respite was over ; shelling had recommenced. It was a strange coincidence that the target should have been this very spot at this very moment. Overhead cables collapsed. Civilians fell to the pavement. The air was thick with choking dust, through which the trucks

plodded steadily on . . . twelve, thirteen, fourteen I counted. Then a terrific crash caused me to duck momentarily.

As the murk cleared truck number fifteen could be seen weaving about the road, but still under control. It pulled into the side and stopped, the driver springing from the cab. He was all right, anyhow. Helpers appeared and the rear doors were flung back.

S. W. SHARP

Of the 20 occupants only two were not seriously injured. Razor-like fragments, piercing the steel bodywork, had done terrific damage among the infantrymen. They were carried to a temporary shelter to await ambulances of the Divisional Advanced Dressing Station, whilst the balance of the convoy, with worried faces peering out at the scene, rolled through and away to its destination.

As the sun slowly sank, the vehicles streamed to location, the "lift" completed. That night Ghent's canal glowed with another radiance, the reflection of the burning chemical factory quivering in its still waters. In the holocaust the remnants of the defenders were being mopped up by the combined team of infantry. On September 11 a Polish armoured brigade relieved the Division, which moved back to Malines for rest.

They Made Me Wield a Pick in Germany

Realization that he had been " had " came to Sgt. Charles Sadgrove, of the Royal Signals, after he had laboured as a prisoner of war in German hands: as he explains in this glimpse of arduous days of picking and shovelling prior to the publication of the Geneva Convention. See portrait in page 477.

I WAS fond of my fountain-pen, and was most reluctant to part with it. Not that it was much use to me in the early period of prisoner-of-war life. At the first big search on entering Germany an English-speaking (and strangely polite) German officer had emptied it of ink. All the same, it was a link with the old days and I liked to carry it with me.

In the end it went up in smoke. A D.C.L.I. sergeant with whom I had become friendly in hospital bartered his precious penknife

for four cheap, tongue-biting Polish cigarettes and offered me a half-share. Such generosity in time of sheer want called for some response. My watch, ring or pen— which should it be ? The pen lost the day— and we smoked.

Well, a pick and a shovel soon took its place. It came as something of a shock when I was sent out on my first working-party, because I had been doing a "reserved" job as typist at Stalag XXA and at the same time acting second-in-command of a

BRITISH P.O.W. AT KLEIN BARTELSEE, near Bromberg, stripped for work in the German gravel pits : the author of the story is the single figure at the back. He was in this " luxury " camp for over two years and, choosing the lesser of two evils, elected to be a labourer—until the arrival of a document " saved his bacon."

H.M.S. LI WO, the gallant little patrol vessel whose valiant commander, Lieut. Thomas Wilkinson, was posthumously awarded the V.C., as described in page 631. In normal times, this 1,000-ton steamer plied as a passenger vessel between Ichang and Chungking on the Upper Yangtse River in China. Under the White Ensign, on February 14, 1942, she fought to the last with a Japanese convoy.
Photo by courtesy of Indo-China Steam Navigation Co.

company of British prisoners. But there was my number, one of 40 on a list, and so I had to undergo the fitting-out, delousing, searching, counting, and all the other preliminaries of a move out from camp to the larger world of working-parties.

We travelled in the cattle-trucks by which we had made our entry into the "greater German Reich." Where we were going nobody really knew, but in the end we landed a road-making job in East Prussia. And from 40 of our countrymen who were there before us we soon learned the ropes— where the cookhouse was (most important), what the rations were like, when to expect the next issue of "Junaks" (Polish cigarettes, of which we now received a small allocation) and the type of work which we would be required to do.

After a few hours' rest on louse-infested palliasses, reveille came all too soon with the dreaded word "Aufstehen!" In the darkness of early dawn we were paraded, marshalled into lorries, and driven some miles out of the town to one of the many sections of the Danzig road at that time undergoing widening and improvements at the hands of British prisoners of war. I remarked upon the number of senior N.C.O.s in the party, but everyone had to work, even the sergeant-major in charge. At that time we had not been allowed to discover the clause in the Geneva Convention which excused senior ranks anything but supervisory duties.

Daily My Blistered Hands Bled

We were each given a pick and shovel, and an officious German civilian measured out for each man a certain stretch of road from which the top surface had to be removed to a depth of six to eight inches. This completed, we moved to another measured stretch, and so on until dusk, the day's toil being relieved with two breaks of half an hour in which we were permitted to light fires around which to sit and eat our rations.

That job brought me nearer to tears than anything experienced before or since. My back used to ache continuously and my blistered hands bled before the day was half through. The road surface was made granite-like by the severe frosts of early winter, so that our picks bounced as we wielded them. In fact, a staff smithy, a civilian, was kept permanently employed with the task of sharpening the points of our picks as we blunted them.

Today I can find amusement in recalling how we spent our evenings in that camp. The first thing was a mad rush to the cookhouse to collect our soup in a bowl that was later used as a drinking vessel for coffee (ersatz) and then as a wash-basin. Someone would then produce an old pack of cards, and with these we would play in the dim light of a paraffin lamp until first one and then another started scratching. A shirt would be removed for closer inspection, and then another—until, finally, the game of cards would deteriorate into a general bout of delousing.

By November winter had set in with a vengeance, and it was decided that 80 men was too many for the work available. Our employer selected those who were to stay (presumably the best workers) and those who were to go. I am proud to relate that I was considered among the slackers. The next day found us marshalled into the cattle-trucks once again, and soon we were back among the hordes at the stalag.

Within a fortnight I was out again—this time one of a party of 500 en route to Klein Bartelsee, near Bromberg, where we were the first to occupy a specially-built camp. After the last place, it was a veritable "Butlin's," with well-appointed kitchen, lavatories, wash-places, and even showers. The beds were well-constructed two-tier bunks, mostly with spring mattresses and white sheets and blue check blanket covers and pillow cases.

A Surprise From the Red Cross

The camp was alongside a huge pine wood, and I was lucky enough to stay there for over two years. There were tradesmen and labourers in that camp and I chose to be a labourer, which meant anything from trench digging to pipe laying. I did both at different times, but the best job was in the gravel pits. We changed shifts each week—from five till twelve and twelve to seven—and a lorry took us from the camp to the working site and back again. In the summer we stripped down to shorts and boots, and in the intervals between the filling of skips and the shunting of the next lot into position we had ample time for sun-bathing. We teamed up, two and sometimes three men to a skip, with generally ten skips to a train-load.

At last, thanks to the Red Cross, copies of the Geneva Convention began to circulate among the camps. One came to us at Klein Bartelsee—with disastrous results for the Germans. The compulsory labour among senior N.C.O.s was found to be contrary to international law. Those who wished could volunteer for further work; otherwise nothing but supervision was obligatory. I need hardly say that I did not volunteer!

NEW FACTS AND FIGURES

AFTER more than 18 months of "standing down" the Royal Observer Corps was from January 1, 1947, completely re-organized on a peacetime basis. A nucleus of permanent officers is provided, and 28,500 spare-time volunteers are being enrolled, drawn initially from men and women with wartime experience of identifying and plotting aircraft in the Royal Observer Corps.

"MULBERRY harbour" at Arromanches is to be preserved as a war memorial to the British by the French Government. Through this small Normandy resort (see illus. page 559) poured 600,000 British troops on their way to the Rhine and Germany. Tanks, guns, and blockhouses will remain in place.

FOUR Normandy battlefields are to be turned into State-owned sites by the French Tourist office. They are Utah and Omaha beaches, where the Americans first landed, Arromanches and Courseulles, where Montgomery and De Gaulle landed. People will not be allowed to acquire property there, and removal of abandoned war material is forbidden. Hitler's Atlantic Wall will also be preserved.

STRENGTH of the Polish Army and Re-settlement Corps in November 1946 was as follows: in the United Kingdom, 108,958; in Germany, 20,479; in Italy, 18,662; in the Middle East, 6,369; in France, 5,229. Of the total of 159,697, women and child dependents made up 6,834. To November 1946 some 55,000 Poles had been repatriated, 3,749 had emigrated to countries other than Poland, and 3,834 were on leave for relegation to reserve for civilian employment. It was stated that the British Army was prepared to take up to 10,000 Polish troops under 30 years of age.

THE British Zone of Germany is crowded with homeless Germans from the East and displaced persons. Into an area which before the war had a population of 19,750,000, some 22,750,000 persons have been crammed. As 49 per cent of dwellings were destroyed by the war, men, women and children are accommodated in every available farmhouse, disused office and cellar. Living space is eight square metres per person, compared with 11 to 12 square metres in the Russian Zone, and 12 to 13 in the French.

THE 13th and 14th Dickin Medals (Animals' V.C.) to be awarded to dogs (other recipients being pigeons) have been won by Punch and Judy, Boxer dogs belonging to two officers of Army H.Q., Palestine. In Jerusalem on August 5, 1946, they raised the alarm when a terrorist armed with a sub-machine gun approached the house and in attacking him both sustained injuries, Punch having four bullet wounds. Their action prevented what might have been a tragic incident. The dogs were treated at the Jerusalem hospital of the People's Dispensary for Sick Animals, which has continued to function throughout the war and subsequent civil disturbances, treating sick animals of Jew and Arab alike.

FORMER gun factories in the U.S.S.R. in 1946 manufactured goods for civilian use to the value of more than 1,500,000,000 roubles, two and a half times more than in 1945. The Soviet Armaments Minister stated that about 15 per cent of production consisted of consumer goods.

German Strongpoint Becomes Dutch Home

PILL-BOX AT WESTKAPELLE, Walcheren Island, serves as a temporary home for this girl who, wishing to get married and impatient of delay in obtaining a house, decided with her fiancé to appropriate the former German strongpoint on the sand dunes. Friends, inspired by their example, erected a wooden hut for themselves on the concrete roof, and now both families are waiting for more conventional premises to become available. Much of the island's inundated land has now been reclaimed. See also page 542.

Photo, New York Times Photos

Printed in England and published every alternate Friday by the Proprietors, THE AMALGAMATED PRESS, LTD., The Fleetway House, Farringdon Street, London, E.C.4. Registered for transmission by Canadian Magazine Post. Sole Agents for Australia and New Zealand : Messrs. Gordon & Gotch, Ltd. ; and for South Africa : Central News Agency, Ltd.—January 31, 1947.   S.S   *Editorial Address* : JOHN CARPENTER HOUSE. WHITEFRIARS. LONDON. E.C.4.

Vol 10 *The War Illustrated* Nº 252

SIXPENCE

FEBRUARY 14, 1947

I WAS THERE

COLOURS OF THE 1st BATTALION THE LONDON SCOTTISH were handed over for safe-keeping to Dr. R. F. V. Scott, of St. Columba's Church of Scotland, on Jan. 12, 1947. The Battalion will remain in a state of " suspended animation " until recruiting for the new Territorial Army commences on April 1, 1947, when the London Scottish will form a part of the 44th (Home Counties) Division. St. Columba's, Pont Street, Chelsea, London, is the Regiment's place of worship. *Photo, G.P.U.*

Edited by Sir John Hammerton

NO. 253 WILL BE PUBLISHED FRIDAY, FEBRUARY 28

War Leaders Caught by Our Roving Camera

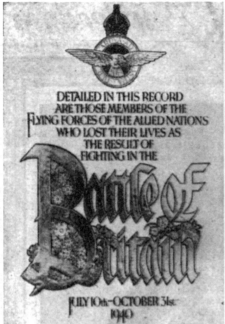

TITLE PAGE (left) of the Roll of Honour to be deposited in Westminster Abbey in memory of the fallen in the Battle of Britain.

BRITISH SERVICE CHIEFS were decorated by the French Ambassador at an investiture held in London on January 15, 1947.

MARSHAL STALIN (right) received Field-Marshal Montgomery at a reception at the Kremlin, Moscow, on Jan. 10, 1947. Lord Montgomery afterwards described his conversation with the Soviet leader as "great."

NORWEGIAN TROOPS (right) embarked for Germany in January 1947. This was the first time in history that Norway had sent occupation troops abroad. The force, wearing British uniforms, went to the British Zone.

SEA-MINE-DETONATING CRAFT, known as "egg-crates," brought to Mumbles, Swansea Bay, to await demolition, were constructed in America for the Royal Navy in order to detonate a special type of sea-mine used by the Germans during the latter part of the war. Fitted with water-tight bulkheads for buoyancy and open compartments to allow free access to the sea, they created a tremendous disturbance under water over a wide area as they were towed by powerful tugs. They measure 120 feet by 60 feet, with 22 feet draught, but when afloat only two feet of their cumbersome hulls appeared above water.

Photos, Central Press, P.A. Reuter, Pictorial Press, I.N.P.

The Dramatic Liberation of Amsterdam

By
L. MARSLAND GANDER

who, as The Daily Telegraph War Correspondent, entered Amsterdam with the first British troops of the 1st Canadian Army on May 7, 1945.

ALTHOUGH the surrender of General Blaskowitz's 21st German Army in Holland seemed a secondary affair in the great collapse of May 1945 it brought in train surprises, joy turning to terror, and exciting, strenuous days for the war correspondents attached to the 1st Canadian Army. The war was over. Yet on that fateful May 7, when all Amsterdam was wild with hysterical relief, war broke out again in its cruellest form. I became involved in one of the most dangerous situations I had experienced in four years' reporting of five campaigns.

The surrender conference was held at the battered little village of Wageningen, between Arnhem and Utrecht. Here the opposing battle-lines had frozen, and for some days before the final surrender food lorries had been passed through to succour the starving civilians of western Holland. We had our first surprise when the massive, grunting Blaskowitz acknowledged that he had 110,000 men under command. Our Intelligence had not expected more than 60,000 or 80,000. This great army had been contained and pressed back by an Anglo-Canadian force greatly inferior in numbers, while the main offensive tide flowed northwards and north-west into Germany.

Into the Last German Strongholds

We had two divisions only on this section of front, and were therefore outnumbered by about four to one. Our moral and material superiority had been equal to the task up to the standstill, when Germany's armies on all other fronts were melting away fast. The only question was whether this comparatively small force could effectively control the situation and preserve order in an area which contained so many armed Germans, surrounded by a starving, persecuted population who hated their oppressors with cold, concentrated fury.

My own concern was to get into Amsterdam at the earliest possible moment. I was teamed with John Redfern, of The Daily Express. We scouted around and found that at dawn on May 7 the tape barriers at Wageningen—which were all that separated us from the defeated enemy—would be removed and armoured cars of the 49th (West Riding) Reconnaissance Regiment, leading the 49th Division, would advance into the last German strongholds of western Holland. "B" squadron, commanded by Major Hamish Taite, of Lutterworth, near Rugby, would be in the van.

It must be confessed that there was a certain amount of good-natured rivalry between the British and Canadian elements in the 1st Canadian Army; the British felt that it was not generally realized that they were fighting in the Canadian Army. These reconnaissance boys had achieved many daring feats during the advance into Holland, and they sensed that at last here was a deserved "piece of cake," a fitting climax to their war record. When two tame war reporters came along anxious to be taken into Amsterdam, or as near to it as we could get, the troops were hugely delighted.

Major Taite agreed to attach us to a troop consisting of 30 men in four armoured cars and six carriers, under the command of Lieut. George Bowman, of Scarborough, and Lieut. John Rafferty, of Cardiff. Most of these troops had landed in France soon after D-Day. In the early hours of May 7, Redfern and I piled into our jeep, with our French-Canadian conducting officer and driver, and slung our bed-rolls and typewriters into the trailer. We wedged our vehicle, by arrangement, between two armoured cars and waited in the traffic jam at the Wageningen tape. There was no official "starter," no ceremony. Suddenly we began to roll forward—and we were in the midst of the German army.

New Dutch Flags Were Everywhere

The first German I saw was walking sulkily along the road with a stick grenade in his hand. He took no notice of us, and we swept on. Then a couple more passed, on bicycles, rifles slung across their backs. But the Germans were only slinking back into their camps, barracks, and concentration areas. Soon we hardly noticed them, for the population went wild with delight, their welcome mounting in enthusiasm with every yard we progressed. They shouted, danced, and ran—anything to let off steam. I saw girls leaping into the air clapping their hands above their heads as if they were doing Swedish drill. New Dutch flags floated everywhere from the houses.

My scarcely legible notes are eloquent. They read: "lilac, tulips, people cycling like mad, comic hats, statuesque figures in toppers, orange dresses, flags, streamers, Japanese lanterns, people shouting 'good-bye,' 'welcome,' 'hullo.'" In Utrecht and Hilversum the police managed to keep a road free through the dense throngs. As we passed the old ramparts of Naarde people

IN THE DAM SQUARE, AMSTERDAM, many people were killed and wounded when German Marines opened fire without warning shortly before Canadian troops occupied the city early in May 1945. The author of this story was mobbed there by a wildly excited crowd just before the tragedy occurred. The Royal Palace, originally used as the Town Hall, overlooks the Dam. Beside it is the new Church, where lie some of the Netherlands' most illustrious dead, including the famous Admiral de Ruyter.   PAGE 675   *Courtesy of Royal Netherlands Govt.*

with tears streaming down their cheeks bombarded us with flowers and illuminated addresses. At last, after one or two hold-ups at blown bridges, we were running between flooded fields into the outskirts of Amsterdam. What we had already experienced should have prepared us ; but we were hardly ready for the tumultuous reception in the Dam Square, the heart of the old city.

Excited Crowds in Dangerous Mood

The jubilant people simply engulfed us. There were a dozen laughing, half-hysterical girls on the bonnet of our jeep, and a score of demonstrative youths and boys on the trailer. They thought the whole British Army had arrived—instead of which it was only 30 men, while the main liberating force of Canadians was 40 or 50 miles away.

A few score German troops who had apparently been on street duty and were fully armed, made a sheepish, half-hearted attempt to push the milling mob back with their rifles before they, too, were overwhelmed. So far the crowd, intoxicated with joy, was in carnival mood. But it was an inflammable situation. We were completely stuck. I felt most uneasy, not only because one shot would have caused a massacre, but also because our force was far too small to control the town which we knew contained at least 3,500 regular German troops, unknown numbers of the hated Grünpolizei, and thousands of the brave Dutch Resistance forces, who were now pouring out into the open with their Sten guns.

Another point was that it was my professional duty to get a dispatch rider away with the story of the Liberation. I talked earnestly to Lieutenants Bowman and Rafferty,

counselling a withdrawal in the hope that our departure would calm the excited crowds. They agreed, but we could not move. So with persuasion and expostulation, having autographed hundreds of identity cards and distributed scores of cigarettes. we removed most of our would-be passengers and began slowly to bulldoze our way out. At first only two of the armoured cars and our jeep got away from the square. It was fatal to stop again and wait—as we did on the Amstel Dijk beside the river—for we were immediately surrounded again by cigarette beggars and hero worshippers.

Killed in Panic Act of Terrorism

The other cars and jeeps struggled out to join us at a farmhouse on the outskirts. There Bowman wirelessed back to headquarters while Redfern and I wrote our stories and sent them off by dispatch rider. We did not know that terrible events had occurred immediately we withdrew. Exactly how it all started must remain a mystery, but as I pieced it together later it appeared something like this. German officers were hustled in the crowd, whose mood changed from minute to minute, ranging from the heights of hilarity to raging anger. Some Dutch Resistance men—acting contrary to the armistice terms—attempted to disarm a German, who resisted. Somebody fired a shot—whether Dutchman or German I do not know. Thereupon German marines, who were holding the De Groote Club building, overlooking the Dam, in some strength, opened fire.

Between 20 and 30 people, including old women and tiny children, were killed outright in this ruthless, panic act of terrorism.

I saw some of their bodies with terrible wounds, later. How typical of the Germans to fire into the crowd instead of firing warning shots overhead ! Shooting also broke out near the railway station. Immediately, the Dutch Resistance forces, their only uniforms blue overalls, encircled the Germans in the De Groote Club and the railway station.

That was the situation when we received radio orders at the farmhouse to return into Amsterdam. This time I went in an armoured car, but as there was no room inside I had to cling precariously to the outside, feeling most unpleasantly conspicuous. We nosed cautiously through the maze of narrow streets and waterways round the Dam Square. Bullets were flying, but it was not easy to decide who was shooting at whom or what. Blue overalled men crouched in doorways with weapons at the ready.

People shouted at me, "Keep your head down, sir !" and I felt most unhappy. For the war was over, and to be killed now. . ! Rafferty and Bowman held a conference. Should we turn our 37-mm. guns on the murderers in the De Groote Club ? It was a great temptation. Yet we felt that it would not check the useless slaughter and might easily develop into a minor battle. We decided to retire again and ask for further instructions. After all, what could a handful of men in four light Humber reconnaissance cars do but aggravate matters ?

Period of Troubled Truce

It so happened that while we deliberated, the gallant commander of the Dutch Resistance forces, Major Overhoff, president of the Amsterdam Stock Exchange, was taking dramatic steps to stop the bloodshed. Under a flag of truce he drove in a motor-car into the Dam for a parley. Unhappily, his driver was shot dead, but Overhoff was spared and induced the Germans to cease fire pending the arrival of the British. The trouble was that while the Germans were prepared to surrender to the British they would not do so to the Dutch Resistance forces.

Meanwhile, outside the city, we were joined by Major Taite and the rest of "B" Squadron, making, if memory serves, ten armoured cars altogether. So for the third time that momentous day I found myself being whisked into Amsterdam. Through darkening, deserted streets, where fearful faces peered from the doorways, we drove straight to the Burgomaster's office in the Prinsenhof Stadhuis. Major Taite took Redfern and me into a room where we met Major Overhoff, the Burgomaster, Mr. de Boer, and several other Dutch Resistance leaders. It was heavily furnished and dimly lighted by an oil lamp. The atmosphere was tense, and outside an unnatural quiet brooded over the city that had lately been so boisterously happy.

MAJOR TAITE took command of the situation in a calm and confident manner. He telephoned for the German commander, Lieut.-Colonel Schroeder, who came in five minutes. Schroeder offered his hand, which the Major refused. Then, looking sheepish and uncomfortable, the German sat mute, making pencil notes of Major Taite's orders, which were that after curfew his men were to proceed to certain concentration areas. They were no longer to be scattered in "penny packets" all over Amsterdam.

So ended the tragic battle of Amsterdam, though for days the electrical situation lasted while the Germans remained in their barracks heavily guarded by their own armed sentries, and Dutch Resistance forces roamed the streets arresting Fifth Columnists and openly displaying their arms, which they had kept hidden for months or years. At night, we frequently heard outbursts of firing, and the atmosphere did not become easy until the arrival of the Canadians in force two or three days later.

DRIVING TO THE ZUIDER ZEE, Bren carriers of the 49th Division's Reconnaissance Regiment halted outside Kampen, near the mouth of the River Ijssel, on April 19, 1945. Tumultuous welcome was accorded the British and Canadians by the jubilant population. The area was practically free of German troops, and the historic old town was unharmed. PAGE 676 *War Office photo*

We Bid Farewell to Two Famous Ships of Battle

AFTER THIRTY YEARS SERVICE H.M.S. WARSPITE, "Grand Old Lady of the Royal Navy," is being scrapped. In January 1947 she was in Portsmouth Dockyard (1), where her gun mountings and other installations were removed (see also page 6). The ship's cat, "Stripey" (2), has served in her for 8 years. The Implacable (3, right), formerly the Duguay-Trouin, captured from the French on Nov. 4, 1805, and for years used as a training ship, lowered her colours for the last time on Jan. 14, 1947, also at Portsmouth. PAGE 677 *Photos, Topical, Central Press, Keystone*

How the Glowworm's Light Went Out at Last

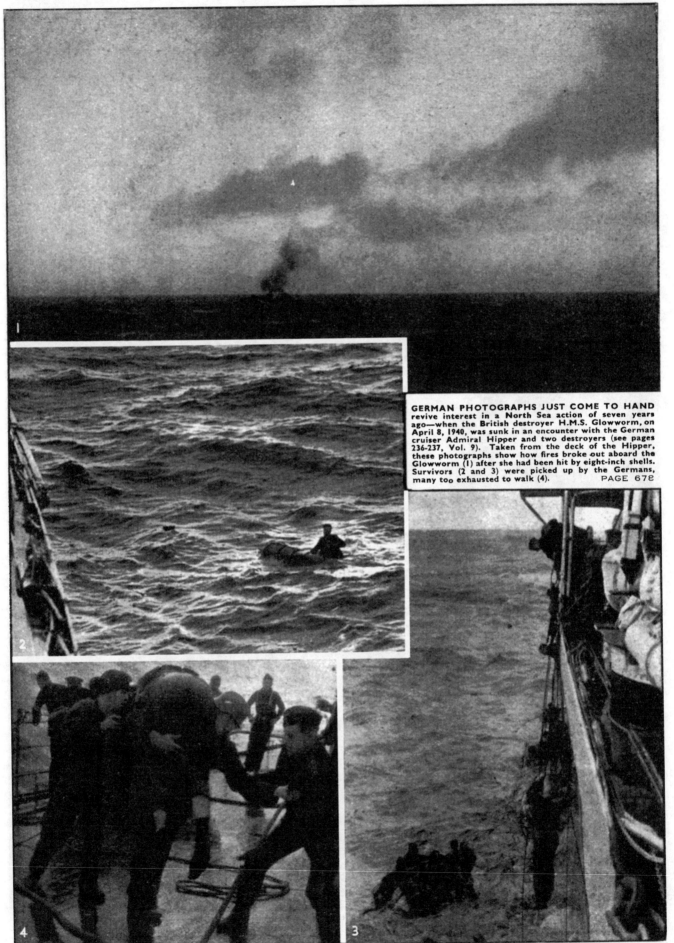

GERMAN PHOTOGRAPHS JUST COME TO HAND revive interest in a North Sea action of seven years ago—when the British destroyer H.M.S. Glowworm, on April 8, 1940, was sunk in an encounter with the German cruiser Admiral Hipper and two destroyers (see pages 236-237, Vol. 9). Taken from the deck of the Hipper, these photographs show how fires broke out aboard the Glowworm (1) after she had been hit by eight-inch shells. Survivors (2 and 3) were picked up by the Germans, many too exhausted to walk (4). PAGE 678

Field of Alamein is Now a Place of Pilgrimage

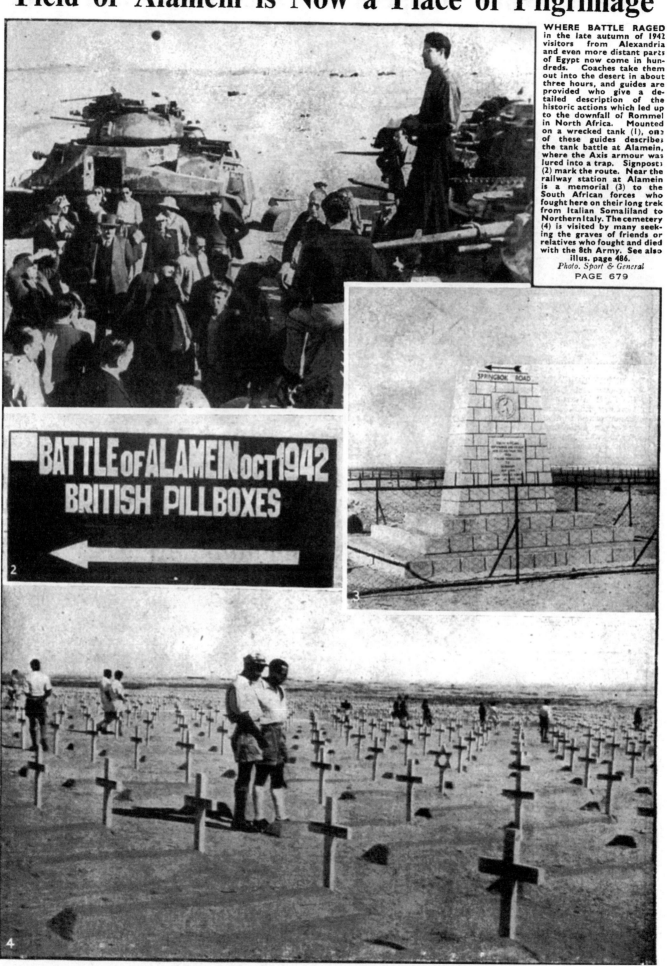

WHERE BATTLE RAGED in the late autumn of 1942 visitors from Alexandria and even more distant parts of Egypt now come in hundreds. Coaches take them out into the desert in about three hours, and guides are provided who give a detailed description of the historic actions which led up to the downfall of Rommel in North Africa. Mounted on a wrecked tank (1), one of these guides describes the tank battle at Alamein, where the Axis armour was lured into a trap. Signposts (2) mark the route. Near the railway station at Alamein is a memorial (3) to the South African forces who fought here on their long trek from Italian Somaliland to Northern Italy. The cemetery (4) is visited by many seeking the graves of friends or relatives who fought and died with the 8th Army. See also illus. page 486.

Photo. Sport & General

BATTLE of ALAMEIN OCT 1942
BRITISH PILLBOXES

SPRINGBOK ROAD

This is What Happens to Discovered Nazi Loot

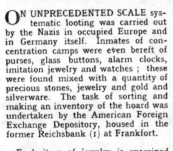

ON UNPRECEDENTED SCALE systematic looting was carried out by the Nazis in occupied Europe and in Germany itself. Inmates of concentration camps were even bereft of purses, glass buttons, alarm clocks, imitation jewelry and watches; these were found mixed with a quantity of precious stones, jewelry and gold and silverware. The task of sorting and making an inventory of the hoard was undertaken by the American Foreign Exchange Depository, housed in the former Reichsbank (1) at Frankfort.

Each item of jewelry is examined by an expert (2). One storeroom contains over 300 gold and silver articles (3). Roughly packed in wooden boxes are hundreds of clocks (4). Even more important are vast deposits of gold and silver bullion of all countries which were discovered by the Americans in 1945 at Marker's Mine, to the north of Kassel. Counting and valuing banknotes (5).

Exclusive to THE WAR ILLUSTRATED

R.A.F. Regiment Patrols Keep the Peace in Berlin

AT THE GATOW R.A.F. STATION, BERLIN, is a detachment of No. 2777 Squadron of the R.A.F. Regiment, which maintains a constant patrol in the environs of the aerodrome. Humber armoured cars, manned by a crew of three, leave by the main gate (1) to patrol the streets of Gatow (2) for an hour, the area including the shores of the Havel (3), a lake that was formerly one of the Berliners' playgrounds. The unceasing vigilance of the crews, their turnout and the smartness of their vehicles, has earned them the respect of the German civilians. Before proceeding on patrol the crews and cars are inspected (4), and during the winter months the men wear windproof tank suits. Hardly a day passes without some minor incident, the most common crime being the stealing of food or fuel from military camps. PAGE 681 *Exclusive to* THE WAR ILLUSTRATED

HIS MAJESTY'S SHIPS   H.M.N.Z.S. Kiwi

THE Kiwi was one of three large trawlers of special design built at Leith for the Royal New Zealand Navy at the beginning of the war, the other two being named Moa and Tui. Of 600 tons displacement, armed with one 4-inch, several smaller guns and depth-charge equipment, they were originally rated as corvettes. They were launched in 1941 and delivered in the Pacific the following year—in good time to take part with other Allied naval forces under American command in the struggle to drive the Japanese out of the Solomon Islands and adjacent territories.

On the night of January 29, 1943, the Kiwi and Moa were on patrol in the Solomons when they intercepted a large Japanese submarine, the I.1, of nearly 2,000 tons. She was armed with two 5·5-inch and some smaller guns and on paper should have been more than a match for the two New Zealand craft; but after a fierce struggle on the surface, the enemy vessel was driven aground on a shoal and destroyed, an action for which the captains and other officers and men of the Kiwi and Moa were decorated. Unfortunately the Moa did not long survive this engagement. On April 7 following she foundered off Guadalcanal as the result of damage sustained in action with Japanese aircraft.

The third ship of the class, the Tui, also distinguished herself. On August 19, 1943, she sank a still larger Japanese submarine, I.17, of 2,180 tons, off New Caledonia, being aided in the hunt by American shore-based aircraft.

The Worcestershire Regiment

By Major H. P. E. Pereira

IN August 1939 the Worcestershire Regiment was composed of two Regular and two Territorial battalions: the 1st stationed in Palestine, the 2nd at Sialkhot, India. The 7th and 8th Territorial battalions were at their annual camp and in the process of "doubling," which resulted in the formation of the 9th and 10th Battalions. (The 3rd and 4th, Regular Battalions, raised in 1900, were disbanded after the 1914-1918 war. The 5th and 6th represented the old Militia and had ceased to exist.) Such was the set up of the Regiment when the Second Great War broke out. In 1940 two new battalions, the 11th and 12th, were raised.

The 1st Battalion moved to the Sudan just before war was declared and formed part of the 5th Indian Division patrolling the border between the Sudan and the Italian possessions in East Africa ; the mortar detachment was mounted on camels to facilitate patrolling with the Sudan Defence Force. At the end of 1940 the Italians invaded the Sudan, and the fight was on. With the 29th Brigade of the 5th Indian Division the Battalion began the long battle into Eritrea. At Gogni and Barentu the Italians were routed, retreating to the mountain fortress of Keren that barred the way to Eritrea. The 4th and 5th Indian Divisions laboriously seized the lower spurs as a start line for an assault on the high peaks, with the object of working along the summits until they could dominate Keren Gorge, the only passage through this formidable barrier.

Guard of Honour at Amba Alagi

More than once the Regiment won to the key heights, only to leave their dead there when fierce counter-attacks hurled the assailants back down the slopes. The objective of the 1st Battalion was Falestoh—one of the towering peaks. B and C Companies reached the crest on the left of Falestoh and a fierce bomb fight ensued. The rest of the Battalion, forsaking caution, rushed across the open in support and arrived in time to stem a counter-attack by an Alpini battalion. The Battalion had achieved its objective but was precariously established, with enemy posts all around. The enemy realized this and concentrated their fire on the salient, and our ammunition began to run out. Attempts to drop supplies by air went astray.

As the Battalion had been out of touch with Brigade all day, owing to the fire that signals attracted to Brigade H.Q., the commanding officer went back to report on the situation. When he returned it was with orders to retire—casualties had been heavy, and in the Battalion's present condition there could be no hope of maintaining the position won, unless supports could be brought up ; success and Keren were so near, yet there was not a fresh unit in the whole force. The 29th Brigade had been the last throw. That night the 1st Battalion was withdrawn, after evacuating the wounded. They then held a line of hills behind the fort from which they could watch the final forcing of the pass a week later by the other two brigades of the Division. Their advance so surprised the Italians that when the Battalion's turn came to capture Zeban, on the third day after the attack, the enemy had withdrawn. The advance was continued on to Amba Alagi, where the Italian Viceroy finally surrendered

THE 250th anniversary of the raising of the Regiment by Colonel Farrington was celebrated in February 1944 by the 1st Battalion (29th Foot); the 2nd Battalion (36th Foot) was raised eight years later—in 1702. In 1794, detachments of the 29th (Worcestershire) Regiment of Foot served as Marines on board Earl Howe's fleet at the battle of the Glorious First of June, and for this action the Regiment was later granted the honour of bearing a Naval crown upon its Colours. Its many battle-honours were added to during the 1914-18 war, when the Regiment increased to 22 battalions and served on four fronts and in Egypt and Persia.

on May 19, 1941. The 1st Battalion formed part of the guard of honour when the garrison, led by the Viceroy, the Duke of Aosta, marched out with the due honours of war.

LIEUT.-COL. J. PARKES, M.C., D.C.M. (right), commanded the 7th Battalion in France during the 1939-40 campaign. He had served as a private with the Regiment in the First Great War.

Meanwhile, Rommel's panzers were sweeping on and the 5th Indian Division was moved to the Western Desert. In the Knightsbridge fighting of May 1942 the 1st Battalion held a "box" at Point 187, holding up and destroying the German armour until overrun by sheer weight of numbers. The attack was made by 60 panzers supported by infantry in lorries. From the beginning the Germans concentrated their fire on the guns inside the box while the infantry tried to work around the flanks. At four o'clock the Germans broke through the forward positions and the Battalion went for them with Bren guns, bombs and bayonets. When they were nearly surrounded, the survivors, 500 of the 700 who had commenced the action, were ordered to fight their way out. This they eventually succeeded in doing, leaving 20 German tanks knocked out.

Unexplained Tragedy of Tobruk

The Battalion was then withdrawn into Tobruk. When the Germans' onslaught fell on that fortress in June it was the Worcestershires and the Coldstream Guards who bore the brunt of the first attack. What happened afterwards has never been officially explained, but, in the words of their commanding officer, "in good heart and with their tails well up " the Battalion were ordered to destroy their guns and stores and cease fighting. The majority of the Battalion were made prisoners, though a small party under the adjutant managed to escape in transport. From the survivors of this tragedy, and reinforcements already at the base, it was proposed to re-form the 1st Battalion, but higher authority decreed otherwise, and a small cadre returned to England to re-form.

On January 1, 1943, the Battalion was re-formed on this cadre by disbanding the 11th Battalion and drafting the personnel to the 1st Battalion. On January 5, their colours, which had gone with the Battalion to Palestine and were brought back by the cadre, were laid up in Worcester Cathedral for safe keeping until Victory. The reconstituted Battalion carried on with the training

WORCESTERS AND CAMERONS who broke out of Tobruk before the surrender of the port in June 1942, and escaped in a captured truck. After the Battle of Knightsbridge the 1st Battalion The Worcestershire Regiment was withdrawn into the fortress, and received orders to cease fighting; but some fought their way back to the British lines. PAGE 683 *War Office photographs*

that the 11th Battalion had been doing with the 1st and the 9th Armoured Divisions and then the 24th and 33rd Guards Independent Brigade Groups. Shortly afterwards the Battalion was posted to the 43rd (Wessex) Division. Training went on until D-Day, and the Battalion crossed to France about 10 days after the first wave. One of their first actions, which resulted in the capture of Mouen, in the region of Caen, was described by the divisional commander as "one of the slickest attacks of the war."

Every Man Went Into Battle

After the breakout came the spectacular drive to the Seine with the 43rd Division in the lead—100 miles in three-and-a-half days. At dawn on August 26 part of the Battalion crossed the river and held a firm bridgehead after severe fighting. In the evening more assault troops crossed under smoke and strong machine-gun support. They were met with intense fire and for several hours the situation was critical. At first light the next morning a second attempt succeeded. The Battalion established itself on the wooded heights overlooking the river and stood firm to prevent enemy interference with the bridging. Next day the Battalion was ordered to extend the bridge-head by working along towards Tilly, which involved a clash with Tiger tanks.

To stem the counter-attacks that the Germans mounted all day every man in the Battalion went into battle—drivers, clerks, orderlies and signallers. This fierce fighting gave cover to the armoured drive into Belgium and Holland. After a spell of comparative quiet the Battalion set out again, driving up into Holland to try to relieve the gallant men of Arnhem. The fighting to keep the supply corridor open was some of the fiercest the Battalion had experienced. Three company commanders were killed in action around the Neder Rijn. The month of

October 1944 was spent "resting" in Holland in precarious discomfort.

The next move came in November, towards the Siegfried Line, and the Division took on left-flank protection to the Americans breaking out towards Julich and Duren. After capturing Tripsrath, the Battalion felt the full weight of the heavy guns in the Siegfried Line, and eventually was relieved—too tired almost to care. When the Germans tried their last desperate throw in the Ardennes the Battalion was in reserve and was able to celebrate a very passable imitation of Christmas. January 1945 saw some fighting in the Tripsrath area, and early in February the Battalion moved up into the Eindhoven area. Preparations were on foot for rolling up the Siegfried Line, and the 1st put up a very fine show in their battle to capture the Goch escarpment. After the battle, the Corps Commander, General Horrocks, sent to the Regiment a special message of praise.

The Triumphal End in Germany

The Battalion was not in the first crossing of the Rhine but followed up in the area of the Highland Division. Trying to break out from the bridge-head they came across fanatical paratroopers entrenched on an unfinished autobahn. The battle was costly, but was won. The breakout proper found the Battalion in the van of the Brigade and the vanguard company, mounted on tanks, made a fruitless dash to try to prevent a bridge over the Twete canal being blown. One tank was actually on the bridge when the latter was destroyed. The advance continued, and as victory drew near the Battalion prepared to clear up Bremen, then moved on—and VE Day found them in an area north of Lüneburg. So ended the progress of the 1st Battalion from Normandy to Germany. It had won five D.S.O.s, seven M.C.s, two D.C.M.s, 20 M.M.s, one B.E.M., one Croix de Guerre, 19 C.-in-C.'s Certificates for

Colours : *Yellow Arrow on Black Circle*

7TH (INDIAN) DIVISION

MOBILIZED in the spring of 1942, this Division in 1943 received special training in jungle warfare, Major-General F. W. Messervy assuming command in July of that year. Later in 1943 it was operating in the Arakan with the 5th Indian Division. In February 1944 the 7th was surrounded in the region of the Ngakyedauk Pass, where it put up a magnificent fight until relieved by the 5th Division on February 23.

In the following month the 7th assumed the offensive, capturing Buthidaung, and took part in the repulse of the Japanese attacks at Kohima and Imphal. In December it began a march of 400 miles to the south, the leading troops crossing the Irrawaddy at Nyaungu on February 14, 1945. Pagan was seized two days later ; and there was heavy fighting during the Japanese attempts to eliminate the bridge-head.

ITS next task was the recapture of the oilfields in the Chauk and Yenangyaung areas, successfully accomplished during April. It was then engaged in intercepting parties of the enemy endeavouring to escape across the Irrawaddy. After the surrender of the Japanese the 7th was flown into Siam, where it disarmed and concentrated 113,000 Japanese troops. It rescued and evacuated some 20,000 British and Australian prisoners of war and took charge of 25,000 coolies brought from Malaya by the Japanese.

From December 1944 to February 1946 Major-General G. C. Evans commanded the Division, whose composition was continually changing ; but the infantry brigades were the 33rd, the 89th and 114th. The infantry, between August 1943 and December 1945, was made up at one period or another by battalions of the Queen's, King's Own Scottish Borderers, Somerset Light Infantry, South Lancashire Regt., Punjab Regt., Sikhs, Jats, Gurkhas and the 1st Burma Regiment.

Gallantry, and 20 officers and men were mentioned in dispatches.

Throughout this period the Battalion was supported in great style by a battery of the 179 Field Regiment, R.A.—which was raised in 1942 from the 12th Battalion The Worcestershire Regiment. The 12th had been raised in June 1940, and when trained did duty on the beaches in South Wales, and in the early summer, 1941, went to Iceland and took over the defences of the North-West Sector. Returning to England towards the end of the year they were stationed at Gravesend and had an anti-invasion role. At this time it became necessary to convert several infantry battalions to various types of gunners, and the 12th was one of the two battalions specially selected for conversion to a field regiment. And so on March 1, 1942, the 12th Battalion ceased to exist and was transformed into the 179 Field Regiment, Royal Artillery.

AT A CEREMONY OF INCORPORATION at Harrow School, Middlesex, on Jan. 1, 1943, the 11th Battalion was merged in the 1st Battalion, the main body of the latter having been captured at Tobruk. The reborn unit, as the 1st Battalion, was inspected by the Colonel of the Regiment, Brig. Gen. G. W. St. G. Grogan, V.C., C.B., C.M.G., D.S.O.   PAGE 684   *War Office photograph*

Through Burma with The 2nd and 7th Worcesters

FIGHT AND ADVANCE—that was the watchword of the 2nd and 7th Battalions The Worcestershire Regiment in Burma. They entered the campaign early in 1944 and endured its horrors and hardships until its victorious conclusion in August 1945. Humour helped them along the road, which in those days appeared to stretch so far into the distant future. At Stonehenge Camp, between Imphal and Kohima, the Worcesters erected a signpost (1) to mark a staging point on the road to Tokyo. One of the ancient stones from which the camp took its name can be seen on the left of this photograph.

Major F. G. Burrell, of the 7th Battalion, received the Military Cross from Lt.-Gen. Sir Oliver Leese, Bt., K.C.B., D.S.O., C.-in-C. Allied Land Forces South-East Asia, at an investiture at Calcutta on April 26, 1945 (2).

The 7th Battalion performed a wonderful feat of endurance in marching 120 miles in 20 days across central Burma. Assembled on Mount Popa, an extinct volcano to the west of Meiktila, a little crowd gathered round the wireless set (3) to hear news of the "other war," in which in April 1945 the Allies were poised ready for the kill.

War Office photographs
PAGE 685

IN SHATTERED HOUSES OF BENNEVILLE, Normandy, a section of the 1st Battalion searched for snipers during the advance of the 43rd (Wessex) Division towards Aunay-sur-Odon at the beginning of August 1944. The man kneeling at the window is covering the entry of comrades, and is protected by the man behind him. *War Office photograph*

Two battalions of the Regiment fought in South-East Asia with the 14th Army. The 2nd was in India at the start of the war and after a spell on the North-West Frontier was employed on internal security. Joining the 19th Indian ("Dagger") Division, the 2nd set about various types of training—with Burma as the end in view. The 7th Battalion had already seen fighting in France, with the 2nd Division, and were evacuated from Dunkirk ; they then re-formed and went to India with the rest of the division.

Two Battalions Advanced on the Japs

The story of the Regiment in Burma began in 1944. Throughout it was a tale of fight and advance—never once was either the 2nd or the 7th Battalion forced back. At the time, IV Corps was cut off in Imphal from the rest of India by the Japs who held, among other places, Kohima, the mountain stronghold. To open the only road between Imphal and India, Kohima had to be captured ; and the task was given to the 2nd Division. One action among many is memorable—it was at Merema that the 7th Battalion evicted in 36 hours a Jap force that had been ordered to hold on for ten days. With the fall of Kohima the road from India to Burma was opened, and the 2nd Division flooded down to the Burma border before taking a well-earned rest.

In the last months of the year the two Worcestershire Battalions advanced on the Japs, taking different routes. The 7th, without hindrance from the enemy, reached and crossed the Chindwin River at Kalewa. From there they marched across the sandy plain of Central Burma towards Shwebo, covering the last 120 miles in 20 days which included some fighting. Shwebo is a famous name now in the Regiment ; in the Regimental Museum is a lacquered bowl presented by the inhabitants to the 7th in gratitude for their deliverance from the Japs.

Meantime the 2nd had performed one of the greatest of Burma forced marches through forests, jungles and valleys, over hills, gorges and rivers. Keeping up the tradition of their predecessors, the old 36th Foot, who were known in the Peninsular War as "The Marching 36th," in six weeks they covered 400 miles from the Chindwin, stopping to build an airstrip and have two small fights with the Japs on the

way. First moving eastwards, they turned south to advance on Shwebo. In their first scrap with the Japs they captured two swords which are now in the Regimental Museum. The two Battalions met in Shwebo in the village square ; the 7th, first to arrive on the scene, laid dinner for their comrades, in the open air, using parachutes as tablecloths.

Between Shwebo and the Irrawaddy, which covered the entrance to Mandalay, lay 120 miles of hot, dry plain covered with scrub. The Japs pulled back to hide in the hills at Sagaing or behind the barrier of the Irrawaddy. The 7th gave chase. Down along the banks of the Irrawaddy the 7th grouped with their comrades of the Camerons, Dorsets and Royal Welch Fusiliers for the crossing of that great river. Disaster nearly overtook them when they started the assault—their boats were rotten and leaked furiously. Under a heavy fire the boats sank and their occupants swam or waded ashore. Happily the casualties were few; but the 7th had to wait impatiently until the other battalions could spare their boats. The bridge-head was made in short time, and fighting through elephant grass and sniper-ridden country they joined the

Camerons and Royal Welch Fusiliers in the Nagazun bridge-head, enlarged it and broke out towards Mandalay.

Meanwhile, the 2nd fought their battle for Mandalay. They had turned east with the 19th Division, made towards Kyaukmymayaung, and helped to establish the first 14th Army bridge-head across the Irrawaddy, at Singhu, against fanatical Jap resistance. Gradually this bridge-head, a vital one held only by a small force, was secured and widened, thus allowing the 14th Army's advance on Mandalay to continue. At Mandalay the 2nd Battalion helped to encircle Fort Dufferin while the Air Forces tried to blast holes in the massive walls. On March 19 our troops were astonished to see an Anglo-Burman come out of one of the gates carrying a white flag. The Japs had fled ! Advanced troops of the 19th Indian Division and the 2nd Division met in the Fort, and the Union Jack and the flag of the 19th Division were hoisted. The 2nd Division claimed to have wiped up more than half the escaping garrison, and the 7th Battalion included several cars in their bag. The 7th saw no further serious fighting, but the 2nd Battalion had the task of clearing up the Japs who were scurrying back to what they thought was safety. After VJ Day the 7th Battalion was depleted by drafts of homegoing men for release, but they were brought up to strength again and are employed on internal security duties in India. The 2nd Battalion is at Maymyo, in Burma.

The 10th in "Exercise Big Bobs"

The 8th Battalion went to France early in 1940 with the 48th Division, which was composed of Midland Territorials, and for a short time occupied outposts in front of the Maginot Line. Then came the advance into Belgium and the subsequent withdrawal to Dunkirk ; on June 1, 1940, a party from the 8th Battalion was taken off the beaches by H.M.S. Worcester, and that day these men were among those who manned the A.A. guns and helped to bring down several Heinkels. After Dunkirk the Battalion re-formed and carried out an anti-invasion role and later became a training battalion drafting to other battalions. Late in 1945 the 8th entered into "suspended animation."

The 9th and 10th Battalions, offshoots from the 7th and 8th, were in the 61st Division and trained in Northern Ireland, preparing for the assault on Europe. This, however, was not to be, and the 9th and 10th had to find drafts to make good the wastage in battle of other battalions, as well as rehabilitating wounded and returned prisoners of war. The 10th took on recruit training for a while, and before and after D-day played an important role with exercise "Big Bobs"—which consisted in assembling and maintaining a fleet of dummy landing craft at Dover, Folkestone and on the Orwell near Ipswich. This deception played a large part in keeping the German army in the Pas de Calais when they would have been invaluable to the army fighting in Normandy.

THE 10th found itself going into "suspended animation," while the 9th were once again a combatant battalion training for a special role in the Far East. The collapse of the Japs put an end to this, and the 9th, too, went into "suspended animation." The fortunes of the 11th and 12th have already been recounted : one became the nucleus of the 1st Battalion, after Tobruk, and the other Battalion a Field Regiment of the Royal Artillery.

PTE. FORMAN, of London, was with the 1st Battalion in the first British offensive on German soil. It started on Nov. 18, 1944, when the 2nd Army attacked in the Geilenkirchen sector, north of Aachen.
War Office photograph

Life in Britain's Largest Training Ship Afloat

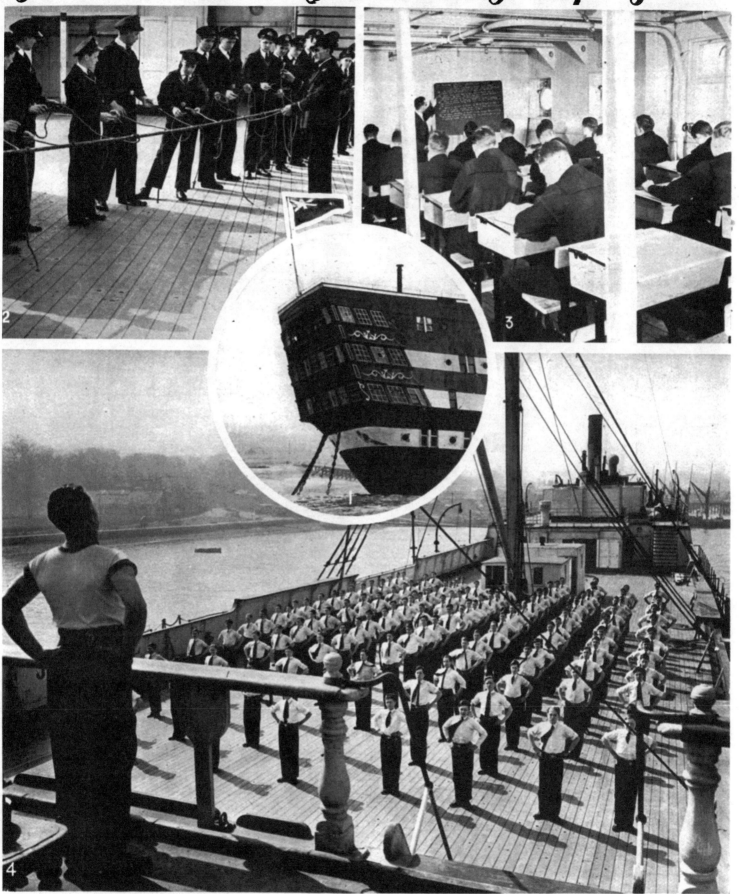

Built for the L.C.C., the former Exmouth, new training ship of the Thames Nautical Training College, has now been renamed H.M.S. Worcester, the stern of which is shown (1), for the sake of tradition and to preserve the continuity of this famous name. She is moored off Greenhithe, Kent, and was specially built as a training ship, the classrooms being light and airy (3). The curriculum provides for a general education as well as instruction in nautical subjects, such as tying knots (2). Physical training (4) and drill are carried out on the spacious upper deck. *Exclusive to* THE WAR ILLUSTRATED

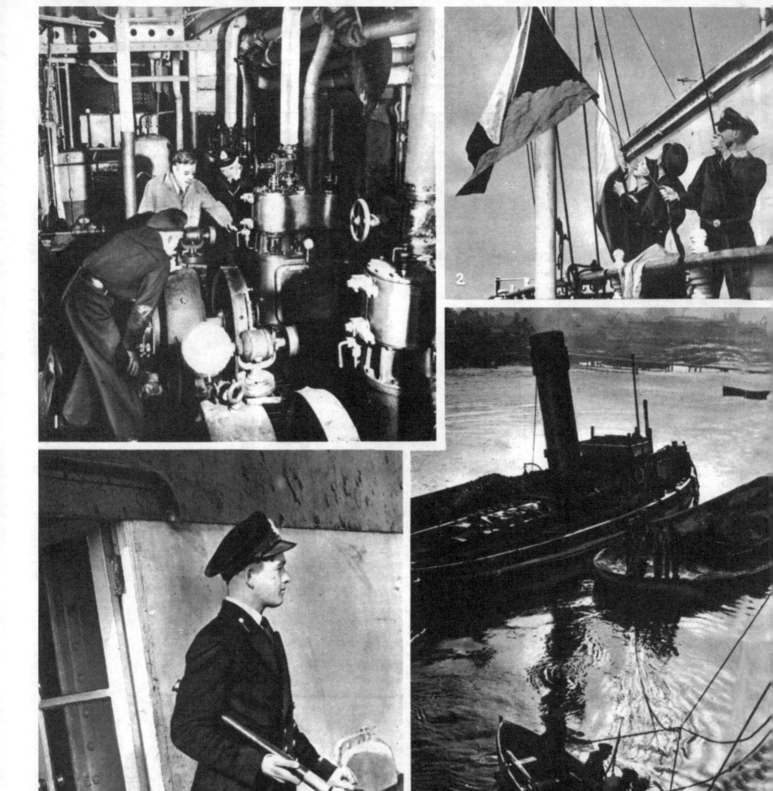

Cadets Trained in the Ways of the Sea

Below decks the boys are shown how to handle marine engines (1). Every ship's officer must be something of an engineer, as a modern ship is a mass of complex machinery. All vessels speak an international language with flags, and the cadets must learn to make and read signals (2). The ability to remain alert during a lonely watch is acquired (4); while a not too pleasant duty of which the technique must be mastered is that of coaling ship (5).

Exclus
THE WAR I

Young Seadogs Work Hard and Play Hard

There is considerable rivalry between the boats' crews (3) and to be the winners of the annual boat race is accounted a signal honour. Taught to pull an oar and handle a small boat in all weathers, the cadets will be able to do these things better than the men they command when they become officers of the Merchant Navy. H.M.S. Worcester is a floating replica of a modern school; and the lengthy decks take the place of the customary grounds (6).

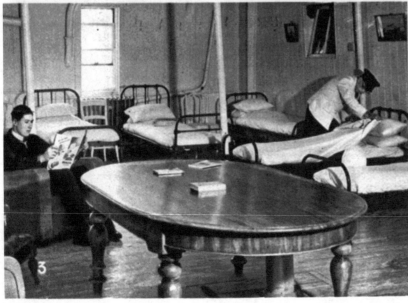

Home of 200 Cadets

Having a gross displacement of 6,000 tons and a length of 346 feet, with a beam of 53 feet, the new Worcester can well accommodate her normal complement of 200 cadets and an instructional staff of 50. The boys join between the ages of 13½ and 16, the leaving age being 17. The fees are £150 a year, and qualified cadets have little difficulty in obtaining appointments in the Merchant Navy. The Commander is Captain Gordon Steele, V.C., R.N. (Retired), an old Worcester boy. After the passing out examinations of the Senior Term, the top cadet is chaired by his term mates (4). There is a fine library (1); a dignified little chapel (2); and a well-equipped sick bay (3).

EAST and WEST AFRICANS in BURMA

By HARLEY V. USILL

Tʜᴇ decision to send African troops to the Far East demanded the most careful consideration. Both East and West Africans had performed magnificently against the Italians in the Abyssinian campaign (see pages 243 and 275), but how would they react to the Japanese ? Then there were the questions of health and the effect of separation from their native land. Early in 1942 it was decided to take the risk, and a Brigade of East Africans sailed for Ceylon. The West Africans were then still needed to protect West Africa from attacks which might develop through Vichy-controlled territory.

The East African Brigade arrived too late to be employed in the defence of Burma, and for many months they helped to defend Ceylon, undergoing hard jungle training. In 1943 this Brigade was increased to a Division ; later, two independent Brigades were sent to the Far East over and above this Force. This decision meant that East Africa Command assumed a new responsibility in the provision of fighting men and services against the Japanese. Commenting on this task Lieut.-General Sir Kenneth A.N. Anderson, General Officer Commanding-in-Chief, East Africa Command, said :

"Training was the keynote. The Askari, thousands of whom answered the recruiting calls of the Government, had to be trained along new lines. Fighting in the jungles of the Far East demanded a specialized type of warfare ; tactics which proved their value in North African deserts and Tunisian mountains, the fast-moving, mechanized warfare which brought Nazi Germany to her knees, were impossible over Burmese jungle terrain. So officers who had fought in Burma, and were therefore conversant with jungle warfare, were brought to the East Africa Command to give battalions the benefit of their experiences.

"Complete Japanese bunker positions and Burmese villages were built in the African bush ; Askari sweated on the slopes of Kilimanjaro and Mount Kenya, or in dense country miles from the nearest town and its prying eyes, as they learnt the kill-or-be-killed tactics of the jungle . . . And in due course the East African forces went overseas to battle once again."

Meanwhile, in West Africa, the danger from Vichy having gone, preparations were in train for sending two complete Divisions to fight in the Far East. The 81st Division was completed in April 1943, and the 82nd Division in the following October. On its arrival in India the 81st West African Division went into training for a short period, and by the end of the year it was on the Burma frontier, deployed ready to strike.

West Africans Go Into Action

In December 1943 the main body of West Africans started out from " Christmas Camp," in the little Bengal town of Chiringa, in an attempt to reach the valley of the Kaladan River—cutting a track, later called the " West African Way," through the jungle. The job was done in six weeks, and by January 17, 1944, about 80 miles of the road had been driven through to the upper waters of the Kaladan, across some of the worst country in Burma. By January 24 the Division reached and occupied Paletwa, and by-passing Kaladan village advanced to their main objective, the road and river centre of Kyauktaw. Here the Gold Coast Brigade struck off to the west to come down the Pi Chaung River which joins the Kaladan just in front of Kyauktaw.

Everything now appeared to be ready for a further advance across the Kaladan. This had actually commenced when the whole situation changed. A strong force of Japanese attacked the few troops which had been left behind, and on March 2 reoccupied

Fɪɢʜᴛɪɴɢ in' the jungle through the monsoon, participating in amphibious operations, and airborne with the Chindits, native troops from East and West Africa, under British officers and senior N.C.O.s, gained distinction in the Burma victorious campaigns of 1944 and 1945.

Kyauktaw. Instructions were received to get back on to the Kaladan River and destroy the Japanese forces which had reoccupied Kaladan village and were using " West African Way " for their advance. Kaladan village was retaken on April 3, contact was made with an Indian battalion garrisoning Paletwa, and the road to the north was at last cleared. The columns reached India with the loss of only one lorry. Commenting on this first campaign of the West Africans, Brigadier C. M. Findly of the Army Medical Corps said, " No other troops, European or

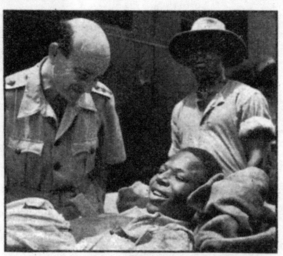

WOUNDED FROM BURMA arrived at Accra, Gold Coast Colony, in August 1945. The 81st West African Division built up a magnificent reputation fighting the Japanese.
British Official photograph

Indian, could possibly have undergone the same physical exertions as the Africans and come out of the Kaladan still smiling."

While the West Africans were fighting in the Kaladan, the 11th East African Division had completed training in Ceylon. It moved to Burma in August 1944 to become part of the 14th Army under General Slim and to join in the advance which was driving the Japanese down from Imphal into northwest Burma. Through the mud and rain of the monsoon it fought its way down the Kabaw Valley, the " Valley of Death," taking Kalemyo and Kalewa, and establishing a bridge-head over the River Chindwin opposite Kalewa before being relieved by the 20th Indian Division. " The 11th East African Division," said General Slim, " had with the 5th Indian Division the honour of achieving what had up to then been considered impossible. It was thought that no major formation could move or fight in the worst jungle country through the monsoon. They did it."

Gᴇɴᴇʀᴀʟ Sʟɪᴍ's next objective was Mandalay and in this the 28th East African Brigade played an important role. The East African Brigade led the secret march of the IV Corps to the Irrawaddy. It was this Corps which established such a grip on Meiktila that the XXXIII Corps was able to break from its bridge-head below Mandalay and storm southwards. For the Japanese, caught in an encircling movement, there was no

escape, and with the capture of Mandalay the battle of Central Burma was won.

Before dealing with the final phases of the Burma campaign, special mention must be made of the West African Reconnaissance Regiment which, on the Maungdaw coast in March 1944, landed in sampans to give valuable support to the British and Indian troops operating to the west of the Mayu range. Sailing at night in river steamers and small boats they made more than 150 patrols and commando-like landings on enemy-held beaches to destroy stores and communications, and returned with valuable information. Then there was the Nigerian Brigade with the famous Chindits. This, the Third Brigade of the 81st West African Division, had been specially chosen as part of the long-range penetration group operating with General Wingate in Central Burma. In the campaign for the capture of Rangoon both West and East Africans were prominent. Once again the 81st West African Division started from Chiringa, and in September 1944 made their way over the high ridge into the Kaladan, reaching Kyauktaw at the beginning of January 1945, running into some heavy fighting. By the end of the month they captured Nyohaung, and there were relieved by the 82nd West African Division which had recently arrived in India. This advance, by the latter Division, of 150 miles had an important effect on the operations to the west, which were designed to cause the fall of Akyab in the Arakan.

Before the final advance on Rangoon could take place, the Arakan had to be cleared of the Japanese, in order that its airfields could be utilized by the Allies. The campaign began on December 10, 1944, with the 25th Indian Division advancing astride the Mayu Mountains. On its left the 82nd West African Division reoccupied Buthidaung and moved down the east bank of the Mayu River, while the 81st West African Division was marching southward again in its old familiar tracks. The pressure on the Japanese was intense, and their attempt to escape along the coast was harassed by the West Africans who were pushing eastwards, and by seizing the ferry at Kyauktaw across the Kaladan they compelled the Japanese to carry out long flanking marches in an attempt to avoid destruction, and reach the important strategic position at the village of An.

Proud Record in the Far East

If Rangoon were to be taken before the monsoon broke, the Japanese had to be prevented from reaching this objective. It was then that the decision was taken to launch an amphibious operation against Ramree Island. In these operations one of the East African Brigades took part, and by February 22, 1945, Ramree Island was cleared.

With the plains of Mandalay cleared of the enemy and the Arakan firmly held, General Slim received orders to press on to Rangoon. The East and West Africans took no prominent part in these later stages of the Burma campaign, but their record in the Far East is one of which they can be proud. There were no spectacular advances of a thousand miles in a month as in the Abyssinian campaign, but in Burma they were up against a far more formidable enemy than the Italians, and were fighting in conditions totally unlike anything which they had encountered in the African continent. They had fully justified the decision to send them to the Far East, and rewarded the British officers and N.C.O.s who turned these unsophisticated men into fine fighting units of a mechanised army.

From Grievous Disability to Skilled Employment

"AND SO TO WORK" was the title of an exhibition opened on Jan. 8, 1947, at a site in Oxford Street, London. Organized by the Ministries of Labour and National Service, Health and Pensions, it showed the process of rehabilitation and resettlement from hospital to training centre—and so to work. Loss of a limb no longer carries the threat of unemployment. One disabled man operated a lathe (1). Another worked at a loom (2) for treatment of shoulder and spine injuries. A brick fireplace (3) was built by men from a Government centre. Two ex-Servicemen (4) made nursery furniture and perambulators. Articles of wrought iron (5) showed a high standard of training. See also illus. pages 496-498, Vol. 9.　　　　　PAGE 692

Restoring Canterbury's Stained Glass Glory

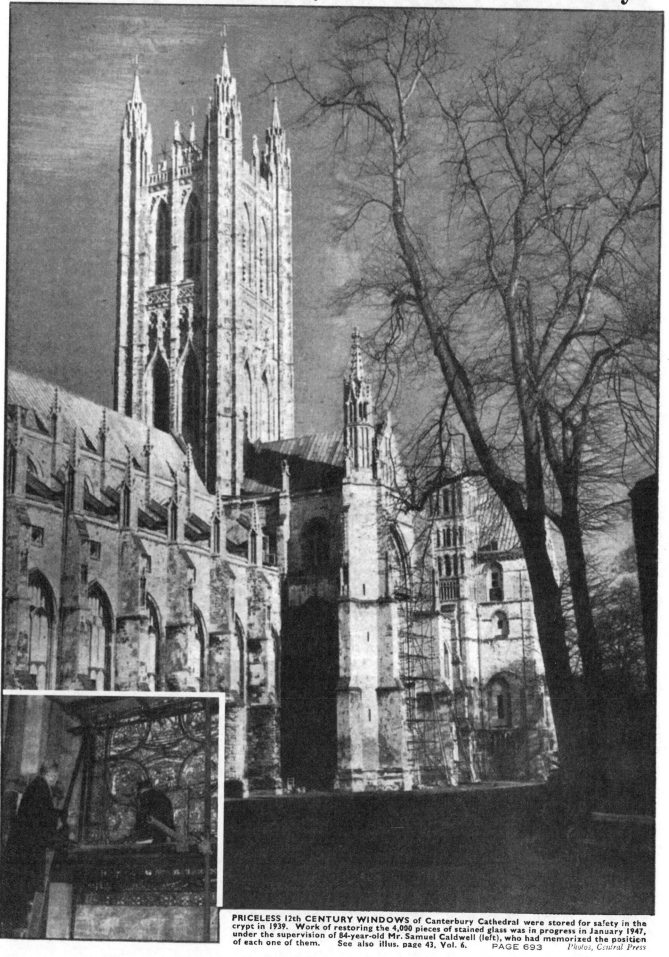

PRICELESS 12th CENTURY WINDOWS of Canterbury Cathedral were stored for safety in the crypt in 1939. Work of restoring the 4,000 pieces of stained glass was in progress in January 1947, under the supervision of 84-year-old Mr. Samuel Caldwell (left), who had memorized the position of each one of them. See also illus. page 43, Vol. 6.

Photos, Central Press

Europe's Wartime Capitals in 1947

REYKJAVIK

By NORAH GOURLIE

ICELAND's capital is her centre for shipping and industry. Here the Althing (Parliament) has met since 1845 in a dignified grey stone building backed by a garden and facing the principal square. Flanking it lies the simple, white, Lutheran Cathedral, 150 years old, a fitting association when it is remembered that Christianity was adopted by an act of the Althing for the whole country in A.D. 1000. The Presidential Residence Bessastsdir lies some miles outside the town.

Iceland already had Home Rule in 1904, and from then the standard of living rose rapidly. There was, however, a strong feeling that the ruler of the State should be an Icelander, and this increased when the country was cut off from her King in Denmark in 1914 and again in 1940. For a year after the latter date the regal authority was exercised by the Icelandic Government, but this was found impractical and a Regent was appointed.

Ceremony on Plain of Thingvellir

In May 1944 a general referendum was held 95 per cent of Icelandic citizens who had attained their majority voting for a revival of the Republic of Iceland. The Hon. Sveinn Björnsson, who had already acted as Regent, was returned unopposed as President, and on June 17 the Republic of Iceland was formally proclaimed. The ceremony took place on the Plain of Thingvellir, on the spot where the first session of the Althing was held in A.D. 930 and where it continued to meet till Reykjavik was found to be more convenient. The separation from Denmark was carried out amicably and the King sent his former subjects a message of good wishes. Sveinn Björnsson, a loved and respected President, is rendering his country great services.

The town of Reykjavik has grown up round the harbour flanked by two hills over which it has spread. On the opposite side of the wide bay is the beautiful Esja, a long mountain range sloping nearly sheer into the sea, of which splendid views can be had from almost every street. The snow-capped Snaefell glacier can also be seen. The University and the Roman Catholic Cathedral both command dominant sites and are visible far out at sea. Architecturally they are simple and imposing.

As everything has to be imported except fish, sheep, cattle and horses, the harbour is busy with big ships from Great Britain, the U.S.A., Denmark, Norway and other European countries. There is also much lively traffic at the large aerodrome built during the war a couple of miles outside the town. Planes for Scotland, Denmark, Sweden, and the U.S.A. leave several times a week.

The population of Iceland is 130,000 and of Reykjavik 50,000. Here the numbers have risen tremendously during the war years owing to the huge demand for even unskilled labour made by the Allied troops. Although these have now left, the people drawn to the capital show no desire to follow suit and the housing shortage is acute. Nissen hut camps have been taken over for civilian use till housing accommodation is sufficient. During the last three years approximately 700 houses have been built of concrete, roughcast over with native gravel which gives an attractive, soft broken-grey finish. The houses are of modern design, mostly of a two-storey type, semi-detached and surrounded by a good garden. There are a few larger blocks.

All lighting and cooking is done by water-generated electricity, and the greater number of the factories are powered by this means. It is estimated that four million horse-power is available, and it is planned to carry electricity throughout the country. Reykjavik kitchens would be a paradise to the average British housewife, with their well-planned sinks, cupboards, refrigerators, electric wringers and washers.

One of the first things to strike a foreigner is the absence of smoke and the resultant cleanliness ; 96 per cent of the houses have heating and hot water laid on from the natural hot springs 12 miles outside Reykjavik. The town today easily claims to be the best and most cheaply warmed city in Europe. In many places where there are hot springs they have been utilized to heat glasshouses, where flowers, tomatoes, cucumbers, grapes, and even bananas are grown. The fruit, however, is not very successful.

There are no queues in Reykjavik. All food is unrationed with the exception of sugar and butter. There is plenty of everything, except fruit and green vegetables in winter, but the cost is high, although prices are nominally controlled. There is a fixed tariff in restaurants and in some of them monthly terms can be made for one meal a day or full board at a reduced price. Clothing is very expensive and of not very high quality or finish ; most of the garments are of British " utility " manufacture.

Luxury Cars Jostle Each Other

Iceland has had trade relations with Britain since the days of King Alfred, and in 1810 an order was issued that "Icelanders should be considered in no case alien enemies but as stranger friends." The chief exports are fish and their by-products. During the war Britain imported practically all the Icelandic catch, which averages 900 billion pounds a year. About half of this is herring, taken in summer ; the winter catch is principally cod. Iceland is one of the countries with the greatest foreign trade per capita ; between 1939-45 she rose to the top of the list. The result of this is plainly visible in Reykjavik, where luxury cars jostle each other and in the residential quarters litter the streets, garage space being even shorter than housing.

The health standard can be said to be high and the death rate is lower than in any European country or the U.S.A. A special

REYKJAVIK'S PARK is famous for its trees, which are very scarce on the island owing to lack of soil and the terrific storms that blow nearly all the year round. PAGE 694

campaign is being conducted against tuberculosis. In 1945, 45 per cent of the population was voluntarily examined, and in 1946, 98·8 per cent. Strict control is exercised over all persons engaged in handling food or in teaching. Reykjavik has two fine modern hospitals, one supported by the State and the other by the Catholic Order of St. Joseph. The infant mortality rate is lower than in most countries. There are three efficient day nurseries in the capital which cater for children from the age of two weeks to seven years.

Main Traffic is Carried by Sea

Owing to the Gulf Stream, Iceland, particularly in the south, is not really cold. In Reykjavik, January is the coldest month with a mean temperature of about 33 degrees Fahrenheit. The summers are, on the whole, cool, the thermometer rarely rising to more than 70 degrees. The worst aspect of the climate is the brusque changes, for within five hours there can be nearly as many variations of weather. But worse than cold or rain is the wind which rises with sudden violence and works up to great strength. On the whole the air is dry and invigorating. In October 1946 herbaceous borders were still gay and even at the end of the month good, green lettuce was growing.

The Reykjavik University is a fine modern building with a good library. A beautifully equipped School of Domestic Science is housed in the basement. The University has a roll of about 400 students. The State is generous in awarding scholarships to students of subjects beneficial to the development of Icelandic interests. The faculties are theology, law and economics, philosophy and philology, medicine, engineering. All school and University education is free and books are published at cost price for students. The general standard of education is high.

Roads in Iceland, though still poor, have been greatly improved during the war years and bus traffic is on the increase. There is a local air service, but the principal traffic is still carried by sea. An efficient State Tourist Bureau supplies free information and arranges delightful group tours. It is absolutely necessary for persons who wish to visit Reykjavik or tour the country to book in advance owing to the shortage of hotel accommodation.

THERE is no unemployment in Iceland but rather a shortage of labour of every sort. The influx of people to the capital has had the serious effect of depleting the farms of labour and as, apart from fishing, agriculture is the main support of the country, the cost of living is bound to go on increasing unless the situation balances in the near future. The Icelandic people are tough and hardy, not afraid of hard work and are at present enjoying a prosperity hitherto unknown in the history of Iceland. This is the only country which can be said to have profited from the war by entirely fair means ; and in spite of being under Allied protection the Icelandic Red Cross observed strict neutrality and carried on, proportionately to its size, as big a programme of humanitarian help as any of the other countries.

During and since the end of the war Iceland has contributed in money, food and clothing the equivalent of almost half a million pounds for relief in Denmark, Finland, Norway, Poland, Germany, Holland, France and Belgium, including regular payments to U.N.R.R.A., of which Iceland was a member from the outset. This is an enormous sum in proportion to the population, amounting to almost £4 per head.

Iceland's Capital Far in the Northern Seas

IN THE HARBOUR AT REYKJAVIK ocean-going vessels can lie at anchor (1), and nearly all the island's exports and imports are handled at the port. The inner harbour is protected by sea walls against the violent gales that rage so frequently. The National Library (2, left) contains some 40,000 volumes and has also a valuable archaeological collection. Next to it is the National Theatre which was begun in 1928 and used as a depot for stores by the Royal Navy during the war. The whitewashed Lutheran cathedral (3) is close to the Senate House, and beside it is a statue of the Icelandic patriot, Jon Sigurdsson, who paved the way for the island's independence and died in 1879. Main thoroughfare is the Austurstraeti (4), with unpretentious shops, many of them built of wood. PAGE 695

The Roll of Honour
NCO's &MEN
1939—1946

So great has been the response of readers to our invitation to submit portraits for our Roll of Honour that no more can now be accepted. But senders may rest assured that all those so far received will be published.

A/B W. H. E. BROWN
Royal Navy.
Act: N. Atlantic. 15.11.42.
Age 23. (London)

Pte. J. ADAMS
No. 11 (Scot.) Commando.
Action : Syria. 9.6.41.
Age 22. (Perth)

Spr. W. J. BULL
Royal Engineers.
Act.: N. Africa. 25.4.43.
Age 24. (Ascot)

Cpl. C. BATCHELER
Queen's Royal Regt.
Action : Burma. 13.6.45.
Age 31. (Peasmarsh)

L/Cpl. G. BEAUMONT
R.A.S.C.
Action : At Sea. 27.3.43.
Age 26. (Chatham)

Dvr. C. BOWLING
Royal Signals.
D/W : St. Valery. 1941.
Age 27. (Willesden)

Rfn. G. W. BARKER
Cameronians.
Act. : Caumont. 30.7.44.
Age 26. (Leeds)

Gdn. A. CARPENTER
Grenadier Guards.
Action : Anzio. 31.1.44.
Age 20. (Cinderford)

A/B D. CLARIDGE
H.M.S. Barham.
Action : Medit. 25.11.41.
Age 18. (Thornton Heath)

Pte. A. CHERRY
King's Own Royal Regt.
Action : Anzio. 26.2.44.
Age 28. (Lancaster)

Spr. F. COHOON
Royal Engineers.
Action : Italy. 31.10.43.
Age 32. (Newhey)

Sgt. C. COLBOURN
Royal Air Force.
Action : France. 18.5.40.
Age 26. (London)

Gdn. R. G. CROWE
Coldstream Guards.
Action : Dunkirk. 30.5.40.
Age 24. (Wellington)

Sgt. F. DANIELS
Royal Artillery.
Action : Burma. 22.5.44.
Age 24. (Halifax)

Pte. E. R. DAINTON
Royal Welch Fusiliers.
Died of wounds. 22.10.44.
Age 22. (Bradford-on-Avon)

Pte. A. L. DEWBERRY
Black Watch.
Action : Tunisia. 15.4.43.
Age 32. (London)

Pte. R. DOVEY
Royal Warwickshire Regt.
M'n'vres:Warwick. 12.6.45.
Age 18. (near, Dudley)

Pte. T. H ECCLES
R.A.S.C.
Act. : Flanders. 29.5.40.
Age 21. (Birmingham)

A/B A. GILMOUR
H.M.S. Firedrake.
Act. : Atlantic. 17.12.42.
Age 22. (Linlithgow)

Cpl. W. E. GREEN
D. of Wellington's Regt.
Died of wounds. 9.4.44.
Age 37. (Hazelbury Bryan)

Pte. J. T. GREEN
Gordon Highlanders.
Died of wounds. 18.8.44.
Age 23. (Sheffield)

Pte. D. A. L. HALL
Royal Norfolk Regt.
Action : Caen. 8.7.44.
Age 24. (Salisbury)

C/Rad/O. HUMPHREYS
S.S. Halfried.
Action : At Sea. 31.10.43.
Age 23. (Bridgend)

Mne. R. J. KEOUGH
Royal Marine Commando.
Act. : Osnabruck. 4.4.45.
Age 21. (Coventry)

Pte. G. W. LAYTON
Parachute Regiment.
Act. : Arnhem. Sept. '44.
Age 25. (Grantham)

Pte. A. LIGHTFOOT
Royal Pioneer Corps.
Action : France. 3.11.44.
Age 44. (Hanley)

Mne. F. D. LITTLE
H.M.S. Repulse.
Action : At Sea. 10.12.41.
Age 23. (Ilford)

L/Bdr. G. McDONALD
Royal Artillery.
Action : Libya. 16.4.43.
Age 21. (Faringdon)

Pte. G. MOTT
Suffolk Regiment.
P.O.W. : Siam. 23.7.43.
Age 29. (Bury St. Edmunds)

Cpl. E. OSBOURNE
Lancashire Fusiliers.
Action : Italy. 16.5.44.
Age 21. (Portsmouth)

L/Cpl. D. QUINN
Royal West Kent Regt.
Action : Italy. 13.4.45.
Age 25. (Croydon)

Pte. H. ROBINSON
Green Howards.
Action : Sicily. 21.7.43.
Age 23. (Barnsley)

Tpr. F. SHARPE
Reconnaissance Corps.
D/Wds. : Anzio. 19.5.44.
Age 27. (Manchester)

Tpr. K. RUSSELL
Reconnaissance Corps.
Action : Caen. 11.8.44.
Age 20. (Bradford)

Pte. W. H. SLATER
Royal Inniskilling Fus.
Act. : N. Africa. 18.1.43.
Age 25. (Cropwell Bishop)

A/B J. J. STEVENS
S.S. Empire Amethyst.
Action : At Sea. 14.4.42.
Age 22. (Paddock Wood)

L/Cpl. B. STOKES
Royal Engineers.
Action : Tunisia. 25.1.42.
Age 28. (Sheffield)

Pte. W. J. TURNER
R.A.S.C.
Died : B'ham. 9.3.43.
Age 30. (Birmingham)

I was a Liaison Officer with Lord Gort

Eight junior officers with Lord Gort in 1940 saw more of the fast-moving, confused battle, and the factors which led to Dunkirk, than perhaps any other subalterns in the B.E.F. A swift glimpse of that hectic period is given by one of them—Peter Tewson, late The Bedfordshire and Hertfordshire Regiment and General Staff.

THE crack of A.A. guns awoke me on a May morning of 1940 in my billet in the pleasant little town of Wambrechies, Northern France. Dressing rapidly, I hurried over to 42nd Divisional Headquarters in the château beside the river. All was excitement and bustle : Hitler's troops had crossed the Belgian, Dutch, and Luxembourg frontiers early that morning, and the British Expeditionary Force was preparing to carry out "Plan D"—the advance to the River Dyle in Belgium.

But I was not to remain with the Division, to which I had been attached as liaison officer. I was to report back immediately to G.H.Q. in Arras. My little open Austin made good speed down the magnificent straight Route Nationale, through Lille and Lens to Arras. Parking the car near the Cathedral I ran into the Palais St. Vaast, General Headquarters of the B.E.F. in France. A Guards sentry pointed out the rooms occupied by General Staff Operations Branch, and in a moment I was reporting to the G.S.O.1, Lieut.-Col. P. Gregson-Ellis.

I was told that I had been selected, with seven other second-lieutenants, as junior liaison officer to General Gort, the Com-mander-in-Chief. My first task was to begin at once. I was to take a wireless detachment to the French 7th Army on the left flank of the B.E.F. for liaison duties with G.H.Q. Command Post. I have no space to describe in detail the events of the next ten days with the 7th Army, commanded by the famous General Giraud. The threat to the First Group of Armies round Sedan robbed the 7th Army of their commander and most of their infantry. Belgian troops were progressively taking over the sector in face of the reduced German threat. My task was finished, and I was ordered back to join the Command Post at Wahagnies, south of Lille, to which it had withdrawn from its most forward position at Renaix in Belgium.

As the B.E.F. was Forced Back

Things were very different on my return to the ugly industrial district north-east of Lille, which I had grown to know so well during the months before Hitler struck. There were signs of bomb-damage in the drab streets, wrecked vehicles lay in the ditches, some riddled with machine-gun bullets. In one village a French Army convoy of horse-drawn vehicles had been caught in the street.

Dead horses, burnt-out limbers, and scarcely recognizable fragments of humanity lay in a ghastly chaos ; all that had been done was the clearing of a passage for vehicles through the wreckage.

I found the Command Post established in a red-brick house in the little town of Wahagnies. Here was the nerve-centre of the B.E.F., from which the Commander-in-Chief and a small staff endeavoured to control the fast-moving and confused battle as the British Army was forced back in conformity with its Allies. The Command Post was, in fact, what in later campaigns would have been called a Tactical Headquarters, the great bulk of G.H.Q. Main being far to the rear, since its unwieldy size rendered it difficult to move at short notice.

THE other junior liaison officers all had tales to tell of their adventures on every sector of the British front. The crumbling communications meant that urgent operational orders and appreciations had to be taken by hand, and these specially trained young officers had been kept busy. The rest of the Operations staff looked tired but unperturbed, taking their cue from the C.-in-C., whose tall, bulky figure appeared fitfully in the intervals of his almost incessant visits to every part of the front line.

General Viscount Gort, V.C. of the First Great War, believed in seeing for himself, and a major concern of his staff was to keep him out of the danger to which daily he exposed himself. One of our tasks, when not

GENERAL HEADQUARTERS IN FRANCE during the winter of 1939-40 was at the Palais St. Vaast, Arras, and here Lord Gort (leading figure on right) the C.-in-C. of the B.E.F., is seen in the grounds with General Pownall, the Chief of General Staff to the B.E.F., on his right. The author of the accompanying story reported at G.H.Q. before setting out to contact the French 7th Army. May 10, 1940, ushered in a confused, rapidly changing war of movement, in which commanders lost contact with their troops except through liaison officers. PAGE 697 *War Office photograph*

Motto: "Nobody Unprepared"

NO. 78 SQUADRON

DISBANDED on December 31, 1919, the Squadron was re-formed at Boscombe Down, Wilts, on November 1, 1936, and was equipped with Whitley aircraft in the following year. It made its first operational sortie in July 1940, carrying out 46 raids in that year. Targets were in Germany, Italy, France and the Netherlands, and included marshalling yards, aerodromes, oil refineries, railways and naval bases. Attacks were also made on the German battleship Scharnhorst at Kiel and on the French "invasion" coast.

On April 14, 1941, the Squadron flew from Middleton St. George, Yorks., to bomb the Scharnhorst and Gneisenau, at Brest. In 1942 the unit was re-equipped with Halifax aircraft and, besides taking part in an attack on St. Nazaire and in the 1,000-bomber raid on Cologne, it was engaged in many hazardous mine-laying sorties.

IT fought in the great battle of the Ruhr during 1943 and attacked the German experimental station at Peenemünde from a height of only 7,000 feet. It was at Peenemünde that the pick of Germany's scientists developed the V-weapons, and the bombing considerably delayed the introduction of these missiles into the war. In the early part of 1944 the Squadron was principally engaged in wrecking communications in Germany, France, Belgium and the Netherlands, and later in the year Caen, Falaise, St. Lo, coastal guns and flying-bomb sites were attacked.

The beginning of 1945 witnessed a successful attack on Ludwigshafen, and daylight raids on the Ruhr and in Central Germany. During the course of the war the Squadron flew 6,337 sorties, dropped 17,000 tons of bombs and lost 182 aircraft. Total number of operational flying hours was 35,000.

---

came out on to the lawn, and slept in the bright spring sunshine, the slight Admiral dwarfed by the colossal figure of General Ironside and the only slightly smaller form of the C.-in-C.

Shortly afterwards, the rapidly deteriorating situation made further withdrawal of the Command Post necessary, and we moved to a small country house in its own grounds at Premesques, between Lille and Armentieres. Now we junior liaison officers entered into the most hectic period of our existence. Normal times for food and sleep were forgotten; we snatched a handful of bully and biscuits and a cup of coffee when we could, and flopped down to sleep as soon as a task was completed, only to be awakened a little later and dispatched on yet another urgent errand. More than anything in the world at that time I longed for sleep, and it was only by taking turns

PETER TEWSON

with my driver at the wheel that we were able to keep going. Attacks by enemy aircraft became more frequent, and we developed a lightning drill for stopping the car, leaping out and diving for the ditch as Stukas roared down or Messerschmitts sped along the straight roads only a few feet above the ground.

Another difficulty was caused by shortage of maps, and it was this that reduced our numbers from eight to seven. Gordon Elms, Royal Sussex, was sent to the map depot at Doullens in order to replenish our stock. We did not see him again, and it was many months later that we learned he had found Doullens in the hands of the enemy, and after several days spent in hiding had been captured while trying to make his way back to the British lines. The result was that a map became a treasure, and the majority of ours were taken for the use of senior officers. Fortunately we

had received special training in the art of route recognition and prided ourselves on our ability to remember roads once covered. In any case, one travelled in those days largely by guess-work.

When sent out on a job, we studied the operations map closely so as to be able to answer the questions of the worried divisional or brigade commander whom we were to visit; at the same time we discovered the last recorded location of the headquarters concerned and any details of recent enemy moves in the area. Frequently we found that not only had the headquarters disappeared into the blue but that enemy tanks had established themselves in towns and villages en route, necessitating long detours and heart-breaking searches before we reached our goal.

On the Last Lap to the Coast

But by now it was obvious even to a junior second-lieutenant that the French campaign was on the point of collapse. General Gort was as taciturn and unruffled as ever, and even found time to make personal inquiries as to when the most junior members of his staff—ourselves—had last eaten or slept. But the faces of the General Staff officers were set and serious, and a jumpy atmosphere prevailed whenever the C.-in-C. disappeared on one of his long absences from his headquarters. At last came the day when I was sent on what was to prove my last task as a liaison officer in France. This was to find out the situation with Frankforce, the composite Division which had fought so gallantly on the Arras Canal.

ON my return to Premesques, after a long and fruitless journey, I found a scene of desolation. During my absence the Command Post had removed itself on the last lap to the coast, where it was established at La Panne, east of Dunkirk, and from where General Gort, on the insistence of the British Government, reluctantly left his Army and sailed for England.

I never found the Command Post again; naturally enough they did not advertise their whereabouts. Three days later, after the harrowing experiences of the Dunkirk beaches, I was on a Fleet minelayer homeward bound.

Seventy-Two Hours' Blissful Leave

Readers' memories of similar spells of "freedom" will be stirred by John Fortinbras' fleeting stay, in the summer of 1945, at the most popular of the rest camps in the British Occupied Zone in Germany: the XXX Corps Centre at Bad Harzburg in the Harz Mountains.

THE bad Reich side roads, pitted here and cobbled there, didn't worry us. As our jeep passed through Hildesheim, a bomb-shattered industrial city, and along the avenues fringed with oak and apple trees to Goslar, our interest was excited by harnessed teams of red-spotted oxen, called "Rotschecken" by their teamsters. Absurdly docile beasts they seemed. Some drew carts and wagons piled with wood fuel; others, often with a horse as consort, hauled ploughs and harrows over the flat North German loams. These novelties heightened our sense of freedom—from night patrols in search of curfew-breakers and raids to check looting Poles and other Displaced Persons.

Then, at the foot of a ridge of fir-covered mountains, nestling between two hills, we saw the red-roofed, timbered town of Bad Harzburg. So peaceful it looked—not a vestige of debris, not a tile displaced, not a sign of war damage anywhere—it seemed like a dream-world far remote from present-day Germany. Authority received from the Commander of XXX Corps allowed troops whilst on leave in this town (banned to all other non-duty personnel) to suspend the usual courtesies between ranks.

A placard displaying this no saluting concession met us outside the Reception Office. Here we were allotted our rooms: my driver billeted at a former sanatorium, myself at the Harzburger Hof, a virtual Lama's palace in wood used during the war as a nursing home for wounded Wehrmacht officers. As I drew up at the entrance, a civilian valet grasped my belongings. A German porter bowed me courteously into the hall, where I booked in, then conducted me to a first-class bedroom suite, with bathroom adjoining.

Sport of All Kinds—and Free

As the Reception Clerk advised, I went early to the Information Room to see what was on the cards. What did I wish to do? Go Riding? Lively hunters awaited in the Camp's Riding School. Go fishing? There was trout fishing in the Oker, rods, tackle, transport and luncheon provided. Play tennis? Rackets and balls were available, and the hard courts were said to be in good trim. Or pot at clay pigeons? Guns and cartridges were at call. Not a pfennig to pay for anything. And to everyone, from Colonel to Sanitary Duties man, the same facilities. My driver, a New Forest boy, whose father kept pony stables down Lyndhurst way,

---

employed on liaison duties, was to assist in the marking-up of the operational maps; frequently, as one put back the red chinagraph lines on the talc, and filled in the ever-lengthening blue arrows indicating German thrusts, one would find the C.-in-C. at one's side, silently taking in the details of changes in the general situation which had occurred since his last leaving his headquarters. Then he would disappear into a small room with his Chief of Staff and other officers, and shortly afterwards some of us liaison officers would be sent for to take urgent instructions to this or that Corps or Division, or to find out the exact situation in some remote part of the fighting line.

On the afternoon that I arrived the Command Post was visited by General Ironside, C.I.G.S., and by Admiral Sir Roger Keyes, special liaison officer with the King of the Belgians. After a conference, the three men

TO THE "LAMA'S PALACE," formerly a nursing-home for German wounded, come men on short leave from XXX Corps in the British Occupied Zone of Germany. The sanatorium is at Bad Harzburg, a lovely little town in the Harz Mountains, and it owes its nickname to its peculiar style of architecture. Over the building flies the famous leaping boar—XXX Corps sign.

went instinctively to the Riding School, where he assisted the German manager, a much worried man at the time, to recover several of his best mounts which had vanished after leaving their riders kicking in thin air.

As sedatives to the heat wave I had the happy choice between the "Schwimmbade," a fine modern pool in Elysian surroundings, where one could loiter in borrowed swimsuit all day long, and the hotel's excellently stocked bar.

Prices here seemed a little astonishing if one remembered comparative costs in England—draught beer at 50 pf. (3d.) a glass; red wine, white wine and brandy at 1 mark (6d.) a glass; gins 1 mark 50 pf. (9d.) a glass; 2 marks (1s.) for a double whisky, and white Rheinwein or Graves at 10 marks (5s.) the bottle. In the kitchen the German chef excelled himself, the speisekarte (menu) for dinner listing five stimulating courses.

Each morning at half-past seven a chambermaid knocked at the door with a cup of German-brewed English tea; perhaps not so sweet as Army char, but good. And if one spoke German it was possible to get two cups in as many minutes. These civilian courtesies, after a world of khaki brusqueness, renewed in one all the hankerings for civilization.

By day I decided to try the hills, putting in some bare footslogging (astonishing how pleasant it is to walk barefoot in areas reasonably stoneless), ignoring the prescribed tourists' tracks. I avoided the Brocken, the Harz's highest and most tempting hill, for good reasons. It lay in the Russian sector, and since smuggling human beings from Russian territory into the British zone seemed to have become a useful trade for some Ger-

man guides, Russian patrols sent out to stop the racket were prone to shoot first and examine credentials at their leisure. Life was too sweet risk straying within their range.

On either side of Harzburg, trekking over pine-covered hills, I came across old women laboriously collecting sticks and logs; others stooped over the ground in search of wood mushrooms, and I passed one small gang of tree-fellers. In the main, I found the hills silent and deserted. The wind moved through some of the richest timber forests in Europe, a vast paper supply, if someone would but set the wheels in motion. At night, the rutting cry of battling stags broke out. Owls added a dismal commentary. By moonlight a black squirrel skipped across my path, as fortunate an omen as a black cat.

WITH the weather remaining gloriously fine, I felt "in the pink." Clay pigeons tossed into the air mechanically in a quarry by the Radau waterfall were elusive and I thought disappointing "birds." Their velocity seemed more V2-like than pigeon-like! Most of us missed, dismally. But there was an R.A.F. pilot who downed five birds out of 6 shots; actually he blew them to pieces.

There was a shopping arcade open to all ranks, highlights of which were a gift shop where you could buy first-class German hunting knives for 3 marks 50 pf., eau-de-Cologne for 6 marks a bottle, face-creams, lipsticks, and scale models of jeeps, tanks and lorries equally cheap. . . . Seventy-two hours is but a short sojourn. When it was time to pack I left reluctantly, conscious of a spaciousness in living not met in one's everyday life, and of having had a millionaire's holiday for precisely nothing!

in the picture by means of radio contact with battalion or brigade H.Q. The decision to make the V.C.P. airborne for Arakan operations was taken in February 1945, when units of XV Corps were successfully keeping the Japs on the hop by a series of brilliantly executed amphibious operations against their coastal supply routes.

I Meet the "Spirit of Winship"

My R.A.F. opposite number, Flt.-Lieut. R. W. E. Duke (subsequently killed in action in Java), picked up a L.-5 (U.S. light aircraft) from Akyab, then the base for operations, and flew it down to the mainland near Ruwya, a small village at the head of one of the many Arakanese waterways, and the scene of recent landing operations by the 25th Indian Division. I received orders to bring along the rest of the unit in landing craft and rendezvous with him at a newly constructed light plane strip adjacent to the bridge-head. I had my first big shock on arrival at the strip. The plane was there, all right—or rather what was left of it. A bystander told me that not five minutes after Duke had landed it two days earlier a lone Jap heavy gun had opened up on it and a dozen shells had done their worst.

I SPED up the dust-strewn track to Divisional H.Q. for further orders, and was told to rendezvous with Duke at first light next morning and render as much aid as possible to an Indian brigade that was to put in a big attack against strong Jap positions in the hills beyond Tamandu. We were to work to another ground V.C.P. unit that would be up with our forward troops. There was to be any amount of air support both against specific targets and also waiting ready for our calls to go in and strike any targets that our reconnaissance might reveal.

Next morning, clutching a map and aerial photos in one hand and a pair of borrowed binoculars in the other, I waited on the strip as the first tints of day chased away the darkness. A drone became a roar and an L.-5 clattered down on the strip beside me. That was my first introduction to Spirit of Winship, a light aircraft sponsored by the pupils of the Winship school, Detroit, U.S.A.

A hasty pow-wow with Duke as to our plan of action, and we took the air. Below us was a scene of movement as troops, tanks and guns began to move. Where the green-clad columns ended I got out my binoculars and gazed down on the dusty highway that led to Tamandu. It was the task of some of our battalions to push on along that track and link-up with West African troops pushing down from the north, while other units were to make a series of hooks through the jungle and assault the enemy positions on high ground to the east of Tamandu.

Chasing Japs With Smoke and Fire

In the Burma campaigns light aircraft earned many tributes for operations in varying fields, not least being their use as Flying Visual Control Posts. Their work in the Arakan in 1945 is typified by the "Spirit of Winship," as described by Bernard T. Ridgway (portrait in page 510).

IN a country deemed the worst fighting terrain in the world, ordinary ground Visual Control Post units were sometimes little more than useless. Like the Forward Observation Officer of the gun battery, the V.C.P. officer must be as far forward as possible and have a commanding view of the target, so that when the close support aircraft arrive on the scene he is able to give them a clear idea of the target's

location and, if necessary, call on smoke mortars to put down rounds on the target as a greater aid to pilots.

The normal constitution of a V.C.P. was one R.A.F. officer and several operators who contacted all aircraft through a V.H.F. (Very High Frequency) set, either portable or mounted in a jeep, and one Army captain and staff who kept the R.A.F. component

FARMERS USE OXEN rather than horses in many parts of Germany. Slow and docile, the white breed is usually to be seen in the north German plain. See facing page.

FLIGHT-LIEUT. DUKE (left), who was subsequently killed in Java, and Bernard T. Ridgway, the author of the accompanying story, beside the "Spirit of Winship."
Photo, S.E.A.C.

I had already made contact with our ground element when Duke called me up on the inter-com to tell me that he was going down to scout around the Jap fortifications on a position known to our people as "Strong." With the glasses glued to my eyes I searched the hilltops, spotting a faint, irregular streak that snaked its way through the thick undergrowth—slit trenches. We had four aircraft available at the time and we hastily called up Napier, our ground station, and gave instructions for the four aircraft (Hurribombers) to follow us in to attack.

As we manoeuvred for position I saw the Hurribombers getting into the circuit with us and gave Duke the tip-off. Down we went over the target, waggled our wings and climbed away. Looking back I saw the attacking aircraft go down and the bombs detach themselves as the planes pulled out of their dive. Flames enveloped the whole feature and a column of black smoke rose high into the air. Our first strike looked successful, but you could never be too sure in that thick jungle that the Japanese positions were right underneath your bombs.

We flew away down the Tamandu road to see how our troops were progressing. We passed over what was left of Tamandu, the gaunt outlines of burned-down huts, and a few miles to the south came across our most forward elements. Troops were pinned down on the roadside and tanks were lobbing shells over into the jungle some distance up the road. Napier confirmed that there was trouble ahead from enemy posts bordering the road, and asked could we help?

OUT came the binoculars again, and I searched for the tell-tale marks of Jap trenches and foxholes. We had to go down really low to find them, so low, in fact, that Duke suddenly whipped the plane all over the sky as a stream of light Ack-Ack came up to meet us. We were determined to get that bunch below, if we had to go down to nought feet to do it. This time we tried an approach from the rear, and suddenly I saw what we had been looking for—a series of foxholes along the forward slope of a small hill. Position was hurriedly pinpointed on my map and wirelessed down to the ground. A few minutes later a hail of gun and mortar shells began to fall around the position.

We decided to follow this up with what air support we had around at the time—two cannon-equipped Spitfires. As before we guided the aircraft in; but this time we had the mortars put down the necessary smoke shells on the target for the Spitfire boys. Via the ground we asked the Spit merchants to follow up their attacks with a dummy run on the target, to keep the Japs' heads down when our troops went forward to the attack. We stayed around to watch that attack, and in a few minutes our troops had gained the position and were swallowed up in the thick jungle.

A Mass of Burning Undergrowth

Later that afternoon news came to us that the attacks on "Strong" and other hill features were being fiercely resisted and it was believed that the enemy was rushing up reinforcements along the road leading from An. Our job was to keep a look-out for troop movements to and from the battle area. It looked like a real Hell's Kitchen when we passed over at 1,000 feet, heading for the east. The hills were a mass of burning undergrowth and shells were raining down on the area. Although I did not have my glasses to my eyes at the time I suddenly

saw a number of men on the twisting, turning road that headed east from the hills.

I leaned forward to touch Duke, and pointed below. He followed my finger, and suddenly put the Winship's nose right down. I had no time to get my glasses up, but I recognized that the men were Japs and that they were moving away from the hills. The air was alive for the next few minutes as we gave all the gen to Napier. "Important message for you, Nobby" (our own call-sign) came through to us just as the Japs we had been following reached cover. Brigade had decided to hit the party with everything they had and we were to control the fire. First, the Naval sloop Narbada, anchored some miles down the chaung, was to register on the target, and then we were to range some Army 25-pounders on to the area. The first shells from the sloop fell short into the river and it was a fairly easy task to correct on those. Then it was the turn of the 25-pounders, and that was not so easy.

Let the Gunners Have Their Fling

For miles the jungle was a mass of fire and smoke and to pick out individual shell-bursts was wellnigh impossible. By persuading the guns to increase the range we managed to put a shell into the river and after that it was not too difficult to get in corrections. We were asked to go in and see if the enemy was still milling around the little feature where we had last seen them. As we orbited I saw a figure suddenly dash for the safety of a tree, and that was good enough for us to let the gunners have their fling. Shell after shell hit the area, and then we directed two fighter bombers on to the target.

Discussing the matter of smoke indication with Duke a few days later, we hit on the idea of carrying our own smoke markers in the aircraft. Army phosphorous grenades we decided were ideal for the task, and we took a box up with us on our first try-out. Small rock formations that dotted the sea-shore off Ramree Island were to be our range. It seemed all very primitive as I opened the back hatch and waited for Duke to give me the word to drop the grenade. Presently, away it went, twisting and turning in its fall. We waited for what seemed minutes, then decided that we must have been miles off the target. Duke said we would have another shot, and he lined Winship up fair and square on the target. Then we saw a column of smoke drifting up from the rock. We had achieved a bull's-eye.

VISUAL CONTROL POSTS were vital links in the chain of communication between troops in the front line and the aircraft giving them close support. Beside a burned out Indonesian tank a V.C.P. is in a state of readiness (left) to contact troops of the 5th Indian Division in Surabaya, Java, in January 1946. At the request of the assaulting units Mosquitoes and Thunderbolts have been called up, and their attacks on the designated targets are being watched by the post (right).

Air Ministry photographs

All-Seeing Eyes Feared By the Japs in Burma

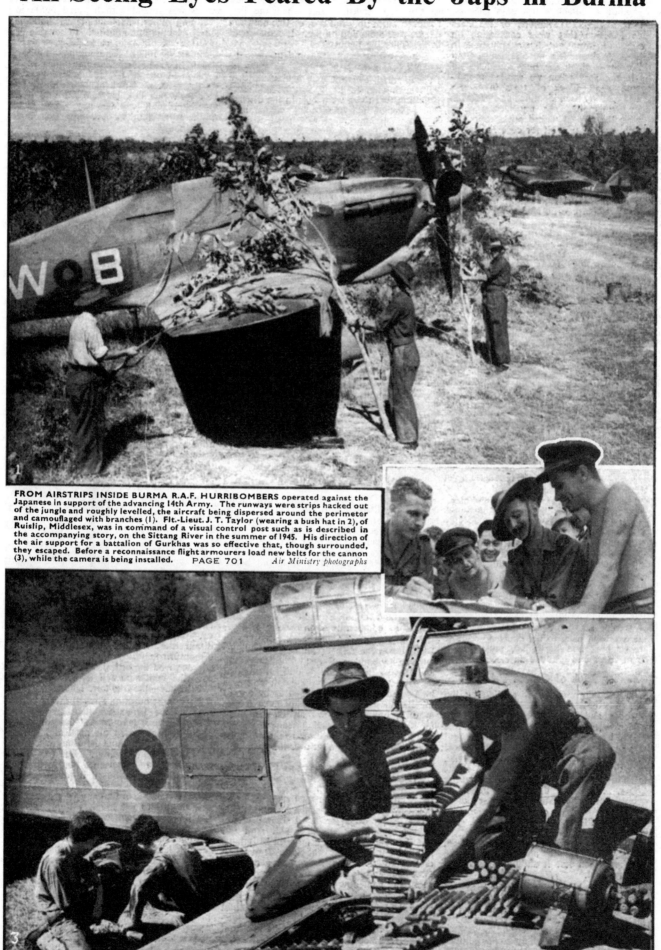

FROM AIRSTRIPS INSIDE BURMA R.A.F. HURRIBOMBERS operated against the Japanese in support of the advancing 14th Army. The runways were strips hacked out of the jungle and roughly levelled, the aircraft being dispersed around the perimeter and camouflaged with branches (1). Flt.-Lieut. J. T. Taylor (wearing a bush hat in 2), of Ruislip, Middlesex, was in command of a visual control post such as is described in the accompanying story, on the Sittang River in the summer of 1945. His direction of the air support for a battalion of Gurkhas was so effective that, though surrounded, they escaped. Before a reconnaissance flight armourers load new belts for the cannon (3), while the camera is being installed. PAGE 701 *Air Ministry photographs*

We had the opportunity of trying out our new method of attack a few days later as we flew ahead of battalions of the 26th Indian Division that were converging on Taungup, an important Jap supply base in the lower Arakan. We were returning from a dawn recce along the only semblance of road in the area when we spotted a well-prepared road block of trees in a part that had recently been identified as a probable enemy strongpoint. As my glasses came down on the scene I picked out a couple of Japs making a blind bolt for cover.

My Grenades Right on the Target

Hastily we called up our ground element to find if there were any aircraft in the area that we might use to hit the position. Back came the reply to hang around for a few minutes as some fighters were being whipped up. Four Hurricanes were soon orbiting the position we had given, and I hastily opened the window and held the two grenades ready. Duke took Winship down to 500 ft. before giving the signal to release. The two grenades went down together and we waited anxiously for the smoke. It did not seem so long this time, and when we saw it we gave a whoop of joy. It was right on the target.

We gave the Hurris the signal to go in, and leaned back with satisfaction as we saw the cannon shells bursting all around the smoke-filled area. We used smoke on nearly every attack after that; we even used it to burn down the undergrowth around Jap positions if we could not be too certain

that they were occupied or not. Many times we saw Japs scuttling out when the fire began to warm up. But only on one occasion did we ever see a Jap on fire. It came about in the following manner.

A Jap P.O.W. had given Intelligence the rough location of his Brigade H.Q. We were to keep watch over the area at first and last light each day, to try to get definite confirmation that there were Japs in the district. Our suspicion fell on a small village in a clearing; in four days we never saw a sign of life there to show that it was inhabited. That in itself was suspicious. We felt certain there were Japs hiding in the huts and nearby jungle. So as not to frighten them away we had to play a game of hide and seek, passing directly over the village on a journey to the south at dusk and dawn, to give the impression that we were off on a distant recce.

WE discovered what we wanted after a long waiting game. One morning my binoculars rested on a Jap racing from one hut to another. That afternoon we headed back to the area, this time with two squadrons of Hurricanes as our companions. I dropped a clutch of grenades and watched them burst on the village. From the doorway of a hut dived a Jap with smoke pouring from him. He suddenly veered from the trees and headed for a small stream, then disappeared from view. Subsequently we learned that the Hurricanes had done their work well and in that bomb-wrecked village the Jap brigade commander and his staff had joined their honourable ancestors.

Frenzied Italians Rushed Our Boats

Three hundred miles north-east of Ascension Island, in the Atlantic, an unseen submarine sank the liner Laconia on Sept. 12, 1942. Homeward bound from India, she was carrying many British passengers—and a large number of Italian prisoners who promptly panicked. The thrilling events are recalled by Purser Claude Jones.

THE alarm gongs were sounding and men, women and children were hurrying to the companion ladders. The life was dying out of the ship, for the engines were in course of being stopped. There was no indication of her sinking quickly, although no one could be sure that the unseen submarine would not slam another torpedo into her. I was in no rig suitable for a voyage in an open boat, even in the tropics, and that was the prospect conveyed by the signal to abandon ship. So instead of joining the throng swarming up the companion ladders I went back to my quarters, donned a reefer coat and life-jacket, pulled on a pair of shoes and grabbed an electric torch.

Milling Mob of Crazed Prisoners

The Laconia was slowly settling by the head. My emergency station was Number 2 lifeboat, and it was up to me to go there by the shortest route and assist with whatever had to be done. A babel of voices and shuffling of feet suggested what is most dreaded in a crowded, sinking ship—panic. The moment I gained the open deck I was caught in a milling mob of frenzied, shouting Italians. I had to fight to avoid being knocked down and trampled on. By violent effort I broke clear, only to discover that Number 2 lifeboat, badly damaged, was hanging uselessly from a single davit. I turned back along the darkened deck, evading crazed Italians and refraining from using my torch lest it should be snatched from my hand.

The task of abandoning ship was becoming increasingly difficult. The confusion among the prisoners was serious, and another adverse factor was that the Laconia was not only settling deeper but taking a gradual list to starboard. Struggling Italians jammed the ladders, and I took a chance by climbing

a stanchion to gain the boat-deck near Number 8 lifeboat; it was necessary to hold them at bay whilst the women and children were placed in the boats. I was ordered to help in keeping a space clear. The prisoners came at us like howling dervishes in their efforts to rush the boat. We used only our fists and feet, but elsewhere aboard the sinking ship shots were being fired by the Polish guards. Throughout the whole nerve-racking ordeal the British women and children made no fuss and obeyed all commands in an orderly manner.

An officer urged us to "get going," and I slid down the falls of Number 8 lifeboat, burning my hands red-raw and bruising body and legs against the ship's hull. I alighted between the thwarts in the boat, and was hammered flat on the floorboards by one of the Italians crashing on top of me. It was meant to hold 75. More than 100 were piled in it, and the frenzied prisoners started scrapping among themselves again, with the result that a number went over the side.

IN a dazed kind of way I was aware of someone shouting "Shove off! Shove off!" The overcrowded boat had very little freeboard and was in imminent danger of being holed by bumping against the Laconia's side in the heavy ocean swell. I scrambled up, helped to unhook the falls and fend off, and the boat was rowed clear with 14 Italians in the water clinging to the sides. It was then discovered that our rudder was missing. Four seamen plied a pair of oars, and elbow room had somehow to be made for them.

When the boat rose high the Laconia showed as a dark silhouette against the night sky—until her boilers burst and she disappeared below the waves. Lamps and torches denoted the position of other boats

and the rafts, and one area of the dark waters was spread with tiny red lights like gleaming rubies. Modern life-jackets have a small red lamp attached to enable the position of the wearers to be seen in the darkness of night. The coloured lights we saw marked the men who had failed to find a place in one of the undamaged boats or on the rafts. A jacket of kapok and canvas was their one link between life and death. Our Number 8 boat was now riding so low in the water that we had only four inches of freeboard.

Schoolgirls Took Turn in Baling

The night seemed unending and daybreak found only two other boats in sight; we drew within hailing distance and all set a course eastward for the African coast. A count was made of the number in our boat— 102 survivors, including many women, several children between the ages of eight and fifteen, and two babies in arms. Our breakfast consisted of a biscuit, a small cube of chocolate, a Horlick's tablet and an egg-cupful of water. Two or three Italians still alongside were hitched to the boat with grab-lines under their seats, and fed with similar fare in the same quantity.

The sea rose under a freshening wind. We were all drenched to the skin, and the boat had to be baled out constantly. Even the schoolgirls with us took turn with the baling cans, and their youthful spirits transformed a grim ordeal into a semblance of gay adventure. Slow progress was made, and anxiety became acute the following night owing to a slightly heavier sea. Work at the oars took severe toll of our strength owing to the meagre rations; and those Italians hitched alongside had a grim passage, although the sea was warm. We did all we could for them short of taking them aboard, for any such attempt would have been madness, with over 100 lives at stake; nor were the other boats in any better position to help. There was no callousness toward them, quite the reverse; and happily I am able to say that they endured the intense discomfort manfully and survived the ordeal. Other Italians with

CLAUDE JONES

us in the boat were well treated and lived to tell the tale—the true tale, I hope.

Early next morning a naval rating huddled next to me bemoaned the slow progress. "The breeze is favourable," he said, "what about trying to step the mast and spread a sail?" The job could be done in less than half-an-hour in harbour. But out on the ocean in our tightly-packed boat with a bare four inches of freeboard it took the entire day. The mast was under the thwarts, and slow, systematic reshuffling of many people was needed to get it out without upsetting the lifeboat. Then, with extreme care, one end had to be lifted and the mast dragged back inch by inch. Finally, at even greater peril, it had to be raised while the boat was kept head-on and rode its switchback course over the Atlantic rollers.

The mainsail was eventually clewed to the mast and gradually hoisted, while those taking no active part in rigging the boat sat tensely in expectation of being flung into the sea at any moment. Sail was set without mishap, and a seaman remained by the halliards ready to let go instantly should a squall

TORPEDOED BY A GERMAN U-BOAT in the Atlantic on Sept. 12, 1942, the Cunard liner Laconia was the scene of a ghastly panic when terrified Italian prisoners fought to seize the lifeboats. The author of the story in these pages escaped in an overcrowded boat and had the unusual experience of seeing both Italian and German submarines succour the survivors.

threaten or the improvised steering with an oar fail to keep the boat on a safe course. We parted company from the other boats. Good progress was made in fair weather during the night, and hopes ran high of reaching the African coast. But our boat never made a landfall.

Once again an issue of rations was made. I sat in the stern squeezed between a R.A.F. officer and a Chief Petty Officer of the Royal Navy, and received my fair whack like the rest of the tightly packed mob. That breakfast of a biscuit, small cube of chocolate, a Horlick's tablet and eggcupful of water was not my idea of a meal to start the day. My mind's eye conjured a vision of ham and eggs with buttered rolls and fragrant coffee. The remarkable thing was how the women and children who had endured the ocean ordeal for so long remained outwardly cheerful in spite of ever-present danger. No one knew how long the voyage must continue, or how soon the weather would break with disastrous result to all.

We Awaited the Grim Finale

Suddenly the indigo sea was disturbed by a white flurry of foam. All except the sleeping babes-in-arms stared wide-eyed as a grey-green object thrust itself above the surface like the snout of some prehistoric monster. It was the conning-tower of a submarine, and within a matter of seconds part of the hull loomed into view with the sea rolling from it in hissing cascades. The markings on it were unrecognizable; at least, no one was able to identify the nationality of the craft. We gazed, hypnotized, as it surfaced a couple of cables' lengths away on the port beam. One or two seamen of the Laconia's crew were first to recover the use of their tongues; but one guess was as good as another.

The submarine cruised along slowly on a parallel course to our own. No ensign was flown, but the general appearance of the men who came out of the hatches and their guttural tones suggested that the vessel was German.

I looked at the R.A.F. officer next to me and read my own thoughts reflected in his eyes. We expected our lifeboat to be machine-gunned. There was a period of heart-searing suspense. Already in the Atlantic the sea-wolves had carried out the Nazi orders to "sink without trace." Cramped and helpless, we awaited tensely the grim finale to another tragedy of the sea while the Germans stood by the guns.

No further threatening move was made, however, and we began to breathe more freely. The submarine drew ahead, then slowed down and manoeuvred nearer. The commander could be seen plainly—a young man with a downy beard, wearing dark-blue battle-dress and armed with a Mauser pistol. After scrutinizing us in silence for a time, he hailed our boat in fluent English : " I am going to stop. Take down your sail and come alongside ! "

The C.P.O. seated beside me gave the order " Lower away ! " and expressed the general feeling when he added, " There's no sense in disobeying the swab." We moved cumbrously alongside the U-boat, which had hove-to. The German commander looked down from the conning-tower bridge, but did not see the Italians. These had squirmed under the thwarts, where they remained hidden ; the two or three still in the water were at the far side of the lifeboat and also concealed from view.

Those prisoners were scared stiff of the Huns, their allies. They knew that if taken aboard the U-boat the German captain would endeavour to repatriate them—and they wanted no more active soldiering after their experience in the Western Desert. So they kept out of sight, fearing rescue by their Hun " friends " more than anything else that might befall them.

Harangue from Conning Tower

After a prolonged survey of us, the submarine commander brusquely asked : " How many are in the boat ? " Someone told him the number—102. The German raised his eyebrows and, addressing our packed boat-load in general, remarked : " English seamen are all right—but ach, your Government ! Why don't you British give up the war, causing all this suffering ? " He spoke with disarming sincerity, apparently unaware of the irony conveyed to us victims of ruthless submarine attack. " By hokey ! " the C.P.O. muttered. " That's rich, if you like ! "

Like others, I was wondering whether this might be the same U-boat which had sunk the Laconia without warning. The truth about this, however, was never discovered. The U-boat commander stroked his beard and expressed his sympathy. Using his conning-tower bridge as a " soap-box," he made a speech in which he attributed our plight solely to a vicious Government who had misled the British public at the instigation of " their overlords." He blamed us victims only for our own blindness and folly. His speech was the familiar Nazi rigmarole such as Dr. Goebbels, Lord Haw-Haw and others broadcast repeatedly. Of course, he ignored the black record of the Nazi regime and the acquiescence of the German public in the overrunning of Poland and other ill-defended countries.

We were wet, cramped and weakened and in no mood for political argument—not that it is ever much good arguing with the fellow who has a machine-gun to back his opinions. We were mightily relieved when he got down to brass tacks. " Your perfidious Government has got you into trouble," he said, " but I will give you what help I can. You will come on board a few at a time. And I will give you good food."

(Continued in No. 253)

NEW FACTS AND FIGURES

DURING 1946 the Salvation Army found accommodation for 41,941 people in shelters and hostels, supplied 34,000,000 meals, found jobs for over 68,000 people and cared for 5,012 children in 123 homes. These facts are given in the Salvation Army Year Book (1947) which contains many interesting details of wartime and post-war activities of this great organization all over the world.

IN Denmark, Norway, the Netherlands, Belgium and France—where Salvation Army operations had been suspended to a greater or less degree during enemy occupation—1946 saw a great revival and the reopening of many social institutions. In ex-enemy countries, corps and outposts were reopened. In Vienna open-air meetings were resumed after being banned for 12 years. In Germany, where many corps had been bombed out, British Salvationists engaged in relief work, and the Army's 305 German officers began a drive to win young people after a lapse of many years.

SALVATION ARMY reports from the Far East relate that in China, where Children's Homes were kept going throughout the war, ex-internees gave valuable aid in relief work with U.N.R.R.A. In Japan, 60 corps and 20 social work centres were in action in 1946. In Malaya, after work was forbidden by the Japanese, underground activities continued, and at the liberation of Singapore the S.A. flag, drum and song-

books were brought out from hiding. During the occupation of Burma a native officer, Adjutant Saw Kee Doe, when all his uniform had gone, had the Salvation Army crest tattooed on his arm so that he might continue to testify to his beliefs.

AT Thanbyuzayat in Lower Burma, starting point of the Burma-Siam railway, ceremonies were held on December 18, 1946, to commemorate the men who died during the construction of the railway by the Japanese. In an Allied military cemetery 1,728 British, 1,103 Australian and 691 Dutch P.O.W. are buried. Altogether nearly 15,000 British, Australian and Dutch prisoners and some 150,000 Burmese, Indians, Chinese and Siamese lost their lives in the building of the 240-mile railway. The Bishop of Rangoon and the Bishop of Singapore conducted the Christian service, and a Buddhist memorial ceremony was held near by.

ACCORDING to information available to the United Nations War Crimes Commission at the beginning of December 1946; persons to the number of 24,365 had been tried in Europe for war crimes in British, U.S., French, Greek, Norwegian, Czechoslovak and Polish courts. The last two included also persons accused of collaboration and treachery. Of this total, 1,432 received the death penalty, 16,413 were sentenced to varying terms of imprisonment, and 6,520 were acquitted.

Full-Rigged Prize of War in Tasman Sea

Photo, Central Press

OUTWARD-BOUND FROM NEW ZEALAND, the barque Pamir made a majestic picture as she raced on the last 200 miles to Sydney, New South Wales. A vessel of 2,500 tons displacement, she formerly sailed under the Finnish flag and was seized by the New Zealand authorities at the outbreak of war with Finland on Dec. 6, 1941. She rendered valuable service at a time when there was grave shortage of shipping and was still being operated by the New Zealand Government in 1947.

Photo, Central Press

Printed in England and published every alternate Friday by the Proprietors, THE AMALGAMATED PRESS, LTD., The Fleetway House, Farringdon Street, London, E.C.4. Registered for transmission by Canadian Magazine Post. Sole Agents for Australia and New Zealand: Messrs. Gordon & Gotch, Ltd.; and for South Africa: Central News Agency, Ltd. February 14, 1947. S.S. *Editorial Address :* JOHN CARPENTER HOUSE, WHITEFRIARS, LONDON, E.C.4.

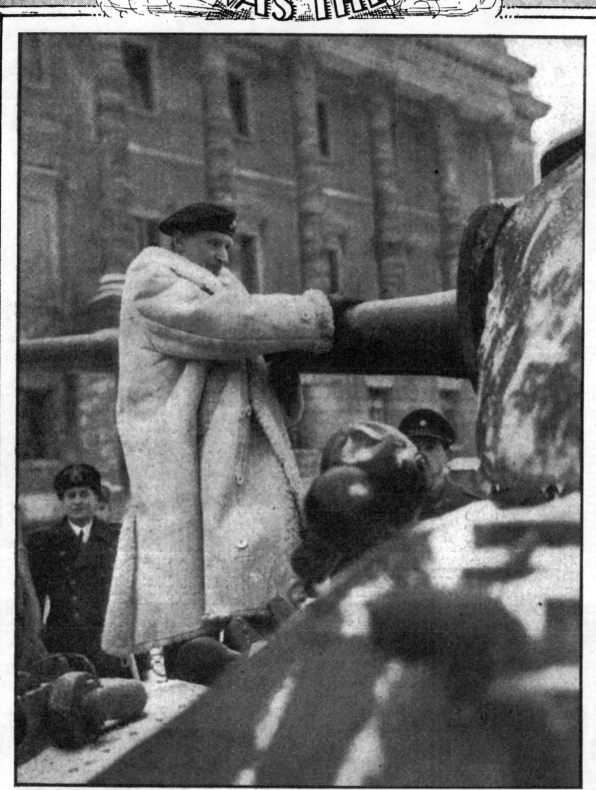

AT THE STALIN MILITARY ACADEMY for armoured and mechanized troops Field-Marshal Lord Montgomery inspected a Stalin tank during his visit to Moscow early in January 1947. He and his Soviet hosts exchanged views on the employment of tanks in battle; and the Chief of the Imperial General Staff had a discussion with Marshal of Tank Troops Rybalko, a Russian tank expert in the Second Great War. On his return to England Field-Marshal Montgomery announced that Russian would be taught at our Royal Military Academy, Sandhurst. See also page 709.
Photo, Planet News

Edited by Sir John Hammerton

Glimpsed by Our Roving Camera

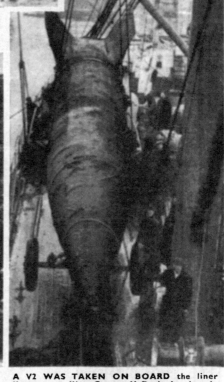

SCIPIONE AFRICANO, an Italian cruiser, may be allotted to one of the Allies under the Peace Treaty signed in Paris, Feb. 10, 1947. Names of the vessels to be surrendered were kept secret, to avoid possible sabotage.

A GEORGE CROSS award was made to Sqdn.-Leader H. Dinwoodie, O.B.E., M.C. (above), on Feb. 4, 1947, for defusing a German bomb which was surrounded with high explosives. His action, on Aug. 20, 1946, saved the German port of Lübeck from devastation. Eleven hundred tons of bombs were being unloaded from two trains into ships for disposal at sea when a 120-pound bomb was dropped and exploded, killing six persons and injuring 12. There was grave danger that other bombs would also detonate, and blow up the trains. Dinwoodie proceeded to dismantle one, to ascertain, if possible, the cause of the explosion. He found that the accident was due to defective German workmanship or design, the fusing devise having moved. In the light of this knowledge the Squadron-Leader, assisted by Corporal Garred, who received the George Medal, was able to render harmless the remaining bombs. At the time it was not known whether the action of defusing the bombs would in itself cause a detonation. L.A.C. J. W. Halton, who also gave valuable assistance, was granted the British Empire Medal.

UNUSED BARBED WIRE stacked at Taplow, Bucks., is to be exported to Canada, where it will be smelted. In February 1947 there were several such "mountains," estimated to be worth about 600,000 dollars. Every coil was made for defence purposes; now it all goes as salvage.

A V2 WAS TAKEN ON BOARD the liner Karamea at King George V Dock, London, in February 1947, for shipment to Australia, where it will be placed on exhibition in the War Museum at Canberra.

SURVIVORS OF THE JERVIS BAY met at a re-union dinner held at the Marylebone Station Hotel, London, on Feb. 1, 1947. A wreath commemorated those who died in the gallant action fought with the German warship Admiral Scheer in mid-Atlantic on Nov. 5, 1940, while protecting a merchant convoy.

FERGUSON TRACTORS, of revolutionary design, are being manufactured in large numbers at the former wartime shadow factory of Standard Motors, Coventry. These agricultural machines, which are intended mainly for export, will help to overcome the world food shortage.

Photos Planet, A.P., Keystone, G.P.U., Central Press

How the Australians Took Sattelberg

By KENNETH HARE-SCOTT

In February 1943 the 9th Australian Division, which had launched the first attack in the Allied thrust at El Alamein, sailed from Suez for Australia. On board ship they were told to forget the art of desert warfare and learn the craft and guile of the jungle. Other divisions, including the 6th, had already returned and were engaging the enemy on the beaches and in the jungles of the Papuan promontory of New Guinea. By then the holding war in the South Pacific was at an end for the Allies (see article in pages 195-196).

The Japanese had planned to capture Port Moresby, an ideal base for launching and maintaining an assault upon Australia. They planned its capture for September 1942, but by that time it had become the indispensable base through which the great Australian—and later American—counter-offensive gained its life-blood in supplies and reinforcements. In the first eight months of the counter-offensive the Allies recaptured all strategic points as far as the Huon Gulf, and by September 1943 the Japanese defenders had massed their main forces in the Huon Peninsula. Here lay the next objective in the reconquest of New Guinea, and the greater aim—the destruction of the Japanese Army still menacing the security of Australia.

Initial Assault at Scarlet Beach

Lae, in the Huon Gulf, was captured by the 7th Australian Division on September 16 and plans, already prepared, were immediately set in motion for the 9th Australian Division to carry out an amphibious operation against the harbour of Finschhafen on the Huon Peninsula. The landing was made on September 22, six miles north of Finschhafen, at a spot which came to be known as Scarlet Beach, about 90 miles sea distance from Lae. A little way inland from Scarlet Beach a coral track beginning at Heldsbach ran south to Finschhafen, passing through Salankaua coconut plantation to the Kakakog area, a narrow spur between the coast and the steep foothills, believed to be occupied in some strength by the enemy.

A single Brigade group, making the initial assault, was greeted by heavy fire as the frail craft rode into the beach to discharge the crouching troops over whose heads roared the continuous fire of the Naval guns covering the landing. Having cleared the beach area the drive towards Finschhafen, six miles to the south, began. Three days later the Bumi River was crossed, at heavy cost. Stiffening enemy resistance and the vulnerability of the lengthening supply line began to cause anxiety. An enemy stir in the Sattelberg region inland from Scarlet Beach spelt some concentration of strength.

Enemy patrols began feeling their way towards beach defences and prodding the life-line of the force to the south. Clearly time was to be the deciding factor and reinforcements would be needed. The push on Finschhafen continued in face of almost impossible ground conditions with enemy resistance growing stronger every hour, and it was a force of little more than two-company strength which delivered the final artillery bombardment and later the assault upon the harbour. Finschhafen fell to the bayonet-fighting Australians on October 2.

The success of the operation now depended upon the tactical envelopment of the enemy, and his eventual destruction. Reinforcements—one battalion—which had now landed at Scarlet Beach proved to be timely arrivals, as the Japs had concentrated a considerable force for an attack upon the beach area. The seven-days bitter struggle which followed

that attack remains outstanding among the highlights of the New Guinea fighting— the Australians battling with their backs to the beach against a desperate enemy who had already cut their link with their comrades to the south, in Finschhafen. The arrival of the balance of the Division tipped the scales and the Jap was driven, although fighting tooth and nail, from his position astride the dispersed Australian force. With the threat to the beach gone and a general withdrawal of enemy forces, the next objective needed no searching.

Sattelberg, the centre of Japanese resistance in the area, remained the one stronghold to be captured before the tide of advance might roll the Jap to the north and eventually tip him into the sea. In the days of the Lutheran missionaries the Settlement had been a Mission and Convalescent Centre which, apart from its position—perched on a rocky height with a difficult approach— possessed no other claims to be the southern pivot of enemy resistance. With massed aircraft and heavy artillery it would have been easy to reduce. But our Australians were fighting light and the assault on Sattelberg depended upon their skill at beating the enemy the hard way.

The capture of Sattelberg depended upon the occupation of two features: one 2,400 feet high just south-east of the Mission, which we shall call "2400," and another about 1,000 yards east called "2600." The 2/48 Battalion was to attack along the main Jivevaneng-Sattelberg road, forming the centre of the thrust, having the 2/23 Battalion on the left flank moving north from Kumawa, and the 2/24 Battalion on the right flank advancing north-west up the slopes of the "2600" feature. For the first time tanks were to reinforce the assault—a squadron of British Matildas having been landed and a week earlier concealed in the jungle growth beside the road on the axis of the 2/48 Battalion's advance (see illus. page 596, Vol. 7).

They were to be a surprise for the enemy, and in order to muffle the sound of their movements an artillery shoot was planned

in as noisy a manner as possible—full use being made of the echoing depths of the valleys and rocky cliffs. By November 15 it was reasonable to assume that the main enemy concentration was at Sattelberg and to the north, whilst the forces located across the Song River west of the track to Wareo were doubtless supply and lines of communication troops.

The attack was launched on November 17 with an artillery barrage, and a general advance with intense fighting among the dense bamboo thickets where the Jap had skilfully concealed himself in well-prepared foxholes with overhead cover. During the night of the 19th the enemy had become tank-conscious and had laid traps and mines which further hindered progress. A Jap counter-attack was broken that evening, and the enemy's resulting disorganization was exploited to the full. The following day "2400" was taken by the 2/23 Battalion and a junction made by them with 2/48 Battalion on the main road. Much equipment and many weapons were captured and enemy casualties were heavy. Meanwhile, the column moving on "2600" was tied down by superior forces, and at this stage the Australians decided to attack the enemy's supply line on the Wareo-Bonga track—a carefully planned move which proved completely successful.

Standing High on Mountain Ranges

With the artillery and Air Force harassing the enemy's rear areas and other known positions, the advance along the Sattelberg road was continued on November 22. The main drive followed the road, with an out-flanking movement in the tangled undergrowth about 300 yards west of the road. The Japanese Air Force had been active daily since November 19 but with little damaging effect. November 23 was devoted to preparatory reconnaissance on the whole approach to Sattelberg, and on the next day the assault was launched.

On the road the enemy was in strength on one of the last ridges below the scarp, but a flanking movement to the east destroyed a strong post and enabled the force to reach the edge of the kunai grass which

AUSTRALIAN INFANTRY entered Sattelberg on Nov. 25, 1943, to find the town had been devastated by aerial and artillery bombardment, though at least one Japanese strongpoint had survived the pounding. As the assault could be made from one direction only the defenders held every advantage. Sattelberg stands on a rocky height in north-eastern New Guinea.

Photo, Australian Official

marked the southern end of the plateau. The Mission itself was in a cleared kunai patch standing high on the mountain ranges rising to the inland heights of the peninsula. The cleared plateau gave the enemy choice at will of defensive posts, but it also offered an opportunity for our troops to engage the Jap in open country. The flanking movement east of the road inspired the enemy to mount an expensive counter-attack. It was repulsed, and at last light our troops were within 150 yards of Sattelberg crest.

In order to visualize the situation it is necessary to bear in mind the nature of the country in the vicinity of Sattelberg. The only possible approach to the town lay through the open kunai patch situated directly beneath the top of the cliffs. The enemy had taken full advantage of his superior position, entrenching himself with carefully concealed and well-directed machine-guns against which one particular platoon, commanded by Sgt. Thomas Derrick, had fought all day in face of intense machine-gun fire and grenades, making little appreciable progress. The position seemed invulnerable, and orders had been given for a withdrawal for the night when Derrick pleaded for and was given another 20 minutes for a last attack. And this is what happened, in the words of the official citation of the action :

"MOVING ahead of his forward section he personally destroyed with grenades an enemy post which had been holding up this section. He then ordered his second section around on the right flank. This section came under heavy fire from L.M.G.s and grenades from six enemy posts. Without regard for personal safety he clambered forward well ahead of the leading men of his section, and hurled grenade after grenade, so demoralizing the enemy that they fled, leaving weapons and grenades. By this action alone the Company was able to gain its first foothold on the precipitous ground.

"Not content with the work already done, he returned to the first section and, together with the third section of his platoon, advanced to deal with the three remaining posts in the area. On four separate occasions he dashed forward and threw grenades at a range of six to eight yards, until these positions were finally silenced. In all, Sgt. Derrick had reduced ten enemy posts. From the vital ground he had captured the remainder of the Battalion moved on to capture Sattelberg the following morning.

"Undoubtedly Sgt. Derrick's outstanding gallantry, fine leadership and refusal to admit defeat in the face of a seemingly impossible

FINSCHHAFEN, on the Huon Peninsula, New Guinea, was captured by the Australians prior to the assault on Sattelberg in November 1943. Map shows the area covered by these operations.

situation resulted in the capture of Sattelberg. His outstanding gallantry and thoroughness were an inspiration to his platoon and to the remainder of his Company, and served as a conspicuous example of fearless devotion to duty throughout the whole Battalion."

SATTELBERG fell at 9 a.m. on November 25, 1943. For his gallant action, "conspicuous courage, outstanding leadership and devotion to duty" Derrick was awarded the V.C. (see illus. pages 707 and 760, Vol. 7). His name will forever be associated with the action which I have tried to describe. The battle continued into the heart of Japanese controlled New Guinea, until eventually the Australians destroyed their enemies there and moved on to the recapture of other islands of the Pacific battlefield.

Derrick received his Commission on November 25, 1944. Six months later he died in action at Tarakan, the oil island off the north-east coast of Borneo. He was hit by a machine-gun burst on the morning of May 23, 1945, when the Japs counter-attacked positions from which the Australians, led by Derrick, had driven them in a fearless assault. The enemy held the positions strongly, but Derrick's men attacked the first crest and made way for another platoon's occupation of the knoll. His platoon cut the track between the knolls and established a block, while another group attacked the second feature. Seeing that a direct assault was essential if success was to be achieved before night, Derrick moved his platoon and took command of the force. He lined sixteen Owen-gunners and six men

with Bren guns almost shoulder to shoulder and ordered them to attack targets of opportunity. Inspired, the men charged forward firing from the hip. Derrick ran among the section, indicating targets, organizing and giving encouragement. Carrying a rifle he stood up fully exposed and fired over the heads of his crouching, advancing men. The Jap defenders were killed or driven off.

The Australians consolidated in preparation for enemy attacks in overwhelming numbers on the third knoll. About 3.30 a.m. the enemy attacked, and a machine-gun burst wounded Derrick in the body and legs as he sat up to organize resistance. Despite his wounds he gave orders repulsing the attack. It was impossible to get the wounded out until daylight, and when he was being carried out Derrick said, "Well, we lost good men getting that hill. Don't pull out now. Tell my wife I went down fighting. It's curtains for me, but I'm happy." Twenty-one bodies were found around the knoll.

MATILDA TANKS, which surprised the Japanese at Sattelberg, tore tracks through the jungle over which the wounded could be evacuated. The battle for the stronghold began on Nov. 17, 1943, and Japanese resistance was overcome eight days later.

Monty an Honoured Five-Day Guest in Moscow

"CHALK-TALK" ON ALAMEIN by Field-Marshal Montgomery (1) to the students of the Voroshilov Military Academy was among the highlights of his five-day visit to Moscow in January 1947. He attended the ballet, with Marshal Vassilievsky (2). At the Frunze Military Academy (3) he delivered another lecture. Clad in a squirrel-lined great-coat, a gift from the Soviet Army, he inspected the guard of honour (4). See also illus. page 705.

PAGE 709   *Exclusive to* THE WAR ILLUSTRATED

How Dover's Radio Jammed German Radar

FROM THE NAVAL POINT OF VIEW the success of D-Day depended to a great extent on the efficiency of R.C.M., or Radio Countermeasures, in "blinding" a watchful enemy established on the northern coast of France. The object of R.C.M. was to stop the Germans using effectively their own radar equipment. It was in March 1941 that the Royal Navy began to take active radio countermeasures against German batteries on the French coast that were firing on British coastal convoys as these passed through the Straits of Dover.

One way to give protection was to stop the Germans on the far shore seeing the ships in the dark with radar. Radio experts stationed at posts along the south coast of England listened for enemy radar signals as our ships passed, and jammed them as soon as they were heard. So well did the operators and scientists follow every German move that when the large convoys were passing through the Straits for the invasion of Normandy only about six ships of some 2,000 were hit by enemy gunfire.

To mystify the enemy, German radar in the area where the invasion was to occur was jammed; and in certain other places, where no landings were intended, the enemy was made to detect on his radar screens indications that suggested the approach of an assault force. The transmitting-room of one of the Dover jamming stations (2) had a Wellsian appearance, and the aerials (3) might have been tubular steel scaffolding. The aerials of the monitoring receivers (4), which listened to the enemy's signals. Further countermeasures had to be devised to combat the German radio-controlled bombs; scientists invented equipment (1) that enabled a ship's wireless operator to jam the radio control and no ship so fitted was hit by one of those missiles. This successful warfare waged against the enemy's radar was always a race against time, and the scientist behind the fighting man should have a large share of the credit. More often than not he was told the enemy had perfected some device and the countermeasure was required within a few hours. He managed it, somehow.

Admiralty photographs

Preserving Law and Order at the Zone Frontier

CAUGHT BY OUR GUARDS NEAR HELMSTEDT, young Germans (1) had made a foray into the Russian zone in search of food. Sgt. J. Tarnopolski (2), interpreter at the frontier post, is seen giving directions to a Russian officer on his way to Frankfort. The changing of the guard (3) carried out on the autobahn, with Lieut. R. E. Prosser, of London, taking the parade. Everybody's papers are checked by an officer or N.C.O. ; a French officer (4) is subjected to friendly interrogation. German lorries, usually towing a trailer and laden with food (5) for Berlin, constitute the bulk of the traffic. See also illus. page 736.   PAGE 711   *Photos, Pictorial Press*

BERLIN 117 MILES AND THE FAR EAST

REPORT HERE

BRITISH ZONE

HIS MAJESTY'S SHIPS   H.M.S. Arethusa

Motto: "Swiftly Audacious"

SEVENTH bearer of a famous name, H.M.S. Arethusa is a cruiser of 5,220 tons, launched at Chatham in 1934. She is adopted by the City of Swansea. Her first important service during the war of 1939-1945 was in the Norwegian campaign of 1940. She was again in Norwegian waters the following year for the Lofoten Islands raid. Thence she proceeded to the Mediterranean, to engage in various operations against the Italians. In March 1942, immediately after escorting a convoy to Malta, she was attacked by German aircraft which hit the ship with a torpedo. This tore open one of the fuel tanks and set the oil on fire. Burning oil showered around, starting further fires, which in spite of every effort threatened to envelop the forward magazine.

Owing to broken connexions, the emergency system for flooding the magazine could not be used, and catastrophe seemed imminent. Yet no explosion followed. When at last the flames were under control, it was found that the torpedo had laid the magazine open to the sea and so saved the ship. After 3½ days the Arethusa reached Alexandria in so precarious a state that it seemed miraculous that she could have remained afloat. Temporary repairs were executed, and she proceeded to a U.S. Navy Yard for refit.

On D-Day in 1944 the Arethusa led the bombarding forces; and on June 16 she had the honour of carrying H.M. the King across the Channel. A little later she was put out of action by a magnetic mine, which twisted her propeller shafts out of shape. Repaired on the Clyde, she returned to the Mediterranean Station in time for the German surrender in 1945.

The Royal Engineers

By Brigadier
C. C. PHIPPS, C.B.E., M.C.

THERE are many different types of R.E. units, which may be classified under main headings according to the type of work done. Field units form part of every division, whether infantry, armoured or airborne, and are included in Corps and Army troops. In attack they have to advance with the leading troops to clear minefields and other obstacles, and build bridges, roads, and prepare routes generally. In defence they have to construct concrete pill-boxes, gun emplacements, lay minefields and demolish bridges and other installations. In both attack and defence they have to arrange water supplies.

Assault Engineer Squadrons are provided with tanks fitted with special devices for clearing minefields, breaching anti-tank obstacles, and destroying road blocks and pill-boxes. These tanks, known as A.V.R.E. (Assault Vehicle, R.E.), may carry bulldozer blades, dischargers for projecting demolition charges, and bridges which can be launched by the tank without exposing the crew to fire. Other armoured vehicles, known as Arks, are used for crossing anti-tank ditches. These vehicles drive into the ditch and are so designed that other tanks can cross over the top of them.

Lines of Communication units have to carry out all engineering work at bases and on the L. of C. Such work includes the building of depots, workshops, hospitals and other accommodation, construction of roads

THERE are many early historical records of military engineers, and Edward III formed a Corps of Engineers for the siege of Calais in 1346. In 1716 the first permanent Corps of Royal Engineers was formed, of officers only; the first permanent unit of other ranks, formed at Gibraltar in 1772, was known as Soldier Artificers. In 1856 these were combined under the present title of Corps of Royal Engineers. The R.A.F. began life as the Air Battalion R.E. Mechanical transport was started by the R.E., who used steam traction engines during the Boer War. The original Tank Corps, formed in France in 1916, was commanded by an Engineer officer, and "Signals" was one branch of the R.E. until formed into a separate Corps in 1920. Submarine mining was the responsibility of the R.E. until 1905. The varied activities of the Corps, brought into prominence in the 1914–18 war, help to explain why the Second Great War was so often called a "Sapper's War."

〰〰〰〰〰

and bridges, repair and operation of electric power stations, water and sewage plants, and so on. Transportation units have to construct, repair and operate ports and railways.

Airfield construction in the field is mainly an R.E. responsibility, assisted by units of the Royal Pioneer Corps. In the later stages of the war the R.A.F. also provided airfield construction units to deal with the very large number of airfields required in France and Holland. R.E. units are also engaged in chemical warfare, bomb disposal, survey

work and the making of camouflage. Certain duties of a non-technical nature are also carried out by special branches, such as control of the movement of all personnel and stores by rail or water and the staffing of the Army post offices, though mails are delivered in the field by the Royal Army Service Corps. R.E. units are, trained to fight, and have on many occasions taken their place in the line in an infantry role. The Second Great War, more than any previous war, was one of movement; often under most difficult conditions, including millions of mines, demolition of hundreds of bridges, flooding of enormous areas, and most elaborate types of defences constructed over a period of many years regardless of labour and expense. It was the principal task of the Royal Engineers to overcome such obstacles and keep the Army on the move.

SPACE does not permit of detailed description of the many wonderful achievements of the Corps in all parts of the world. Only main activities in each theatre of operations can be mentioned, very briefly. Some idea of the magnitude of the work involved is grasped when it is realized that in Italy over 2,500 Bailey bridges were constructed, while in the advance from Normandy to the Rhine over 1,000 bridges were built on the British front alone, including several of over 2,000 feet across the Rhine and the Meuse, and at least one of 4,000 feet over the Meuse and its flooded approaches. These outstanding triumphs were made possible by the invention of the Bailey bridge, designed at the Engineer Experimental Bridging Establishment.

The main works in Burma were the construction of airfields, roads and bridges. The jungle conditions meant very heavy labour in connexion with the two former, and the wide and fast-flowing rivers and the long

HUGE CEMENT-MIXING PLANT IN THE WESTERN DESERT was erected by R.E. when they were constructing new additions to the British defences in December 1940. Once the campaign in the Desert had developed into a tug-of-war that swayed backwards and forwards across Cyrenaica, the clearing of minefields became the most important task of the Engineers. Mine detectors at that time were crude and unreliable and flail tanks were unknown, so mines had to be located by prodding through the sand with a bayonet.

Photo, British Official

JAPANESE BOMBS used as mines on the road to Mount Popa had to be cleared by the Royal Engineers ; here a 250-pounder is being dealt with. The mountain, in central Burma, was taken by troops of the British 2nd Division on April 20, 1945.

roads, often little better than tracks, made bridging operations extremely difficult. The Irrawaddy river had to be crossed by ferrying. It was 1,500 yards wide at the site selected for the crossing, and more than 10,000 vehicles were ferried over in about 12 days. A Bailey pontoon bridge with a span of over 1,000 feet was built over the Chindwin river, and later replaced by a more permanent structure.

INDIA was the main base for supplies and for the training of troops for the Far East. The principal R.E. work here consisted in providing accommodation for personnel, stores, workshops, and the construction of airfields. Persia became important in 1942

as a supply route to Russia. An R.E. force was sent there to improve the roads and railways. Many miles of new roads were constructed, and some 100 miles of new railway line were laid, as well as miles of new sidings. In addition to the constructional work on the railways, R.E. personnel were employed on the operating side to assist the Persian authorities. In 15 months they increased the capacity of the railway, in a northerly direction, from 1,800 to 43,000 tons a quarter.

IN Libya and Cyrenaica a considerable amount was done on the coast road, but bridging was not much required. Many airfields were constructed, but the most important R.E. task was clearance of mines. In those earlier days the special tanks with flails and other means of destroying mines, which were later used in north-west Europe, were not available, although it was here that first experiments with these types were made. Mine detectors were in their infancy and few in number ; most of this work had to be done by prodding for the mines while crawling on hands and knees ! In 1941, Lieut. Bhagat of the Bombay Sappers and Miners,

LAYING NEW TRACKS was part of the work of the R.E. Railway Construction and Operating Companies in North Africa, Italy and North-West Europe. Majority of the men had been railway workers in peacetime.

Indian Army, was the first engineer officer in the Second Great War to win the V.C., for most conspicuous gallantry in clearing mines (portrait in page 760, Vol. 4).

WATER supply was a difficult problem. Old Roman aqueducts were repaired and used and a pipe-line constructed from the Nile to near Sidi Barrani. First large-scale use of camouflage as a means of deception was carried out by the camouflage units of the Royal Engineers before the battle of Alamein. Collapsible dummy tanks and other vehicles were constructed and used to represent an armoured division. The enemy was completely deceived as to the location of our real tanks by this method.

R.E. work in Algeria and Tunisia consisted mainly in the construction of airfields and roads and a number of Bailey bridges. Heavy rain throughout the winter of 1942-43 made this work very difficult. Port reconstruction was a most important and vital task immediately after Tripoli, Bizerta and Tunis had been captured. In spite of the most elaborate and effective demolitions by the

BY THE SEIZURE OF TARANTO on Sept. 9, 1943, the Allies obtained this great Italian port as a base depot, and special Dock Companies of R.E.s were soon at work unloading supplies. The Sappers had assault squadrons clearing the path of the attacking infantry, as well as units carrying out important duties behind the front line.   PAGE 714   *Photos, British Official*

R.E. Everywhere Sped Advance of Our Armies

FIRST BRITISH BRIDGE ACROSS THE RHINE was a Folding Boat Bridge built at Xanten by VIII Corps Troops, R.E., on March 24, 1945. Fifteen hundred feet long, it was built in 13 hours. This was quickly followed by several of the heavier Bailey Pontoon Bridges (1). To speed the advance of the Army in Burma the Sappers rebuilt many bridges, such as the one near Pinwe (2). In Tunisia and elsewhere a dangerous task was the demolition of damaged German tanks ; the placing of a demolition charge is followed by a dash for cover (3). PAGE 715 *Photos, British Official*

ON THE FROZEN ELBE AT HAMBURG shipping ploughs through the ice which threatens to close the port. Like the rest of north-west Europe, Germany experienced bitter weather in January 1947, a number of people in Hamburg dying from the intense cold and more than 100 being admitted to hospital suffering from frost-bite. The freezing of the inland waterways added to the difficulties of transporting coal from the Ruhr, and the British authorities instituted "warming" centres in buildings, such as cinemas and schools, for the civilian population, the majority being without fires in their homes.

GAPS CLEARED OF MINES were marked at night by shaded lights. This Sapper of the 8th Army, near the Mareth Line in March 1943, carries lamps for this purpose.
Photo, British Official

Germans, these ports were all partially re-opened within a few days of their capture.

In Sicily and Italy, R.E. work included a vast amount of mine clearance, and a very extensive programme of road making and bridge building. Altogether over 2,500 Bailey bridges were built and many hundreds of timber bridges. The landings at Salerno and Anzio provided useful lessons for the future operations in Normandy, although in neither of the former cases were the obstacles or the defences on the beaches nearly so formidable as in Normandy. Extensive port reconstruction work had to be carried out at Naples and other ports.

IN the greatest invasion operation of all time the Royal Engineers played a very prominent part in initial landings. The special R.E. assault companies, with their A.V.R.E., cleared lanes through numerous obstacles on the beaches and the exits from them. Their task was to clear the minefields, cut lanes through obstacles of steel and concrete, and deal with hundreds of pill-boxes and concrete gun emplacements. All of which, however, would have been of little value without means of landing the thousands of tons of ammunition, supplies and vehicles required to keep the attack going—and this was made possible by the Mulberry Harbour. Many persons had a hand in this wonderful achievement, including civilian workers at home who produced a mass of material in a very short time, and, of course, the Royal Navy and the Merchant Navy, who were responsible for transporting all the parts across the Channel and for the erection of parts of the breakwater. But the Royal Engineers were responsible for most of the initial experimental work, for the design of most of the parts and actual construction of a number of them, and for the erection of much of it, including all the long piers, pier-heads and a considerable portion of the breakwater.

Once Le Havre, Boulogne, Calais, and Antwerp had been captured, these ports had to be repaired and quays put in working order. The Germans had destroyed everything, except at Antwerp. Sunken ships had to be blown up, quays repaired, new cranes erected, electric power and water supplied, and all this in a matter of days. Although the cross-Channel pipe-line known as Pluto

(see illus. in pages 120, 533, Vol. 9) was not a R.E. project, the Engineers, assisted by Pioneer Corps units, were responsible for the continuation of the line across Europe to Germany. The R.E. were also responsible for ship-to-shore pipe-lines and for most of the larger pumping stations.

Mention has already been made of well over 1,000 Bailey bridges built from Normandy to the Rhine and the Elbe. Hundreds of miles of railway lines and many railway bridges had also to be constructed; altogether nine road bridges, of an average length of 1,400 feet, were built over the Rhine on the British front alone, and a railway bridge 2,360 feet long. Another important task was the construction of airfields, the majority being made by Airfield Construction Groups, consisting of R.E. and Pioneer Corps personnel. Additional airfields were constructed by R.A.F. Airfield Construction Groups.

THE ROYAL ENGINEERS were responsible for the improvement and provision of accommodation for British troops and Americans in the U.K. and Northern Ireland. In addition to housing the personnel, hospitals, supply, ordnance and ammunition depots and workshops had to be constructed, and many training facilities, such as tank and anti-tank ranges, artillery and rifle ranges, provided. Amongst the many engineering works carried out entirely by military labour was the construction of two large new ports in Scotland, complete with railway sidings. These were not only constructed, but also operated, entirely by Royal Engineers and Pioneers. One of these ports, at Gareloch, north of Glasgow, had six deep-water berths for ships up to 30 feet draught, and a large lighter berth. The other, near Stranraer, had five deep-water berths and also a lighter berth. Work commenced on both ports in the spring of 1941, and Gareloch was operating in the

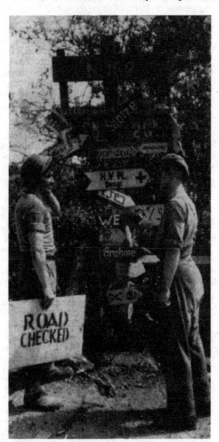

ROAD CHECKED signs denoted that this highway, near Thury Harcourt, Normandy, had been cleared by R.E. in Aug. 1944. The puzzle here is to find a vacant space on the signpost —already overcrowded with German signs.
Photo. The Times

Colours: Yellow on Red

8TH (INDIAN) DIVISION

FORMED in the Secunderabad area in 1940, by Major-General C. O. Harvey, the Division took part in 1941 in the operations in Iraq and Persia. During 1942 the 18th Brigade was rushed to Libya to help stem Rommel's advance, but was overrun and destroyed by German tanks. Early in 1943 the Division, now commanded by Major-General D. Russell, moved into Syria, being transferred to Egypt in June.

It landed in Italy in September 1943 and forced the crossings of the Trigno and Sangro rivers. In May 1944 it broke the German line on the Rapido river and advanced steadily northwards, Florence being entered on August 12.

THE Gothic Line was pierced on September 15, and a prolonged battle began for the passes over the Apennines. For two months the Division fought its way slowly across the watershed, finally executing the turning movement that cleared the way for a general advance. In December two brigades were rushed to the Serchio valley, on the U.S. 5th Army front, where they blocked a threatening German advance. During April 1945 the Division made two more bitterly opposed river crossings —those of the Senio and Santerno— then took part in the dash to envelop the town of Ferrara.

It headed next for Padua and Venice; but the German collapse was now imminent and the Divisional Reconnaissance Regiment, racing forward, caught up with one of the Division's toughest opponents, the German 1st Parachute Division, and received the surrender of 11,000 men. As a Division this formation never failed to take its objective. It was adjudged to be one of the finest in the Mediterranean theatre. Up to June 1945 four Victoria Crosses had been won by members of the Division, and the number of approved honours and awards had by then reached a total of 635, convincing proof of the formation's distinguished record.

summer of 1942 and Stranraer later. This great engineering achievement was of the utmost value in training personnel to repair damaged ports in Europe. (See page 173, Vol. 9).

On the Home Front the great bravery and skill shown by the Bomb Disposal Companies, R.E., will not be forgotten. Work on bombs often had to be carried out in most confined and awkward spaces and false movement might have meant instant death. When there was no further risk of invasion of this country Bomb Disposal Companies were employed in lifting and making safe hundreds of thousands of British mines which had been laid on the beaches as anti-invasion defences; numbers had become very sensitive, and the work entailed was extremely hazardous. Bomb Disposal personnel were also trained as divers, for removing under-water demolition charges at captured ports and assisting with under-water repairs.

They Now Bear the Title 'Royal'

IN December 1946 a Special Army Order announced that in recognition of their past services His Majesty the King had been graciously pleased to approve that the following Regiments and Corps should in future enjoy the distinction of "Royal." Their distinguished 1939-1945 records are here briefly outlined.

The Royal Hampshire Regiment

AT the outbreak of the Second Great War the 1st Battalion was stationed at Mersa Matruh, having been moved there from Palestine as a precautionary measure, and mechanized subunits took part in the attack on the Italians at Sidi Barrani in December 1940. Soon after the conclusion of General Wavell's offensive the 1st moved to Malta, there breaking all records for time taken to unload ships. It fought throughout the Sicilian campaign, and also in the landings on the Italian mainland in September 1943, before being sent to England to refit and train for D-Day. The 1st Battalion was among the first troops to storm the Normandy beaches, and after the break-out had the honour to be the first infantry to enter both Belgium and the Netherlands.

The 2nd Battalion served in France and Belgium during the 1939-40 campaign and greatly distinguished itself during the retreat and the evacuation at Dunkirk. Landing with the 1st Army in North Africa in November 1942, it won fame at Tebourba, Tunisia, on Nov. 30, 1942, in what has been described as one of the greatest infantry engagements of the war. It landed at Salerno on Sept. 9, 1943, and fought throughout the Italian campaign, except for a short period spent in Greece.

THE 1/4th, 2/4th and 5th Battalions, forming 128 Infantry Brigade, landed in North Africa in January 1943 and engaged in the operations that brought about the surrender of the Axis forces. The 5th Battalion gained much fame by their outstanding fight at Sidi Nsir. All these units fought at Salerno and remained in Italy until they went to Greece in 1944. The 1/4th and 5th Battalions returned to Italy after a short tour of duty, leaving behind the 2/4th.

The 7th Battalion did not see active service until June 1944, when it went to France with the 43rd (Wessex) Division. It was in the heavy fighting in Normandy and at the crossing of the Seine. Early in 1945 actions were fought on the River Waal, near Nijmegen, and during the advance to the Siegfried Line. Crossing the Rhine in the following March, the 7th Battalion was the vanguard of the 43rd Division and reached the line Hamburg-Bremen before the unconditional surrender of Germany.

Among the many decorations awarded to members of the Regiment were three V.C.s. The recipients of this honour were Major H. W. Le Patourel (portrait page 59, Vol. 7); Major R. Wakeford (portrait page 216, Vol. 8); and Lieut. G. Norton (portrait page 478, Vol. 8). In recognition of its outstanding record the Freedoms of Winchester, Aldershot, Bournemouth and Southampton were conferred upon it. Representative parties of all battalions attended these ceremonies and, on each occasion, were under the command of Lieut.-Col. J. M. Lee, D.S.O., who successively commanded the 7th, 2nd, 1st and 1/4th Battalions.

In conferring the title "Royal" on the Regiment in December 1946, His Majesty the King gave great pleasure and satisfaction to the inhabitants of Hampshire and to those who had taken their part in the grand services rendered by the County Regiment.

The Royal Lincolnshire Regiment

THE 1st Battalion was in India at the outbreak of war on Sept. 3, 1939, and engaged in operations on the North-West Frontier until the end of 1941. It moved to Bengal in 1942 and took part in the first offensive in the Arakan in January 1943. It was the only battalion engaged in the attack to reach its objective at Akyab, and covered the retreat of the main body during the withdrawal to India. The Arakan offensive was resumed in January 1944, and in the following March the Regiment relieved the 7th Indian Division, which had been surrounded by the Japanese at Ngakyedauk Pass. In this battle the Commanding Officer, Lieut.-Col. Sinker, was given the immediate award of the D.S.O., and Major Charles Hoey the immediate award of the posthumous V.C. (see portrait page 216, Vol. 8). In 1945 the 1st Battalion was engaged in a series of amphibious operations on the coast of Burma, seizing Ramree Island on Jan. 21 and leading the assault on Rangoon on May 2.

The 2nd Battalion formed part of the Expeditionary Force sent to France in 1939 and was in action in Belgium and during the retreat in 1940. On returning to England it took its place in the Field Army and began training for the invasion of Europe. It landed with the assault troops of the British 2nd Army on the Normandy beaches on June 6, 1944, and was involved in the heavy fighting at Caen. After advancing through northern France, distinction was won in the Battle of the Escaut Canal in September, this success being followed by victory at Overloon, Holland, on Oct. 12, 1944. The 2nd was in the prolonged fighting to clear the west bank of the Rhine in February and March 1945, and fought its way across north-west Germany to reach the port of Bremen as the war ended.

THE 4th Battalion was dispatched to Norway in April 1940, and after the termination of this ill-starred campaign formed a part of the Iceland Occupation Force until September 1942. It landed in Normandy with the rest of the 49th Division in July 1944, and fought in the operations preceding the Battle of Caen. After crossing the Seine it distinguished itself at the capture of Le Havre on Sept. 12, 1944, and further enhanced its reputation in Belgium and southern Netherlands. In 1945 it came under the command of the 1st Canadian Army, and captured Arnhem on April 15, 1945.

The 6th Battalion went to France with the Expeditionary Force at the beginning of the war and was in most of the major engagements up to the evacuation at Dunkirk. In 1942 it was sent to Tunis as part of the 1st Army, and saw hard fighting before the surrender of the Axis forces in May 1943. With other units of the Anglo-American 5th Army the 6th landed at Salerno, where it was almost wiped out. It was re-formed, and subsequently was engaged in important actions of the Italian campaign. In one of these Capt. J. H. C. Brunt was awarded a posthumous V.C. (portrait page 24, Vol. 9)

The Royal Leicestershire Regiment

VARIOUS battalions of The Royal Leicestershire Regiment saw active service in Norway, France, North Africa, Crete, Syria, Italy, Greece, Burma, Belgium, the Netherlands and Germany. A Regular battalion left India for Malaya shortly before the Japanese landings in December 1941. Fighting against overwhelming odds, it fell back to Singapore, where it was involved in the surrender of Feb. 15, 1942. Another battalion landed in France early in July 1944 and gave magnificent service in the advance to the Seine. It was present at the surrender of Le Havre on Sept. 12, and subsequently saw much fighting in Belgium and the Netherlands.

A second Regular battalion was stationed in Palestine at the outbreak of war, and was soon in action against the Italians with General Wavell's Army of the Nile, driving back the enemy 200 miles in six weeks. It fought with distinction at Sidi Barrani, Buqbuq, Sollum and Bardia. Sent to Crete as a forlorn hope, it was forced eventually to evacuate the island, and after taking part in the relief of Tobruk the battalion was sent to Syria for the brief campaign against the Vichy French forces, June 1941. In 1942 this unit was transferred to India, and later to Burma, where it joined the Chindit Force under General Wingate. Another battalion took part in Wingate's airborne invasion of Burma in 1944, capturing Taungni Bum and seizing and holding the Kyusanlai Pass.

A TERRITORIAL battalion, sent to work behind the lines in France in 1940, was drawn into the fighting line and fought its way most gallantly to Dunkirk. After a period of training in England, it joined the 1st Army in its invasion of North Africa. This battalion took the full weight of the first heavy German attacks at Sedjenane, Green Hill, Hunt's Gap and Thala. After the defeat of the enemy in N. Africa, it was amongst the units that assaulted the beach at Salerno and won a reputation during the advance north in Italy, storming Mondaino and breaking through the Gothic Line. Of the Mondaino action the Divisional Commander wrote: "The storming of Mondaino was indeed a Tigers' battle and will rank high among the many feats of arms of the Leicestershire Regiment."

Royal Army Educational Corps

IT would be difficult to over-estimate the importance of the work carried out by the Royal Army Educational Corps; the Second Great War proved that without the right mental attitude physical courage could not endure. Enforced inactivity that followed Dunkirk and the attendant problem of keeping men's minds interested and alert led to the recall of members of the Corps

(Continued in page 723)

War Service of the New 'Royals'

Signposting in the Western Desert was carried out by the Corps of Royal Military Police. Cut from petrol tins, these signs in a " shop " (1) were set up along tracks and trails to aid transport drivers. Traffic control was another task of the M.P. ; an identity card is examined in Teheran in 1942 (2). In the Middle East (3) an Egyptian sheep dog of the Dog Section—an Ermenti —receives attention. See page 723.

When the Royal Pioneer Corps was the Auxiliary Military Pioneer Corps (AMPS) ; an old soldier with his squeeze-box (4) leads a sing-song in Britain in 1940. In Tunisia in 1943, with native labour to assist, Pioneers at this enormous dump (5) handled 500 tons a day, working in shifts the clock round to do it.

Photos, British Official, Fox

Uplift and Instruction in Intervals of War

With The Royal Leicestershire Regiment in Italy in 1943 : the 2/5th Battalion took its turn in carrying supplies through the mountains (1) to front-line units of the 5th Army.   Tommy-gun instruction (2) in 1944 for Leicesters in the Middle East.   The Royal Army Educational Corps is as expert in putting over workshop lessons (3) as in lecturing in the field (4) on current events and other topics not necessarily connected with the art and craft of soldiering.

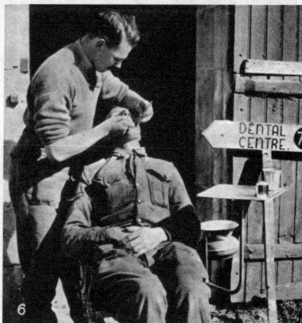

Time Off from Battle to Visit the Dentist

As well as permanent centres at bases, the Royal Army Dental Corps has mobile field units such as this (5) in the Western Desert. There were over 600 men of the Corps in the Middle East giving dental treatment of all kinds to British and Allied troops. Tents and equipment can be swiftly transported and set up. At an advanced dressing station just behind the line in Normandy, during the Liberation of Europe, the Dental Corps were still busy (6).

Lincolns and Hampshires

Officers of the 2nd Battalion The Royal Lincolnshire Regiment engaged in 3rd Division exercises (1) in the St. Pol area in March 1940. More than four years later, members of the 4th Battalion made pets of two goats (2) which they found in the ruins of Willemstad, Holland, liberated on Nov. 7, 1944. Seventh Battalion The Royal Hampshire Regiment occupied a German slit trench (3) south of Caumont, Normandy, in 1944. Bren carriers of the Hampshires (4) in Sicily in 1943.

Photos, British Official

(*Continued from page 718*)

from the military duties to which they had been dispersed at the outbreak of war. It became obvious that what the troops needed was an opportunity to discuss the topics of the day. By the autumn of 1941, such discussions, based on informative pamphlets issued by the newly created Army Bureau of Current Affairs, had become a recognized part of unit training.

THE winter scheme of education launched in 1942 represented a more systematic approach and survived, with various additions and alterations, until the end of hostilities in Europe. Three hours of training time were allocated each week to educating the man as a soldier, citizen and individual. Members of the Corps also assisted in physical, mental and moral rehabilitation in military hospitals and prisons and broadened the general education of youths in the Young Soldiers' Battalions. From 1943 onwards basic education courses were arranged, and text books, suitable for illiterate adults, were published to combat illiteracy in the Army. By the end of the war basic education centres existed in every Command, and illiteracy was almost non-existent.

Experience in the field showed that the soldier still required some form of mental stimulus even when operating under the most arduous conditions. Education staff officers were with divisions in Iceland, Egypt and India ; and, following the invading forces into North Africa, Sicily and Italy, formed education centres behind the front line. D-Day saw A.E.C. officers and instructors in Normandy with divisions and beach groups, and for the first time in military history their daily commentaries brought reliable information to the rank and file.

With demobilization came greatly increased activity. Local and centralized courses, ranging from engineering to languages and from musical appreciation to carpentry and designed to facilitate the released soldier's transition to civilian life, were arranged according to demand. The correspondence courses were expanded, and libraries of specially selected books were issued to every major unit. The Formation Colleges, foreshadowed by those already established at Perugia and Haifa, provided specialized residential courses in the sociable atmosphere which is an essential part of education.

Royal Army Dental Corps

DURING the Second Great War this Corps attained a maximum strength of 2,300 officers and 3,500 other ranks, including A.T.S., and provided comprehensive facilities for dental treatment to soldiers in every location and particularly in the forward areas of operational theatres. Dental officers, who were all qualified dental surgeons and assisted by skilled technicians, were employed with independent, mobile and static dental units both at home and overseas. They were also attached for duty with the majority of medical units, including Parachute and Airborne Landing Field Ambulances. Inestimable service was also given by specialist dental surgeons in treatment of jaw injuries and facial disfigurements.

By lectures, demonstrations, instructional films and posters the Corps impressed upon the soldier the importance of oral hygiene and made him fully aware of the value of dental treatment to his physical fitness. This branch of the medical services contributed in no inconsiderable measure to the high standard of health obtaining in the Army. How vast was its task can be gauged from the fact that attendances for treatment alone numbered 20 millions, while teeth conserved totalled 15 millions as against 8 millions extracted. The Corps also supplied, repaired or remodelled 1¾ million dentures. Much of this invaluable work was done by small mobile units, carrying out their duties in specially equipped vehicles in forward areas often under fire ; one mobile surgery might have to deal with as many as from 500 to 600 patients a month, the surgeon being responsible for some 2,000 men.

Royal Pioneer Corps

THE badge of the Corps is symbolic of the fact that without this military labour force behind the front lines no victories could have been achieved. Units of the Corps were to be found in every theatre of operations as well as in certain island outposts, such as the Faroes, Iceland and the Azores, where construction of airfields and preparation of defences were essential means of preventing invasion by Axis forces.

The men who went to France for labour duties with the first contingent of the Expeditionary Force in 1939 were Army reservists, and it was from them that the first units of Auxiliary Military Pioneer Corps, as it was then called, were formed. Although Pioneers were at that time only 25 per cent armed many of them did sterling work in the defence of Boulogne and Dunkirk, and on one memorable occasion they wrecked the tracks of German tanks with picks and shovels. The Corps became fully combatant when it was re-formed after Dunkirk. From a force of approximately 25,000 men in July 1940, it had expanded to an army of more than 160,000 U.K. personnel and over 270,000 non-U.K. personnel by May 1945.

PIONEERS contributed in great measure to the build-up of the Army in preparation for D-Day, by the construction of depots, airfields, roads, railways and defences and the handling of tens of thousands of tons of ammunition and supplies. They helped to build the Mulberry Harbour and Pluto, and provided specially trained smoke units for screening vital areas from air attack. The fire-watching sections saved quantities of valuable stores and much property from destruction, and a special force was formed for the clearance of debris during the intensive bombing of London and other cities.

The Pioneers sometimes fought with infantry units, acquitting themselves well. During the critical battle of the Kasserine Gap in Tunisia they did sterling work in manning the defences. They landed with the first waves of assault troops at Salerno and Anzio during the Italian campaign, and carried out such strenuous tasks as portering supplies to forward troops in mountainous country, often under fire and in appalling weather. Their work at Anzio was specially commended by General Mark Clark, G.O.C. 5th Army, when the discharge of over 5,000 tons of supplies daily for three days constituted a record then unequalled.

They were also employed as stevedores, dockyard workers, stretcher-bearers and guards for P.O.W. camps. In the Middle East many races and creeds were represented in the Corps. Cypriot and Palestinian Companies took part in the operations in Greece and Crete and suffered heavy casualties. Other units were employed on the construction of defences, harbour works and the water pipe-line through the desert behind the advancing 8th Army.

ON D-Day, Pioneers landed "wetshod" on the Normandy beaches with the infantry, and distinguished themselves at Caen, the crossing of the Orne River, at Walcheren and Nijmegen. Pioneers operated as airborne troops for the first time at Arnhem. The great smoke screen that concealed the preparations of the British 2nd and 1st Canadian Armies for the crossing of the Rhine was maintained by units of the Corps. Their proudest moment probably came at the Victory March in Berlin where, while British tanks and troops paraded down the Unter den Linden, the route was lined by Pioneers. Of the men of this Corps it was said by Col. H. Greenwood, V.C., one of their commanders throughout the war : " When trouble came they were too old to run away. They fought with what they had where they were. And usually they were never heard of again."

Corps of Royal Military Police

IN September 1939 the Corps had a strength of about 3,500, and 720 struggled with the Provost problems of the B.E.F. in 1940. Traffic control had been revolutionized by mechanization, and the confusion caused by streams of refugees and wholesale pilfering of Army stores showed the need of expansion. In 1940 and 1941 three new branches were formed : the C.M.P. (S.I.B.), Special Investigation Branch, the C.I.D. of the Army ; the C.M.P. (T.C.), the Traffic Control Companies ; and the C.M.P. (V.P.), police for the guarding of Vulnerable Points—mainly huge ammunition and supply dumps that were scattered all over the British Isles. Ports, too, had their special companies.

Hundreds of miles of desert track were marked for the 8th Army ; and Sappers and Military Police led the attack through the minefields at Alamein. Beach Provost Companies were formed for the invasion of North Africa in November 1942, and the police landed with the assault troops. This new branch of the C.M.P. developed rapidly and formed part of the British spearhead at Salerno and Anzio. All wings of the Corps were represented in vast numbers in the final campaign that took them from the Normandy beaches to Hamburg and Berlin.

Special Gurkha, Indian, Cingalese and African companies were formed and served with distinction against the Japanese. At the end of the war the Corps was some 35,000 strong, and this figure does not include the Indian and Colonial units. Its casualty list was lamentably long ; and it proved itself to be indispensable to all commanders, whether at home or in the field.

A Dog Section was formed during the war. The animals were used for patrolling military supply depots both at home and overseas, thereby releasing many of the police for more urgent duties. The dogs proved remarkably efficient, one making 83 "arrests" during two years' service in Palestine and Egypt.

SIR ARTHUR (BOMBER) HARRIS HITS OUT

IN twelve bold and concise chapters Sir Arthur Harris sets out in Bomber Offensive (Collins, 21s.) to prove how the defeat of Germany was largely achieved by the indispensable part played by the Command which will for ever be associated with his name. He not only maintains that without the help of Bomber Command the invasion of Europe would have been "the bloodiest campaign in history, unless, indeed, it had failed outright—as it would undoubtedly have done," but asserts that there would have been no need for the invasion if men, aircraft and equipment, both British and American, were not "always being diverted from the main offensive by the demands of other Services."

It is only human nature to be cynical when you don't have your own way, and for a man with a personality like "Bomber" Harris, who combined all the qualities of great resourcefulness and ability with sound judgement but strong convictions, his task often seemed irksome. In almost every chapter he comments in trenchant style on the obscurity or obliquity of vision shown on matters that affected the war effort in general and his work in particular. He dismisses leaflet raids as ridiculous and a complete waste of time. He attributes the lack of speed and efficiency in getting things done when there is an emergency to the fact that the matter is argued about "by all sorts of junior officers at the Ministries concerned and then once again by all sorts of irresponsible and very often operationally ignorant officials."

OUR incendiary attacks, he says, would have been vastly more efficient and effective " if the armament and production authorities had not bungled everything as they did." He then describes how, after three years of bitter dispute and argument, he despaired of getting a serviceable and useful 5-inch gun-turret through official channels and went and ordered direct from a firm "which can do anything without any fuss and with a comparatively minute staff in the design and drawing office." As a result one whole Group of his Command was equipped in less than a year with a first-class turret of revolutionary design.

But the real importance of the book lies not so much in the value of any carping criticism that the Air Marshal has wanted to get off his chest, but in the undisputed record of the achievements of Bomber Command which he so ably directed for three years. When he took over in February 1942 there were only 69 heavy bombers serviceable with crews. (The education of a member of a bomber crew was the most expensive in the world, he says. It cost some £10,000 for each man.) In 1943 the average number of heavy bombers was 570 and during 1944 this figure was almost doubled, although it fell far short of the 4,000 heavy bombers he had asked for as a front line strength.

New and Untried Weapon Proved

Sir Arthur shows himself throughout his book to be a man with a fixity of purpose, backed by an unflinching will of his own. His belief that the bomber was the predominant weapon for the task of destroying the enemy's war potential amounted to almost monomania. It was heavy bombers he wanted, bombers which could carry about three times the load of a medium type, but still requiring only one pilot. Having watched the burning of London he was convinced that a bomber offensive of adequate weight and with the right kind of bomb would, if continued long enough, be something that no country in the world could endure. But he wanted to use his force to fight the war by itself. "The same principle of strategy that made England a sea power in the past,"

MARSHAL of the R.A.F. Sir Arthur Harris, G.C.B., C.B.E., A.F.C., looks back from retirement to his active war days and nights in an outspoken book entitled Bomber Offensive, which is here reviewed by Derek Adkins.

he writes, "had only to be applied to the new weapon which had rendered obsolete the old one, the battleship."

His first task was to convince those in power that bombing could really be a decisive weapon. He first had to dispose of any wishful thinking engendered by optimistic forecasts of what might be done, and to make clear the grounds of his complete confidence in a bomber offensive if this was given a real chance. The 1,000-bomber raid on Cologne in May 1942 provided the answer. At the time it was planned and carried out complete success was far from being assured, but Sir Arthur had such faith in the strategic consequences of similar operations on a large scale that he was prepared to risk everything in a single battle. He reveals that half-trained crews and air-

SIR ARTHUR HARRIS forged Bomber Command into an offensive weapon of devastating power, contributing materially to the collapse of Germany in 1945. *Photo, Fox*

craft from Operational Units and Conversion Units were needed to bring the strength up to the requisite figure, but he adds that " we should never have had a real bomber offensive if it had not been for the 1,000-bomber attack on Cologne, an irrefutable demonstration of the power of what was to all intents and purposes a new and untried weapon."

It is evident that the two main contributions to the implementation of his broad plan and programme were, first, the development of non-visual aids to navigation and, second, radio counter-measures to jam the enemy's early warning system, his ground control stations, and communication between his night fighters and the ground. Sir Arthur's description of the very elaborate ways in which deception was practised provides one of the most illuminating revelations of warfare that has yet been published. He lays stress in particular on the dropping of metallized strips of paper, known as "Window," which completely confused the enemy's radar.

"Searchlights waved aimlessly in all directions," he writes, "the gunfire was inaccurate, and in England the stations which intercepted the enemy's wireless traffic were

immediately aware of hopeless confusion in the German ground control stations." The jamming war, he adds, "was eventually to develop to such a point that it became a major factor in deceiving the enemy about our intentions and action by air, sea, and land on D-Day."

When Sir Arthur went to Bomber Command the few scientists who were able to devise new navigational aids were entirely preoccupied with defensive measures, and the author comments that "whereas in 1940 and 1941 it often happened that more aircraft and crews were lost by crashing in England on the return flight than over Germany, in 1942 the wastage had become almost insignificant." He explains how this was largely due to target-finding and target-marking aids which he caused to be developed under the names of "Gee," "Oboe," "H2S" and "GH" (see page 444, Vol. 9), and to the formation of the famous Pathfinder Force.

A complementary requirement for the success of the offensive, however, was the provision of cameras in all aircraft of his Command, so that a complete and accurate assessment of any operation could be made. This was not completed until the autumn of 1942 when, he says, "with the long deferred expansion of strength at last becoming effective, I was ready to start." Meanwhile, he had had other problems to solve.

Saved the Flower of Our Youth

High explosive bombs were found to be too small, and Sir Arthur describes the 250-lb general-purpose bomb as "a ridiculous missile," although the 4-lb incendiary bomb he rates "the best weapon for destroying large industrial areas." The policy decision to destroy Germany's industrial cities, and the factories in them, was calculated to be the best way of destroying Germany's capacity to produce war material, and by saying that "the surest way to win a war is to destroy the enemy's war potential" Sir Arthur reaffirms that he has always belonged to this school of thought. But he makes it clear that he did not invent "area bombing" or insist on carrying it out "in the face of the natural reluctance to kill women and children that was felt by everyone else." To correct the widespread impression that he was not only the author but executor of the bomber offensive, and possibly to vindicate himself, Sir Arthur takes pains to point out that such decisions " are not in any case made by Commanders-in-Chief in the field but by the Ministries, by the Chiefs of Staff Committee and by the War Cabinet."

Throughout the 280 pages of his book and throughout the significant period of his valuable service with Bomber Command, the image of total warfare is reflected in the mirror of his thoughts. It was even more clear as he directed his bomber offensive which, as he puts it, "saved the flower of the youth of this country and of our Allies from being mown down by the military in the field." In his view the wholesale destruction of property was always justified if it was calculated to save casualties and not cause casualties. He recognizes that bombing will inevitably cause civilian casualties, but argues that the bombardment of any city as a whole is still a normal practice.

As a Service chief Sir Arthur Harris was a virile leader with a dynamic flair for getting things done ; as an author writing in the tranquillity of Rhodesia he displays a surprisingly acrimonious nature : and as a man who cannot suffer easily the shortcomings of others he cannot complain if his book earns him the indictment, coined many years ago about someone else, of being "intolerant of suggestion and unyielding in negotiation."

To the Honour and Glory of H.M.S. Lively

SUNK BY ENEMY AIRCRAFT in the eastern Mediterranean on May 11, 1942, H.M.S. Lively (1, and badge, 2) and company were commemorated by the unveiling, on Feb. 2, 1947, of a stained glass window (3) in St. Margaret's Church, Liverpool. The ceremony (4) was performed by Admiral Sir Harold Burroughs, K.C.B., D.S.O., C.-in-C. the Nore. Lively was a destroyer of 1,920 tons, with main armament of six 4·7-in. guns and speed of 36 knots. Her captain, Lieut.-Commander W. F. C. Hussey, D.S.C., R.N., and 75 of the ship's company were lost, the destroyer sinking within four minutes of being hit. See also page 302, Vol. 5.

Photos, Admiralty, H.M.S.O., Liverpool Daily Post, Topical

L.A.C. R. ARNELL
Royal Air Force.
Accident. M. East. 2.12.41.
Age 31. (Felling-on-Tyne)

From its inception on page 88 of this volume, up to page 568, our ROLL OF HONOUR appeared regularly as a single page. In order to accommodate the large number of portraits accepted, this space has now been increased to two pages in alternate issues.

The ROLL of Honour
1939—1946
NCOs & MEN

Pte. D. BRENCHLEY
Royal Armoured Corps.
P.O.W. Siam. 29.8.45.
Age 27. (Greenwich)

L/S. F. BAILEY
Royal Navy.
Died. 6.8.46.
Age 23. (Macclesfield)

Sgt. A. BAYLISS
Royal Artillery.
Action : Cassino. 8.11.43.
Age 22. (Liverpool)

Pte. W. BORROW
Cheshire Regt.
Action : Caen. 6.6.44.
Age 25. (Middlesbrough)

L/S J. H. BRYANT
Royal Navy.
Act. : Channel. 12.10.40.
Age 21. (Lowestoft)

Rfmn. M. BRYCE
Rifle Brigade.
Action : Calais. 1940.
Age 33. (Haswell)

A/B BRACKENRIDGE
H.M.S. Aldenham.
Action : Aegean. 14.12.44.
Age 18. (Johnstone)

L/Cpl. R. T. BURT
Shropshire L.I.
Action: Tunisia. 24.4.43.
Age 22. (Guernsey)

Fus. D. CASEY
Royal Fusiliers.
Action : Cassino. 14.5.44.
Age 19. (Cheshunt)

Pte. A. W. CLARK
Suffolk Regt.
P.O.W. Formosa. 11.2.43.
Age 27. (Braintree)

Pte. S. COLLINS
Royal Sussex Regt.
P.O.W. Germany. 24.6.40.
Age 32. (Brighton)

A.C.I J. CLARKSON
R.A.F.V.R.
Off Sumatra. 18.9.44.
Age 34. (Birmingham)

Pte. T. J. S. COOPER
Somerset L.I.
Action : Goch. 17.2.45.
Age 19. (Bristol)

L/S. V. CROCKER
Royal Navy.
Act.: Nr. Tobruk. 26.3.42.
Age 21. (Wincanton)

L/Sto. B. CROSS
H.M.S. Atherstone.
Action : Margate. 12.9.40.
Age 23. (Banbury)

Pte. J. CURRAN
Royal Leicestershire Regt.
Action : Italy. 14.10.44.
Age 29. (Stockport)

Pte. T. DAVISON
K.O.S.B.
Act.: N.W. Europe. 16.7.44.
Age 25. (Newcastle/Tyne)

Pte. N. DEWIS
Beds. & Herts. Regt.
Action : Italy. 18.7.44.
Age 28. (Bedworth)

Sgt. D. J. DOUGLAS
Scots Guards.
Action : Libya. 29.12.41.
Age 25. (North Shields)

A/B T. DUNCALF
H.M.S. Royal Oak.
Act. : Scapa Flow. 14.10.39.
Age 28. (Ormskirk)

Sgt. J. A. G. FIRTH
Royal Air Force.
Action : Charleroi. 7.5.42.
Age 23. (Llanrhaiadr)

Sgt. T. A. FIRTH
Royal Air Force.
Died. 3.7.44.
Age 22. (Llanrhaiadr)

Rfn. A. FULLERTON
Royal Irish Rifles
Action : Dunkirk. 29.5.40.
Age 20. (Gilford)

Fus. E. GALSTON
Royal Fusiliers.
Action : Italy. 27.7.44.
Age 19. (Manchester)

A/B S. GOLDSMITH
H.M.S. Janus.
Act.: Off Nettuno. 23.1.44.
Age 19. (Strood, Kent)

A/B R. GOODCHILD
H.M.S. Isis.
Action : At Sea. 20.7.44.
Age 19. (Dagenham)

A/B J. GREATBATCH
H.M.S. Rawalpindi.
Action : At Sea. Oct. '39.
Age 41. (Daventry)

Sgt. J. D. GREEN
Royal Air Force.
Action : Berlin. 15.11.40.
Age 20. (Fitzwilliam)

Bdr. C. V. HARRIS
Royal Artillery.
D/W. : Cleve. 24.3.45.
Age 35. (Campden, Glos.)

L/Cpl. H. HOTCHKIN
E. Riding Yeomanry
Action : Caen. 8.7.44.
Age 28. (Beverley).

Sgt. I. A. JERVIS
R.A.F.V.R.
Action : Holland. 23.5.43.
Age 19. (Clowne)

Fus. T. JODDRELL
Royal Welch Fusiliers.
Action: Belgium. 17.9.44.
Age 19. (Stockport)

Fus. L. JOHNSON
Royal Scots Fusiliers.
D/W. : France. 11.9.44.
Age 23. (Feltham)

Cpl. S. KEEN
Wiltshire Regt.
Action : Caen. 22.7.44.
Age 27. (Streatham)

Gnr. F. KNOTT
Royal Artillery.
Action : Italy. 8.5.44.
Age 24. (Manchester)

L/Cpl. H. KAYE
Beds. & Herts. Regt.
D/W. 18.10.44.
Age 23. (Huddersfield)

Gnr. C. KENYON
Royal Artillery.
D/W. : Libya. 25.12.42.
Age 33. (Stratford/Avon)

The NCOs Roll of Honour & MEN
1939—1946

Fus. E. LEWIS
Royal Welch Fusiliers.
Action : Holland. 7.12.44.
Age 18.   (Penycae)

Sgt. J. LEWIS
Royal Air Force.
Action : France. 24.6.44.
Age 22.   (Lampeter)

Pte. J. W. LARKIN
Gloucestershire Regt.
Action : Burma. 23.11.44.
Age 22.   (Salford)

Gnr. E. G. LANG
Royal Artillery.
Action : Burma. 25.2.45.
Age 21.   (Port Talbot)

Pte. G. E. LAY
Royal Hampshire Regt.
D/W. : N. Africa. 7.8.43.
Age 23.   (Woodbridge)

Fus. J. O. MELLOR
Royal Fusiliers.
D/W. : Italy. 11.9.44.
Age 24.   (Audenshaw)

Gnr. J. MANSELL
Royal Artillery.
Action : Malta. 19.4.42.
Age 34.   (Dagenham)

Mne. R. MARSHALL
H.M.S. Arethusa.
Action : At Sea. 18.11.42.
Age 30.   (Romford)

A/B J. METTRICK
H.M.S. Prince of Wales.
Act. : Off Malaya. 10.12.41.
Age 25.   (Huddersfield)

Pte. A. MORGAN
The Royal Scots.
Accident : Italy. 23.8.45.
Age 34.   (Cardiff)

L/Cpl. D. MILLER
R.A.S.C.
Action : At sea. 26.4.41.
Age 33.   (Haworth)

Sgt. E. N. PERKINS
Royal Air Force.
Action : France. 4.2.43.
Age 19.   (London)

F/Sgt. W. F. PERKINS
Royal Air Force.
D/W. : Java. 21.2.42.
Age 21.   (London)

Pte. G. PETTIGROVE
Dorset Regt.
Act. : N.W. Europe. 10.7.44.
Age 21.   (Birmingham)

Pte. T. PRUDEN
Oxf. & Bucks (Airborne).
Act. : Germany. 24.3.45.
Age 24.   (Coseley)

F/Sgt. J. M. REID
R.A.F. Bomber Command.
Act. : Brunswick. 13.8.44.
Age 20.   (Dalkeith)

Pte. R. RICHARDSON
Herefordshire Regt.
Act. : Germany. 10.4.45.
Age 24.   (Horsham)

Pte. P. J. ROGERS
K.S.L.I.
D/W.   7.8.44.
Age 23.   (Whitchurch)

Sgt. W. J. ROWE
Royal Air Force.
Action : Holland. 8.5.42.
Age 25.   (Crewe)

F/Sgt. V. RAYMOND
Royal Air Force.
Action : France. 24.3.44.
Age 21.   (Newark)

L/Sgt. R. RYAN, M.M.
Queen's Royal Regt.
Action : Italy. 9.9.44.
Age 25.   (London)

L/Bdr. A. V. SEABY
Royal Artillery.
P.O.W. : Far East. 12.9.44.
Age 29.   (Twickenham)

L/Cpl. E. SHEARER
Seaforth Highlanders.
D/W.   25.5.43.
Age 21.   (Portmahomack)

A/B F. R. SIMPSON
H.M.S. Bullen.
Action : At Sea. 6.12.44.
Age 21.   (Whaley Bridge)

F/Sgt. E. J. SHARP
Royal Air Force.
Act. : Hungary. 20.10.44.
Age 21.   (Droylesden)

L/Cpl. J. J. SMITH
Queen's Royal Regt.
Act. : Salerno. 9.9.43.
Age 26.   (London)

L/Stwd. V. STAFRACE
H.M.S. Barham.
Action : Medit.   1941.
Age 37.   (Valetta, Malta)

L/Cpl. H. TAYLOR
East Yorks Regt.
Action : France. 29.5.40.
Age 26.   (Ashington)

A/B S. TAYLOR
H.M.S. Royal Oak.
Act. : Scapa Flow. 13.10.39.
Age 18.   (Ashington)

Tpr. D. TOY
Royal Tank Regt.
Action : Libya. 27.5.42.
Age 21.   (Falmouth)

L/Sgt. J. WALKER
Black Watch.
Act. : N. Africa. 26.4.43.
Age 25.   (Wakefield)

Sgt. J. WAREHAM
Manchester Regt.
Action : Italy. 28.7.44.
Age 31.   (Manchester)

L.A.C. R. WATTS
Royal Air Force.
P.O.W. Far East. 29.7.45.
Age 29.   (Offley)

Sgt. R. E. WATTS
Royal Air Force.
Act. : Germany. 2.1.44.
Age 33.   (Mkt. Harborough)

Sgt. D. H. WARNER
Royal Air Force.
Action : Medit. 29.10.41.
Age 26.   (Harrow)

L/Cpl. G. WATTAM
King's Own Royal Regt.
Action : Ramleh. 17.8.42.
Age 29.   (Kirkby Lonsdale)

Sgt. J. C. WEBBER
Royal Air Force.
Over Germany. 21.1.44.
Age 19.   (Southall)

AC/1 D. WILLINGHAM
Royal Air Force.
Act. : Normandy. 22.6.44.
Age 18.   (Earls Colne)

Walrus Aircraft Engage in Chasing the Whale

ABOARD THE BALAENA, 25,000-ton whaling-factory ship (1), when she sailed from Southampton in October 1946, were three Walrus amphibian aircraft to act as whale spotters. They can be catapult-launched and picked up (3) after a flight. Far out of sight of the parent ship the spotters flash back reports which enable the small, whale-catching craft to be directed to their quarry. The interior of the Balaena resembles a factory, one section being crammed with machinery for separating the whale oil (2). Masses of material covered the decks (4) on sailing, including timber for platforms on which the whales are cut up. It is hoped that the present season, ending in April 1947, will yield 1,000,000 barrels of oil from the ships of the whole fleet. A record catch will go a long way towards easing the fat-ration situation. By the spring, too, whale steaks should be entering many British homes. See also illus. page 212.

Photos, Central Press, Planet News PAGE 728

'Up the Micks!' at Djebel Bou Aoukaz

At four o'clock in the afternoon of Tuesday, April 27, 1943, the 1st Battalion The Irish Guards attacked the Djebel Bou Aoukaz, the last hill left to the Germans west of Tunis. Their task was to take its most important feature, Hill 212, and hold it while the guns, tanks and infantry of the 8th and 1st Armies launched the final attack on Tunis. How the Micks acquitted themselves is told by Major D. J. L. Fitzgerald, then with the Regiment.

HILL 212 is really a long, barren ridge, rising steeply from the flat plain, with a knob on either end, Point 212 on the west, Point 214 on the east. In full view of the Germans the Companies waded slowly through the waist-high green corn and the tall red poppies, unchecked by the rain of shells. Less than half of them reached the olive grove at the foot of the ridge.

We lay down beneath the trees to wait till nightfall before scaling the hill. It was not long before the German big guns and those abominable machines the six-barrel mortars came into action. They pounded the olive-grove systematically from end to end, working up and down the lines of stumpy trees. The ground had just been ploughed by some industrious French colonist, but unfortunately for us the furrows ran the wrong way, so that while we could press our heads and legs down below ground level our middles were protruded. But, of course, no cover was of any use against the heavy shells; the Regimental Sergeant-Major, for instance, and the tree he was sheltering under both disappeared in one explosion.

One hundred and twenty men out of the four Rifle Companies and Battalion H.Q. reached Hill 212 that night. The rest lay down in the corn or in the grove calling to the stretcher-bearers, or silent and marked only by a rifle butt silhouetted in the glow of burning Arab huts. The top of the ridge was bare rock, with only a few pockets of earth. We worked all night, digging, hacking and shifting boulders, to get slit-trenches built before dawn. Down below in the plain the carriers ran a shuttle-service from the Battalion's old position, bringing ammunition, rations and cans of water up to the foot of the ridge and taking the casualties back to the Aid Post. The Germans, too, were busy.

WE could hear the clank and clatter of their "half-tracks" ferrying up fresh troops, and we suspected that they were passing groups round behind us. That was exactly what they were doing. Every now and then there was a confused brush in the dark, the flare of a Verey light and a burst of wild firing. We expected a counter-attack at dawn. When none came, fatigue-parties went down the hillside to pick up the dumped stores. They managed to collect some twenty boxes of ·303, three or four sacks of bread and bully, a large bag of cigar-ettes and some cans of water and tea before the Germans put a stop to these expeditions. We then took stock of our position.

We were stuck out on a barren hill, separated from the nearest British troops by over a mile of open plain. We had enough small arms ammunition to be going on with, and as long as our one wireless—an 18 set—worked we could call for artillery support. None of the mortars had reached the hill, and now it did not seem that they ever would until another attack opened a clear way up the hill. Till then, though a few small parties might—and in fact did—slip through to join us, the duty of holding this vital hill fell on 120 men, armed with Brens, rifles and bayonets and two grenades per man.

At midday the Germans set to work to soften-up Hill 212. Salvos from the six-barrel mortars screamed through the air like Green Line buses and crashed in quick succession along the ridge. About two o'clock, 88-millimetre guns and tanks in the olive-grove opened up on the crest. This fire was heavy, most unpleasant and very accurate. With their telescopic sights and at such close range the Germans could snipe an individual man with solid armour-piercing shot. The main force was withdrawn to the top of the reverse slope, leaving look-outs in the best trenches. Both then and throughout the following day casualties were terribly heavy amongst these look-out men, but there was never any lack of volunteers for the task.

At three o'clock the German fire intensified. The look-outs shouted "Here they

ON HILL 212 IN TUNISIA is a white cross dedicated to men of the 1st Battalion The Irish Guards who fought and died there. The photograph was taken from Point 214 at the conclusion of the memorial service held in July 1943; and Point 212 can be seen behind the cross Germans retook Point 214, and it was there that the Guardsmen made their magnificent charge, which is described by the author of the stor he was one of the 1st Battalion's 72 survivors in the Battle for the "Bou".

Motto: "Strength by Night"

NO. 149 SQUADRON

DISBANDED in August 1919, the Squadron was re-formed at Mildenhall, Suffolk, in April 1937, when it was equipped with Heyford aircraft. In February 1939 it received Wellingtons and made its first sortie on September 4, 1939—a daylight attack on the German fleet near Heligoland. This was followed by months of reconnaissance flights, leaflet dropping and attacks on targets in enemy-occupied territory.

In August 1940 the Squadron made its first operational flight to Berlin, and by January 1941 it had engaged such targets as Turin, Milan, Genoa and Venice, in addition to the vital German centres of Bremen, Kiel, Wilhelmshaven and Munich. Converted to a Stirling squadron, it raided Lübeck in daylight on July 16, 1942. It was also one of the busiest mine-laying squadrons of Bomber Command, and in Dec. 1943 it introduced a new technique of high-level mining.

DAYLIGHT bombing became a regular operation during the last twelve months of the war ; targets included flying-bomb sites, Channel ports, oil and petrol installations, dykes and concentrations of enemy troops and armour. The Squadron's last bombing mission was carried out against Bremen on April 22, 1945. In the final days of the war supplies of food were dropped for the starving population of the Netherlands.

Perhaps the Squadron's best work was on special missions, some of which, such as the dropping of agents and supplies to the Maquis, were not divulged until some time after the end of the war. All these sorties required expert navigation ; also it was highly dangerous work, the unescorted bombers running the gauntlet of the enemy's fighters and ground defences, and the routes to the dropping zones being long and intricate.

The Germans had run away from us, and from then on no-one for one moment doubted our ability to thrash and to go on thrashing the Germans.

After this attack, the mortar and shell fire began again and went on steadily till the Friday night. I cannot remember any time when we were not being shelled or mortared, and later machine-gunned and sniped as well. But the worst of all was the thirst. We had only some half-dozen jerricans of water and two petrol tins of cold tea. The water was strictly rationed, and by the end we were all croaking harshly. The tea we kept for the wounded.

IT rained for half an hour on Thursday night and we caught a little muddy but very welcome water in groundsheets. The only other source of supply was the Germans ; after dark, men used to crawl forward and unhook the water-bottles from the dead bodies down the slope. One man got down to a wrecked carrier at the foot of the hill and brought back three tins of canned peaches. He brought them to me for the

ridge at maximum elevation and minimum range, with alternative switches to left and right. We could judge the effect from the screams which followed each burst.

No. 4 Company and part of No. 1 slipped forward and destroyed the leading Germans who had been cut off from their friends by the mortar fire. The Germans then retired for the night, and in the darkness we could hear them collecting their dead and wounded in the plain below. Their roll was loudly called by what seemed to be a very bad type of sergeant-major ; we were glad to note that he was deficient in a good half of his names.

The Germans did not attack again till nine o'clock the following morning. This was a mass attack, all along the ridge from 212 to 214, including both points. On the right, by Point 212, Lance-Cpl. Kenneally, V.C., broke up that half of the attack by going forward to meet it, firing a Bren gun from the hip. On the left the Germans drove an armoured car up the eastern slope of the hill. Lieut. Keigwin stopped it by firing four armour-piercing bullets into the engine. The crew baled out, but tried to salvage

GERMANS CAPTURED BY IRISH GUARDS on Hill 212, in the Medjez sector, in April 1943, march back to the rear. They could not face the accurate small-arms fire and bayonets of the Guardsmen, and in a series of attacks and counter-attacks a handful of indomitable Irishmen captured and held this key position.
Photo, British Official

---

wounded, and for the next three days I doled out the juice spoonful by spoonful to dying men. It was the only physical comfort we had to offer them.

At six o'clock that evening the Germans began to work round the left of the ridge, into a gully below Point 214. At seven they attacked again, this time trying to scale the ridge from the east. No. 2 Company ran along the reverse slope and caught the enemy in the flank, but even so a large number of Germans reached the top of Point 214. Life on the ridge would have been intolerable, if not impossible, if the Germans had held this point. They could not hold it. A bayonet and tommy-gun charge swept them off it back down the hill. However, the Germans continued to press their attack on that part of the ridge and had dug themselves in only a few yards from the top of it.

It was by now getting dark, and the situation looked serious. At this very moment a sergeant and three men came running along the reverse slope, carrying the parts of a three-inch mortar. They had just rescued it from the bottom of the hill—how I do not know. They now assembled it in record time and shot 20 bombs over the

their machine-gun. A section of Guardsmen caught them with it half-way out of the car, and fired a volley which completely disposed of the crew.

After a few hours respite, fresh German troops made another attack. By this time everybody was getting used to them. As usual, the Germans were driven off, but this time we launched a small counter-attack across a gully beyond 214, captured two machine-guns on a neighbouring hill, and turned one of them on to the retiring enemy. We had not enough men to hold this hill as well as our own, so the counter-attack force came back, draped with belts of ammunition, and bringing one machine-gun with them.

The rest of the afternoon we spent shooting their own ammunition at German infantry who were following up the tank attack on the plain below us. As a result of this attack German tanks got round to the rear of the ridge and opened fire along the reverse slope. We were now under fire from all sides. Just before dawn (Friday the 30th) Battalion Rear H.Q. managed to get some ammunition and food up to the base of the ridge. Unfortunately, the Germans started activities at the same time, and only a very small portion of the stuff could be got up, for everybody

---

come !'' Germans were climbing the slope from the front on the left half of the ridge. This was the first opportunity the Guardsmen had had of engaging the enemy personally, and they took it eagerly. Two small groups of men—we still called them Nos. 3 and 4 Companies—moved up the crest as soon as the shell fire slackened, and halted the Germans half-way up with rifle and Bren gun fire.

When the Germans were already wavering, two Brens and a section of No. 1 Company came over the right flank and joined in. This increase in the volume of fire had a splendid effect. The Germans turned and ran back down the hill. We were astonished at this sight, but soon recovered and went forward and shot down the fugitives. Two German officers who tried to rally their troops were picked off by riflemen, and our own guns, called down by the 18 set, completed the rout. Naturally, we were all elated by this success.

who tried to get it was killed by snipers. At eleven o'clock that morning the Germans made their last attack.

They came on in greater numbers and with greater persistence than ever before. There was with them a higher percentage of officers than I have ever seen with any troops—half were in front leading (these were easily picked off), and half were behind (these were harder to hit). They swept over Hill 214 and along the top of the ridge—and the Guardsmen were ready for them. Each man fired a couple of steady aimed shots and then jumped out of his trench and rushed at the nearest German. This spontaneous charge shattered the enemy and the whole line of Guardsmen swept forward, cheering and shouting "Up the Micks!" It was the most remarkable thing I have ever seen.

They chased the Germans half-way down the ridge, shooting into the thick mass and bayoneting the less fleet-footed. It was with great difficulty that the two surviving officers stopped the Guardsmen from going downright into the cornfields. This last and complete failure of their biggest attack must have broken the Germen's spirits for they never launched another one, though throughout the day they continued to work their way up in small groups only to be shot down.

THAT afternoon the plain behind was cleared of enemy and we were joined by a company of Grenadiers. Hill 212 was safe. Just before dawn the following morning we were relieved by a new battalion. Of the 120 men who had reached the top of the hill on Tuesday night and the few parties who had joined us during the following days, 72 came down on Saturday morning. The remainder who stayed there are commemorated by a great white cross, standing proudly on the ridge they died to hold. It was an honour to have served with such men.

Night-Fighter Versus Flying Bombs

As a Lieutenant (A), R.N.V.R., on loan to the R.A.F. for operational night-fighter duties, L. F. Thompson was given various tasks that could scarcely be considered Naval. Among them was the shooting down of Hitler's V weapons. His experiences with VIs—variously known as flying bombs, buzz-bombs and doodle-bugs—in July 1944 are recorded here.

L. F. THOMPSON

FROM 7,000 feet up the French coast shone clearly below us in the light of the full moon. Our patrol line took us south from Cap Gris Nez to Saint Valery and then back again at 6,000 feet. We did the northward trip at a different height so as to lessen the chance of collision with one of our fellow-patrollers on the opposite course.

We had to stooge up and down just off the French coastline and wait for the flaring white light that meant another load of death and destruction was on its way to London. In mid-Channel, we knew, were other night-fighters on the same job as ourselves; while others, we suspected, were actually inside France, also on the job. Across the Channel to the north in England thousands of gunners and searchlight crews stood ready for the same purpose of shooting down the VIs.

Sandy, my pilot, didn't go much on this business. Nor did I. We had been taken off intruding to help in this anti-V1 campaign, in which the tactics were as follows. On sighting the V1 the pilot placed his aircraft above the line of flight, as near as he could judge, and switched his navigation lights on to warn other aircraft that he was in the chase. Thus positioned, the pilot would wait until the V1 passed in front of and below him. Then he opened the throttles and put the nose of the Mosquito down, using the extra speed gained in the dive to hold the small target in range for long enough to shoot it down. My job, as observer, was to read out the ranges to Sandy as they appeared on the radar screen. There was a gun-sight evolved later for single-seat fighters, but in our aircraft it was unnecessary as the radar set was equally accurate. Some form of range-taking was essential since, by night, the exhaust flame of the buzz-bomb looked just as near at widely different ranges. I helped where possible with the judging of the enemy's line of flight, which, however, was no easy matter.

I was watching a rather spectacular raid which Bomber Command was putting on just inside the coastline when, looking back, I saw a light. "That looks like one, Sandy!" I exclaimed. "Just down to port." Sandy turned slightly to port to look more closely. "I think you're right," he said, and swung the Mosquito out from shore a little. We turned starboard again and had another look back for it. Then happened what we had seen many times. Before anyone could get on its tail the V1 toppled over and the light went out in the waters of the Channel.

We turned northward and prepared to make our way back to Gris Nez. But that dud was the herald of many live ones. Soon they were crossing the coast at several points, and the sky seemed full of the red, green and white navigation lights on the pursuing fighters. We spotted another that looked within our range. Out we charged again, throttles well open. When we judged that we were on the line of flight and over our target, we looked for it. It was not below us on my side and Sandy couldn't see it on his, and we wondered if it had gone into the "drink." I craned my head backwards and saw it still coming along. We waited for it to overtake us. But it came no closer.

"Must be one of those slower ones," said Sandy. For doodle-bugs came in two main speed categories. One lot, the more numerous, tore through the sky at about 400 m.p.h. The others, either through defect or intentionally, reached only about 250 m.p.h. We turned back, throttling down, and keeping the target carefully in sight. Sandy eased the Mosquito in behind it and down to its level, some 2,000 feet above the sea. The ranges came down and down on my radar set. I read them out, 1,000 feet, 900, 800, 700, 600 . . . As I said "six" I looked up from my set, knowing that Sandy would fire at that range. He aimed at the flaring light right in front of us. As the aircraft shook to the thump of the cannons I saw the little flickering white lights from around the flying bomb's jet, which told of strikes on our target. Then a great shower of red sparks mingled with the white glow of the jet.

SANDY pulled out, and we waited for the V1 to fall into the sea, its fuel tank, as we thought, holed by our cannon shells. But nothing happened, so we went in again. Once more the flicker of the strikes, again the red shower from the exhaust light. Again Sandy pulled the Mosquito aside: too many of our squadron's aircraft had come back to base battered and torn by the terrific blast of a buzz-bomb's explosion at close range. Others had never come back but had perished from unknown causes. Altogether, the squadron had lost more aircraft and crews on this type of operation than in a similar period on the apparently more dangerous job of night intruding. So Sandy turned aside once more. But again nothing happened and again we

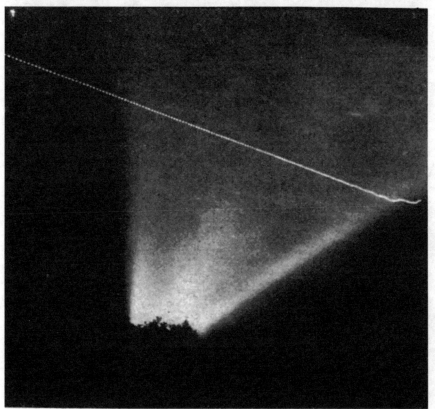

PATH OF A FLYING BOMB over England, as seen by a camera, appears as a white line drawn across the night sky. The speeding doodle-bug is held in the beam of a powerful searchlight to attract the attention of the pilots of patrolling night-fighters who might be unable to see the weapon's exhaust flame, so easily observable from the ground. PAGE 731 *Photo, Associated Press*

This Way Our Tempests Destroyed Flying Bombs

ONLY THE FASTEST AIRCRAFT could shoot down flying bombs, and Tempests were among the most successful. Diving on a VI (top), the pilot would fire a burst and then turn away (bottom) to escape the terrific blast when the missile exploded. Mosquitoes also intercepted VIs over the Channel, and bursts of A.A. fire were often used to indicate the course of the target to a pilot. (See story beginning in page 731.) The reproductions above are from paintings by Roy Nockolds (top) and W. T. Monnington, now in the Imperial War Museum, London. PAGE 732 *Crown Copyright*

went in. This time to closer range, 400 feet. Sandy put his sights on the target, pressed the firing button and we saw the strikes. Then, suddenly, the V1 seemed to stand still in mid-air, so violently did it slow down. We passed it close on our starboard side, my side of the Mosquito, as Sandy and I sat side by side in the nose of the aircraft. For one ghastly moment we were dead level with it. There, almost at our wing-tip, was the buzz-bomb, and I could see every detail of it as clear as day, for it was glowing a fiery red. I thought, "It's going to explode right in my face!" With a gulp I found my voice.

"Hard port, Sandy!" I yelled. "Turn hard port!" He did so, and as I looked back I saw our hard-hit target topple over in a stall and plunge into the Channel. "Well," I said to my pilot, "you've shot one down at last. But if you're going to give me another scare like that, you'd better find yourself another observer!"

I Lent a Hand with Mighty Mulberry

In the M.T.C., driving for the Ministry of Supply, Miss Gwen Croft was one of the unknown number of men and women who helped to make possible the great prefabricated harbour that was towed over to Normandy for the Invasion. See also pages 430-434 and 710, Vol. 8.

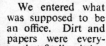

GWEN CROFT

ON the evening of April 21, 1944, my friend Miss Eileen M. Ward and I were told to prepare to leave the next morning for Southampton, on a very hush-hush job. We spent the evening getting things ready, and next morning, before leaving London, we were warned that on no account were we to divulge to anyone the nature of our task. Well, that was easy; we had yet to discover it for ourselves! We arrived at Southampton about lunchtime, and were told to report at King George V Dock, where we were warmly welcomed by the man in charge.

We entered what was supposed to be an office. Dirt and papers were everywhere. We discovered later that finding it impossible to work satisfactorily in a tiny hut, these people had decided that the railway offices were more suitable, and they had moved in a day or so before our arrival, and there was no time for cleaning up. But then there was hardly time for them to eat. We concluded that something must be done, and whilst Miss Ward took her car into the town for brooms, buckets, soap and disinfectant, I swept up as much dirt as I could find and lit a fire in a room containing a cooking-range. Between us we cleaned up, much to the amusement of the staff. But that wasn't what we had been sent to Southampton for.

Later, over a cup of tea, they told us that we had been fixed up in a hotel at Brockenhurst, a very delightful spot. And the job? It was to drive around men in charge of various parts of the building and construction of Mulberry! Hence all the secrecy. Conveyance had been almost impossible to find for these men who had to go from place to place where Mulberry's parts were being built: the caissons at Marchwood, the pontoons at Bosham and elsewhere.

THE pierheads built at Conway (Caernarvonshire) were towed to Southampton, where the spuds (anchors) were fitted. These were 60 feet high. It was indeed a fascinating sight to see the little tugs towing huge pierheads down the river, then pushing this way, pulling that, and finally guiding them gently alongside the quay. As soon as they were alongside the workmen were on deck with their equipment. Not a second was wasted. Speed and yet more speed was the cry, and from daylight until dark the work went on.

When we were not driving we did our best to eliminate the hasty sandwich lunch washed down with a cup of almost cold tea. We managed to get hold of stools and tables, and arranged them in what we now called our kitchen, bought crockery and cutlery and proceeded to serve a decent meal to the staff, 18 in all. It was surprising how many other people happened to find their way to the office kitchen when the teapot was on the go!

WHEN MULBERRY HARBOUR WENT TO FRANCE it was the first time in history that an invading force had taken its own prefabricated harbour with it. The spud pontoons, one of which is seen on tow at the Gareloch (upper), were 60 feet high. Several of the huge concrete caissons, weighing more than 6,000 tons each, are shown under construction at Marchwood, near Southampton (lower). The Germans knew nothing of this great project, though their reconnaissance aircraft flew over the southern port where much of it was assembled.

VICHY FRENCH CRUISER GLOIRE took on board survivors of the torpedoed liner Laconia after she had been summoned to a rendezvous in the Atlantic by the commander of a German submarine (story below). The Gloire, seen with H.M.S. Waveney at Saigon Docks, French Indo-China, in October 1945, was built in 1935. Her displacement is 7,600 tons, main armament nine 6-inch guns, speed 31 knots. The cruiser joined the Allied navies on the adherence of French West Africa to the Allies in November 1942.
Photo, Sport & General

One day I crossed to the Isle of Wight, in connexion with rehearsal of troop-carrying craft, and was amazed at the sight of so many ships, little and big, that smothered the sea. We almost had to squeeze our way through them. Sometimes Jerry would come over during the day, but he always kept his distance, at a great height—spotting, so the men said. There were heavy raids at night, but not once did they hit the docks.

Every man now was working at top pressure, for D-Day was in the air. There were plenty of guesses at the date, and nobody seemed keen on being in Southampton on the particular day—especially on the docks ! We knew by this time what Mulberry was for and how it would look when completed. We were shown over one of the completed pier-heads. Its stairways and passages were very narrow, and the crew had great difficulty even in getting into their bunks. Down below there were steel supports every-where, and at each corner was encased mechanism that worked the spuds up and down ; when the pier-head was in position the spuds were lowered, anchoring it.

We were very glad to get up on deck again, though the siren was going and everyone was thinking the same thing—Jerry was sure to make a mass attack soon and this might be it. But it wasn't; only one enemy plane approach-ing, and the All Clear soon sounded. A few days later I went back to London for 48 hours and when I returned to Southampton the sea was still covered with ships, and the pier-heads were still in the King George V Dock. But early the next morning everything was gone—and my part of the job was finished.

We Were Guests of the Sea-Wolves

In this story which began in page 702 Claude Jones, purser in the liner Laconia, told how his ship was torpedoed in the Atlantic. While the over-crowded lifeboat in which he found himself was making progress towards Africa it encountered a U-boat, whose commander invited the survivors to come on board a few at a time for a meal.

This was a surprise indeed, and many of us were still suspicious. A U-boat commander in the role of Good Samaritan and his ship providing a hostel for British survivors ! What he said, or his kindly tone, so impressed two of our Italians that they changed their mind about lying doggo. They came from under the thwarts and allowed themselves to be " rescued " ; but the others stayed out of sight. The pair that surrendered for the sake of getting a meal were taken aboard the U-boat, and to do them justice they did not squeal on their comrades.

The women and children were lifted out of the lifeboat and given something to eat and drink by the Germans. Other small parties went aboard in turn, and were fed from large bowls of soup placed on the steel deck for'ard of the conning-tower. The soup and bread were a godsend, but what I enjoyed even more was the chance to stretch my cramped limbs. On this occasion the sea-wolves had not run true to form ! They had assumed sheep's clothing. Nevertheless, I suspected an ulterior motive by reason of what occurred while I and some of my ship-mates were being fed.

One of the Germans came through the conning-tower hatch and handed a small cine-camera to the young commander, who

leaned over the bridge and shot a reel of film to record the scene on the foredeck. There was little doubt in my mind that this pictorial record was intended for the dual purpose of proving that a successful attack had been made against a British transport and for propaganda by demonstrating the humanity of German U-boat crews towards their victims.

Refreshed by the food and comparative freedom we returned to our boat, the submarine standing by. Then the German commander addressed us again. "It is bad," he said, "that women and children should suffer for the sins of a criminal Government. They have permission to come on board the Unterseeboot again. I will give them more food, and they may dry the clothes. You can trust me," he added, when no one stirred. "I give my word of honour they shall be well cared for."

After some discussion the invitation was accepted. The women and children were transferred again to the U-boat, and that gave blessed relief to the rest of us. It was good to be able to stretch the legs and move about without fear of capsizing. We raised sail, and the submarine cruised slowly near us. During the short tropic twilight the young commander reappeared on his bridge and made another announcement that caused us some anxiety. "I am going to dive," he said. "Your women and children will stay with me to rest tonight. Tomorrow morning I will give them back. You must sail slowly and keep the course you are on now."

The C.P.O. demanded, "What are you going to do after that?" To this the German answered that he intended to radio a signal and try to arrange for a ship to make a rendezvous and take all of us aboard. With that we had to be content. And the Italians who were still in the water and had remained unseen were more than content when the U-boat submerged and we hauled them into our boat. Those fellows had got on our nerves. We had been inclined to hand them over to the Jerries, but they had pleaded desperately to be allowed to stay where they were. Now they were curling up in the boat, catching up with much-needed sleep.

Nothing at all was seen of the U-boat during the hours of darkness. When daybreak came we scanned the sea for a sight of her periscope, wondering if the German would keep his promise and return. The sun lifted above the horizon and gilded the waves. Then, suddenly, one of our seamen, whose pre-war service had been in a whaling ship, drew attention to a burst of foam: "There she blows !" The submarine had kept her tryst.

Whatever ruthlessness the German commander and crew were capable of in active warfare was now hidden beneath a veneer of good will. It is only fair to record that we and the survivors in two other lifeboats received generous consideration that was as gratifying as it was exceptional. Once more we were allowed to board the submarine, in batches, and fed with stew in the lee of a 4·7 gun while the seawater sluiced over our feet. Our women and children were returned dry and rested to the lifeboat, and the fact that they were soon drenched again with spray was nobody's fault. Finally, we were given some rations, water, cigarettes and matches, and the German commander ordered us to proceed on an easterly course and wished us luck before sheering off.

Our lifeboat made progress on an easterly course, switchbacking over the long Atlantic rollers. Packed like sardines, we spent a restless, uncomfortable night but enjoyed a fair breakfast, thanks to the extra rations. Haze made visibility poor, and we had no expectations of sighting a sail when, quite startlingly, at eleven o'clock in the morning, a grotesque shadow loomed into view. A ship ! Rescue at last ! That was the instant reaction. The vessel came nearer, and with fading hopes we saw it was another submarine.

Tide of Luck Again in Our Favour

"It's a 'guinea' !" a seaman ejaculated, using the Merchant Navy slang meaning an Italian. He was correct. The approaching craft unfurled an ensign from the short staff abaft the conning-tower bridge, and suspense was almost unbearable as the enemy hove-to and signalled for us to moor alongside. Here were sea-wolves of a different tribe. We could hardly expect this encounter to pass off as the previous one had, especially with Italians among us who might give a garbled account of what had occurred to many of their compatriots when the Laconia had been torpedoed. But again our prisoners went to cover under the thwarts, even less inclined for rescue by their own countrymen than by the Germans.

The Italian submarine commander spoke English, and his first question did nothing to relieve our anxiety. "Have you seen any Italian prisoners?" he demanded. The Naval C.P.O. acted as our spokesman. "No," he replied. He feared, like the rest of us, that if these submariners suspected loss of life among Italian prisoners the consequences might be serious for us.

The commander looked down upon our crowded boat and asked the name of the ship that had been sunk. He repeated the question, but no one told him. He shrugged his shoulders, and put another query about the nationality of the attacker. "We were torpedoed by a German," the C.P.O. told him. We could not be sure of this, but it proved a good answer, because the Italian captain responded with an exclamation of disgust before interpreting to a younger officer standing by his side. One doubt kept me on tenterhooks during this second encounter. Would the Italians in our boat remain hidden and silent? They never stirred a finger or said a word—and all was well. The tide of luck again ran in our favour ! Kegs of water, flasks of Chianti, boxes of biscuits and cigarettes were produced from the submarine's hatches and handed into our lifeboat. The spectre of

hunger and thirst was banished once more, and the real dread now was lest the weather should worsen.

When the Italian submarine left us to continue its interrupted patrol, we exchanged farewells with a friendliness curiously inconsistent as between enemies ; the years of political misunderstandings and military combat were bridged in an hour or so by compassion on one side and gratitude on the other. Discomfort and anxiety attended the further voyaging of our boat until the sixth day, which held another surprise for us. From a seemingly empty ocean our old "friend" reappeared—the U-boat with her young bearded commander. He knew nothing of our meeting with the Italian craft, and no one enlightened him. His first concern was for the women and children, whom

he took aboard again, thereby giving the rest of us a chance to move about.

"Now I will give you a tow," he said. "You will be made prisoners of war. Ja, it is for your own sakes, because the weather may change and you might founder. I have made a signal by radio for a French warship to meet me. Always we Germans are humane." There was nothing we could do about it, and we made fast a rope and were towed for a couple of hours while the women and children sat on the U-boat's after-deck.

Presently, to our joy, we saw four or five of the Laconia's lifeboats. That German sea-wolf had been ranging like a sheep-dog to round them up, and amid emotional scenes numbers of relatives and friends were reunited for the first time since the transport was torpedoed. Then the U-boat took the boats in tow and proceeded on a different course all night and part of the following day. At last the lifeboats were cast off, and the German commander made his final speech through a megaphone.

Gloire Keeps a Glad Rendezvous

"Here you must wait," he announced. "Soon you will be rescued, I think, but I warn you that there will be bad trouble if you try to sail away !" When the women and children had been returned to our lifeboat, the submarine moved off and dived—and that was the last we saw of her. The boats kept together and drifted on the tide, but we were not left long in suspense. Smoke smudged the horizon and a ship hove in sight —the Vichy warship Gloire keeping the rendezvous in response to the U-boat's signals.

The transfer of everyone from the lifeboats took some time because many were unable to mount the rope-ladders and had to be hoisted in slings. Again there were glad reunions, for the Gloire had picked up many other survivors elsewhere at sea. Our lifeboats were sunk by gunfire, and the warship steamed direct for Dakar ; and I for one was mighty glad she arrived without "catching a packet" from Allied air-patrols. In contrast to the open boats, our voyage was a holiday. Yet the accommodation for the men was vile, the food poor and insufficient, and we had to sleep on the steel decks without bedding, and no pillows other than our own damp life-jackets. Treatment by the French guards varied according to individual allegiance to the Vichy regime or sympathy with the Allied cause—but no open display of sympathy was made.

From Dakar some of us were taken to Casablanca, then to a grim prison camp under the ramparts of the Atlas Mountains. They gave us cubes of tough meat that the Vichy French guards called boeuf, veau or mouton, but which were easily recognized for what they were—goat. And we had a "high" tea consisting of black bread and hard-boiled eggs. The only privileges we received at this wretched camp were accorded secretly by De Gaullists among the guards. What with dysentery and skin troubles our lot was indeed unenviable, and then prolonged gunfire from the direction of the coast one morning set us all seething with excitement.

After much suspense, we came to learn the truth of a stupendous event. The Allies had landed in North Africa ! Jeeps came roaring down the rough road outside our compound. "The Yanks ! The Yanks are here !" We yelled ourselves hoarse. It was November 11, 1942, a red-letter day in our lives. We were taken to Casablanca, feasted aboard transports and cargo-carriers, and all arrangements made for our repatriation. I returned to England via Norfolk, Virginia, and New York ; and another red-letter day for me came a bit later at Liverpool when I was provided with a brand-new uniform and appointed purser in the ocean-going steamship Wanderer.

British-Soviet Frontier Post in Germany

Printed in England and published every alternate Friday by the Proprietors, THE AMALGAMATED PRESS, LTD., The Fleetway House, Farringdon Street, London, E.C.4. Registered for transmission by Canadian Magazine Post. Sole Agents for Australia and New Zealand : Messrs. Gordon & Gotch, Ltd. ; and for South Africa : Central News Agency, Ltd.—March 14, 1947.   S.S.   *Editorial Address :* JOHN CARPENTER HOUSE, WHITEFRIARS, LONDON, E C.4.

ON THE AUTOBAHN NEAR HELMSTEDT is the British-Soviet frontier control point in Germany. Helmstedt is a small town 21 miles east of Brunswick and about 117 from Berlin, and the post is one of the busiest on the Russian line. Night and day a British sentry is on guard beside the red-and-white pole which can be lowered across the road as a barrier. The soldier on duty (above) is Pte. F. Kendrick, of Walsall, serving with the 2nd Battalion The South Staffordshire Regiment. See also page 711.

Exclusive to THE WAR ILLUSTRATED

Vol 10 The War Illustrated N° 254

SIXPENCE

I WAS THERE

MARCH 28, 1947

AT STIRLING CASTLE men of the 2nd Battalion The Argyll and Sutherland Highlanders paraded in a snowstorm on Feb. 5, 1947, for the first ceremony of its kind in Scotland. The occasion marked the passing of the Battalion into " suspended anima-tion." Major-General G. H. A. Macmillan, C.B., C.B.E., D.S.O., M.C., Colonel of the Regiment, took the salute, and the Colour Party, headed by the Pipes and Drums (above), placed the Colours in the Castle, there to remain until the 2nd Battalion is restored to the active list in 10 or 12 years' time. In the meantime the men will be drafted to other Highland regiments. *Photo. G.P.U.*

Edited by Sir John Hammerton

NO. 255 WILL BE PUBLISHED **FRIDAY, APRIL 11**

Personalities Smile for Our Roving Camera

SOUTH AFRICAN WAR VETERANS were greeted by General Sir Ian Hamilton (left centre) when members of the Defence of Ladysmith Association laid a wreath at the statue of Field-Marshal Sir George White in Portland Place, London, on March 2, 1947.

BELGIAN MINISTER OF NATIONAL DEFENCE, Col. de Fraiteur (left), arrived at Victoria Station, London, on March 5, 1947, and was greeted by Mr. H. Hynde, Parliamentary Private Secretary to Mr. A. V. Alexander, Britain's Minister of Defence.

APPOINTED U.S. AMBASSADOR IN LONDON on Feb. 26, 1947, Mr. Lewis Williams Douglas, aged 53, is President of the English-Speaking Union of the United States. He was a member of Congress from 1927 to 1933. Representing Arizona State.

VISCOUNT MOUNTBATTEN OF BURMA, President of King George's Fund for Sailors, opened the campaign for Sailors' Day (April 15) at Admiralty House, London, on Feb. 19, 1947. Lord Mountbatten assumed office as Viceroy of India in March 1947.

Photos, G.P.U., Keystone

How Germany Came to Grief at Sea

By
FRANCIS E. McMURTRIE

THE reasons that led to the ultimate defeat of Germany at sea are explained in three documents of enemy origin released by the Admiralty at the end of January 1947. One is a summary of papers relating to the supersession of Grossadmiral Raeder as Commander-in-Chief of the German Navy by his subordinate, Karl Doenitz, in January 1943 ; a second is a review by Doenitz of the whole course of the naval war ; the third a somewhat acid commentary on the general conduct of the war at sea, produced by two anonymous writers of the German Naval Staff.

All three are in general agreement that the causes of German failure to accomplish more in the naval sphere were mainly political. It was apparently the genuine belief of Hitler and his chief advisers that Britain would not go to war when Poland was invaded in September 1939. This was typical recklessness on Hitler's part, for the strength of his fleet was admittedly inadequate for such a conflict. Though submarine construction had been resumed, the number of U-boats available at the outbreak of war was wholly insufficient. Doenitz intimated that to give the submarine campaign real assurance of success, 1,000 U-boats should have been at his disposition in 1939. Actually he had about 50, with 20 more nearing completion.

Naval War Staff Advice Unheeded

Throughout the struggle the co-operation of the Luftwaffe with the navy was no more than half-hearted. "It could not achieve the right conception of naval warfare, and thought primarily on a military basis. Its ideas were superficial, and the navy's advice on the finer points of naval tactics, etc., were unheeded." Raeder is contrasted as "an experienced leader of sound judgement" with the supreme head of the Luftwaffe, Goering, who is stigmatized as "a narrow-minded dilettante." Nor could a solution be reached by arbitration when their views disagreed, owing to lack of specialized

knowledge on the part of the Commander-in-Chief of the Wehrmacht, the only authority who could decide between them.

At every crisis the opinion and advice of the Naval War Staff went unheeded by the Supreme Command. Though Raeder was an extremely able man from the professional aspect and highly esteemed by Hitler in that capacity, his personal characteristics put him at a disadvantage when presenting to the Supreme Command the unpopular viewpoint of the Naval War Staff. He was not gifted with a persuasive manner, nor with the tenacity to force his opinions on his listeners.

Assumed Britain Would Be Neutral

Not only did this have a deleterious effect on co-operation between the navy and the Luftwaffe, but it severely limited Raeder's influence over Hitler. It is true that when alone with the Fuehrer, Raeder would occasionally succeed in convincing his chief of the wisdom of the naval arguments ; but as soon as he had left, other influential persons, such as Goering, would very quickly bring Hitler round to the opposite view. This actually occurred when the question of the conduct of the war in the Mediterranean was in question, and again over the possibility of French collaboration.

Doenitz was on much better terms with Hitler, and his appointment as Raeder's successor caused no surprise. Not only did he enjoy the full support of the younger officers, especially those in the U-boat service, but he possessed the qualities of ruthlessness and persuasiveness that Raeder lacked, though he was his inferior as a master of naval warfare in all its aspects. Doenitz himself declares that the German Navy was inadequate from the outset, the proportions of the armed forces having been planned for a purely Continental war, on the assumption that Britain would remain neutral. This was partly due to the fact that the navy

was but weakly represented in Germany's highest councils.

After Dunkirk, the possibility of ending the war quickly by an early invasion of England was mooted. Owing to the unexpectedly rapid development of the war in the Low Countries and France, no kind of preparation for such an operation had been made. It was not possible to produce suitable landing-craft in large numbers in time to participate in the invasion of 1940, so it became necessary to utilize the available tugs and barges of the coastal and inland water transport systems. A considerable number of these craft were modified for landing purposes, but their seaworthiness was limited and few were self-propelled, involving the necessity of relying upon towage for the passage across Channel. Detailed reports on landing conditions in the south of England and on currents and weather in the Channel were prepared, and troops were trained in landing operations.

It was clear that the German navy was far too weak to protect the landing forces against the British fleet, the full weight of which would have to be encountered. This protection must be furnished by the Luftwaffe. But first the Luftwaffe would require to wipe out all air opposition, and render untenable any ports near the projected landing places which might serve as bases for British naval forces.

Invasion Prospects Became Dim

Ordered in July 1940 to prepare his forces for an invasion while good weather could be expected, Raeder informed Hitler that the navy would be ready to do its part by September 15. As the defeat of the British air defence was not achieved, the prospects of success became dim, and the invasion was first deferred and then abandoned. It was urged by the Naval Staff that the resources assembled for invasion purposes should be devoted to securing control of the Mediterra-

OFF THE NORTH CAPE on Dec. 31, 1942, British destroyers commanded by Capt. R. St. V. Sherbrooke, D.S.O., R.N., engaged a vastly superior German force and beat off an attack on the convoy, which reached Russia unharmed, though the British destroyer Achates was sunk and Onslow damaged. The failure of this German attempt to destroy a convoy infuriated Hitler and "spelled the end of the High Seas Fleet." Capt. Sherbrooke was awarded the V.C. for his great gallantry in the action.   PAGE 739   *From the painting by Charles Pears, Crown copyright*

ncan theatre. Ignoring this recommendation, the Supreme Command had decided by the end of 1940 to summon all its strength for an attack upon Russia, whose attitude had been causing increasing uneasiness to the Reich.

It was found impossible to obtain even temporary command of the sea in the Mediterranean in face of the offensive spirit displayed by the British Fleet under Sir Andrew Cunningham. No realization was shown by the enemy of the strategic importance of Malta. Against Crete the German airborne assault met with success, that island's geographical situation rendering it peculiarly open to this form of attack.

Involving Risk of Heavy Losses

Doenitz describes the Italian navy as badly led, insufficiently trained, suffering from "inferior technical equipment and lack of offensive spirit." Except in the Aegean, the German navy was unable to play much part in the Mediterranean operations, so the direction of sea warfare in this area was largely in the hands of the Italian fleet, over whose operations only limited influence could be exerted by the Germans.

is attributed to the "unfortunate decision" of Captain Langsdorff to make a raid on shipping in the Plate estuary, which led him into the encounter with Commodore Harwood's squadron.

At the end of 1941 it was decided to withdraw the Scharnhorst, Gneisenau and Prinz Eugen from Brest and to employ them in conjunction with the Tirpitz and other ships in attacks upon Allied convoys bound for North Russia. Though the Gneisenau received such serious damage that she never operated at sea again, the other two ships duly appeared in Norwegian waters and added materially to the perils of the Arctic convoy route.

Doenitz, while commanding the submarine service, appears to have expressed dissatisfaction at the demands made by the large surface warships upon dockyard resources, on which he considered the U-boats should have had first claim. It is observed by the authors of the Naval Staff paper that Doenitz evidently "failed to acknowledge the tactical and strategical significance of the battleships, particularly

rewarded by the V.C., beat off every enemy attack (portrait in page 544, Vol. 6). Not only did he partially disable the heavy cruiser Admiral Hipper, but a large German destroyer, the Friedrich Eckoldt, was sunk.

Hitler's fury was not easily quenched. After violently abusing the naval personnel concerned, and comparing them unfavourably with their British opponents, he proclaimed that "the whole thing spelled the end of the High Seas Fleet." Raeder was sent for and told peremptorily that, apart from such ships as might be required for training, the whole German surface fleet must be put out of commission. Though Raeder commented that the ships might just as well be scuttled, the Fuehrer overruled his objections and refused any reprieve. The resignation of Raeder was the immediate sequel.

Actually the course followed by Doenitz on taking over the chief command on January 30, 1943, was less drastic than the Fuehrer had originally ordered, for both the Tirpitz and Scharnhorst remained in commission in the waters of North Norway until their ultimate destruction. Otherwise the admiral continued to devote his energies to the energetic prosecution of the U-boat campaign, ordering new submarines of greatly improved design for which he was able to secure priority, though, as it proved, too late to influence the issue of the war. Doenitz attributes the sinking of the Scharnhorst in December 1943 to "a misjudgement of the local situation," and observes that "the superiority of British radar became very evident." To radar-equipped aircraft he attributes in large measure the defeat of the U-boat campaign in the same year.

Sunk by Mistake by the Luftwaffe

Failure to repel the invasion of Normandy is ascribed to lack of suitable mines. "The precautionary laying of mines, apart from those already laid, was rejected so as not to paralyse prematurely our own freedom of movement in the narrow coastal waters still unmined, and to prevent the limited number of mines fitted with new fusing devices being laid in wrong positions, whilst the laying of mines equipped with old type fuses, which could be easily swept, seemed to serve no useful purpose." This somewhat lame excuse is bolstered up with the remark that "the new type fuses, considered unsweepable, had been brought into operation in isolated cases only with the greatest precaution, so as to prevent their falling into the hands of the enemy and being copied by him. The use of these mines in the shallow waters of the Baltic would have had a catastrophic effect."

REAR-ADMIRAL R. L. BURNETT, C.B., O.B.E., CONGRATULATED THE SHIP'S COMPANY of H.M.S. Onslow for their gallantry in the action off the North Cape, on their return to Scapa Flow in February 1943. The destroyer has a displacement of 1,550 tons, main armament of four 4·7-in. guns, speed of 32 knots and complement of 230.   *Admiralty photograph*

By implication, the handling of the Russian Black Sea Fleet is also criticized. It is pointed out that it possessed an overwhelming superiority over the few units of the Rumanian navy, which were poorly trained and without sea experience. German reinforcements amounted to only half-a-dozen U-boats of the 250-ton type and a number of landing-craft, trawlers, and small auxiliaries. The conquest of the Crimea and the advance into the Caucasus in 1942 forced the Russian Fleet into the extreme south-east corner of the Black Sea, where it was almost impotent. When the tide turned in 1943-44 the Soviet navy was given a good chance to fall upon the German sea communications with Sebastopol across the Black Sea, yet "the activity of the Russian Fleet, in comparison with its size, was remarkably small." During the evacuation of the Crimea in June 1943 "Russian naval forces again appeared only in small numbers."

Doenitz points out that the German surface forces could not embark on a battle for sea supremacy on account of their inferior numbers. For the same reason, any attempt to protect German sea traffic was impossible. With the whole focus of the war at sea turned to submarine attack upon shipping, it was obvious that surface forces must as far as possible be devoted to the same task, involving the risk of heavy losses. Instances cited are the sinking of the Admiral Graf Spee and the Bismarck. The loss of the Graf Spee

for creating a diversion from the war in the Far East. He had considerable influence over Hitler, though it cannot be stated definitely how far the representations he made influenced the decision of the Supreme Command to remove the battleships from Brest." Hitler appears to have feared a British landing in North Norway, and had "an unwarranted faith in the suitability of battleships for repelling such a landing."

Hitler Distrusted His Own Ships

In December 1942 the climax came with news that a German surface squadron was in action against a British convoy off the North Cape. For over 48 hours no further reports were received, driving the Fuehrer into a state of frenzy. Raeder rightly refused to agree to ships being asked to break their wireless silence, exciting Hitler into the taunt that "big ships were useless," and the suggestion that the older officers who commanded them lacked ability and daring. Recalling the events of 1918 the Fuehrer proceeded to describe large surface ships as "breeding ground for revolution."

Ultimately a message came from Norway revealing utter failure of the attempt to destroy the convoy. Though a British destroyer had been sunk and various ships damaged, the gallant and skilful handling of the destroyer escort by Captain R. St. V. Sherbrooke, R.N., whose fine service was

BOMBING of industrial targets in Germany did no more than slow up the production of war material until the autumn of 1944. In fact, the maximum output of the war industries was achieved in May 1944. The output of U-boats did not reach the desired figure of 30 a month until then. The first industry to show a fall in production was steel, and this was partly the result of the loss of Upper Silesia. By January 1945 German communications had become the target for intensive air attack, starting the collapse of the armaments industry.

An interesting footnote refers to the mysterious loss of the destroyers Leberecht Maass and Max Schultz in the North Sea in February 1940. It had generally been supposed in British naval circles that these two ships had run into a minefield; but it is now revealed that the German court of inquiry into their loss decided that they were sunk by mistake by the Luftwaffe—yet another instance of its failure to co-operate effectively with the navy.

The foregoing is a mere summary of the more important matters referred to in the German documents, which occupy 139 foolscap pages of typescript.

Anglo-French Pact at Dunkirk of Solemn Memory

TREATY OF DUNKIRK, binding France and Great Britain in a 50-year military and economic alliance, was signed on March 4, 1947, by Mr. Bevin, British Foreign Minister (top, right), and M. Bidault, French Foreign Minister (top, left), in the sub-prefecture, which was the only public building in Dunkirk left undamaged by the war. Afterwards the two Ministers visited the beaches (lower) where, nearly seven years earlier, the B.E.F. had made its magnificent stand against overwhelming German onslaught and experienced the "miracle of deliverance." PAGE 741 *Photos, G.P.U., Keystone*

The 'Skins' Return Home to Omagh in Tyrone

LED BY SAFFRON-KILTED PIPERS the cadre of the 2nd Battalion The Royal Inniskilling Fusiliers (the "Skins") came home to Omagh, Co. Tyrone, Northern Ireland (1), on Feb. 11, 1947. Under the scheme for the reorganization of the Infantry this Battalion has been placed in "temporary suspended animation." Madagascar, Persia, Syria, Sicily, Italy and finally Austria were among the countries visited by it during the war, and smiling faces at the carriage doors and windows (2) testified to pleasure at homecoming. Lieut.-Col. T. T. Macartney Filgate, O.B.E. (3), commanding the Battalion, handed over the Colours, which were laid up in the Officers' Mess (4) at the Regimental Depot in Omagh. The Battalion had previously been disbanded in 1922, but was re-formed in 1937. See also pages 459-462.

Photos, International News Photos

From Monty's H.Q. to Ancient Village Church

UNION JACK WHICH FLEW ON LUNEBURG HEATH, at the H.Q. of Field-Marshal Montgomery, after the German surrender in May 1945, now hangs in the church of Englishcombe village, near Bath. The Field-Marshal presented it, in Jan. 1947, in response to an appeal by the Vicar of Englishcombe, who made it known that in the old church were hanging three war-tattered flags—ensigns of the Royal Navy, R.A.F. and Merchant Navy; the Army was not represented. And now has arrived this honoured trophy. See also illus. page 79, Vol. 9. PAGE 743   *Photo, Topical*

Our Fight to Mitigate Hardship and Peril of

DISRUPTING Britain's industrial and home affairs as never before, snow and intense cold and shortage of coal led to such serious constrictions of power, light and warmth in February and March 1947 that the general activities of the country were brought almost to a standstill. Northern England was cut off from the South by snowdrifts : jet aircraft engines (1) were used to clear the railway between Brecon and Newport, Mon. The R.A.F. dropped bread in containers (2) to snowbound villagers of Longnor, Staffs. Fisheries Patrol Protection vessel H.M.S. Mariner (3) kept watch on ice floes in North Sea shipping lanes. Girl farm-worker (4) at Lawford, Essex, was one of many who used a pickaxe for lifting turnips from the frozen ground. German P.O.W. helped to clear the Scarborough-Bridlington road (5). The intensity and duration of the cold spell, and its incidence over the whole of Great Britain, made this one of the most severe winters in the last 70 years.

Photos, G.P.U., I.N.P., Keystone
PAGE 744

—Fuel Crisis and Prolonged Freeze-Up Combined

BLIZZARDS and tremendous seas had to be faced by colliers from north-east coast ports to bring coal to the Thames, where it was discharged into barges and towed (1) to London's power-stations. Some 3,000 troops helped with transport : at Bolsover Colliery, Chesterfield, the first coal-laden military vehicle left the pithead (2) on February 17. Coal wagons were icebound (3). Coal from the Army reaches gasworks at Saltley, Birmingham (4). Westminster (South) Area Committee, appointed to consider the staggering of working hours in that part of London, met by candlelight (5), owing to cuts imposed on the use of electric lighting in offices and other industrial undertakings. During this Arctic spell the lowest temperature was that taken on the night of Jan. 28-29, when 41 degrees of frost were registered on the grass on the outskirts of London.

Photos, Planet News, Associated Press, G.P.U., Topical Press

HIS MAJESTY'S SHIPS   H.M.I.S. Bengal

A FLEET minesweeper of 650 tons, with a speed of 15 knots, armed with one 4-inch and a few smaller guns, H.M.I.S. Bengal was built in Australia for the Royal Indian Navy in 1942. Soon after being commissioned by Lieut.-Commander W. J. Wilson, R.I.N.R., she was escorting the Dutch motorship Ondina, a valuable tanker of 6,341 tons gross, built in 1939, across the Indian Ocean.

On Nov. 11, 1942, two Japanese armed merchant cruisers were encountered about 1,000 miles S.W. of Java. These were the Kikoku Maru, a new ship of 10,000 tons gross, and the Kunikawa Maru, 6,863 tons gross, built in 1937. Each was armed with six 5·5-inch guns, besides torpedo-tubes, and carried seaplanes. Immediately on sighting the enemy the captain of the Bengal headed for the larger of his opponents, to enable the Ondina to escape ; but the Dutch master preferred to fight. A hit from the Bengal set the Kikoku Maru on fire, and ultimately there was a magazine explosion which destroyed the after-part of the raider. She ceased fire and foundered by the stern. Though both ships had received a number of hits, the Bengal sustained only slight damage and no casualties.

Meanwhile, the Ondina, in action with the Kunikawa Maru, had suffered severely, her brave master being killed. With ammunition exhausted, the crew abandoned ship, whereupon the Japanese machine-gunned the lifeboats, killing the chief engineer and three Chinese. Having fired a torpedo into the tanker, the Japanese ship made off rather than continue the action with the Bengal. Thereupon the Ondina's second officer, third engineer and gunlayer (an Australian naval rating) returned on board with three members of the crew. The engines being undamaged, the remainder of the crew were embarked and the ship was able to proceed.

Indian Official photograph

The Welsh Guards

By Authority of the Officer Commanding, Col. Sir ALEXANDER B. G. STANIER, Bart., D.S.O., M.C.

AT the outbreak of war in 1939 the Regiment had two battalions : the 1st in Gibraltar as part of the garrison on the Rock, the 2nd Battalion, recently formed, doing guard duty at the Tower of London. On October 30, 1939, the 1st Battalion received orders to move to France ; on November 7 it embarked on the troopship Devonshire, rounded the Europa point and headed for Marseilles. There followed a triumphal march through Paris, and a great welcome was given to them by the Parisians. The next day the Battalion moved to Doullens and then to Izel le Hameau, as part of G.H.Q. troops.

Meantime, the 2nd Battalion had received warning orders to proceed to Norway, but these were changed and the Battalion came under command of the newly formed 20th Guards Brigade. On May 10, 1940, Germany invaded Holland and Belgium. Part of the 2nd Battalion was immediately formed into a Composite Battalion with the 2nd Battalion Irish Guards to proceed to the Hook of Holland, the plan being to hold the Hook and then to advance to The Hague to render such assistance as required. On May 12, the Composite Battalion embarked from Dover and next day formed a bridge-head around the Hook. The advance to The Hague was found to be impracticable, so the Battalion held on to the bridge-head to cover the evacuation of the British Embassy Staff and the Dutch Royal Family. This done, they returned to England.

Whilst that was happening the 1st Battalion was concentrated inside Arras, to guard

RAISED during the First Great War, on February 26, 1915, the 1st Battalion Welsh Guards was in action at Loos, in France, in the following September. It fought in the battle of the Somme and took part in actions at Ginchy, Flers, Courcelette and Morval in 1916. After the third battle of Ypres, Aug.-Sept. 1917, it was engaged at Cambrai. In 1918 the Welsh Guards fought in the critical battles of March and April and in the final Allied victories, including the battle of Bapaume, the crossing of the Canal du Nord and the attack at Bavai five days before the Armistice. They formed part of the Army of Occupation in Germany and returned to England in March 1919. There was also a Reserve Battalion which was absorbed into the 1st Battalion in March 1919. The 2nd Battalion was formed on May 18, 1939.

G.H.Q., on which the enemy were advancing. The 1st held out in the town, against air and ground attacks, until the early morning of May 24, when they were ordered to withdraw to join G.H.Q. in its new location. One road only was open, and along this the Battalion moved. During the withdrawal the column came under fire near St. Nicholas, a suburb of Arras. The carrier platoon engaged the enemy, and by their action the further successful withdrawal of the Force was made possible. For his leadership and gallantry in this action, Lieutenant the Hon. Christopher Furness was posthumously awarded the Victoria Cross (portrait in page 103). From

Arras the 1st Battalion moved to Douai, Premesque and then to Cassel. On May 28 it was ordered to move to counter an enemy threat south of Bergues. Positions were taken up and the Battalion, with elements of the 48th Division, was the last rearguard in this section south of the canal. It had a severe task. The position was outflanked, and after a sterling defence during which Number 2 Company had to fight its way out of a chateau at West Cappel, the Battalion withdrew to the beaches at Bray Dunes and embarked for England.

The 20th Guards Brigade in England, under command of Brigadier W. A. F. L. Fox-Pitt, D.S.O., M.C., a past Commanding Officer of the 1st Battalion, was ordered to Boulogne to hold up the German advance along the coast. The 2nd Battalion took part in this operation. For two days and two nights they held the Germans at bay, until orders to withdraw were received. A last stand was made on the docks before the final evacuation took place. Remnants of Number 3 Company held out until May 25, when owing to shortage of food and ammunition, they were eventually overrun.

THE 1st and 2nd Battalions both back in England, the great task of reorganization and training began. The Guards Armoured Division was formed, and the 1st Battalion became the first lorry-borne battalion in the Division. The 2nd Battalion was converted into an Armoured Battalion in September 1941, and training began on Salisbury Plain.

In February 1942 the 3rd Battalion was training, outside London, with the 33rd Guards Brigade. This training continued for nearly a year, when on January 8, 1943, orders were received to mobilize. And on February 26 the Battalion sailed for North Africa to join the 1st Guards Brigade, commanded by Brigadier F. A. V. Copland

MARCHING THROUGH PARIS to the music of their drum and fife band on Nov. 12, 1939, the 1st Battalion Welsh Guards were accorded a very warm welcome by the Parisians. From the French capital the 1st went to Doullens, 17 miles S.W. of Arras ; and the latter town was defended by them in May 1940 to cover the withdrawal of British G.H.Q. In 1941 the Guards Armoured Division was formed, and the 1st Battalion became part of the lorry-borne infantry of that formation.

Photo, Associated Press

HOSPITALITY AT ST. NICHOLAS, a suburb of Arras, was freely offered by the people and gladly accepted by men of the 1st Battalion Welsh Guards in May 1940, and regimental M.O.s acted, in emergency, as family doctors (below). An officer of the Battalion won the V.C. here during the withdrawal towards the end of the month. *Photos, British Official*

Colours: Yellow on Red Background

19TH (INDIAN) DIVISION

FORMED in the Secunderabad area in October 1941, the original number of the famous "Dagger" Division was 18, and it was commanded while on active service by Major-General T. Wynford Rees. At a time when the threat of a Japanese invasion of India was only too real it was entrusted with the defence of a part of Southern India, remaining there for three years.

The Division went into action in Burma on December 4, 1944, when it began to advance in extremely bad country between the Chindwin and Irrawaddy rivers. At Leiktu, on the edge of the Shwebo Plain, it fought its first set battle, which lasted for five days; and on Jan. 8, 1945, Shwebo was entered. The main crossing of the Irrawaddy was made at Kyaukmyaung, 46 miles north of Mandalay.

THE Japanese counter-attacked the bridge-head with two divisions, but all the attacks were held, and early in March the 19th broke through the Japanese lines, thrusting southwards along the east bank of the river to Mandalay. On March 8, 1945, the outskirts of the city were reached, but the Japanese made a very determined stand, holding on grimly to Mandalay Hill and Fort Dufferin. On the hill the Japanese troops barricaded themselves in a tunnel beneath the great reception hall; they were burned out by rolling petrol drums into the tunnel and flinging grenades after them to ignite the oil. The end came on March 20, but most of the garrison had managed to slip away during the night. The British 2nd Division and 20th Indian Division now joined the 19th, and the city was cleared after a few days.

In the meantime a detached brigade had driven the enemy out of Maymyo and cut the railway to Lashio. The Division then moved south and took Toungoo; again a brigade column was detached, having as its task the liberation of Kalaw. This was accomplished during the second week of June, in the face of bitter opposition.

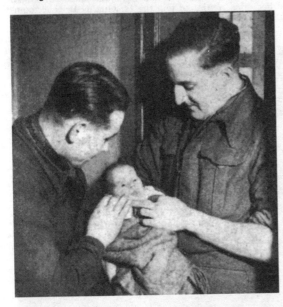

Griffiths, D.S.O., M.C., the Commanding Officer of the 1st Battalion in 1939-1940. The 3rd moved up towards Tunis, and in April had its first major battle, at Fondouk, in the final effort to break Rommel's forces who were retreating up the coast in front of the 8th Army.

The Battalion, now in the 6th Armoured Division, took part in the final attack on Tunis, and a few days later carried out a highly successful attack on Hammam Lif, thus sealing off the German forces in the Cap Bon peninsula—which resulted in their ultimate annihilation and capitulation. After the capitulation of the German forces, in Africa in May 1943, the 3rd Battalion settled down to a long period of waiting, until on February 4, 1944, they were ordered at two days' notice to embark for Italy.

They were soon in action in the mountains north and west of the Garigliano, south of Cassino, and later in Cassino itself in a defensive role, occupying the ruined houses with the enemy 50 yards or less away. But there were few casualties and no actual brushes with the enemy. On May 18 the Germans abandoned the town, and the 3rd Battalion were able to move out of their positions and follow the sweep up the Liri valley.

On May 26 the 3rd Battalion attacked Monte Piccolo. Number 2 Company, on the left, met heavy opposition and suffered a large number of casualties, including all its officers. But the hill was taken, the way to Rome lay open—and this important city fell on June 4. Seven days later the 3rd Battalion carried out another series of attacks, near Perugia, and on July 15 were in a successful Brigade battle for the heights guarding Arezzo, the town falling the next day. Although well below strength, the 3rd continued on and took up positions opposite the Gothic Line.

FROM October 2 to November 19, the 3rd Battalion was holding positions on Monte Battaglia feature, 2,000 feet above the sea. The cold was intense, the mud thick, the positions were exposed, and considerable hardship was experienced. These operations were continued until February 1945, when the 1st Guards Brigade were withdrawn into reserve prior to the final offensive. On April 9 this offensive began, the 3rd Battalion taking a prominent part in it, crossing the River Po, following up the enemy and capturing many prisoners. May found the Battalion in Carinthia after the German

forces had surrendered, and in June the Battalion was ordered home to England. The 3rd was later disbanded.

While the North African and Italian campaigns were taking place, the 1st and 2nd Battalions were training in England with the Guards Armoured Division, the 2nd Battalion taking on the new role of an Armoured Recce Battalion. About two weeks after D-Day, both Battalions landed in Normandy and were soon in action, first in operation "Goodwood," the armoured drive north and east of Caen, fighting in the Bocage country, the attack on Montchamp, and in August on the village of Le Bas Perrier. All these actions were carried out successfully, although at Montchamp the enemy put in a strong counter-attack with the 9th S.S. Panzer Division.

Then came the advance to Brussels, the advance that will be recorded in history as

Welsh Guards 3rd Battalion Triumphant in Italy

FROM TUNISIA THE 3rd BATTALION arrived in Italy in February 1944. Before going into action all weapons, including Vickers machine-guns (1), were overhauled. In the Arezzo area in July 1944 choir practice on a grand scale was held (2). After the capture of Cassino on May 18, 1944, the Battalion advanced up the valley of the Garigliano, or Liri, river to Arce, some of the men riding on Sherman tanks (3). The seizure of Monte Piccolo on May 26 by the 3rd Battalion opened the way to Rome.

Photos. British Official

WELSH GUARDS 1st AND 2nd BATTALIONS on the road to Caen (left), where they engaged in heavy fighting. They landed in Normandy with the Guards Armoured Division in June 1944, and at the end of August came the crossing of the Seine and the epic advance—probably unequalled for speed—which took the Armoured Division through Amiens, Arras and Douai and into Brussels on Sept. 3, 1944. A 2nd Battalion tank (right) on the way to the Belgian capital, cheered by the populace.
Photos, British Official, Central Press

the finest ever made by an Armoured Division. The 1st and 2nd Battalions were formed into one group, tanks and lorry-borne infantry working as one. The Group were the first to liberate Arras, the 1st Battalion having been the last troops to leave the town in 1940 ; they were first into Brussels, where a tremendous reception was given to them by the populace of the liberated capital. The advance

continued on into Holland. Heavy fighting took place at Hechtel, where the 1st Battalion launched a series of attacks supported by tanks of the 2nd Battalion. The village was finally captured on September 13.

Five days later the 2nd Battalion resumed their advance. They crossed the Nijmegen bridge on September 21, the day of its capture by the Grenadier Guards Group, but failed,

owing to the waterlogged country, to reach Arnhem and to relieve the 1st Airborne Division. After a series of engagements in "The Island" between Nijmegen and Arnhem, the Guards Division moved to Sittard, a quieter sector ; but on Christmas Day 1944 both Battalions were ordered to move down to Namur to hold the bridge there against Rundstedt's last great counter-offensive, but this offensive failed and the Battalions were not committed.

In February 1945 the Division returned to the Nijmegen area to take part in operation "Veritable," planned to drive the Germans back beyond the Rhine. The Regimental Group fought actions at Hassum and Bonninghardt, both highly successful. On March 23 the 1st Battalion was relieved by the 2nd Battalion the Scots Guards and returned to England. The 2nd Battalion at the end of March took part in operation "Plunder," the last great advance of the war.

THE 2nd Battalion crossed the Rhine and led the Division through Germany, moving via Lingen and Menslage to Cappelen, then across the main autobahn between Bremen and Hamburg. At Vesselhovede, a counter-attack was launched against the leading Squadron and Battalion H.Q. ; this involved a two-hour ordeal of what became almost hand-to-hand fighting. The counter-attack was eventually beaten off and the advance was continued. The 2nd Battalion was in Cuxhaven, on the North Sea, on VE Day.

So ended the war in Europe. The 2nd Battalion remained in Germany, and is now stationed at Lübeck on the Baltic. The 1st Battalion embarked for Palestine on October 6, 1945, and are still there as part of the 1st Guards Brigade. A brief mention should be made of the Training Battalion, which was formed on October 1, 1939, and for most of the war was stationed at Sandown Park, Esher. It was responsible for training men before they went to a Service battalion. The admirable way in which this was carried out was proved by the great achievements in battle of the three Service Battalions of the Regiment.

AT CUXHAVEN, after the German surrender at Luneburg, advanced elements of the Guards Armoured Division were met by the German commandant, who rode back on a British tank (above) to surrender the town, at the mouth of the River Elbe. The 2nd Battalion Welsh Guards was in Cuxhaven on VE Day, May 8, 1945. PAGE 750
Photo, British Official

Five Peace Treaties Signed at Last

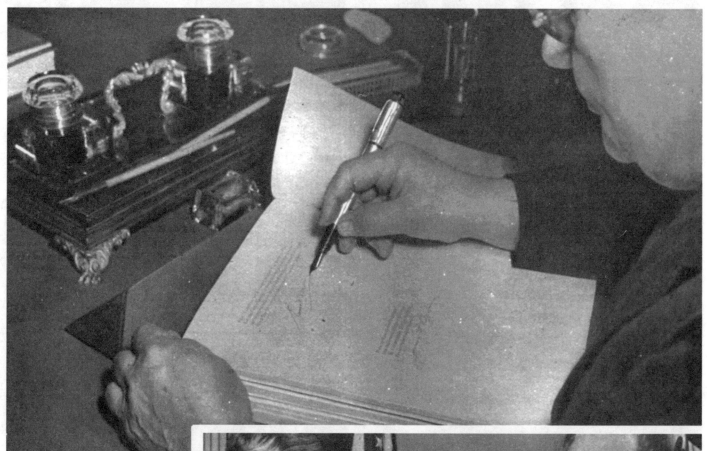

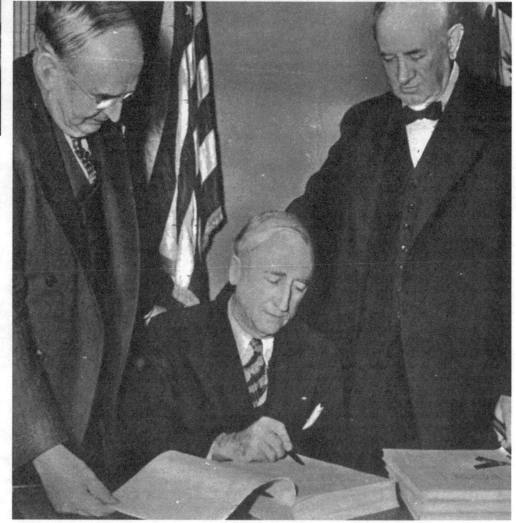

MONTHS of difficult preparatory work came to fruition in February 1947 with the signing of peace treaties between 21 Allied Nations and ex-enemy States (see also illus. pages 303-306 and 513). At the Foreign Office, London, on February 4, Mr. Ernest Bevin, our Foreign Secretary, placed his signature to the treaties with Italy, Finland, Rumania, Hungary and Bulgaria. On the one he is signing above is seen also the signature of Mr. James F. Byrnes, for the U.S.A.

As his last official act as U.S. Secretary of State, before he resigned that office for health reasons, Mr. Byrnes (right) signed, in Washington, four of the five treaties—the U.S.A. had not been at war with Finland. They were then taken by air to Moscow where Mr. Molotov, Soviet Minister for Foreign Affairs, signed all five. After Mr. Bevin, in London, had added his signature (these three signing as the ones responsible on behalf of their respective governments for negotiating the treaties) the documents were removed to Paris for the official ceremony on February 10.

Photos, Associated Press, I.N.P.

Ceremony in Paris Seals Solemn Pacts With—

At the Foreign Office on the Quai d'Orsay in Paris on February 10, 1947, the peace treaties were signed again, by accredited representatives of the Allied Nations, including Mr. Duff Cooper (1), the British Ambassador there : Mr. Bogomolov (2) for U.S.S.R. ; Mr. Masaryk (3), Czechoslovakian Foreign Minister. A welcoming address had been delivered by M. Bidault, French Foreign Minister, to delegates assembled in the Salon de l'Horloge (4), the famous Clock Room,

—States That Waged War as Hitler's Satellites

Italian Ambassador in Paris, the Marchese di Soragna (5) signed for his country; Karl Enckell (6) for Finland; M. Obbov (7) for Bulgaria; Mr. Gyongyossi (8) for Hungary; Mr. Tatarescu (9) for Rumania. Thus one more important stage in the post-war settlement was reached. Just one month ahead was the Moscow conference, opening on March 10, 1947, for the framing by the Big Four Foreign Ministers of the German and Austrian peace treaties.

Japanese Nightmare

Australian artist Murray Griffin (4) in a P.O.W. camp in Malaya set down in nearly 100 paintings and drawings some of the gross brutalities of the Japanese and the sufferings of his fellow prisoners during the enemy occupation. Recently exhibited in Melbourne, Victoria, their nightmarish quality is exemplified in reproductions in this page. To safeguard his pictures he adopted ingenious ruses—his portrayal of captives labouring on a railway bridge (1) was concealed from his guards between sheets of tin used to patch the leaky roof of his hut. A working party returns to Changi camp (2) carrying oddments of wood for a fire to heat-up their meagre rice rissoles. Ghastly scene in a camp hospital ward (3).

BRITISH WEST INDIES AND BERMUDA

By HARLEY V. USILL

LONG association with Great Britain has developed a loyalty in the West Indies (see page 104) which is in many respects more intense and personal than that found in many other Colonies, and when war broke out the whole of the Caribbean rallied their full resources. As stated in a previous article (page 147), one of the major problems was the feeding of the widely scattered populations. The West Indies are primarily agricultural communities, and with the exception of Trinidad and British Guiana they have not developed mineral resources.

Their pre-war economy was built on growing for overseas markets, sugar, bananas and other primary products, and importing in exchange foodstuffs, clothing and machinery. By a gigantic effort the whole balance of this economy was changed, and by an intensive production of locally grown food much valuable shipping space was saved. By the middle of 1944 the British West Indies had contributed over £750,000 to the United Kingdom for general war purposes, nearly £400,000 for war charities, and had given over £425,000 for the purchase of aircraft for the Royal Air Force. Their Governments and peoples had lent over £1,400,000 free of interest.

MOBILE canteens provided by the West Indies served in London and other towns during the air raids on Britain. They also contributed to the funds of the "Queen's Messengers," the mobile food convoys which helped to feed people in bombed towns. Gifts in kind were on an equally generous scale: lime juice and honey from the Bahamas, 80,000 lb. of cocoa for H.M. Forces from Grenada, hospital supplies and clothing comforts from little St. Kitts, and so on. In a number of the islands clubs and canteens were maintained for men of the Royal Navy and the Merchant Navy. The Government and people of Bermuda by September 1944 had given over £235,000 for general war purposes, and had lent over £1,000,000 free of interest. In addition, over £55,000 was contributed to war charities, and over £35,000 to buy aircraft. In spite of all this effort, however, the British West Indies felt a very serious sense of frustration. There was a great desire to form fighting battalions to serve overseas, but for a long time the War Office refused to allow this to be done. In December 1943, however, the War Office relented, and it was agreed that a West Indian contingent should move to the Mediterranean as soon as possible.

THE Regiment duly left the West Indies for the United States, where it carried out training; the first British unit to train on American soil since the War of Independence. In July 1944 it landed safely in Italy. The Battalion still required some months of training before being fit to go into battle, and in the autumn, as the weather had become too cold, they were sent to Gaza in the Middle East. In the spring of 1945 the Regiment was ready to move back into Italy, but before this could be effected German resistance had collapsed; and the West Indians after all had no opportunity of fighting, at least as a separate entity.

Back in the West Indies the situation had to some extent changed. The building of the American bases in the West Indies and Bermuda had led to the recruitment of considerable labour forces. In addition to Bermuda, the other Colonies affected were

A QUICK survey of the wartime activities of the Caribbean area, with which this series detailing our Colonies' war efforts concludes, indicates the magnitude and complexity of the assistance given by the British West Indies and Bermuda to Great Britain and the Allied cause.

the Bahamas, Jamaica, Antigua, St. Lucia, Trinidad and British Guiana, and much energy which had previously sought an outlet in military service was absorbed in the building of this network of offensive and defensive bases. Although, at first, labour troubles arose owing to varying rates of wages and the tendency of the Americans to apply the colour bar in British territories, these difficulties were eventually ironed out and the work proceeded without serious trouble.

One of the outstanding features of the West Indian war effort was the determination of the men and women to break through officialdom and by hook or by crook, even at their own expense, to get into the fighting zone. More than 4,000 men and women

PHYSICAL TRAINING WITH LOGS engaged these West Indian recruits to the R.A.F. in 1944. They were inspected at a training centre in northern England by Col. Oliver Stanley (in mufti), Secretary of State for Colonies, and Air Marshal Sir Arthur Barratt, K.C.B., C.M.G., M.C., A.O.C. Technical Training Command. *Photo, Keystone*

from the Islands and from British Honduras and British Guiana left their homes to join the British and Canadian forces. A contingent from the Bermuda Volunteer Rifle Company came to the U.K. in 1944 to join the Lincolnshire Regiment, with which the Bermuda unit has old-established connexions.

It was the R.A.F., however, which made the greatest appeal, and many men from the West Indies served with distinction as members of air crews, and others as R.A.F. tradesmen. Close association with the Royal Navy and the Merchant Navy over several centuries (and all but two of the Colonies being islands) has developed a special interest in the sea. Many West Indians served in these Services. Contingents of the West Indian A.T.S. came to Britain, and others served at home and in the U.S.A.

Another very welcome addition to the war effort was the several hundred technicians from Jamaica, including welders, riveters, fitters and motor mechanics, who volunteered to come to Britain to work in war factories. And there was the Forestry Unit of 900 men from British Honduras who served for two years in Scotland, and the 4,000 farm workers from the Bahamas, and over 9,000 from Jamaica who went to help with the 1943

harvest in America. In 1944 the number from Jamaica was nearly doubled, and in addition 3,000 went from Barbados.

And so we could go on, but enough has been written to indicate the unflinching loyalty of the British West Indies and Bermuda to Great Britain in particular and to the Allied cause in general. Although frustrated in their main endeavour to get to grips with the enemy as a Caribbean Force, West Indians, both men and women, played their part nobly in every task which they were called upon to perform.

WE have now come to the end of the story of the war effort of the British Colonial Empire. Taken as a whole it is a record of which all concerned may be justifiably proud, and although there is no justification for the indiscriminate use of such terms as "loyalty" and "patriotism," the fact remains that no other Metropolitan Power succeeded in achieving such a result. It may be that the West African who wrote the following to a Gold Coast newspaper summed up the feelings of many people of the Colonies:

" To show that we are fit to lead a better life, higher life, we are contributing our best to the British cause, which is our cause too, to ensure victory. We are not called upon to contribute to an aircraft purchasing fund because we are a subject people. The contribution is voluntary and we have undertaken it as an intelligent deed to register our disapproval of Hitlerism and all that is connected with it."

In the West Indies and Bermuda the main difficulty was to utilize to the full the desire of so many to enter the fighting zones. Now the impact of war has given rise to renewed claims for a greater degree of self-government within the British Commonwealth and Empire. Those Colonies occupied by the Japanese raise one of the most important questions of Colonial administration. Few would deny the basic principle of British Colonial policy that Colonial peoples should be nurtured in the arts of peace, but the acceptance of such a policy implies the ability of Great Britain to provide defence for Colonies, whose people are not temperamentally fitted for soldiering. Ceylon has every reason to consider her part in the war as worthy of adult nationhood, and even during the war conversations were proceeding in an attempt to formulate a new constitution which, with certain Imperial safeguards, would give her control of her own affairs. In the Mediterranean, Malta has the twofold problem of repairing the appalling devastation occasioned by constant bombardment at the same time as she is considering a new constitution. Cyprus suffered little material damage, but she is in the throes of political controversy revolving round the Enosis (union with Greece) movement. Gibraltar, reasonably free from political problems, has the task of housing her population and developing social services.

THE war, then, had the effect of accelerating political and social problems and making Colonial peoples increasingly aware of the outside world; there is evident a real determination to have a greater share in the management of their own affairs. In some cases progress may be rapid, in others it must be slow. The degree of understanding which Great Britain displays will determine the future of more than 60 million people of many races and diverse colours and creeds.

Terrorists Strike Again in Uneasy Jerusalem

IN THE MOST DARING ATTACK since the King David Hotel explosion (see illus. page 295) terrorists blew up the British Officers' Club (1), Jerusalem, on March 1, 1947, killing 13 and injuring 14. This was one of a series of lawless acts designed to enforce the establishment of an independent Jewish state. Explosives were taken to the site in an Army truck (2). Many people were removed for questioning (3). Jewish civilians were searched for arms (4), and the R.A.F. Regiment manned a post (5) overlooking the Damascus Gate. PAGE 756 *Photos, Planet News I.N.P., Keystone*

Union Jack Flutters Down at Mustapha Barracks

AT ALEXANDRIA THE MUSTAPHA BARRACKS were handed over to Egyptian troops on Feb. 8, 1947, in furtherance of our policy for the military evacuation of Egypt. Egyptian troops arrived in Bren carriers (1) to take over the barracks, which had been occupied by British troops for 64 years. Brigadier Horlington and General Abdul Azim Ibrahim (2) took the salute at the march past. The Union Jack (3) was lowered, and the Egyptian flag hoisted on the tower (4) of the so-called dungeon. See also illus. page 264.

Great Italian Naval Base Passes to Yugoslavia

UNDER THE TERMS OF THE ITALIAN PEACE TREATY, Pola, beside the Adriatic, 86 miles by rail south of Trieste, was awarded to Yugoslavia, and by the end of February 1947 about 2,000 Italian nationals were leaving the city (population 32,000) every three or four days. For hours they queued at the emigration office (1) for permission to enter Italy. Movable possessions accompanied them, including cattle (2) and household chattels (4). Food had to be purchased (3) for the journey before boarding the steamer (5).

Photos, Keystone

Welsh Industries Shine in London's Limelight

FIRST SHOW of Welsh manufactures to be held in London opened on Jan. 1, 1947, at the Royal Horticultural Hall, Westminster. It was organized by the National Industrial Development Council of Wales and Monmouthshire to demonstrate that "Wales can make it—and sell it." Stands of some of the 83 exhibitors are seen (1). The multi-coloured wedge shoes (2) are the only shoes of their kind made in Britain. Members of the Welsh Ladies' Choir tried on ball-bearing roller skates (3) from a factory on the Treforest Trading Estate. Artistic metal furniture (4) was displayed, and steel yachts (5) were among the toys. A wide range of aluminium utensils (6) attracted attention.

Photos, Planet News, P.A.-Reuter

The Roll of Honour
NCOs & MEN
1939—1945

Spr. F. AUSTIN
Royal Engineers.
D/W. : Libya. 27.1.42.
Age 25. (Ellesmere)

Since its inception on page 88 of this volume our Roll of Honour has displayed 950 portraits. It is regretted that no more can be accepted. A final 78 will appear in No. 255. Attention is drawn to the announcement in page 767.

O/S S. BATES
Royal Navy.
Act. : Atlantic. 2.10.42.
Age 19. (Overseal)

L/Cpl. W. BENNETT
Royal Welch Fusiliers.
Act. : Normandy. 19.8.44.
Age 27. (Heswall)

Pte. W. J. BOWL
Dorset Regiment.
Act. : N.W. E'pe. 8.6.44.
Age 18. (Hornchurch)

W/O R. BRYANT
R.A.F.V.R.
Act. : Pas de Calais. 24.6.44.
Age 30. (Colchester)

Pte. G. CARHART
Wiltshire Regiment.
D/W. : Nijmegen. 3.10.44.
Age 26. (Warminster)

L.A.C. W. CHAMBERLIN
Royal Air Force.
Act.: Istres Airfield. 5.9.45.
Age 20. (Nottingham)

Sto. CAWTHRA, D.S.M.
H.M. submarine Salmon.
Action: At Sea. 14.7.40.
Age 30. (Castleford)

Cpl. C. T. COOK
Oxford & Bucks L.I.
Act. : France. 13.8.44.
Age 19. (Dartford)

Pte. A. CLARE
6th Airborne Division.
D/W. : Rhine. 25.3.45.
Age 21. (Lte. Totham)

Pte. W. A. COOPER
Herefordshire Regt.
Act. : Eudem. 27.2.45.
Age 18. (Beeston)

Sgt. R. COZENS
Royal Air Force.
Act. : Brunswick. 22.5.44.
Age 19. (York)

Pte. A. E. DALBOCK
S. African Eng. Corps.
Died : Egypt. 12.6.41.
Age 24. (East London, S.A.)

Pte. C. E. DIXON
Royal Hampshire Regt.
Act. : Italy. 25.6.44.
Age 20. (Southampton)

L.A.C. P. DYER
Royal Air Force.
D/W. : Egypt. Nov. 1941.
Age 29. (Watford)

Pte. F. C. E. ELLIS
Suffolk Regiment.
P.O.W. : Siam. 25.11.43.
Age 27. (Herongate)

F/Sgt. W. A. FOWLER
Royal Air Force.
Middle East. 25.6.45.
Age 21. (Offord D'Arcy)

Pte. R. HODGES
The Buffs.
D/W. : Alamein. 30.9.42.
Age 19. (Welling)

Sgt. G. W. HOLFORD
R.A.F. Bomber Command.
Act. : England. 24.7.44.
Age 20. (Brentford)

Sgt. D. JOHNSON
Royal Artillery.
P.O.W. : Far East. 12.9.44.
Age 24. (Brockley)

F/Sgt. I. JAMES
Royal Air Force.
Act. : Greece. Oct. '44.
Age 21. (Caio, S. Wales)

Pte. J. H. KEANE
The King's Regiment.
Act. : Burma. 6.3.44.
Age 32. (Castleton)

L/Cpl. A. LAMB
Loyal Regiment.
Act. : Anzio. 30.5.44.
Age 25. (Lancaster)

L/Cpl. A. E. LEE
Rifle Brigade.
Act. : Normandy. 31.7.44.
Age 22. (Ilford)

Sgt. D. McASSEY
Cameron Highlanders.
Act. : Burma. 10.6.44.
Age 26. (Liverpool)

F/Sgt. E. NEWMAN
R.A.F. Bomber Command.
Act.: Nuremberg. 19.10.44.
Age 28. (Blundellsands)

Pte. F. NOTTLE
D.C.L.I.
Act. : Normandy. 3.8.44.
Age 25. (Bodmin)

F/Sgt. A. PARRATT
R.A.F. Coastal Command.
Act. : Off Norway. 13.10.41.
Age 20. (Birmingham)

L/Cpl. N. PERKINS
S. Wales Borderers.
Action : Italy. 1942.
Age 28. (Blackwood)

Sto. I. PICKLES
Royal Navy.
Action : At Sea. 1.11.44.
Age 19. (Colne)

W/O R. E. RALPH
Royal Air Force.
Act. : Germany. 14.1.45.
Age 24. (Margate)

Cpl. J. F. RIPPIN
Rifle Brigade.
Action : Italy. 11.1.45.
Age 25. (Walthamstow)

Dvr. W. ROBERTS
Royal Army Service Corps.
Action : Caen. 21.7.44.
Age 24. (Birmingham)

Spr. A. SMITH
Royal Engineers.
Act. : N.W. E'pe. 29.10.44.
Age 20. (Manchester)

F/Sgt. R. SMITH
Royal Air Force.
Act. : Biscay. 18.3.44.
Age 22. (Newport, Mon.)

A/S.M. G. STANLEY
18th Division.
Off Malaya. 5.2.42.
Age 29. (Seaton)

Sgt. J. STARSMORE
R.A.F.V.R.
Act. : Frisian Is. 29.8.44.
Age 19. (Worksop)

O/Tel. L. TURRELL
H.M.S. Penelope.
Act. : Off Naples. 18.2.44.
Age 23. (Barking)

Knocking Around in the Indian Ocean

An Ordinary Seaman in the cruiser Caledon, later transferred to the aircraft carrier Illustrious, M. C. Hyde looks back on busy and perilous months in 1942. In both the first and second expeditions to Madagascar, in May and September of that year, the Illustrious was prominent.

I LEFT England in January 1942, in the crowded troopship Strathmore, with 200 other very raw Naval recruits intended to form the nucleus of a Fleet replacement pool at Colombo, Ceylon. We arrived on March 10, and were promptly dispatched to the Naval barracks at the converted St. Joseph's College, which was full of survivors from Singapore and the many ships sunk since the wave of Japanese aggression had swept across the East Indies. Two weeks later I joined the cruiser Caledon, and the following day we were visited by the C.-in-C. of the Eastern Fleet, Admiral Sir James Somerville, who told us what was going to happen to the Japs should we get at them. Unfortunately the Japs turned up shortly afterwards with a much stronger fleet.

After sinking the cruisers Dorsetshire and Cornwall and the carrier Hermes, and delivering to Colombo its first air attack, they looked around for the rest of the Fleet. But having refuelled at a remote atoll south of Ceylon and having picked up survivors from the two cruisers, we were making a strategic withdrawal in the direction of East Africa. It was obvious that Ceylon was too near the Japs and too short of effective aircraft defence to provide any reasonable sanctuary for us.

MOMBASA was to be our new base, and it soon took on the air of an old-established Naval port. Canteens appeared, and most of the best hotels and restaurants were put out of bounds to ratings, and Fleet exercises and manoeuvres became regular features of our lives. Towards the end of April 1942 it became apparent that some operation was pending. Rumours were as numerous as they were fantastic. Singapore, Rangoon and the Andaman Islands were all included in the speculations, but not until the Fleet had put to sea was it made known that our objective was Madagascar. This was to be our first offensive move in the Far Eastern war, even though we were not going to attack the Japs themselves. Japanese military and naval missions had been in Madagascar negotiating with the Vichy French for the use of the island—and we were going to forestall them.

Mad With Relief at Being Spotted

On leaving Mombasa the Fleet split up. The aircraft carrier Indomitable with other units joined the carrier Illustrious and the large convoy of troops that had set out from England. The Caledon, with the carrier Formidable and other ships, was to patrol the north Madagascan coast to ward off any surprise Japanese counter-attack, while the rest of the Fleet went to cover the actual landing operations. I was serving as an Ordinary Seaman, and my action station was in the shell handing room—an unenviable position, as on those old cruisers armour-plating left much to be desired. The presence of oil tanks and magazines in adjacent compartments did not add to my sense of security, and the magazine gunner, knowing I was raw, delighted in telling me of magazine crews who had gone to the bottom with their ships.

Whilst we were closed up at action stations in the early hours of May 5, the Commandos were storming the beaches of Courrier Bay, which lies about 8 miles west of the port of Diego Suarez. They reached Diego Suarez 12 hours later, without having met much opposition. The main objectives of Antsirane and the harbour were captured 48 hours later. An ultimatum from Rear-Admiral Syfret, leader of the expedition, on May 5 had been immediately rejected. Shortly after the Commando landing at Courrier Bay, bomber aircraft from the Illustrious and Indomitable attacked the airfield, shipping and harbour installations. The auxiliary cruiser Bougainville and a submarine were sunk and a destroyer beached. In a later attack the submarine Le Héros was sunk. Swordfish torpedo-bombers dropped leaflets explaining the object of the attack and calling on the French to surrender. Dummy parachutes were also dropped, to give the impression of an assault by paratroopers. During these operations we were maintaining our patrol north of Madagascar and meeting no opposition.

Following the capture of Diego Suarez, though not equipped with anti-submarine devices we spent arduous weeks on submarine patrol with two other old cruisers, the Dragon and Danae, for Jap submarines were very active on the Cape Town, Durban and Mombasa run. One night in June 1942, whilst watch-keeping on the bridge during the first watch (8 p.m. to midnight), I heard shouts, apparently from the sea on the port bow. I reported, and the Caledon slowed down to half-speed ahead, and the water was swept by the ship's searchlight. Presently, about 100 yards distant, we saw three men clinging to what appeared to be a spar or broken mast. They shouted and waved to us, obviously mad with relief at being spotted. We moved closer to pick them up, but before we had completed a half-circle the most frightful and nerve-racking cries pierced the still night. In the beam of our searchlight was just a broken mast. Death had come suddenly to those three seamen. Exhausted by long exposure they had been washed from their handhold by our wake. Later it was learned that the victims of this tragedy were from a torpedoed Greek merchant vessel.

SHORTLY after that I was transferred to the carrier Illustrious, and on the same day, July 17, we left for Colombo. I had known nearly everyone of the Caledon's small company; the Illustrious, with its complement of over 1,400, seemed more like a barracks. I had a good watch-keeping billet, in harbour and at sea, as member of an Oerlikon anti-aircraft gun's crew on the island (the bridge), but because of an injury to my right foot I was transferred to the

BRITISH ASSAULT CRAFT REACHED THE SHORE AT TAMATAVE, a port on the east coast of Madagascar, on Sept. 18, 1942. Aircraft carrier Illustrious was among the vessels forming the naval covering force (story above). There was no fighting at Tamatave, the French garrison surrendering after a few shells had been fired by our warships. Lessons learnt by each of the Services in the landings on Madagascar were applied to later amphibious operations undertaken by the Allies.

Photo, British Official

captain's office to do clerical work, retaining my action station on the gun.

We spent a few days in the Bay of Bengal on an offensive sweep, brought down a Jap seaplane, and after a brief sojourn at Colombo returned to Mombasa. On arrival our air arm squadrons were sent ashore, as was the usual practice in harbour, to maintain their high standard of efficiency. Towards the end of August we began to comment on the large number of troop and supply ships that came to Mombasa and it was not long before word went round that we were off to capture the southern part of Madagascar.

With the battleship Warspite, veteran of Narvik and Matapan, and the rest of the Fleet we sailed en route to Madagascar ; aircraft from the Illustrious occupied an airfield on the Comoro Islands, west of Diego Suarez. Whilst we lay off Majunga on September 10, large-scale landings were taking place down the entire western coast. Majunga and Morondava, two major west ports, were occupied on September 11. From Majunga the 19th King's African Rifles began their march to Tananarive, the capital, some 250 miles distant. Most of the way had to be hacked through dense jungle and across raging streams with barely a bridge left intact

by the retreating French ; supporting aircraft from the Illustrious helped clear French pockets of resistance holding up our troops.

With the capture of Majunga we sailed for Diego Suarez, where we lay for a few days, with opportunity for shore leave. The magnificent harbour is one of the largest and deepest in the world. It has a narrow entrance, is surrounded by thick jungle and verdant hills, and as the water is always rough the journey ashore in a small ship's motor pinnace is hazardous. I was drenched to the skin before stepping on to the jetty, but soon dried under the blazing sun. The main street, Rue Colbert, possessing many cafés and drinking houses, proved to be the sole attraction. Not knowing its potency, I drank two glasses of absinthe. . . . Many sailors who drank too much of it passed out without warning.

We left Diego Suarez to cover further landings at Tamatave, a large port on the east coast, on September 18. Our envoys, under the white flag, were fired upon and their demands rejected. After a further time limit had expired British warships fired a few shells on the town, The echo of their explosions had scarce died away when the white flag of surrender was hoisted.

With the occupation of Tulear on the southwest coast on September 29 hostilities were brought to an end, and an armistice was signed on November 5. Immediately after the capture of Tamatave we left the landing forces, and to our great joy made our way to Durban for a short refit period—the first civilized port I had visited for nearly a year.

In January 1943 the Illustrious left for England. It was a comfortable feeling when passing through the Mozambique Straits in a hurricane to know that Madagascar on our port side was not a haven of Jap submarines !

Wartime Life in the Lonely Falklands

The loyal inhabitants of the most southerly of our Crown Colonies gave warm hospitality to their wartime Naval visitors. Life in this outpost, where roads and railways are non-existent, is described by Kenneth J. Buckley, who was stationed there from 1943 to 1945.

By July 1943 I had finished my training as a Coder and was patiently waiting at the Royal Naval Signal School, Devonport, for my first draft. At last my name was called ; with nine others I had been detailed for H.M.S. Pursuivant, which we later discovered was not the name of a ship but the R.N. Shore Station at Port Stanley, Falkland Islands, South America.

We sailed from Liverpool and travelled via Freetown to Montevideo. The luxuries

and pleasures of this great South American city were unbelievable after wartime Britain, and we were fortunate enough to stay there for two weeks before continuing our voyage to Port Stanley in a 500-ton packet steamer. This last stage of the journey was very bad indeed. The little ship tossed and rolled, and each day, as we approached Cape Horn, became stormier and colder.

On November 11 we sighted the bleak brown cliffs of the Falkland Isles, passed the

Pembroke Lighthouse—the most southerly in the world—and entered Port Stanley harbour. Although it was spring in that half of the hemisphere the day was bitterly cold, and a gale was blowing. We were to find out later, however, that this was normal Falkland Islands weather. We went ashore and were taken to our comfortable naval quarters, which were to be our home for the next two years. The first few days were spent in learning more about the Islands, and we were pleased to find that life in Port Stanley was not unlike village life in England.

The Falkland group, most southerly outpost of the Empire, consists of several islands of which the East and West Falklands are the biggest. These two are each approximately 100 miles in length and 50 miles wide, and the population of the whole area is only

Colours: Black on Green

25TH (INDIAN) DIVISION

FORMED at Salem, Madras, in August 1942, at a time when a Japanese invasion on the Madras coastline was considered highly probable, the 25th (Indian) Division moved to the Arakan in February 1944, under the command of Major-General H. L. Davies, C.B.E., D.S.O., M.C., and took over from the 36th (Indian) Division in the area of Buthidaung-Maungdaw, being allotted the task of guarding the XV Corps' southern flank.

As soon as the monsoon ended, the 25th, now commanded by Major-General G. N. Wood, O.B.E., M.C., assumed the offensive, the Mayu Peninsula being cleared by the end of December. The Division was now to undertake a series of amphibious operations. On Jan. 3, 1945, it landed unopposed at Akyab and began a long advance southwards. Five days later it took part in landings on the Myebon Peninsula. Advancing inland it was engaged in the protracted struggle for Kangaw.

FIGHTING continued from Jan. 22 to Feb. 18, the Japanese realizing that Kangaw, lying as it did on the direct supply route and line of retreat of their forces operating farther north, had to be held at all costs. Tanks of the 19th Lancers—the first Indian tanks to take part in a sea landing—did some magnificent work in this area, where the main Japanese escape route from the Arakan was cut.

On Feb. 16, units of the Division landed at Ruywa, which was speedily captured. In March came the seizure of Tamandu, which made a valuable supply base. There was extremely heavy fighting here, and when the mopping-up had been completed the 25th was transferred to India, where it was remustered in the newly-formed XXXIV Corps for the invasion of Malaya. It landed at Port Swettenham, 25 miles S.W. of Kuala Lumpur, after the unconditional surrender of Japan and took part in the rounding-up and disarming of the Japanese forces.

ground beyond the Liri, sent this message, "I send my greeting and congratulations to your magnificent fighting men, your fearless tank crews and your admirable infantry."

These Suffolk men, like their comrades in North-West Europe, made friends with the country people. One writer said of the Italians, "Notwithstanding their grievous poverty they made generous hosts, even when the home was but a one-roomed hovel with only a few sticks of furniture, the most treasured possession a sewing machine. The visitor was always pressed to share the family meal of oily batter, spaghetti, or some other unusual dish, and neither refusal nor payment was accepted."

Dancing was a favourite pastime for the troops when, later, time and circumstances permitted. The fair signorinas were strictly chaperoned, not merely by mother or an aged

DRUMS OF THE SUFFOLK REGIMENT were played again at Haecht, 16 miles north-east of Brussels, in February 1945, after having been left in Roubaix in May 1940. They were hidden there by French civilians during the German occupation, and three (in the front rank above) were restored to the 1st Battalion shortly before Christmas 1944. *Photos, British Official*

aunt but by several generations of the family. The chief attraction of the dance, if organized by the soldiers, was the food : no sooner had the buffet been opened when it was cleared, and no sooner cleared when a homeward trek of Italian guests would begin !

The Second Great War proved once again how invaluable to the Army are the traditions of a great regiment. Minden, the greatest battle honour of The Suffolk Regiment, was celebrated on every First of August, wherever any unit of the Regiment was serving ; and every detached officer or soldier proudly wore a rose in his head-dress on that day, no matter what other regimental badge he might, temporarily, be wearing.

ON MINDEN DAY, Aug. 1, 1945, a party of the 1st Suffolks, which is one of the "Minden" regiments, visited the monument in Germany erected to commemorate that great battle. Each wore the traditional rose in his cap, and Lieut.-Col F. A. Milnes, the commanding officer, standing on the steps of the memorial, related the history of the battle.

From Normandy to Gibraltar with The Suffolks

AFTER THE ATTACK NEAR CAEN on July 18, 1944, a party of the 1st Battalion The Suffolk Regiment converted a crater (1) outside Troarn into a platoon H.Q. In the following October the Battalion moved up (2) to attack Venray, Holland. At Gibraltar, in June 1945, a detachment of the 31st Battalion formed part of the escort (3) at the funeral of Lieut.-Gen. Hawkesworth, C.B., D.S.O., former commander of X Corps in Italy. Dugouts (4) for the 1st Battalion on the Maas in November 1944. Returned from patrol to a smoke and rest (5). PAGE 781 *Photos. British Official*

particular, had had a glorious history in the 1914-1918 war and were determined to add more pages to it.

But those four battalions were dispatched along with the rest of the 18th Division to Singapore, where they were involved in the surrender. Many months followed in Japanese captivity, under the most dreadful conditions. Almost all the prisoners of war were employed on the construction of the Burma-Siam railway and suffered the most callous and brutal treatment. There was a disastrous death roll from cholera, malaria, starvation and exhaustion. Though these battalions won no battle honours, the display of heroism, fortitude, self-sacrifice and, above all, the good humour so typical of the British soldier, had no equal in any other Army in any campaign during 1939-1945. They proved themselves the finest type of British soldier.

The history of the remaining first-line unit, the 7th Suffolk, is happier. During the earlier months of the war after the evacuation from Dunkirk, like other battalions of the Regiment it was employed on coast defence. Then as the production of tanks increased it was converted into a tank regiment, becoming the 142nd Regiment, R.A.C. But the men were Suffolk soldiers, and they never forgot it. They painted the names of Suffolk battle honours on some of their tanks, and on others the names of distinguished officers of the

Regiment. A year after they had been converted from Infantry they were fit to take the field and were sent with their Churchill tanks to North Africa.

There they went straight into battle, helping the 78th Division and the sorely-pressed American and French to hold on to what they had gained during the first onrush. At first the Regiment was split up into squadrons but later fought as a unit in the desperate battles round Medjez-el-Bab, which ended in the victorious advance to Tunis. During this fighting the few Churchills had proved of the greatest moral value. Tanks were comparatively rare in the early stages of this campaign and the Churchill was the most powerful British tank in the field.

THE 142nd Regiment, R.A.C., the old 7th Suffolk, sailed for Italy in time to take part in the assault on the Adolf Hitler line and the advance to Rome. There they were in support of the 1st Canadian Division, which proved a great partnership. After the successful assault of the German lines the Commander of the Canadian Division wrote that he hoped the Regiment would for the future paint on their tanks a maple leaf emblem in remembrance of the assistance the Suffolks had been to the Canadians.

And the Commander of the French forces, who had watched the fighting from high

REGIMENTAL TELEPHONE EXCHANGE of the 1st Battalion The Suffolk Regiment was in a private house (1) at Bouvines, France, in February 1940, and the men were billeted in barns (2). The 7th Battalion, in England during 1941, engaged as infantry in anti-invasion exercises (3) at Sandbanks, near Bournemouth : by 1943 they had become familiar with the intricacies of wireless telephony (4) and were operating their tanks in the Medjez-el-Bab area, Tunisia. Men of the 1st Battalion waiting to go forward (5) at Overloon, Holland, in October 1944. PAGE 780 *Photos, British Official*

The Suffolk Regiment

By Colonel
W. N. NICHOLSON,
C.M.G., D.S.O.

IN September 1939 there were two Regular Battalions of The Suffolk Regiment. The 1st had recently returned to England from Malta and the 2nd was stationed on the Indian North-West Frontier, at Razmak. The two Territorial Battalions, the 4th Suffolk and the 1st Cambridgeshire, had each formed a second battalion earlier in that year, these being the 5th Suffolk and the 2nd Cambridgeshire, respectively. It speaks well for the strong Regimental feeling in these East Anglian Territorials that they were the first in England to recruit their quota of men for two additional units.

These six battalions all saw active service. One other, the 7th Suffolk, became a first-line unit. The 8th Suffolk was in due course a Home Defence unit and later, when the urgency of Home Defence faded, a reinforcement battalion, supplementing holding battalions in the training of recruits. The only other Suffolk battalion, the 9th, expanded in due course into the 30th and 31st Battalions, composed largely of old soldiers employed on garrison duties, and the 70th (Young Soldiers') Battalion, consisting of boys too young to be conscripted, but a first-class contingent. Behind the Regiment stood the Home Guard, its battalions filled with a great many old soldiers, recruiting their strength from Suffolk, Cambridgeshire and the Isle of Ely.

In the following brief account of the Regiment's history during the Second Great War only the fighting battalions can be mentioned. The 1st Battalion was with the original expeditionary force as a part of Montgomery's 3rd Division, "the Iron Division," with which it served throughout the war. The 2nd Battalion was in India, first at Razmak, then on "Internal Security," and finally in Burma. The four

FORMERLY the 12th Foot, the Regiment originated in a company established to garrison Windsor Castle in 1660, this company being formed into a regiment in 1685. It served under William III in Ireland and Flanders and was at Dettingen in 1743. The 12th was one of the six British regiments at Minden, took part in the last siege of Gibraltar, 1779-83, and shared in the storming of Seringapatam, 1799. Further battle honours were gained in the Kafir War, 1851-53, the New Zealand War, 1863, and the Afghan War, 1878-80. The Regiment served in the South African War and had a large number of battalions engaged in the First Great War.

Territorial Battalions were in the ill-fated 18th Division, engulfed at Singapore. The 7th became a tank unit and fought as such with the 1st Army in Tunisia and later in Italy. Thus the Regiment was fully represented in all the principal theatres of operation.

The Suffolk Regiment has rarely, if ever, had a greater battalion than the 1st. Good fortune is of paramount importance in war, where ill-luck may blight the most promising career: and good fortune favoured the 1st Battalion. It formed part of a great Division, and it had the best possible commanding officers, sometimes Suffolk, sometimes "foreign"; above all, it was a great team. The retreat to Dunkirk blooded the men. They came back to England convinced they were better than the Germans. They trained unceasingly. The 3rd Division was one of the assault divisions on D-Day, and the 8th Infantry Brigade, with the 1st Battalion The Suffolk Regiment, was the assault Brigade for the landing, being the first on the Normandy beaches. In the strenuous fighting that followed the 1st Battalion did all that was expected of it—and much had been expected. But perhaps the hardest fighting of all was in Holland, in the five-days' battle for the village of Overloon, in October 1944, where against the stiffest possible resistance and in the most difficult country their tenacity eventually won victory.

Flown Over the Jungle to Imphal

Luck, which favoured the 1st Battalion, was not so kind to the 2nd Battalion in India. The 2nd won a fine reputation on the North-West Frontier, taking part in two punitive expeditions ; but for months afterwards it was scattered on "Internal Security," during which time many of the best officers, N.C.O.s and men were drafted off on duties from which they never returned to the Battalion. Then, at short notice, the 2nd left for the Arakan, in Burma, where all speedily learned that good as the Japanese were at jungle fighting the British soldier could be even better.

From the Arakan they were flown over the jungle to Imphal, and took part in the fighting there and at Kohima. In Burma they fought as part of the fine 5th Indian Division. But sickness and disease took a big toll. Reinforcements were not forthcoming, and after the defeat of the Japanese before those two towns the 2nd Battalion returned to India.

The fluctuating fortunes of the 2nd Battalion were as nothing compared with the disastrous fate of the 4th and 5th Suffolk and the 1st and 2nd Cambridgeshire. These battalions had shown the finest promise during training in England and Scotland. The great majority of officers and men were East Anglian, and their Regimental enthusiasm was very high. The Cambridgeshire, in

AT THE MARCH PAST OF THE 7th BATTALION at Sandbanks, near Bournemouth, in November 1941, Lieut.-General Sir E. C. A. Schreiber, K.C.B., D.S.O., then commanding V Corps, took the salute. This was the Battalion's last ceremonial parade as infantry before being transferred to the Royal Armoured Corps. Equipped with Churchill tanks, they landed in North Africa with the British 1st Army 12 months later and gained a magnificent reputation both there and in the Italian campaign.

Photo. British Official

HIS MAJESTY'S SHIPS   H.M.S. Belfast

BUILT by Messrs. Harland & Wolff in the city after which she is named, H.M.S. Belfast of 10,000 tons, with main armament of twelve 6-inch guns and speed of 32 knots, was the most modern cruiser afloat when completed in August 1939. Quite early in the war she had the misfortune to be heavily damaged by a magnetic mine. Only the soundness of her construction saved her from sinking, and she had to be practically rebuilt.

In 1943 she hoisted the flag of Vice-Admiral (now Sir Robert) Burnett for duty in escorting convoys bound to North Russia. On the morning of Dec. 26, 1943, the Belfast, together with the cruisers Norfolk and Sheffield, was stationed on the starboard bow of a large convoy (flagship of Rear-Admiral Bey) was sighted. Without hesitation Vice-Admiral Burnett about 150 miles to the northward of North Cape when the German battleship Scharnhorst steered a course towards the enemy, which so disconcerted the German Admiral that the Scharnhorst turned away and disappeared in the semi-darkness. Later the enemy battleship approached the convoy from another direction, only to find the British cruisers again between the attacker and his prey.

Contriving to keep touch with the elusive enemy, Vice-Admiral Burnett must have felt highly satisfied when at 4.30 that afternoon the battleship Duke of York (flagship of Admiral Sir Bruce Fraser), accompanied by the cruiser Jamaica, arrived and engaged the Scharnhorst. It then became the Belfast's duty to illuminate the German ship by star-shell for the benefit of the Duke of York's gunners. After temporarily drawing away, the enemy was re-engaged and sunk. At the close of the war the Belfast was again operating under Admiral Sir Bruce Fraser, this time in the Pacific Fleet against Japan.

Photo, Wright and Logan

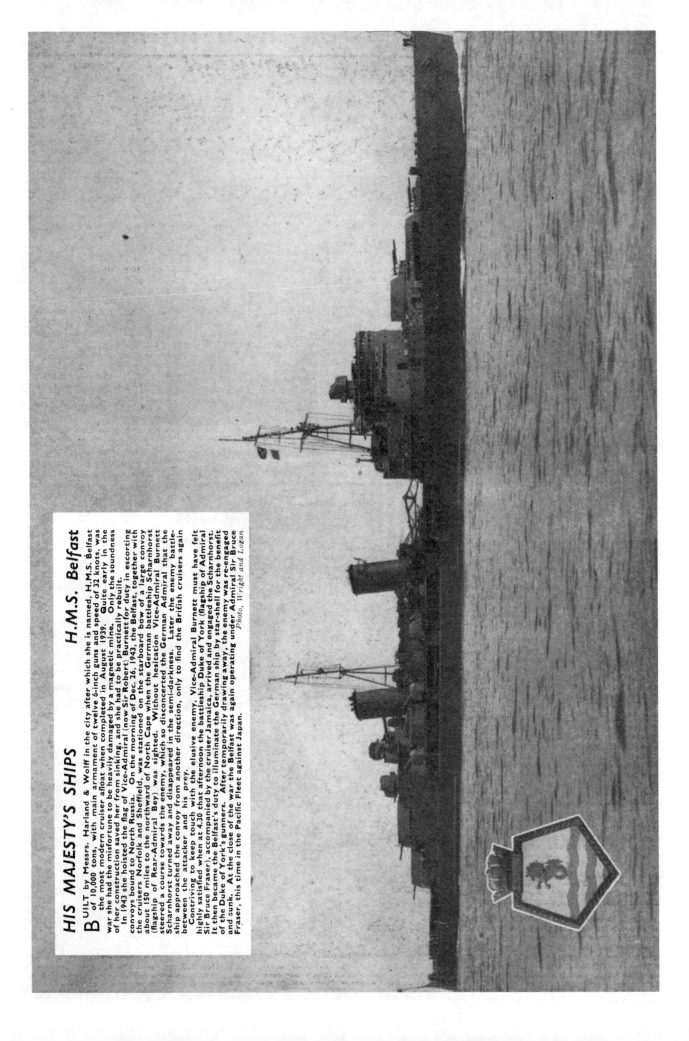

How We Fought by Night With Invisible Rays

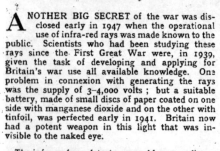

ANOTHER BIG SECRET of the war was disclosed early in 1947 when the operational use of infra-red rays was made known to the public. Scientists who had been studying these rays since the First Great War were, in 1939, given the task of developing and applying for Britain's war use all available knowledge. One problem in connexion with generating the rays was the supply of 3–4,000 volts ; but a suitable battery, made of small discs of paper coated on one side with manganese dioxide and on the other with tinfoil, was perfected early in 1941. Britain now had a potent weapon in this light that was invisible to the naked eye.

The infra-red ray detector resembles an ordinary telescope except that inside, between the lenses, is a special device which converts the infra-red rays into green light, which is visible to the user of the detector. The infra-red image converter thus enables an object illuminated by the invisible rays to be seen by the human eye.

FIRST operational use of the new weapon was in the Mediterranean in 1941, when Commandos, equipped with infra-red signalling sets, maintained contact with parent ships offshore. Infra-red binoculars (1) and headlamps (2) were fitted to tanks and transport vehicles (4) to enable them to move freely at night, unobserved by the enemy. As a navigational aid during the Rhine crossing in March 1945 the transport of the British 79th Armoured Division was fitted with this equipment.

An infra-red sight for automatic weapons (3) was also developed, enabling an enemy to be picked off in complete darkness at a range of 30 yards. Night-fighters and bombers of the R.A.F. (5) were equipped with infra-red sets, and the tails of friendly fighters carried infra-red identity lights. Midget submarines, which attacked the German battleship Tirpitz in September 1943, used infra-red rays, and again when they cut the submarine cables at Hongkong and Saigon.

A simple instrument was produced to detect the use of infra-red equipment by the enemy, and extensive reconnaissance was carried out from the air over enemy-occupied territory. Infra-red devices, however, were not used by the Germans on the Western Front, although their limited employment was reported against the Russians.

Photos, British Official

China's Young Sailors Schooled by Royal Navy

VETERAN BATTLE-CRUISER H.M.S. RENOWN became a school in February 1947, when 600 Chinese sailors arrived at Plymouth to undergo a course with the Royal Navy. Physical training (1) starts their day's work. Signallers receive instruction in semaphore (2) from a British Petty Officer. In the engine room stokers are shown how to feed and maintain boilers (3). Ratings learn to read the compass and use English text books (4), and to handle small boats (5). Parade on the Renown's quarter-deck (6) under a Chinese officer. See also page 202. PAGE 776

Communal Conflict Sets the Punjab in Tumult

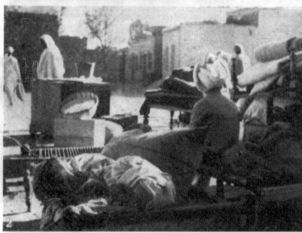

INDIA'S DEEP-ROOTED religious and political differences were emphasized at the beginning of March 1947 by the situation in the Punjab, where the Moslem League's theory of Pakistan—a separate State for a combination of all the Provinces having a Moslem majority—was put to the test amid bloodshed and communal conflict.

Rioting began in Lahore on March 4, following the refusal of the Hindu and Sikh leaders to support the Moslem League ministry in the Legislative Assembly; there, Moslems attacked Hindus and Sikhs, many being killed and hundreds injured (1). At Mandra the Hindu quarter was sacked; survivors piled their remaining possessions in the street (2). Amritsar suffered more severely than Lahore; refugees, including Afghan traders (3), streamed out of the city. Bhim Sen Sachar (4, under the flags), Finance Minister in the Punjab Government, addressed a meeting. Streets in Amritsar were guarded (5) to prevent looting.

Martial Law for Sake of Peace in Palestine

FINDING A SOLUTION to Palestine's problems sorely tried the powers of the British Government, and on Feb. 18, 1947, Mr. Ernest Bevin announced that conferences with Arab representatives and consultations with the Zionist Organization having failed it had been decided to ask the United Nations to suggest a settlement. Following Jewish attacks on March 1 (see illus. page 756) martial law was imposed in some of the principal Jewish areas of the country.

A Bren gun post (1) covered a barrier on the Jaffa road at Tel Aviv. No motor vehicles, except for essential workers, were allowed on the streets ; queer vehicles appeared (2), and the few buses were stormed (3). A military cordon was flung round Tel Aviv on March 2, and citizens lined up (4) for permission to return to their homes. Martial law ended at noon on March 17, when thousands flocked to the barbed wire in Jerusalem to greet their friends (5).　PAGE 774

Moscow Deliberations on Germany and Austria

TO COMMENCE FRAMING THE GERMAN AND AUSTRIAN PEACE TREATIES the "Big Four" Foreign Ministers—Mr. Bevin (Britain), Mr. Molotov (Soviet Union), Gen. Marshall (U.S.A.), M. Bidault (France)—met in Moscow on March 10, 1947. Mr. Molotov (1, second from right) at a reception attended by Mr. Bevin (2, right). The Council of Ministers in session (3) with advisers. Gen. Marshall (4, centre) chatted with M. and Mme. Bidault. U.S. Deputy for Austria, Gen. Clark (5, extreme right), and Russian Deputy for Austria, Mr. Gusev, with Marshal Koniev.

tons. They were so flexible that the roadway could twist vertically until one end was at an angle of 40 degrees to the other, and yet still carry the heaviest equipment at a speed of 25 m.p.h. It was composed of separate panels loosely bolted to the cross members. The supports for the spans consisted of pontoons of steel plate or reinforced concrete; these were known by the code name of Beetles. Those Beetles which were always to remain afloat, even at low tide, were constructed of precast concrete panels 1¼ ins. thick, and were joined by concrete ribs cast *in situ*. Other Beetles were built of steel sheeting. Roadway lengths of 500 feet could be towed in one section; that is in six spans made up of five spans and the shore ramp float.

CONSTRUCTION was undertaken with that of the pierheads, contracts for the two schemes combined—known as Whale—being placed in June 1943, through the normal channels of the Ministry of Supply under the Director General, Mechanical Equipment, Sir Geoffrey Burton.

It had been decided at the Quebec Conference in 1943 that the main breakwaters should be composed of reinforced concrete caissons, and that *immediate* shelter would be provided by means of breakwaters formed by several old ships that would be sunk as block-ships. This line of block-ships was known by the code name Gooseberry. The ships used were old Merchant Navy and Royal Navy vessels, still seaworthy and in some cases still in use. They were to be the first to arrive, and were to be sunk by explosive charges by their Naval and Merchant Navy crews, who were then to return to Britain. This operation was successfully completed in the first five days after D-Day, and provided very valuable initial shelter.

Sole Failure in Vast Programme

A further outer floating breakwater was to be established to give shelter to ships larger than those of the Liberty type, which were the biggest that the port could accommodate. This floating breakwater, the design and production of which was undertaken by the Admiralty, was the only failure in the whole ambitious programme. Its component units, referred to as bombardons, were destroyed in the storm.

The concrete caissons, known under the code name of Phoenix, were designed like ships, because they would be subjected to similar wave action and would require the

same stability as ships in calm or stormy seas. Design was as near box-like as the conditions would permit, but to obtain the lowest towing resistance they were provided with swim ends, not unlike Thames barges.

Lack of time precluded prototypes of the caissons being built, but models were made and tested at the National Physical Laboratory at Teddington for towing and sinking and for the effect of wave action. As a result of these tests no alteration of the design was found to be necessary. Although the design of the caissons was not commenced until October 1, 1943, construction was actually put in hand on many sites before the end of the month. One hundred and forty-seven units were to be built in six different sizes, with displacements ranging from 6,044 tons to 1,672 tons. Total length of the caissons added up to approximately 5½ miles. Under a subsequent programme a further 66 units were constructed.

Blitz Rubble Played a Part, Too

The project was undertaken by 24 leading public works contractors, at 14 different sites around the English coast. This task was controlled by a special department of the Ministry of Supply directed by the late Sir John W. Gibson, who received his knighthood for his work in connexion with Mulberry (portrait in page 430, Vol. 8).

Construction took place in the Graving Docks at Middlesbrough, Goole, Southampton, and of the Port of London Authority at Tilbury. Several units were built in an entrance lock at Plymouth, and in the floating dock there. Two London Docks, the East India and South Dock, were de-watered after precast concrete block dams had been constructed in the entrance locks, and 18 units were built on these two sites, where hundreds of thousands of cubic yards of blitz rubble were used to make construction beds on the dock bottoms. Twenty-three units were constructed on slipways built on the foreshore at Stokes Bay, Stone Point, and Langston Harbours in the Portsmouth and Southampton areas. Here the caissons were constructed to about 60 per cent of completion and were then towed to jetties where the remainder of the construction was carried out.

At the suggestion of the Ministry of Supply, shallow basins were excavated in open land alongside the River Thames. But here the depth of excavation was limited by the ground water-level, and the units could only

be constructed up to a certain height, after which they were floated out and completed. Sufficient of these basins were dug to enable 40 units to be constructed at a time. Altogether, 98 were commenced in these basins, some being completed in other sites. The most suitable dock—the King George V Dry Dock at Southampton—at which many batches of caissons could have been built, was not available as the Admiralty were using it for construction of bombardons.

THIS vast programme of construction was an outstanding example of co-operation between various Government departments and the British Public Works Contractors. The contractors provided the site organization, key men and supervision, while the Government provided the materials and labour. Men were directed from all parts of the country to the London area and other sites, where they toiled on objects about which they knew nothing; nor could they find out anything in regard to the ultimate use of what they were working on. Guesses, which were numerous, included " A causeway across the English Channel," "A floating aeroplane base," and "Blockades for docks and canals."

In all, 212 caissons were built, of which 147 were ready before D-Day. The remainder, which were used as additional breakwaters and as replacements, were completed before August 1944. This was indeed a remarkable accomplishment, as is further shown by the following quantities of materials involved: 545,000 cubic yards of reinforced concrete; 66,000 tons of reinforcing steel; 9,000 standards of timber; 440,000 square yards of plywood; and 97 miles of steel wire rope.

Grand Tribute to Our Engineering

Maximum number of men employed was about 20,000; this total included 10,500 labourers, 1,000 scaffolders, 5,000 carpenters, and 770 steel fixers. The War Office issued more than 130,000 prints of working drawings dealing with the construction of the caissons.

That Mulberry—code name used to embrace all the details of the great scheme—was constructed and assembled in the British Isles in such a short space of time in the fifth year of the Second Great War was an astonishing performance. That such an operation as the Normandy landings was successful was a glowing tribute not only to thoroughness of the military planning but also to the British engineering industry.

BOMBARDONS FORMED A FLOATING BREAKWATER outside the main harbour to give shelter to large vessels. These hollow steel structures, unfortunately, did not stand up to the severe gale that raged for several days during the middle of June 1944: this worst June storm for 40 years enforced the abandonment of the Mulberry Harbour for the Normandy beaches used by the invading Americans (see page 430, Vol. 8). The Admiralty were responsible for production of the bombardons, constructed in the King George V Dock at Southampton. PAGE 772 *Photo, Admiralty Official*

The Building of Mulberry Harbour

By MICHAEL F. KENNARD

VITAL build-up in reinforcements and supplies of the successful landings in France in June 1944 was made possible by the unique construction methods employed to produce two complete harbours in the British Isles, and to transport them in sections across the English Channel to the French coast. The harbours were designed to be established at Vierville-sur-Mer and at Arromanches, on the coast of Normandy. That for the former, known as Mulberry A, was intended for American use but had to be abandoned after the very severe storm on D-Day + 13 in favour of the French port of Cherbourg which became available earlier than had been expected. The British harbour, Mulberry B, which was in a more sheltered position, was used right through the autumn and winter and into 1945.

At Arromanches, the site chosen for Mulberry B, the sea bed was shallow and sandy, and a small reef—the Calvados Reef—offshore partially sheltered the area. At one time French engineers had proposed a permanent harbour here, but the difficulties were considered insurmountable. The actual planning of Mulberry B was based on French charts, though the final siting was dependent on soundings taken on D-Day.

VERY simple in composition, the harbours comprised only three parts, (1) the pierheads and quays, (2) the floating roadways, (3) the breakwaters. The initial decision to construct them was taken at the Quebec Conference in 1942, when instructions for the design of the pierheads and floating roadways were given. At the 1943 conference, also at Quebec, it was decided to proceed with the design and construction of the concrete caissons which formed the breakwaters.

The design and main research work on the pierheads or landing pontoons was undertaken by Messrs. Lobnitz & Co., Ltd., of Renfrew. This firm's association with the scheme came about through the intervention of Brigadier Sir Bruce White, K.B.E., R.E. (director of the scheme for the Quartermaster-General), who had knowledge of a dipper dredger of Lobnitz construction having safely ridden a severe storm in the West Indies several years previously. The problem confronting the designers was summed up by Mr. Winston Churchill thus : " Piers for use on beaches :—They must float up and down with the tide. The anchor problem must be mastered—let me have the best solution worked out. Don't argue the matter. The difficulties will argue for themselves." The Churchillian manner !

That was in the autumn of 1942. The prototype was in the Solway Firth by April 1943. This original pierhead, which required over 1,000 tons of steel, was there thoroughly tested for many months, and was found to be entirely satisfactory—an amazing achievement considering the magnitude of the undertaking and the short time available.

The pierheads consisted of a steel pontoon with four steel legs or spuds which were power-operated and when driven hard against the sea bed caused the pontoon to rise. Hence the pierheads could be adjusted to maintain a fairly constant height above sea-level ; alternatively, they could float with the tide, sliding up or down the legs.

SPUD PONTOONS, the pierheads of Mulberry Harbour, were tested early in 1943 by ships bumping against them (above), the movement noted being 6 inches. Mr. Lobnitz (left, in mufti), whose firm was responsible for the design of the pontoons, inspected a prototype in the Gareloch area, Scotland, in April 1943. See also page 733. *Photos, British Official*

After completion of the tests, approval was given to about 200 firms throughout the country for the large-scale manufacture of the piers and pierheads. A waste stretch of ground at Leith was very soon transformed into erection berths where the majority of the construction took place. Other sites were at Conway, North Wales, managed by Messrs. Jos. Parkes & Son, of Northwich, and at the Military Port No. 1 at Cairnryan (see page 173, Vol. 9), where the Army entirely undertook the erection.

The roadways were designed so that they could be towed for about 100 miles and be able to stand up to such weather as is common in the English Channel in the summer months. They comprised 80-foot bridge spans, supported on floats. Each span consisted of two 30-foot girders and a 10-foot wide road, and weighed about 30

Sgt. W. LOCKLEY
Royal Lincolnshire Regt.
Action : Burma. 24.4.43.
Age 36. (Birmingham)

Right
Pte. O. LOMAS
East Lancs. Regt.
Action : Belgium. 7.1.45.
Age 32. (Barnsley)

L/Cpl. W. McKELVEY
Glasgow Highl. (H.L.I.).
Act. : N.W. E'pe. 2.11.44.
Age 20. (Laurencetown)

Right
Cpl. D. McLEOD
Long Range Desert Group.
Action : Rimini. 6.10.44.
Age 25. (Helensville, N.Z.)

Gnr. R. MAPLEY
Royal Artillery.
D/W : Italy. 29.7.44.
Age 22. (Doncaster)

Fus. A. MARKLAND
Royal Welch Fusiliers.
Act.: Madagascar. May '42.
Age 32. (Swindon)

Pte. A. MOCHAR
Argyll & Sutherland H.
Act. : N. Africa. April '43.
Age 33. (Falkirk)

Cpl. F. W. P. MOTT
Royal Tank Regiment.
Action : Tunisia. 7.4.43.
Age 26. (Hurst Green)

Spr. G. W. MOUZER
Royal Engineers.
P.O.W.: Germ'y. 11.4.45.
Age 25. (Woolwich)

Gnr. H. P. NASH
Royal Artillery.
Act. : Tobruk. 26.11.41.
Age 26. (North Weald)

F/Sgt. J. L. OAKLEY
R.A.F. Coastal Command.
Action : Medit. 11.5.43.
Age 29. (Huddersfield)

L/Bdr. E. OCKENDEN
Royal Artillery.
P.O.W. : Siam. 23.9.43.
Age 24. (Worthing)

Dvr. P. PAUL
Royal Signals.
Nr. Hanover. 14.4.46.
Age 25. (Banchory-Devenick)

Gnr. W. PAYNE
Royal Artillery.
D/W. : Italy. 27.9.44.
Age 39. (Farnworth)

Pte. T. E. PEARSON
South Lancs. Regt.
Pres. K. Burma. 25.5.44.
Age 27. (London)

Dvr. H. J. PLUMMER
Royal Army Service Corps.
D/W. Italy. 11.9.44.
Age 26. (S. Wales)

A B D. PULLIN
Royal Navy.
Died : Sydney. 30.11.45.
Age 20. (Loughton)

Rfln. L. READ
King's Royal Rifle Corps.
Act. : Alamein. 27.10.42.
Age 28. (Enfield)

Sgt. R. J. RENYARD
Royal Air Force.
Off Scotland. 22.8.42.
Age 20. (Lewisham)

Tpr. A. ROBERTS
Reconnaissance Regt.
Action : France. 23.7.44.
Age 31. (Bury)

Gdsmn. T. ROBERTS
Grenadier Guards.
Action : Anzio. 26.1.44.
Age 27. (Meir, S.O.T.)

Pte. R. RUNDLE
6th Australian Div.
Action : Libya. 21.3.41.
Age 27. (Burnie, Tasmania)

L/Cpl. C. SCRIVEN
Queen's Royal Regt.
Act. : Normandy. 18.6.44.
Age 28. (Troedyrhiw)

Cpl. R. SWAINSTON
R.A.O.C.
Died : Egypt. 26.7.44.
Age 25. (Thornaby-on-Tees)

F/Sgt. S. SWIFT
Over Marseilles. 24.3.44.
Age 23. (Penge)

Sgt. E. SLATER
R.A.F.V.R.
Over Germany. 25.8.44.
Age 21. (Oldham)

Pte. J. W. TAYLOR
Manchester Regt.
Died Burma. 26.5.43.
Age 31. (Oldham)

Pte. C. THOMPSON
2/5 Inf. Bn. A.I.F.
Act. : New Guinea. 6.6.45.
Age 33. (Preston, Australia)

Pte. W. THOMPSON
Northamptonshire Regt.
Act. : Tunisia. 17.2.43.
Age 23. (Kettering)

Sgt. M. A. TOWERS
Royal Leicestershire Regt.
Act. : Belgium. 21.10.44.
Age 32. (Leicester)

A.C.2. R. UMNEY
Royal Air Force.
Nr. Cirencester. 16.8.42.
Age 19. (Hanslope)

F/Sgt. W. B. WARR
Royal Air Force.
Over Dortmund. 2.2.45.
Age 22. (Gillingham)

Pte. D. W. WATKINS
2, 12 Field Ambulance.
Act. : Amboina. 20.2.42.
Age 29. (Stroud Rd., N.S.W.)

L/Sto. W. WEBBER
H.M.S. Glorious.
Action : At sea. 9.6.40.
Age 22. (Exeter)

H. WHEATCROFT
Merchant Navy.
Act. : At sea. 25.8.40.
Age 55 (Hull)

Spr. WHITTINGHAM
Royal Engineers.
Act. : Germany. 22.4.45.
Age 25. (Derby)

Sgt. F. H. WILLIAM
R.A.F.V.R.
Act. : Mulheim. 23.6.43.
Age 22. (Malvern)

E.R.A. R. WILLIAMS
H.M. sub. Stratagem.
Act. : Malacca St. 22.11.44.
Age 23. (Warwick)

Gnr. C. C. YEOMAN
S. African Artillery.
Act. : Sarteano. 28.6.44.
Age 20. (Durban, S.A.)

Sto. D. W. ZANDER
H.M.N.Z.S. Leander.
Act. : Alexandria. 7.6.41.
Age 21. (Hamilton, N.Z.)

Europe's Wartime Capitals in 1947

ROME

By F. L. SHEPLEY

ROME was untouched by the war because even to the Nazis its name was somehow more powerful than tactics ; and war went around Italy's capital. The traveller today often has not the time to go and look for the two or three isolated areas where bombs fell, towards the outskirts of the city. Thus, Rome strikes the visitor as an oasis of standing houses, untouched palaces, undisturbed roads amidst a desolation of stricken towns and villages.

Trajan's column in his Forum may still be surrounded by a wartime protection of bricks, certain other treasures may still be walled up, but that is not because there is a priority on masons for the reconstruction of dwelling houses. It is rather because no one has yet thought of taking down those baffle-walls. And one cannot, in Rome, escape the impression that there is indeed no hurry, that time is not only measured in years but in centuries.

This may explain why a dictatorship which lasted a mere generation seems, on the surface at least, to have left no visible trace. The Rome of speeches from balconies, of multi-colonnaded edifices in the new "imperial" style, of stadia and swimming pools all groaning with fasces—the triumph of Rome "resurgent" and often of bad taste : where is it now ? These things still stand out in other Italian towns. But Rome seems to have rid herself in a few months of all those spurious excrescences.

Mussolini's Palace Now a Museum

Some things have remained, but without the significance they were meant to have. Since the Mussolini Forum lost its name it has become just another forum. It is now a harmonious part of the hill on which it is built, and it blends with the widespread umbrella pine trees surrounding it. The Palazzo Venezia, Mussolini's own palace, the one with the famous balcony, is no longer a forbidding stronghold defended by black-uniformed guards. Once more it is a museum, and if small crowds sometimes gather in the piazza it is to listen to an Allied military band.

In the busy crowded streets there is much quick-moving traffic. Though most of the Allied military vehicles have gone and the official civilian petrol ration is niggardly, the roads are streaming with cars. Black petrol is just a question of money ; you can fill your tank at any garage at an average price of 1,000 lire a gallon (the official rate of exchange is 900 lire to a £). One in every six cars you see has a bogus log-book and its ownership has not got a very clear pedigree. It was recently calculated that over 50,000 cars had officially "disappeared" since Italy's collapse. After dark cars may not always be stolen—but they are nearly sure to lose some or all of their tires. A second-hand tire is worth 50,000 lire.

BUT the average Roman never had a car and has always had to cover the big distances in Rome by bus and trolley bus and tram. The German army took most of the buses. Some were recovered minus their tires. And trolley buses need tires, too. Today the infrequent buses and trolley buses groan away up the hills with scores of people hanging on to the outside—the young and healthy people who managed to prevail in the free-for-all fight at the last stop. Fortunately a host of enterprising individualists took the problem of transport into their own hands.

Three-wheeled delivery vans, light lorries, transformed cars, anything with an engine on wheels, however small, however rickety and unsafe went into service, on routes self-appointed but somehow rationally distrib-uted. They had no permit, no licence, and of course were not entitled to petrol. Allied Military Police stepped in. The Italian Police took parallel action. They were stopped ; and the town was completely paralysed. So the police took no more notice. Those who consider these ramshackle vehicles unsafe go by bicycle—you can buy one for 20,000 lire.

Twenty thousand lire is a very good salary for a bank manager. It is double the monthly wage of a clerk or a good shorthand typist, or of a skilled worker in a factory. You can obtain this sum by changing 12 pounds. With this sum you can buy 40 lb. of sugar or 35 lb. of butter, or three pairs of average shoes, or a bad suit of clothes, or 20 very good meals in a restaurant. Black market, of course. They call it the "free" market and the terminology is perhaps more exact, for there is nothing secret or underground about its transactions. You can buy all these things in the shops, over the counter,

WEEPING MEN AND WOMEN gathered at the tomb of Italy's Unknown Warrior in Rome when the Italian Peace Treaty was signed in Paris on Feb. 10, 1947. Demonstrations took place throughout the country. *Photo, Keystone*

or in one of the big open market-places, such as the famous and colourful Campo dei Fiori in the centre of the town.

At times the police prosecute the "free" merchants and confiscate their goods. The most important immediate result when that happened on a large scale quite recently was a steep increase in the "free" prices. And the consumers complained bitterly. The reason ? Rations are insufficient and the black market is, in fact, at least as important a medium of food distribution as the official channels.

The main topic of conversation of the average man or woman is the day's price of bread or spaghetti or olive oil. For them, insecurity literally means not knowing how much they will be able to afford to eat the next day. Invitations to dinner, once the normal thing for these most hospitable people, now form a subject avoided with studious care only too painfully transparent. The problem of living is further made difficult by

the rationing of electricity (two days per district in turn each week without power during the hours of daylight) and of gas (just over two hours daily at subnormal pressure). As most Romans live in blocks of six or seven floors, the rationing of electricity means non-working lifts and many a weary climb.

WITHOUT a doubt the clerks and civil servants who constitute the majority of Rome's workers are the worst off—they do not join in the ring of black marketeering and they have no subsidiary activity like many workmen. You can see some of them, having lost their jobs, standing at street corners among the numerous vendors of cigarettes, with the frayed collars of their once smart coats turned up against the cold. And you will sometimes see a timid, elderly woman, a typical middle-class mother, holding out her furtive hand to beg. That means she has already sold the clothes she is not wearing, her few jewels and her mattresses.

More likely than not she will be standing in front of one of the smart restaurants, or in Rome's "Bond Street," Via Condotti, waiting for the new-rich customers as they step into their cars. Past her brush elegant women, and young men studiously dressed in the latest Hollywood fashion. They pause and gaze in at the windows where are displayed with great taste every article which you could possibly wish for, produced by the artist-craftsmen of Italy's artisan industries. Some shops, of course, are being redecorated, many glittering American Bars are temporarily closed to acquire the latest pastel tint and the last word in daylight illumination. But the destitute bourgeois is not shocked at these contrasts which appear fantastic to the English visitor. The idea of fair distribution is Utopia—"it is nowhere"—as they disbelievingly listen to your own account.

Problems of Swollen Population

There is a terrible shortage of houses. It does not pay to build dwelling houses, as rents are pegged ; and there are many ways for the business man to double his capital in a few weeks by shrewd buying of commodities. By acquiring a third interest in a heavy lorry plying twice a week between Milan and Rome, a man can keep his family in comparative luxury. With all this, Rome still has a population which is about one million greater than it was pre-war. They came from all over the peninsula—"The Pope is the best A.A. defence," they used to say. There was a regular invasion of people who fled before the German retreat ; and when the fighting line went north of Rome, a steady trickle of refugees went through the lines.

TODAY, many cannot go back because their homes have been destroyed. Others have settled down profitably in Rome and will not leave. And there are thousands of mysterious foreigners, mostly displaced persons from Yugoslavia and Poland, with more than a sprinkling of racial refugees, ex-P.O.W., Allied deserters. If you loiter around the column in Piazza Colonna, a voice may ask in bad Italian, "Pounds, Swiss Francs ?" You are now in the "free" stock exchange.

All the while Romans pass by, many shabby, some undernourished, a few haughty "signori," seemingly supercilious and indifferent, but all of them giving an impression of vitality and energy. Most of it is expended on the task of living. But this is important : the Romans are not passive. And when, leaving the busy streets behind, you look over the capital from the Pincio, you will perhaps decide that Rome is eternal indeed and that its sores will soon be healed.

Rome By-passed by War Feels the Pinch of Peace

SMARTLY-DRESSED ROMAN CITIZENS crowd on to privately-owned lorries and trucks (1) which augment the city's scanty transport services. Distributing alms to homeless beggars (2) from Italy's war-damaged regions, a common sight on the streets. Olive oil (3), basis of Italian cookery, is severely rationed, and is eagerly sought on the "free" or black market. Repatriates from P.O.W. and concentration camps are fed and housed (4). A brisk trade in top-price flour at the black market in Piazza Vittoria (5). See facing page. PAGE 787 *Photos, New York Times Photos, Keystone*

War-Buildings are Being Blown Up in Berlin

DEMOLITION of concrete air-raid shelters in the British sector of Berlin is being carried out by order of the Allied Kommandatura, the international governing body, as part of the plan for the destruction of German fortifications and buildings erected for war purposes. This is being undertaken by the Royal Engineers.

Heavy explosive charges have to be skilfully placed in the shelters (1) to secure maximum effect. One in the Tiergarten area goes up in a tremendous column of dust and smoke (2). Some refuges (3 and 4) were immensely strong, but the huge slabs of concrete did not give the Berliners immunity from our block-buster bombs. In the background (4) is the huge Zoo "bunker," which had shelters underground and anti-aircraft guns mounted on the roof. During the Battle of Berlin thousands of people lived for days on end in the shelters.

Photos, Associated Press, Planet News

Flying Mercy Missions Over Sumatra

Immediately after VJ Day, Liberator aircraft based on Ceylon took off for the Netherlands East Indies to parachute supplies to Allied prisoners. Flight-Lieut. Sydney Moorhouse (portrait in page 284), then Public Relations Officer with No. 222 Group, R.A.F., describes one of these long flights.

WE in Ceylon had greeted the news of the Japanese capitulation with delight—especially those, like myself, who had but few months to wait for the expiration of overseas duties. The suddenness of the collapse, however, caught us in an awkward position, with one foot well off the ground to give the Japs a good kick with an invasion of Malaya. Part of the expedition was already at sea. At Minneriya, an airfield carved out of thick Ceylon jungles, aircrews and ground staffs of a couple of Liberator squadrons had been working day and night supplying the secret Malayan guerilla army with arms and ammunition across 1,500 miles of the Bay of Bengal. In no other theatre of war had guerillas been supplied at so long a range.

Now the aircraft which had been breaking records for long-distance flying were to be switched to a new task—the taking of Red Cross parcels and medical supplies to thousands of Allied prisoners of war and civilian internees, in camps throughout Malaya and the Netherlands East Indies.

A FEW days after VJ Day I drove through the thick Ceylon jungles to Minneriya. Darkness falls early in the tropics, and it was nearly midnight when I got to the camp, but there were flares on the runway and dark figures were still working on the phantom-like Liberators which were to take off in a few hours' time with the first parcels for Sumatra. It would be the first time for nearly four years that R.A.F. aircraft had carried out a peaceful mission over the Netherlands East Indies.

Shortly before five a.m. I climbed into the aircraft. Huge containers had been loaded into the bomb bay, and near the beam gunners' posts were other packages. There was even a supply of copies of SEAC—the Forces' own newspaper in the East—and periodicals from Home which had been gathered together by airmen in all parts of the camp. Dawn was just breaking as we climbed above the jungle airfield. It was not the first time I had left Ceylon at such an early hour and seen the sun mount the sky above the long line of serrated peaks which forms the interior of the island.

Heaving Indian Ocean Lay Below

On other occasions I had been in an aircraft loaded with depth-charges and carrying ammunition as it set out to hunt for enemy submarines or keep guard over some vital convoy. This time there were Red Cross parcels instead of depth-charges, and the beam gunner, looking at the empty ammunition racks, remarked, "I hope the Japs know the war is over and don't send up any Zeros after us!" The crew I was flying with had been mainly concerned with dropping arms to the guerilla armies in Malaya and only the skipper, Flight-Lieut. F. F. R. Charlton, had been on a mission to Sumatra before.

For five hours we flew through low cloud and occasional rain-showers. A thousand feet below us was the grey, heaving mass of the Indian Ocean. "The times 've gazed into that blooming mass and thought I saw a periscope!" one of the crew remarked. "Now when it's all over I suppose we shall be told the Japs never had any perishing submarines here—or something silly."

I thought of the hectic days of August 1944—only a year before—when every time I looked in at the operations room at Group Headquarters the sea around the Maldive Islands seemed full of lifeboats being plotted. Catalinas of 222 Group, R.A.F., were responsible for detecting over 150 survivors from torpedoed ships at that time. And that had been the Japs' final fling as regards submarine warfare in the Indian Ocean.

Soon after nine o'clock the wireless operator, Flying-Officer G. L. Bakes, announced that we were passing the extremity of the Nicobars. I looked out of the beam gunner's opening but could see nothing of the islands through the mist. However, the radar "eye" had spotted them all right and enabled the navigator, Flying-Officer J. A. d'Alpuget, to set his course for Sabang, the little fortified island which lies off the northern tip of Sumatra.

Another hour passed. Some of us slept, others read. There was no need for the vigilant look-out now. Suddenly interest was aroused by sight of the conical-shaped hills of Sabang ahead. Fifteen months earlier the enemy naval base there had been raided by carrier-borne aircraft of the then Eastern Fleet. Eighteen months before that it had been bombed by Catalinas operating from Koggala, Ceylon's flying-boat station, in one of the most daring operations of the war. Not until many months afterwards was the identity of the raiding aircraft disclosed; the Japs were led to believe that we still had a carrier at large in Eastern waters. Today as we flew over Sabang we saw British warships of the East Indies Fleet anchored in the harbour and the White Ensign fluttering in the breeze.

ON, then, at low height across the narrow straits and over Sumatra itself. From the air it looked as green as Ceylon. We passed over jungle-clad hills, over fields of paddy, and over dismal stretches of mangrove swamp. "What a spot for a forced landing!" one of the crew remarked. For a couple of hours we were flying over the island. Villagers and farmers came out and looked up at us, some waving, and a couple of men in a sampan flourished their paddles as we passed.

Soon, Flying-Officer d'Alpuget announced that we were approaching the target. Parcels

FROM THIS AIRSTRIP AT MINNERIYA, Ceylon, flew R.A.F. Liberators to supply the guerilla armies of Malaya. After VJ Day aircraft regularly travelled between 2,500 and 3,000 miles to drop Red Cross supplies to P.O.W. camps in the Netherlands East Indies. Minneriya was the starting point of the flight described in this story. PAGE 789 *Photo, R.A.F. Official*

AT MEDAN IN SUMATRA were many P.O.W., and aircraft from Ceylon flew over there (left) soon after the Japanese capitulation. Streets were thronged with waving, cheering crowds, and in the P.O.W. camp (right) the occupants gesticulated wildly as the aeroplane circled round to identify the dropping zone for supplies so sorely needed by the half-starved men, women and children. Unfortunately, the prisoners had still to undergo the horrors and trials of the Indonesian uprising against the Netherlands Government.
Photos, R.A.F. Official

and packages were arranged for the "dropping." It reminded me of the day—twelve months before—when I went out in a Dakota to drop supplies to the 14th Army, fighting its way to the Chindwin, but then, of course, we had to keep our eyes open for enemy fighters. There *were* enemy fighters to be seen today—50 or 60 of them, arranged on either side of the runway of Medan airfield. The rear gunner was looking at his empty cartridge racks again. "Yes, it looks as though they know the war is over now," he remarked, thoughtfully.

THE spot for the dropping was a large open space easily distinguishable by an ornamental fountain at one end. Close by was the Roman Catholic College in which the prisoners were believed to be housed. As soon as the Liberator began circling the inhabitants of the town rushed out, and before long we were flying over roads crammed with people. Tablecloths, garments and flags were waved in wild delirium. Whatever the later reactions of the Indonesians, there is no doubt that they were overjoyed at the idea of liberation from the Japanese.

The pilot pressed a buzzer, which was a signal for dropping to begin, and we pushed the packages out through the exit in the floor behind the beam gunner. Each had a parachute cord attached to a stronger cord running across the opening ; as they entered the slipstream the cords reached breaking point and the parachutes opened to send the goods sailing to earth. As the first batch touched the ground I saw people running across the open space to collect them.

IT was great fun sending down those packages. We had a sense of satisfaction that never came with the dropping of bombs or the shooting-up of transport. We made three runs over the target, and each time we passed over the town the crowds seemed denser than ever. As we pulled out again I was glad to see that every package had landed safely in the prescribed area and all were being loaded into a car. Evidently, the "agents" (who had been busy organizing

a guerilla force only a few days before) had got things well tied-up with the Japs.

We flew back to Ceylon through rainstorms and low cloud. As we put down at Minneriya the ground crews, who had been working throughout the previous night, were there to see us come back. "How's it gone, sir ?" I heard one of them ask the

skipper. "Grand !" was the reply. The ground staffs hurried off to bed. Tomorrow they would be loading more parcels into the Liberators. For this operation continued for several weeks, and not until plans were well under way for the prisoners and internees to be repatriated did those R.A.F. lads get the respite they so richly deserved.

How We Breached the Atlantic Wall

With grenade and bayonet and tommy-gun Royal Marine Commandos went in from the sea and attacked on D-Day . . . Here is a close-up of swift-moving battle against Germans entrenched behind "impregnable" defences. The vivid recollection is by Major W. R. Sendall, R.M.

THE night before D-Day was the longest I have ever known. Our little L.C.I., bearing half the H.Q. of the 4th Commando Brigade, heaved and rolled on her slow progress across the Channel to the intense discomfort of all on board. Dawn of the great day revealed a leaden sky overhanging grey sea whipped into a sullen swell by the wind.

Overhead I heard the roar of hidden bombers, and saw on the skyline a low coast from which, at intervals, church spires needled up through a bank of smoke. The bombardment was in full swing, but we could see little of it. We stooged about in the swell for an interminable time till we saw a long line of little assault craft, bearing The North Shore Regiment of Canada, pitching and tossing as they passed us. Someone waved from one of the packed craft and we waved back. Excitement quickened and the seasickness was forgotten. In the wake of The North Shores our craft turned in towards the distant beach.

I went below to collect up my maps, and by the time I returned to the deck the yellow beach of St. Aubin was just ahead—and the sea-wall, festooned with barbed wire. Beyond was a row of villas, one blazing furiously, bright orange of the flames glaring through the black smoke pall. Fully rigged, we lay down on deck, making for the beach at full speed. What happened to the left and right

during the following minutes I never knew. As if in blinkers, all I could see was a section of yellow beach, a piece of sea-wall with its barbed wire frieze, red-tiled villas and the bright orange fire rushing towards us.

The craft grounded. Long narrow ramps shot out, and the first men sprang up from the deck to go over. I heard no bullets in the confusion of noise, only the surge and crash of the sea and a sharp crackling that might have been the fire, but the leading man collapsed at the head of the ramp and two or three of his comrades flattened out beside him. I ran forward crouching, but men rose in front of me, pulling the wounded from the head of the ramp. Then over we went, staggering heavy-laden into the waist-deep surge that was heaving great baulks of timber like matchsticks to and fro.

MY sodden boots sank into the soft wet sand as I struggled into the shelter of the sea-wall. Both our craft were beached and the men were struggling to get bulky signals equipment down the ramps that were swinging wildly in the waves. We rushed back to hold them steady, and saw mortar bursts appearing in the sea just astern of the craft ; and the Naval ratings, firing heavy Oerlikons over our heads, were blasting the enemy in the row of villas. In a few minutes we were all ashore, filing along under the sea-wall to a gap in the minefields and through this on to a road. Pushing forward through a dense blanket

Commandos Surge Ashore Under Fire at St. Aubin

ROYAL MARINES 4th COMMANDO BRIGADE headquarters landed at St. Aubin, Normandy (upper), on June 6, 1944, and met with desperate resistance from the German defenders who remained out of sight in prepared positions. Author of the story in facing page is the third figure from the right (upper), assisting with motor-cycle. As assault troops the Commandos had no heavy transport with them, but jeeps, hand-carts and light and heavy motor-cycles had to be manhandled ashore for the advance inland (lower).

Photos. British Official

Motto : "Strike and Return"

NO. 460 SQUADRON

AN all-Australian Squadron, No. 460 began training at Breighton, Yorks, in January 1942, equipped with Wellington aircraft. Operational sorties were carried out in the following March, the first against Emden. In May it took part in the 1,000-bomber raid on Cologne, and undertook many mine-laying missions. In August 1942 it was converted to Halifaxes, these being replaced by Lancasters in November.

Spezia and Stettin were among targets attacked during February 1943. In the following month the Squadron moved to Binbrook, Lincs. The Australians were in the Battle of Hamburg in July and also bombed Cologne and Turin. The experimental station at Peenemunde was attacked in August, and Berlin eight times in November and December.

OF nine major attacks made in January 1944, six were on the German capital. Fortifications on the French coast and communication centres were targets during the weeks immediately preceding D-Day. The veteran Lancaster, G for George, having completed 90 trips, was presented to the War Museum at Canberra, Australia. The Squadron gave close support to the British 2nd Army in Normandy during July and August, by night and by day.

In February 1945 the German town of Cleve was almost totally destroyed in a night attack that cleared the way for the advancing British and Canadian troops. Chemnitz and Dresden were bombed in March to assist the Russian armies. By April 10, 1945, the Squadron had carried out 5,000 sorties, dropped nearly 24,000 tons of bombs, and flown 4,000,000 miles. At the end of the war it was engaged in flying food to the Netherlands and picking up released P.O.W. for repatriation.

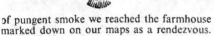

of pungent smoke we reached the farmhouse marked down on our maps as a rendezvous.

Shedding my heavier equipment here, I made contact with the H.Q. of 48 Royal Marine Commando, which had landed on our left. The Commando had been exposed to the full fire of the St. Aubin strongpoint, against which the North Shores were still hammering, and had suffered heavily. Many of them had swum ashore considerable distances, though the strong undertow had swept even powerful swimmers away. Nevertheless, the leading troop had already set out down the coast road for the next village, Langrune, which was their objective.

I followed cautiously but saw no sign of the enemy in the shattered streets, though an occasional bullet wailed overhead. I reached the big church in Langrune without incident and, as there seemed to be little resistance, returned to Brigade in St. Aubin, looking in on the way at the Canadians who

were still battering at the tough strongpoint, smashing their way through a huge barricade of logs with which the enemy had blocked the narrow street.

IT was not until late in the evening that I heard of the sharp check the Commando had encountered when attempting to force their way through the narrow defiles of the mined and barricaded streets to attack the strongpoint on the Langrune seafront. The attack could not be renewed that night, as information came of an expected enemy counter-attack. As we were the only troops between the enemy in Douvres La Delivrande and the crowded beaches, and were very thin on the ground, every available man was ordered into the line.

I spent most of the night scratching for myself a weapon-pit under the church wall on the outskirts of St. Aubin, using an entrenching tool with a rough improvised

ADVANCE OF THE ROYAL MARINE COMMANDOS and The 1st Battalion The North Shore Regiment of Canada was held up at Langrune by a German strongpoint and an anti-tank wall. But our tanks (above) and a self-propelled gun cleared the way. The field beyond the low hedge was thickly strewn with mines.
Photo, British Official

handle that quickly raised blisters, occasionally straightening my aching back to watch the quick streams of coloured tracer that flamed up from the beaches to beat off enemy sneak raiders coming in low overhead. The anticipated counter-attack never came, and in the morning I went back to Langrune, where the assault on the strongpoint was being renewed.

THE only approach to this hedgehog was by way of two narrow streets, both enfiladed by German snipers firing from the roofs of reinforced houses on the front. One of these was hopelessly blocked by mines and wire and swept by machine-gun fire, so the attack had to be directed down the other street. This terminated in a cross-roads in the centre of which was a concrete machine-gun cupola and, beyond, a thick, heavily reinforced concrete anti-tank wall. On the previous day the Marines had penetrated as far as the cross-roads and knocked out the machine-gun, but the wall barred all further progress.

As I came up, the leading troop was clearing the houses up to the cross-roads once more, operating through back gardens where they had some cover from the German riflemen. As I stood in a gap between these houses, beside an officer of the Army Film

Unit, one of those riflemen put a bullet through the "bellows" of the camera slung around my companion's neck. We dived into cover with some promptness, and with my rifle I put three bullets through the hole in the roof-top indicated to me as the sniper's hide-out, with what success I never discovered—for an armoured M.10 self-propelled gun, just then moving cautiously down the street, swung round to bear upon the house and demolished it with a couple of 75-mm. shells.

THAT gun, loaned by the Canadians, was our battering ram. The Marines cleared a path for it by exploding some of the mines, and it sat down near the cross-roads to hammer at point-blank range at the wall, huge chips flying off in all directions as each shell smashed into the concrete. Meanwhile, the Germans were dropping a continual rain of mortar shells into the back gardens as our men probed forward. For 90 minutes the S.P. gun battered the wall. By the time its ammunition was exhausted a breach had been made barely practicable for a storming party. A Sherman from the Royal Marine Armoured Support Group then moved up to carry on with the work.

When the upper part of the wall was demolished, the assault troop of the Commando, waiting crouched in the gardens, was ordered in. They dashed across the bullet-swept road to seize possession of the two reinforced houses on each side of the wall. This jump forward was executed in a few minutes and was a first lodgement within the defences. The Marines discovered beyond the wall a deep ditch that prohibited the introduction of a tank, so another troop, armed this time with picks and shovels and high explosive, dashed across to lay charges in the captured houses.

I WAITED for the explosion, lying flat in the road beside the Sherman. With a roar, half a house went up and a shower of brickbats hurtled down upon us through the thick dust cloud, and I pressed myself hard against the ground, trying to squeeze as much of my body as I could under my steel helmet. The Marines then proceeded to shovel the debris from the demolished houses into the trench, to form a causeway across which the tank could make its way.

All this while, slowly but surely, the assault troop had been driving the Germans from one house after another, forcing them back on to their seaward defences. When the causeway was complete I nipped out of shelter to signal forward the Sherman that was sitting closed up in the middle of the cross-roads. I had just recovered the shelter of the houses when a bullet from ever-vigilant snipers chipped a piece of brickwork from the corner I had just rounded. The maddening thing about this harassing fire was that we could never see the enemy. They had tunnelled from cellar to cellar of the houses and could pass unseen from one to another, so that by the time we could open fire on one position the German rifleman had moved elsewhere. The first sure sight of a German I had was when they were driven out and surrendered.

The Sherman slowly lumbered forward over the rubble that filled the ditch, to debouch on to the wide promenade of the sea-front. At this point one track slipped into a slit trench, and the armoured monster lurched over at an awkward angle. But it was still possible to bring its Browning machine-gun to bear, and with this it blasted the promenade.

BEHIND its spray of bullets the Marines went in with a cheer to drive the enemy from his last refuges, the honeycomb of trenches and dug-outs overlooking the beach. With grenade, bayonet and tommy-gun our men went forward ; and the Germans had no stomach for such close-quarters stuff with some of the best bayonet fighters in the British forces. They streamed up with their hands above their heads. And so the Marine Commandos made an end to one of the bastions of the Atlantic Wall.

buy, then—poof, they are all gone ! Yes ? At the front our soldiers have many of these things, and you too must suffer discomfort sometimes. It is the war, yes ? "

"Herr Directeur," I replied bluntly, "when we were fighting we expected to rough it. But when we were captured we were told that for us the war was over. You want the men to work for you. They have no choice about that. But they'll make up their beds in the road before they sleep in here ! "

P.O.W. CAMP COMMANDER at Deutsch Eylau, in East Prussia, was this burly feld-webel (sergeant)—his job no sinecure. He had to be ever on his guard against efforts of his British charges to outwit him.

Brisk Battle of Wits in Stalag XXB

During the two years that he was British Camp Leader in Stalag XXB the narrator of these experiences, Sgt. C. J. Sadgrove, of the Royal Signals, participated in notable victories over domineering and tricky Huns in such matters as conditions of labour and personal comfort. See also page 670.

IT was in April 1943 that I became a camp leader among British P.O.W. For two and a half years prior to that I had been first a worker, then (with the discovery of the Geneva Convention under which senior N.C.O.s are excused anything but supervisory work) one of a number of party leaders in a large camp at Klein Bartelsee, near Bromberg.

The work we had been doing had seemed innocent enough at first—trench digging, pipe laying, and so on, for a big new factory in the woods. As the plans developed, machinery was introduced and camouflaging of the buildings was undertaken on a large scale. Our suspicions were aroused. Was this job of ours as innocent as it had seemed ? It was not. Gunpowder and other explosives were to be produced in the factory.

QUESTIONS were asked by the sergeant-major in charge of us, confidential reports were sent to our Chief Man of Confidence in Thorn, and finally we were moved. It was a big transfer, involving our own camp of about 500 men and at least three others of similar size. The move was effected in

cattle-trucks, and some 2,000 men of Stalag XXA found themselves on the lists of Stalag XXB, with its H.Q. in Marienburg.

We did not all travel to the same place ; the train distributed groups over a wide area. My party of 58 arrived in the little town of Deutsch Eylau, in East Prussia. Eight were chosen to work in a dairy, and the main body (later doubled in number) moved on across the town, over the river on the bank of which a huge chimney was pointed out to us as denoting the sawmill where the men were to be employed. Our billet was a two-storeyed house on the waterside and within a minute's walk of the factory. The place was filthy, the beds swarmed with bugs. I sought out our commandant, the German control officer and a director of the firm.

" We can't sleep here ! " I told them in my best post-Dunkirk German. " The place is alive. Come and see for yourselves." They picked their way gingerly through the dirt and rubbish that littered the floor. " Oh, a few little bugs—that's nothing," said the director, naturally anxious to treat the matter lightly. " I will some disinfectant

That did it ! Commandant, control officer, and director were all trying to speak at once. We were to be sent back to Stalag for punishment, we were to be shot for our impudence, everything was to happen to us. In the end we moved out for a fortnight while wooden partitions were taken down and burned, floorboards prised up and replaced, ceilings and walls stripped and renewed, beds and blankets cleaned, and the whole building redecorated and disinfected throughout.

I WON'T pretend we saw no more bugs. Their demise was to come nearly two years later, when the Russians shelled the place. But we felt we had gained our first victory in Deutsch Eylau. We had, but the director tried to get me returned to Stalag for refusing to work. My interpretation of the Geneva Convention was not enough for him. He had to hear it from the authorities before I was allowed to stay.

We had many victories on that working party. One concerned the breakfast break of 20 minutes. This left our men insufficient time to return to the billet for a snack (which included the brewing of Red Cross tea—when we had any), and so an application for a further ten minutes was made—and granted.

The new arrangement was to operate from the following Monday, I told the fellows when we were assembled for roll-call that week-end. They passed on the information to the civilians with whom they worked, and were laughed at. They, the civilians, had been at the factory for 25 years and in all that time had never had more than 20 minutes for breakfast, and it wasn't likely the change would be made for prisoners of war. How wrong they were !

Another victory came about through football. Seldom a week-end passed without a match against a neighbouring working

SEATED WITH THE MEN HE LED as a working party when a prisoner at Stalag XXB, Marienburg, West Prussia, Sgt. C. J. Sadgrove is in the centre of the front row. The photograph was taken in 1943, and the healthy appearance of the men is due rather to the Red Cross parcels they received than to the German rations.

party. One camp which interested us more than most was eight or nine miles away, and we had to march there and back. "Why not get one of the firm's lorries?" someone suggested. We thought he was joking. But the day of the proposed match would be a holiday, so the lorry would be free, and we had our own drivers, so no civilians need be involved. Chancing to meet the control officer at the station after a trip into stalag, I tackled him on the subject.

He laughed, too, at first ; but we got the lorry. It involved several interviews with the firm's director, interviews in which I was told that all the men weren't working as hard as they might, and that such kindness as we were receiving didn't come the way of German prisoners. But we were quite hardened to such propaganda, and listened calf-like to anything that brought results in our favour.

I HAD that lorry thrown up at me a few weeks later, following a complaint I had made to the Chief British Man of Confidence regarding work some of my men were expected to do. My report reached the local control officer by a devious route, and one day he arrived at the camp almost foaming at the mouth.

"When it's a favour you want—a lorry to go to a football match—you stop in the street to speak to me ! " he stormed. "When it's a complaint you have to make, you go behind my back and report it to stalag. What sort of a fool have you made me look in the eyes of the authorities?" I sought to explain my action, but he ordered the commandant and me to accompany him to the factory. In the carpeted office of the director I stated my case, which concerned the cutting and packing by prisoners of veneer wood which we knew (but were unable to prove) was being used in the production of aeroplane propellers.

For Propellers and Block-Houses

The firm's reply was that the final destination of the wood was unknown to them ; and that, even if it were being used for propellers as I suggested, the prisoners were not making them, and were therefore not being directly employed on the production of equipment for war. And so victory on that occasion went to the other side, but we levelled the score a few weeks later. This time our complaint concerned wood which German soldiers were bringing to the mill in the form of tree-trunks, and which our men were expected to cut up into planks by means of a block-band saw. Naturally, our men cribbed at having to work with the German soldiers, but within a day or two they had learned what they wanted : the wood was being used in the construction of block-houses. I complained to our commandant, a fatherly old man who wished us no harm, but he was too fearful of his position to argue our case. So I went direct to the head of the firm, told him that the work the men were doing was a direct breach of the Geneva Convention and that I would have to make a further report to stalag. It was largely bluff, but it worked. After that, when uniformed Germans brought wood into the mill, our men stood by while the Germans cut it.

construction of an all-weather highway from Alice Springs (see map in page 486, Vol. 5).

Looking at last to her defences in the Pacific, Australia dispatched her 8th Division to Malaya late in 1941. It was considerably weakened by the loss of the 23rd Brigade which was detached to Darwin. It in turn detached one battalion to Rabaul in New Britain and the remainder of the brigade stood by, not for the defence of Darwin but to be dissipated over an even greater area. Their role, on the outbreak of war in the Pacific, was to move in and safeguard vital Dutch and Portuguese bases on essential lines of communication to Singapore.

THE Pearl Harbour disaster was their signal to move, one battalion proceeding to Koepang, in Dutch Timor, another to Amboina ; simultaneously, a company of Commandos landed at Dilli in Portuguese Timor and took over the undefended airfield despite loud protestations from neutral Portugal which dispatched troops to take over from the Australians—but before they had completed the lengthy sea voyage from Portugal to Timor the Japs were in occupation. Dilli soon became a busy air base for Japanese bombers hammering Darwin.

With the myth of the impregnability of the Singapore fortress exploded, these isolated Australian garrisons—in hundreds where thousands would have been inadequate—were enveloped in the mighty flood of the Japanese advance. Rabaul was engulfed even before Singapore fell, and Amboina seized about the time General Percival was forced to surrender. Timor was next on the list of Japanese invasion.

On the morning of February 15, 1942, a convoy of Australian and American ships slipped out of Darwin harbour carrying reinforcements of men and material in an attempt to bolster up the Koepang garrison to meet the threatening blow. There was one regiment of United States artillery which had not been able to reach the Philippines, an odd battalion of Australian pioneers and a few other bits and pieces.

On the Eve of the Great Debacle

Two days later, with Timor in sight, after beating off heavy enemy air attacks the convoy received orders from General Wavell's headquarters in Java to about-turn and return to Darwin. Just after noon on February 18 the convoy nosed its way into the crowded harbour. Troops disembarked immediately, but their equipment was left on board pending orders regarding future movement. That was the confused situation on the eve of the Darwin debacle. There was no radar in the area, no fighters based on Darwin. The solitary 3·7-in. anti-

I Saw the Terror That Came to Darwin

Directly threatened by the Japanese southward drive, the northern Australian port of Darwin was lamentably unprepared for the air attack which wrecked its harbour and airfield on February 19, 1942. The story of the disaster is told by Roy Macartney, Major A.I.F., who investigated the incident for the Military History Section of the Australian Army.

DARWIN harbour was a shipping grave-yard when our Sunderland flying-boat touched down on its waters in early May 1942. Mast-tops just showing above the water and rusting hulks littering the shores bore silent witness to the first shattering Japanese air raid of February 19. Security had drawn a veil across the Japanese success scored the first time bombs fell on Australian soil. For a time I, like every other man in the area, was so busy preparing to repel invasion should it come that I learned only a few details of what happened during that first sensational surprise raid.

Then the Military History Section of the Australian Army contacted me and asked me to investigate the raid and narrate as accurately as possible, for historical purposes, exactly what happened. From my investigations emerged a story of a disaster which in many ways resembled that of Pearl Harbour. Ill-prepared as were the Darwin defences, what forces there were on February 19, 1942, had been caught napping. Despite half an hour's warning that Japanese bombers were approaching, these were over the town before the alarm was given and when the skies cleared of enemy aircraft the crowded Darwin harbour had been practically cleared of shipping—a dozen merchantmen had been lost and hundreds of American and Australian sailors killed in the terrible holocaust which swept the harbour.

HERE is the story of the debacle as I was able to piece it together. Before the war Australia maintained a small garrison manning six-inch coastal batteries guarding the Darwin harbour, and there were a few hundred infantry and ancillary troops. They were housed in the commodious modern Larrakia Barracks, standing on a headland overlooking the harbour and about as easy to camouflage as the Empire State Building,

New York. With similar short-sightedness the R.A.A.F. had constructed a £2,000,000 airport just outside Darwin, with airmen's billets standing high on piles in serried ranks. The piles defeated the enemy white ant but presented the two-legged enemy from the north with a bombardier's dream of a target.

Darwin was practically dependent on sea lines of communication, there being little more than an embryo track across the thousand-mile stretch of desert between the northern port and Alice Springs in the middle of the continent. During the first two years of war, while Australia was concentrating on her overseas expeditionary forces, little was done to prepare Darwin for war beyond the commencement of the

CAPSIZED AFTER A DIRECT HIT by a Japanese bomb, this cargo vessel lay beside the twisted jetty, which was also severely damaged during Japanese attacks on Port Darwin, Northern Australia, on Feb. 19, 1942. The scanty and unprepared defences could do little to protect the town or the mass of shipping then in the harbour.

Photo, Planet News

WRECKAGE OF A JAPANESE ZERO FIGHTER shot down during the attack on Port Darwin just missed the barracks, which also had been damaged by bombs. The buildings are set on piles to escape the ravages of white ants. Two attacks on the Australian port, as described in these pages, left it without means of defence.
Photo, Planet News

aircraft battery defending the harbour had done only one shoot with full-charge ammunition. The town had practically no A.R.P. slit trenches, and shelters were few. February 19 was D-Day for the Japanese at Koepang and Dilli. To cover these operations Darwin had to be neutralized.

Early that morning, nine American Kittyhawks took off from Darwin for Koepang. They had arrived the previous night from Sydney on their way north to help stem the Japanese tide. The Americans were not far out across the Arafura Sea when Koepang signalled that the weather was too bad to land. R.A.A.F. operations room accordingly called the Americans back. Not long afterwards, a message was received by pedal wireless from Father McGrath, Roman Catholic Missionary on Bathurst Island, advising that a large force of aircraft had been sighted overhead flying towards Darwin. It was again the story of Pearl Harbour. R.A.A.F. operations room for nearly half an hour took no action on the warning, believing the priest had sighted the American fighters returning.

With Little Fuel and No Height

Seven of the nine Kittyhawks had landed when the enemy force hove in sight. It consisted of 17 heavy bombers in formation, 54 dive-bombers and 18 Zero fighters. The Zeros made quick work of the two still airborne Kittyhawks, caught with little fuel and no height. The formation of heavy bombers was nearly over the town when the alarm was given, and the 3.7-in. anti-aircraft guns opened fire. Flying in their favourite shallow V-formation the enemy planes pattern-bombed the foreshore, scoring a direct hit on the jetty, killing 20 labourers and isolating two ships lying at the end.

Meanwhile, the Zeros had dealt with the other seven American fighters which all struggled gamely to take the air. With the enemy waiting to pounce with their advantage of height, not one of the Americans gained a thousand feet. Although the buildings along the foreshore had been reduced to rubble around them, the anti-aircraft gunners stuck to their guns and the "green" crews got off hundreds of rounds in the crowded 50 minutes of the first raid. Dive-bombers picked off all the ships in the harbour, one by one, as Australians and Americans fought back with light automatic machine-guns. The Barossa and Neptuna, caught tied to the jetty, were soon in flames.

Oil from a punctured oil-line drained into the sea. Soon it caught fire and the water around the wharf blazed fiercely. The British Monarch, an oil tanker, was another early hit and set alight. Burning oil from her tanks spread over the waters of the harbour. Men drowned in the heavy oil, or burned where the flames held sway. Dive-bombers methodically, almost leisurely, added Zeelandia, Meigs, Mauna Loa, and Port Mar to their list of victims. The American destroyer Peary, fighting furiously, could not slip her rear moorings before she received a direct hit which disabled her. Drifting helplessly she fought to the last, two-thirds of her complement going down with the ship.

For 50 minutes the slaughter continued, while dive-bombers also concentrated on the R.A.A.F. airfield. Hangars went up in flames while Zero fighters raced back and forth at only 50 feet, machine-gunning the station. Men lay helplessly in slit trenches, longing for just one Bofors ; but there wasn't a single one in the area. A wing commander, standing in the open with a Lewis gun to his shoulder, was killed by a cannon shell.

At last the skies cleared, hungry flames still licking the sheet of oil covering the waters of the harbour. The townsfolk emerged from where they had sheltered, and numbed, bewildered, set to work to get their casualties and the burned survivors from the harbour to hospital. There was apprehension throughout the town, but no panic. Men wanted arms to fight, but none were available. They wanted direction, and strong leadership at this stage might have prevented the terror which later in the day gripped the populace. Shortly after noon Japanese bombers launched a second heavy attack, 54 high-level bombers this time destroying what was left of the R.A.A.F. station. Again the A.A. gunners toiled manfully, increasing their bag to two bombers and three fighters, plus five probables.

Ordered to Disperse to the Bush

Following this second raid which the unarmed, unsheltered civilians had helplessly witnessed, many panicked. They thought invasion imminent and, to escape capture, most headed south on the 1,000-mile trek to Alice Springs (see page 701, Vol. 5). On the R.A.A.F. station, men had been caught at mess by the second raid. An order was issued that they should disperse to the bush, where they would be fed safe from the danger of again being caught in mess queues. Communications had broken down, however, and the order had to be passed from mouth to mouth. In the prevailing excitement it soon grew to "Take to the bush. Every man for himself."

Nightfall found Darwin in a terrible state. Wounded were still limping up from the harbour lit by the fitful glow of fires. Garrison troops stood fast to their posts, but with all air cover gone, no supply lines on which to depend, Darwin was ripe for the picking. However, the enemy was not then ready to seize the foothold on the Australian mainland. During the ensuing days battle-tried veterans from the Middle East returned to Australia and were rushed to the north. American equipment and planes poured into the country and soon their engineers, with Australian assistance, had ripped new airstrips out of the bush, erected radar equipment and honeycombed the area with A.A. guns of all calibres.

Armies of Australian Servicemen and civilians sweated to complete the 1,000-mile all-weather road across the desert and soon the Darwin force was fed by a grand supply line. Within two months the Australians were ready to repel almost any invasion attempt. In the same period, American fighter pilots wrested aerial supremacy over Darwin from the enemy still trying to batter the port into submission.

End of a Long Story

The Editor Says Good-Bye to His Readers

Photo, Howard Coster

With this number THE WAR ILLUSTRATED is brought to an end, not from any lack of interesting pictorial and literary matter wherewith it might have been continued through several more volumes, but simply because, having arrived at the conclusion of its tenth volume, we may claim to have covered every happening of any importance in the whole course of the Second World War, and for almost two years of the strangely uneasy Peace. In closing down the publication it is impossible to say, with any pretence to foreknowledge, whither the world is heading : towards a new era of true peace and reconstruction, or towards the incalculable catastrophe of a third and final world war.

One thing seems clear : the threat, almost the certainty of wars in the Far East. On these matters of fearful importance we may each have our own opinions, and one man's guess is as good as another, but although nearly sixteen years of my editorial life have been devoted to chronicling the events of the two greatest wars with which innumerable historians of a future day will have to concern themselves, universal bewilderment, in which the aftermath of the second has left all the nations and their elected or imposed leaders, has left this editor at least with no confidence to offer any opinion or to attempt a forecast.

Back in 1920. I was less reticent in both respects, when producing the *Universal Encyclopedia.* Accused by a stupid critic of being unfair to "our late enemies," I retorted in my editorial notes of July 27, 1920 : "I am fully persuaded that 'our late enemies' are also our present potential enemies, and that they will be our inevitable future enemies," which almost put me amongst the prophets !

But it was not part of THE WAR ILLUSTRATED'S function to anticipate, far less to prophesy : our business has been from week to week and later on when paper restrictions limited us to fortnightly issues, to record and to illustrate the war news after it had been verified and censored. And this, despite unforeseen and unprecedented difficulties, we have contrived to do through all those dreadful years of war. The ten volumes which we have now completed are unique in the world today. Those of our readers who have collected and bound the whole series may congratulate themselves on possessing a pictorial and literary record of a kind which can never be rivalled and could only have been brought into existence by a method of publishing that had stood the test of time, under the same editorship, throughout the First World War. Our ample indexes to each of the volumes enable the reader to trace down almost every incident from Hitler's attack on Poland, Sept. 1, 1939, to the Nazi surrender at Rheims on May 7, 1945, and the end of Japanese resistance on August 14, 1945.

Beyond these years of actual hostilities there were the long-drawn-out proceedings at Nuremberg—the reader may compare the shrunken figure of the sinister Ribbentrop there awaiting his doom with the smiling Ribbentrop shown on page 29 of our first volume, shaking hands with Stalin on concluding the Nazi-Soviet pact which was the signal for the war to begin. In our thousands of actual photographs the reader has the richest wartime collection of war photographs that could ever be gathered within the compass of ten volumes, and endless instruction may be obtained by contrasting those of one year with those of another.

Every aspect of the war can be studied in our picture pages, from the first air raid on Great Britain (Firth of Forth, Oct. 16, 1939) seen in an exclusive photograph published on page 297, Vol. 1, to the havoc of one of the last V2s that fell on London's Farringdon Market (page 61, Vol. 9) ; the whole course of the U-boat war ; Montgomery's epic advance, first with the 8th Army from El Alamein to Tunis and on into Italy, then with 21st Army Group from Normandy to the Baltic ; but these are only details of the whole immense and complicated story as it may be traced here in picture and prose. And that story for the largest part of the time was the continuous concern of Maj.-Gen. Sir Charles Gwynn, K.C.B., D.S.O., who mainly confined himself to elucidating the ever-changing movements of the armies, while Mr. F. E. McMurtrie, A.I.N.A., the naval expert, told in each successive number the story of the war at sea, and Capt. Norman Macmillan, M.C., A.F.C., wrote so interestingly and expertly on the development of the aerial war. To all three, and many others too numerous to mention, I am deeply indebted for their highly skilled collaboration and the authority which their expert contributions brought to our pages.

Correspondents innumerable throughout the British Empire and Commonwealth have written letters of congratulation and encouragement during those laborious and exciting years. To the hundreds of thousands of faithful readers who have stayed the long and trying course I now say "Good-bye," and give thanks for such loyal support, while expressing the hope that there may be no future occasion for such a recording of comparable events in the lifetime of the youngest amongst us. As I write there are many ominous clouds still overhanging a world distressed, but

" My own hope is, a sun will pierce
   The thickest cloud earth ever stretched."

J. A. Hammerton

Printed in England and published every alternate Friday by the Proprietors, THE AMALGAMATED PRESS, LTD., The Fleetway House, Farringdon Street, London, E.C.4. Registered for transmission by Canadian Magazine Post. Sole Agents for Australia and New Zealand :: Messrs. Gordon & Gotch, Ltd.; and for South Africa : Central News Agency, Ltd. April 11, 1947. S.S. *Editorial Address :* JOHN CARPENTER HOUSE. WHITEFRIARS. LONDON. E.C.4.

FAMILY
ROLL OF HONOUR

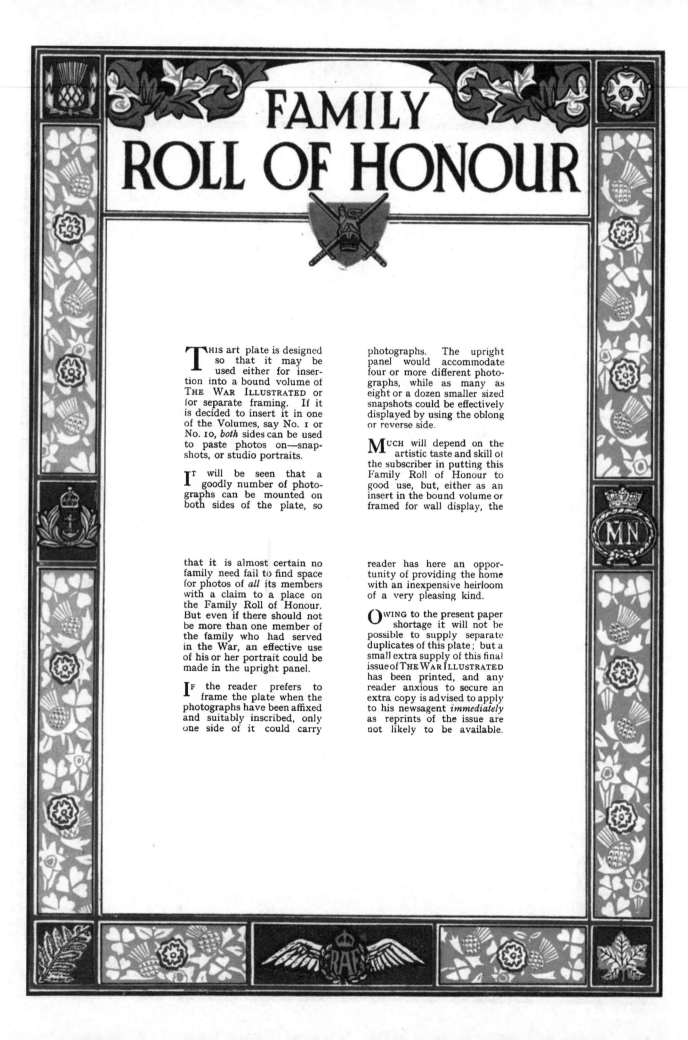

THIS art plate is designed so that it may be used either for insertion into a bound volume of THE WAR ILLUSTRATED or for separate framing. If it is decided to insert it in one of the Volumes, say No. 1 or No. 10, *both* sides can be used to paste photos on—snapshots, or studio portraits.

IT will be seen that a goodly number of photographs can be mounted on both sides of the plate, so

that it is almost certain no family need fail to find space for photos of *all* its members with a claim to a place on the Family Roll of Honour. But even if there should not be more than one member of the family who had served in the War, an effective use of his or her portrait could be made in the upright panel.

IF the reader prefers to frame the plate when the photographs have been affixed and suitably inscribed, only one side of it could carry

photographs. The upright panel would accommodate four or more different photographs, while as many as eight or a dozen smaller sized snapshots could be effectively displayed by using the oblong or reverse side.

MUCH will depend on the artistic taste and skill of the subscriber in putting this Family Roll of Honour to good use, but, either as an insert in the bound volume or framed for wall display, the

reader has here an opportunity of providing the home with an inexpensive heirloom of a very pleasing kind.

OWING to the present paper shortage it will not be possible to supply separate duplicates of this plate; but a small extra supply of this final issue of THE WAR ILLUSTRATED has been printed, and any reader anxious to secure an extra copy is advised to apply to his newsagent *immediately* as reprints of the issue are not likely to be available.

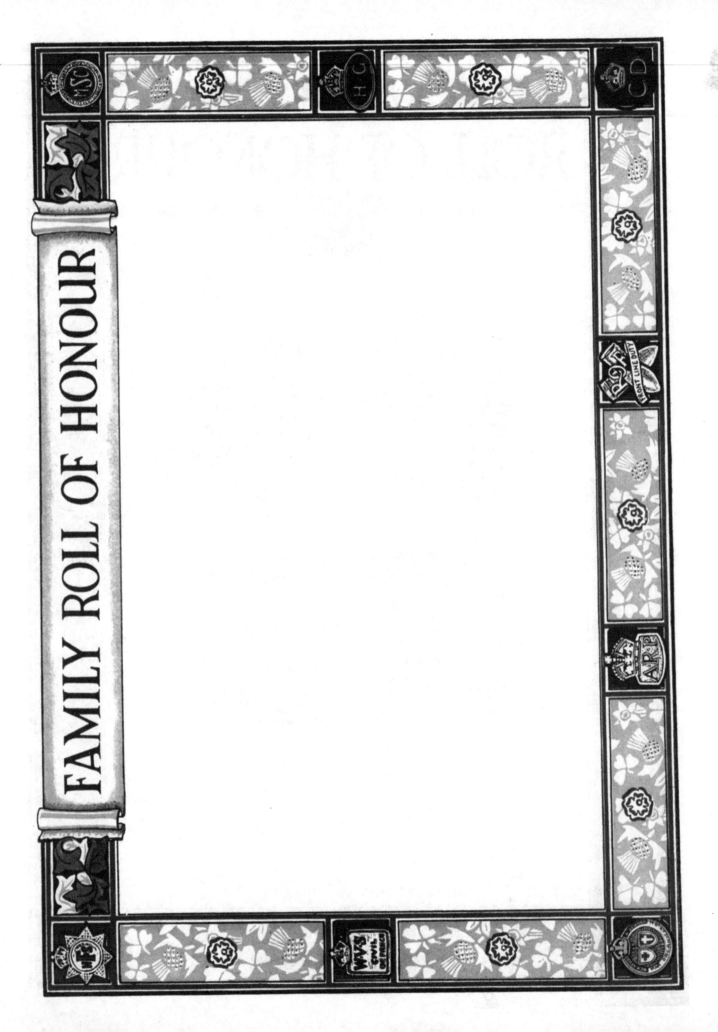

FAMILY ROLL OF HONOUR

'In Darkest Germany'

HAMILTON FYFE reviews a notable book of THE AFTERMATH

O NE of the most popular features of THE WAR ILLUS-
TRATED was the long series of reviews of vital War
Books contributed by Mr. Hamilton Fyfe, but in
asking him to review " In Darkest Germany " for our
final number we have not done so because of the literary
interest of the book, which has no literary merit, but
because of its immediate importance to the proper study
of world affairs. Mr. Gollancz is a loyal, earnest, and
distinguished member of British Jewry, and his personal
examination of social conditions in the British Zone of
Germany has attracted wide and deserved attention.

What the reviewer says is not to be assumed as representing the opinion of THE WAR ILLUSTRATED, whose Editor
has never encouraged any denigration of the British
officials who are placed there in the discharge of a most
difficult task and are entitled to have not less than " the

comforts of home," and perhaps more than these count
up to at the present time. Above all, we consider it would
be foolish of them to carry out their duties without making
it clear to the German people that Germany *lost* the appalling
war which she forced upon the peace-loving nations.

We should like to see a similar criticism by a Russian
Jew of the conditions obtaining in the Russian Zone of
Germany, where we have the best of reasons for believing
that every effort is being put forth to sweep the Germans
there into the sphere of Communism. But that is a book
which there is no free Russian Jew alive to write. One
would also like to see more evidence from our loyal
British Jews of their sympathy with Britain in the shameful machinations of America's anti-British Zionists, which
have made Palestine the plague spot of the world nearly
two years after the destruction of Nazi power.—EDITOR

L ET us suppose that someone wrote a
book during the war predicting what
the Germans would do if they defeated
us and occupied our country. This book
would have shown how they would keep us
on semi-starvation rations with the result
that we should suffer from various painful
and enfeebling diseases, how they would
destroy our industry, make some of our
finest ports useless, dismantle factories, take
away essential machinery and machine-tools,
force us to send coal out of the country while
millions of us were shivering with cold.

The book would also have warned us that
the officers of the German Army of
Occupation and the civilians who shared the
job of keeping us down would behave in a
haughty, unfriendly way towards us. Many
of us would be turned out of our homes to
make room for these "master-folk" and
in many cases be compelled to leave our
furniture, even our beds, for them. They
would build spacious, well-appointed clubs
for themselves while numbers of us had to
herd together in cellars or ruins. They would
eat well, while we were always hungry.

Had you read such a book you would have
said, "Yes, that's how they would treat us,
the brutes ! Thank God we aren't like that !
We are democrats, we believe in Christianity
even if we don't go to church. It is un-
imaginable that we could ever set deliberately
to work to ruin a nation in such a callous,
devilish manner."

Soothing Assurances Examined

Now, in one respect that complacency
would have been justified. We should
not act "deliberately" in that way. We
should not "callously" aim at wrecking the
lives of millions of our fellow human beings.
But if you will read my friend Victor
Gollancz's book recently published, titled In
Darkest Germany, the Record of a Visit
(Gollancz, 8s. 6d.), you will discover that
we are doing just that, through muddling,
dunderheaded disregard of human values,
unimaginative blindness to human suffering.

You will probably say, having read so
far, that Gollancz must be exaggerating.
You cannot believe men of British stock
would lay themselves open to such charges.
Soothing assurances given in the House of
Commons have convinced you of the
humanity with which Germans are treated.
Well, Gollancz deals with some of those.

For example, we have been told that the
re-housing of Germans bombed out of their
homes goes on "as quickly as possible."
How does this square with the figures of
building workers employed on repairs in
Hamburg, which fall very far short of the
many thousands forced to construct "a sort

of garden city" for members of the Control
Commission and their families in a part of
the city almost undamaged by bombing?
The German families who lived there have
been turned out.

There is also in Hamburg a very large
and in appearance magnificent Victory
Club ; its photograph is included in the
collection of 143 pictures which illustrate
and corroborate the text. Here are restaurants, lounges, ballrooms, rest-rooms, bathrooms, and so on—for the "master-folk"
only. Care is taken to keep British and
Germans as far as possible apart. The
difference between British and German
conditions is "far greater than it need be."

Costing us £100,000,000 a Year

Many will reply that there ought to be
this difference between the way our people
live and the German way (though a good
many Germans are not at all badly off in
the matter of dwellings and food, Gollancz
says). The Germans provoked war twice,
and they well deserve to be made to suffer for
it. Yes, retorts Gollancz :

I am never likely to forget the unspeakable
wickedness of which the Nazis were guilty ;
but when I see the swollen bodies and living
skeletons in hospitals ; when I look at the
miserable "shoes" of boys and girls in the
schools, and find they have come to their
lessons without even a dry piece of bread for
breakfast ; when I go down into a one-roomed
cellar where a mother is struggling, and
struggling very bravely, to do her best for a
husband and four or five children—then I
think not of Germans but of men and women.

Then he longs to see our "inefficient
totalitarianism" dropped and in its place
"a little liberalism or Christianity" given a
trial. "Inefficient" will seem to the readers
of his book an under-statement. Between
them the Governments of Britain, the
United States and Russia have made a
complete mess of the "liberation" of
Germany. We have made the Germans
hate us all. We have taken the heart out of
them. "The uncertainty of life—no one
knows what may happen to him next week
or month or year—grows increasingly
desperate." We have made young men and
women "bitter, cynical, hostile to us and all
our works." "For God's sake don't make
us Nazis," a student at Hamburg said to
Gollancz. Yet that is what we shall certainly
do if our methods are not changed.

Gollancz is a Labour adherent, but he
says angrily that the British Government
have no policy. A dozen, a hundred different
policies are being clumsily carried out.
We blow up shipbuilding yards. We
"dynamite into masses of shapeless metal"

very fine overhead cranes and electric motors,
which could have been used to great advantage in Britain, if they could not be left
where they were. Military authorities give
absurd or contradictory orders, making it
impossible to reconstruct industry, which we
proclaim to be our idea. Our occupation
of Germany is costing us *one hundred million
pounds* a year, and all we obtain for this
enormous expenditure, this war indemnity
which we are paying to the enemy we brought
low, is the knowledge that "a mania for
destruction" is making the confusion worse
confounded, "filling the German people with
despair rather than with hope."

That is the substance of Gollancz's
indictment, and he supports it with an
appalling array of evidence gathered by
himself. He touches on all aspects of German
life—if it can be called life. He mentions
as a proof of the general weakness and
weariness due to under-feeding that, "if
you are in a car you are always in danger
of running them down, they drift about with
such lassitude." He cites also the plight
of a university professor who sold some law
books for butter, to nourish his ailing wife.
"He had no further use for the volumes
anyhow, he said, as he was too feeble to read."

Eyewash—or Mere Silliness ?

Even those who have strength and spirit
enough to read are able to get very few books.
There is a ridiculous censorship, applied
to public libraries as well as publishers.
There is a famine of paper. Our talk about
"re-educating" the Germans and making
them "good Democrats" was either eyewash
(that is the German view) or mere silliness,
which is the more likely.

If men are to have the chance of becoming
democrats, they must breathe the spacious air
of personal freedom and intellectual responsibility. If you censor a man's reading, you
make him a slave and therefore excellent
raw-material for the first shoddy fanatic that
may be out to manipulate him. If you forbid
a man any decent employment and deprive
him of his pension (because he was a Nazi
Party member), it isn't likely he will become a
useful and contented member of society.

S TOP the process known as de-Nazification,
urges Gollancz. It does more harm than
good. The same criticism applies to a great
many of the other methods we have fumbled
with in Germany. The book shows plainly
which these are, and makes suggestions for
altering them. These are supported by
many Conservative M.P.s. One, who has
also visited Germany, wrote in the Daily
Mail that Gollancz's "record of tragedy
and horror, of missed opportunities, of
terrible and perhaps irretrievable mistakes"
—this was Major Guy Lloyd's own phrase—
is "every word of it true."

The Roll of Honour
NCOS & MEN
1939—1946

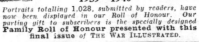

Portraits totalling 1,028, submitted by readers, have now been displayed in our Roll of Honour. Our parting gift to subscribers is the specially designed **Family Roll of Honour** *presented with this final issue of* THE WAR ILLUSTRATED.

Gdsmn. J. K. ALVEY
Grenadier Guards.
Action : Holland. 31.3.45.
Age 25. *(Duckmanton)*

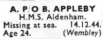

A. P/O B. APPLEBY
H.M.S. Aldenham.
Missing at sea. 14.12.44.
Age 24. *(Wembley)*

L/Bdr. M. BAIGENT
Royal Artillery.
P.O.W. Saigon. 30.4.42.
Age 22. *(Newbury)*

Pte. L. BARKER
13th Parachute Regt.
D/Wounds. 28.6.44.
Age 20. *(Luton)*

Pte. J. BENNETT
1st Airborne Division.
Shot P.O.W. Ger. 13.10.44
Age 20. *(Hayes)*

A/B R. BONSIR
H.M.S. Fidelity.
Act. : Atlantic. 1.1.43.
Age 25. *(Hinckley)*

W/O C. E. BOWDEN
Merchant Navy.
Act. Atlantic. 18.2.42.
Age 51. *(Cardiff)*

Fus. A. BROADHEAD
Royal Fusiliers.
Action : Italy. 15.12.43.
Age 26. *(London)*

Sgt. C. A. BRYANT
Royal Air Force.
Honnington. 30.10.39.
Age 24. *(Thetford)*

Gdsmn. R. CATTERALL
Grenadier Guards.
D/W : Brussels. 4.9.44.
Age 19. *(Orrell)*

Tpr. T. COLLETT
Reconnaissance Regt.
Action : Italy. 6.2.45.
Age 19. *(Isleworth)*

Pte. G. J. COPE
N. Staffs Regt.
Act. : Tunisia. 23.4.43.
Age 20. *(Stone)*

A.C.2. M. DAVIDSON
R.A.F.V.R.
Died : London. 19.2.45.
Age 42. *(London)*

Mne. C. DEWBERRY
Royal Marine Commando.
D/W : Normandy. 2.2.45.
Age 20. *(Clapton)*

Gdsmn. B. DEARDEN
Coldstream Guards.
Action : Italy. 20.3.45.
Age 29. *(Bolton)*

Pte. J. ELLIS
King's Own Regiment.
Action: Burma. 15.10.43.
Age 34. *(Trawsfynydd)*

A.C.2. A. H. FELLOWS
Royal Air Force.
Act. : E. Anglia. 16.5.41.
Age 27. *(Birmingham)*

Gnr. D. H. FIELD
8th Division, A.I.F.
P.O.W. : Siam. 28.7.43.
Age 25. *(Mackay, Qnsld.)*

Gnr. P. FLETCHER
Royal Artillery.
Action : Bayrue. 19.7.44.
Age 19. *(Halifax)*

Sgt. A. J. E. FROST
Essex Regiment.
Action : Italy. 2.11.43.
Age 28. *(Southend-on-Sea)*

A/B J. O. GRIFFITHS
Royal Navy.
Act. : Adriatic. 21.8.44.
Age 20. *(Bl. Festiniog)*

Sgt. H. F. GULLERY
Royal Air Force.
Nr. Scunthorpe. 4.2.43.
Age 33. *(Blackpool)*

Pte. D. HARBONE
R. Warwickshire Regt.
Act. : W. E'pe. 10.7.44.
Age 19. *(Birmingham)*

Pte. W. HARBONE
S. Wales Borderers.
D/W. : W. E'pe. 30.8.44.
Age 22. *(Birmingham)*

Sgt. W. HARRIS
R.A.F. Coastal Command.
Act. : N. Ireland 27.8.43.
Age 28. *(W. Norwood)*

Sgt. F. HASLEMORE
Royal Air Force.
Action : Kiel. 27.6.41.
Age 21. *(Riverton, N.Z.)*

Pte. W. HATCH
Lorne Scots (Can.).
Act. : France. 25.11.44.
Age 23. *(Oshawa, Ont.)*

Sto. J. HENDERSON
H.M.S. Dorsetshire.
Act. : Ind. Ocean. 5.4.42.
Age 21. *(Gateshead)*

Sgt. D. M. HERBERT
R.A.F.V.R.
Over Austria. 20.8.44.
Age 20. *(Hastings)*

L/Cpl. W. HILL
E. Lancs. Regt.
Act. : W. E'pe. 14.4.45.
Age 19. *(Warrington)*

G. E. HUGGINS
Cf. Can. Man. N.A.A.F.I.
Act. : Portland. 8.7.40.
Age 36. *(Portsmouth)*

Pte. C. HUMPHREYS
K.O.Y.L.I.
Act. : N.W. E'pe. 3.9.44.
Age 21. *(Yorks)*

L/ACW. HUTCHISON
W.A.A.F.
Act. : Scotland. 16.4.45.
Age 24. *(Gateshead)*

Bugler J. INGALL
Royal Marines.
Act. : At sea. 25.11.41.
Age 19 *(Rushden)*

Sgt. E. F. JARRETT
Royal Air Force.
Act. : N. Africa. 22.8.43.
Age 21. *(Wimborne)*

Gnr./Sig. D. JONES
Royal Artillery.
Act. : Malaya. 1.3.42.
Age 27. *(Llanharan)*

Sgt. A. LANGTON
Royal Air Force.
Act. : Kiel. 13.10.42.
Age 21. *(Gt. Yarmouth)*

Tpr. F. J. LINDSAY
Border Regiment.
D/W : India. March '44.
Age 31 *(Liverpool)*